D1067917

WRITING

Annotated Teacher's Edition

JAMES L. KINNEAVY
JOHN E. WARRINER

Introductory Course

Holt, Rinehart and Winston

Harcourt Brace Jovanovich HBJ

Austin • Orlando • San Diego • Chicago • Dallas • Toronto

Critical Readers

Ron Dorsey
Hadley Middle School
Wichita, Kansas

Shirley Foley
Steinbeck Middle School
San Jose, California

Betty Harmon
DuBose Middle School
Summerville, South Carolina

Becky Holditch
Deerpark Middle School
Austin, Texas

Pamela Kimelberg
Niskayuna Middle School
Niskayuna, New York

Sandra Nielsen
Washington Middle School
Brainerd, Minnesota

Sandie Smith
Lewis Central Middle School
Council Bluffs, Iowa

Printed in the United States of America

ISBN 0-03-047152-4 3 4 5 6 062 94

Authors

James L. Kinneavy, the Jane and Roland Blumberg Centennnial Professor of English at The University of Texas at Austin, directed the development and writing of the composition strand in the program. He is the author of *A Theory of Discourse* and coauthor of *Writing in the Liberal Arts Tradition.* Professor Kinneavy is a leader in the field of rhetoric and composition and a respected educator whose teaching experience spans all levels—elementary, secondary, and college. He has continually been concerned with teaching writing to high school students.

John E. Warriner developed the organizational structure for the Handbook of Grammar, Usage, and Mechanics in the book. He coauthored the *English Workshop* series, was general editor of the *Composition: Models and Exercises* series, and editor of *Short Stories: Characters in Conflict.* He taught English for thirty-two years in junior and senior high school and college.

Professional Essays

Donald M. Murray is Professor Emeritus of English at The University of New Hampshire, where he served as director of Freshman English and as English Department Chairperson. As a journalist, he won a number of awards including the Pulitzer Prize for editorial writing on the *Boston Herald* in 1954.

Lee Odell has a Ph.D. in English and Education from The University of Michigan. A former middle school and high school teacher of English, he now teaches writing at Rensselaer Polytechnic Institute. He has published frequently on the teaching of writing and is interested in the processes of writing, talking, and thinking.

Maxine C. Hairston has a Ph.D. in English from the The University of Texas at Austin, where she served as Director of Freshman English. She is the author of several texts on writing theory and the teaching of writing, including *A Contemporary Composition.*

Barbara J. Shade has a Ph.D. in Educational Psychology from The University of Wisconsin-Madison. She is a Professor and Dean of the School of Education at The University of Wisconsin-Parkside. She specializes in the social and psycholôgical attributes of people with high academic achievement with an emphasis on African Americans. She has written extensively on culture and its impact on learning and achievement. She also served as consultant for this series.

Wanda B. Schindley has an Ed.D. in Composition and Rhetoric from East Texas State University. She teaches at Northeast Texas Community College and serves as coordinator and curriculum specialist for the Workplace Partnership program. She coauthored a teacher's resource series, *The English Teacher's Guide to the Essential Elements.*

Charles W. Leftwich has an Ed.D. in Educational Administration from Harvard University. He is a professor in the Department of Educational Administration at East Texas State University. He worked in public schools for over twenty-five years as a teacher, a vice-principal, a principal, and a superintendent.

Patricia G. Tweeddale has an Ed.D. in Educational Administration from East Texas State University. She has taught at-risk students in high school and has written about the impact of public education policy on such students. She is a partner in an educational consulting service that focuses on helping teachers to teach at-risk student populations.

Norbert Elliot has a Ph.D. in English from The University of Tennessee. A director of the writing program at New Jersey Institute of Technology, he is a specialist in test development and writing assessment.

Karen L. Greenberg has a Ph.D. in Linguistics from New York University. She is an Associate Professor of English at Hunter College of The City University of New York, where she directs the Developmental English Program and teaches courses in writing and linguistics. She is the director of the National Testing Network in Writing, and she has authored numerous books and essays on writing instruction and assessment.

David A. England has a Ph.D. in English from Indiana University. He is the Associate Dean of Teacher Education at Louisiana State University. A former high school English teacher, he has been active in the National Council of Teachers of English and was active in the National Writing Project.

Writers and Editors

Kelis Berry has an M.Ed. in English from East Texas State University. She teaches English at Southeastern Oklahoma State University at Durant, Oklahoma. She is engaged in research on revision practices with computers. She is a published author of poetry and short fiction.

Patti Day-Miller has an M.A. with a Reading Endorsement from Indiana University. She has been the reading consultant for the Bartholomew Consolidated Reading Corporation of Columbus, Indiana and has written educational material for composition and literature textbooks.

H. Edward Deluzain has a Ph.D. in English Education from Florida State University. He teaches at A. Crawford Mosley High School in Panama City, Florida, where he is also a writer of educational material in composition and literature.

Jan Freeman has a B.A. in English from Vassar College and an M.A. in English with a concentration in creative writing from New York University. A published poet, she is a freelance writer and editor in Massachusetts.

Peter Harris has a Ph.D. in English literature from Texas Tech University. He is an Associate Professor of English at West Virginia Institute of Technology in Montgomery, West Virginia.

Deborah Taylor-Simpson has an M.A. in English from East Texas State University. She teaches English at Roane State Community College in Harriman, Tennessee.

Acknowledgments

We wish to thank the following teachers who participated in field testing of pre-publication materials for this series:

Susan Almand-Myers
Meadow Park Intermediate School
Beaverton, Oregon

Theresa L. Bagwell
Naylor Middle School
Tucson, Arizona

Ruth Bird
Freeport High School
Sarver, Pennsylvania

Joan M. Brooks
Central Junior High School
Guymon, Oklahoma

Candice C. Bush
J. D. Smith Junior High School
N. Las Vegas, Nevada

Mary Jane Childs
Moore West Junior High School
Oklahoma City, Oklahoma

Brian Christensen
Valley High School
West Des Moines, Iowa

Lenise Christopher
Western High School
Las Vegas, Nevada

Mary Ann Crawford
Ruskin Senior High School
Kansas City, Missouri

Linda Dancy
Greenwood Lakes Middle School
Lake Mary, Florida

Elaine A. Espindle
Peabody Veterans Memorial High School
Peabody, Massachusetts

Joan Justice
North Middle School
O'Fallon, Missouri

Beverly Kahwaty
Pueblo High School
Tucson, Arizona

Lamont Leon
Van Buren Junior High School
Tampa, Florida

Susan Lusch
Fort Zumwalt South High School
St. Peters, Missouri

Michele K. Lyall
Rhodes Junior High School
Mesa, Arizona

Belinda Manard
McKinley Senior High School
Canton, Ohio

Nathan Masterson
Peabody Veterans Memorial High School
Peabody, Massachusetts

Marianne Mayer
Swope Middle School
Reno, Nevada

Penne Parker
Greenwood Lakes Middle School
Lake Mary, Florida

Amy Ribble
Gretna Junior-Senior High School
Gretna, Nebraska

Kathleen R. St. Clair
Western High School
Las Vegas, Nevada

Carla Sankovich
Billinghurst Middle School
Reno, Nevada

Sheila Shaffer
Cholla Middle School
Phoenix, Arizona

Joann Smith
Lehman Junior High School
Canton, Ohio

Margie Stevens
Raytown Middle School
Raytown, Missouri

Mary Webster
Central Junior High School
Guymon, Oklahoma

Susan M. Yentz
Oviedo High School
Oviedo, Florida

Contents in Brief

Table of Contents

PROFESSIONAL ESSAYS

A TEACHER'S GUIDE TO ELEMENTS OF WRITING

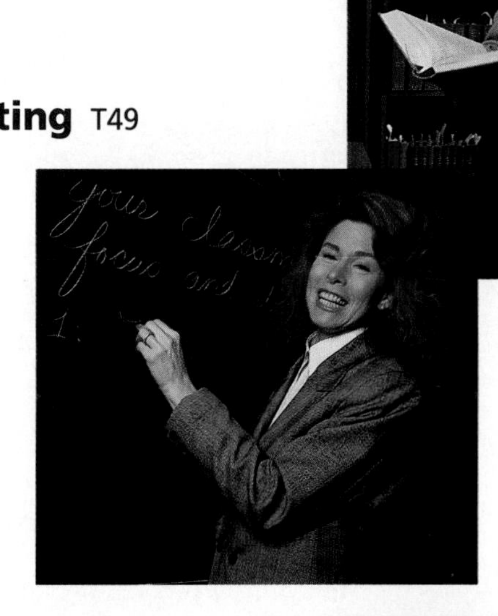

PART ONE WRITING

CHAPTER 1 WRITING AND THINKING

CHAPTER 2 LEARNING ABOUT PARAGRAPHS

CHAPTER 3 EXPRESSIVE WRITING

CHAPTER 4 USING DESCRIPTION

CHAPTER 5 CREATIVE WRITING

CHAPTER 6 WRITING TO INFORM

CHAPTER 7 WRITING TO PERSUADE

CHAPTER 8 WRITING ABOUT LITERATURE

CHAPTER 9 WRITING A REPORT

what?
who?
when?
how?
where?
why?

What Lava Is
2
magma = hot liquid rock deep in earth
lava = magma when it erupts from volcano—
mixed with gas & steam
1,300°–2,200° F. Glows red to white.
p. 89

CHAPTER 10 WRITING EFFECTIVE SENTENCES

CHAPTER 11 ENGLISH: ORIGINS AND USES

CHAPTER 12 THE SENTENCE 338

Subject and Predicate, Kinds of Sentences

CHAPTER 13 THE PARTS OF SPEECH 367

Mask, Bassa Peoples, Liberia. Wood, pigment, bone or ivory, iron. H. $9\frac{1}{2}$" W. $5\frac{3}{4}$" D. $4\frac{1}{2}$". National Museum of African Art, 95-5-1. Photograph by Jeffrey Ploskonka.

CHAPTER 14 THE PARTS OF SPEECH 390

CHAPTER 16 COMPLEMENTS 437

N600D
N30GM

WAYNE PIERCE

CHAPTER 19 USING PRONOUNS CORRECTLY 502

Spanish Governor's Palace

Riverwalk

CHAPTER 20 USING MODIFIERS CORRECTLY 525

Comparison of Adjectives and Adverbs

Horace Pippin, 1935, "After Supper, West Chester". Gridley/Graves © 1991/Collection Leon Hecht and Robert Pincus-Witten, New York City.

CHAPTER 23 PUNCTUATION 586

End Marks, Commas, Semicolons, Colons

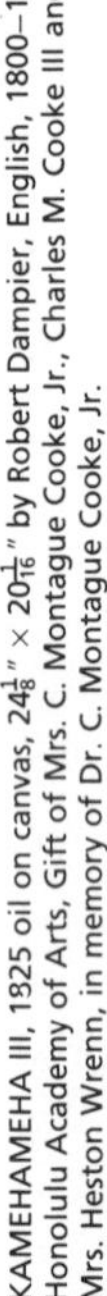

KAMEHAMEHA III, 1825 oil on canvas, $24\frac{1}{8}$" × $20\frac{1}{16}$" by Robert Dampier, English, 1800–1874 Honolulu Academy of Arts, Gift of Mrs. C. Montague Cooke, Jr., Charles M. Cooke III and Mrs. Heston Wrenn, in memory of Dr. C. Montague Cooke, Jr.

人形

PART THREE RESOURCES

CHAPTER 26 SPEAKING 664

CHAPTER 27 LISTENING 676

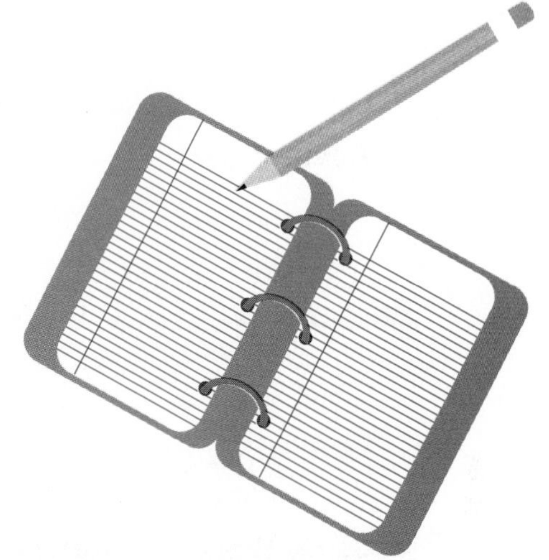

CHAPTER 28 THE LIBRARY/MEDIA CENTER 684

CHAPTER 31 LETTERS AND FORMS 706

Style and Contents

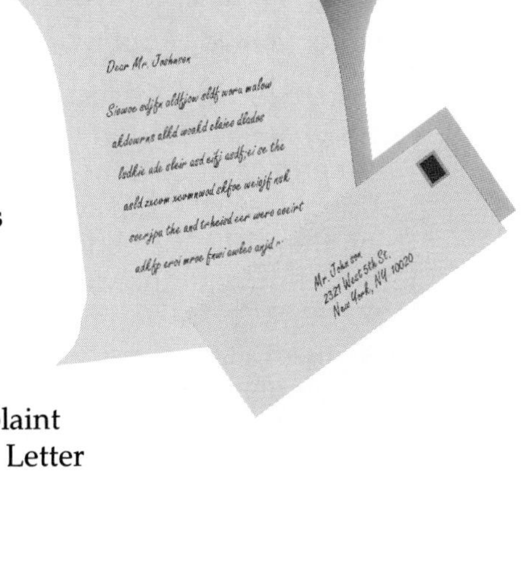

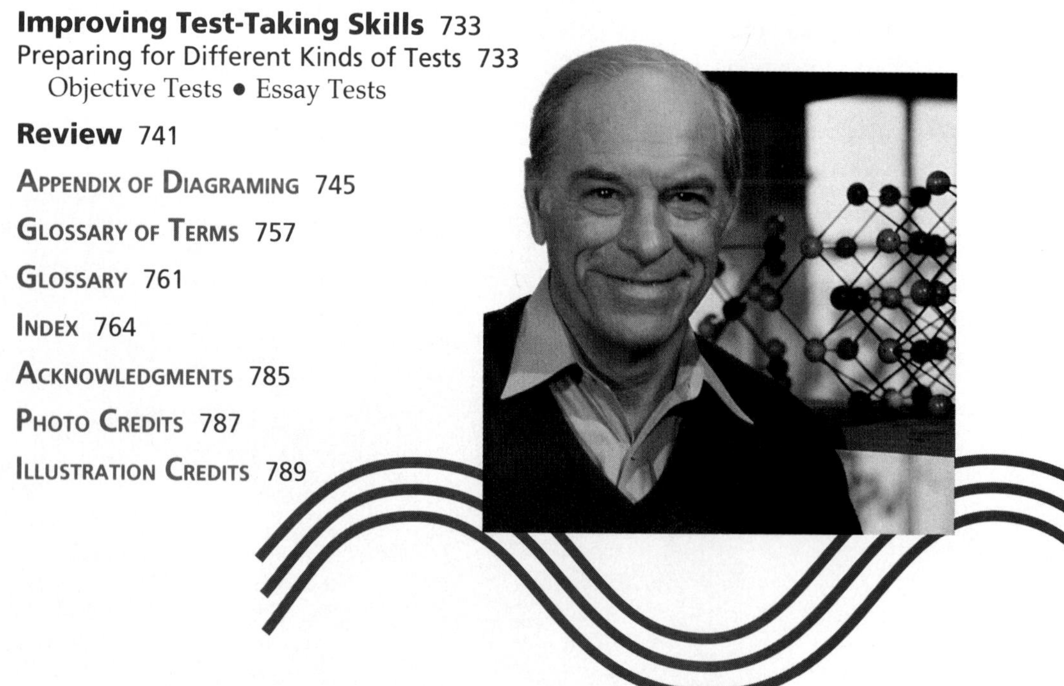

Models

Fiction

Rudolfo A. Anaya, *Tortuga*
Terry Brooks, *The Sword of Shannara*
Beverly Cleary, *Ramona Forever*
Ernest J. Gaines, "The Sky Is Gray," *Bloodline*
Edward Hoch, "Zoo," *Sudden Twists*
Julius Lester, "Brer Billy Goat Tricks Brer Wolf," *Further Tales of Uncle Remus*
Keith Robertson, *Henry Reed, Inc.*
Cynthia Rylant, "Boar Out There," *Every Living Thing*
Lee Smith, *Oral History*
Eva-Lis Wuorio, "You Can't Take It With You," *Escape If You Can*

Nonfiction

Isaac Asimov, *How Did We Find Out About Coal?*
Beverly Cleary, *A Girl from Yamhill: A Memoir*
Joanna Cole, *A Cat's Body*
Kathy Darling, *Manatee on Location*
Margery Facklam, *Wild Animals, Gentle Women*
Harry Gersh, *Women Who Made America Great*
Don Herbert, "Banana Surprise," *Mr. Wizard's Supermarket Science*
E. Adamson Hoebel, "Massasoit," *The World Book Encyclopedia*, 1991 ed.
Cheng Hou-tien, *Scissor Cutting for Beginners*
Tatsuo Ishimoto, *The Art of the Japanese Garden*
Patricia Lauber, *Volcano: The Eruption and Healing of Mount St. Helens*
"Lava and Magma," *Compton's Encyclopedia*, 1990 ed.
Paula Morrow, "Making a Flying Fish," *Faces*
Donald M. Murray, *Expecting the Unexpected*
Huynh Quang Nhuong, *The Land I Lost*
Joanne Settel and Nancy Baggett, "How Can Water Striders Walk on Water?," *How Do Ants Know When You're Having a Picnic?*
Paul Robert Walker, *Pride of Puerto Rico—The Life of Roberto Clemente*
Ralph Whitlock, *Rabbits and Hares*
Laurence Yep, *The Lost Garden*

Poetry

A Limerick, *Beastly Boys and Ghastly Girls*
James Berry, Riddle #11, *When I Dance*
Langston Hughes, "Poem"
Naomi Shihab Nye, "The Rider"
Agnes T. Pratt, "Fragments of Spring" and "So Quickly Came the Summer," *The Whispering Wind: Poetry by Young American Indians*
William Jay Smith, *Laughing Time: Nonsense Poems*

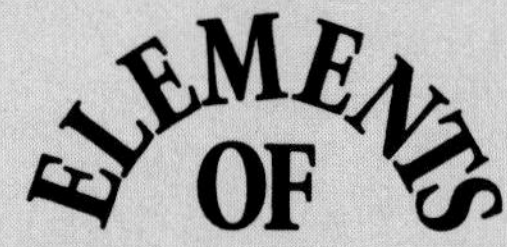

A Teacher's Guide to ELEMENTS OF WRITING

CONTENTS

JAMES L. KINNEAVY

DONALD MURRAY

KAREN GREENBERG

LEE ODELL

BARBARA SHADE

MAXINE HAIRSTON

NORBERT ELLIOT

PATRICIA TWEEDDALE
CHARLES LEFTWICH

WANDA SCHINDLEY

HOW DARE THEY?

. . . IN THE SPIRIT OF MAINTAINING THE LASTING VALUES AND STANDARDS OF THE SERIES . . .

Certainly when teachers saw a new name listed as a coauthor with John E. Warriner, some of you must have said, "How can the editors dare do this?" Like the editors, I am fully aware that Warriner has been a legendary name in high school English composition and grammar books since 1941, the year of the first edition of his series, till the present. His high school textbooks have changed somewhat through the decades, but they have stood the test of half of a century—despite many educational trends and fashions—because they have incorporated important values and standards. I am aware of all of this, aware that Warriner's texts have almost a biblical authority.

But even the Bible is translated anew for different generations. So it is in the spirit of maintaining the lasting values and standards of the series while bringing a few further changes that this new edition of the series is published with a new name listed as coauthor. I was properly flattered when the company's editors asked me to be the consultant for the composition sections of the books in the new series. But I was also in awe of this long tradition of excellence and can only hope that this tradition can be upheld.

Like John E. Warriner, I have a long and varied experience as a teacher. He taught in junior high, high school, and college. I have taught in elementary school, high school, and college. He taught for many years; I have been teaching since 1941 and continue to teach today. For the past twenty-five years I have given workshops to high school students involved in statewide competitive contests in extemporaneous writing. Like Warriner, I have attempted to keep up with the profession and to reflect in my writings what we have learned and continue to learn about teaching the language arts. I have trained students to teach at all grade levels from elementary school through graduate school. I have also observed student teachers for years at the high school and college levels.

You will find in this series, therefore, an attempt to maintain the best values of the Warriner series and to add to it a few new features that teachers, administrators, scholars, and editors think will make it an even better set of books.

THE TEACHER'S EDITION IS A *GREAT* HELP

I know that teaching school combines the blue and white collar syndromes: You're there at 8:00 and leave at 4:00; then you take on extra-hour professional chores in the evening and on weekends of correcting papers, reading to keep up professionally (which you are doing right now), working on extracurricular activities,

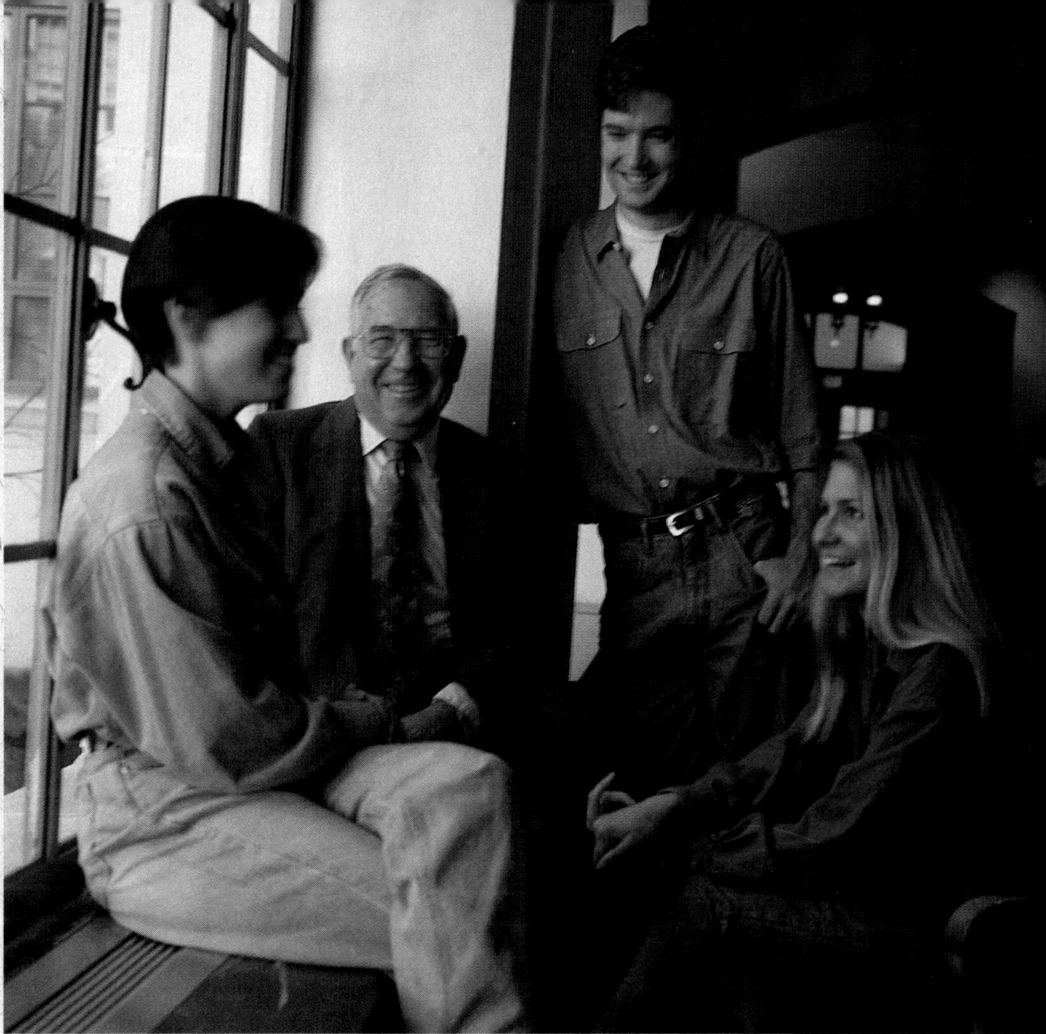

JAMES KINNEAVY, WITH STUDENTS AT THE UNIVERSITY OF TEXAS AT AUSTIN.

attending conventions, etc. You need all of the timesavers you can find.

You will find many of them in this edition. On each page you will find that your objectives, your lesson plan, and your resources are packed around the student text. Questions you can ask the students are provided (with answers). Vocabulary items are defined. Adaptations to more-advanced students, to less-advanced students, and to ESL students are suggested. Special exercises supplementing those in the textbook are provided. Student responses to questions are foreseen and reactions suggested. Applications to critical thinking and to cooperative learning are continually provided.

All in all these helps are a treasure trove. Before spending hours looking up supplementary materials for a class, look in your teacher's edition. Someone else may have done your work already and saved you hours. When I look at the wealth of all of these materials and contrast them to what I had to teach with in my early teaching years in both elementary and high school, I am green with envy.

Beginning teachers especially should exploit these materials, built upon the experiences of hundreds of their predecessors. These experiences can help new teachers avoid some all-too-common problems. Let me point out some of them.

RELATIONSHIP BETWEEN COMPOSITION AND GRAMMAR

You will find in the new series the same close relationship between composition and grammar that has characterized the series since its inception. You can see this by simply looking at the table of contents.

Such a look makes quite clear that the primacy and the preponderance of attention is given to writing, and that grammar is a handmaid to writing. But both are covered extensively.

Given the increasing importance of rhetoric in public schools and in college, you will find more depth in the composition section of this textbook. There is a more discernible structure to the various chapters on writing. These chapters reflect the concern for certain important kinds of writing—concerns that are reflected in many state writing tests. Thus, there is a chapter devoted to each of the major aims of writing: to inform, to persuade, to explain, to prove, to entertain, and to allow the students to express themselves. Each of the modes of writing usually gets a chapter at each grade level: narrating, describing, classifying and defining, and evaluating. This structure is more explicit in the new series than it was in the earlier ones.

In each of these chapters, however, the close relationship between composition and grammar

> WHAT THIS TEXTBOOK DOES NOT WANT TO DO IS TO ENCOURAGE THE ISOLATED TEACHING OF GRAMMATICAL SKILLS IN A ROTE MANNER.

is maintained. There is a grammatical issue covered in each chapter, particularly relevant to the kind of writing being covered. Thus, a chapter on persuasion can consider the problem of fragments, often seen in advertisements. A chapter on description can consider the importance of adjectives and adverbs. Finally, nearly all of these chapters refer to the grammar chapters for coverage of issues that relate to the kind of writing under consideration.

This careful attempt to relate grammar to composition was explicit in the longtime title of this series, which has linked grammar to composition for years.

This linkage is confirmed by seventy years of *empirical research.* Studies at all levels, from elementary school through college, confirm that grammar is learned best when taught in conjunction with composition, as well as with speaking and with literature. These studies have been made in the United States, in Canada, in the British Isles, and in Australia. What this textbook does not want to do is to encourage the isolated teaching of grammatical skills in a rote manner. This is called the formal teaching of grammar. Sometimes, it has to be done. But most of the time, the grammar is linked to a writing assignment and even motivated by it. For instance, consistent fragments in a formal paper suggest a lesson in the sentence, emphasizing its elements and its completeness. This improves the composition and also teaches the grammar in a manner that gives it meaning.

THE PROCESSES OF COMPOSING

In keeping with the emphasis in the schools and in college writing courses, you will find a continuation of the unremitting concern with the processes of writing in every writing chapter of the series—a concern begun several years ago. The stress on process will be evident in the structuring of the chapters by the stages of the writing process; in the frequent use of support groups of students to react to each other's plans, drafts, and papers; and in teacher and peer interventions in the writing process. The idea that writing is a solitary, sedentary process, as a poet once said, is not at all adhered to in this textbook. Rather writing is viewed as a collaborative and cooperative action.

> THIS *DOMINANCE OF THE WHOLE OVER THE PARTS* EXPLAINS THE GENERAL STRUCTURE OF THE BOOK. THE WRITING CHAPTERS COME AT THE BEGINNING OF THE BOOK, AND THE GRAMMAR, USAGE, AND MECHANICS MAKE UP THE LAST SECTION OF THE BOOK.

A COOPERATIVE ATMOSPHERE

The process view of writing that sees the writing place as a happy, cooperative workshop rather than a silent dungeon enables the students to get support and help from one another and from the teacher.

The students are usually divided into *peer support groups* of three or four, all working on similar projects, and all trying to help each other turn out better work. The members of the groups help one another plan the papers, critique each other's rough drafts, and provide a real audience for the final version. The members of the group are like a miniature research group working on a common project.

The *teacher* moves from group to group, helping in the planning, discussing problems, critiquing rough drafts, and grading the final drafts. Like the members of the peer support groups, the teacher fulfills different functions: at times the teacher is a motivator, a source of ideas, a theorist who has general ideas that apply to the current situation, a careful listener, a constructive critic of plans and rough drafts, a sympathetic reader and grader of the final version, and above all, a fellow writer.

With this view of the writing process, the teacher with a *heavy paper load* can find help from the students. The teacher isn't the only person who reads a student's paper. The other members of the support group can assist the teacher with useful feedback to the author at any level of the writer's concerns with mechanics, with word choice, with organization, with ideas, and with style. If the teacher trains support groups to be helpful and constructively critical, a good deal of the drudgery of grading papers can be avoided.

Finally, the writing process often results in some kind of *publication*, possibly in a public speech (or in a performance in the case of creative writing), sometimes in a class newspaper put out by desktop publishing on a computer, sometimes in a school newspaper, or maybe just in a permanent portfolio that the student keeps of his or her better work.

THE WHOLE AND THE PARTS

Another motif that you will see given more prominence from the very beginning and running through all of the writing chapters is the insistence on the relationship between the whole and the parts in the composing process. A theme is like a sentence: It is made up of parts that are uttered in a chronological sequence, but the whole is greater than the parts because it also includes the relationships among the parts and with the whole. We don't begin a sentence with no idea where it is going to end or what it is going to say; we begin with a whole and choose the parts to articulate it. We may change our minds halfway through a sentence and adjust to our new idea; the same phenomenon often happens with a whole theme.

In other words, a theme begins with a vague but somewhat distinct idea of a whole and looks around for the parts that will embody that idea. The parts are single words, phrases, sentences, paragraphs, even large sections of the theme.

Consequently, in the writing chapters, each of these parts is treated as a part of a whole. A composition is not an expanded word or phrase or paragraph. An expanded paragraph is a big paragraph, just as an expanded wheel is just a big wheel, not suddenly a complete automobile. To use another metaphor, a student setting out to write a composition is like an architect who draws up a plan of the whole building; it's going to be a home or a department store or a restaurant or a sports coliseum or whatever. But the architect doesn't haphazardly gather bricks and steel and staircases and chimneys and just throw them together.

With this idea of the dominance of the whole over the parts, each of the writing chapters pursues the writing process through to the production of a complete theme. There are writing activities throughout addressing the parts, but they are all orchestrated to the final whole.

This *dominance of the whole over the parts* explains the general structure of the textbook. The writing chapters come at the beginning, and the grammar, usage, and mechanics make up the last section.

In fact, the suggested treatment for writing encourages the students to write rapidly and enthusiastically in their first plans, sketches, and drafts, without stopping to check spelling, word choice, or grammatical purity. The idea is to support the writing process as a creative surge in the beginning. The mechanical matters are often better handled in revision.

THE IDEA IS TO SUPPORT THE WRITING PROCESS AS A CREATIVE SURGE IN THE BEGINNING. THE MECHANICAL MATTERS ARE OFTEN BETTER HANDLED IN THE REVISION.

AIMS AND MODES AS WAYS OF THINKING

The close connections among the aims and modes of writing and rather different ways of thinking have been emphasized in the introduction to the student's edition, so these will not be repeated here in any detail. But at the heart of the series is the notion that writing involves thinking all of the time; and different ways of writing involve different ways of thinking. Expressive writing is quite different from expository writing, and some students can do one type better than another. Nevertheless, a minimum competence in each aim and mode is necessary to the development of a full mental life. You are encouraged to reread the **"Introduction to Writing"** chapter to see the development of this notion.

THE AIMS OF WRITING AND DIFFERENT DIALECTS

You will undoubtedly notice that different levels of formality are suggested with the different aims of writing. In the chapters on expressive writing, a casual, personal, and familiar style is suggested. At the other extreme, in the chapters on information and proof, a more formal sense of grammar and word choice is expected. This is true in real life and in the classroom. In between self-expression and these types of expository writing, there are various shades of formality in persuasive, creative, and exploratory writing.

The model adopted here is that of Martin Joos, whose book *The Five Clocks* distinguishes five different levels of formality that nearly all of us use, depending on the circumstances. Joos calls these the intimate, the colloquial, the consultative, the formal, and the ritual levels. We speak to our family members (and sometimes our pets) in the familiar dialect. We speak to our friends in an ordinary conversation on the colloquial level. We adopt the consultative tone usually when we are teaching class. We use our formal dialect when we are giving speeches at a convention. And we use the ritual level of formality when we are at church or are graduating or are being initiated into a society.

But teachers are not the only people who have their five levels of formality. Teenagers also have their own dialects for intimacy—I say dialects because girls have a different intimate dialect than do boys. Teenagers also have their own colloquial, consultative, formal, and ritual dialects. Mature people have their own five levels. Finally, the elderly have their own five dialects, often quite different from the other age levels.

Being aware of the different purposes for writing and the various levels of formality also helps the teacher be more aware of *minority dialects*, such as those used by Hispanic, Asian, and African Americans. The use of these dialects in expressive and sometimes in creative writing is often to be encouraged. On the other hand, the dialect of the targeted audience is to be encouraged in persuasion. In expository writing, there is more emphasis on the standard dialect.

WRITING AND LITERATURE

While you are teaching this book on handling writing and grammar, you are also using a separate textbook for literature. But the necessity of putting the major readings in different literary genres covered in the sixth grade in a special book should not at all imply a separation of the study of literature from that of writing or grammar. All through the literature book, there are writing assignments that cover the same purposes that are taught in the writing book. Students are asked to react expressively, persuasively, creatively, and informatively to literary selections. Thus the literature textbook resonates the same tones and rhythms as the writing textbook.

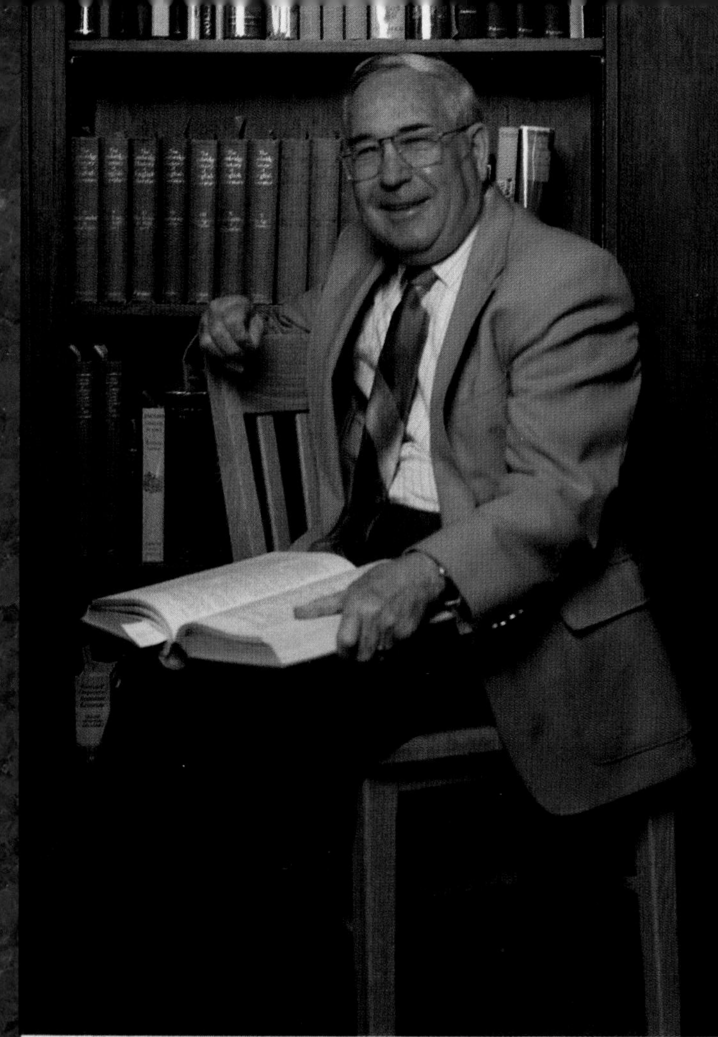

Conversely, this series is permeated with reading and literature. Each writing chapter includes models of the type of writing that is being studied. Many samples are drawn from the literary canon. In one of the textbooks, for instance, to illustrate the aims of writing, there is an excellent poem by William Stafford. Nearly every chapter in the student's edition contains similar material. Of course, all of these selections are annotated.

Further, in this edition, in each chapter of the book there are **Literature Links**, which take common literary selections and relate them to the material being studied in the chapter. Besides the **Literature Links**, there is the **Quotation for the Day**, a writing prompt drawn from literature.

Some writing chapters are almost completely devoted to literary writing, especially the chapters on creative writing, narration, and description.

Thus writing and literature are highly integrated by a common underlying philosophy of language.

WRITING AND THE OTHER LANGUAGE ARTS

In addition to being highly integrated with literature, this writing textbook is also tightly integrated with reading, speaking, and listening.

Each chapter contains several reading samples of the type of writing being studied. These are carefully analyzed by the students by means of questions after each selection. These questions are usually answered in an oral forum. The oral emphasis continues throughout the chapter because each stage of the writing process is carried out by means of small support groups of three or four students helping each other in planning, organizing, writing, and revising, as explained above. Frequently the publication of the paper takes an oral form. Thus persuasive speeches are delivered in front of the class.

The support group is clearly as much of a listening group as it is a speaking group. Students learn to listen carefully to each other in order to make constructive suggestions for improvement.

Thus the four language arts are carefully interwoven into the structure of each chapter at each stage of the writing process.

WRITING AND NEW TECHNOLOGIES

Whenever possible, teachers should take advantage of the new technologies that are increasingly becoming available at the high school level. Consequently, throughout this edition, there are continual reminders of these possibilities. Let us mention a few of them.

Networking with Computers

Some high schools have word processors available for use in teaching some writing classes. A few of these are even networked to allow student interactions with each other, either with the entire class or with selected support groups. The simultaneous writing reactions of all members of the class to a common reading assignment is one of the most effective methods to insure one hundred percent participation in group discussions, especially if the right questions are asked. And the use of computers to set up small support groups for the different stages of the writing process is also an exceptionally efficient technique of using small groups in teaching writing.

Revising and Word Processors

Even without networking, however, the use of word processors is to be commended whenever possible, particularly because of the manner in which revising is accomplished on computers. Students who formerly hated to revise now see revision as an easy and enjoyable manner to improve their work, not just at the level of vocabulary or mechanics, but even at the level of full discourse changes.

Spelling, Vocabulary, Grammar, and Word Processors

Word processors also bring substantial help to the poor speller and to the student having trouble finding the right word. Nearly all word-processing programs have some type of spell-check feature that shows students which words are incorrectly spelled. Thus each student can keep a list of his or her own problem words. This is acknowledged by nearly all spelling research as the single best way to improve spelling. Most spell-check programs are accompanied by programs that properly hyphenate words at the end of a line. This is an additional bonus for students who use word processors.

In addition, most word processors now come with a thesaurus of some size. This enables the students to look for options in vocabulary, even while working at the computer.

Thirdly, some word processors now have grammar programs that can check tense, case, subject-verb agreement, fragments, etc. These are not as common as spell-check features or thesauruses, but they are becoming available.

Publishing and Word Processors

Even if there is not a full classroom of word processors, it is possible to use a word processor as a desktop publisher to enable students to see some of their writings in elegant print and format. These can be put into portfolios for permanent records. Frequently throughout the annotated teacher's edition you are reminded of this option as one method of publishing the students' papers.

A FINAL WORD: USE YOUR OWN PERSONAL STAFF

Possibly after reading this essay, which brings together many of the rather complex tasks of the writing teacher, you may have been somewhat intimidated. But luckily you don't have to solve all of these problems overnight. The teaching of writing is a slow and cumulative process. Each chapter of this textbook focuses on a very specific issue and tries to teach just that particular skill. Following chapters build on the skill just learned. The student is slowly building up a range of abilities, not suddenly moving from barbarism to literacy.

Of course, in the preceding grades, your predecessors have worked with the students whom you now face, just as your colleagues will pick up where you leave off. And you are not alone at the present time: Your current colleagues are working with the same students in other classes.

In other words, just as writing is a cooperative endeavor among the students with each other and with you in your classroom, so also is it a cooperative endeavor among a sequence of teachers from year to year and among a group of teachers one year at a time. In many cases, parents are also willing cooperators.

Put Your Staff to Work

This textbook adds several more dimensions of helpmates. The authors are seasoned professionals who have faced many of the issues of these chapters before. These authors draw on other textbooks with which they are familiar. They also draw heavily on scholars that they have consulted. Thus, when I said earlier that the best way for a poor speller to improve spelling skills was to keep a journal list of personal mistakes, add to it when new mistakes are made, and consult this personal list regularly, this statement was drawing on ten years of research at two major universities with thousands of students. The marketing staff of this series is also made up of seasoned professionals who make it their business to find out what teachers want in a textbook. The teaching consultants who tried out the materials for these chapters were chosen because of their experience and knowledge. Finally, the editors of this series are acknowledged masters in their field—they have marketed the best-selling series in writing and grammar for almost half of a century.

Thus, you the teacher are backed by a phalanx of authors, scholars, market experts, teacher consultants, and editors all trying to assist you as you work with your students and other teachers. They are really your own personal staff. Use this book intelligently and this staff springs to life at your command. Donne's statement particularly can be applied to teachers: "No teacher is an island."

This textbook tries to put you in touch with all of these other helpers in the business of education. It can take a good deal of the loneliness out of teaching.

No One Does A More Important Job

Finally, you should be assured that your task is at the top of educational priorities. No one does a more important job than the teacher of writing. Throughout history, people who can write have been considered educated. Writing, in fact, has been the hallmark of the educated person in antiquity, in the Middle Ages (they were called clerks at that time), and in the modern period as well. A person who teaches students how to write is at the forefront of the educational enterprise. Such a person is also teaching students how to think in ways that will enable them to cope with a complex modern society as full human beings.❦

ELEMENTS OF WRITING addresses the *aims* and *modes* of writing and the *writing process* in the following ways:

Pupil's Edition

Demonstrates and teaches writing skills, focusing on the aims (the *why*) and the modes (the *how*) of writing

Provides an organized, easily understood approach that allows students to gain and sharpen writing skills

Annotated Teacher's Edition

Gives instructional strategies on how to teach the aims and modes

Offers lesson plans based on each stage of the writing process

Teacher's ResourceBank ™

Offers materials keyed to the writing process that assist students in achieving the aims and modes

By Donald M. Murray

Use Genre as Lens

"We write about what we don't know about what we know."

Students are usually introduced to each genre—essay, narrative, poem—in isolated units, as if one form of writing would contaminate another. But each genre is a lens, a way to observe, record, and examine the world. Students should be encouraged to use each genre to explore a single important experience.

Student writers and their teachers should begin the exploration with a personal experience—an event, a person, a place—that holds a significant mystery for them. Mystery is the starting place for most writing, what Grace Paley described when she said, "We write about what we don't know about what we know." Invite your students to explore a moment in their lives to which they keep returning in memory, the way the tongue seeks the missing tooth.

Encourage your students to play with the fragments of language connected with that experience in their minds and on paper to discover a line, a phrase, or a word that contains a tension or conflict within the experience. The "line" might be a word—*Christmas*—that might have special implications for a student with a Catholic mother and a Jewish father. It might be a phrase—*the debts of Christmas*—to a person whose family spends too much money to make up for their true family feelings. The "line" could be a sentence—"Each Christmas I remember my sister who will never grow old"—for someone who lost a sister years before. Each "line" has a tension and mystery the writer needs to understand by writing.

Before your students begin, it is important to remind them that all writing is experimental, that experimentation implies failure, and that failure is instructive. It is not possible they will fail; it is imperative that they fail. We do not improve our writing by avoiding failure, but by making use of it.

To guarantee failure, urge students to write the first draft fast. Velocity is as important in writing as it is in bicycle racing. Speed will produce the accidents of language, connection, and insight that will propel the draft forward towards meaning. And velocity allows students to escape, for the moment, the censor that demands premature correctness.

They should allow their drafts to instruct them. The evolving text will take its own course, exploring the experience as it is relived. If they are patient, receptive, and open to surprise, the text will tell them what they have to say. You may want to write two statements by E. M. Forster on the chalkboard:

Think before you speak is criticism's motto; speak before you think creation's.

and

How do I know what I think until I see what I say?

Students should write out loud, hearing the text as they write it. They may actually do this—it is your classroom—or read silently but *listen* to the text. As they tune their voices to the story being told, the voice—angry, nostalgic, humorous, sad, analytical, instructive, argumentative, poetic, even narrative—will reveal the meaning of the draft to the writer.

I invite you to stand beside me at my workbench and to observe me

AT HOME ON A WINTERY MORNING, DON MURRAY ENJOYS HIS FAVORITE TIME OF THE DAY.

as I use genre to explore an experience of mine.

THE ESSAY

I prefer the term *reflective essay* to *personal essay* because the writer reflects on personal experience, or on a topic of personal interest. The essay is neither a simple narrative of experience nor of thought unanchored by experience, but a combination of thought and experience, an effort to discover and share meaning in experience. The essay is a demonstration of critical thinking.

Some notes on the craft of the essay.

- Narrow the territory to be explored so you can achieve depth.
- Be specific. The specific will instruct. The more specific you are, the more universal your audience will be.
- Work locally; the paragraph you have just written contains the seed of the next paragraph. For example, if you have said the experience was important, show how it was important in the next paragraph.
- Answer the reader's questions. Writing is a conversation between reader and writer.
- When the draft surprises you, pay attention. Develop the surprise to discover its meaning.

On April 21, while visiting a daughter and her husband in their new home, I got up early without the alarm, as is my habit, and ended up sitting at the top of the stairs waiting for my family to wake, and I found mystery in the experience. It was a moment full of emotion, and I needed—not wanted, but needed—to explore that moment through writing.

I made a few notes in my daybook:

I can remember myself as a small boy in Doctor Denton's trying to be quiet sitting at the head of the stairs (night) waiting for the family to get up

I can remember my own daughter's impatient waiting

Sunday morning I sit at the head of the stairs a good place to read, a good place legs waiting, wife, behind me in the room, my wife

It is 8 AM and they plan on rising 9 AM, I've been up at 5:33, explored town, coffee, read Sunday NY Times

The next day I wrote the column that was published in *The Boston Globe*, April 30, 1991:

I am once again a small boy in Dr. Denton's sitting at the top of the stairs waiting for the snoring to stop and another day to begin.

I am, at the same time, an old man sitting at the top of the stairs in the new home of a daughter and her husband, waiting once more for the snoring to stop and a new day to begin.

Minnie Mae and I, on our first visit, have taken their bed, and they sleep on the hide-a-bed in the living room. They work in the theatre and have agreed to get up early—at 9 o'clock on Sunday morning—because the old folks are here.

But I followed the custom of many old men and was up at 5:33 AM. I tiptoed downstairs, went out to the car, explored Mount Kisco, sipped a cup of coffee at Dunkin Donuts—yes, and had a doughnut, and yes, juice to get down my six pills I take because of previous doughnuts—bought the Sunday *New York Times*, sat in the car reading it, and now, at eight AM sit at the head of the stairs where I can stretch my legs, flex my football knee, and read my book and wait.

It has been a good morning, and I feel little guilt that I have not been able to sleep in. They will laugh at my compulsion to be up and doing, and I will tease them for their laziness, but they will not understand the joy I, like many over sixties, experience when I am up in the lonely hours of dawn.

I ruminate—early morning is ideal for rumination—on the fact that as a child I was always up early when I could lose myself in a book—no TV then—explore the backyard or the vacant lot where the morning glories grew.

Awake before the grown-ups, I could be what I needed to be: Lindbergh crossing the Atlantic alone, Admiral Byrd isolated in his tiny room under the Antarctic ice, the unnamed Indian scout watching the palefaces land on the Maine coast.

As a teenager I bicycled my route for Gallagher's News Agency in Quincy finishing before the sun was up, drove Miller's grocery truck to market in Boston or cleaned the vegetables and laid them out in rows on the boxes balanced in front of the small store on Beach street.

Only now I confess that when I nicked myself trimming the lettuce that was packed in ice, my hands numb and clumsy, I would turn that lettuce head so the blood did not show. I was apprentice to Miller's game: profit through deceit.

I still remember playing grown-up early in the morning, the grocer's apron twice tucked so it did not sweep the sawdust strewn floor. The profit would be Miller's not mine, but I anticipated the customers who might, this Depression Saturday, pay cash. That anticipation would last until midnight when Mr. Miller would go out and scan the street right and left and reluctantly, when no one was on the street, give the command to close.

In combat I preferred the early morning patrols, guard duty when I was alone to watch the theatre of morning's change from dark to light, the promise of a new day even when the landscape was littered with last night's dead.

After college I worked for a morning newspaper and liked the mystery and companionship of the night worker, enjoyed the coming home at dawn. Eventually I returned to days, and morning became my best writing time as it is for most writers.

Goethe advised, "Use the day before the day. Early morning hours have gold in their mouth." John Hersey testified that "To be a writer is to sit down at one's desk in the chill portion of every day, and to write." A few years ago poet Donald Hall said, "I get up at 5 without an alarm. This morning I didn't get up until 5:45, because I stayed up until 11:15 watching the NCAA basketball. But in summer I'll be up at 4:30, make coffee, let out the dog, go pick up *The Boston Globe*. Then I write."

> THIS MORNING I DIDN'T GET UP UNTIL 5:45, BECAUSE I STAYED UP UNTIL 11:15 WATCHING THE NCAA BASKETBALL. BUT IN SUMMER I'LL BE UP AT 4:30, MAKE COFFEE, LET OUT THE DOG, GO PICK UP *THE BOSTON GLOBE*. THEN I WRITE."

In retirement I, like so many other over sixties, still get up early when there are no cows to milk, no commuter train to meet, no factory shift to join. It is habit, but for me a habit built not from compulsion but delight.

Sitting at the top of the stairs waiting for the young—and the not-so-young Minnie Mae—to wake, I try to define the strange emotion I feel. At last it comes to me. I am, after a lifetime of chasing the carrot, content.

I have another day to celebrate. Sitting here alone, I can enjoy the feeling of this house that is turning so quickly into a home. I am comfortable in this home and know that soon my wife will wake with a groan and a smile, and downstairs I will hear conversation and music, smell coffee and we will all make plans for the day not too far off when a grandchild will sit where I sit, perhaps beside me, waiting for another day to begin.

The grandchild has arrived. His name is Joshua. I have not yet sat beside him at the top of the stairs but I will.

THE NARRATIVE

There are many wonderful ways to tell stories, but I suggest student fiction writers begin with the scene.

Conrad is supposed to have said that a novel is a series of scenes of confrontation. The writer experienced in nonfiction tells *about* the story; the fiction writer *reveals* the story. That is an enormous difference, and the writing of a scene is the best way to cross the divide. Students can draw on their experiences with TV and film. The reader observes a room with the fourth wall removed; the action within the room tells the story and the reader discovers its meaning. As the short-story writer Becky Rule points out, students think that fiction has no rules, but the rules come from the story, and they are established early; if Hamlet is an indecisive prince he can suddenly become a king but not a decisive one.

Some notes on the craft of narrative.

- Start with character, not theme. The story and its meaning are revealed through the interaction of the characters.
- Write in the third person. It gives you more room and detachment.
- Dialogue is action, what the characters do to each other. Joan Didion says, "I don't have a very clear idea of who the characters are until they start talking."
- Point of view is where the camera is positioned to record the scene. In the beginning, stick with one point of view, perhaps entering into one head but not jumping in and out of every head. If you are in one sister's head, you don't know Frank is in the freezer; in the other sister's head, you do.
- Kurt Vonnegut counsels, "Don't put anything in a story that does not reveal character or advance the action."

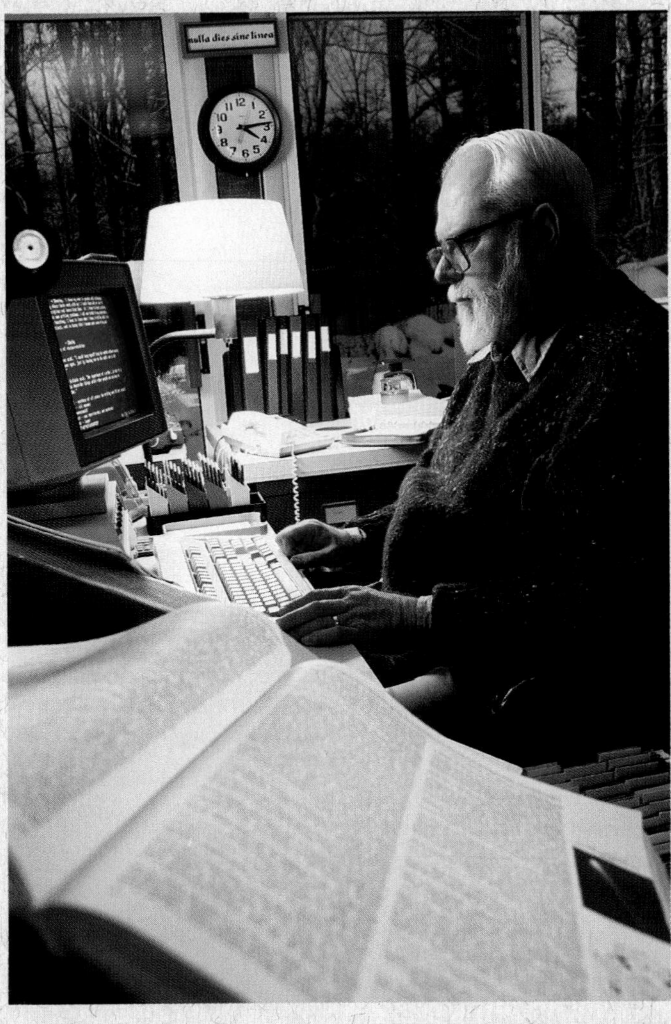

In writing a draft of my novel, I found myself stealing the experience from my own essay and began a scene:

Melissa found lain sitting in the shadows at the top of the stairs, "It's 5:30 in the morning."

He nodded.

"On guard duty?"

"In a way. I often sit here in winter, watch the light just before dawn, the woods, the field that goes down to the lake."

She thought for a moment of what it would be like to be a spy to your life, always on guard and asked, "You said last night that wherever you are, you see a field of fire, are aware of where to dig in, put the machine guns, even after all these years?"

"I'm not proud of it, Melissa. It's just my geography, an infantryman's geography."

"Do you always see a geography of war?"

"Always first, then I can make it go away. Most times. It's natural, just the way I see things. The doctor sees you as kidney or a colon; I'm an old soldier, I see a field of fire, where the attack would come from."

"That's sad."

"Tedd's a soldier too, Melissa."

They hear the key probe for the lock, at last find it, and hurried down the stairs....

That is just a small fragment of narrative, and yet you can see how the story is revealing itself dramatically to the writer and the reader.

THE POEM

Poetry is the most disciplined and difficult form of writing. It is also the most fun. Experience is distilled by the writing of poetry. Poetry is always play—play with image and language so that meaning is revealed directly without rhetoric getting between the writer and reader or between experience and reader. Inexperienced poets often write with adjectives and adverbs, trying to describe their own feelings. The experienced poet writes with information, revealing specifics, provocative details, and compelling images that make the reader feel and think. The meaning is rarely stated but always there. In the poem, even more than fiction, the meaning is implied. The poem is the stimulus to the reader's thinking.

Some notes on the craft of poetry.

- Forget, for the moment, rhyme, meter, and traditional verse forms.

• Brainstorm images and other specifics, creating a list that may become a poem.
• Draft lines—not sentences but fragments of language—that capture an event, person, or place.
• Rearrange the lines until they reveal a meaningful pattern.
• Pay attention to the line breaks, trying to end on a strong word that causes the reader to read on.

The morning I wrote the column, I also wrote, on the computer, what might become a poem for my poetry group that was meeting that Thursday evening. I pasted this in my daybook:

Sitting at the top of the
stairs
I listen to the silences
to understand Grandma's
war with Mother

Sitting at the top of the
stairs
I tune
train myself to l
elinesss

Later that day I made a handwritten note I also cut out and pasted in the daybook:

I lived at the top of the
stairs, behind the living room
couch, under the dining room
table, the tent of tablecloth–
in the apple tree, under the
porch,

And still later I drafted a poem that went through one radical and three or four extensive revisions (periods of word play) until it became the following completed poem:

Childhood Espionage

Spy to my life, I lived at the
top of the stairs, recorded
silence, mapped how hurt was
done. Under the porch, at the
bedroom door, behind living
room

sofa, I filled notebooks with
what was not said, not done,
escaped to the sidewalk, tried
to read the shades drawn
against my life. It must be
Mother's shadow

sitting on the edge of the
double bed, must be father's
kneeling to pray. I cannot be
sure, circle the block,
listen to the neighbor's opera
of argument , stand under

an open window where
conversation will pour over me
Once I saw my friend's older
sister. She never pulled the
shade. The dogs learned my
smell

and let me patrol back yard,
alley, vacant lot, in silence. I
found the room where the
Beckers kept the boy with the
enormous head, watched
comfort flow

from a priest's dancing hands
as he gave the last rites to
Vinnie's grandma, swayed to
the rhythm of the Mitchells'
bedroom dancing, lying down.
Late, I returned to the home

of closed doors where we
passed each other without
touching. We never raised our
voices, never stood between

light and shade, never let a
secret fall out a window.

Students should be encouraged to take central experiences from their lives—Willa Cather said, "Most of the basic material a writer works with is acquired before the age of fifteen"—and explore them with an array of genre, using each lens—essay, narrative, poem—and then examining the subject through other genre, perhaps argument, report, screenplay, or news story, to discover the many meanings in their lives.❦

Sources quoted include Grace Paley, Joan Didion, and Kurt Vonnegut cited in the following work: Donald M. Murray, *Shoptalk: Learning to Write with Writers*, Boynton/ Cook Publishers, Inc., 1990.

ELEMENTS OF WRITING addresses the *aims* and *modes* of writing and the *writing process* in the following ways:

Pupil's Edition
Demonstrates and teaches writing skills, focusing on the aims (the *why*) and the modes (the *how*) of writing
Provides an organized, easily understood approach that allows students to gain and sharpen writing skills

Annotated Teacher's Edition
Gives instructional strategies on how to teach the aims and modes
Offers lesson plans based on each stage of the writing process

Teacher's ResourceBank ™
Offers materials keyed to the writing process that assist students in achieving the aims and modes

By James L. Kinneavy

Meet the Aims and Modes of Writing

The place to start (and end) the teaching of writing is to have students see what written language can do for them.

Why Write? Where Do I Begin?

Writing is a very complex activity, and so is the teaching of writing. I admit these facts, and I have been teaching writing for fifty years. You may be teaching your first class this year, and you probably have the same problem: In the face of this complex process, where do you start?

Some teachers recommend what may seem to be a very simple and logical approach: Start with the simple building blocks of writing and gradually work up to more complex blocks. In other words, teach students some elementary things about words, then move up to phrases, afterwards teach sentences, eventually work up to paragraphs, and finally, have students write full themes. Some say that this is how children learn to use language orally. At first blush this theory has a kind of plausible simplicity to it. Years of research, however, have shown that it doesn't work and that it isn't the way children learn language.

Language Gets Things Done

Babies see that family members around them accomplish things by using language, and they quickly learn to use it themselves to get food, drink, or attention. This is the motivation behind all language acquisition and usage, from cradle to grave—language gets things done.

Consequently, if we can keep this elementary driving force behind our attempts to teach writing (or any language art for that matter), we can draw on a basic incentive that even babies understand. But when language teaching is divorced from getting things done, students rightly find it boring and uninteresting.

For this reason, the place to start (and end) the teaching of writing is to have students see what written language can do for them. What can writing do? In one introductory chapter, we attempt to get students to look around and see what language is getting done. We call language-users the hidden agents behind many of the miracles of our age, we say that language is where the action is, and we call language-users the movers and shakers of the world.

We focus the student's attention on the different kinds of things that language accomplishes, using very concrete examples. But the principle is the same at every grade-level and on into the college educations, careers, and adult lives of our graduates: The central concept in the teaching of writing at every level is an awareness of the aims or purposes of writing.

The Four Major Aims of Writing

Luckily for you, as well as for the students, these aims are not infinite, unpredictable, and unmanageable. They can be reduced to a few basic categories, and both you and the students have a good deal of practical experience with the categories in general. For example, one kind of language experience with which you are very familiar has to do with attempts to explain to or inform an audience about something of which it is partially or totally ignorant. You do this daily in the classroom and the students are the targets of this use of language. Other examples of this kind of writing are news stories in newspapers and magazines, encyclopedia articles, reports, textbooks, discussions, proposed solutions to problems, research studies, etc. The emphasis is always on the subject matter, considered more or less objectively. *This kind of writing is generically referred to as expository writing.*

As a teacher, you are only too aware of a second kind of writing that places more emphasis on the writer. In this case, the writing reveals the feelings of the writer, allows the writer to voice his or her aspirations or reactions to something in a quite personal way, or gives the writer a chance to articulate important beliefs. Examples of this kind of writing are journals, diaries, myths, prayers, credos, and protests. Of course, some of this writing may also overlap with other kinds. The major emphasis in this kind of writing is on the writer. *This kind of writing is often called expressive writing.*

As a teacher, you often try to convince your students of the importance of an education and of their duties as citizens. As a matter of fact, in our culture we are bombarded with attempts to get readers to vote a certain way, to change attitudes or beliefs, to buy certain products, to switch allegiances, etc. Examples of such writing are advertising, political speeches, legal oratory, editorials, and religious sermons. In all of these cases, the focus of the use of language is on the receiver of the message. *Usually, this kind of writing is called rhetorical or persuasive writing.*

A fourth kind of writing, probably your favorite, is literature. This type of writing is given an honored place in English classes. We read selections of literature. They are intended to delight us and sometimes to teach us lessons. Examples of literature range from simple jokes, funny stories, ballads, small poems, and TV sitcoms to serious dramas, movies, novels, and epics. We try to get students to write this way when we teach creative writing. *Although all writing involves originality, we usually reserve the term* creative writing *for this kind of writing.*

THE COMMUNICATION BASIS OF THE AIMS OF WRITING

As a perceptive reader, you may have noticed as we went through the four major aims of writing that each one emphasized a different element of the communication process. It is not accidental that the major purposes of writing generally can be reduced to four. The structure of the written communication process is based on a writer, a reader, a language, and the subject matter; you may have seen these elements presented in a graphic form, such as the communication triangle shown below.

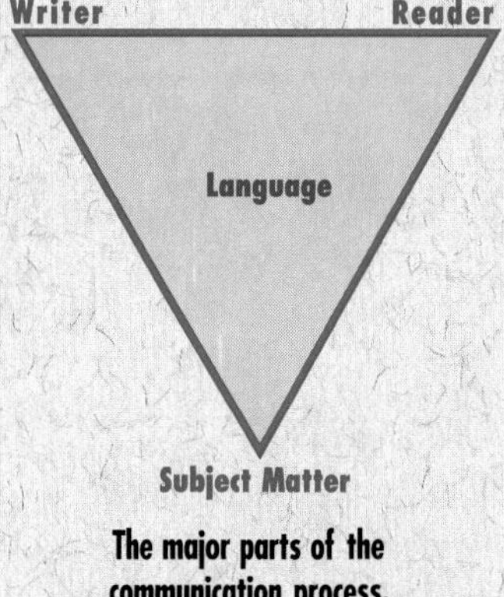

The major parts of the communication process.

You will find that students usually recognize that these four elements all play an important role in the writing process, but it is more difficult to get them to see that the role of each element changes in the different aims of writing.

CHANGING ROLES OF ELEMENTS IN DIFFERENT AIMS

In the expressive aim, as we pointed out above, the major focus of the attention is on the writer; the reader, language, and subject matter take on secondary roles. In persuasion, on the other hand, the reader takes center stage; the writer, though present, wants to get the message acted upon and uses language and subject matter to achieve this end.

In expository writing, the subject matter is given the lead role in the communication drama; the writer, reader, and language are subordinate to the explanation, proof, or communication of information that is involved. In literature, finally, the emphasis is on the beauty of the literary craftsmanship as an object of delight to the reader; the subject matter and the author, though present, are not as important as the literary object. When we are studying *Huck Finn*, the novel is more important than either Mark Twain or life on the Mississippi as experienced by a young white boy and a black man.

To assist you to get students to see these differing roles, the relationship between the elements of the communication process and those of the aims of discourse is expressed graphically below (the major aims of writing and the main parts of the communication process).

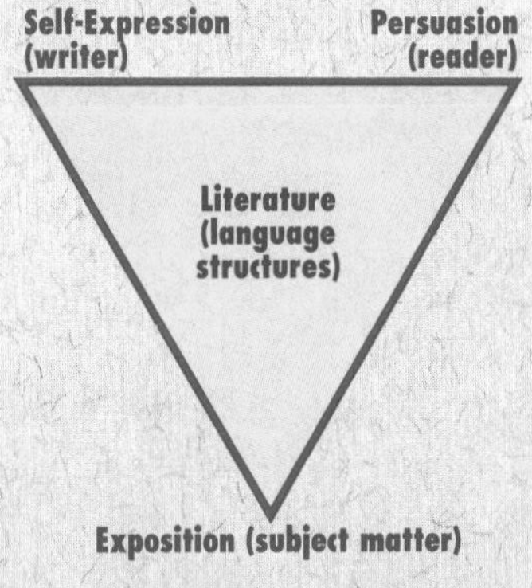

The major aims of writing.

Consequently, from aim to aim there is a continual shifting of roles in the communication process. The lead role determines the major purpose of the writing and the other roles become subordinate. Many teachers have found that this simple diagram enables students to grasp the changing dynamics of language use.

AS A TEACHER, YOU OFTEN TRY TO CONVINCE YOUR STUDENTS OF THE IMPORTANCE OF AN EDUCATION . . .

DOMINANT AIMS AND OVERLAP

As a teacher, you have probably written one or two of these different kinds of writing, but you may not have written all of them. In your own writing you are certainly aware that most writing does not attempt to achieve all of these aims at the same time. A specific piece of writing usually has a single dominant aim, subordinating the others to avoid conflicts and confusion. Though subordinate, the other aims are still present. Thus, movie ads in the newspaper contain important information about actors, actresses, directors, titles, show times, etc., but the information is there to persuade people to come to the movies.

Similarly, a scientific report proving that smelters of Sudbury, Ontario, affect the ecology of the area emphasizes in an objective way the evidence for this hypothesis. But there is clearly the implicit notion that something ought to be done about it (a persuasive strain). Indeed, all the aims overlap each other.

WHY ARE THE BASIC AIMS IMPORTANT?

Despite overlaps, however, it is quite important to distinguish the various aims. It is crucial that both teachers and students understand why.

As a teacher, you are very aware that the criteria by which one kind of discourse is judged are different from the criteria by which another kind of discourse is judged. You know and try to impress upon your students that expository writing is judged on the basis of objective evidence; the appeal of the writer as such is not relevant to the final proof or explanation, nor is the use of emotion or humor. For this reason, you know that when you teach expository writing, it is important to discourage the use of these other kinds of appeal—they are, in fact, considered inappropriate in news stories, scientific reports, or textbooks. Thus the pedagogy of expository writing follows from the nature of this kind of writing.

But when you switch to teaching other kinds of writing, these other appeals are positive and important. In persuasion, for example, the emphasis is on the appeal of the writer and the appeal to the interests of the audience. The differences among exposition, persuasion, literature, and self-expression force you to emphasize different criteria when teaching these different kinds of writing. There is no single criterion of aim which makes all writing good. That is why the different aims are taught separately.

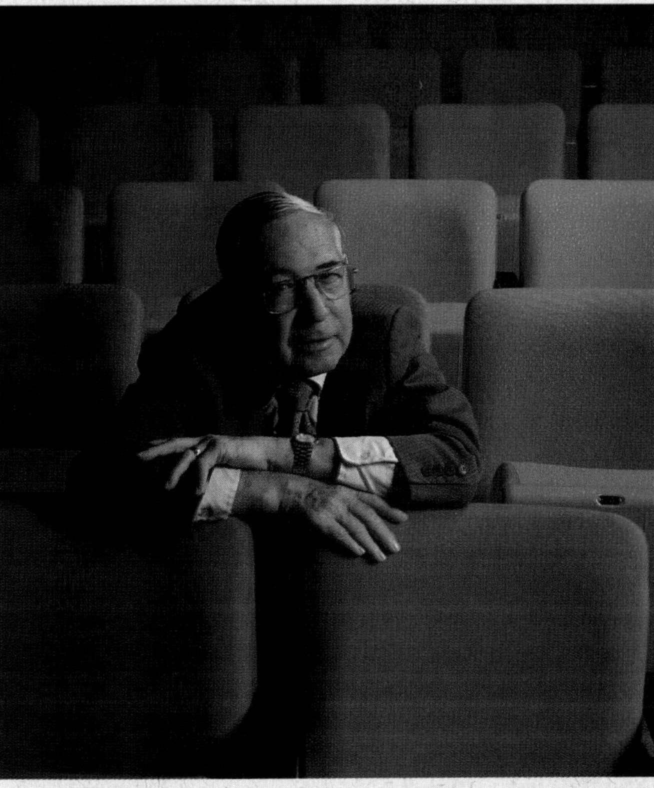

JAMES L. KINNEAVY
AUTHOR OF
ELEMENTS OF WRITING

THE MODES OF WRITING

After all this talk about the aims of writing, you, as a teacher, might very well say to me, "Well, Mr. Kinneavy, all this may be very true. But are you maintaining that if I get students to pay attention to the aims of their writing, all other problems will disappear? There are many other facets of the process of writing to which we teachers have to pay attention. Grammar is clearly a persistent concern, as are spelling, vocabulary, sentence structure, paragraphing, genres of writing (letter, report, story, poem, speech, ad, etc.), subject matter, and last but not least, the modes. What do you propose to do with all of these issues?"

I recognize all of these concerns and reply that they will be given close and continuous attention throughout the entire course, but in this introduction I would like to stress the last dimension, that of the modes of writing.

This dimension bridges the two mentioned just before it—genre and subject matter, and it implicates a major concern of all writing teachers—organization. More than any other aspect of writing, modes determine overall organization. This particular essay, for example, is a series of classifications and definitions.

At times in the history of writing, modes have been given almost as much attention as the aims, but most of the time they have been a serious second candidate. The modes are listed differently in various books. In this textbook we call narration, description, classification, and evaluation the modes. They could be called the genres of writing, and they could be called ways of looking at subject matter.

USE THE NEWSPAPER TO DISPLAY THE MODES

When I want to introduce students to the modes, I use a newspaper. I ask students to find examples of news stories (narratives). I ask them to find classifications, especially in the classifieds, as they are called. I ask the students to examine individual items within each section of the classifieds and to tell me what the details are. It becomes clear to them that there are hundreds of specific descriptions of cars, houses, lost dogs, jobs, etc., in the classifieds. Finally, I have the students check reviews of books, movies, television programs, concerts, football games, etc. These are all evaluations. Modes are as ubiquitous as the aims of writing.

Like the aims, the modes have to be taught separately. What makes a good narrative is not what makes a good evaluation or a good description or a good classification. The rules of defining are not at all the rules of narrating. As with the aims of writing, the modes of writing are different in nature and require different pedagogies. Consequently, the modes are given careful consideration in the following chapters.

THE PHILOSOPHIC BASIS OF THE MODES

You are probably wondering if there is a neat graphic structure that you can use to help students with the modes. Yes, there is. But, before it can be presented, let us ask the preliminary question, "What is a mode?"

WHAT IS A MODE?

A mode is a different perspective on a given subject matter. Take George Washington or a razor, two very different kinds of subject matter. I can write a history of George Washington or a history of the development of a given razor. I can describe the individuating characteristics of both. I can classify George Washington or a razor from several different viewpoints. Finally, I can evaluate George Washington, and I can evaluate the razor. Each of these discourses is a very different kind of writing.

What explains the differences? In other words, what differentiates narration from description, for example? Narration is always dynamic; it is concerned with change, whereas description is static. A narrator looks at the changing aspects of something, whereas a describer looks at the static aspects of the same thing.

When you are trying to get students to see the difference between description and classification, ask them what a description of Washington entails and what a classification of Washington would require. In description, the individuating characteristics of his personality are stressed (the father of our country, for example), but a classification of Washington pays attention to the different roles he assumed (president, general, husband, etc.). Both pay attention to Washington as static, and are therefore not like narration.

When you are trying to get students to differentiate narration from evaluation, first have someone tell a little of the history of Washington at Valley Forge. Then have someone evaluate Washington as a general. They will see that narration as such, simply details change in something, whereas evaluation considers that thing's performance against some norm and makes a judgment of approval or disapproval. Both narration and evaluation are dynamic: Narration details change, and evaluation considers performance.

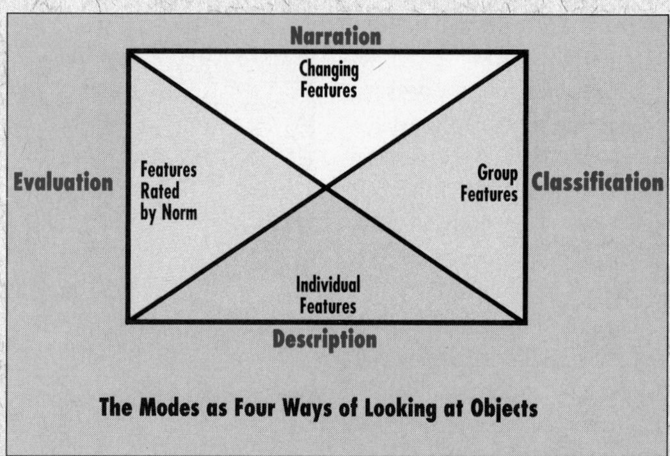

The Modes as Four Ways of Looking at Objects

These differences are shown above in **The Modes as Four Ways of Looking at Objects**.

In the textbook, these four modes will be continuously related to the aims. Anything that is written will always involve both an aim and a mode. Together, they solve nearly all of the organizational problems of writing, for either the aim or the mode determines the way the theme is laid out, as the following chapters will show. The aim especially determines the style, as will be made clear in each chapter. Thus, the aim and the mode of a given piece largely determine the main ideas, the overall organization, and the direction of the style.❦

ELEMENTS OF WRITING addresses the *aims* and *modes* of writing in the following ways:

Pupil's Edition
Demonstrates and teaches writing skills, focusing on the aims (the *why*) and the modes (the *how*) of writing
Provides an organized, easily understood approach that allows students to gain and sharpen writing skills

Annotated Teacher's Edition
Gives instructional strategies on how to teach the aims and modes

Teacher's ResourceBank ™
Offers materials keyed to the writing process that assist students in achieving the aims and modes

By Lee Odell

Showing vs. Telling:

Using Models in Teaching Writing

Make us see what you're talking about.

For some time now, teachers of writing have made a point of exhorting students to make their writing "show, not tell." Don't just tell us your reactions or opinions, we say to them. Make us see what you're talking about. If you're trying to describe a person, let us see facial expressions, details of clothing, mannerisms, actions; let us hear exactly what the person says. Or, if students are trying to write persuasively, we insist: Don't just give us your generalized conclusions. Give us some specific information that lets us see what you base your judgment on and that lets us decide for ourselves whether your judgment makes sense.

This advice is not an infallible, inflexible rule. Writers can't elaborate on everything. Furthermore, readers sometimes let a generalization pass unchallenged because it seems to ring true or because writers have sufficient authority for us simply to take their word on the matter. But if we are judicious in asking students to "show, not tell," the phrase constitutes good advice for writers and excellent advice for teachers. If we want students to make significant progress as writers, we will have to show them—not just tell them, *show*

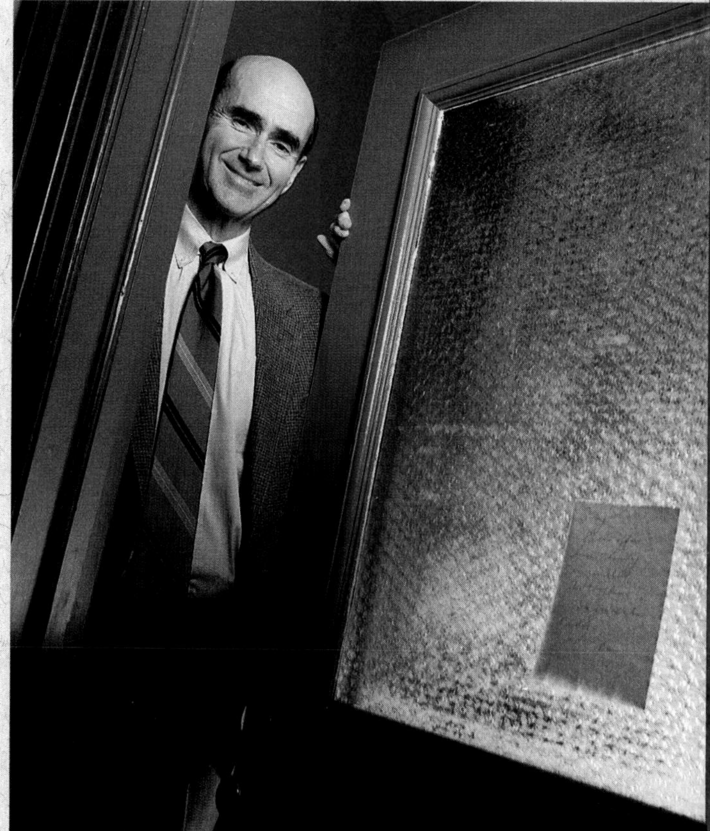

Lee Odell opens his classroom door at Rensselaer Polytechnic Institute.

them—what we mean. In effect, we need to make sure they have models, not just of the kinds of writing they will do but of the writing processes.

There is, of course, a long history to the practice of working with models. For centuries, teachers of rhetoric and writing have required students to study the works of great writers, sometimes having students copy model texts word for word or asking students to imitate the sentence structures they found in these works. Indeed, a version of this practice persisted through the middle 1980s in the form of sentence combining. This system did not ask students to emulate one specific writer, but it did show them frequently used sentence patterns in the works of highly admired professional writers so students could construct their own sentences based on a wide variety of these patterns.

Traditional approaches to using models have their uses, but these approaches are not what I'm talking about here. I'm suggesting that we depart from traditional practice in several ways. For one thing, the model should come not solely from famous authors but rather from books and magazines students read willingly and have readily accessible. Also, teachers don't have to provide all the models; students should be asked to bring in articles or excerpts from books that they personally find engaging and effective. Finally, these models should not be treated as though they are sacred; they are, instead, objects for analysis—for criticism as well as for praise. We and our students need to examine entire models where writers have used successful strategies that students might incorporate into their own writing, as the occasion warrants. But we and our students also need to identify things that don't work and maybe even to collaborate on devising ways to improve the model.

There are several ways we might use models, but my favorite is to use them to help students solve their own writing difficulties. For example, a number of my students can't figure out how to begin a piece of writing, what Donald Murray would refer to as a "lead." When this is a problem, I ask students to bring in copies of the first pages of articles that they somehow found themselves reading, even though the topics might not normally have concerned them.

For example, one student brought in an article entitled "Hell on Wheels," which began this way:

Almost from the time the downtown No. 4 subway train began its 21-mile run below New York City at 11:38 p.m. on the night of Tuesday, Aug. 27, something seemed amiss. Heading from the Bronx to Manhattan, the train overshot the platform at a couple of stations. At times it slowed to a crawl and then accelerated to breakneck speeds. The conductor contacted the motorman, Robert Ray, 38, several times on the intercom to find out if everything was all right. Ray replied that he was fine. But that was clearly not the case....

This article begins, of course, with a claim about a specific event ("something seemed amiss") and then illustrates this claim with a series of incidents. It mentions specific, troubling things that happened (for example, the train "slowed to a crawl and then accelerated to breakneck speeds"); it reports what people said to each other; and then it challenges what one of the people said ("But that clearly was not the case...."). In this last sentence, the author creates a conflict that engages the reader and lets the reader know what the rest of the article will be about (i.e., it will show how the driver's claim was "not the case").

> I DON'T WANT STUDENTS TO THINK THERE IS JUST ONE WAY TO BEGIN A PIECE OF WRITING.

Other articles brought in by the students began quite differently—by citing troubling statistics, for example, or by describing general trends in society that a reader was almost certain to know and be concerned about. These differences are important. I don't want students to think there is just one way to begin a piece of writing. Consequently, I photocopied a variety of examples and asked students to talk them through to identify the strategies writers had used to engage readers. My goal was to help students recognize some of the options that are open to them in doing their own writing.

In addition to bringing in models written by professionals, it can be extremely useful for us to bring in copies of our own efforts to do the same kind of writing students are working on. And once we have developed an atmosphere of trust, it can be useful to bring in effective examples of student work, continually asking such questions as these: What did the writer do here? How did he or she go about capturing our interest and letting us know what to expect in the rest of the text? Is there anything that this writer is doing that you might profitably do? Again, the goal is not to provide recipes or rules chiseled on tablets of stone but to get students to see what is possible.

MODELING THE COMPOSING PROCESS

Thus far, I have been describing ways we might use written products as models. In addition, we also need models of the composing processes of writers. This modeling can be as sophisticated or as rudimentary as our students need. It can focus on the work of an individual writer as Donald Murray shows in his "Use Genre as Lens" essay or on the efforts of peers as they revise their initial drafts. That is, we need to let students see the processes professional writers and students go through in doing their own writing and even in responding to classmates' writing.

There are several activities teachers can use that allow students to observe their peers' writ-

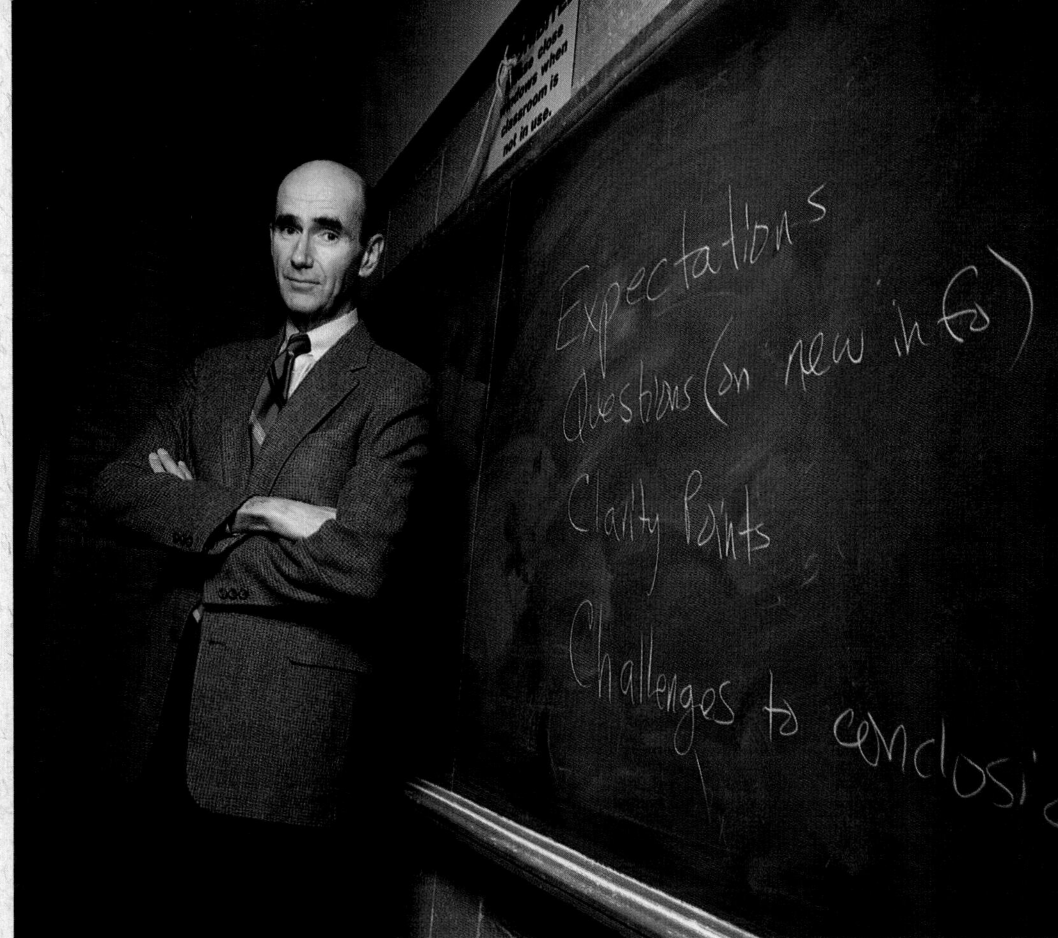

ing processes. For example, a colleague was concerned that her tenth-graders would have difficulty passing the state basic competency test that is required for high school graduation. Knowing that one of the questions on that test was likely to require students to report information in a well-organized form, she could have concentrated on paragraph form and the proper use of transitions. But suspecting that her students' difficulties were more profound than that, she decided that her students weren't paragraphing because they did not understand that certain kinds of expository paragraphs require writers to group facts by setting up categories that the paragraphs would be about.

Consequently, she asked students to watch a videotape of a movie that she was fairly certain they would find moving, an account of the difficulties encountered by a child who had been classified as mentally retarded but who had, nonetheless, a number of good traits and who was personally likable. After students had watched the videotape, she asked them to write down every fact they could remember from the movie and to collaborate as a class to make the list as complete as possible. That night she typed a complete list of facts, made an overhead transparency of them, and then cut the transparency into strips, each strip containing one fact.

The next day, she asked students to collaborate on ways to group these facts. For instance, students noticed that many of the facts pertained to ways people reacted to the young boy, while others could be grouped under such headings as the boy's reactions to other people or his abilities. As students discussed ways of grouping facts, the teacher reflected what they were saying by moving the transparency strips around on the overhead projector. She was showing, not telling, her students about the basic process they needed to create one type of organized paragraph.

Another approach to modeling the composing process comes from a ninth-grade teacher concerned that her students' descriptive writing was bland. She believed their real problem was not a lack of descriptive adjectives and adverbs but that students weren't really looking closely at the people or objects they were describing.

She also knew that television programs routinely provide excellent examples of the process of observing. That is, as a rule, television cameras do not stay in one spot to observe everything from the same angle and distance. Instead, the cameras change position to vary the angles and the distances from which they view things. For example, one detective program began with a close-up shot of a ringing phone. Then the camera moved back so that the viewers could see a well-dressed man hurrying across an elegant apartment toward the phone. Next, the camera moved in to focus on the man's trembling hands as he nervously dried his sweaty palms on his handkerchief before picking up the phone. Finally, the camera shifted focus again, to show the head and shoulders of a burly, unshaven man speaking into a pay phone. These shifts in focus set the scene for the entire episode.

To help students understand this process of observing by shifting focus, the teacher asked students, as part of their homework, to watch one of their favorite TV programs and to count the number of times the camera shifted its focus in a two-minute period. She also asked them to make notes about the different things they saw every time the camera shifted focus. The next day they discussed these episodes and concluded that a program in which the camera did not shift focus would almost certainly be dull.

To help students see how this process applied to writing, the teacher gave students the following description:

She probably has false teeth and wears glasses. She wears her hair up in a bun and wears dresses from the 1930s. She has a habit of tapping her pencil on her desk.

Students readily agreed that this passage was uninteresting. To help them see why, the teacher asked students to think of the grammatical subject of each sentence as the visual focus of the sentence. (In response to the predictable question, the teacher told students that, for this passage, they could think of the grammatical subject as "how the writer begins each sentence.") Students saw readily that this writer's "camera" was standing in one place, not shifting at all. So the teacher asked students to work in groups to revise the passage so that the grammatical focus reflected changes in visual focus.

As one group collaborated on revising the passage, the following discussion took place:

"OK. Let's start with her false teeth—yeah—write that down."

She has false teeth.

"No, dummy. We gotta start the sentence with 'her false teeth'."

Her false teeth.

"OK, now what?"

"Oh, no. If we start with that we gotta add stuff. Like....'Her false teeth look funny'."

"Yeah, put that down."

"No, you gotta tell what 'funny' means. She'll [the teacher] only ask 'What's funny mean?'"

"I got it." Her false teeth look yellow. *"My grandma's are."*

"Yeah, 'cause they're old, like her."

"Hey. Who's writing?"

"I am." Her false teeth are yellow because they're old.

"That's good."

"OK, now the stuff on glasses. Oh, gosh. We're gonna have to add stuff to everything!"

Indeed, they would. And that was just the point. Their teacher wanted them to see that as they shifted visual focus, they would have to explore their subject further. Not only was their teacher showing these students a fundamental process of observing, but also she was showing them how the process of observing translated into the process of writing.

In addition to modeling the writing process, we also need to model the process of responding to writing. It is true that students can learn to make very helpful comments about their peers' writing. But the important phrase here is *learn to*. As Karen Spear has pointed out in her excellent book *Sharing Writing*, working in response groups is a complex process. It requires that students be able to go beyond uninformative, global comments ("Yeah, it's pretty good." "I guess it's OK.") and do two things: pay attention to specific words, phrases, or ideas and explain why and how they personally react to those things. The ninth-grade class I've just described illustrates one way to model the process of responding. When the teacher asked students to revise the bland description, she was showing them a process they could use in responding to each other's drafts. That is, she was helping them see that when they responded to a classmate's descriptive writing, they might consider whether the student had shifted focus and whether the shifts in focus helped give the reader a clearer visual picture of the person, object, or place being described. Indeed, the teacher made sure students worked as a class to give this sort of response to one or two students' subsequent drafts.

But modeling the response process may not be enough. It may also be necessary to model the processes of listening to and using those responses. Listening can be especially difficult when the response implies that a writer's work is unclear or in need of further effort. In such cases, any writer—and students are no exception—may well become defensive, more eager to prove that responses are invalid or irrelevant than to listen to those responses and consider the uses they might have. In other words, students may need to learn how to respond to responses.

If so, teachers may need to model the way we want student writers to react to their classmates' comments. Specifically, we should bring in our own efforts to do some of the same writing students are doing and ask students to respond to it. Where is it clear or unclear? What sort of personality or attitude is our writing conveying? At what points have we said things that seem appropriate or inappropriate for the audience we are addressing? My experience in doing this sort of work with students is that if they trust us, they can be very perceptive and painfully direct. If they don't get it, they can tell us so in no uncertain terms. In doing so, they give us a chance to show how a writer listens to readers, not by arguing but by attempting to find out why readers react as they do and then using that information to revise a subsequent draft.

The process of modeling is, like everything else about teaching writing, a slow business. One example rarely does the trick. But if we are persistent in showing students what is involved in producing good writing through the writing process, we can usually count on results. But if we don't model, we should expect our distinction between *showing* and *telling* to fall on deaf ears. If we don't follow our own advice, why should they?❦

ELEMENTS OF WRITING addresses the ***writing process*** and ***cooperative learning*** in the following ways:

Pupil's Edition

Provides students with detailed instruction for each stage of the writing process

Provides numerous activities and exercises in the writing chapters for students to work cooperatively

Annotated Teacher's Edition

Offers lesson plans based on each stage of the writing process

Offers *COOPERATIVE LEARNING* features that suggest activities for teaching writing and grammar

Teacher's ResourceBank ™

Furnishes materials that can be used for peer evaluation

BY MAXINE HAIRSTON

THE JOY OF WRITING

STUDENTS NEED TO GET SOME FUN OUT OF WHAT THEY'RE DOING.

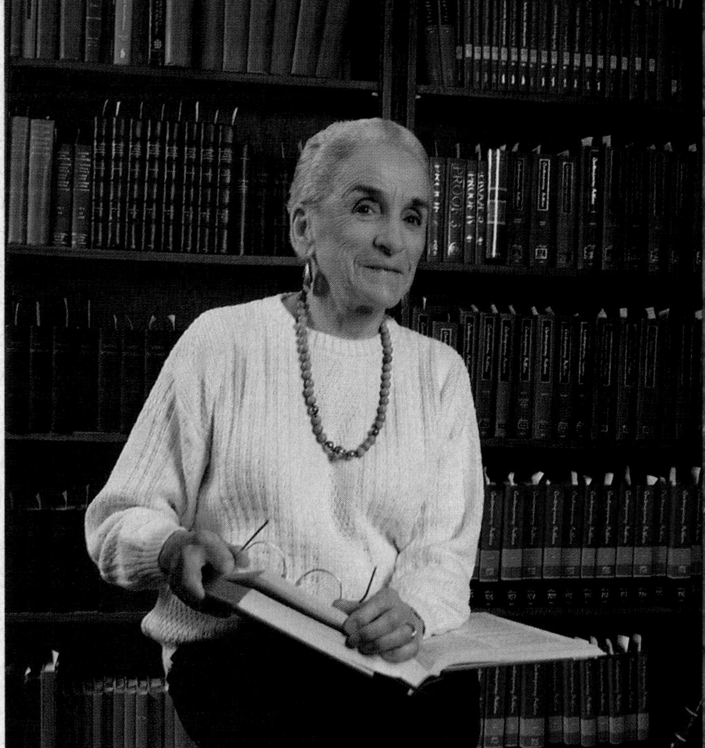

MAXINE HAIRSTON TAKES A BREAK FROM CLASSES.

In recent years I have come to believe that the most important job I can do as a writing teacher is to help my students enjoy writing. I say this because I'm convinced that unless students find some pleasure in their writing classes, most of them will not be willing to invest the time and energy required to turn out work that they—and we, as their teachers—can be proud of. Few adults are disciplined and determined enough to drudge away at some project—whether it's exercising or learning Spanish verbs—simply because someone else tells us that it will be good for us in the long run. We just won't stay with such projects unless there's some satisfaction in the process itself. How much harder it is, then, for youngsters to whom college or even next fall seems light years away to subject themselves to the hard work of learning to write if they get no pleasure from it at the time. Deficit motivation, working to avoid penalties or simply for a passing grade, isn't enough; students need to get some fun out of what they're doing. Fortunately, given what we now know about teaching the writing process, it's quite possible to create a writing classroom in which many students work from growth motivation; that is, they work at their writing because they enjoy doing it for its own sake.

Cognitive studies, ethnographic studies about writing, and the national projects argue that four characteristics define the congenial writing classroom, the kind in which students are likely to enjoy writing and to flourish as writers.

First, teachers provide a low-risk environment that encourages students to write without fear. Second, teachers have students develop their papers through a series of drafts and revisions. Third, teachers honor the students' right to their own writing, allowing students to choose their own topics and encouraging them to write about their interests. Fourth, teachers create and support a collaborative learning environment.

ESTABLISHING A LOW-RISK CLASSROOM

Creating a low-risk environment in the writing classroom may seem like a formidable challenge, and indeed it can be at the beginning of a new term when many students are as wary as stray cats. They're nervous for fear someone is going to try to trap them. In the first week of a writing class sometimes I feel as if I want to wear a banner across my chest, emblazoned with "Trust me! It's going to be all right!" But I can understand students' anxiety. Students who have come from writing courses with a heavy emphasis on rules and form, courses in which they did badly, have good reason to see a composition course as a high-risk situation. No wonder they start out by trying to stay in the safety zone of rules and formulas.

The humanistic psychologist Abraham Maslow theorizes that all people have two sets of forces operating within them: a need for safety and a fear of risk on one hand and an urge toward growth and autonomy on the other hand. Maslow also believes that every individual has an innate urge to create, to grow, to discover new abilities and talents. I agree; I think all children want to communicate, to write something that catches the interest and attention of others, but most will hesitate if they think they will be punished for breaking rules. As Maslow points out, "Safety needs are prepotent over growth needs....[and] in general, only a child who feels safe dares to grow forward healthily" (49). He adds, "Only the [teacher] who respects fear and defense can teach; . . . " (53).

The writing teacher's challenge is to foster the low-risk environment that will encourage creativity and expression but at the same time to work toward helping students master the writing conventions that they must know to be accepted as writers. There are several ways teachers can do this. First, of course, is to emphasize that we write in stages; we plan, we draft, we read and reread, and we revise. Final details matter when a writer gets ready to publish, but the most-productive writers learn how to suspend their error monitors in the early stages.

I have found it helps me to suspend my own error monitor when reading early drafts if I can put down my pencil and force myself to read strictly for content, good practice for trying to become a courteous reader. I ask myself, what is this writer trying to express? Why? How? Then I make only a large-scale response, focusing on being positive and on asking questions that could help the next draft. I emphasize that I hope to see substantial change and development in that draft. It would waste time even to mention error at this stage. When students realize that I really am not looking for mistakes in their drafts, they begin to relax and become more venturesome.

On second drafts, I still try to avoid writing on the paper, but focus on more specific suggestions for improvement. I also make checks in the margins to indicate potential trouble spots that the writers need to be aware of when they begin to polish their papers, sometimes adding a comment that the writer should be alert for problems with commas, subject-verb agreement, or whatever area seems most troublesome. This gives the writer specific areas to concentrate on at proofreading/editing time.

Probably one of the best ways to reduce risk in the writing classroom is to set up a portfolio system that allows students to draft a variety of papers over a period of time and then to choose a limited number to develop fully and submit for final evaluation. This method has become increasingly popular for a number of reasons. For one, student writers can work more as adult working writers do. They can attempt different kinds of writing, can stay with those projects that go well and, putting the others aside, they can invest as much as they like in them. It also gives students more control over the evaluation process. They decide which pieces they want evaluated; the teacher doesn't even have to see the others. There is considerable literature on the portfolio system if you find it an attractive option. (See also Elliot and Greenberg's essay "The Direct Assessment of Writing: Notes for Teachers.")

A final specific suggestion for reducing your students' anxieties is to establish a hierarchy of errors. We know from research that not all errors are created equal. Some are truly damaging: for instance, wrong verb forms, egregious sentence fragments, double negatives, and faulty parallelism. Errors like these set off alarms for most readers. Others, such as split infinitives, comparison of absolutes, or misusing *lie* and *lay* cause scarcely a riffle with most audiences. We should be lenient about such lapses and reduce the number of things our students have to worry about.

IN THE FIRST WEEK OF A WRITING CLASS SOMETIMES I FEEL AS IF I WANT TO WEAR A BANNER ACROSS MY CHEST, EMBLAZONED WITH "TRUST ME! IT'S GOING TO BE ALL RIGHT!"

We should also remember that the more a writer attempts, the more mistakes he or she is likely to make. But if we are encouraging growth, we need to let student writers know that we regard such mistakes as the natural accompaniment of growth and as less important than the students' fresh ideas.

TEACHING THE WRITING PROCESS THROUGH A SYSTEM OF DRAFTS

Because this textbook so strongly emphasizes that drafting, evaluating, and revising are essential parts of the writing process, I don't feel I need to build an elaborate case for having students develop their papers in drafts. Fortunately, with most writing teachers and curriculum supervisors embracing the concept of writing as a process, students accept drafting as a routine practice. I hope so, because students write more freely and more confidently when they know that their readers view their drafts as "work in progress," not as finished products to be critiqued and judged. Under such a system, knowing they're not irrevocably committed to what they've written, writers can afford experiments. Writing tentatively, they can count on getting help from their readers to help them work out their ideas. That's very reassuring, particularly to students who haven't written much and aren't sure they have anything to say.

The less articulate, inexperienced writers are probably those who get the most out of numerous drafts because they have the opportunity to improve first attempts substantially before they must submit the papers for evaluation. They also have the chance to get feedback *during* the writing process, feedback that is far more valuable than comments on a paper that has already been graded. We know that many students, perhaps even most, pay scant attention to comments written on graded papers, especially negative comments. But when they get comments—both written and oral—on drafts, they are likely to pay attention because they use them to real advantage.

> WRITING CAN BECOME A GENUINE JOY FOR GOOD WRITERS WORKING AT THEIR PEAK.

Good students also benefit from drafts, although sometimes they may resist doing them because the system requires more work than they've usually had to do in order to get good grades. But for some good writers, developing a paper through drafts can be a heady experience as they tap into talent they didn't know they had and then earn new recognition from their peers. Writing can become a genuine joy for good writers working at their peak.

In my opinion, the worse possible system for having students write papers is to give a fresh assignment each week, have everyone write the paper only once and turn it in for a grade, and then return the graded papers and repeat the process. Under such circumstances, the anxiety level skyrockets for all but the most able students, writers get no help during the process (when they need it most), and teachers never learn what most students can really do. Even when students write in class, those papers should be drafts that they can work on again during the next class periods. Only then are students likely to develop their potential.

LETTING STUDENTS CHOOSE THEIR OWN TOPICS FOR WRITING

After several years of having students choose their own writing topics, I am committed to the practice because it has several invaluable benefits. First, most students have never had an opportunity to write about matters they're genuinely interested in and can write about with authority. Too often they see traditional assignments that ask everyone to write on the same topic as meaningless exercises in which the teacher seems to be forgetting that students are individuals.

Second, students are more likely to put time and energy into their writing when they can explore topics that interest them. When students are writing on their own topics, they may also discover a potent truth: Writing is a powerful tool for learning, one that will serve them well.

Third, when students choose their own topics, a rich diversity can develop as they write about their own special interests. Some students may write about family rituals that come from their ethnic heritages or about unusual people in their families; others may write about living in another country or on a military base; others may write about hobbies—bicycling or scuba diving or canoeing. The possibilities are almost endless. In many schools, a rich multicultural tapestry can emerge as students from diverse backgrounds and cultures read each other's work and share stories.

Fourth, students will become more confident writers because they have more control over their writing. As they develop their expertise in some area, they begin to realize how much they know about something, whether it's car stereos or cooking hamburgers. They can take on a new identity in the class and find that people pay attention to what they have to say. That's good for all of us.

Finally, when students choose their own writing topics, the class simply becomes more interesting for everyone. Students may cover a remarkable range of subjects, and even those writing on similar topics bring different perspectives to them. Boredom drops quickly because everyone is constantly learning directly from other people's experiences. Perhaps the greatest bonus is to teachers, who not only garner a wealth of information about their students, but also over a period of years become mini-experts on numerous topics. Furthermore, they are spared trying to think up a good writing topic and then having to read fifty papers on that topic.

I BELIEVE STRONGLY IN PEER GROUPS AND COLLABORATIVE LEARNING IN WRITING CLASSES.

It does take considerable class time to help select topics, since many students will protest that they have nothing to write about, but such obstacles can be overcome in a few days of brainstorming and group work in class. As teacher, you can come in with a list of possible topics and then work with the class to generate subtopics. Or ask everyone to bring in a list of fifteen things to write about, encouraging the concrete and specific rather than large, abstract categories.

I have had good success with asking students to choose a general topic to write on for the whole term and then to pick subtopics for individual papers. That way they get into their topics in some depth and eliminate the process of having to work through choosing a fresh topic for each paper. You may want to specify the kinds of papers students write within their topics—informative, expressive, persuasive, and so on—to focus the class within the formats they're learning from the textbook.

ESTABLISHING A COLLABORATIVE-LEARNING CLASSROOM

I believe strongly in peer groups and collaborative learning in writing classes. Perhaps their greatest advantage is that they give students an immediate sense of audience, something that's hard to achieve when the teacher is the only reader for the drafts. Usually they respect each other's opinions; in fact, they may take their peers' responses more seriously than they do the teacher's because they feel closer to peers and they genuinely want to communicate.

Students also begin to see how useful collaboration can be for generating ideas. Most students in writing groups readily admit how much their classmates have contributed to the final versions of their papers. Each class period when I hand back graded papers, I pick two or three of the best ones to read aloud and then ask the writer and the writer's group to comment on how the paper developed through drafts. Their accounts are revealing, and the investment they feel in each other's work is truly gratifying.

I favor randomly chosen groups of at least four students so if someone is absent, the discussion doesn't break down. I reorganize groups to allow working with as many writers as possible. This arrangement also enhances every student's exposure to diverse cultural experiences as they get to know other students more closely. Managing groups in the classroom may not be easy, although I suspect trained secondary teachers know considerably more about it than most college teachers do. For the teacher who doesn't feel comfortable with groups, there is considerable literature on the concept. (See the professional bibliography on p. T74.)

Ultimately, groups help to establish the whole class as a community of writers who work together, feel a common sense of purpose, and see writing as a shared enterprise that's important to everyone. We all know intuitively that the most important element for achieving a congenial writing classroom is the teacher's attitude, and for that reason it's important for the teacher to be a part of that community, not to be an outside authority and a judge. Teachers need to write with students during writing workshops and share writing with them—its joys and frustrations. With luck and time, I am convinced that both teachers and students will enjoy being in a writing classroom more than they might have thought possible.

Work Cited

Maslow, Abraham. Toward a Psychology of Being, 2nd ed. New York: D. Van Nostrand Company. 1968.

ELEMENTS OF WRITING addresses students' understanding of the *writing process*, acceleration of learning through *cooperative group work*, and feedback to students through effective *assessment* in the following ways:

Pupil's Edition

Provides detailed instruction for each stage of the writing process

Provides numerous activities and exercises in the writing chapters for students to work cooperatively

Annotated Teacher's Edition

Provides students with detailed instruction for each stage of the writing process

Offers *COOPERATIVE LEARNING* features that suggest activities for teaching writing and grammar

Gives helpful assessment ideas in the *TIMESAVER*, *A DIFFERENT APPROACH*, and *ASSESSMENT* features

Teacher's ResourceBank ™

Offers materials keyed to the writing process that assist students in achieving the aims and modes

Furnishes materials that can be used for peer evaluation

Provides an **Assessment Portfolio** section and **Holistically Graded Composition Models** for the writing chapters

By Barbara J. Shade

Teaching for Learning's Sake

This approach to teaching will empower students as learners.

Helping students incorporate ideas, skills, and concepts that will improve their ability to perform tasks and to solve problems is the ultimate goal of teaching. Teachers who achieve this goal effectively find ways to accommodate students' different learning styles so that the teaching-learning process works more efficiently.

What do we mean by *learning styles*? Over the years, researchers have identified three dimensions in which students have specific learning preferences: (1) their preferences for various environmental factors that influence the learning climate; (2) their preferences about the ways they choose to engage in the learning process (motivational style); and (3) their preferences for the various ways in which they process information (cognitive style).

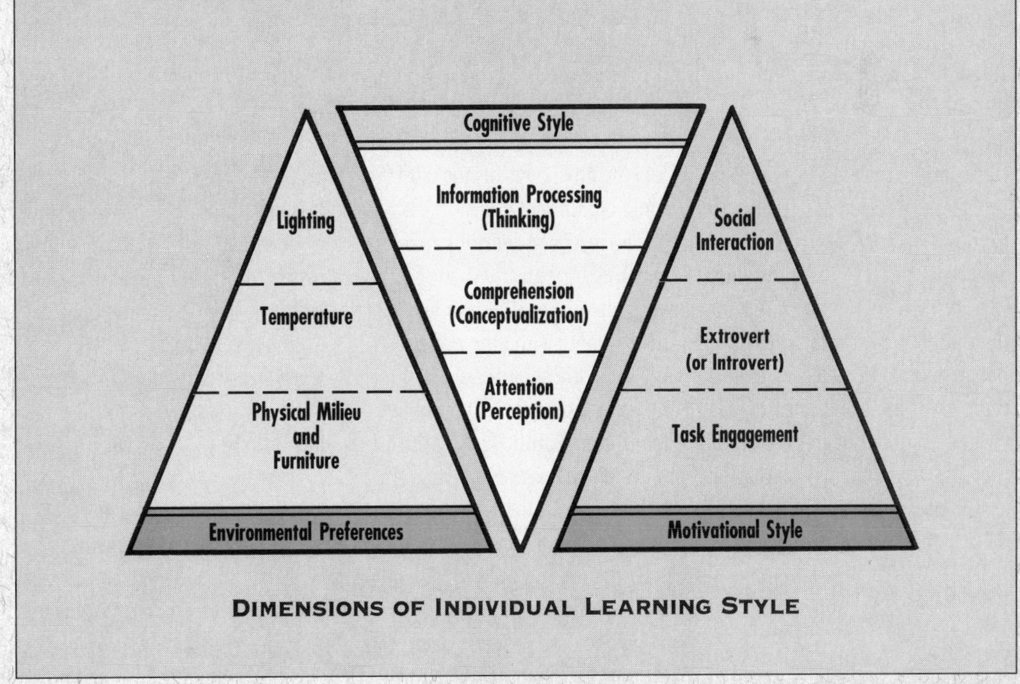

Dimensions of Individual Learning Style

ENVIRONMENTAL PREFERENCES

Individual environmental preferences focus on the lighting, temperature, and furniture used in the learning process. For example, some individuals might prefer bright light while others prefer it muted; some might prefer a warm room while others like it cool. A variation in studying postures has also been noted, with some individuals preferring to sit in a traditional classroom desk while others prefer to stand or recline when engaged in a learning task.[1]

MOTIVATIONAL STYLE

The second dimension of learning style focuses upon the extent to which students take responsibility for their own learning. Teachers often incorrectly assume that students' desire to engage in work is inherent. As with other aspects of learning, the extent to which individuals become involved in work depends upon how they have been socialized to respond to work. Some students, for example, have been taught to rely on others for assistance, to follow directions as given, and to perform the task as modeled. Others have been made more independent of others and have been taught to work alone, to find their own solutions, and to decide whether or not they can complete the work before asking for assistance. Corno and Mandinach refer to this stylistic dimension as a preference for resource management, and students tend to use the approach that makes them feel the most comfortable and the most competent.

The teaching-learning process involves human interaction, and students prefer different levels of involvement with others, depending upon the social and personality development that emanates from their families and communities. Families stressing prosocial behavior encourage children to help, to share, and to work toward benefiting others.

These students are more likely to give and receive assistance in the learning process and to like cooperative-learning ventures. Children trained to be highly individualistic and self-oriented are less likely to cooperate and offer help. Learners with this orientation function well in a competitive setting because they prefer to work alone and are less likely to enjoy cooperative-learning activities unless there is a reward or a method of accommodating their need for individuality.

COGNITIVE STYLE

The least discussed dimension of learning style—that of cognitive style—represents individually preferred ways of perceiving, organizing, and evaluating information so that it can be learned.

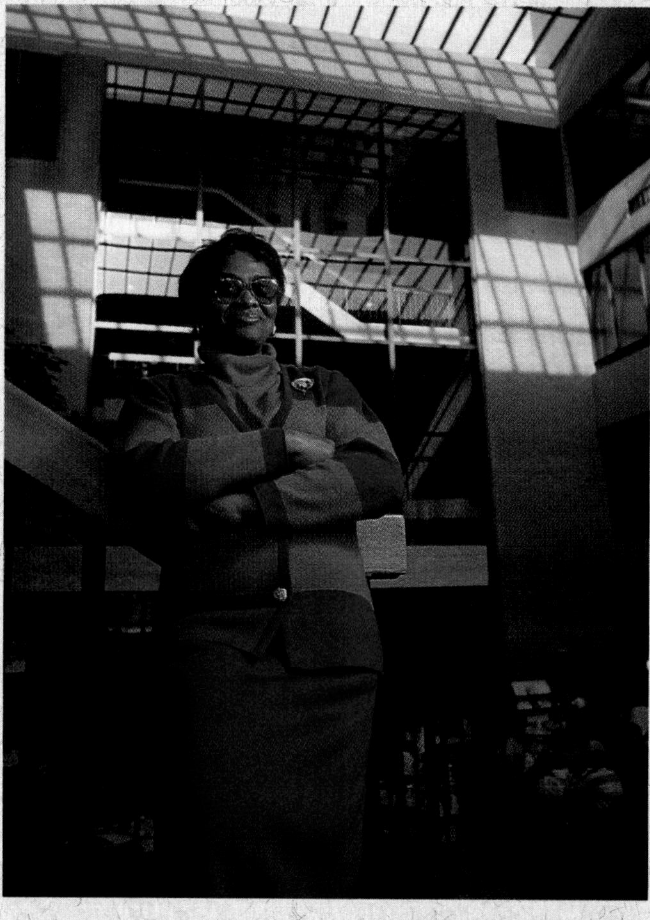

BARBARA SHADE AT UNIVERSITY OF WISCONSIN-PARKSIDE CAMPUS.

Three cognitive processes influence the way individuals acquire and produce knowledge. These are the perceptual, the conceptual, and the evaluative processes.

1. Perceptual Processes: The most recognized area in learning-style literature, this area focuses on the sensory modalities. Through cultural socialization, learners develop a preference for either the visual modality (photographs, graphs, art, texts); the aural modality (records, tapes, lectures); the haptic/kinesthetic modality (group discussions, interactive debates, drama); or some combination of these. Instruction delivered through the preferred modality establishes an instant rapport that allows students to process information more easily.

Different cultures socialize their children to attend to different cues in the environment; therefore, students have selective attention. Some students focus their attention on the task or idea being presented. For others, the people, their peers, their self-evaluation, or even the teacher's reaction to them are the most important elements on which to focus. How children choose to attend to cues is an important dimension of learning, and teachers who wish to ensure cognitive engagement find ways to influence the perceptive focus of the students.

[1] For a more detailed description of the social and physical environment preferences of students, the reader should examine the writings of Kenneth and Rita Dunn.

2. Conceptual Processes: Having focused on an idea that must be learned, students must then classify it based upon prior experiences. The techniques involved include assessing similarities and differences to prior knowledge, as well as determining how best to define or describe the concepts. Again, the extent to which students can manipulate various concepts depends upon whether or not the ideas can be communicated to them using a common language with commonly accepted images.

Some students prefer to have ideas presented in a hierarchical manner, beginning with the big picture followed by the details involved (whole to part). Other students prefer to have the information presented in a more sequential approach, beginning with the minute details and building toward the larger concept (part to whole). Regardless of the technique used, teachers must include methods of helping learners make connections with prior knowledge.

3. Evaluative Processes: The third aspect of cognitive style focuses on the processes of thinking about the information. *Thinking* is difficult to define, but many researchers define it as "comprehension monitoring." The major focus of thinking centers on the individual's ability to plan, monitor, and evaluate his or her learning and understanding about the information he or she is seeking to learn.

Again, teachers should look for variations in the way individuals approach thinking. On one hand, individuals may spend time using their imaginations to create ideas based upon personal views or beliefs. On the other hand, some individuals will engage in a more formal logic, which requires familiarity with the rules in order to select the correct problem-solving strategies. In the first type of information processing, individuals seem to arrive at their decisions rather intuitively, using a process that seems to be generated from an internalized logic. In the second type, the one most influenced by instruction, students learn to organize and review their approach to information or problems through an analytical process.

ACCOMMODATING VARIATIONS IN LEARNING STYLES

When teachers are first introduced to the concept of learning styles, they immediately conjure up visions of having to construct thirty different learning plans to accommodate their students. *Learning styles* is not another euphemism for individually guided education. Instead, it is an entreaty to teachers to provide different approaches and strategies that individuals can use as they work at learning.

In today's classrooms, there are basically *two distinct modes of learning*: the *traditional orientation*, the one to which most instruction is geared; and the *community orientation*, the one more likely to be displayed by African American, Hispanic American, Native American, and immigrant Asian students who identify closely with the culture of their ethnic communities.

Particular suggestions to enhance the instructional process for the community-oriented students who are often ignored in instructional delivery system include the following ones:

Environment Style Accommodation: For the community-oriented students, the classroom should become inviting and supportive as an experiential setting in which students can use various media to explore concepts that may be foreign to them because they are not prevalent in their communities or because their economic situation does not permit the type of travel or involvement in enrichment activities that is true of the more successful, economically affluent students. Being able to see an enlarged picture of the Eiffel Tower in the classroom can provide an important conceptual image that might be needed to foster comprehension. Because learning centers permit self-exploration, they should also become important aspects of the classroom design for all levels of students in all types of classes.

Motivational Style Accommodation: Having the opportunity to participate in a good class discussion on lesson content motivates community-oriented students, satisfying their needs to share information with others and to obtain feedback. Moreover, it provides them an opportunity to listen to different perspectives. Teachers should note, however, that group discussion is not the same as class recitation in which students are asked to recite facts and information to the teacher from a textbook. For example, it is not enough to discuss nouns as a part of speech without leading students through the concept of a complete sentence and of the purpose of using nouns within sentences and paragraphs. Moreover, students need to be able to identify nouns within the framework of their own speech and written narratives as well as to determine how and why they have used a particular word as a noun.

The key to a good group discussion is a teacher who is an excellent questioner, who is reflective, who can lead students to reflect and inquire, and who has an excellent understanding of the broad structure and relationships within the lesson content.

Information Processing Style Accommodation: Teachers can facilitate the processing of information by students through the use of some of the following techniques:

1. Present concepts with multimedia using a variety of modalities.

THE KEY TO A GOOD GROUP DISCUSSION IS A TEACHER WHO IS AN EXCELLENT QUESTIONER, WHO IS REFLECTIVE, WHO CAN LEAD STUDENTS TO REFLECT AND INQUIRE, . . .

TEACHERS MUST REMEMBER THAT STUDENTS HAVE DIFFERENT PERCEPTIONS OF THE WORLD AND TEACH TO THESE PERCEPTIONS.

❦❦❦

2. Assist the students in identifying the relationships of concepts through cognitive mapping, brainstorming, or reciprocal teaching in which you ask them to predict possible answers in stories.

3. Take time to ensure there is a common understanding of words, concepts, or ideas. Bilingual students should be encouraged to interpret the words in their languages. Students should also be encouraged to develop art projects as representations of the ideas and to use new words in their oral interactions with you.

4. Model the thinking processes that are needed to complete tasks successfully. Most importantly, provide students the time to think about a problem or to complete an assignment so that they grasp the underlying meaning. Students learn best when they can perform a task with the teacher available to provide feedback.

Teachers must remember that students have different perceptions of the world and teach to these perceptions. Assisting students in

The stylistic differences of these two preferences seem to lie along the following continuum:

School-Oriented Students	Community-Oriented Students
Environmental Preferences: Prefer less intense, perhaps earth-oriented colors or plain whites. Seem able to work well in classrooms in which seats are in rows.	*Environmental Preferences:* Prefer warm, bright colors—blues and yellows are particularly soothing. Seem to prefer groupings of desks or tables, which perpetuate cooperation.
Motivational Style: Are individualistic and prefer to work alone on tasks. Are competitive and self-regulated in resource management.	*Motivational Style:* Are prosocial, more cooperative, and prefer to work with others on tasks. Are more dependent and like to have help from peers with constant reinforcement from the teacher or adult.
Cognitive Style: Learn well through auditory senses and function well with print media. Are able to focus attention on a specific task or object. Can focus on a single task for a sustained period of time. Understand American English used in textbooks, magazines, newspapers, and television, which facilitates comprehension. Backgrounds are closer to the writers of the curriculum materials, which facilitates meaning. Prefer or can handle material well when presented in a linear-sequential manner. Have been taught to use formal logic, algorithms, and analytical thinking. Are more likely to present written and spoken thoughts in a sequential manner. Are likely to function in a low-context fashion and to explain all variations of meanings because they assume the meaning is not shared.	*Cognitive Style:* Prefer visual material to emphasize oral presentation. Like group discussions, debates, and projects. Prefer to constantly scan room or object for new features, nonverbal cues, or contextual features. Prefer a variety of tasks in a relatively short time to maintain attention. Can focus on several tasks at one time. Likely to speak dialect or community-oriented language or are bilingual, which creates different orientation to words and meanings. Backgrounds usually differ from that of texts, requiring reinterpretation of the material within the context of the communities from which students come. Prefer to have material presented in a holistic, relational, or contextual manner, a presentation from whole to part. Are more intuitive and synergistic and may not have been taught to use formal logic to approach objects and problems. Have been exposed to more observational learning. Are more likely to present thoughts in a spiral or episodic fashion. Are likely to function in a high-context fashion and to assume that the meaning is shared by all individuals with whom they are communicating.

learning requires lots of talking—talking between students and teachers and between students. Expressing ideas orally allows better processing and comprehension.

When considering the use of learning styles, teachers must confront three important perceptions. First, teachers should understand that the identified style preference should not and cannot be used as evidence of deficiencies. Being different does not mean that the child is deficient in ability. Second, teachers should not think that the community-oriented style reflects all members of a group. It is merely behavior that is most likely to be found within the community. Third, teachers who use the concept of learning styles should do so as indicators of approaches to lesson design and to the selection of methods of instruction, not as the basis for judging intellectual potential.

A FINAL CAVEAT

Developing a successful learner is the ultimate goal of a successful teacher, and ensuring that children become successful learners requires that teachers see themselves not as the ultimate purveyors of knowledge, but as guides through the learning process. This approach to teaching will empower students as learners. By incorporating various learning-style approaches in the classroom and in the curriculum, teachers will assist students to maximize the energy they spend in the learning process. This permits students to approach the learning process in their own words and to use the information as a bridge. When learners grasp the ideas and really know that they know, their sense of self-worth and confidence and their intellectual strength improve tremendously. It is at this point teachers know they, too, have been successful. What a great sense of accomplishment! ❦

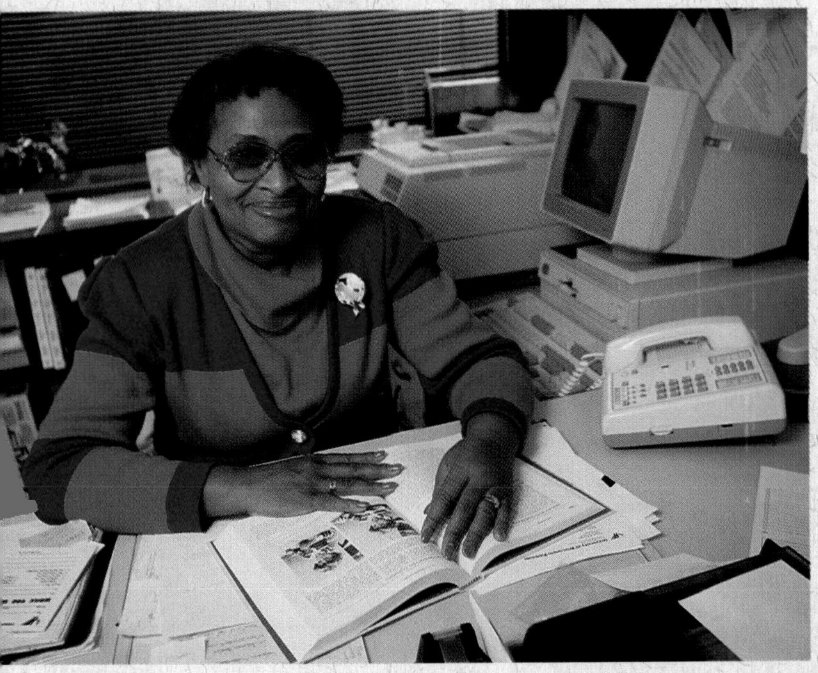

Additional Readings

Grossman, Herbert. *Educating Hispanic Students.* Springfield, Illinois: Charles C. Thomas Publisher, 1984.

Henson, Kenneth T. *Theory Into Practice: Matching Teaching and Learning Styles*. Columbus, Ohio: Ohio State University, 1984.

Shade, Barbara J. *Culture, Style, and the Educative Process*. Springfield, Illinois: Charles C. Thomas Publisher, 1989.

Tharp, Roland and Ronald Gallimore. *Rousing Minds to Life*. New York: Cambridge University Press, 1988.

Trueba, Henry T., Lila Jacobs and Elizabeth Kirton. *Cultural Conflict and Adaptation: The Case of Hmong Children in American Society*. New York: Falmer Press, 1990.

ELEMENTS OF WRITING addresses the needs of America's diverse student populations and the range of students' *learning styles* in the following ways:

Pupil's Edition

Represents a wide range of ethnically diverse cultures in the literary models and a broad selection of topics in the exercises and examples

Accomodates a range of learning styles by providing a variety of student activities

Offers teachers a flexible program that can be easily adapted to suit a variety of situations

Annotated Teacher's Edition

Provides specific *MEETING INDIVIDUAL NEEDS* features such as *Learning Styles, Less-Advanced, Advanced, Students with Special Needs, LEP/ESL,* and *At-Risk*

Suggests ways for language teachers to address language diversity in the multicultural classroom

Teacher's ResourceBank ™

Meets individual needs of students with graphic organizers and reinforcement practice activities

WANDA B. SCHINDLEY

INTEGRATING THE LANGUAGE ARTS

INTEGRATING THE TEACHING OF THE LANGUAGE ARTS CREATES THE MAGIC THAT HELPS STUDENTS LEARN.

Thirty-five years ago in a rural classroom, a creative woman integrated the teaching of reading, writing, speaking, listening, and even math. Her second-graders built a playhouse-size cardboard post office, made block-letter signs, wrote and read letters, counted tokens to buy and sell stamps, and spoke and listened as postmaster and customer. That teacher had not read research on the integration of skills or on using whole-language methodologies, but she knew intuitively what worked. I don't remember much about my experiences in kindergarten, first grade, third grade, or even fourth grade, but I remember well that second-grade classroom; I remember the magic of learning.

Integrating the teaching of the language arts creates the magic that helps students learn. It creates a context for developing language proficiency and relevancy for reading, writing, speaking, and listening activities. Students grow through active participation in language activities. Although categorizing the language arts may be necessary for describing curricula, in the classroom language skills are best learned through doing—through seeking meaning from texts, through writing and revising, and through sharing ideas and opinions.

WANDA SCHINDLEY IS A SPECIALIST FOR THE WORKPLACE PARTNERSHIP.

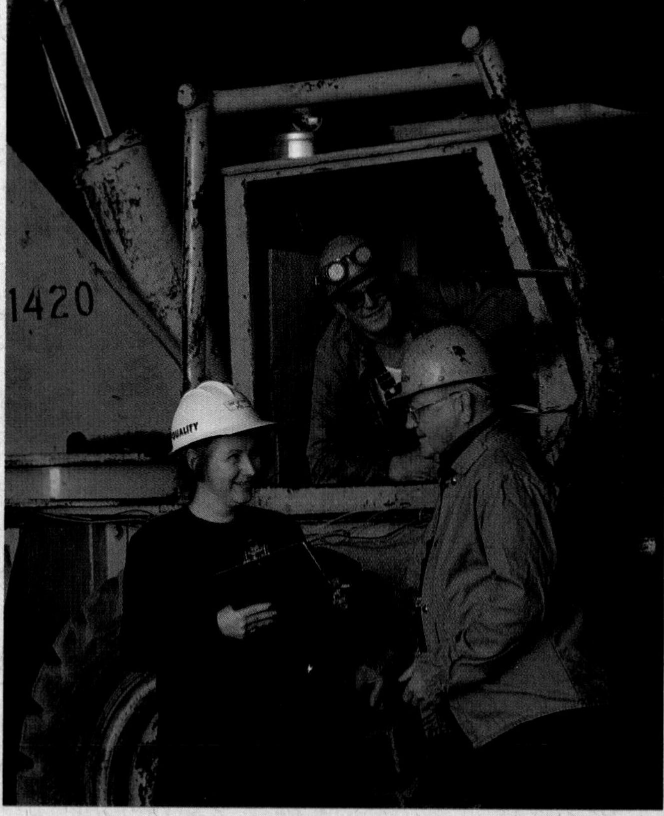

WANDA STILL LIVES IN THE RURAL AREA WHERE SHE WENT TO SCHOOL AS A CHILD.

SUGGESTIONS FOR INTEGRATING THE LANGUAGE ARTS

- Involve students in prereading activities such as discussion, writing, research, and sometimes, vocabulary development. Creating a context for reading involves discussing themes and related issues, making predictions, recalling prior knowledge and related experiences, and searching out related information.
- Involve students in prewriting activities such as discussion of possible topics and details, reading model essays, searching out and reading informative pieces, reading literary writing, interviewing others, and sentence-combining or sentence-revision activities. Like the writing process itself, development of language proficiency involves a recursive practice in reading, writing, thinking, speaking, and listening.
- Make writing assignments relevant by having students write for and share with real audiences for meaningful purposes. Have students share their writing with peers.
- Relate correctness—development of conventional usage, spelling, grammar, and punctuation—to the revising and proofreading stages of the writing process. Correctness becomes important to students when it helps them communicate their ideas clearly. Class review of grammar, usage, and mechanics can be done with sentences from student papers and with sentence-combining, sentence-manipulation, and vocabulary activities.
- Approach standard usage in speech as appropriate for use in business and academic situations, not as a replacement for all vernacular expression.
- Encourage student involvement in class discussion, team study groups, cooperative research projects and presentations, group creative writing, and role playing.
- Foster an atmosphere in which students feel free to respond to, to evaluate, and to critique literature.
- Act as facilitator in students' discovery processes through activities that encourage creative and critical thinking—decision making and problem solving—and allow students to take more responsibility for their own learning.
- Create an atmosphere of cooperation, caring, and high expectations.

LIKE THE WRITING PROCESS ITSELF, DEVELOPMENT OF LANGUAGE PROFICIENCY INVOLVES A RECURSIVE PRACTICE IN READING, WRITING, THINKING, SPEAKING, AND LISTENING.

USING THE TEXTBOOK IN AN INTEGRATED APPROACH

Literature selections are provided in each chapter to give students opportunities to read before writing. However, this book can be used in a literature-driven approach as the springboard to writing by incorporating into the study of each chapter ample readings from literature anthologies, magazines, and student papers. The features in each chapter of the *Teacher's Edition* contain suggestions for integrating additional literature selections **(Integrating the Language Arts: Literature Link)**, using a variety of group activities **(Cooperative Learning)**, and encouraging students to use higher-level thinking skills to contribute to class discussion **(Critical Thinking)**.

Throughout, the textbook guides students through the prewriting, writing, evaluating, revising, proofreading, and publishing phases of the writing process. It also instructs students in the dynamics and behavior involved in group work with ample opportunities for group writing, revising, speaking, and listening activities. The chapters on speaking and listening help students develop skills that will serve them throughout their school years and later as citizens.

The **Common Error** and **Integrating the Language Arts** features in each chapter of the *Teacher's Edition* contain suggestions for integrating the teaching of grammar, usage, and mechanics into the stages of the writing process, as do the suggestions for integrating the language arts in the introduction of each composition chapter.

Sample Integrated Lesson Plan

A lesson on creative writing might begin with a class discussion about stories and poems.

Guiding questions encourage students to share attitudes (What kinds of stories/poems do you like?)

—in order to recall prior knowledge about the structure of stories (What happened toward the end of a favorite story? How did you feel as your read? What name do we use for the most exciting or scary part of the story?)

—and of poems (Can you think of a favorite poem? What do you like about the poem?)

—and to synthesize knowledge about fiction and poetry (What characteristics do stories and poems have in common? What other forms might a writer use to tell about an event or to express an idea?)

Students might then read the stories and poems and discuss their responses and evaluations of each. Volunteers might bring their favorite stories, poems, or lyrics to share with the class before beginning to write original stories and poems.

Teachers can use group stories and poems as guided practice and as a non-threatening introduction to creative writing. Students working in groups to create story lines and to describe characters and setting will quickly learn literary terminology to use within the group. A group activity in which students write noun poems might begin informal grammar instruction as the class brainstorms a list of words that name people, places, things, or ideas. Small groups can then choose from the list of topics for noun-metaphor poems.

Example: Dreams are
Envelopes of hope,
Fluffy clouds that
disappear in daylight,
Stars to reach for.

As groups begin to revise and proofread their poems for class presentation, teachers might focus on the use of commas and end marks.

When students begin the creative writing assignments, they are again given opportunities to write, discuss, read, think, talk, revise, and so on. Instruction in usage and mechanics can be provided to the class as the need arises, to partners as they debate an issue of correctness, and to individuals in one-on-one conferences.

Finally, students share their work with the class—perhaps anonymously at first, but eventually as accomplished and proud authors who share a firsthand knowledge of the creation of literature and a greater understanding of language.

ELEMENTS OF WRITING addresses the *integration* of the various aspects of language in the following ways:

Pupil's Edition

Connects the study of writing to reading, speaking, listening, grammar, usage, and mechanics

Reinforces in the language-structure chapters the fundamentals of effective communication, stressing application and proficiency.

Annotated Teacher's Edition

Provides features that give a variety of strategies to link every aspect of language diversity instruction—*INTEGRATING THE LANGUAGE ARTS: Literature Link, Library Skills Link, Mechanics Link, Grammar Link, Usage Link, Technology Link*

Teacher's ResourceBank ™

Offers supplemental materials on every aspect of the language arts

By Charles W. Leftwich & Patricia G. Tweeddale

Accepting the Differences:

Teaching the At-Risk Student

...IT IS UNLIKELY THAT AT-RISK STUDENTS WILL LEAVE SCHOOL WITH THE BASIC SKILLS OUR EDUCATION SYSTEM SHOULD PROVIDE.

Teachers are facing a growing population of students for whom a minimal success such as completing high school is not probable. These students comprise the group known as at-risk, a label that can be acquired for reasons ranging from a person's socioeconomic background to being a teenage parent or coming from a single-parent home, from having a parent or sibling incarcerated to being a latchkey child. Whatever the reason for the categorization, it is unlikely that at-risk students will leave school with the basic skills our education system should provide.

The task of teaching the at-risk student must begin with knowledge of individual student characteristics that are relevant to the instructional objective at hand. A focus upon stereotypical characteristics denies attention to the in-

Patricia Tweeddale and Charles Leftwich in their office.

Charles and Patricia Pose with a favorite quotation and their canine friend Spriger.

"FEAR OF DIFFERENCE
IS DREAD OF LIFE
ITSELF."
- mary parker
follett
TEACHING
&
LEARNING

dividual learner and what that student brings to the classroom. Because teaching and learning are highly interactive social encounters, the efficacy of any given encounter may be dependent upon the emotional response of both parties to their first contact.

The initial response by a teacher is often conditioned by previous exposure to learners similar to the one in question. Positive previous exposure leads to a sense of confidence in the ability to successfully foster and facilitate learning. However, if a teacher has had negative previous exposure, the quality of the initial encounter may be tainted by the teacher's lack of confidence in effecting learning or establishing a positive social interaction.

There are at least two sources for interference in the initial interaction between the teacher and the at-risk student, the vicarious and the real. Vicarious sources are grounded in images created by other teachers, the school organization, and community expectations, as well as portrayal in print and electronic media by editorial and entertainment entities.

The real source of interference in the initial interaction may well be so subtle as to escape recognition, and yet it seems to be pervasive. It is a basic misunderstanding of differences. The nonverbal language exhibited by the at-risk student is different or at least unfamiliar, and this may reinforce the teacher's sense of being called upon to do an impossible task. The student's verbal language may also be unfamiliar, and the clash between assumptions of what students ought to sound like and what the teacher actually hears further frustrates and impedes the teaching process.

Interaction between the teacher and the learner should focus upon the individual student's characteristics with the intention of discovering what sets that individual apart from others. New learning is built upon old learning, and new knowledge is supported by old; therefore, the teacher of the at-risk student must concentrate on discovering what the student knows. Often this can be a difficult task since that knowledge may be communicated in a different mode. The teacher should be aware of some characteristics of the at-risk student: negative self-image, a heavy dependence upon and rigid adherence to a distinct mode of concrete thinking, unique ideolect spoken language, low motivation, and a lack of positive response to constructive criticism. Any at-risk student may exhibit one or all of these characteristics in varying degrees. What is important is to recognize and appreciate the student as an individual. Whatever the individual's characteristics, they are an integral part of the learner and as such must be taken

FOR THE TEACHER TO INTERACT SUCCESSFULLY WITH THE AT-RISK STUDENT, A SENSE OF TRUST AND ACCEPTANCE MUST BE ESTABLISHED.

into account in structuring interaction. And that structuring is solely the responsibility of the teacher; the structure must be the product of informed assessment rather than reactive judgment.

For the teacher to interact successfully with the at-risk student, a sense of trust and acceptance must be established. The student must suspend any suspicions of the teacher's intentions, which is no small accomplishment given the student's probable historical experience with schools. The teacher must overcome any negative preconceptions of the nature of the at-risk student that may stem from some students' demeanor. In fact, teacher response to the demeanor of the at-risk student may be a much larger barrier to a positive interaction than any of the student's other characteristics. The student cannot help but sense rejection by the teacher and will respond in kind. The student, being less sophisticated, frequently manifests inner anger and frustration by overt, socially unacceptable behavior. Administrators and teachers may deal with this behavior as if it were the real problem rather than a symptom. However, if the teacher is well aware of the differences that are brought to the classroom and can accept them, there can develop an interaction in which the teacher and the student are focused on, rather than distracted from, their respective tasks—teaching and learning.

Another difficulty in developing meaningful interaction is overcoming the sense of hopelessness that some students feel. Some students know they are at-risk; they have been told this from the beginning. Innumerable sights and sounds reinforce an absence of control over their environment. Hopelessness often pervades the neighborhoods in which they live. Previous experiences may have taught them that high hopes and effort more often than not lead to disappointment and heartbreak. The challenge for the teacher is to identify the students' strengths though they be disguised or denied beneath the protective facade of bravado and coolness, and to try to inspire and motivate students who have little or no expectation of success and who outwardly signal an intense desire to be left alone. To meet this challenge, the teacher more than ever before must be a thinker, a planner, and a decision maker. Then, drawing on a rich professional knowledge base, the teacher can serve as a model and mediator.

It is one thing to understand intellectually that at-risk students bring to the classroom with them entirely different bents and behaviors. It is another, however, to confront these differences and to view them as starting points for teaching. If we are to succeed in teaching this segment of our student body, we have to understand and accept these differences and to exercise our expertise as planners and implementers of instruction.

Successful teaching continues to hinge on the characteristics of the learner, the material to be learned, the specific tasks to be mastered, and the strategies utilized by the teacher. No one ever said it would be easy. Surprisingly though, many have found it to be professionally fulfilling and personally rewarding.

ELEMENTS OF WRITING addresses the needs of America's diverse student populations and the range of student *learning styles* in the following ways:

Pupil's Edition

Represents a wide range of ethnically diverse cultures in the literary models and a broad selection of topics in the exercises and examples

Accomodates a range of learning styles by providing a variety of student activities

Offers teachers a flexible program that can be easily adapted to a variety of situations

Annotated Teacher's Edition

Provides specific *MEETING INDIVIDUAL NEEDS* features such as *Learning Styles*, *Less-Advanced, Advanced, Students with Special Needs, LEP/ESL*, and *At-Risk*

Suggests ways for language teachers to address diversity in the multicultural classroom

Teacher's ResourceBank ™

Meets individual needs of students with graphic organizers and reinforcement practice activities

BY NORBERT ELLIOT & KAREN GREENBERG

THE DIRECT ASSESSMENT OF WRITING:

Notes For Teachers

HOW CAN ASSESSMENT STRATEGIES BE MODIFIED TO HELP BOTH TEACHERS AND STUDENTS?

Teachers spend a great deal of time assessing students' writing; they correct errors, offer suggestions, and assign grades. This process can be exhausting to teachers and discouraging for students. How can assessment strategies be modified to help both teachers and students?

Instruction and assessment can be aligned so that the two work together. To enable instruction and assessment to complement each other, teachers have turned to two relatively new methods of direct assessment: holistic scoring and portfolio assessment.

HOLISTIC SCORING

One of the most common methods of scoring writing samples is holistic scoring, a procedure based on the responses of concerned readers to a meaningful whole composition. Holistic scoring involves reading a writing sample for an overall impression of the writing and assigning the sample a score based on a set of consistent scoring criteria. Most holistic scoring systems use a scoring scale, or guide, that describes papers at six or eight different levels of competence.

Holistic scoring has many advantages:

1. It communicates to students that writing is a process leading to a unified, synergistic piece of writing.

2. Writing samples that have been holistically scored provide students with clear information about the quality of their writing, but they are less intimidating than grades or written critiques.

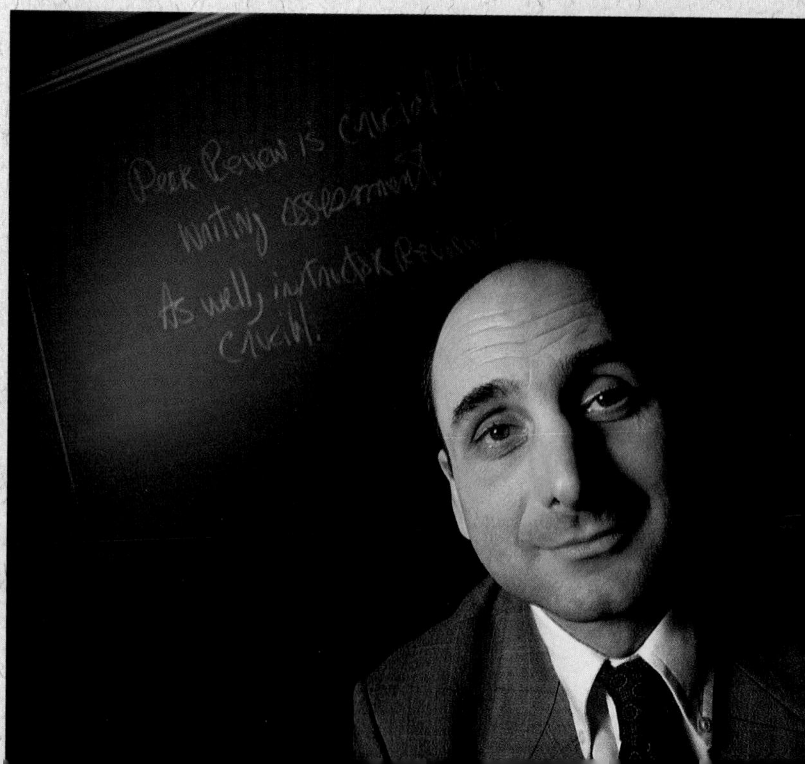

NORBERT ELLIOT, DIRECTOR OF THE WRITING PROGRAM AT THE NEW JERSEY INSTITUTE OF TECHNOLOGY.

3. Holistic scoring is rapid. Readers spend only minutes judging the total effect of a paper.
4. The criteria on a holistic scoring scale give teachers a vocabulary to use in discussing essays with students and their parents.
5. The process of developing holistic scoring guides and scoring writing samples enables teachers to share their unique responses to writing, as well as their evaluative criteria. If an entire department uses the same scoring guide, students will realize that effective writing has definable features upon which all of their English teachers agree.

Nevertheless, there are weaknesses to this method. It alone cannot, for instance, provide diagnostic information about specific writing proficiencies and deficiencies. The score cannot substitute for a teacher's detailed responses to an essay—the provocative notes in the margin, the encouraging comments at the end, etc. This weakness, however, can be overcome if teachers review papers with their students in light of the scoring criteria.

Another weakness is more serious. Using holistic scoring, teachers often consider only one piece of writing during assessment. If only one sample of writing is evaluated, then teachers may not get a representative idea of students' writing ability, because this ability does not exist in a vacuum but varies from day to day and across the aims and modes of writing. In response to this concern, teachers have investigated a second method of direct assessment.

KAREN GREENBERG, DIRECTOR OF THE NATIONAL TESTING NETWORK IN WRITING.

PORTFOLIO ASSESSMENT

Portfolio assessment allows writing teachers to evaluate various samples of students' work, taken at various times under various conditions. Consequently, portfolio assessment can provide a fuller portrait of writing abilities.

To begin portfolio assessment, teachers develop a series of writing assignments that express the goals of a course. For instance, a group of teachers might require their students to write papers based on each of James Kinneavy's aims: expressive writing (a journal entry), informative writing (a summary of a news article), literary writing (a short story), and persuasive writing (an editorial). Over time, students work on these papers both at home and in class. Portfolios can include other forms of communication that students have produced, such as artwork, audio recordings, or videotapes.

Teachers need not assess everything that is included in a portfolio. In fact, it is often preferable not to evaluate every piece of a student's writing. This strategy allows teachers to separate instruction and response from formed evaluation. Portfolio assessment, therefore, can be based on samples that the teacher, the student, or both consider to be the student's best writing.

Clearly, there are advantages to this method:
1. Because multiple samples are assessed, portfolio assessment is a valid, authentic evaluation.
2. Because the authenticity of the assessment is increased, the curriculum becomes enriched.

As teachers plan tasks, they debate curricular values and strategies, devise workable instructional schemes for the classroom, and design thoughtful evaluative criteria for assignments.

With portfolio assessment, students gain a more positive attitude toward writing. Because they invest in their writing, students seek both teacher and peer response, create multiple drafts, and revise for their readers. Over time, a school's entire writing program can become an exciting adventure in communication and critical thinking.

CONCLUSION

There is still much to be investigated about the evaluation of writing. What kind of assessment best suits the multiple literacies on which our democratic society rests? What kind of local assessments will best supplement large-scale assessment? How can assessment reveal more about effective teaching? Answers will have to come from those who know students best: their teachers.❦

ELEMENTS OF WRITING addresses *holistic evaluation* and *portfolio assessment* in the following ways:

Annotated Teacher's Edition
Offers a wide variety of assessment ideas in the *TIMESAVER, A DIFFERENT APPROACH*, and *ASSESSMENT* features

Teacher's ResourceBank ™
Provides an **Assessment Portfolio** section and **Holistically Graded Composition Models** for the writing chapters

BY DAVID A. ENGLAND

PROFESSIONAL BIBLIOGRAPHY

COMPOSING PROCESSES

Belanoff, Pat, Peter Elbow, and Sheryl I. Fontaine, eds. *Nothing Begins with N*. Carbondale and Edwardsville, IL: Southern Illinois University Press, 1981. An overview of what we know about the uses of freewriting in the classroom, with major sections on strategies and benefits for teachers and students.

Berthoff, Anne E. *The Making of Meaning*. Upper Montclair, NJ: Boynton/Cook Publishers, Inc., 1981. Suggesting that classrooms can become philosophical laboratories, Berthoff shows the way to practical approaches for thoughtful teachers.

Brannon, Lil, and C.H. Knoblauch. *Rhetorical Traditions and the Teaching of Writing*. Upper Montclair, NJ: Boynton/Cook Publishers, Inc., 1984. Staying with the theory and history provided in this book's early chapters rewards readers who come to understand better the basis and rewards of teaching in nontraditional ways.

Caplan, Rebekah, and Katherine Keach. *Showing-Writing: A Tutoring Program to Help Students to be Specific*. The University of California, Berkeley, CA: Bay Area Writing Project Publications. This nicely focused monograph is itself a good illustration of "showing, not telling," and it explains how the author tested her program for helping students learn to be more specific in their writing.

Dellinger, Dixie Gibbs. *Out of the Heart: How to Design Writing Assignments for High School Courses*. The University of California, Berkeley, CA: Bay Area Writing Project Publications. The author provides several examples of assignment sequences, each reflecting a solid discourse theory, for teachers who want to move beyond disconnected assignments in writing classes.

Kinneavy, James L., William J. McCleary, and Neil Nakadate. *Writing in the Liberal Arts Tradition* (2nd ed.). New York, NY: Harper & Row, 1990. This book is the basis for the writing chapters in the *Elements of Writing* series.

Kirby, Dan, and Tom Liner. *Inside Out: Developmental Strategies for Teaching Writing*. Upper Montclair, NJ: Boynton/Cook Publishers, Inc., 1981. *Developmental* aptly describes the authors' approach as they explain and demonstrate teaching strategies designed to help writers at all levels of sophistication improve their writing processes.

Kutz, Eleanor, and Hephzibah Roskelly. *An Unquiet Pedagogy: Transforming Practice in the English Classroom*. Upper Montclair, NJ: Boynton/Cook Publishers, Inc., 1991. This seminal book will challenge traditional assumptions about learners and literacy as it explores how imagination and learner-constructed knowledge undergird any meaningful writing in classes where the development of true literacy is the goal.

Mohr, Marian M. *Revision: The Rhythm of Meaning*. Upper Montclair, NJ: Boynton/Cook Publishers, Inc., 1984. This book defines and exemplifies revision in terms that teachers will understand, adapt, and use as they help their students improve initial drafts.

Murray, Donald M. *Learning by Teaching*. Upper Montclair, NJ: Boynton/Cook Publishers, Inc., 1982. The author connects his process model for writing his thoughts on the processes of teaching writing in a readable text with useful examples and illustrations from the author's experiences as a teacher and writer.

———. *A Writer Teaches Writing* (2nd ed.). Boston, MA: Houghton-Mifflin, 1974. This early "writing process" work was designed to show how real writers write and to make that knowledge useful and powerful for teachers of writing.

Romano, Tom. *Clearing the Way: Working with Teenage Writers*. Portsmouth, NH: Heinemann, 1987. Especially helpful chapters on conferencing and evaluation distinguish this book, which is written in a lively style and which is supported with examples of students' writing and clear insights into a writing teacher's learning.

Willis, Meredith Sue. *Personal Fiction Writing: A Guide for Writing from Real Life for Teachers, Students, and Writers*. New York, NY: Teachers & Writers Collaborative, 1989. An experienced writer and teacher shares classroom-tested ideas on helping students to describe places, people, and action; to write dialogues and monologues; to create structure; and to revise what they have written.

Ziegler, Alan. *The Writing Workshop*, Vol. 1. New York, NY: Teachers & Writers Collaborative, 1981. This description of a workshop method for individualizing writing instruction includes ample references to students' work and sharp observations by the author.

———. Vol. 2. New York, NY: Teachers & Writers Collaborative, 1984. This is an excellent catalog of assignments exemplified by students' responses to them, along with the author's observations—a sequel to Vol. 1, which describes a writing environment conducive to such assignments and approaches.

Cooperative Learning

Elbow, Peter. *Writing Without Teachers*. New York, NY: Oxford University Press, 1973. The title of the book should not suggest that teachers are not necessary, but rather that they assume different roles in nurturing students' group processes and peer-response activities.

Eubanks, Ilona M. "Nonstandard Dialect Speakers and Collaborative Learning." *The Writing Instructor* Vol. 10 (Spring 1991): 143-148. This article examines features of the traditional language-and-writing classroom that lead to difficulty, frustration, and often failure for speakers of nonstandard dialects.

Golub, Jeff, ed. *Focus on Collaborative Learning: Classroom Practices in the Teaching of English 1988*. Urbana, IL: National Council of Teachers of English, 1988. In compiling this collection of best practices, the editor includes pieces from teachers who describe general collaborative-learning skills before moving to others who discuss how these skills are applied in literature study and various writing activities, from prewriting through revision.

Healey, Mark K. *Using Students' Writing Response Groups in the Classroom*. The University of California, Berkeley, CA: Bay Area Writing Project Publications. In a monograph that realistically assesses problems often associated with response groups, the author provides practical suggestions on how to help students become more helpful in fostering growth in peers' writing.

Rabkin, Eric S., and Macklin Smith. *Teaching Writing That Works*. Ann Arbor, MI: The University of Michigan Press, 1990. In a step-by-step process for breaking the cycle of one individual student writing for a teacher, the authors move from the development of ideas in group settings through group editing and evaluation. Writing designed to help students accomplish "real work" is central to all group activities.

Spear, Karen. *Sharing Writing*. Upper Montclair, NJ: Boynton/Cook Publishers, Inc., 1988. This most practical guide to forming and nurturing response groups could only have been written with the benefit of this teacher's broad and thoughtful experience with response groups in writing courses. The book begins with an honest and promising appraisal of "challenges in peer response groups."

Individual Needs/Language Diversity

Allaei, Sara Kurtz, and Ulla Maija Connor. "Exploring the Dynamics of Cross-Cultural Collaboration in Writing Classrooms." *The Writing Instructor* 10 (Fall 1990): 19-28. After reviewing what is known about cross-cultural writing, the authors provide guidelines and recommendations for establishing collaborative groups in multicultural writing classes.

Brooks, Charlotte K., ed. *Tapping Potential: English and the Language Arts for the Black Learner*. Urbana, IL: National Council of Teachers of English, 1985. In addition to explaining why many African American children have not responded to the standard curriculum taught in traditional ways, contributors to this collection offer specific suggestions for classroom practices.

Cleary, Linda Miller. "A Profile of Carlos: Strengths of a Nonstandard Dialect Writer." *English Journal* 77 (September 1988): 59-64. A case study in which the language barriers and biases faced by one writer prove instructive for his teachers and for all teachers.

Daniels, Harvey, and Marcia Farr. *Language Diversity and Writing Instruction*. New York, NY: ERIC Clearinghouse on Reading and Communication Skills, National Council of Teachers of English: 1986. This book succeeds in providing just enough theory and background of teachers seeking to improve the writing of students who are native speakers of nonstandard dialects.

Gonzalez, Roseann Duenas. "When Minority Becomes Majority: The Changing Face of English Classrooms." *English Journal* 79 (January 1990): 16-23. Even though the recommendations in this article are for all the language arts, applications to writing instruction will be easy and crucial to teachers in multicultural classes.

Marik, Ray. *Special Education Students Write: Classroom Activities and Assignments*. The University of California, Berkeley, CA: Bay Area Writing Project Publications. Case studies of students with special learning needs are the bases for the author's advocacy of well-sequenced, developmentally appropriate writing activities for all learners.

Rose, Mike. *Lives on the Boundary*. New York, NY: Penguin Books, 1989. The author's experiences as a remedial student contributed to his sensitive understanding of the educational underclass about which he writes so effectively.

Shade, Barbara J. Robinson, ed. *Culture, Style and the Educative Process*. Springfield, IL: Charles C.Thomas, 1989. This book provides insight into various cultures' learning styles as well as methods for enhancing students' retention by addressing their learning styles.

Shaughnessy, M.P. *Errors and Expectations: A Guide for the Teacher of Basic Writing.* New York, NY: Oxford University Press, 1977. The author's strategies for unlocking expression and clarity for basic college writers are helpful to high school writers as well.

Stottlar, James, ed. *Teaching the Gifted*. Urbana, IL: National Council of Teachers of English, 1988. Ways to identify students with special talents in the language arts, to individualize instruction to meet their needs, and to encourage independent thinking in academically advanced students are among topics in this collection.

Urzua, Carole. "'You Stopped Too Soon': Second Language Children Composing and Revising." *TESOL Quarterly* 21 (June 1987): 279-304. This research report shares what six months of careful observations of Southeast Asian students' writing taught teachers about how second-language children learn to write.

Assessment

Belanoff, Pat, and Marcia Dickson. *Portfolios: Process and Product.* Portsmouth, NH: Heinemann, 1991. In a good blending of theory and practice in how to use writing portfolios for assessment in many settings, this book allows teachers to plan strategies unique to their own purposes.

Clay, Marie M. "Research Currents: What Is and What Might Be in Evaluation." *Language Arts* 67 (March 1990) : 288-298. After discussing problems and limitations of standardized testing, the author makes recommendations toward more useful assessment models and philosophies across the language arts and into high school.

Holmes, Ken. *Perspectives on Teaching and Assessing Language Arts.* Urbana, IL: National Council of Teachers of English, 1990. These essays include a rationale for multiculturalism in reading materials as well as a timely consideration of assessment in whole-language approaches.

Najimy, Norman C. *Measure for Measure: A Guidebook for Evaluating Students' Expository Writing.* Urbana, IL: National Council of Teachers of English, 1981. By using examples of students' writing, this guide suggests how teachers' responses can enhance instruction instead of threatening students.

Posner, Richard. "Life Without Scan-Tron: Tests as Thinking." *English Journal* 76 (February 1987): 35-38. This author demonstrates how six types of written, in-class tests improve his students' writing, thinking, and mastery of subject matter.

Robinson, Joy L., et al. *Creating Writers: Linking Assessment and Writing Instruction*. White Plains, NY: Longman, 1990. This book helps students and teachers agree on attributes of good writing and has scoring guides that help link instruction to assessment.

Responding to Writing

Belanoff, Pat, and Peter Elbow. *Sharing and Responding*. New York, NY: Random House, 1989. This book provides useful examples of students' responses to peers' writing along with clear rationales and activities designed to increase the value of peer responses.

Freedman, Sarah Warshauer. Response to Student Writing. Urbana, IL: National Council of Teachers of English, 1987. This research report on the state of the art in response to writing not only indicates what teachers do and how students feel about it, but offers clear ideas on best practices in providing students with feedback.

Harris, Muriel. *Teaching One-to-One: The Writing Conference*. Urbana, IL: National Council of Teachers of English, 1986. The author provides a strong justification for one-on-one conferencing in the writing classroom and provides useful strategies and insights that can help writing teachers at all levels.

Sommers, Nancy. "Responding to Student Writing." *College Composition and Communication* 33 (May 1982): 148-56. The author encourages teachers to respond to the ideas, meanings, and purposes in students' papers before error hunting in order for students to engage in meaningful revision.

Sullivan, Patrick, "Responding to Student Writing: The Consequences of Some Common Remarks." *English Journal* 75 (February 1986): 51-53. The author describes the hidden messages behind four types of comments teachers frequently make in responding to students' writing.

Whole Language/Integration

Cronin, Hines, David Meadows, and Richard Sinatra. "Integrating Computers, Reading, and Writing Across the Curriculum." *Educational Leadership* 48 (September 1990): 57-60. Good illustrations suggest how visual maps can be constructed via computers to enhance students' thinking and organizational skills in all school subjects.

Kroll, Barry M., and Roberta J. Vann. *Exploring Speaking-Writing Relationships: Connections and Contracts*. Urbana, IL: National Council of Teachers of English, 1981. A precursor of many whole-language texts and approaches, these essays provide instructive analysis of how speaking and writing can be composed and contrasted toward better understanding and teaching of both.

Martin, Nancy, et al. *Writing Across the Curriculum*. Portsmouth, NH: Boynton/Cook Publishers, Inc., 1983. Each pamphlet in this series suggests ways to integrate the teaching of writing by "writing to learn" in various school subjects.

Newkirk, Thomas. *Only Connect: Uniting Reading and Writing*. Upper Montclair, NJ: Boynton/Cook Publishers, Inc., 1986. An excellent middle section on "Reading, Writing, and Interpreting" will help teachers see possibilities for reading in the writing classroom and vice versa.

Peterson, Bruce T., ed. *Convergences: Transactions in Reading and Writing*. Urbana, IL: National Council of Teachers of English, 1986. This collection of essays cuts across several fields in contemporary writing theory and research to explain the logic of integrating reading and writing in the classroom.

Shuman, Baird R., and Denny Wolfe. *Teaching English Through the Arts*. Urbana, IL: National Council of Teachers of English, 1990. In this "Theory and Research into Practice" (TRIP) booklet, the authors provide teachers with classroom-tested ways to connect reading and writing in English classes to popular culture and traditional art forms.

Self, Judith. *Plain Talk About Learning and Writing Across the Curriculum*. Urbana, IL: National Council of Teachers of English, 1987. Teachers of different subjects demonstrate how writing can provide a helpful way for students to think about content and experiences in all subjects.

Writing Across the Curriculum

Fulwiler, Toby. *Teaching with Writing*. Upper Montclair, NJ: Boynton/Cook Publishers, Inc., 1987. An especially strong chapter on writing and testing helps make this treatment of process writing in the content areas valuable for teachers in all subject areas.

Gere, Anne Ruggles, ed. *Roots in the Sawdust: Writing to Learn Across the Disciplines*. Urbana, IL: National Council of Teachers of English, 1985. The editor has compiled essays on how writing can improve thinking and enhance learning in all the traditionally included subjects such as science and math with the added bonus of thoughtful essays on writing in art and foreign-language classes.

Kiniry, Malcolm, and Ellen Strenski. "Sequencing Expository Writing: A Recursive Approach." *College Composition and Communication* 36 (May 1985): 191-202. Though the model described here is based on a college program, the rhetorical strategies and discipline-specific approaches to writing are applicable to high school writers.

Talbot, Bill. "Writing for Learning in School: Is It Possible?" *Language Arts* 67 (January 1990): 47-57. The author describes his experiences in observing students who were learning how to use writing for learning and raises both concerns and hopes based on his observations. ❦

ELEMENTS OF WRITING

A Full Range of Components to Meet Your Students' Needs

The materials that accompany ***Elements of Writing*** have been designed to help teachers in real classrooms—where the demands on their time and energy are great—to deal with each student as an individual. Regardless of your students' learning styles, ***Elements of Writing*** has a variety of materials to meet their needs.

Pupil's Editions

The *Pupil's Editions* for ***Elements of Writing*** combine the latest educational research with practical teacher input. Extensive surveys of both teachers and students, as well as field testing across the nation, were used to verify and validate the instructional design.

Annotated Teacher's Editions

The *Annotated Teacher's Editions* that accompany each level of ***Elements of Writing*** suggest lesson plans and a variety of teaching strategies for all types of students.

Teacher's Resource Banks™

The blackline-masters in the *Teacher's ResourceBanks* provide practice and reinforcement for every chapter in the *Pupil's Editions.* Each binder is divided into nine sections which correspond to specific chapters in the *Pupil's Edition:* Process and Structure, Aims for Writing, Language and Style, Grammar, Usage, Mechanics, Resources, Holistically Graded Composition Models, and Assessment Portfolio.

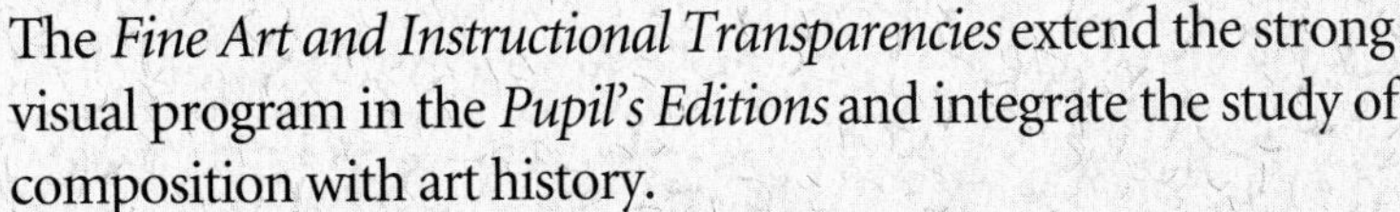

Fine Art and Instructional Transparencies

The *Fine Art and Instructional Transparencies* extend the strong visual program in the *Pupil's Editions* and integrate the study of composition with art history.

For each grade level, there are three types of transparencies: *Fine Art Transparencies, Graphic Organizer Transparencies,* and *Revision Transparencies.* Each transparency is supported by *Teacher's Notes* which suggest ways to use the transparencies in the classroom.

Vocabulary Workshop, Grades 6-12

Vocabulary Workshop is based on the word lists included in the *Teacher's ResourceBanks.* Each level of *Vocabulary Workshop* uses a variety of new student-centered activities to help students develop their ability to understand new and unfamiliar words.

Holt Writer's Workshop 1 and 2

The *Holt Writer's Workshop* is a software program for IBM® PC and Compatibles and Macintosh® computers that provides students with opportunities to develop expository, persuasive, expressive, and literary writing. *Holt Writer's Workshop 1* is designed to be used with Grades 6-8 and *Holt Writer's Workshop 2* is designed to be used with Grades 9-12.

Test Generators

The *Test Generators* are user-friendly software programs that enable teachers to create customized worksheets, quizzes, or tests for each grammar, usage, and mechanics chapter in the text. The *Test Generators* are available for Apple® II Series, IBM® PC and Compatibles, and Macintosh® computers.

ELEMENTS OF WRITING

JAMES L. KINNEAVY
JOHN E. WARRINER

Introductory Course

Holt, Rinehart and Winston

Harcourt Brace Jovanovich

Austin • Orlando • San Diego • Chicago • Dallas • Toronto

Critical Readers

Grateful acknowledgment is made to the following critical readers who reviewed pre-publication materials for this book:

John Algeo
University of Georgia
Athens, Georgia

Aileen Bonin
Harrison Middle School
Albuquerque, New Mexico

Anthony Buckley
East Texas State University
Commerce, Texas

Betsy Bunte
East Cobb Middle School
Marietta, Georgia

Norbert Elliot
New Jersey Institute of Technology
Newark, New Jersey

Elaine A. Espindle
Peabody Veterans Memorial High School
Peabody, Massachusetts

Sherry Evanofski
Heskett Middle School
Bedford, Ohio

Sheeran Flournoy
Moody Middle School
Richmond, Virginia

Nancy Fuleihan
Southwest Middle School
Orlando, Florida

Ruth Hall
Hillsborough County Schools
Tampa, Florida

Kim Holbrook
Griffiths Middle School
Downey, California

Printed in the United States of America

ISBN 0-03-047139-7

3 4 5 6 7 8 9 062 95 94

Authors

James L. Kinneavy, the Jane and Roland Blumberg Centennial Professor of English at The University of Texas at Austin, directed the development and writing of the composition strand in the program. He is the author of *A Theory of Discourse* and coauthor of *Writing in the Liberal Arts Tradition*. Professor Kinneavy is a leader in the field of rhetoric and composition and a respected educator whose teaching experience spans all levels—elementary, secondary, and college. He has continually been concerned with teaching writing to high school students.

John E. Warriner developed the organizational structure for the Handbook of Grammar, Usage, and Mechanics in the book. He coauthored the *English Workshop* series, was general editor of the *Composition: Models and Exercises* series, and editor of *Short Stories: Characters in Conflict*. He taught English for thirty-two years in junior and senior high school and college.

Writers and Editors

Ellen Ashdown has a Ph.D. in English from the University of Florida. She has taught composition and literature at the college level. She is a professional writer of educational materials and has published articles and reviews on education and art.

Jan Freeman has an M.A. in English from New York University. She has taught college composition classes. A published poet, she is a contributing editor to *The American Poetry Review*.

Mary Hix has an M.A. in English from Wake Forest University. She has taught freshman composition courses. She is a professional writer and editor of educational materials in language arts.

Madeline Travers-Hovland has an M.A. in Teaching from Harvard University. She has taught English in elementary and secondary school and has been an elementary school librarian. She is a professional writer of educational materials in literature and composition.

Alice M. Sohn has a Ph.D. in English Education from Florida State University. She has taught English in middle school, secondary school, and college. She has been a writer and editor of educational materials in language arts for twelve years.

Raymond Teague has an A.B. in English and journalism from Texas Christian University. He has been children's book editor for the *Fort Worth Star-Telegram* for more than ten years and has been a writer and editor of educational materials for seven years.

PART ONE

WRITING

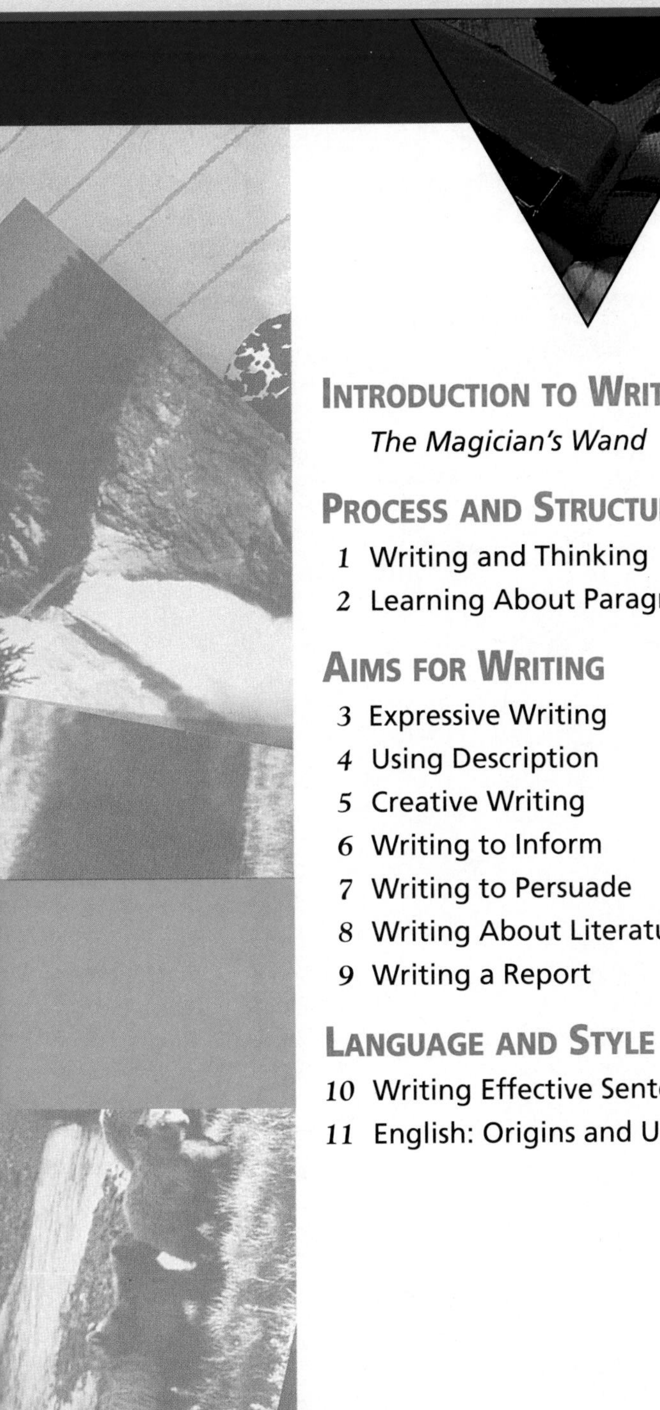

Introduction to Writing

The Magician's Wand

Process and Structure

1 Writing and Thinking

2 Learning About Paragraphs

Aims for Writing

3 Expressive Writing

4 Using Description

5 Creative Writing

6 Writing to Inform

7 Writing to Persuade

8 Writing About Literature

9 Writing a Report

Language and Style

10 Writing Effective Sentences

11 English: Origins and Uses

HIDDEN AGENTS *(pp. 2–17)*

OBJECTIVES

- To explore the ways writers and writing affect the world
- To identify and analyze the aims of writing
- To compare and contrast the aims of writing

USING THE INTRODUCTION TO COMPOSITION

This introduction to composition is just that—an introduction. It starts by talking briefly about the power of writing in peoples' lives rather than by discussing writing as schoolwork. Next, it touches upon the two central focuses of the writing chapters in the book—the "how" of writing (the

INTRODUCTION TO WRITING

THE MAGICIAN'S WAND

James L. Kinneavy

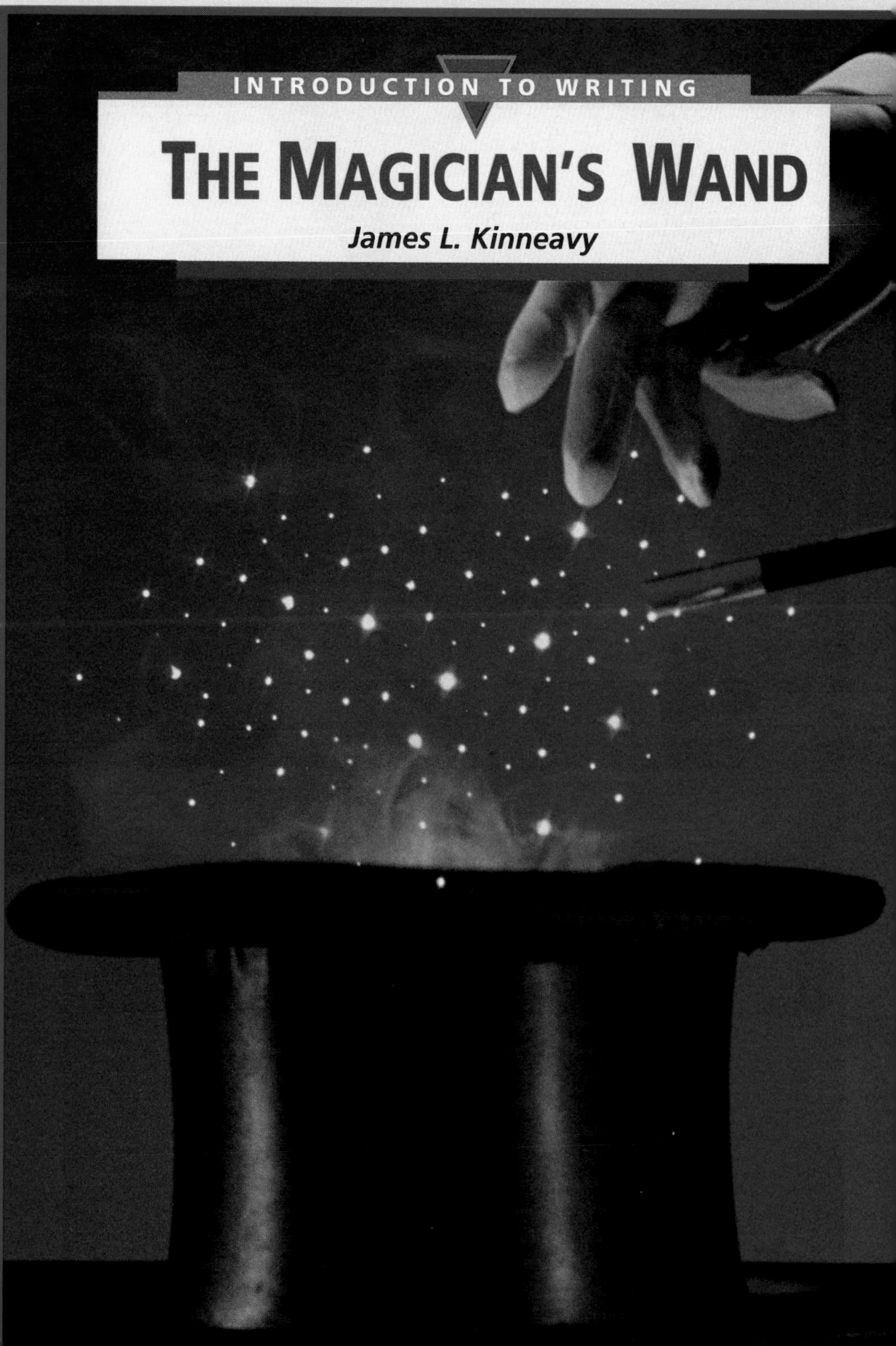

writing process) and the "why" of writing (aims).

The communication triangle on p. 5 graphically reflects the four major aims of Kinneavy's theory of discourse. For more information, refer to the essay in the front of this book, **"Meet the Aims and Modes of Writing,"** or to Dr. Kinneavy's two books, *A Theory of Discourse* and *Writing in the Liberal Arts Tradition.* ■

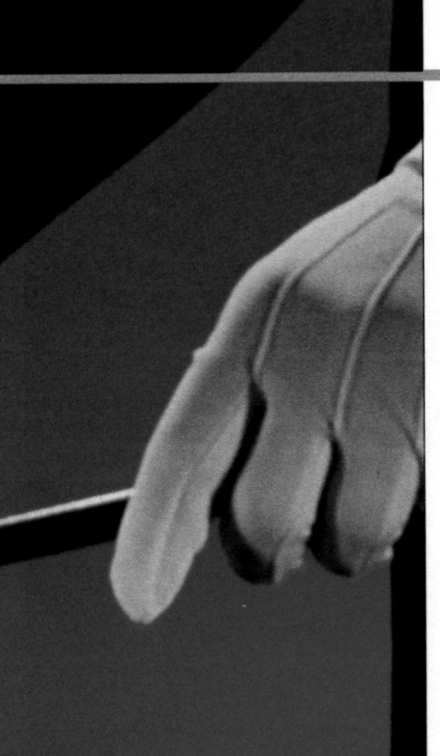

The tall, mysterious magician strides onto the stage, silk cape swirling. Suddenly, he stretches out his arm and points a slender wand at a dirt-filled flower pot. Presto! Flowers bloom. He shakes out a silk handkerchief, rolls it up, points the magic wand. Eureka! Birds fly from the silk. His assistant disappears into a small box. The **magician** waves the magic **wand** and points to the back of the auditorium. Presto! There's the assistant!

What amazing powers magicians appear to have. But did you know that some of the world's most powerful magicians don't wear capes or perform on stage? Yet they make things happen all around you. With their magic wands they explain mysteries (even magic tricks), build whole cities, fill theaters with laughter. Astounding!

Who are these people? What are their magic wands?

Who Are These Magicians?

These magicians are writers and their magic wands are words. Their words give them the power to make things happen and appear. What things? All the things that fill your life.

With their magic wands they tell how to build a skyscraper and how to repair your bike. They give instructions for new video games and explain black holes in space. They scare you and delight you with movies and TV shows. They convince you to recycle cans and buy new jeans. They say what mattered to them when they were your age.

Take a quick look around you. These word magicians have been at work everywhere. They've created computer software, dictionaries, and newspaper comics. They've made all sorts of things appear: textbooks, billboards, magazines, the song lyrics for your favorite hits—even baseball cards!

How important are these word magicians? Just stop for a minute and imagine the world without a single written word. It's a very empty stage, isn't it? Thank goodness for the people who fill our world with the power of words!

What's the Magic?

Writers really do have a special power: the power of communication. They have something to write about (a ***subject***), someone to say it to (an ***audience***), and a way to say it (a ***language***). You can have this power, too. Think of these magic elements as a communication triangle. Notice that language—both written and spoken—is at the center of the triangle.

How Do Writers Write?

The Writing Process

Writers even have a magic formula for what they do. But this formula is not a trick, and it's not a secret. It's a series of steps called the ***writing process.*** It helps writers develop their ideas and communicate them clearly. Different writers use the process in different ways, but it's a basic formula for making things happen on paper.

Prewriting	Thinking and planning; thinking of a subject to write about, a purpose, and an audience; collecting ideas and details; making a plan for presenting ideas
Writing	Writing a first draft; putting ideas into sentences and paragraphs; following the writing plan
Evaluating and Revising	Reading the draft closely; deciding what to keep and what to take out; making changes to make the draft better
Proofreading and Publishing	Looking for and fixing mistakes; writing a final copy; finding ways to share it with an audience

Why Do Writers Write?

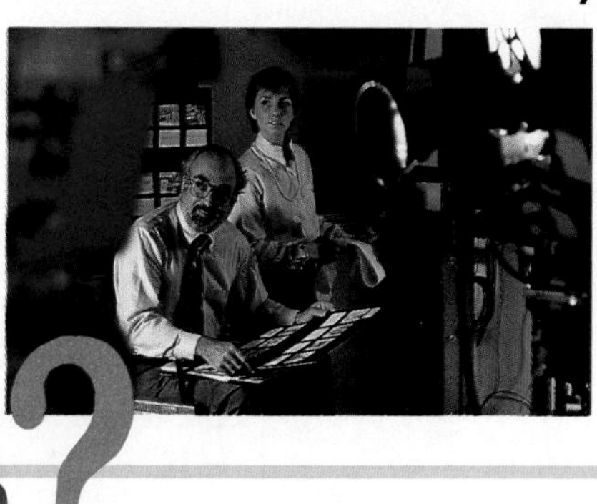

The Aims of Writing

Writers have four main reasons, or ***aims,*** for writing. They write to inform someone, to persuade someone, to express themselves, or to be creative. Sometimes a writer has only one aim, but other times a writer might combine two or more aims. Part of a writer's power comes from knowing the basic aim before starting to write.

To Inform	Writers give facts and other information, or explain something.
To Persuade	Writers also try to convince others to think or act in a certain way.
To Express Themselves	Writers sometimes just want to express their own thoughts and feelings.
To Be Creative	Writers may also write to create something new with language. They create stories, poems, songs, and plays.

Next you'll read four models about a man named Basil. Each model has a different aim. As you read, think about each writer's reason for writing.

INFORMATIVE WRITING

Local Millionaire Dies

Basil Northampton, 72, of 12 Axminster Court, died Tuesday of natural causes. He was born and lived most of his life in Surrey.

The son of working-class parents, Mr. Northampton made a fortune mining gold in the Transvaal. He was one of the ten richest men in England and was well known in financial circles for his wise investment decisions.

Mr. Northampton never married. Surviving family members include sisters Clotilda Greystone, Bernice Walton, and Maud Scarborough; brothers Cecil, Charles, and Lionel Northampton; and several nieces and nephews. At Mr. Northampton's request, family members will attend a private funeral. Distribution of his vast estate is not known.

Reader's Response

1. Why do you think newspapers print obituaries (death notices)? Do you think it's natural, or odd, to read obituaries about people you *don't* know? Why?
2. Can you think of any information to add to this obituary? Can you tell from reading it what the writer thinks and feels? Explain your answers.

ANSWERS

Reader's Response

Answers may vary.

1. Newspapers print obituaries to inform readers of recent deaths or to pay respect to the deceased. The first thing readers might look for is someone they know or know of. It seems natural to read obituaries about unknown people, probably out of curiosity.
2. There is no absolutely necessary material to add. There is only room for factual material here. The reader cannot tell what the writer's thoughts and feelings are because this obituary is designed strictly to inform.

EXPRESSIVE WRITING

July 1—The whole bunch of phony mon
grabbers was here today for my birthda
Ha! What they'd really like to celebrate
I hope I live forever jus

July 1—The whole bunch of phony money-grabbers was here today for my birthday. Ha! What they'd really like to celebrate is my death day. I hope I live forever just to spite them.

That lazy wimp Percival had the nerve to ask me to buy him some fancy new car. Why should it be up to me to give him a car he'd probably just wreck? I told him to get a job and buy his own car. "You can't take it with you, you know," he whined. That's all he knows.

They think I can't hear. They go around acting all lovey-dovey even while they're saying mean things about me. They call me names and say I'm stingy. Why shouldn't I be stingy with them? Not one of them deserves even a part of what I have. Letitia's still pouting because I won't buy her a new fur coat. They never ask for anything sensible. Well, it's my fortune. I earned it. I'll decide where it goes.

Thanks to Verner, my plan is working. He's the only relative who doesn't want to bleed me dry. And he's the only one who never says I can't take it with me. We will see, won't we? Ha!

READER'S RESPONSE

1. Who do you think wrote this journal entry?
2. What is on the writer's mind? What feelings does the writer express?

ANSWERS

Reader's Response

1. Basil Northampton
2. The writer is upset because his family members seem only interested in his money. He also seems to want to hurt them. He expresses feelings of dislike—even hatred—and superiority.

ANSWERS

Reader's Response

Answers may vary.

1. A person's decision about inheritance shouldn't necessarily *always* be honored. Sometimes it can be entirely unfair. Sometimes a person can be coerced into leaving certain things to certain people.
2. Students might say they would sign. As Bernice says, there is plenty of money to go around; no one will be hurt by sharing it. Her strongest argument involves saying everyone will benefit and no one will be hurt by sharing.

PERSUASIVE WRITING

Dear Charles,

As you know, Basil has announced that he won't split up his fortune when he dies. Of course, this means that one of us will get millions and the rest of us will get nothing. This is a situation that could hurt any one of us very much. But I have a plan that will help us all. We should draw up an agreement stating that whoever receives the money will share it equally with the rest. Anyone interested in fairness will surely sign it.

We have all been equally kind and loyal to Basil. We deserve to be rewarded. We also have to admit that Basil has gotten a little odd in recent years. He may have decided who should get the money when he wasn't thinking clearly. I'm sure he really wants all of us to share it. Most important, there is plenty of money to go around. Everyone will benefit from sharing it, and no one will be hurt.

I will have my lawyer write the agreement. To protect your interests, you should sign it. It's completely to your advantage.

Your loving sister,
Bernice

Reader's Response

1. Someone could leave a fortune to a goldfish. Should a person's decisions in a will *always* be honored? Or can that be unfair? What do you think?
2. If you were Charles, would Bernice's letter convince you to sign the agreement? Why or why not? What do you think is Bernice's strongest reason?

CREATIVE WRITING

You Can't Take It with You

by Eva-Lis Wuorio

There was no denying two facts. Uncle Basil was rich. Uncle Basil was a miser.

The family were unanimous about that. They had used up all the words as their temper and their need of ready money dictated. Gentle Aunt Clotilda, who wanted a new string of pearls because the one she had was getting old, had merely called him Scrooge Basil. Percival, having again smashed his Aston Martin for which he had not paid, had declared Uncle Basil a skinflint, a miser, tightwad, churl, and usurer with colorful adjectives added. The rest had used up all the other words in the dictionary.

"He doesn't have to be so parsimonious, that's true, with all he has," said Percival's mother. "But you shouldn't use rude words, Percival. They might get back to him."

"He can't take it with him," said Percival's sister Letitia, combing her golden hair. "I need a new fur but he said, 'Why? it's summer.' Well! He's mingy, that's what he is."

"He can't take it with him" was a phrase the family used so often it began to slip out in front of Uncle Basil as well.

"You can't take it with you, Uncle Basil," they said. "Why don't you buy a sensible house out in the country, and we could all come and visit you? Horses. A swimming pool. The lot. Think what fun you'd have, and you can certainly afford it. You can't take it with you, you know."

Uncle Basil had heard all the words they called him because he wasn't as deaf as he made out. He knew he was a mingy, stingy, penny-pinching screw, scrimp, scraper, pinchfist, hoarder, and curmudgeon (just to start with). There were other words, less gentle, he'd also heard himself called. He didn't mind. What galled him was the oft repeated warning, "You can't take it with you." After all, it was all his.

He'd gone to the Transvaal when there was still gold to be found if one knew where to look. He'd found it. They said he'd come back too old to enjoy his fortune. What did they know? He enjoyed simply having a fortune. He enjoyed also saying no to them all. They were like circus animals, he often thought, behind the bars of their thousand demands of something for nothing.

Only once had he said yes. That was when his sister asked him to take on Verner, her somewhat slow-witted eldest son. "He'll do as your secretary," his sister Maud had said. Verner didn't do at all as a secretary, but since all he wanted to be happy was to be told what to do, Uncle Basil let him stick around as an all-around handyman.

Uncle Basil lived neatly in a house very much too small for his money, the family said, in an unfashionable suburb. It was precisely like the house where he had been born. Verner looked after the small garden, fetched the papers from the corner tobacconist, and filed his nails when he had time. He had nice nails. He never said to Uncle Basil, "You can't take it with you," because it didn't occur to him.

Uncle Basil also used Verner to run messages to his man of affairs, the bank, and such, since he didn't believe either in the mails or the telephone. Verner got used to carrying thick envelopes back and forth without ever bothering to question what was in them. Uncle Basil's lawyers, accountants, and bank managers also got used to his somewhat unorthodox business methods. He did have a fortune, and he kept making money with his investments. Rich men have always been allowed their foibles.

Another foible of Uncle Basil's was that, while he still was in excellent health he had Verner drive him out to an old-fashioned carpenter shop where he had himself measured for a coffin. He wanted it roomy, he said.

The master carpenter was a dour countryman of the same generation as Uncle Basil, and he accepted the order matter-of-factly. They consulted about woods and prices, and settled on a medium-price, unlined coffin. A lined one would have cost double.

"I'll line it myself," Uncle Basil said. "Or Verner can. There's plenty of time. I don't intend to pop off tomorrow. It would give the family too much satisfaction. I like enjoying my fortune."

Then one morning, while in good humor and sound mind, he sent Verner for his lawyer. The family got to hear about this and there were in-fights, out-fights, and general quarreling while they tried to find out to whom Uncle Basil had decided to leave his money. To put them out of their misery, he said, he'd tell them the truth. He didn't like scattering money about. He liked it in a lump sum. Quit bothering him about it.

That happened a good decade before the morning his housekeeper, taking him his tea, found him peacefully asleep forever. It had been a good decade for him. The family hadn't dared to worry him, and his investments had risen steadily.

Only Percival, always pressed for money, had threatened to put arsenic in his tea but when the usual proceedings were gone through Uncle Basil was found to have died a natural death. "A happy death," said the family. "He hadn't suffered."

They began to remember loudly how nice they'd been to him and argued about who had been the nicest. It was true too. They had been attentive, the way families tend to be to rich and stubborn elderly relatives. They didn't know he'd heard all they'd said out of his hearing, as well as the flattering drivel they'd spread like soft butter on hot toast in his hearing. Everyone, recalling his own efforts to be thoroughly nice, was certain that he and only he would be the heir to the Lump Sum.

They rushed to consult the lawyer. He said that he had been instructed by Uncle Basil in sane and precise terms. The cremation was to take place immediately after the death, and they would find the coffin ready in the garden shed. Verner would know where it was.

"Nothing else?"

"Well," said the lawyer in the way lawyers have, "he left instructions for a funeral repast to be sent in from Fortnum and Mason. Everything of the best. Goose and turkey, venison and beef, oysters and lobsters, and wines of good vintage plus plenty of whiskey. He liked to think of a good send-off, curmudgeon though he was, he'd said."

The family was a little shaken by the use of the word "curmudgeon." How did Uncle Basil know about that? But they were relieved to hear that the lawyer also had an envelope, the contents of which he did not know, to read to them at the feast after the cremation.

They all bought expensive black clothes, since black was the color of that season anyway, and whoever inherited would share the wealth. That was only fair.

Only Verner said that couldn't they buy Uncle Basil a smarter coffin? The one in the garden shed was pretty tatty, since the roof leaked. But the family hardly listened to him. After all, it would only be burned, so what did it matter?

So, duly and with proper sorrow, Uncle Basil was cremated.

The family returned to the little house as the housekeeper was leaving. Uncle Basil had given her a generous amount of cash, telling her how to place it so as to have a fair income for life. In gratitude she'd spread out the Fortnum and Mason goodies, but she wasn't prepared to stay to do the dishes.

They were a little surprised, but not dismayed, to hear from Verner that the house was now in his name. Uncle Basil had also given him a small sum of cash and told him how to invest it. The family taxed him about it, but the amount was so nominal they were relieved to know Verner would be off their hands. Verner himself, though mildly missing the old man because he was used to him, was quite content with his lot. He wasn't used to much, so he didn't need much.

The storm broke when the lawyer finally opened the envelope.

There was only one line in Uncle Basil's scrawl.

"I did take it with me."

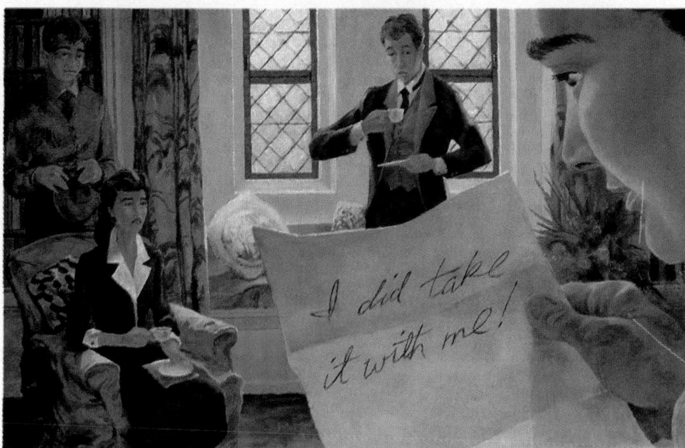

Of course there was a great to-do. What about the fortune? The millions and millions!

Yes, said the men of affairs, the accountants, and even the bank managers, who finally admitted, yes, there had been a very considerable fortune. Uncle Basil, however, had drawn large sums in cash, steadily and regularly, over the past decade. What had he done with it? That the men of affairs, the accountants, and the bank managers did not know. After all, it had been Uncle Basil's money, ergo, his affair.

Not a trace of the vast fortune ever came to light.

No one thought to ask Verner, and it didn't occur to Verner to volunteer that for quite a long time he had been lining the coffin, at Uncle Basil's behest, with thick envelopes he brought back from the banks. First he'd done a thick layer of these envelopes all around the sides and bottom of the coffin. Then, as Uncle Basil wanted, he'd tacked on blue sailcloth.

He might not be so bright in his head but he was smart with his hands.

He'd done a neat job.

Reader's Response

1. Basil's family considered him mean and stingy. How would you describe him? Why?
2. Stories with a surprise ending, or twist, are popular. Do you like them? Did you guess the ending? (If so, what clues did you use?) Besides the ending, what was your favorite part of the story?

ANSWERS

Reader's Response

Answers may vary.

1. Students may think he is mean and stingy. He has plenty of money but is not willing to part with it. The money will do him no good when he dies, but he prefers destroying it to allowing others to enjoy or benefit from it.
2. Most people like stories with surprise endings. Some students may guess the ending. The main clue was the size of the coffin along with the repeated statement, "You can't take it with you." An interesting part other than the ending was hearing about Basil's not using telephones or the mail.

Writing and Thinking Activities

1. Discuss these questions with two or three classmates.
   - **a.** In which model does the writer try to convince the reader to do something? How?
   - **b.** Which model is mostly about the writer's own thoughts and feelings?
   - **c.** Which model gives mostly factual information about Basil?
   - **d.** Which model tells a story? What creative ending does the story have?
2. Did you ever think about the ways you communicate? On one ordinary day of your life, jot down the ways you use language. Make a note when you write, read, speak, and listen to words. Decide what your aim is each time: to inform, persuade, express yourself, be creative—or some mixture? Then talk over your day with two or three classmates. Which aims appear most often for each of you?
3. Bring a magazine or newspaper to class. With a group, try to find examples of the four types of writing: informative, persuasive, self-expressive, and creative. Which type do you find most often? Compare your findings with another group's. Do different publications focus on different types of writing?
4. What do you think of as creative writing? Probably novels, short stories, poems, and plays. They take a lot of imagination. But can other writing be creative, too? What about Bernice's letter to Charles? Or Uncle Basil's journal entry? In what ways are Bernice and Basil being creative in those writings? Find something you've written that is not a story or poem but that you feel is creative in some way. Explain why.

ANSWERS

Writing and Thinking Activities

Answers may vary.

1a. In the letter from Bernice to Charles, Bernice lists strong arguments for splitting the fortune. She appeals to Charles's sense of fairness.

b. the journal entry

c. the obituary notice

d. "You Can't Take It with You" tells a story. At the end Basil has found a way to take it with him or, more accurately, a way to see to it that no one else benefits from it.

2. Students will probably be surprised at how often they communicate with a specific purpose in mind.

3. Yes, different publications focus on different types of writing. News magazines and newspapers are primarily informative, but their editorials and advertisements are persuasive. Fiction magazines primarily involve creative writing. Many magazines and newspapers publish commentaries and narratives that are self-expressive. Have students look for all four kinds of writing.

4. All writing can be creative in the sense that the term is used here. Bernice's letter to Charles involves a creative plan to solve the family's problem about Basil's money. Basil's journal entry shows creativity as he struggles to arrive at a plan to keep anyone but himself from having his money. It also shows his attempt to put his feelings on paper. Finally, it shows his creativity in labeling members of his family.

Chapter 1

WRITING AND THINKING

OBJECTIVES

- To identify ideas and to associate them with a writing topic
- To record and group ideas related to a topic
- To select material appropriate for the purpose and audience
- To organize and draft a paragraph from selected material
- To evaluate and revise a paragraph by adding, cutting, replacing, and reordering words and ideas
- To proofread a paragraph for usage and mechanical errors
- To identify ways of publishing writing

Motivation

Start a class discussion about the kinds of reading students enjoy. Begin by asking questions about the subject matter and authors they prefer. List students' favorite subjects and authors on the chalkboard and ask what makes each author interesting to read and how the students think authors get their ideas.

Introduction

Briefly review with students the list of subjects they have generated. As students begin to discover the variety of subject matter mentioned, explain that there are as many kinds of writing ideas as there are people to write about them.

Lead students in a discussion of the kinds of writing they have done that they enjoy. Direct questions to the discovery of a reason and an audience for their writing. What was the writing meant to do? What was its aim? Who was the reader to be? Help students to differentiate the four aims of writing: (1) expressing feelings, (2) telling stories, (3) explaining facts, and (4) influencing readers. With this introduction, students should be able to relate to the ideas the poet Naomi Shihab Nye has about writing.

Integration

This chapter introduces the writing process and will be useful in helping students organize their thinking and writing across the curriculum. If they are studying poetry, you may want them to compare other poets' descriptions of how they get ideas with how Naomi Shihab Nye describes her process.

If you are teaching critical-thinking skills, refer students to the analysis, synthesis, and evaluation skills required in selecting information, organizing a paragraph, and critiquing it.

Basic research skills used in the prewriting stage **(Exercise 7)** will be helpful to students as they begin science and social studies projects. Strategies for note taking **(Critical Thinking Exercise)** will also be helpful in other areas of study. Critical-listening skills will help students prepare for test taking.

The chart on the next page illustrates the strands of language arts as they are integrated into this chapter. For vocabulary study, glossary words are underlined in some writing models.

QUOTATIONS

All **Quotations for the Day** are chosen because of their relevance to instructional material presented in that segment of the chapter and for their usefulness in establishing student interest in writing.

INTEGRATING THE LANGUAGE ARTS

Selection	Reading and Literature	Writing and Critical Thinking	Language and Syntax	Speaking, Listening, and Other Expression Skills
"The Rider" by Naomi Shihab Nye **20-22** from ***Expecting the Unexpected*** **55**	Applying interpretive and creative thinking **23, 27, 30, 38, 40, 43, 46** Reading with a focus **35** Gathering information using research skills **35** Selecting appropriate sources to locate information **35** Taking notes **36** Using mass media to obtain information **36** Recognizing irrelevant statements **38, 46** Making judgments and using logical reasoning **38, 40, 41, 43, 46** Recognizing facts and supporting details **38, 41, 43, 46** Sequencing ideas **40** Categorizing ideas **40, 41, 43, 46** Forming critical judgments and evaluating writing **50**	Exploring personal experience and knowledge **23, 27, 29, 30** Generating and recording ideas **23, 30** Generating ideas from imagination **23, 27, 40** Writing a journal entry **27** Using freewriting techniques and looping **29** Generating cluster diagrams **31** Using questions to explore ideas **33, 55** Taking notes from reference material **35, 36** Limiting information for audience and purpose **38, 40, 46** Organizing ideas for writing **40, 41, 43, 46** Choosing method of organization for audience and purpose **40** Including details for audience and purpose **40** Charting information **43** Writing a topic sentence **45** Writing a paragraph **46** Revising paragraphs **50** Proofreading paragraphs **52** Generating publishing ideas **53** Writing letters to request information **55**	Using a dictionary for spelling and usage **52** Using a grammar handbook for revising **52**	Expressing opinions, feelings, and ideas **30, 50** Observing details by viewing and listening **36** Using mass media to obtain information **36** Sharing writing with peers **50** Creating cartoons that communicate information **54**

CHAPTER 1

SEGMENT PLANNING GUIDE

Whether you are planning for a quick review of a writing concept or preparing an extended lesson on composition, you can use the following Planning Guide to adapt the chapter material to the individual needs of your class.

	SEGMENT	PAGES	CONTENT	RESOURCES
1	*Looking at the Process*	*19-23*		
	Literary Model **"The Rider"**	20-22	Guided reading: a model of a writer's process	
	Reader's Response	23	Model evaluation: responding to literature and analyzing the poet's words and ideas	
2	*Aim and Process*	*24-25*		
3	*Prewriting*	*26-43*		Freewriting 1 Brainstorming 2 Clustering 3 Asking Questions 4 Thinking About Purpose and Audience 5 Chronological Order and Spatial Order 6 Charts and Diagrams 7
	Finding Ideas for Writing	26	Guidelines: finding ideas for writing	
	Chart: Prewriting Techniques	26	Guidelines: analyzing prewriting techniques	
	Writer's Journal	26-27	Guidelines: making journal entries	
	Exercise 1	27	Applied practice: starting a journal	
	Freewriting	27-28	Guidelines: examining criteria for freewriting	
	Exercise 2	29	Applied practice: using freewriting	
	Brainstorming	29	Guidelines: listing ideas	
	Exercise 3	30	Cooperative learning: brainstorming and recording ideas	
	Clustering	30-31	Guidelines: making a cluster map	
	Exercise 4	31	Applied practice: creating a cluster diagram	
	Asking Questions	32-33	Guidelines: finding facts and ideas	
	Exercise 5	33	Applied practice: generating *5W-How?* questions	
	Exercise 6	33	Cooperative learning: writing "What if?" questions	
	Reading and Listening	34	Introduction: gathering information	
	Reading with a Focus	34	Guidelines: reading for specific information	
	Exercise 7	35	Applied practice: reading to find answers	
	Listening with a Focus	35	Guidelines: listening for specific information	
	Critical Thinking: Observing Details	36	Explanation: watching and listening for details	
	Critical Thinking Exercise	36	Cooperative learning: observing details and taking notes	
	Thinking About Purpose and Audience	37	Guidelines: analyzing and selecting appropriate purpose and audience	
	Exercise 8	38	Applied practice: choosing appropriate details	
	Arranging Ideas	39	Introduction: choosing a method of order	
	Chart: Arranging Ideas	39	Guidelines: examining ways of arranging information	

All the resources listed in this chapter are located in the *Teacher's ResourceBank™*.

SEGMENT	PAGES	CONTENT	RESOURCES
Critical Thinking: Arranging Ideas	40	Guidelines: deciding how to arrange information	
Critical Thinking Exercise	40	Applied practice: using criteria to decide order	
Using Visuals	41-42	Explanation: making charts and diagrams	
Exercise 9	43	Applied practice: making a chart to organize notes	
4 *Writing*	*44-46*		Writing a First Draft 8
Writing a First Draft	44	Guidelines: using criteria and examining a model	
Writing Note	44	Writing suggestion: using a natural voice	
Critical Thinking: Synthesizing Ideas	45-46	Guidelines: combining main ideas with details	
Critical Thinking Exercise	46	Applied practice: combining ideas in a paragraph	
5 *Evaluating and Revising*	*47-50*		Practicing Peer Evaluation 9 Revising: Adding and Cutting 10 Revising: Replacing and Reordering 11
Chart: Guidelines for Peer Evaluation	48	Guidelines: examining tips for peer evaluation	
Chart: Guidelines for Evaluating and Revising	49	Guidelines: applying evaluation and revision techniques	
Exercise 10	50	Cooperative learning: evaluating and revising	
6 *Proofreading and Publishing*	*51-53*		Proofreading 12
Chart: Proofreading	51	Guidelines: examining criteria for proofreading	
Exercise 11	52	Cooperative learning: proofreading a paragraph	
Publishing	52	Publishing ideas: reaching an audience	
Chart: Form of a Paper	53	Guidelines: examining criteria for good form	
Exercise 12	53	Applied practice: brainstorming publishing ideas	
Chart: Symbols for Revising and Proofreading	53	Guidelines: examining symbols for revision and proofreading	
7 *Making Connections*	*54-55*		
Creating a Cartoon About Writing	54	Cooperative learning: identifying and expressing writer's block	
Asking a Writer Questions	55	Applied practice: writing to an author	
Literary Model ***Expecting the Unexpected***	55	Guided reading: considering where a writer writes	
WHOLE-CHAPTER RESOURCE Chapter Review			

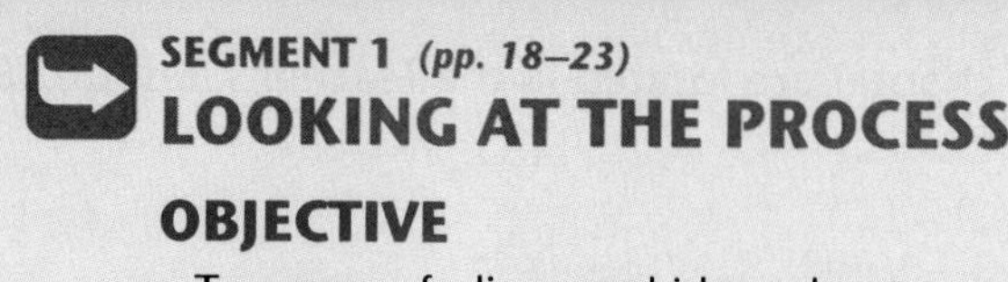

SEGMENT 1 *(pp. 18–23)*

LOOKING AT THE PROCESS

OBJECTIVE

- To express feelings and ideas about writing

TEACHING THE LESSON

Begin a discussion of the relationship between writing and thinking. Ask students what tools they use to write. [Students might mention pencils, paper, erasers, desks, or computers.] Point out that although these are needed, ideas are even more important to writing. Have volunteers read the introduction aloud. Ask students if the writing

VISUAL CONNECTIONS
Berta

About the Artist. Warren Brandt was born in 1918 in Greensboro, North Carolina. He started drawing when he was thirteen, and he studied art in New York after he graduated from high school. Brandt later worked with animation for Walt Disney in California, but his art was put on hold when he volunteered for military service in 1940. After serving with the military in World War II, Brandt returned to art school and graduated with honors from Washington University in St. Louis, Missouri.

Warren Brandt's work is characterized by strong, stable compositions that give the viewer a sense of movement within a fixed framework. Noted for his powerful use of color and texture, Brandt's main influences have been artists such as Beckmann, Matisse, and Cézanne.

Ideas for Writing. Discuss the prewriting stage of the writing process with students. Then ask them to make notes on the thoughts and feelings that Brandt's picture inspires in them. Let the students choose the prewriting techniques they like best for their notes. Some students may take their notes through the other stages of the writing process to create poems, journal entries, essays, or short stories.

1 WRITING AND THINKING

problems seem familiar. Have students mention what they find difficult about writing. Point out that writing is capturing ideas and that it is difficult to find just the right words to express one's thoughts.

After students have read Naomi Shihab Nye's poem silently, you can read it aloud and continue with Nye's thoughts about writing. Ask the class to listen for ways the poet generates her ideas.

Looking at the Process

What's your reaction to writing? Maybe you're not sure. You don't *love* writing and you don't *hate* writing. It's just that sometimes the **process** of writing isn't easy.

Writing and You. Maybe it takes you forever to get an idea for writing. Or, you have great ideas but get stuck when you're choosing the right words. Well, you're not alone. Every writer faces trouble like that. It's all part of the *writing process:* the steps that you take to get from blank paper to finished paper. Did you realize that you and "real writers"—even *poets*—go through the same process?

As You Read. In the poem on the next page, Naomi Shihab Nye says that poets are "regular people." Read her poem and her thoughts about writing. Where does she get her ideas? What does she think of blank paper?

Berta, Warren Brandt (1967–68). Oil on canvas. 36″ × 40″. Collection Dr. & Mrs. Arnold D. Kerr, Wilmington, DE. © 1988 the artist. Reproduced by permission of Hudson Hills Press.

QUOTATION FOR THE DAY

"Memory is the mother of imagination, reason and skill . . . [Memory] is the tutor, the poet, the library with which you travel." (Mark Van Doren, 1894–1972, American writer and teacher)

Explain that writers often gather ideas from material they read, from conversations they overhear, or from events they witness. Students might brainstorm lists of ideas for future writings and start collections of unusual or interesting things they see, hear, or read.

LEP/ESL

General Strategies. Ask students to share examples of writing found in their daily lives and list these on the chalkboard. [Examples include billboards, magazines and newspapers, comic books, personal letters, graffiti, and textbooks.] Encourage students to discuss the following questions: Why can't people rely solely on oral communication? Is writing valuable? How can writing help students?

GUIDED PRACTICE

The first four **Reader's Response** questions provide an opportunity for continued class discussion and guided practice. Encourage a variety of responses to the questions.

INDEPENDENT PRACTICE

You may want to assign the last **Reader's Response** question as independent practice. The question could serve as a prompt for a short essay.

The Rider

by Naomi Shihab Nye

A boy told me
if he rollerskated fast enough
1 his loneliness couldn't catch up to him,

the best reason I ever heard
for trying to be a champion.

What I wonder tonight
pedaling hard down King William Street
is if it translates to bicycles.

A victory! To leave your loneliness
panting behind you on some street corner
2 while you float free into a cloud of sudden azaleas,
3
4 luminous pink petals that have never felt loneliness,
no matter how slowly they fell.

USING THE SELECTION
The Rider

1
The writer uses personification in this poem—loneliness is a quick-moving companion who pursues the poet unless she moves fast enough to escape.

2
azaleas: shrubs with showy flowers

3
luminous: full of light; glowing

4
A play on words with bicycle *pedals* and azalea *petals* emphasizes the differences in images.

ASSESSMENT

Assess students' understanding by evaluating their ability to produce a variety of responses to the **Reader's Response** questions.

CLOSURE

Ask students to explain what good writing involves. Make sure they include the relationship between writing and thinking. Survey the class for ways to get writing ideas, and list the responses on the chalkboard. You may want to classify them as Nye did—from people, experience, quotations, and imagination.

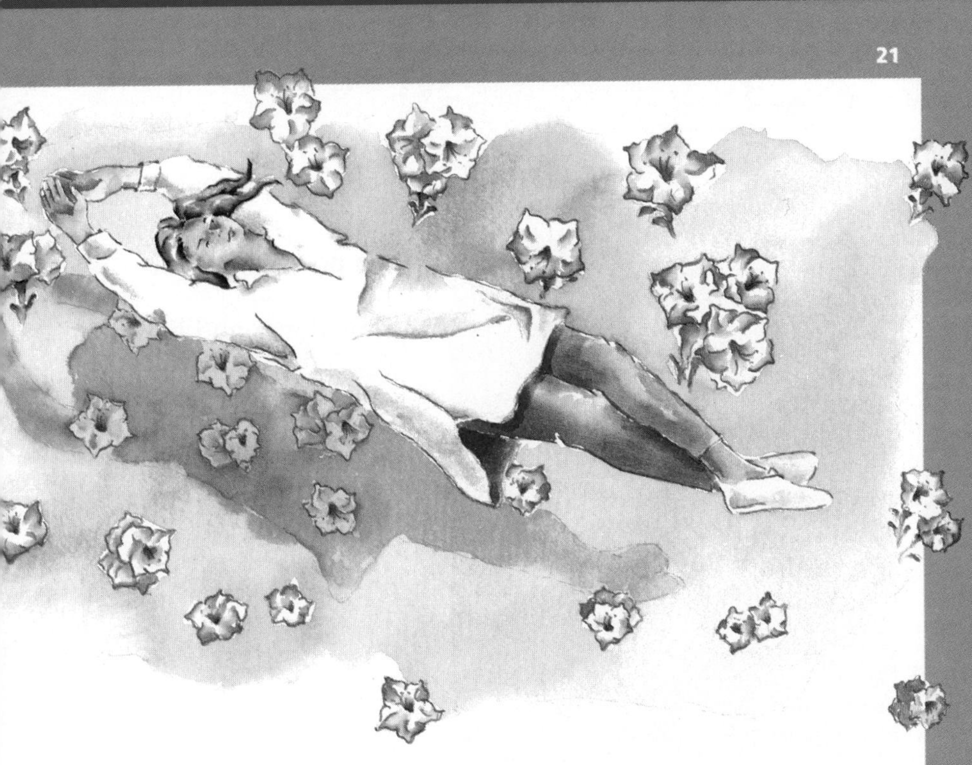

"For me poetry has always been a way of paying attention to the world. We hear so many voices every day, swirling around us, and a poem makes us slow down and listen carefully to a few things we have really heard, deep inside. For me poems usually begin with 'true things'—people, experiences, quotes—but quickly ride off into that other territory of imagination, which lives alongside us as much as we will allow in a world that likes to pay too much attention to 'facts' sometimes. I have always had a slight difficulty distinguishing where the 'true' part ends and the 'made-up' part begins, because I think of dreaming and imagining as being another kind of *true.* Once I made up a song that ends, 'You tell me what's real, what I see or what I feel?', and I think that corresponds to the poems we make out of our lives."

COOPERATIVE LEARNING

Divide the class into groups of five or six and have each group think of as many sources of writing ideas as they can. Use Nye's ideas about people, experiences, and quotations to get the students started. Challenge each group to find the most sources. Have a student from each group read the ideas aloud.

EXTENSION

Suggest students illustrate portions of the poem, contrasting the literal portions with the imaginative. Some students might prefer finding other poems to illustrate. ■

VISUAL CONNECTIONS

Exploring the Subject. Naomi Shihab Nye was born in St. Louis, Missouri on March 12, 1952. She has written six books of poetry.

SELECTION AMENDMENT

Description of change: excerpted

Rational: to focus on the concept of the connection between writing and thinking presented in this chapter.

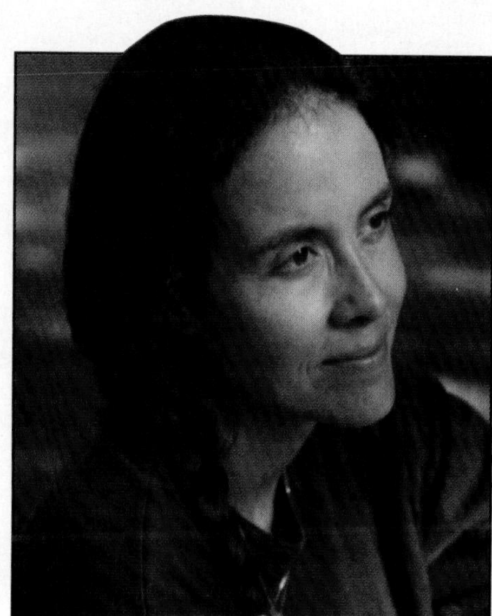

"...a poem makes us slow down and listen carefully to a few things we have really heard, deep inside."

"Sometimes there's no one to listen to what you really might like to say at a certain moment. The paper will always listen. Also, the more you write, the paper will begin to speak back and allow you to discover new parts of your own life and other lives and feel how things connect."

"Poets are explorers, pilgrims. Most of the poets I know are not in the least bit frilly. Poets are also regular people who live down the block and do simple things like wash clothes and stir soup. Sometimes students ask, 'Are you famous?', as if fame is what would make a poet happy. I prefer the idea of being invisible, traveling through the world lightly, seeing and remembering as much as I can."

Reader's Response

1. Naomi Shihab Nye's poem puts into words what it feels like to ride (or run or skate or swim) *very hard.* When you're moving all-out, do you leave "loneliness panting behind"? Do you "float free"? What words would you use to describe how you feel when you do the following:
   When I ride my bike I ______.
   When I swim I ______.
   When I skate I ______.
2. Writing ideas come from "people, experiences, quotes" for Naomi Shihab Nye. Where do you get your best ideas?
3. She also says that dreaming and imagining are "another kind of *true.*" What do you think she means? In your writing, how do you use your imagination? Give an example.
4. Nye says "the paper will always listen" and after a while it will "speak back." Have you ever tried writing out your thoughts, just for yourself? Do you sometimes surprise yourself when writing—maybe coming up with a word or idea you didn't expect?
5. Do you agree that being invisible would be good for your writing? Why or why not?

LOOKING AHEAD

In this chapter you'll learn some writing techniques. They'll help you with your own writing process. And many of them are fun. You'll get to practice all parts of writing, from finding topics to publishing. As you try out your writing, remember that

- writing and thinking go together
- the writing process isn't just rules—you'll be able to make the process fit *you*

ANSWERS

Reader's Response

Responses will vary.

1. Most students will say that hard physical activity allows them to feel free and alive. Words students might use include *escape, fly,* and *glide.*
2. Encourage varied responses. Have students give examples of how they get ideas.
3. Responses will vary. Students may say that Nye means dreaming and imagining are valid human activities.
4. Encourage students to think about ideas they discovered as they were writing.
5. Some students might suggest it would be good to be invisible to observe the world without disturbing it.

SEGMENT 2 *(pp. 24–25)*

THE "WHY" AND "HOW" OF WRITING

TEACHING THE AIMS

To assist students in understanding the reasons for writing, display and discuss several types of reading that they enjoy.

Have a volunteer read the opening paragraphs and discuss the **Why People Write** chart. Ask students for examples of each writing purpose. Assess identification of the purposes by presenting various samples of writing and having students tell what purpose each has.

SOFTWARE CONNECTION

Holt Writer's Workshop 1 interactive software for grades 6–8 guides students through each stage of the writing process and offers a wide variety of assignments for each of the writing aims. The program provides a word processor; a built-in spell check feature; and an on-line grammar, usage, and mechanics handbook. *Holt Writer's Workshop 1* can be purchased separately.

Aim—The "Why" of Writing

It may seem like there should be as many individual purposes for writing as there are people who write. But there are really just a few.

WHY PEOPLE WRITE	
To express themselves	To explore their ideas and feelings; to learn more about themselves
To share information	To tell others about things they need or want to know; to give knowledge and information to others
To persuade	To cause others to think or do something
To create literature	To write something creative or unique

Whatever people write has one of these four purposes. However, sometimes more than one of these four purposes shows up in a single piece of writing at the same time. For example, a writer may want to express himself or herself, to persuade you to think a certain way about a topic, and to create a piece of literature—all at the same time.

No matter what country or language a writer writes in, every time a writer writes, it's for at least one of these same four purposes.

Process—The "How" of Writing

Wouldn't it be great if you had an Instant Perfect Writing pen? You could sit right down and turn out a guaranteed "A" paper in five minutes. And the pen would do all the work. Unfortunately, there's no

To help students think about writing as a process, have them discuss projects that require following steps such as making model cars or baking bread. How did they begin? Did they follow set steps? Explain that writing is also a process of set steps and that writing skills improve with practice.

Discuss the chart and the steps involved in good writing. Assess understanding by giving examples from each stage and by having students name the stage. ■

such magic writing tool. Good writing takes time and a great deal of thinking.

Most writers go through a whole process, or series of steps, shown in the following diagram. Notice that each stage in the writing process requires thinking.

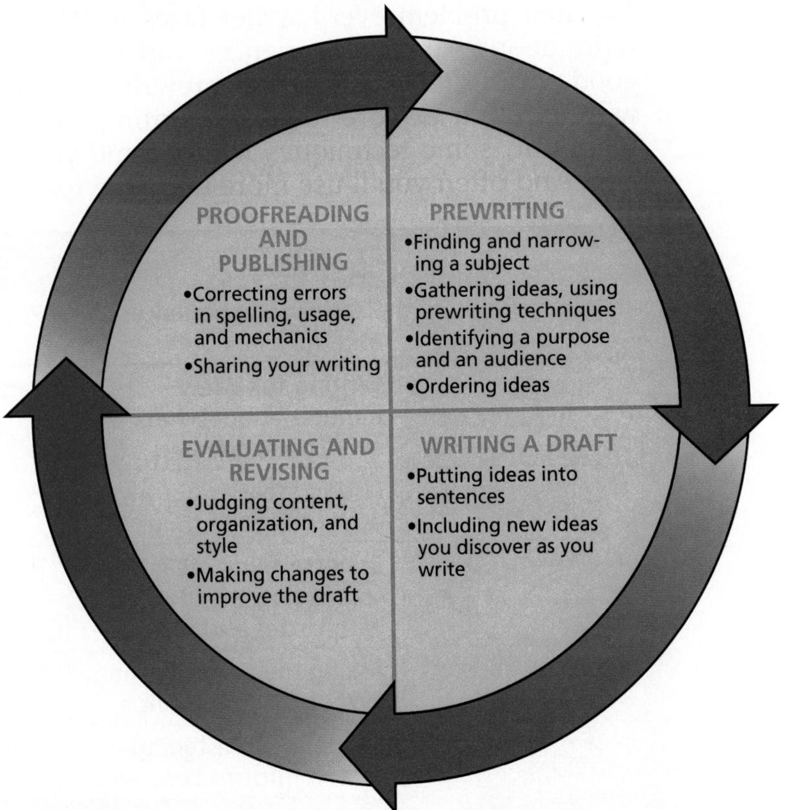

Each time you write, the process may be a little different. Sometimes you work straight through the stages, but at other times you may go back and forth between stages. Suppose you're entering a Mother's Day writing contest. You write an entry that gives three reasons why your mom should win. But when you reread it, you decide it needs examples of what your mom does and says. Then you would go back to the prewriting stage to think of examples.

COOPERATIVE LEARNING

To help students relate the writing process to familiar operations, divide the class into four groups and assign each group a project idea. Have each group chart four stages of development, similar to the stages of writing. Ideas you might use include playing on a championship baseball team, performing in a school play, cooking for a birthday banquet, or swimming in a meet. Have a spokesperson from each group tell how the project follows the same stages as writing.

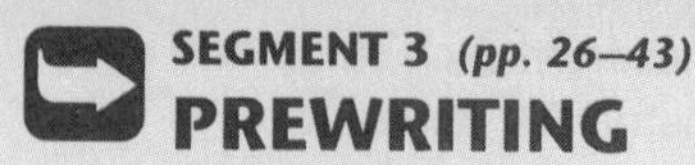

SEGMENT 3 *(pp. 26–43)*

PREWRITING

OBJECTIVES

- To record personal experiences in a journal
- To select and limit a topic and to freewrite about the topic
- To brainstorm and record ideas
- To group ideas related to a topic
- To design questions for exploring ideas
- To generate ideas from the imagination
- To research a topic to answer questions

Teacher's ResourceBank™

RESOURCES

PREWRITING

• Freewriting	1
• Brainstorming	2
• Clustering	3
• Asking Questions	4
• Thinking About Purpose and Audience	5
• Chronological Order and Spatial Order	6
• Charts and Diagrams	7

QUOTATION FOR THE DAY

"There is an art of reading, as well as an art of thinking, and an art of writing." (Isaac D'Israeli, 1766–1848, English writer)

You may want to discuss what students think the arts of reading, of thinking, and of writing might include. List these three categories on the chalkboard and have students make suggestions. Help them become aware of their commonalities such as imagination and experience.

Prewriting

Finding Ideas for Writing

The first problem every writer faces is "What will I write about?" Your experiences and interests make good writing topics. These six prewriting techniques will help you explore ideas for writing. As you try them out, some techniques will become your favorites. And often you'll use more than one for a paper.

PREWRITING TECHNIQUES		
Writer's Journal	Recording experiences and thoughts	Page 26
Freewriting	Writing for a few minutes about whatever comes to mind	Page 27
Brainstorming	Listing ideas as quickly as you think of them	Page 29
Clustering	Brainstorming ideas and connecting the ideas with circles and lines	Page 30
Asking Questions	Asking the *5W-How?* and "What if?" questions	Page 32
Reading and Listening	Reading and listening to find information	Page 34

Writer's Journal

Fill your ***writer's journal*** with experiences, feelings, and thoughts. You can have a section called "Things I Like." You can put in cartoons, quotations, song lyrics, and poems that have special meaning for you. Keep your journal in a notebook or file folder.

MOTIVATION

To continue the emphasis on the connection between thinking and writing, ask students to think of their brains as idea banks that store old memories and create new thoughts. Tell them that to help them get their best ideas from their brain banks onto paper, they should use several prewriting methods. Explain that these techniques can help a writer remember past details and generate new ideas. You may want to draw a chart on the chalkboard to represent this.

- Try to write every day, and date your entries.
- Write as much or as little as you want. Don't worry about spelling, punctuation, or grammar.
- Give your imagination some space. Write about dreams, daydreams, and far-out fantasies.

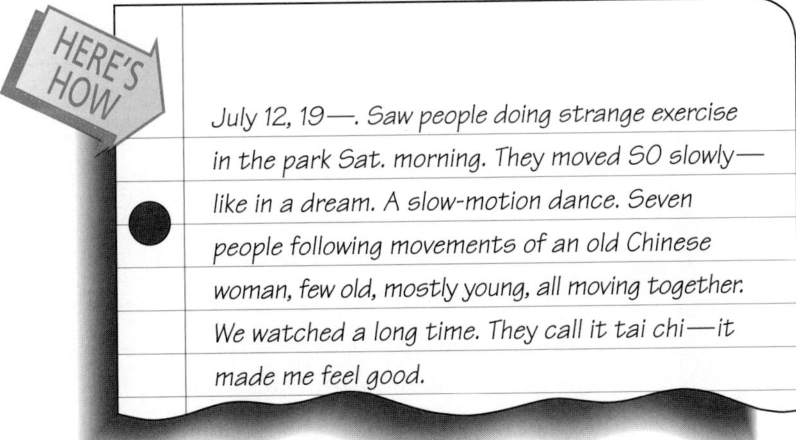

HERE'S HOW
July 12, 19—. Saw people doing strange exercise in the park Sat. morning. They moved SO slowly—like in a dream. A slow-motion dance. Seven people following movements of an old Chinese woman, few old, mostly young, all moving together. We watched a long time. They call it tai chi—it made me feel good.

EXERCISE 1 **Starting a Writer's Journal**

You can write about anything, but here's one possible idea: your early-morning routine. Do you jump right out of bed in the morning? Or do you want to keep snoozing? Are you organized or always searching for your shoes? Describe how you got ready and came to school this morning.

Freewriting

Freewriting means just that—writing freely. You begin with a word or phrase and then write whatever comes to mind. Time yourself for three to five minutes, and keep writing until the time is up.

LEP/ESL

General Strategies. Although students might feel comfortable with oral communication, many of them might be anxious and uncomfortable about their writing abilities in English. Having them work with peers may ease their transition into this area of study.

ANSWERS

Exercise 1

Journal entries will be as individualistic as the students, but all entries should focus on the prompt.

TEACHING THE LESSON

This segment may require several days to teach, depending upon your class structure and needs. Some students may be familiar with prewriting techniques. If they are, you may want to briefly discuss several techniques and follow up with exercises. If not, you may want to spend more time on each method.

Two **Critical Thinking Exercises** are interspersed in the segment. They use prewriting techniques, but also require synthesis and evaluation skills.

Give students an overview of the segment by guiding the reading of the introduction and the **Prewriting Techniques** chart. Refer to the chart on p. 25 and remind students that prewriting is the planning stage.

Students with language problems have difficulty putting ideas on paper. You may want to eliminate some of the assignments in this segment and concentrate on the development of ideas in the ones you assign.

For example, give more structure to journal writing by providing students with prompts such as "When I wake up in the morning I am ____."

- Write your topic first. Then write whatever the topic makes you think of.
- Don't stop or pause. If you can't think of anything to write, keep writing the same word or phrase until something pops into your head.
- Don't worry about spelling, punctuation, or complete sentences.

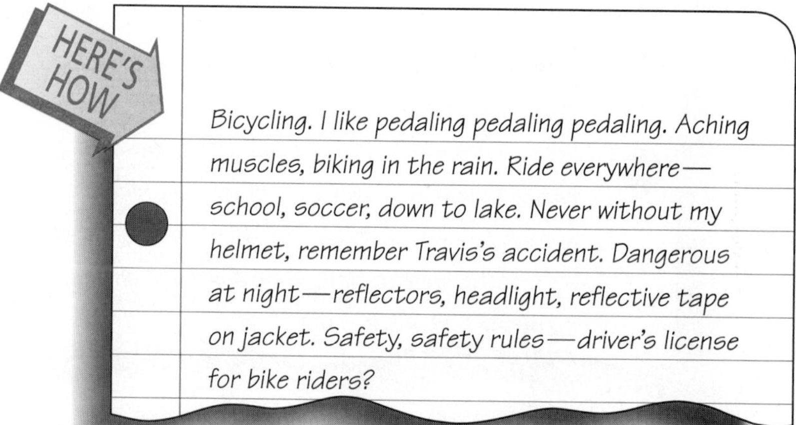

HERE'S HOW
Bicycling. I like pedaling pedaling pedaling. Aching
muscles, biking in the rain. Ride everywhere—
school, soccer, down to lake. Never without my
helmet, remember Travis's accident. Dangerous
at night—reflectors, headlight, reflective tape
on jacket. Safety, safety rules—driver's license
for bike riders?

In ***focused freewriting*** (or ***looping***), you begin with a word or phrase from freewriting you've already done. You might choose "biking in the rain," for instance, and do three minutes of freewriting on this limited topic.

Explain that over the next several days they will learn how to use the techniques.

Ask volunteers to read the prewriting ideas. Discuss the **Here's How** sections and generate further samples with the class, as needed.

After students have become familiar with the prewriting techniques, they should be ready to learn about purpose and audience. Show them how deciding on what to write depends on why they want to write. Give students plenty of examples of writing to serve each purpose.

To illustrate the importance of keeping their audiences in mind while they write, remind students that people speak differently to different people. They wouldn't speak to a teacher the same way they speak ☛

EXERCISE 2 **Using Freewriting**

Think of six activities you really like to participate in or watch. (Consider bicycling, dancing, listening to music, skating, reading, or playing ball.) Choose one activity, and freewrite for three minutes about it.

Brainstorming

When you ***brainstorm,*** your thoughts fly out in all directions. You start with a subject. Then you quickly list everything the subject makes you think of. You can brainstorm alone, but it's also fun to brainstorm ideas with a group.

- Write any subject at the top of a piece of paper or on a chalkboard.
- Write down every idea that occurs to you. If you're brainstorming in a group, one person should record the ideas.
- Don't stop to judge what's listed.
- Don't stop until you run out of ideas.

Here are some brainstorming notes on the subject "astronauts." Notice the silly ideas. When you're brainstorming, it's OK to list silly ideas. You can always cross them off your list later.

HERE'S HOW

Astronauts

Sally Ride
Neil Armstrong
walking on the moon
space shuttle
spacesuits, diving suits
Astroturf
astrodome
"lunar rover" vehicles
space explorers
floating without gravity
cramped space, food in tubes
Challenger explosion
man in the moon
woman in the moon

ANSWERS

Exercise 2

There are no rules for freewriting, so the ideas in your students' responses may not be complete.

to classmates and vice versa. Tell them it's the same with writing.

When the class is ready to discuss arranging ideas, you may want to set up some demonstrations to illustrate the types of order. You can use the students' daily schedule to explain chronological order, and you can describe the classroom to explain spatial order. Order of importance and logical order may be the hardest for the students to understand. You can use examples like job application information to explain order of importance, where education is more important than interests and hobbies. To help students understand logical order, ask them what TV shows they watch regularly. Then have them group the shows together through classification

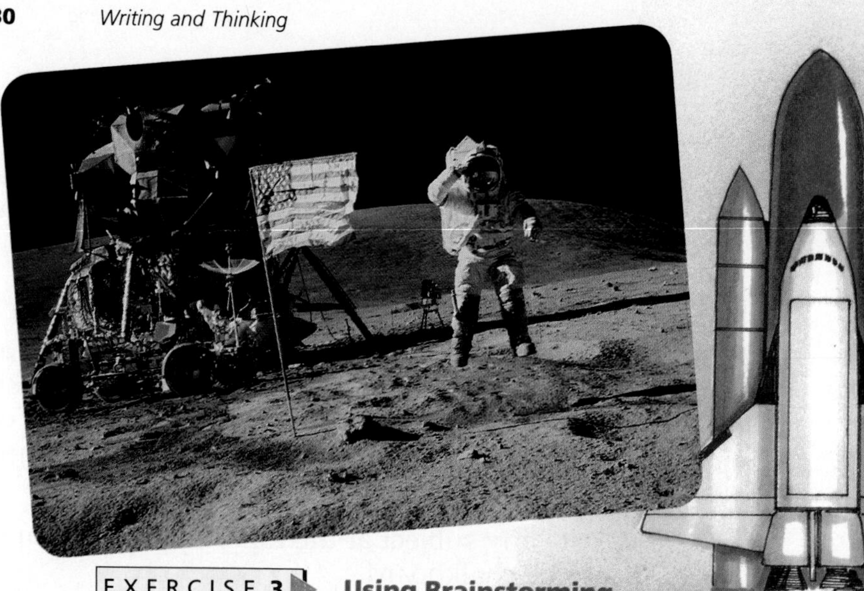

ANSWERS

Exercise 3

Any evaluation of brainstorming should disregard the quality of the ideas. The more ideas the students generate, the better they have done at brainstorming.

EXERCISE 3 **Using Brainstorming**

Brainstorming is like flipping through the files in your brain to see what's stored there. With two or three classmates, choose one of the following subjects or one of your own. Brainstorm as fast as you can and have someone record every idea.

1. movies
2. musical groups
3. brothers and sisters
4. summer vacations
5. computer games
6. scary experiences

Clustering

Clustering is sometimes called *mapping* or *webbing* (because the diagram looks like a spider web). It's a visual kind of brainstorming.

- Write your subject in the center of your paper, and then circle it.
- Around the subject, write related ideas that you think of. Circle these, and draw lines to connect them with the subject or with each other.
- Keep going. Write new ideas, circle them, and draw lines to show connections.

(cartoons, sports programs, comedies, and so on).

Encourage students to save their work on the exercises in notebooks or files that they can refer to when they are stuck for ideas. This process can also help students to become aware of their progress.

GUIDED PRACTICE

During this stage of learning, students might benefit from directed practice on the prewriting techniques. Using the **Here's How** sections as guides, work with the students to generate class samples. Assign volunteers to work at the chalkboard while other students supply ideas. As students make suggestions, guide the work and point ☛

Here's a cluster diagram on the topic of Hispanic grocery stores, or *bodegas*.

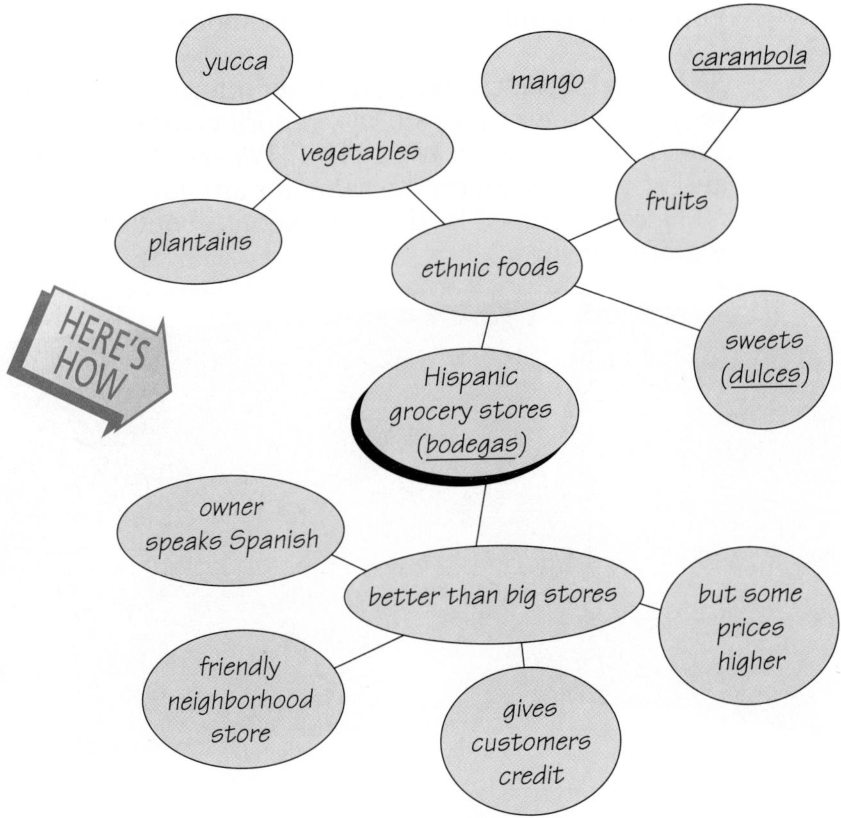

EXERCISE 4 **Using Clustering**

See if you can make a cluster diagram that has enough ideas and connections to look like a spider web. First, select a subject. You might use one of the subjects that were listed for Exercise 3 (page 30) but that you didn't use yet. You could also think of a subject of your own that you could use to develop ideas and connections.

LEARNING STYLES

Visual Learners. Some students will probably benefit most from clustering because it is a visual arrangement of ideas. However, many visually oriented students will prefer making their own visual hierarchies and will be very concerned with the way their arrangements look on paper. They might want to make lists and arrange them in related boxes, color-code their ideas, or integrate drawing and writing with a simple chart or diagram.

ANSWERS

Exercise 4

Evaluate students' clusters for the number of ideas presented and for the connectedness of the relationships shown.

out alternative ways of recording and grouping ideas.

Since each of the exercises involves a different technique, you may want to have students work on the exercises in class with your assistance. Although journal writing, freewriting, clustering, and questioning are independent in nature and require independent thinking, students need encouragement as well as guidance at this stage. Brainstorming requires group participation and monitoring may benefit the activity.

Asking Questions

Do you ever talk to yourself? Do you ever answer? You can find facts and ideas for writing by asking yourself two different kinds of questions.

5W-How? Questions. To gather information when they write their news stories, reporters often ask the ***5W-How?*** questions: *Who? What? Where? When? Why?* and *How?* You can do the same for any topic.

Here are some *5W-How?* questions about the photographs below.

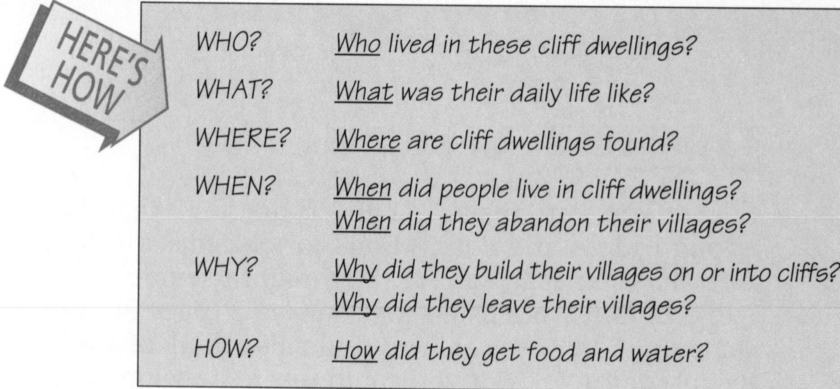

WHO?	Who lived in these cliff dwellings?
WHAT?	What was their daily life like?
WHERE?	Where are cliff dwellings found?
WHEN?	When did people live in cliff dwellings? When did they abandon their villages?
WHY?	Why did they build their villages on or into cliffs? Why did they leave their villages?
HOW?	How did they get food and water?

INDEPENDENT PRACTICE

Many of the exercises in this segment lend themselves to independent practice. Students might enjoy researching the encyclopedia independently and completing **Exercises 8** and **9** as homework.

ASSESSMENT

Evaluate students' understanding of prewriting by looking over their responses to the exercises. Evaluate the ideas generated and students' ability to group and organize them. Look for creative rather than complete ideas at this stage.

"What if?" Questions. What if you could be anyone you wanted to be for a day? What if you could travel through time into the future or past? What if you happened to find a diamond ring on the seat beside you in a movie theater or on a city bus? Asking questions like these can help you think of creative writing ideas.

- *What if I could change one thing in my life?* (What if I could make myself invisible? What if I had a car and a driver's license?)
- *What if some everyday thing did not exist?* (What if the earth had no moon? What if radios hadn't been invented?)
- *What if I could change one thing about the world?* (What if everyone in the whole world had enough food and a home? What if animals could really talk with people?)

EXERCISE 5 Asking *5W-How?* Questions

You've been chosen to interview an athlete for an article for the school paper. Choose a real athlete, and write some *5W-How?* questions you would ask him or her.

EXERCISE 6 Asking "What if?" Questions

You and a partner are writing a short story for a magazine contest. Here's your idea: Two friends are helping a neighborhood group with a project to clean up a vacant lot. Write four "What if?" questions to develop this story idea.

EXAMPLES *What if the friends found a box full of money?*
What if they argued about what to do with the money?

ANSWERS

Exercise 5

Questions will vary. Here are some possibilities:

Who helped you the most in your career?

What advice would you give young players?

Where did you first play?

When did you start playing?

Why do you like your sport?

How many years have you played at your present position?

ANSWERS

Exercise 6

Questions will vary. Here are some possibilities:

What if they uncovered a fossilized bone?

What if the bone turned out to be from a dinosaur?

What if some other kids stole the bone?

What if they found out the stolen bone was worth lots of money?

RETEACHING

Some students might have trouble generating ideas quickly because they are too critical of their work and want their writing to be correct. Reemphasize the free flow of ideas in the prewriting stage by playing a word-association game with the class. Write a word on the chalkboard and have students add a word that the last word listed made them think of.

For students who are having difficulty seeing possible relationships with words and ideas, extend the activity by drawing overlapping circles around related words or by rewriting the words under topic headings that students suggest.

VISUAL CONNECTIONS

Exploring the Subject. For more than 60 years Ellis Island served as a U. S. immigration station. Over 12 million immigrants passed through the island's facilities on their way to new homes in the United States. Located in New York Harbor about one mile southwest of Manhattan, Ellis Island is now part of the Statue of Liberty National Monument.

INTEGRATING THE LANGUAGE ARTS

Library Link. Exercise 7 requires research, and some research may be helpful with other exercises. Have an encyclopedia index available and let students suggest what listings they would look under to find information about pollution, animal habitats, or earthquakes. Familiarize students with cross-references for further ideas. Have students work in groups to look up the topics. Discuss how to use headings to narrow a focus and how to scan for information. Have them record three facts that interest the group.

Reading and Listening

Suppose you need to write about what it was like for immigrants to arrive at Ellis Island, New York, in the 1890s. How can you find out? For a topic like this, you'll *read* or *listen* to gather information.

Reading with a Focus. When you look for information in books, magazines, and newspapers:

- Find your topic in a book's table of contents or index. Turn to the pages listed.
- Don't read every word. Skim pages quickly, looking for your topic.
- When you find information on your topic, slow down and read carefully.
- Take notes on main ideas and important details.

If students have difficulty choosing appropriate sentences for an audience, select sentences from a variety of sources (nursery rhymes, short stories, song lyrics, or comic books). Have students suggest another way to say the same thing for a different audience or purpose.

Cont. on p. 37

EXERCISE 7 Reading with a Focus

Do you recognize any of these names: Mauna Loa, Mount Saint Helens, Mount Fuji, Krakatau, Mount Vesuvius, Tambora, Mount Pelée, Nevado del Ruiz? If you lived near one, you would—they're all volcanoes. Choose one volcano, and look it up in an encyclopedia, almanac, or other source. Find and write down answers to these questions.

1. Where is the volcano?
2. How tall is it?
3. When did it last erupt?
4. What danger resulted from the last eruption?

Listening with a Focus. You can find information by listening to radio and TV programs, audiotapes, and videotapes. You may even be able to interview someone who knows something about your topic. Before you listen, write out some questions about your topic. Then listen for answers to your questions and take notes.

REFERENCE NOTE: For more information on listening, see pages 676–681. See pages 678–679 for more about interviewing.

ANSWERS

Exercise 7

Answers will vary. Each student should write answers to all four questions as applied to the volcano he or she chooses.

CRITICAL THINKING

Evaluation

Have students determine which prewriting techniques work best for them by writing down the five methods and listing what they like or dislike about each. Have them defend their choices.

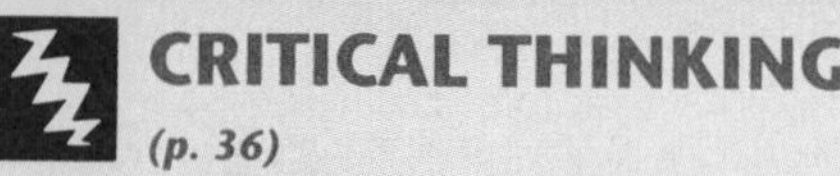

CRITICAL THINKING

(p. 36)

OBJECTIVE

- To observe and record details of a TV program and to formulate and compare statements of fact from notes

TEACHING *OBSERVING DETAILS*

Ask students to discuss other media that make the world available to people [newspapers, magazines, radio]. Give students note-taking practice by reading an article from a newspaper or magazine to them while they take notes.

MEETING INDIVIDUAL NEEDS

Students with learning disabilities might have trouble taking notes. Teach them several strategies. Tell them to write key words and any related ideas they remember. Ask them to draw illustrations or to cluster ideas. Simple reminders about having what they need on hand are helpful.

ANSWERS

Critical Thinking Exercise

Students' notes will vary, but they should be reflective of the nature of the television shows they were taken from. New facts should also be such that you wouldn't expect your students to have known them before they watched the television program.

CRITICAL THINKING

Observing Details

If you watch and listen carefully, you can collect information from educational programs and videotapes. A videotape can show you details you can't learn from a book. For example, if you watch a videotape on alligators, you can see how they swim and listen to the sounds they make.

CRITICAL THINKING EXERCISE:

Watching and Listening for Details

With a partner, decide on an educational TV show you are both going to watch this week—a program about nature, science, or history. As you watch and listen, take notes on important details. Write at least five new facts you learned. Then compare your notes with your partner's.

Cont. from p. 35

CLOSURE

Ask students to recite the prewriting techniques [writer's journal, freewriting, brainstorming, clustering, asking questions, reading and listening]. Then ask them to name the purposes for writing [to express yourself, to be creative, to explain, to persuade]. Finally, ask students to recite the types of order for arranging information [chronological, spatial, importance, logical].

Thinking About Purpose and Audience

What do you want your writing to *do*? If you don't have a clear idea of the *purpose* for your writing, it may not have the effect you want. Here are the basic writing purposes and some forms you might use.

MAIN PURPOSE	FORMS OF WRITING
To express yourself	Journal entry, letter, personal essay
To be creative	Short story, poem, play
To explain, inform, or explore	Science or history report, news story, biography
To persuade	Persuasive composition, letter to the editor, advertisement

The readers of your writing—your *audience*—are also important to think about. When you express your ideas on a specific topic to your friends at school, you probably talk differently than you do when you're talking to your parents about the same topic. Most of us do this automatically, adjusting what we're saying to fit whoever we're talking to.

You'll need to think about your audience when you're writing, too. How would you define the word *self-respect* for your six-year-old cousin? Would you use the same definition for a test question for your teacher? When you write, ask yourself these questions about your audience:

- What do my readers already know about the topic? What will I need to explain?
- What will interest them?
- What kinds of words (easy or difficult) should I use?

INTEGRATING THE LANGUAGE ARTS

Speaking Link. To help students become aware that what and how they write depends on their audiences, have them role-play situations involving different audiences. Ask volunteers to act out a scenario in which a student has lost something valuable. Have the student first explain that loss to his or her parents, then to a classmate or friend.

Point out how the two situations differed in terms of vocabulary, tone of voice, selection of details, and body language. Remind students that the audience controls much of what a speaker (and writer) says and does.

EXTENSION

Tell students that they are the inventors of machines that generate ideas for writing about different subjects. Have students draw their machines churning out ideas about any subjects they choose. Have students show how the machine arranges ideas.

ENRICHMENT

Have students recall an environmental concern that they have read or heard about—air or water pollution, the depletion of the ozone layer, oil spills, or others. Have each student list five questions he or she would research if appointed to an environmental clean-up committee. ■

EXERCISE 8 Thinking About Purpose and Audience

You're writing a factual report on Chamizal National Memorial in El Paso, Texas. It will be part of a travel guidebook for your school library. Which sentences are appropriate for your report? Which ones aren't?

1. The park honors the Chamizal Treaty of 1963.
2. The treaty settled a 99-year-old boundary dispute between the United States and Mexico.
3. Two years ago my uncle went to the Border Folk Festival in Chamizal. He met his wife-to-be there.
4. More than 225 different fine arts and folk art programs are held in Chamizal each year.
5. My favorite Mexican foods are tacos and burritos.

1. appropriate **2.** appropriate **3.** not appropriate **4.** appropriate **5.** not appropriate

Arranging Ideas

If you were writing the report on Chamizal National Memorial, what would you discuss first? As soon as you had gathered some details and ideas, you would need to choose what order to put them in. Deciding what will come first, second, and third in your paper is the next writing step.

Types of Order

Here are four common ways that you can arrange information. The chart below shows you each of these four ways to arrange ideas and tells you some of the kinds of writing that use each method.

ARRANGING IDEAS		
TYPE OF ORDER	DEFINITION	EXAMPLES
Chronological Order	Describes events in the order they happen	Story, narrative poem, "how-to" paper
Spatial Order	Describes details according to their location (near to far, left to right, top to bottom, and so on)	Description of place, room, object
Order of Importance	Gives details from least to most important, or the reverse	Persuasive writing, descrip-tion, book report
Logical Order	Groups related details together	Definition, comparison and contrast

CRITICAL THINKING
Synthesis

Before students arrange their ideas in a particular type of order, they need to select the details that they are going to include in their compositions. Remind students that during the pre-writing stage they should look over the information they have generated and eliminate any ideas that don't fit their purposes and audiences. This will help keep their writing unified and will make the process of arranging information easier.

CRITICAL THINKING
(p. 40)

OBJECTIVE

- To determine the best organizational method for details, considering topic, purpose, and audience

TEACHING *ARRANGING IDEAS*

Go over the **Arranging Ideas** chart and discuss the terms. Generate more examples of each type of order with students. Remind them of the relationships between topic, purpose, and audience before having them complete the exercise.

LESS-ADVANCED STUDENTS

Some students will be unfamiliar with terms for the types of order. Spend time defining terms and showing examples of each. Read several paragraphs illustrating each type of order and have students determine which order was used and why.

ANSWERS

Critical Thinking Exercise

1. order of importance
2. spatial
3. chronological
4. logical

CRITICAL THINKING

Arranging Ideas

How do you choose an order for your writing? Let your subject, purpose, and details guide you.

Suppose you're writing about Sacagawea, the Shoshone woman who guided the Lewis and Clark expedition. Your purpose is to inform your classmates about her life. It's natural to tell about a person's life from birth to death, so you arrange your details in ***chronological order,*** the order that they happened.

But suppose your purpose is to explain how Sacagawea helped the expedition. In that case, you might use ***order of importance.*** First, you could discuss the most important thing she did. Then you could tell the next most important, and so on.

CRITICAL THINKING EXERCISE:
Deciding How to Arrange Information

Study the writing examples below. Think about each topic, purpose, and audience. Next, imagine the kinds of details you'd probably include. Last, use the chart on page 39 to decide the order you'd use.

1. You are writing a letter to the editor of your local paper. You give three reasons why your city should have a new park with a zoo and recreational facilities.
2. You're writing a letter to a friend. You describe the stage setting you helped create for a school skit.
3. In your journal, you're writing about how you spent your birthday.
4. For a social studies report, you're comparing and contrasting two women governors.

Using Visuals

"A picture is worth a thousand words," the old saying goes. And sometimes a chart or diagram can even help you see the meaning of your own notes better.

Charts. A *chart* groups together details that are alike in some way. Look at your notes, and decide which details belong together. Write a heading for each group. Here's an example.

HERE'S HOW

Inuit Stone Prints		
History	How They're Made	What They Show
Cape Dorset, Canada Long history of sculpture and carving, no experience with printing In 1950s taught about printing by James Houston	Carve slabs of native stone. Ink the surface. Press paper against stone.	Scenes of daily life Animals Dreams and visions Myths

Shoroshiluto/Reproduced with permission of West Baffin Eskimo Co-Operative Ltd., Cape Dorset, NWT

Venn Diagrams. A ***Venn diagram*** uses circles to show how two subjects are alike (comparison) and different (contrast). Each subject has its own circle, but the circles overlap. In the overlapping part, you write details that are the same for both subjects. In the parts that don't overlap, you write details that make these subjects different.

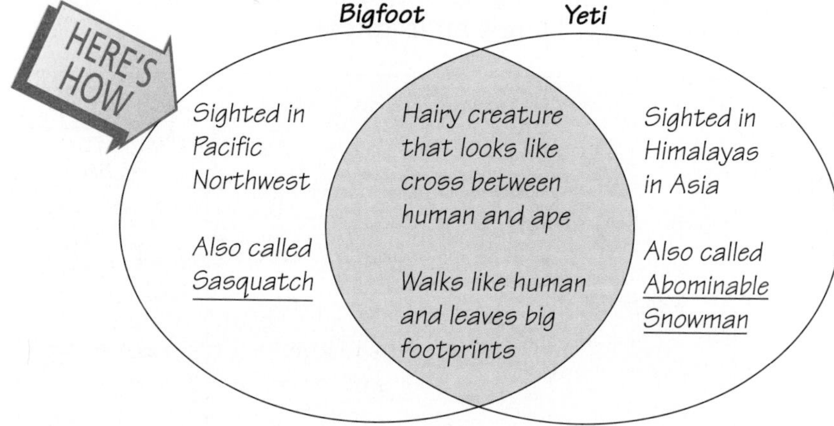

EXERCISE 9 **Making a Chart**

Study the following notes about "Nessie," a mysterious monster. Nessie supposedly lives in Loch Ness, a deep lake in northern Scotland. Organize the following notes under these two headings: Description and Sightings.

Has long neck and small head D
First sighting in A.D. 565; hundreds of sightings since S
Sonar investigations—large, moving object in Loch Ness S
One or two humps on its back D
1960 film shows dark shape moving in lake S
About 30 feet long D
1970s—researchers took photographs S

COOPERATIVE LEARNING

Because classifying details requires higher-level thinking skills, you may want to have students work in groups of three or four for **Exercise 9.** Make sure the groups are balanced, with advanced and less-advanced students in each group.

VISUAL CONNECTIONS

Exploring the Subject. The earliest known report of a strange creature in Loch Ness was made in A.D. 565. Since then there have been numerous reports of sightings of what many believe to be a dinosaur-like reptile.

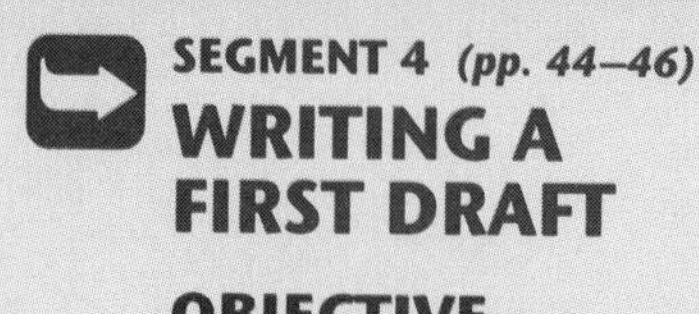

SEGMENT 4 *(pp. 44–46)*

WRITING A FIRST DRAFT

OBJECTIVE

- To read a model first draft and to note problems

TEACHING THE LESSON

Read with students the **Writing Note** and **Here's How** sections. Have students recall reminders from the lesson as you list them on the chalkboard. You might want to include them with the ones in the **Critical Thinking** section on a chart or a bulletin board. ■

Teacher's ResourceBank™

RESOURCES

WRITING A FIRST DRAFT

- Writing a First Draft 8

QUOTATION FOR THE DAY

"I've been to a lot of places and done a lot of things, but writing was always first. It's a kind of pain I can't do without." (Robert Penn Warren, 1905–1989, American writer)

Use the quotation to remind students that writing is a difficult, ongoing process and that the aim of writing a first draft is not to produce a flawless, finished product, but to create a draft the writer can change, improve, and polish later in the writing process.

VISUAL CONNECTIONS

Exploring the Subject. Thurgood Marshall was born July 2, 1908, in Baltimore, Maryland. As a lawyer, he successfully argued before the U.S. Supreme Court, in the historic *Brown v. Board of Education* case (1954), that racial segregation in public schools was unconstitutional. He later became the first African American to be named U.S. solicitor general (1965) and went on to be the first African American to serve on the U.S. Supreme Court (1967).

Writing a First Draft

Remember the magic Instant Perfect Writing pen that doesn't exist? At this stage in the writing process, any old pen, pencil, typewriter, or word processor will do. That's because you already have everything you need to write your first draft.

Some people write quickly, zapping their notes into sentences. Others write more slowly, laboring over each sentence. Whatever works for you is fine.

- Follow your prewriting plans as you write.
- If you come up with new ideas, include them.
- Don't worry about spelling and grammar; you'll correct mistakes later. Just keep writing.

Beginning writers sometimes try to use difficult-sounding words and long sentences. That's a mistake. Your writing should sound like your own voice—not someone else's. Try to express your ideas clearly, simply, and naturally.

On the next page is a first draft of a paragraph from a paper about Thurgood Marshall, the first African American Supreme Court Justice. The paragraph tells a family story about Justice Marshall's grandmother. You'll see that the paragraph isn't perfect. The writer will make changes later.

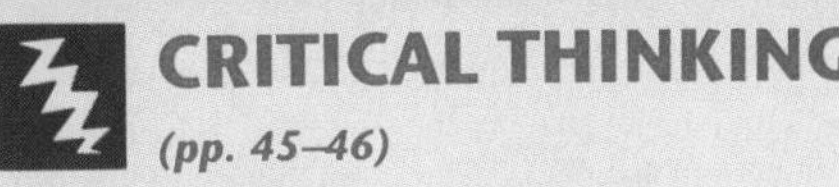

CRITICAL THINKING

(pp. 45–46)

OBJECTIVES

- To analyze prewriting notes and to select appropriate information
- To write a paragraph from selected information

TEACHING *SYNTHESIZING IDEAS*

Write the word *synthesize* on the chalkboard and tell students that it comes from a Greek word that means "to combine or put together." Have a volunteer read the introduction. Go over the guidelines with students and list reminders on the chalkboard. Monitor students' progress as they write their paragraphs.

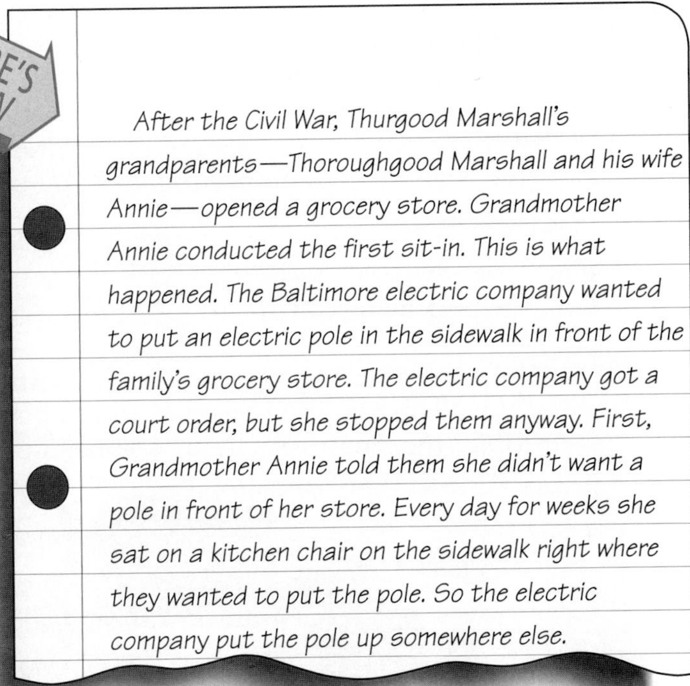

After the Civil War, Thurgood Marshall's grandparents—Thoroughgood Marshall and his wife Annie—opened a grocery store. Grandmother Annie conducted the first sit-in. This is what happened. The Baltimore electric company wanted to put an electric pole in the sidewalk in front of the family's grocery store. The electric company got a court order, but she stopped them anyway. First, Grandmother Annie told them she didn't want a pole in front of her store. Every day for weeks she sat on a kitchen chair on the sidewalk right where they wanted to put the pole. So the electric company put the pole up somewhere else.

CRITICAL THINKING

Synthesizing Ideas

Synthesizing means creating something new from separate parts. Musicians can use an electronic synthesizer to put sounds together and create music. Songs, salads, patchwork quilts, paragraphs—all these are new wholes made from separate parts. To synthesize a paragraph:

- Look over your prewriting notes. Think about your main idea, and then write a sentence that states this main idea.

LEP/ESL

General Strategies. Students may need help deciding which pieces of information to use to describe the albatross's flying abilities. If possible, you may want to pair ESL students with more advanced students or discuss the information available with them yourself to help them get started.

- Choose the details that best support your main idea. List the details in an order that makes sense to you.
- Write a draft of the paragraph. Express your ideas as clearly and naturally as you can.

CRITICAL THINKING EXERCISE:
Writing a First Draft

Draft a paragraph based on these prewriting notes about the albatross, the largest of all sea birds. Make your topic "the albatross's flying abilities." You won't use all the information.

Lives on oceans; goes to land to lay single egg
Eats squid and small sea creatures; drinks salt water
Long flights—months—with brief rests
Wingspan of six to eleven feet
Glides on nearly constant air currents
Alternates flapping and gliding
Glides for hours without flapping its wings
Zigzags against wind currents to reach a certain spot
Can fly hundreds of miles

ANSWERS
Critical Thinking Exercise

Paragraphs will vary. Here is a sample:

The albatross is an amazing ocean bird. When it flies, it alternates flapping and gliding. It can glide for hours without flapping its wings. Albatrosses have wingspans of from six to eleven feet wide that help them make use of the nearly constant air currents. The albatross zigzags across the wind to reach its destination and can fly hundreds of miles.

SEGMENT 5 *(pp. 47–50)*

EVALUATING AND REVISING

OBJECTIVES

- To critique writing by assessing strengths and weaknesses
- To revise a paragraph

TEACHING THE LESSON

Introduce this segment by showing students the roles they play in producing good writing. To come up with ideas, they must become explorers. To put ideas on paper, they must become artists. The next role they will play is one of the most critical ones, the judge. Ask volunteers to read the

Evaluating and Revising

Until they figure out what's wrong, doctors can't cure patients and mechanics can't repair cars. The same is true for writing. Before you can improve your first draft, you have to decide what needs fixing.

Evaluating

Evaluating means judging. You evaluate writing by judging what's good and what needs improving. You'll evaluate your own writing and that of your classmates.

Self-Evaluation. Try these techniques whenever you evaluate your own writing.

- Take some time. Set the draft aside for a day or two. You'll be able to see it from a fresh viewpoint.
- Read and reread. Read your paper carefully more than once. Focus on both ideas and wording.
- Read your paper aloud. Listen for awkward or unclear spots.

Teacher's ResourceBank™

RESOURCES

EVALUATING AND REVISING

- Practicing Peer Evaluation 9
- Revising: Adding and Cutting 10
- Revising: Replacing and Reordering 11

QUOTATION FOR THE DAY

"I am an obsessive rewriter, doing one draft and then another and another, usually five." (Gore Vidal, 1925–   , American writer)

Lead students to understand that revision is a necessary step in creating work that is as good as it can be. Tell students not to be discouraged or to think they have failed when they or other students find things to change in their writing. Encourage students to think of evaluation and revision as opportunities for improving their work.

lesson aloud and have them pause when you want to emphasize main points.

You may want to prepare a chart showing the techniques and guidelines in the textbook. Discuss how self-evaluation differs from peer evaluation. Emphasize constructive criticism and the need for specific comments. Point out the revision techniques used.

GUIDED PRACTICE

To help students analyze the evaluation process, use the drafted paragraph on p. 50. Note what has been added, cut, replaced, and reordered. Quiz students about how the change improved the writing.

MEETING INDIVIDUAL NEEDS

LEP/ESL

General Strategies. If at all possible, spend time with each student, emphasizing the positive aspects of their drafts and making encouraging comments. It might also be helpful to begin this segment with a class discussion differentiating the two terms *evaluating* and *criticizing*. Create two columns on the chalkboard and ask students to give examples from daily life that typify these behaviors. Emphasize that when students evaluate each other's work, they need to make a special effort to deliver comments in a positive way.

INTEGRATING THE LANGUAGE ARTS

Literature Link. Have students read the Gwendolyn Brooks poem "Narcissa." In a discussion of the poem, tell the class about the Greek myth of Narcissus and ask the students how Brooks has revised that myth in her poem. [Narcissus fell in love with his own reflection and wasted away while staring at it. Narcissa uses her imagination to create new experiences.]

Peer Evaluation. A peer is someone who is your equal. In this case, it's your classmate. When you do peer evaluation, you trade papers with one of your classmates. You read the paper carefully and take notes about it. Then you tell your classmate what you think was good about the paper and what parts could be improved.

When you do peer evaluation, you'll have two roles. You'll be a writer (listening to your classmate's evaluations of your writing). And you'll also be a reader (evaluating your classmate's writing).

GUIDELINES FOR PEER EVALUATION

Tips for the Writer

1. List some questions for the reader. Ask about parts of your paper that you feel especially unsure about.
2. Take your classmate's comments seriously, but don't get hurt feelings. Everyone's writing can be improved.

Tips for the Reader

1. First, remember to tell the writer what's good about the paper.
2. Make suggestions and criticisms politely. Asking questions is usually a good way. For example, you might say, "Can you give a specific example here?"
3. Suggest something specific the writer can do to improve the paper.

Revising

Once you figure out what needs fixing, do it. You'll use these four basic revision techniques: ***adding, cutting, replacing,*** and ***reordering.***

On the following page are some general guidelines that fit all types of writing.

INDEPENDENT PRACTICE

Have students choose partners for completing **Exercise 10** independently. Have them work first in pairs and then alone to evaluate and rewrite their paragraphs.

ASSESSMENT

As students work, walk around the classroom and monitor the conversations. Listen for criticisms to see if the comments are considered in the rewriting. Look for additions, deletions, reorderings, and replacements.

GUIDELINES FOR EVALUATING AND REVISING

	EVALUATION GUIDE	REVISION TECHNIQUE
1	Is the writing interesting?	**Add** examples, a brief story, dialogue, or details.
2	Are there enough details?	**Add** details, facts, or examples to support the main idea.
3	Is every sentence related to the topic?	**Cut** unrelated ideas.
4	Are ideas and details arranged in a clear order?	**Reorder** ideas and details to make the meaning clear.
5	Are the connections between ideas and sentences clear?	**Add** transition words—*because*, *for example*, and so on. (See pages 66–68.)
6	Is the language appropriate for the audience and purpose?	**Replace** difficult words with easier ones for younger readers. For experienced readers, use more difficult words. **Replace** slang and contractions in formal writing.

Now take another look at the draft paragraph about Thurgood Marshall's grandmother. It's been revised using the four revision techniques. To understand what the handwritten marks mean, see the chart of proofreading and revising symbols on page 53. To

COOPERATIVE LEARNING

To provide practice in analyzing revision techniques, divide the class into small groups. Have each group examine a rewritten paragraph and its first draft. Tell them to search for words or ideas that were cut, added, replaced, or reordered in the revision. Have each student serve as a reader, discussion leader, recorder, or reporter. Have each group report the revision techniques and results to the class.

CLOSURE

Ask students to name the four basic revision techniques [adding, cutting, replacing, reordering]. ■

ANSWERS

Exercise 10

Evaluations and revisions will vary. Students' revised paragraphs should have a clearly stated topic and details that support the topic. The ideas should be arranged clearly. Here is a sample revision:

The albatross is an amazing ocean bird that can glide for hours without flapping its wings. Albatrosses have wingspans of up to twelve feet, which help them make use of the nearly constant ocean winds and air currents. When the wind blows the wrong way, the bird zigzags across the wind to reach its destination. An albatross may fly hundred of miles in one day.

understand why the writer made the changes, use the guidelines in the chart on page 49.

After the Civil War, Thurgood Marshall's grandparents—Thoroughgood Marshall and his wife Annie—	
opened a grocery store (in Baltimore). (Justice Marshall says that) Grandmother	add/add
Annie conducted the first (successful) sit-in (in Maryland). ~~This is~~	add/add/cut
~~what happened.~~ The ~~Baltimore~~ electric	cut/cut
company wanted to put an electric pole in the sidewalk in front of the family's grocery store. The electric company got a court order, but	
~~she stopped them anyway.~~ (Annie Marshall wouldn't be stopped.) ~~First,~~	replace/cut
Grandmother Annie told them she didn't want a pole in front of her store.	reorder
Every day for weeks she sat on a kitchen chair on the sidewalk right	
where they wanted to put the pole. ~~So~~	cut
the electric company (finally gave up and) put the pole ~~up~~ somewhere else.	add/cut

EXERCISE 10 **Evaluating and Revising a Paragraph**

With a partner, evaluate the paragraphs you wrote about the albatross (page 46). Write some evaluation comments for each other. (Review the guidelines on page 48.) Take turns telling the comments, then discuss them. Later, evaluate your paragraph on your own. Using your partner's suggestions along with your ideas, revise your paragraph.

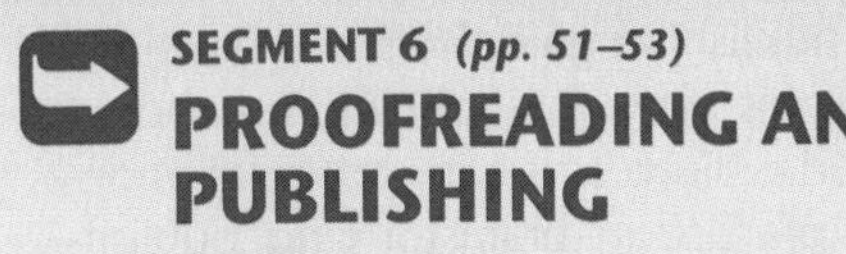

SEGMENT 6 *(pp. 51–53)*

PROOFREADING AND PUBLISHING

OBJECTIVES

- To proofread paragraphs for errors
- To brainstorm ideas for publishing

TEACHING THE LESSON

Read through the **Guidelines for Proofreading** chart and review the pages suggested to help students think about what to look for.

Write a few sentences on the chalkboard for students to proofread. (Use examples from students' writing.) As students find the errors, refer to the **Guidelines for** 

Proofreading and Publishing

After you've revised your paper, it's time to give your writing its finishing touches. Then you can share it with an audience.

Proofreading

Give yourself a break. A little time away from your writing usually makes it easier to come back to it later with fresh eyes. Then you can proofread your paper. When you proofread, you read your paper carefully to spot any mistakes in spelling, grammar, usage, and punctuation.

The secret of proofreading is to slow your reading down to a crawl. Focus on one line at a time, and read it word by word. If you find something that you think looks weird, check it in a dictionary or grammar handbook (see pages 336–661). Double-check your proofreading by exchanging papers with a classmate.

GUIDELINES FOR PROOFREADING

1. Is every sentence a complete sentence? (See pages 303–305.)
2. Does every sentence begin with a capital letter and end with the correct punctuation mark? (See pages 564–565 and 587–591.)
3. Do singular subjects have singular verbs? And do all plural subjects have plural verbs? (See pages 456–470.)
4. Are verb forms and tenses used correctly? (See pages 476–495.)
5. Are the forms of personal pronouns used correctly? (See pages 503–520.)
6. Are all words spelled correctly? (See pages 636–661.)

Teacher's ResourceBank™

RESOURCES

PROOFREADING AND PUBLISHING

- Proofreading 12

QUOTATION FOR THE DAY

"...you must discover what there is in you, this bottomless fountain of imagination and knowledge." (Brenda Ueland, 1891–1985, American writer)

As students come to the final stage of the writing process, use the quotation to assure them that they will never run out of writing ideas. Students might brainstorm lists of future writing topics by completing several sentences, each starting with "I know about . . ."

LEP/ESL

General Strategies. You may want to assign short and easily understood literary excerpts for students to read for enjoyment. In the long run, this strategy may prove more beneficial than requiring students to correct passages that are faulty.

Proofreading chart. Use **Exercise 11** for independent practice.

In discussing publishing, you may want to refer to the examples you used in talking about processes earlier in the chapter so that students realize publishing is the culmination of a process. As you read this part of the segment, tell students to keep the ideas in mind for publishing their work. Go over the publishing guidelines and have students discuss why finished writing should look good. Allow students time for independent practice in brainstorming publishing ideas.

ANSWERS

Exercise 11

Have you ever thought of making a mobile for your room? A mobile is made of hanging shapes that move in a current of air. You can use any shape, though many people like fish, birds, butterflies, or other animal shapes. As the shapes move, they come close and then pass each other. The shapes seem to dance in a wobbly sort of way.

EXERCISE 11 Proofreading a Paragraph

What's wrong with this paragraph? Work with a partner to find and correct five mistakes. Use a dictionary and the **Handbook** on pages 336–661.

Have you ever thought of makeing a mobile for your room? a mobile is made of hanging shapes that move in a current of air. You can use any shape, though many people likes fish, birds, butterflys, or other animal shapes. As the shapes move, they come close and then pass each other, The shapes seem to dance in a wobbly sort of way.

Publishing

Now you're ready to publish or share your writing. Here are a few of the many ways to find an audience.

- Start a class newspaper with news, brief reports, and creative writing. It can be handwritten, typed, or done on a computer.
- Post class writing on a bulletin board in the classroom or in the hall. Change the writing every week.
- Create a class booklet with one piece of writing from each student. Lend your book to other classes and the school library.

When you publish your writing, it should look good. Be sure to proofread your final copy.

CLOSURE

Ask students to name potential audiences for their writing. List the suggestions on the chalkboard. Ask why the way a paper looks is important. List these ideas also. ■

GUIDELINES FOR THE FORM OF A PAPER

1. Use only one side of a sheet of paper. Write in blue or black ink, or type. Double-space if you type.
2. Leave margins of about one inch at the top, sides, and bottom of each page.
3. Include your name, the date, your class, and the title of your paper. Your teacher will tell you where to place this information.
4. Indent the first line of each paragraph.

EXERCISE 12 **Publishing Your Writing**

Brainstorm ideas for sharing or publishing your writing. Research information (addresses, requirements, deadlines) about contests or magazines that publish student writing.

SYMBOLS FOR REVISING AND PROOFREADING

SYMBOL	EXAMPLE	MEANING OF SYMBOL
≡	spanish class (s marked ≡)	Capitalize a lowercase letter.
/	my older Brother (B marked /)	Use lowercase letter.
∧	by∧front door (the inserted)	Add a word, letter, or punctuation mark.
℘	"Hi," he he said. (second he deleted)	Leave out a word, letter, or punctuation mark.
∽	easliy (l and i transposed)	Change the order of the letters or words.
¶	¶The street was empty.	Begin a new paragraph.
⊙	Mrs⊙Martinez	Add a period.
∧ (comma)	Yes∧I'll go with you.	Add a comma.

ANSWERS

Exercise 12

Responses will vary. Here are some possibilities:

Start a class magazine.

Make topical booklets for the library on other subjects studied in school.

Create storybooks with colorful illustrations for younger readers.

Post student work on a bulletin board.

Select favorite compositions to share with family members. Design a cover and leave a page for the family to comment.

Addresses of magazines:

Scholastic Scope
Scholastic Magazines, Inc.
730 Broadway
New York, NY 10003

Odyssey
21027 Crossroads Circle
P.O. Box 1612
Waukesha, WI 53187

Writing Awards and Contests for Young People:
Scholastic Writing Awards
Scholastic Magazines, Inc.
730 Broadway
New York, NY 10003

"Achievement in Writing Program"
National Council of Teachers of English
1111 Kenyon Road
Urbana, IL 61801

SEGMENT 7 *(pp. 54–55)*

MAKING CONNECTIONS

CREATING A CARTOON ABOUT WRITING

OBJECTIVE

- To create a cartoon to express a writing problem

CREATING A CARTOON ABOUT WRITING

Teaching Strategies

You may want to have students think about what problems they want to illustrate and then divide them into small groups to brainstorm cartoon ideas.

GUIDELINES

Cartoons or comic strips will vary, but they should clearly communicate a specific writing experience.

MAKING CONNECTIONS

Creating a Cartoon About Writing

Can you identify with Snoopy's problem? Do you have a hard time ending a paper—or is your worst problem trying to get started? Or does revising give you a headache? Create your own cartoon or comic strip about a problem you have with writing. If you like, work with a partner or small group.

ASKING A WRITER QUESTIONS OBJECTIVE

- To write a letter to a favorite author and to use questions to collect information about writing

Asking a Writer Questions

"Where do you write best?" a student asked Donald M. Murray. Murray, a teacher and writer, has published many books about how to write. Here's his surprising answer:

> The ideal writing environment for me would be a busy lunchroom. I like a lot of noise and confusion that doesn't involve me. I can't stand quiet. And if I'm in my office under the porch I play records, tapes, or the radio. I do a lot of writing in the living room, on the porch, and in the car.
>
> Donald M. Murray, *Expecting the Unexpected*

Choose a writer you admire—perhaps the author of a favorite book or a comic strip. You might even choose a newspaper reporter. Make up five questions you'd like to ask the person about how he or she writes. Include your questions in a letter to the writer. You can send your letter in care of the book or newspaper publisher. If you get a response (and most writers are very busy, so you may not), share it with the class.

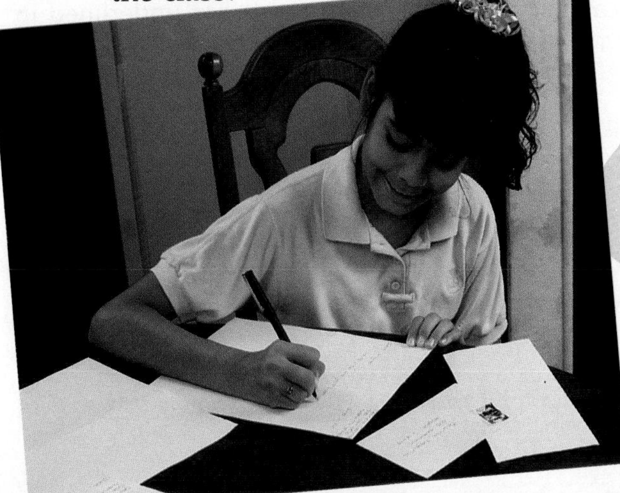

ASKING A WRITER QUESTIONS

Teaching Strategies

Ask students to name favorite books, cartoon strips, or other reading materials. Then lead them in a discussion of some favorite authors, focusing on why they like the authors.

GUIDELINES

Questions will vary. Here are some possibilities:
What is your biggest problem with writing?
How do you deal with the problem?
Do you write just when you feel like it, or every day?
Where do you get your ideas?
How often do you revise your writing?
Do you enjoy writing?
What tips would you give a beginning writer?

SELECTION AMENDMENT
Description of change: excerpted
Rationale: to focus on the concept of a writing environment presented in this chapter.

Chapter 2 LEARNING ABOUT PARAGRAPHS

OBJECTIVES

- To respond in a journal entry to paragraphs from a book
- To analyze the paragraphs of a selection from a book
- To identify different kinds of paragraphs
- To identify topic sentences and main ideas
- To collect supporting details for a main idea of a paragraph
- To identify transitions
- To develop four kinds of paragraphs: description, narration, comparison-contrast, and evaluation
- To identify and use spatial order, chronological order, logical order, and order of importance
- To give a two-minute evaluative speech
- To write paragraphs for different purposes: to express, to inform, to persuade, and to create

Motivation

You may want to introduce writing to your students by asking them what kinds of writing they have done in the past year. You will probably have to start by asking them about school work, notes, letters, lists, and telephone messages—writing they may do without even thinking of it as writing. After having established that just about everybody does writing of some kind, explain that the paragraph is a way of organizing that writing to make it clear to the reader.

Introduction

Emphasize the importance of logically organized paragraphs by taking a good paragraph and changing the order of the sentences. You might take a paragraph from the textbook and retype it without transitions, without a topic sentence, and in a mixed-up order. Ask the students to read the paragraph and to tell what they think is wrong with it. Point out that it does make a difference how a writer puts information together.

Tell students that textbook suggestions for good paragraph writing don't apply only to school writing. Ask the students to bring favorite magazines, books, or newspaper stories to class on the day that you will begin this chapter to show that professional writers do the same things that you will be teaching your students.

Integration

To write well, students must understand how to create paragraphs. You may want to make the point that if they learn this lesson well, the lengthier writing assignments in later chapters will be easier. Understanding paragraphs will also make the students better readers. When they understand how to find the topic sentence or main idea, for example, they will be less likely to miss the main point of a paragraph. Understanding paragraphs can help in all school subjects requiring reading or writing.

If you want the students to have an oral activity, use one or more of the **Making Connections** features to assign speeches instead of writing. Prewriting activities then become prespeaking activities, and students plan their speeches in much the same way as they plan their paragraphs.

The chart on the next page illustrates the strands of language arts as they are integrated into this chapter. For vocabulary study, glossary words are underlined in some writing models.

QUOTATIONS

All **Quotations for the Day** are chosen because of their relevance to instructional material presented in that segment of the chapter and for their usefulness in establishing student interest in writing.

INTEGRATING THE LANGUAGE ARTS

Selection	Reading and Literature	Writing and Critical Thinking	Language and Syntax	Speaking, Listening, and Other Expression Skills
FROM ***Volcano*** by Patricia Lauber **58-59** ***Wild Animals, Gentle Women*** by Margery Facklam **61** ***A Cat's Body*** by Joanna Cole **63** ***Pride of Puerto Rico*** by Paul Robert Walker **64** ***How Did We Find Out About Coal?*** by Isaac Asimov **64** ***Women Who Made America Great*** by Harry Gersh **67** ***The Art of the Japanese Garden*** by Tatsuo Ishimoto **70** ***Ramona Forever*** by Beverly Cleary **71** ***Scissor Cutting for Beginners*** by Cheng Hou-tien **72** ***Rabbits and Hares*** by Ralph Whitlock **74**	Applying interpretive and creative thinking **60, 65, 70-71, 74, 76, 80-81** Drawing conclusions and making inferences **60, 63** Analyzing paragraphs **60, 63-64** Identifying the topic sentence **63-64** Identifying main ideas **63-64** Identifying transitions **68**	Recognizing different kinds of paragraphs **60** Writing about a personal experience **60, 76** Writing a journal entry **60** Analyzing paragraphs **60, 63-64** Identifying main ideas and topic sentences **63-64** Collecting details for a paragraph **65-66, 70, 74** Listing details **65-66, 70-71** Identifying transitions **68** Using spatial order to develop paragraphs **70-71** Using chronological order **73** Using narration to develop paragraphs **73** Using comparison and contrast to develop a paragraph **74** Using order of importance **75** Writing an expressive paragraph **76-77** Writing a paragraph to inform **77-78** Writing a paragraph to persuade **79-80** Writing a creative paragraph **80-81**	Identifying transitional words and phrases **68** Proofreading for errors in grammar, usage, and mechanics **77, 79, 80, 81**	Writing a group story **73** Giving an evaluative speech **75** Listening to an evaluative speech **75** Evaluating peers' narratives **75**

CHAPTER 2

SEGMENT PLANNING GUIDE

Whether you are planning for a quick review of a writing concept or preparing an extended lesson on composition, you can use the following Planning Guide to adapt the chapter material to the individual needs of your class.

	SEGMENT	PAGES	CONTENT	RESOURCES
1	*Looking at the Parts*	*57-60*		
	Literary Model from ***Volcano***	58-59	Guided reading: a model of paragraph writing	
	Reader's Response/Writer's Craft	60	Model evaluation: responding to literature and analyzing paragraph writing	
2	*The Parts of a Paragraph*	*61-69*		Main Ideas and Topic Sentences 17 Supporting Sentences and Details 18 Transitions 19
	Literary Model from ***Wild Animals, Gentle Women***	61	Guided reading: examining main idea, topic sentence, and supporting sentences	
	The Topic Sentence	62-63	Guided reading: identifying the topic sentence	
	Exercise 1	63-64	Applied practice: identifying main ideas and topic sentences in model paragraphs	
	Literary Model from ***A Cat's Body***	63	Guided reading: identifying main ideas and topic sentences	
	Literary Model from ***Pride of Puerto Rico***	64	Guided reading: identifying main ideas and topic sentences	
	Literary Model from ***How Did We Find Out About Coal?***	64	Guided reading: identifying main ideas and topic sentences	
	Supporting Sentences	65	Guided reading: identifying supporting sentences	
	Exercise 2	65-66	Applied practice: choosing a main idea and listing details	
	Words That Connect Ideas	66	Guided reading: relating details to main ideas	
	Chart: Transitional Words and Phrases	66	Guidelines: examining transitional words and phrases	
	Literary Model from ***Women Who Made America Great***	67	Guided reading: examining the use of transitional words to connect ideas	
	Exercise 3	68	Applied practice: finding and listing transitions in a paragraph	
	Ways to Develop Paragraphs	69	Introduction: examining ways to develop paragraphs	
	Chart: Ways to Develop Paragraphs	69	Guidelines: examining ways to develop paragraphs	
3	*Description*	*69-71*		Description 20
	Literary Model from ***The Art of the Japanese Garden***	70	Guided reading: examining spatial order of details	
	Exercise 4	70-71	Applied practice: choosing a subject and listing and arranging details	

All the resources listed in this chapter are located in the *Teacher's ResourceBank™*.

	SEGMENT	PAGES	CONTENT	RESOURCES
4	*Narration*	*71-73*		Narration 21
	Telling a Story	71	Introduction: examining a narrative paragraph of fiction	
	Literary Model from ***Ramona Forever***	71	Guided reading: examining a narrative paragraph	
	Writing Note	72	Writing suggestion: using chronological order in a paragraph	
	Explaining a Process	72	Guidelines: examining the order of a paragraph	
	Literary Model from ***Scissor Cutting for Beginners***	72	Guidelines: examining chronological order in a process	
	Exercise 5	73	Cooperative learning: writing a narrative	
5	*Comparison and Contrast*	*73-74*		Comparison and Contrast 22
	Literary Model from ***Rabbits and Hares***	74	Guided reading: examining logical order in comparison and contrast	
	Exercise 6	74	Applied practice: using comparison or contrast to develop paragraphs	
6	*Evaluation*	*75*		
	Evaluation	75	Guidelines: supporting an opinion	
	Exercise 7	75	Cooperative learning: evaluating a food	
7	*Making Connections*	*76-81*		
	Writing Paragraphs for Different Purposes: Writing a Paragraph to Express Yourself	76-77	Guidelines: using sentence starters to write a paragraph Applied practice: writing about thoughts or feelings	
	Writing a Paragraph to Inform	77-79	Guidelines: using a chart to write a paragraph Applied practice: writing an informative paragraph	
	Writing a Paragraph to Persuade	79-80	Guidelines: using a given sentence to write a paragraph Applied practice: writing a persuasive letter to the school board	
	Writing a Paragraph That Is Creative	80-81	Guidelines: imagining a scene Applied practice: writing a story prompted by a picture	

WHOLE-CHAPTER RESOURCE
Chapter Review

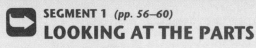

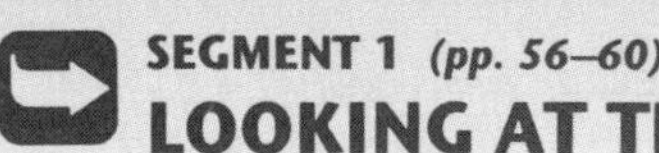

SEGMENT 1 *(pp. 56–60)*

LOOKING AT THE PARTS

OBJECTIVES

- To respond with personal writing in a journal to paragraphs from a book
- To analyze the paragraphs of a selection from a book

MOTIVATION

Type a short selection twice—once with paragraph indentions and once without. Ask students to read the unindented version first. Then ask them to read the indented version. They will probably find it much easier to identify main ideas in this version. Point out the importance of paragraphing.

VISUAL CONNECTIONS

Exploring the Subject. Jigsaw puzzles were originally maps that were cut apart in order to teach students geography. The first puzzles appeared in the 1700s; soon after that, puzzle makers began using other pictures for their puzzles. None of the early jigsaw puzzles had interlocking pieces, but by the late 1800s interlocking pieces were common.

Although the first jigsaw puzzles were wooden, by World War I, manufacturers switched to cardboard because it was less expensive. Today, custom-made puzzles like the one shown here are handcrafted in the old tradition, using wood. These puzzles are trickier than mass-produced cardboard puzzles. For example, the 500-piece puzzle to the right has three layers, and there are few straight edges to guide the puzzle solver.

Ideas for Writing. Discuss with students how writing a paragraph is similar to solving a puzzle. Point out that each sentence in a paragraph must connect with the other sentences just as a piece in a puzzle fits with the other pieces. Ask students how they might get their sentences to interlock. [Transition words are especially effective for connecting ideas.]

2 LEARNING ABOUT PARAGRAPHS

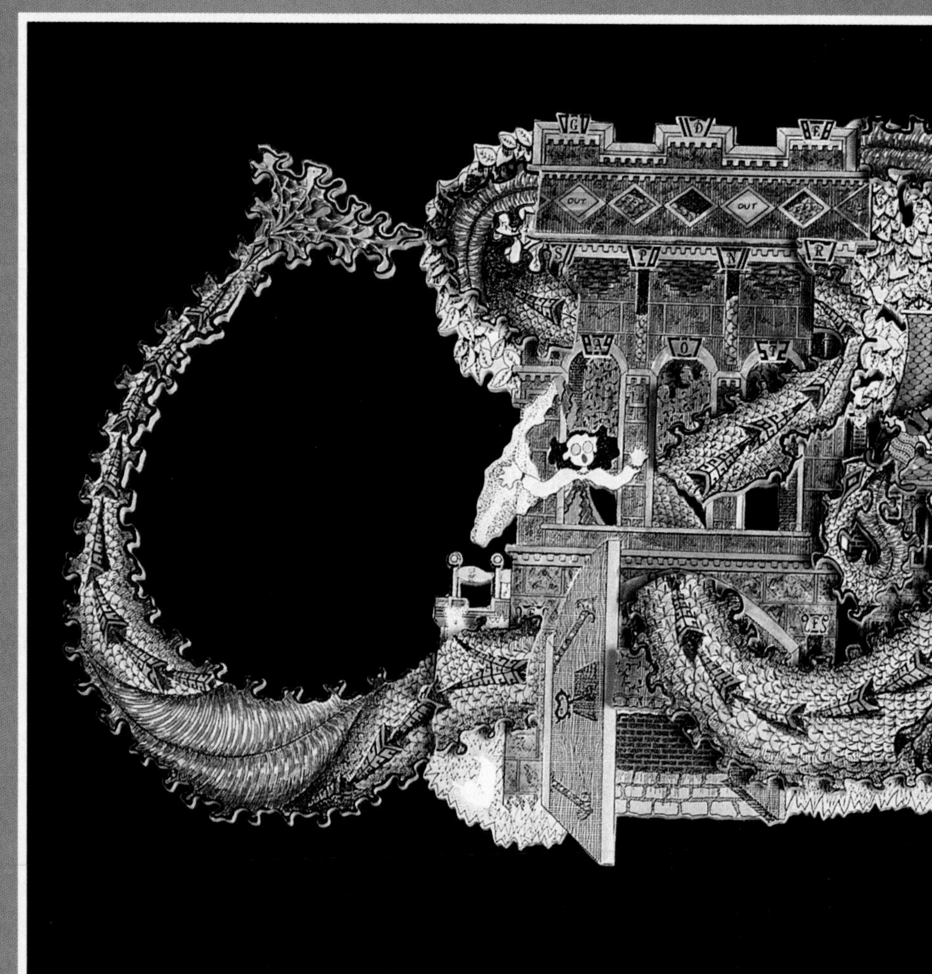

TEACHING THE LESSON

You could read the selection from *Volcano* on pp. 58–59 aloud as the class follows in their textbooks. Ask students to identify the main idea or topic sentence for each paragraph, guiding them to notice that each paragraph presents different information.

After this analysis, you could ask students to record in their journals their answers to the **Reader's Response** questions. Then give students the opportunity to share their ideas. You could then guide discussion of questions 3 and 4 in **Writer's Craft.** For question 5, ask students to find examples of very short paragraphs to bring to class for discussion the next day.

Looking at the Parts

Have you flown a kite? A kite has several **parts.** It has a frame and paper stretched over it. It also has some kind of a tail. But kites aren't all alike. Some are big, and some are small. Some have fancy designs, and others don't.

Paragraphs are like kites. They may have the same parts but be very different. Some are long, and some are short. Some can stand alone, and others can't.

Writing and You. Writers usually connect paragraphs together in a story, an article, a letter, or even a book. When you write, you may use paragraphs this way, also. Do you think about paragraphs as you read and write?

As You Read. The following paragraphs are about a volcano named Mount Saint Helens. As you read, look for different kinds of paragraphs.

QUOTATION FOR THE DAY

"The paragraph is a convenient unit; it serves all forms of literary work. As long as it holds together, a paragraph may be of any length—a single, short sentence or a passage of great duration." (E. B. White, 1899–1985, American humorist, essayist, and novelist)

Ask students to use this quotation to think of short definitions of the word *paragraph.* [A possible response is "a literary unit of varying length with one main idea."]

LEP/ESL

General Strategies. Why bother with paragraphs? What real function do they serve? Why not write one ongoing composition instead of dividing it into parts? Students might profit from a discussion of the usefulness of paragraphs, especially if concrete examples are introduced that underscore the importance of breaking a whole into parts to achieve greater clarity. Any kind of collection, such as seashells, stamps, or coins, can be enjoyed and viewed more clearly if the parts are not heaped one on the other, but rather are displayed as separate components.

ASSESSMENT

You will be able to assess students' understanding by their participation in the class discussions. You can also evaluate the journal entries from **Reader's Response.**

CLOSURE

You may want to ask students what a paragraph is. After listing several of their ideas on the chalkboard, point out the facts about paragraphs in **Looking Ahead** on p. 60. ■

USING THE SELECTION

***from* Volcano**

1

The topic sentence introduces a descriptive paragraph that tells what Mount St. Helens looked like in 1980, right after the eruption.

2

Details are given to show what Mount St. Helens looked like.

FROM

VOLCANO

By Patricia Lauber

Mount Saint Helens erupted on May 18, 1980. These paragraphs describe the mountain as it appeared a few months later.

1 In early summer of 1980 the north side of Mount St.
2 Helens looked like the surface of the moon—gray and lifeless. The slopes were buried under mud, ground-up rock, pumice, and bits of trees. Ash covered everything with a thick crust. The eruption had set off thunderstorms that wet the falling ash. The ash became goo that hardened into a crust. The slopes looked like a place where nothing could be alive or ever live again. Yet life was there.

With the coming of warm weather, touches of green appeared among the grays and browns. They were the green of plants that had survived the force and heat of the eruption.

Some plants had still been buried under the snows of winter on May 18 [when the volcano had erupted].

3 Huckleberry and trillium sprang up among the fallen forest trees. So did young silver firs and mountain hemlocks.

In other places, where the snow had melted, the blast swept away the parts of plants that were aboveground. But roots, bulbs, and stems remained alive underground. They sprouted, and hardy shoots pushed up through the pumice and ash. Among these was fireweed, one of the first plants to appear after a fire.

A few plants were even growing in blocks of soil that had been lifted from one place and dropped in another.

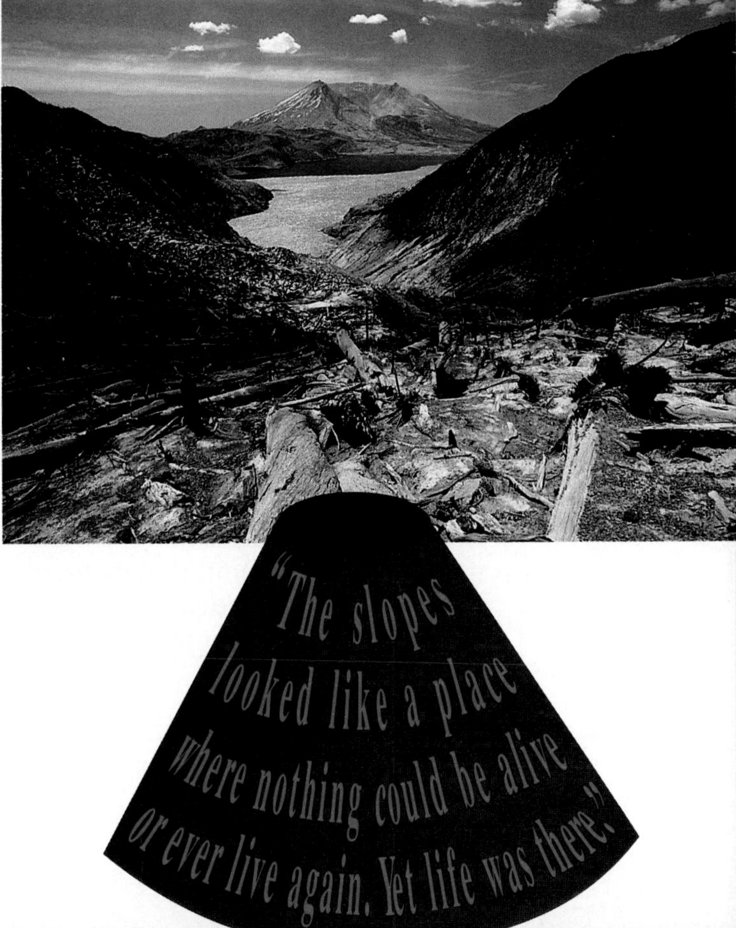
"The slopes
looked like a place
where nothing could be alive
or ever live again. Yet life was there."

3

huckleberry: a shrub that produces a small berry resembling a blueberry

MEETING
INDIVIDUAL
NEEDS

LESS-ADVANCED STUDENTS

To help students identify main ideas and supporting details, you may want to provide study questions. Here are some questions you might provide ahead of time for the first paragraph of the reading selection:

1. When did Mount St. Helens recently look as if there were no life on it—no plants, no trees, no flowers? [in early summer of 1980]
2. What did it look like? [the surface of the moon]
3. What covered the slopes? [mud, ground-up rock, pumice, and bits of trees]
4. What made a thick crust over everything? [ash]
5. What happened to Mount St. Helens to make it appear so dead? [a volcanic eruption]

In a variation of this activity, you could ask the students to write questions, trade papers, and answer each other's questions.

SELECTION AMENDMENT

Description of change: excerpted
Rationale: to focus on the concept of paragraph analysis presented in this chapter

ANSWERS

Reader's Response

1. Whether or not the student would like to visit Mt. St. Helens, insist that reasons be given for the response.
2. Although the question suggests several sentences written in a journal, you may want to encourage students to record a more complete memory.

Writer's Craft

3. The fifth paragraph has one sentence.
4. The rest of the book is probably about what happened at Mount St. Helens before and after the latest big eruption. The book probably is about only this one volcano since the title is singular, not plural.
5. The really short paragraphs are usually set apart to emphasize the importance of a statement so the reader can't miss it. They also may come in dialogue when the writer indents for each change of speaker.

READER'S RESPONSE

1. Would you like to visit Mount Saint Helens? Explain why or why not.
2. The author describes Mount Saint Helens after the volcano erupted. What is a place, person, or object that you've seen and remember well? Write several sentences about it in your journal.

WRITER'S CRAFT

3. The first paragraph has seven sentences in it. How many sentences does the shortest paragraph have?
4. These few paragraphs come from a book. What do you think the rest of the book is about?
5. Some paragraphs can be as short as one or two words. Look for some really short paragraphs in stories or magazine articles. How do they work?

LOOKING AHEAD

In this chapter, you'll learn what paragraphs do and how they're put together. As you work, keep in mind that a paragraph

- is usually part of a longer piece of writing
- usually has a main idea
- may have supporting details to explain or prove the main idea
- may be developed in one of four basic ways

SEGMENT 2 *(pp. 61–68)*

THE PARTS OF A PARAGRAPH

OBJECTIVES

- To identify main ideas and topic sentences
- To collect supporting details for a main idea of a paragraph
- To identify transitions

MOTIVATION

Write the words *apple, lips, valentine,* and *stop sign* on the chalkboard and ask students what these words have in common [the color red]. Explain that *red* is the main idea and the other words are supporting details. Remind students that most paragraphs have both a main idea and supporting details.

The Parts of a Paragraph

Paragraphs aren't all alike, but many of them have the same three parts. One part is the ***main idea.*** This is the big idea of the paragraph. Most paragraphs have a main idea. The main idea may be in a ***topic sentence,*** which is the second part of some paragraphs. A third part consists of the ***supporting sentences.*** These sentences add details about the main idea. Here's an example of a paragraph with all three parts.

Topic sentence
Main idea
Supporting sentences

Chimpanzees are very social animals. They enjoy being with each other. When they meet, they greet each other with kisses, hugs, pats on the back, and hand-holding. Grooming—the gentle parting of the hair, combing, and touching—is an important social function. It is peaceful, relaxing, friendly physical contact.

Margery Facklam, *Wild Animals, Gentle Women*

Teacher's ResourceBank™

RESOURCES

THE PARTS OF A PARAGRAPH

QUOTATION FOR THE DAY

"The house praises the carpenter." (Ralph Waldo Emerson, 1803–1882, American poet, essayist, and philosopher)

Ask students to compare the essential parts of a paragraph and the essential parts of a house [main idea, roof; supporting evidence, walls].

SELECTION AMENDMENT

Description of change: excerpted
Rationale: to focus on the concept of paragraph organization presented in this chapter

TEACHING THE LESSON

Since the explanations of the various parts of a paragraph are brief, you may want to read them aloud to the class and then ask the class to read the example paragraphs silently before discussing them. Emphasize to students that a main idea is what a paragraph is about and that each paragraph should have just one main idea. Every sentence in the paragraph should tell something about the main idea. Remind them that each paragraph should be indented. To reinforce this lesson, you or the students could make posters that show the parts of a paragraph. Students can then use the posters as a reference.

INTEGRATING THE LANGUAGE ARTS

Literature Link. You may want to show students that paragraphs in books really do have topic sentences and supporting details. Have students read a piece of nonfiction writing and ask them to notice how the paragraphs are put together. Ask students to write the topic sentences of at least three paragraphs in a selection such as "The Land I Lost" by Huynh Quang Nhuong. Beneath each topic sentence, ask students to list the supporting details in the paragraph.

The Topic Sentence

When a paragraph has a topic sentence, it is often the first or second sentence. But not always. Sometimes it comes in the middle or at the end. In the following paragraph, the topic sentence comes at the end. Notice how the other sentences all support the main idea in the topic sentence.

> He thought he had failed in his life's work. Others agreed with him. He died poor and bitterly disliked. To us today, this rejection seems strange. He had helped to free five South American countries from Spanish rule. He had won major victories on the battlefield. He was anything but a failure. Over time, people began to accept the truth. Monuments were built to honor him. People started to celebrate his birthday. Today, Simón Bolívar is regarded as one of Latin America's greatest heroes.

GUIDED PRACTICE

To help students begin **Exercise 1,** use the examples to show how the parts of a paragraph function. For example, when discussing the paragraph on chimpanzees, ask the students to explain why the underlined sentence is the main idea. Continue with the other examples. If students can explain why the underlining is correct, they should understand the main idea.

For **Exercise 2,** work through the first main idea together and list suggested details on the chalkboard. Then let students choose one of the remaining two main ideas for independent practice.

A topic sentence helps a writer stick to the topic. But remember that not all paragraphs have topic sentences. You'll see many good paragraphs that don't. Often a paragraph has a main idea but no topic sentence. The details all fit together, however, and support, or prove, the main idea.

EXERCISE 1 Identifying Main Ideas and Topic Sentences

How good are you at identifying main ideas and topic sentences? Each of the following paragraphs has one main idea. Read each paragraph, and try to identify its main idea. If the paragraph has a topic sentence, tell what it is. If there isn't a topic sentence, state the main idea in your own words.

1. Whenever cats are together, they have ways of communicating with each other. They make faces to express feelings like anger, fear, and contentment. They also use body language. Switching the tail can mean "I am annoyed." Holding the tail straight up means "I am happy and friendly." Cats also "talk" to each other with sounds. They meow, hiss, growl, chirp. These noises can mean many things, from "hello" to "don't come any closer."

Joanna Cole, *A Cat's Body*

STUDENTS WITH SPECIAL NEEDS

You may want to give students with comprehension disabilities that hamper their reading a few straightforward paragraphs for practice before assigning **Exercise 1.** Give students paragraphs with clearly stated topic sentences. A few initial successes will bolster students' confidence and prepare them for the more complicated paragraphs in **Exercise 1.**

SELECTION AMENDMENT
Description of change: excerpted
Rationale: to focus on the concept of paragraph organization presented in this chapter

INDEPENDENT PRACTICE

Use **Exercises 1, 2,** and **3** to give students an opportunity to demonstrate that they can identify the parts of a paragraph: main idea, topic sentence, supporting details, and transitions.

ASSESSMENT

Ask students to take the work they did on **Exercise 2** and develop the collected details into complete paragraphs. Their performance on this activity should indicate their level of mastery.

COOPERATIVE LEARNING

You could let students work all three paragraphs in **Exercise 1** at the same time in groups, with each student writing the answers. Then have them compare answers and come up with an accurate set. Tell them to make sure that they can explain why these answers are correct.

When they are done, ask one member from each group to report on the group's answer to each question.

TIMESAVER

When students work in groups, you might give the same grade to every member of the group. In this way, they all feel responsible for doing good work, especially if they don't know which student's work you will select to grade.

AMENDMENTS TO SELECTIONS

Description of change: excerpted
Rationale: to focus on the concept of paragraph organization presented in this chapter

M.I.—As a boy, future baseball star Roberto Clemente had poor playing conditions and primitive equipment.

2. It was a warm tropical evening in Puerto Rico. Roberto Clemente was playing with a group of boys on a muddy field in Barrio San Antón. It was nothing at all like the great stadium in San Juan. There were bumps and puddles, and the outfield was full of trees. The bat in Roberto's hand was a thick stick cut from the branch of a guava tree. The bases were old coffee sacks. The ball was a tightly-knotted bunch of rags.

Paul Robert Walker, *Pride of Puerto Rico*

3. <u>Some types of wood gave more light than others did</u>. There were the kinds that contained soft, gummy substances called *resin.* Such wood burned with a brighter flame that made it possible to see at night. The wood of certain evergreen trees such as pines and cedars burned brightly for this reason and such wood was used as torches.

Isaac Asimov, *How Did We Find Out About Coal?*

RETEACHING

Divide the class into groups of four or five students. Assign each group one of the following topics:

baseball	music	pizza
toys	zoos	vacations

Have each group write a topic sentence, a main idea, and three or four details about the topic. Provide time for groups to share their paragraphs.

Supporting Sentences

Supporting sentences have details that support, or prove, the main idea. These may be facts, examples, or other kinds of details. In the following paragraph, notice how the supporting sentences reinforce the main idea. This idea is stated in the first sentence.

Topic sentence — Details — Example/Facts

> Icebergs come in different shapes and sizes. An iceberg may be domed, with a rounded top like that of an old mountain. It may be blocky, a great squared slab of floating ice. Or it may be tabular, almost like a tombstone on its side adrift at sea. Some icebergs are small, but many are huge. In 1956, a naval icebreaker in the Antarctic measured a tabular iceberg at about 12,500 square miles. That's two and a half times the size of the state of Connecticut.

EXERCISE 2 **Collecting Details**

Perhaps you collect details about the life of your favorite movie or TV star. In the same way, you can collect details about your main idea for a paragraph. Choose one of the following main ideas. Then make a list of three or four details that support it.

LESS-ADVANCED STUDENTS

If some students need more practice in identifying the parts of a paragraph, provide more examples of good paragraphs from magazines, books, or newspapers for students to analyze. They will probably learn better by working in small groups at first, with you as leader. With this support, students can gradually work with more independence.

LEARNING STYLES

Kinetic Learners. Some students may learn the parts of a paragraph more easily if you give them copies of a paragraph with each sentence written on a separate strip of paper. (Advanced students might help you prepare the activity.) Then ask the students to read the strips of paper and to arrange them in a logical order, labeling each main idea, topic sentence, or supporting detail.

To teach transitions, ask students to cut some small strips of paper and to write one transition from the list on p. 66 on each strip. Then give students copies of a paragraph with the transitions left out and ask the students to insert the strips of paper in the proper places.

CLOSURE

You could conduct a quick review by asking the purpose of each part of a paragraph: the main idea [to announce the subject], the topic sentence [to narrow the subject], the supporting details [to inform, explain or make clear], and the transitions [to show how the ideas are connected].

EXTENSION

Once the students have identified the parts of a paragraph, you may want them to write one or more paragraphs on topics of their choice. Then ask them to exchange papers and to label the parts of each other's paragraphs. Be sure to allow time for them to discuss what they find.

MEETING INDIVIDUAL NEEDS

LEP/ESL

General Strategies. When teaching **Transitional Words and Phrases,** you could provide an opportunity to expand students' vocabulary. Pair students. Have them look up the expressions listed in both a bilingual dictionary and in an ordinary English dictionary. Have them use bilingual dictionaries to record native-language definitions in the word banks of their journals. The standard English dictionary should be used to record one synonym or short definition. There are dictionary publications designed specifically for younger students that could be particularly useful.

ADVANCED STUDENTS

Ask students to find other examples of paragraphs to bring to class to analyze in terms of finding the main idea, topic sentence, supporting details, and transitions. They could use either materials supplied by you or materials from home.

ANSWERS

Exercise 2

Answers will vary. Details should support the main idea chosen by the student.

1. examples of skateboarding skills needed
2. details about how the room looks
3. reasons why you don't like the thing

EXAMPLE *Main Idea: Stamp collecting is a useful hobby.*
Details: (1) It makes geography interesting. (2) Stamps teach you something about history. (3) The value of your stamps may go up in time.

1. Skateboarding (or another sport) requires skill.
2. My room is always messy.
3. Snakes (or spiders, worms, lightning storms) are one thing I can't stand.

Words That Connect Ideas. A good paragraph makes sense. When you read it, you see that all its details relate to the main idea.

Sometimes you can easily tell how ideas are related. In a story, for example, one event usually follows another. This order helps you understand what happens in the story.

But many times, special words help to show how ideas are related. These words are called ***transitional words and phrases.*** They are *connectors.* They may connect one idea to another, one sentence to another, or one paragraph to another.

TRANSITIONAL WORDS AND PHRASES

Showing Likenesses	Showing Differences	Showing Causes and Effects
also like and too another in addition	although but however instead	as a result because since so
Showing Time	**Showing Place**	**Showing Importance**
after next before second finally then first when	above down across into around there behind under	first last mainly most important

ENRICHMENT

Have students provide an example of writing that has been divided into paragraphs from an outside source such as a magazine, newspaper, book, or encyclopedia. Have students underline the main idea in each paragraph. You might display their work on a bulletin board to show students that paragraphs have the same parts in all kinds of writing. ■

The following paragraph is about Babe Didrickson Zaharias, a great woman athlete. In 1932, she was the entire winning track "team" for an insurance company in Dallas, Texas. Notice how transitional words connect ideas in this paragraph.

> Even as they entered the stadium, the loud speakers were calling the teams for the parade onto the field. When the Illinois Women's Athletic Club was called, twenty-two athletes marched forward. A second club fielded fifteen girls, another twelve. All in all there were more than 200 female athletes on the field. Then they called the team of the Employers' Casualty Insurance Company of Dallas, Texas. And one lonely girl marched bravely down the field. The crowd roared.
>
> Harry Gersh, *Women Who Made America Great*

CRITICAL THINKING
Evaluation

After students have completed **Exercise 2,** ask them to exchange papers and to evaluate the supporting details that have been listed. They can underline each main idea or topic sentence and then check each supporting detail to see whether or not it pertains to the subject of the paragraph.

SELECTION AMENDMENT
Description of change: excerpted
Rationale: to focus on the concept of paragraph organization presented in this chapter

A DIFFERENT APPROACH

You could give the students a paragraph with quite a few transitions and ask students to change the transitions so that the meaning is changed. Students may come up with some far-fetched statements, but they will see clearly how the transitions function. It may be more helpful to have them complete this activity in groups and read their creations aloud.

EXERCISE 3 **Identifying Transitions**

How do you bake a potato? Why might a polar bear's fur look green? The transition words in the following paragraphs can help you answer those questions. Find and list the transitions in each of the paragraphs. Use the chart on page 66 to help you.

1. It's easy to bake a potato. First, preheat the oven to 425° F. Then, choose a potato that's the right type for baking, such as an Idaho. Next, wash and scrub it thoroughly. Dry the potato, and grease it lightly with butter. Puncture the skin with a fork to allow steam to escape while baking. Bake the potato for approximately one hour. When it's done, serve it with a topping. For a healthful dish, use yogurt or cottage cheese.
2. A polar bear's fur looks white, but it isn't. Instead, each hair is a transparent tube. When the hairs are clear, the bear appears to be white. But sometimes tiny green plants called algae grow inside the hairs. As a result, the bear looks green.

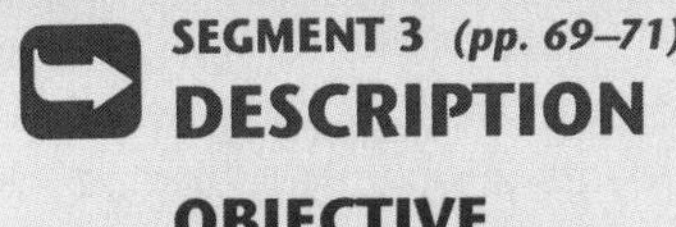

SEGMENT 3 *(pp. 69–71)*

DESCRIPTION

OBJECTIVE

- To use description to develop paragraphs

TEACHING THE LESSON

You could teach **Ways to Develop Paragraphs** by having the class suggest possible paragraphs about a current or well-known movie. Possible paragraphs include description (what the characters and sets looked like), narration (the story of the movie), comparison/contrast (comparing it

Ways to Develop Paragraphs

You often use the same parts (main idea, topic sentence, and supporting sentences) in writing paragraphs. But you don't develop all paragraphs the same way. Here are four ways to develop a paragraph.

WAYS TO DEVELOP PARAGRAPHS	
Description	Looking at details about a person, place, or thing
Narration	Looking at changes over time in a person, place, or thing
Comparison/ Contrast	Finding likenesses and differences in a person, place, or thing
Evaluation	Judging the value of someone or something

Description

What does your street look like when it rains or snows? What's your lunch like today?

When you want to tell what something is like or looks like, you use description. ***Description*** calls for details. Sometimes they are *sensory details*. ***Sensory details*** come from your five senses: sight, sound, smell, taste, touch. You may describe how your cousin looks, how the bakery smells, or how a peach tastes.

Details for a description are often arranged in spatial order. With ***spatial order,*** you organize details by their location. To describe a scene, for example, you might give details as your eyes move from left to right or right to left. You might also arrange details from far away to close up or close up to far away.

As you read the following paragraph about Japan, notice the spatial order of details. The writer begins at the top of the mountain and moves down.

Teacher's ResourceBank™

RESOURCES

DESCRIPTION
- Description 20

QUOTATION FOR THE DAY

"Words, when well chosen, have so great a force in them that a description often gives us more lively ideas than the sight of things themselves." (Joseph Addison, 1672–1719, English journalist, playwright, and poet)

You may wish to ask a volunteer to tell about a time when someone described something so clearly that the volunteer could easily see a picture in his or her mind. Students might brainstorm lists of sensory details to describe assigned subjects such as ice cream, a sunny day, a snowstorm, cafeteria food, and so forth.

to another movie), and evaluation (telling what was good or bad about the movie).

Then ask them to read the explanatory material on description, looking for the meaning of *sensory details* and *spatial order.* You can use the paragraph by Tatsuo Ishimoto to illustrate the use of both strategies.

CLOSURE

After doing **Exercise 4,** you may want to ask several students to volunteer to read their lists of details for their chosen subjects. As each student reads, you could ask the rest of the class to say whether each type of sensory detail appeals to sight, smell, sound, taste, or touch. ■

MEETING INDIVIDUAL NEEDS

LEP/ESL

General Strategies. Exercise 4 is an excellent opportunity for students to work with peers in a collaborative effort. Make sure, however, that ESL students are integrated with mainstream students. Some students benefit more from a collaborative, rather than a competitive, learning environment.

STUDENTS WITH SPECIAL NEEDS

Students with problems in written expression will benefit from creating or finding illustrations for their descriptive compositions before they begin writing their first drafts. Students can then use the illustrations as prompts for their writing.

A DIFFERENT APPROACH

List the names of various objects on the chalkboard. Have one student at a time give a brief oral description of one of the items. Record some of the descriptions on the chalkboard, or ask the class to choose their favorites and to state why they selected them.

SELECTION AMENDMENT
Description of change: excerpted
Rationale: to focus on the concept of paragraph organization presented in this chapter

Mountains dominate the landscape. Down their slopes rush many swift streams and rivers, cascading in waterfalls, pausing in hillside pools and small lakes. The mountains are not only forested, they are rocky. In the high mountains are stands of fir, larch, hemlock, spruce—also azaleas, dwarf bamboo, dwarf birch and dwarf pine. On the lower slopes grow oak, elm, magnolia, also linden, birch, cherry—all trees familiar to Americans although the species differ from the native species of the United States. In the lowlands are the gardener's favorites—black pine and red pine and the tall bamboos. And always, not far away, is the sea.

Tatsuo Ishimoto, *The Art of the Japanese Garden*

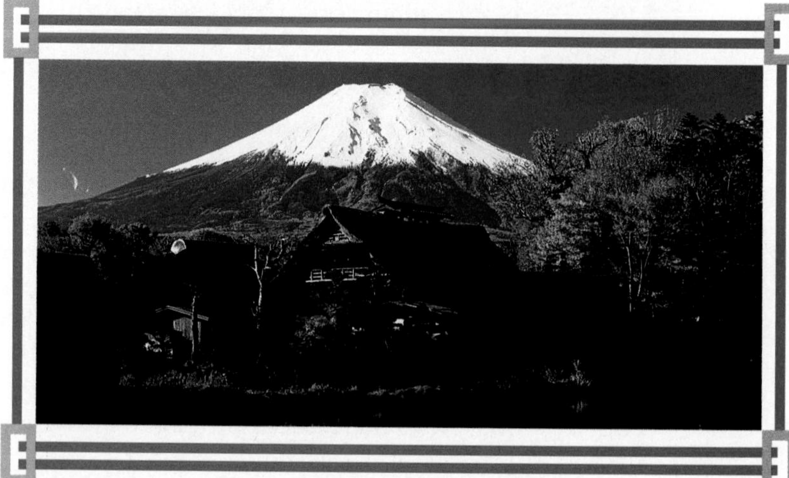

EXERCISE 4 **Using Description to Develop Paragraphs**

How would you describe the lizard that slithers across your driveway? Choose one of the following subjects. Then list the details you would use to describe it. Try to use sensory details of sight, sound, smell, taste, and touch. Arrange the details in spatial order.

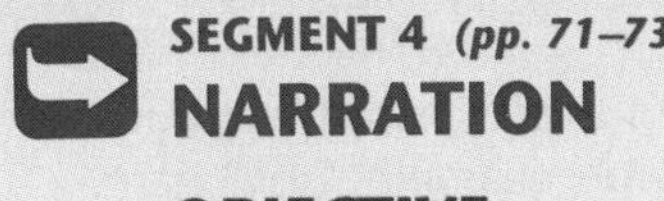

SEGMENT 4 *(pp. 71–73)*

NARRATION

OBJECTIVE

- To use narration to develop paragraphs

TEACHING THE LESSON

You could give students the following list of words and phrases to identify in the lesson on narration: *narrating, chronological order, telling a story, fiction, explaining a process,* and *step-by-step order.* Then ask students to read silently and to write definitions.

You can use the students' work from **Exercise 5** to assess their learning.

1. what you think the planet Mars is like
2. one person or creature in your favorite video game
3. a shopping mall when it's very busy
4. a city (or country) street in the middle of the day
5. your dirty tennis shoes

Narration

What happens to the characters in your favorite movie? How does an eagle build its nest?

When you answer these questions, you're narrating. ***Narrating*** means telling what happens over time. You may tell a story. You may tell how to do something or explain a process.

When you narrate, you often arrange events in chronological order. With ***chronological order,*** you put events in the order in which they happen.

Telling a Story. Some stories are true, and some are made up. Either kind of story is a narrative. The following narrative paragraph is from a book of fiction.

> Strangely, when Ramona's heart was heavy, so were her feet. She trudged to the school bus, plodded through the halls at school, and clumped home from the bus after school. The house felt lonely when she let herself in, so she turned on the television set for company. She sat on the couch and stared at one of the senseless soap operas Mrs. Kemp watched. They were all about rich people—none of them looking like Howie's Uncle Hobart—who accused other people of doing something terrible; Ramona didn't understand exactly what, but it all was boring, boring, boring.
>
> Beverly Cleary, *Ramona Forever*

ANSWERS

Exercise 4

Descriptions will vary. Students will have satisfactorily completed this exercise if they have chosen one of the five subjects, listed the details called for, and arranged the details in spatial order. Students should be prepared to explain the rationale for their ordering of sentences.

Teacher's ResourceBank™

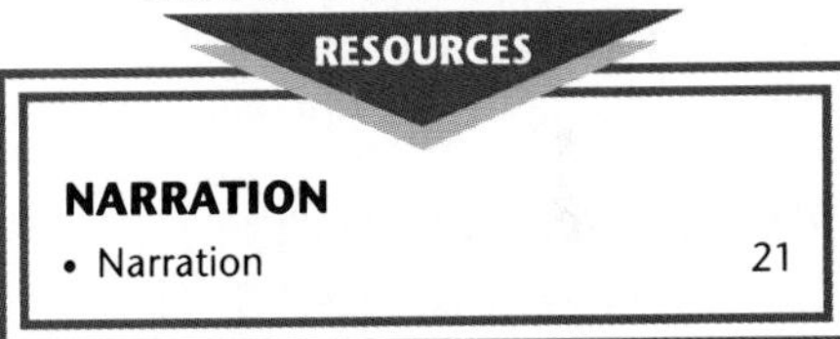

NARRATION

- Narration 21

QUOTATION FOR THE DAY

"I think the whole glory of writing lies in the fact that it forces us out of ourselves and into the lives of others." (Sherwood Anderson, 1876–1941, American writer)

You may wish to use the quotation to address students' ideas about what a writer is or does. Ask students to brainstorm some ways writing "forces" them "into the lives of others."

SELECTION AMENDMENT

Description of change: excerpted
Rationale: to focus on the concept of paragraph development presented in this chapter

Start a story and then move around the room, asking each student to add one sentence in chronological order to the story.

CLOSURE

Ask students the following questions:

1. What are two examples of narration? [telling a story and telling how to do something or explaining a process]
2. What is the name for putting events in the order in which they happen? [chronological order]

LEP/ESL

General Strategies. To clarify the concept of chronological order, ask the class if anyone knows the origin of the word *chronological.* What part of speech is it? [It is an adjective.] On the chalkboard, write the Greek root word from *chronos,* meaning "time." Then write the noun form, *chronology.* Explain that chronology is the order of occurrence of events in time. Ask several students to give brief chronologies of their days' events. The strategy is to bring abstract concepts to a concrete level.

INTEGRATING THE LANGUAGE ARTS

Technology Link. You may want to pair students to complete the second part of **Exercise 5.** Have each pair brainstorm to develop a list for their chosen narrative strategy. Explain that they should collaborate to type, rearrange, and proofread the list on a computer. Each pair should make three printouts, one for each partner and one for you. Remind students that most word processing programs provide the option of printing multiple copies.

SELECTION AMENDMENT
Description of change: excerpted
Rationale: to focus on the concept of paragraph development presented in this chapter

Paragraphs that tell a story usually don't have a main idea. But events in the paragraph do follow one another. That makes the paragraph easy to understand.

Explaining a Process. When your friend explains how to make a dog sit, she's explaining a process. She puts her instructions in step-by-step order. It's the same as chronological order.

Notice how the writer uses chronological order in the following paragraph. He explains how to begin the Chinese art of paper cutting.

> First, cut up paper squares about the size of the palm of your hand. Make a model using any paper. When you have the right size, use it to cut colored paper. If you are going to cut a word, make sure the squares are all the same size.
>
> Cheng Hou-tien, *Scissor Cutting for Beginners*

3. What is the name for putting instructions in step-by-step order? [explaining a process] ■

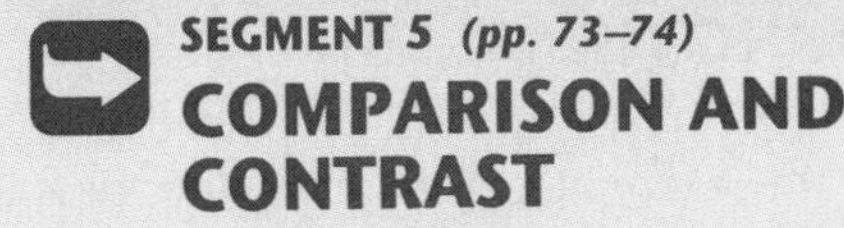

SEGMENT 5 (pp. 73–74)

COMPARISON AND CONTRAST

OBJECTIVE

- To use comparison or contrast to develop paragraphs

EXERCISE 5 Using Narration to Develop Paragraphs

It's fun to tell a story. It's easy to explain a process. The following exercises will help you develop those skills.

1. Write a group story. Work as a whole class or in smaller groups. Begin with one of the following "starters" or with one of your own. Then take turns adding a sentence to the story. Be sure the events of the story are in chronological order.
   - **a.** Every day promptly at 5:00 P.M., Ms. Arrigo set the burglar alarm on the main bank vault.
   - **b.** It all began when a scarecrow appeared in the shopping mall and shouted, "Show time!"
   - **c.** The long gray car came sputtering into the gas station. A white poodle climbed out from behind the steering wheel.
2. Choose one of the following processes. Then list three or more steps in doing it. List the steps in chronological order (in the order they happen).
   - **d.** how to get to the principal's office from your classroom
   - **e.** how to use the telephone to report an emergency
   - **f.** how to choose a pair of sneakers

Comparison and Contrast

How are you and your brother or sister alike? What's the difference between football and soccer?

To answer these questions, you need to ***compare*** or ***contrast*** things. You tell how they are alike and how they are different. When you compare and contrast, you use logical order. With ***logical order,*** you group related ideas together in a way that makes sense.

Read the following two paragraphs. How are rabbits and hares alike? How are they different?

ANSWERS

Exercise 5

1. Accept all responses, but make sure that each sentence follows chronological order.
2. Be prepared to help students with chronological order. Here are possible answers:

   d. Go out the door. Walk down the hall going south. Stop in front of the door marked "Principal."
   e. Lift the receiver. Listen for the dial tone. Dial or push the buttons for 911.
   f. Look at different styles to choose the one you want. Ask the salesperson if the sneakers are available in your size. Try on the sneakers.

Teacher's ResourceBank™

RESOURCES

COMPARISON AND CONTRAST

- Comparison and Contrast 22

TEACHING THE LESSON

Have students read the text and discuss the examples. Then give the class practice by leading them in a comparison-contrast discussion of two items they know about such as cafeteria food and home cooking, reading and writing, movies and books, or football and basketball.

CLOSURE

After students have made their lists for **Exercise 6,** ask students to use that information to write brief paragraphs. Ask students to read their paragraphs to the class. After each reading, ask the class if they can think of any other comparisons or contrasts the writer might have used. ■

QUOTATION FOR THE DAY

"That was the chief difference between literature and life. In books, the proportion of exceptional to commonplace people is high; in reality, very low." (Aldous Huxley, 1894–1963, English-born author and philosophical essayist)

Explain that Huxley's quotation contrasts the difference between literature and life. Students might write journal entries in which they compare and contrast their lives to those of fictional characters from stories, books, plays, movies, or television programs.

ANSWERS

Exercise 6

Answers may vary. Students may have never thought about differences between seeing movies on television and in a theater. You may have to help them start by pointing out that a movie in a theater involves a larger screen and louder sound. You might also discuss the effect of commercials interrupting movies.

SELECTION AMENDMENT

Description of change: excerpted
Rationale: to focus on the concept of paragraph development presented in this chapter

Comparison

To look at, rabbits and hares are very like each other. Both have long ears, big eyes and short, white, tufty tails which show up when they are running away. Both live by eating plants. Both can run very fast.

Contrast

Their habits, however, are very different. Hares live alone in open fields. Rabbits are gregarious, which means that they like crowding together. They dig a maze of underground tunnels, in which lots of them live.

Ralph Whitlock, *Rabbits and Hares*

EXERCISE 6 **Using Comparison or Contrast to Develop Paragraphs**

Think about yourself one year ago. How are the two "you's" alike? How are they different? Try the same thing with one of the following topics. First, make a list of likenesses between the two animals, pizzas, or movies. Then make another list of differences.

1. a dog and a cat as pets
2. the best and the worst pizza you've ever had
3. movies on television and movies in a theater

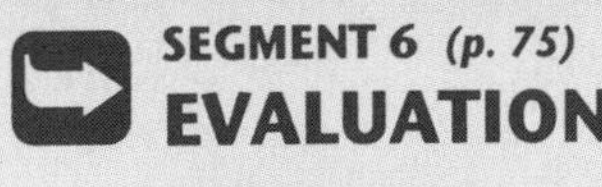

SEGMENT 6 *(p. 75)*

EVALUATION

OBJECTIVES

- To evaluate a food
- To make a two-minute evaluative talk to the class, using order of importance to organize the talk

TEACHING THE LESSON

Guide students through **Exercise 7** on the chalkboard, having them choose subjects, form opinions, and suggest reasons to support their evaluations.

Close the lesson by having students suggest how they might use evaluation throughout the course of the day. ■

Evaluation

What's the best dish your school lunchroom serves? What movie is a waste of time? When you answer these questions, you're ***evaluating.*** You're deciding the value, or worth, of things.

When you evaluate, it's important to give reasons to support your opinion. You can organize your reasons by ***order of importance.*** You can either begin or end with the most important reason.

In the following paragraph, the writer gives an opinion about bottled apple juice. Notice the reasons the writer gives for this opinion. Where is the most important reason?

Opinion	I love apples, but not bottled apple juice.
Reason	My low opinion of bottled apple juice is based mainly on taste. This juice tastes like sugar, not like apples.
Reason	Second, there isn't much nutrition in bottled apple juice. About all a glass of it offers is a hundred empty calories.
Reason	Finally, most bottled apple juice just doesn't *look* very good. Its pale yellow color is sickly compared to orange juice or grape juice. For apple lovers like me, the choice is fresh-pressed apple cider.

EXERCISE 7 **Speaking and Listening: Evaluating a Food**

President George Bush once made headlines by declaring, "I hate broccoli!" Choose a food that you like or dislike very much. Then list at least three reasons for your opinion. Begin with the most important reason. Share your evaluation with your class in a two-minute talk. Compare your evaluation with those of your classmates. Which foods do your classmates like most? least?

QUOTATION FOR THE DAY

"Everyone complains of his memory, but no one complains of his judgment." (Duc François de La Rochefoucauld, 1613–1680, French writer)

You may wish to write the quotation on the chalkboard and assure students that having strong opinions often gives writers an extra tool. Students might create lists of statements that begin "I think that. . ." or "I believe in. . ." Explain that each statement could be used as a topic sentence when evaluating paragraphs.

ANSWERS

Exercise 7

Evaluations will vary. Make sure that students move from the most important to the least important reason. Encourage students to think about how the foods appeal to senses other than taste.

SEGMENT 7 *(pp. 76–81)*

MAKING CONNECTIONS

WRITING PARAGRAPHS FOR DIFFERENT PURPOSES

OBJECTIVE

- To write expressive, informative, persuasive, and creative paragraphs

WRITING A PARAGRAPH TO EXPRESS YOURSELF

Teaching Strategies

To help students plan this expressive paragraph, you may want to review the modes they have learned—description, narration, comparison and contrast, and evaluation. You might use the first suggested topic to show that any or all of the four modes could be used: description to describe what you like about that time of day, narration to tell what is done at that time of day, classification to compare and contrast the parts of a day; or evaluation to give reasons why that time of day is best.

Then you could ask them to follow the writing process for this assignment, and to let you see the prewriting notes, at least one rough draft, and a final draft.

GUIDELINES

You could ask volunteers to share their paragraphs with the class, but because these paragraphs are often highly personal, students should not be forced to read them aloud.

MAKING CONNECTIONS

In this chapter you've learned what makes a paragraph. Now you can try making your own. Remember that the basic purposes of writing are to express yourself, to inform, to persuade, and to be creative.

WRITING PARAGRAPHS FOR DIFFERENT PURPOSES

Writing a Paragraph to Express Yourself

Writing about your own thoughts and feelings is called personal, or *expressive,* writing. Expressive writing is often private. For example, you might write about your private thoughts and feelings in a diary or journal.

Write a paragraph telling how you feel or think about something. Use one of the following sentence starters or create one of your own.

- My favorite time of the day (week, year) is ____.
- I've always thought it would be fun to ____.
- A person who seems like a real hero to me is ____.
- Something that always annoys me is ____.

Prewriting. If you're trying to find ideas, you may want to make some notes first. Try listing, clustering, or brainstorming for ideas. (For more help with these prewriting techniques, see pages 29–31.)

Writing, Evaluating, and Revising. If you're only writing for yourself, write just one draft. But if you'd like to share your paragraph, reread it first. Did you express your thoughts and feelings clearly? Did you arrange your ideas in an order that makes sense? Make changes to improve your paragraph.

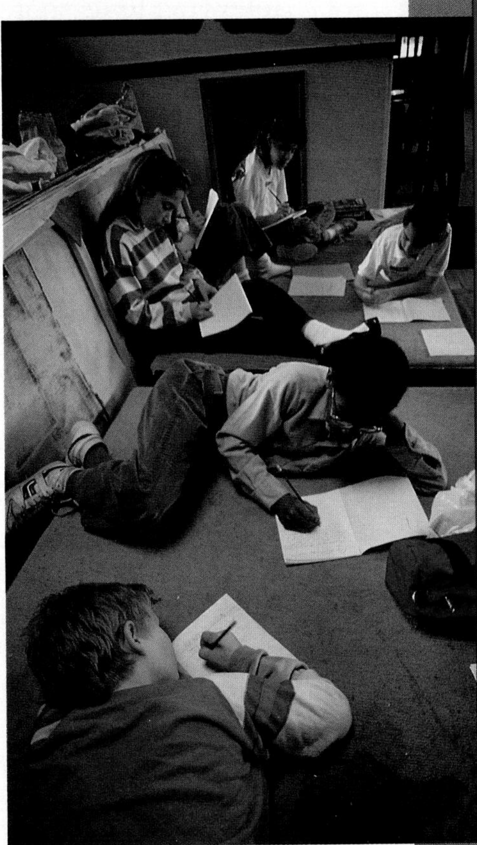

Proofreading and Publishing. If you share your paragraph, proofread it first. Correct any mistakes. (See the Guidelines for Proofreading on page 51.)

Writing a Paragraph to Inform

You get and give information all the time. For example, you get information from books, newspapers, and magazines. You also get information from television and radio. You give information when you give directions to your house or explain how to fold a paper crane.

WRITING A PARAGRAPH TO INFORM

Teaching Strategies

To help students start, you may want to go over the chart on p. 78 to make sure they understand it. Then ask them to write paragraphs using the suggested topic sentence. You may want the students to work in small groups on this project. They should follow the instructions in the textbook for the writing process from prewriting through publishing.

GUIDELINES

Students will have satisfactorily completed this exercise if they have written an informative paragraph, using information from the chart concerning life spans and including good topic sentences and four or five supporting sentences.

The following chart gives information about life spans for different animals. Use this information to write a paragraph for your classmates. You might not use all the information in the chart. You can use the following topic sentence.

Topic Sentence: Large animals often have longer life spans than small ones.

LIFE SPANS	
Animal	Longest Life Span
mosquito	30 days
rat	3 years
dog	12–15 years
gorilla	50 years
whale	60 years
elephant	65 years

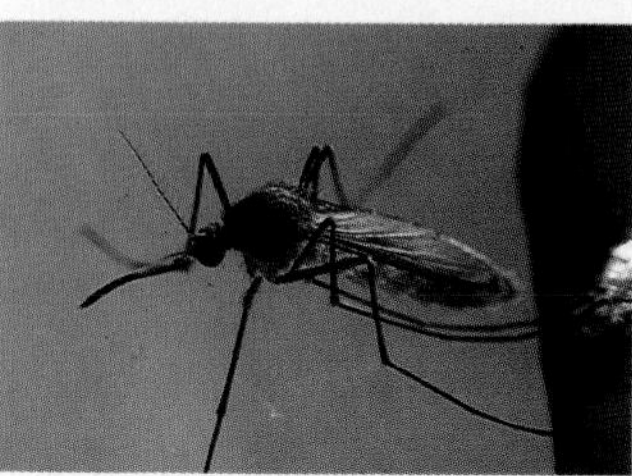

Prewriting. Start with the topic sentence on page 78. Decide how you will use the figures in the chart. Will you use them all? Will you summarize some of the information? You might write, for example, "The biggest animals, such as the elephant and the whale . . . "

Writing, Evaluating, and Revising. Write two or three supporting sentences to go with the topic sentence. Then write a sentence that sums up what you have said; just say the topic sentence in different words. Are your details clearly arranged? Do you use transitional words to show how the details are related? After you have written your paragraph, evaluate it and revise it.

Proofreading and Publishing. Check over your writing one last time. Look for mistakes in spelling, punctuation, or usage. Share your writing with the other students in your science class. Can the science teacher help you find out why larger animals usually live longer?

Writing a Paragraph to Persuade

People use persuasion all the time. You persuade a friend to lend you a new CD. A teacher persuades you to join the computer club at your school. In order to persuade, you need to give reasons to support your belief.

In most schools, students take physical education. Suppose you want to persuade your school board to change some P.E. (physical education) classes in your school. You think everyone should take swimming. Here are possible reasons:

Swimming is a good choice for P.E. because it
- exercises every muscle in the body
- can be a year-round activity with an indoor pool
- could save your life some day

WRITING A PARAGRAPH TO PERSUADE

Teaching Strategies

You may want to remind students of the four basic purposes of writing. They need to decide which mode(s) will be most effective: description, narration, classification, or evaluation.

Ask them to follow the instructions in the textbook for the writing process. You could ask the students to also present their ideas orally.

GUIDELINES

Students will have satisfactorily completed this exercise if they have written persuasive paragraphs recommending to their school board the addition of a specific physical activity to the curriculum, and have shared the paragraphs with others in some way.

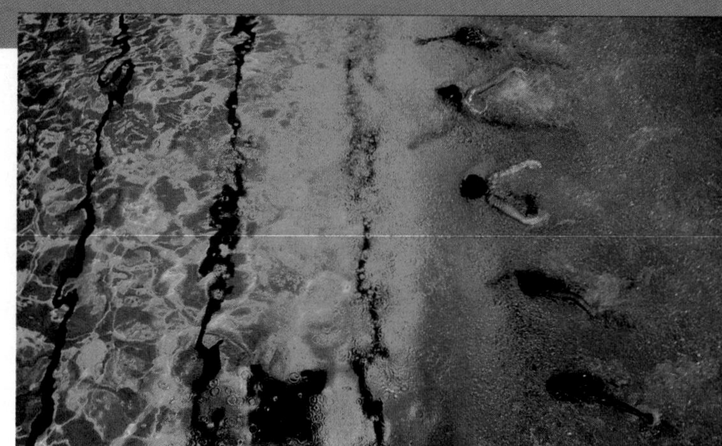

Write a paragraph to persuade your school board to add a specific activity to your school's P.E. program. Begin by writing a topic sentence like this one. Just substitute your activity for *swimming.*

The school board should add swimming to the school's P.E. program.

Prewriting. Think of at least three good reasons that will convince the school board. List the most important reason first.

Writing, Evaluating, and Revising. Read over your reasons. Are they the best ones? Are they clearly arranged? Revise your paragraph to make it more convincing.

Proofreading and Publishing. Be sure to correct any errors in usage, spelling, or punctuation. Then share your paragraph with other readers. Ask your readers if they were convinced.

Writing a Paragraph That Is Creative

When you create, you use your imagination. You invent something that didn't exist before. Creative writing seems difficult to many people. "Where do you get your ideas?" they ask writers. One novelist,

WRITING A PARAGRAPH THAT IS CREATIVE

Teaching Strategies

You may want to ask students to write these creative paragraphs in pairs so they can brainstorm to create an imaginative situation. To generate ideas, you might call for several ideas for stories suggested by the picture. Then the pairs can work together, following the writing process instructions in the textbook.

Ernest Gaines, replied that he gets his ideas by putting a character on a road. Then he starts his story from there.

Imagine that you're in the picture at the right. Imagine that you're standing at the base of the steps, looking upwards. Write a paragraph that tells what happens next.

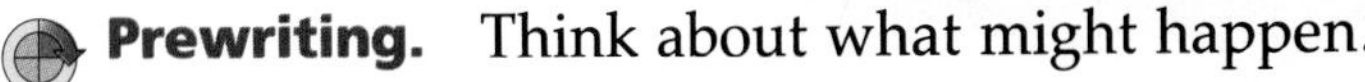

Prewriting. Think about what might happen.

- Is there a strange figure at the top of the steps?
- At the top of the steps, do you find an old, creaky door that you try to open?
- Do you try to walk away but find that you can't move?

Use your imagination! Think about what might happen on or near these steps. Jot down your ideas.

Writing, Evaluating, Revising. Write a narrative paragraph telling what happens. Put in lots of action. Then exchange papers with a classmate. What happened in your classmate's paragraph? Which story do you prefer? What ideas does your classmate have for improving your paragraph?

Proofreading and Publishing. Correct any errors in spelling, punctuation, or usage. Take turns reading your paragraphs aloud in a group or in your class. Whose paragraph is the most exciting?

GUIDELINES

Make sure that what students write in some way logically follows from what they see in the picture. Sometimes, while exercising their imaginations, they will forget the original assignment.

Chapter 3

EXPRESSIVE WRITING

OBJECTIVES

- To identify the purpose of expressive writing and to examine its characteristics
- To analyze the parts of a strong personal narrative
- To select a topic for a personal narrative and to write a description of that topic
- To gather details for a personal narrative
- To organize details for a personal narrative and to write a draft
- To evaluate and revise a personal narrative
- To proofread a personal narrative and to prepare it for publication

Motivation

Lead students in a discussion about the different ways that expressive writing can allow them to reveal their thoughts, feelings, and experiences. Start by asking students questions that enable them to share their experiences. Then encourage students to talk about what these experiences show about their lives. For example, you could ask students to describe their last birthdays. As students respond, point out that the details they use emphasize their likes and dislikes, as well as what and who is important to them.

Introduction

Using the students' descriptions of their experiences, explain that expressive writing allows writers to share their lives with others. Tell students that they can use expressive writing in personal narratives, letters, journals, and stories. You may find it useful to have the class talk about the differences between expressive, informative, persuasive, and literary writing. With this introduction, students should be prepared to appreciate the experiences, feelings, and thoughts expressed in the excerpt from ***The Land I Lost***.

Integration

You can use this chapter as a springboard for other activities in your classroom. If students are reading stories such as Maya Angelou's "Life Doesn't Frighten Me," you can have them compare the expressive writing in the excerpt from Beverly Cleary's ***A Girl from Yamhill: A Memoir*** with the stories they are reading.

The chart on the next page illustrates the strands of language arts as they are integrated into this chapter. For vocabulary study, glossary words are underlined in some writing models.

QUOTATIONS

All **Quotations for the Day** are chosen because of their relevance to instructional material presented in that segment of the chapter and for their usefulness in establishing student interest in writing.

INTEGRATING THE LANGUAGE ARTS

Selection	Reading and Literature	Writing and Critical Thinking	Language and Syntax	Speaking, Listening, and Other Expression Skills
from ***The Land I Lost*** by Huyn Quang Nhuong **84-86** from ***A Girl from Yamhill: A Memoir*** by Beverly Cleary **99-100**	Applying creative and interpretive thinking **87** Drawing conclusions and making inferences **87** Interpreting information **87, 96-97, 101, 108-109** Finding details **87, 96-97, 101, 108-109** Identifying author's thoughts and feelings **87, 101, 108-109** Evaluating author's experience **87, 101, 108-109** Finding the main idea **101**	Analyzing and evaluating author's experience **87, 101, 108-109** Recalling and evaluating details **87, 90, 97, 101, 103, 108-109** Analyzing personal experience **87, 94-95, 97, 101, 108-109** Analyzing a personal narrative **87, 101, 104-105** Choosing a topic **90** Writing dialogue **94-95** Writing a draft of a personal narrative **103** Analyzing revisions **104-105** Revising a draft of a personal narrative **104-105** Evaluating a personal narrative **105** Proofreading and publishing a personal narrative **107** Writing a journal entry **109, 110** Writing a journal entry from the viewpoint of a historical figure **110**	Proofreading for errors in grammar, usage, and mechanics **107**	Sharing a narrative with others **87** Talking and listening to others **90, 94-95, 101, 105** Sharing dialogue **94-95** Discussing details **96-97** Drawing a cartoon about an experience **111**

SEGMENT PLANNING GUIDE

You can use the following Planning Guide to adapt the chapter material to the individual needs of your class. All the Resources listed in this chapter are located in the *Teacher's ResourceBank™*.

SEGMENT	PAGES	CONTENT	RESOURCES
1 ***Discovering Yourself***	***83-87***		
Literary Model from ***The Land I Lost***	84-86	Guided reading: a model of expressive writing	
Reader's Response/ Writer's Craft	87	Model evaluation: responding to literature and analyzing expressive writing	
2 ***Ways to Express Yourself***	***88***		
3 ***Prewriting***	***89-97***		Writing a Personal Narrative Recalling Details 28
Choosing an Experience	89-90	Guidelines: selecting an experience for a narrative	
Writing Assignment: Part 1	90	Applied practice: selecting a topic for a personal narrative	
Planning Your Personal Narrative	91	Introduction: organizing ideas and memories	
Thinking About Purpose and Audience	91	Explanation: understanding purpose and audience	
Recalling Details	92-93	Guidelines: analyzing and selecting sensory and action details	
Writing Note	94	Writing suggestion: using chronological order in a narrative	
Exercise 1	94-95	Cooperative learning: writing dialogue for situations	
Critical Thinking: Evaluating Details	95-96	Explanation: evaluating details	
Critical Thinking Exercise	96-97	Cooperative learning: evaluating and listing details	
Writing Assignment: Part 2	97	Applied practice: charting details	
4 ***Writing***	***98-103***		Writing a Personal Narrative 29
The Parts of a Personal Narrative	98	Guidelines: identifying and examining the elements of a personal narrative	
Literary Model from ***A Girl From Yamhill: A Memoir***	99-100	Guided reading: examining basic elements in a model of expressive writing	
Exercise 2	101	Cooperative learning: examining and responding to expressive writing	
A Writer's Model for You	101	Introduction: examining parts and purpose in a model	
Writer's Model	101-102	Guided reading: analyzing a sample narrative	

For **Portfolio Assessment** see the following pages in the *Teacher's ResourceBank™*:
Aims For Writing—pp. 27–32
Holistically Graded Composition Models—pp. 379–384
Assessment Portfolio—pp. 421–445

SEGMENT	PAGES	CONTENT	RESOURCES
Chart: Framework for a Personal Narrative	103	Guidelines: structuring a personal narrative	
Writing Assignment: Part 3	103	Applied practice: writing a first draft	
5 *Evaluating and Revising*	*104-105*		Writing a Personal Narrative 30
Chart: Evaluating and Revising Personal Narratives	104	Guidelines: applying evaluation and revision techniques	
Exercise 3	104-105	Applied practice: analyzing a writer's revisions	
Writing Assignment: Part 4	105	Cooperative learning: evaluating and revising a narrative	
6 *Proofreading and Publishing*	*106-107*		Writing a Personal Narrative 31
Proofreading	106	Guidelines: proofreading a paper	
Usage Hint	106	Writing suggestion: using personal pronouns	
Publishing	107	Publishing ideas: reaching an audience	
Writing Assignment: Part 5	107	Applied practice: proofreading and publishing a narrative	
7 *Writing Workshop*	*108-109*		
A Journal Entry	108	Explanation: using personal narrative in a journal entry	
Model/Questions	108-109	Examining techniques: analyzing a journal entry	
Writing a Journal Entry	109	Applied practice: applying skills to journal writing	
8 *Making Connections*	*110-111*		
Writing Across the Curriculum: A Day in the Life of a Historical Figure	110	Guidelines: writing a journal entry Applied practice: writing an imaginative historical journal entry	
Mass Media: A Cartoon or Comic Strip	111	Guidelines: drawing a cartoon strip Applied practice: creating a cartoon or comic strip from a personal experience	
WHOLE-CHAPTER RESOURCE A Writing Process Log, A Writing Prompt, Holistically Graded Models, Assessment Portfolio Materials			

SEGMENT 1 *(pp. 82–87)*

DISCOVERING YOURSELF

OBJECTIVES

- To examine the characteristics of expressive writing
- To identify the expressive elements in a literary model
- To recall personal experiences

TEACHING THE LESSON

Tell students that expressive writing describes a writer's feelings, experiences, and thoughts. Before beginning the model, explain that the experience the writer shares takes place in Vietnam. As students read the narrative, suggest that they look and listen for details expressing the writer's feelings.

VISUAL CONNECTIONS

The Starry Night

About the Artist. Vincent Willem van Gogh was born on March 30, 1853 in the Netherlands. Van Gogh's artistic career was very short, lasting only the ten years from 1880 to 1890. Although Van Gogh is arguably the most famous of modern artists, he was virtually unknown during his lifetime.

Van Gogh's work is unique in its use of line, color, and distinctive brush strokes. He respected the visual, external aspects of his subjects, but could not suppress his feelings about them as he painted. His work is thus partly expressionist and partly symbolist.

Related Expression Skills. Allow students to draw or paint their own impressions of the night sky or some other subject. Encourage them to try to get their drawings and paintings to express moods or feelings. When they have finished, open a class discussion on being expressive. Lead the students to understand that while in painting there are many ways to express mood or feeling, in writing, there is only the use of words. The challenge is to be able to use words the way Van Gogh used line, color, and brushstrokes to be expressive.

3 EXPRESSIVE WRITING

GUIDED PRACTICE

Tell students that expressive writers use details to show feelings. Before they read the model, have students list details that could show fear [palms sweating, knees shaking, teeth chattering]. After reading the model, you could ask the class to identify details in the narrative that show that the speaker is afraid. Answer the first **Reader's Response** question and the first **Writer's Craft** question with students in an open discussion.

Discovering Yourself

Remember when you learned to ride a bicycle? You thought you'd never keep that wobbly bike straight. But you did. You've discovered you can do many things. And there's more you can **discover about yourself.** You can do this with expressive writing.

Writing and You. You've probably watched *The Cosby Show.* It's about the experiences of a make-believe family. But did you know that Bill Cosby writes about his own family? He tells about funny things that happen between parents and children. He expresses himself in writing. When have you put your feelings in writing?

As You Read. The author of the following selection writes about a scary experience. What are his thoughts and feelings?

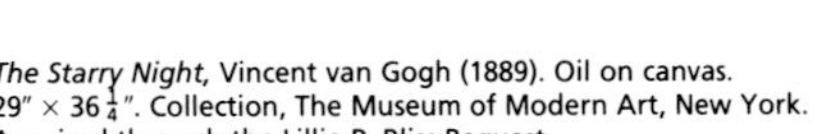

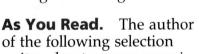

The Starry Night, Vincent van Gogh (1889). Oil on canvas. 29" × 36¼". Collection, The Museum of Modern Art, New York. Acquired through the Lillie P. Bliss Bequest.

QUOTATION FOR THE DAY

"The need to write comes from the need to make sense of one's life and discover one's usefulness." (John Cheever, 1912–1982, American author)

Write the quotation on the chalkboard and have students discuss other needs that writing serves [to communicate, to record, to entertain]. How does expressive writing fit in with these needs?

LEP/ESL

General Strategies. It is important to note that some students may be from cultures in which personal disclosure is discouraged, or even forbidden. In this case, all speaking activities should initially focus on reports, information gathering, and low-risk, non-personal content. Students should never be forced to share values, beliefs, or feelings orally if they are clearly uncomfortable doing so.

INDEPENDENT PRACTICE

Have students independently answer the other **Reader's Response** and **Writer's Craft** questions. Encourage them to use exact details from the narrative and their own lives when answering the questions.

ASSESSMENT

You can assess students' reading comprehension by checking that they have used specific details from the text and their own experiences when answering the questions. Criteria for evaluating students' answers can be based on the quantity and quality of details they used to describe feelings and experiences.

LEARNING STYLES

Visual Learners. Drawing can help students become comfortable with expressing experiences, feelings, and thoughts. Have students draw a picture that shows a scary experience they've had. Ask them to use lots of color and details to express their thoughts and feelings about the experience.

INTEGRATING THE LANGUAGE ARTS

Library Link. Ask students to go to the library and locate Vietnam in a world atlas. Then have them draw maps of Vietnam. You could also have students locate pictures of Vietnam and share the pictures with their classmates.

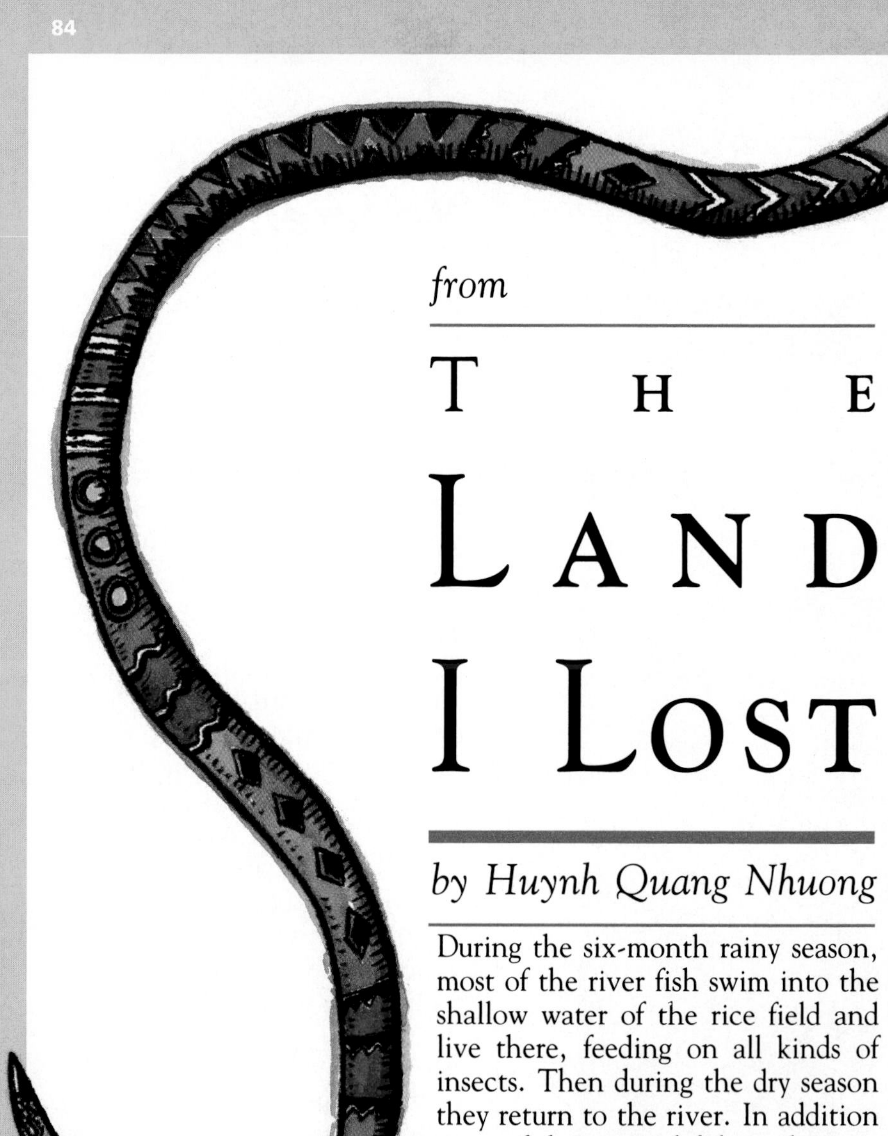

from

THE LAND I LOST

by Huynh Quang Nhuong

During the six-month rainy season, most of the river fish swim into the shallow water of the rice field and live there, feeding on all kinds of insects. Then during the dry season they return to the river. In addition most of the tropical fish in the area also have the ability to live out of the water for more than two hours, staying on paths and dikes where they can find more insects at night.

My cousin and I liked to go out into the field and catch fish at

CLOSURE

Have students identify what expressive writing is dependent on [personal experience]. ■

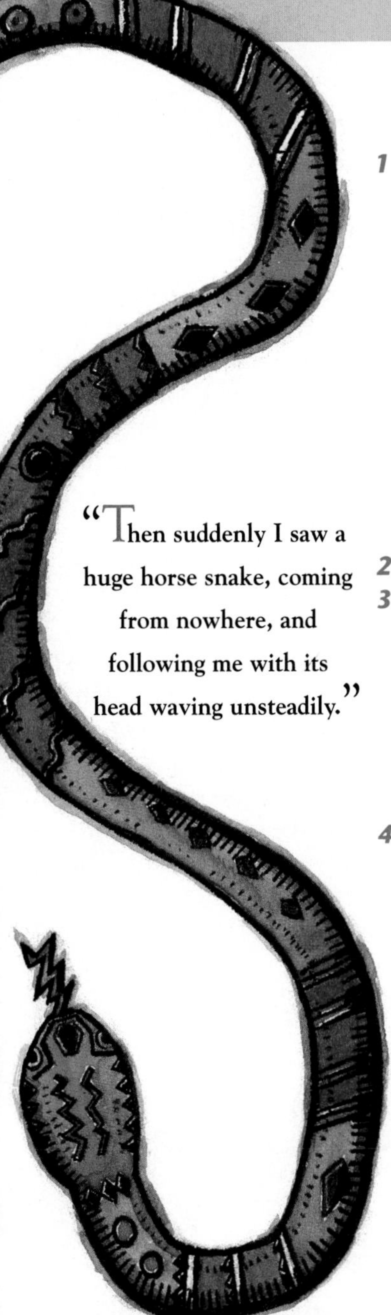

"Then suddenly I saw a huge horse snake, coming from nowhere, and following me with its head waving unsteadily."

night. Whenever we went out we
1 always carried a hogfish oil lamp. Since I could not catch fish as well as my cousin, who was ten years older, I carried the lamp and a bucket to put the fish in, and my cousin carried a long knife to kill any fish that we found near the edge of the water. But he preferred to catch them alive.

One evening when we were in the field, my cousin began teasing me, saying that since I carried the
2 hogfish oil lamp, a horse snake
3 would follow us home. I knew that he was teasing, but I was frightened and looked back every so often to make sure that there was no horse snake following us. Then suddenly I saw a huge horse snake, coming from nowhere, and following me
4 with its head waving unsteadily. I was so terrified that I couldn't speak; I could barely drag my feet. Luckily my cousin stopped and tried to catch a fish lying in the middle of the path. I bumped into him and almost knocked him over. Surprised at my unusual clumsiness, he looked back and saw the horse snake behind me. He was terrified too, but instinctively he swung his knife and struck the snake in the head. We dropped everything and ran home as fast as we could, more frightened than ever by the great noise the snake made behind us.

USING THE SELECTION

***from* The Land I Lost**

1

The lamp used oil made from hogfish.

2

The horse snake is a large snake native to Vietnam.

3

How does the writer show that he was frightened? [He keeps looking back.]

4

What details show the writer's feelings? [He couldn't talk or walk.]

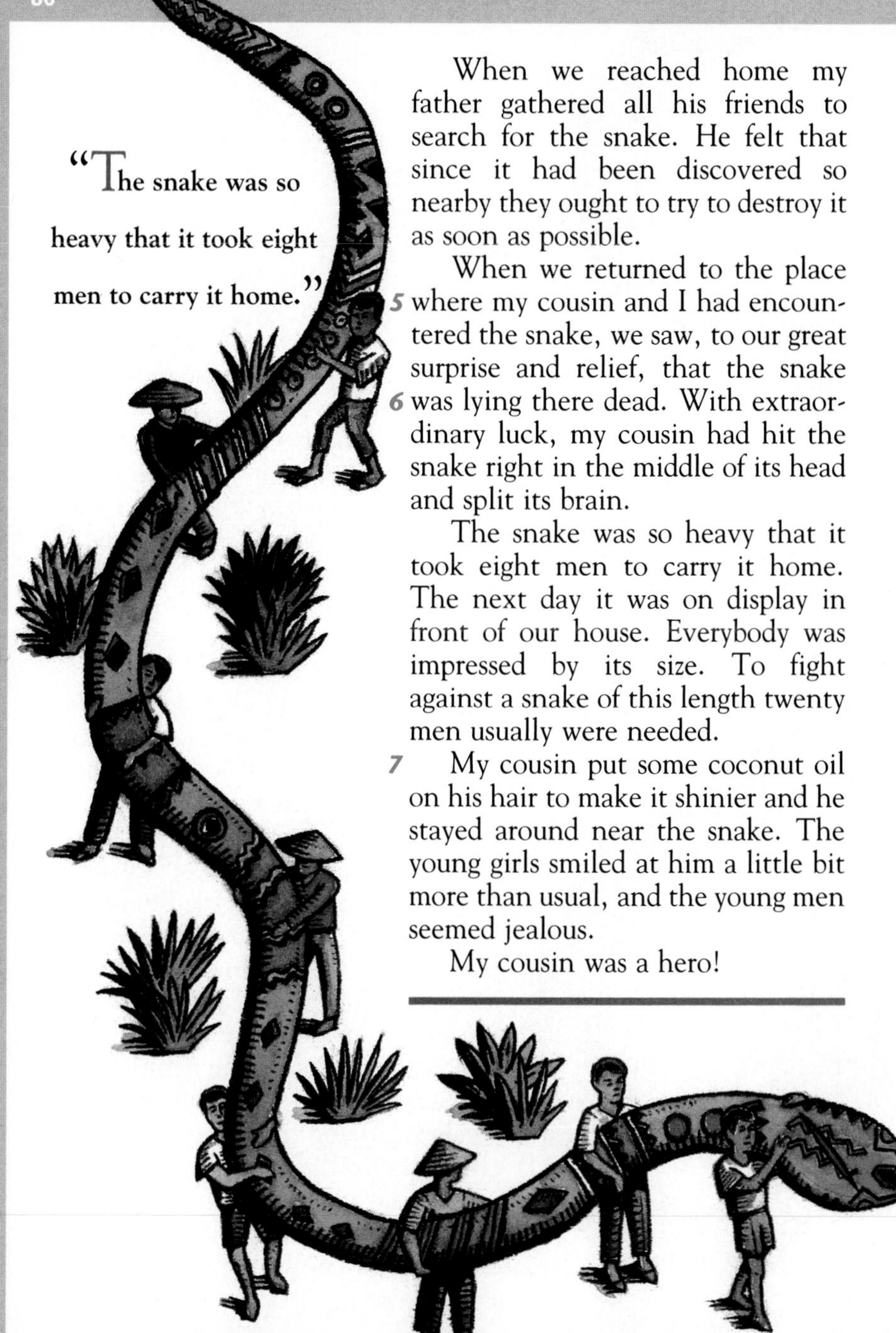

"The snake was so heavy that it took eight men to carry it home."

When we reached home my father gathered all his friends to search for the snake. He felt that since it had been discovered so nearby they ought to try to destroy it as soon as possible.

When we returned to the place
5 where my cousin and I had encountered the snake, we saw, to our great surprise and relief, that the snake
6 was lying there dead. With extraordinary luck, my cousin had hit the snake right in the middle of its head and split its brain.

The snake was so heavy that it took eight men to carry it home. The next day it was on display in front of our house. Everybody was impressed by its size. To fight against a snake of this length twenty men usually were needed.

7 My cousin put some coconut oil on his hair to make it shinier and he stayed around near the snake. The young girls smiled at him a little bit more than usual, and the young men seemed jealous.

My cousin was a hero!

5
encountered: met

6
extraordinary: special

7
Why would the cousin want to stay near the snake? [He is proud of himself and he is showing off his great accomplishment.]

SELECTION AMENDMENT
Description of change: excerpted
Rationale: to focus on the concept of expressive writing presented in this chapter

Reader's Response

1. This narrative is about the writer's experiences in the jungles of Vietnam. How are they different from experiences you might have? How are they similar?
2. Have you ever been frightened by something? How did you behave? Tell classmates about your experience.

Writer's Craft

3. In a good narrative, the writer shows you the experience. What are some details that show you how the horse snake looks?
4. What are some details that show how frightened the writer is?

ANSWERS

Readers Response

Responses will vary.

1. Most students will not have lived in the jungle, gone night fishing, and been followed by a deadly snake. All students will have experienced fear.
2. Most students will say they have been frightened. Behavior will vary. Try to elicit specific details from students.

Writer's Craft

Responses will vary.

3. Answers may include details such as "huge"; "head waving unsteadily"; "it took eight men to carry it home"; and "it usually took twenty men to fight a snake this length."
4. Answers may include the speaker looking back periodically, his inability to speak, his difficulty walking, his knocking into his cousin, and his running home as fast as possible.

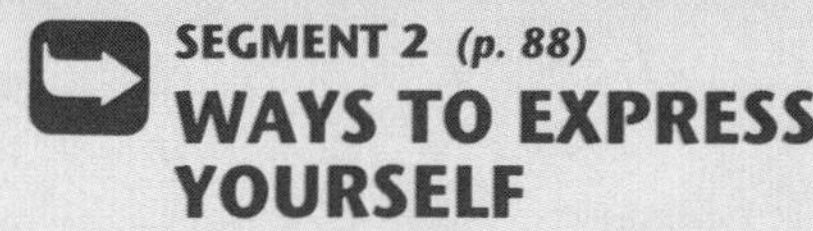

SEGMENT 2 *(p. 88)*

WAYS TO EXPRESS YOURSELF

TEACHING THE MODES

This section will give students an overview of the uses of expressive writing and the modes that they can use to develop expressive writing. You may want to begin by defining *narration, description, classification,* and *evaluation.* You could then have students discuss the different ways that each mode can be used in expressive writing. Encourage students to use personal examples when talking about the uses of each mode. ■

Ways to Express Yourself

You express yourself in letters to friends and relatives, in messages on greeting cards, in notes to classmates, and in journal entries. Writing is expressive when you focus on your own experiences, thoughts, and feelings. Huynh Quang Nhuong expressed his feelings in a narrative. A narrative is one of four ways to develop expressive writing.

- **Narration:** telling what happened on your first day of school this year; writing about the time your parents restricted you to the house.
- **Description:** describing to a friend the unusual snakes your science teacher has in a jar; in your journal, describing your brand-new soccer uniform and how proud it makes you feel.

Classification: expressing your thoughts about the good times you've had this year; in a letter to your cousin, comparing your feelings about two friends.

Evaluation: in a letter, expressing your feelings that your town is the perfect place to live; writing in your journal about the movie you think is the best.

LOOKING AHEAD

In the main part of this chapter, you'll use narration to write about a personal experience. In the workshop, you'll use description to write about a special place. Keep in mind that a good personal narrative

- tells about events in a clear order
- has details that show the experience
- tells why the experience is important

COOPERATIVE LEARNING

Divide the class into groups of four. Assign each group a feeling such as happiness, sadness, excitement, or fear. Then tell each group to use the four different modes to express its assigned feeling. Suggest that students relate their own personal experiences when using each mode. For instance, one student might use description to tell about an exciting moment when riding the rickety roller coaster at a local amusement park. Another student might use classification to compare the excitement felt when riding in an airplane with the excitement felt when sledding at top speed down a hill.

INTEGRATING THE LANGUAGE ARTS

Speaking Link. Ask students to write short speeches in which they use at least two modes to tell about funny experiences they've had. Encourage students to use interesting details to express their thoughts and feelings. Have students present their speeches to the class.

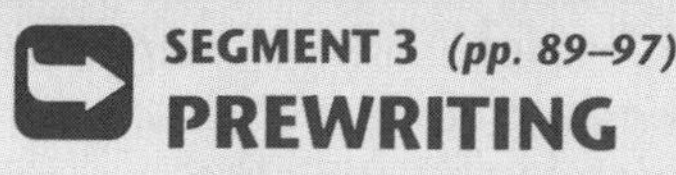

SEGMENT 3 *(pp. 89–97)*
PREWRITING

OBJECTIVES

- To select a topic and organize information for a personal narrative
- To identify purpose and audience
- To evaluate details for a narrative
- To work with others to create dialogue

Writing a Personal Narrative

Prewriting

Choosing an Experience

Did you ever sprain an ankle and go to the emergency room? Maybe you sat, frightened, until a doctor could see you. Or did you ever earn an A on a big test or make the soccer or baseball team? Have you ever been lost and scared?

Teacher's ResourceBank™
RESOURCES

PREWRITING
- Recalling Details 28

QUOTATION FOR THE DAY

"[Writers] tend to have a lot of stories available to them just because they are human beings." (Robert Penn Warren, 1905–1989, American author and poet)

Use the quotation to help students understand that they have already had many experiences worth exploring in expressive writing. You may want to have students make up lists of experiences they have had that might serve as topics for expressive papers.

TEACHING THE LESSON

To help students choose experiences to write about, guide them through a discussion of the introductory material. You could then list the following prewriting steps on the chalkboard:

1. Choose an important experience you want to share.
2. Write a brief description of the topic.
3. Plan the information to be included.
4. Determine purpose and audience.
5. Recall details.
6. Evaluate details.

Students might find it useful to work on their personal narratives with partners. You could ask students to volunteer

LEP/ESL

General Strategies. Students may need help with organizing their writing, dissecting the whole image that they have in mind so that the parts are more apparent, and arranging these parts (or facts) sequentially so that they support the whole. If possible, meet with students individually and have them talk to you about what they intend to write. As they talk, take notes about what you perceive to be their main ideas and the parts that contribute to these ideas. Share your perceptions with the students and see if they agree. Have them create an outline based on this information.

STUDENTS WITH SPECIAL NEEDS

A concrete, visual approach to **Exercise 1** (p. 94) might be beneficial for students. Allow them to base their dialogues on pictures rather than the situations described. Provide several appropriate drawings or photos clipped from magazines and have students use the pictures as prompts for their dialogues.

You don't have to be chased by a snake to have something important to write about. What's happened that's changed your life? or changed the way you feel about yourself or others? What experience have you had that sticks out strongly in your memory? What experience would you like to share with others? Here are some points to help you choose an experience for your narrative.

- *Choose an experience you remember.* You'll have details about the experience stored in your memory. (Remember that you want to tell your readers about your experience. You can't if you don't remember details about it.)
- *Choose an experience that's important to you.* You probably haven't ridden your skateboard around the world. But the small, quiet things you do are important, too. (Remember that you don't have to write about a big adventure—just an experience that means something to you.)
- *Choose an experience you can share.* If the experience is private, write about it in your journal. (Remember that you want to be comfortable sharing the experience with your readers.)

PART 1:
Choosing a Topic for a Personal Narrative

Have you climbed a mountain? Or have you climbed the stairs to receive an award? If you still don't have a topic idea, try brainstorming to draw out what's stored in your own mind. Talk to friends, family, and classmates to recall experiences you have shared. Write down your topic ("the day my family moved to El Paso"; "the scariest storm I ever saw"). You can change it later if you think of a better one. It's not carved in stone!

examples of each prewriting step as you explain the material to them.

Remind students to keep their audiences in mind as they plan their narratives. In most cases, their audiences will consist of fellow students, but even then careful consideration may be needed. For example, students from foreign cultures may be unfamiliar with certain aspects of the experiences students will be writing about, and will thus need explanations that are more detailed. The **Critical Thinking Exercise** in this segment will help students decide on the proper details to include in their narratives.

To help students select their topics for **Writing Assignment: Part 1,** list sample experiences on the chalkboard. Make sure

Planning Your Personal Narrative

When you write a science report about penguins, you have to look for facts. Then you have to develop ideas about how to present the facts you've found. But for a personal narrative, ideas are already in your mind. Should you just start writing? Minds are funny, and your memories probably aren't in an order that makes sense. Spend some time planning before you write.

Thinking About Purpose and Audience

Have you ever had a nightmare? Didn't it feel good to tell someone about it and feel the fear going away? That's the *purpose* of a personal narrative—to share an experience with others. And writing about it helps you understand your feelings.

Your first *audience* will probably be your teacher and classmates. To understand your experience, what details do they need? What details will make the experience seem interesting to them?

COOPERATIVE LEARNING

Divide the class into groups of four or five. Have each group of students brainstorm a list of experiences that they have had together, such as taking a test, attending an athletic event, eating lunch in the cafeteria, participating in a school assembly, or watching a school play.

Ask students to choose one experience that they all remember well and to share their memories about that experience. Have each student contribute one action and one sensory detail that describes his or her memory of the experience. Then have students write the details on a piece of paper.

the topics are memorable, important, and capable of being shared.

To help students with **Exercise 1,** you may want to take one of the three suggested situations and develop a dialogue for it with the help of the class. Or, you could suggest a different situation and lead the class to develop a dialogue for it.

When students are ready for the **Critical Thinking Exercise,** take either the action details or the sensory details and lead the class to understand in an open discussion which details are not important to the visit and why. You can model the **Writing Assignment: Part 2** by making a chart for details of one of your own personal experiences on the chalkboard.

A DIFFERENT APPROACH

Ask students to think about an experience that everyone in the class will be familiar with such as watching fireworks on July Fourth, going to a doctor's office, or feeling shy at a party. Have each student write the experience down on a piece of paper, fold the paper, and put it in a box. Pass the box around the classroom and have each student pick one paper from it. Then have each student use the experience he or she has selected as the topic for listing action and sensory details.

INTEGRATING THE LANGUAGE ARTS

Speaking Link. Divide the class into small groups and ask students to tell each other about the experiences they selected for their topics. As they describe their experiences, encourage students to ask each other questions about the topics. Point out that speaking about experiences can help students remember sensory and action details. If students think of new details as they are speaking, encourage them to jot them down immediately.

Recalling Details

Think of watching a movie with half the screen blank. You wouldn't enjoy it as much because many details would be left out. That's how readers feel when a personal narrative lacks details.

There are many ways you can recall details for your narrative. You can brainstorm or cluster. You can talk to others who were part of the experience. Or you can close your eyes and replay the time in your mind. Think about two kinds of details: *sensory details* and *action details.*

Sensory details help you relive the experience so that you almost see, taste, smell, hear, and touch again.

> *my baby sister's tiny feet, the hot and melting cheese, the rotten garbage, the sharp cries, a cool fall day*

Action details tell what happened and how it happened.

> *I rushed to the bus and climbed on board. Two minutes later I noticed we were going down a strange street. I was on the wrong bus.*

Action details may also be the words that people say. These words are called ***dialogue.***

> *Crying, I asked the driver, "Would you please help me?"*

 **REFERENCE NOTE:** For more help on writing and punctuating dialogue, see pages 157 and 615–621.

Students should do **Writing Assignment: Part 1, Exercise 1, Writing Assignment: Part 2,** and the **Critical Thinking Exercise** as independent practice after responses to these exercises have been modeled.

ASSESSMENT

Assess students' lists of experiences by checking that they are described clearly. Assess the choice of topics by determining if the circled experience is important, clearly remembered, and one that can be shared with the class. Sensory details should describe basic sensory perceptions that can be expanded with development. Action 

INTEGRATING THE LANGUAGE ARTS

Literature Link. You could have students read another selection of expressive writing, such as "Life Doesn't Frighten Me" by the contemporary African American writer Maya Angelou. Tell students that expressive writing is used in stories and poems as well as in personal narratives.

Have students describe the feelings and thoughts that Maya Angelou expresses as she describes her experience. Then ask students if they have had thoughts, feelings, or experiences similar to those described in "Life Doesn't Frighten Me."

Sensory and action details about people, places, and events will make your personal narrative livelier. You might use a chart like this one as you try to recall details.

Topic: The day I took the wrong bus	
ACTION DETAILS	*SENSORY DETAILS*
At age 8 took bus downtown alone for first time	*inside bus—hot, humid, noisy; whoosh of electric door opening and closing*
Got on wrong bus coming home; crying; saying to driver, "Would you please help me?"	*smell of wet clothes; people pushing; tears stinging chapped face*
Changed buses and got home; people probably thinking, "Dumb kid"	*best sight ever was my snow-covered street*

details should describe the basic actions involved in the experience.

The dialogues generated in **Exercise 1** will vary but should be related to the chosen situation.

Cont. on p. 97

ANSWERS

Exercise 1

Responses will vary. Here are some examples:

1. "I've always loved Ellie's dog. If we don't take her, she could wind up starving!" I exclaimed.

"You know our home is too small for a big dog," my mother said.

"But Ellie's home is much smaller than ours. Please, can't we adopt it? I promise I'll take care of it."

2. "Okay," I said, "if you scream for help, I'll pound on the floor."

"No," my brother whispered, "if I scream, they'll all think I'm a chicken. Hey, is that a shadow or a ghost?"

3. "I'm never gonna learn how to ride a bike. I wanna go home," my cousin whined.

"I fell a hundred times when I was learning how to ride," I said. "You have to keep trying."

Think about a time you told a friend about a movie. You probably said what happened first, second, next, and so on. You used *time order* to tell about events. Events in a narrative are often arranged in time order. You might want to use time order for events in your own narrative.

EXERCISE 1 **Speaking and Listening: Practice in Writing Dialogue**

As you try to recall your experience, you may not be able to remember exactly what people said. When that happens, it's important to try to recreate what was said. You may have to use a little imagination or guesswork. To practice your guesswork, get together with two or three classmates. Then choose one of the situations in the following list. Work together to write the words the people in the situation might say. Think about *how* they speak, as well as *what* they say. When you finish, share your dialogue with the rest of the class.

EXAMPLE

Situation Jesse, Cari, and Jon plan to start a band. Jesse and Cari have been working on their music all summer. Jon has been playing baseball instead. Cari is angry.

Dialogue "How can we start a band if you goof off all the time?" Cari shouted.

"I know it was stupid," Jon yelled back. "But it'll be okay. We can still make the talent show."

1. Your parents don't like big dogs very much. A friend of your is moving. She needs to find a home for her black Labrador. You really like the dog and want to adopt it. Write what you and your parents might say.

CRITICAL THINKING

(pp. 95–97)

OBJECTIVES

- To determine the most important part of an experience
- To identify the important part of a sample personal narrative and to evaluate the details

TEACHING *EVALUATING DETAILS*

Before students begin working in small groups, make sure that they understand the purpose of evaluating. Point out that evaluating details will enable students to think about their experiences and to understand why the experiences are important and memorable. Then point out that by identifying the important parts in

2. You and your brother are exploring the attic in your grandmother's house. The wind blows the attic door shut and it locks. It's dark and creepy, and you're both scared. Write what the two of you might say.
3. You're trying to teach your five-year-old cousin how to ride a bike. Things aren't going too well. Write what you and your cousin might say.

CRITICAL THINKING

Evaluating Details

If you look at bikes to buy, you think what's good and bad about each one. You decide which one has more value for you. Judging the value of something is called ***evaluating.***

After you jot down details for your narrative, evaluate them. Begin by asking yourself what was important about your experience. Suppose you went on a camping trip with your family. Maybe the most important part was seeing animals like deer and bears. Or, maybe it was learning to have fun without watching TV and playing video games.

LEARNING STYLES

Visual Learners. Students may benefit from drawing a picture in which they incorporate the sensory and action details listed in the **Critical Thinking Exercise.** Visualizing the experience through drawing may enable students to evaluate the details with greater ease and clarity. As they are drawing, encourage students to focus their attention on the important details and leave out the unimportant ones.

COOPERATIVE LEARNING

Ask students to form small groups to look at photographs together. Have each group discuss the action and sensory details that seem particularly important in its photograph. Then ask each group to talk about the experience that is taking place in its photograph, and have the group list the three most important details that convey the experience.

experiences, they will be able to express the experiences clearly and powerfully.

After students complete the evaluating exercise in small groups, you could generate a class discussion about recognizing the differences between important and unimportant details.

To conclude, you could use several important details from the exercise and write a paragraph with students that describes a visit to the Tigua Indian Reservation. Ask each student to add an additional sentence to the paragraph. Tell students to use at least one more important detail from the exercise in each of their sentences.

Now you can evaluate your details. You can decide which details show readers what was important about the experience. If the most important part of a camping trip is the animals, most of your details should be about animals. If the most important part is having fun without TV, details may be about many different activities.

CRITICAL THINKING EXERCISE: Evaluating Details

On the next page there are some details about a visit to the Tigua Indian Reservation near El Paso, Texas. The most important part of the visit is learning about the history and culture of the Tiguas. Discuss the details with two or three classmates. Which details show the important part of the visit? Which details don't? Make a list of the details that show the most important part of the visit—what the writer learned about the history and culture of the Tiguas.

ANSWERS

Critical Thinking Exercise

Important Action Details: took tour of reservation, saw old mission church, had Indian bread at lunch

Unimportant Action Details: brother sprained his foot, car had flat tire on the way home

Important Sensory Details: smooth pottery decorated with designs, soft voice of woman making pottery, warm taste of Indian bread, bright sun hitting on adobe houses

Unimportant Sensory Details: delicious hamburger on the way home, sound of my favorite rock music on car radio

Cont. from p. 94

CLOSURE

Ask students to list the three elements to consider when choosing a topic for a personal narrative [topic is clearly remembered, is important to the writer, and can be shared]. ■

Action Details
took tour of reservation
saw an old mission church
brother sprained his foot
had Indian bread at lunch
car had flat tire on way home

Sensory Details
delicious hamburger on the way home
smooth pottery decorated with designs
soft voice of woman making pottery
warm taste of Indian bread
bright sun hitting on adobe houses
sound of my favorite rock music on car radio

PART 2:
Recalling Details

Elephants may never forget, but humans often do. Try to recall both sensory details and action details about your experience. Collect them in a chart like the one above. If you recall some dialogue, put it in the chart, too. After you've collected several details, take time to evaluate them. Cross out any details that are not really important to your experience.

How our brain loses things along the way.

LESS-ADVANCED STUDENTS

Give students more one-on-one attention as they are selecting an experience for their personal narratives. Help them uncover topics by asking them direct questions that will help trigger their memories. For instance, have they ever helped rescue an animal or person from a dangerous situation? Have they ever done something so embarrassing they wanted to disappear into thin air?

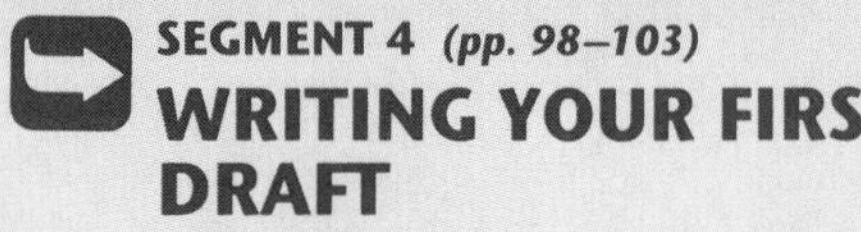

SEGMENT 4 *(pp. 98–103)*

WRITING YOUR FIRST DRAFT

OBJECTIVES

- To analyze the basic parts and the organization of a personal narrative
- To write a draft of a personal narrative

TEACHING THE LESSON

To begin, review the basic parts of a personal narrative and ask students to keep these elements in mind as they read the models. Then tell students how they can use dialogue, action, and description to reveal feelings in their narratives.

Read the **Professional Model** with students and have them discuss the questions

Teacher's ResourceBank™

RESOURCES

WRITING YOUR FIRST DRAFT

- Writing a Personal Narrative 29

QUOTATION FOR THE DAY

"My yesterdays walk with me. They keep step, they are gray faces that peer over my shoulder." (William Golding, 1911–   , English novelist)

Use this quotation to remind students that they already have all the information necessary to produce personal narratives. To help them remember details they have forgotten, you may want to have the students tell each other their stories before they begin to write.

VISUAL CONNECTIONS

About the Subject. Beverly Cleary is the author of many books for young readers. She has received many honors for her books, including a Newbery Medal and the American Library Association's Laura Ingalls Wilder Award. Ms. Cleary was born in McMinnville, Oregon. Until the age of six she lived on a farm in Yamhill, Oregon.

Writing Your First Draft

The Parts of a Personal Narrative

A personal narrative may be one paragraph or several. That's up to you. But most personal narratives have these parts:

- a **beginning** that grabs the reader's interest and tells the topic
- a **body** that presents the events in an order that makes sense (usually time order)
- an **ending** that tells why the experience was important

Writers don't usually wait until the end to tell their thoughts and feelings. They include them in the body of the narrative. Sometimes they tell them directly.

> I was really afraid.

Sometimes they reveal them by their words or actions—what they say or do.

> I shivered and pulled my coat tighter around me. "What's going on?" I asked. Was my voice really shaking?

The following passage is from a memoir (a kind of autobiography) by Beverly Cleary. In this passage, Cleary tells about something that happened to her when she was a small child. Even though this is a part of a book, it has the three basic parts of a narrative—a beginning, a middle, and an end.

in small groups. Then have students read the **Writer's Model** independently. When discussing the **Framework for a Personal Narrative** feature, return to the **Writer's Model** to show how the framework helps organize the writer's thoughts and feelings.

GUIDED PRACTICE

You may want to lead the class in a discussion of one of the questions in **Exercise 2** to show students what kind of answers are expected. To help students with **Writing Assignment: Part 3**, suggest a sample experience and let them ask you questions about it. Use your answers to those questions to develop sentences for a narrative. ☛

A PASSAGE FROM A BOOK

from A Girl from Yamhill: A Memoir

by Beverly Cleary

BEGINNING

First actions

Sensory details

At Christmas I was given an orange, a
rare treat from the far-off land of California. I sniffed my orange, admired its
color and its tiny pores, and placed it
beside my bowl of oatmeal at the breakfast
table, where I sat raised by two volumes of
1 Mother's *Teacher's Encyclopedia.*

BODY

Dialogue

Action details

Thoughts

Father picked up my orange. "Did you know that the world is round, like an orange?" he asked. No, I did not. "It is," said Father. "If you started here"—pointing to the top of the orange—"and traveled in a straight line"—demonstrating with his finger—"you would travel back to where you started." Oh. My father scored my orange. I peeled and thoughtfully ate it.

USING THE SELECTION

***from* A Girl from Yamhill: A Memoir**

1

a very thick book

INDEPENDENT PRACTICE

After discussing one question as a class, assign the remaining questions in **Exercise 2** as independent practice. Let students discuss the questions first in small groups, and then have them share their responses as a class.

Students should be able to complete **Writing Assignment: Part 3** by themselves. Let them know that it's all right to talk to friends or classmates for ideas, but the actual writing should be done individually. You might want to suggest they find quiet places where they can be alone to write.

2
What details create a picture of the writer's surroundings? ["big field," "barnyard," "too wet to plow"]

3
Where in Sam Hill? is an expression that means "Where in the world?"

SELECTION AMENDMENT
Description of change: excerpted
Rationale: to focus on the concepts of sensory and action details presented in this chapter.

Thoughts / Events in order / Sensory details

I thought about that orange until spring, when wild forget-me-nots suddenly
2 bloomed in one corner of our big field. The time had come. I crossed the barnyard, climbed a gate, walked down the hill, climbed another gate, and started off across the field, which was still too wet to plow. Mud clung to my shoes. I plodded on and on, with my feet growing heavier with every step. I came to the fence that marked the boundary of our land and bravely prepared to climb it and plunge into foreign bushes.

ENDING / Dialogue / Sensory and action details

My journey was interrupted by a shout. Father came striding across the field in his
3 rubber boots. "Just where in Sam Hill do you think you're going?" he demanded.

"Around the world, like you said."

Father chuckled and, carrying me under his arm, lugged me back to the house, where he set me on the back porch and explained the size of the world.

Mother looked at my shoes, now gobs of mud, and sighed. "Beverly, what will you think of next?" she asked.

ASSESSMENT

Responses to **Exercise 2** should indicate how well the students have grasped the concepts of sensory and action details. The real proof of their understanding, however, will be the first drafts they develop for **Writing Assignment: Part 3.** Their drafts should each have a beginning, body, and an ending, and each should adequately relate a personal experience.

EXERCISE 2 **Analyzing a Personal Narrative**

Get together with two or three classmates, and talk over these questions.

1. Beverly Cleary understands her father when he compares the earth to an orange. But he forgets to tell her how big the earth is. Can you remember a time when you misunderstood something about the world? What was it?
2. What sensory details does Cleary use in this narrative? How does she describe the orange? How does she describe her walk across the field?
3. Does Beverly Cleary's experience seem real to you? Why or why not?
4. Since this passage is part of a whole book, Cleary doesn't stop at the end and tell us how she felt about the experience. However, she does tell us some of her thoughts and feelings earlier in the passage. What are they?

A Writer's Model for You

Beverly Cleary is a professional writer. She wrote her narrative as an adult. Your writing might be more like the following shorter model. As you read, notice that this writer's model has the same parts as Cleary's narrative. It also has the same purpose.

A WRITER'S MODEL

BEGINNING
Attention grabber/Topic

I was so scared my legs were shaking. It was my first day at Oakridge School. As a "new kid," I was afraid to speak to anyone. No one spoke to me either, but two girls smiled at me.

BODY
Action details

The principal gave me a class schedule and a locker number. Then she called a boy

ANSWERS

Exercise 2

Any answer that may vary is indicated by an asterisk (*).

*1. Students may remember believing that if they began digging a hole in the earth, they could dig straight through to China.

2. She sniffs the orange and looks at its color and its pores. Forget-me-nots bloom in the field; she plods across the wet land, mud clinging to her shoes; her feet become heavier and heavier as she moves across her family's property.

*3. Many students will think it seems real because her reaction to the orange and her hike across the field are believable. The story may remind some students of similar experiences they have had. Some students from urban environments may think this seems unreal because the landscape is unfamiliar.

4. She is curious about the orange and it seems to make her happy. She thinks about the similarity between an orange and the world. She thinks about walking around the world. She feels brave as she prepares to climb over the fence into foreign territory.

CLOSURE

Ask students to name the three parts of a personal narrative [beginning, body, ending]. ■

LEARNING STYLES

Auditory Learners. You could have students dictate their experiences into a tape recorder before they begin writing their drafts. Then tell students to listen to the tapes to make sure that they've revealed their experiences in a clear, interesting, and organized way. Encourage students to jot down changes they want to make as they listen to the tapes. Then have students write their narratives.

AT-RISK STUDENTS

Meet with students individually to help them develop frameworks for their narratives and to get them started on **Writing Assignment: Part 3.** Offer students encouragement about their writing and the experiences they are revealing. If the experiences will be unfamiliar to their classmates, tell them how important their experiences are and emphasize how much the rest of the class will learn from their narratives.

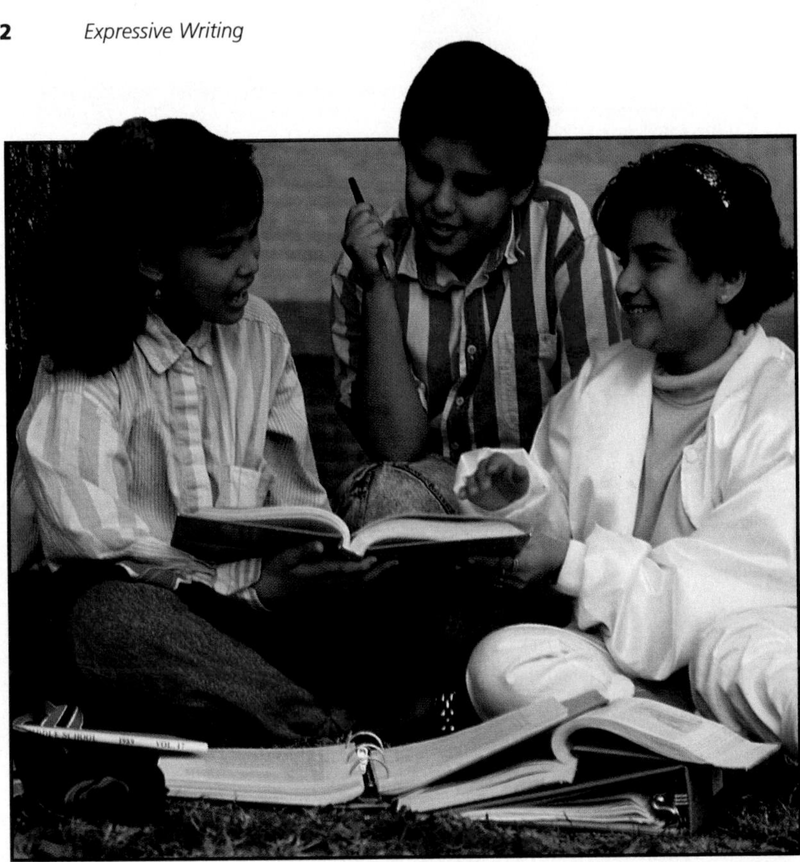

Dialogue into her office and said, "Sam will be your guide today, Rosa. He lives in your apartment building. I thought you'd like to meet a new

Feelings friend and neighbor." I was embarrassed and

Sensory details couldn't speak because my throat felt so dry. Sam rescued me by asking which apartment I lived in and if I had any brothers or sisters. It felt good to meet someone who wanted to know me.

ENDING Now Sam is one of my best friends. I have

Meaning of experience many other friends, too. Being a "new kid" is painful for a while, but it doesn't last very long. Then the hurt goes away. I guess everyone's a new kid some time.

The narrative you've just read uses this framework. You might want to follow it as you write your own first draft.

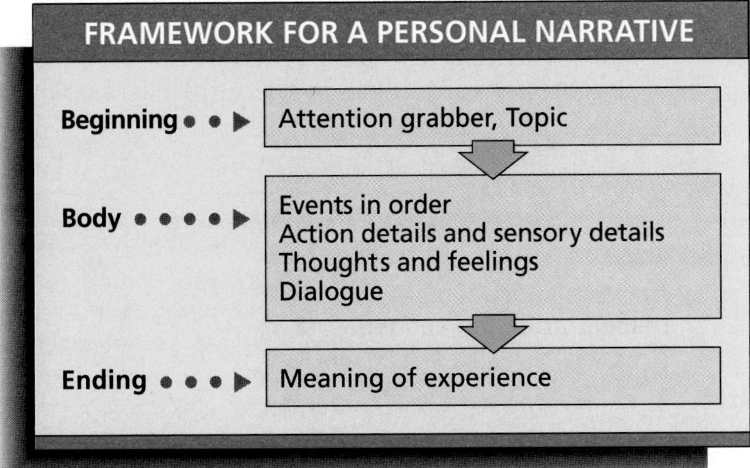

FRAMEWORK FOR A PERSONAL NARRATIVE

Beginning ▶	Attention grabber, Topic
Body ▶	Events in order Action details and sensory details Thoughts and feelings Dialogue
Ending ▶	Meaning of experience

As you write your draft, remember to

- use action details, sensory details, and dialogue
- put events in order
- tell the meaning the experience has for you

PART 3:
Writing Your First Draft

It's time to turn your notes (from Writing Assignment, Part 1, page 90, and Part 2, page 97) into sentences and paragraphs. If you have trouble getting your ideas on paper, try telling your experience to a friend or classmate. Ask him or her to ask questions about the experience. Then use your answers to develop your narrative.

TIMESAVER

To make it easier to check that students are using their frameworks, have students draw boxes around the beginning, middle, and end of their narratives. You could also have students underline the important information and details in each section to make sure that their narratives are well-organized and filled with interesting and important details.

INTEGRATING THE LANGUAGE ARTS

Vocabulary Link. Point out that writers choose words and expressions that they know their audience will relate to and understand. Encourage students to keep their audiences in mind when they are choosing words to express their thoughts, feelings, and experiences.

Speaking Link. If students wish to use dialogue in their narratives suggest that they read the dialogue aloud as they are writing. Point out that this will help them create dialogue that is natural and believable.

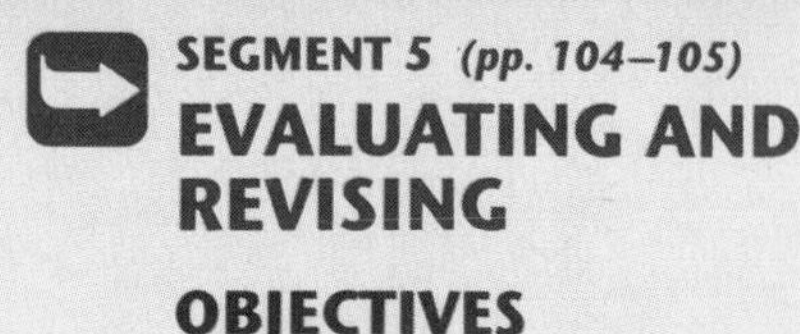

SEGMENT 5 *(pp. 104–105)*

EVALUATING AND REVISING

OBJECTIVES

- To analyze a writer's revisions
- To evaluate and revise a personal narrative

TEACHING THE LESSON

Use the **Evaluating and Revising Personal Narratives** chart to evaluate the professional model to show students how to use the guide and the listed techniques. Have students use the chart while independently completing **Exercise 3** and **Writing Assignment: Part 4.**

Teacher's ResourceBank™

RESOURCES

EVALUATING AND REVISING

- Writing a Personal Narrative 30

QUOTATION FOR THE DAY

"Experience is a hard teacher because she gives the test first, the lesson afterward." (Vernon Law, 1930– , major league baseball player, pitcher for the Pittsburgh Pirates 1950–1967)

Write the quotation on the chalkboard and use it to initiate a discussion on how expressive writing allows a writer to reexamine the lessons learned from personal experiences.

ANSWERS

Exercise 3

Answers may vary. Here are some possibilities:

1. It shows what the writer was feeling. It makes a reader curious to know what the narrative is going to be about. It introduces the topic.
2. It isn't an important detail that relates to the topic of the narrative.
3. It offers an important detail and creates a fuller picture.

Evaluating and Revising

This chart will help you improve your first draft. Ask yourself the questions in the left-hand column. Then use the revision ideas in the right-hand column.

EVALUATING AND REVISING PERSONAL NARRATIVES

	EVALUATION GUIDE	REVISION TECHNIQUE
1	Does the beginning get readers' attention and tell the topic?	**Add** sensory details to the beginning. **Add** a sentence that says what experience you are telling about.
2	Do action and sensory details show readers the experience?	**Add** details about people, places, and actions. **Add** dialogue to show what you and other people said.
3	Does the writer tell or show the meaning of the experience?	**Add** your thoughts and feelings to the body. **Add** a sentence or two at the end that tells the meaning of the experience to you.

EXERCISE 3 **Analyzing a Writer's Revisions**

The following sentences from the narrative about being the new kid at school show changes the writer made. See if you can figure out why the writer made the changes. Then answer the questions.

ASSESSMENT

Make sure that students answer the questions in **Exercise 3** thoroughly. You can then use the **Evaluating and Revising Personal Narratives** chart to assess the quality of their responses.

CLOSURE

Ask students what they can add to their personal narratives to make them better [sensory details; a sentence explaining the experience; people, place, and action details; dialogue; thoughts and feelings; and a sentence about the meaning of the experience]. ■

I was so scared my legs were shaking. It was my first day at Oakridge School. ~~The name Oakridge is from the streets, Oak and Ridge.~~ As a "new kid," I was afraid to speak to anyone. No one spoke to me either, but two girls smiled at me.

add

cut

add

1. Why did the writer add a new beginning sentence?
2. Why did the writer cut the second sentence? [Hint: Review pages 95–97.]
3. Why did the writer add *No one spoke to me either, but* to the last sentence?

PART 4:

Evaluating and Revising Your Personal Narrative

You probably made some changes as you wrote your first draft. Now, think about your finished draft. How can you improve it? Start by using the evaluating and revising chart on page 104. You might also exchange papers with a classmate and evaluate each other's narrative. Think about your evaluation and your classmate's. Finally, make changes that will improve your narrative.

LEP/ESL

General Strategies. Because self-evaluation is an important metacognitive strategy, all students must eventually participate in and become comfortable with that process. However, you must determine if their language proficiency level realistically allows them to do this. Will they profit from making the attempt, or will they simply experience further frustration? If you find that some of your ESL students are not ready for self-evaluation or peer evaluation, it is crucial to meet with them privately and provide as much individual attention as possible.

LESS-ADVANCED STUDENTS

You may want to work closely with students to help them identify the strengths and weaknesses in their drafts and to show them ways to improve their narratives.

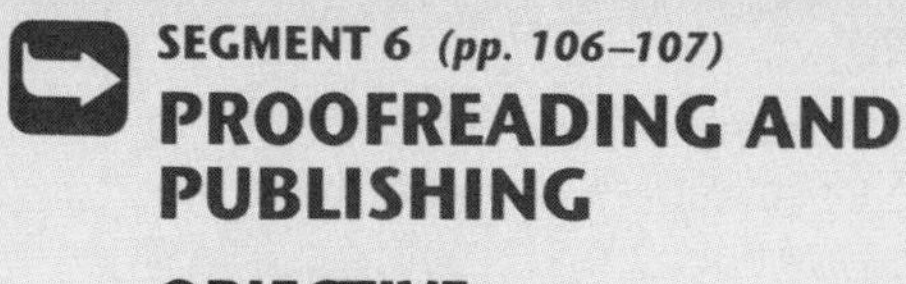

SEGMENT 6 *(pp. 106–107)*

PROOFREADING AND PUBLISHING

OBJECTIVE

- To use proofreading strategies to prepare a personal narrative for publication or sharing

TEACHING THE LESSON

Direct your students' attention to grammar, usage, or mechanics areas that they have difficulty with. Then assign **Writing Assignment: Part 5.** Lead the class in an open discussion on how their personal narratives can be shared or published.

Teacher's ResourceBank™

RESOURCES

PROOFREADING AND PUBLISHING

QUOTATION FOR THE DAY

"One of the advantages of the kind of writing I do is that you are your own boss. You shoot your own stock, choose all the scenes, cast all the characters. You're your own everything, really—and the product, then, is yours." (John Updike, 1932– , American author)

Use this quotation as a motivation for students to take care in proofreading. Just as the product belongs to the writer, so does the responsibility to make that product as good as it can be. Proofreading is one process by which this goal is met.

Proofreading and Publishing

Proofreading. What if you received an award, and your name was spelled wrong? You'd wonder why someone wasn't more careful. ***Proofreading*** is being careful of your writing. It's finding and correcting mistakes in grammar, usage, and mechanics.

USAGE HINT

Using Personal Pronouns

When you write about yourself, you use the pronoun *I*. This pronoun has a subject form and an object form.

Use the subject form when the pronoun is the subject of the sentence.

I didn't realize the mountain was so high.
I am always ready to climb, as my friends will tell you.

ASSESSMENT

To evaluate students' proofreading skills, check the personal narratives for grammatical, mechanical, and usage errors.

CLOSURE

Ask students to define *proofreading* [finding and correcting mistakes in grammar, usage, and mechanics] and *publishing* [sharing your writing]. ■

Use the object form when the pronoun is an object.

Direct object:	The climb exhausted **me.**
Indirect object:	The ledge gave **me** a place to rest.
Object of a preposition:	My parents bought a little trophy for **me.**

REFERENCE NOTE: For more about personal pronouns, see pages 374–376 and 503–520.

Publishing. After proofreading, the final step is ***publishing***—sharing your narrative with the class. Or you might want to share it only with a trusted friend or adult. Here are two ideas.

- Use the experience you wrote about in a short story. You can change the experience any way you want. You can change the time and place. You can change how the experience turns out. You can even make the characters Martians, if you want to. Let your imagination run wild!
- Share your narrative with yourself a year from now. Put it in a box in the back of a closet. One year later, read it again. Or put it in your writing portfolio and pull it out in three or four months. How have you changed? Does the experience still have the same meaning for you? What do you think about putting pieces of your writing aside to read later?

PART 5:
Proofreading and Publishing Your Personal Narrative

Make your writing shine! Check it carefully for errors. Then choose a way to share it. Use one of the ideas above or one of your own.

LEP/ESL

Spanish. Spanish-speaking students may have difficulty with positioning direct object pronouns within sentences. In Spanish, the direct object pronoun comes before the verb. Also, when the direct object denotes a person in Spanish, the preposition *a* is placed before it. Students may transfer this rule to English.

Make sure your students understand how direct object pronouns are treated in English and monitor their writing for these particular grammatical problems. If needed, offer extra practice in this area.

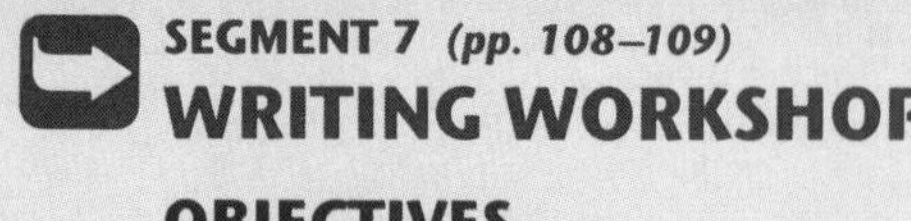

SEGMENT 7 *(pp. 108–109)*

WRITING WORKSHOP

OBJECTIVES

- To analyze the expressive writing used in a journal entry
- To use expressive writing in a journal

TEACHING THE LESSON

Read the model journal entry with students and answer one of the questions with them in an open discussion. Then have them answer the other questions independently. Ask students to write their own journal entries about a special place.

QUOTATION FOR THE DAY

"Writers write for themselves and not for their readers." (Rebecca West, 1892–1983, Irish writer)

Let this quotation open a discussion between those students who agree with West and those who don't. Matters of contention might include the attention most writers give to audience (though keeping an audience in mind does not necessarily mean that one writes for that audience) and types of writing (a journal entry is definitely for the writer since the writer and audience are the same).

LEARNING STYLES

Visual Learners. Have students create visual journal entries by drawing people, places, and activities. When they complete their drawings, have students write brief captions that give extra information about what is happening in each picture.

WRITING WORKSHOP

A Journal Entry

Personal narratives are expressive writing that you usually share with someone. A journal entry is a form of private expressive writing. It's a chance to explore your ideas and feelings without worrying about other people. That also means you don't have to worry about correct usage and punctuation unless you just want to.

Here's a journal entry about a favorite place in a city park. As you read, notice the details the writer uses to describe the park. Notice how the writer's feelings are part of the entry, too.

I had a bad day today. I made a D on that dumb test. This afternoon, I sat at the fountain in Fairmont Park. It has trees and benches all around it. The sun was shining, and lots of people were there. Mothers and fathers and kids walk around. The kids like to stick their hands and feet in the fountain. Today, I saw a big black dog jump in. When he jumped out, he shook water all over everybody. Just being there made me feel better. There's more to life than a D on a test. But I'll try harder next time.

ASSESSMENT

Assess the quantity and quality of the details students give when they answer the questions that follow the model. Assess journal entries by checking that students have completed the assignment.

CLOSURE

Ask students to tell what a journal entry is [a form of private expressive writing]. ■

Thinking It Over

1. How does this writer feel about his day? Have you ever felt the way he does? When?
2. If this writer keeps his journal, he may reread this paragraph ten or fifteen years from now. What details in the paragraph will help him recall what his day was like?

Writing a Journal Entry

Prewriting. What's a special place to you? Do you like to walk on the beach or just sit on your front steps? Do you still like your old treehouse? What do you do at your special place? Why is it special? Is it somewhere you take your problems? Or is it somewhere you always have a good time? Do you share it with others, or is it a private place? Write a journal entry about this special place. Use sensory details to describe it.

Writing, Evaluating, and Revising. A journal can be anything you write in. People have kept journals on scraps of paper, on walls, even on the backs of their own hands. A journal is different from a personal narrative. You don't have to write about events in order. You can skip around if you want to. Write what's on your mind.

Proofreading and Publishing. You don't have to share your journal entries. You can lock your journal up so no one can ever read it. But remember what fun it is to look at photographs of yourself when you were younger. A journal can be like those photographs. It gives you a record of yourself through the years. Many people enjoy keeping their journals and reading them many years later.

ANSWERS

Thinking It Over

Answers may vary. Here are some possibilities:

1. The writer seems unhappy about the D he received on his test, but he feels better when he watches the people and the dog at the fountain. Most students will remember feeling badly about something in the not-too-distant past. Perhaps they did poorly on a test or didn't perform well in an athletic meet. Many students will also remember feeling better after taking a walk, watching people, looking at nature, or talking with friends.
2. Getting a D on a test, sitting at the fountain at Fairmont Park, watching children stick their hands and feet into the fountain, and watching a dog shake water onto people are all vivid details that will probably help the writer remember the day.

SEGMENT 8 *(pp. 110–111)*

MAKING CONNECTIONS

WRITING ACROSS THE CURRICULUM

OBJECTIVE

- To use expressive writing skills to write a journal entry for a historical figure

WRITING ACROSS THE CURRICULUM

Teaching Strategies

Tell students to brainstorm details about the persons and the historical events that they have chosen for their journal entries. Point out that the details will make the entries seem real. Before students begin to write, suggest that they close their eyes and imagine that they have become their subjects.

When students complete the assignment, have them share their journal entries with the rest of the class. Students could tell classmates who their historical figures are before they read their entries, or the class could guess the identity of each historical figure.

GUIDELINES

Journal entries will vary. Check that the language is believable and that students use interesting details to describe the feelings of their subjects after the historical events.

MAKING CONNECTIONS

WRITING ACROSS THE CURRICULUM

A Day in the Life of a Historical Figure

Sacagawea was a Shoshone woman who accompanied Lewis and Clark. They were the men who explored the northwest part of this country in 1804–1806. What might Sacagawea have written in a journal the day she began the long trip? What if George Washington really did cut down the cherry tree? What would he have written in his journal? Use your skills in expressive writing to "capture" a famous moment from history. Begin by choosing a famous person you know about. Think of a major event in his or her life. Here are a few ideas.

- Vasco Núñez de Balboa—the day he first sees the Pacific Ocean
- Amelia Earhart—the day she becomes the first woman to fly alone across the Atlantic Ocean
- Jackie Robinson—the day he becomes the first African American elected to the National Baseball Hall of Fame

Or choose some other historical figure you know about or can find out about. "Step into the shoes" of that person. Write a journal entry about the event.

MASS MEDIA
OBJECTIVE

- To draw a cartoon or comic strip based on a personal experience

MASS MEDIA

A Cartoon or Comic Strip

Do you read cartoons or comic strips? Usually, they tell about funny experiences. Some, like *Family Circus,* come from the artist's own life. This cartoon, for example, is about parents and children on a camping trip. Have you ever had an experience like this?

THE FAMILY CIRCUS® **By Bil Keane**

"This is our vacation and you're going to enjoy it whether you like it or not."

Drawing cartoons is a form of personal expression. Think of a funny experience you've had. Draw a cartoon or comic strip about it. Draw with pencil so you can make changes easily. When you're happy with it, go over the pencil lines with ink. Then, if you want to, fill in with colored pencils or markers.

MASS MEDIA
Teaching Strategies

Have students look at the *Family Circus* cartoon and discuss the characters and the action that is taking place within it. Ask students to talk about personal experiences that the event in the comic strip reminds them of.

Then generate a class discussion about different kinds of funny experiences that students have had with their friends or families. Point out that drawing can be a good way to express personal experiences. Then ask each student to choose one funny experience and to draw a cartoon or a comic strip about the experience. When students complete their cartoons or comic strips, you could display them in your classroom so that all students can enjoy them.

GUIDELINES

Students drawings will vary, but each comic strip or cartoon should include characters doing something funny.

Chapter 4

USING DESCRIPTION

OBJECTIVES

- To identify the purposes of description and to analyze the characteristics of descriptive writing
- To choose a subject and to write a description that expresses feelings about that subject
- To select and organize sensory details
- To identify similes and metaphors and to use them in description
- To organize and draft a description
- To evaluate and revise the organization and wording of a description
- To proofread and publish a description
- To analyze a descriptive poem
- To write, evaluate, and revise a descriptive poem
- To write a paragraph that describes a place

Motivation

Ask students which of the following descriptions is more effective in catching their interest and communicating the excitement of the moment described. Then ask students what makes that description better.

1. The stands were full of students dressed in their school colors. The students waved their flags and shouted as the fullback scored.

2. When the fullback broke three tackles and scored, the stands became a roaring ocean of blue and yellow waves dashing against each other.

Discuss the descriptions and write on the chalkboard any differences students point out. Explain that the second description is more effective due to the image of the ocean and to the specific words that appeal to the reader's senses.

Introduction

Ask the students what kinds of writing they think of when they hear the term *description*. Do they think of short stories? Novels? Poems? News stories? Editorials?

Remind students that description can serve many purposes: to express feelings by recapturing a moment, to persuade others to accept a view or to buy a product, or to set the mood or the scene for action in a story or play. Ask students to mention descriptions they have heard or read recently. What were the purposes of the descriptions? To get students started, have them think about stories they have read recently.

Integration

Students may use the examples in this chapter to help identify the kinds of description used in any form of writing and the possible purposes of the authors of the works. **Exercise 3** will help students understand that description can reveal an author's purposes.

The exercises in this chapter will help students to see that including description in their writing will help to make it more effective, regardless of the aim.

The chart on the next page illustrates the strands of language arts as they are integrated into this chapter. For vocabulary study, glossary words are underlined in some writing models.

QUOTATIONS

All **Quotations for the Day** are chosen because of their relevance to instructional material presented in that segment of the chapter and for their usefulness in establishing student interest in writing.

INTEGRATING THE LANGUAGE ARTS

Selection	Reading and Literature	Writing and Critical Thinking	Language and Syntax	Speaking, Listening, and Other Expression Skills
"Fragments of Spring" by Agnes T. Pratt **114** **"So Quickly Came the Summer"** by Agnes T. Pratt **115** from **"Tortuga"** by Rudolfo A. Anaya **127-128** **"The Toaster"** by William Jay Smith **137**	Applying interpretive and creative thinking **116** Identifying sight words **116, 128, 132, 137** Identifying sound words or rhyming words **116, 132, 137** Identifying a comparison used to describe **116, 128, 132** Using similes and metaphors **116** Identifying sensory words and exact words in a literary selection **116, 128, 137**	Writing a journal entry to describe a season **116** Identifying the uses of description **116** Analyzing a description **116, 128** Observing, recalling, imagining, and listing details **116, 122, 123, 124, 128, 138** Planning a description **119, 123** Choosing details and organizing by spatial order or order of importance **124** Using exact words **130** Writing a descriptive paper **130** Evaluating a writer's revisions **131** Evaluating and revising a description **132** Writing, evaluating, and revising a poem **137-138** Writing a description of a historic site **140-141** Writing a travel description **141**	Proofreading for errors in grammar, usage, and mechanics **135, 138**	Making a chart of sensory details **122** Sharing lists with classmates **122** Evaluating the descriptions of others **132** Publishing a descriptive paper **135, 138**

SEGMENT PLANNING GUIDE

You can use the following Planning Guide to adapt the chapter material to the individual needs of your class. All the Resources listed in this chapter are located in the *Teacher's ResourceBank™*.

	SEGMENT	PAGES	CONTENT	RESOURCES
1	***Creating Pictures and Images***	***113-116***		
	Literary Model **"Fragments of Spring"**	114	Guided reading: a model of descriptive poetry	
	Literary Model **"So Quickly Came the Summer"**	115	Guided reading: a model of descriptive poetry	
	Reader's Response/ Writer's Craft	116	Model evaluation: responding to literature and analyzing descriptive writing	
2	***Uses of Description***	***117***		
3	***Prewriting***	***118-124***		Writing a Description Collecting Details 34
	Planning a Description	118	Introduction: creating a clear description	
	Thinking About Subject, Purpose, and Audience	118-119	Guidelines: analyzing and selecting appropriate subject, purpose, and audience	
	Writing Assignment: Part 1	119	Applied practice: choosing a topic and writing to express feelings	
	Gathering Details	120	Guidelines: observing, recalling, and imagining details	
	Writing Note	120	Writing suggestion: combining real details with imaginary details	
	Critical Thinking: Observing Details	121	Guidelines: examining a chart of sensory details	
	Critical Thinking Exercise	122	Applied practice: making a chart and inferring sensory details from a picture	
	Exercise 1	122	Applied practice: observing and listing sounds	
	Writing Assignment: Part 2	123	Applied practice: observing and listing details in a chart	
	Choosing and Organizing Details	123	Guidelines: choosing and organizing details	
	Choosing Details	123	Guidelines: choosing specific details	
	Organizing Details	123-124	Guidelines: examining spatial order and order of importance	
	Writing Assignment: Part 3	124	Applied practice: choosing and organizing details	
4	***Writing***	***125-130***		Writing a Description 35
	Using Exact Words	125	Guidelines: creating a word bank	
	Chart: A Word Bank	126	Guidelines: creating a word bank	
	Writing Note	126	Writing suggestion: using a thesaurus	

For **Portfolio Assessment** see the following pages in the *Teacher's ResourceBank™*:
Aims For Writing—pp. 33–38
Holistically Graded Composition Models—pp. 385–390
Assessment Portfolio—pp. 421–445

SEGMENT	PAGES	CONTENT	RESOURCES
Using Similes and Metaphors	127	Explanation: examining similes and metaphors	
Literary Model from **"Tortuga"**	127-128	Guided reading: examining sensory and exact words in a model	
Exercise 2	128	Cooperative learning: analyzing a description for sensory words	
A Writer's Model for You	129	Introduction: using a model of descriptive writing	
Writer's Model	129	Guided reading: examining description in an essay	
Writing Assignment: Part 4	130	Applied practice: writing a draft	
5 ***Evaluating and Revising***	***131-132***		Writing a Description 36
Chart: Evaluating and Revising Description	131	Guidelines: applying evaluation and revision techniques	
Exercise 3	131-132	Applied practice: evaluating a writer's revisions	
Writing Assignment: Part 5	132	Cooperative learning: evaluating and revising a first draft	
6 ***Proofreading and Publishing***	***133-136***		Writing a Description 37
Mechanics Hint	133	Writing suggestion: using commas with adjectives	
Publishing	134	Publishing ideas: reaching an audience	
Writing Assignment: Part 6	135	Applied practice: proofreading and publishing essays	
Writer's Model	135-136	Sample: examining detail in a student essay	
7 ***Writing Workshop***	***137-138***		
A Poem That Describes	137-138	Explanation: using description in poetry Applied practice: writing a descriptive poem	
Literary Model **"The Toaster"**	137	Guided reading: analyzing detail and word sounds in poetry	
8 ***Making Connections***	***139-141***		
Description Across the Curriculum: Describing Historic Sites	139-140	Guidelines: examining description in a paragraph Applied practice: writing a descriptive paragraph	
Description and Persuasion: Writing a Travel Description	140-141	Guidelines: examining persuasive description in a paragraph Applied practice: writing a persuasive description	

WHOLE-CHAPTER RESOURCES
A Writing Process Log, A Writing Prompt, Holistically Graded Models, Assessment Portfolio Materials

SEGMENT 1 *(pp. 112–116)*

CREATING PICTURES AND IMAGES

OBJECTIVES

- To analyze how pictures and images appeal to the reader through the senses
- To identify and list sight and sound words the poet uses to describe seasons
- To write descriptive words for a favorite season
- To identify a comparison used to describe the earth

VISUAL CONNECTIONS
Los Pescados Peña

About the Artist. Amado Peña was born and reared in Laredo, Texas. He received his B.A. degree from Texas A&I University in Kingsville and spent three years teaching high school in Laredo before returning to school. After earning his M.A. in 1971, Peña moved to Crystal City, Texas, to work as a teacher and art consultant. During this time, he also was active in the Chicano art movement.

Peña's work, mainly done in acrylic paints, in noted for its bright colors and repeated forms. He often uses flat, two-dimensional figures outlined for effect.

Ideas for Writing. Tell students who don't speak Spanish that *pescado* means *fish.* Ask students to examine the fish in this picture and to describe what is unusual about them. Point out that imagination often plays an important part in description. Tell students to imagine strange sea creatures and to write short descriptions of the animals. Remind students that their readers will not be able to envision the creatures if they, the writers, do not include all the details they can think of.

4 USING DESCRIPTION

TEACHING THE LESSON

Read the selections from ***The Whispering Wind*** (p. 114) expressively. Ask students to analyze the possible purposes of the author and to identify ways the descriptions appeal to the senses and call upon personal memories. Then lead students in a discussion of the information and feelings conveyed in the pictures and images. List the images on the chalkboard.

Guide students through the **Reader's Response** questions. Monitor the journal entries and reinforce lesson concepts by pairing students and having them check each other's entries for sensory images.

Have students answer the **Writer's Craft** questions independently. Oral review 

Creating Pictures and Images

A messy closet: Can you see it? The crunch of a crispy apple: Can you hear it? Writers use words to create **pictures and images** in your mind. You can see, hear, taste, smell, and touch what they describe.

Writing and You. A novelist describes a rattlesnake so vividly that you are afraid of it. An advertiser describes a cereal so invitingly that you want to buy it. These writers don't tell you about their subjects; they show them to you. When have you used words to show a subject to readers?

As You Read. Description is important in poems as well as stories and ads. What pictures and images of spring and summer do the following poems create in your mind?

Los Pescados Peña, Amado Peña (1978). Serigraph. 25″ × 38″. Courtesy of the artist and El Taller Publishing, Austin, TX.

QUOTATION FOR THE DAY

"'What is the use of a book,' thought Alice, 'without pictures or conversations?'" (Lewis Carroll, 1832–1898, English writer and mathematician)

Write the quotation on the chalkboard and use it to initiate a discussion about written description. Lead students to understand that the quotation from *Alice's Adventures in Wonderland* might contain some truth about a reader's expectations. Painting pictures with descriptive words and writing dialogue so that readers can hear imaginary conversations are two ways writers show rather than tell.

of students' answers to these questions will help assess how well students have understood the lesson.

CLOSURE

Ask students to write down a definition of *description* and to explain why sensory words and specific images are effective in communicating feelings to readers. ■

LEARNING STYLES

Auditory Learners. Although all students will benefit from an expressive reading of these poems, auditory learners will benefit most. Read the poems through at least twice with great attention to emphasis and rhythm.

USING THE SELECTION

***from* The Whispering Wind**
Poetry by Young American Indians

1

bold: bold in conduct and bold in colors

2

emeralds: the most brilliant green, sparkling like a gem

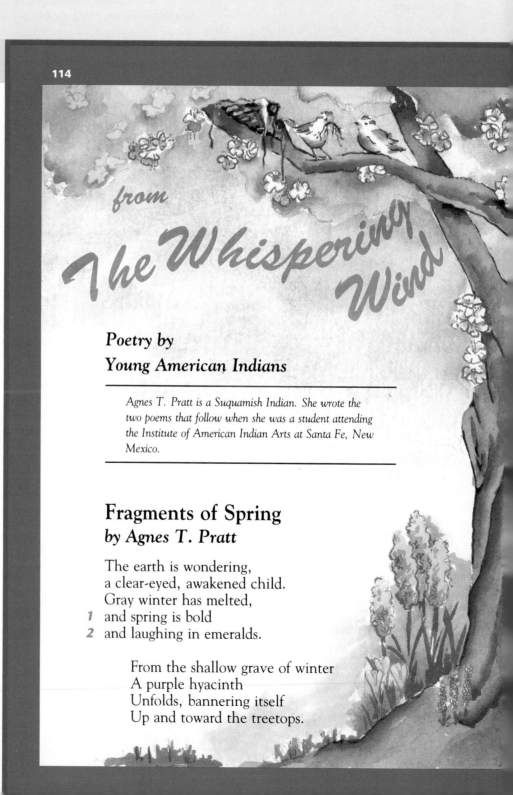

from

The Whispering Wind

Poetry by Young American Indians

Agnes T. Pratt is a Suquamish Indian. She wrote the two poems that follow when she was a student attending the Institute of American Indian Arts at Santa Fe, New Mexico.

Fragments of Spring
by Agnes T. Pratt

The earth is wondering,
a clear-eyed, awakened child.
Gray winter has melted,
1 and spring is bold
2 and laughing in emeralds.

From the shallow grave of winter
A purple hyacinth
Unfolds, bannering itself
Up and toward the treetops.

So Quickly Came the Summer

by Agnes T. Pratt

3 Night laid itself down beside the horizon,
The mountain wrapped itself in clouds,
Forest sighed through yellowing leaves
Hushed in mourning for dying spring.
So quickly came the summer
When spring departed, she left
A young boy strumming a guitar,
The moon sighing along its strings,
As he slowly walked down the hill.

CRITICAL THINKING

Analysis

Put students in groups of four to analyze the use of concrete and sensory details in the poems. Ask them to identify all senses used in each image.

When students finish analyzing the poems, ask them to name characteristics of accurate description in poetry. [The images are specific and may involve more than one of the senses. They are also sometimes related to word sounds and may use figures of speech.]

A DIFFERENT APPROACH

Some students may wish to sketch or paint their impressions of the poems. Encourage students to share their works with the class.

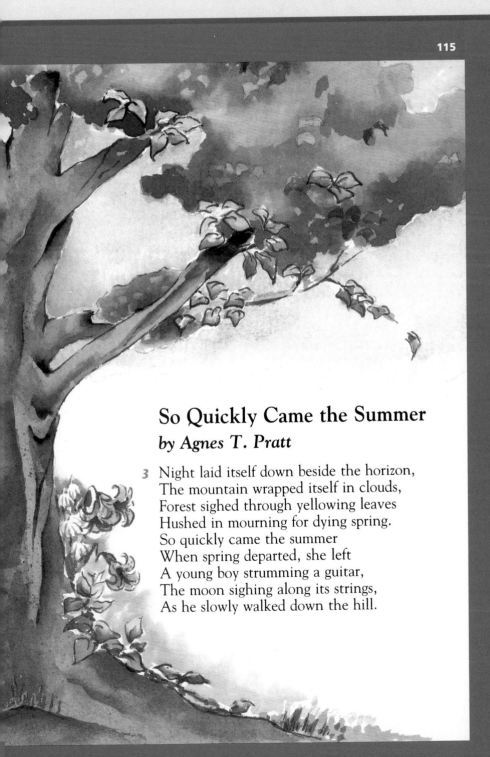

3

The device of personification is used in almost every line.

ANSWERS

Reader's Response

Responses will vary.

1. Students should include sensory words in their descriptions.
2. Each journal entry should include words describing a season as well as words describing the student's feelings.

Writer's Craft

3. Answers may vary, but students should be able to explain why they think the sight or sound words describe spring and summer.
4. a clear-eyed, awakened child

Reader's Response

1. Agnes T. Pratt says that "spring is bold and laughing in emeralds." Write down some words that show what spring looks like to you.
2. These two poems are about seasons. Which is your favorite season—spring, summer, fall, winter? Why? Write a few words in your journal to describe your favorite season and how you feel about it.

Writer's Craft

3. The writer uses several sight words to create a picture of spring and summer. What are they? She also uses some sound words. What are they?
4. Sometimes you can describe one thing by comparing it to another. In "Fragments of Spring," what does the writer compare the earth to?

Happily may I walk.
May it be beautiful before me.
May it be beautiful behind me.
May it be beautiful below me.
May it be beautiful above me.
May it be beautiful all around me.
In beauty it is finished.

NAVAJO CHANT

SEGMENT 2 (p. 117)

USES OF DESCRIPTION

TEACHING THE AIMS

After a volunteer reads aloud **Uses of Description,** ask students to give examples of how description might be used to accomplish each aim.

Ask students to identify the purposes in the following situations:

1. the opening of a short story [creative]
2. description of an amoeba [informative]
3. an editorial describing needed changes in welfare laws [persuasive]
4. description of what you would eat if you had your choice [expressive]

Uses of Description

All writers of description want to plant an image in your mind. They want you to see, hear, feel, taste, or smell what they describe. But writers use description for many reasons. Here are some purposes you might have for writing description.

To Express Yourself: in a journal entry describing an awful new haircut; in a letter to a friend describing your weird party costume.

To Persuade: describing your old baseball glove so your parents will buy you a new one; describing school ground litter to convince students to pick it up.

To Inform: describing your lost starter jacket so others can help you find it; describing your favorite dish to your grandparent, who's cooking your lunch.

To Be Creative: in a short story describing a haunted house; in a poem about nighttime describing the shining green eyes of a cat.

Descriptions are everywhere: in newspapers, books, magazines, or even menus. Descriptions are used to create a clear picture in your mind.

LOOKING AHEAD

In the main assignment in this chapter, your basic purpose will be to express yourself or be creative. As you plan and write your description, remember to

- use details of sight, sound, taste, touch, and smell
- use exact words
- organize your ideas so they're easy to follow

INTEGRATING THE LANGUAGE ARTS

Literature Link. Description is a major component of fiction, and it may serve several purposes within a story. If the book is available in your library, ask students to examine "The Phantom Tollbooth" by Norton Juster. Guide students to see that specific images set the scene and establish the mood throughout this fanciful story, which would otherwise be unbelievable.

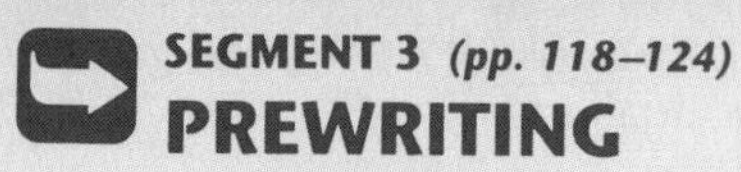

SEGMENT 3 *(pp. 118–124)*

PREWRITING

OBJECTIVES

- To choose a subject for a description and to choose and organize details for that subject
- To observe and list sounds that create a feeling about a topic

TEACHING THE LESSON

Tell students that good descriptions do not just happen; they are the result of an orderly process. List the following steps on the chalkboard and guide students through them:

1. Select a subject.
2. Select a purpose and an audience.
3. Gather, select, and organize details.

Teacher's ResourceBank™

PREWRITING

- Collecting Details 34

QUOTATION FOR THE DAY

"I am convinced more and more day by day that fine writing is next to fine doing, the top thing in the world." (John Keats, 1795–1821, English poet)

Write the quotation on the chalkboard and ask a few volunteers to restate the quotation in their own words. Then students might write journal entries about whether they agree or disagree that writing can be an admirable activity.

Writing a Description

Planning a Description

Perhaps you've seen an inspiring picture of the Statue of Liberty gleaming in New York Harbor. You can create a description in words that is just as clear as a photograph. But it takes careful planning.

Thinking About Subject, Purpose, and Audience

Subject. If a tarantula crawled across your wall, wouldn't you describe it to your friend? You don't have to think about finding a *subject* at a time like this. You already know what subject you want to describe. When you write a description in school, though, you may wonder at first what you could possibly describe. Just think about things you see often. You can write about animals (that scary spider, for example), your favorite people, or even your own yard.

Purpose. In this chapter, you have a choice of *purposes.* Would you like to write a description to express yourself, to show how you feel about something? You might write a description of your little brother that shows how you feel about the way he follows you around. Or would you rather write a description that is totally creative? Perhaps you'd like to write a description of a haunted place that you could later use in a scary story. For either purpose, creating feelings about your subject will be important. If you do a good job, your readers will feel that your little brother is pesky but lovable or the place is horrible.

Use textbook discussions to define terms and to explain prewriting steps.

GUIDED PRACTICE

Use **Writing Assignment: Part 1** for guided practice. Have students brainstorm for five minutes, and then have them get into groups of four to share ideas.

Audience. Your *audience* is important, too. Think about what your readers need to know. For example, if your readers have already seen a dolphin, they probably know about its color and shape. But if they haven't ever seen a dolphin, they will probably need to know these details.

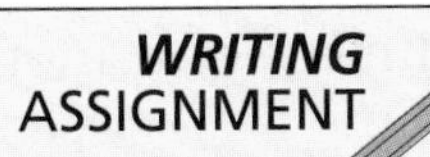

PART 1:
Choosing a Subject

What would you like to describe? It's time to decide. You can choose one of the following subjects, or brainstorm for ideas of your own. When you have made a choice, write down the name of your subject. Then think how you feel about the subject and how you want your readers to feel. Write two or three sentences telling about those feelings.

1. the kitchen of your home on a holiday
2. a pet or an animal that frightens you
3. a jacket or other piece of clothing you wear all the time
4. a creepy old house
5. your backyard late at night or during a rainstorm

LEP/ESL

General Strategies. In English, most verbs are modified by adverbs. An important exception to this rule includes the sensory verbs *taste, look, feel, sound,* and *smell,* which are followed by predicate adjectives. You may want to give your students practice with the following sentences:

1. The spines on a cactus . . . .
2. Perfume . . . .
3. Spaghetti . . . .
4. Before a storm, the sky . . . .
5. Some rock music . . . .

Supply students with the five verbs listed above. Ask them to fill in the appropriate verb and to provide a predicate adjective for each sentence.

COOPERATIVE LEARNING

If three or four students have chosen the same topic for **Writing Assignment: Part 1,** allow them to work together to compare and discuss the feelings they have listed. Each of the students might have feelings that others may not have.

INDEPENDENT PRACTICE

Have students complete **Writing Assignments: Parts 2** and **3** for independent practice.

ASSESSMENT

Ask students to underline all details that would help create a clear picture in the reader's mind and to put an *S* over each sensory detail. You can then evaluate students' performance by checking the details students have marked.

CRITICAL THINKING

Analysis

Show students several good descriptive paragraphs. These may be in stories in their literature textbook or may be taken from other sources and put on a transparency.

Ask students to analyze the readings to identify both the order in which the details are arranged and the feeling created by the details. Then ask students to identify the most important details and to determine which senses they appeal to.

Gathering Details

Some descriptions sizzle. Others just simmer. The details make the difference. You can gather details by observing your subject. You can also *recall* and *imagine* it.

Observing. If your subject is nearby, take a close look at it. Suppose your subject is an old pair of sneakers. Pick them up, feel them, look at them carefully, turn them over—take a whiff if you dare! Observe all the details you can.

Recalling. If your subject is real but not close by, take time to recall it. Close your eyes and picture your subject. Bring it to the attention of each of your senses in turn. How does it look, sound, feel, taste, or smell?

Imagining. Perhaps your subject is fantasy, such as a character in a science fiction story. In that case, take time to imagine it. Let your ideas float freely. Then sharpen the focus until more and more details become clear.

Even if your subject is imaginary, you still want it to seem real. One way you can do this is to combine made-up details with ones from real life. Think about the little alien E.T., for example. (You can see his picture on page 121.) The writers who made up this movie character added details to show E.T. as a strange creature from outer space. For instance, he is able to use special powers to do things like make a bicycle fly. But the writers also combined in E.T. feelings that are like a human's. E.T. loves Elliot, the little human boy he lives with. He also feels sad when he can't return to his own home.

CRITICAL THINKING
(pp. 121–122)

OBJECTIVE

- To observe details and to list the details in a chart

TEACHING *OBSERVING DETAILS*

To make students more aware of all the senses, bring to class items that appeal to several senses. For example, a ripe pineapple is rough to the touch, has distinctive colors and visual patterns, can be smelled and tasted, and produces sounds when handled. Remind students that they can sense these

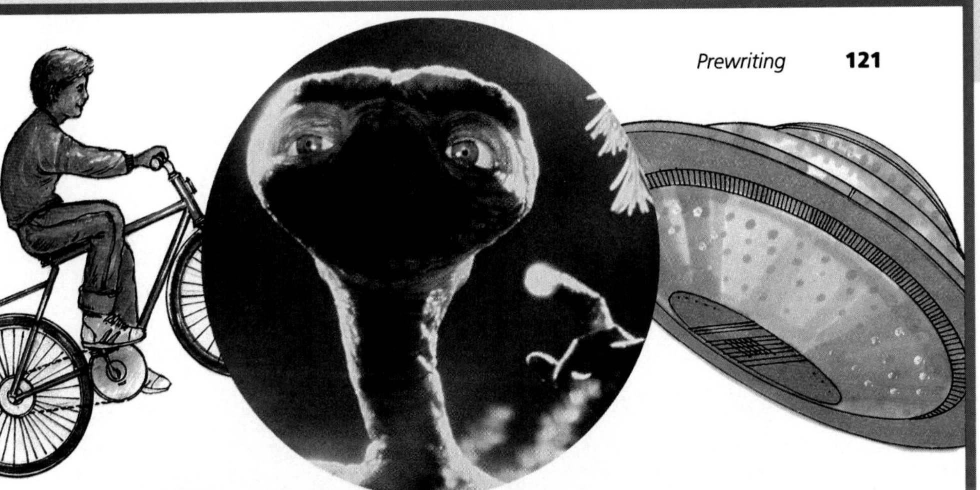

CRITICAL THINKING

Observing Details

Sensory details—details of sight, sound, taste, touch, and smell—make descriptions come alive. Does your subject make noise? Does it have a smell? How does it feel when you touch it? Is there a taste? You can't use *all* of your senses to describe every subject, but you should be able to use at least two or three.

You could make a chart of details as you observe them. Here's an example of a chart one writer created after observing the activities at a playground.

SIGHT	TOUCH	SOUND
swings	rough canvas seats	"Higher! Higher!"
monkey bars	sticky grips	laughing
barefoot boy	hot cement underfoot	"Ouch!"
seesaw	sharp splinters	creaky
water fountain	icy water	gurgling

COOPERATIVE LEARNING

Divide the class into groups of four or five. Each group should brainstorm for three minutes on a topic (perhaps a common food) for details to mention when describing it to a friend. Ask for a volunteer in each group to record the descriptive details mentioned by the group.

When time is up, ask the groups to discuss the types of details they have listed. Are they all the same kind of details, or are some different? How are they different? [Types of details could include sensory details or details that evoke a specific feeling.]

LEP/ESL

General Strategies. The **Critical Thinking Exercise** lends itself to a small-group format and will likely prove more productive if ESL students are well integrated into groups with native speakers. To limit confusion, you may want to suggest that only one person in each group do the actual writing, while all members engage in brainstorming and generating ideas.

things at a distance by memory—and so can their readers if they provide the details.

Ask several volunteers to give sensory details about one of the things brought to class.

To close, ask students to list the five senses and to provide sensory details for one of the many things in the picture of the farmer's market. Ask volunteers to share answers.

VISUAL CONNECTIONS

Exploring the Subject. Many large cities have cooperative farmers' markets where farmers gather to sell the goods they produce. Sometimes farmers drive more than 200 miles to take produce to market, but they can make a profit because customers are willing to pay more for goods they know are fresh. Almost every major city has a farmer's market.

ANSWERS

Critical Thinking Exercise

Charts will vary. Students should mention specific sizes, colors, textures, smells, and flavors.

ANSWERS

Exercise 1

Lists will vary. The sounds should be specific, perhaps associated with a particular object, person, or action, or compared effectively with another sound. If possible, the word that describes the sound should be onomatopoeic.

CRITICAL THINKING EXERCISE:
Observing Details

What can you see in this picture? What might you hear, feel, taste, and smell? Make a chart like the one on page 121. Fill in as many details as you can. Then get together with a partner and compare your lists.

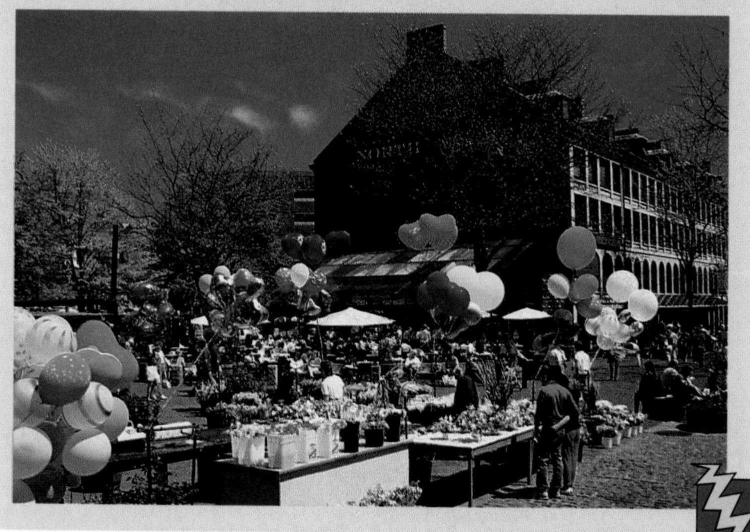

EXERCISE 1 Speaking and Listening: Observing Sounds

Writers train their senses to be alert. They don't just see a cat; they see a spotted Cheshire with a twitching tail. They don't just hear the drone of noises in a classroom; they hear the squeak of chalk on the chalkboard and the buzz of a pesky fly.

You can do the same thing. Practice on just one sense for now: your hearing. During lunchtime at your school cafeteria, list at least ten sounds that you hear. Afterward, share your list with a classmate. In what ways do your lists differ? If you put your lists together, how many sounds are there?

RETEACHING

Write a broad topic on the chalkboard. Ask students to discuss the prewriting steps they would follow to develop a description for that topic. Make sure students know why the topic must be limited. List each prewriting step on the chalkboard and allow students to provide specific responses related to the topic.

CLOSURE

Ask students to volunteer details they would use to describe a thing or place with which they are all familiar. Write the details on the chalkboard. Then ask students to identify the sensory details and to suggest what feelings the details convey. ■

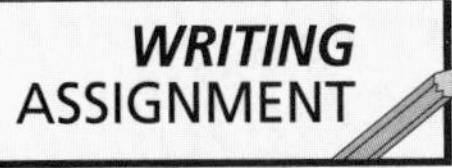

PART 2:
Gathering Details

How good an observer are you? Observe firsthand the subject you chose in Writing Assignment, Part 1 (page 119) or call it to mind. Let each one of your senses "check it out." Write down details that tell what your eyes see, what your nose smells, what your ears hear, and so on. It may help to write your details in a chart like the one on page 121.

Choosing and Organizing Details

Choosing Details. Now you have a list of details. But you might not use all of them. Think about the feeling you want readers to have. Should the rat you are describing give them the creeps? Do you want them to feel how sad rainy days make you? Choose details that will give readers a specific feeling.

Organizing Details. You usually list details as you think about them. You may have details about a rat's whiskers and then details about its tail. To help readers follow your description, you can arrange details in *spatial order* or *order of importance.*

ADVANCED STUDENTS

Students might plan an editorial that uses descriptive details to influence a particular audience. As part of the prewriting, ask them to name their audience, to analyze the audience, and to list descriptive details that would be likely to influence it. Students should also specify the effect that each of the details would be intended to have.

LEARNING STYLES

Kinetic Learners. Kinetic learners may find it easier to describe things they can operate, touch, hold, or feel. They may need to learn words to express particular motions and to describe textures or other physical features of things. It may be a helpful strategy for them to have physical contact or interaction with objects they must describe from a distance.

LESS-ADVANCED STUDENTS

In **Writing Assignment: Part 3,** students may have problems with the concept of order of importance. Check that each student has stated a single purpose and that the student knows that a detail's importance has to do with how well it creates the feeling the writer wants.

A DIFFERENT APPROACH

To demonstrate the importance of having well-chosen concrete details in a logical order, ask each student to think of an animal and to prepare a list of ten concrete details that could be used to describe it.

After arranging the list in either spatial order or order of importance, each student should recopy it neatly and trade papers with another student without saying what animal the details describe. From knowledge of the descriptive details and the order, each student should try to guess what the partner's animal is.

TIMESAVER

When students finish arranging lists in **Writing Assignment: Part 3,** let them trade papers to judge each other's lists. Ask them to consult you if they disagree.

Spatial order arranges details according to their location. For example, your eye might move in order from the tip of the rat's nose to its tail. In your description, you'd arrange details about the rat this way: whiskers, teeth, eyes, ears, body, tail.

With ***order of importance,*** give the most important detail first or last for greatest impact on your readers. If you want your readers to feel the rat's cold, glaring eyes, start or end your description with its eyes.

Here's how one writer chose details for a description. Notice how he crossed out details that wouldn't create the feeling he wanted. He then numbered the other details in the order he would use them.

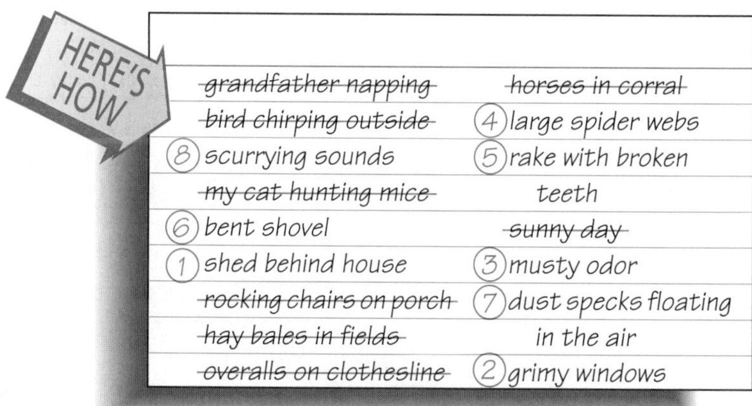

WRITING ASSIGNMENT

PART 3:
Choosing and Organizing Details

Read over the list of details you gathered for Writing Assignment, Part 2 (page 123). Think about how you want your readers to feel about your subject. Cross off details that don't show this feeling. (If the rat is supposed to be scary, don't tell about its soft, gray fur.) Next, decide how to organize your details. Will you use spatial order or order of importance? Number your details in the order you'll use them.

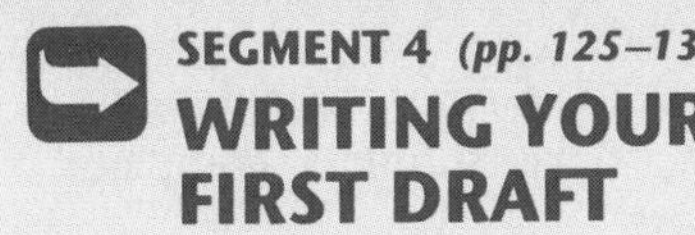

SEGMENT 4 *(pp. 125–130)*

WRITING YOUR FIRST DRAFT

OBJECTIVES

- To analyze a description
- To write a draft of a description

MOTIVATION

Ask several students to name favorite books or stories and to tell what they remember best from the stories. Make sure students realize that effective description of action, places, or persons makes these works memorable.

Writing Your First Draft

Have you ever seen a 3-D movie? You wear a special pair of glasses. Then people and places seem so real they almost come off the screen. You can make your descriptions as real as a 3-D movie if you choose your words carefully.

Using Exact Words. A camera that's not in focus takes a blurry picture. As you focus the lens, the picture becomes sharper. Using exact words is like putting a camera in focus. Vague words create blurry images. But exact words create bright, clear pictures.

Exact words say just what you mean. An exact word to describe the color of a person's eyes might be *chocolate* or *sandy,* not just *brown.* You might describe a *bald-headed eagle* or a *sparrow,* not just a *bird.* A snake doesn't just *move* through the grass, it *slithers* or *glides.*

Sometimes it's hard to come up with the exact word that says what you mean. Using a word bank can help. In your journal, you might want to start a word bank like the one on page 126. Then you'll have a list of words when you need them. Don't forget to leave room for more words.

Teacher's ResourceBank™

RESOURCES

WRITING YOUR FIRST DRAFT

- Writing a Description 35

QUOTATION FOR THE DAY

"Summer afternoon—summer afternoon; to me those have always been the two most beautiful words in the English language." (Henry James, 1843–1916, American writer)

You may wish to use the quotation to introduce a brainstorming activity. Ask students to list their favorite words—words that are beautiful or ugly, happy or sad, scary or soothing. Explain that words represent specific things or ideas, but they also carry connotations because of feelings, memories, and associations they stir within individuals.

TEACHING THE LESSON

If you have students who read well, ask one to read the excerpt from **"Tortuga"** expressively. Ask everyone to listen carefully to notice the two kinds of details (sensory details and details that give a specific feeling) and their effects. [Some details convey the narrator's feelings, but only the sensory and exact details let readers experience for themselves the strong physical presence of the tortoise.] To reinforce the differences in different types of details, have students complete **Exercise 2** in class.

MEETING **INDIVIDUAL** NEEDS

LEP/ESL

General Strategies. Encourage students to enter the word bank for sensory details in their journals. Pair each student with a peer tutor and make sure each pair has access to a dictionary (ESL students may need to use a bilingual dictionary, as well). Ask ESL students to write native-language definitions for each of these words and, with the help of their peer tutors, to create original sentences in English by using this vocabulary.

WRITING NOTE

There are thesaurus publications designed specifically for younger students and these publications could be particularly useful. Explain to students how to use a thesaurus. Then assign several simple words and ask students to record two synonyms for each item. Students' performance on this activity should indicate their level of understanding.

WORD BANK	
Sight Words	shiny, golden, freckled, torn, short, wrinkled, bumpy, narrow, plastic
Touch Words	fuzzy, slippery, hard, lumpy, scratchy, cool, damp, dry, rough
Sound Words	shriek, blare, whisper, shout, cry, moan, cackle, screak, whoop
Smell Words	smoky, fresh, spicy, spoiled, stink, perfumy, reek, sniff, decaying
Taste Words	sweet, salty, greasy, sour, sugary, rotten, syrupy, cool, fishy

A *thesaurus* can help you find the exact words you want. Every library has at least one. When you want to replace a vague word, look it up in the thesaurus. You'll find an entire list of words that you can choose from. For example, if you look up the word *fast,* a thesaurus might offer you words like these: *swift, rapid, dashing, snappy, zippy, like a flash, like greased lightning, supersonic.* Take your pick!

GUIDED PRACTICE

Go through **"Tortuga"** with the students. Have them identify the two kinds of details. To reinforce the point that the two kinds of details must work together, go over **A Writer's Model** as a whole-class activity.

INDEPENDENT PRACTICE

Have students complete **Writing Assignment: Part 4.** Monitor their progress and encourage good use of sensory and exact details.

Using Similes and Metaphors. You can show readers your subject by comparing it to something they know. *Similes* and *metaphors* help you make these comparisons. A ***simile*** uses *like* or *as.*

His hair was as orange *as apricots.*
He snuck away *like an alley rat.*

Metaphors make a direct comparison. They don't use the word *like* or *as.*

Her long brown hair was *a veil she hid behind.*
The dog, far ahead, was *just a black dot on the horizon.*

Here's a description of a tortoise, or turtle, from a short story. As you read, look for sensory words and exact words. Notice that the writer names his subject in the first sentence.

A PASSAGE FROM A SHORT STORY

1 *from* Tortuga
by Rudolfo A. Anaya

. . . There in the middle of the narrow path
lay the biggest tortoise any of us had ever
Subject 2 seen. It was a huge monster which had
Metaphor crawled out of the dark river to lay its
eggs in the warm sand. I felt a shiver, and
3 when I breathed the taste of copper
drained in my mouth and settled in my
queasy stomach.
The giant turtle lifted its huge head and
looked at us with dull, glintless eyes. The
tribe drew back. Only I remained facing
4 the monster from the water. Its slimy head
dripped with bright green algae. It hissed a

LESS-ADVANCED STUDENTS

Students may have trouble differentiating between metaphors and similes. Remind them that a simile is always introduced by *like* or *as.* Because providing examples is one of the best ways to help students internalize difficult concepts, give a few additional examples of metaphors and similes.

A less-advanced student who enjoys drawing might have fun learning about metaphors by illustrating several metaphors such as the examples in the textbook.

USING THE SELECTION

***from* Tortuga**

1

Tortuga is a Spanish word meaning "turtle."

2

The blending of *dark* and *warm* appeals to sight and touch in the same sentence.

3

This is probably not literally the taste of copper, but a way of providing a sensory, concrete image that conveys the idea of extreme fear.

4

From here on, images that appeal to sense of touch such as *slimy, dripped, wet, leathery, clung, crushed,* and *encrusted* put the reader at the scene.

ASSESSMENT

Ask students to underline descriptive details in their descriptions.

Mark each well-used detail with a check and each detail that needs work with a question mark. Give feedback on the overall effect of the descriptions.

RETEACHING

Write a general word such as *tree, bike,* or *lake* on the chalkboard and ask students to supply five sensory details and one detail that evokes a specific feeling.

Sensory words and exact words

warning. It had come out of the water to lay its eggs, now it had to return to the river. Wet, leathery eggs fresh from the laying clung to its webbed feet, and as it moved forward it crushed them into the sand. Its gray shell was dry, dulled by the sun, encrusted with dead parasites and green growth; it needed the water.

VISUAL CONNECTIONS

Ideas for Writing. Because they are slow and can provide a large quantity of meat, many large land and sea turtles are in danger of extinction. Students might wish to look up material about extinct and currently endangered species of tortoises and to write reports to share with the class.

ANSWERS

Exercise 2

Answers may vary.

1. Students may feel fear or loathing ("shiver," "taste of copper," "queasy stomach," "glintless eyes," "hissed a warning," "slimy head"), amazement or awe ("huge monster," "biggest tortoise . . . ever seen") or pity ("it needed the water").
2. Students may say that it is called a monster because it is so big and strange looking.
3. Head: huge, dull, glintless eyes, slimy, dripped with bright green algae. Shell: gray, dry, dulled by the sun, encrusted with dead parasites and green growth.
4. Taste: the taste of copper drained in my mouth and settled in my stomach. Touch: wet, leathery, fresh from the laying, clung to its webbed feet.

SELECTION AMENDMENT
Description of change: excerpted
Rationale: to focus on the concept of descriptive words presented in this chapter

EXERCISE 2 Analyzing a Description

Get together with two or three classmates. Then answer these questions about the description of the tortoise.

1. How does this description make you feel about the tortoise? What words make you feel that way?
2. A giant tortoise is not really a monster. Why does the writer compare it to one?
3. What are some sensory words that help you see and touch the tortoise's head? Which ones help you see its shell?
4. What words help you taste what the writer feels in his mouth? What words help you touch the turtle eggs?

CLOSURE

Ask students to define *sensory, audience, spatial order,* and *order of importance.* Students should give an example of each concept. They might need to use comparison and contrast to make some points clear.

EXTENSION

Let students go to the library to look up animals in which they are interested. Have each student write down ten sensory details about the animal.

Ask students to follow the prewriting sequence and to include the descriptions in letters to friends. 

A Writer's Model for You

You might not be quite ready to match the skill of Rudolfo A. Anaya. But here's a model you could match. It's shorter and the words are a little easier.

A WRITER'S MODEL

Subject

Simile

Sensory words and exact words

An old shed stands behind my grandfather's house. Its rotten boards lean against each other like tired people. Inside, it's very dark because the grimy windows keep the sunlight out. I can smell a musty odor. Hanging down from the rafters are large spider webs. These sticky webs sometimes brush against my face. I brush the webs away and leave swarms of dust specks floating in the air. A broken shovel and a rake with bent teeth slouch against the side of the shed. In the corner, I hear soft, scurrying sounds.

CRITICAL THINKING

Analysis

Ask students to analyze the order in which details are arranged in **A Writer's Model** [spatial order]. Why is this order appropriate? [When someone comes upon any structure, he or she must start with the outside before moving inside; therefore, the outside is natural starting place for arranging the details in this case.]

VISUAL CONNECTIONS

Ideas for Writing. Students who have visited farms have probably seen or entered such a shed. On farms where chickens are not caged, hens often seek such places to nest. Students who have visited old farms might like to write brief narrations of part of what they did and saw on their visits. They should each include a description of at least one object or animal.

When you write your description

- choose details to show a specific feeling about your subject
- organize details so your readers will be able to follow your description
- use sensory words and exact words

PART 4:
Writing a Draft of Your Description

Now paint your own picture with words. Using your prewriting notes, write the first draft of your description. Begin by naming your subject. Then use sensory words and exact words to show it to readers. And don't forget that special feeling you want your readers to have!

SEGMENT 5 *(pp. 131–132)*

EVALUATING AND REVISING

OBJECTIVES

- To analyze and evaluate a writer's revisions of a description
- To evaluate and revise the first draft of a description

TEACHING THE LESSON

Tell students that before revising, the writer must evaluate the composition to decide what parts to improve. Revision involves adding, taking out, moving, or changing words, sentences, or paragraphs to improve a written work.

Use the **Evaluating and Revising Description** chart to guide students through 

Evaluating and Revising

It's important to evaluate and revise your description, and the chart below can help you do it. To use the chart, ask yourself each question in the left-hand column. If you find a problem, the ideas in the right-hand column will show you how to fix it.

EVALUATING AND REVISING DESCRIPTION

	EVALUATION GUIDE	REVISION TECHNIQUE
1	Do sensory words and exact words make the subject real for readers?	Observe, recall, or imagine your subject. **Add** details that let readers see, hear, feel, taste, or smell it.
2	Would a simile or metaphor add spice to the description?	**Add** a simile or metaphor if it makes the description livelier.
3	Are the details organized in the best order?	**Reorder** details so they make sense and help create a specific feeling for your readers. Use spatial order or order of importance.

EXERCISE 3 **Evaluating a Writer's Revisions**

The following sentences are from the description of the old shed. Try to figure out why the writer made the changes you see. Use the evaluating and revising chart, above, to help you decide.

Teacher's ResourceBank™

RESOURCES

EVALUATING AND REVISING

- Writing A Description 36

QUOTATION FOR THE DAY

"Being specific sometimes involves no more than choosing the right word or phrase." (Ronald Munson, American author and teacher)

Write the quotation on the chalkboard and remind the class that being specific in description involves including details. Encourage students to check for details while they revise their essays.

LEP/ESL

General Strategies. Before students begin **Writing Assignment: Part 5,** remind them of the difference between evaluating and criticizing. Create two columns on the chalkboard and ask students to give examples from daily life that are examples of these behaviors. Emphasize that when students evaluate each other's work, they need to make a special effort to deliver comments in a positive way.

Exercise 3. To show why revisions were needed, help students compare and analyze the first drafts with the revised versions. Then let students work independently on **Writing Assignment: Part 5.**

By monitoring students as they complete their revisions, you can assess their mastery of revision techniques.

CLOSURE

Ask students to tell what they think they have done best in their descriptions and what was most helpful about the evaluation and revision process. ■

VISUAL CONNECTIONS

Related Expression Skills. Students who enjoy drawing or painting might want to create their impressions of the inside of this old shed, based on the description given.

ANSWERS

Exercise 3

1. *Shed* is more specific. A building could be beautiful or rich.
2. The writer doesn't want the reader to see the shed as a cozy place.
3. Most students will say that the change is appropriate for spatial order because the speaker begins by looking at the outside.
4. Most students will say the additions help show what the shed looks like. The comparison suggests the shed is about to fall.

COOPERATIVE LEARNING

As students evaluate each other's work in **Writing Assignment: Part 5**, they should put two column heads, "Specific" and "Vague," on sheets of paper and record each image under the appropriate head. If a student finds too few images, the description either needs more images or the editor might need a clearer definition of what an image is. Images tagged *vague* should be evaluated and replaced with specific images.

An old ~~building~~ shed stands behind my — **replace**
grandfather's house. ~~It's where~~ — **cut**
~~Tabatha's new kittens sleep.~~ Inside, it's
very dark because the grimy windows keep — **add**
the sunlight out. Its rotten boards lean — **reorder**
against each other like tired people. — **add**

1. The writer replaced the word *building* with *shed*. Which word helps you see the subject better?
2. Why did the writer cut the second sentence? [Hint: What feeling does the writer want to express?]
3. Why did the writer move the last sentence? [Hint: Review page 124.]
4. Why did the writer add the word *grimy*? the words *like tired people*? How do these words help you see the shed?

PART 5:
Evaluating and Revising Your Description

Can readers see, hear, feel, taste, and smell your subject? Use the chart on page 131 to help you evaluate your first draft. Then trade descriptions with a classmate and evaluate each other's work. Think about your own and your classmate's evaluation. Finally, make changes that will *show* your subject to readers.

SEGMENT 6 *(pp. 133–136)*

PROOFREADING AND PUBLISHING

OBJECTIVE

- To use proofreading strategies to prepare a description for publication

TEACHING THE LESSON

Inform students that books and magazines often contain factual and grammatical errors that are very costly for publishing companies to correct.

Students may have no financial reason to make work correct, but they have other reasons to proofread carefully before

Proofreading and Publishing

Proofreading. When you proofread, you look for mistakes in capitalization, punctuation, spelling, or usage. Once you've corrected any errors, your readers will be able to read your description more easily.

MECHANICS HINT

Using Commas with Adjectives

You often use adjectives to make a subject seem real. Separate two or more adjectives before a noun with commas.

> The small, grimy windows keep the sunlight out.
> I hear soft, scurrying sounds.

Don't separate an adjective and the noun it describes with a comma.

INCORRECT An old, mangy, dog slept in the corner.
CORRECT An old, mangy dog slept in the corner.

REFERENCE NOTE: See pages 595–596 for more about using commas with adjectives.

Teacher's ResourceBank™

RESOURCES

PROOFREADING AND PUBLISHING

- Writing a Description 37

QUOTATION FOR THE DAY

"Of all the needs a book has the chief need is that it be readable." (Anthony Trollope, 1815–1882, English author)

Write the quotation on the chalkboard and use it to emphasize audience as students complete the proofreading and publishing stage of the writing process. Explain that carefully correcting mechanical errors at this point will help the audience read and understand the published work more easily.

MECHANICS HINT

Tell students to try inserting the word *and* when they are in doubt about whether to put a comma after an adjective. If the sentence does not make sense with the *and* in place, a comma does not belong there.

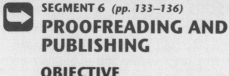

publishing, such as pride and the desire to have their ideas understood.

Assign **Writing Assignment: Part 6.** Focus the students on the specific problem areas you noted on their papers as you monitored revisions and look for changes in these areas as you evaluate the final drafts.

CLOSURE

Ask how many students caught errors as they proofread their work. Then ask students why proofreading and publishing are important in the writing process. ■

LEP/ESL

Spanish. The **Mechanics Hint** on p. 133 concerns the use of commas with adjectives. There are additional grammatical features related to adjective usage that may prove problematic for some students. In Spanish, an adjective follows the noun it modifies. Another interference problem lies in the fact that in Spanish, an adjective agrees with the accompanying noun in both number and gender. In reviewing students' compositions, you may want to remain alert to these possibilities and to offer extra practice as needed.

VISUAL CONNECTIONS

Related Expression Skills. Have students use a tape recorder or a video camera as they practice delivery of their descriptive writing. Then let them evaluate their own deliveries to find weaknesses and to turn them into strengths. The cassettes or videotapes can be duplicated and taken home or shared with other classes.

Publishing. Why go to so much work on a description if you're not going to share it? Here are two publishing ideas for descriptions.

- With your classmates, produce a class "radio show" by taping all of your descriptions. When it's your turn, try to capture the feeling of your writing in your voice. Speak slowly so your audience won't miss any details.

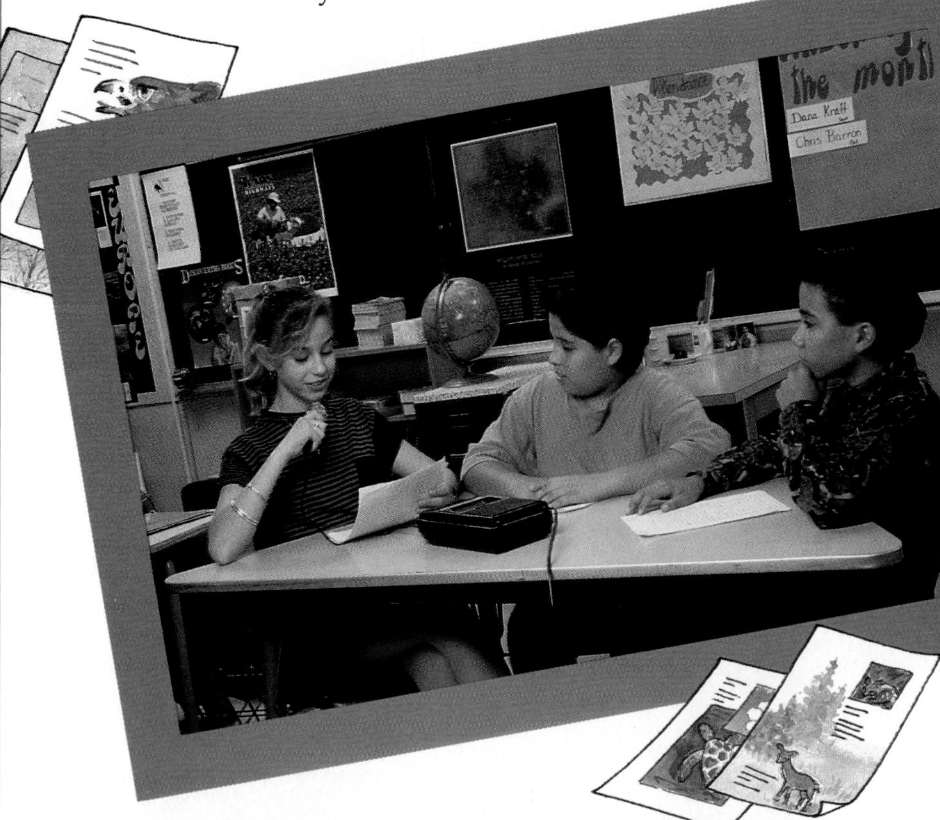

- Illustrate your work with drawings or other artwork or with magazine photos. Try to capture the feeling you have about your subject. Your teacher might display your work in the classroom, or you might get together with some classmates and bind your work together in a booklet.

WRITING ASSIGNMENT

PART 6:
Proofreading and Publishing

A diamond doesn't shine brightly until it's properly cut and polished. Proofread your description and correct any errors to make it shine. Then use one of the ideas you have read about to publish it. Or use an idea of your own.

A STUDENT MODEL

Description comes in handy in all kinds of writing, as Jenny Boscamp's paper shows. A student at Frost Elementary School in Chandler, Arizona, Jenny describes a snow leopard to help us learn about it. Jenny says the hardest thing about writing this paper was arranging "the details so they sounded good and made sense." As you read, notice how the details she includes create a picture of the snow leopard.

INTEGRATING THE LANGUAGE ARTS

Listening Link. You may suggest that students read through their papers aloud at least once during this stage. Because punctuation should occur only at natural pauses in thought, careful listening to the rhythm of each sentence will often catch incorrect punctuation.

STUDENTS WITH SPECIAL NEEDS

The prospect of seeing their best work attractively printed or prominently displayed on a bulletin board will often provide motivation for students to do their best work.

A STUDENT MODEL

Evaluation

1. Jenny's exact words, such as "thick and long," "cunning cleverness," "deadly consequences," and "quick speed" help give the reader a clear description of the snow leopard.
2. Jenny's description is made livelier by the use of two metaphors, "It attacks its prey like a race car" and "it makes its attack like stealing candy from a baby."
3. Jenny uses order of importance to arrange the details to help the reader follow her description. She gives the most important detail her first for greatest impact.

Snow Leopard—The Predator!
by Jenny Boscamp

The snow leopard seems calm from far away, but a run-in with one could lead to deadly consequences. The snow leopard's fur is not sleek, but it is thick and long which makes it easier for the snow leopard to adapt to the cold climate it lives in. The tropical leopard and many big cats have large ears in proportion to the size of their heads, but the snow leopard's ears are small. Its tail is also longer than other big cats' tails. The snow leopard's tail is three feet long and is used as a blanket in its cold habitat when it is sleeping.

The snow leopard is a predator. If it weren't for its cunning cleverness and its quick speed, the snow leopard's diet would be plants, bugs, and other small animals. It attacks its prey like a race car passing the finish line. It runs and runs until it gets there and attacks the prize. The snow leopard's movement is so quick that it makes its attack like stealing candy from a baby.

SEGMENT 7 *(pp. 137–138)*

WRITING WORKSHOP

OBJECTIVE

- To write, evaluate, revise, and prepare a descriptive poem for publication

TEACHING THE LESSON

Read the poem expressively to allow students to appreciate what the poet has done. Tell students that they may write something just as effective by using simple words.

It is important that each student begin with a specific physical object and let

WRITING WORKSHOP

A Poem That Describes

Writing a paragraph is one way to describe something, but you can also describe in a poem. In a descriptive poem, you need to use sensory details, just as you used them in your descriptive paper. In addition, descriptive poems sometimes use word sounds. The following poem uses sensory details and word sounds—rhyming words—to describe a common object, a toaster.

The Toaster

by William Jay Smith

A silver-scaled Dragon with jaws flaming red
Sits at my elbow and toasts my bread.
I hand him fat slices, and then, one by one,
He hands them back when he sees they are done.

Think about the sensory details in this poem. The word *silver-scaled* helps you see the toaster's silver sides. The words *flaming red* help you see and feel its hot insides. Try writing your own poem that describes an object. If you like, make your poem a riddle, also.

QUOTATION FOR THE DAY

"If everybody became a poet, the world would be so much better. We would all read to each other." (Nikki Giovanni, 1943–   , American poet.)

You may wish to use the quotation to prepare students to respond to poetry in this section. Initiate a discussion about poetry. Ask students if they agree or disagree with Giovanni about the powers of poetry.

his or her imagination build an event around it and find a meaning in it.

To make sure students use sensory words, ask them to underline sensory words and to label the senses involved. Similes or metaphors should be labeled also.

To assess students' work, check underlining and labeling. As a closure, ask students to explain how sensory details create mental images. ■

LEP/ESL

General Strategies. Students might need continued practice with present-tense verbs because students frequently omit the *s* in the third person singular. Both of the short poems in **Writing Workshop** use this tense form throughout. Photocopy these poems after taking out the verbs. Have students provide the correct verb forms of any verbs that fit the meaning. You may also want to suggest that students adhere to the present tense when writing their poems.

CRITICAL THINKING

Analysis

Remind students of the definitions of *metaphor* and *simile* they learned earlier in this chapter. Ask students to analyze the figures of speech that control this poem [metaphor, personification]. Does this dragon act differently than might be expected? [Yes, it does. No knight in shining armor would need to fight this domesticated dragon.]

Writing a Descriptive Poem

Prewriting. Think of some object you see every day. You might choose your bicycle, the refrigerator, or even your closet. Imagine this object as a creature. Brainstorm for sensory details. How might it look or sound? Does it have a smell or taste? How does it feel to touch it?

Writing, Evaluating, and Revising. If you like, follow the pattern of "The Toaster." For example, you might write about the space under your bed where you push things when you clean your room in a poem like this one:

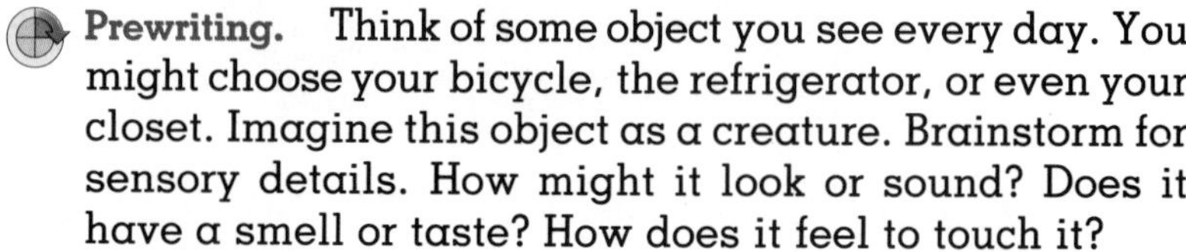

A horrid great bedrumph with never a mutter
Lives under my bed and holds all my clutter.
I throw things under, and he keeps them there
And asks for more, till my room's clean and bare.

You can make any lines rhyme in the poem that you want. Or you can decide to have no words that rhyme. Just revise the poem until it *sounds* good when you read it out loud.

Proofreading and Publishing. Commas and periods don't always go at the end of lines in poetry. Put them where your voice pauses or stops. And be sure to check for misspelled words; you don't want them to spoil the fun for readers. To share your poem, write or type it in the center of unlined paper. For the final touch, draw a picture of the object or creature.

SEGMENT 8 *(pp. 139–141)*

MAKING CONNECTIONS

DESCRIPTION ACROSS THE CURRICULUM

OBJECTIVE

- To use details in writing a short description of a historic site

MAKING CONNECTIONS

DESCRIPTION ACROSS THE CURRICULUM

Describing Historic Sites

Historic sites are places where people's lives or feelings have been changed or touched. You can't always visit a historic site. But by reading a good description, you can "see" the site and share the experience. Here's a description that helps you share the experience of seeing a famous site.

The Statue of Liberty stands on her own island in the New York Harbor. She's green from head to toe. Her right arm is raised straight in the air, lifting the torch of freedom. Sunlight gleams off the torch like sparks of fire. Tugboats, sailboats, and barges pass her. Seagulls circle her crown. The Statue of Liberty is a huge shining emerald in the middle of the water.

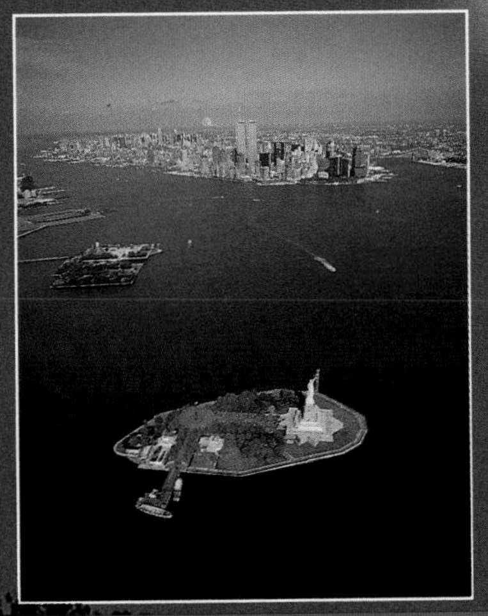

DESCRIPTION ACROSS THE CURRICULUM

Teaching Strategies

Tell students to select sites about which they know enough to supply specific details that will express their feelings. Remind students that selected specific details are the key to good writing. If possible, allow students to visit the library to find background information on the sites they have selected.

GUIDELINES

Responses will vary. Stress accuracy and the inclusion of specific details (sensory, subjective, and historical) that are appropriate to the site.

DESCRIPTION AND PERSUASION OBJECTIVE

- To write a descriptive paragraph that will convince an audience to visit a place

DESCRIPTION AND PERSUASION

Teaching Strategies

Remind students that it is difficult to be enthusiastic about a place one does not like or to be persuasive about a place one does not know much about. Details and enthusiasm are both essential in a persuasive travel description.

Knowing the intended audience is very important. Writing to a youthful audience the writer might stress contact with nature through hiking, camping, and similar activities. Perhaps an audience with families would be more interested in details describing picnic areas and first-aid stations. But the writer should not exhaust the topic. Leaving something for the reader to discover is a good tactic.

This writer tried to express her feelings about the Statue of Liberty. Can you remember the feelings you had when you visited or read about some historic site? It could be a battlefield, statue, memorial—even a historic building in your own town. Write a short description of the historic site. Select details that will help you share your feelings about it.

DESCRIPTION AND PERSUASION

Writing a Travel Description

Have you ever noticed the travel section of the Sunday newspaper? Take a look sometime. You'll find all kinds of ads, and you'll also find some articles written by travel writers. Travel writers describe places they have visited. Sometimes they just share information, but often they try to persuade their readers to visit the sites they're describing. Here's an example of a persuasive description of the Grand Canyon. Does it make you want to go there?

> If you're interested in time and space travel, visit Grand Canyon National Park in Arizona. A good way to start is floating down the Colorado River on a raft. It took the river millions of years to carve out the canyon. Or take a ride on a mule, down six or seven thousand feet from the rim to the bottom of the canyon. While there, take another look at the past and visit the ruins of adobe houses built hundreds of years ago by the Pueblo Indians. From the rim itself, look out over the canyon and watch the colors of the rocks change with the varying light of the sun. And if you want to get a true sense of space, rent a seat on one of the planes that fly out over the canyon. Its vastness and majesty are unforgettable.

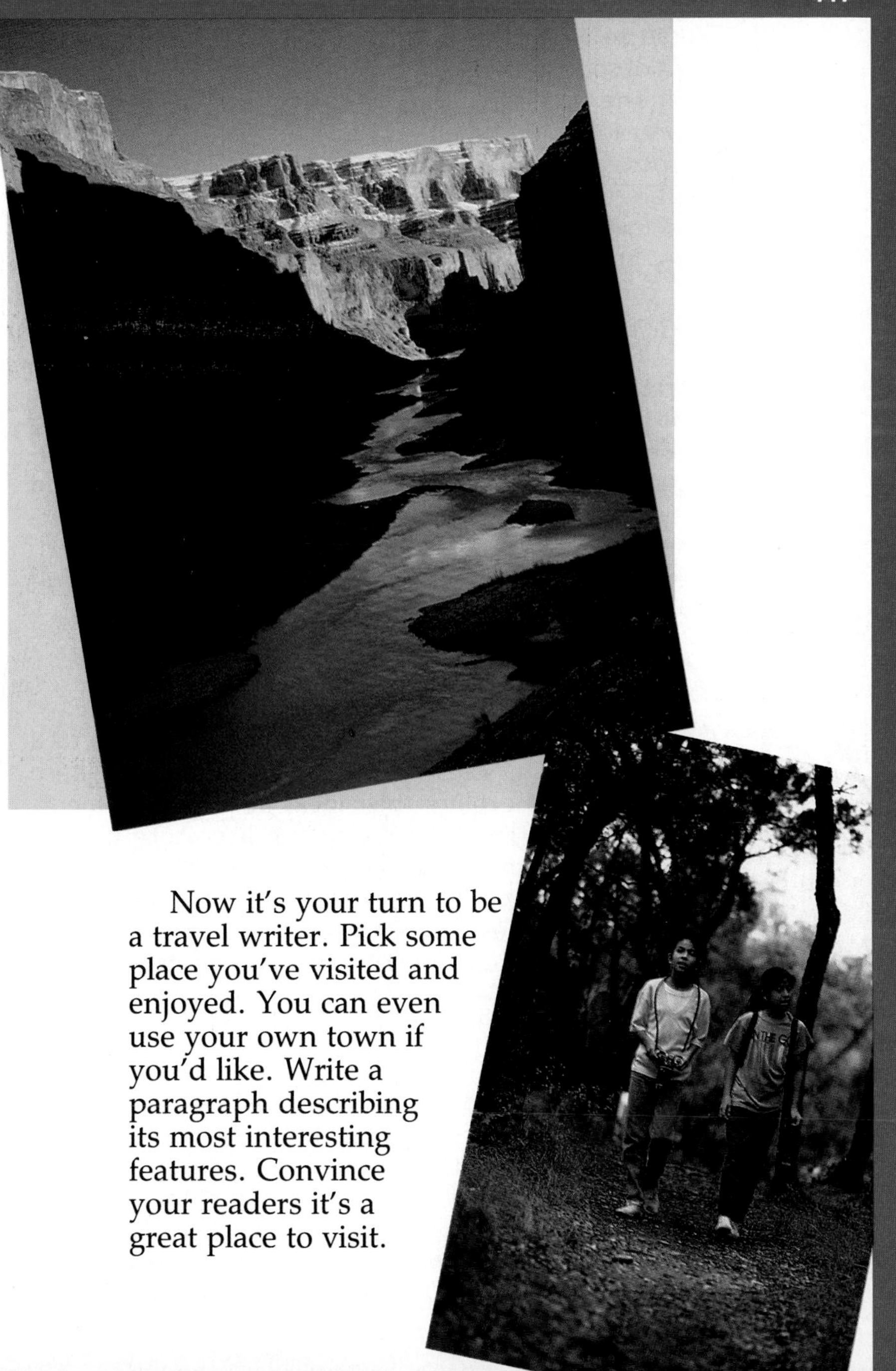

Now it's your turn to be a travel writer. Pick some place you've visited and enjoyed. You can even use your own town if you'd like. Write a paragraph describing its most interesting features. Convince your readers it's a great place to visit.

GUIDELINES

Responses will vary. Stress inclusion of specific details that would motivate the audience to want to visit the place.

VISUAL CONNECTIONS

Ideas for Writing. According to various groups, the Grand Canyon is threatened by air pollution. A student who is interested in environmental issues might want to research this story and present to the class a report on how serious the threat is.

Chapter 5

CREATIVE WRITING

OBJECTIVES

- To generate ideas for possible stories based on situations given in the text
- To generate ideas for a story with at least one character and a problem
- To write a draft of a story
- To evaluate and revise a draft of a story
- To proofread and publish a story
- To write a limerick, a skit, and a sports story

Motivation

Most students love stories. Many sixth-graders are good storytellers, and some of your students may write stories for their own enjoyment. On the day you start this chapter, ask your students to share with the class the stories they remember best from their childhood. Tell the class that the stories are the result of thinking and planning by the people who made them up and that the class will learn how to plan and write stories in this chapter.

Introduction

The largest portion of this chapter is an application of the stages of the writing process to the task of writing a short story. After a literary model of a folk tale, the chapter takes up the prewriting tasks of finding a story idea, planning a story by imagining a setting and characters, and creating a plot by developing a plot map. During the writing stage each student writes a draft of a story and then learns how to evaluate and revise the draft. Finally, students are asked to proofread and publish their finished stories.

The next portion of the chapter deals with writing a limerick as an example of a simple poem. Limericks are concrete and relatively easy to compose, and students usually enjoy the humor that is characteristic of limericks. In the **Making Connections** features students are asked to write skits and to write stories based on the lives of sports heroes.

The primary aim of creative writing is literary expression, but students can write creatively for other purposes. For example, a story set in a culture that readers are unfamiliar with can have the secondary aim of informing readers about the traditions of the culture. A story about the harmful effects of pollution on animal life can help persuade readers to get involved in an environmental campaign.

The most important mode of writing used in short stories is narration, but description also plays an important part. In poems and other forms of creative writing students can employ the classification mode by comparing objects and people through figures of speech, and they can use the evaluative mode by relating the characteristics of a true friend or a beautiful sunset. In short, creative writing offers opportunities to use the full range of aims and modes of writing.

Integration

This chapter can be used as a natural follow-up to a literature unit on short stories. It provides a chance for students to explore their ideas about the elements of fiction that they studied in the literature unit by using the ideas in their writing.

The chart on the next page illustrates the strands of language arts as they are integrated into this chapter. For vocabulary study, glossary words are underlined in some writing models.

QUOTATIONS

All **Quotations for the Day** are chosen because of their relevance to instructional material presented in that segment of the chapter and for their usefulness in establishing student interest in writing.

INTEGRATING THE LANGUAGE ARTS

Selection	Reading and Literature	Writing and Critical Thinking	Language and Syntax	Speaking, Listening, and Other Expression Skills
"Brer Billy Goat Tricks Brer Wolf" retold by Julius Lester **144-146** **"Zoo"** by Edward D. Hoch **158-162** Limerick by William Jay Smith from ***Laughing Time: Nonsense Poems*** **170** Anonymous limerick **170**	Applying creative and interpretive thinking **146, 149-150, 152, 162, 164, 171, 172** Drawing conclusions and making inferences **146, 162** Identifying character traits, conflicts, and sources of suspense in a folk tale **146, 162** Analyzing setting **146-162** Analyzing setting, characters, and plot **146, 162** Writing a journal entry **146** Analyzing dialogue **146** Analyzing plot **162** Analyzing the basic parts of a story **162** Analyzing a limerick **171** Reading about a sports hero **173**	Brainstorming story ideas **150** Imagining characters and setting **150, 152, 164** Analyzing causes and effects in the plot of a story **154** Planning a story **155, 164** Making a plot map **155** Using description and dialogue **158** Writing the first draft of a story **164** Evaluating and revising a draft of a story **168** Analyzing a writer's revisions **168** Proofreading and publishing a story **169** Writing a limerick **171** Writing a skit **172** Writing a sports story **172-173**	Using verb tenses correctly **169** Proofreading for errors in grammar, usage, and mechanics **169** Identifying stressed syllables in a limerick **171**	Brainstorming details in story starters **149** Sharing and comparing information with others **154, 168** Making a plot map **155** Working with a group to rewrite a passage **158** Reading aloud and listening to others read aloud **158, 168** Working with a classmate to analyze a short story **162, 168** Reading a limerick aloud **171** Listening to identify stressed syllables in a limerick **171** Listening to identify the rhythm of a limerick **171**

CHAPTER 5

SEGMENT PLANNING GUIDE

You can use the following Planning Guide to adapt the chapter material to the individual needs of your class. All the Resources listed in this chapter are located in the *Teacher's ResourceBank™*.

	SEGMENT	PAGES	CONTENT	RESOURCES
1	***Imagining Other Worlds***	***143-146***		
	Literary Model from **"Brer Billy Goat Tricks Brer Wolf"**	144-146	Guided reading: a model of creative writing	
	Reader's Response/ Writer's Craft	146	Model evaluation: responding to literature and analyzing literary writing	
2	***Ways to Write Creatively***	***147***		
3	***Prewriting***	***148-155***		Writing a Story Finding a Story Idea 40 Imagining Characters 41 Imagining Setting 42 Planning a Plot 43
	Finding a Story Idea	148	Introduction: imagining characters and problems	
	Starting with People	148	Guidelines: imagining characters	
	Starting with Problems	149	Guidelines: imagining plot	
	Exercise 1	149-150	Cooperative learning: brainstorming ideas from story starters	
	Writing Assignment: Part 1	150	Applied practice: brainstorming for a story idea	
	Planning Your Story	151	Introduction: developing characters, setting, and plot	
	Thinking About Purpose and Audience	151	Guidelines: writing for a specific audience	
	Imagining Characters	151	Guidelines: using criteria for lively characters	
	Imagining Setting	151	Guidelines: using criteria to plan a setting	
	Writing Assignment: Part 2	152	Applied practice: writing a description of characters and setting	
	Exploring Your Plot	153	Guidelines: using criteria to plan a plot map	
	Critical Thinking: Analyzing Causes and Effects	154	Explanation: learning causes and effects in a plot	
	Critical Thinking Exercise	154-155	Cooperative learning: creating a cause-and-effect chain	
	Writing Assignment: Part 3	155	Applied practice: making a plot map	
4	***Writing***	***156-164***		Writing a Story 44
	Writing Your First Draft	156	Introduction: writing a story	
	Combining the Basic Parts of a Story	156-157	Guidelines: analyzing the elements of a story	
	Exercise 2	158	Cooperative learning: adding description and dialogue to passages	
	Looking at a Short Story	158	Introduction: examining a short story	

For **Portfolio Assessment** see the following pages in the *Teacher's ResourceBank*™:
Aims For Writing—pp. 39–47
Holistically Graded Composition Models—pp. 391–396
Assessment Portfolio—pp. 421–445

SEGMENT	PAGES	CONTENT	RESOURCES
Literary Model **"Zoo"**	158-162	Guided reading: examining a short story	
Exercise 3	162	Cooperative learning: analyzing the parts of a short story	
Using a Story Framework	162	Introduction: examining structure in a model	
Writer's Model	163-164	Guided reading: examining a sample short story	
Writing Assignment: Part 4	164	Applied practice: writing a first draft	
5 ***Evaluating and Revising***	***165-168***		Writing a Story 45
Evaluating and Revising	165	Introduction: improving a first draft	
Writing Note	165	Writing suggestion: creating a title	
Chart: Evaluating and Revising Short Stories	166	Guidelines: applying evaluation and revision techniques	
Grammar Hint	167	Writing suggestion: using verb tenses	
Exercise 4	168	Cooperative learning: analyzing a writer's revisions	
Writing Assignment: Part 5	168	Cooperative learning: evaluating and revising	
6 ***Proofreading and Publishing***	***169***		Writing a Story 46
Publishing	169	Publishing ideas: reaching an audience	
Writing Assignment: Part 6	169	Applied practice: proofreading and publishing	
7 ***Writing Workshop***	***170-171***		
A Limerick	170	Explanation: examining a limerick	
Literary Model/Questions from ***Laughing Time: Nonsense Poems***	170	Guided reading: examining a limerick	
Writing a Limerick	171	Applied practice: applying skills to the writing process	
8 ***Making Connections***	***172-173***		
Writing a Skit	172	Guidelines: using criteria for skit writing Cooperative learning: writing and presenting a skit based on a folk tale	
Writing Across the Curriculum: Writing Sports Stories	172-173	Guidelines: using criteria for nonfiction writing Applied practice: writing a nonfiction story	
WHOLE-CHAPTER RESOURCE A Writing Process Log, A Writing Prompt, Holistically Graded Models, Portfolio Assessment Materials			

SEGMENT 1 *(pp. 142–146)*

IMAGINING OTHER WORLDS

OBJECTIVE

- To analyze the characters, plot, and sources of suspense in a folk tale
- To write personal responses to literature

TEACHING THE LESSON

Julius Lester's retelling of Joel Chandler Harris's folktale **"Brer Billy Goat Tricks Brer Wolf"** is relatively simple, and students should have little trouble understanding what happens in the story.

Much of this story's charm lies in the language, and a good oral reading can be a memorable experience for students. For

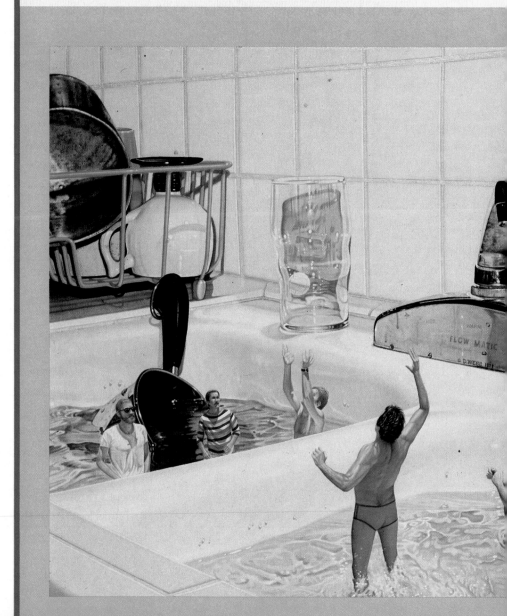

5 CREATIVE WRITING

VISUAL CONNECTIONS
Kitchenetic Energy

About the Artist. Doug Webb is a surrealist painter who follows many of the traditions of the surrealist movement. Surreal art usually combines a realistic painting style with imaginary subject matter, resulting in a dreamlike effect. Webb rearranges size and context in his paintings, and he often uses commonplace settings for his uncommon scenes.

Ideas for Writing. Have students work as a class to tell a funny story, each student taking a turn and adding a sentence or two. Then have each student evaluate, revise, proofread, and publish a copy of the class story independently. Have several volunteers read their final drafts aloud. Point out that the evaluating and revising stage of the writing process often requires as much creative thinking as the prewriting and writing stages.

Related Expression Skills. To help students think creatively, have them work in small groups to make surreal collages. Remind students that they can play with size, color, and context to achieve the surreal effect.

this reason, you may want to read the story aloud. If you have students read it aloud, work with the readers to help them get the rhythms and pronunciations right.

GUIDED PRACTICE

You can use the **Reader's Response** questions and question 3 in **Writer's Craft** for guided practice. For question 1, make a chart on the chalkboard with columns for Brer Billy Goat and Brer Wolf. Ask the students to consider both characters and

Imagining Other Worlds

Quick! Think of the perfect world. Would rutabaga be the national vegetable? Or would stuffed animals do chores for their owners? You've just **imagined another world.**

Writing and You. That's what writers of stories, poems, plays, and TV shows do. They create other worlds with their imaginations. Their worlds may be happy—like the Cosby family's warm world. Or they may be scary—like Frankenstein's creepy world.

But all writers try to make the people, places, and events of their worlds seem real. Have you noticed that an imaginary world can even help explain the real world?

As You Read. The world in the following African American folk tale is make-believe. But it seems real, too. What could the folk tale explain about life?

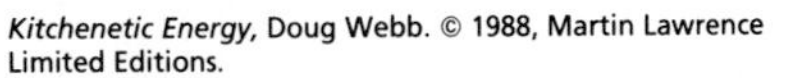

Kitchenetic Energy, Doug Webb. © 1988, Martin Lawrence Limited Editions.

QUOTATION FOR THE DAY

"I've found a good place to start in the search for ideas is with your own interests and enthusiasms." (James Cross Giblin, 1933– , American editor and nonfiction writer)

Have students make lists of their interests. Remind them that writing about things they know and care about will be easier than writing about something they have no interest in. You may want to lead a class discussion on why this is so.

AFRICAN AMERICAN

Brer Billy Goat and Brer Wolf are among the many characters that have come to us from the oral tradition of African Americans. Joel Chandler Harris (1848–1908) became acquainted with African American slaves when he worked for a plantation owner in Georgia. He listened to the wonderful tales that the slaves told and learned the language of the story teller and the customs that the stories preserved. Harris recorded many of these tales in his Uncle Remus stories, keeping alive the language of the African American dialect.

to suggest details of both characters' personalities for you to write in the proper column.

INDEPENDENT PRACTICE

Writer's Craft questions 4 and 5 should provide sufficient independent practice. These questions will force students to reread the story, and this should aid their comprehension.

USING THE SELECTION

Brer Billy Goat Tricks Brer Wolf

1

Brer Wolf was hungry.

2

condominium: an apartment building in which the apartments are owned by the tenants

Brer Billy Goat *Tricks* Brer Wolf

as told by Julius Lester

1 rer Wolf was going along the road one day and Ol' Man Hungriness was on him. Brer Wolf made up his mind that the first thing he saw, he was going to eat it, regardless.

No sooner was the thought thunk than Brer Wolf rounded a bend and there was Brer Billy Goat standing on top of a rock. This was not one of your little rocks. This rock was as big and broad as a house, and Brer Billy Goat was standing on the top like he owned it
2 and was thinking about turning it into a condominium.

Brer Wolf didn't care about none of that. He charged up the rock to find out what goat meat tasted like.

Brer Billy Goat didn't pay him no mind. He put his head down and went to acting like he was chewing on

"Brer Wolf made up his mind that the first thing he saw, he was going to eat it, regardless."

ASSESSMENT

Your students' answers to the questions in the exercises at the end of the story should give you a good idea of how well they understand the story and of how well students are able to analyze the characters and the plot of the folktale.

RETEACHING

If you had your students read the story silently, you can try reading it to them with appropriate expression to enhance their comprehension. If you read it to them in the first place, have them read it silently and then discuss the questions at the end with them.

something. Brer Wolf stopped. He stared at Brer Billy Goat, trying to figure out what he was eating. Brer Billy kept on chewing.

Brer Wolf looked and looked.

Brer Billy Goat chewed and chewed.

Brer Wolf looked close. He didn't see no grass. He didn't see no corn shucks. He didn't see no straw and he didn't see no leaves.

Brer Billy Goat chewed and chewed.

Brer Wolf couldn't figure out to save his life what Brer Billy Goat was eating. Didn't nothing grow on a rock like that. Finally Brer Wolf couldn't stand it any more.

"How do, Brer Billy Goat? I hope everything is going well with you these days."

Brer Billy Goat nodded and kept on chewing.

"What you eating, Brer Billy Goat? Looks like it tastes mighty good."

Brer Billy Goat looked up. "What does it look like I'm eating? I'm eating this rock."

Brer Wolf said, "Well, I'm powerful hungry myself, but I don't reckon I can eat rock."

CLOSURE

Have the students write a list of main characters for the story [Brer Wolf and Brer Billy Goat] and a plot summary [Brer Billy Goat fools Brer Wolf and keeps himself from being eaten].

ENRICHMENT

If your students liked **"Brer Billy Goat Tricks Brer Wolf,"** you may want to introduce them to some of the other tales of Joel Chandler Harris. His *Uncle Remus, His Songs and His Sayings* is a famous collection. ■

3

Goats are ruminants. That means they can rechew what they eat after they have swallowed it. The cud is what the food is called when it is rechewed.

ANSWERS

Reader's Response

Responses will vary.

1. Students will probably say the two characters do remind them of real people because they have human personality traits. Words that students might use to describe Brer Wolf include *hungry, mean,* and *scary;* words to describe Brer Billy Goat may include *tricky, smart,* and *brave.*
2. Journal entries will vary.

Writer's Craft

3. Brer Wolf is hungry and wants to eat Brer Billy Goat. Brer Billy Goat does not want to be eaten.
4. The rock was "big and broad as a house."
5. One possibility is Brer Billy Goat's offer to break off a piece of the rock for Brer Wolf to eat.

SELECTION AMENDMENT
Description of change: excerpted
Rationale: to focus on the concept of characterization presented in this chapter

"Come on. I'll break you off a chunk with my horns. There's enough here for you, if you hurry."

Brer Wolf shook his head and started backing away. He figured that if Brer Billy Goat could eat rock, he was a tougher man than Brer Wolf was. "Much obliged, Brer Billy Goat. But I got to be moving along."

"Don't go, Brer Wolf. This rock is fresh. Ain't no better rock in these parts."

Brer Wolf didn't even bother to answer but just kept on going. Any creature that could eat rock could eat wolf too.

Of course, Brer Billy Goat wasn't eating that rock. He
3 was just chewing his cud and talking big.

You know something? There're a lot of people like that.

READER'S RESPONSE

1. Do Brer Wolf and Brer Billy Goat remind you of real people? Why? What words would you use to describe them?
2. Brer Billy Goat was "talking big" to save himself from Brer Wolf. Can you think of a time when you saw someone talking big? How did it turn out? In your journal, write about what happened.

WRITER'S CRAFT

3. In most stories, a problem makes the characters act. What is the problem in this story?
4. The place where Brer Billy Goat is standing is very important to the story. What details describe this place?
5. What do you think was the most convincing thing Brer Billy Goat said to fool Brer Wolf?

SEGMENT 2 *(p. 147)*

WAYS TO WRITE CREATIVELY

TEACHING THE MODES

Have students develop other examples of the kinds of writing that fit under each mode. To provide guided practice, develop these examples orally with the whole class by writing the material on the chalkboard. For independent practice, let students work alone or in small groups. How well students' examples fit the modes should tell you how well students understood the modes. Have the class recite the modes at the end of the discussion. ■

Ways to Write Creatively

In this chapter, you'll write a story and a poem, two types of creative writing. Creative writing always starts with imagination, but it can have many different forms. Writers create plays, song lyrics, movie scripts, and fairy tales. They use words in many different ways—like musicians playing different instruments. Here are some ways writers use words and imagination to write creatively.

Narration: in a movie script, telling what happens to a child who gets separated from her parents at an amusement park; telling a story about a boy who trains his dogs for a dog-sled race in Alaska.

Description: writing a poem showing how a kitten's fur looks and feels; in a story about summer camp, describing the inside of the cabins.

Classification: in a song, showing how a father and son are different; in a poem, comparing fog to "little cat feet."

Evaluation: in a play, showing how hard work leads to an athlete's victory; in a poem, judging what makes a good friend.

LOOKING AHEAD

In the main assignment in this chapter, you'll use the strategy of narration to create a story. As you think and write, keep in mind that a good short story

- entertains the reader
- includes a problem, or conflict
- presents lifelike characters, clearly described places, and interesting events

INTEGRATING THE LANGUAGE ARTS

Vocabulary Link. You can help students remember what each of the modes means by giving students words students can associate with each term. For example, explain that *narration* implies a person who tells a story, *description* requires the writer to describe something, and *classification* involves putting things into classes. Finally, *evaluation* tells the value of something.

Classification may present problems. Explain that when someone shows how a father and son are different, the person shows how the father and son belong to different categories.

A DIFFERENT APPROACH

If you're using this chapter as a follow-up to a literature unit, ask your students to go review the literature they've studied to assign each work to one of the modes. Some works may contain elements of more than one mode. For example, a short story is primarily narrative, but it may contain elements of description. In addition, the story's theme may be related to the evaluation mode.

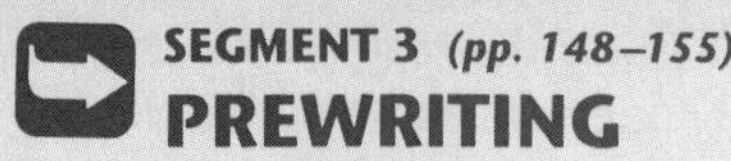

SEGMENT 3 *(pp. 148–155)*

PREWRITING

OBJECTIVES

- To find story ideas based on a character or a problem given in the text
- To find an idea for an original story
- To invent characters and a setting for an original story
- To create a plot map for an original story

Teacher's ResourceBank™

RESOURCES

PREWRITING

• Finding a Story Idea	40
• Imagining Characters	41
• Imagining Setting	42
• Planning a Plot	43

QUOTATION FOR THE DAY

"Through trial and error, I evolved something of a system that has helped me. The key phrase is *know your people.* Do a biography of them before you begin to write your story." (Mary Higgins Clark, 1929– , American novelist)

Have students follow Clark's advice by having them develop several short biographies of possible characters for their stories. Biographies should include things like age, place of birth, number of siblings, occupations, interests, and so on.

Writing a Story

Prewriting

Finding a Story Idea

Have you ever seen two kids whispering to each other and imagined what they were saying? Maybe they're deciding where to bury a treasure. What about seeing a car stranded with a flat tire? You might imagine it's Michael Jordan—on his way to a big Bulls game! Will he make it in time?

These are great starting ideas for stories. And how did you get them? Just notice any person or problem. Then let your imagination take off.

Starting with People. Think about people you see on the news, read about in the newspaper, or see on the street. Imagine them as ***characters*** in a story. What problems might they have? You see an article about your town's mayor and imagine that she's being held hostage by a creature from another planet. You notice the big ring on your next-door neighbor's finger and imagine that it suddenly disappears.

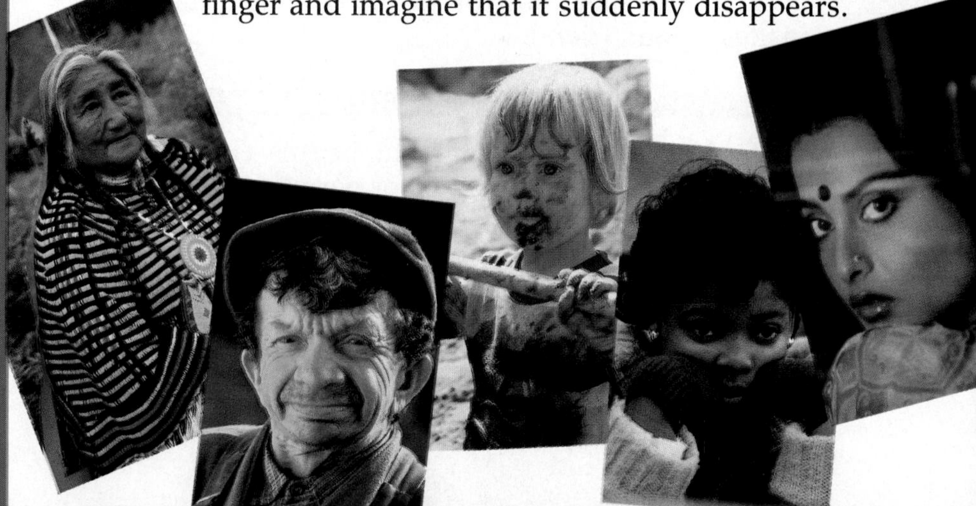

TEACHING THE LESSON

This segment is divided into three sections of approximately equal length, and you may want to spend all or part of a class period on each section. The first section involves finding story ideas, and it culminates in the first part of the writing assignment when students are asked to find ideas for their own stories. **Exercise 1** is designed as a warm-up activity for **Writing Assignment: Part 1,** so you may want to assign **Exercise 1** as a classroom activity and the first part of the writing assignment as additional work for the same period or as homework. The second and third sections deal with planning a story and outlining a plot, respectively.

Starting with Problems. Listen to friends, family, or people on the news talk about ***problems.*** Are you curious about how the problems might turn out? One of your friends has to move to another state, and you imagine a teenager having trouble making friends. You read about a two-year-old trapped in a well and imagine a boy coming to the rescue.

EXERCISE 1 **Exploring Story Ideas**

It's time to rev up your imagination! Following are three story starters—details about a possible character or about a problem someone has. With each story starter, there is a question for you to answer about the problem or the characters. Work with a small group and brainstorm as many ideas as you want.

EXAMPLE **1. A Person**: A twelve-year-old boy who is small for his age and not very strong. **What is the problem?**

1. *Chim will be grounded if he's late getting home. He can make it if he takes the shortcut through the alley. But he's scared of the dark alley and a big mean dog.*

1. **A Person**: A teenage circus performer who has never lived outside the circus. Her parents are great acrobats with the circus.

   What is the problem?

ANSWERS

Exercise 1

Responses will vary. Here are some possibilities:

1. The girl probably has interacted with few people her own age. She may have a problem with how to dress like other teenagers, how to understand and use teenage slang, what to do if she goes to a regular school, and how to make friends with teenagers she meets in the towns the circus visits.
2. Some of the people who may be in the mall food court on a Friday night include a girl or boy who is alone, waiting for friends; a tourist who isn't familiar with the layout of the mall; and people who panic in the dark.
3. Some of the characters who might be on the camping trip include experienced campers who know just what to do in the storm, inexperienced campers who panic when the storm blows their tent away, people who aren't equipped for bad weather, and a family with small children who need to be protected from the storm.

This segment contains information on developing characters, setting, and plot, including conflicts (which the text calls problems). If you're using this chapter as a follow-up to a literature unit, your students may already be familiar with these concepts. If they aren't, the text provides ample explanation for the purpose of the chapter.

GUIDED PRACTICE

Provide guided practice on the three parts of the writing assignment by working through a few examples for each part of the assignment on the chalkboard. If this isn't enough, you can circulate to help individuals while students are working.

LEP/ESL

General Strategies. For those students with little experience with the situations given in **Exercise 1,** call their attention to the pictures that accompany the exercise and discuss each picture's content. If necessary, you can change the situations to fit students' experiences. For example, you can have them consider a teenager who must live in a foreign country and learn a new language.

ADVANCED STUDENTS

Point out that descriptions of characters should focus on the parts of the characters' appearances that are relevant to the their personalities. This means attention to detail. For example, to say that a character always wears a T-shirt doesn't tell much about the character, whereas to say a character always wears concert souvenir T-shirts might shed light on the character's personality.

2. **A Problem**: The lights suddenly go off in a noisy, crowded food court at the mall on a Friday evening.

   Who is (are) the character(s)?

3. **A Problem**: A big storm develops on a camping trip. The tent begins to leak and fall down.

   Who is (are) the character(s)?

PART 1:
Finding a Story Idea

Now you're ready to find your own story ideas. Brainstorm until you find an idea for your story. Your idea should include a problem and at least one character. Remember: You might pick up a hint of an idea from a real person or problem, but you need to use your imagination to go beyond that hint to an original story idea.

INDEPENDENT PRACTICE

The exercise and the three parts of the writing assignment should provide sufficient independent practice. The parts of the assignment provide a structured plan students can follow in creating their stories.

ASSESSMENT

You can use the work your students do in **Exercise 1** and **Writing Assignment: Parts 1, 2,** and **3** to assess how well they're able to handle the concepts in the text.

Prewriting

Planning Your Story

Now you can think about your purpose and audience and can gather material for your characters, setting, and events.

Thinking About Purpose and Audience. When you write a story, one *purpose* is to be creative. Another purpose is to entertain your *audience.* Maybe you'll write a scary story about aliens or a funny story about talking ducks. Just think about what your readers would enjoy.

Imagining Characters. You may start with an idea drawn from a real person and experience—for example, your neighbor and the ring on her finger. But how do you go from there to the characters in your story? Try to form a mental picture. Will they have black shiny hair like your friend Wen Yu? Maybe they'll dress like your favorite band. Use the following questions to bring your characters to life.

- How old is my character?
- What does she or he look like? dress like? talk like?
- How does the character act—mean? silly? brave? kind?

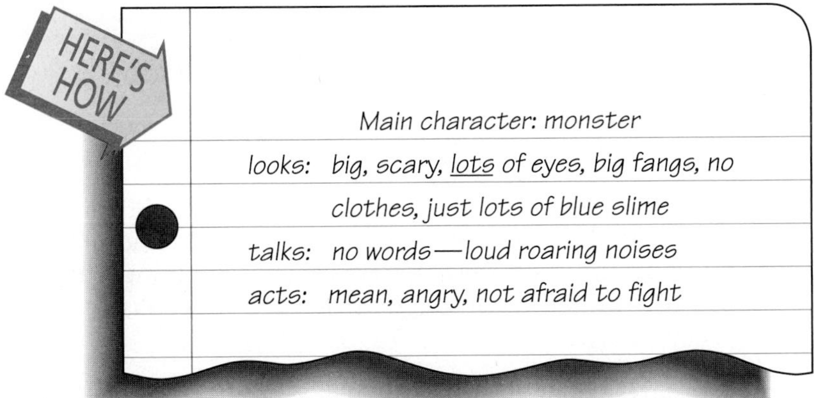

HERE'S HOW
Main character: monster
looks: big, scary, lots of eyes, big fangs, no clothes, just lots of blue slime
talks: no words—loud roaring noises
acts: mean, angry, not afraid to fight

A DIFFERENT APPROACH

You can point out to students that their story ideas don't have to be completely imaginary. Someone can develop a story idea based on something that really happened. One prewriting technique that may be helpful if they base their stories on real experiences is the "What if?" question. The answers can become their story ideas.

INTEGRATING THE LANGUAGE ARTS

Literature Link. If it is available in your library, have students read the short story "Mowgli's Brothers" by Rudyard Kipling before they consider the settings of their stories. The setting of this story contributes to the conflict of the plot and may serve as a model for your students.

RETEACHING

If your students need reteaching on one or more parts of the segment, try having them visualize real-life events that they can develop for their stories. Point out that many writers use their own experiences as the basis for their work.

CLOSURE

Ask students to name three important prewriting steps they need to do before they begin writing stories [finding story ideas, imagining characters and settings, and creating plot maps].

CRITICAL THINKING
Application

Suspense is an important part of many stories, and one way that a writer can create suspense is by using dramatic irony. Dramatic irony occurs when the reader knows something important that one or more of the characters doesn't know. For example, in a story about a monster, the narrator of the story can let the reader know that the monster is in a house without letting the character who is about to go into the house know this. The reader wonders what will happen when the character gets inside with the monster, and this creates suspense.

Imagining Setting. The place and time of your story are the ***setting.*** A setting can create a problem or a mood. Suppose your setting is a burning building with people inside. That's quite a problem! A dark cave in a storm would also create a mood of fear.

The setting doesn't always create a problem or a mood. Maybe it's as ordinary as the school ball field. But your readers will need to see the setting in their minds so they can understand your story. Use these questions to plan your setting.

- Where will my story take place—in a house or a bus? under the sea? in a city or on a farm?
- When will my story take place? at what time of day? during the spring, summer, fall, or winter?

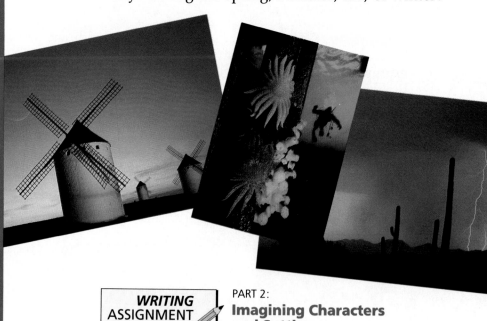

WRITING ASSIGNMENT PART 2: **Imagining Characters and Setting**

Can you close your eyes and picture your characters? How about your setting? To spark your imagination, use the questions on pages 151 and above. Write your ideas down.

ENRICHMENT

Bring some old magazines to class and let the students find pictures of people who resemble characters from their stories in the advertisements. Have them cut out the characters and paste them on poster board with brief captions of identification. ■

Exploring Your Plot. All stories have ***plots,*** and they start with a ***problem*** (sometimes called a ***conflict***). The problem sets a ***series of events*** in motion. These events happen in chronological order, with one event causing the next.

The events build in excitement or interest to the reader until they reach a ***high point.*** That's when the problem is settled, one way or another.

The part of the story that occurs after the problem is settled is called the ***outcome.*** It shows how everything works out and answers all the questions readers might have.

When you developed your original story idea, you built it around a problem. Now, all you have to do is take that problem and build the rest of your plot. To plan your plot, ask yourself these questions:

- What series of events does my problem begin?
- What happens first, second, later?
- What event will settle the problem (the high point)? How will it be settled?
- Will my readers have any questions about what happened at the end of the story? How could I answer those questions (the outcome)?

One way to plan a story is to complete a map. Here is how a writer did a map of a story about a monster.

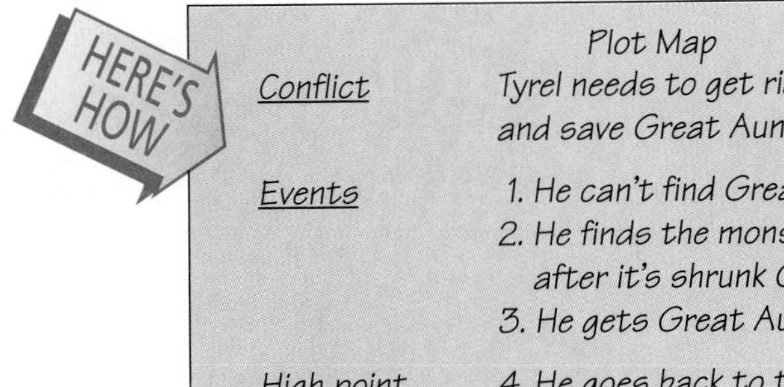

Plot Map

Conflict	*Tyrel needs to get rid of the monster and save Great Aunt Bernice.*
Events	*1. He can't find Great Aunt Bernice.* *2. He finds the monster in the kitchen after it's shrunk Great Aunt Bernice.* *3. He gets Great Aunt Bernice outside.*
High point	*4. He goes back to the monster and destroys it.*
Outcome	*5. It's a dream.*

A DIFFERENT APPROACH

You can point out to students that a plot map is like an outline. Sometimes writers get ideas as they're writing that didn't occur to them when they were making their outlines, and they change the outlines by adding the new ideas. Students should feel free to do the same thing with their plot maps. The plot maps are intended to help facilitate the writing process; they shouldn't prevent the writer from using new ideas.

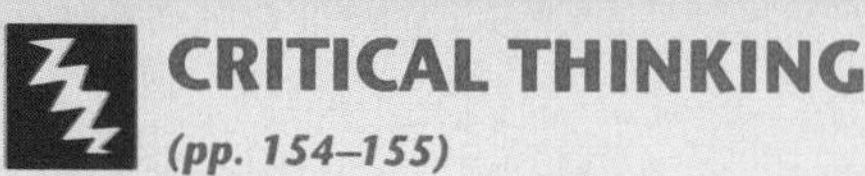

CRITICAL THINKING

(pp. 154–155)

OBJECTIVE

- To create cause-and-effect chains of events for events given in the text

TEACHING *ANALYZING CAUSES AND EFFECTS*

After students have read the material in this segment, but before they attempt the exercise, let them practice analyzing causes and effects by making a flowchart like the one in the feature for **"Brer Billy Goat Tricks Brer Wolf."** You can

LEP/ESL

General Strategies. Some students may come from cultural traditions in which magic plays an important part in storytelling. In such traditions, some events in stories don't have logical causes. You can point out that even if students may want to use magical occurrences in their stories, they should concentrate on events that cause other events—without relying on magic—when they work on the **Critical Thinking Exercise.**

To plan a good story

- use your imagination to develop your characters
- imagine a setting that creates a problem or a mood, or that helps your readers understand the story
- explore the conflict or problem and map out a series of events, a high point, and an outcome

CRITICAL THINKING

Analyzing Causes and Effects

When you analyze causes and effects, think about how one thing leads to another. In a story one event should cause another event. If something happens without an obvious cause, the story seems fake. Have you ever seen a movie where the hero crawls out of a flooding river and then pulls a dry match out of his pocket to light a fire? How did he happen to have that dry match? To write a good story, you have to connect effects with causes.

CRITICAL THINKING EXERCISE:
Analyzing Causes and Effects

Figure out causes and effects with a little help from your imagination. Look at the following example and notice how it begins with one event that causes a chain of events. After studying the example, get together with a partner and create a cause-and-effect chain for the three events listed below the example. Then compare your chains with those of other students. Is there an obvious cause for every effect?

create this flowchart on the chalkboard with the whole class. [The basic ingredients include Brer Wolf gets hungry, and he confronts Brer Billy Goat. Brer Billy Goat pretends to be eating the rock, and Brer Wolf leaves Brer Billy Goat alone.]

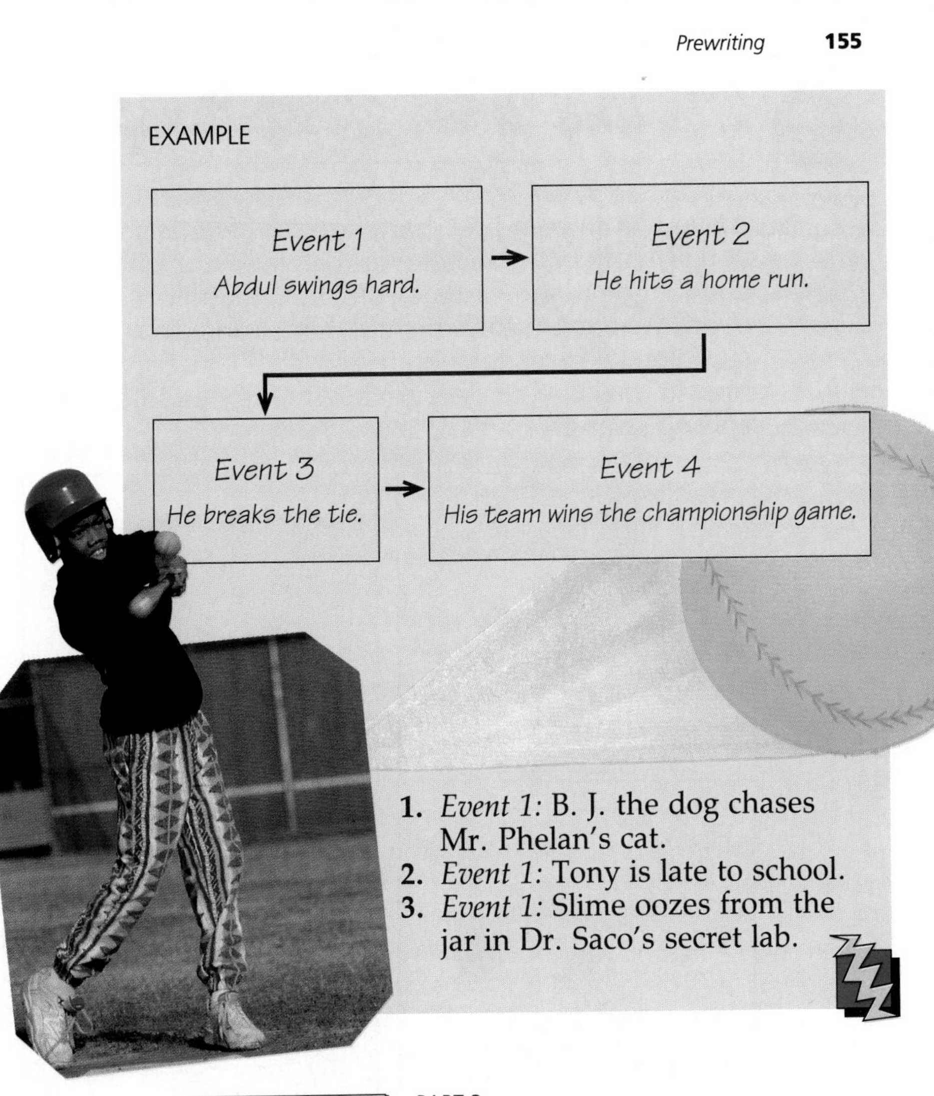

1. *Event 1:* B. J. the dog chases Mr. Phelan's cat.
2. *Event 1:* Tony is late to school.
3. *Event 1:* Slime oozes from the jar in Dr. Saco's secret lab.

WRITING ASSIGNMENT

PART 3:
Planning Your Story

Gather together the main events for your story. Then make your own plot map just like the one on page 153. Put this map together with the notes you made about your characters and setting in Writing Assignment, Part 2 (page 152). That's it—you have a good plan for your story!

ANSWERS

Critical Thinking Exercise

Responses will vary. Here are some possibilities:

1. Event 1: B. J. the dog chases Mr. Phelan's cat.
   Event 2: Mr. Phelan's cat runs up a tree.
   Event 3: Mr. Phelan complains to B. J. the dog 's owner.
   Event 4: B. J. the dog has to wear a leash.
2. Event 1: Tony is late for school.
   Event 2: He misses a history test.
   Event 3: His grades go down.
   Event 4: His parents make him go to bed one hour earlier.
3. Event 1: Slime oozes from the jar in Dr. Saco's secret lab.
   Event 2: The slime gets on Dr. Saco's hands.
   Event 3: Dr. Saco's hands begin to glow in the dark.
   Event 4: People think Dr. Saco is a monster.

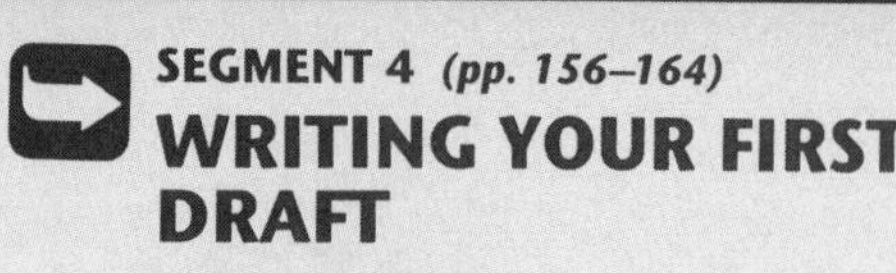

SEGMENT 4 *(pp. 156–164)*

WRITING YOUR FIRST DRAFT

OBJECTIVES

- To use description and dialogue to rewrite story situations
- To analyze the parts of a short story
- To write the first draft of a short story

Teacher's ResourceBank™

RESOURCES

WRITING YOUR FIRST DRAFT

- Writing a Story 44

QUOTATION FOR THE DAY

"While I am writing, I am listening to the story; I am not listening to myself." (Madeleine L'Engle, 1918– , American novelist)

Lead a class discussion on why listening to oneself while writing might not be a good idea. [One of the most important things in writing a first draft is to get the whole story down on paper. Listening to oneself instead of the story might be distracting and interrupt the flow of the story.]

Writing Your First Draft

As you write your first draft, you may feel as if part of you is living in the secret world of your story. That's a good sign. It shows that your imagination is taking over. Wherever your imagination leads you, make sure you keep readers interested. Following are some tips to make your story's beginning, middle, and ending strong.

Combining the Basic Parts of a Story

Beginning. Get your reader hooked right away. Introduce the conflict early, so the reader wants to find out what happens. Gabriella loses her sister Elena's new bracelet. Can she find it before Elena misses it?

TEACHING THE LESSON

This is a fairly long segment, so you may want to devote more than one day to it in class. On the first day have your students read the introductory material to prepare them to work **Exercise 2.** Because **Exercise 2** requires group work, you'll probably want your students to work on this exercise in class.

The second part of the segment consists of the short story **"Zoo"** by Edward D. Hoch and **Exercise 3.** You can have your students read the story for homework or in class and then have them work in pairs on the exercise. The last part of the segment leads up to the assignment to write a draft of an original story.

Middle. Use *suspense* to keep your readers wondering what will happen next. Elena says she can't wait to show her bracelet to a friend. How will Gabriella stall Elena?

Also keep events and characters lively with these two techniques:

- **Use description.** Don't just say, "Gabriella acted nervous." Does she jump up from the table and talk in a loud voice? Is her face red? Remember to *show*, not tell, your readers what's happening.
- **Use dialogue.** The words a character uses add life, too. "Gabriella tried to stop her sister" is pretty dull. See how much better this dialogue is: "Wait, wait!" she shouted. "You can't, I mean, don't get the bracelet. Not yet, OK? Have more spinach!" Try to make dialogue sound natural, as people actually talk. You can use short phrases, contractions, and slang.

REFERENCE NOTE: For help in punctuating dialogue, see pages 615–621.

Ending. Solve your conflict, and tie up any loose ends. Make the outcome believable. If Gabriella finds the bracelet before Elena discovers it's missing, the conflict is over. But have you explained how and where Gabriella found it? Be sure to satisfy your readers' curiosity.

LEP/ESL

General Strategies. One way you can help students cope with writing the first drafts of their short stories is to allow them to write the drafts in their native languages. In the drafting stage of the writing process, students should try to get something on paper quickly so they will have something to work with later when they revise. Trying to write the drafts in English may slow some students down and force them to limit their word choices to what may be a rather limited English vocabulary. After they've drafted their stories, they can rewrite the stories in English during the rest of the writing process.

LEARNING STYLES

Visual Learners. Some visual learners may have trouble writing dialogue that sounds natural. You can suggest that any students with this problem read dialogue out loud to another student in the tone of voice he or she imagines the characters would use. If the lines don't sound natural to the other student, or if they seem out of character, the student who wrote them can work on them until they sound like natural speech.

Some of your students may have trouble getting started on their drafts, even after they've done all the prewriting activities. The drafts will be revised later, so you can suggest students start with the traditional "Once upon a time . . . " opening. Later, after they've written the drafts, they can find more-interesting openings. You can also point out that many short stories start with a description of the setting. This is true of **"Zoo"** and of the student model in this segment.

ANSWERS

Exercise 2

Answers may vary. The description in the rewrites should be clear and should help readers develop a mental image of the characters, setting, and events. The dialogue should sound natural, and it should reveal the personalities of the characters.

TIMESAVER

You can save time grading **Exercise 2** by moving from group to group as students are reading their rewritten story situations. You can assess how well they are able to use description and dialogue on the basis of their reading.

EXERCISE 2 **Speaking and Listening: Using Description and Dialogue**

Working with a group, rewrite the following passages. Use description and dialogue to make them come alive. Working with another group, take turns reading your passages aloud. What are your favorite parts?

1. Angela's mother told her to get off the phone. Angela ignored her and kept talking. Then her mother got mad.
2. The coach called Deven off the bench as relief pitcher. The other players shouted support as he ran to the mound. Deven felt nervous.

Looking at a Short Story

No two stories are exactly the same. Writers use characters, setting, and plot in many different ways. The following science fiction story begins with a description of the setting. It also starts off with strong suspense. Can you guess the ending as you read?

A SHORT STORY

Zoo

by Edward D. Hoch

BEGINNING

Setting

Main character

The children were always good during the month of August. This was especially so when it began to get near the twenty-third. For every year on the twenty-third of August, Professor Hugo's Interplanetary Zoo came to the Chicago area. The great silver spaceship would settle down in a huge parking area. It would remain there during its annual six-hour visit.

GUIDED PRACTICE

You can provide guided practice for **Exercise 2** by using the story situation given in the first item and working through it with students. For **Exercise 3,** answer the first two questions with the students in an open discussion. For **Writing Assignment: Part 4,** you may want to provide students with copies of a first draft of a short story you have written.

Suspense

Characters

MIDDLE
Event 1

Setting

Description

Long before daybreak large crowds would gather. Lines of children and adults, each one clutching his or her dollar, would wait restlessly to see the Professor's Interplanetary Zoo. Everyone was eager to see
1 what race of strange creatures the Professor had brought this year.

In the past they had been treated to three-legged creatures from Venus. Or tall, thin men from Mars. Or snake-like horrors from some even more distant planet.

This year, as the large silver spaceship settled down to earth in the huge parking area just outside of Chicago, the children watched with awe. They saw the sides of the spaceship slide up to reveal the usual cages made of thick bars. Inside the cages were some wild, small, horse-like animals that moved with quick, uneven motions and kept chattering in a high-pitched tone.

Description

The citizens of Earth clustered around as Professor Hugo's crew quickly collected a dollar from everyone in the audience. Soon the good Professor, himself, made an appearance. He was wearing his many-colored cape and top hat.

USING THE SELECTION
"Zoo"

1
What does the word *race* imply about the creatures in the zoo? [It implies that the creatures aren't earth animals (perhaps not animals of any kind) and that the creatures may be the inhabitants of another planet.]

INDEPENDENT PRACTICE

You can let students work on the exercises for independent practice. Even if you use item 1 of **Exercise 2** for guided practice, you can have students do this item again with their own ideas. Assign the last two questions of **Exercise 3** as independent practice. Students will also get ample independent practice writing their drafts.

2
Why does Professor Hugo say *peoples* instead of *people?* [Professor Hugo is referring to all of the races and ethnic groups on earth. A "people" in his sense of the word is a distinct group.]

3
Kaan: a fictional planet

Dialogue

2 "Peoples of Earth," he called into his microphone.

The crowd's noise died down and he continued. "Peoples of Earth," he went on, "this year we have a real treat for your dollar. Here are the little-known horse-spider
3 people of Kaan—brought to you across a million miles of space at great expense. Gather around the amazing horse-spider people of Kaan. See them, study them, listen to them. Tell your friends about them. But hurry! My spaceship can remain here for only six hours!"

Conflict/ Suspense

Event 2

And the crowds slowly filed by, horrified and fascinated by these strange creatures that looked like horses, but ran up the walls of their cages like spiders. "This is certainly worth a dollar," one man remarked. "I'm going home to tell my wife."

Dialogue

All day long it went like that. Finally, ten thousand people had filed by the barred cages which were built into the side of the spaceship. Then, as the six-hour time limit ran out, Professor Hugo once more took the microphone in his hand.

Event 3

Dialogue

"We must go now," said the Professor, "but we will return again next year on this date. And if you enjoyed Professor Hugo's Interplanetary Zoo this year, phone your friends in other cities. Tell them about it. We will land in New York tomorrow. Next week we go on to London, Paris, Rome, Hong Kong, and Tokyo. Then we must leave for other worlds!"

He waved farewell to them. And, as the ship rose from the ground, the Earth peoples agreed that this had been the very best Zoo yet. . . .

ASSESSMENT

Students' answers to the questions in the two exercises can serve as a basis for assessment of how well students are able to rewrite story situations by using description and dialogue and of how well they can analyze a short story.

To assess students' first drafts, determine if they have followed the framework suggested by the models. Each draft should include a setting, characters, a problem or conflict, a high point or climax, and a resolution of the conflict.

ENDING
Event 4
Setting

Two months and three planets later, the silver spaceship of Professor Hugo settled at last onto the familiar jagged rocks of Kaan. The horse-spider creatures filed quickly out of their cages. Professor Hugo was there to say a few parting words to them. Then the horse-spider creatures

Description

scurried away in a hundred different directions as they began seeking their homes among the rocks.

Event 5

4 In one, the she-creature was happy to see the return of her mate and little one. She babbled a greeting in the strange Kaan language. Then she hurried to embrace

Dialogue/ Suspense

them. "You were gone a long time," she said. "Was it good?"

The he-creature nodded. "Our little one enjoyed it especially," he said. "We visited eight worlds and saw many things."

Description/ Dialogue

The little one ran up the wall of the cave. "The place called Earth was the best.

4
she-creature: a female horse-spider

RETEACHING

Try giving students a model of how a story situation can be rewritten. To do this, select a brief story and write a story situation based on it. Then show the students the original story and point out the differences between it and the story situation. You can reteach draft writing by pointing out to students where their stories deviate from the framework offered by the models and by suggesting how improvements can be made.

Conflict
High point

The creatures there wear garments over their skins, and they walk on two legs."

"But isn't it dangerous?" asked the she-creature.

"No," the he-creature answered. "There are bars to protect us from them. We stay right in the ship. Next time you must come with us. It is well worth the nineteen commocs it costs."

Outcome/Surprise Ending

5 The little one nodded. "It was the very best Zoo ever. . . ."

EXERCISE 3 **Analyzing the Parts of the Short Story**

Think about the parts of "Zoo." Then, with a partner, answer the following questions.

1. Do you like this story? What is your favorite part of the story?
2. Is the setting of the story important? Why or why not?
3. Who are the characters in the story?
4. "Zoo" is unusual because there is a small conflict—whether everyone in line can see the horse-spider people—that is solved pretty easily. But then, POW! A surprise ending makes you see the events in a different way. What do you learn at the end?

Using a Story Framework

"Zoo" is filled with odd characters, strong descriptions, and a funny surprise ending. Your own story may not be as long and tricky, but it can be just as entertaining. Read the following Writer's Model and notice how the writer gets right to the conflict. Does the beginning make you curious? Does it make you want to keep on reading?

5
Why is the ending a surprise? [The Earth people thought the horse-spiders were a curiosity, but the horse-spider creatures thought the same thing about the people. Instead of considering themselves exhibits in a zoo, the horse-spiders thought of themselves as visiting a zoo.]

ANSWERS

Exercise 3

1. Answers may vary. Most students will like the story; many will consider the last paragraph their favorite part.
2. The parking lot setting isn't that important, but the silver spaceship is. The spaceship establishes the story as science fiction. The setting on Kaan at the end is important because it shows that the horse-spider creatures are intelligent visitors from space.
3. The characters are Professor Hugo, the people who visit the Interplanetary Zoo, and the she-creature, he-creature and young horse-spider creature from Kaan.
4. At the story's end the reader learns that the horse-spider creatures were on an adventure to see creatures in the zoos on other planets. This suggests that people on Earth are just as strange to creatures from space as these creatures are to Earth people.

CLOSURE

Ask students to recite the three parts of a story [beginning, middle, and ending]. ■

A WRITER'S MODEL

Soap to the Rescue

BEGINNING
Characters/ Setting
Event 1

After school Tyrel went to his Great Aunt Bernice's house. He went there every Tuesday to see if she needed anything. She was his favorite relative. When he knocked on the door, he heard a weird roaring noise. He opened the door and looked around. He didn't see Great Aunt Bernice anywhere. He did see tons of gigantic blue footprints.

Conflict/Suspense
Description
Event 2
Character/Description

Tyrel went down the hall and saw a huge space monster standing in the kitchen. He didn't see Great Aunt Bernice anywhere. The monster looked very fierce. It had five gigantic eyes that popped out of its head. It had two fangs sticking out of its mouth. It was covered in blue slime, and it smelled bad.

MIDDLE
Event 3
Dialogue/ Suspense

Tyrel was about to run for help. Then suddenly one of the monster's eyes shot out of its head and saw him. Tyrel said, "Yi! Yi! Yi!" He jumped into the air and zoomed to the other side of the kitchen. Suddenly he saw a little glass jar on the table. Great Aunt Bernice was inside it. She was trying to jump out of the jar.

INTEGRATING THE LANGUAGE ARTS

Reading Link. The story in the **Writer's Model** is another example of a science fiction story that has a surprise ending. Encourage your students to jot down any questions and answers that occur to them during their reading. The following questions are examples:

1. What's making the weird roaring noise Tyrel hears?
2. What could have made the gigantic blue footprints?
3. How could Great Aunt Beatrice have gotten inside the jar?
4. Why would a stinky monster be afraid of soapy water?

Event 4

Tyrel grabbed the jar and jumped out the kitchen window. He put Great Aunt Bernice on the ground. Then he ran around and went back inside the house. In science class he had learned that space monsters were scared of soap. He filled a bucket with soapy water and ran back to the kitchen.

ENDING
High point/ Description

Outcome

The monster was roaring, and blue slime was all over. Tyrel said, "Take this, Stinky!" He threw the soapy water onto the monster. It roared even louder, and all its eyes popped out. Then it shrank to the size of a bug. When Tyrel looked up, he saw Great Aunt Bernice. She was shaking him. He had dreamed the whole thing.

PART 4:
Writing Your First Draft

Now it's your turn. Use your notes and plot map to guide your writing. But don't try to stop your frisky mind. If you have new ideas for characters, setting, or plot, use them. Be creative with the outcome of your story. The model used a dream. What other kind of ending could you try?

SEGMENT 5 *(pp. 165–168)*

EVALUATING AND REVISING

OBJECTIVES

- To analyze a writer's revisions
- To evaluate and revise a draft of a short story

TEACHING THE LESSON

The five items in the **Evaluating and Revising Short Stories** chart offer guidance for students to evaluate and revise their work. You can guide their practice by working with individuals or small groups or by preparing a handout of a story and working through the items with the whole class.

Evaluating and Revising

One tough part of writing a story is over. You made it all the way through! Now you can do some finishing touches. Could you make your characters more real? your plot more exciting? By evaluating your story, you'll find spots that could be better. When you revise, you'll fix those weak spots, so your story will be really fantastic.

The chart on the next page will help you evaluate and revise. If you answer no to any of the questions in the left-hand column, try out the suggestions in the right-hand column.

Don't forget an important finishing touch to your story: the title. The title is an invitation to the reader. If it's snazzy in some way, the reader may accept the invitation and start reading. You can create an inviting title by thinking about an important character, the setting, or the plot. The writer focused on the way Tyrel destroyed the monster. Doesn't "Soap to the Rescue" make you curious about how and what soap could rescue? Try to create a title your reader can't resist.

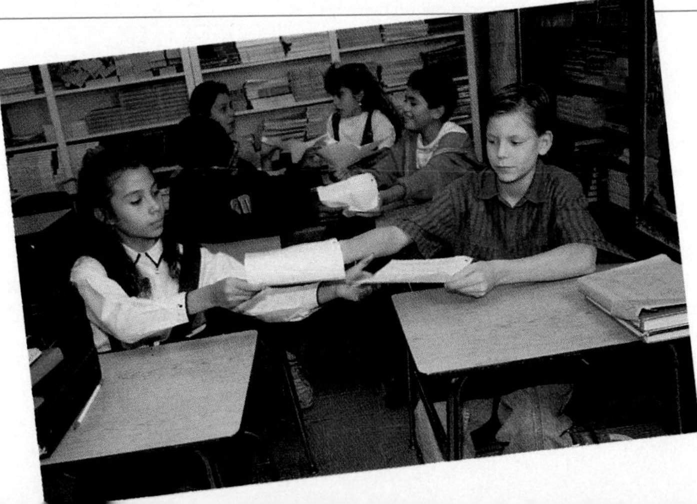

Teacher's ResourceBank™

RESOURCES

EVALUATING AND REVISING

- Writing a Story 45

QUOTATION FOR THE DAY

"Motivation makes the difference between actions seeming real or staged." (Stewart Bronfeld, 1929– , American television and nonfiction writer)

Explain to students that motivation is the reason behind a person's actions, and discuss how motivations can often be traced to basic human needs. Have students list the motivations for the actions of the characters in their stories. Explain that the evaluation and revision stage is a good place to check their characters' motivations and to improve the motivations if necessary.

You may want to let your students work on their drafts independently.

The **Grammar Hint** deals with consistency of verb tense. Use a few examples from your students' stories to illustrate this concept on the chalkboard or overhead projector. **Exercise 4** gives students an opportunity to apply evaluation skills to a piece of writing.

ASSESSMENT

You can assess how well your students revise their stories by comparing the final versions to their drafts. If you noted potential revisions on the drafts, check to see how students handled these. The key is whether the revised story is clearer, more appealing, and more suspenseful than the draft was. Also, responses to the questions

LEP/ESL

General Strategies. Students who are learning to speak and write English may need help with idioms. You can have a special workshop session in small groups to point out passages in their stories that would be expressed by idioms in English. An explanation of the idioms should help students improve their abilities to write English dialogue.

INTEGRATING THE LANGUAGE ARTS

Technology Link. Encourage students who use computers or other word processors for their writing to print hard copies of their stories before they begin revising them. Having the whole story printed out usually makes revision easier than trying to work with the small segment of the story that appears on the monitor. It's also a good idea to have hard copy available in case the text or some part of it is inadvertently erased in the computer.

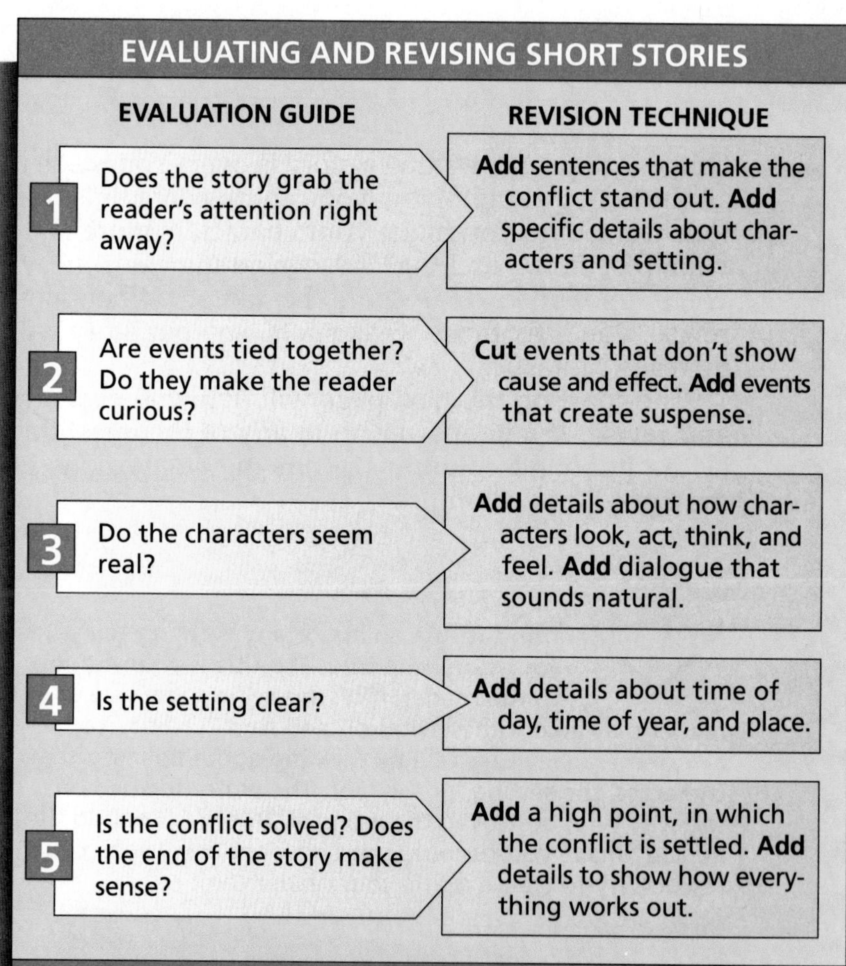

EVALUATING AND REVISING SHORT STORIES

	EVALUATION GUIDE	REVISION TECHNIQUE
1	Does the story grab the reader's attention right away?	**Add** sentences that make the conflict stand out. **Add** specific details about characters and setting.
2	Are events tied together? Do they make the reader curious?	**Cut** events that don't show cause and effect. **Add** events that create suspense.
3	Do the characters seem real?	**Add** details about how characters look, act, think, and feel. **Add** dialogue that sounds natural.
4	Is the setting clear?	**Add** details about time of day, time of year, and place.
5	Is the conflict solved? Does the end of the story make sense?	**Add** a high point, in which the conflict is settled. **Add** details to show how everything works out.

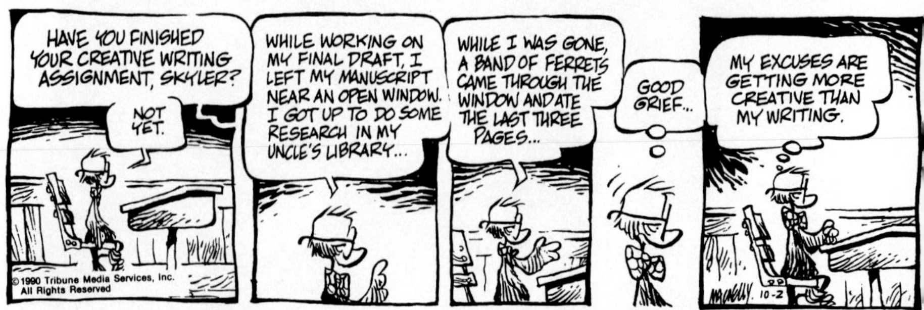

Shoe, by Jeff MacNelly, reprinted by permission: Tribune Media Services.

in **Exercise 4** should indicate students' understanding of the purpose of revision.

CLOSURE

Ask students what they can add to stories in the revision stage. [They can add specific details about characters and setting, events that create suspense, dialogue that sounds natural, details about time and place, a high point in which the conflict is settled, or details that show how everything works out.] ■

GRAMMAR HINT

Using Verb Tenses

To describe action in a story, you usually use the past tense: "They **slurped** and **burped.**" Be careful not to switch from past tense to present tense. Be consistent by using one tense. (Remember that past tense shows what has already occurred. Present tense shows what is occurring now.)

TENSES SWITCHED The monkey **threw** the coconut out of the tree. It **hits** the sand and **rolls** down to the water. The fisherman **picked** it up and **puts** it in his sack.

TENSES CONSISTENT The gigantic bug **crawled** to the door and **pushed** it open. It **knocked** over a table and **moved** toward the cat food. The cat **scrambled** out of the way.

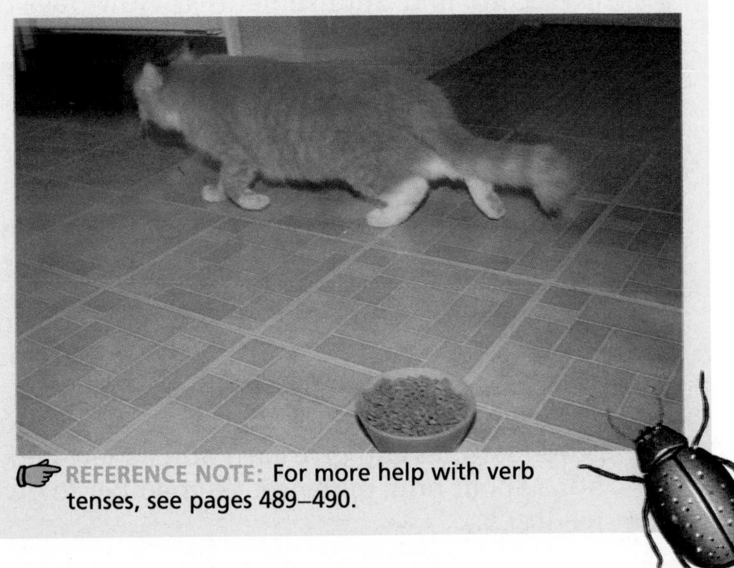

REFERENCE NOTE: For more help with verb tenses, see pages 489–490.

INTEGRATING THE LANGUAGE ARTS

Grammar Link. The material in the **Grammar Hint** may be new to many students. You may find it worthwhile to spend some time working with a few examples from students' stories in which they've failed to use a consistent tense.

ANSWERS

Exercise 4

1. The sentence was added to establish a cause-and-effect relationship between what Tyrel says and how the monster responds. This helps the story by creating suspense and by adding details about how a character acts.
2. Answers may vary, but most students will probably think the revision is a good change because it makes the monster's appearance after the soaping clearer and more vivid.

A DIFFERENT APPROACH

When your students do the analysis required in **Exercise 4,** have them match each revision to one of the revision techniques in the **Evaluating and Revising Short Stories** chart. [The first revision is related to item 2 in the chart. The added material creates a cause-and-effect relationship between what Tyrel says and how the monster responds. The second revision is related to item 3. It gives a clearer picture of how the monster looks after it's splashed with soapy water.]

EXERCISE 4 Analyzing a Writer's Revisions

Here is a draft of the last paragraph of "Soap to the Rescue." It shows the changes the writer made to revise the first draft. Working with a classmate, take turns reading the paragraph aloud. Study the writer's changes. Then answer each of the questions about the writer's revisions. Your answers may help you revise your own story.

> The monster was roaring, and blue slime was all over. Tyrel said, "Take this, Stinky!" (He threw the soapy water onto the monster.) It roared even louder, **add**
> and all its eyes popped out. Then it ~~got very small~~ (shrank to the size of a bug.). When Tyrel looked up, he **replace**
> saw Great Aunt Bernice. She was shaking him. He had dreamed the whole thing.

1. Why did the writer add a sentence between the second and third sentences? How does this help the story?
2. Do you think replacing *got very small* with *shrank to the size of a bug* is a good change? Why?

PART 5:
Evaluating and Revising Your Story

It's time to evaluate and revise your own story. Read it over carefully and use the evaluating and revising chart on page 166 to help you out. When you're finished, trade stories with a classmate. Read each other's stories and give each other a few good suggestions about how to revise. (Remember to give helpful feedback.)

SEGMENT 6 *(p. 169)*

PROOFREADING AND PUBLISHING

OBJECTIVE

- To proofread and publish a short story

TEACHING THE LESSON

Encourage students to proofread their stories for errors in grammar, usage, and mechanics.

Ask the students to recite the steps of writing a story [prewriting, writing, evaluating and revising, and proofreading and publishing]. ■

Proofreading and Publishing

Now that you've revised your story, it's time to clean it up. Are words spelled correctly? Are verb tenses consistent? Correct all the errors you can find.

Then, get together with classmates and make a list of ideas for publishing or sharing your story. Here are two ideas to get you started.

- Have a lunchtime story hour, and invite students from other classes to hear you read the stories aloud in the cafeteria.
- Make your own book and illustrate the important events in your story. When you're finished, give the book to someone special.

PART 6:
Proofreading and Publishing Your Story

Carefully go over your revised story and proofread it. Publish your story or share it with some classmates, friends, and family.

Teacher's ResourceBank™

RESOURCES

PROOFREADING AND PUBLISHING

- Writing a Story 46

QUOTATION FOR THE DAY

"Clarity is the cornerstone of effective communication—and effective communication is the foundation of good writing." (David Petersen, 1946– , American writer and editor)

Remind students that errors in grammar, usage, or mechanics can distort or obscure meaning and inhibit effective communication. You may want to have students keep lists of errors they find while proofreading.

LEP/ESL

General Strategies. Some ESL students may need individual help with proofreading. If you have already identified specific grammar, usage, and mechanics skills for students to concentrate on, you'll probably want to make sure they correct errors in these areas. If your approach has been more general, you may want to concentrate on idiomatic expressions, dialogue, and colloquial aspects of the language.

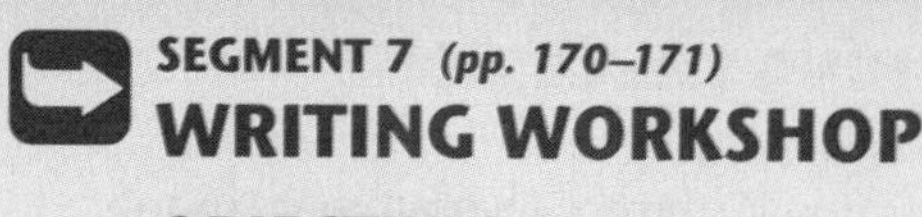

SEGMENT 7 *(pp. 170–171)*

WRITING WORKSHOP

OBJECTIVES

- To analyze a limerick
- To plan, write, evaluate, revise, proofread, and publish a limerick

TEACHING THE LESSON

You can help students learn the pattern and structure of limericks by having volunteers read some examples aloud. When they read, encourage them to emphasize the stressed syllables. The suggestions under **Prewriting** can get your students started, but they may need additional help from you or each other. You

QUOTATION FOR THE DAY

"Nine-tenths of the best poetry of the world has been written by poets less than thirty years old; a great deal more than half of it has been written by poets under twenty-five." (H. L. Mencken, 1880–1956, American author and critic)

Share the quotation with the class to encourage the young writers as they begin work on their first drafts.

SELECTION AMENDMENT

Description of change: some words and parts of words are capitalized

Rationale: to focus on the concepts of limericks and stress in poetry presented in this chapter

WRITING WORKSHOP

A Limerick

A ***limerick*** is a funny rhyming poem that tells a story. Most limericks are about characters who do very silly things, like the ones in this limerick:

> There was a Young Lady named Rose
> Who was constantly blowing her nose;
> Because of this failing
> They sent her off whaling
> So the whalers could say: "Thar she blows!"
>
> William Jay Smith, *Laughing Time: Nonsense Poems*

All limericks have five lines. The first, second, and fifth lines rhyme with each other. The third and fourth lines also rhyme with each other.

Each line in a limerick has a certain number of stresses. A ***stress*** is a strong beat—an emphasis in your voice. In the next limerick, the stresses are shown with capital letters. Read the limerick aloud. You'll hear that the first, second, and fifth lines have three stresses. The third and fourth lines have two stresses.

Many limericks are like jokes. They travel all around the world by word of mouth. Have you heard the one about the girl who threw eggs?

> There WAS a young GIRL of AsTURias,
> Whose TEMper was FRANtic and FURious.
> She USED to throw EGGS
> At her GRANDmother's LEGS—
> A HABit unPLEASant, but CURious.
>
> Anonymous

may want to handle this segment as the kind of writing workshop where students are allowed to consult with one another for ideas and help.

CLOSURE

Ask students to tell how many lines there are in a limerick [5] and which lines rhyme. [Lines 1, 2, and 5 rhyme, as do lines 3 and 4.] ■

Thinking It Over

1. What makes this limerick funny?
2. Do you know anyone who acts like this girl? Do you think that she's supposed to seem real?
3. What words rhyme at the end of lines one, two, and five?
4. What words rhyme at the end of lines three and four?

Writing a Limerick

Prewriting. Can you think of a silly character for your limerick? You might begin by finishing this line: "There once was a . . . " Brainstorm a few ideas. Then jot down notes with some funny details you want to try.

Writing, Evaluating, and Revising. Listen to the limerick rhythm a few times. Get the singsong beat in your head. Then start writing. When you've finished writing your limerick, read it to yourself aloud. Is it silly enough? Do the right words rhyme? Swap limericks with a classmate and give each other a few helpful suggestions. Revise your limerick and read it once more to make sure that it's as goofy as possible.

Proofreading and Publishing. Proofread your limerick carefully to catch mistakes. Then publish your limerick. Perhaps you can read it aloud for a class "Who Can Be Silliest?" contest.

LEP/ESL

General Strategies. Some students who aren't native English speakers, as well as some who are, may have trouble coming up with rhymes. This may be a good time to introduce students to rhyming dictionaries. Your school librarian may be able to help you find one to bring to class and have on hand as a resource for students who wish to use it.

ANSWERS

Thinking It Over

1. Responses will vary. Many students will find the absurdity of someone throwing eggs at her grandmother's legs funny.
2. Responses will vary. Students might know someone with a frantic and furious temper, but may not think this girl seems real because she throws eggs at her grandmother's legs.
3. Asturias, furious, and curious
4. eggs and legs

SEGMENT 8 *(pp. 172–173)*

MAKING CONNECTIONS

WRITING A SKIT
OBJECTIVE

- To write and perform a skit based on a folk tale

WRITING A SKIT

Teaching Strategies

Your students will be working in groups on the script for their skit, so you can have one student serve as the reader for each group. This student can read the folk tale sentence by sentence, and the other students in the group can discuss how they would like to dramatize each part. If you think the story is too long for students to use the whole piece for a skit, have groups focus on one of the scenes.

Another way to handle this assignment is to have your students create a script for Reader's Theater. This kind of script can have a narrator who fills in the part of the story that isn't contained in the dialogue and the action.

GUIDELINES

You'll probably want to emphasize creativity in your evaluation of the scripts your students create. However, the scripts should also be true to the story, contain dialogue and action, and preserve the language of the folk tale.

MAKING CONNECTIONS

WRITING A SKIT

Another good way to tell a story is to act it out. You can do that by writing a ***skit,*** or very short play. When you write a skit, you tell a story through dialogue and action.

Many folk tales and fairy tales make good skits. The folk tale gives you characters, plot, and some dialogue. With a little imagination, you can create a skit. How should the characters speak? Will they move in funny ways? Will you need scenery to show the setting?

Try writing a skit to perform for your class based on "Brer Billy Goat Tricks Brer Wolf" on pages 144–146. With other students as co-writers, read the story again. Try to picture how you could act it out. Ask yourself these questions before writing.

- Can we use all the dialogue that's in the story?
- Will we need to write more dialogue for the characters?
- What parts of the story can we show through action?

WRITING ACROSS THE CURRICULUM

Writing Sports Stories

Many of the things you learned about writing make-believe stories can be used to write stories about real people and real events. To write a true story about a real sports hero, you need to

WRITING SPORTS STORIES
OBJECTIVE

- To write a true story about a real sports hero

- show how the person walks, talks, and acts
- show how the person faces a real problem or conflict
- create suspense for the reader
- let the reader know the outcome of the story

Who is your favorite sports hero? Is it Jackie Joyner-Kersee, Muhammad Ali, Babe Ruth, or Gertrude Ederle? Think of a great athlete you admire. Then read about your sports hero in the newspaper, a book, or an encyclopedia. You might even be able to find a video about this person.

Look for a problem this person had to solve in his or her life—a childhood illness, an accident, a failure in some important contest, or a lack of confidence. Write a story showing how your hero overcame the problem. Perhaps your physical education teacher would like to read it when you're finished.

WRITING SPORTS STORIES
Teaching Strategies

Point out that the assignment in this section requires each student to write a story about a true event in a real person's life. However, students should use the same techniques, such as dialogue and suspense, that they used in writing their short stories. They will have to find sports heroes who have overcome a major problem in their careers. You may want to let groups of four or five students write about the same sports hero. These groups can discuss the problem the hero overcame, and the members can help one another decide how they should approach the assignment.

GUIDELINES

When you assess students' performance on this assignment, consider how well they were able to use fictional techniques (description, plot, suspense, dialogue, and resolution of the conflict) in their stories. Your basic question can be, "Do the stories read like fiction while presenting fact?"

Chapter 6
WRITING TO INFORM

OBJECTIVES

- To write a journal entry to generate writing ideas and to share ideas with other students
- To discuss the necessary resources and the role of chronological order in a process paper
- To brainstorm ideas for a "how-to" paper
- To choose a process to explain
- To generate a list of steps and materials necessary for a process
- To gather and organize information for a "how-to" paper
- To evaluate details in a process paper to determine whether they are necessary
- To analyze a "how-to" explanation
- To write a draft of a "how-to" paper
- To explain and follow a process by speaking and listening
- To analyze a writer's revisions
- To evaluate, revise, proofread, and publish a "how-to" paper
- To use the writing process to create a "how-to" paper that gives travel directions
- To choose a process riddle and to ask classmates to guess the answer
- To write the steps for a first-aid process and to prepare a class demonstration

Motivation

To motivate students for process writing, begin by discussing how processes affect everyday life. Explain to students that a process is a series of steps one takes to repair something, to make something, to get from one place to another, and even to do homework. You may want to have students brainstorm on the other ways that process writing affects their lives and to list the suggestions on the chalkboard. Point out to students that many people use processes in their jobs. "How to" papers provide information to explain processes. For example, a nurse would need to know how to take a blood-pressure reading and how to apply fresh bandages.

Introduction

Through this discussion, help students realize the importance of learning to give good directions. Have students decide what makes directions hard to follow.

Take this opportunity to help students realize how many times a day they are asked to follow instructions. Discuss the difference between explaining a process in which directions to complete a task are given, and informative writing in which information is given but no directions are provided for achieving a goal.

Integration

You may want to integrate this chapter with other aspects of the language arts. For example, a discussion of the imperative sentence is necessary to help students understand process writing and to avoid redundancy. To apply this chapter across the curriculum, discuss how important process writing is to the study of science. By now, students will have probably performed experiments in science class. You may want to ask students to look at scientific reports that illustrate process writing. Students should readily see how the skills in this chapter will help them in a variety of areas.

The chart on the next page illustrates the strands of language arts as they are integrated into this chapter. For vocabulary study, glossary words are underlined in some writing models.

QUOTATIONS
All **Quotations for the Day** are chosen because of their relevance to instructional material presented in that segment of the chapter and for their usefulness in establishing student interest in writing.

INTEGRATING THE LANGUAGE ARTS

Selection	Reading and Literature	Writing and Critical Thinking	Language and Syntax	Speaking, Listening, and Other Expression Skills
"Banana Surprise" by Don Herbert **176-177** **"Making a Flying Fish"** by Paula Morrow **186-188** from ***The Sword of Shannara*** by Terry Brooks **198** from ***When I Dance*** by James Berry **200**	Responding personally to a selection **178, 189, 195, 199** Applying interpretive and creative thinking **178, 195, 200** Determining tools necessary for a process **178** Examining steps in a process **178, 183, 184-185, 189, 193-194, 195** Examining details in a paragraph **178, 195** Examining details in a process paper **189, 193-194, 195** Examining basic steps in a process paper **189, 193-194, 195** Analyzing illustrations in a process paper **189** Analyzing travel directions **197, 199** Examining details in a selection **199** Analyzing a process riddle **200**	Writing a journal entry **178** Evaluating details **178, 183, 184-185, 189, 193-194, 195, 200** Brainstorming ideas for a topic **181** Choosing a process to explain **181** Writing a topic sentence **181** Making a list of steps and materials **183, 201** Gathering and organizing information **185, 199** Creating a chart of pertinent details in chronological order **185** Writing a draft of a "how-to" paper **191, 200** Analyzing a writer's revisions **195** Drawing conclusions and making inferences **195, 198-199, 200** Evaluating and revising a "how-to" paper **195, 199** Proofreading and publishing a "how-to" paper **196, 199** Using the writing process to write travel directions **199** Analyzing a process riddle **200**	Proofreading for errors in grammar, usage, and mechanics **199**	Developing listening, collaborative, organizational, and management skills **181, 193-194, 201** Working with a classmate to make a list of steps and materials **183** Working with a classmate to analyze a "how-to" explanation **189** Demonstrating speaking skills by presenting a process **193-194, 201** Publishing a process paper **196, 199** Making illustrations to show information **199**

CHAPTER 6

SEGMENT PLANNING GUIDE

You can use the following Planning Guide to adapt the chapter material to the individual needs of your class. All the Resources listed in this chapter are located in the *Teacher's ResourceBank™*.

SEGMENT	PAGES	CONTENT	RESOURCES
1 ***Working and Playing***	***175-178***		
Literary Model **"Banana Surprise"**	176-177	Guided reading: a model of process writing	
Reader's Response/ Writer's Craft	178	Model evaluation: responding to literature and analyzing process writing	
2 ***Ways to Inform***	***179***		
3 ***Prewriting***	***180-185***		Writing a "How-to" Paper Listing Steps and Materials 50
Choosing a Process to Explain	180	Guidelines: writing for audience and purpose	
Exercise 1	181	Cooperative learning: brainstorming ideas	
Writing Assignment: Part 1	181	Applied practice: writing a main-idea sentence	
Gathering and Organizing Information	182	Introduction: preparing to write a process paper	
Listing Important Steps and Materials	182	Guidelines: gathering information and materials	
Arranging Your Information	182-183	Guidelines: arranging steps in chronological order	
Exercise 2	183	Applied practice: listing steps and materials	
Critical Thinking: Evaluating Details	184	Guidelines: using criteria to evaluate details	
Critical Thinking Exercise	184-185	Applied practice: determining appropriate details	
Writing Assignment: Part 2	185	Applied practice: charting details in order	
4 ***Writing***	***186-191***		Writing a "How-to" Paper 51
Literary Model from **"Making a Flying Fish"**	186-188	Guided reading: examining process in a model	
Exercise 3	189	Cooperative learning: analyzing a "how-to" explanation	
Writing Note	189	Writing suggestion: drawing pictures for a process paper	
Following a Basic Framework for a "How-to" Paper	189	Introduction: examining structure in a model	
Writer's Model	189-190	Guided reading: examining a sample essay	
Writing Note	191	Writing suggestion: using signal words	
Chart: Framework for a "How-to" Paper	191	Guidelines: structuring a "how-to" paper	
Writing Assignment: Part 3	191	Applied practice: writing a first draft	

For **Portfolio Assessment** see the following pages in the *Teacher's ResourceBank™*:
Aims For Writing—pp. 49–54
Holistically Graded Composition Models—pp. 397–402
Assessment Portfolio—pp. 421–445

SEGMENT	PAGES	CONTENT	RESOURCES
5 *Evaluating and Revising*	*192-195*		Writing a "How-to" Paper 52
Evaluating and Revising	192	Guidelines: improving a first draft	
Chart: Evaluating and Revising Process Papers	193	Applied practice: applying evaluation and revision techniques	
Exercise 4	193-194	Cooperative learning: explaining and following a process	
Grammar Hint	194	Writing suggestion: using different kinds of sentences	
Exercise 5	195	Applied practice: analyzing a writer's revisions	
Writing Assignment: Part 4	195	Applied practice: evaluating and revising a "how-to" paper	
6 *Proofreading and Publishing*	*196*		Writing a "How-to" Paper 53
Publishing	196	Publishing ideas: reaching an audience	
Writing Assignment: Part 5	196	Applied practice: proofreading and publishing a process paper	
7 *Writing Workshop*	*197-199*		
Travel Directions	197	Guidelines: giving travel directions	
Literary Model/Questions from ***The Sword of Shannara***	198	Examining techniques: analyzing a sample model	
Writing Travel Directions	199	Applied practice: applying techniques to the writing process	
8 *Making Connections*	*200-201*		
Process in Literature: Riddle Poems	200	Applied practice: sharing a riddle	
Literary Model from ***When I Dance***	200	Guided reading: solving a riddle in a poem	
Speaking and Listening: Science and Health	201	Guidelines: administering first aid Cooperative learning: writing and presenting first-aid instructions	

WHOLE-CHAPTER RESOURCES
A Writing Process Log, A Writing Prompt, Holistically Graded Models, Assessment Portfolio Materials

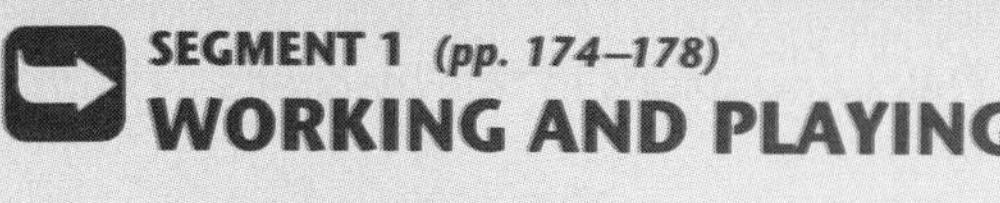

SEGMENT 1 (pp. 174–178)

WORKING AND PLAYING

OBJECTIVES

- To write a journal entry to generate writing ideas, and to share ideas with other students
- To discuss the role of chronological order in a process paper

MOTIVATION

You may want to bring to class the ingredients to make a peanut butter and banana sandwich. As you make the sandwich, ask students to follow what you are doing, and to list the steps in chronological order. After you have finished, explain to students that they have just described a process.

VISUAL CONNECTIONS

Exploring the Subject. There are many kinds of paper airplanes. Some planes fly for a long time, while others do aerobatic tricks. Different designs produce paper airplanes with differences in speed, flight distance and duration, and aerobatics.

Every paper airplane, however, relies on the same principles of aerodynamics to fly. There are four forces that act on a flying object: gravity, which pulls the object down; lift, which pushes the object up; drag, which pulls the object back; and thrust, which propels the object forward. Designers of paper airplanes seek to balance these forces so that planes will fly effectively.

Ideas for Writing. Have students study the illustrations and directions for this paper airplane. Ask students to list the steps shown and write the process in paragraph form. Then have them exchange their written directions with a partner and use each other's instructions to make the plane. Discuss with the class the most common difficulties of writing and following instructions, and have students note solutions that they can use in writing future process papers.

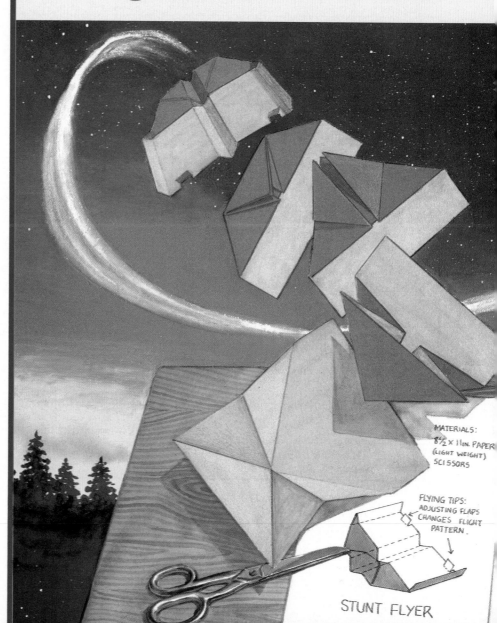

6 WRITING TO INFORM

TEACHING THE LESSON

Emphasize to students that clear, precise explanations of processes are necessary in everyday life. Students must acknowledge and follow processes every day at school. Even at home, students follow instructions for processes. They might put together a toy for a younger sibling or microwave a dinner. You might let students follow the process of **"Banana Surprise"** by bringing bananas to class and trying the trick. Students should understand that important, clear, concise instructions are necessary if the reader is to follow the process.

Working and Playing

Have you asked any questions today? Have you gotten any answers? Have you found out something? You probably have. We want and get information every single day of our lives. And because **working and playing** fill so many hours, we're often finding out about *processes*—how to do something or how something works.

Writing and You. Writers give you information about processes all the time. One tells you how to build a model plane. Another explains how glaciers move. What processes have you read about lately? Did you learn to do something new?

As You Read. Mr. Wizard, whose real name is Don Herbert, explains "how-to" processes in science and makes them fun. As you read "Banana Surprise," notice that his information contains careful steps.

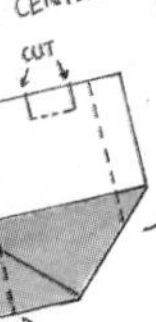

QUOTATION FOR THE DAY

"So before writing, learn to think." (Nicolas Boileau-Despréaux, 1636–1711, French critic and poet)

Write the quotation on the chalkboard and ask students to consider how the quotation applies to a writer who explains a process.

LESS-ADVANCED STUDENTS

Some students might have difficulty putting steps in chronological order. To help students, suggest they write out the steps on cards and experiment with the order until it appears to be a logical and reasonable sequence. Then have students repeat the steps verbally to friends to see if the steps are in order and to make sure that none have been left out.

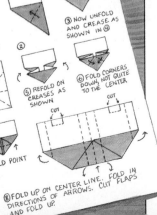

GUIDED PRACTICE

Work through the first question of **Reader's Response** with the class, and then have students work in small groups to swap journal entries and to write ideas for the second question. Monitor the groups and offer guidance when necessary. Then discuss students' answers as a class.

INDEPENDENT PRACTICE

Have students answer the **Writer's Craft** questions independently. Students should focus on numbering the steps of a process in chronological order and discussing the materials or resources necessary to follow the process.

COOPERATIVE LEARNING

Divide the class into groups of four. Ask the groups to write process papers explaining how to do something. You might have them use one of the following ideas:

1. how to polish shoes
2. how to make sun tea
3. how to plant flowers
4. how to clean a fish tank

Allow the groups to choose a topic for writing. After students have finished, call on one student from each group to present the group's process paper to the class.

BANANA SURPRISE

BY DON HERBERT

IMAGINE the amazement of a friend when you hand him a banana, which he peels only to find it has already been sliced into pieces! How can you slice the inside of a banana and not the outside?

ASSESSMENT

To assess students' comprehension, discuss the **Writer's Craft** questions as a class.

RETEACHING

To reteach this lesson, bring or ask students to bring boxed or canned food items from home. Have students write down the instructions for preparation. Remind students that the instructions must be followed in chronological order.

INSERT a threaded needle into one of the ridges on the peel and push it through under the skin to the next ridge. Pull the needle through, leaving a few inches of the tail end of the thread sticking out of the banana. Reinsert the needle into the same hole, and run it under the skin again to the next ridge. Pull the needle through again, leaving the thread in both the first and second holes. Continue around the banana like this until the needle comes out of the first hole you made. The thread now circles the banana under the skin. Gently pull the two ends of the thread, slicing the banana as neatly as with a knife. The more cuts like this you make, the more surprised your friend will be to find the banana sliced under the skin.

from *Mr. Wizard's Supermarket Science*

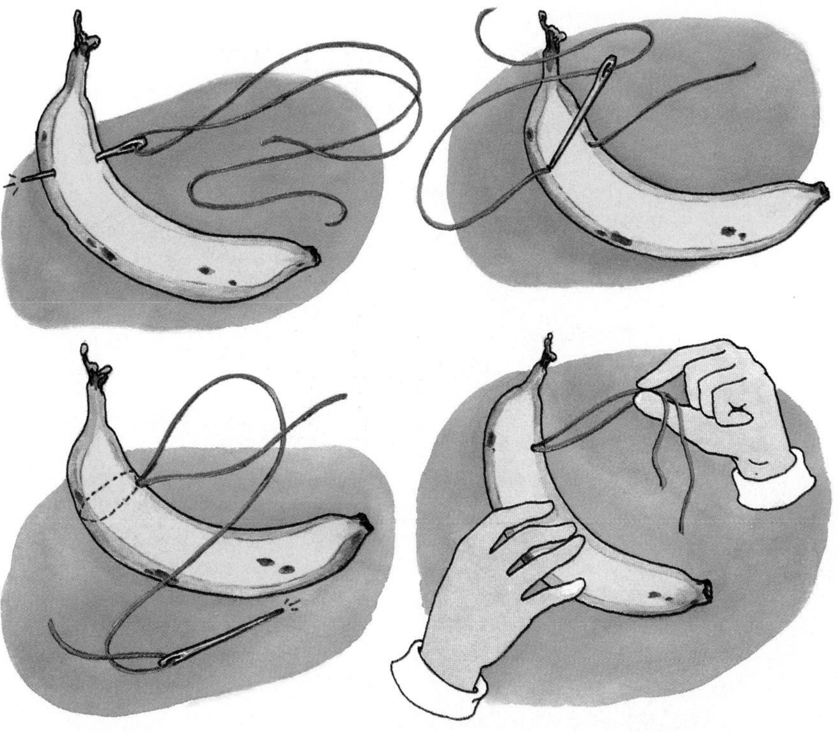

CRITICAL THINKING

Application

Ask students to work in pairs and to take turns explaining processes. To help students think in terms of chronological order, give students thirty seconds to turn to their partner and explain a process. You might suggest topics such as mailing a letter, mowing a lawn, making toast, or making a bed.

After the speaker has finished, the listener should point out any obvious steps the speaker has left out.

SELECTION AMENDMENT

Description of change: excerpted

Rationale: to focus on the concept of process writing presented in this chapter

CLOSURE

Close this lesson by discussing the following questions:

1. What is a process paper? [It is a "how-to" paper.]
2. How is a process paper ordered? [It should be in chronological order.]
3. Why is mentioning tools and materials necessary in a process paper? [This will help the reader follow your instructions completely.]
4. What processes do you use every day? [Students might say they follow instructions when doing things in school or when following a recipe.] ■

ANSWERS

Reader's Response

Answers may vary.

1. Students may or may not want to perform the trick. Students might say they would react with astonishment and curiosity to Banana Surprise.
2. The trick that students write about in their journals should be described in a clear, ordered manner.

Writer's Craft

3. A threaded needle and a banana are needed.
4. **(1)** Insert a threaded needle into one of the ridges of a banana peel and push it through under the skin to the next ridge. **(2)** Pull the needle through, leaving a few inches of the tail end of the thread sticking out of the banana. **(3)** Reinsert the needle into the same hole, and run it under the skin again to the next ridge. **(4)** Pull the needle through again, leaving the thread in both the first and second holes. **(5)** Continue around the banana in this fashion until the needle comes out of the first hole you made. The thread now circles the banana under the skin. **(6)** Gently pull the two ends of the thread, slicing the banana as neatly as with a knife.
5. Mr. Wizard says that the more cuts made to the banana, the more surprised people will be to find the banana sliced under the skin.

READER'S RESPONSE

1. Would you like to do this trick? Would you want it done *to* you? Describe how you think you would react to Banana Surprise.
2. In your journal, describe the funniest trick you ever played on someone—or someone played on you. If you like, swap stories with others. You may get ideas!

WRITER'S CRAFT

3. When you give information about a "how-to" process, materials and tools are usually important. What "tool" do you need for Banana Surprise?
4. The steps of a process should be given in the order you do them in—one, two, three, and so on. Are the steps of this trick in order? Give numbers to them.
5. Mr. Wizard ends his explanation with a final hint. What is it?

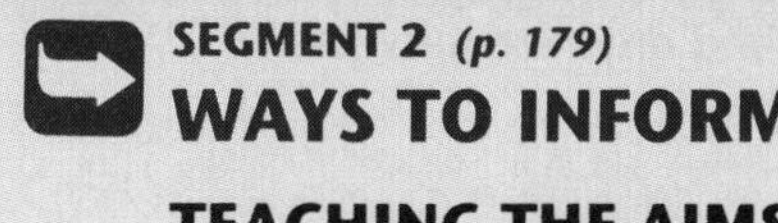

SEGMENT 2 *(p. 179)*

WAYS TO INFORM

TEACHING THE AIMS

Explain to students that the four main ways to inform are narration, description, classification, and evaluation. Go through the examples of how to use each way to inform. To check comprehension, ask students to think of additional examples for each. To close this lesson, give students an example of each way to inform and ask students to determine which way you are describing. ■

Ways to Inform

Your main writing in this chapter will be explaining a process. To do that, you use a kind of writing called narration: telling about something as it happens, step by step. But you often share information in other ways, too. Here are examples of the four main ways you can inform.

Narration: writing directions for a friend so she can find the new library; in school, explaining how Newton put the law of gravity into words.

Description: describing poisonous oleander so your friends won't pick the flowers; describing your cat in a lost-and-found ad.

Classification: explaining how break dancing and gymnastics are alike and different; for a science project, telling which birds in your yard eat seed, suet, or both.

Evaluation: telling your friends which of your new video games is the biggest challenge; in a book review, telling how realistic the setting was.

In the main assignment in this chapter you'll be writing a paper telling how to do something. Your basic purpose will be to inform. As you practice and then write, keep in mind that a "how-to" paper

- includes all of the necessary materials, tools, and steps
- gives the steps in the order that you need to do them in

LESS-ADVANCED STUDENTS

Some students might have difficulty understanding the differences between the ways to inform. Draw a simple map on the chalkboard with all roads leading to a central location. label the central location "Process." Label each road with the possible ways to inform. Explain to students that all ways will lead to the same destination—explaining a process. Explain to students that the road used will depend on the way the writer decides to inform and the audience the writer wants to reach.

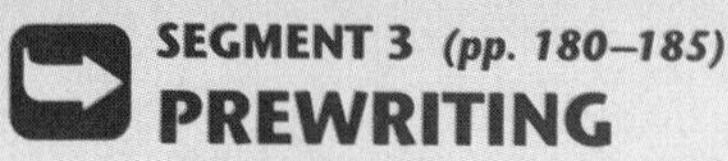

SEGMENT 3 *(pp. 180–185)*

PREWRITING

OBJECTIVES

- To brainstorm ideas for a "how-to" paper
- To choose a process for explaining
- To list steps and materials necessary for a process
- To gather and organize information for a "how-to" paper

Teacher's ResourceBank™

RESOURCES

PREWRITING

- Listing Steps and Materials 50

QUOTATION FOR THE DAY

"We are wiser than we know." (Ralph Waldo Emerson, 1803–1882, American author)

Write the quotation on the chalkboard and use it to initiate a discussion. You may wish to remind students that each day they complete many processes that have become automatic. Ask students in small groups to brainstorm lists of processes they go through regularly. Lists might include making a bed, mailing a letter, or preparing a sandwich. The ideas students list can be used later as the subjects of how-to papers.

Writing a "How-to" Paper

Prewriting

Choosing a Process to Explain

All day long you learn how to do things in school and at home. Here's your chance to teach other people how to do something.

Start by brainstorming a list of things you like to do and do well. Have you trained your cat to fetch a ball of paper? Can you patch bicycle tires? Are you good at playing chess?

Also look for something that your *audience,* or readers, will want to learn. Remember the *purpose* of a "how-to" paper. You are sharing information about a process so that other people can do the process themselves. Let's say you want to write about how to double Dutch jump rope. Some readers will be interested, but others may not be. If your audience doesn't want to know how to jump rope, you need to find another process.

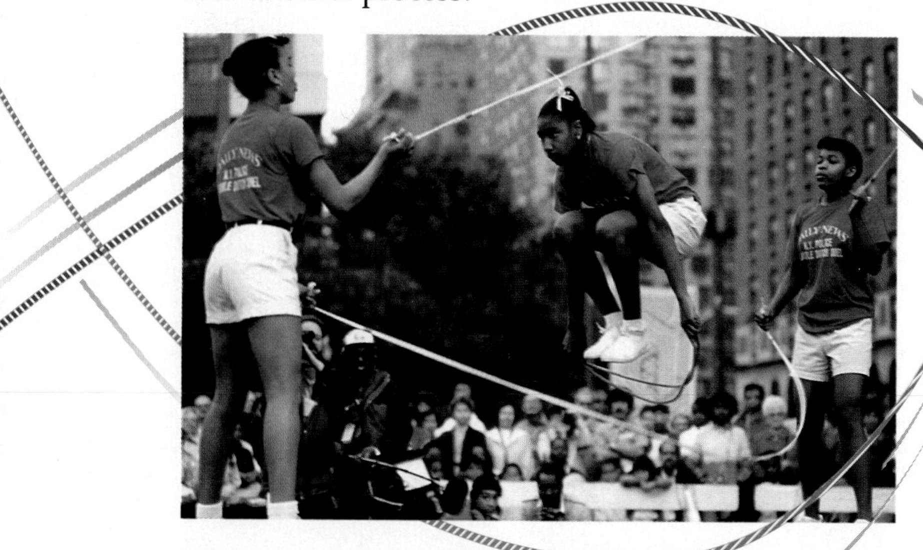

MOTIVATION

Explain to students that they have been following processes their entire lives. For example, having older siblings teach them to ride a bicycle and learning to print their names in kindergarten both involved processes. Ask students to name several other processes they have mastered in their lives.

TEACHING THE LESSON

To teach this lesson, you will need to discuss audience and purpose with students. If their audience for a paper were a group of first-graders, they would not want to write about the complicated process of making candles. However, they could describe the process involved in making fruit cubes (placing fruit juice in an ice cube tray and freezing it). 

EXERCISE 1 Exploring Possible Topics

Get together with two or three classmates to brainstorm ideas for "how-to" papers. You may have a million ideas, but if you're feeling blank, start with subjects like "games," "crafts," and "cooking." Then narrow the subject to a specific process like "how to play chess" or "how to make a pizza." When you have some topics, talk about them. Would you like to learn one of these processes? Can it be covered in a paragraph or two?

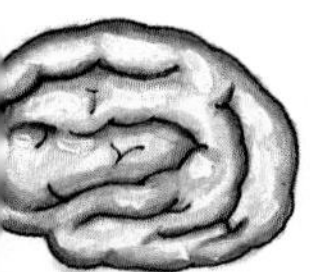

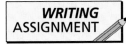

PART 1:
Choosing a Process to Explain

The group brainstorming may have given you the perfect topic. But if not, think about your skills and thrills. Are you good at something other people might not know how to do? What's really fun to do? After you've picked your topic, write one sentence telling what it is.

ANSWERS

Exercise 1

Students should each have at least one topic in mind that can be covered in a paragraph or two.

LEP/ESL

General Strategies. You may want to do **Exercise 1** as a class activity in order to activate relevant knowledge and vocabulary. Using cooking as the subject, get as many ideas as possible and write them on the chalkboard. Then have students narrow the topic to one food, list ways to prepare it, and tell what's needed to do so. They can use this exercise as the basis for the **Gathering and Organizing Information** section. Encourage students to consider writing a "how-to" paper about preparing traditional dishes or crafts from their cultures.

COOPERATIVE LEARNING

For **Exercise 1,** give groups of four students a large piece of poster board and a few colored markers. Ask each group member to contribute at least three topics to a list of possible topics. Post these lists at the front of the room for all class members to see. This will help students generate ideas for writing.

Remind students to keep their topics appropriate and interesting for their audience. For example, they would not want to describe the process involved in purchasing a snake to a person who has a fear of snakes.

GUIDED PRACTICE

Write the topics "games," "crafts," and "cooking" on the chalkboard to get groups started with their brainstorming in **Exercise 1.** Stress to students the importance of choosing processes with which they are already familiar.

INTEGRATING THE LANGUAGE ARTS

Literature Link. You might want to read Garrison Keillor's "How to Write a Letter" to students. Then put students into groups of four and assign each group a different section of the essay. Each group should list in chronological order the process steps mentioned in its section. When the groups have completed their lists, have a representative from each group present its list, following the chronological order of Keillor's process. List the steps on the chalkboard and discuss with students whether or not they think this process would help them write letters. Is the process clearly presented? Has Keillor left out any steps?

You could extend this activity by having students follow Keillor's process to write letters to friends, relatives, or persons they admire.

Prewriting

Gathering and Organizing Information

What happens if you forget to tell your readers to put soap in the water? They can't blow bubbles. To make sure you don't forget any necessary information, plan carefully. Identify every important step, the materials you will need, and the best way to arrange the information.

Listing Important Steps and Materials

In a "how-to" paper, you need two types of information: the steps in the process and the materials and tools you need for the process.

Here's one way to gather the information. Imagine yourself doing the process on a "how-to" TV program. You do each step carefully and with great skill. You yourself didn't know you could do it so well! As you watch yourself, jot down two things: what each step is and what materials you need for it.

Arranging Your Information

Usually, the first thing your readers want to know is what materials or tools they'll need. Then they need the steps of the process in the order in which they need to be done. That's usually ***chronological order,*** or time order. Always check to be sure you don't put a step too early or too late. That might confuse your readers.

Remember, too, that every detail you use should help your readers understand the process. This is a good time to cross out any details that just get in the way.

On the next page is an example showing how one writer listed information for a paper about teaching a dog to heel. Notice that the steps are in the order you have to do them in.

INDEPENDENT PRACTICE

Students can work independently on **Writing Assignment: Part 1,** each writing one sentence describing the topic for his or her "how-to" paper. Students could work in pairs to complete **Exercise 2** and the first part of **Writing Assignment: Part 2.**

ASSESSMENT

Use **Exercises 1** and **2** and **Writing Assignment: Parts 1** and **2** to monitor students' progress.

How to Teach Your Dog to Heel on a Leash

Materials: six-foot leash and a training collar

Steps:

1. *Get a leash and a training collar called a choke chain.*
2. *Put the training collar on your dog.*
3. *Get into the correct starting position.*
4. *Say "Heel," and start walking.*
5. *Jerk the collar when the dog makes a mistake.*

To plan a "how-to" paper

- list the steps in the process
- jot down the materials needed for each step
- make sure the steps are in chronological order
- take out details that aren't necessary

EXERCISE 2 **Listing Steps and Materials**

Here is a list of steps for making a Chinese papercut. Only the first two steps are in the right order. Working with a partner, number the other steps in order. Finally, list the materials and tools needed for this process.

1. Using tracing paper, copy your design.
2. Put the traced design on top of two or three sheets of colorful tissue paper.
6 Tape your papercuts to a window, so light will shine through them.
5 Last of all, cut the outline of the design.
3 Staple around the edges of the sheets so they can't move.
4 Using a sharp scissors, start cutting from the center of the design.

ADVANCED STUDENTS

Some students might enjoy writing "how-to" papers after researching an unfamiliar topic in the library rather than writing on a topic with which they are familiar. Exploring an unfamiliar topic would allow students to learn and share new knowledge and skills.

Students might also write a process, putting the steps on separate pieces of paper. Then have another student reassemble the steps in the correct order.

ANSWERS

Exercise 2

Materials: tracing paper, two or three sheets of colorful tissue paper, and tape
Tools: stapler and scissors

CLOSURE

Ask students the following question: Why is it necessary that you be knowledgeable about your topic? [You need to be able to list the steps and required materials accurately.] ■

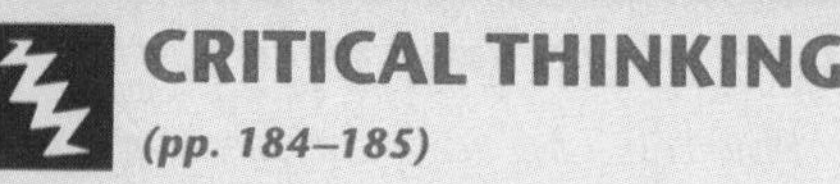

CRITICAL THINKING

(pp. 184–185)

OBJECTIVE

- To evaluate details in a process paper to determine whether they are necessary

LEP/ESL

General Strategies. Discuss with students how the salsa made from the given recipe might taste. Did students expect lime juice to be in a sauce? What consistency do they think the sauce might have? Write relevant vocabulary on the chalkboard during the discussion, along with more familiar sauce ingredients. Then, divide the class into small groups and have each group create an original recipe for a sauce. The groups can exchange and evaluate recipes for clarity of detail and the class can vote on the sauce they think would be the tastiest.

COOPERATIVE LEARNING

Have students work in groups of three or four to compile the steps in the process for making salsa. Have them list the steps on a piece of poster board, excluding unnecessary details. After they have finished, display the posters at the front of the room and discuss each one with the class. Students should be prepared to discuss why they left details in or took details out.

CRITICAL THINKING

Evaluating Details

When you write a "how-to" paper, it's easy to get carried away. Sometimes you know so much about the topic that many more details than you need crowd into your mind. It's important to get rid of unneeded details. They just confuse your readers. To ***evaluate,*** or judge, whether to keep a detail, ask yourself:

- Is this information that my audience already knows? (If it is, cross it out!)
- Is this detail a helpful hint? Does it keep readers from making a mistake? (If it does, keep it!)

CRITICAL THINKING EXERCISE:
Evaluating Details

One writer jotted down the following notes for making salsa, a Mexican sauce. The audience is a class of sixth-graders. Which details do you think could be crossed out?

TEACHING *EVALUATING DETAILS*

Model the evaluation techniques in the **Critical Thinking Exercise** by examining a "how-to" paper written by a former student.

To assess if students comprehend this exercise, ask students to jot down the details from the salsa recipe that can be omitted. Discuss the answers as a class.

To close this lesson, ask students the following question:

What questions must you ask yourself when deciding to keep details in your paper? [Is this information something my audience already knows? Are these details helpful? Do they keep the reader from making a mistake?]

You need 1 ripe tomato, 1 small onion, 1 peeled garlic clove, 1 or 2 chile peppers, 1/2 teaspoon salt, and 1 teaspoon lime juice.
Use serrano or jalapeño peppers. I like jalapeños best.
Also find measuring spoons, a knife, a cutting board, a mixing spoon, and a bowl.
My grandmother has a mixing bowl she bought in San Diego.
Chop the tomato, onion, garlic, and peppers very finely. Be careful not to cut yourself while you're chopping. You may want an adult to help you.
You can chop all the vegetables on the same cutting board since they'll be mixed up together anyway.

Put the chopped vegetables in a bowl and mix in the salt and lime juice.
Let the mixture sit for about half an hour, so the flavors can combine.
Serve with fajitas, tacos, or eggs. Salsa makes a plain egg fantastic.

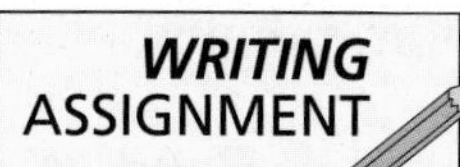

WRITING ASSIGNMENT

PART 2:
Gathering and Organizing Information for Your Paper

Now you're ready to plan your own "how-to" paper. First, create a chart like the one on page 183. Remember to double-check for chronological order and to cross out details readers don't need.

ANSWERS

Critical Thinking Exercise

Generally, the following details are unnecessary:

1. I like jalapeños best.
2. My grandmother has a mixing bowl she bought in San Diego.
3. You can chop all the vegetables on the same cutting board since they'll be mixed up together anyway.
4. Salsa makes a plain egg fantastic.

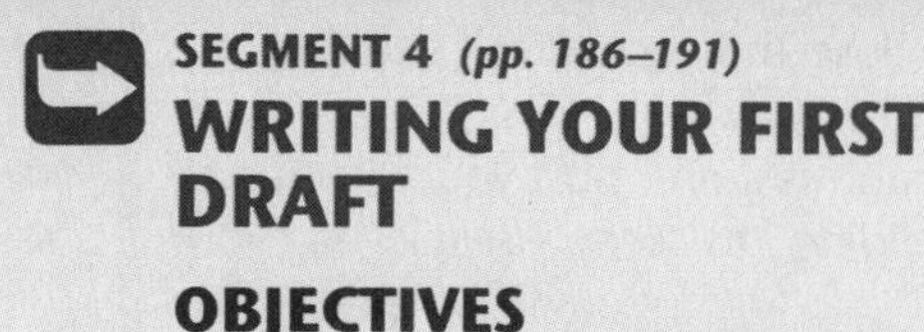

SEGMENT 4 *(pp. 186–191)*

WRITING YOUR FIRST DRAFT

OBJECTIVES

- To analyze a "how-to" explanation
- To write a draft of a "how-to" paper

MOTIVATION

Ask students if they know what a flying fish is. [A flying fish is a fish with long, wing-like fins that give it the illusion of flight when it leaps out of the water.] Then tell them that they are going to learn about another kind of flying fish—one that they can make. Explain to students that they will learn a process for making a *koinobori,* a

Teacher's ResourceBank™

RESOURCES

WRITING YOUR FIRST DRAFT

- Writing a "How-to" Paper 51

QUOTATION FOR THE DAY

"Writing is manual labor of the mind: a job, like laying pipe." (John Gregory Dunne, 1932– , American writer)

Use the quotation to remind students that writing a first draft, like any physical chore, is best completed by rolling up the shirt sleeves and getting to it. Any draft can be polished and improved in the revision stage, but first the draft must be written.

Writing Your First Draft

Here are some tips for writing your first draft.

- In the very beginning, try to catch your readers' interest. [Hint: Why is this process fun or important?]
- List the materials.
- Discuss the steps in order.
- End with a helpful tip or another example showing why the process is fun or important.

The explanation that follows tells one way to celebrate Children's Day. It's a national holiday in Japan. Do you think you could follow the writer's directions?

A MAGAZINE ARTICLE

Making a Flying Fish

by Paula Morrow

Attention grabber

Japanese boys and girls have their own special day each year on May 5. It is called Children's Day and is a national holiday. This is a time for families to celebrate having children by telling stories, feasting, going on picnics, or visiting grandparents. . . .

Process to be explained

A special feature of Children's Day is the *koinobori* that families display in their yards—one for each child in the family. A tall pole is placed in the garden. . . . Fish made of cloth or strong paper are attached to the pole. Each fish has a hoop flying fish the Japanese make in honor of Children's Day, a national holiday in Japan. Ask students to help list on the chalkboard items they make for holidays in their own cultures. Point out to students that in many cultures processes are handed down from one generation to the next.

TEACHING THE LESSON

You will need to define the terms *koinobori, carp,* and *eaves* and to guide students through the reading of the process for making a flying fish. Point out to students that the professional model includes explanations accompanying the steps and reasons for some steps.

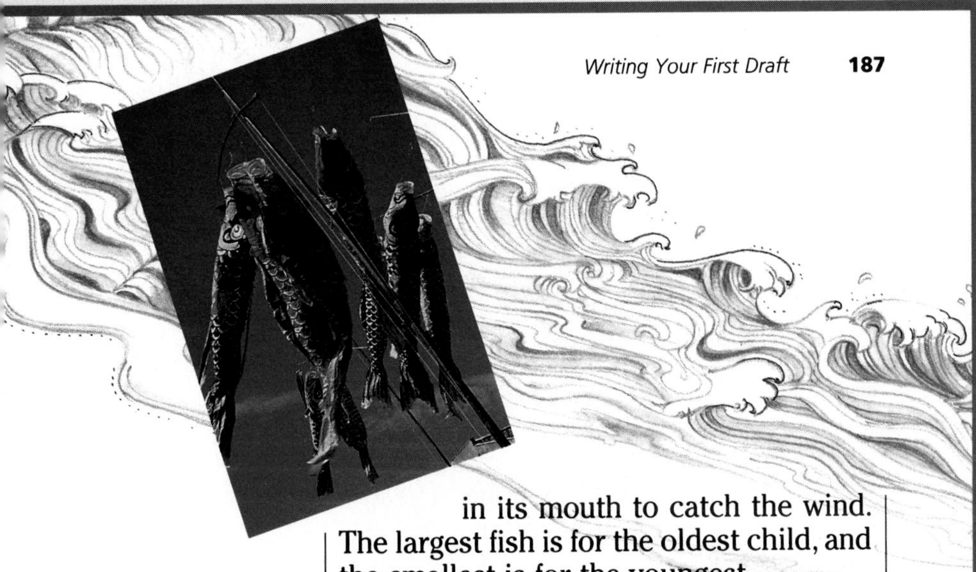

in its mouth to catch the wind. The largest fish is for the oldest child, and the smallest is for the youngest.

1 These fish represent a kind of carp known as a strong fighter. These carp battle their way upstream against strong currents. When the koinobori dance in the wind, they remind the children of carp leaping up a waterfall. This is supposed to inspire children to be equally brave and strong.

Reason for learning process

You can make your own koinobori and fly it from a pole or hang it from your window on May 5. In that way, you can share Children's Day with the boys and girls of Japan.

List of materials

You need an 18- by 30-inch piece of light-weight cloth (cotton, rayon, or nylon), felt-tip markers, a needle and thread, scissors, a narrow plastic headband, and string.

Step 1

Step 2

First, choose a piece of cloth with a bright, colorful pattern or decorate it yourself with felt-tip markers. Fold the fabric in half lengthwise, with the bright side on the inside. Sew a seam 1/2 inch from the long (30-inch) edge, making a sleeve.

USING THE SELECTION

Making a Flying Fish

1

carp: any of a group of freshwater fish living in ponds or other tranquil waters and widely cultivated in Europe and Asia for food

LEP/ESL

General Strategies. Due to cultural and language differences, students might be uncertain about how to catch an American audience's attention. References to people, places, events, and ideas that are important or interesting to Americans, and expressions such as "I'll bet you've never . . . .", "Have you ever . . . ?" and "What would you do if . . . ?" tend to catch young American readers' attention. You could offer examples of attention-grabbing introductions from various pieces of children's writing and explain how the introductions catch the reader's attention.

GUIDED PRACTICE

Ask for class responses to **Exercise 3.** Before discussing the questions as a group, allow students to spend a few minutes discussing the questions with a partner.

INDEPENDENT PRACTICE

Students can work independently on **Writing Assignment: Part 3.** Students should use their charts of steps and materials and the basic framework as guides.

LEARNING STYLES

Auditory Learners. Some students could use tape recorders to record their steps for a "how-to" explanation. As students listen to their tapes, they can check to make sure that all the steps are present and in chronological order.

Visual Learners. Some students might benefit from illustrating each step in their "how-to" explanations. This will help students see that all steps are present and in chronological order.

2
eaves: the lower edges of a roof, usually projecting beyond the sides of a building

SELECTION AMENDMENT
Description of change: some sentences have been deleted
Rationale: to focus on the concept of writing to inform presented in this chapter

Step 3 — On one end of the sleeve, make a 1-inch-wide hem by turning the right side of the fabric over the wrong side. Then, sew the hem, leaving three 1-inch-wide openings about 5 inches apart.

Step 4 — Make cuts 5 inches deep and 1 inch apart all around the unhemmed end of the sleeve to form a fringe. Explanation — This is the fish's tail.

Step 5 — Next, turn the sleeve right side out. With . . . a felt-tip marker, add eyes near the hemmed (head) end Explanation — (away from the fringed tail).

Step 6 — Thread the narrow plastic headband into the hem through one of the openings. Continue threading it until the open part of the headband is hidden.

Step 7 — Then, tie a 12-inch-long piece of string to the headband at each of the three openings. Tie the loose ends of the strings together.

Step 8 — Finally, hang your windsock from the strings on a tree limb, a clothes pole, or the eaves[2] of your house. Repeat of reason — On windy days, it will dance like a carp swimming upstream against a waterfall!

Faces

ASSESSMENT

To assess students' mastery, monitor **Writing Assignment: Part 3** by asking students to label their papers, following the examples in the professional model. Students should label the attention grabber, process to be explained, reason for learning process, list of materials, steps, and needed explanations or reasons. You can quickly check student labels to make sure most of these elements are present in students' papers.

EXERCISE 3 **Analyzing a "How-to" Explanation**

Before you make your own flying fish, take a closer look at the process. Get together with a partner to discuss the following questions.

1. Paula Morrow writes a long introduction before talking about the "how-to" steps. What interesting details does she give?
2. What are the basic steps in making koinobori? Can you follow all of them? If not, where do you need help?
3. Do the pictures help you understand the process better? Explain.

Think about drawing pictures for your "how-to" paper. Sometimes they make following a process easier.

Following a Basic Framework for a "How-to" Paper

Don't think you have to write a "how-to" paper like Paula Morrow's. The following writer's model is more like what you'll write. Your paper may even be shorter than the model. You may need only one or two paragraphs to explain your process.

A WRITER'S MODEL

Attention grabber Is your dog a daredevil? Does it chase cars or fight other dogs? To control your daredevil,
Reason train it to "heel" on a leash.

List of materials You will need a six-foot leash. You'll also need a special training collar called a choke

ANSWERS

Exercise 3

Any answer that may vary is indicated by an asterisk (*).

*1. Here are some possibilities: Japanese boys and girls have their own special day each year on May 5; Children's Day is a national holiday; families celebrate Children's Day by telling stories, feasting, going on picnics, or visiting grandparents; families display koinobori on Children's Day; each koinobori represents a child in the family.

2. The basic steps are as follows:
   a. Choose a piece of cloth with a bright, colorful pattern or decorate it yourself with felt-tip markers.
   b. Fold the fabric in half lengthwise with the bright side on the inside. Sew a seam 1/2 inch from the long (30–inch) edge, making a sleeve.
   c. On one end of the sleeve, make a 1-inch-wide hem by turning the bright side of the fabric over the dull side. Then, sew the hem, leaving three 1-inch-wide openings about 5 inches apart.
   d. Make cuts 5 inches deep and 1 inch apart all around the unhemmed end of the sleeve to form a fringe.
   e. Turn the sleeve right side out. With a felt-tip marker, add eyes near the hemmed head-end and away from the fringed tail.
   f. Thread the narrow plastic headband into the hem through one of the openings. Continue threading it until the open part of the headband is hidden.

RETEACHING

Have students write each step on a separate slip of paper so that they can more easily put the steps into chronological order. If necessary, help them sequence the steps. Then have them write the transitions to link the steps.

CLOSURE

Ask students to answer the following questions about their own papers:

1. What interesting details do you include in the introduction?
2. What are the basic steps in your process?
3. What added information did you include to help the reader avoid mistakes?

g. Tie a 12–inch-long piece of string to the headband at each of the three openings. Tie the loose ends of the string together.

h. Hang your windsock from a tree limb, a pole, or the eaves of your house.

*3. Students might respond by saying that the pictures add a visual dimension which make the complicated steps easier to follow.

INTEGRATING THE LANGUAGE ARTS

Grammar Link. Because students are directing someone to do something in their "how-to" papers, their writing will probably involve the use of imperative sentences. You may want to review this type of sentence with students and explain that the subject is always *you* in an imperative sentence, even though it may not actually appear in the sentence.

Step 1 **Helpful hint**	chain. Before you get the collar, measure your dog's neck. The best collar size is about two inches longer than the dog's neck.
Explanation **Step 2** **Step 3**	A choke chain has a ring at each end. To make it work, attach the leash to one ring. Hold the other ring in your right hand. With your left hand, double the chain. Then put the doubled chain through the ring you're holding. This makes a loop. To start training, put the loop over your dog's head.
Helpful hint **Step 4** **Step 5**	The starting position is important. Stand with your dog at your left. Hold the end of the leash in your right hand. Your left hand holds the leash close to the choke chain. Say "Heel" in a firm voice, and begin walking, left foot first.
Step 6 **Explanation** **Helpful hint**	If the dog gets ahead or behind, jerk the leash with your left hand. Say "Heel." Your dog will learn that a tight collar means "Uh, oh, mistake!" Of course, be sure to say "Good dog" when your dog walks right.
Repeat of reason	That's one way to be your dog's best friend. Teach it to heel!

4. Would illustrations help your reader understand the process better?

ENRICHMENT

The professional model in this segment focuses on Japanese culture and tradition. Ask students to go to the library and research a process that is followed during a special holiday in another culture. Encourage students to share their findings with the class. ■

Transition words like *before, first, next,* and *then* signal a new step. They help your readers follow along, as these examples show.

Before you get the collar, measure your dog's neck.
First attach the leash to one ring.

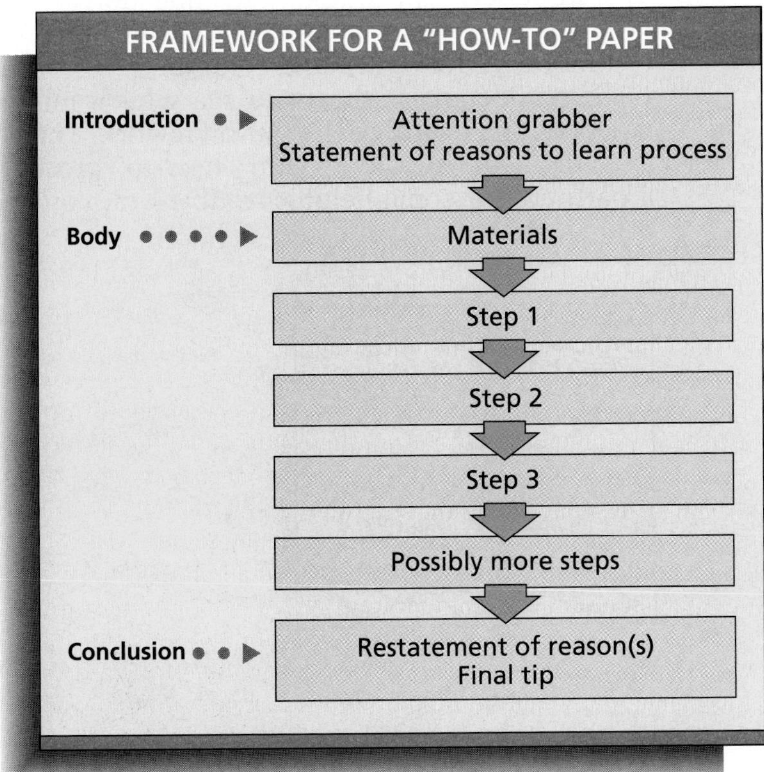

PART 3:
Writing a Draft of Your "How-to" Paper

Put your own process on paper, using your chart of steps and materials as a guide. Look at the framework above whenever you need to know what comes next.

CRITICAL THINKING
Analysis

Ask students to form groups of four. To encourage them to think critically, ask students to analyze each draft in their group and to check for clarity and completeness. Have students make written comments and suggestions before they return the papers to their owners.

SEGMENT 5 *(pp. 192–195)*

EVALUATING AND REVISING

OBJECTIVES

- To explain and follow a process
- To analyze a writer's revisions
- To evaluate and revise a "how-to" paper

MOTIVATION

Explain to students that the evaluating and revising stage in writing helps to improve writing by giving the writer an opportunity to check for mistakes. This stage is similar to the one in which coaches watch replays of games to determine problems and how they can be solved.

Teacher's ResourceBank™

RESOURCES

EVALUATING AND REVISING

- Writing a "How-to" Paper 52

QUOTATION FOR THE DAY

"If [the audience is] satisfied with your poor performance, you will not easily make it better." (Ralph Waldo Emerson, 1803–1882, American author)

Write the quotation on the chalkboard and use it as the basis for a discussion of peer editing. Ask students what they like or dislike about sharing their work with other students, what kinds of comments they find beneficial, and what they would like to change about their peer-editing sessions. Lead students to understand that showing their partners ways to improve their papers is an important role in the writing process.

Evaluating and Revising

As Garfield the cat likes to say, "Nobody's perfect." Everybody makes mistakes, especially in a first draft.

Use the chart on the next page to look more closely at your paper. Ask yourself each question on the left. When you honestly answer a question no, use the technique in the right-hand column.

Sometimes it isn't easy to see what's missing or what sounds confused in your own work. That's why it's a big help to evaluate your "how-to" process with a partner. For some helpful feedback on your paper, also use Exercise 4 on pages 193–194.

TEACHING THE LESSON

Read over the **Evaluating and Revising Process Papers** chart with students to make sure they understand what the chart is suggesting they do to improve their writing. Point out to students that each revision technique begins with a verb, which suggests that they take action to correct problems. Students will be working with partners in **Exercise 4** to improve rough drafts. Explain to students that all comments should be constructive. You may want to present both the original paragraph and the revised paragraph in **Exercise 5** on a transparency to aid in the class discussion.

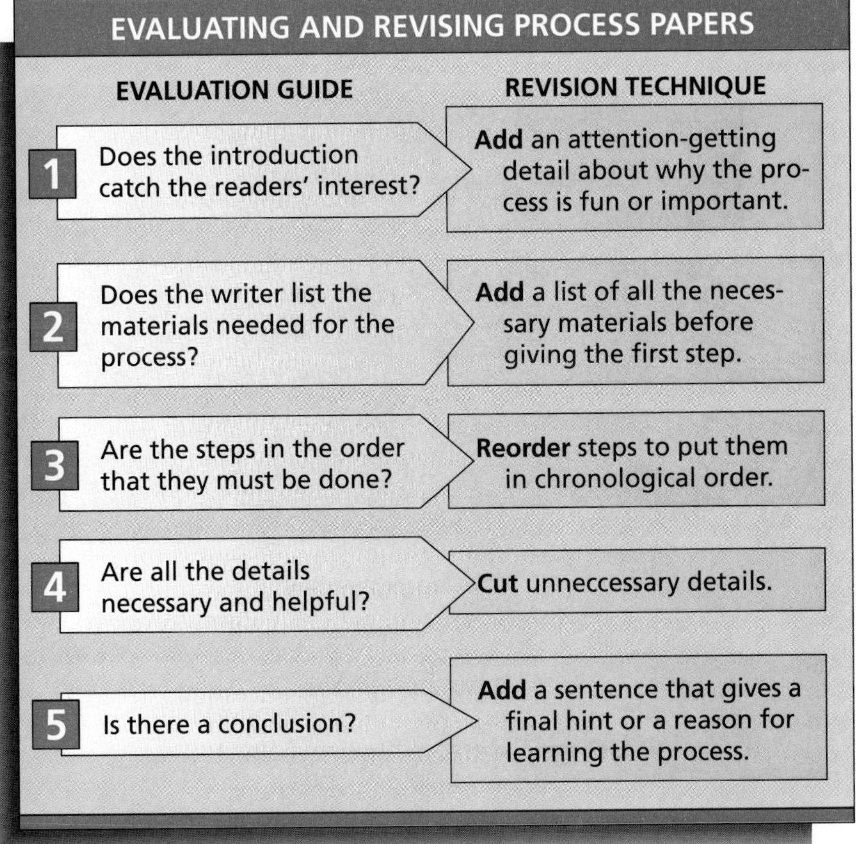

EVALUATING AND REVISING PROCESS PAPERS
EVALUATION GUIDE
REVISION TECHNIQUE
1 Does the introduction catch the readers' interest?
Add an attention-getting detail about why the process is fun or important.
2 Does the writer list the materials needed for the process?
Add a list of all the necessary materials before giving the first step.
3 Are the steps in the order that they must be done?
Reorder steps to put them in chronological order.
4 Are all the details necessary and helpful?
Cut unneccessary details.
5 Is there a conclusion?
Add a sentence that gives a final hint or a reason for learning the process.

EXERCISE 4 Speaking and Listening: Explaining and Following a Process

Will your process make sense to readers? Let's find out. Get together with two classmates. You'll read your draft aloud. One classmate will be the "actor" and pretend to act out your process as you read. The other will be the "director." The director jots down the materials when you read them. Then, if the actor needs something you haven't listed, the director stops the process. The director also stops the process whenever a step doesn't go right. He or she makes

MEETING
INDIVIDUAL
NEEDS

LEP/ESL

General Strategies. Whenever students exchange papers for peer evaluation, you may want to make sure that two ESL students do not trade essays. Every bit of feedback they can get from native speakers will be helpful to their language-acquisition process. It may also be helpful to suggest that students should check for one type of error at a time while evaluating.

ANSWERS

Exercise 4

Students will have completed this exercise when all students have participated as reader, actor, and director. You may want to grade on effort and attitude in addition to quality of presentation.

GUIDED PRACTICE

Use student papers from **Exercise 4** to model revision techniques for the class. You may want to focus on evaluating methods such as adding necessary materials, reordering steps or placing them in chronological order, and omitting unnecessary details.

INDEPENDENT PRACTICE

Students should work independently to complete **Writing Assignment: Part 4.** Using the model in **Exercise 4** and following the evaluating and revising chart, students should evaluate, revise, and write clean drafts of their papers.

INTEGRATING THE LANGUAGE ARTS

Mechanics Link. To help students who have difficulty spelling words that contain the letter combinations *ei* and *ie,* review these few basic spelling rules:

1. Write *ie* when the sound is long *e,* except after *c.* Exceptions are *either, neither, seize, weird,* and *leisure.*
2. Write *ei* when the sound is not long *e,* especially when the sound is long *a.* Exceptions are *friend, mischief, kerchief.*

Then ask students to apply the rules by spelling the following words correctly: *piece, ceiling, freight, reign, niece, relief, piece, brief,* and *height.*

GRAMMAR HINT

The **Grammar Hint** teaches students to use imperative sentences in a variety of ways. Write the following sentences on the chalkboard and ask students to restate them:

1. Don't forget to butter your hands before you pull taffy.
2. Don't stop pulling the taffy once you've started.
3. Don't slow down or the taffy will harden.

[Here is a possible revision: Remember to butter your hands before you pull homemade taffy. Keep pulling the taffy once you've started or the taffy will harden.]

notes about problems. Make sure everyone has a chance to be reader, actor, and director.

GRAMMAR HINT

Using Different Kinds of Sentences

When you write a "how-to" paper, it's easy to use too many *imperative sentences. **Imperative sentences*** are commands: Do this! Do that! To avoid sounding too pushy, try to vary your sentences.

IMPERATIVE SENTENCES	**Don't let your pet decide where you go. Don't let it get ahead or behind. Jerk the leash with your left hand.**
VARIED SENTENCES	**You shouldn't let your pet decide where you go. If it gets ahead or behind, jerk the leash with your left hand.**

REFERENCE NOTE: **For more information on sentence variety, see pages 311–318.**

ASSESSMENT

While students are revising, check one paragraph from each paper to make sure that students are following the instructions for revision.

To assess students' mastery, you will need to check their rough drafts and revised copies to see that they have made the necessary changes.

CLOSURE

Discuss the following questions:

1. Why are revisions necessary? [Revisions make writing easier to follow and help ensure proper organization.]
2. Name the four parts of a "how-to" paper [attention grabber, materials, ordered steps, and conclusion]. ■

EXERCISE 5 **Analyzing a Writer's Revisions**

Here's the way the writer revised the fourth paragraph in the model on pages 189–190. After you've studied the changes, answer the questions that follow the paragraph.

The starting position is important. Hold the end of the leash in your right hand. ~~You may be left-handed, but~~	cut
~~that doesn't matter.~~ ~~Hold~~ the leash	add
close to the choke chain ~~in~~ your left	add/cut/reorder
hand. Stand with your dog at your left.	reorder
Say "Heel" in a firm voice, and begin walking, left foot first.	add

1. Why did the writer move the fifth sentence to the beginning of the paragraph?
2. Why did the writer cut the third sentence?
3. What's the reason for changing the fourth sentence to begin *Your left hand holds . . .*? [Hint: See page 182.]
4. At the end, is *in a firm voice* a good detail to add? Why do you think so?

PART 4:
Evaluating and Revising Your "How-to" Paper

You probably have some ideas for improving your paper from the actor-director exercise (pages 193–194). Now, use the evaluating and revising chart on page 193 for more help. After you've made all your changes, make a clean copy. Then, have your partners evaluate the paper one final time.

ANSWERS

Exercise 5

1. The starting position is with the dog at your left.
2. It is an unnecessary detail.
3. Beginning the sentence in the revised way helps the trainer start the next step in the proper position.
4. Yes, it will make a difference as to the effectiveness of the dog trainer's command.

CRITICAL THINKING
Synthesis

To help students understand that processes are an important and necessary part of everyday life, ask them to keep diaries of all the processes they encounter in one day. Students should briefly list the steps involved in each process. The following day, they can share their diaries with their classmates.

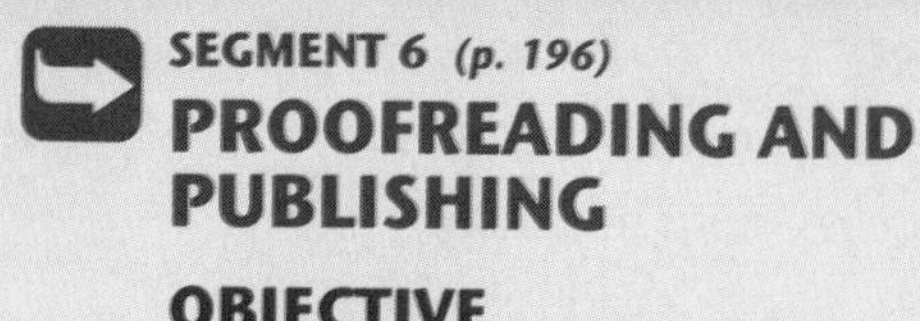

SEGMENT 6 *(p. 196)*

PROOFREADING AND PUBLISHING

OBJECTIVE

- To proofread and publish a "how-to" paper

TEACHING STRATEGIES

Ask groups of four students to look over each paper in their group one final time.

To assess these final drafts, use the evaluation guide on p. 193 as a checklist. ■

Teacher's ResourceBank™

RESOURCES

PROOFREADING AND PUBLISHING

- Writing a "How-to" Paper 53

QUOTATION FOR THE DAY

"It's not who does the most tricks, but the total package." (Brian Orser, 1962– , Canadian Olympic ice skater)

Write the quotation on the chalkboard and ask students to discuss what they think it means. Lead them to understand that informative writers are obligated to give their readers all the information they can, and that the proofreading and publishing stage of the writing process is when the final touches are put on a package of writing.

A DIFFERENT APPROACH

To engage the interest of students in process writing, you could ask some workers in your community to visit your classroom and discuss processes that they use every day. Some people you might consider are bakery workers, postal employees, store clerks, chefs, secretaries, pilots, flight attendants, hairdressers, or repairpersons.

Proofreading and Publishing

Proofreading. You always need to proofread a "how-to" paper carefully. A tiny mistake can ruin the whole process. Think about the koinobori "how-to" article. Suppose the author had told you to get an **8-inch** by 30-inch piece of cloth instead of an **18-inch** by 30-inch piece. Your koinobori would end up looking more like a snake than a fish!

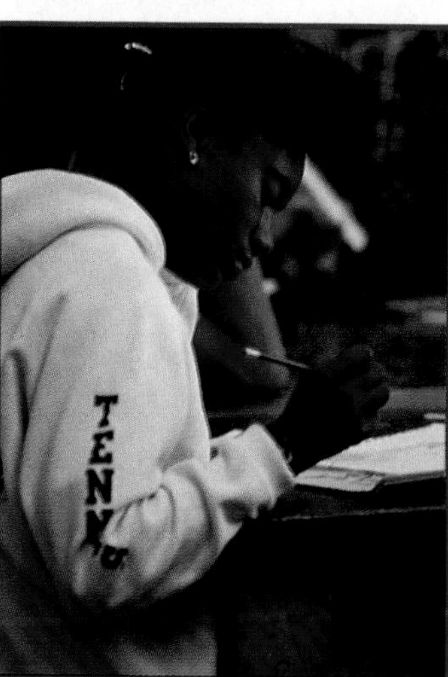

Publishing. Any "how-to" paper is meaningless unless someone reads it and tries to follow the process. Here are some suggestions for publishing a "how-to" paper.

- If you are explaining how to do a craft, hobby, or game, you might send a copy to the director of a retirement center or a day-care center.
- If you are explaining how to do a science project, give a copy to your science teacher.
- If you are explaining how to cook something, get together with a friend to try out the recipe.

PART 5:
Proofreading and Publishing Your Paper

After you've checked your paper for mistakes, make a clean copy of it. Then find a way to share it. Use one of the ideas above or an idea of your own.

SEGMENT 7 *(pp. 197–199)*

WRITING WORKSHOP

OBJECTIVE

- To use the writing process to write a "how-to" paper that gives travel directions

MOTIVATION

Give the class a series of clues and locations in the room that lead to a prize. Explain to students that they have just followed directions on how to get from one place to another, and they will explore a professional model that gives travel directions.

WRITING WORKSHOP

Travel Directions

You can give different kinds of information in process papers—such as explaining how to do something. You can also explain how to get from one place to another using landmarks. A landmark is anything that can be seen easily—a big tree, a street corner, or a high building. In travel directions, words like *right, north, up,* and *near* help people understand where to go. They are *geographical* directions. Details about the distance between landmarks can help, too.

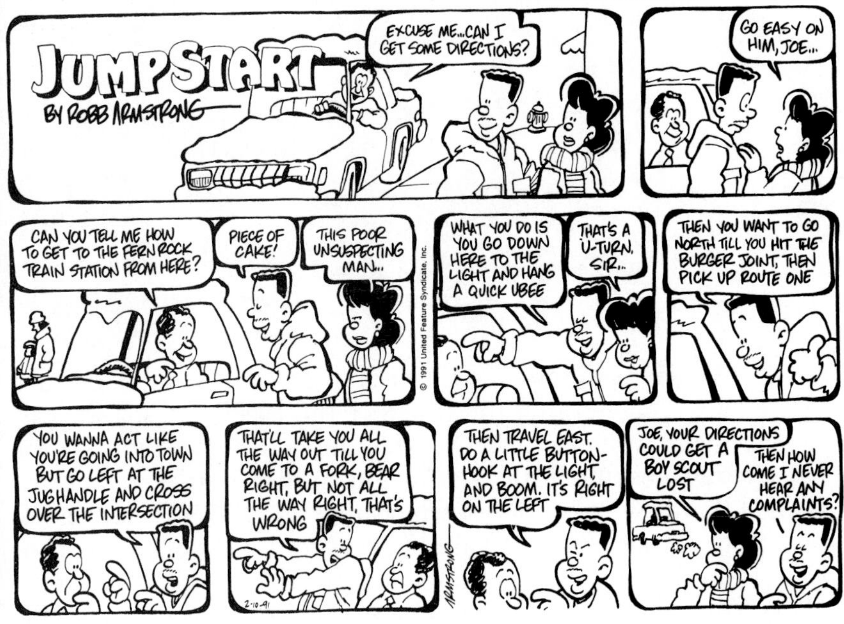

In the following passage from a fantasy adventure book, three characters are on a journey. Menion is giving his friends directions for getting to the Anar Forests. What landmarks does he mention?

QUOTATION FOR THE DAY

"If you reject the food, ignore the customs, fear the religion and avoid the people, you might better stay home." (James A. Michener, 1907– , American writer)

Have students restate the quotation in their own words and spend a few minutes responding to the quotation in writing. Explain that writing, like travel, requires students to learn new ways of thinking and new ways of expressing themselves.

LEP/ESL

General Strategies. Before assigning the **Writing Workshop** exercise, you may want to create a set of directions as a group. Choose a place close to school and ask students to give you directions to it. Draw a map on the chalkboard and mark the path as they give you directions to help them visualize the importance of clear directions.

TEACHING THE LESSON

You may want to spend some time with students brainstorming possible uses for travel directions and reasons why accurate directions are important. Point out that directions can incorporate travel by land, sea, or air. For guided practice, demonstrate how to give a new student directions to the school cafeteria or library, and write the information on the chalkboard.

For independent practice, students should work independently to write travel directions.

LESS-ADVANCED STUDENTS

You may need to review geographic directions with some students to help them give accurate locations. You could also have students work with partners. In addition to peer tutoring, you might recommend to students that they use travel directions to destinations with which they are familiar.

ADVANCED STUDENTS

Some students might want to focus on locations that perhaps exist only in their imaginations, or they might want to do a little research in their library to guide travelers to a place the writers have never experienced but would like to visit.

LEARNING STYLES

Kinetic Learners. Some students might want to move around the room as they create their maps, to help them visualize the steps.

SELECTION AMENDMENT
Description of change: excerpted
Rationale: to focus on the concept of travel directions presented in this chapter

from The Sword of Shannara
by Terry Brooks

"Well, at least we've made it this far," he declared cheerfully. "Now for the next leg of the trip!"

He sat up and began to sketch a quick map of the area in the dry earth. Shea and Flick sat up with him and watched quietly.

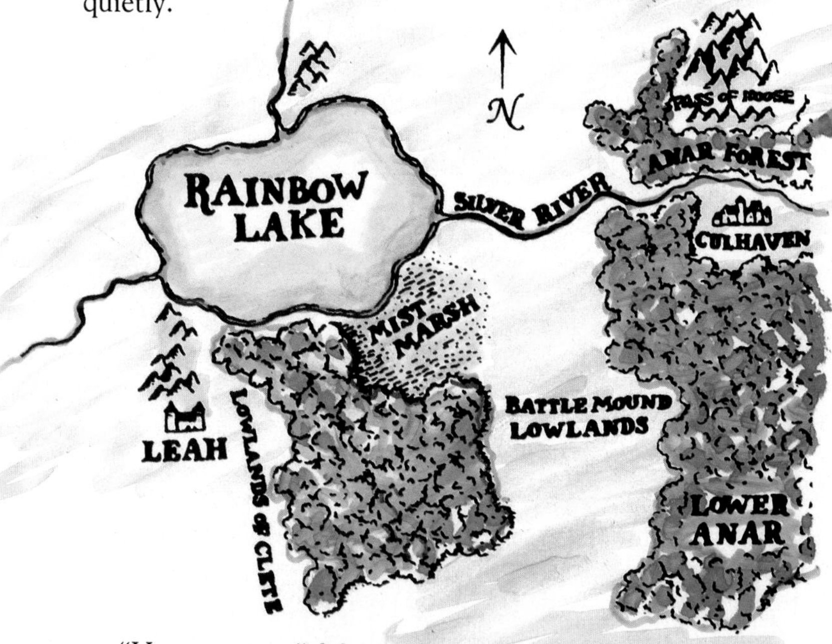

"Here we are," Menion pointed to a spot on the dirt map representing the fringe of the Black Oaks. "At least that's where I think we are," he added quickly. "To the north is the Mist Marsh and farther north of that the Rainbow Lake, out of which runs the Silver River east to the Anar Forests. Our best bet is to travel north tomorrow until we reach the edge of the Mist Marsh. Then we'll skirt the edge of the swamp," he traced a long line, "and come out on the other side of the Black Oaks. From there, we can travel due north until we run into the Silver River, and that should get us safely to the Anar."

ASSESSMENT

Ask each student to evaluate a partner's map, using the instructions in the **Writing, Evaluating, and Revising** step. Ask students to attach the evaluations to their partners' maps. You can then quickly assess how students are doing by comparing the two maps.

CLOSURE

Read one student's paper aloud and then ask the following questions:

1. What details give information about geographical directions and landmarks?
2. Where is the starting place, and what is the final destination? Did the writer make these locations clear? ■

Thinking It Over

1. How does the map help Shea and Flick understand Menion's directions?
2. Find some details that give you information about geographical directions and landmarks.
3. Which part of this trip would you enjoy? Can you find hints that the journey will be dangerous?

Writing Travel Directions

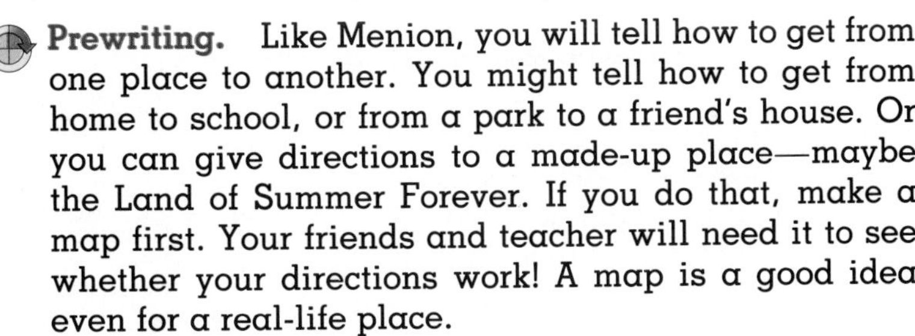

Prewriting. Like Menion, you will tell how to get from one place to another. You might tell how to get from home to school, or from a park to a friend's house. Or you can give directions to a made-up place—maybe the Land of Summer Forever. If you do that, make a map first. Your friends and teacher will need it to see whether your directions work! A map is a good idea even for a real-life place.

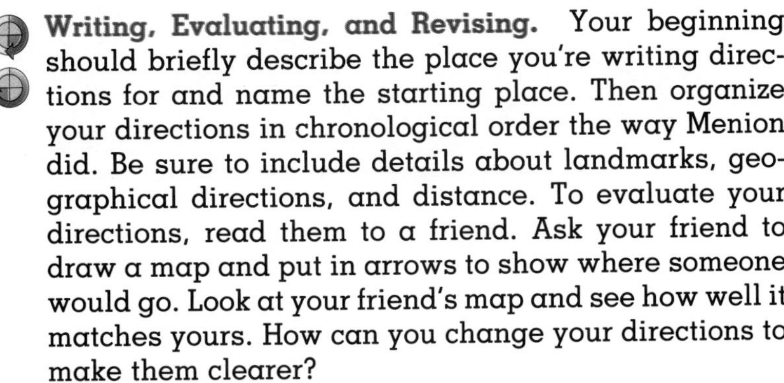

Writing, Evaluating, and Revising. Your beginning should briefly describe the place you're writing directions for and name the starting place. Then organize your directions in chronological order the way Menion did. Be sure to include details about landmarks, geographical directions, and distance. To evaluate your directions, read them to a friend. Ask your friend to draw a map and put in arrows to show where someone would go. Look at your friend's map and see how well it matches yours. How can you change your directions to make them clearer?

Proofreading and Publishing. Be sure to check your punctuation, capitalization, and spelling before setting someone off on a journey. Is your landmark a *hill* or a *mill*? It makes a difference! You could swap neighborhood directions with others who live near you. Or you could play a draw-the-map game—as suggested in the paragraph above—with a small group.

ANSWERS

Thinking It Over

Any answer that may vary is indicated by an asterisk (*).

1. The map shows the starting point, important landmarks, and important bodies of water.
2. To the north is Mist Marsh. Farther north of that is Rainbow Lake, out of which the Silver River runs east, to the Anar Forest.

*3. Some hints that traveling might be dangerous are "Our best bet is to travel north," "we'll skirt the edge of the swamp," and "that should get us safely to the Anar."

COOPERATIVE LEARNING

Divide the class into groups of four and take them outdoors or to a location in the school where they can quietly talk without disturbing other students. Before leaving the classroom, give each group a compass and instructions for using it, and ask them to describe what they see to the northwest, northeast, southwest, and southeast.

SEGMENT 8 *(pp. 200–201)*

MAKING CONNECTIONS

PROCESS IN LITERATURE OBJECTIVE

- To choose a process riddle and ask classmates to guess the answer

PROCESS IN LITERATURE

Teaching Strategies

Explain to students that the words used in riddles often have more than one meaning and the writer may try to use a particular meaning to confuse the audience. You may want to discuss famous riddles in literature. Many of Emily Dickinson's poems are written as riddles, so you could have students read some of her poetry.

GUIDELINES

Students' riddles should describe processes.

COOPERATIVE LEARNING

Have groups of students write their own riddles. Arrange the riddles into a bulletin board display. Challenge students to guess the answers to the other groups' riddles.

MAKING CONNECTIONS

PROCESS IN LITERATURE

Riddle Poems

Here's a riddle from *When I Dance* by Jamaican writer James Berry. Can you figure out the answer?

Riddle my this, riddle my that—
guess my riddle or perhaps not.
Hill is my pillow, I have my own bed,
I stretch out, then I roll
side to side—
what am I?

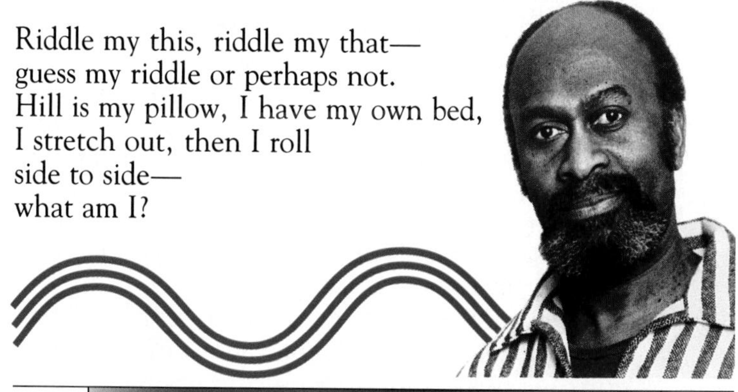

"What am I?" riddles like this often describe a process. When you figure out the process, you know the riddle's answer. But the process may be written in a tricky way! Words may have more than one meaning, like river *bed* in James Berry's riddle poem.

You can find many other riddles that make you figure out a process. Ask people in your family if they know any riddles, or look for "What am I?" riddles in the library. Choose the process riddle you like best. Then see if your classmates can guess the answer.

Answer: A river from its source to meeting and mixing with the sea.

SPEAKING AND LISTENING OBJECTIVE

- To write the steps for a first-aid process and to prepare a class demonstration

SPEAKING AND LISTENING

Science and Health: First Aid

In emergencies, you hope that someone knows how to give first aid. If no one else knows what to do, *your* first-aid skills may save someone's life.

Most first-aid instruction is a clear list of steps. For example, here's what to do if someone is choking.

1. Stand behind the person.
2. Put your arms around the person's waist.
3. Place your fist against the middle of the person's waist. The right place is just below the ribs.
4. With your other hand, grab your fist.
5. Pull your fist in. Use a quick, upward motion.

Fortunately for Sparky, Zeke knew the famous "Rex maneuver."

Get together with two classmates. Choose one of the following emergencies: burn, sprain, cut, nosebleed, or bee sting. Together, find out the first-aid process for helping the injured person. You can look for information in scout handbooks, Red Cross manuals, health books, and encyclopedias. Write down the first-aid steps for the emergency, and prepare a class demonstration.

SPEAKING AND LISTENING

Teaching Strategies

Emphasize to students that the steps in this process must be very clear because first aid is usually administered in an emergency situation. You may want to suggest that students include injuries that are unique to your area, such as frostbite, snakebite, or dehydration. Students should work in groups to present class demonstrations of emergency procedures. You may want to ask students to prepare a handout for their classmates. When students have all completed their handouts, they can make a first-aid manual.

GUIDELINES

The first-aid process should include a clear list of the steps involved.

Chapter 7

WRITING TO PERSUADE

OBJECTIVES

- To analyze persuasive writing and to freewrite a response
- To write about ways to persuade in a journal entry
- To analyze a call to action in persuasive writing
- To explore and choose a possible persuasion topic
- To write an opinion statement
- To number supporting evidence in order of importance
- To use a chart to gather support for an opinion statement
- To test support in a small-group situation
- To identify facts and opinions
- To analyze persuasive writing in a magazine article
- To write a draft of a persuasive essay
- To analyze a writer's revisions
- To evaluate and revise a persuasive essay
- To proofread and publish a persuasive essay
- To determine audience for a persuasive letter
- To identify a statement of opinion in a persuasive letter
- To use the writing process to write and summarize support in a persuasive letter
- To recognize and identify the use of bandwagon and testimonial appeals in advertisements
- To create a presentation to convince city voters to build a historical museum

Motivation

To motivate students for this chapter and to help students begin thinking about persuasion, ask students to freewrite responses to the following prompts:

1. Think of the last time you tried to convince someone to do something for you. Describe how you went about convincing the person to do it.

2. How successful were you in getting results?

3. Why do you think he or she refused or accepted your request?

After students have responded, discuss the answers with the class. Students will discover that persuasion is used in many ways and in many different places.

Introduction

As students share their experiences, help them understand that convincing people is not an easy task. To persuade others to agree with an opinion, a person needs strong arguments that listeners will accept. The arguments must be carefully planned and well said. Convincing others often involves appealing to their emotions.

Integration

This chapter has many opportunities for students to use persuasion across the curriculum. Students will have the opportunity to complete a project to convince city voters to build a historical museum.

Students will integrate this chapter with grammar by examining ways to combine sentences and by learning when to use *since* or *because* to make ideas clearer and writing smoother.

Students will be encouraged throughout the chapter to integrate composition skills with public concerns. After completing the activities in this chapter, students will have had an opportunity to develop an awareness of what is going on in their school and community.

The chart on the next page illustrates the strands of language arts as they are integrated into this chapter. For vocabulary study, glossary words are underlined in some writing models.

QUOTATIONS
All **Quotations for the Day** are chosen because of their relevance to instructional material presented in that segment of the chapter and for their usefulness in establishing student interest in writing.

INTEGRATING THE LANGUAGE ARTS

Selection	Reading and Literature	Writing and Critical Thinking	Language and Syntax	Speaking, Listening, and Other Expression Skills
from ***Henry Reed, Inc.*** by Keith Robertson **204-206** from ***Manatee on Location*** by Kathy Darling **218-219**	Applying interpretive and creative thinking **207, 212, 216, 220, 223, 229** Identifying and analyzing supporting reasons in writing **207, 220, 223-224, 225** Examining a call to action in a persuasive essay **207, 230** Responding personally to writing **207, 220, 223-224** Examining persuasive language **207, 220, 223-224, 225, 232** Drawing conclusions and making inferences **211, 216, 220, 223, 225, 229** Examining reasons and facts in a persuasive essay **220, 223, 225** Using the framework for a persuasive essay **222** Recognizing persuasion in the media **232**	Writing a journal entry **207** Analyzing persuasive language **207, 220, 223-224, 225** Brainstorming ideas for persuasive writing **212** Choosing a topic **212** Writing an opinion statement **212** Determining order of importance **216, 217** Analyzing audience **217** Identifying facts and opinions **220** Writing a persuasive essay **222, 232-233** Choosing a title **222** Analyzing a writer's revisions **223-224** Evaluating and revising a persuasive essay **225, 232-233** Proofreading and publishing a persuasive essay **226, 232-233** Evaluating propaganda techniques **232** Evaluating emotional appeal in an advertisement **232**	Proofreading for errors in grammar, usage, and mechanics **226, 230** Assessing the impact of emotionally charged words on a listener or a reader **232** Recognizing propaganda in persuasive writing **232**	Brainstorming, writing, and discussing opinion statements in a small group **212** Testing opinion statements and lists of support in a small group **217** Analyzing persuasive writing in a small group **220, 230** Analyzing a writer's revisions with a classmate **223-224** Choosing a medium for delivering a persuasive message **226** Proofreading with a classmate **226** Recognizing the use of persuasive techniques in media **232** Creating a persuasive presentation with a small group **232-233** Examining emotional appeals in an advertisement **232**

CHAPTER 7

SEGMENT PLANNING GUIDE

You can use the following Planning Guide to adapt the chapter material to the individual needs of your class. All the Resources listed in this chapter are located in the *Teacher's ResourceBank™*.

SEGMENT	PAGES	CONTENT	RESOURCES
1 ***Taking a Stand***	***203-207***		
Literary Model from ***Henry Reed, Inc.***	204-206	Guided reading: a model of persuasive writing	
Reader's Response/ Writer's Craft	207	Model evaluation: responding to literature and analyzing persuasive writing	
2 ***Ways to Persuade***	***208***		
3 ***Prewriting***	***209-217***		Writing a Persuasive Paper Supporting an Opinion 56
Choosing a Topic	209	Introduction: finding a good topic for persuasion	
Finding a Topic That Matters	209	Guidelines: selecting a suitable topic	
Focusing Your Opinion	209	Guidelines: writing an opinion statement	
Critical Thinking: Identifying Facts and Opinions	210-211	Guidelines: examining facts and opinion statements	
Critical Thinking Exercise	211	Applied practice: distinguishing facts from opinion statements	
Exercise 1	212	Cooperative learning: brainstorming possible topics	
Writing Assignment: Part 1	212	Applied practice: writing an opinion statement	
Planning Your Paper	213	Introduction: planning a persuasive paper	
Thinking About Purpose and Audience	213	Guidelines: focusing on audience	
Finding Support for Your Opinion	213-214	Guidelines: using reasons, facts, and opinions of experts	
Organizing Your Ideas	215	Guidelines: using order of importance	
Exercise 2	216	Applied practice: arranging statements in order of importance	
Writing Assignment: Part 2	217	Applied practice: supporting an opinion	
Exercise 3	217	Cooperative learning: testing support statements	
4 ***Writing***	***218-222***		Writing a Persuasive Paper 57
The Basics of Persuasion	218	Guidelines: examining the basic elements of persuasion	
Literary Model from ***Manatee on Location***	218-219	Guided reading: analyzing an annotated model of a persuasive passage	
Exercise 4	220	Cooperative learning: analyzing supporting statements	
Writing Note	220	Writing suggestion: using emotional words	

For **Portfolio Assessment** see the following pages in the *Teacher's ResourceBank™*:
Aims For Writing—pp. 55–60
Holistically Graded Composition Models—pp. 403–408
Assessment Portfolio—pp. 421–445

SEGMENT	PAGES	CONTENT	RESOURCES
A Simple Framework for Persuasion	220	Introduction: structuring a persuasive essay	
Writer's Model	221	Guided reading: examining structure in a sample essay	
Chart: Framework for a Persuasive Paper	222	Guidelines: structuring a persuasive essay	
Writing Note	222	Writing suggestion: using transitional words	
Writing Assignment: Part 3	222	Applied practice: writing a first draft	
5 *Evaluating and Revising*	*223-225*		Writing a Persuasive Paper 58
Evaluating and Revising	223	Introduction: improving a first draft	
Exercise 5	223-224	Cooperative learning: analyzing a writer's revisions	
Chart: Evaluating and Revising Persuasive Writing	224	Guidelines: applying evaluation and revision techniques	
Grammar Hint	225	Guidelines: combining sentences with *since* and *because*	
Writing Assignment: Part 4	225	Applied practice: evaluating and revising an essay	
6 *Proofreading and Publishing*	*226-227*		Writing a Persuasive Paper 59
Publishing	226	Publishing ideas: reaching an audience	
Writing Assignment: Part 5	226	Applied practice: proofreading and publishing	
Student Model	227	Sample: deciding effectiveness of persuasion in a student essay	
7 *Writing Workshop*	*228-230*		
Writing a Persuasive Letter	228	Introduction: writing a persuasive letter	
Model/Questions	228-229	Examining techniques: analyzing a sample letter	
Writing a Persuasive Letter	229-230	Applied practice: applying skills to the writing process	
8 *Making Connections*	*231-233*		
Persuasion in Advertising: Language Arts	231-232	Guidelines: examining emotional appeal Applied practice: collecting bandwagon and testimonial ads	
Persuasion Across the Curriculum: Social Studies	232-233	Guidelines: making a presentation Cooperative learning: creating a presentation of persuasion	

WHOLE-CHAPTER RESOURCES
A Writing Process Log, A Writing Prompt, Holistically Graded Models, Assessment Portfolio Materials

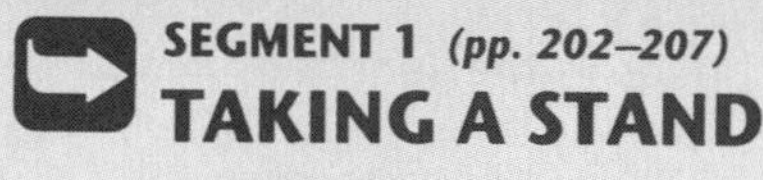

SEGMENT 1 *(pp. 202–207)*

TAKING A STAND

OBJECTIVES

- To analyze persuasive writing and to freewrite a response
- To write about ways to persuade in a journal entry
- To list reasons supporting an opinion
- To analyze a call to action in persuasive writing

VISUAL CONNECTIONS

Ideas for Writing. This picture shows one way wildlife is endangered by humans. Have students brainstorm other facets of human behavior that threaten animals. Then discuss with the class what could be done to protect animals. Emphasize the importance of considering not only preventative but also reparative actions. Interested students can use their notes from the discussion to write persuasive papers focusing on protecting specific animals.

Related Expression Skills. Posters like this one have been effective persuasive tools throughout American history. Discuss with students the elements of this poster, and have them work individually or in groups to create persuasive posters following the model of this illustration. Display the posters in the classroom.

7 WRITING TO PERSUADE

PROTECT
OUR
WILDLIFE

MOTIVATION

Ask students how they would convince their parents or guardians to let them go to a party. Have them discuss the persuasive reasons they might use to convince their parents.

TEACHING THE LESSON

Discuss how Midge Glass pursued her hope of being allowed to join a business by addressing the following important aspects of persuasion:

1. Who did Midge use as a resource to convince Henry Reed he needed a co-worker? [Midge used her father.]

Taking a Stand

When you feel strongly about something, you **take a stand.** You say, "Listen. This is what I believe, and why I believe it." Then you try to persuade others to think or feel the same way. Notice how the poster on these pages tries to persuade you.

Writing and You. There are different ways to persuade. You can give logical reasons. Or you can try to use words that will affect people's feelings. Usually, people do a little of both. The government urges you to recycle; advertisers try to convince you to buy a certain brand of hair gel or jeans; your parents try to get you to study harder; and you try to convince them to let you go to a party. Have you taken a stand lately?

As You Read. In the following story passage, Midge Glass tries to persuade Henry Reed that her brains will help him with his business.

QUOTATION FOR THE DAY

"The chief danger in life is that you may take too many precautions." (Alfred Adler, 1870–1937, Austrian psychiatrist)

Write the quotation on the chalkboard and ask students to freewrite for a few minutes about what Adler's quotation means. Use the quotation to encourage students not to be afraid to take stands or to have strong opinions.

LESS-ADVANCED STUDENTS

For the **Reader's Response,** encourage students to write dialogues that describe situations in which they felt strongly about something and tried to persuade others to think or feel the same way. By encouraging students to write about something meaningful in their daily lives, you will facilitate their active involvement in the material.

Explain to students that often experts are used to back up an opinion or a statement of fact in persuasive writing.

2. After reading the excerpt, why do you think audience is very important in persuasion? [You must appeal to one person or one group's emotions and sense of reasoning.]

GUIDED PRACTICE

Discuss the first **Reader's Response** question with the class before students begin to freewrite.

A DIFFERENT APPROACH

You may want to show students an advertisement for a product they might use, such as an athletic shoe, a soft drink, or a backpack. Ask students how the advertiser is trying to convince the consumer to purchase the product. [The advertiser tries to convince the consumer that he or she will be in style, more popular, a better student, a better athlete, and so on.]

INTEGRATING THE LANGUAGE ARTS

Literature Link. Have students read and examine "The Emperor's New Clothes" by Hans Christian Andersen. In this story, two weavers persuade the emperor that only worthy men can see the new garments. Discuss the following questions with students after they have finished the story:

1. How do the two weavers persuade the emperor to buy their clothes? [The weavers tell him that what they make will be invisible to everyone who is unfit for office.]
2. What attitude does the emperor have toward clothing that the weavers use to their advantage? [The emperor wants to own the finest clothes.]

SELECTION AMENDMENT
Description of change: excerpted
Rationale: to focus on the concept of persuasion presented in this chapter

from

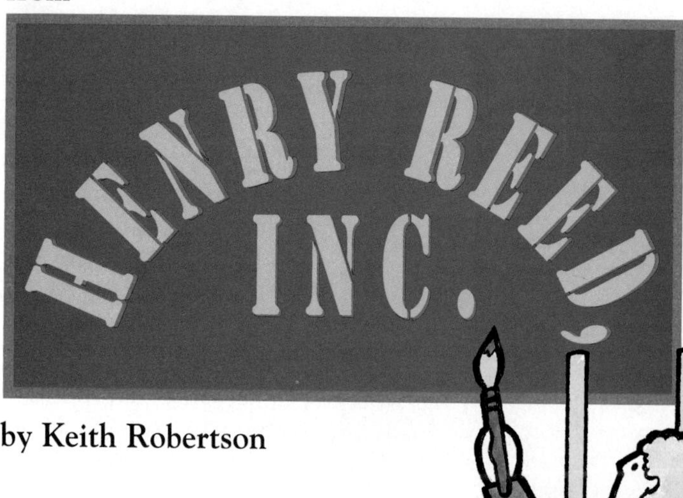

by Keith Robertson

"Why should I?"

"Teamwork," she answered. "Teamwork's the thing these days in research. My father says things have gotten so complicated that one man alone can't discover much any more."

I thought this over for a minute while I kept working on my sign. If her father was a research chemist like she said, she probably knew quite a bit about how research organizations work, and also with the whole summer ahead of me I figured it might be nice to have someone to talk to, even if it was a girl a year and a half younger than I. I turned around and sat down on the ladder.

INDEPENDENT PRACTICE

Students should answer **Reader's Response** question 2 and all of the **Writer's Craft** questions independently. These questions will check for comprehension of the persuasive aim.

ASSESSMENT

To assess students' comprehension, read through responses to **Writer's Craft** questions 3–5. You may also want to discuss the answers in class to allow students to hear and understand the correct answers.

"What are you going to put into the business?" I
1 asked. "I've got the property here, the building, a lot of pigeons which are inside, and one turtle." I waved my hand up at the half-finished sign, which was pretty good. "I'm even furnishing the sign."

"I'll furnish brains," she said.

Even though I always try to be polite, I laughed out loud at that, but she didn't seem to mind.

"Brains are the most important part of any research organization. My father says so."

"He's probably right," I admitted. "But the question is who has them? What grade are you in?"

"Seventh," she replied.

"There you are," I said. "I'm in the eighth grade so I've had more education. I've had more experience, too. I'm a teen-ager and you're only twelve."

"That's no advantage," she said. "Who are all these <u>delinquent</u> children you read about in the papers? Teen-agers—that's you. Me, I'm not a teenager so I must be a respectable, law-abiding citizen."

USING THE SELECTION

***from* Henry Reed, Inc.**

1

Is Henry's response persuasive?
How? [Henry provides examples to show that he possesses the equipment necessary for the business, so Midge's presence will not be necessary to make the business a success.]

COOPERATIVE LEARNING

Have students work in groups of three to brainstorm ways that persuasion can be used in advertising. Discuss how advertisers want people to think that they need their products because it will benefit them personally in some way. Give each group at least three advertisements and ask them to report findings to the class.

1. What does the advertisement want you to do or buy?
2. How does the advertisement convince you that you need the product?
3. Is this an effective advertisement? Why or why not?

CLOSURE

Discuss the following questions:

1. Why is knowing your audience important in persuasive writing? [You must appeal to the emotions of a certain group or individual.]
2. Name at least three places to find persuasive writing [radio, television, newspapers, and billboards].
3. When is persuasion encountered in everyday life? [It is used in advertising and when people try to convince someone to believe or to do something.]

She started laughing like an idiot again. I don't know what about, since her remark didn't even make any sense. I climbed down the ladder and put my can of paint and brush on a box. I sharpened my pencil and started toward the ladder again.

"I could also contribute a pair of rabbits," she said. "We could raise rabbits, and they use a lot of rabbits in research to test serum and drugs and feeds and things like that."

I thought this over for a minute. I've never had any rabbits because we have never lived anyplace where there was room enough. "What kind of rabbits?" I asked.

2 "Checkered Giants," Midge replied. "They're great big white rabbits with black spots."

"That might not be a bad idea," I said, "to have a few rabbits."

"You could just make that 'Reed and Glass, Inc.,' " she said, pointing up at my sign.

I had just finished painting the words "Henry Reed" and I didn't care much for the idea of changing my sign before it was half finished. "Let's see the rabbits first," I suggested.

2
How has Midge's use of description helped to persuade Henry? [She is able to give some information about the kind of rabbits she could provide to the business.]

EXTENSION

Ask students to make journal entries as if they were writing to their principal. In the entries, students should convince the principal of something such as the need for a larger cafeteria, an additional course, or a new type of sport at their school. ■

Reader's Response

1. If you were Midge, would you give different answers to "Why should I?" If you were Henry, would you ask Midge other questions? Pretend you are either character, and freewrite what you would say to the other. You could also work up a skit with a friend.
2. Can you think of a time when you wanted someone to let you join in or tag along or share something? What did you say or do? What do you *wish* you had said or done? Write about it in your journal.

Writer's Craft

3. What reasons does Midge give Henry to convince him?
4. He thinks two of the reasons are pretty good ones. One reason makes him laugh. Explain his reactions.
5. Persuasion that asks you to do something ends with a ***call to action:*** a suggestion for a specific act. What does Midge try to get Henry to do (probably so he can't easily change his mind)?

ANSWERS

Reader's Response

Responses will vary.

1. Midge might want to add other benefits for Henry; for example, he could take a vacation if he had a partner to work with, customers would see that he is willing to work with others and capable of handling a lot of work, or someone could always be at the business in case Henry had to leave.
2. Encourage students to include examples of persuasion in their journal entries.

Writer's Craft

3. Teamwork is needed in research; she can contribute intelligence; as a twelve-year-old she is a respectable, law-abiding citizen; and she could contribute rabbits.
4. Henry likes the idea of having a partner to talk to, and he likes the idea of Midge contributing rabbits. Henry laughs when Midge says she will contribute intelligence. His reaction is based on the fact that she is younger than he is, so he feels he should know more about running a business.
5. Midge suggests that Henry add her name to the sign that he has been painting, which would show that he has agreed to let her become his business partner.

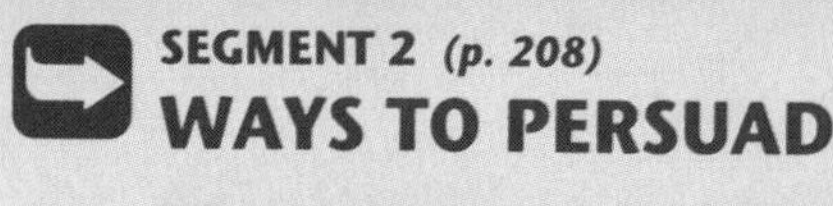

SEGMENT 2 *(p. 208)*

WAYS TO PERSUADE

TEACHING THE MODES

This segment teaches students the various forms that persuasion can take. Explain that the modes—narration, description, classification, and evaluation—can all lead to the persuasive aim. After discussing modes, ask students to write a brief example of each mode.

To assess student comprehension, quiz students orally over what they have learned. ■

COOPERATIVE LEARNING

Divide the class into groups of three or four. Have students act out each of the four modes in skits. The class should be able to determine the mode by examining the content of each skit. Discuss each skit's mode to make sure all students have mastered the concepts.

CRITICAL THINKING

Synthesis

To give students practice in using the persuasive modes, ask each student to create an example of at least one mode for the class to identify. Students can use the suggestions in the textbook as models.

Ways to Persuade

Persuasion has many different forms and messages. You can recognize it in sermons and songs as well as in articles and books. The goal is always the same, though: to convince someone to believe or act a certain way. Here are some examples of ways to persuade.

Narration: writing about a chess tournament to convince students to start a chess club; telling your cousins a story about your grandmother's childhood to persuade them to come to a family reunion.

Description: describing a piñata to persuade your art teacher to let you make one; describing a homeless kitten to persuade your parents to let you keep it.

Classification: defining the word *friend* to convince a friend to help you baby-sit your three young neighbors; comparing ravioli and lasagna to persuade your brother to try lasagna.

Evaluation: evaluating a new television show and trying to persuade your family to watch it; forming an opinion about a tutoring program and trying to convince classmates to help tutor second-graders.

LOOKING AHEAD

In this chapter, you will use the strategy of evaluation to write a persuasive composition and a persuasive letter. As you develop your writing assignments, keep in mind that effective persuasion

- states an opinion clearly
- gives convincing support for the opinion

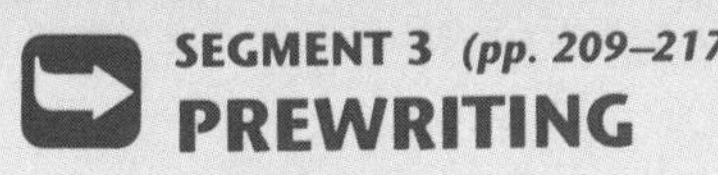

SEGMENT 3 *(pp. 209–217)*

PREWRITING

OBJECTIVES

- To number supporting evidence in order of importance
- To use a chart to gather support for an opinion statement
- To test support in a small group situation

MOTIVATION

Ask students to respond to the following statements on paper with *A* for agree or *D* for disagree:

1. I think everyone should own at least one dog.
2. The best dessert is hot apple pie.

Cont. on p. 211

Writing a Persuasive Paper

Prewriting

Choosing a Topic

You hear on the news that the city council is considering this law: No one under the age of fourteen can be on the street after 9 P.M. on school nights. You don't want this curfew law to be passed, but some other people think it's a good idea. This would be a good topic for persuasion.

Finding a Topic That Matters. What makes you mad? Litter on your street? What do you think should be changed in your school? Dress rules? If you care about something and have a strong opinion about what should be done, you can write about it.

Of course, it's also important that some other people disagree with you. If everyone has the same opinion about litter, you don't have anyone to persuade. Make sure you choose a topic about which people have different opinions.

Focusing Your Opinion. Sometimes you're not sure exactly what you think until you try to put something into writing. What do you really think should be done about your school's dress rules? No rules at all? Rules for Friday but not for Monday? To focus your opinion, write a sentence saying exactly what you believe. This *opinion statement* is the starting point of your paper. Here are some examples:

The curfew law should not be passed.
Our school lunchroom should have a salad bar.
Writing a pen pal is a great way to learn about another country.

Teacher's ResourceBank™

RESOURCES

PREWRITING

QUOTATION FOR THE DAY

"The vital, successful people I have met all had one common characteristic. They had a plan." (Marilyn Van Derbur, former Miss America)

Use the quotation to illustrate the importance of the prewriting stage of the writing process. As students begin thinking about audience and purpose, selecting and narrowing a topic, and asking questions and finding sources, remind them that having a plan will make their work much easier and their finished products much better.

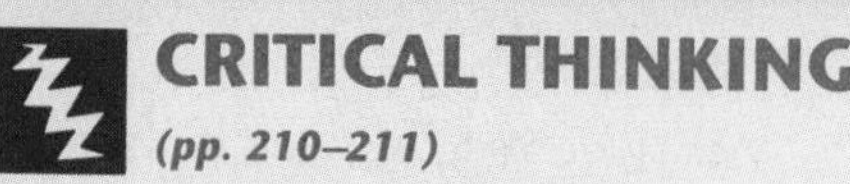

CRITICAL THINKING
(pp. 210–211)

OBJECTIVE
- To identify facts and opinions

TEACHING *IDENTIFYING FACTS AND OPINIONS*

To help students understand the difference between fact and opinion, explain that facts do not vary but opinions vary from person to person, creating the possibility of persuasion. You may want to find cassettes or videotapes of political or motivational speeches to help students understand how

LEP/ESL

Spanish. Having students work in small groups reinforces the value that some cultures place on collective, cooperative efforts rather than on individual, competitive ones. In assigning the **Critical Thinking Exercise,** encourage students to compare mental notes about the statements of fact and opinion. Have students complete the evaluation as a team.

CRITICAL THINKING
Application

Ask students to monitor all advertisements they see and hear for one day and to write down how facts are manipulated to support opinions. Have each student present one example to the class. Have the class discuss whether or not the persuasive tactics were effective for the product.

VISUAL CONNECTIONS

Ideas for Writing. Ask each student to write three facts and three opinions about his or her favorite athlete or sports team. Students can share their work with partners or with the class.

CRITICAL THINKING

Identifying Facts and Opinions

A *fact* is a statement that can be tested and proved true. Facts can be checked in books and other sources.

FACTS The moon has many craters on its surface.
Nolan Ryan is the third pitcher in baseball history to strike out three hundred men in back-to-back seasons.

An *opinion* states a personal belief. Opinions can't be proved or checked in books. Notice that opinions often contain "judgment words," such as *good, best, worst, least, most, should, ought.*

OPINIONS The United States should build a space station on the moon.
The best name for our new ball field is Nolan Ryan Park.

facts and opinions can be used persuasively. Explain that although facts are constant, people can manipulate facts to echo opinions. Point out that the most persuasive papers rely on opinions for emotional appeal and on facts to support these opinions.

Cont. from p. 209

3. Every school should have a dress code.
4. We rely on gravity to stay on the earth.
5. George Washington was the first president of the United States.

Explain to students that statements that cannot be supported with facts are opinion statements. (Statements 1–3 are opinion statements.) Statements that can

In persuasion, you need to be able to tell facts from opinions. Here's why:

- Your opinion statement expresses a belief. You aren't trying to persuade others of facts.
- You support your opinion statement with facts. These facts help you convince other people that your opinion is right.

CRITICAL THINKING EXERCISE:
Identifying Facts and Opinions

Decide which statements below are facts and which are opinions. Then decide whether each statement would make a good topic for persuasive writing. Explain your thinking.

O 1. Dogs make the best pets.
F 2. Bicycles produce less air pollution than cars.
O 3. Our club should sell tacos at the Spring Fair.
O 4. Zoos are cruel to animals and should be closed.
F 5. The Atlanta Braves baseball team has the best hitters.
F 6. Sunburns cause skin cancer.
F 7. Wearing seat belts saves lives.
F 8. Crocodiles are an endangered species.

ANSWERS
Critical Thinking Exercise

Numbers **2**, **5**, **6**, **7**, and **8** are not good topics because the facts can be proven and there would be no reason to persuade.

1. Students might say that this could become an emotional issue and that supporting evidence could be found easily.
3. Some students might say this is a good topic because they will be trying to convince other club members or perhaps the school principal of the benefits from this type of fund-raising; some students might say that there would be few opponents to this subject.
4. Students might say that this would be a very emotional topic for writing and that they could find examples of cruelty to support their opinion statements; this would be an excellent topic for a persuasive essay because students could convince an audience of zoo enthusiasts that people who really care about animals would not want them to suffer.

be supported with evidence and that do not vary from person to person are statements of fact. (Statements 4 and 5 are statements of facts.) Ask students how fact and opinion statements are important to persuasive writing. [Opinion statements offer a starting point, while facts are intended to make the opinion believable and convincing.]

TEACHING THE LESSON

List on the chalkboard the stages of writing a persuasive paper so that students can clearly see how the steps fit together.

1. exploring possible topics
2. choosing a topic
3. writing an opinion statement

LESS-ADVANCED STUDENTS

You may need to give some students additional guidance in selecting topics. Sometimes students tend to choose topics that are too broad or too narrow. To help students avoid this problem, ask them if they can write at least three topic sentences for their subjects. If they can, then their subjects are probably specific enough and can probably be covered adequately in short persuasive essays.

ADVANCED STUDENTS

Suggest that students look to outside sources for information on their subjects for writing. For example, if students are writing to their city council to convince the city to build another city pool, you may want to suggest that students visit a city council meeting to find out how decisions are made. If students are trying to convince their parents to allow them to have pets, students can contact a local veterinarian's office to find out how much caring for the puppy will cost in the first year.

ANSWERS

Exercise 1

Students will have successfully completed **Exercise 1** when they have each chosen two topics and written two opinion statements. Have the class discuss writing potential for each topic.

When you choose a topic for persuasive writing

- find a topic you care about
- make sure everyone doesn't already have the same opinion about it
- write one sentence that clearly states your opinion

EXERCISE 1 **Exploring Possible Topics**

In a small group, brainstorm possible persuasion topics. (You can start with general subjects like the environment, schools, the homeless, movies, and TV. But also remember that you'll need to narrow down any general subjects.) Each person then chooses two of the topics and writes opinion statements for them. Discuss your statements. Who disagrees? Which topics create interest?

WRITING ASSIGNMENT PART 1: **Choosing a Topic**

Will you write about a topic from the brainstorming you did in your small group? Will you take a stand on something else? Your journal and newspapers are also sources for topics you care about. Choose one and write your opinion statement.

4. determining purpose, audience, and tone
5. distinguishing fact from opinion
6. stating reasons and evidence to support the thesis statement

Make sure students understand that fact and opinion are necessary to write persuasive essays. Explain that opinions cannot be proved or checked in books.

GUIDED PRACTICE

Students will work in small groups to complete **Exercise 1.**

Complete **Exercise 2** with the class so that students will have a clear understanding of order of importance before they complete **Writing Assignment: Part 2** independently.

Planning Your Paper

Suppose you're facing your audience in person. You have stated your opinion. But the people in the audience just sit there, looking doubtful. "Why should we believe you?" they ask. To persuade them, you have to build a convincing answer.

Thinking About Purpose and Audience

Your *purpose* is always to persuade your *audience* to agree with you. You want your readers to think or to feel the same way you do about something. Sometimes, too, you'll add a *call to action* that asks them to do something. For instance, you may want them to vote for building a school taco stand or to volunteer for cleaning the schoolyard.

Think ahead about your audience. Ask yourself, *What do my readers think about my topic? What reasons will appeal to them? Will I ask them to take an action?*

Finding Support for Your Opinion

Suppose you've been studying about nutritious meals and you think people shouldn't eat doughnuts for breakfast every day. You can't just write "Don't do it. It's bad for you." To support your opinions, you can use *reasons, facts,* and *the opinions of experts.* Here are some examples:

- **Reasons:** Doughnuts are fattening.
- **Facts:** A yeast doughnut has about 235 calories. That's more than four times the calories in a serving of strawberries.
- **Expert opinions:** Mrs. Capo, the cafeteria manager, says that doughnuts are high in sugar and fat, not protein.

LEARNING STYLES

Visual Learners. Advertisements provide excellent examples of persuasion. Have students choose a TV or magazine ad and have them think about the use of pictures, symbols, music, colors, and words. To help them analyze the ad, have them complete the following statements:

1. This ad makes the reader think or feel . . .
2. The advertisers chose these pictures or symbols because . . .
3. This ad is persuading people to . . .

CRITICAL THINKING

Analysis

To help students understand audience, write the following opinion statements on the chalkboard and have the class discuss why and how the persuasive supporting evidence will change to appeal to each audience.

1. Our school should buy more computers. (audiences: students, parents, teachers)
2. Students need a longer lunch period. (audiences: students, cafeteria personnel, teachers)
3. Our town should sponsor a carnival to honor outstanding citizens. (audiences: Chamber of Commerce, parents, business owners)

INDEPENDENT PRACTICE

Students should work independently in **Writing Assignment: Part 1** to establish topics. Students may refer to journal entries, newspapers, or other sources for topics. Then each student should write one opinion statement. After students have discussed **Exercise 2** as a class, they should apply what they have learned to complete **Writing Assignment: Part 2** independently.

INTEGRATING THE LANGUAGE ARTS

Writing and Mechanics. Students who are using expert opinions might need to use quotations in their persuasive essays. You may want to give students a few reminders on how to punctuate quotations correctly.

1. A direct quotation is set off from the rest of the sentence by commas or by a question mark or exclamation point in addition to quotation marks.
2. Commas and periods are always placed inside closing quotation marks.

Write the following sentence on the chalkboard and ask students to punctuate it correctly:

Principal Smith explained School funds to buy new textbooks are not possible now because the school has a leaky roof that must be fixed. [Principal Smith explained, "School funds to buy new textbooks are not possible now because the school has a leaky roof that must be fixed."]

Sometimes you'll be able to think of reasons and facts by yourself. For some topics, though, you'll need to find support in books, magazines, and other library resources. These sources will also give you expert opinions to quote. But don't forget about people in your school or community who know something about your topic. You can quote them, too.

There's no magic number of reasons when you're writing persuasion. But two or three items of support are probably fine for a short paper. Here's how one writer gathered reasons, facts, and expert opinions for a paper.

OPINION:	*Our city should have a tree-planting program.*
AUDIENCE:	*The city council*
SUPPORT:	*1. Trees are pretty.* *2. Trees give off oxygen (helps fight pollution).* *3. Trees make shade.* *4. They lower traffic noise that can damage hearing. (Yori Matsuo, pres. Arbor Club)*

ASSESSMENT

To assess students' comprehension for **Writing Assignment: Part 1,** ask students to read their opinion statements aloud. If you find that an opinion statement is too general or unclear, brainstorm as a class to focus the statement. To assess **Writing Assignment: Part 2,** read over students' charts. You may want to ask students to use the right margin to label each supporting detail as a reason, a fact, or an expert's opinion. Remind students that they need a variety of support to be persuasive.

Organizing Your Ideas

Some reasons and facts are more convincing than others. Look at these reasons for not riding your bicycle into a wall:

1. You could leave a scuff mark on the wall.
2. You could bend your wheel.
3. You could break your head.

Probably the first reason is totally unimportant to you—hardly worth mentioning. The second reason is more important, and the last one is most important of all.

A good way to arrange your support is ***order of importance:*** from least important reason to most important, or the opposite. Either will work. In persuasion, you can start with a strong punch or end with one.

CLOSURE

Discuss the following questions with your class:

1. What is the first step in writing a persuasive essay? [finding an issue that matters to the writer]
2. What is the difference between a fact and an opinion? [Opinions cannot be proved true. Facts can be proved true or false.]
3. How can you find information to support your opinions? [by talking to experts, by using facts, and by providing reasons] ■

Reminder

To plan a persuasive paper

- support your opinion with reasons, facts, expert opinions
- choose support you think will convince your audience
- arrange your support in order of importance

EXERCISE 2 **Using Order of Importance**

"Just *try* to convince me," says the audience. Think about the following opinion statement, specific audience, and support. Choose the reasons you think will be most convincing to this audience. Then number the reasons in order of importance, with 1 as most important. Be ready to explain your thinking.

OPINION: Neighborhood businesses should hire kids to pick up litter from the streets.
AUDIENCE: Neighborhood Merchants Association
REASONS:
a. City employees will have less work to do.
b. People like to shop in an area with clean streets.
c. Picking up litter teaches kids good citizenship habits.
d. Kids will have more money to spend in the neighborhood stores.

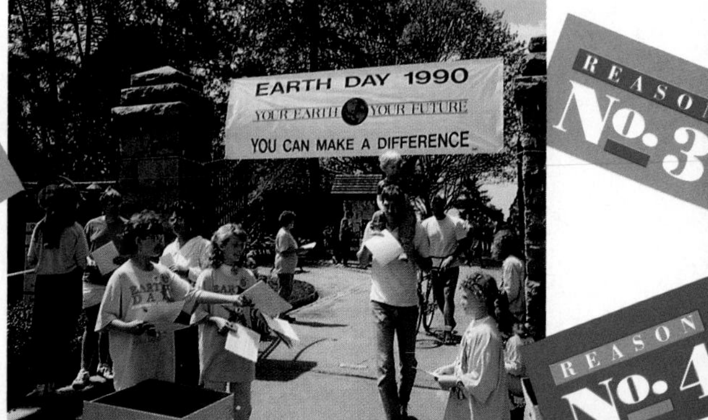
EARTH DAY 1990
YOUR EARTH YOUR FUTURE
YOU CAN MAKE A DIFFERENCE
REASON No. 3
REASON No. 4

REASON No. 1
REASON No. 2

ANSWERS

Exercise 2

Order of importance will vary, but most students will find that this order is logical: b, d, c, a. Explain that although learning good habits is important, merchants will be looking for direct benefits from having clean streets.

VISUAL CONNECTIONS

Related Expression Skills. Ask students to brainstorm other ways that they can help improve the environment and also receive personal benefits. To help students share their ideas, ask them to illustrate their ideas for display in the classroom. Students may want to use these ideas for their persuasive papers.

PART 2:
Supporting Your Opinion

Use a chart like the one on page 214 to gather support for your opinion. Be sure to identify your audience. Then ask yourself, *Why should they believe me?* Jot down all the reasons and facts you can think of. If your support seems weak, use the library or talk to experts on your topic. Finally, number your support in the order of importance to your audience.

EXERCISE 3
Speaking and Listening: Testing Your Support

In a small group, test the strength of your supporting ideas. First, identify your audience. Your listeners will then pretend to be that audience. Read your opinion statement and list of support once. Next, read everything again. This time your audience can stop you to ask questions or even to argue! Answer as best you can, and also make notes about good ideas. Finally, before you change roles, discuss which parts of your support were strong and which seemed weak. And don't forget what the "arguers" said—you may get ideas for other support.

INTEGRATING THE LANGUAGE ARTS

Library Link. Students may want to use the school library to create charts of supporting evidence for **Writing Assignment: Part 2.** In this library session you may need to focus on helping students locate subject information in a card catalog or a library computer system.

TIMESAVER

To save time grading **Writing Assignment: Part 2,** ask students to label their supporting evidence as reasons, facts, or expert opinions. You can quickly assess students' information and make sure they have used a variety of support.

ANSWERS

Exercise 3

Students will have successfully completed **Exercise 3** when they have tried out their support in small groups. You may want to make students responsible for keeping lists of ideas so they will not forget what the audience suggested.

SEGMENT 4 *(pp. 218–222)*

WRITING YOUR FIRST DRAFT

OBJECTIVES

- To analyze persuasive writing in a magazine article
- To write a draft for a persuasive essay

MOTIVATION

Ask students how their favorite film or book begins and discuss why the beginning is interesting. Explain that the person reading the book or watching the film should be interested from the start. Explain that students' papers must begin in an interesting way if they want their audience to continue to pay attention.

Teacher's ResourceBank™

RESOURCES

WRITING YOUR FIRST DRAFT

- Writing a Persuasive Paper 57

QUOTATION FOR THE DAY

"Nothing is ended with honour which does not conclude better than it began." (Samuel Johnson, 1709–1784, English writer)

You may wish to write the quotation on the chalkboard to use as the basis for a discussion about endings of persuasive essays. Explain that attention-grabbing introductions, supporting middle paragraphs, and well-written endings all work together to build a convincing case.

SELECTION AMENDMENT
Description of change: excerpted
Rationale: to focus on the concept of persuasion presented in this chapter

Writing Your First Draft

The Basics of Persuasion

You have an opinion statement and some support for it. But how do you put this together in a persuasive essay? Just keep these basic parts in mind:

- **The Beginning.** Grab your readers' attention with a question or surprising fact. Present your opinion statement.
- **The Middle.** Present your support in the order that will be most convincing to your audience. Hit them with your best support right away, or save it for the final punch.
- **The Ending.** Close with power. Restate your opinion or call your readers to action. Tell them what you want them to do.

The following example of persuasion is from a book about an endangered sea animal, the manatee. What is the writer trying to persuade you to do or to think? Is she successful?

A PASSAGE FROM A BOOK

from Manatee on Location

by Kathy Darling

Opinion statement — Saving the manatee is an American challenge—one that we should be able to meet.

Reason — Manatees are adaptable. Facts — They can live in fresh or salt water. They can eat a variety of plants. They do not require big wilderness areas. Where they are not hunted they have no fear of humans and can coexist even in heavily populated areas.

TEACHING THE LESSON

Before students read the passage from *Manatee on Location,* point out the basic parts of a persuasive essay and ask students to keep these elements in mind as they read. After students have completed the reading and the questions that follow, show them how to write an attention grabber. Then explain to students that they must support each topic sentence with evidence in a body paragraph. Point out that although there is no exact number of supporting statements, they should have enough support to explain their topics thoroughly.

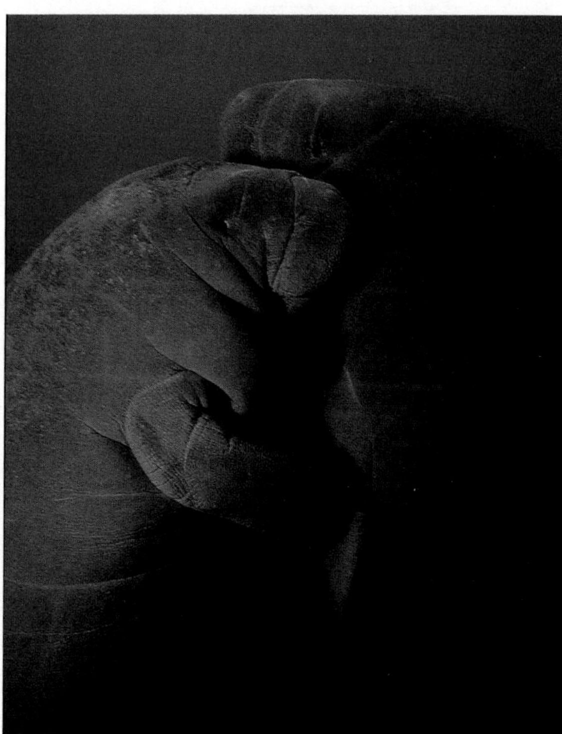

Reason//Fact

But it is beyond their power to adapt to speeding boats and crushing barges, which account for one third of all deaths. Only humans can prevent boat collisions or accidents in flood-control gates.

Reason

Not as dramatic, but perhaps the biggest threat of all is the increasing destruction of the sea-grass beds the manatees need for food. Laws prohibiting dumping, dredging, or filling of these underwater pastures are urgently needed.

Opinion

Opinion statement

With our help the manatees can survive. By saving an endangered species in our own country, we can help the world to see how important—and effective—animal protection can be.

Reason

VISUAL CONNECTIONS

Exploring the Subject. The manatee is a large gray water mammal often called a sea cow. Its front legs are paddle shaped, and its tail is rounded. Manatees are found in the Caribbean Sea, the southeastern United States, the Amazon, and the coastal waters of western Africa. Manatees have been hunted for their flesh, hides, and oil.

LEP/ESL

General Strategies. In the passage from *Manatee on Location,* the author uses some powerful and emotional words and phrases. Point out one or two examples and then have students find others. Ask students why they think writers use strong phrases in persuasive writing and whether or not the phrases are effective. [The strong phrases engage the reader and make the article's concern more personal to the reader.] To help students understand how a selective word choice can involve readers in what they read, ask students to list synonyms for the examples of emotional words they find in the passage and to determine how the synonyms might change the effectiveness of the persuasive passage.

GUIDED PRACTICE

After students have read **A Writer's Model,** use the annotations to initiate a discussion of the essay's organization. Use the example thesis sentence and evidence started in the **Prewriting** segment to demonstrate how a **Framework for a Persuasive Paper** may be used.

INDEPENDENT PRACTICE

Students could work independently to complete **Exercise 4** and **Writing Assignment: Part 3.** They should refer to their planning charts when writing drafts of persuasive essays.

ANSWERS

Exercise 4

1. Responses will vary. Most students will be unfamiliar with manatees until they are told the more common name—sea cow.
2. She is attempting to convince the reader that people should try to prevent boating accidents and should pass laws prohibiting misuse of underwater pastures.
3. Reasons: Manatees can be saved because they are adaptable. However, there are some things that humans are doing—using power boats and barges recklessly, destroying sea-grass—that manatees can't adapt to. They should be saved to create an example for the world.
   Facts: Manatees can live in fresh or salt water, can eat a variety of plants, and do not require big wilderness areas. Boats and barges account for one third of all deaths.
4. Responses will vary. Answers should be supported with specific evidence from the passage.

EXERCISE 4 **Analyzing Persuasive Writing**

Discuss the excerpt from *Manatee on Location* with two or three classmates. Then answer the following questions.

1. What did you know about manatees before you read this material? How did you feel about them?
2. Kathy Darling's opinion—what she's trying to convince you to believe and do—has three parts. One part is that we should save the manatees, even though she never says this directly. What are the other two parts of her opinion?
3. What reasons does she give to support her opinion? What facts does she give to support her opinion?
4. Does the support convince you? Explain why or why not.

The words you choose are important in persuasion. You can appeal to your readers' emotions with words like "hottest hockey star" or "unfair curfew." But don't go overboard. If you're too negative ("lousy idea") or excited ("worldwide favorite"), readers may not trust your opinion.

A Simple Framework for Persuasion

On the next page is a persuasive paper that follows a simple plan. You might want to organize your own first draft in the same way. The writer's audience is the city council.

ASSESSMENT

To assess students' comprehension, monitor students as they write and then have them answer the following questions about their drafts.

1. Who is your audience?
2. What kind of attention grabber are you using?
3. What is your opinion statement?
4. What are your topic sentences?
5. What is your call to action?

A WRITER'S MODEL

Trees Help Humans

Attention grabber	When you think of a city, do you picture buildings, concrete, and cars? Trees belong in that picture, too.
Opinion statement	Our city council needs to start a tree-planting program.
Reason	Everybody agrees that trees are pretty, but they have other benefits, too.
Reason	For one thing, their shade makes the city cooler in the summer.
Reason	They also cut traffic noise and help people's health.
Expert opinion	Yori Matsuo, president of the Arbor Club, says trees lower loud traffic sounds that raise people's blood pressure and even damage their hearing.
Fact	Most important, trees actually fight pollution by giving off oxygen.
Fact	That's a great benefit for streets full of car fumes.
Summary of reasons	The city council can help make our city prettier and healthier this spring.
Call to action	Please vote to start a tree-planting program at your meeting on February 11.

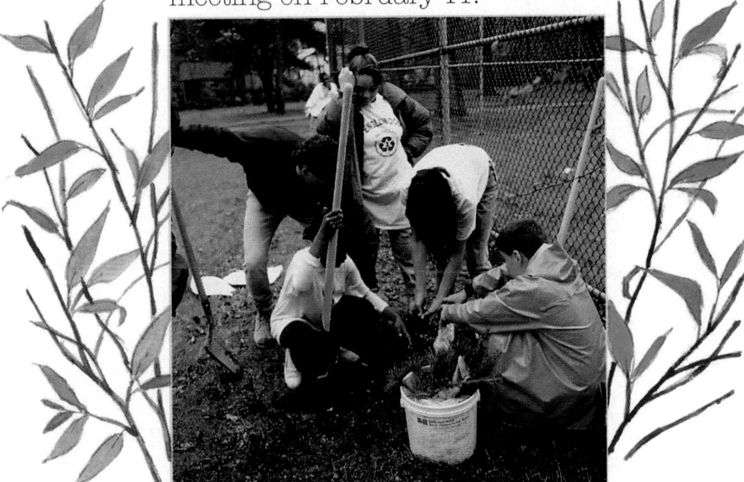

LEARNING STYLES

Visual Learners. To help students follow the framework for persuasive essays, have them highlight each part in a different color. Make sure students know the parts: beginning (attention grabber), middle (support), and ending (restatement of opinion or call to action). Marking each part with a different color will help students organize their papers because they will clearly see where each part of the framework begins and ends.

INTEGRATING THE LANGUAGE ARTS

Literature Link. Students should be encouraged to look for persuasion in literature. For example, students could read "The Sneetches" by Dr. Seuss and discuss the persuasive tactics of Sylvester McMonkey McBean and the emotional appeal used by Mr. McBean to convince the sneetches to buy his product. Discuss with students the specific reasons Mr. McBean used as supporting evidence. Ask students to describe similarities between Mr. McBean's persuasion and the persuasion found in television commercials or billboard advertisements.

CLOSURE

Ask students to provide the answers to the following questions:

1. What are two ways that a persuasive paper might begin? [a question or a surprising fact]
2. How are persuasive papers usually organized? [in the order that will be most convincing to the audience]
3. How can you write a good ending for your persuasive paper? [restate your opinion or call readers to action] ■

TIMESAVER

To save time grading rough drafts, ask each student to label in the side margin the attention grabber, the statement of opinion, the support (students should be specific about what type of support), and the restatement of opinion or call to action. After these parts have been labeled, you and the students can readily see that no parts are missing and that the paper is organized and easy to follow.

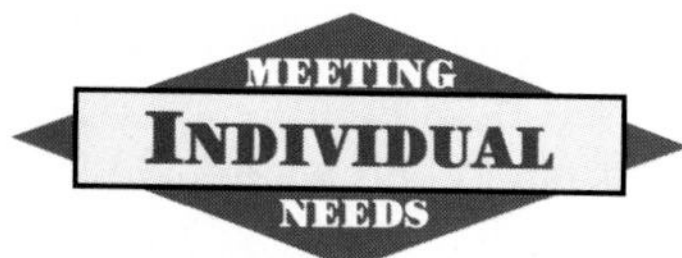

LEARNING STYLES

Auditory Learners. Students might benefit from hearing their persuasive essays read aloud. Ask students to record their drafts from **Writing Assignment: Part 3** on a cassette recorder and to listen to what they have written. Students may have a better understanding of what their support sounds like to an audience and will know if any changes need to be made in the supporting statements.

The writer's model you've just read follows the framework given below. You might want to refer to this framework as you write your first draft.

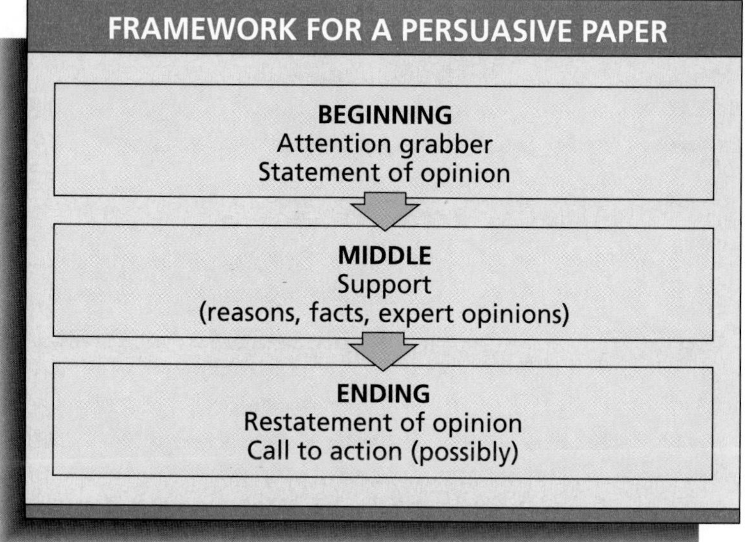

FRAMEWORK FOR A PERSUASIVE PAPER
BEGINNING
Attention grabber
Statement of opinion
MIDDLE
Support
(reasons, facts, expert opinions)
ENDING
Restatement of opinion
Call to action (possibly)

WRITING NOTE In persuasive writing, it's important for your readers to follow your reasoning. Transitional words will help them follow along. Try using words like *first, next, also, finally, most important,* and *for example* to guide your readers through your paper.

PART 3:
Writing a Draft of Your Persuasive Paper

Use your planning chart to draft a convincing paper. Don't waste words. Be as clear and as forceful as you can. This is a good time to choose a title for your paper. Think of one that will interest your audience in your topic and will make them want to read on.

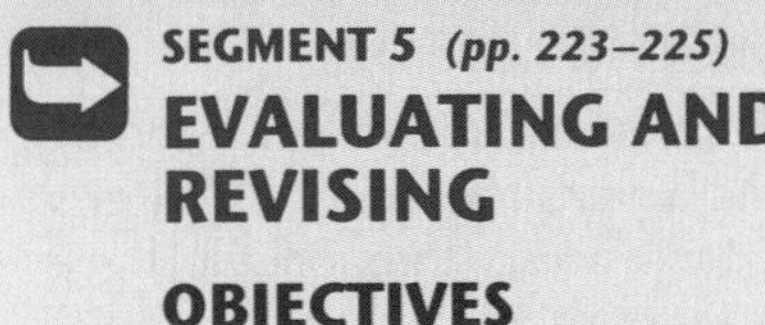

SEGMENT 5 *(pp. 223–225)*

EVALUATING AND REVISING

OBJECTIVES

- To analyze a writer's revisions
- To evaluate and revise a persuasive paper

MOTIVATION

Write the following paragraph on the chalkboard:

My class is making a booth for our school's fund-raising event. We need some paint. Please donate some to us.

Have the class discuss ways to make the paragraph more persuasive by asking the following questions:

Evaluating and Revising

How often have you come away from an argument thinking, "I *should* have said . . . ?" By then, of course, it's too late. When you write a persuasive paper, however, it's not too late. You can take time to get your reasoning just right.

You can try your persuasion out on other people. Then you can use the evaluating and revising chart on page 224 to help you find problems in your paper and fix them. Ask yourself each question in the left-hand column. When you answer no to a question, use the revision technique in the right-hand column.

EXERCISE 5 **Analyzing a Writer's Revisions**

Here is a draft of the second paragraph in the writer's model on page 221. Study the changes with a partner. Use the evaluating and revising chart on page 224 to help you answer the questions that follow.

Everybody agrees that trees are pretty, but they have other benefits, too. [For one thing,] Their shade makes the city cooler in the summer. **add** [Most important,] Trees actually fight pollution by giving off oxygen. That's a great benefit for streets full of car fumes. **add/reorder** They also cut traffic noise and help people's health. [Yori Matsuo, president of the Arbor Club, says] Trees lower loud traffic sounds that raise people's blood pressure and even damage their hearing. **add**

Teacher's ResourceBank™

RESOURCES

EVALUATING AND REVISING

- Writing a Persuasive Paper 58

QUOTATION FOR THE DAY

"There should be no distinction between what we write down and what we really know." (Allen Ginsberg, 1926– , American poet)

Write the quotation on the chalkboard and remind students that part of the evaluating and revising stage of the writing process is checking for truth, making sure that the audience will not be misled when they read what is written.

1. What is the purpose of the paragraph?
2. Who is the intended audience?
3. What reasons does the writer use to persuade the reader?

TEACHING THE LESSON

Guide students through this lesson by discussing the writer's revision of **A Writer's Model** and by working through the three questions in **Exercise 5** with the class. Then read through the evaluation and revision guidelines.

Students should work independently to complete **Writing Assignment: Part 4.**

ANSWERS

Exercise 5

1. The writer moved the third and fourth sentences to the end of the paragraph so that the support is arranged in an effective order and the ending is strong.
2. The addition is good because the audience will clearly know the writer's most important point. The statement also adds order of importance to the paragraph.
3. The comments by Mr. Matsuo make the paragraph convincing because he is an expert on trees.

LEP/ESL

General Strategies. Because cultural identity is so closely tied to written expression, a great deal of sensitivity is required in guiding students towards standard usage. You may want to explain that nonstandard English (which may include rich metaphorical and idiomatic expressions) is more appropriate in self-expressive, creative writing. Informative writing, on the other hand, generally demands standard expression.

1. Why did the writer move the third and fourth sentences to the end of the paragraph?
2. Is *Most important* a good addition? Why or why not?
3. How does the addition about Yori Matsuo help make the paper more convincing?

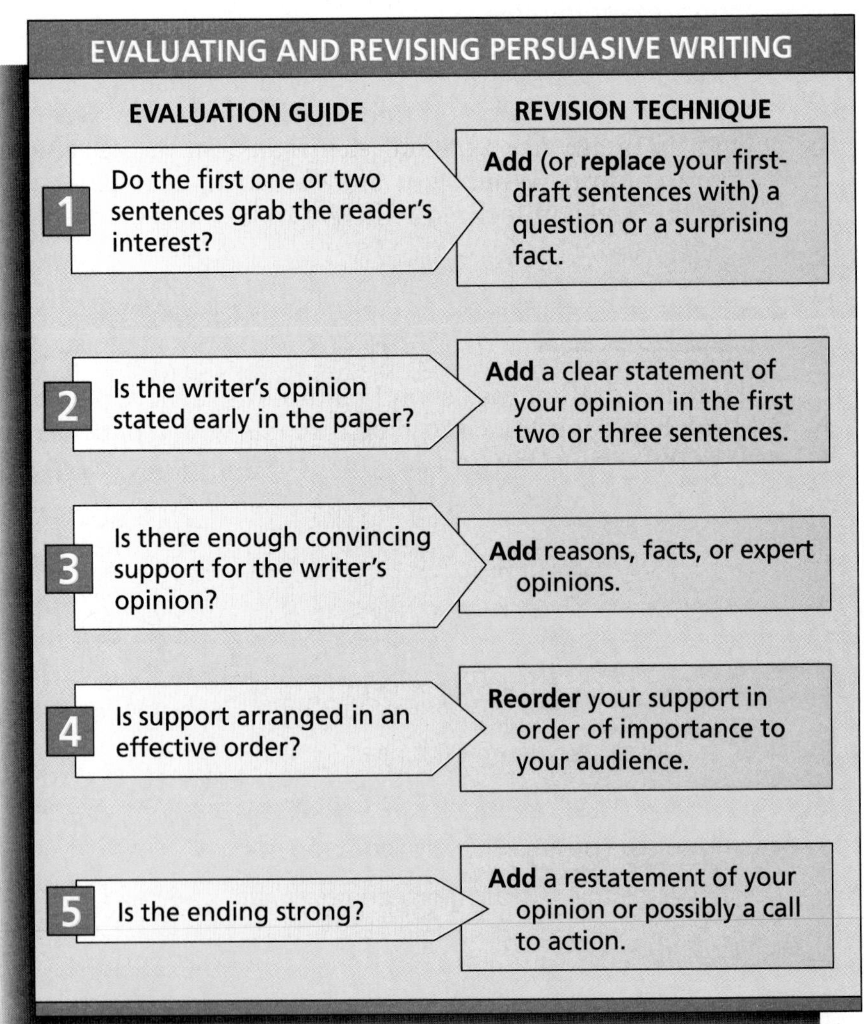

EVALUATING AND REVISING PERSUASIVE WRITING

	EVALUATION GUIDE	REVISION TECHNIQUE
1	Do the first one or two sentences grab the reader's interest?	**Add** (or **replace** your first-draft sentences with) a question or a surprising fact.
2	Is the writer's opinion stated early in the paper?	**Add** a clear statement of your opinion in the first two or three sentences.
3	Is there enough convincing support for the writer's opinion?	**Add** reasons, facts, or expert opinions.
4	Is support arranged in an effective order?	**Reorder** your support in order of importance to your audience.
5	Is the ending strong?	**Add** a restatement of your opinion or possibly a call to action.

You may want students to use colored pens or pencils for revisions.

CLOSURE

Ask students to discuss the following questions:

1. How do you revise a beginning that does not grab the reader's attention?
2. How do you revise a paper that is lacking in supporting details? ■

GRAMMAR HINT

Combining Sentences with *Because* and *Since*

When you give reasons in persuasion, you are trying to show your readers *why* they should accept your opinion. Often you can combine sentences that explain *why* by using the words *since* or *because*. The new sentence makes your idea clearer and your writing smoother.

TWO SENTENCES: In-line skating is good for you. The movements tone your muscles.

I'll do better in math. Mr. García will be tutoring me.

COMBINED SENTENCE: In-line skating is good for you **because** the movements tone your muscles.

I'll do better in math, **since** Mr. García will be tutoring me.

REFERENCE NOTE: For more information on combining sentences, see pages 311–318.

PART 4
Evaluating and Revising Your Persuasive Paper

Read your first draft aloud to yourself, and try to hear it as your audience would. To check your paper carefully, use the guidelines on page 224. If you answer no to questions on the left, use the techniques on the right to make improvements in your paper.

CRITICAL THINKING
Evaluation

Have students document what they feel they have learned from their writing experience in this chapter. Ask each student to list at least one thing he or she would like to improve for the next writing assignment and one thing he or she has now mastered. Students should then list strategies for improving the writing weakness they mentioned. This critical-thinking assignment will help students evaluate their writing, see how it has improved, establish what they need to work on, and acknowledge what they are doing well.

TIMESAVER

To save time grading on the evaluating and revising step of the writing process, copy the evaluation and revision guide for students to attach to the fronts of their essays. For each revision strategy, give the student a number from one to five, five being the highest. Scores recorded on their copy of the guide will indicate to students how well they have evaluated and revised each part.

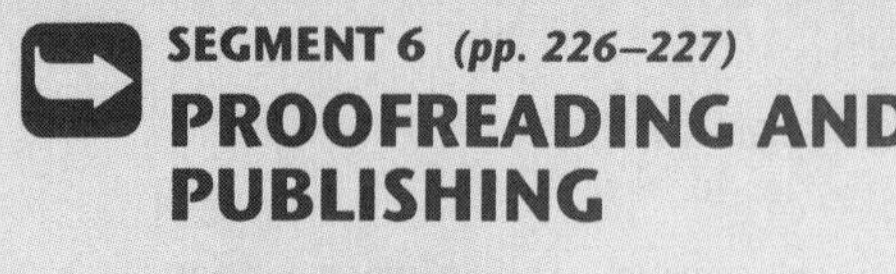

SEGMENT 6 *(pp. 226–227)*

PROOFREADING AND PUBLISHING

OBJECTIVES

- To proofread a persuasive essay to correct all errors
- To publish a persuasive essay

TEACHING THE LESSON

Ask students to consider what would happen if books, newspapers, billboards, and maps were not proofread for mistakes. Students can probably think of many ways that readers could be confused. Explain to students that they must also proofread their work carefully because mistakes often confuse the reader and a confused reader

Teacher's ResourceBank™

RESOURCES

PROOFREADING AND PUBLISHING

- Writing a Persuasive Paper 59

QUOTATION FOR THE DAY

"A good book is the best of friends, the same today and forever." (Martin Tupper, 1810–1889, English writer)

Write the quotation on the chalkboard and ask students to copy it into their journals. Students might write an entry about the very first book they read and enjoyed or about a book or story they have read again and again.

LEP/ESL

General Strategies. You may find that placing too much emphasis on correct spelling, mechanics, and usage can block students' ability to take risks with creative expression. Instead of marking each grammar error on the students' papers, you may want to make notes on the kinds of errors they consistently make. Assign extra practice in those areas that seem problematic.

Proofreading and Publishing

On a radio, interference and static can drown out the music. That's the same way annoying errors keep your message from getting to readers. Proofread your paper carefully to find and correct all mistakes in punctuation, spelling, and usage.

Here are two suggestions you can use to publish your paper:

- Mount your paper on construction paper, and hang it where your audience is sure to see it. You might hang it on a class bulletin board, on the family refrigerator, or on a community bulletin board.
- Give (or send) a copy of your paper to someone who could actually do what you would like to have done—the mayor, the school principal, or the President of the United States, for example. Perhaps you will even be surprised with a response!

WRITING ASSIGNMENT

PART 5:
Proofreading and Publishing Your Paper

Proofread your paper carefully to correct all errors. Try having a partner read it aloud while you follow along silently looking for errors. Make a clean copy of your corrected paper, and find a way to publish or share it.

will probably not be persuaded.

To close this lesson, you may want to have students discuss ways that they have improved their writing by careful proofreading. Sharing proofreading experiences will help students improve writing through modeling.

Encourage students to publish their essays by sending them to their intended audience. Students might also want to display their essays on a bulletin board. Students might have a better understanding of the complete writing process if you display the other writing steps with the finished essays. This should help students see that writing a good essay takes time and effort and that all stages of the writing process are equally important. ■

A STUDENT MODEL

You can be convincing about all kinds of topics, as Cameron Kuehne shows in his persuasive paragraph. Cameron, a student at Sunnyside Elementary School in Clackamas, Oregon, supports a four-day workweek for students and teachers. To Cameron, "picking which topic to write about was easy because I knew exactly what I wanted." Does Cameron convince you?

A Four-day Workweek
by Cameron Kuehne

Which would you rather have, a four-day workweek, or a five-day workweek? I know a four-day workweek would be better for teachers and students, and even for the schools! Teachers would get more rest and have more time to prepare better lessons. Students would have resting time, time to practice extra on instruments, more study time, and more time for classroom reports. The schools would save energy, and the buses would save a tank of gas a week. There would be less garbage from school lunches, and there wouldn't be as much stress or pressure on students. Students could even improve in grades! Better grades, better lessons, more rest, and even helping to save the earth—let's have a four-day workweek!

INTEGRATING THE LANGUAGE ARTS

Speaking Link. Write out issues that currently concern your school or community on strips of paper and ask each student to draw an issue out of a hat or bowl. Then have students try to convincingly voice their opinions on how the issues should be handled in their school or community. You may want to let peers evaluate how convincing each speaker's reasons were.

A STUDENT MODEL

Evaluation

1. Cameron begins his paper with an interesting question to grab the reader's attention.
2. Cameron's opinion is clearly stated in the second sentence.
3. He lists several specific reasons such as more study time, better lessons, and saving the environment to convince his audience.
4. The last sentence presents a strong ending by restating Cameron's opinion.

SEGMENT 7 *(pp. 228–230)*

WRITING WORKSHOP

OBJECTIVE

- To use the writing process to write a persuasive letter

MOTIVATION

Show students copies of letters to the editor from a local newspaper. Write the modes or ways to persuade on the chalkboard—narration, description, classification, and evaluation. Ask students to place each issue addressed in the letters under the proper mode.

QUOTATION FOR THE DAY

"All Poets believe that [thinking that something is true makes it so], and in ages of imagination this firm persuasion removed mountains." (William Blake, 1757–1827, English poet)

You may wish to use the quotation to prompt students to write journal entries. Ask each of them to write about a time when believing in an opinion or a concept brought about positive results.

LEP/ESL

General Strategies. Contact your local newspaper to request a donation of recent back issues of the editorial section, one for each student. After discussing the letter to the editor in the **Writing Workshop** and the questions that follow, divide the class into small groups. Each group should select a letter from one of the donated newspapers and answer the same four questions.

WRITING WORKSHOP

A Persuasive Letter

Letter writing is often persuasive writing. You may write a friend to convince her you *didn't* blab a certain secret that everybody now knows. You may write a clothing company with a good reason for a refund: After washing, your new shirt is small enough to fit your hamster.

Then there are public letters—ones published in magazines and newspapers. These "letters to the editor" are really written for readers. Often they give opinions. The writer wants a specific group of readers to believe a certain idea or take a certain action. Here's a letter published in a local newspaper.

To the Editors:

This year the School Board will vote on whether students can wear shorts. We believe the change in the dress code should be approved.

First, shorts aren't really different from other clothes now allowed. Some people say shorts are too casual. But they're no more casual than jeans, which kids wear all the time. Also, there's no rule about the length of skirts. If girls can wear short skirts, why can't people wear shorts?

But the main reason to let students wear shorts is that they're cooler. It gets very hot in Florida, and shorts are more comfortable than pants. Some classes are air-conditioned, but some are not. When you're hot, it's hard to concentrate.

Changing the dress code is fair and will actually help students at our school. We hope you'll agree and call the School Board at 555-3261.

Mr. Deloach's Sixth-Grade Class

TEACHING THE LESSON

Remind students when they write their persuasive letters that although they might be writing friendly letters to people they know, they must concentrate on writing persuasively. Ask students to rely on their knowledge of their audience to find reasons that will be emotionally appealing.

GUIDED PRACTICE

Write a brief persuasive letter on the chalkboard or on an overhead transparency for the students to use as a model. You may want to pick an issue that the students will be familiar with. Ask students to identify the opinion statement, supporting evidence, and call to action.

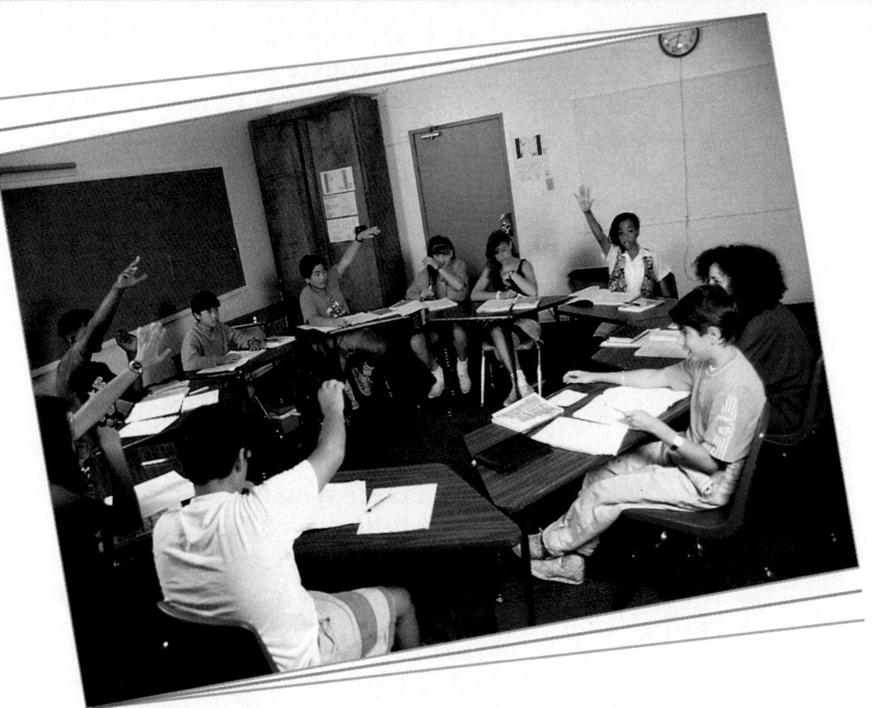

Thinking It Over

1. Who is the audience for this letter?
2. Which sentence gives the writers' statement of opinion? What is the writers' call to action?
3. Summarize the support for the opinion.
4. Do you think the letter will convince people to call? Which parts of it do you think are strongest?

Writing a Persuasive Letter

Prewriting. You have a choice of audiences in the letter you will write. Do you want to write about a topic that is between you and one other person? Maybe you want your cousin to come visit over the Thanksgiving holiday. Or do you want to write about a topic that is important to many people? Perhaps you want the police department to give tickets to people who speed

ANSWERS

Thinking It Over

1. The audience is the public—readers of the newspaper.
2. The statement of opinion is "We believe the change in the dress code should be approved." It is restated just before the call to action, "We hope you'll agree and call the School Board at 555–3261."
3. Answers may vary. Students may summarize by saying that shorts aren't really different from other clothes now allowed and that they are cooler.
4. Responses will vary. Students might say that people will call because of two strong points made—comparing shorts to short skirts and the point that it is too hot to concentrate.

INDEPENDENT PRACTICE

After reading the model and examining your letter on the chalkboard, students should be prepared to write their own persuasive letters. Assess students' comprehension by evaluating their letters.

CLOSURE

To close this lesson, ask students why it is essential to know who their audience is. [To be persuasive you must appeal to a particular audience.] ■

CRITICAL THINKING

Synthesis

Engage pairs of students in a role-playing activity that will involve persuasion. Ask one student from each pair to pretend that he or she is a customer returning an item to a store. The partner will be a manager at the store. Ask the student who plays the customer to describe why it became necessary to return the item and why he or she feels a refund is appropriate. Give each student a chance to play both roles. You may want volunteers to role-play other situations involving persuasion in front of the class.

INTEGRATING THE LANGUAGE ARTS

Mechanics Link. Students might need to be reminded of a few guidelines for writing a business or friendly letter. Discuss the following rules for punctuating letters:

1. Use a colon after the salutation of a business letter.
2. Use a comma after the salutation of a friendly letter and after the closing of any letter.
3. In the heading, use a comma between the city and the state and between the day of the month and the year.

near your school. First, decide on your topic and the person or people you want to convince.

Now, find your support. What facts or reasons will be convincing, and what's the best way to arrange them?

Writing, Revising, and Evaluating. Be sure you state your opinion and support it clearly. If, like Mr. Deloach's sixth-grade class, you're writing a letter to the editor, be *brief*. Newspapers and magazines may shorten long letters. Then, have someone else read over your letter to help you evaluate it. You can ask each other the following questions.

1. What is the writer's opinion? Who is the audience?
2. What reasons does the writer give? In what order does he or she present them?
3. Does the letter contain a call to action? If so, what is it?

Proofreading and Publishing. After you correct all errors, make a clean copy. Follow the format for a friendly letter if you're writing to a friend or relative. Follow the format for a business letter if you're writing to a business or to the editor of the newspaper (see pages 709–713). Mail your letter to the person or group you're trying to persuade. If you get a reply, share your reply with the class.

SEGMENT 8 *(pp. 231–233)*

MAKING CONNECTIONS

PERSUASION IN ADVERTISING

OBJECTIVE

- To recognize and identify the use of bandwagon and testimonial appeals in advertisements

MAKING CONNECTIONS

PERSUASION IN ADVERTISING

Language Arts

Reasons and facts appeal to your brain. Emotional appeals are aimed at your feelings. Advertisers are good at emotional appeals. They try to persuade you that their brand of soap, jeans, and sneakers will make you happy and popular. Following are two ways they do it.

- **Bandwagon.** The idea behind the bandwagon appeal is "Everybody loves it, so join the crowd." If you *don't* "jump on the bandwagon," you'll feel left out, different, and peculiar.

EXAMPLE Rubber socks! The fashion craze that's bouncing across the nation!

PERSUASION IN ADVERTISING

Teaching Strategies

To teach this lesson, ask students to brainstorm things they really need in life and things they simply want. Students will readily find that their needs are simple and their wants are great. Explain to them that advertisers often try to convince consumers that they need a product when they may not. As students work to collect advertisements that use bandwagon and testimonial appeals, you may want to bring in examples yourself to guide students. Bring in a sample or two daily and discuss the type of emotional appeals that are used in the advertisements.

VISUAL CONNECTIONS

Related Expression Skills. Ask students to look at the picture of kids in rubber socks and the picture of Wanda Wonder endorsing cereal on p. 232. Ask them to analyze the ads for effective persuasion and then to think of their own products and ad slogans. They could design advertisements using bandwagon or testimonial techniques of persuasion.

PERSUASION ACROSS THE CURRICULUM OBJECTIVE

- To create a presentation to convince city voters to build a historical museum

- **Testimonial.** This appeal uses a famous person to "testify" that a product is good. Because you like the person, you're supposed to like the product.

EXAMPLE What keeps Wanda Wonder going when she's on a concert tour? A big bowl of Breakfast Chunks every morning.

Can you spot bandwagon and testimonial appeals in ads? For a week collect examples of ads from television or magazines. Cut out the magazine ads if you can; make notes on the TV ads. Try to find ten ads that show either bandwagon or testimonial appeals. Share your ads in a small group, and see if you agree on the emotional appeals used in each one.

GUIDELINES

Students will have successfully completed this assignment when they have collected examples of ads from television or magazines. Students will share ads in groups and discuss the use of emotional appeals.

PERSUASION ACROSS THE CURRICULUM

Social Studies

Should your community build a historical museum? You think so, but city voters have to decide. You need to convince them that your community has a history worth preserving and sharing.

PERSUASION ACROSS THE CURRICULUM

Teaching Strategies

Ask students to focus on the advantages of having a historical museum in their community. Remind students that their presentations need to prove that the community has a history worthy of a museum. To begin this activity and to motivate students, invite guests to your classroom who have extensive knowledge of the community's history.

With a group of classmates, create a presentation to convince the voters. Begin by digging up some unusual facts about the history of your community. Look in the library, write to state historical societies, and interview older residents. You might find facts in the earliest issues of a local newspaper.

Present the history you find in a persuasive way. You might tell stories, read from old letters, and play taped interviews. You might show photographs and present skits. Use any format you like. Just prove that your community has a fascinating history worth celebrating in a museum.

GUIDELINES

Before students begin this activity, give them grading criteria so that they know what is expected of them.

Chapter 8 WRITING ABOUT LITERATURE

OBJECTIVES

- To identify the process aim and to analyze the characteristics of writing responses to literature
- To select an appropriate story and to write a statement of opinion about that story
- To assemble supporting evidence for an opinion statement
- To organize and draft a response to a selected story
- To evaluate and revise the content and organization of an essay about literature
- To proofread a response essay and to prepare it for publication

Motivation

Discuss the variety of reading material that students look at every day. Begin by asking students about what they read daily. Discuss newspapers, textbooks, fiction—anything that interests the students. Have volunteers share favorite books or comic strips. Discuss the differences between reading for pleasure and reading for information. If you have students who complain about reading, ask them about their favorite topics and suggest books that might address those interests.

Introduction

Use a discussion of students' reading interests to help the class see that learning to evaluate and support an opinion involves the use of reasoning and textual evidence. Find everyday activities in which students must support their opinions. Then help the students differentiate the ways in which they can respond to a piece of literature, a movie, or a television show. The class might identify the reasons for writing a letter to a newspaper editor [persuasive], a letter to a friend [expressive], a letter to a relative about something learned in school [informative], or a letter to a television network about an idea for a new program [creative].

Integration

Help students realize the importance of learning to read critically and emphasize why they need to respond to their reading. Students should realize that reading critically is a valuable tool in judging whether an idea is worthwhile or practical. Discuss the necessity for students to read fiction with a willing suspension of disbelief.

Take this opportunity to help students realize how many times a day they are asked to read or how many times a day each student reads voluntarily. What criteria do students have for choosing what they read? How do students convince other students to read a book or a comic strip? Have students share ways in which they can communicate their like or dislike of a book, movie, song, or comic strip. This discussion is a good preparation for Yep's excerpt on the kinds of books he likes to read (p. 236).

This chapter can be used as a resource for subjects across the curriculum. For example, your students need to know how to read science and history textbooks critically. Students need to be aware of how authors successfully put words together to communicate messages and of how writers command the attention of their audience. Students also need to be aware of how what they read can be applied to their daily living and how stories, comics, or other pieces of literature can have a universal message. It is also important for students to understand how and why people try to convince others to read pieces of literature.

The chart on the next page illustrates the strands of language arts as they are integrated into this chapter. For vocabulary study, glossary words are underlined in some writing models.

QUOTATIONS

All **Quotations for the Day** are chosen because of their relevance to instructional material presented in that segment of the chapter and for their usefulness in establishing student interest in writing.

INTEGRATING THE LANGUAGE ARTS

Selection	Reading and Literature	Writing and Critical Thinking	Language and Syntax	Speaking, Listening, and Other Expression Skills
from ***The Lost Garden*** by Laurence Yep **236-238** **"Boar Out There"** by Cynthia Rylant **242-245** **"Poem"** by Langston Hughes **267**	Applying creative and interpretive thinking **239, 246, 250-251, 253, 254, 259, 265, 267-268, 269** Drawing conclusions and making inferences **239, 246, 250-251, 259, 260, 265, 267-268, 269** Evaluating a story **239, 246, 253, 254, 269** Responding personally to literature **239, 246, 253, 264-266, 267-268** Reading for details **239, 250-251, 256, 264-265, 269** Understanding the elements of stories **251, 253, 256, 269** Taking notes **251, 256**	Writing an opinion statement **246, 254, 269** Writing a journal entry **246** Creating dialogue **246, 265-266** Drawing conclusions and making inferences **250-251, 265, 266, 268, 269** Listing and evaluating support **251, 256** Writing a topic sentence **254** Writing a draft of an evaluation **258** Writing effective paragraphs **258, 269** Analyzing a writer's revisions **259-260** Analyzing a story evaluation **260** Evaluating and revising a story evaluation **260** Proofreading and publishing a story evaluation **262** Evaluating a scene from a play **264-265** Applying creative and interpretive thinking **265, 266, 268, 269** Writing a scene for a play **265-266** Proofreading and publishing a scene from a play **266**	Proofreading for errors in grammar, usage, and mechanics **262, 266** Writing dialogue **266**	Creating dialogue **246** Evaluating a story in a group **253** Working with a classmate to analyze a writer's revisions **259-260** Working with a classmate to evaluate and revise **260, 266** Publishing a story **262** Using art to respond to a poem **267-268** Working with a group to evaluate school lunches **268**

CHAPTER 8

SEGMENT PLANNING GUIDE

You can use the following Planning Guide to adapt the chapter material to the individual needs of your class. All the Resources listed in this chapter are located in the *Teacher's ResourceBank*™.

	SEGMENT	PAGES	CONTENT	RESOURCES
1	***Reading and Responding***	***235-239***		
	Literary Model from ***The Lost Garden***	236-238	Guided reading: a model of literary analysis	
	Reader's Response/ Writer's Craft	239	Model evaluation: responding to literature and examining a literary analysis	
2	***Purposes for Writing About Literature***	***240***		
3	***Prewriting***	***241-256***		Evaluating a Story Taking Notes on a Story 62
	Starting with Response	241	Introduction: responding to a story	
	Literary Model **"Boar Out There"**	242-245	Guided reading: responding to a model	
	Chart: Ways to Respond Personally	245	Guidelines: examining ways to respond to literature	
	Exercise 1	246	Applied practice: responding to a story	
	Exercise 2	246	Cooperative learning: creating dialogue	
	Writing Assignment: Part 1	246	Applied practice: choosing a story and writing a personal response	
	Looking Closely at a Story	247	Introduction: reading critically	
	Understanding Elements of Stories	248	Guidelines: examining character, plot, and setting	
	Chart: Elements of Stories	248	Guidelines: examining elements of stories	
	Taking Notes on a Story	248-249	Guidelines: reading critically and taking notes	
	Critical Thinking: Making Inferences	250	Guidelines: making inferences about stories	
	Critical Thinking Exercise	250-251	Applied practice: making inferences	
	Writing Assignment: Part 2	251	Applied practice: taking notes on character, setting, and plot	
	Thinking About Purpose and Audience	252	Guidelines: evaluating purpose and audience	
	Evaluating a Story	252-253	Guidelines: using criteria to evaluate a story	
	Exercise 3	253	Cooperative learning: evaluating a story	
	Deciding on Your Main Idea	254	Guidelines: writing a main idea statement	
	Writing Assignment: Part 3	254	Applied practice: writing a main idea statement	
	Supporting Your Evaluation	255-256	Guidelines: examining various kinds of details	
	Writing Assignment: Part 4	256	Applied practice: rereading and taking notes	

For **Portfolio Assessment** see the following pages in the *Teacher's ResourceBank™*:

Aims For Writing—pp. 61–66
Holistically Graded Composition Models—pp. 409–414
Assessment Portfolio—pp. 421–445

SEGMENT	PAGES	CONTENT	RESOURCES
4 *Writing*	*257-258*		Evaluating a Story 63
Writing Your First Draft	257	Guidelines: writing a literary analysis	
Writer's Model	257-258	Guided reading: examining elements in a model	
Writing Assignment: Part 5	258	Applied practice: writing a first draft	
5 *Evaluating and Revising*	*259-260*		Evaluating a Story 64
Chart: Evaluating and Revising Story Evaluations	259	Guidelines: applying evaluation and revision techniques	
Exercise 4	259-260	Cooperative learning: analyzing a writer's revisions	
Writing Assignment: Part 6	260	Applied practice: evaluating and revising essays	
6 *Proofreading and Publishing*	*261-263*		Evaluating a Story 65
Mechanics Hint	261-262	Writing suggestion: using quotation marks	
Publishing	262	Publishing ideas: reaching an audience	
Writing Assignment: Part 7	262	Applied practice: proofreading and publishing	
Student Model	263	Sample: examining a student essay	
7 *Writing Workshop*	*264-266*		
A Scene for a Play	264-265	Guidelines: turning a story into a play	
Model/Questions	264-265	Examining techniques: analyzing a sample scene	
Writing a Scene for a Play	265-266	Applied practice: applying skills to the writing process	
8 *Making Connections*	*267-269*		
Responding to Poetry	267-268	Guidelines: responding to poetry	
Literary Model **"Poem"**	267	Guided reading: responding to poetry	
Writing Across the Curriculum: Health	268-269	Guidelines: making a chart to evaluate school lunches Applied practice: evaluating healthy lunches	
Writing About Characters and Plot	269	Guidelines: using criteria for character analysis Applied practice: writing a character analysis	
WHOLE-CHAPTER RESOURCES A Writing Process Log, A Writing Prompt, Holistically Graded Models, Portfolio Assessment Materials			

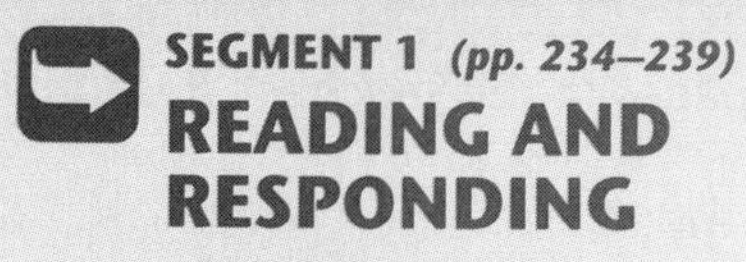

SEGMENT 1 *(pp. 234–239)*

READING AND RESPONDING

OBJECTIVE

- To read, analyze, and respond to an article about books

TEACHING THE LESSON

Read the first two paragraphs of Yep's excerpt. Have students share the ways in which the Oz books transport people to new lands and discuss how each character adapts to a new culture. (This is a good opportunity to involve students from other cultures by having them discuss what it is like to be transported into another culture.)

VISUAL CONNECTIONS
Libraries Are Appreciated

About the Artist. Jacob Lawrence is an African American painter from Atlantic City, New Jersey. Lawrence has used the library as the subject of many paintings and has painted several historical series as well. Known for his use of stylized patterns, abstract design, and bright colors, Lawrence often explores the theme of the perseverence of the human spirit to overcome adversity.

Exploring the Subject. The importance of libraries to students increases as students' education progresses. The sooner your students become familiar with libraries, the better. You might want to plan a field trip to the school or community library. Students could prepare for the trip by reviewing **Chapter 28: "The Library/ Media Center"** and by choosing specific authors, stories, or subjects to locate in the library.

8 WRITING ABOUT LITERATURE

Clarify for students what science-fiction books are. Ask for examples with which they are familiar, and then read the rest of the essay. Discuss the variety of exotic worlds to which reading can transport us. Have students share their experiences with books that successfully transported them to a different time or place.

GUIDED PRACTICE

Use the **Reader's Response** questions and the first of the **Writer's Craft** questions for guided practice. These questions can be answered by students in a class discussion.

Reading and Responding

When you're **reading and responding,** thoughts and feelings are perking inside you. You respond to everything you see and hear, too. A cartoon makes you laugh—or yawn. This year's most popular song puts you to sleep. "But wait a minute," someone might say, "that's a *good* song." Each person's response is different.

Writing and You. You talk to friends about songs and TV shows. You can also talk on paper. Writing down your response helps you understand it. What good—or bad—song, book, or comic strip could you write about?

As You Read. The author of the following excerpt writes about the kinds of books he used to like. As you read, see if you can tell how he felt about the books.

Libraries are Appreciated, Jacob Lawrence (1943). Gouache & watercolor on paper. Philadelphia Museum of Art: The Louis E. Stern Collection. © the artist/VAGA, New York 1992.

QUOTATION FOR THE DAY

"All good books are alike in that they are truer than if they really happened and after you are finished reading one you will find that all that happened to you and afterwards it belongs to you . . . ." (Ernest Hemingway, 1899–1961, American writer)

Share the quotation with the class and ask students to write journal entries about a book or story they've read that made them feel as if they were part of the story's imaginary world.

LEP/ESL

General Strategies. Chances are that few ESL students have ever read an Oz book or works by Homer Price or Andre Norton. Check the school library or local public library for copies of these books. Making such publications available to your students may open new worlds that they have never had the opportunity to explore.

Allow and encourage students to read for pleasure, without the burden of assignments or expectations.

INDEPENDENT PRACTICE

Use the second of the **Writer's Craft** questions as independent practice. You can assign it as a one-paragraph homework assignment or as an in-class activity.

ASSESSMENT

Students' responses to the **Reader's Response** and **Writer's Craft** questions should indicate their ability to respond to material they've read.

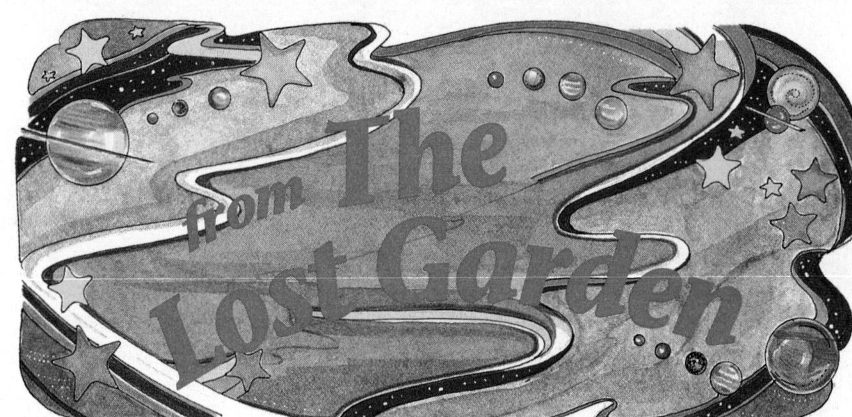

by Laurence Yep

Though I really couldn't have put my feelings into words at the time, I think I loved the Oz books because
1 they seemed far more real to me than the Homer Price books. The Oz books gave me a way to think about myself.

In the Oz books, you usually have some child taken out of his or her everyday world and taken to a new land where he or she must learn new customs and adjust to new people. There was no time for being stunned or for complaining. The children took in the situation and adapted. Unlike the Homer Price books, the Oz books talked about survival. They dealt with the real mysteries of life—like finding yourself and your place in the world. And that was something I tried to do every day I got on and off the bus.

2 From fantasy, it was natu-
3 ral to begin reading science fiction. At that time, every science-fiction book was marked by a rocket ship on the spine; and I would go through

USING THE SELECTION
***from* The Lost Garden**

1
The Homer Price books were written by Robert McCloskey, and the series deals with everyday events. The hero, Homer Price, solves mysteries in his town.

2
fantasy: literary or dramatic fiction characterized by fanciful or supernatural effects

3
science fiction: literature in which science plays an integral role

CLOSURE

Ask students to fill in the blanks in the following statements:

1. Everyone's response to things heard or read is ____. [different]
2. Writing down your response helps you ____ it. [understand]

ENRICHMENT

Provide students the opportunity to bring their favorite books to class and orally defend the reasoning behind their selections. Have students use a formal speech format in which they have two to three minutes to present their material in an organized fashion. ■

the children's room at the Chinatown and North Beach branches as well as the Main Library, looking for anything with a blue rocket on its spine. I moved quickly on to the young adult science-fiction books. Robert Heinlein was an author I liked because his characters were so funny and memorable.

4 However, Andre Norton was a special favorite because she could evoke whole new worlds with a kind of sadness and wonder. Up until then, I had not really thought that much about stars because I saw only a few in the night sky. San Francisco's lights were too bright and hid most of them. On some of our expeditions, my mother had taken me to
5 Morrison Planetarium in the park to see stars; but I did not see the real thing until my first trip to Disneyland. We took the train, called the Lark, to Los Angeles and slept in a
6 Pullman car. Kept awake by the clackety-clack of the train wheels, I leaned over from my berth and peeked out under the shade. For the first time in my life, I saw a blaze of stars spilled out over the black sky. I didn't sleep

4
Andre Norton originally began writing under the pseudonym of Mary Alice Norton. Norton's books are based on space adventures.

5
Morrison Planetarium: San Francisco planetarium near the Golden Gate Bridge

6
Pullman car: a railroad sleeping car

much that night between the noise, the excitement of seeing Disneyland, and the display of stars.

Unfortunately, stars were something that people had to drive to see. I only saw them when I went on camping trips, either with my parents to Yosemite or with the Boys' Club.

Anyway, the real appeal of Norton's books was not the stars themselves but the exotic worlds she created with their mysterious, half-ruined cities. I already knew what it was like to see an area that had been abandoned. Half the fun of her books wasn't so much the plot or the characters but the universe itself she created. And through that sad, tragic landscape ran outlaws and outcasts with whom I could identify.

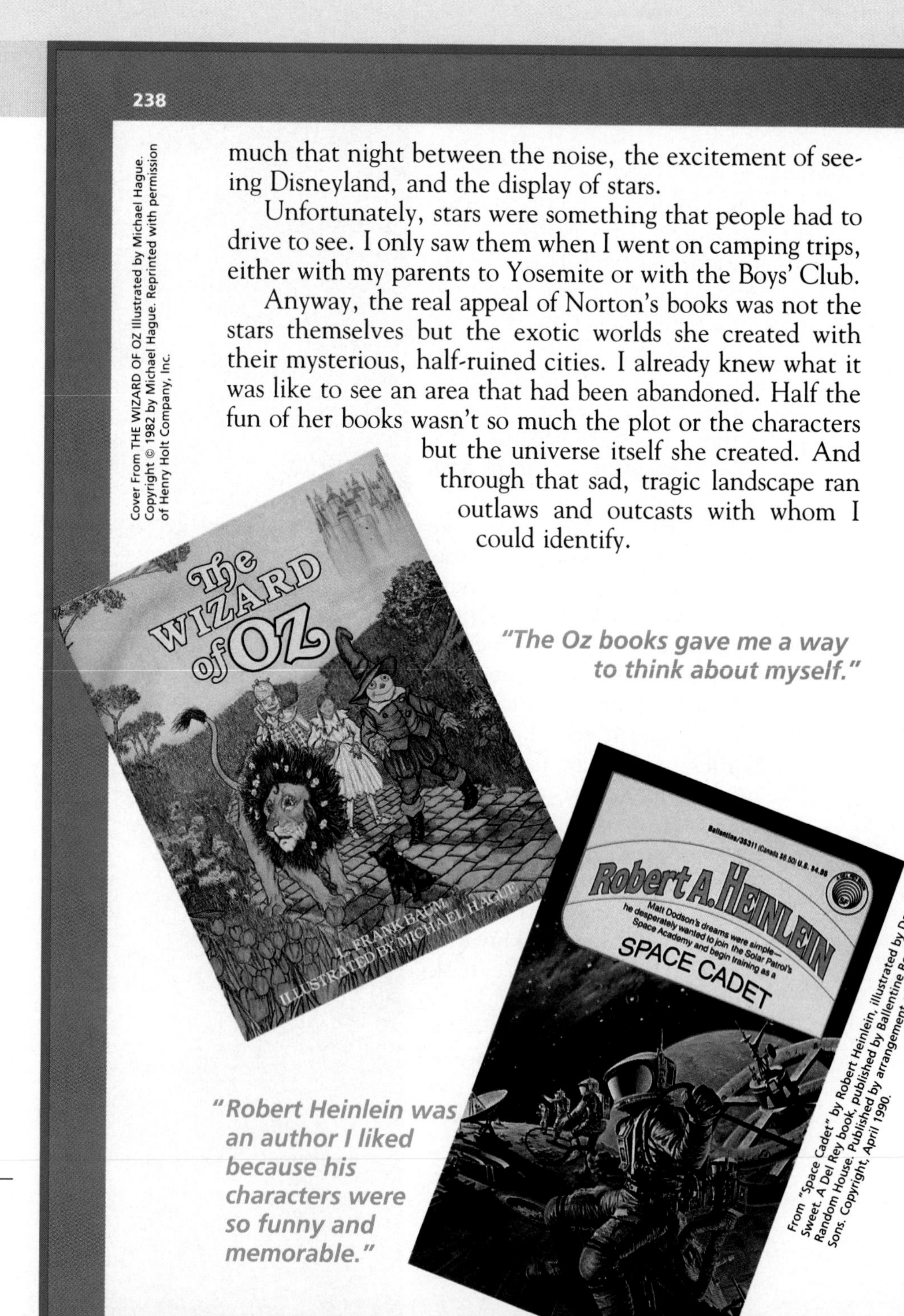

"The Oz books gave me a way to think about myself."

"Robert Heinlein was an author I liked because his characters were so funny and memorable."

SELECTION AMENDMENT

Description of change: excerpted
Rationale: to focus on the concept of evaluation presented in this chapter

Reader's Response

1. Laurence Yep liked fantasy and science fiction. What's your favorite kind of book? Tell why you like it.
2. Have you read an Oz book, a Homer Price book, or anything by Andre Norton? If you have, tell why you like or don't like that kind of story.

Writer's Craft

3. Did Laurence Yep like the Oz books or the Homer Price books better? How do you know?
4. Why does the author like science fiction by Andre Norton?

"...Andre Norton was a special favorite because she could evoke whole new worlds with a kind of sadness and wonder."

Author Laurence Yep

ANSWERS

Reader's Response

1. Answers will vary. Students should list some of the things they like about their favorite kinds of books.
2. Responses will vary. Encourage students to be as specific as they can in explaining why they like or dislike the kinds of stories discussed in the literary model.

Writer's Craft

3. Laurence Yep liked the Oz books better. He states, "I think I loved the Oz books because they seemed far more real to me than the Homer Price books. The Oz books gave me a way to think about myself."
4. Andre Norton could "evoke whole new worlds with a kind of sadness and wonder" for Yep, which is why he chose Norton as a favorite author.

VISUAL CONNECTIONS

Exploring the Subject. Lawrence Yep was born on June 14, 1948, in San Francisco, California. A writer of short stories and novels, Yep creates characters who struggle against prejudice and injustice while seeking a personal identity. As a third-generation Chinese-American who grew up in a black ghetto and attended school in San Francisco's Chinatown, Yep is no stranger to cultural alienation and racial conflict.

SEGMENT 2 *(p. 240)*

PURPOSES FOR WRITING ABOUT LITERATURE

TEACHING THE MODES

Help students define *self-expression, persuasion, information,* and *creativity.* Ask them to give further examples of how each mode might be used in writing or speaking about literature.

Assess students' understanding of the modes by having them find one piece of response-writing and give a specific example of how it works effectively (persuasion, exposition, self-expression). ■

COOPERATIVE LEARNING

Arrange students in groups of three and provide them with copies of a short story or poem. Have each student develop an outline of responses his or her group has to each mode of writing in the copied selection. When the members of every group have had a chance to respond personally to the selection, ask a spokesperson from each group to report the group's ideas.

Purposes for Writing About Literature

Laurence Yep wrote about the kinds of books he liked when he was growing up. You write about literature, too—and not just in English class. When you write about literature, you usually have one of these four purposes.

To Express Yourself: writing in your journal about how you're like a character in a TV movie; writing a letter to your favorite author telling why you like his or her books.

To Persuade: telling friends why they should read your favorite book; writing about *Dragon* magazine so the librarian will buy it for the library.

To Inform: telling your grandfather what you learned about Cherokees from reading a book by a Native American; comparing the monster in a story with the same monster on TV.

To Be Creative: telling how you wish a book or movie had ended; writing a skit that shows your favorite story character meeting a real person.

LOOKING AHEAD

In the main assignment in this chapter, you'll evaluate a story. Your purpose will be to inform your readers. As you work, remember that a good evaluation

- evaluates one or more story elements, or parts
- gives details to support the evaluation

SEGMENT 3 *(pp. 241–256)*

PREWRITING

OBJECTIVES

- To read short stories and write responses to them
- To create dialogue for a fictitious event
- To take notes on description, action, and dialogue in a story and to use them to support an evaluation
- To evaluate a short story
- To compose a sentence that states the main idea of an evaluation of a short story

Writing a Story Evaluation

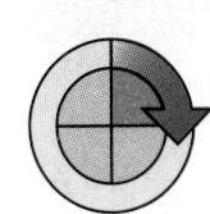

Prewriting

Starting with Personal Response

You're crazy about rock music. Your best friend loves Top-40 songs. Some people are die-hard fans of country, rap, metal, reggae, or soul. Each person responds in a different way to music.

Each person responds differently to stories, too. One reader loves a detective story. She says, "It was fun to figure out 'whodunit' before I got all the clues." That same story bores another reader. "I had to force myself to finish it," he says. Ask ten other readers how they feel about that story. You're likely to get ten different responses. When it comes to personal response, there's no right or wrong.

Here's a story about a girl and a wild boar. Read it and see how you respond.

"When I write... I think of the books on library shelves, without their jackets, years old, and a countryish teen-aged boy finding them, and having them speak to him."

John Updike

Teacher's ResourceBank™

RESOURCES

PREWRITING

- Taking Notes on a Story 62

QUOTATION FOR THE DAY

"Sure, you use things—you even use yourself and try not to tell yourself about it. You use whatever you can get your hands on, but you're not really using a person; you use something attached to a person—some suggestion, some episode, some quirk or trait of character." (Robert Penn Warren, 1905–1989, American author and poet)

Share the quotation with students and open a discussion on how an evaluator uses things in much the same way a writer does.

SELECTION AMENDMENT

Description of changes: excerpted, some words have been replaced with ellipses

Rationale: to focus on the concept of responding to literature

MOTIVATION

Students should be aware by now of the importance of writing about literature. Understanding why we write about literature helps students to become more aware of aspects of a text. Discuss ways in which authors make characters real for the reader. How does an author create excitement for the reader? Talk about how students learn to be better writers by imitating authors they enjoy reading.

A SHORT STORY

Boar Out There

by Cynthia Rylant

Everyone in Glen Morgan knew there was a wild boar in the woods over by the Miller farm. The boar was out beyond the splintery rail fence and past the old black Dodge that somehow had ended up in the woods and was missing most of its parts.

Jenny would hook her chin over the top rail of the fence, twirl a long green blade of grass in her teeth and whisper, "Boar out there."

And there were times she was sure she heard him. She imagined him running heavily through the trees, ignoring the sharp thorns and briars that raked his back and sprang away trembling.

1 She thought he might have a golden horn on his terrible head. The boar would run deep into the woods, then rise up on his rear hooves, throw his head toward the stars and cry a long, clear, sure note into the air. The note would glide through the night and spear the heart of the moon. The boar had no fear of the moon, Jenny knew, as she lay in bed, listening.

USING THE SELECTION

Boar Out There

1

By imagining the boar with a golden horn, Jenny turns the boar into a mythical beast.

TEACHING THE LESSON

Have students read silently the first four paragraphs of **"Boar Out There."** When students are finished, ask for predictions concerning the story. For example, will Jenny ever see the boar? What will happen if she does? Write the responses on the chalkboard. Then have students read the rest of the story and discuss how accurate the predictions turned out to be.

Go over the Ways to Respond Personally chart on p. 245 with students. Have them respond to the questions and use **"Boar Out There"** as the basis for their answers. Then discuss characters, setting, and plot. Ask students to describe these story elements in **"Boar Out There."** List the characters on the chalkboard and ask students to ☛

One hot summer day she went to find the boar. No one in Glen Morgan had ever gone past the old black Dodge and beyond, as far as she knew. But the boar was there somewhere, between those awful trees, and his dark green eyes waited for someone.

Jenny felt it was she.

Moving slowly over damp brown leaves, Jenny could sense her ears tingle and fan out as she listened for thick breathing from the trees. She stopped to pick a teaberry leaf to chew, stood a minute, then went on.

Deep in the woods she kept her eyes to the sky. She needed to be reminded that there was a world above and apart from the trees—a world of space and air, air that didn't linger all about her, didn't press deep into her skin, as forest air did.

Finally, leaning against a tree to rest, she heard him for the first time. She forgot to breathe, standing there listen-
2 ing to the stamping of hooves, and she choked and coughed.

Coughed!

And now the pounding was horrible, too loud and confusing for Jenny. Horrible. She stood stiff with wet eyes and knew she could always pray, but for some reason didn't.

He came through the trees so fast that she had no time to scream or run. And he was there before her.

2
Jenny's cough alerts the boar to her presence.

supply descriptions for each one. Ask volunteers for descriptions of the setting and list them on the chalkboard too. Finally, draw a plot diagram as students identify the separate events of the story.

Look at the **Taking Notes on a Story** section on p. 248 and discuss this section with students to determine ways students can use note taking in their daily reading. Use the **Critical Thinking** feature to help students understand how to make inferences.

Now you should be ready to discuss evaluating a story with the class. Ask volunteers to tell what their favorite stories are. You can pick one or two of the stories and have the volunteers tell about the characters, settings, and plots. Lead a discussion of the differences and similarities between students'

His large gray-black body shivered as he waited just beyond the shadow of the tree she held for support. His nostrils glistened, and his eyes; but astonishingly, he was silent. He shivered and glistened and was absolutely silent.

Jenny matched his silence, and her body was rigid, but not her eyes. They traveled along his scarred, bristling back to his thick hind legs. Tears spilling and flooding her face,
3 Jenny stared at the boar's ragged ears, caked with blood. Her tears dropped to the leaves, and the only sound between them was his slow breathing.

3
The boar's actual appearance is much different from the way Jenny imagined he would look.

Then the boar snorted and jerked. But Jenny did not move.

High in the trees a bluejay yelled, and, suddenly, it was over. Jenny stood like a rock as the boar wildly flung his head and in terror bolted past her.

Past her. . . .

And now, since that summer, Jenny still hooks her chin over the old rail fence, and she still whispers, "Boar out there." But when she leans on the fence, looking into the trees, her eyes are full and she leaves wet patches on the splintery wood. She is sorry for the torn ears of the boar and sorry that he has no golden horn.

favorite stories and **"Boar Out There."** Then ask students whether they think **"Boar Out There"** is as good as, better than, or not as good as the other stories.

If students have trouble evaluating **"Boar Out There,"** have them concentrate on the character of Jenny. Ask them if they can relate to her. Does she seem real even though she is only a fictitious character? Remind students that evaluations focus on how well authors develop the elements of a story.

4 But mostly she is sorry that he lives in fear of bluejays and little girls, when everyone in Glen Morgan lives in fear of him.

4
This is an example of irony because everyone is afraid of the boar, and the boar is afraid of everyone.

What was your personal response to "Boar Out There"? You can respond to a story in different ways.

WAYS TO RESPOND PERSONALLY

- Pretend you're the main character in the story. Write about what happens to you after the story ends.
- Make up some details about the main character. What does he or she do for fun? What's the character's favorite food? How does he or she feel about school?
- How does the ending of the story make you feel? You don't like the ending? Make up a new one.
- Think about what happens in the story. Pretend it's made into a TV movie. You're in charge of finding background music for it. What music would you pick?

GUIDED PRACTICE

You can use one of the events in **Exercise 2** as guided practice by letting the class help construct a dialogue. The students can then choose one of the remaining two events to use when writing their own dialogues.

INDEPENDENT PRACTICE

Exercises 1 and **2** offer students the opportunity to evaluate and to respond to literature. Because these exercises involve discussion among students, the assignment can be prefaced with class discussion. **Writing Assignment: Parts 1, 2, 3,** and **4** should also be done independently.

ANSWERS

Exercise 1

Responses will vary. Encourage students to explore their ideas fully, instead of giving short answers.

ANSWERS

Exercise 2

Answers will vary. Since this is a group exercise, allow students to act out their responses. Give each group time to write their responses and perform them for the class.

EXERCISE 1 Responding to a Story

How did you like "Boar Out There"? Do you think Jenny was foolish to go into the woods? Would you rather the story ended in a different way? Pick one of the personal-response ideas you read about on page 245. Then write your response in your journal, or share it with a classmate.

EXERCISE 2 Speaking and Listening: Making Up Dialogue

You're the author! Here are three events that might have happened in "Boar Out There." With two or three classmates, choose one event. Make up the words the two characters say to each other. Have one classmate write down the lines. When you finish, share your work with the rest of the class.

1. Jenny takes a friend into the woods with her and they are together when the boar runs toward them. What do they say to each other?
2. At school the next day, Jenny tells her best friend about her experience. What do Jenny and her friend say to each other?
3. Twenty-five years have gone by and Jenny tells the story of the boar to her twelve-year-old daughter. What do they say to each other?

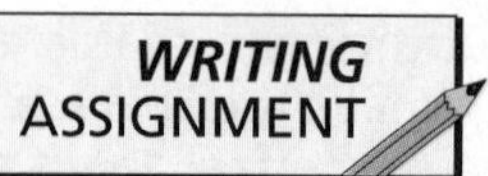

PART 1:
Choosing a Story for Response

Choose a story in your literature book. Or look for stories in the library, and choose one of those. (And remember: If you still can't think of a story to read, one of your friends might be able to suggest one to you.) Read the story, and then write your response in your journal. Tell how the story makes you feel.

ASSESSMENT

Assess students' mastery of the various elements of a short story by evaluating their responses to **Exercises 1, 2,** and **3** and to the **Writing Assignment: Parts 1, 2, 3,** and **4.**

RETEACHING

Ask each student to think of an event that happened to him or her recently at school. Then have students write three descriptive paragraphs about the events. The first paragraph should be a description of the people involved, the second paragraph should be a description of the setting, and ☛

Prewriting

Looking Closely at a Story

You read some stories just for fun. Then, your personal response is all you care about. Sometimes, though, you need to read a story more closely. Your teacher may ask you to write about a story for English class. Maybe you want to tell someone why you loved a story—or why it put you to sleep.

LEP/ESL

General Strategies. Using the small-group format with exercises and activities in this chapter whenever possible should prove beneficial. A focus on cooperative learning has two distinct advantages, especially for the ESL student. When students can talk with each other, they have more frequent opportunities to practice English, both in areas of comprehension and composition; and when ESL students use English to problem-solve in group discussions with native speakers, they work harder to make themselves understood.

LESS-ADVANCED STUDENTS

You may wish to work closely with students to ensure that they are able to take notes while reading. This is most easily done by reading sections aloud as a group and deciding together what notes to make. Though time-consuming, note taking is a skill vital to the educational success of students.

the third paragraph should be a description of the event itself.

After the paragraphs are written, have students exchange papers and evaluate the descriptions. The fact that the students are familiar with the characters, setting, and possibly the events should help them evaluate each other's writing.

When they are through with their evaluations, let the students confer among themselves about the strengths and weaknesses they found in each other's descriptions. Or, you may want to ask for volunteers to share their evaluations with the class.

When this activity has been completed, send the students back to the short story **"Boar Out There"** and have them take a new set of notes on it after another close reading.

COOPERATIVE LEARNING

To help students understand the elements of stories, divide the class into groups of three and let the groups develop the elements for their own stories. One student in each group will be responsible for characters, one student will be responsible for setting, and one student will be responsible for plot. Encourage students to make the elements as compatible as possible.

When the groups are through, let them share their elements with the class. Ask the class which stories sound the most interesting and why.

CRITICAL THINKING

Analysis

Tell students that although every story has its own conflict, conflicts in stories can be divided into three basic types. These are a person or persons against nature, a person or persons against another person or persons, and a person against him- or herself.

Understanding the Elements of Stories

To talk or write about a story, you need to know about its elements. ***Elements*** are what something is made of. They are like the materials—wood, paint, metal, and nails—that make up a skateboard.

The following chart gives you three important elements that make up a story. You can refer to this chart as you work through this chapter.

ELEMENTS OF STORIES
CHARACTERS. The people and animals in a story are its ***characters.*** Sometimes, even plants or things or imaginary creatures can be characters. Heath, a bronze, winged dragon, is an important character in the science fiction story "The Smallest Dragon Boy."
SETTING. The ***setting*** is the place and time of the story. For example, a story's setting may be a city in an African country during the 1300s. Another story's setting might be a Caribbean island in the 1980s.
PLOT. What happens in a story is called the ***plot.*** In a good story, one event leads to another. What makes a plot interesting is ***conflict.*** That's some kind of problem or fight. There is ***suspense:*** you keep wondering and worrying how the conflict will turn out. By the end of the story, you know how the problem is solved or who wins the conflict.

Taking Notes on a Story

Taking notes while you read a story helps you write about it later. Following are some notes you might take while reading part of Cynthia Rylant's story "Boar Out There." Each of the notes is about character, setting, or plot. Some of the notes are questions that you might ask yourself. As you read, try to answer your questions.

CLOSURE

Ask students to name the elements of a story [characters, setting, plot]. Then ask them what an inference is [an educated guess]. Finally, ask what the purpose of a story evaluation is [to tell how well the story is written].

ENRICHMENT

Ask students to illustrate **"Boar Out There"** by using their notes on characters and setting. ■

A MODEL OF NOTE TAKING

Reading Passage	**Close-Reading Notes**
Everyone in Glen Morgan knew there was a wild boar in the woods over by the Miller farm. The boar was out beyond the splintery rail fence and past the old black Dodge that somehow ended up in the woods and was missing most of its parts.	*A wild boar? Is this the conflict?* *Are the woods the setting?*
Jenny would hook her chin over the top rail of the fence, twirl a long green blade of grass in her teeth and whisper, "Boar out there."	*Who's Jenny? I wonder why she's so interested in the boar. A conflict between Jenny and the boar?*
And there were times she was sure she heard him. She imagined him running heavily through the trees, ignoring the sharp thorns and briars that raked his back and sprang away trembling.	*Jenny must be the main character. There aren't any other characters yet.*
She thought he might have a golden horn on his terrible head. The boar would run deep into the woods, then rise up on his rear hooves, throw his head toward the stars and cry a long, clear, sure note into the air. The note would glide through the night and spear the heart of the moon. The boar had no fear of the moon, Jenny knew, as she lay in bed, listening.	*She's really curious about the boar, fascinated even.* *I think Jenny's going to run into this boar someplace. How? Will she get hurt?*

Like the reader of this passage, you can ask and answer questions as you read along.

SELECTION AMENDMENT
Description of change: excerpted
Rationale: to focus on the concept of taking notes on a story presented in this chapter

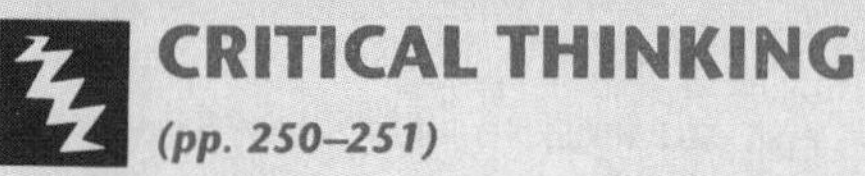

CRITICAL THINKING
(pp. 250–251)

OBJECTIVE

- To make inferences about character, setting, and place

TEACHING *MAKING INFERENCES*

Discuss how students often judge things or people by the way they look or by what someone says. Ask students to share other clues they look for when they are judging something. Write these ideas on the chalkboard.

Use one or two of the questions in the **Critical Thinking Exercise** as guided practice

LESS-ADVANCED STUDENTS

If students are having trouble with the idea of inferences, remind them that making inferences is nothing new. People do it all the time when they judge others, predict the outcome of sports events, or try to guess what someone else is going to do. Tell students that the best way to make correct inferences is to pay close attention to details.

CRITICAL THINKING

Making Inferences

Inferences are educated guesses. When you read a story, you need to make educated guesses about the characters, the setting, and the plot. To make inferences, you look for clues that the writer gives you. Sometimes these clues are in the actions or words of the character. They may also be in details or words that describe the setting or the action in the story.

CRITICAL THINKING EXERCISE:
Making Inferences

To practice the critical thinking skill of making inferences, look back at "Boar Out There." Then answer the following questions to make inferences about the story.

1. From the first sentence of the story, "Everyone in Glen Morgan knew there was a wild boar in the woods. . . ," you can infer that
   a. the people in Glen Morgan like to gossip
   b. Glen Morgan will be important in the story
   (c.) the boar will be important in the story
2. When you read that Jenny looks over the fence and whispers, "Boar out there," you can infer that she
   a. has had a bad experience with a wild boar
   (b.) is curious about the wild boar
   c. likes wild animals
3. When you read that the "pounding was horrible" and Jenny "stood stiff with wet eyes," you can infer
   (a.) that Jenny is frightened
   b. that the boar is going to hurt Jenny
   c. that Jenny thinks her father will be angry

to show students how to use details in the text of a story to make an inference. You can assign the other questions as independent practice, either as homework or as an in-class assignment.

Remind students that inferences are guesses and can be misleading. Some pieces of literature use readers' inferences to keep them from determining the resolution until the final outcome. In real life, inferences can cause problems when they lead to the wrong conclusions. Discuss how incorrect judgements on people, places, and things are made because of inferences.

4. When Jenny notices the boar's "scarred" back and "ragged ears, caked with blood," you can infer that she
 (a.) is beginning to feel sorry for the boar
 b. knows that the boar has been in a fight with the dog her neighbor owns
 c. is terrified of the wild boar

PART 2:
Looking Closely at a Story

You wrote your personal response to the story you picked. Now, take a closer look. Read the story again. This time take notes on it. Try to have notes about each element: character, setting, and plot.

MEETING **INDIVIDUAL** NEEDS

STUDENTS WITH SPECIAL NEEDS

Students with learning or emotional disabilities often find writing very stressful. Thus, it is important to provide motivation. One way to accomplish this is to show a videotaped version of a piece of literature. Before showing the video, give the students a list of key vocabulary words and read them aloud. Also, discuss any concepts or background knowledge necessary to understand the story. Interrupt the video periodically and ask the students to write about the story. Remind them to focus on ideas rather than grammar and punctuation during prewriting activities.

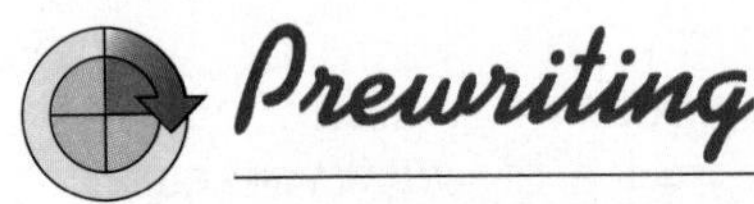

Planning a Story Evaluation

You've read a story and thought about it carefully. Now it's time to plan the paper you're going to write.

Thinking About Purpose and Audience

The *purpose* of a story evaluation is to tell how well the story is written. Evaluating a story helps you think more deeply about it. You may evaluate a story just for yourself—because you want to understand it better. Or your *audience* may be your teacher, classmates, relatives, pen pals, or friends who are looking for a good story.

Evaluating a Story

To ***evaluate*** something, you rate it. That means you judge it against a set of standards. For instance, judges at a dog show look closely at each dog's coat. A thick, healthy coat is one of the standards used to evaluate dogs. There are also standards for rating such things as TV shows, video games, bicycles, clothes, and restaurants.

People use standards to evaluate stories, too. The standards for stories are based on the elements. Here are some questions about story elements. You can use the questions to evaluate a story.

- Do the characters act and talk like real people?
- What details about the setting do you notice? Do these details make the story seem real?
- Is the plot believable? Is there a problem or a conflict? Does the author create suspense and make you wonder what will happen next?

Most stories are not all bad or all good. A story may have great characters that are really believable. Yet that same story may not have a very interesting plot. Don't be surprised if you find that the author has done a better job with some story elements than others.

EXERCISE 3 **Evaluating a Story**

Get together with some classmates to evaluate "Boar Out There." Use the questions given above. After you have answered the questions, decide on your overall evaluation of the story. Is it great, average, weak—or something else? Does everyone in the group agree on the evaluation?

ANSWERS
Exercise 3

Evaluations will vary, but students should have definite reasons for their opinions.

A DIFFERENT APPROACH

To help students develop their main ideas for their evaluation papers, have them list the important elements of their stories. Which character or characters are the most important? In which setting does the most or most important action take place? Which event is the most important for the development of the story?

When they have these questions answered, ask the students to then choose the most important of the three. Which element do they feel their stories depend upon the most? When they think of their stories, which element comes to mind first? The answers to these questions should help students develop their main idea statements.

Deciding on Your Main Idea

By now you've made a judgment about the story. You probably think it's great, terrible, or something in between. Now you need to write a main idea statement that expresses your evaluation of the story. Here are some example main idea statements about "Boar Out There."

> "Boar Out There," by Cynthia Rylant, is one of the best stories I have ever read.
>
> The plot of "Boar Out There," by Cynthia Rylant, has suspense and an interesting conflict.
>
> In "Boar Out There," by Cynthia Rylant, the character is interesting and believable.

Notice that two of these main idea statements are about only one story element. They are more realistic for a short paper. It would be difficult to write about all the story elements in a paragraph or two.

Once you've written your main idea statement, you can use it as a guide for planning. Later you may use it, or some version of it, in your paragraph.

REFERENCE NOTE: For more information on main idea statements, see pages 61–63 of Chapter 2, Learning About Paragraphs.

PART 3:
Evaluating Your Story

Are you ready to evaluate the story you picked? Get set by looking back at the close-reading notes you took. Jot down answers to the questions on page 253. Use your answers to help you decide which element to write about. Then write a sentence that states your main idea—for example, "The characters seem like real people." Or you might write, "The plot is interesting and suspenseful."

Supporting Your Evaluation with Details

To back up your evaluation, you need details from the story. You'll need to read the story again. This time, keep your main idea statement in mind. Hunt for details in the story that support it. Here are examples of three kinds of details from "Boar Out There." They support this main idea statement: In "Boar Out There" the plot has suspense and a strong conflict.

Action (what characters do)	"One hot summer day she went to find the boar."
Dialogue (what characters say)	"Jenny would . . . whisper, 'Boar out there.' "
Description	"Jenny stood like a rock as the boar wildly flung his head and in terror bolted past her."

On the next page you'll see notes one writer jotted down to support an evaluation of the plot in "Boar Out There." Notice that the writer uses a quotation from the story, and that most notes are in the writer's own words.

VISUAL CONNECTIONS

Exploring the Subject. The figure of Atlas originated in Greek mythology. Atlas was one of the Titans overthrown by Zeus. In punishment for his role in the war, Zeus made Atlas hold up the heavens on his shoulders.

The figure of Atlas holding the world was first used by a Flemish mapmaker in the sixteenth century. The figure was used as an illustration for a book of maps. Since that time, the term *atlas* has been used to mean a collection of maps.

SELECTION AMENDMENT
Description of change: excerpted
Rationale: to focus on the concept of supporting evaluations with details presented in this chapter

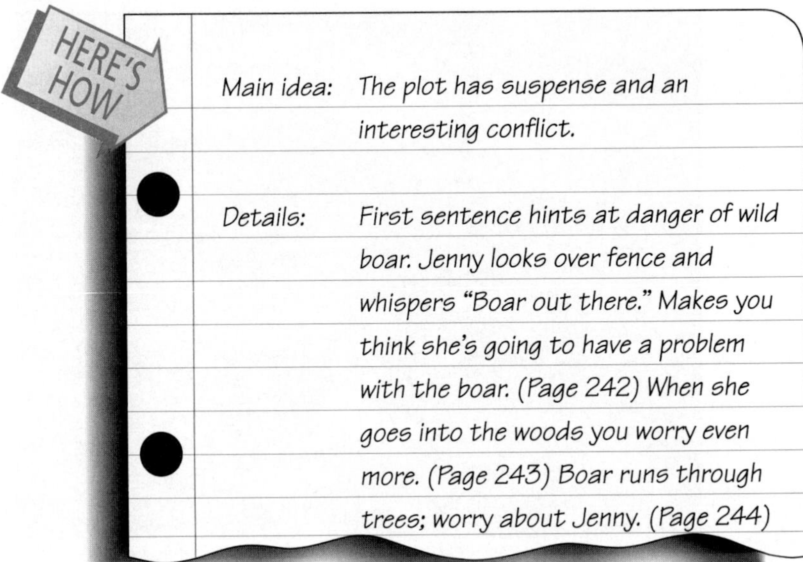

HERE'S HOW
Main idea: The plot has suspense and an interesting conflict.
Details: First sentence hints at danger of wild boar. Jenny looks over fence and whispers "Boar out there." Makes you think she's going to have a problem with the boar. (Page 242) When she goes into the woods you worry even more. (Page 243) Boar runs through trees; worry about Jenny. (Page 244)

To plan a paper evaluating a story

- evaluate the characters, setting, and plot
- decide which element to write about
- write a main idea statement of your evaluation
- take notes on the story to support your main idea

PART 4:
Gathering Details to Support Your Evaluation

It's time for the final prewriting step. Get out the evaluation and main idea statement you wrote in Writing Assignment, Part 3. Now, read the story one more time. Look for description, actions, and dialogue that support your evaluation. You're judging. Make notes about each of these elements like the notes you've just read.

SEGMENT 4 *(pp. 257–258)*

WRITING YOUR FIRST DRAFT

OBJECTIVE

- To write a draft of an evaluative essay

TEACHING THE LESSON

Ask volunteers to tell in simple sentences what happens in their stories. When the plots have been distilled to basic events, have the students choose the most important. Then ask the students why the events took place. When the reasons for the actions are linked with the actions in statements, the students will have adequate summaries of ☛

Writing Your First Draft

You're just about ready to write your first draft. The paper you write about the story you've read will have these four parts:

- the story's title and author
- a sentence or two telling your readers what the story is about
- your evaluation of an element in the story (your main idea)
- details from the story that support your evaluation

If you like, you can also give your personal response to the story. (In fact, your response might give your readers some new ideas or feelings about the story.) Here's a model paragraph that evaluates the plot in "Boar Out There." As you read, look for the four parts.

A WRITER'S MODEL

A Frightening Meeting

Title/Author
Summary
Main idea/Evaluation
Details to support evaluation

"Boar Out There," by Cynthia Rylant, is about a young girl who faces a wild boar. The plot of this story keeps you interested and in suspense. The suspense starts with the beginning of the first sentence: "Everyone in Glen Morgan knew there was a wild boar in the woods. . . ." You soon start to wonder if Jenny, the young girl, will look for the boar. She keeps looking over the fence and whispering "Boar out there." When she goes into the woods, you are afraid she will meet the

Teacher's ResourceBank™

RESOURCES

WRITING YOUR FIRST DRAFT

- Evaluating a Story 63

QUOTATION FOR THE DAY

"To note an artist's limitations is but to define his talent." (Willa Cather, 1873–1947, American writer)

Write the quotation on the chalkboard and tell students that when they write about a piece of literature, they should notice its weak points as well as its strong points. Explain that analyzing a piece of literature for its good and bad qualities helps the reader create a more balanced main idea and allows for a greater use of supporting details.

the stories and should be ready to write their drafts as instructed in **Writing Assignment: Part 5.**

Use students' drafts to assess how well they have understood the concept of the evaluative essay.

CLOSURE

Ask students to name the four parts and the optional feature their essays should contain [story's title and author, a summary of the story, evaluation of one of the story's elements, supporting details and a personal response to the story]. ■

LEP/ESL

General Strategies. Writing a first draft may be the most difficult part of the writing process for some students. Before they begin writing, meet with them individually and discuss the items in the following checklist:

1. Summary—Have them tell you briefly what the story is about.
2. Evaluation—Ask them to specify which element (character, setting, or plot) they are evaluating.
3. Main idea—Encourage them to tell you if they liked the story and why or why not. Have them comment on the element they are targeting.

This process should serve as a good warm-up and should bring the students' ideas into sharper focus.

boar; and she does. He comes running through the trees and she doesn't have "time to scream or run." Then, just as you think the boar will charge, he runs past her. The story is exciting, but it made me feel sorry for wild animals. The boar was scared, too.

Personal response

PART 5:
Writing Your First Draft

You already have most of the information you need for your first draft. All you need to do is shape your notes into sentences. You're writing about one element, so you may have just one paragraph. As you work, remember what you've learned about writing paragraphs. (For more information about the parts of paragraphs, see Chapter 2.)

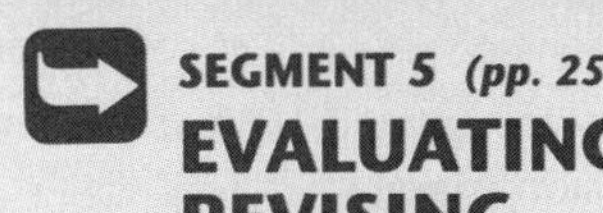

SEGMENT 5 *(pp. 259–260)*

EVALUATING AND REVISING

OBJECTIVES

- To analyze a writer's revisions
- To evaluate and revise an essay

TEACHING THE LESSON

Discuss with students the problems they may have with their papers and the solutions to those problems.

Use **Exercise 4** to show students how a writer revises. Stress the importance of revision and explain why writers make revisions.

Assign **Writing Assignment: Part 6** as independent practice and use student 

Evaluating and Revising

Once you've written your draft, you need to start thinking about how to improve it. This evaluating and revising chart can help you. Ask yourself the questions in the left-hand column. If you find problems, try the ideas in the right-hand column.

EVALUATING AND REVISING STORY EVALUATIONS

	EVALUATION GUIDE	REVISION TECHNIQUE
1	Does the paper give the author and title and a brief summary of the story?	**Add** the author and title. **Add** a sentence or two about what happens in the story.
2	Does the writer state the main idea of the paper?	**Add** a sentence or two that states your evaluation of one element. Use the standards for a story (page 253).
3	Does the writer give details to support the evaluation?	**Add** details from the story. Use quotations or put details in your own words.

EXERCISE 4 **Analyzing a Writer's Revisions**

The following rough draft shows how the writer revised the beginning of the evaluation of "Boar Out There." Working with a partner, answer the questions to tell why the writer made the changes. Use the evaluating and revising chart to help you.

Teacher's ResourceBank™

RESOURCES

EVALUATING AND REVISING

QUOTATION FOR THE DAY

"I found that, having started writing books, I was always having to write one more to kind of make up for the deficiencies of the one I'd just completed." (John Dos Passos, 1896–1970, American author)

Use the quotation to remind students that almost all writers recognize the need to improve their work. Encourage the class to remember that even the work of professional authors needs to be evaluated and revised.

responses to assess their understanding of the evaluating and revising stage of the writing process.

CLOSURE

Ask students to explain what is involved in the revision stage. [Revision is the process of improving a manuscript. In this lesson, it means ensuring that the essays contain titles and authors, story summaries, main ideas, and supporting details.] ■

ANSWERS

Exercise 4

1. The writer replaced *This story* with *"Boar Out There"* to identify the exact story being evaluated.
2. The writer cut the sentence *I've never seen a real wild boar* because it has nothing to do with the evaluation of the story.
3. The writer added the quotation to show how suspense is created in the story. The sentence improves the evaluaton by adding a detail from the story to support the writer's assertion.

LEP/ESL

General Strategies. You may find it necessary to work with some students on **Writing Assignment: Part 6.** If so, photocopy their papers so that each of you has a copy to refer to. Cite specific examples from their paragraphs to help them understand whether they are meeting the necessary criteria. ESL students want and need to know if they are doing the work correctly; however, they may feel too shy to ask for guidance.

"Boar Out There,"
~~This story~~, by Cynthia Rylant, is about a young girl who faces a wild boar. The plot of this story keeps you interested and in suspense. ~~I've never seen a real wild boar~~. The suspense starts with the beginning of the first sentence: "Everyone in Glen Morgan knew there was a wild boar in the woods...." You soon start to wonder if Jenny, the young girl, will look for the boar.

replace

cut

add

1. In the first sentence, why did the writer replace *This story* with *"Boar Out There"*?
2. Why did the writer cut the sentence *I've never seen a real wild boar*? [Hint: What's the purpose of an evaluation?]
3. Why did the writer add the quotation in the next-to-last sentence? How does adding that sentence improve the evaluation?

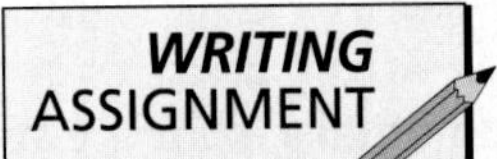

PART 6:

Evaluating and Revising Your Story Evaluation

You've just evaluated a story. Now it's time to evaluate your own writing. You can work with a classmate to evaluate and revise your paper. First, use the chart on page 259 to evaluate your own work. Then, exchange papers and evaluate your partner's work. (Remember that the Peer-Evaluation Guidelines on page 48 give you hints on how to help your classmates improve a piece of writing.) Make suggestions if you can think of ways to fix problems in your partner's work. After you've thought about your partner's suggestions, make changes to improve your paper.

SEGMENT 6 *(pp. 261–263)*

PROOFREADING AND PUBLISHING

OBJECTIVE

- To proofread an essay in preparation for publication

TEACHING THE LESSON

You may choose to focus the students' attention on one or two specific problem areas in grammar, usage, and mechanics. Make a note of the mistakes made on the last papers and deal with those mistakes at this time.

Now is also a good time to discuss difficult mechanics questions such as when, 

Proofreading and Publishing

Proofreading. Don't let your audience read your paper now! You still have to ***proofread*** it. Check your work for errors in grammar, usage, and mechanics.

MECHANICS HINT

Using Quotation Marks

You often use quotation marks in a story evaluation. Put quotation marks before and after the title of the story itself. You also need quotation marks before and after words you take from the story. Use quotation marks even when a character isn't speaking. Use single quotation marks to show someone speaking within a quotation.

Teacher's ResourceBank™

RESOURCES

PROOFREADING AND PUBLISHING

- Evaluating a Story 65

QUOTATION FOR THE DAY

"Proofreading is like the quality-control stage at the end of an assembly line." (John R. Trimble, American writer and teacher)

Write the quotation on the chalkboard and remind students that just as a faulty product is a bad reflection on the manufacturer, so is faulty writing a bad reflection on the writer.

where, and how to use quotation marks. Students are often confused about when to use quotation marks and where the punctuation goes at the end of a quotation. After you have discussed proofreading with students, assign **Writing Assignment: Part 7** as independent practice.

You may also want to discuss publishing. Could the students publish their essays for people who might be interested in reading their stories? Is the library interested in a collection of critical essays written by students about some of its stories?

LEP/ESL

General Strategies. Depending on their levels of proficiency, some students will not yet have developed the requisite skills to proofread for grammar, usage, and mechanics. It may be useful to assign peer tutors to help your ESL students. Once they have proofread the papers together, note the areas in which most errors occur. Provide students with further explanation and extra practice in their particular problem areas.

SELECTION AMENDMENT

Description of change: excerpted
Rationale: to focus on the concept of using quotation marks presented in this chapter

EXAMPLES *Story Title:* **"Boar Out There" has a strong, suspenseful plot.**

Quotations from Story: **The suspense builds when you read that the boar "came through the trees so fast that she had no time to scream or run."**

Quotation Within a Quotation: **"Jenny would hook her chin over the top rail of the fence, twirl a long green blade of grass in her teeth and whisper, 'Boar out there.' "**

REFERENCE NOTE: For more information on quotation marks, see pages 615–622.

Publishing. Here are two ways to share your story evaluation:

- Make a bookmark for the book that has your story in it. Use marking pens to make a colorful design at the top of a narrow strip of paper. Neatly write or type your evaluation on the front and back of the strip.
- With others who write about the same element, make a bulletin board display. Draw pictures to display along with your paper. If your paper evaluates a story's setting, for example, draw a picture showing a place in the story.

PART 7:
Proofreading and Publishing Your Story Evaluation

You'll be happy to hear this: You're almost finished with your assignment! Just proofread your final draft carefully and correct your mistakes. Finally, share it with others, and be proud of your work!

CLOSURE

Ask students what kind of errors they should look for when proofreading [errors in grammar, usage, and mechanics]. ■

A STUDENT MODEL

What you say about a story sometimes makes other people want to read it. David Sierra, a student at Hillview Junior High School in Pittsburg, California, writes about Mark Twain's story "Dentistry." Here's what David suggests when you're writing about a story: "Take notes as you go along and write little comments to put in your essay." He also says, "Don't rush it."

"Dentistry"
by David Sierra

The story I evaluated was "Dentistry" by Mark Twain. I enjoyed reading it. At first it was boring, but toward the middle it became great. It was great how Twain expressed how Tom Sawyer felt. The story also gave me the feeling that I was right at the bedside with Tom when his aunt pulled out his tooth. It really caught my attention when Tom was trying to find a way to stay home from school. I think it reminded me of myself. Twain made Tom's aunt sound really mean because of how she pulled out his tooth, but I guess they didn't have dentists like us. I think Twain used very good dialogue and really made the characters come to life. I would highly recommend this story to people who like to laugh.

A STUDENT MODEL
Evaluation

1. In the first sentence, David states the title and author of the story he evaluated.
2. To support his evaluation, David includes statements about the characters of the story and about how Twain's writing made him feel as a reader.

SEGMENT 7 *(pp. 264–266)*
WRITING WORKSHOP

OBJECTIVES

- To analyze a scene for a play based on a short story
- To write a short play based on a story

TEACHING THE LESSON

Begin by talking about the differences between a short story and a play. Discuss how the author of a play must write from an objective point of view and use stage directions, scenery, and dialogue to inform the audience. The author of a short story, on the other hand, can tell the reader what a

QUOTATION FOR THE DAY

"There are many reasons why novelists write—but they all have one thing in common: a need to create an alternative world." (John Fowles, 1926– , British novelist)

Use the quotation to reemphasize that the need to create alternative worlds applies to all creative writers, dramatists included.

SELECTION AMENDMENT
Description of change: excerpted and adapted to read like a scene from a play
Rationale: to focus on the concept of adapting stories to plays presented in this chapter

WRITING WORKSHOP

A Scene for a Play

One way to respond to literature is to be creative yourself. Have you ever tried turning a story into a play? Stories and plays have many things (characters, settings, and plots) in common. Here's an example of a scene for a play. It's based on the story you read earlier in this chapter, "Boar Out There." (The words in brackets are stage directions.)

Scene 1: [The front porch of a house]

[The wooden porch has a railing around it. At the top of the stairs is a middle-aged man wearing jeans, a lightweight jacket, and boots. He has a water jug in his hand and a blanket thrown over his arm. He looks frantic as he starts to run down the porch stairs. Then a young girl runs on stage from the right.]

Mr. Carmona: [in a panicked voice] Jenny! Where have you been? I've been looking everywhere for you!

Jenny: [almost breathless from running] Dad, you'll never guess--just saw. . .

Mr. Carmona: [angrily] Jenny, I've been scared to death! Where were you for the last four hours?

Jenny: In the woods. I saw the wild boar.

Mr. Carmona: You saw the boar? He didn't hurt you?

Jenny: [sadly] No, Dad. He ran past me when he heard a bluejay yell. He was afraid of me.

character is thinking and uses words to describe how and why characters do things.

Ask students if they have ever seen a play. If possible, take them on a field trip to a play or ask your high school drama department to perform a short play. Discuss the things actors must do to communicate ideas and thoughts to their audience.

Use the **Thinking It Over** questions in a class discussion to prepare students for writing their own play scenes.

Thinking It Over

1. Where does the writer tell what the setting is?
2. Where does the writer describe the characters?
3. How does the writer tell what the characters are doing?
4. What does this scene have in common with the story? How is it different?

Writing a Scene for a Play

Prewriting. Find a story you like, or use the one you evaluated earlier in this chapter. Use the story and your imagination to create a scene for a play.

"The All American Slurp"
"All Summer in a Day"
"A Secret for Two"
"Becky and the Wheels-and-Brake Boys"

There are two ways you can create your scene. You can change an event in the story into a scene, or you can imagine another event that might happen to one of the characters in the story. Either way, you should limit your scene to two characters. You'll probably have to use your imagination to make up some dialogue (the conversation) between the characters. You'll also have to make some notes about stage directions to describe the setting and what the characters are doing.

ANSWERS

Thinking It Over

1. The writer tells what the setting is in the first set of stage directions.
2. The writer also describes the characters in the beginning stage directions.
3. In the beginning stage directions, the writer tells what the characters are doing by describing their actions. Then he gives more stage directions before each character's dialogue.
4. The scene from the play and the story have in common the same basic plot. They are different in that the scene from the play is entirely dialogue while the story has no dialogue; and the story contains considerably more description, more emotion, and is in general fuller and richer than the scene from the play.

LEP/ESL

General Strategies. Reassure students by explaining that writing scenes for a play is easier than other types of writing because elements such as setting, action, and dialogue are separate in plays. Encourage students to find stories from their native countries that would make good subjects for scenes. This will make their task easier and will enlighten their classmates about other cultures when the scenes are shared with the class.

CLOSURE

Ask students how stories and plays are similar. [They both have characters, settings, and plots.] ■

COOPERATIVE LEARNING

When students have completed the assignment, you may want to divide the class into groups to act out some of the scenes.

Writing, Evaluating, and Revising. Begin with the setting and stage directions. Then write your dialogue. Don't forget to put in directions that will tell what the character looks like or sounds like when speaking. When you've finished writing, exchange scenes with a classmate. Help each other find ways to improve the scene. Then, using your classmate's suggestions and your own ideas, revise your scene.

Proofreading and Publishing. First, make sure that your punctuation and capitalization help to show who's speaking and what is happening. Next, find some other students to act out the parts in your scene. You get to be the director. Have your classmates practice their parts. Be sure to give them suggestions about where to stand and how to speak. Finally, have your play performed in front of the whole class. Congratulations, Director!

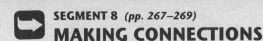

SEGMENT 8 *(pp. 267–269)*

MAKING CONNECTIONS

RESPONDING TO POETRY
OBJECTIVE

- To write a personal response to a poem

MAKING CONNECTIONS

Responding to Poetry

Here's a poem about two friends, one leaving another behind. As you read, think about your own personal response.

Poem
by Langston Hughes

I loved my friend.
He went away from me.
There's nothing more to say.
The poem ends,
Soft as it began—
I loved my friend.

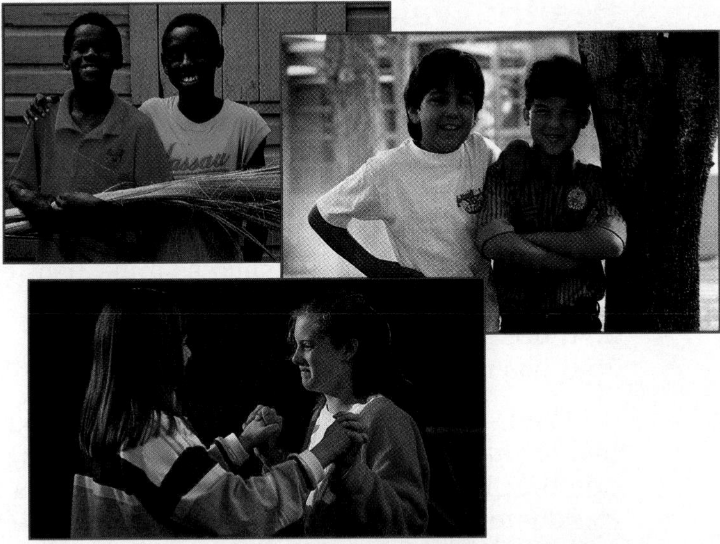

RESPONDING TO POETRY
Teaching Strategies

Have students discuss their reactions to Hughes' poem. Many students have experienced the death of a loved one or have lost a friend who has moved away. Discuss the feelings these students have over their losses and have the students apply those feelings to the poem. Does Hughes recreate some memories and feelings for these students? Ask students to freewrite about how they would feel if their best friend moved away.

WRITING ACROSS THE CURRICULUM OBJECTIVE

- To evaluate what students eat for lunch with respect to nutrition

GUIDELINES

Student responses will vary. If students chose to write a note from Jenny, they should try to keep it consistent with that character's personality as established in Cynthia Rylant's story, "Boar Out There." If students chose to find a song they feel is comparable to Hughe's poem, it should probably be something soft and somber.

WRITING ACROSS THE CURRICULUM

Teaching Strategies

Discuss with students how evaluation can be used in every subject area and why being able to evaluate things will help them in their studies. [If students learn to evaluate information, they will not have to spend as much time studying. Students will also be able to make inferences about what point an author is trying to make, what idea is important in a section of material, or how to follow a set of guidelines.]

How does this poem make you feel? Think about some times when you felt the same way.

Here are some ways to respond to this poem. Try one.

- What would Jenny (in "Boar Out There") say? Write a note she might send to the poem's speaker.
- Find a song that gives you the same feeling as "Poem," by Langston Hughes. Or, if you play an instrument, make up a rhythm and a melody for the poem.
- Convey your feelings through art. What pictures, colors, or designs express your response to the poem? Make a collage using your own drawings or photographs and pictures from magazines and newspapers. Or use paints or colored pencils to create an abstract design.

WRITING ACROSS THE CURRICULUM

Health: Evaluating School Lunches

Get together with a few classmates and evaluate what students at your school eat for lunch. First, make a list of standards for a healthful lunch. You can find information in a textbook. Or you can use this list.

1. A healthful lunch has fruit, bread or a roll, and some kind of protein (such as milk, fish, eggs, red beans and rice, or peanut butter).
2. It doesn't have much fat or sugar.
3. It has milk or juice, not a carbonated drink.

Then, ask several of your classmates what they had for lunch yesterday. You can use a chart like the one that follows and check off the columns as your classmates answer your question. Have one row for each student.

WRITING ABOUT CHARACTERS AND PLOT

OBJECTIVE

- To write a paragraph that analyzes the effect of a character on the plot of a favorite story

This chart shows that one student had a somewhat healthful lunch. Another student had a lunch that wasn't very healthful.

Fruit	Bread or roll	Protein	Low in fat and sugar	Milk or juice
✓		✓		✓
		✓		

Once you've filled out your own chart, look to see what you've learned. You can tally up how many students ate fruit, how many ate protein, and so on. (You can even change your tallies into percentages: What percentage of the students you surveyed ate fruit? ate protein? and so on.) Did most students have a lunch that was healthful? Can you write a sentence or two that presents your evaluation of what students at your school eat for lunch?

WRITING ABOUT CHARACTERS AND PLOT

Have you ever thought about how the plot—what happens in a story—might be different if one of the characters were different? If Captain Hook hadn't been so crazy, how might the movie *Hook* have been different? How would "Boar Out There" have been different if the boar hadn't been frightened?

Reread one of your favorite stories and think about these questions:

1. What is the character like? What does he or she enjoy? dislike? believe? care about? want?
2. How does this character affect what happens in the story?

Now write a paragraph explaining what you've discovered. You and your classmates might enjoy comparing your ideas.

GUIDELINES

Responses will vary depending on which students are interviewed and what they eat for lunch. Encourage students to interview a wide variety of their schoolmates. All responses should be in the form of a chart as shown.

Chapter 9

WRITING A REPORT

OBJECTIVES

- To write a report by using library research skills
- To choose an appropriate topic for a research report
- To take notes from research materials as an aid to report writing
- To organize information and to create an outline for a report
- To write a book report by using the writing process
- To present an oral report

Motivation

Many students are intimidated by the idea of writing a report. To relieve their anxiety and to acquaint them with the material in this chapter, have students brainstorm lists of topics or subjects that are of interest to them. List the students' topic ideas on the chalkboard. Explain to students that report writing involves exploring a topic that the writer finds interesting.

Introduction

Through a discussion of a specific topic possibility, help students to see that research is the process of discovering facts and information about a topic. The actual report is the method students use to share the information they find as a result of their research. Help students understand the various possibilities for developing their research reports. You may want to discuss how these reports will differ by emphasizing that students are able to focus on the aspects of their topics that most fascinate them.

With this basic introduction to report writing, students should be prepared to appreciate **"How Can Water Striders Walk on Water?"** by Joanne Settel and Nancy Baggett.

Integration

This chapter may be used to enhance other activities in your classroom. For example, the **Evaluating and Revising a Report** chart on p. 294 may be useful for any writing assignment. It clearly outlines steps useful for evaluation and revision.

Also, if you are emphasizing oral presentations or participation, both activities in the **Making Connections** segment may be used for this purpose. Although this chapter emphasizes research, the same ideas could be used without research for oral practice alone.

Finally, if students are reading nonfiction informative essays, you may want to compare the essays with **"How Can Water Striders Walk on Water?"** This chapter can easily be integrated with any assignments from other courses that require students to share information.

The chart on the next page illustrates the strands of language arts as they are integrated into this chapter. For vocabulary study, glossary words are underlined in some writing models.

QUOTATIONS

All **Quotations for the Day** are chosen because of their relevance to instructional material presented in that segment of the chapter and for their usefulness in establishing student interest in writing.

INTEGRATING THE LANGUAGE ARTS

Selection	Reading and Literature	Writing and Critical Thinking	Language and Syntax	Speaking, Listening, and Other Expression Skills
"How Can Water Striders Walk on Water?" by Joanne Settel and Nancy Baggett **272-274** **"Lava and Magma"** from *Compton's Encyclopedia*, 1990 ed. **285** **"Massasoit"** by E. Adamson Hoebel **285-286**	Responding personally to a selection **274, 293, 297-299** Reading critically **274, 278, 282-283, 285, 286, 297-299, 301-302** Locating information **274, 285, 286, 297-299, 301-302** Applying creative and interpretive thinking **277, 280, 282, 286, 288, 293, 297, 300, 302** Analyzing information **278, 282, 285, 286, 288, 299, 301-302** Drawing conclusions and making inferences **282, 286, 288, 293, 297, 300** Recognizing revisions in writing **293**	Analyzing sources **274, 282-283** Choosing and narrowing a topic **277-278, 301-302** Developing questions **280-281, 300** Listing sources **283, 289, 292, 299** Taking notes **285, 286, 299, 301-302** Paraphrasing information **285, 286, 297-299** Locating information in research materials **285, 286, 299, 301-302** Organizing information **288, 299** Outlining ideas and supporting facts **288** Writing a draft of a research report **292** Analyzing a writer's revisions **293** Evaluating and revising a report **294** Preparing an oral report **295** Analyzing an introductory paragraph **297-299** Analyzing the purpose of writing **297-299** Writing a book report **297-299**	Proofreading for errors in grammar, usage, and mechanics **295, 296, 299** Underlining titles **299**	Asking questions to obtain information **280-281, 300** Considering and answering oral questions **280-281, 294** Exploring nonprint information sources **280-281, 300** Sharing writing with classmates **294, 296, 299** Presenting an oral report **295** Creating a group display **295, 299** Creating a television news report **300**

CHAPTER 9

SEGMENT PLANNING GUIDE

You can use the following Planning Guide to adapt the chapter material to the individual needs of your class. All the Resources listed in this chapter are located in the *Teacher's ResourceBank™*.

	SEGMENT	PAGES	CONTENT	RESOURCES
1	***Exploring Your World***	***271-274***		
	Literary Model from **"How Can Water Striders Walk on Water?"**	272-274	Guided reading: a model of report writing	
	Reader's Response/ Writer's Craft	274	Model evaluation: responding to literature and analyzing a report	
2	***Ways to Develop a Report***	***275***		
3	***Prewriting***	***276-288***		Writing a Report Narrowing Your Subject 68 Asking Questions 69 Finding and Listing Sources 70
	Choosing and Narrowing a Subject	276-277	Introduction: planning a report	
	Exercise 1	277-278	Applied practice: narrowing subjects for a report	
	Writing Assignment: Part 1	278	Applied practice: choosing and narrowing a subject	
	Planning Your Report	279	Introduction: planning a report	
	Thinking About Audience and Purpose	279	Guidelines: examining criteria for preparing an appropriate report	
	Asking Questions	279-280	Guidelines: examining *5W-How?* questions	
	Exercise 2	280-281	Cooperative learning: practicing questioning skills	
	Finding Sources	281	Guidelines: finding print and nonprint sources	
	Critical Thinking: Evaluating Sources	281	Guidelines: using criteria to evaluate sources	
	Critical Thinking Exercise	282	Applied practice: evaluating and choosing appropriate sources	
	Listing Sources	283	Guidelines: listing research sources	
	Taking Notes	284-285	Guidelines: examining criteria for note cards	
	Literary Model **"Lava and Magma"**	285	Guided reading: reading an entry for note taking	
	Exercise 3	285-286	Applied practice: making note cards	
	Literary Model **"Massasoít"**	285	Guided reading: taking notes	
	Writing Assignment: Part 2	286	Applied practice: writing the *5W-How?* questions	
	Organizing and Outlining Your Information	287	Introduction: grouping and outlining information	
	Grouping Notes	287	Guidelines: organizing notes	
	Outlining	287-288	Guidelines: writing main ideas and arranging notes	

For **Portfolio Assessment** see the following pages in the *Teacher's ResourceBank™*:
Aims For Writing—pp. 67–74
Holistically Graded Composition Models—pp. 415–420
Assessment Portfolio—pp. 421–445

SEGMENT	PAGES	CONTENT	RESOURCES
Writing Assignment: Part 3	288	Applied practice: outlining main ideas and supporting facts	
4 *Writing*	*289-292*		Writing a Report 71
Understanding the Parts of a Report	289	Explanation: understanding the structure of a report	
Writing Your Report	289	Introduction: analyzing structure in a model essay	
Writer's Model	290-292	Guided reading: examining a sample essay	
Writing Assignment: Part 4	292	Applied practice: writing a first draft	
5 *Evaluating and Revising*	*293-294*		Writing a Report 72
Evaluating and Revising	293	Guidelines: improving a first draft	
Exercise 4	293	Applied practice: analyzing a writer's revisions	
Chart: Evaluating and Revising Your Report	294	Guidelines: applying evaluation and revision techniques	
Writing Assignment: Part 5	294	Applied practice: evaluating and revising a report	
6 *Proofreading and Publishing*	*295-296*		Writing a Report 73
Publishing	295	Publishing ideas: reaching an audience	
Mechanics Hint	296	Writing suggestion: using underlining and quotation marks	
Writing Assignment: Part 6	296	Applied practice: proofreading and publishing	
7 *Writing Workshop*	*297-299*		
A Book Report	297	Guidelines: writing a book report	
Model/Questions	297-299	Examining techniques: analyzing a sample essay	
Writing a Book Report of a Biography	299	Guidelines: applying skills to the writing process	
8 *Making Connections*	*300-302*		
Speaking and Listening: Giving a Television News Report	300	Guidelines: using criteria to prepare and present a news report Cooperative learning: writing and presenting a news report	
Research Across the Curriculum: Mathematics	301-302	Guidelines: using criteria to research and to write about mathematics Applied practice: researching and writing a report	
WHOLE-CHAPTER RESOURCES A Writing Process Log, A Writing Prompt, Holistically Graded Models, Assessment Portfolio Materials			

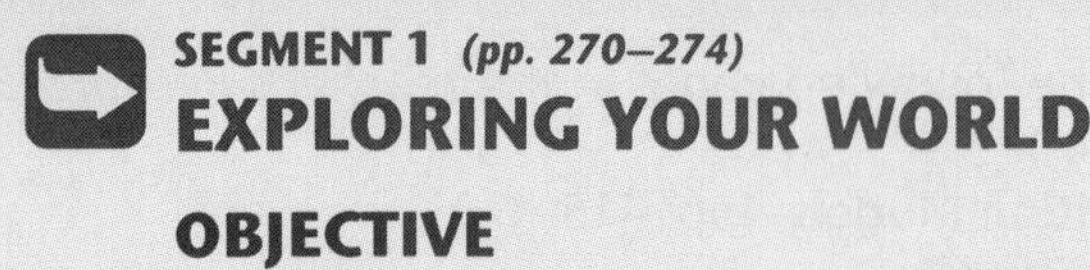

SEGMENT 1 *(pp. 270–274)*

EXPLORING YOUR WORLD

OBJECTIVE

- To respond to and analyze a model report

TEACHING THE LESSON

Ask students where they might find information on topics that interest them. They might mention sources such as magazines, books, or television shows. You may also want to discuss which of these sources students have used recently, and why. Finally, have students look through some magazines popular among adolescents.

VISUAL CONNECTIONS

Exploring the Subject. This is a panel from *The Book of the Dead of the Scribe Ani,* one of the best preserved of such papyruses from the time of the Pharaohs. The heiroglyphic text contains incantations, prayers, and hymns meant to help the soul of Ani, a minor palace official of ancient Egypt, in its journey to the underworld. The papyrus dates from about 1250 B.C.

Ideas for Writing. Ask each student to choose a character from mythology and have them write notes on what they already know about their characters. Then allow students to work with each other in pairs to generate lists of questions that can be answered through research. Interested students might want to take these prewriting notes and develop short research papers to present to the rest of the class.

9 WRITING A REPORT

Point out reports that required research. What kind of research was done?

Have a volunteer read the introductory paragraphs of the chapter aloud. After discussing the nature of reports, students should be able to describe the reports they have read recently.

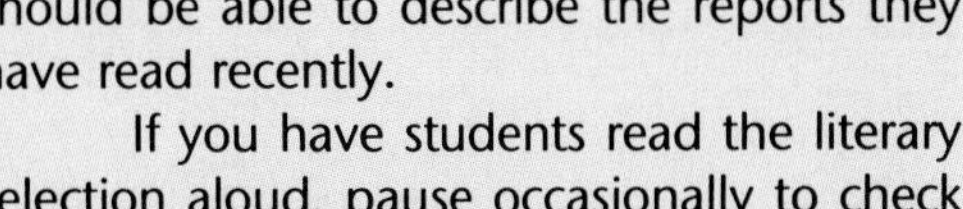

If you have students read the literary selection aloud, pause occasionally to check students' understanding of the vocabulary and concepts. After they have read the selection, ask students if they have ever seen a water strider. Students may want to share stories of other interesting animals or insects they have seen.

Exploring Your World

Through research—looking for information—you can find out almost anything you want to know. You can **explore** the deepest underground caves. You can decipher ancient Egyptian hieroglyphics. You can discover how a music video is made.

Writing and You. **Reports** are summaries of information, and they're everywhere. On TV, journalists report happenings all over the world. In books, historians write reports about the American Civil War. And in magazines, sports writers report the most exciting moments of a champion's life. Have you read an interesting report recently?

As You Read. As you read this science report, you'll learn a surprising fact: one insect does the impossible—walks on water. How does the first paragraph grab your attention?

Detail of *Book of the Dead of the Scribe Ani,* circa 1250 B.C. Egyptian 19th dynasty. Collection of British Museum, London. Bridgeman Art Library/Superstock, Inc.

QUOTATION FOR THE DAY

"Man cannot live without seeking to describe and explain the universe." (Sir Isaiah Berlin, 1909– , Russian-born British philosopher and historian)

Write the quotation on the chalkboard and ask students to brainstorm lists of ways writers describe and explain the world. Lead students to understand that reports are one method used by writers to explore the world.

LEP/ESL

General Strategies. Students might find the report on water striders more comprehensible if they have a corresponding visual reference. A short field trip to a nearby pond or botanical garden would be ideal. Another possibility is to borrow from a science teacher a film strip or video on aquatic insects.

Before having students read or write about the report, examine the topic through the students' listening and speaking skills. Ask if any students have seen or tried to capture water striders. Try to relate the material to the students' own experiences.

GUIDED PRACTICE

Use the **Reader's Response** questions and the first of the **Writer's Craft** questions as guided practice. Emphasize the importance of facts and information in the report. Point out that facts can be interesting as well as informative. The second **Reader's Response** question may help in guiding students to choose appropriate topics for their reports.

HOW CAN Water Striders Walk on Water?

by Joanne Settel and Nancy Baggett

If you could step off a stream bank and skate on the water's surface, you'd be a candidate for *The*
1 *Guinness Book of World Records*! Amazingly, however, this <u>feat</u> is so easy for the insects known as water striders that they spend most of their lives gliding around on ponds and streams.

Water striders, which look sort of like float-
2 ing daddy longlegs, not only catch their insect <u>prey</u> and eat it on the water, they also meet mates and carry out their courtship there as well. In addition, once a pair of striders has mated, the female even deposits her eggs on a floating leaf, piece of bark, feather, or other object. Clearly, water striders haven't much need to go on land. As a matter of fact, they don't go unless rain or strong wind stirs up the water surface or the water drops below 32 degrees Fahrenheit.

One reason water striders can so easily "walk" on their liquid environment is that they have specially designed bodies and legs. Their bodies are covered with water-repellent scales so they won't get heavy with water and sink. Also, their middle and back legs, which are the ones striders use for rowing and steering, are long and widely

USING THE SELECTION

How Can Water Striders Walk On Water?

1

This is a book dedicated to reporting record-setting statistics.

2

daddy longlegs: an arachnid (spider) with a small, rounded body and long, slender legs

INDEPENDENT PRACTICE

Have students complete the second **Reader's Response** question and the second **Writer's Craft** question independently. You may need to explain what is meant by *sources* before students complete the assignment.

ASSESSMENT

Use students' responses to the **Reader's Response** and **Writer's Craft** questions to assess their understanding of the lesson.

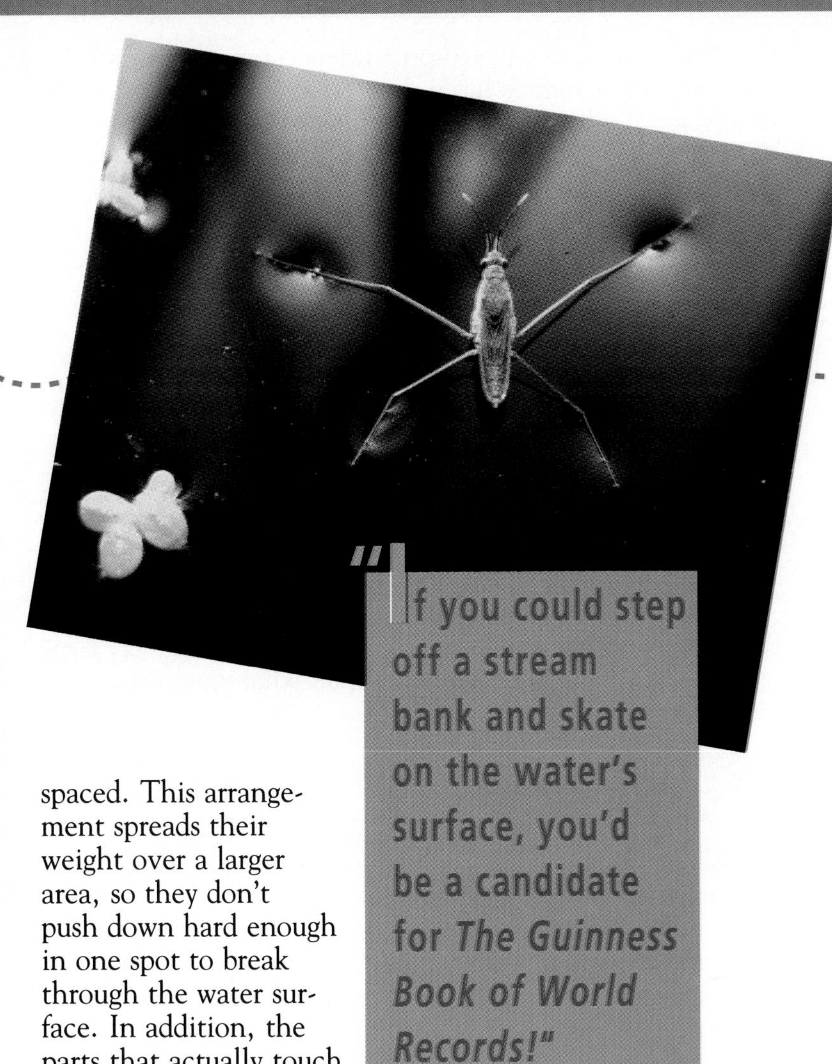

"If you could step off a stream bank and skate on the water's surface, you'd be a candidate for *The Guinness Book of World Records!*"

spaced. This arrangement spreads their weight over a larger area, so they don't push down hard enough in one spot to break through the water surface. In addition, the parts that actually touch the water, the feet and lower legs, are covered with unwettable hairs. These tiny hairs trap bubbles of air and work like mini-life preservers to <u>buoy</u> the striders up.

VISUAL CONNECTIONS

Exploring the Subject. All water striders, except for those of the genus *Halobates,* are found in fresh water. The marine insects have been seen many miles from land in tropical and subtropical waters.

SELECTION AMENDMENT
Description of change: excerpted
Rationale: to focus on the concept of reports presented in this chapter

CLOSURE

Ask students to tell what a report is [a summary of information]. You may want to have volunteers mention topics they are considering for their reports. ■

ANSWERS

Reader's Response

Responses will vary. Here are some possibilities:

1. Water striders walk on water; they deposit their eggs on floating objects; they only go on land when forced off the water; they have specially designed bodies and legs.

   Students may be surprised by the description of the water striders' unwettable hairs.

2. elephants, alligators, cats, dogs, frogs, snakes; sports, other countries, movies, television, video games

Writer's Craft

Answers may vary. Here are some possibilities:

3. They begin answering the question with the sentence "One reason water striders can so easily 'walk' on their liquid environment is that they have specially designed bodies and legs." The answer to the question in the title is concluded at the end of the selection with the description of how the water itself helps the water striders to walk on its surface.
4. encyclopedias, magazines, books on insects, dictionaries

Another important reason striders can walk on water is that the water surface has a thin, strong, elastic film. Normally you don't see this film, but it's still there, helping to keep the striders afloat. The film forms because the very tiny parts, or molecules, that make up water tend to stick together when they contact the air.

from *How Do Ants Know When You're Having a Picnic?*

READER'S RESPONSE

1. What new facts did you learn? Which facts surprised or interested you most?
2. Name another animal you're curious about. If "animals" isn't your favorite topic, what would you rather read about?

WRITER'S CRAFT

3. Where do the writers begin to answer the question of the title? Where does the answer end?
4. Some reports, like this one, don't tell where the writer found the information. Yet, in school reports, you'll be asked to list your sources. What are some sources the writers of this report might have used?

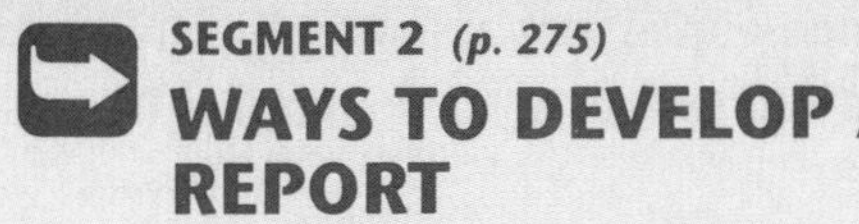

SEGMENT 2 *(p. 275)*

WAYS TO DEVELOP A REPORT

TEACHING THE AIMS

Students may be unfamiliar with the terms *narration, description, classification,* and *evaluation.* You may need to refer to previous writing assignments or sample essays to help clarify these purposes in writing.

To assess students' understanding of the aims of report writing, have them locate reports that are representative of each of the aims. They might use newspapers, magazines, or encyclopedias. ■

Ways to Develop a Report

Every day you can learn new facts from reports. You can rent a videotape about how to paddle a sea kayak. You can listen to cassette tapes that describe life on a Mississippi River boat when Mark Twain was a boy. And you can find out the latest news by reading reports in newspapers and magazines or by listening to TV and radio.

The report on water striders was developed with description. Here are some other examples of the many different ways you can develop a report.

- **Narration:** writing about a football player's teenage years; reporting on the battle of the Alamo.
- **Description:** describing the conditions on a slave ship that carried captured Africans to the West Indies; describing the stages in the life cycle of a butterfly.

Classification: comparing professional baseball in Japan and in the United States; grouping poisonous snakes and telling the features of each group.

Evaluation: reporting on the advantages and disadvantages of mountain bikes; telling whether a new video game is better than similar games.

LOOKING AHEAD

In the main assignment in this chapter, you'll write a short, informative report. You'll use narration or description to share information with your audience. The report that you write will

- give factual information about a topic
- use both print and nonprint sources
- list the sources of information

CRITICAL THINKING

Evaluation

Write the following list of possible topic ideas on the chalkboard:

1. computers in the classroom
2. the Queen of England
3. hurricanes
4. skateboarding tricks

For each topic, have students suggest several ways they could develop reports. Write their suggestions next to the appropriate topic. After listing the ideas, have students evaluate the methods. Ask students which reporting method they think would be most effective for each topic and why.

INTEGRATING THE LANGUAGE ARTS

Literature Link. Have students read a nonfiction report such as Charlene Billings's "Microchip: Small Wonder." Have students pause while reading to analyze the purpose of different sections of the writing.

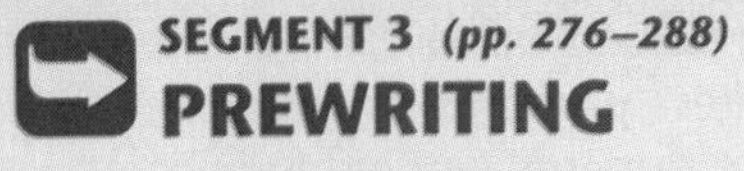

OBJECTIVES

- To narrow general subjects to topics suitable for a five-paragraph essay
- To choose and narrow an appropriate topic for a research report
- To compose questions about topics
- To take appropriate notes from research sources
- To organize information and to create an outline for a report

Teacher's ResourceBank™
RESOURCES

PREWRITING

- Narrowing Your Subject 68
- Asking Questions 69
- Finding and Listing Sources 70

QUOTATION FOR THE DAY

"We wholly conquer only what we assimilate." (André Gide, 1869–1951, French writer)

Explain to students that an important part of writing a report is gathering facts about the subject. You may also wish to explain that writers then assimilate the information they collect for use in their own informative reports. To help students understand this concept, have them freewrite descriptions of their school and ask a few volunteers to read their descriptions aloud. Have the reader pause after each sentence to allow other students to determine which sentences are factual and which express opinions.

Writing a Report

Choosing and Narrowing a Subject

Who invented basketball? How does a telephone work? Where did our number system come from? Maybe you don't know the answers to these questions, but you can find out. Then you can tell other people about the information in a report.

Choosing a Subject. Think about your hobbies and what you like to read about. Would you enjoy an article about secret codes? Do bald eagles fascinate you? Do you wonder how ancient sailors navigated across the seas? A good report topic should be something that really interests you.

But "my pet turkey, Gobbler"—no matter how fascinating to you—isn't a good report topic. You will do research for this report, and you won't find anything about your pet in the library.

In the library's nonfiction books and magazines, though, you may find topic ideas. For example, a book about the things young people can do to save the earth may give you an idea for a report on "recycling." Or, a magazine article on wildlife in rain forests may give you an idea for a report on iguanas.

Narrowing a Subject. Suppose you've decided on a subject that interests you—perhaps "baseball" or "volcanoes." These subjects are too broad for a short report. In fact, entire books have been written about each subject! You need to narrow your subject to a topic that can be covered in a report of five or six paragraphs.

TEACHING THE LESSON

This segment is divided into three subsections: **Choosing and Narrowing a Subject, Planning Your Report, and Organizing and Outlining Your Information.**

As a student volunteer reads the introductory paragraphs on choosing and narrowing a subject aloud, occasionally ask the students to suggest a topic as an example to illustrate the process of narrowing topics. For instance, if one of the students suggests "skateboarding" as a topic, you might suggest "skateboards" as more narrow and "how skateboards are made" as a properly narrowed topic. The **Writing Note** on p. 278 may help students realize the importance of budgeting their time. Some students will have more difficulty budgeting their time ☛

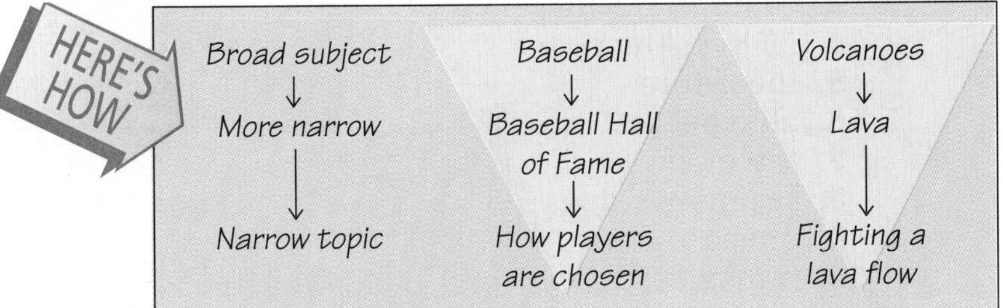

EXERCISE 1 Narrowing Subjects for a Report

Practice thinking smaller and smaller and smaller. Narrow each of the following ten general subjects to a topic for a five-paragraph report. Try using an upside-down pyramid chart like the one in the Here's How above. You might want to get together with one or two classmates and compare your work. Was any subject particularly easy to narrow down? Was any really hard to narrow down? Why do you think so?

1. teenagers
2. exercising

LEP/ESL

General Strategies. Cooperative learning activities are excellent for promoting student interaction and alleviating anxiety. You may want to use this same strategy when assigning encyclopedia research. Suggest that pairs of students work together in gathering information relevant to their respective reports. Depending on their language proficiency and research skills, ESL students may profit greatly from peer tutors' help in using the encyclopedia.

LESS-ADVANCED STUDENTS

Some students may have difficulty narrowing their topics sufficiently. You may need to suggest possible narrow versions of their topic ideas to prevent an overwhelming research experience.

than others, especially while researching and taking notes.

You may want to read the introductory paragraphs of **Planning Your Report** to your class. Pause to clarify and provide examples as needed. The questions about audience on p. 279 could be used on a sample topic as a class activity.

As you discuss how to find sources with your students, you may want to show them some examples of different types of sources. While students might be used to using print materials, nonprint sources may be new to them.

Listing sources and taking notes are steps many students often find difficult. They sometimes do not recognize the importance of clearly recording and labeling information.

ANSWERS

Exercise 1

Responses will vary. Here are some possibilities:

1. the early life of a specific teenage movie star
2. the design of running shoes
3. the creator of the first computer game
4. hunting methods of the Sioux
5. energy sources of the future
6. Olympic swimmers
7. the first moonwalk
8. training seeing-eye dogs
9. Disney movie songs
10. the early history of trains

A DIFFERENT APPROACH

For some students, the most difficult step of this research report will be choosing a topic. To help students who can't decide on a topic, assign each student a letter from the alphabet. Students should then spend a specified period of time not to exceed twenty minutes looking for topic ideas that begin with their assigned letter. They might look in the card catalogue, encyclopedias, dictionaries, or other indexes.

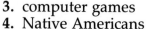

3. computer games
4. Native Americans
5. the future
6. athletes
7. the moon
8. seeing-eye dogs
9. music
10. transportation

WRITING ASSIGNMENT

PART 1:

Choosing and Narrowing a Subject

What general subject are you interested in? If you don't have one in mind, skim through some books and magazines in your library. Then narrow your subject to a specific topic. Remember, you'll spend several days with your topic, so pick one you'll have fun exploring. Don't forget: It can't be personal, and it can't be too big.

Writing a report takes time. Don't start late and try to finish in a day or two. Make yourself a schedule, and stick to it. You'll need time for six activities:

1. finding information
2. taking notes
3. organizing your notes
4. writing your first draft
5. evaluating and revising the draft
6. proofreading and publishing your final report

As you read over the explanatory information, you may want to provide several samples for the class. The numbered suggestions for taking notes on p. 284 clearly outline the steps students should follow with each source and item of information.

Students might not be ready to begin **Organizing and Outlining Your information** at the same time because of different research needs. You may want to have students begin this section independently as they finish their research. If students follow the steps as outlined in the text, they should be prepared to begin writing their first drafts in the next segment.

Planning Your Report

You can't build a treehouse until you gather the wood, nails, and tools. And before you start building, you need to figure out how to put it together. Just where will the doorway be? You need to do the same kind of planning for your report.

Thinking About Purpose and Audience. Your *purpose* in writing a report is to share interesting facts about your topic. You might include the opinion of an expert, but your own opinions do not belong in a factual report. Remember this difference:

- A ***fact*** is a piece of information that experts have checked and believe is true.
- An ***opinion*** is a belief or a feeling that cannot be proven.

The main *audience* for your report will probably be your teacher and classmates. To prepare for your audience, ask yourself these questions:

1. What do my readers already know about my topic?
2. What basic information do they need to know?
3. What information will they find most interesting?

Remember that your readers will enjoy your report more if they learn something new when they read it.

REFERENCE NOTE: See pages 210–211 for more about facts and opinions.

Asking Questions. What do you want to find out about your topic? Plan your research by writing some questions you'd like to answer in your report. The

STUDENTS WITH SPECIAL NEEDS

Because students with learning and emotional disabilities often have poor motivation, it is crucial to help them find topics that are of high interest to them. Provide structure by giving them a list of the steps necessary to complete the assignment. Ask them to organize their ideas graphically. Remember that many students with learning disabilities are poor readers and may need extra time to read and organize their material.

GUIDED PRACTICE

When assigning **Exercise 1,** demonstrate the use of the upside-down pyramid chart on p. 277 for your students with one or two of the general subjects.

Exercise 2 provides students the opportunity to develop questions about their topics. To provide guided practice for this exercise, you could use some of the narrowed topics from **Exercise 1** as subjects for your questions. You may want to assign partners for the activity on the basis of topic ideas. Students with similar topics could share question ideas.

To show students how to complete **Exercise 3,** bring to class enough copies of an encyclopedia article for all students and write the notes you take from it on the

INTEGRATING THE LANGUAGE ARTS

Literature Link. To prepare students for writing reports, have them read an informative essay such as Ann Waldron's "True or False? Amazing Art Forgeries." In this essay, the author carefully supports each main point with a variety of details. To give students practice, tell each student to select three or four main ideas and to outline the supporting information provided for each.

TIMESAVER

To provide for timely completion of these reports, hold conferences with individual students at each stage of the research process. Requiring students to meet with you to discuss topic choice, research methods, and organization will help you to guide students' efforts more closely, thereby preventing last minute difficulties.

5W-How? questions—questions that begin with *Who, What, Where, When, Why,* or *How*—work well.

If you don't know much about your topic, you can start by reading an encyclopedia article or looking quickly at a book about your topic. These sources will give you ideas for questions. Here are some questions one writer prepared on the topic of "karate."

Who invented karate?

What was the original purpose of karate?

Where and when did karate start?

How is karate different from other kinds of martial arts?

Why is karate studied today?

EXERCISE 2 **Speaking and Listening: Asking Questions About a Topic**

Practice your questioning skills by exploring this topic. One morning a Russian tank on display in Prague, Czechoslovakia, had turned a shocking pink. If you were a newspaper reporter, what questions would you ask to find out what happened? With a classmate, take turns pretending you are newspaper chalkboard. Be sure to show students how to rephrase the important information in their own words.

Cont. on p. 283

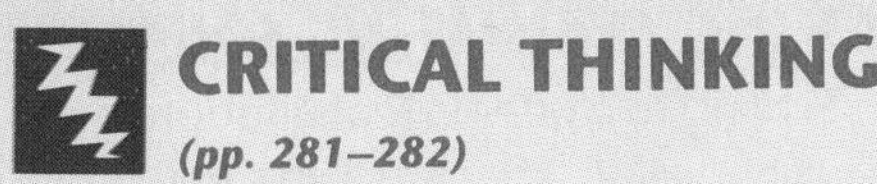

CRITICAL THINKING

(pp. 281–282)

OBJECTIVE

- To evaluate sources for usefulness

reporters. Give your partner your topic as a newspaper story "assignment." Your partner (the reporter) has to come up with *5W-How?* questions to ask you. Once you answer your partner's questions (use your imagination to come up with answers), it's your turn to be the reporter. Think of several *5W-How?* questions to ask your partner about his or her topic.

Finding Sources. When you research, look for at least three good sources of information. You'll find ***print sources*** (books, encyclopedias, magazines, microfilm) in your library. Be sure to explore ***nonprint sources,*** also. TV and radio programs, videotape documentaries, and interviews may give you new facts.

REFERENCE NOTE: See pages 684–692 for more about using library resources for research.

CRITICAL THINKING

Evaluating Sources

When you *evaluate* a source, you decide how useful it is. Use these questions to evaluate possible sources for your report.

1. **Is the source nonfiction?** Don't use short stories or novels when you're looking for facts.
2. **Is the information up to date?** Check the copyright page of a book and the date of a magazine. For a current topic, such as "protective gear for Little Leaguers," use a source that's recently published.
3. **Can you trust the source?** Don't believe everything you read. Avoid gossipy magazines and newspapers and sources that present only one side of an issue. Encyclopedias, almanacs, and books written by experts can usually be trusted.

ANSWERS

Exercise 2

Responses will vary, but each student should include at least one question for each of the *5W-How?* questions. Each question should deal with a specific topic, not a general, vague idea.

COOPERATIVE LEARNING

You may want to divide the class into groups of three to four students to complete the **Critical Thinking Exercise.** In their groups, students should discuss the merits of each source listed. Students should then write brief explanations of why the source would or would not be an effective research tool.

TEACHING *EVALUATING SOURCES*

Explain to students that all sources are not equally useful. After students have read the guideline questions, you may want to pause to ask why fiction or older sources might not be as effective as more recent or more authoritative citations.

You can use the exercise as a group activity, discussing the usefulness of each of the sources listed. 

ANSWERS

Critical Thinking Exercise

Students' explanations of choices will vary. Here are some possibilities:

Source #1 is an up-to-date encyclopedia article. It is current and probably trustworthy.

Source #2 is fiction and should not be used for a research report.

Unless your aunt is an expert in dolphin communication, **Source #3** will probably not provide too much factual information and probably should not be used.

Source #4 is a good factual source, but it will probably be useful only as a source of such background information as dolphin anatomy because it is dated.

Source #5 is a current, factual report dealing specifically with the topic.

CRITICAL THINKING EXERCISE: **Evaluating Sources**

You are writing a report on the most recent research into humans communicating with dolphins. Which of the following sources would you use? Explain your answers.

1. "Dolphin" by H. Dean Fisher in the 1992 edition of *The World Book Encyclopedia*.
2. *A Ring of Endless Light* (1980) by Madeleine L'Engle, a novel about a girl who can communicate with dolphins.
3. An interview with your aunt, who once swam with a dolphin on the Florida Keys.
4. *The Audubon Society Field Guide to North American Fishes, Whales, and Dolphins*, edited by Herbert T. Boschung, Jr., and others, published by Alfred A. Knopf in 1983.
5. "If You Need Me, Whistle," by Peter Tyac, an article about dolphin communication, in *Natural History Magazine*, August 1991.

Cont. from p. 281

INDEPENDENT PRACTICE

Students should complete **Exercises 1, 2,** and **3** on their own or with partners after you have demonstrated what is required. **Writing Assignment: Parts 1, 2,** and **3** provide students the opportunity to apply the segment's concepts to their reports. Before you assign **Writing Assignment: Part 1,** each student must have a general topic in mind. You may want to discuss students' general topics before they begin the assignment.

Depending on students' individual research needs and skills, completion time for **Writing Assignment: Part 2** will vary. You may want to work closely with students who have less research experience and to ☛

Listing Sources. You'll need to keep track of where your information comes from by giving each source a number. You can write the ***source number*** and the following information on a note card or a sheet of paper:

INFORMATION ON SOURCES
1. **Books:** author, title, city of publication, publisher, copyright year.
2. **Magazine articles:** author, title of article, magazine, date, page numbers.
3. **Encyclopedia articles:** author (if given), title of article, encyclopedia, edition (year).
4. **Videotapes:** title, director or writer (if given), publisher, year.

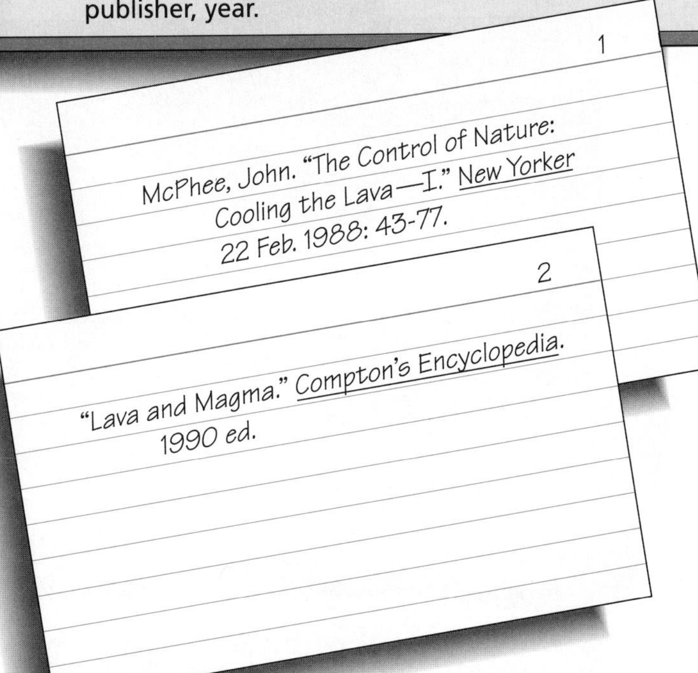

1
McPhee, John. "The Control of Nature:
Cooling the Lava—I." New Yorker
22 Feb. 1988: 43-77.
2
"Lava and Magma." Compton's Encyclopedia.
1990 ed.

INTEGRATING THE LANGUAGE ARTS

Library Link. Even your advanced students may not know how to utilize the nonprint resources available at your school. Your librarian may be willing to present a short session explaining how such sources are used. Students might want to look at public television programming, video programs, and filmstrips. They could even attend local lectures if possible.

Technology Link. Many databases are now available for all types of computers and all levels of skill. You may want to check the computer facilities available in your district to see if computers could function as a research tool for your students.

guide them to useful sources. Once they have sources, they can do the actual research independently.

Finally, before assigning **Writing Assignment: Part 3,** specify the type of outline (formal, less formal, planning outline) students should develop.

ASSESSMENT

Assess students' mastery of the segment concepts through an evaluation of **Exercises 1, 2,** and **3.** Assess their progress on the reports by evaluating the **Writing Assignment: Parts 1–3.** Because these parts build on each other, students should master each one before continuing to the next.

AT-RISK STUDENTS

When assigning research requirements and deadlines for completion, keep in mind that some of your students may have limited access to research conducted outside of class time or outside of the school building. You may need to allow students extra class time for research in the school library. Furthermore, students may need frequent progress assessments. If you assign only a final deadline, they may find themselves with too much work to do at the last minute. Short, frequent deadlines will help them stay on top of their workload.

Taking Notes. As you look through your sources, you'll use your research questions. You'll need to write down facts that help answer these questions. Here are some suggestions for taking notes:

1. Use 4″ × 6″ note cards or separate sheets of paper.
2. Write the source number at the top of each card. You'll need it later.
3. Write a *label* (a word or phrase) that tells what the note card is about.
4. Write notes in your own words. If you copy someone's exact words, put quotation marks around the quote. (Writers' words are protected by law. You are guilty of ***plagiarism*** if you use someone else's words without quotation marks.)
5. At the end of each note, write the page numbers where you found the information.

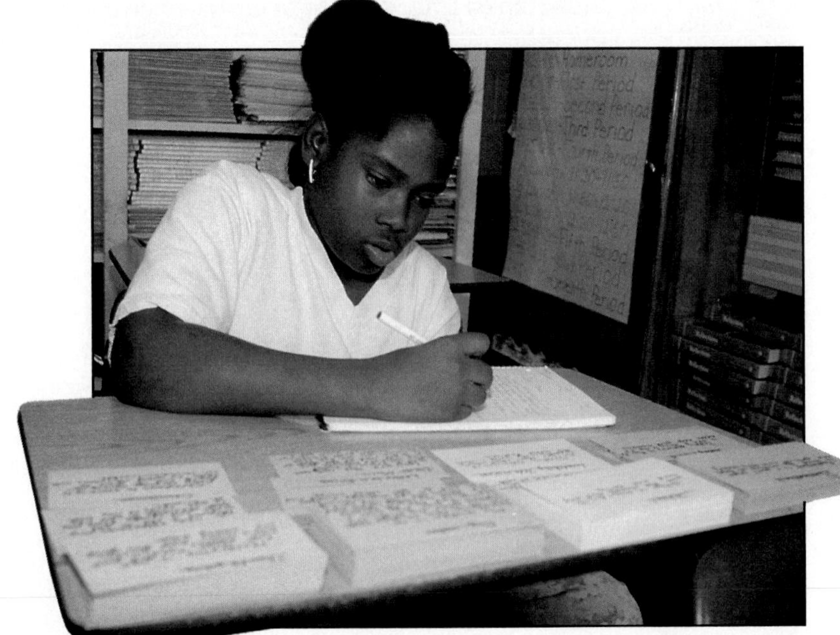

On the next page there is a paragraph from an encyclopedia article about lava and magma and a sample note card.

RETEACHING

Give students a very specific topic and lead them through all of the research steps, from narrowing the topic and conducting research, to taking notes and organizing the information. To better aid students, you may want to have pertinent articles already chosen so that you may demonstrate how to take notes from the sources.

CLOSURE

Ask students to repeat the six steps involved with writing a report [finding information, taking notes, organizing notes, writing a first draft, evaluating and revising, and proofreading and publishing]. Then ask students to define *fact* and *opinion* ["a verifiable piece of information" and "a belief or feeling," respectively]. Finally, ask students to ☛

LAVA AND MAGMA. Molten, or hot liquefied, rock located deep below the Earth's surface is called magma. When a volcano erupts or a deep crack occurs in the Earth, the magma rises and overflows. When it flows out of the volcano or crack, usually mixed with steam and gas, it is called lava. Fresh lava ranges from 1,300° to 2,200° F (700° to 1,200° C) in temperature and glows red hot to white hot as it flows.

Compton's Encyclopedia, 1990 ed.

What Lava Is 2 — label/source number

magma = hot liquid rock deep in earth
lava = magma when it erupts from volcano—
mixed with gas & steam
1,300°–2,200° F. Glows red to white. — note written in your own words

p. 89 — page number

EXERCISE 3 **Taking Notes**

You're writing a report on how the Native Americans helped the Pilgrims. Read the following encyclopedia article, and write two note cards that answer these questions: **(1.)** Who was Massasoit? **(2.)** How did he help the Pilgrims? Be sure to use your own words.

Massasoit, *MAS uh* SOYT (1580?–1661), was a chief of the Wampanoag tribe of Indians which lived in what is now southern Massachusetts and Rhode Island. He made a treaty with Governor John Carver of Plymouth

COOPERATIVE LEARNING

Before students begin taking notes from their research sources, you may want to explain the problem of plagiarism. After discussing plagiarism, you may find the following cooperative activity helpful in reinforcing the message.

Develop a short, one-page report based on two or three library sources. Be sure to plagiarize in a few places. Divide your class into groups of two or three students and have them check your report for plagiarism. Students must look up the sources used and mark out any sentences or ideas copied directly from the sources. The groups must then rewrite the offending sections. A few of the groups might then read their versions to the class.

SELECTION AMENDMENT
Description of change: excerpted
Rationale: to focus on the concept of note-taking presented in this chapter

name one method of presenting organized information [outline]. ■

ANSWERS

Exercise 3

1. Who Massasoit Was — source #
   –chief of Wampanoag Indians
   –lived in southern Massachusetts and Rhode Island
   page #
2. How Massasoit Helped — source # Pilgrims
   –after Pilgrims landed, he set up a treaty with the governor, John Carver, of Plymouth
   –promised not to harm them
   –maintained peace
   page #

SELECTION AMENDMENT

Description of change: excerpted
Rationale: to focus on the concept of note taking presented in this chapter

Colony in the spring of 1621, shortly after the Pilgrims landed in America.

He agreed that his people would not harm the Pilgrims as long as he lived. In turn, the Pilgrims guaranteed to protect the Indians and their rights. Massasoit kept the peace all his life.

E. Adamson Hoebel, from *The World Book Encyclopedia*, 1991 ed.

When you're gathering information for your report

- keep in mind what your audience wants and needs to know about your topic
- look for both print and nonprint sources
- give publishing information and assign a number for each source
- use your research questions to take notes

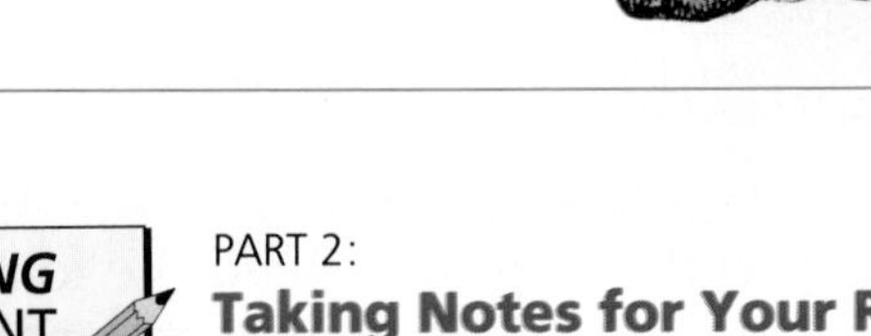

Researching facts is like hunting for treasure. First, make up *5W-How?* questions on your topic. Next, search through books, magazines, encyclopedias, and videotapes. You might also talk to an expert. Find at least three sources. Then, take notes for your report.

Organizing and Outlining Your Information

Before you start writing, you'll need to sort through your notes and organize them. You'll group notes together and then decide on an order for the groups.

Grouping Notes. First, you'll group the note cards into stacks that have the same or a similar label. For a report on "the beginning of basketball," you might have one stack that tells about basketball's inventor. Another stack might be about the game's first rules. (Some notes may not fit into groups. You can leave them out at first, but you may find a use for them later.)

Each of your note stacks should be about one main idea (for example, "the inventor of basketball"). Then each main idea can become one paragraph in your report.

Outlining. Next, you can put your information into a plan, or outline, for your report. You'll create the main headings in your outline by writing down the main idea of each of your groups. You can then take these steps:

1. Decide how to order the main headings: stack 1, stack 2, and so on. Write your main headings on a sheet of paper. Be sure to leave several line spaces between main headings.
2. Go through the cards in each stack, and put them in an order that makes sense. The main facts in each stack are the outline's subheadings. Write the subheadings under the main headings.

Once you've created your plan, or ***informal outline,*** you can use it as a guide as you write your report. But remember, you may change your mind

LEARNING STYLES

Visual Learners. Some of your students might benefit from a classroom display that graphically depicts the steps necessary for the completion of the research assignment. Divide a board into six areas and label each with one of the six writing activities (finding information, taking notes, organizing notes, writing a first draft, evaluating and revising, and proofreading and publishing). As students complete each step, they could place a small sticker on the area finished.

Auditory Learners. Activities that require individual reading and writing can be very frustrating for auditory learners. Therefore, you may want to have a peer-conference area available. In this area, students can meet to quietly discuss each other's ideas and writing. To manage the peer conference area, have students sign up for a limited time slot.

about some things as you write and revise. Maybe you'll decide to add some information or leave something out. Just jot down the change on your planning outline. Later, your teacher may ask you to make a ***formal outline.*** Here's a formal outline one writer created for a report on lava.

Controlling Lava Flow

I. Using bombs
   A. 1935--lava threatening Hilo, Hawaii
   B. Bombs dropped on lava source
   C. Lava stopped in 30 hours
II. Using sea water
   A. 1973--lava threatening harbor at Heimaey, Iceland
   B. Sea water sprayed from pipes for three weeks
   C. Lava flow cooled and stopped
III. Using barricades
   A. 1983--lava threatening ski resort at Mount Etna, Sicily
   B. Walls of volcanic ash and stone built at diagonal to lava flow
   C. Lava flow dynamited
   D. Lava flow changed direction

REFERENCE NOTE: For more help with outlining, see page 729.

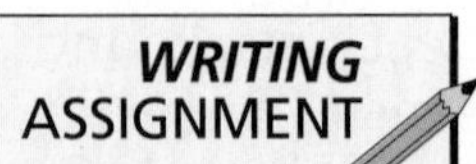

PART 3:
Organizing Your Notes and Making an Outline

You've collected many facts. Do they seem like a jumble? Read through your notes and sort them into stacks that have the same main idea. Then outline the main ideas and supporting facts.

SEGMENT 4 *(pp. 289–292)*

WRITING YOUR FIRST DRAFT

OBJECTIVE

- To write a first draft of a research report

TEACHING THE LESSON

Explain to students that they have already completed the most-difficult steps. They should already have all of their information organized. They just need to write it in report form.

Students should be familiar with the concepts of introduction, body, and conclusion. The only new part is the list of sources. 

Writing Your First Draft

Understanding the Parts of a Report

Like every composition, a report has three main parts. It also has a fourth part, a list of sources.

The ***introduction*** is the beginning of your report. It tells what the report is about. To grab the reader's attention, you can use a question, a brief story, an interesting quotation, or a surprising fact.

The ***body*** presents the report's main ideas and specific details. Each paragraph develops one main idea.

The ***conclusion*** is the last paragraph. A strong conclusion ties together the ideas in the report. It also brings the report to a clear, definite ending.

The ***list of sources*** is a separate page at the end of your report. It tells where you found your information. Your readers might be interested in your topic and might want to read more about it. They can use your list of sources to find the sources you used in your report.

You'll start with the list you made before you took your notes. (See page 283.) Alphabetize the sources by the author's last name. If there's no author, alphabetize by the title. You can follow the form in the sample list on page 292 or another that your teacher shows you.

Writing Your Report

As you draft your report, you'll use your note cards and outline as guides. Remember that you can always change the order of ideas and drop or add information.

You might want to use the following report as a model for your own report. Notice how each paragraph in the body has a topic sentence that states the paragraph's main idea.

Teacher's ResourceBank™

RESOURCES

WRITING YOUR FIRST DRAFT

- Writing a Report 71

QUOTATION FOR THE DAY

"Nothing goes by luck in composition. It allows of no tricks. The best you can write will be the best you are." (Henry David Thoreau, 1817–1862, American writer)

Write the quotation on the chalkboard and ask students to write journal entries about how writing well relates to them being their best. [Students might discuss how good writing demands a certain honesty, the same way being the best at anything demands real ability and not tricks or gimmicks.]

You may need to provide several examples to demonstrate what is meant by a list of sources.

As volunteers read the model report aloud, you may want to pause occasionally to discuss the author's main points and supporting details.

ASSESSMENT

Writing Assignment: Part 4 may be used to assess students' understanding of report writing. Careful monitoring of students' progress as they write their first drafts will help prevent problems as well as allow for continual assessment of student work.

LEP/ESL

General Strategies. Before writing lists of sources, students may need extra practice with bibliographical form. Create several erroneous bibliographies for *Controlling Lava.* One version could have entries scrambled alphabetically. Another version could have neither book nor journal titles underlined. A third version could omit necessary punctuation, and so on. Have students correct the versions by comparing them to the original.

LESS-ADVANCED STUDENTS

Some students may have difficulty providing enough supporting details in the body paragraphs of their reports. You may want to require that each student provide at least three separate details to support the topic. With a specific number as a goal, students will know when they are able to effectively end one section of the body and begin writing the next.

A WRITER'S MODEL

Controlling Lava

INTRODUCTION

Lava is the red-hot, boiling, melted rock that comes out of an erupting volcano. What would you do if a fiery stream of lava--at least 1,100 degrees F--was aimed at your doorstep? You would probably run fast. People have always done that. But scientists have been fighting back. They have tried different ways to stop lava flows or turn them.

BODY
Main topic:
Using bombs

At first, scientists bombed a volcano. In 1935 Mauna Loa erupted in Hawaii. A wide stream of lava was near the city of Hilo and came a mile closer every day. An American scientist, Thomas Jaggar, had a daring plan. Ten U.S. Army planes dropped powerful bombs on the lava flow high up on the side of Mauna Loa. A little more than a day later, the lava stopped, just twelve miles from Hilo.

Main topic:
Using sea water

Another plan used sea water to cool a lava flow. In Heimaey, Iceland, in 1973, a volcano erupted. The eruption went on for more than

CLOSURE

Ask students to name the four main parts of a written report [introduction, body, conclusion, and list of sources]. ■

five months. Lava and ash covered almost four hundred homes and threatened to fill up the city's harbor. Workers used forty-seven giant pumps and nineteen miles of pipes to dump four thousand tons of sea water a day on the lava flow. After three weeks, the wall of lava cooled from 1,800 degrees F to 215 degrees. The lava changed from a liquid to a solid—and it stopped.

Main topic: Using barricades

Scientists have also changed a lava flow's direction. They have built barriers at a diagonal to the lava flow. In Sicily in 1983, for example, lava from Mount Etna destroyed parts of a ski resort. Workers built huge walls of volcanic ash and stone. They also dynamited the lava flow. The lava flow turned away from the ski resort.

CONCLUSION

Trying to control lava is difficult and dangerous work. Yet as long as people live in the shadows of volcanoes, scientists will look for new ways to control lava. Bombs, sea water, and barriers are the first attempts. Maybe someone like you will think of a better way.

VISUAL CONNECTIONS

Exploring the Subject. Volcanoes can be divided into two types: fissure volcanoes, which occur along fractures in the earth's crust and which are relatively quiet and less dangerous; and central volcanoes, which are cone-shaped and often very explosive. Lava buildup in the latter type of volcano led to the violent explosion of Mount St. Helens in 1980. Thousands of the world's volcanoes are dormant (sleeping) or dead.

LIST OF SOURCES

The MLA calls for a 5-space indent. For the typeface used in this book, the 5-space indent translates into a printer's measure that is slightly different.

List of Sources

Cashman, Katharine V. "Volcano." The World Book Encyclopedia. 1991 ed.

"Lava and Magma." Compton's Encyclopedia. 1990 ed.

McPhee, John. "The Control of Nature: Cooling the Lava--I." New Yorker 22 Feb. 1988: 43-77.

Nature: The Volcano Watchers. Videotape. Dir. Ned Kelly. Thirteen/WNET and BBC-TV, 1987.

Volcano. Alexandria: Time-Life Books, 1982.

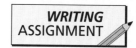

PART 4:
Writing Your First Draft

All right, researcher, it's time to share your knowledge. Sit down with your outline and note cards and write! When you've finished your draft, write a list of sources. Follow the style in the writer's model.

SEGMENT 5 *(pp. 293–294)*

EVALUATING AND REVISING

OBJECTIVES

- To study the changes made in a revised paragraph
- To evaluate and revise a first draft

TEACHING THE LESSON

After the class reads over the segment's introductory material, you may want to complete **Exercise 4** as a group activity. As you call on students to answer the questions, you can assess and guide their understanding of the revision process.

Writing Assignment: Part 5 allows students the opportunity for peer evaluation. 

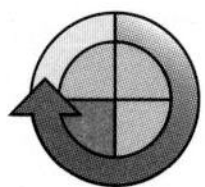

Evaluating and Revising

If you've followed your schedule, you should have time to put your draft away for a while. Then you can look at it with a fresh eye. This will help you recognize the strengths and weaknesses of your draft.

You can *evaluate* by asking yourself the questions on the left side of the chart on page 294. You can also ask a partner to read your report and make suggestions. You may find that you need to go back and look for additional information or reorganize some of your ideas. The chart on page 294 will also give you help with revising.

EXERCISE 4 **Analyzing a Writer's Revisions**

Study the changes the writer made when she revised the second paragraph of "Controlling Lava."

At first, scientists bombed a volcano. In 1935 Mauna Loa erupted in Hawaii. An American scientist, Thomas Jaggar, had a daring plan. A wide stream of lava was near the city of Hilo and came a mile closer every day. *Ten* U.S. Army planes dropped powerful bombs on the lava flow *high up on the side of Mauna Loa*. A little more than a day later, the lava stopped, just twelve miles from Hilo.

add

reorder

add

add

1. Why did the writer add a new first sentence?
2. Why did she move the second sentence?
3. Where did the writer add facts? How do they make the report better?

Teacher's ResourceBank™

RESOURCES

EVALUATING AND REVISING

- Writing a Report 72

QUOTATION FOR THE DAY

"Thinking is our greatest sport." (Robert Rauschenberg, 1925– , American artist)

Write the quotation on the chalkboard and use it to open a discussion on how thinking could be considered a sport. [Students might say it requires effort, can be fun, and is usually improved with practice.]

ANSWERS

Exercise 4

Answers may vary. Here are some possibilities:

1. The new sentence grabs the reader's attention and introduces the topic.
2. She wanted all of the information about the volcano to be in one part of the report and all of the information about the scientist and his plan in another part so that the information in the report is clearly organized.
3. She added the number of planes and the exact location where they dropped the bombs in the next to the last sentence. The additional clarity and detail help present supporting facts for the main idea.

You may want to use the questions from the **Evaluating and Revising Reports** chart to better direct the groups' discussions.

CLOSURE

Ask students what they will do to improve their drafts [add, cut, replace, and move words]. ■

LEP/ESL

General Strategies. If possible, meet with each of your ESL students to explain the evaluation guidelines. Photocopy their reports for reference purposes. Isolate specific examples from their reports to help them understand the evaluation guidelines and to determine whether they are meeting the necessary criteria.

Attention and individualized instruction are crucial to the students' successful completion of the assignment.

TIMESAVER

If you are planning to read the drafts as well as the final papers, you may want students to highlight changes in the drafts before writing their final copies. Not only will this help you to identify student revisions, it will also help students to identify improvements they made in their writing.

EVALUATING AND REVISING REPORTS

	EVALUATION GUIDE	REVISION TECHNIQUE
1	Does the introduction grab the reader's interest? Does it tell what the report is about?	**Add** an attention-getting question, brief story, or fact. **Add** a sentence that tells the report topic.
2	Does the body present the main ideas and supporting facts?	**Add** topic sentences to paragraphs. **Add** facts to support main ideas.
3	Is the information in the report clearly organized?	**Reorder** sentences or paragraphs until the organization of your ideas is clear.
4	Does the report have a conclusion?	**Add** a paragraph that ties together the main ideas and brings the report to a definite end.
5	Is the list of sources on a separate sheet at the end?	**Add** a list of your sources in the correct form (see page 292).

***WRITING* ASSIGNMENT**

PART 5:

Evaluating and Revising Your Report

Two heads—or three or four—are usually better than one. Share your first draft with a small group of classmates. Ask for their suggestions, and consider them carefully. Then evaluate your draft yourself. Make changes based on all these evaluations.

SEGMENT 6 *(pp. 295–296)*

PROOFREADING AND PUBLISHING

OBJECTIVE

- To proofread a report for errors and to share the finished product with an audience

TEACHING THE LESSON

Explain to students that it is easy to miss spelling and punctuation errors as they read over their reports. Although they may have read the reports several times, there may still be errors. To find such mistakes, they must read very slowly and carefully. They should pay little attention to the content, but concentrate on spelling and

Proofreading and Publishing

Proofreading. When you proofread, slow your reading down. Check every word and every sentence. Look for mistakes in spelling, punctuation, capitalization, and usage—and fix them.

Publishing. Now's the time to think of a good title for your report. You'll need to make a clean copy to share it with some readers. Here are two suggestions for publishing your report:

- Get together with other students whose reports are in the same general area as yours (biography, science, sports, and so on). Each group can create a display with reports, drawings, photographs, and objects.
- Give an oral report based on your report. Don't just read your report, but *tell* your audience what you've learned. Volunteer to give your talk to a class or club that would be interested in your topic.

Teacher's ResourceBank™

RESOURCES

PROOFREADING AND PUBLISHING

- Writing a Report 73

QUOTATION FOR THE DAY

"He who hesitates is sometimes saved." (James Thurber, 1894–1961, American humorist, cartoonist, and author)

Write the quotation on the chalkboard and divide the class into small groups. Ask each group to create a scenario for which Thurber's quotation could be a title or a moral. Have representatives from each group share their results. Explain that writers who allow themselves time to carefully proofread their work are able to correct any mistakes before their papers are published.

punctuation. Careful proofreading takes time and concentration but results in improved reports and higher grades.

When assigning **Writing Assignment: Part 6,** emphasize the importance of neat, clean final papers.

CLOSURE

Ask students which type of mistakes they should look for in the proofreading stage [mistakes in spelling, punctuation, capitalization, and usage].

MEETING INDIVIDUAL NEEDS

LEP/ESL

General Strategies. Remind students that content is not changed during the proofreading process. The objective of proofreading is to check for minor problems such as spelling errors, improper use of apostrophes and commas, problems with subject-verb agreement, and so on. Emphasize that even professional writers receive help in checking their final drafts.

INTEGRATING THE LANGUAGE ARTS

Spelling Link. Students might find it difficult to check their papers for spelling errors. It is easy to get preoccupied in a paper's content and not to see a misspelled word. To solve this problem, have students read the papers word for word. They should start at the ends of the papers and read backwards. This activity forces proofreaders to concentrate on the individual words.

Underlining and Quotation Marks

Underline the title of each book, magazine, encyclopedia, or videotape in your list of sources. Use quotation marks for the titles of articles in magazines or encyclopedias.

EXAMPLES **Book:**

Smith, Kathie Billingslea. Martin Luther King, Jr. New York: Simon and Schuster, 1987.

Magazine:

Scott, David. "Submarine Power Lines." Popular Science Feb. 1990: 76–78.

 REFERENCE NOTE: For more information on underlining and quotation marks, see pages 613–614 and 622.

PART 6:
Proofreading and Publishing Your Report

You're almost finished! Copy your report on clean paper and proofread it. Then share your report, using one of the ideas on page 295 or an idea of your own.

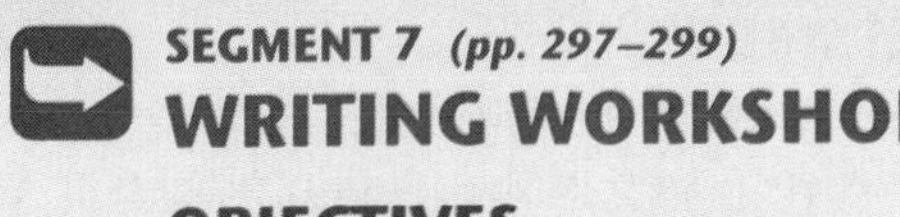

SEGMENT 7 *(pp. 297–299)*

WRITING WORKSHOP

OBJECTIVES

- To analyze a sample book report
- To write a book report of a biography

TEACHING THE LESSON

Begin by sharing several examples of biographies with your students. Biographies of popular sports figures or other prominent people might be of interest. You may want to discuss the analytical questions in relation to the sample books.

The **Thinking It Over** questions provide students the opportunity to see and

WRITING WORKSHOP

A Book Report

You've probably read dozens of books. You've liked some and disliked others. When you write a ***book report***, you tell what the book is about and what you think of it. You say exactly what you like or dislike about it.

A ***biography*** tells the life story of a real person. Here are some questions about biographies. They will help you give good reasons why you like or dislike a biography you have read.

1. Does the book tell about the most important events in the person's life?
2. Does the book include interesting details about the person's life and personality?
3. Does the book give a clear picture of the person's character? Does it make you care about the person?

As you read the following sample book report, look for information about events in the life of Martin Luther King, Jr.

Martin Luther King, Jr., a Man of Dreams

Have you ever dreamed of righting some wrong in the world? Martin Luther King, Jr., was a courageous leader who did just that. Margaret Davidson's biography I Have a Dream: The Story of Martin Luther King helps readers share in King's dream.

Davidson's biography describes King's childhood in Georgia, his many years of education, and his career as a minister and civil rights leader. King believed in nonviolent resistance. He tried to change unfair laws by

QUOTATION FOR THE DAY

"I have always come to life after coming to books." (Jorge Luis Borges, 1899–1986, Argentine writer)

Share the quotation with the class and ask several volunteers to restate the quotation in their own words. Lead students to understand that some books can change peoples' moods, teach them lessons, or show them how to deal better with the problems in their lives. Designate a special place on the classroom chalkboard where each student may write the title and author of a book, story, or poem that the student especially enjoyed.

discuss what makes a book report effective. The writing steps may take some students longer than others, especially if a lengthy biography is chosen. Keep reading levels in mind as students choose their books and as you set deadlines.

ASSESSMENT

It should benefit students' performance if each step of the writing process is assessed for accuracy and clarity. You may want to use the **Thinking It Over** questions as an evaluation guide.

MEETING INDIVIDUAL NEEDS

LEP/ESL

General Strategies. Encourage students to choose biographies about individuals whose life experiences are somehow relevant to their own—someone with whom they can identify—for their book reports. The challenge is to make biographies of appropriate people available to ensure that students have access to interesting publications appropriate to their reading levels.

INTEGRATING THE LANGUAGE ARTS

Literature Link. You may want to have your students read autobiographical or biographical essays such as Russell Freedman's "A Backwoods Boy," selections from Anne Frank's *A Diary of a Young Girl,* or Susy Clemens's "My Papa, Mark Twain." Have students evaluate their selections. If you feel that guided practice is necessary, help the class write a miniature book report on one of the selections.

peacefully disobeying them. To protest the unequal treatment of African Americans, he led boycotts and marches.

King was arrested, his life was threatened, and his home was bombed, yet he never stopped believing in peaceful methods. King received the Nobel Peace Prize in 1964 for his work in the civil rights movement. But in 1968, he was shot and killed in Memphis, Tennessee. He was thirty-nine years old when he died.

Davidson's book helps readers come to know and admire Martin Luther King, Jr. Through many details and incidents, Davidson shows King's courage and strength. This biography will inspire you. It will help you understand what a great man Martin Luther King, Jr., was.

CLOSURE

Ask students what a book report should convey [what the book was about and what the report writer liked and disliked about the book] and what a biography is [the life story of a real person]. ■

Thinking It Over

1. What information do you learn in the introductory paragraph?
2. What purpose does the body of the report serve?
3. What does the writer think of the book? What reasons does the writer give for the opinion?

Writing a Book Report of a Biography

Prewriting. Think of a person you'd like to learn more about—perhaps a favorite sports star or someone you have read about in your history class. If you can't think of anyone, look through the biography shelves of your library. As you read the biography you have chosen, take notes to help you summarize the book.

Writing, Evaluating, and Revising. Begin your introduction with an interesting fact or question. Tell whom the biography is about and why that person is important. The introduction should also give the title and the author of the biography. In the body, summarize some important events in the person's life. Then, write a conclusion that tells what you think of the biography. Be sure to give specific reasons why you did or didn't like the book.

To make your report better, reread it several times. Ask a classmate to read it, too. Think about what your classmate says. Then, add your own ideas and make changes.

Proofreading and Publishing. Make a clean copy of your book report and proofread it carefully. Remember to underline the title of the book. Make a "Heroes and Heroines" display of class reports. You could also present the display to other classes and let the students sign a list to check out and read a report.

ANSWERS

Thinking It Over

Answers may vary. Here are some possibilities:

1. Martin Luther King, Jr., was a courageous leader who worked to right wrongs in the world. Margaret Davidson wrote a biography, *I Have a Dream: The Story of Martin Luther King.*
2. It tells of the major events in King's life and the beliefs that helped to shape his life.
3. The writer thinks the book helps readers to know and admire King. The writer feels that the book's details show King's strength and courage.

A DIFFERENT APPROACH

It often helps students to better understand the grades they receive if they participate in the grading process. You may want to provide students with your grading criteria. To demonstrate the evaluation method, the class could evaluate the sample book report on Martin Luther King, Jr. Then each student could evaluate his or her writing, and make any needed improvements before turning in the report for final evaluation.

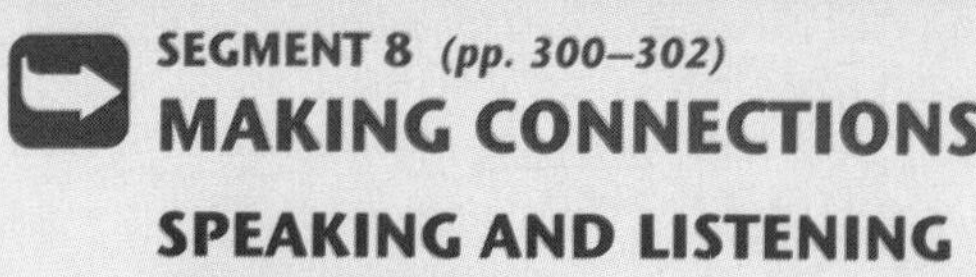

SEGMENT 8 *(pp. 300–302)*

MAKING CONNECTIONS

SPEAKING AND LISTENING OBJECTIVES

- To take notes of local events
- To prepare and cooperatively present news reports based on them

SPEAKING AND LISTENING

Teaching Strategies

Students should not choose the same local events for their news reports. You could act as the producer and assign various events so that an entire news show could be presented. Some students might report on school events, some on local sports, some on community events, and some students on special activities.

If possible, videotape the reports so students can watch their television news program. Before the taping, you might have a practice run with peer evaluations to raise students' confidence in their reporting.

GUIDELINES

Students should attend the events they are covering with questions already prepared. The final reports should be ordered very clearly, should be brief, and should highlight the main happenings at the events.

MAKING CONNECTIONS

SPEAKING AND LISTENING

Giving a Television News Report

Turn on your television early in the morning or around dinner time, and you're bound to see a news program. If you were a TV reporter, you'd give reports all the time. Why not see how you'd like it?

Form a TV news team with two other classmates. Choose a local event to give an oral report on. For example, you might choose a holiday parade, a school basketball game, or a parent-teacher organization meeting. Remember to choose an event that your classmates will want to know about. Then follow these steps:

1. Before the event, watch several TV news reports. Notice the kinds of information reporters present. Then work with your team to prepare a list of *5W-How?* questions about your local event.
2. Each person on the team should attend the event and take notes. Remember that you're trying to answer your *5W-How?* questions.
3. After the event, compare notes and agree on the information for your report. Then prepare final note cards and put them in a clear order. Come up with an interesting way to begin and end.
4. Choose one member of your team to present the report. If you're the presenter, practice the report in front of your teammates.
5. Give your report to the entire class as though you were a reporter on a TV news program. If your school has videotaping equipment, you can also tape your report and present it to other classes.

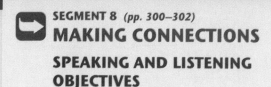

RESEARCH ACROSS THE CURRICULUM OBJECTIVES

- To use research skills to find out about the history of mathematics
- To prepare and present a report on the subject

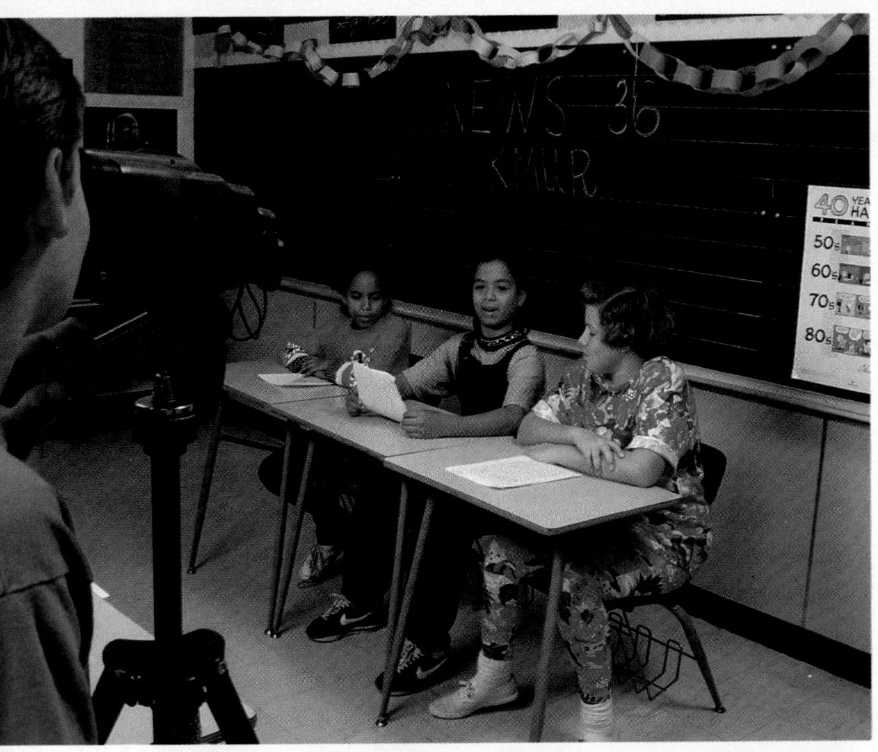

RESEARCH ACROSS THE CURRICULUM

Mathematics

You probably know something about mathematics. But do you know how mathematics began? Use your research skills to find out about the history of mathematics. Choose a topic from the following questions or decide on a topic of your own.

1. Where did the idea of zero come from? If we had no zero, how would our number system have to change? What do you call the kind of numbers in this list (1, 2, and so on)?
2. What kinds of number systems did the ancient Egyptians and Mayas use? How did they record numbers?

RESEARCH ACROSS THE CURRICULUM

Teaching Strategies

To provide more topic ideas for students, you may want to see what students are currently studying in mathematics. Mathematics teachers might have ideas for helpful research topics.

Because all students will be researching the same general topic, they may need to share research sources. You may want to have half of your class working on the news report and half on the mathematics report. When students complete their first project, they can begin the second.

Remind students that they are not writing formal papers. Instead, they are preparing oral presentations. Each student must concentrate on developing an interesting beginning, clear information, and a concise closing.

GUIDELINES

Each oral report should be clearly directed toward answering a specific question or set of questions. Each report should have a clear introduction, body, and conclusion. Also, students should tell what sources were used in finding their information.

1. The zero was invented independently by the Mayas (300 A.D.) and Hindus (600 A.D.). If we had no zero, our number system could not be based on 10. The numbers in the list are called numerals or integers.
2. Ancient number systems were probably simple straight marks for small numbers with some special mark for 10. Numbers were recorded by putting notches in sticks, scratches on stone, marks on pottery, and so on.
3. The ancient Romans used letters to record numbers. These are still used in outlines.
4. An abacus is an ancient counting device or calculator. It works by the manipulation of beads on wires or rods and was probably invented around the sixth century B.C.

3. Describe how the ancient Romans recorded numbers. Where in this chapter did you use their system?
4. What is an abacus? How does it work, and when was it invented?

Besides using the library, you might ask your math teacher about sources of information. From your notes, prepare a report to share with your math class. You can make it fun, too. Perhaps you can challenge others to solve problems using another number system.

Chapter 10 WRITING EFFECTIVE SENTENCES

OBJECTIVES

- To identify and revise sentence fragments and run-on sentences
- To identify and revise stringy sentences
- To combine sentences by inserting words and word groups, by joining subjects and verbs, and by joining sentences

Motivation

After students have written drafts of paragraphs or longer compositions, collect their papers to find examples of sentence fragments, run-on sentences, stringy sentences, and sentences that should be combined. On the day you begin this chapter, distribute the example sentences in a handout or write them on the chalkboard. Tell students that the sentences come from their work and that they are going to learn why the sentences need revision and how to revise the sentences. Explain that the skills they learn in this chapter will be used to revise their compositions.

Introduction

The first three segments of this chapter are relatively independent of one another, and this gives you considerable flexibility in how you can use the chapter. One way to teach the chapter is to deal with it as a separate unit. Most sixth-graders probably aren't skilled in the concepts in the chapter, and you can treat it as an introduction to sentence fragments, run-on sentences, and so on.

A second way to handle the chapter—especially if your students have been exposed to the concepts—is to treat it as a resource for students who are having problems with one or more of the sentence faults. For example, if some of your students consistently write sentence fragments, you can work with the students in a small group on the segment on fragments. If others continually write stringy sentences, you can assign the section on stringy sentences to them.

A third way to use this chapter is to concentrate on one sentence fault at a time as your students are revising compositions written in conjunction with the other composition chapters.

One question that might come up (especially with advanced students) concerns the use of sentence fragments by professional writers. A good way to handle this is to acknowledge that while fragments can be useful in achieving certain effects, students must be able to recognize and revise fragments in their own writing so they don't write them when they don't intend to use them for effect.

Revision is an essential part of the writing process for any writing aim or mode. This chapter will help students sharpen their skills in expressive, informative, persuasive, and creative writing. It will also help improve their skills in narration, description, classification, and evaluation.

Integration

You can use this chapter in conjunction with a unit on public speaking, as well as with any unit or assignment that involves writing. Sometimes students use long, stringy sentences in informal speeches, and you can make your students aware of this problem by referring them to the segment that deals with stringy sentences.

The chart on the next page illustrates the strands of language arts as they are integrated into this chapter. For vocabulary study, glossary words are underlined in some writing models.

QUOTATIONS

All **Quotations for the Day** are chosen because of their relevance to instructional material presented in that segment of the chapter and for their usefulness in establishing student interest in writing.

INTEGRATING THE LANGUAGE ARTS

Selection	Reading and Literature	Writing and Critical Thinking	Language and Syntax	Speaking, Listening, and Other Expression Skills
	Reading to detect short, choppy sentences **313-314, 318-319**	Identifying complete sentences **305-306** Identifying sentence fragments **305-306** Identifying and revising sentence fragments **306** Identifying and revising run-on sentences **308-309** Identifying and revising stringy sentences **309-310** Revising fragments, run-ons, and stringy sentences **310-311** Combining sentences by inserting words **313-314** Combining sentences by inserting word groups **315-316** Combining sentences by joining subjects and verbs **317** Combining complete sentences **318-319** Revising a paragraph by combining sentences **319** Reconstructing a message by adding missing words **320**	Identifying components of a complete sentence **305-306** Attaching a fragment to a preceding or following sentence **306, 310-311** Using coordinating conjunctions to revise run-on sentences **308-309, 310-311** Using commas correctly to join independent clauses **308-309, 310-311, 314** Identifying stringy sentences **309-310** Identifying compound subjects and verbs **317-318**	

CHAPTER 10

SEGMENT PLANNING GUIDE

Whether you are planning for a quick review of a writing concept or preparing an extended lesson on composition, you can use the following Planning Guide to adapt the chapter material to the individual needs of your class.

SEGMENT	PAGES	CONTENT	RESOURCES
1 *Sentence Fragments*	*303-306*		Sentence Fragments 75
Writing Clear Sentences	303	Introduction: identifying unclear sentences	
Sentence Fragments	304-305	Guidelines: identifying and revising sentence fragments	
Writing Note	305	Writing suggestion: attaching fragments to other sentences	
Exercise 1	305-306	Applied practice: identifying sentence fragments	
Exercise 2	306	Applied practice: identifying and revising sentence fragments	
2 *Run-on Sentences*	*307-311*		Run-on Sentences 76 Stringy Sentences 77
Run-on Sentences	307	Guidelines: identifying and revising run-on sentences	
Mechanics Hint	308	Writing suggestion: using commas correctly	
Exercise 3	308-309	Applied practice: identifying and revising run-on sentences	
Stringy Sentences	309	Guidelines: revising stringy or rambling sentences	
Exercise 4	309-310	Applied practice: revising stringy sentences	
Review A	310-311	Applied practice: revising fragments, run-ons, and stringy sentences	
3 *Combining Sentences*	*311-319*		Inserting Words and Word Groups 78 Combining with *And, But,* and *Or* 79
Combining Sentences	311-312	Guidelines: examining combined sentences in a model	
Inserting Words	312	Guidelines: combining sentences by inserting a key word from one sentence into another	
Chart: Using the Same Form/Changing the Form	312	Example: combining two sentences into one	
Writing Note	313	Writing suggestion: forming adjectives and adverbs	
Exercise 5	313-314	Applied practice: combining sentences by inserting words	

All the resources listed in this chapter are located in the *Teacher's ResourceBank™*.

SEGMENT	PAGES	CONTENT	RESOURCES
Inserting Groups of Words	314-315	Guidelines: combining sentences by inserting phrases	
Exercise 6	315-316	Applied practice: combining sentences by inserting phrases	
Using Connecting Words	316-317	Guidelines: combining sentences by using *and, but,* or *or* to join subjects and verbs	
Exercise 7	317	Applied practice: combining sentences by joining subjects and verbs	
Joining Sentences	318	Guidelines: creating compound and complex sentences by using connecting words	
Exercise 8	318-319	Applied practice: joining complete sentences	
Review B	319	Applied practice: revising a paragraph by combining sentences	
4 *Making Connections*	*320*		
Reconstruct a Message	320	Applied practice: reconstructing a message by adding missing words	
WHOLE-CHAPTER RESOURCES Review Form A, Review Form B			

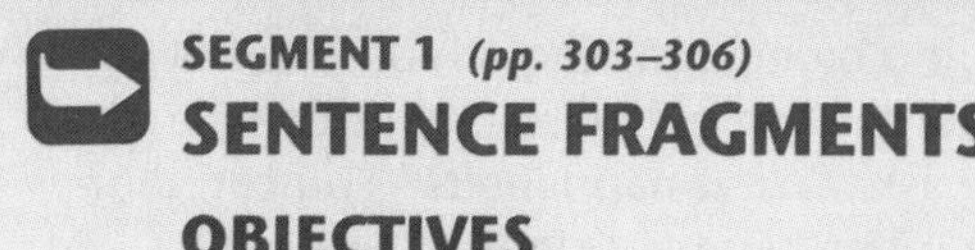

SEGMENT 1 *(pp. 303–306)*

SENTENCE FRAGMENTS

OBJECTIVES

- To use the three-part test to identify sentence fragments
- To revise sentence fragments

TEACHING THE LESSON

If students have a clear understanding of the terms *subject* and *verb,* you can probably proceed with the lesson by having them read the text and do the exercises. Otherwise, you'll probably want to spend time reviewing the terms.

If you're using this chapter as a resource for students during the revision

Teacher's ResourceBank™

RESOURCES

SENTENCE FRAGMENTS

- Sentence Fragments 75

QUOTATION FOR THE DAY

"The greatest part of a writer's time is spent in reading in order to write: a man will turn over half a library to make one book." (Samuel Johnson, 1709–1784, English writer and scholar)

Write the quotation on the chalkboard and use it as the basis for a discussion of ways reading and writing are connected. Lead students to understand that reading books, magazines, and newspapers lets them see how other writers create clear sentences.

10 WRITING EFFECTIVE SENTENCES

LOOKING AHEAD

Have you ever polished a car or a tabletop until it gleamed? You can add "polish" to your sentence style, too. That's what you will learn to do in this chapter. You will practice

- writing clear sentences
- combining sentences for smoothness and variety

Writing Clear Sentences

A clear sentence gives your reader just enough information. It doesn't leave out any important pieces, and it doesn't run together or string together too many ideas at once. You can learn how to spot three enemies of clear writing: *sentence fragments, run-on sentences,* and *stringy sentences.*

stage of the writing process and don't want to break the momentum of the lesson with a review of grammar, you can try teaching students to read sentences in a way that will help them recognize sentence fragments. For example, try reading the fragment "Because I wasn't in school yesterday" aloud as though it were an introductory clause. Exaggerate your reading by maintaining a high pitch at the end of the expression so that listeners naturally ask, "What happened?" You can indicate other fragments in the same way.

Exercise 1 introduces the three-part test, which will help students recognize sentence fragments. **Exercise 2** gives students the opportunity to revise fragments after they recognize them.

LEP/ESL

General Strategies. If students are having trouble recognizing the differences between complete sentences and sentence fragments, give them more examples orally. Some students are better at hearing the differences than recognizing them in print. For example, you could give pairs like "the girl with the red shoes" and "I saw the girl with the red shoes." After students practice orally, give them written pairs and have them decide which are fragments and which are sentences.

INTEGRATING THE LANGUAGE ARTS

Mechanics Link. Point out to students that commas are never used before the word *because* in sentences like the example in the **Writing Note.** However, if the sentence were changed to "Because he wants to try out for the basketball team, Mark is practicing his hook shot," the comma after *team* is necessary.

Sentence Fragments

What kind of sentence could you write about this picture?

You might write something like this:

> The fearless climber crawls inch by inch up the steep cliff.
>
> *or*
>
> Look at the size of that rock!
>
> *or*
>
> How does she know where the handholds are?

These groups of words say different things, but they have something in common. Each is a complete sentence. A ***complete sentence*** is a group of words that expresses a complete thought.

A part of each thought is expressed by the verb: *crawls, look, does know.* Another part is expressed by the subject: *climber, you, she.* [The *you* is understood in the second sentence even though it isn't expressed: (You) Look at the size of that rock!]

A ***sentence fragment*** is a part of a sentence that is punctuated as if it were a complete sentence. A fragment is confusing because it doesn't express a complete thought. The following word groups are the example sentences you just read—with some important words left out. Notice how unclear the word groups are when written as fragments.

You can use the first two or three items in **Exercises 1** and **2** for guided practice by writing them on the chalkboard and working through them with the class.

Exercises 1 and **2** can be assigned as homework or as a classroom activity. If students need more independent practice, use fragments from their writing or create fragments from sentences from exercises in other chapters.

Crawls inch by inch up the steep cliff. [The subject is missing. *Who* or *what* crawls?]
At the size of that rock. [The verb and the understood subject are missing. *What about* the size of the rock?]
Where the handholds are. [This word group has a subject and a verb, but it doesn't express a complete thought. *What about* the location of the handholds?]

Sometimes a fragment is really a part of the sentence that comes before or after it. You can correct the fragment by attaching it to the sentence it belongs with.

FRAGMENT Mark is practicing his hook shot. **Because he wants to try out for the basketball team.**
CORRECT Mark is practicing his hook shot because he wants to try out for the basketball team.

When you attach a fragment to a sentence, be sure to check your new sentence for correct punctuation.

EXERCISE 1 **Recognizing Fragments**

Use this simple three-part test to help you figure out which of the following word groups are sentence fragments and which are complete sentences.

1. Does the group of words have a subject?
2. Does it have a verb?
3. Does it express a complete thought?

If the group of words is a complete sentence, write *S*. If it is a fragment, write *F*.

1. We visited the pet shop in the mall. **1.** S
2. A bright-eyed hamster chewing on pieces of carrot. **2.** F
3. Named him Mustard. **3.** F

A DIFFERENT APPROACH

When students do **Exercise 1**, you may want to have them list the subjects and verbs in the sentences if you've spent time reviewing these concepts. This should reinforce understanding of the three-part test and the ability to recognize fragments. [**(1)** We, visited; **(2)** not a complete thought; **(3)** not a complete thought; **(4)** not a complete thought; **(5)** pouches, are; **(6)** not a complete thought; **(7)** not a complete thought; **(8)** He is, has; **(9)** not a complete thought; **(10)** you, decide.]

COOPERATIVE LEARNING

You may want to let students work in pairs on **Exercise 2.** Have each pair produce two revised versions of each fragment, with each student responsible for one of the versions. This should help students see that there are many ways to revise fragments.

ASSESSMENT

You can assess how well students can identify and revise sentence fragments by evaluating how well they complete **Exercises 1** and **2** and **Review A.**

CLOSURE

Ask the class to recite the three things they should look for when checking to see if a sentence is complete [subject, verb, and complete thought]. ■

4. Has pouches inside each fat cheek. 4. F
5. The pouches are for carrying food. 5. S
6. Newspaper in lots of little shreds. 6. F
7. Making his cage quite comfortable. 7. F
8. He is plump and has white and tan fur. 8. S
9. A diet of mostly fruit, vegetables, and grain.
10. If you decide to raise hamsters. 9. F 10. F

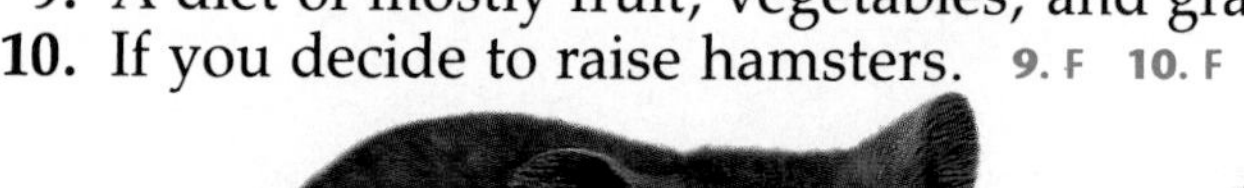

EXERCISE 2 **Revising Fragments**

Some of the following groups of words are sentence fragments. First, identify the fragments. Then, revise each fragment by (1) adding a subject, (2) adding a verb, or (3) attaching the fragment to a complete sentence. You may need to change the punctuation and capitalization, too. If the word group is already a complete sentence, write *S*.

1. Was watching TV Wednesday night.
2. A movie about aliens invading from space.
3. Suddenly, the lights went out on the whole block.
4. Because the batteries in the flashlight were dead.
5. A strange noise in the backyard.
6. After our dog started to bark.
7. Crept slowly to the door and looked out.
8. Two small, glowing eyes in the dark.
9. When I saw it was just the cat from next door.
10. Maybe I should stop watching so many scary movies.

ANSWERS

Exercise 2

Answers may vary. Here are some possibilities:

1. I was watching TV Wednesday night.
2. I was watching a movie about aliens invading from space.
3. S
4. I had to light a candle because the batteries in the flashlight were dead.
5. I heard a strange noise in the backyard.
6. After our dog started to bark, I began to wonder what was outside.
7. I crept slowly to the door and looked out.
8. I saw two small, glowing eyes in the dark.
9. I laughed when I saw it was just the cat from next door.
10. S

SEGMENT 2 *(pp. 307–311)*

RUN-ON AND STRINGY SENTENCES

OBJECTIVES

- To identify and revise run-on sentences
- To identify and revise stringy sentences

TEACHING THE LESSON

If you cover run-on and stringy sentences together, be sure to emphasize that while run-ons and stringy sentences are related, they are two different kinds of sentence faults. Start the lesson by reading aloud several run-on sentences in a way that emphasizes the confusion they cause. Stringy sentences can be demonstrated in ☛

Run-on Sentences

A *run-on sentence* is actually two or more sentences run together into one sentence. It's often hard to tell where one idea in a run-on ends and the next one begins.

Like sentence fragments, run-on sentences usually appear in your writing because you are in a hurry to get your thoughts down on paper. You may leave out the correct end punctuation (period, question mark, or exclamation point) or use just a comma to separate the sentences.

There are two good ways to revise run-on sentences. You can break the run-on into two complete sentences, or you can link the two ideas with a comma and a coordinating conjunction (*and, but, or*).

RUN-ON
Sally Ride's mission began on June 18, 1983 she had to train for many months before then.

CORRECT
Sally Ride's mission began on June 18, 1983**.** **S**he had to train for many months before then.

or

Sally Ride's mission began on June 18, 1983**, but** she had to train for many months before then.

Teacher's ResourceBank™

RESOURCES

RUN-ON AND STRINGY SENTENCES

QUOTATION FOR THE DAY

"You've got to know when to turn around." (John Roskelley, mountain climber)

Write the quotation on the chalkboard and ask students to freewrite for a few minutes about how the quotation might relate to sentence construction. Remind students that for a writer, the time to turn around occurs when he or she writes past a complete thought and creates a run-on or stringy sentence.

much the same way if you read them at a faster-than-normal pace with breaks for an exaggerated breath where necessary. Emphasize that stringy sentences contain too much information.

Use items 1 and 3 in **Exercise 3** and items 1 and 2 from **Exercise 4** to provide guided practice. Call on students to read the sentences as you demonstrated and then ask the class to explain what's wrong with each sentence and how it should be fixed. You can do the same with faulty sentences taken from students' writing.

Exercises 3 and **4** should provide sufficient independent practice at identifying and revising run-ons and stringy sentences. If your students need more reinforcement of these concepts, you can

MEETING INDIVIDUAL NEEDS

LEP/ESL

General Strategies. Previewing vocabulary for students should make the grammar exercises less difficult. Give students lists of the more difficult words and phrases for each segment and have the students find the words in the text. Then tell students to copy the sentences containing these words into notebooks and to underline the difficult words or phrases. Finally, ask students to use a dictionary to determine the correct definitions for the words in context and have them write these definitions in their notebooks as well. If the students are writing journals, they could keep the words, sentences, and definitions there.

TIMESAVER

You can save time grading papers if you have students underline all of the changes they make as they complete **Exercise 3.** The underlining will catch your eye and help you find the relevant words.

MECHANICS HINT

Using Commas Correctly

A comma alone is not enough to link two complete ideas in a sentence. If you use just a comma between two complete ideas, you create a run-on sentence.

RUN-ON Sally Ride was the first American woman in space, she was a member of a shuttle crew.

CORRECT Sally Ride was the first American woman in space. She was a member of a shuttle crew.

REFERENCE NOTE: For more about using a comma between two complete ideas, see page 597.

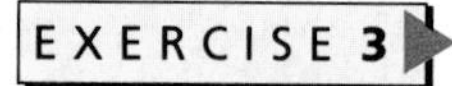

EXERCISE 3 **Identifying and Revising Run-on Sentences**

Decide which of the following groups of words are run-ons. Then revise each run-on by (1) making it into two separate sentences or (2) using a comma and a coordinating conjunction. You may have to change the punctuation and capitalization, too. If the group of words is already correct, write *C*. Revisions may vary.

1. Someday you may not live on Earth you may live in a space colony.
2. Space colonies will be important. They will be sources of raw materials and energy. 2. C
3. Space colonies will be enclosed otherwise people couldn't live in the alien climate.
4. If materials for the colony come from the moon and asteroids, construction will be difficult. 4. C
5. Electricity could come from solar cells, the cells would collect energy from the sun's rays. 5.

create additional exercises by rewriting sentences from exercises in other chapters.

ASSESSMENT

Base your assessment of students' understanding of run-on and stringy sentences by how well they do on **Exercises 3** and **4. Review A** offers an additional opportunity for assessment.

6. The space station's orbiting platform could be covered with millions of solar cells. 6. C
7. The energy collected could be beamed to Earth^ then it could be used here for electricity. 7. , and
8. Some people will build platforms,^some will grow food. 8. and
9. Computer chips could even be manufactured in a space station. 9. C
10. A space colony is still many years away^it is fun to imagine the future. 10. , but

Stringy Sentences

For variety, you'll sometimes want to join sentences and sentence parts with *and*. But if you string many ideas together with *and*, you create a ***stringy sentence***. Stringy sentences ramble on and on. They don't give the reader a chance to pause between ideas.

STRINGY The ostrich is the largest living bird and it stands nearly eight feet tall and it weighs over three hundred pounds when it is fully grown and this speedy bird can run up to forty miles an hour!

BETTER The ostrich is the largest living bird. It stands nearly eight feet tall, and it weighs over three hundred pounds when it is fully grown. This speedy bird can run up to forty miles an hour!

In the revised version, only two ideas are linked by *and*. These ideas can be joined in one sentence because they are closely related. However, notice that a comma was added before the *and*. The comma is necessary to show a slight pause between the two complete ideas.

EXERCISE 4 **Identifying and Revising Stringy Sentences** Revisions may vary.

Some of the following sentences are stringy. Revise each stringy sentence by breaking it into two or more sentences. If a sentence is already correct, write *C*.

INTEGRATING THE LANGUAGE ARTS

Mechanics Link. Students sometimes overuse one method of revising run-ons. For example, if they consistently correct run-ons by dividing them into separate sentences, the result may be a series of short, choppy, monotonous sentences.

Remind students that good writing uses a variety of sentence structures. Encourage students to try to find the method of revision that works best for the particular run-on. Some run-ons will be better as separate sentences (when the ideas involved aren't too closely connected), and others will be better as one sentence joined by a comma and coordinating conjunction (when the ideas involved are closely connected).

COOPERATIVE LEARNING

Your students can work in pairs on **Exercise 4.** If they do, ask that each pair produce two different ways in which each stringy sentence can be revised.

CLOSURE

Ask students to recite the two ways of revising run-on sentences [by making two complete sentences or by adding a comma and a coordinating conjunction] and how to revise stringy sentences [by breaking them into separate sentences]. ■

REVIEW A

OBJECTIVE

- To revise fragments, run-ons, and stringy sentences

1. Thomas and José were playing softball at school and Thomas hit the ball very hard and then he saw it roll under the steps of the library.
2. Thomas peered under the dark steps to recover his ball and when he reached for it he saw a giant raccoon and Thomas wasn't sure what to do next!
3. José told Thomas that raccoons are fierce fighters and then José warned him not to anger the raccoon and by this time, other softball players had gathered to offer advice.
4. Thomas finally rolled the ball out from under the steps with a baseball bat. The raccoon stayed completely still, and it hissed and looked fiercely at the group. Then Thomas saw why the raccoon was behaving so strangely. 4. C
5. Five baby raccoons were hiding behind the mother and they were too small to protect themselves and that's why the mother raccoon was trying to frighten the softball players away!

REVIEW A **Revising Fragments, Run-on Sentences, and Stringy Sentences**

Decide which of the following word groups are fragments, run-ons, or stringy sentences. Then revise each of these word groups to make it clear and complete. Remember to add correct capitalization and punctuation. If a word group is already clear and complete, just write *C*.

1. An ordinary person goes into a dressing room a clown comes out.
2. Creates a special face.
3. Clown makeup starts with white greasepaint, and the greasepaint looks like a mask, and a special cream must be used to remove it.
4. After painting bright colors above the eyes, the clown adds eyebrows high on the forehead.

ANSWERS

Review A

Answers may vary. Here are some possibilities:

1. run-on; An ordinary person goes into a dressing room, but a clown comes out.
2. fragment; Each clown creates a special face.
3. stringy; Clown makeup starts with white greasepaint. The greasepaint looks like a mask, and a special cream must be used to remove it.
4. C

SEGMENT 3 *(pp. 311–319)*

COMBINING SENTENCES

OBJECTIVE

- To combine sentences by inserting words or word groups and by joining subjects, verbs, and sentences

TEACHING THE LESSON

This segment of the chapter is longer than the others, so you may want to spread it out over two or more days. The concepts are relatively easy, however, and most students should have little difficulty with them.

This textbook uses the grammatical terms *subject* and *verb.* You may want to 

5. A lot of red is used around the mouth, and the mouth is very important, and it determines the personality of the clown.
6. Some clowns wear a large red nose, it is fitted over the person's own nose.
7. A tight-fitting cap can make a clown look bald on each side the cap sometimes has funny, wild-looking hair.
8. Since a funny costume adds to the effect.
9. Baggy pants and a big shirt with a ruffled collar come next.
10. Floppy shoes the outfit.

Combining Sentences

Good writers usually use some short sentences, but they don't use them all the time. An entire paragraph of short sentences makes writing sound choppy. For example, notice how dull and choppy the following paragraph sounds.

Quicksand is really just sand. The sand is wet. The sand is loose. You can sink in quicksand. It won't actually suck you down. You might get caught in quicksand. You can lie on your back. You can float. Then you can roll or wriggle. Your movements must be slow. You can get to solid ground this way.

5. stringy; A lot of red is used around the mouth. The mouth is very important. It determines the personality of the clown.
6. run-on; Some clowns wear a large red nose. It is fitted over the person's own nose.
7. run-on; A tight-fitting cap can make a clown look bald. On each side the cap sometimes has funny, wild-looking hair.
8. fragment; A clown's clothes are important since a funny costume adds to the effect.
9. C
10. fragment; Floppy shoes complete the outfit.

Teacher's ResourceBank™

RESOURCES

COMBINING SENTENCES

- Inserting Words and Word Groups 78
- Combining with *And, But,* and *Or* 79

spend a little time reviewing these concepts, but students can probably handle the exercises by noting the pattern given in the examples.

This segment discusses four methods of combining sentences: (1) inserting words, (2) inserting word groups, (3) joining subjects and verbs, and (4) joining sentences by using *and, but,* or *or.* An exercise follows discussion of each method and provides students with practice for that method.

QUOTATION FOR THE DAY

"Writing is exploration. You write to find out what you're writing." (E. L. Doctorow, 1931– , American writer and editor)

After you write the quotation on the chalkboard, ask students to respond to Doctorow's ideas. In what ways do writers find out what they're writing about when they combine sentences?

Now, see how the writer has revised the paragraph by combining some of the short sentences. Notice how sentence combining has helped to eliminate some repeated words and ideas. The result is a smoother paragraph with much more variety.

> Quicksand is really just wet, loose sand. You can sink in quicksand, but it won't actually suck you down. If you're caught in quicksand, you can lie on your back and float. Then you can slowly roll or wriggle to solid ground.

You can combine sentences in several different ways. Sometimes you can insert a word or a group of words from one sentence into another sentence. Other times you can combine two related sentences by using a connecting word.

Inserting Words

One way to combine two sentences is to pull a key word from one sentence and insert it into the other sentence. Sometimes you can just add the key word to the first sentence and drop the rest of the second sentence. Other times you'll need to change the form of the key word before you can insert it.

USING THE SAME FORM	
ORIGINAL	Martin Luther King, Jr., was a civil rights leader. He was an American.
COMBINED	Martin Luther King, Jr., was an **American** civil rights leader.
CHANGING THE FORM	
ORIGINAL	He was famous for his brilliant speeches. His fame was international.
COMBINED	He was **internationally** famous for his brilliant speeches.

GUIDED PRACTICE

If you are using this segment as part of instruction in revision, you may want to draw some examples from students' papers to use for guided practice. The examples from the text and at the beginning of each exercise can be used for additional guided practice. If you find it necessary to provide more guided practice than the examples afford, you can work with the first item in each exercise in the same way you used the examples.

When you change the forms of the key words, you often add endings such as *–ed, –ing, –ful,* and *–ly* to make adjectives and adverbs.

EXAMPLES			
	skill	→	skilled
	crash	→	crashing
	use	→	useful
	quiet	→	quietly

EXERCISE 5 **Combining Sentences by Inserting Words**

Each of the following items contains two sentences. Combine the two sentences by taking the italicized key word from the second sentence and inserting it into the first sentence. The directions in parentheses will tell you how to change the form of the key word if you need to do so.

EXAMPLE

1. Chief Joseph was a Nez Percé Indian chief who fought for his people. He was a *brave* fighter. (Add *–ly*.)

1. *Chief Joseph was a Nez Percé Indian chief who fought bravely for his people.*

LEP/ESL

Spanish. Adding key words that are adjectives may be confusing to some Spanish speakers. In Spanish, descriptive adjectives usually come after the nouns they modify, and those that can come either before or after the noun often have different meanings in each position. You can help resolve the confusion by using **Exercise 5** as an oral activity with the class and by focusing on the placement of adjectives in relation to the nouns they modify.

VISUAL CONNECTIONS

Exploring the Subject. Chief Joseph was the head of a band of Nez Percé in eastern Oregon. When gold was discovered on their ancestral lands, the U.S. government tried to forcibly reduce by three-quarters the territory assured the Nez Percé by treaty. Chief Joseph and his people resisted, and the government waged war against them. After the war, Chief Joseph, who had been educated by white missionaries, became a spokesperson for Native Americans.

INDEPENDENT PRACTICE

Exercises 5, 6, 7, and **8** can be used for independent practice, as can **Review B.** They can be assigned as homework or completed independently in the classroom.

If your students need more independent practice, create sentences for them from exercises in other chapters. These can be broken down into their component kernel sentences and then recombined by your students. Or students could break different sentences down into single concepts, trade these with each other, and recombine them.

INTEGRATING THE LANGUAGE ARTS

Punctuation Link. The question of when to set off words and groups of words with commas can be a difficult one for students. Point out that commas are used around word groups that can be left out of the sentence without changing the meaning. For example, in the sentence "The boy who ate the pie was late," commas are not used because *who ate the pie* tells which of several boys was late. However, in the sentence "George, who ate the pie, was late," the phrase *who ate the pie* is set off with commas because the boy has already been identified by name.

1. The name *Joseph* was given to him by ^ missionaries. ~~The missionaries were *white*.~~ **1. white**
2. His ^ name means "thunder traveling over the mountains." ~~That is his *Nez Percé* name.~~ **2.** ***Nez Percé***
3. Chief Joseph ^ fought the United States Army to defend his people's homeland. ~~The fighting was *fierce*.~~ (Add *–ly.*) **3. fiercely**
4. When he realized he could not win, he led the ^ Nez Percé band more than one thousand miles. ~~The band was in *retreat*.~~ (Add *–ing.*) **4. retreating**
5. Chief Joseph's ^ surrender speech is famous. ~~It is *moving*.~~ **5. moving**

Inserting Groups of Words

Often, you can combine two related sentences by taking an entire group of words from one sentence and adding it to the other sentence. When the group of words is inserted, it adds detail to the information in the first sentence.

ORIGINAL The sailboats raced. They raced in the bay.
COMBINED The sailboats raced **in the bay.**

ORIGINAL The sailboats were beautiful. The sailboats were docked in the marina.
COMBINED The sailboats **docked in the marina** were beautiful.

ORIGINAL The boats are all built alike. These are boats in one-design sailboat races.
COMBINED The boats **in one-design sailboat races** are all built alike.

Sometimes you'll need to put commas around the group of words you are inserting. Ask yourself whether the group of words renames or explains a noun or pronoun in the sentence. If it does, use a comma or commas to set off the word group from the rest of the sentence.

ASSESSMENT

The way students perform on **Exercises 5, 6, 7,** and **8** will indicate how well they're able to combine sentences. The work in **Review B** can also be used for assessment, especially since that exercise doesn't contain any of the clues that some of the other exercises have.

The best assessment of students' sentence-combining skills comes when they use the skills to revise their own writing.

ORIGINAL We'll watch the race from the marina. The marina is the best spot to see the race.

COMBINED We'll watch the race from the marina**, the best spot to see the race.**

ORIGINAL The catboat has only one sail. It is a popular racing boat.

COMBINED The catboat**, a popular racing boat,** has only one sail.

REFERENCE NOTE: For more about using commas in sentences, see pages 594–603.

After you combine two sentences, be sure to read your new sentence carefully. Then ask yourself the following questions:

- Is my new sentence clear?
- Does it make sense?
- Does it sound better than the two shorter sentences?

EXERCISE 6 Combining Sentences by Inserting Word Groups

Combine each of the following pairs of sentences by taking the italicized word group from the second sentence and inserting it into the first sentence. Be sure to add commas if they are needed.

EXAMPLE **1.** Martha read *The Island of the Blue Dolphins* for her book report. Martha is *a girl in my English class.*

1. *Martha, a girl in my English class, read* The Island of the Blue Dolphins *for her book report.*

1. *The Island of the Blue Dolphins* is an exciting adventure story. It is *by Scott O'Dell.* **1.** by Scott O'Dell.
2. It is about Karana, a girl who lived alone. She lived alone *on an island.* **2.** on an island.
3. Karana built a shelter and found food. Karana was *a self-sufficient girl.* **3.** , a self-sufficient girl,

RETEACHING

If students still have difficulty with sentence combining after reading the material in the textbook, supply them with sentences and let them break the sentences into basic concepts. For example, "The big, yellow butterfly floated gracefully on the gentle breeze," would be reduced to the following basic concepts: The butterfly was big. The butterfly was yellow. The butterfly floated. The floating was graceful. The floating was on the breeze. The breeze was gentle.

You can get sentences for this activity from a piece of literature or you could let students make them up. Working at sentence combining backwards might help students grasp the concept behind the process.

LEARNING STYLES

Kinetic Learners. To help kinetic learners with sentence combining, choose several sentences from the exercises or from some other source and transfer the words to note cards, one word per card. Then let students combine the sentences by rearranging the cards and discarding those words no longer needed. Don't forget to supply cards with *and, but,* and *or.*

LEP/ESL

General Strategies. Students may need help understanding the relationship that must exist between sentences, subjects, and verbs joined by *and, but,* and *or.* Explain that in general, *and* is used when the two things to be combined are similar, *but* is used when they are different, and *or* is used when there is a choice between the two.

To give students practice in picking out which conjunction to use, give students a few compound sentences with the coordinating conjunctions left out and let them supply the conjunctions.

4. She waited [4. many years] for a ship to rescue her. ~~She waited *many years.*~~
5. Your library probably has a copy of *Island of the Blue Dolphins* [5. , an award-winning novel.] ~~It is *an award-winning novel.*~~

Using Connecting Words

Another way you can combine sentences is by using connecting words called *conjunctions.* Conjunctions allow you to join closely related sentences and sentence parts.

Joining Subjects and Verbs

Sometimes two sentences are so closely related that they have the same subjects or verbs. If two sentences have the same subject, you can combine them by making a ***compound subject.*** If the sentences have the same verb, you can combine them by making a ***compound verb.***

The conjunction you use is important. It tells your reader how the two subjects or verbs are related to one another.

Use *and* to join similar ideas.

ORIGINAL Drawing is fun. Painting is fun.
COMBINED **Drawing and painting** are fun. [compound subject]

CLOSURE

Ask students to recite the four ways of combining sentences [inserting words; inserting word groups; joining subjects and verbs with *and, but,* or *or*; and joining complete sentences with *and, but,* or *or*]. ■

Use *but* to join contrasting ideas.

ORIGINAL Mike will cook the main course. Mike will buy the dessert.

COMBINED Mike will **cook** the main course **but buy** the dessert. [compound verb]

Use *or* to show a choice between ideas.

ORIGINAL Sara Tallchief may be elected president of the Student Council. Frances O'Connor may be elected president of the Student Council.

COMBINED **Sara Tallchief or Frances O'Connor** may be elected president of the Student Council. [compound subject]

EXERCISE 7 Combining Sentences by Joining Subjects and Verbs

Use *and, but,* or *or* to combine each of the following pairs of sentences. If the sentences have the same verb, make one sentence by joining the two subjects. If the sentences have the same subject, make one sentence by joining the two verbs. The hints in parentheses will help you.

EXAMPLE **1.** Beans are grown on that farm. Tomatoes are grown on that farm. (Join with *and.*)
1. *Beans and tomatoes are grown on that farm.*

1. Florida produces many citrus products. Florida exports many citrus products. (Join with *and.*)
2. Oranges are grown in Florida. Grapefruits are grown in Florida. (Join with *and.*)
3. Grapefruit looks sweet. It tastes sour. (Join with *but.*)
4. The orange will be chosen the Citrus Fruit of the Year. The grapefruit will be chosen the Citrus Fruit of the Year. (Join with *or.*)
5. The orange could win the contest. The grapefruit could win the contest. (Join with *or.*)

ANSWERS

Exercise 7

1. Florida produces and exports many citrus products.
2. Oranges and grapefruits are grown in Florida.
3. Grapefruit looks sweet but tastes sour.
4. The orange or the grapefruit will be chosen the Citrus Fruit of the Year.
5. The orange or the grapefruit could win the contest.

Joining Sentences

Sometimes you may want to combine two related sentences that express equally important ideas. You can connect the two sentences by using a comma and *and, but,* or *or.* The result is a ***compound sentence.***

ORIGINAL Dad's favorite dog is a cocker spaniel. Mom's favorite dog is a collie.

COMBINED Dad's favorite dog is a cocker spaniel**, but** Mom's favorite dog is a collie.

Other times you may want to combine two sentences that are related in a special way. One sentence helps explain the other sentence by telling *how, where, why,* or *when.* A good way to combine these sentences is to add a connecting word that shows the special relationship. In this kind of sentence combining, you create a ***complex sentence.***

ORIGINAL The drawbridge was pulled up. The enemy knights could not get into the castle.

COMBINED **When** the drawbridge was pulled up, the enemy knights could not get into the castle.

Some connecting words that you can use are *after, although, as, because, before, if, since, so that, until, when, whether,* and *while.* The word that you choose will depend on what you want your sentence to say.

EXERCISE 8 Combining Complete Sentences

Following are five sets of short, choppy sentences that need improving. Make each pair into one sentence by using the connecting word given in parentheses. Be sure to change the capitalization and the punctuation where necessary.

EXAMPLE **1.** Planets move. Stars stay in their places. (but)
1. *Planets move, but stars stay in their places.*

1. I would like to learn more about stars. They are interesting and beautiful. (because)

ANSWERS

Exercise 8

1. I would like to learn more about stars because they are interesting and beautiful.

REVIEW B

OBJECTIVE

- To revise a paragraph by combining sentences

2. Planets do not give off light of their own. Stars do. (but)
3. Some stars are fainter than our sun. Some are many times brighter. (and)
4. Our sun will change. The change will be slow. (but)
5. We must continue to study the stars and planets. We will understand how we fit into our vast universe. (so that)

REVIEW B **Revising a Paragraph by Combining Sentences**

The following paragraph sounds choppy because it has too many short sentences. Use the methods you've learned in this section to combine some of the sentences. You'll notice how much better the paragraph sounds after you've revised it.

Many lizards defend themselves by playing tricks on their attackers. For example, the horned lizard frightens off its enemies by squirting a thin stream of blood. The lizard squirts the blood from its eyes. Another kind of lizard fools attackers with its long, brittle tail. This kind of lizard is the glass snake. Sometimes an enemy grabs the glass snake's tail. The lizard just breaks off the tail. The lizard crawls away. The tail keeps wriggling. The attacker doesn't see the lizard escape. The attacker keeps struggling with the tail.

2. Planets do not give off light of their own, but stars do.
3. Some stars are fainter than our sun, and some are many times brighter.
4. Our sun will change, but the change will be slow.
5. We must continue to study the stars and planets so that we will understand how we fit into our vast universe.

ANSWERS

Review B

Paragraphs will vary. Here is a possibility:

Many lizards defend themselves by playing tricks on their attackers. For example, the horned lizard frightens off its enemies by squirting a thin stream of blood from its eyes. Another kind of lizard, the glass snake, fools attackers with its long, brittle tail. Sometimes an enemy grabs the glass snake's tail, but the lizard just breaks off the tail and crawls away. The tail keeps wriggling, and the attacker doesn't see the lizard escape. The attacker keeps struggling with the tail.

SEGMENT 4 (p. 320)

MAKING CONNECTIONS

RECONSTRUCT A MESSAGE OBJECTIVE

- To apply skills learned in the chapter to reconstruct a message

RECONSTRUCT A MESSAGE

Teaching Strategies

This activity requires students to use the pieces of sentences to reconstruct complete sentences. Let students work in pairs on the assignment; one student can read a sentence while the other suggests possible additions to complete the meaning. They can alternate sentences, and each one can initial his or her individual contributions.

In evaluating the work, make sure there are no sentence fragments, run-on sentences, stringy sentences, or short, choppy sentences that could be combined. Also, the ideas inserted in the message have to make sense in the context.

ANSWERS

Making Connections

Sentences will vary. Here is one example of how students can reconstruct the message:

I am stranded on a small island near you. I haven't seen another human being in two years! I've sent many messages but never got an answer. I'm building a small boat, and I will try to find you. Light a bonfire so I can see where you are.

Reconstruct a Message

You have been shipwrecked on a tiny, uncharted island. You've built a sturdy shelter and have plenty of fish, coconuts, and sea vegetables to eat. But after being stranded for a month, you're eager to be rescued. You scratch a message on a piece of tree bark telling where your ship was lost. Then you stuff the bark into a bottle and send it out to sea.

A week later, you see the bottle bobbing in the water close to shore. The current has carried back a message! Excited, you bring the bottle to shore, pull out the cork, and find this message written in berry juice:

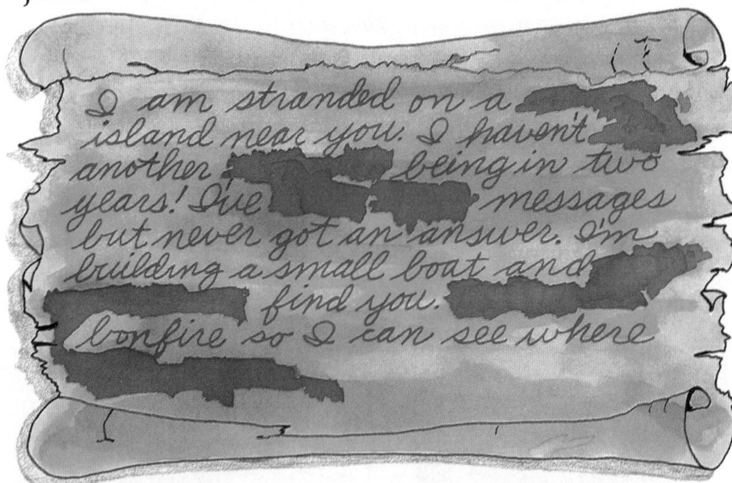

Oh, no! A few drops of water leaked into the bottle and washed away some of the writing! Try to piece together the original, complete sentences from the blurred fragments. What is the message? What does the person want you to do?

Chapter 11

ENGLISH: ORIGINS AND USES

OBJECTIVES

- To match words with their original spellings and meanings
- To research word origins
- To analyze characteristics of a dialect
- To use formal and informal English appropriately
- To recognize connotations
- To write an informal, descriptive postcard
- To write a formal report about an imaginary creature

Motivation

To show how people adapt language to fit an audience, tell students about an imaginary event at school such as a fight or an argument of some kind. Relate the incident in very informal English and ask students to identify the speaker and the audience. Then relate the incident in standard English and again ask students to identify the speaker and the audience. Finally, relate the story in very formal English and ask students to identify the speaker and the audience.

You might introduce the concept of connotation by showing students a picture of an object. First, tell them to imagine that this is a picture of an object that they like. Ask students how they might describe the object. Then ask them to imagine that this is a picture of an object that they do not like. Ask students how they might describe the object differently. Point out the connotative meanings of the words in both the positive and negative descriptions.

Introduction

Discuss with students the power that comes from the ability to use language well. Lead students to see that language influences how listeners respond to a speaker. Tell students that this chapter will help them to understand better how flexible and useful language can be.

Then ask students how they think language happens. Where did it come from? Does it change? How does a speaker know which word to choose when two words mean almost the same thing? Encourage students to notice language development by asking them to think of modern words that were not a part of English vocabulary in 1900 or that did not mean the same things they mean now. They may suggest such words as *atomic bomb, computer, beeper, calculator, fax,* and *instant replay.*

Integration

Skills learned in this chapter should be useful when students are studying literature. For example, when students are learning about point of view, you could ask them to rewrite a story by using another point of view that demands a shift from standard English to nonstandard English, the addition of slang or colloquialisms, or the use of a particular dialect. Similarly, when students are studying characters in a story, you could have the students analyze the characters' language as one way of learning more about the characters. The class might also notice that sometimes language alone reveals how one character responds to another.

The chart on the next page illustrates the strands of language arts as they are integrated into this chapter. For vocabulary study, glossary words are underlined in some writing models.

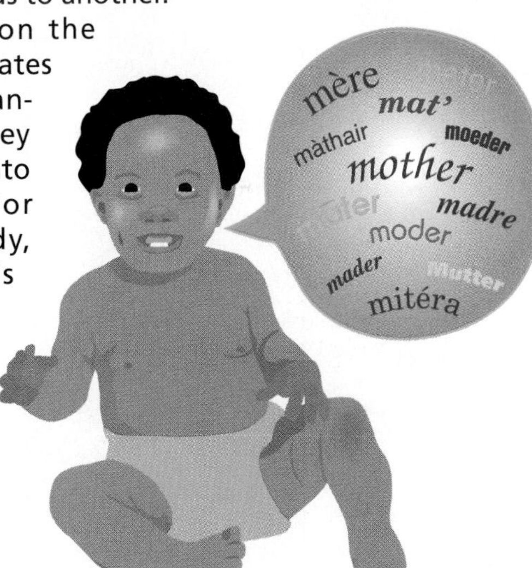

QUOTATIONS

All **Quotations for the Day** are chosen because of their relevance to instructional material presented in that segment of the chapter and for their usefulness in establishing student interest in writing.

Integrating the Language Arts

Selection	Reading and Literature	Writing and Critical Thinking	Language and Syntax	Speaking, Listening, and Other Expression Skills
from *Oral History* by Lee Smith **328** from **"The Sky Is Gray"** by Ernest J. Gaines **329**	Reading dialect **328, 329**	Drawing conclusions and making inferences **326, 329** Describing a scene in dialect **329** Writing an informal letter **332** Writing a postcard **334-335** Writing a formal report **334-335**	Matching words with their original spellings and meanings **326** Using a dictionary to research word origins **326** Understanding the nature of dialect **329** Recognizing standard and nonstandard English **329** Identifying the differences between formal and informal English **329, 332** Recognizing word connotations **333** Assessing the impact of connotative words **333**	Reading dialect aloud **329** Comparing word connotations with classmates **333** Drawing an illustration for a postcard **334**

CHAPTER 11

SEGMENT PLANNING GUIDE

Whether you are planning for a quick review of a writing concept or preparing an extended lesson on composition, you can use the following Planning Guide to adapt the chapter material to the individual needs of your class.

SEGMENT	PAGES	CONTENT	RESOURCES
1 *The Growth of English*	*321-326*		How Words Change 87 Where Words Come From 88
Looking Ahead	321	Introduction: learning the origins and uses of English	
The Growth of English	322	Guidelines: learning the history of English	
Changes in Pronunciation and Spelling	323	Guidelines: examining changes in pronunciation and spelling	
Changes in Meaning	324	Guidelines: examining how word meanings have changed through history	
How New Words Enter English	325	Introduction: examining borrowed words and words from names	
Borrowed Words	325	Explanation: examining words borrowed from other languages	
Words from Names	325	Explanation: examining the origin for the word *frisbee*	
Exercise 1	326	Applied practice: matching words with their original spellings and meanings	
Exercise 2	326	Applied practice: researching word origins	
2 *Choosing Your Words*	*327-333*		Formal and Informal English 89 Denotation and Connotation 90
Dialects of American English	327	Introduction: describing regional and ethnic dialects	
Regional Dialects	327-328	Explanation: examining characteristics of regional dialects	
Style Note	328	Writing suggestion: using dialect to capture the personality of a character	
Literary Model from ***Oral History***	328	Guided reading: examining dialect in a model	
Ethnic Dialects	328	Explanation: examining ethnic dialects	
Exercise 3	329	Applied practice: reading a dialect	
Literary Model from **"The Sky Is Gray"**	329	Guided reading: examining dialect in a model	
Standard American English	329-330	Explanation: comparing standard and nonstandard English	

All the resources listed in this chapter are located in the *Teacher's ResourceBank™*.

SEGMENT	PAGES	CONTENT	RESOURCES
Formal and Informal	330	Guidelines: using English appropriately	
Colloquialisms	330-331	Guidelines: defining and examining colloquialisms	
Slang	331	Explanation: defining and examining slang	
Style Note	331	Writing suggestion: using slang appropriately	
Exercise 4	332	Applied practice: using formal and informal English	
Denotation and Connotation	332-333	Guidelines: examining emotional effects of words	
Style Note	333	Writing suggestion: choosing synonyms	
Exercise 5	333	Applied practice: recognizing connotations	
3 *Making Connections*	*334-335*		
Name a Newly Discovered Animal	334-335	Guidelines: writing a postcard and a report Applied practice: writing an informal postcard and a formal report	
WHOLE-CHAPTER RESOURCES Review Form A, Review Form B			

SEGMENT 1 *(pp. 321–326)*

THE GROWTH OF ENGLISH

OBJECTIVES

- To match words with their original spellings and meanings
- To research word origins

MOTIVATION

Ask students to name words they sometimes use that adults don't understand. The discussion will probably include slang words that students use. Point out changes in their language by asking them what recently popular expressions are now considered to be outdated.

11 ENGLISH: ORIGINS AND USES

LOOKING AHEAD

You know more words and word combinations than you could ever list. With its huge vocabulary (over 600,000 words!), English offers you many different ways to express your thoughts, observations, and feelings. How did English become such a rich, expressive language? How can you choose the best words for saying what you mean? This chapter will give you some answers to these and other questions about your language. You will learn

- where English comes from
- how English has grown and changed
- what the varieties of English are
- how to choose appropriate words for different situations

Teacher's ResourceBank™

RESOURCES

THE GROWTH OF ENGLISH

QUOTATION FOR THE DAY

"How amazing that the language of a few thousand savages living on a fog-encrusted island in the North Sea should become the language of the world." (Norman St. John-Stevas, Member of British Parliament)

To help students understand that the English language is constantly growing and changing, have students work in small groups to brainstorm lists of new words that are used mainly in their age group or in their school. Explain that over the centuries, thousands of new words have entered the English language.

TEACHING THE LESSON

Have students read one section of this segment at a time and discuss with them the most important points made in each section. You could write two or three of the most important points for each section on an overhead transparency or on the chalkboard.

GUIDED PRACTICE

You may want to match the first item of **Exercise 1** as a class. For **Exercise 2,** have students look up the first two words and guide them through the process of finding what language or name the words come from.

LEP/ESL

General Strategies. To gain students' interest in word origins, have them think of words in their native languages that sound similar to words in English. Let students work in pairs to look these words up in dictionaries for similarities or differences in origins and meanings.

ADVANCED STUDENTS

Bring to class a dictionary with historical information, such as the Oxford English Dictionary. (If your school library doesn't have one of these dictionaries, you might be able to borrow one from a high school or local library.) Show students how each entry gives the history of the word. Tell students that this type of dictionary is useful when they want to know how a particular word has been used in the past as well as how it is used now.

TRANSLATION OF *BEOWULF*

Beowulf spoke (on him his breast-plate shone, a defensive network stitched together by the skill of the smith): 'To thee Hroðgar, hail!'

The Growth of English

No one knows exactly when or how English got started. We do know that English and many other languages come from an early language spoken thousands of years ago. The related languages still resemble that parent language, just as you resemble your parents. For example, notice how similar the words for "mother" are in the following modern-day languages.

ENGLISH	**mother**	ITALIAN	**madre**
FRENCH	**mère**	SWEDISH	**moder**
SPANISH	**madre**		

About fifteen hundred years ago, a few small tribes of people settled in the area that is now England. These tribes, called the Angles and Saxons, spoke the earliest known form of English. Their English was very different from ours. For example, look at the following passage from *Beowulf,* a poem which was probably written more than 1,100 years ago.

Beowulf maðelode, on him byrne
scán, searo-net seówed smiðes
orþancum: Wes þú, Hróðgár, hál.

English has changed in many ways since it was first spoken and written. But some of our most basic words have been around in one form or another since the beginnings of the language.

PRESENT-DAY FORM	**hand**	**daughter**	**answer**	**leap**
EARLY FORM	**hand**	**dohtor**	**andswaru**	**hleapan**

INDEPENDENT PRACTICE

Have students complete **Exercises 1** and **2** to identify word changes and word origins. For **Exercise 2,** each student will need a dictionary with etymologies. If the classroom dictionaries lack this information, you might allow students to work in the library.

ASSESSMENT

Use students' answers to **Exercises 1** and **2** to assess their understanding.

Changes in Pronunciation and Spelling

If you traveled back in time a few hundred years, you'd probably have a hard time understanding the English being spoken. English words used to be pronounced differently from the way they're pronounced today. For example, in the 1200s, people pronounced *bite* like *beet* and *feet* like *fate.* They also pronounced the vowel sound in the word *load* like our word *awe.*

You've probably wondered why English words aren't always spelled as they sound. Changes in pronunciation help account for many strange spellings in English. For example, the *w* that starts the word *write* wasn't always silent. The *w* sound was gradually dropped, but the spelling lagged behind. The *g* in *gnat* and the *k* in *knee* were once part of the pronunciations of the words, too.

However, the spellings of many words have changed over time. Some changes in spelling have been accidental. For example, *apron* used to be spelled *napron.* People mistakenly attached the *n* to the article *a,* and *a napron* became *an apron.* Here are some more examples of everyday English words and their early forms.

PRESENT-DAY FORM	jail	look	sleep	time
EARLY FORM	jaile	locian	slæp	tima

Pronunciations and spellings still vary today. For instance, the English used in Great Britain differs from the English used in the United States. In Great Britain, people pronounce *bath* with the vowel sound of *father* instead of the vowel sound of *cat.* The British also tend to drop the *r* sound at the end of words like *copper.* In addition, the British spell some words differently from the way people in the United States do.

AMERICAN	theater	pajamas	labor
BRITISH	theatre	pyjamas	labour

RETEACHING

Students who have difficulty remembering the information in this segment could work in small groups to make a poster of the main headings and the important points for each heading. Assign a student who understands the lesson to help the others determine what should go on the poster.

CLOSURE

Ask students to reread the main points of the lesson. Then have each student work with a partner to write four sentences about how English has grown and changed.

COOPERATIVE LEARNING

Explain to students that in England, some English words are used differently or have a different meaning than the same words in America. Have groups of students look up the following words in the dictionary to find out what each word means in England:

1. pram [baby carriage]
2. queue [line up]
3. flat [apartment]
4. petrol [gasoline]
5. lift [elevator]
6. bonnet [car hood]
7. biscuit [cookie]
8. telly [television]
9. bobby [policeman]
10. lorry [van or truck]

Changes in Meaning

It may be hard to believe that the word *bead* once meant "prayer." Many English words have changed meaning over time. Some of these changes have been slight. Others have been more obvious, as with *bead*. Here are a few more examples of words that have changed meanings:

naughty—Back in the 1300s, *naughty* meant "poor or needy." It wasn't until around the 1600s that *naughty* was used to mean "poorly behaved."

lunch—In the 1500s, a *lunch* was a large chunk of something, such as bread or meat.

corn—The word *corn* was being used as long ago as the 800s. Originally it meant "a grain," as in a grain of sand or salt.

caboose—*Caboose* first entered English in the late 1700s. Back then, the word had nothing to do with trains. It meant "the kitchen of a ship."

Today, the meanings of words may vary from one place to another. For instance, some words mean different things in Great Britain than they do in the United States. A British person might ride the *tube* (subway) to work or put her suitcase in the *boot* (trunk) of the car.

EXTENSION

Tell students that there are many ways words enter the English language. You can discuss onomatopoeia with students by giving them the words *gurgle, buzz,* and *screech* as examples. Encourage students to suggest other examples. [*Boom, hiss, rustle, clink, hum,* and *thud* are some possibilities.] Have students work in groups to research and analyze the origins of some of these words.

How New Words Enter English

English grows and changes along with the people who use it. Four hundred years ago, words like *telescope* and *bicycle* didn't exist in English. The objects these words name hadn't been invented yet.

Over the centuries, people have invented thousands of English words to name new objects, places, ideas, and experiences. They've also borrowed many useful words from other languages.

Borrowed Words

Word borrowings first occurred as English-speaking people came into contact with people from other cultures and lands. Eventually, English speakers began to learn words from the languages of these peoples. Many of these foreign words became part of the English language.

English has borrowed hundreds of thousands of words from French, Hindi, Spanish, African languages, and many other languages spoken around the world. In many cases, the borrowed words have taken new forms.

FRENCH	**ange**	HINDI	**chāmpo**
ENGLISH	**angel**	ENGLISH	**shampoo**
AFRICAN	**banjo**	SPANISH	**patata**
ENGLISH	**banjo**	ENGLISH	**potato**

Words from Names

Many things get their names from the names of places or people. The word *Frisbee* is a good example. In the 1920s, someone in Bridgeport, Connecticut, discovered a new use for the pie plates from the Frisbie Bakery. He turned one upside down and sent it floating through the air. Flipping the pie plates soon became a popular game with local college students. The game sparked the idea for the plastic Frisbees of today.

A DIFFERENT APPROACH

To help students learn more about word origins and to give students an idea of the geographic location of the countries in which these languages are spoken, write these words on the chalkboard:

1. ranch [Spanish]
2. drama [Greek]
3. hamburger [German]
4. waffle [Dutch]
5. sofa [Arabic]
6. okra [West African]
7. cheetah [Hindi]
8. yogurt [Turkish]

Tell students that each of these words was borrowed from another language. Divide the class into five groups and give each group two words to look up in a dictionary to find the languages of origin. Then have groups locate on a map the countries in which these languages would be spoken.

ENRICHMENT

Volunteers might work in pairs to ask teachers in other subject areas what words have been added (or what words have had their meanings changed) in their subject areas since 1900. Then the pairs can either report to the class or create posters presenting the information. If they choose to make posters, they might create one poster of new words for each subject area. ■

LESS-ADVANCED STUDENTS

Before assigning **Exercise 2**, explain how to find a word origin in a dictionary by displaying an example from a dictionary entry. Help students find the lists of language abbreviations in their dictionaries. Then have the students complete the exercise in small groups.

ANSWERS

Exercise 2

1. kayak—Eskimo
2. prairie—French
3. cheddar—Cheddar, a village in England, where it was first made
4. denim—French, from Nîmes, a town in France
5. lasso—Spanish
6. macaroni—Italian
7. pretzel—German
8. jumbo—Jumbo, name of a large elephant exhibited by P. T. Barnum who derived the name from the word *jamba*-of African origin meaning elephant.
9. bloomers—Amelia J. Bloomer, 1818–1894, who first referred to them in a magazine she published
10. skunk—Algonquian (Native American)

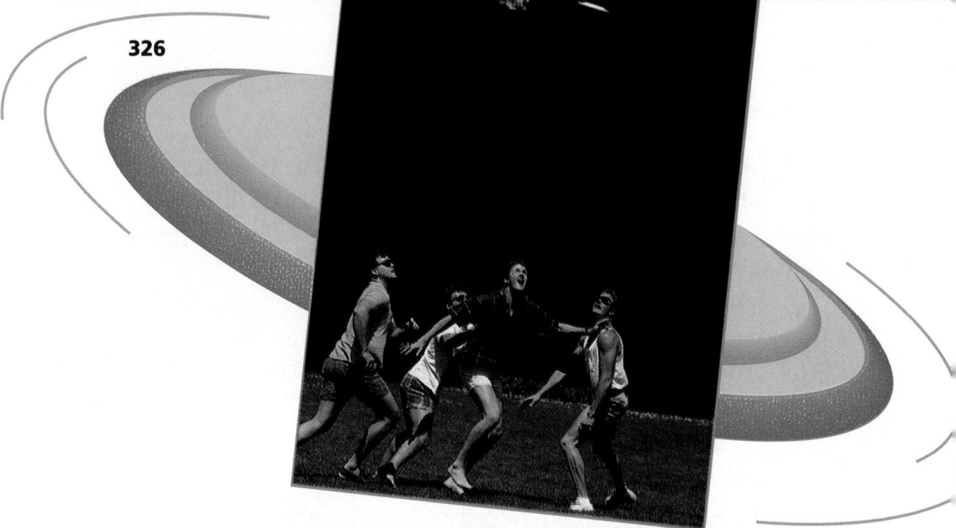

EXERCISE 1 **Matching Words with Their Original Spellings and Meanings**

The words in the left-hand column are English words that came from other languages. See if you can match each word with its original language, spelling, and meaning. [Hint: Use the process of elimination.]

1. pupil 1. d
2. tote 2. a
3. raccoon 3. e
4. tortilla 4. c
5. balloon 5. b

a. Kongo, *tota,* "to pick up"
b. Italian, *pallone,* "a large ball"
c. Spanish, *torta,* "a cake"
d. Latin, *pupillus,* "orphan"
e. Algonquian Indian, *aroughcun,* "one who scratches"

EXERCISE 2 **Researching Word Origins**

Use a dictionary to look up the origin of each of the following words. What language or name does each word come from?

1. kayak
2. prairie
3. cheddar
4. denim
5. lasso
6. macaroni
7. pretzel
8. jumbo
9. bloomers
10. skunk

SEGMENT 2 *(pp. 327–333)*

CHOOSING YOUR WORDS

OBJECTIVES

- To analyze characteristics of a dialect
- To use formal and informal English appropriately
- To recognize connotations

MOTIVATION

Write the words *carbonated drink* on the chalkboard and ask students to think of different synonyms for these words [*soda, pop, soda pop, soft drink,* and *tonic*]. Then ask students to think of all the different names for a very large cold-cut sandwich [*poor-boy, hoagy, submarine, sub,* and *hero*]. Explain to students that these ☛

Choosing Your Words

The variety and flexibility of English allow you to say the same thing in many different ways. Variety keeps the language interesting, but it also makes choosing the right words difficult sometimes. Choosing your words will be easier if you know the different uses and meanings words may have.

Dialects of American English

You probably know some people who speak English differently than you do. Maybe they pronounce some words differently or use them to mean different things. They may even use words you've never heard of before.

Different groups of people use different varieties of English. The kind of English we speak sounds most normal to us even though it may sound "funny" to someone else. The form of English a particular group of people speaks is called a ***dialect.*** Everyone uses a dialect, and no dialect is better or worse than another.

Regional Dialects

Do you *make* the bed or *make up* the bed? Would you order a *sub* with "the woiks" or a *hero* with "the werks"? In the evening, do you eat *supper* or *dinner*? How you answer these questions will probably depend on what part of the country you come from.

Teacher's ResourceBank™

RESOURCES

CHOOSING YOUR WORDS

• Formal and Informal English	89
• Denotation and Connotation	90

QUOTATION FOR THE DAY

"The words! I collected them in all shapes and sizes and hung them like bangles in my mind." (Hortense Calisher, 1911–   , American writer)

Ask students to list ten interesting (polite) words. They might list unusual words, emotional words, or words that they think are fun to say. You may wish to have students share words from their lists and to add words that they like to their collections. Challenge students to use the new words in their writing and to continue to add to their lists when they read or hear new words.

vocabulary differences depend on which type of language is spoken in a particular region or social group.

TEACHING THE LESSON

For each part of this lesson, you might first define the terms *dialect, standard English, nonstandard English, formal English, informal English, denotation,* and *connotation.* After pointing out the textbook examples for these terms, ask students to give examples from their own experiences.

ADVANCED STUDENTS

Students may become more aware of the types of language they see and hear by doing a research project. Have them look through written material such as newspapers, magazines, and pamphlets for examples of major regional dialects in the United States. They could compile these examples into booklets to be displayed for other students.

SELECTION AMENDMENT
Description of change: excerpted
Rationale: to focus on the concept of dialects presented in this chapter

A dialect shared by people from the same area is called a ***regional dialect.*** Your regional dialect helps determine what words you use, how you pronounce words, and even how you put words together.

You can use dialect in short stories to help your reader hear a character's language. As you read the following paragraph, notice how the use of dialect makes the character come alive. Can you tell what part of the country this character comes from?

> I traveled back home acrost the ridge just a-grinning myself. I had a full belly but I was light on my feet as everly. I don't need no light to show me where I'm going, nor a body to lead me the way. I know all the ways there is on Hurricane Mountain.
>
> Lee Smith, *Oral History*

When you write dialogue for a character, think about how your character would really talk. Try to capture the sound as well as the sense of the person's language.

Ethnic Dialects

Your cultural background can also determine the way you speak. A dialect shared by people from the same cultural group is called an ***ethnic dialect.*** Because Americans come from many cultures, American English includes many ethnic dialects. One of the largest ethnic dialects is the Black English spoken by many African Americans. Another is the Hispanic English of many people whose families come from Mexico, Central America, Cuba, and Puerto Rico.

Not everyone from a particular group speaks that group's dialect. Also, an ethnic or regional dialect may vary depending on the speakers' individual backgrounds and places of origin.

GUIDED PRACTICE

To give students practice using different forms of English, you might use the excerpt from ***Oral History*** by Lee Smith on p. 328. Ask students to work in groups to rewrite this brief selection in standard English or in a dialect more familiar to them.

To help students get started using formal and informal English, revise the first sentence of **Exercise 4** with the class.

To check students' knowledge of denotation and connotation, ask them to use the sentence about Coach Carlson in the **Style Note** on p. 333 and to make two columns of words or phrases to describe the coach. One column should list words or ☛

EXERCISE 3 Reading a Dialect

In the following passage, a young African American boy is telling about his experience at a cafe with his mother. Read the passage aloud, pronouncing the words as the writer has spelled them. Does this character's dialect sound different from yours? If it does, tell how you would describe the same scene using your own dialect.

> She take a quarter out the hankercher and tie the hankercher up again. She look over her shoulder at the people, but she still don't move. I hope she don't spend the money. I don't want her spend it on me. I'm hungry, I'm almost starving I'm so hungry, but I don't want her spending the money on me.
>
> She flip the quarter over like she thinking. She must be thinking 'bout us walking back home. Lord, I sure don't want walk home. If I thought it done any good to say something, I say it. But my mama make up her own mind.
>
> Ernest J. Gaines, "The Sky Is Gray"

Standard American English

Every dialect is useful and helps keep the English language colorful and interesting. But sometimes it's confusing to try to communicate using two different dialects. That's why it's important to be familiar with ***standard American English.***

Standard English is the most commonly understood variety of English. It allows English-speaking people from different regions and cultures to communicate with one another clearly. It is the most widely used form of American English.

You can find some of the rules and guidelines for using standard English in the **Handbook** in this text-

ANSWERS

Exercise 3

Responses will vary. Some students will agree that the character's dialect sounds different from theirs, but they will rewrite the passage in different ways. They may tend to rewrite the passage in standard English, so you may want to remind them to write it in their own dialects. One way for them to do this is to make the passage sound as if they were speaking to friends.

AFRICAN AMERICAN

You might help your students to hear the cadences of the African American dialect by reading aloud the passage from "The Sky Is Gray." Then you might read the passage in standard American English. After your readings, discuss with your students the values of each kind of English. Ethnic dialects such as the African American preserve the uniqueness of the rich cultures that make up the United States. Standard American English helps us to communicate in the larger world.

SELECTION AMENDMENT
Description of change: excerpted
Rationale: to focus on the concept of dialects presented in this chapter

phrases with positive connotations, and the other column should list words or phrases with negative connotations.

INDEPENDENT PRACTICE

Use **Exercises 3, 4,** and **5** for independent practice. You could have your students work in pairs so they can discuss possible answers. After they have completed **Exercise 3,** ask the pairs of students to read to the class what they have written.

INTEGRATING THE LANGUAGE ARTS

Literature Link. Let students practice identifying formal and informal English by reading a selection from their literature books and changing one or two paragraphs from formal English to informal English, or vice versa. Discuss the audience's relation to how the selection is written and then how the effect is changed when the letter is rewritten.

book. Language that doesn't follow these rules and guidelines is called ***nonstandard English.***

NONSTANDARD I don't want no more spinach.
STANDARD I don't want **any** more spinach.

NONSTANDARD Jimmy would of gone hiking with us.
STANDARD Jimmy **would have** gone hiking with us.

 REFERENCE NOTE: For more information about the kinds of nonstandard usage shown in the examples, see pages 538–539 and page 549.

Formal and Informal English

Read the following sentences.

Many of my friends are excited about the game tomorrow.
A bunch of my friends are really psyched about the game tomorrow.

Both sentences mean the same thing, but they have different effects. The first sentence is an example of ***formal English.*** The second sentence is an example of ***informal English.***

Formal and informal English are each appropriate for different situations. For instance, you'd probably use the first, more formal example sentence if you were talking to a teacher about the game. But you'd probably choose the informal wording of the second example if you were talking to a classmate.

Colloquialisms

Informal English includes many words and expressions that are inappropriate in more formal situations. The most widely used informal expressions are *colloquialisms.* ***Colloquialisms*** are the colorful words and phrases of everyday conversation. They give our speaking and writing a casual, friendly tone. Many

ASSESSMENT

For a quick way to evaluate the exercise, have students read revised versions of **Exercise 3. Exercise 4** should be turned in independently. For **Exercise 5,** have each pair of students share their word connotations with the class.

RETEACHING

Tell students who have difficulty with the concepts in this segment to restate the definitions in their own words and to create two examples of each concept.

colloquialisms have meanings that are different from the basic meanings of the words.

EXAMPLES I wish Gerald would **get off my case.**
Don't get **all bent out of shape** about it.
We were about to **bust** with laughter.

Slang

Slang words are made-up words or old words used in new ways. Slang is highly informal language. It is usually created by a particular group of people, such as students or artists. Often, slang is familiar only to the groups that invent it. You and your friends may have a slang vocabulary that your parents and teachers don't always understand.

Sometimes slang words become a lasting part of the English language. Usually, though, slang falls out of style quickly. The slang words in the following sentences will probably seem out of date to you.

That was a really **far-out flick.**
Those are some **groovy duds** you're wearing.
I don't have enough **dough** to buy a movie ticket.

Colloquialisms and slang can add zest to language. However, they are acceptable only in the most informal speaking and writing. Don't use colloquialisms or slang in essays, test answers, or reports.

CRITICAL THINKING

Synthesis

Students can discover the difference word choice makes by taking a familiar story such as "Jack and the Beanstalk" and writing it several different ways. You could divide the class into four groups and ask each group to create a different version by writing the story in slang, formal English, informal English, or a familiar dialect.

After the groups have completed the task, ask a volunteer from each group to read its version to the class.

COOPERATIVE LEARNING

Divide the class into groups of three or four. Ask each group to write four sentences—one including colloquialisms, one written in slang, one written in informal English, and one written in formal English.

CLOSURE

Conduct a quick class discussion by asking students where they would expect to read or hear dialects, formal English, slang, or colloquialisms. Ask students to explain the reasons for their answers.

EXTENSION

Students could write brief stories that contain dialect or slang. Brainstorm with the class first on what types of situations would require dialect or slang. ■

ANSWERS

Exercise 4

Letters will vary. The informal letters will probably include colloquialisms and slang words that are not found in the formal letter to Mrs. Domingo.

EXERCISE 4 **Using Formal and Informal English**

You're thinking about starting a coin collection, but you'd like to find out more about coin collecting first. You've already written a formal letter to the woman who is in charge of the coin collection at a local museum. You also want to write to your cousin Dan, who has his own coin collection. Rewrite the formal letter using more informal language, so that it will be more appropriate to send to Dan.

Dear Mrs. Domingo,

I am interested in coin collecting, and I am writing to ask for your assistance. I have not actually started a collection yet. However, I am considering starting one as a hobby, and I would greatly appreciate any information about coin collecting that you could send me.

Sincerely,
[your name]

Denotation and Connotation

Would you rather be described as a *curious* person or a *nosy* person? Both words have the same basic meaning, or ***denotation.*** But they have different *connotations*. A ***connotation*** is the kind of meaning that affects people emotionally.

You probably wouldn't mind if someone described you as *curious*. For most people, the word suggests someone who is interested and eager to learn. But you probably wouldn't like to be described as *nosy*. That word suggests someone who is a busybody—who is *too* interested in other people's business.

It's important to think about the connotations of the words you use. Connotations can have a strong effect on your reader or listener. If you use a word without knowing its connotation, you may send the wrong message to your audience.

Sometimes you will need to choose between *synonyms*—words that have similar meanings. Thinking about the connotations of the words will help you choose the word that says what you really mean. For example, suppose you need to choose a word to fit the following sentence.

> I admire Coach Carlson because her rules are ____ and fair. (*firm, strict*)

Firm and *strict* have similar meanings. But *strict* carries the negative connotation of harshness or rigidness. You'd probably choose *firm* instead, because it has a more positive connotation.

EXERCISE 5 **Recognizing Connotations**

Read each of the following words. What kind of reaction do you have to each word—positive, negative, or neither? Compare your reactions with those of your classmates.

1. fancy
2. bold
3. shy
4. cheap
5. snowstorm
6. coward
7. kind
8. friendly
9. pity
10. flower

ANSWERS

Exercise 5

Answers may vary. Different students will have different associations with some words, so those words can have either positive or negative connotations. For this reason, ask students to explain their answers.

SEGMENT 3 *(pp. 334–335)*

MAKING CONNECTIONS

NAME A NEWLY DISCOVERED ANIMAL

OBJECTIVES

- To write an informal, descriptive postcard
- To write a formal report about an imaginary creature

NAME A NEWLY DISCOVERED ANIMAL

Teaching Strategies

You may want to write the essential information for the assignment on the chalkboard or on an overhead transparency. Discuss with students what may be different in the year 2520 and what the planet Magdon may be like. Be sure students understand the difference between the audiences of a friendly postcard and a formal report and what information should be included in each type of writing.

MAKING CONNECTIONS

Name a Newly Discovered Animal

Throughout history, people have made up names for things that were new to them. For example, when English colonists arrived in the New World, they invented English names for many of the plants and animals they found there. Their language grew along with their knowledge of their new surroundings.

Now it's your turn to give names to some amazing discoveries. The year is 2520. You are on a team of Earthlings sent to explore Magdon, a newly discovered planet in a nearby solar system. After you land on the planet, you notice many strange-looking animals. They are different from any animals you've seen on Earth. As part of the exploration team, you have the honor of giving names to the creatures you find.

I

Write an interstellar postcard to a friend telling about one of the animals you've seen. First, draw a picture of the animal. Then, describe what the animal looks like, how it moves, and what noises it makes. Does it live on land, in the water, or somewhere else? Finally, tell your friend the name you've decided to give to the creature.

Here's a sample postcard written by another member of the exploration team.

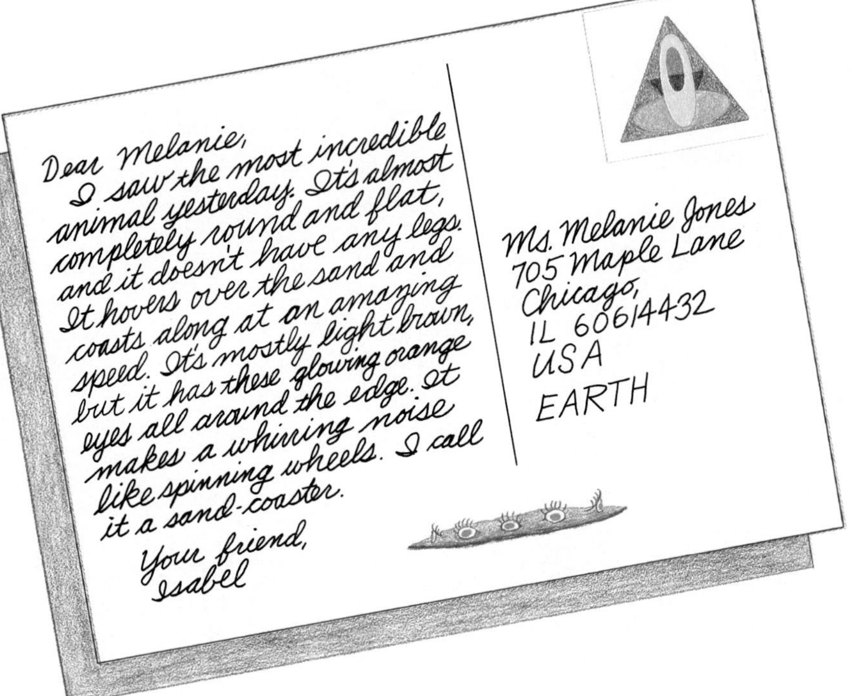

Dear Melanie,
I saw the most incredible animal yesterday. It's almost completely round and flat, and it doesn't have any legs. It hovers over the sand and coasts along at an amazing speed. It's mostly light brown, but it has these glowing orange eyes all around the edge. It makes a whirring noise like spinning wheels. I call it a sand-coaster.
Your friend,
Isabel
Ms. Melanie Jones
705 Maple Lane
Chicago,
IL 60614432
USA
EARTH

II

You've returned to Earth after several months on Magdon. The Council for Understanding Magdonian Creatures asks you to give a formal report on the animal you described in your postcard. Using your drawing as a guide, write the report you will present to the council. Make sure your description is clear and precise.

ANSWERS

Postcards will vary, but each should be written in a casual, friendly tone and should include details describing the creatures. The pictures should include the visible details described in the postcards.

COOPERATIVE LEARNING

After the initial discussion of **Parts I and II,** divide the class into groups of three or four. You may want to give each group a list of tasks to help students get started and keep working.

Students should divide responsibilities within their groups. For example, one student might take notes, another might draw the picture and the remaining two might write the drafts for the postcard and the report. However, the entire group should work together during the prewriting stage as well as when evaluating and revising.

ANSWERS

Reports will vary, but they should have a more serious tone than the informal postcards in **Part I.** They should also include formal words and expressions not often used in ordinary conversation. The descriptions of the animals should correspond to the descriptions given in the postcards in **Part I.**

PART TWO

HANDBOOK

Grammar

Usage

Mechanics

SEGMENT 1 *(pp. 338–340)*

DIAGNOSTIC TEST

OBJECTIVES

- To identify sentences and fragments
- To identify simple subjects and simple predicates
- To identify simple and compound sentences
- To classify and punctuate sentences according to purpose

Teacher's ResourceBank™

RESOURCES

FOR THE WHOLE CHAPTER

- Chapter Review Form A 105–106
- Chapter Review Form B 107–108
- Assessment Portfolio
  - Grammar Pretests 447–454
  - Grammar Mastery Tests 471–478

CHAPTER OVERVIEW

This chapter begins by contrasting the complete sentence and the sentence fragment. The information also identifies and explains the subject and predicate of a sentence. Following this discussion, which includes verb phrases, the material explores compound subjects and compound verbs and then discusses sentence structure. The chapter ends with a treatment of simple and compound sentences and sentence classification. The following **Review Exercises** give students the opportunity to test their mastery of the sentence.

12 THE SENTENCE

Subject and Predicate, Kinds of Sentences

Diagnostic Test

A. Identifying Sentences

Some of the following groups of words are sentences; others are not. If a group of words is a sentence, add a capital letter at the beginning and an appropriate punctuation mark at the end. If a group of words is not a sentence, write *sentence fragment.*

EXAMPLES
1. the big tree lost some limbs
1. *The big tree lost some limbs.*
2. after the storm yesterday
2. *sentence fragment*

1. leaves all over the front lawn and path 1. frag.
2. what is a black hole?
3. every day this week Felipe practiced the piano.
4. our best score in a basketball game this year 4. frag.
5. mail this letter on your way to school.

B. Identifying Simple Subjects and Simple Predicates

Identify the *simple subject* and the *simple predicate* in each of the following sentences. Be on the alert for compound subjects, compound verbs, and verb phrases.

EXAMPLE **1.** He removed the tire and patched it.
1. *He—simple subject; removed, patched—simple predicate*

6. The program about the Great Wall of China will be shown tonight.
7. On the piano was a bowl of fresh flowers.
8. After a test I check my answers carefully.
9. At the beach my brother and my cousins built a sand castle.
10. Lucky ran to the door and barked loudly at the mail carrier.

C. Identifying Simple Sentences and Compound Sentences

Identify each of the following sentences as *simple* or *compound*.

EXAMPLE **1.** The ship sank, but the crew was saved.
1. *compound*

11. Lucia hunted carefully along the dry riverbed and found a rare fossil. 11. simp.
12. I rang the doorbell several times, but nobody was home. 12. cd.
13. The plane finally landed in Bombay at noon, and the passengers looked for their friends and family members. 13. cd.
14. The storm slowed cars and halted trains. 14. simp.
15. Aretha won the first two games, but Lisa won the match. 15. cd.

GRAMMAR

USING THE DIAGNOSTIC TEST

The **Diagnostic Test** can be used to determine your students' understanding of the sentence or to determine problem areas in students' understanding of various aspects of the sentence. Because the test is constructed in four parts (identifying sentences; identifying simple subjects and simple predicates; identifying simple and compound sentences; classifying and punctuating sentences), you may want to use one part at a time to see exactly where students are having problems.

GRAMMAR

SEGMENT 2 *(pp. 340–342)*

SENTENCE OR SENTENCE FRAGMENT?

Rule 12a

OBJECTIVE

- To identify sentences and sentence fragments and to supply proper capitalization and punctuation for complete sentences

GRAMMAR

Teacher's ResourceBank™

RESOURCES

SENTENCE OR SENTENCE FRAGMENT?

- Identifying Sentences 97

QUICK REMINDER

Write the following words on the chalkboard and ask your students to identify them as complete sentences or fragments:

1. run [sentence]
2. the broken stairs [fragment]
3. be quiet [sentence]
4. for her [fragment]

Remind students that a sentence can consist of a verb and the understood subject *you* (numbers 1 and 3). Ask the students to transform the fragments into complete sentences and to punctuate them correctly.

GRAMMAR

D. Classifying and Punctuating Sentences by Purpose

For each of the following sentences, add the correct end mark of punctuation. Then label each sentence *declarative, interrogative, imperative,* or *exclamatory*.

EXAMPLE **1.** Are you ready
1. *Are you ready?—interrogative*

16. Look at this picture of a Navajo hogan. **16.** imp.
17. What a fantastic display of fireworks this is! **17.** excl.
18. Who is studying Spanish? **18.** int.
19. I always enjoy Independence Day. **19.** decl.
20. What is your favorite holiday? **20.** int.

Sentence or Sentence Fragment?

12a. A ***sentence*** is a group of words that expresses a complete thought.

A sentence begins with a capital letter and ends with a period, a question mark, or an exclamation point.

EXAMPLES Octavio Paz won a Nobel Prize in literature.
Walk in single file.
Do you collect coins?
Imagine me riding on an elephant!

When a group of words looks like a sentence but does not express a complete thought, it is a ***sentence fragment.***

SENTENCE FRAGMENT Alonzo's sisters and brothers. [This is not a complete thought. What about Alonzo's sisters and brothers?]

SENTENCE Alonzo's sisters and brothers planned a surprise party for his birthday.

12a

GRAMMAR

SENTENCE FRAGMENT Visited an old Spanish mission in San Diego. [This is not a complete thought. Who visited the mission?]

SENTENCE On our vacation last summer, we visited an old Spanish mission in San Diego.

SENTENCE FRAGMENT On the way to school yesterday morning. [This thought is not complete. What happened on the way to school yesterday morning?]

SENTENCE On the way to school yesterday morning, I saw Mr. Saunders walking his dog.

NOTE: In speech, people frequently use sentence fragments. Such fragments usually aren't confusing because the speaker's tone of voice and facial expressions help to complete the meaning. Professional writers, too, may use sentence fragments to create specific effects in their writing. However, in your writing at school, you will find it best to use complete sentences.

EXERCISE 1 **Identifying Sentences**

Tell whether each of the following groups of words is a *sentence* or a *sentence fragment*. If a group of words is a sentence, use a capital letter at the beginning and add an end mark of punctuation.

EXAMPLES
1. my aunt and uncle raise shar-pei dogs
1. *sentence—My aunt and uncle raise shar-pei dogs.*
2. Queenie, my favorite of all their dogs
2. *sentence fragment*

1. my aunt, my uncle, and my cousins at their house last weekend 1. frag.
2. after dinner Aunt Marie told me about the history of the shar-pei. 2. sent.
3. bred these dogs in China 3. frag.

LEP/ESL

General Strategies. You may find that some students show little interest in differentiating sentences and sentence fragments. Often, communicative competence (making oneself understood to attain specific objectives) is their top priority, and they do not have to rely on complete sentences to accomplish this.

Remind students that writing is an important form of communication, and that to be competent writers, they must write sentences that have subjects and verbs and that express complete thoughts.

GRAMMAR

SEGMENT 3 *(pp. 342–351)*

THE SUBJECT AND THE PREDICATE

Rules 12b–12e

OBJECTIVES

- To identify simple and complete subjects, complete predicates, verbs, and verb phrases in sentences
- To complete sentences by providing predicates
- To write sentences and to identify subjects and verbs

Teacher's ResourceBank™

RESOURCES

SUBJECT AND PREDICATE

- Complete Subjects and Simple Subjects 98
- Complete Predicates and Simple Predicates 99
- The Verb Phrase 100

QUICK REMINDER

After writing the following short sentences on the chalkboard, ask volunteers to underline the subjects.

1. Rosa gave us these tacos.
2. The green notebook is Michael's.
3. Has Cleo had her puppies yet?

If time permits, you may also ask students to make up their own sentences and state the subject of each.

4. just look at all that loose, wrinkled skin. 4. [*or* !] sent.
5. protected them from injury during a fight 5. frag.
6. gentle and a lot of fun with children 6. frag.
7. playing catch with Queenie 7. frag.
8. on the porch were Queenie's new puppies. 8. sent.
9. have you ever seen such a sight as these puppies? 9. sent.
10. what a good time we had! 10. sent.

Subject and Predicate

Every sentence has two main parts: a *subject* and a *predicate.*

The Subject

12b. The ***subject*** tells whom or what the sentence is about.

EXAMPLES **Lois Lenski** wrote *Strawberry Girl.*
The tooth with a point is a canine.

To find the subject, ask yourself *who* or *what* is doing something or *about whom* or *what* something is being said.

REVIEW A

OBJECTIVE

- To provide complete sentences with proper capitalization and punctuation and to form complete sentences from fragments by adding a subject or a verb

12b

GRAMMAR

EXAMPLES **My best friend** sits next to me in science class. [*Who* sits? My best friend sits.]
Science class is very interesting this year. [*What* is interesting? Science class is.]

The Position of the Subject

The subject does not always come at the beginning of a sentence. It may be in the middle or even at the end.

EXAMPLES After school, **Theresa** went to judo practice.
Under our house was **a tiny kitten.**

EXERCISE 2 **Identifying Subjects**

Identify the subject in each of these sentences.

EXAMPLE 1. The final score was tied.
1. *The final score*

1. Many games use rackets or paddles.
2. Tennis can be an exhausting sport.
3. Badminton rackets don't weigh very much.
4. Table-tennis paddles are covered with rubber.
5. Racquetball uses special rackets.
6. In Florida, citrus trees grow an important crop.
7. After three to five years, fruit grows on the new trees.
8. Does Florida grow all of the citrus fruit in the United States?
9. California also grows oranges and other citrus fruit.
10. From Texas comes the Star Ruby grapefruit.

REVIEW A **Writing Complete Sentences**

Some of the following groups of words are sentences. Write these sentences, adding capital letters and punctuation. If a group of words is not a sentence, add a subject or a verb to make it a sentence.

LEP/ESL

General Strategies. One potentially problematic area for some students is the rule that complete sentences must have stated subjects (excepting, of course, in the imperative form or in an interjection). Especially in conversation, students' sentences sometimes imply subjects but don't directly state them. Students may need extra coaching to help them see that neglecting to state the subjects of their sentences can be confusing to their audience and that the standardization of such rules is in the interest of aiding communication.

GRAMMAR

ANSWERS

Review A

Any answer that may vary is indicated by an asterisk (*).

*1. She sent us a postcard from the Philippines.
2. It was cold at the skating rink.
*3. My big sister helped me with my science project.
*4. A surfer on a huge wave can travel a half mile.
5. How hungry I am at lunch time!
6. It is too late for a game of checkers.
7. Is that Niagara Falls or Horseshoe Falls?
*8. The Cuban family next-door had dinner with us.
9. What time is your mom picking us up?
*10. The governor of my state is a woman.

GRAMMAR

GRAMMAR

EXAMPLES **1. we brought costumes from home**
1. ***We brought costumes from home.***
2. wrote a play
2. ***Our language arts class wrote a play.***

1. sent us a postcard from the Philippines
2. it was cold at the skating rink
3. helped me with my science project
4. a surfer on a huge wave
5. how hungry I am at lunchtime
6. it is too late for a game of checkers
7. is that Niagara Falls or Horseshoe Falls
8. the Cuban family next-door
9. what time is your mom picking us up
10. the governor of my state

Complete Subject and Simple Subject

The ***complete subject*** consists of all the words needed to tell *whom* or *what* the sentence is about. The ***simple subject*** is part of the complete subject.

12c. The ***simple subject*** is the main word in the complete subject.

EXAMPLE **A bright-red cardinal** sat on the windowsill.
Complete subject A bright-red cardinal
Simple subject cardinal

EXAMPLE **The Korean market** is closed today.
Complete subject The Korean market
Simple subject market

If you leave out the simple subject, a sentence does not make sense.

A bright-red . . . sat on the windowsill.
The Korean . . . is closed today.

Sometimes the same word or words make up both the simple subject and the complete subject.

EXAMPLES **Hawks** circled above the canyon. [*Hawks* is both the complete subject and the simple subject.]
Little Rascal is the story of a boy and his pet raccoon. [The title *Little Rascal* is both the complete subject and the simple subject.]

NOTE: In this book, the term *subject* refers to the simple subject unless otherwise indicated.

 EXERCISE 3 **Identifying Complete Subjects and Simple Subjects**

Identify the [complete subject] of each sentence. Then underline the simple subject.

EXAMPLE 1. From the chimney came a thick cloud of smoke.
1. *a thick cloud of smoke*

1. [Tents] were set up in the park.
2. Have [you] heard the new CD by Gloria Estefan?
3. [News] travels fast in our town.
4. Above the fort, [the flag] was still flying.
5. Beyond those mountains lies [an ancient Native American village].
6. [Those reporters] have been interviewing the mayor all morning.
7. On the shelf was [a copy of *Jonah's Gourd Vine*].
8. According to folklore, [Johnny Kaw] invented the catfish.
9. [The blue candles] burned all night long.
10. In the drawer were [some chopsticks].

The Predicate

12d. The ***predicate*** of a sentence is the part that says something about the subject.

EXAMPLES The best program **was about the Amazon River.**
The students **took turns on the new computer.**

GRAMMAR

COOPERATIVE LEARNING

Working together to construct sentences may help students understand the value of having the three elements (subject, predicate, and complete thought) in every sentence.

Divide the class in half. Assign students in one half to write complete subjects and assign students in the other half to write complete predicates. Pair students at random and let them read their joint sentences aloud. Point out that regardless of the humorous content or lack of logic, their combined groups of words are sentences if they express complete thoughts.

GRAMMAR

GRAMMAR

LESS-ADVANCED STUDENTS

Just as your students may have found it difficult to know what types of words go in the complete subject, they might also have difficulty understanding the complete predicate. Ask them to write simple predicates or verb phrases on pieces of paper. Then, using predicates or verb phrases from volunteers, add modifiers one at a time to form complete predicates as a demonstration for the class. After you have done a few, let students complete the rest.

ADVANCED STUDENTS

With your students' help, generate a list of words that can be used in sentences as either nouns or verbs. [Some examples are: *run, picnic,* and *skate*]. Write the list on the chalkboard. Ask each student to write five sentences by using the words as simple subjects and five sentences by using the words as simple predicates. More-creative students may want to write brief narratives by following the above instructions.

GRAMMAR

EXERCISE 4 **Identifying Predicates**

Identify the predicate in each of these sentences.

EXAMPLE **1.** Many people would like to have a robot.
1. *would like to have a robot*

1. Robots are machines with "brains."
2. The robot's brain is a computer.
3. A robot does not always look like a person.
4. Pacemakers are little robots.
5. Pacemakers help control a faulty heartbeat.
6. Many companies use robots.
7. Cars of the future may be guided by robots.
8. Some household jobs can be done by robots.
9. A robot could clean your room.
10. You might like to have a robot to help with your chores.

The Position of the Predicate

The predicate usually comes after the subject. Sometimes, however, part or all of the predicate comes before the subject.

EXAMPLES **Quickly** we **learned the layout of the small Hopi village.**
At the entrance to the science fair were maps of the exhibits.

EXERCISE 5 **Identifying Predicates**

Identify the predicate in each of the following sentences.

EXAMPLE **1.** At noon we went to a Mexican restaurant.
1. *At noon—went to a Mexican restaurant*

1. Our family likes different kinds of food.
2. Last night Dad prepared spaghetti and a salad for supper.
3. Sometimes Mom makes chow mein.

4. With chow mein she serves egg rolls.
5. At the Greek bakery we buy fresh pita bread.
6. Tomorrow Erica will make German potato salad.
7. Lately, tacos have become my favorite food.
8. Carefully, I spoon grated lettuce and cheese into a corn shell.
9. After that come the other ingredients.
10. In the United States people enjoy a wide variety of foods.

GRAMMAR

EXERCISE 6 **Writing Predicates**

Make a sentence out of each of the following groups of words by adding a predicate to fill the blank or blanks.

EXAMPLE 1. ___ the people in this photograph ___
1. *With a spirit of adventure, the people in this photograph are rafting down one of the fastest rivers in the state.*

1. Foamy white water ___
2. The hot summer air ___
3. A strong current ___
4. ___ the eyes of every person on board ___

GRAMMAR

ANSWERS

Exercise 6

Predicates will vary. Here are some possibilities:

1. Foamy white water roars through the canyon.
2. The hot summer air chapped my skin.
3. A strong current pulled the raft.
4. When the raft went over a rock, the eyes of every person on board widened in amazement.
5. The lightweight paddles floated down the river.
6. Around the bend dangerous rocks and swirls threatened the raft.
7. Quick action by everyone prevented a disaster.
8. A sleek, blue rubber raft ran aground.
9. The man in the white helmet and blue life jacket saved the little girl's life.
10. Despite all the problems, everyone arrived safely on shore.

5. The lightweight paddles ___
6. ___ dangerous rocks and swirls___
7. Quick action by everyone ___
8. A sleek, blue rubber raft ___
9. The man in the white helmet and blue life jacket ___
10. ___ everyone ___

Complete Predicate and Simple Predicate

The ***complete predicate*** consists of all the words that are not part of the complete subject.

12e. The ***simple predicate,*** or ***verb,*** is the main word or group of words in the complete predicate.

EXAMPLE The nurse **lifted the patient carefully.**
Complete predicate lifted the patient carefully
Simple predicate (verb) lifted

EXAMPLE I **saw a picture of a Siberian tiger.**
Complete predicate saw a picture of a Siberian tiger
Simple predicate (verb) saw

NOTE: In this book, the simple predicate is usually called the *verb.*

EXERCISE 7 Identifying Complete Predicates and Verbs

Identify the complete predicate of each of the following sentences. Then underline the verb.

EXAMPLE 1. For several years, space travel has fascinated me.
1. *For several years—has fascinated me*

1. My class traveled by train to Houston, Texas.
2. In Houston we visited the Lyndon B. Johnson Space Center.

GRAMMAR

TIMESAVER
To save class time you may want to go over the odd numbers orally in **Exercise 7.** For students who need additional practice, assign the even numbers as written work.

GRAMMAR

12e

3. The center displays moon rocks.
4. At the center, astronauts train for their flights.
5. In one room we saw several unusual computers.
6. On the way home, we stopped at the Astrodome for a tour.
7. The stadium in the Astrodome covers nine-and-a-half acres of land.
8. Several teams play there.
9. Every year the Astrodome attracts thousands of tourists.
10. Actually, I had more fun at the space center.

GRAMMAR

The Verb Phrase

A verb that is made up of more than one word is called a ***verb phrase.***

EXAMPLES Yoshi **will go** to Japan this summer.
The park **is located** near a lake.
We **should have planned** a picnic.

NOTE: The words *not* and *never* and the contraction *–n't* are not verbs. They are never part of a verb or verb phrase.

EXAMPLE Kendra **should**n't **have added** another chile to the sauce.

EXERCISE 8 **Identifying Predicates, Verbs, and Verb Phrases**

Identify the complete predicate in each of the following sentences. Then underline the verb or the verb phrase.

EXAMPLE **1.** The Liberty Bell was cast in London.
1. *was cast in London*

1. I am writing a report on the Liberty Bell.
2. The Liberty Bell was ordered by the Philadelphia Assembly.

A DIFFERENT APPROACH

Students may be better able to grasp the idea of the verb phrase if they start by building a sentence around one. Write some main verbs on index cards labeled *MV.* Then write helping verbs on other index cards and label them *HV.* Group students in twos or threes and give each group one *MV* card and some *HV* cards, with instructions to compose four sentences by using verb phrases made from the verbs on the index cards. Ask volunteers to read their sentences aloud.

GRAMMAR

GRAMMAR

PICTURE THIS

To help students get started, ask them to brainstorm the sights and sounds of a festival. Write a list on the chalkboard as they make suggestions. Perhaps some of your students have been to similar celebrations such as the one in New Orleans. Ask the students what they saw [colorful costumes, crowds, food, parades] and what they heard [music, laughter, fireworks]. Encourage your students who have never experienced a celebration like this to be imaginative.

GRAMMAR

3. It was made by Thomas Lester in London.
4. In 1752, the bell was cracked by its own clapper.
5. American patriots hid the bell from the British Army.
6. The bell was not brought back to Philadelphia until 1778.
7. The Liberty Bell cracked again in 1835.
8. This famous bell has been rung on a number of historic occasions.
9. The bell is exhibited in the Liberty Bell Pavilion.
10. We will be seeing the bell during our class trip to Philadelphia.

Finding the Subject

Sometimes it may be difficult to find the subject of a sentence. In such cases, find the verb first. Then ask yourself *whom* or *what* the verb is referring to.

EXAMPLES **Next semester you may take art or music.** [The verb is *may take. Who* may take? *You* may take. *You* is the subject of the sentence.]

Can your sister drive us to the park? [The verb is *can drive. Who* can drive? The answer is *sister. Sister* is the subject of the sentence.]

PICTURE THIS

You are a writer for a travel magazine. The magazine has sent you to Brazil to cover the carnival in Rio de Janeiro. Surrounded by the crowd shown on the next page, you catch the excitement of carnival fever. As a dutiful reporter, you jot down some notes to help you prepare your article. In your notes, describe the people, things, and events you see. Explain how it feels to be part of this festive celebration. For each

SEGMENT 4 *(pp. 351–356)*

COMPOUND SUBJECTS AND COMPOUND VERBS Rules 12f, 12g

OBJECTIVES

- To identify compound subjects, compound verbs, and verb phrases in sentences
- To complete sentences by supplying compound subjects and compound verbs

sentence in your notes, underline the simple subject and circle the verb.

Subject: the carnival in Rio
Audience: readers of a travel magazine
Purpose: to inform and entertain with description

Compound Subjects and Compound Verbs

Compound Subjects

12f. A ***compound subject*** consists of two or more connected subjects that have the same verb. The parts of the compound subject are most often connected by *and* and *or.*

VISUAL CONNECTIONS

Exploring the Subject. *Carnaval* is the most important social event in Rio de Janeiro. Although its roots can be traced back to ancient Egypt, Greece, and Rome, *Carnaval's* major source of origin is Portugal's pre-Lenten festivals that began in the fifteenth and sixteenth centuries to mark the end of winter. The celebration is a four-day event that occurs in February or March (depending on the dates of Ash Wednesday and Easter).

Teacher's ResourceBank™

RESOURCES

COMPOUND SUBJECTS AND COMPOUND VERBS

QUICK REMINDER

Write the following sentences on the chalkboard:

1. Marco and Anna played their guitars.
2. Anna played her guitar and sang for us.
3. Marco and Anna played their guitars and sang for us.

Ask the class to identify the verb in the first sentence [played]. To find the subject, tell the students to ask who or what played [Marco, Anna]. Remind students that *and* is a connecting word, not part of the subject. Ask the students to identify the compound verb in the second sentence [played, sang] and the compound subject and compound verb in the third sentence [Marco, Anna; played, sang]. Have the students compose original sentences with compound parts.

LEP/ESL

General Strategies. Giving students a chance to use grammatical structures in a familiar context that personally interests them is a strategy that might help them master the use of compound subjects and compound verbs. Ask students to write short descriptive paragraphs about their favorite TV programs. Have them use as many compound subjects and compound verbs as possible. Tell students to omit the name of the series. When

GRAMMAR

EXAMPLES **Minneapolis** and **St. Paul** are called the "Twin Cities." [The two parts of the compound subject have the same verb, *are called.*]

Mrs. Jones or **Ms. Lopez** will chaperone our field trip. [The two parts of the compound subject have the same verb, *will chaperone.*]

Flutes, clarinets, and **oboes** are woodwind instruments. [The three parts of the compound subject have the same verb, *are.*]

REFERENCE NOTE: Notice that commas are used to separate three or more parts of a compound subject. For more about this use of commas, see pages 594–595.

EXERCISE 9 Identifying Compound Subjects

Identify the compound subjects in each of the following sentences.

EXAMPLE 1. October and June are my favorite months.
1. *October, June*

1. Wild ducks and geese migrate south from Canada each year.
2. Stars and planets form a galaxy.
3. In the Tower of London are famous jewels and crowns.
4. Baseball and soccer are the two most popular sports at my school.
5. Eggs and flour are two necessary ingredients for pancakes.
6. Every year bugs and rabbits raid our vegetable garden.
7. Pizza or ravioli will be served.
8. At a party, balloons or horns always make the best noisemakers.
9. Dachshunds, Chihuahuas, and Pekingese are small dogs.
10. Someday dolphins and people may be able to talk to each other.

12g

Compound Verbs

12g. A ***compound verb*** is made up of two or more connected verbs that have the same subject. A connecting word such as *and* or *but* is used to join the verbs.

EXAMPLES Ben **overslept** but **caught** his bus anyway.
Conchita **sings** or **listens** to the radio all day long.
My father **bought** a Chinese wok and **cooked** vegetables in it.

EXERCISE 10 **Identifying Compound Verbs**

Identify the compound verbs and verb phrases in the following sentences.

EXAMPLE **1.** I proofread my paper and made a final copy.
1. *proofread, made*

1. Mai and her parents left Vietnam and arrived in California.
2. The Greek restaurant has closed but will reopen soon.
3. Every week our band practices together and writes songs.
4. Before supper I usually set the table or peel the vegetables.
5. Floyd asked for a watch but received a bike instead.
6. We gathered firewood and headed back to camp.
7. Last week everyone gave a speech or recited a poem.
8. The referee will call a rain delay or postpone the game.
9. I remembered the bread but forgot the milk.
10. Julie received good grades and made the honor roll.

GRAMMAR

the paragraphs are completed, ask students to read their paragraphs aloud and let the class guess which television program each paragraph describes.

LESS-ADVANCED STUDENTS

Some students may benefit from doing the exercises in this segment when paired with others who better understand the material. Assign an exercise to groups of two or three students. Encourage them to talk about the sentences and to analyze the problems they have in comprehending the sentences. You may want to walk about the room to verify that the information is being explained adequately.

GRAMMAR

REVIEW B

OBJECTIVE

- To identify subjects and verbs in sentences

ANSWERS

Exercise 11

Compound subjects and compound verbs will vary. Here are some possibilities:

1. Jake and Max are beginning a stamp collection.
2. Mr. Wu and Ms. Jones were my favorite teachers last year.
3. The creature from outer space hugged the president and kissed the governor.
4. At the end of the play, the cast bowed and waved to the audience.
5. Last week actors and directors were interviewed on a television talk show.
6. In the garage are tools and tires.
7. During the storm, we drank hot apple cider and talked about our vacation.
8. At the front door were Lou and Nell.
9. After school, my friends play tennis or fly kites.
10. Before the birthday party, he blew up balloons and iced the cake.

GRAMMAR

GRAMMAR

EXERCISE 11 **Writing Compound Subjects and Compound Verbs**

Make sentences by adding compound subjects or compound verbs to fill in the blanks in the following groups of words.

EXAMPLES
1. ____ are coming to the party.
1. *Fran and Terry are coming to the party.*
2. At the mall, we ____.
2. *At the mall, we ate lunch and went to a movie.*

1. ____ are beginning a stamp collection.
2. ____ were my favorite teachers last year.
3. The creature from outer space ____.
4. At the end of the play, the cast ____.
5. Last week ____ were interviewed on a television talk show.
6. In the garage are ____.
7. During the storm, we ____.
8. At the front door were ____.
9. After school, my friends ____.
10. Before the birthday party, he ____.

REVIEW B **Identifying Subjects and Verbs**

Identify the subjects and verbs in each of the following sentences. [Note: Some of the subjects and verbs are compound.]

EXAMPLE
1. In the history of African American music are many unforgettable names.
1. *names—subject; are—verb*

1. You probably recognize the man in the picture on the next page.
2. Most people immediately think of his deep, raspy voice.
3. Ray Charles is called the father of soul music.
4. He lost his sight at the age of seven and became an orphan at fifteen.
5. However, misfortune and trouble did not stop Ray Charles.

6. His musical genius turned his troubles into songs.
7. Today, the songs of Ray Charles are heard the world over.
8. Do his songs contain different musical styles?
9. Gospel, jazz, blues, and even pop are all part of his sound.
10. His special style and powerful performances have drawn fans to Ray Charles for nearly fifty years.

GRAMMAR

A sentence may have both a compound subject and a compound verb.

EXAMPLES **Zina** and **I brought** corn and **fed** the ducks. (S S V V)

Carrots and **celery are** crunchy and **satisfy** your appetite. (S S V V)

EXERCISE 12 **Identifying Compound Subjects and Compound Verbs**

Identify the compound subject and the compound verb in each of the following sentences.

GRAMMAR

VISUAL CONNECTIONS

Exploring the Subject. The singer, arranger, and composer Ray Charles was born Ray Charles Robinson on September 23, 1930, in Albany, Georgia. By the age of seven, he was totally blind, and it was while attending a school for the deaf and blind that he learned to play the piano. By the age of fifteen, he was touring with dance bands, and his music career has been going strong ever since. Ray Charles dropped his surname to avoid being confused with the boxer Sugar Ray Robinson.

Ray Charles has won many awards and accolades, including a Bronze Medallion presented by the French Republic, ten Grammy Awards, memberships in the Songwriter's Hall of Fame and Ebony Black Music Hall of Fame, and an honorary life chairmanship in the Rhythm and Blues Hall of Fame.

INTEGRATING THE LANGUAGE ARTS

Technology Link. If students have access to word processors, they might enjoy doing **Exercise 12** by using the delete function to eliminate all sentence parts except those they are asked to identify.

ANSWERS

Review C

1. subject—These creatures; predicate—are known as *Yeti* in the Himalayas and as *Rakshas* in Katmandu
2. subject—Native Americans of the Northwest; predicate—call them *Mammoth*
3. subject—*Sasquatch* and *Bigfoot;* predicate—are other common names for these creatures
4. subject—they; predicate—Since 1818, have been described and filmed by people in the United States and Canada
5. subject—Bigfoot adults; predicate—According to most accounts, are very strong and large and smell very bad
6. subject—Their huge footprints; predicate—have been measured and cast in plaster by eager searchers
7. subject—these reports and bits of evidence; predicate—However, do not convince scientists
8. subject—Not one live Bigfoot; predicate—has ever been seen by either scientists or the general public
9. subject—the Bigfoot; predicate—As a result, is simply a fantasy to most people
10. subject—whole families of these shy creatures; predicate—Yet in pockets of deep wilderness across the country may live

GRAMMAR

REVIEW C

OBJECTIVE

- To identify the complete and simple subjects, the complete predicates, and the verbs in sentences

GRAMMAR

EXAMPLE **1.** Tina and Julia washed the dog and dried it with a towel.

1. *Tina, Julia—subject; washed, dried—verb*

1. Alice and Reiko sang and played the piano.
2. Either Dwayne or I will find the coach and ask his advice.
3. Patrick and she read the same biography of Martin Luther King, Jr., and reported on it.
4. Roses and lilacs look pretty and smell good.
5. The dentist or her assistant cleans and polishes my teeth.

REVIEW C **Identifying Subjects and Predicates**

Identify the complete subject and the complete predicate in each of the following sentences. Then underline the simple subject and the verb. [Note: Some of the subjects and verbs are compound.]

EXAMPLE [1] Reports and legends of huge apelike creatures fascinate many people.

1. *subject—Reports and legends of huge apelike creatures; predicate—fascinate many people*

[1] These creatures are known as *Yeti* in the Himalayas and as *Rakshas* in Katmandu. [2] Native Americans of the Northwest call them *Mammoth*. [3] *Sasquatch* and *Bigfoot* are other common names for these creatures. [4] Since 1818, they have been described and filmed by people in the United States and Canada. [5] According to most accounts, Bigfoot adults are very strong and large and smell very bad. [6] Their huge footprints have been measured and cast in plaster by eager searchers. [7] However, these reports and bits of evidence do not convince scientists. [8] Not one live Bigfoot has ever been seen by either scientists or the general public. [9] As a result, the Bigfoot is simply a fantasy to most people. [10] Yet in pockets of deep wilderness across the country may live whole families of these shy creatures.

SEGMENT 5 *(pp. 357–359)*

SIMPLE SENTENCES AND COMPOUND SENTENCES Rules 12h, 12i

OBJECTIVE

- To identify simple and compound sentences

Simple Sentences and Compound Sentences

12h. A ***simple sentence*** has one subject and one verb.

Although a compound subject has two or more parts, it is still considered one subject. In the same way, a compound verb or verb phrase is considered one verb.

EXAMPLES My **mother** (S) **belongs** (V) to the Friends of the Library. [single subject and verb]

Argentina (S) and **Chile** (S) **are** (V) in South America. [compound subject]

Jeannette (S) **read** (V) *Stuart Little* and **reported** (V) on it. [compound verb]

The **acrobats** (S) and **jugglers** (S) **did** (V) tricks and **were rewarded** (V) with a standing ovation. [compound subject and compound verb]

12i. A ***compound sentence*** consists of two or more simple sentences, usually joined by a connecting word.

In a compound sentence, the word *and, but, or, nor, for, so,* or *yet* connects the simple sentences. A comma usually comes before the connecting word in a compound sentence.

EXAMPLES I forgot my lunch**, but** Dad ran to the bus with it.
She likes sweets**, yet** she seldom buys them.

Notice in the second example above that a sentence is compound if the subject is repeated.

Teacher's ResourceBank™

RESOURCES

SIMPLE SENTENCES AND COMPOUND SENTENCES

- Simple and Compound Sentences 103

QUICK REMINDER

Write the following simple sentences on the chalkboard. Ask your students to combine them to create compound sentences.

1. Markey works with animals. Markey has six dogs of her own. [Markey works with animals, and she has six dogs of her own.]
2. Cindy speaks Spanish fluently. She went to Mexico last summer. [Cindy speaks Spanish fluently, so she went to Mexico last summer.]
3. Jared loves to eat cake. He is dieting this week. [Jared loves to eat cake, but he is dieting this week.]

GRAMMAR

REVIEW D

OBJECTIVE

- To identify simple and compound sentences

GRAMMAR

LEP/ESL

General Stragegies. It may be helpful to students to provide an expanded context in which all of the words used to connect simple sentences are used, thereby contrasting their semantic functions. Write the following paragraph on the chalkboard and list the connecting words to one side. Have students fill in the blanks with the appropriate connecting words. Ask students to explain their choices.

Mario had a soccer game early Saturday morning, ___ [so] he decided to go to bed early. He knew he would get a good night's sleep, ___ [yet] he went to bed feeling uneasy. The next morning Mario woke up late, ___ [for] he had forgotten to set the alarm. Mario had no time to take a shower, ___ [but] he did manage to eat breakfast. Unfortunately, Mario couldn't get a ride to the game from his dad, ___ [nor] could his mom take him; they had already left to go to the mall. He didn't panic, however. Mario realized that he could get a ride with a teammate, ___ [or], if necessary, he could walk to the game.

GRAMMAR

EXERCISE 13 **Identifying Simple Sentences and Compound Sentences**

Identify each of the following sentences as *simple* or *compound*.

EXAMPLE 1. That story by Lensey Namioka is good, and you should read it.
1. *compound*

1. My dad and I like enchiladas, but my mother prefers fajitas. 1. cd. 2. simp.
2. Some trees and shrubs live thousands of years.
3. It rained, but we marched in the parade anyway.
4. Mr. Edwards will lead the singing, for Ms. Cruz is ill. 3. cd. 4. cd.
5. My aunts, uncles, and cousins from Costa Rica visited us last summer. 5. simp.
6. I had worked hard all morning, yet I had not finished the job by lunchtime. 6. cd.
7. Abe peeled and chopped all of the onions and dumped them into a huge pot. 7. simp.
8. We made a doghouse for Reggie, but he will not use it. 8. cd.
9. *Chippewa* and *Ojibwa* are two names for the same Native American people. 9. simp. 10. cd.
10. All ravens are crows, but not all crows are ravens.

REVIEW D **Identifying Simple Sentences and Compound Sentences**

Identify each of the following sentences as *simple* or *compound*.

EXAMPLE 1. Have you seen the movie *The Bridge on the River Kwai*?
1. *simple*

1. My stepbrother is eight, and he is fascinated by bridges. 1. cd.
2. We buy postcards with pictures of bridges, for he collects them. 2. cd.

3. He has several cards of stone bridges. 3. simp.
4. Stone bridges are strong, but they are costly. 4. cd.
5. Many bridges are beautiful, but they must also be sturdy. 5. cd.
6. The Central American rope bridge on the right is one kind of suspension bridge. 6. simp.
7. The modern bridge below is another kind of suspension bridge. 7. simp.

8. Suspension bridges may look dangerous, yet they are safe. 8. cd.
9. Bridges must be inspected regularly. 9. simp.
10. My stepbrother collects postcards of bridges, and I collect postcards of towers. 10. cd.

GRAMMAR

STUDENTS WITH SPECIAL NEEDS

Students with learning disabilities have difficulty with abstract concepts. Thus, it may be necessary when assigning exercises to divide the tasks students are asked to do into smaller, more concrete steps.

To help students understand the elements of sentences, give them lists of subjects and predicates and have them combine items from each list to form sentences.

INTEGRATING THE LANGUAGE ARTS

Literature Link. If your literature book contains John Gardner's short story "Dragon, Dragon," have students read and discuss the story. Then ask them to identify the type of sentences Gardner writes in the second, third, and fourth paragraphs [simple sentences with compound verbs]. You may want to have your students write brief expressive paragraphs about how they might feel confronting a vicious dragon. Tell them to include sentences with compound subjects and compound verbs. Ask volunteers to read their paragraphs aloud.

GRAMMAR

SEGMENT 6 *(pp. 360–363)*

KINDS OF SENTENCES Rules 12j–12m

OBJECTIVE

- To classify sentences as declarative, imperative, interrogative, or exclamatory and to provide the correct punctuation

Teacher's ResourceBank™

RESOURCES

KINDS OF SENTENCES

- Kinds of Sentences 104

GRAMMAR

QUICK REMINDER

Write the following sets of words on the chalkboard:

1. the twenty-seventh floor
2. scary Halloween masks
3. the calico cat
4. northern lights

Ask each of your students to compose a declarative, an imperative, an exclamatory, and an interrogative sentence by using the prompts above (total of four sentences). Tell the students to be sure to punctuate each sentence correctly. Ask volunteers to read their sentences aloud.

LEP/ESL

General Strategies. Students might be able to create different kinds of sentences more easily if you give them one base sentence and ask them to form the other three types of sentences starting from this base. This exercise keeps their attention focused on the form rather than on the content. [Example: The game was exciting.
Was the game exciting?
Please tell me if the game was exciting.
Wow! That game was exciting!]

Remember that function is of more immediate use to some students

GRAMMAR

Kinds of Sentences

12j. A ***declarative sentence*** makes a statement. It is always followed by a period.

EXAMPLES Our media center has several computers**.**
Patrick Henry lived in Virginia**.**

12k. An ***imperative sentence*** gives a command or makes a request. It may be followed by a period or by an exclamation point.

EXAMPLES Stop shouting**!** [command]
Please pass the potatoes**.** [request]

The subject of a command or a request is always *you*, even if *you* never appears in the sentence. In such cases, *you* is called the ***understood subject.***

EXAMPLES **(You)** Stop shouting!
(You) Please pass the potatoes.

12l. An ***interrogative sentence*** asks a question. It is followed by a question mark.

EXAMPLES Did the spacecraft *Apollo* land on the moon**?**
How old are you**?**

12m. An ***exclamatory sentence*** shows excitement or expresses strong feeling. It is followed by an exclamation point.

EXAMPLES What a difficult assignment that was**!**
I got her autograph**!**

 EXERCISE 14 **Classifying Sentences by Purpose**

Write each of the following sentences and the punctuation mark that should follow it. Label the sentence *declarative*, *interrogative*, *imperative*, or *exclamatory*.

WRITING APPLICATION

OBJECTIVE

- To create a comic strip that uses the four kinds of sentences

12 j–m

GRAMMAR

EXAMPLE 1. What a funny show that was
1. *What a funny show that was!—exclamatory*

1. Please help me find my umbrella. 1. imp.
2. How happy I am! 2. excl.
3. Have you been to the new video store? 3. int.
4. Go east for three blocks, and look for a mailbox. 4. imp.
5. My father and I are cleaning the attic. 5. decl.
6. What a delicious salad this is! 6. excl.
7. We toured the garment district in New York City. 7. decl.
8. Do you like barbecued chicken? 8. int.
9. My surprise visit pleased my grandmother. 9. decl.
10. When is your next piano lesson? 10. int.

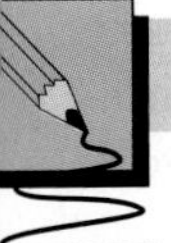

WRITING APPLICATION

Using End Punctuation in a Comic Strip

In any kind of writing, correct end punctuation is important. However, it's especially important in written conversations. The punctuation helps a reader hear how a speaker says something. A sentence can mean very different things when its end punctuation is changed. Try reading the following sentences aloud to hear the difference.

DECLARATIVE He's my hero.
INTERROGATIVE He's my hero?
EXCLAMATORY He's my hero!

WRITING ACTIVITY

As a special project, your social studies class is creating a comic book. Each class member will contribute a comic strip about a particular historical event or historical person. Each strip should be at least one page

LESS-ADVANCED STUDENTS

To give extra practice in using the four sentence types, cut out magazine pictures that are colorful, stimulating, and suitable for writing prompts. Give one to each student with instructions to write a short descriptive paragraph based on what is in the picture. Tell each student to use one interrogative, one imperative, one exclamatory, and at least two declarative sentences in the paragraph.

GRAMMAR

WRITING APPLICATION

This writing assignment provides students with an opportunity to create comic strips based on historical events or persons. Some research may be necessary. You might allow more-advanced students to go to the library to obtain materials for the class.

CRITICAL THINKING
Synthesis

One way to use each of the four kinds of sentences is to present them in dialogue. Because this assignment is to be done in the form of a comic book, a review of the use of quotation marks may not be necessary. However, because the comic book is to be based on a historical event or person, you will want to remind your students to keep the information in their sentences accurate.

GRAMMAR

PREWRITING

It might be helpful for the class to brainstorm various historical events and people. Make a list on the chalkboard of the students' ideas.

WRITING

Remind students that the most important aspect of this stage of writing is to simply get their thoughts on paper. Corrections and improvements will be made later. You may suggest they write on every other line of notebook paper to have sufficient space for revisions.

long. You can draw your own illustrations, cut out pictures from magazines, or make photocopies of pictures you would like to use. In your comic strip, include at least one of each of the four kinds of sentences—declarative, imperative, interrogative, and exclamatory.

GRAMMAR

Prewriting First, jot down some ideas for the characters and story line of your comic strip. You may want to look through your social studies book for ideas. Then, plan the frames of your comic strip. Think about how you could include the four types of sentences in your characters' conversation. For example, what request or command could a character make? What could a character ask a question about or express amazement about?

Writing Use your prewriting notes to help you write a draft of your comic strip. As you write, you may decide to add details. Keep in mind that you'll be able to add details in the pictures that go with the words.

Evaluating and Revising Ask a friend to read your cartoon. Are your characters' conversations clear? Can your friend follow the story line? If not, you may need to add, revise, or rearrange sentences. Make sure you've used only complete sentences in your dialogue. Prepare a final version of your comic strip. Use word balloons to add the dialogue to the pictures.

Proofreading and Publishing Check your comic strip for errors in grammar, spelling, or punctuation. Be sure that you have spelled and capitalized all proper names correctly. Take extra care with end punctuation. Make sure you've used periods, question marks, and exclamation points correctly for each kind of sentence. You and your classmates may wish to make a historical comic book. Photocopy all the comic strips and gather them in a folder for each member of the class.

REVIEW E

OBJECTIVE

- To classify sentences by purpose and to punctuate them appropriately

REVIEW E **Classifying Sentences by Purpose**

For each of the following sentences, add the appropriate end mark of punctuation. Then label each sentence as *declarative, imperative, interrogative,* or *exclamatory.*

EXAMPLE **1. Have you ever seen the Grand Canyon**
1. *Have you ever seen the Grand Canyon?—interrogative*

1. We enjoyed our vacation in the Southwest. **1.** decl.
2. Dad took these photographs when we visited the Grand Canyon. **2.** decl.
3. Our guide spoke Spanish and English. **3.** decl.
4. How pretty the sunset is! **4.** excl.
5. Don't stand so close to the edge. **5.** imp.
6. Did you buy any turquoise-and-silver jewelry? **6.** int.
7. It was quite chilly at night. **7.** decl.
8. What a great movie we saw about the canyon! **8.** excl.
9. Did you take the short hike or the long one? **9.** int.
10. Look at us riding on mules in this canyon. **10.** imp.

GRAMMAR

GRAMMAR

SEGMENT 7 *(pp. 364–366)*

REVIEW: POSTTESTS 1 and 2

OBJECTIVES

- To identify sentences and sentence fragments
- To identify simple subjects and verbs in sentences
- To identify simple and compound sentences

INTEGRATING THE LANGUAGE ARTS

Literature Link. To reinforce the importance of complete sentences in literature, have your class read and discuss Shel Silverstein's poem "Sarah Cynthia Sylvia Stout Would Not Take the Garbage Out." In this poem, Silverstein uses complete sentences to describe Sarah's mess and the consequences of her action. The first and last sentences are similar in tone, rhythm, and message. Ask students to write poems by imitating Silverstein's technique of listing objects.

GRAMMAR

Review: Posttest 1

GRAMMAR

A. Identifying Sentences

If a group of words is a sentence, add a capital letter at the beginning and an end mark of punctuation. If a group of words is not a sentence, label it a *sentence fragment.*

EXAMPLES
1. followed the trail on the map
1. *sentence fragment*
2. the López twins come from Nuevo Laredo, Mexico
2. *The López twins come from Nuevo Laredo, Mexico.*

1. we put up the postcards from our Asian pen pals
2. our neighborhood has a homework hotline
3. mailed the invitations yesterday 3. frag.
4. practice my guitar before dinner 4. frag.
5. the Washington Monument 5. frag.

B. Identifying Simple Subjects and Simple Predicates

Identify the simple subject and the verb in each of the following sentences. [Note: A subject or a verb may be compound.]

EXAMPLE
1. Every year my family travels to Mecca, Saudi Arabia.
1. *family—simple subject; travels—verb*

6. My grandmother plays mah-jongg with my friends and me.
7. The farmers have plowed the fields and will plant potatoes.
8. At night you can rent roller skates at the rink near my house.

- To classify and punctuate sentences
- To identify sentence parts as subjects or predicates and to use them in correctly punctuated complete sentences

9. On the sand lay a beautiful seashell.
10. On Saturday, Amy, Theo, and I walked through Chinatown and took pictures.

GRAMMAR

C. Identifying Simple Sentences and Compound Sentences

Identify each of the following sentences as simple or compound.

EXAMPLE 1. Mom is late, but she will be here soon.
1. *compound*

11. Jaleel learned several African folk tales and presented them to the class. **11.** simp.
12. The dance committee has chosen a Hawaiian theme and will decorate the gym with flowers and greenery. **12.** simp.
13. The school bus stopped suddenly, but no one was hurt. **13.** cd.
14. Raccoons and opossums steal our garbage. **14.** simp.
15. Luis Gonzalez stepped up to the plate, and the crowd roared. **15.** cd.

D. Classifying and Punctuating Sentences by Purpose

For each sentence, add the appropriate end mark of punctuation. Then, label each sentence *declarative*, *interrogative*, *imperative*, or *exclamatory*.

EXAMPLE 1. Have you read this poem by José Garcia Villa
1. *Have you read this poem by José Garcia Villa?—interrogative*

16. Please answer the phone. **16.** imp.
17. What a good time we had! **17.** excl.
18. Has anyone seen the cat? **18.** int.
19. They sat on a bench and played checkers. **19.** decl.
20. Whose book is this? **20.** int.

GRAMMAR

GRAMMAR

ANSWERS

Review: Posttest 2

Sentences will vary. Here are some possibilities:

1. subject—My favorite book is *Treasure Island.*
2. predicate—Mom and I watched a good mystery.
3. subject—The flying saucer landed in a wheat field.
4. subject—The oldest house in town has become a museum.
5. predicate—My neighbor prepares delicious Korean food.
6. predicate—The dog growled and bared its teeth.
7. subject—The shiny red car sped away.
8. predicate—My little sister caught a huge fish.
9. predicate—Can David borrow your skates?
10. subject—The best tacos in town can be found at Rosie's Restaurant.

GRAMMAR

Review: Posttest 2

Writing Sentences

Identify each of the following sentence parts as a *subject* or a *predicate.* Then use each sentence part in a sentence. Begin each sentence with a capital letter, and end it with the correct mark of punctuation. Use a variety of subjects and verbs in your sentences.

EXAMPLE **1. will drive us home**
1. ***predicate—Will your mother drive us home?***

1. my favorite book
2. watched a good mystery
3. the flying saucer
4. the oldest house in town
5. prepares delicious Korean food
6. growled and bared its teeth
7. the shiny red car
8. caught a huge fish
9. can borrow your skates
10. the best tacos in town

SEGMENT 1 (pp. 367–368)

DIAGNOSTIC TEST

OBJECTIVE

- To identify nouns, pronouns, and adjectives in sentences

Teacher's ResourceBank™

RESOURCES

FOR THE WHOLE CHAPTER

• Chapter Review Form A	119–120
• Chapter Review Form B	121–122
• Assessment Portfolio	
Grammar Pretests	447–454
Grammar Mastery Tests	471–478

GRAMMAR

13 THE PARTS OF SPEECH

Noun, Pronoun, Adjective

Diagnostic Test

Identifying Nouns, Pronouns, and Adjectives

Identify each italicized word in the following sentences as a noun, a pronoun, or an adjective. Each sentence contains two italicized words.

EXAMPLE **1.** *Dad* tinkered with the *rusty* lock.
1. *Dad—noun; rusty—adjective*

1. My *best* friend plays *soccer*.
2. *We* went to *Boston* last summer.
3. Help *yourself* to some *Chinese* food.
4. Juana invited *us* to *her* fiesta.
5. What a *beautiful* garden *Mrs. Murakami* has!
6. *My* directions were *accurate*.
7. The jacket on the *chair* is *yours*.
8. A *sharp* knife is *necessary* for making a wood carving.

GRAMMAR

CHAPTER OVERVIEW

This chapter should help students to use nouns, pronouns, and adjectives effectively in their writing. The first part of the chapter defines the word *noun* and explains the difference between proper nouns and common nouns. Next, the chapter focuses on pronouns and their antecedents and discusses the classes of pronouns. The **Writing Application** asks students to create ideas for science fiction movies, while using pronouns that clearly refer to their antecedents. The last section of the chapter explains adjectives. Common, proper, and demonstrative adjectives are discussed.

This chapter may serve as a resource if students are having problems using these parts of speech in their writing.

USING THE DIAGNOSTIC TEST

You can use the **Diagnostic Test** to gauge students' knowledge of nouns, pronouns, and adjectives, but even students who can identify these parts of speech may not use them effectively in their writing. Evaluating actual writing samples should reveal any weaknesses.

TEACHING NOTE

Some of the exercises, reviews, and tests in this chapter may contain possessive or demonstrative pronouns. You may want to discuss with students whether these words should be classified as pronouns or as adjectives.

GRAMMAR

Teacher's ResourceBank™

RESOURCES

THE NOUN
- The Noun 113
- Common and Proper Nouns 114

QUICK REMINDER

Ask students to identify the nouns in the following sentences as you write the sentences on the chalkboard:

1. Maria plays the piano at Concert Hall.
2. With freedom comes responsibility.
3. The boy rode his bike to school.

Have students classify each noun as naming a person, a place, a thing, or an idea. You may also wish to have the class identify each noun as a common or proper noun. [All are common nouns except *Maria* and *Concert Hall.*]

SEGMENT 2 *(pp. 368–373)*

THE NOUN Rule 13a

OBJECTIVES
- To identify nouns in a paragraph
- To classify nouns in sentences as common or proper
- To revise sentences by substituting proper nouns for common nouns

GRAMMAR

9. Almost [*everyone*] in the band takes private music *lessons*.
10. This story, short and *funny*, is my *favorite*.

The Eight Parts of Speech			
noun	adjective	adverb	conjunction
pronoun	verb	preposition	interjection

The Noun

13a. A ***noun*** is a word that names a person, place, thing, or idea.

PERSONS	parents, Scott, teacher, Ms. Vargas, sister, linebacker, baby sitter
PLACES	White House, state, Nairobi, school
THINGS	rocket, desk, ocean, hamster, computer, Newbery Medal, Golden Gate Bridge
IDEAS	anger, freedom, kindness, fear, dream

NOTE: Nouns that are made up of more than one word, like *Rita Rodriguez, Empire State Building,* and *family room,* are counted as one noun.

EXERCISE 1 **Identifying Nouns**

Identify each of the twenty nouns in the following paragraph.

EXAMPLE [1] Clara Barton had two brothers and two sisters.
1. *Clara Barton, brothers, sisters*

• To answer questions with complete sentences and to identify each proper noun used in the sentences

13a

[1] Clara Barton was born in Massachusetts. [2] She was educated in a rural school and grew up with a love of books. [3] She began her career as a teacher. [4] During the Civil War, however, she distributed medicine and other supplies. [5] Later she helped find soldiers who were missing in action. [6] She organized the American Red Cross and was its president for many years. [7] She raised money for the Red Cross and worked with victims of floods and other disasters.

Proper Nouns and Common Nouns

A ***proper noun*** names a particular person, place, thing, or idea. It always begins with a capital letter. A ***common noun*** names any one of a group of persons, places, or things. It is not capitalized.

COMMON NOUNS	PROPER NOUNS
woman	Aunt Josie
teacher	Jaime Escalante
basketball player	Michael Jordan
city	Los Angeles
country	Morocco
continent	Asia
monument	Lincoln Memorial
team	Detroit Tigers
book	*Barrio Boy*
holiday	Chinese New Year
religion	Islam
language	Swahili

Notice that each noun listed above names a person, a place, a thing, or an idea.

REFERENCE NOTE: For more about capitalizing proper nouns, see pages 565–573.

GRAMMAR

AT-RISK STUDENTS

You may wish to use chapter activities in a variety of tutoring situations. Strategies may include cross-age tutoring, peer tutoring, adopt-a-student programs, teacher tutoring, and community volunteers.

Because expectations and student success are directly related, tutors should establish specific timelines and goals for student performance. Clear, prompt feedback along with measurable, valid criteria for evaluation will help build trust and mutual respect and will boost students' self-esteem.

LEP/ESL

Spanish. In Spanish, some proper nouns receive different treatment than they do in English. For example, when discussing a person who is not present, a Spanish speaker will insert the definite article before the person's title. For example "Dr. Hernandez is old" translates as "El doctor Hernandez es viejo." Notice also that titles such as *doctor* (Dr.), *señor* (Mr.), *señora* (Mrs.), and *general* (General) are not capitalized in Spanish preceding a person's name. Therefore, Spanish-speaking students may generate sentences such as "I saw the general Powell on television" instead of "I saw General Powell on television." You may want to emphasize to Spanish-speaking students that the article is omitted in English and that the title is capitalized.

GRAMMAR

COMMON ERROR

Problem. Many students will identify a verb or an adjective as a noun. For example, they might say that *speak* is a noun, since it names a thing that can be done.

Solution. To help students who have difficulty distinguishing nouns, tell them that a word that names a person, place, thing, or idea (unless it is a proper name) can usually be used with *a, an,* or *the.*

Show them that *a speak* doesn't make sense, but that *a conversation* or *a speech* does make sense.

GRAMMAR

VISUAL CONNECTIONS

Ideas for Writing. You may wish to use this photograph as a springboard for having students write and present reports about well-known festivals, perhaps in conjunction with **Chapter 9: "Writing a Report."** After all reports have been presented, have the class discuss which reports were the most interesting and why.

A DIFFERENT APPROACH

Have students bring in newspaper articles or allow them to select articles from newspapers you have in the classroom. Have students make lists of the common and proper nouns in their articles.

Then ask volunteers to display their articles on an overhead projector and have the class find the common and proper nouns. Have the article's owner underline the nouns as they are identified.

GRAMMAR

EXERCISE 2 Identifying Common and Proper Nouns

Identify each of the nouns in the following sentences as *common* or *proper*.

EXAMPLE **1.** The people in Japan celebrate many holidays.
1. *people—common; Japan—proper; holidays—common*

1. This picture is of the Snow Festival in Sapporo.
2. Many groups work together to build these giant sculptures.
3. Do you recognize any of the statues or buildings?
4. Is that the Statue of Liberty made out of snow?

5. In the city of Kyoto each June, you can see a parade of spears.
6. A popular fair in Tokyo offers pickled radishes.
7. Villages are colorfully decorated for the Feast of the Lanterns.
8. Toshiro said his town enjoys the Star Festival in the summer.
9. Several flowers, among them the iris and the lily, have their own special days.
10. The birthday of Buddha is observed in April.

EXERCISE 3 Substituting Proper Nouns for Common Nouns

In the following sentences, substitute a proper noun for each italicized common noun. You may need to change some other words in each sentence. You may also make up proper names to use.

EXAMPLE **1.** The *principal* awarded the *student* the prize.
1. *Ms. Chen awarded Paula Perez the prize.*

1. The *student* is from a *city*.
2. Usually, my *uncle* looks through the *newspaper* after dinner.
3. The *child* watched a *movie*.
4. A *teacher* asked a *student* to tell the class about growing up in Mexico.
5. My *cousin* read that *book*.
6. Surrounded by reporters, the *mayor* stood outside the *building*.
7. Does the *girl* go to this *school*?
8. That *singer* wrote the *song*.
9. My *neighbor* bought a *car*.
10. When he was a college student, the *coach* played for that *team*.

EXERCISE 4 Using Proper Nouns

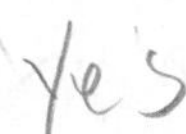

Developers are planning to build a new shopping mall in your neighborhood. They are trying to find out what kinds of stores and other attractions the community would like at the mall. The developers have prepared the following survey. Answer each question with a complete sentence. Underline each proper noun that you use.

<u>New Mall Questionnaire</u>

1. What stores would you most like to see at the mall?
2. What would you be most likely to buy at the mall?

GRAMMAR

ANSWERS

Exercise 3

Responses will vary. Here are some possibilities:

1. Mary is from San Francisco.
2. Usually, Uncle Ned looks through the *New York Times* after dinner.
3. Mike watched *Batman*.
4. Ms. Miller asked Marcos to tell the class about growing up in Mexico.
5. Sarah read *Island of the Blue Dolphins*.
6. Surrounded by reporters, Mayor Brown stood outside City Hall.
7. Does Rosie go to Central High?
8. Michael Jackson wrote "Billie Jean."
9. Mr. Berkowitz bought a Buick.
10. When he was a college student, Coach Johnson played for the Pirates.

ANSWERS

Exercise 4

Responses will vary, but each response should be a complete sentence and all proper nouns should be underlined.

GRAMMAR

REVIEW A

OBJECTIVE

- To identify nouns and to classify them as common or proper

INTEGRATING THE LANGUAGE ARTS

Literature Link. Have students read and discuss John Gardner's "Dragon, Dragon" or another folk tale that uses common nouns rather than proper nouns for its characters. Ask students to consider why the author used common nouns rather than proper nouns for the characters in the story. [Students may say that there were so many characters in the story that it is easier to remember them with descriptive common nouns than with proper nouns.]

COOPERATIVE LEARNING

To give students practice in naming proper nouns, use a team race combined with a social studies topic that students are studying. Divide the class into groups of four. Give each group a category and have the groups write as many proper nouns as possible in two minutes. Award a point for each correct proper noun. For example, you might ask students to list the proper names of states in the United States. Other possible categories are continents, oceans, rivers, countries, capital cities, presidents, battles, and so on.

VISUAL CONNECTIONS

Ideas for Writing. Discuss with students the feelings that soldiers might have during a military conflict and how soldiers might feel about meeting a general. Then ask each student to pretend that he or she is one of the soldiers pictured in the photo and to write a diary entry that a soldier might have written that day.

3. What types of movies would you like to see at the mall theater?
4. What restaurants would you like to have in the mall's Food Court?
5. Would you go to a mall arcade? If so, what games would you play?

REVIEW A **Identifying and Classifying Nouns**

Identify each of the twenty-five nouns in the following sentences as common or proper.

HW! Write out 1-10

EXAMPLE 1. President George Bush gave General Colin Powell a big job.
1. *President George Bush—proper; General Colin Powell—proper; job—common*

1. He appointed Powell to lead the Joint Chiefs of Staff.
2. Powell became one of the top military officers in the United States.
3. Here he's shown talking with soldiers during the Persian Gulf Conflict.
4. Do you think the troops were excited to meet the general?
5. Powell grew up in the Bronx, a neighborhood of New York City.

SEGMENT 3 *(pp. 373–380)*

THE PRONOUN Rule 13b

OBJECTIVES

- To identify pronouns in sentences
- To describe a cartoon scene by writing sentences with pronouns and identifying the pronouns' antecedents
- To rewrite sentences, replacing nouns with pronouns

6. His parents came to the United States from Jamaica.
7. Powell graduated from the City College of New York.
8. It was there he joined the Reserve Officers Training Corps.
9. Did you know that Powell was awarded the Purple Heart during the Vietnam War?
10. In his speeches, he encourages students to graduate from high school.

The Pronoun

13b. A ***pronoun*** is a word used in place of one noun or more than one noun.

In each of the following examples, an arrow is drawn from a pronoun to the noun or nouns it stands for.

EXAMPLES When Cindy Davis came to the bus stop, **she** was wearing a cast.

The trees and bushes are dry; **they** should be watered.

This stable is large. **It** has stalls for thirty horses.

The word that a pronoun stands for is called its ***antecedent.***

EXAMPLES My **aunt** sold **her** car. (antecedent: aunt; pronoun: her)

Anthony, call **your** mother. (antecedent: Anthony; pronoun: your)

Sometimes the antecedent is not stated.

EXAMPLES Call **your** mother. (pronoun: your)

Has **it** been raining? (pronoun: it)

Teacher's ResourceBank™

RESOURCES

THE PRONOUN

QUICK REMINDER

Write the following sentences on the chalkboard. Ask students to name the pronoun in each sentence and to identify each antecedent.

1. Tom gave Maria his book. [*His* refers to *Tom.*]
2. Ron, your teacher called today. [*Your* refers to *Ron.*]
3. These are the pages Mrs. Brown assigned. [*These* refers to *pages.*]
4. The boys sat by themselves at the game. [*Themselves* refers to *boys.*]
5. The apartment was small. It had only one bedroom. [*It* refers to *apartment.*]

LESS-ADVANCED STUDENTS

Because the numerous types of pronouns may be confusing to some students, you may not want to stress the various types of pronouns at this time. Stress instead the general recognition of pronouns.

To give practice in pronoun use, ask students to create sentences by using pronouns based on something in their school, as in "Mac is wearing his red shirt," or "Our class sits by itself at lunchtime." Have students identify the pronoun and its antecedent in each sentence.

In addition, you could have students create charts with examples of different types of pronouns.

LEARNING STYLES

Kinetic Learners. Some students who have difficulty recognizing pronouns on the printed page may understand them more easily with a kinetic approach. Have students work at the chalkboard as you dictate sentences with pronouns. Ask students to circle the pronouns and to draw arrows to the pronouns' antecedents. This activity may aid students' understanding of the relationship between the two parts of speech.

Personal Pronouns

A ***personal pronoun*** refers to the one speaking (*first person*), the one spoken to (*second person*), or the one spoken about (*third person*). Personal pronouns have singular and plural forms.

PERSONAL PRONOUNS		
	SINGULAR	PLURAL
First person	I, me, my, mine	we, us, our, ours
Second person	you, your, yours	you, your, yours
Third person	he, him, his, she, her, hers, it, its	they, them, their, theirs

NOTE: Some teachers prefer to call possessive forms of pronouns (such as *my, your,* and *our*) adjectives. Follow your teacher's instructions regarding possessive forms.

Reflexive Pronouns

A ***reflexive pronoun*** refers to the subject and directs the action of the verb back to the subject.

REFLEXIVE PRONOUNS	
First person	myself, ourselves
Second person	yourself, yourselves
Third person	himself, herself, itself, themselves

EXAMPLES We enjoyed **ourselves** at the party.
She prides **herself** on speaking Spanish well.

EXERCISE 5 Identifying Pronouns

Identify all of the pronouns in each of the following sentences.

EXAMPLE **1. I lent her my camera.**
1. *I, her, my*

1. The dentist washed her hands before examining my teeth.
2. Dad told the mechanics to call him about his bill.
3. Our aunt and uncle have decided that they will visit Guatemala.
4. I asked myself where I could have put my book.
5. He washed the mats and put them in the sun to dry.
6. Here is a postcard from Egypt for you and me.
7. We helped ourselves to tacos and refried beans.
8. You gave us your support when we needed it.
9. He did his math homework before playing soccer with us.
10. I found the weak battery and replaced it.

EXERCISE 6 Using Pronouns

What a mess! Dolly told Jeffy to say *when*. But she didn't say *when* to say *when*! Write five sentences describing this scene. You can write what has happened or what you think will happen next. In each sentence, use a pronoun. Try to use a variety of pronouns in your sentences. Draw an arrow from the pronoun to its antecedent.

EXAMPLE **1.** *Jeffy wanted some juice, but he didn't say how much.*

GRAMMAR

INTEGRATING THE LANGUAGE ARTS

Grammar and Listening. Choose an excerpt from a novel or a pronoun exercise from a resource textbook; then have students list the pronouns and add their antecedents as you read the sentences slowly.

VISUAL CONNECTIONS

Ideas for Writing. Ask students to bring to class favorite cartoons or comic strips, or provide newspapers from which students can make selections. Have each student display a cartoon on an overhead projector and have other students suggest sentences that contain pronouns to describe each cartoon or to tell what they think might happen next. Encourage students to use a wide variety of pronouns in their sentences.

ANSWERS

Exercise 6

Responses will vary, but each should include five sentences describing the scene or telling what may happen next. Each sentence should contain a pronoun with an arrow drawn from it to its antecedent as the example shows.

COOPERATIVE LEARNING

Divide the class into groups of four and give each group an awkwardly written paragraph such as the following example:

The boys were excited about the boys' first day at camp. The boys got lost and wandered around the huge lake. The boys asked a fisherman to help the boys find the boys' way back to the main building.

Ask groups to revise their paragraphs by replacing the repeated nouns with the appropriate personal pronouns.

GRAMMAR

GRAMMAR

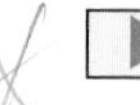

EXERCISE 7 **Substituting Pronouns for Nouns**

In each of the following sentences, replace the repeated nouns with pronouns.

EXAMPLE **1. Viviana set up Viviana's game on the table.**
1. *Viviana set up her game on the table.*

1. The passengers waved to ~~the passengers'~~ friends on shore. **1. their**
2. The test was so long that I almost didn't finish ~~the test.~~ **2. it.**
3. Rachel's neighbors asked ~~Rachel~~ to baby-sit. **3. her**
4. Carlos said that ~~Carlos~~ had already cleaned ~~Carlos's~~ room. **4. he/his**
5. The directions were long, but ~~the directions~~ were clear. **5. they**

Possessive Pronouns

Possessive pronouns are personal pronouns that are used to show ownership. Like personal pronouns, possessive pronouns have singular and plural forms.

POSSESSIVE PRONOUNS		
	SINGULAR	PLURAL
First person	my, mine	our, ours
Second person	your, yours	your, yours
Third person	her, hers, his, its	their, theirs

EXAMPLES Nina stored **her** suitcase under **her** bed.
Is that paper **yours** or **mine**?

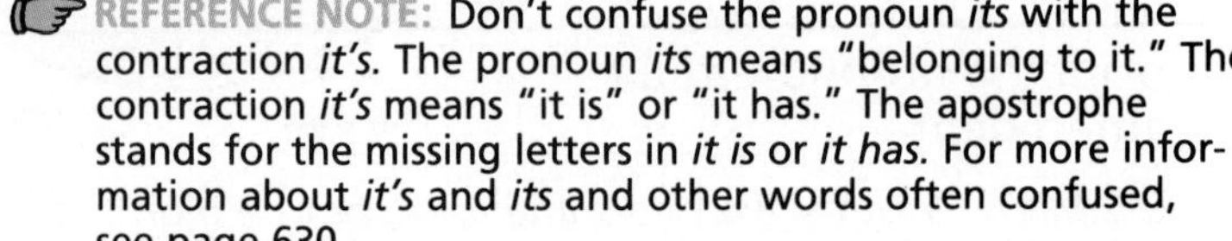

REFERENCE NOTE: Don't confuse the pronoun *its* with the contraction *it's*. The pronoun *its* means "belonging to it." The contraction *it's* means "it is" or "it has." The apostrophe stands for the missing letters in *it is* or *it has*. For more information about *it's* and *its* and other words often confused, see page 630.

Demonstrative Pronouns

A ***demonstrative pronoun*** points out a specific person, place, thing, or idea.

Demonstrative Pronouns			
this	that	these	those

EXAMPLES What is **that**?
This is the uniform once worn by Satchel Paige.
These are the shoes he used to wear.

NOTE: Demonstrative pronouns can also be used as adjectives. When these words tell *which one(s)* about a noun, they are called *demonstrative adjectives.*

PRONOUN **This** is a delicious papaya.
ADJECTIVE **This** papaya is delicious.

REFERENCE NOTE: For more about demonstrative adjectives, see pages 384–385.

Indefinite Pronouns

An ***indefinite pronoun*** does not refer to a definite person, place, thing, or idea.

Common Indefinite Pronouns			
all	each	more	one
any	either	much	other
anybody	everybody	neither	several
anyone	everyone	nobody	some
anything	few	none	somebody
both	many	no one	something

EXAMPLES **Everyone** in the class was invited to the party.
None of the boys knew **much** about camping.

GRAMMAR

COMMON ERROR

Problem. Many students have trouble using the indefinite pronouns *some, any, none, all,* and *most* correctly and often put singular verbs with plural pronouns and vice versa.

Solution. Remind students that these particular pronouns may be singular or plural, depending on the objects of the prepositional phrases that usually follow these pronouns. For example, *none* is singular in the sentence "None of the lemonade has been sweetened," because *lemonade,* the object of the prepositional phrase, is singular. *None* is plural in the sentence "None of the bananas are ripe," because *bananas,* the object of the prepositional phrase, is plural.

REVIEW B

OBJECTIVE

- To identify pronouns in sentences

INTEGRATING THE LANGUAGE ARTS

Literature Link. Have students read and discuss a poem, such as Carl Sandburg's "They Have Yarns," that uses different types of pronouns. Have students identify the pronouns and their antecedents.

Ask students why many poets use pronouns rather than nouns in their poems. [Students may say that pronouns give a universal tone to a poem, thus making it apply to more people; nouns would make the poem more specific.]

Grammar and Writing. After students read and discuss a poem that uses different types of pronouns, have students write poems that contain different types of pronouns. Tell students that the poems may be funny or serious.

After you have collected and read the poems, choose the ones you think are most appropriate and read them to the class. Then display the poems individually on an overhead projector and have the class identify the pronouns and their antecedents.

Students could display their poems in the classroom or in the hall.

GRAMMAR

GRAMMAR

EXERCISE 8 **Identifying Pronouns**

Identify the pronoun or pronouns in each of the following sentences.

EXAMPLE 1. Their car is newer than ours.
1. *Their, ours*

1. Is your puppy losing its baby teeth?
2. This jacket is mine; that one must be yours.
3. Something is different about your hair.
4. Carlota reminded herself to send Luís a card.
5. This is good, but her report is better.
6. Your locker is next to hers.
7. The videotapes on the TV are theirs.
8. They treated themselves to a bucket of popcorn.
9. My sister made her own dress for the Cinco de Mayo celebration.
10. Everyone knows the answer to that.

REVIEW B **Identifying Pronouns**

Identify the pronoun or pronouns in each of the following sentences.

EXAMPLE 1. Everyone in my class likes going on field trips.
1. *Everyone; my*

1. Last week, we really enjoyed ourselves at the National Museum of African Art.
2. It has been part of the Smithsonian Institution in Washington, D.C., since 1979.
3. In 1987, the museum's collection was moved to its present underground facility.
4. Our teacher, Ms. Martínez, told us about the museum before we went there.
5. She said the entrance is made of pink granite.
6. I was surprised by the six domes on top.
7. Everyone had at least one question to ask our museum guide.
8. We enjoyed hearing her lively explanations of the artwork.

WRITING APPLICATION

OBJECTIVE

- To write the plot for a short movie script by using pronouns that clearly refer to their antecedents

9. This is a photograph of one of my favorite objects at the museum.
10. What is your opinion of it?

Mask, Bassa Peoples, Liberia. Wood, pigment, bone or ivory, iron. H. 9½" W. 5¾" D. 4½". National Museum of African Art, 95-5-1. Photograph by Jeffrey Ploskonka.

GRAMMAR

WRITING APPLICATION

Using Pronouns Clearly

Pronouns are some of the handiest words in English. Sometimes, though, personal pronouns can be confusing. To avoid confusion, make sure each pronoun you use refers clearly to its antecedent.

CONFUSING The monster snarled at Reggie as he stepped forward. [Who stepped forward, the monster or Reggie?]

CLEAR As the **monster** stepped forward, **he** snarled at Reggie.

or

CLEAR As **Reggie** stepped forward, the monster snarled at **him**.

GRAMMAR

WRITING APPLICATION

The assignment offers a chance for students to use their imaginations, their senses of humor, and their organizational skills as well as correct pronoun usage.

CRITICAL THINKING

Synthesis

As students write their first drafts, they will be working on plots, character descriptions, costumes, and props. Because of the sophisticated level of thinking and organizational skills in this task, you might encourage students not to be concerned with punctuation or spelling errors at this stage.

GRAMMAR

PREWRITING

Because the idea of writing a spoof may be new to many students, you may want to have students work in groups to brainstorm ideas before they begin working individually.

PROOFREADING AND PUBLISHING

After students have finished their first revisions, have them trade scripts with partners to see if additional work is needed to improve their scripts. The partners should check for spelling, grammar, and punctuation errors and should also make sure that pronouns clearly refer to their antecedents. Have the authors proofread their work a final time.

For the publishing stage, you may want to ask for volunteers to present their movie scripts to the class.

GRAMMAR

WRITING ACTIVITY

Your cousin is taking a filmmaking class at the community center and needs ideas for a project. The theme of the project is "Science Fiction Movie Spoofs." Help your cousin out by writing down an idea for a short movie script. Explain the plot of the movie and describe the characters. Be sure that the pronouns you use refer clearly to their antecedents.

Prewriting In a *spoof,* a writer imitates and makes fun of another work. Imagine several science fiction movie spoofs—for example, *There's an Alien in My Soup* or *Nerds from Neptune*. Choose the idea that you like the best. Then brainstorm some ideas for a simple plot. (For more about developing plots, see pages 153–154.) Jot down brief descriptions of the setting and the characters in the movie.

Writing Use your notes to help you write your first draft. Explain what happens in the movie from beginning to end. Describe each character as you introduce him or her. Keep the props and costumes simple—your cousin is working on a low budget.

Evaluating and Revising Ask a friend to read your movie idea. Is the plot interesting? Is it funny? Can your friend tell which character is performing each action? If not, you may need to revise some details. As you revise, you may think of more suggestions for the script. Add any details that you think will make the movie better or more humorous.

Proofreading Read your script one more time to catch other errors in spelling, grammar, and punctuation. Check to make sure each pronoun refers clearly to its antecedent. Also be sure you've used the pronoun *its* and the contraction *it's* correctly.

SEGMENT 4 *(pp. 381–388)*

THE ADJECTIVE Rule 13c

OBJECTIVES

- To identify adjectives and the words they modify in sentences
- To complete a story by adding appropriate adjectives
- To identify common and proper adjectives in sentences 

13c

GRAMMAR

The Adjective

13c. An ***adjective*** is a word that modifies a noun or a pronoun.

To *modify* a word means to describe the word or to make its meaning more definite. An adjective modifies a noun or pronoun by telling *what kind, which one, how many,* or *how much.*

WHAT KIND?	WHICH ONE OR ONES?	HOW MANY OR HOW MUCH?
gentle dog	**sixth** grade	**two** tickets
foggy day	**these** books	**full** pitcher
scary movie	**other** people	**most** players
purple shoes	**any** CD	**no** work

Adjectives usually come before the words they modify. Sometimes, however, an adjective comes after the word it modifies.

EXAMPLES The dog is **gentle.** [The adjective *gentle* modifies *dog.*]
The tent, **warm** and **dry,** was under the tree. [The adjectives *warm* and *dry* modify *tent.*]

NOTE: The adjectives *a, an,* and *the* are called ***articles.***

EXERCISE 9 **Identifying Adjectives**

Identify the adjective or adjectives in each of the following sentences. Do not include *a, an,* or *the.*

EXAMPLE 1. The sky was clear, and the night was cold.
1. *clear, cold*

1. A silvery moon rode down the western sky.
2. It shed a pale light on the quiet countryside.
3. Long meadows spread out between two hills.

Teacher's ResourceBank™

RESOURCES

THE ADJECTIVE

- The Adjective 117
- Proper, Common, and Demonstrative Adjectives 118

GRAMMAR

QUICK REMINDER

To teach students that adjectives are words that modify nouns or pronouns, write the following list of nouns on the chalkboard and ask students to add words that describe the nouns more specifically:

1. animal [small, large, furry]
2. building [tall, gray, cement]
3. car [new, old, shiny, red]
4. water [warm, cold, deep, shallow]

Point out that *animal* alone could refer to any animal—an elephant, a horse, a mouse—but that adding a descriptive word such as *small* makes the noun more specific.

STUDENTS WITH SPECIAL NEEDS

Help students with learning disabilities to make abstract concepts more concrete. One method is to have students illustrate adjectives. For example, the word *tall* could be written with long, narrow letters. This method will also benefit visual learners.

- To change proper nouns into proper adjectives and to use the adjectives in sentences
- To use adjectives that appeal to the senses to write a first-person description of an event

EXERCISE 9

Teaching Note. Students might identify *my* in the ninth sentence as an adjective. See the **Note** on p. 374.

LEP/ESL

Spanish. In Spanish, an adjective is placed after the noun it modifies. The phrase *the beautiful woman,* for example, is expressed as *la mujer bonita.* Another possible interference from the native language may occur when the adjective modifies a plural noun. In Spanish, adjectives change their form in both number and gender to agree with the noun. For example, *the beautiful women* is expressed as *las mujeres bonitas.* Therefore, in regard to your Spanish-speaking students, you may want to reinforce the correct positioning of adjectives in English and to point out that the adjective form remains the same even when it modifies a plural noun.

GRAMMAR

GRAMMAR

4. The smell of the wild grass was strong.
5. The only sound we heard was the sharp crackle of the fire.
6. Suddenly, several stars came out.
7. I watched until the entire sky was glowing with bright stars.
8. I was lonely and happy at the same time.
9. I finally became sleepy and longed for my comfortable bed.
10. Soon I went indoors and fell into a deep sleep.

EXERCISE 10 **Identifying Adjectives and the Words They Modify**

Identify the adjectives and the words they modify in the following sentences. Do not include *a, an,* or *the*.

EXAMPLE **1.** It costs five dollars to go to that movie.
1. *five—dollars; that—movie*

1. I have a free ticket for the last game.
2. In New Orleans we ate spicy crawfish, and they were delicious.
3. The new neighbor is helpful and nice.
4. The bear, angry and hungry, surprised the campers.
5. Many students compete in the regional Special Olympics.

EXERCISE 11 **Writing Adjectives for a Story**

The following story is about a cave exploration. Complete the story by adding an appropriate adjective for each blank. Underline the adjectives.

Adjectives will vary.

EXAMPLE Exploring caves is [1] ____ on [2] ____ days.
Exploring caves is fun on hot days.

1. real
2. dark
3. scary

Have you ever been in a [1] ____ cave like the one shown on the next page? Would you say it looks [2] ____ and [3] ____? My father and I explored this

[4] ___ cave once. It was [5] ___ but [6] ___, too. We found some [7] ___ rock formations. We also heard [8] ___ sounds. We looked up, and [9] ___ bats flew above our heads. After exploring for about [10] ___ hours, we were ready to see the sky again.

4. huge 5. frightening 6. fun 7. strange 8. weird 9. ten 10. two

GRAMMAR

Proper Adjectives

A ***proper adjective*** is formed from a proper noun and begins with a capital letter.

PROPER NOUNS	PROPER ADJECTIVES
Japan	**Japanese** islands
Christianity	**Christian** beliefs
Maya	**Mayan** art

REFERENCE NOTE: For more about capitalizing proper adjectives, see page 576.

EXERCISE 12 **Finding Common and Proper Adjectives**

Identify all of the adjectives in the following sentences. Then label each adjective as <u>common</u> or <u>proper</u>. Do not include *a, an,* or *the.*

COMMON ERROR

Problem. Many students fail to recognize adjectives that are used to modify pronouns.

Solution. Write the following pair of sentences on the chalkboard:

The girls exercise. They are healthy.

Point out that *healthy* modifies *They* and explain that an adjective in the predicate that modifies the subject is called a predicate adjective.

COOPERATIVE LEARNING

This activity reinforces the concept that adjectives modify nouns or pronouns by telling *what kind, which one, how many,* or *how much.* Divide the class into groups of four. Ask each group to write four sentences with adjectives— one for each of the above categories. When the groups are finished, have each group member write a sentence from each of the categories on the chalkboard. Then have other students identify in which category each sentence belongs.

GRAMMAR

EXERCISE 12

Teaching Note. Students might identify *our* in the eighth sentence as a common adjective.

LESS-ADVANCED STUDENTS

Some students may need help in naming and spelling proper nouns. Have the class suggest proper nouns for each category in **Exercise 13.** List these nouns on the chalkboard before students begin the exercise.

ANSWERS

Exercise 13

Responses will vary. Here are some possibilities:

1. Mexico — Mexican
   Mexican blankets are attractive.
2. India — Indian
   Indian cotton is used to make shirts.
3. Ireland — Irish
   The Irish countryside is beautiful.
4. Paris — Parisian
   We loved the Parisian cafes.
5. Brazil — Brazilian
   David Byrne admires Brazilian music.
6. Hawaii — Hawaiian
   We enjoyed the Hawaiian luau.
7. Asia — Asian
   Asian art often emphasizes nature.
8. Africa — African
   Have you seen an African elephant?
9. Rome — Roman
   We studied Roman mythology.
10. Spain — Spanish
    The cafeteria serves Spanish rice.

GRAMMAR

EXAMPLE 1. The Navajo weaver made a blanket on a wooden loom.
1. *Navajo—proper; wooden—common*

1. Music can express sad or happy feelings.
2. The quartet sang several Irish songs.
3. The gold watch with the fancy chain was made by a Swiss watchmaker.
4. She is a fine Balinese dancer.
5. On vacation, Mom enjoys long, quiet breakfasts.
6. Many Australian people are of British origin.
7. The Egyptian mummies are on display on the first floor.
8. We are proud of our heritage.
9. The movie is based on a popular Russian novel.
10. In Canadian football, a team is made up of twelve players.

EXERCISE 13 Changing Proper Nouns into Proper Adjectives

Think of ten proper nouns. Change each proper noun into a proper adjective. Then use each proper adjective in a sentence. Here are some *types* of proper nouns that you might use. [Note: Some proper nouns, such as *Hopi* and *New England*, do not change spelling when they are used as proper adjectives.]

countries	cities
states	neighborhood names
regions	people's first or last names

EXAMPLES 1. *France—French*
We bought French bread at the bakery.
2. *Jones—Jonesian*
My dad says I have a Jonesian nose like his.

Demonstrative Adjectives

This, that, these, and *those* can be used both as adjectives and as pronouns. When they modify a noun, they are called ***demonstrative adjectives.*** When they are used alone, they are called *demonstrative pronouns.*

ADJECTIVE What are **these** skates doing in the living room?
PRONOUN What are **these** doing in the living room?

ADJECTIVE I prefer **that** brand of frozen yogurt.
PRONOUN I prefer **that.**

REFERENCE NOTE: For more information about demonstrative pronouns, see page 377.

GRAMMAR

PICTURE THIS

Yesterday, you won first prize in a kayaking race. A photographer from a sports magazine was able to capture the most incredible moment of the race on film. Now the editor of the magazine would like you to describe how you felt during this daring plunge down a waterfall. Write a description of this exciting moment for the magazine. In your description, use words that will help your readers see, hear, and feel what you experienced. Include at least five adjectives that appeal to the senses.

Subject: kayaking down a waterfall
Audience: readers of a sports magazine
Purpose: to describe your experience

GRAMMAR

PICTURE THIS

As a prewriting activity, you may wish to discuss what *appeal to the senses* means. Have students name the five senses and discuss how each of the senses could be involved in kayaking down a waterfall.

INTEGRATING THE LANGUAGE ARTS

Technology Link. Many software programs have thesaurus features on them. If you have the appropriate software for this computer-assisted instruction, encourage students to use the thesaurus to find synonyms for adjectives that may be bland or overused. Remind students to double-check word meanings in a dictionary to be sure they are using words with the correct connotations.

REVIEWS C–E

OBJECTIVES

- To identify adjectives in sentences
- To identify nouns, pronouns, and adjectives in sentences

INTEGRATING THE LANGUAGE ARTS

Grammar and Vocabulary. Tell students that well-chosen adjectives can make their writing more interesting. Write the following sentences on the chalkboard. Have students replace the underscored adjectives with vivid, descriptive adjectives without changing the meanings of the sentences.

1. The cold wind made us shiver.
2. Our neighbor has a cute kitten.
3. We all think he is such a nice person.
4. It's a pretty night.
5. She is a good waitress.

A DIFFERENT APPROACH

Have students bring to class pictures from magazines or allow them to select pictures from magazines that you provide. Ask each student to write a paragraph describing one of the pictures and to include at least five adjectives in the paragraph.

Allow classtime for revision and proofreading. Then ask volunteers to read their paragraphs and to show their pictures. You may wish to display the pictures and paragraphs in the classroom or hall.

 REVIEW C **Identifying Adjectives**

Identify the adjectives in the following sentences. Do not include *a, an,* or *the.*

EXAMPLE **1.** I enjoy visiting the large railroad museum in our city.
1. *large, railroad*

1. Museums can be interesting.
2. Large cities have different kinds of museums.
3. Some museums display sculpture and paintings.
4. These museums may focus on one special kind of art.
5. For example, they might specialize in Chinese art or Mexican art.
6. Other museums feature birds, sea creatures, dinosaurs, and other animals.
7. A curator holds an important job in a museum.
8. A curator needs to know many facts about a particular display.
9. Some valuable objects must be displayed in a stable environment.
10. Some people prefer displays of modern art, while others enjoy exhibits of folk art.

REVIEW D **Identifying Nouns, Pronouns, and Adjectives**

Identify all of the nouns, pronouns, and adjectives in the following sentences. Do not include the articles *a, an,* and *the.*

EXAMPLE **1.** Models make a great hobby.
1. *Models—noun; great—adjective; hobby—noun*

1. Do you have a favorite hobby?
2. Models are enjoyable and educational.
3. They require little space.
4. I keep mine on my bookshelf my dad built in my room.

5. Models are packaged in kits.
6. My favorite models are historic ships and antique planes.
7. On my last birthday, my parents gave me two kits of biplanes.
8. They came with directions in several languages.
9. The tiny parts are designed for an exact fit.
10. Bright decals add a realistic look.

GRAMMAR

REVIEW E **Identifying Nouns, Pronouns, and Adjectives**

Identify all of the nouns, pronouns, and adjectives in each of the following sentences. Do not include *a, an,* or *the.*

EXAMPLE 1. Pueblos are practical housing for people in hot, dry regions.
1. *Pueblos—noun; practical—adjective; housing—noun; people—noun; hot—adjective; dry—adjective; regions—noun*

1. The simple building in this photograph contains several individual homes.
2. *Pueblo* is the Spanish name for both a structure like this and a town.

3. This building is located at the Taos Pueblo in New Mexico.
4. Can you tell how pueblos are made?

INTEGRATING THE LANGUAGE ARTS

Literature Link. Have students read and discuss a story such as "The Wise Old Woman" by Yoshiko Uchida, in which descriptive adjectives are used to create a mood or character. Then ask students what mood or type of character is created and which adjectives serve in that creation.

GRAMMAR

VISUAL CONNECTIONS

Ideas for Writing. You may wish to have students research and report on the types of housing and other patterns of living used by Native Americans in different parts of North America before European settlement of the continent. You may wish to use this activity in conjunction with **Chapter 28: "The Library/Media Center."** The project could be a cooperative activity in which group members work on specific parts of the project and each presents some aspect of the report to the class. Reports should connect the geographic location and climate to the types of housing, food, clothing, and customs of the different Native American groups.

SEGMENT 5 *(pp. 388–389)*

REVIEW: POSTTESTS 1 and 2

OBJECTIVES

- To identify nouns, pronouns, and adjectives in sentences
- To write sentences that contain nouns, pronouns, and adjectives

GRAMMAR

GRAMMAR

5. They are built of adobe.
6. People make adobe by mixing mud with grass or straw.
7. They shape the mixture into bricks and dry them in the sun.
8. Buildings made with this material stay cool during the summer months.
9. Anyone who visits the Southwest can find many pueblos similar to this one.
10. Old pueblos built by the Hopi and the Zuñi fascinate me.

Review: Posttest 1

Identifying Nouns, Pronouns, and Adjectives

Identify each italicized word in the following sentences as a *noun,* a *pronoun,* or an *adjective.*

EXAMPLE 1. Her older *brother* has an *important* test today.
1. *brother—noun; important—adjective*

1. The *Roman* emperors built a huge system of aqueducts, *some* of which are still standing.
2. Last summer we visited *Alaska,* which is our *largest* state.
3. Put *yourself* in *my* position.
4. The *Hawaiian* dancers wore *colorful* costumes.
5. The volcano, *inactive* for years, is a popular tourist *attraction.*
6. *Everyone* watched the sun set behind the *mountains.*
7. "*That* notebook is *mine,*" Angela said.
8. *They* made a touchdown just before the final *whistle.*
9. *Colombo* is the capital *city* of Sri Lanka.
10. The pen with the *blue* ink is *hers.*

Review: Posttest 2

Writing Sentences Using Nouns, Pronouns, and Adjectives

Write ten original sentences using the parts of speech given below. In each sentence, underline the word that is the listed part of speech.

EXAMPLE **1. an adjective that comes after the word it describes**
1. *Our guide was very helpful.*

1. a proper noun
2. a possessive pronoun
3. an adjective that tells *how many*
4. a reflexive pronoun
5. a proper adjective
6. a noun that names an idea
7. a third-person pronoun
8. a demonstrative adjective
9. an indefinite pronoun
10. an article

GRAMMAR

CRITICAL THINKING

Synthesis

Prepare index cards based on the list in **Review: Posttest 2.** You could also create other examples. For example, one card might say *a noun that names a place.* Divide the class into two teams and draw a tic-tac-toe form on the chalkboard. Each team in turn draws a card and has to create a sentence by using the part of speech as described on the card. Each correct sentence gives the team a chance to make its mark on the tic-tac-toe form. A winning game earns the team a point. When the stack has been completed, shuffle it and continue.

ANSWERS

Review: Posttest 2

Sentences will vary. Here are some possibilities:

1. The United States is a large nation.
2. It is my homeland.
3. My country has fifty states.
4. It prides itself on its Bill of Rights.
5. The American people are fortunate.
6. Freedom is unknown in some countries.
7. She quotes Jefferson frequently.
8. That student knows her history.
9. All the class respects her.
10. She's an interesting person.

GRAMMAR

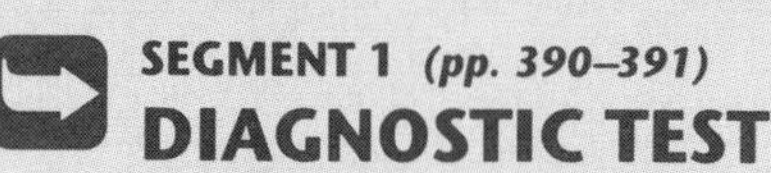

SEGMENT 1 *(pp. 390–391)*

DIAGNOSTIC TEST

OBJECTIVE

- To identify verbs, adverbs, prepositions, conjunctions, and interjections

Teacher's ResourceBank™

RESOURCES

FOR THE WHOLE CHAPTER

• Chapter Review Form A	137–138
• Chapter Review Form B	139–140
• Assessment Portfolio	
Grammar Pretests	447–454
Grammar Mastery Tests	471–478

GRAMMAR

CHAPTER OVERVIEW

This chapter should help students to recognize and understand the function of verbs, adverbs, prepositions, conjunctions, and interjections.

The material in this chapter can be referred to when teaching any of the composition chapters and will be of special help to students when they study **Chapter 12: "The Sentence."**

USING THE DIAGNOSTIC TEST

Use the **Diagnostic Test** to gauge students' familiarity with verbs, adverbs, prepositions, conjunctions, and interjections. Even students who use these parts of speech correctly in their writing may not be aware of the terminology. Therefore, you may wish to evaluate actual writing samples to distinguish students who use these five parts of speech correctly, without being aware of their terminology, from students who can neither identify these parts of speech nor use them correctly.

14 THE PARTS OF SPEECH

Verb, Adverb, Preposition, Conjunction, Interjection

Diagnostic Test

Identifying Verbs, Adverbs, Prepositions, Conjunctions, and Interjections

Identify each italicized word or word group in the following sentences as a *verb,* an *adverb,* a *preposition,* a *conjunction,* or an *interjection.*

EXAMPLE 1. We *visited* a great new water park *on* Saturday.
1. *visited—verb; on—preposition*

1. I *always* have fun *at* a water park. **1.** adv./prep.
2. You *should get* to the park *early* if you can. **2.** v./adv.
3. If you don't, the parking lot *may be* full, and the park itself *uncomfortably* crowded. **3.** v./adv.

SEGMENT 2 *(pp. 391–401)*

THE VERB Rule 14a

OBJECTIVES

- To identify action verbs
- To identify and use transitive and intransitive verbs
- To identify and use linking verbs
- To distinguish between action and linking verbs 

4. You can slide as fast as a bullet down the huge water slide. 4. v./prep.
5. Wow! What a truly exciting ride that is! 5. itj./adv.
6. People land in the water and splash everyone around them. 6. conj./prep. 7. v./adv.
7. Some parks rent inner tubes inexpensively. 8. v./prep.
8. You climb on one and whirl around in the water.
9. You may get tired, but you won't be bored. 9. v./conj.
10. People of all ages enjoy water parks. 10. prep./v.

GRAMMAR

The Verb

14a. A ***verb*** is a word that expresses an action or a state of being.

EXAMPLES We **went** to Boston last April.
Is a firefly a beetle?

Every sentence must have a verb. The verb says something about the subject.

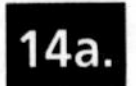 REFERENCE NOTE: For more information about subjects and verbs, see pages 342–357.

Action Verbs

(1) An ***action verb*** is a verb that expresses physical or mental action.

EXAMPLES I **use** a computer in math class.
Please **cook** dinner, Jerome.
Fran **understands** the science assignment.

 EXERCISE 1 **Identifying Action Verbs**

Identify each action verb in the following sentences.

Teacher's ResourceBank™

RESOURCES

THE VERB

• Action Verbs	127
• Transitive and Intransitive Verbs	128
• Linking Verbs	129
• Helping Verbs and Verb Phrases	130

QUICK REMINDER

To give students a review of action verbs, write the following words on the chalkboard:

bend	walk
clap	whisper
smile	wink
talk	yawn

Ask volunteers to perform the actions named by the verbs. You may want to write the words *think* and *remember* on the chalkboard and discuss with students how action can be mental or physical.

GRAMMAR

LEP/ESL

General Strategies. Depending upon the language backgrounds of your students, you may want to point out that the basic order of English sentences is Subject-Verb-Object. Languages such as Japanese and Korean follow a Subject-Object-Verb pattern, and Arabic follows a Verb-Subject-Object pattern. You may want to monitor students' work for this type of interference.

• To identify and use helping verbs and verb phrases

GRAMMAR

VISUAL CONNECTIONS

Exploring the Subject. The Maricopa were originally one of several American Indian groups of the Yuman people. They were primarily an agricultural people who planted along riverbanks. They are accomplished artisans whose pottery is made to be functional.

LESS-ADVANCED STUDENTS

You may want to omit for the moment the concepts of transitive and intransitive verbs. Students may grasp these concepts more easily in connection with **Chapter 16: "Complements."**

GRAMMAR

EXAMPLE [1] The Maricopa people live in Arizona.
1. *live*

[1] The Maricopa make unusual pottery. [2] For this pottery they need two kinds of clay. [3] One kind of clay forms the bowl or platter itself. [4] The other kind of clay colors the pottery. [5] First, the potters mold the clay by hand. [6] Then, they shape it into beautiful bowls and vases like the ones below. [7] With the second type of clay, they paint designs on the pottery. [8] In some cases they make designs with a toothpick. [9] Each family of potters has its own special designs. [10] These designs preserve Maricopa traditions from generation to generation.

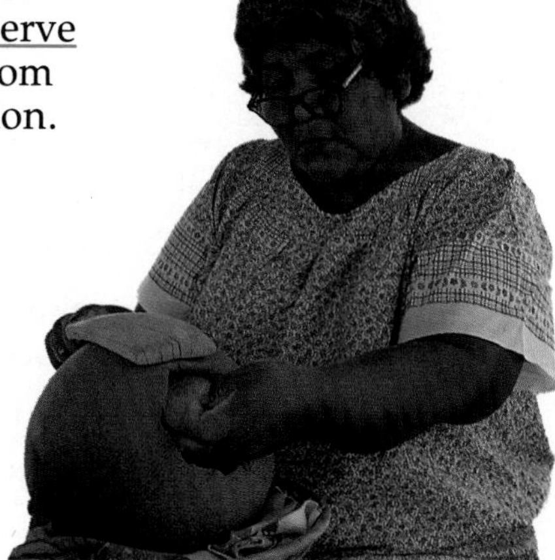

Transitive and Intransitive Verbs

A ***transitive verb*** is an action verb that expresses an action directed toward a person, place, or thing.

EXAMPLES Tamisha **entertained** the child. [The action of *entertained* is directed toward *child.*]
Felipe **visited** San Juan. [The action of *visited* is directed toward *San Juan.*]

Transitive verbs show an action that passes from the doer—the *subject*—to the receiver—the *object.*

REFERENCE NOTE: For more information about subjects and objects in sentences, see pages 342–345 and 438–442.

An ***intransitive verb*** does not pass action to a receiver or an object. It simply expresses an action or tells something about the subject.

EXAMPLES The children **smiled.**
The horses **galloped** across the prairie.

Some verbs may be either transitive or intransitive, depending on how they are used in a sentence.

EXAMPLES My cousin Julio **plays** baseball on a Caribbean League team. [transitive]
My cousin Julio **plays** every week. [intransitive]

Katchina **studies** Chinese each day after school. [transitive]
Katchina **studies** hard. [intransitive]

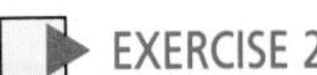

EXERCISE 2 Identifying Transitive and Intransitive Verbs

In each of the following sentences, identify the italicized action verb as transitive or intransitive.

EXAMPLE **1.** Computers *affect* our lives every day.
1. *transitive*

1. Computers *make* calculations incredibly fast.
2. They *perform* many tasks that people find boring and difficult.
3. Many businesses *benefit* from these machines.
4. Home computers *work* in similar ways.
5. They *do* word processing, a useful operation.
6. They also *run* programs for thousands of games.
7. Handy pocket computers *fit* easily into a wallet.
8. My mother *bought* a tiny computer no larger than a credit card.
9. The information in its memory *appears* on the screen at the touch of a button.
10. Addresses, phone numbers, notes, and other information on the screen *help* my mother with her work.

GRAMMAR

COOPERATIVE LEARNING

Have students work in groups of five or six to write paragraphs with sentences containing the following verbs:

arrive	move	stay
play	rise	turn
help	see	use

Have students try to provide a direct object for each of the verbs listed above. Then have students underline each verb for which they cannot provide a direct object. Have students label the underlined words as intransitive verbs.

A DIFFERENT APPROACH

Have each student write a paragraph describing a real or imaginary place he or she would like to visit. Have students use transitive and intransitive verbs and tell them to underline and identify all the verbs as transitive or intransitive.

ANSWERS

Exercise 3

Sentences will vary. The sentences should be based on the picture. Five sentences should contain transitive verbs and five should contain intransitive verbs.

GRAMMAR

LESS-ADVANCED STUDENTS

Students may have difficulty understanding the vocabulary of **Rule 14a** and the definitions of *action verb* and *linking verb.* Provide the following alternative definitions:

1. *verb* — a word that names an action or tells what someone or something is doing
2. *action verb* — a verb that names an action, even if the action can't be seen (such as *thinking*)
3. *linking verb* — a verb that connects the subject to a word telling what someone or something is or is like

ADVANCED STUDENTS

To give further practice in identifying action and linking verbs, have students choose five verbs from the **Other Linking Verbs** chart to use first as action verbs and then as linking verbs.

GRAMMAR

 EXERCISE 3 **Writing Sentences with Transitive and Intransitive Verbs**

It's a busy day on the playground! Some children are playing ball and jumping rope. Others are enjoying hand-held computer games and checkers. Write ten sentences describing these children and their activities. In your sentences, include five of the following verbs. Use each one as a transitive verb and an intransitive verb. Be prepared to identify each verb as transitive or intransitive.

play	stop	win	jump
climb	throw	move	lose
practice	begin	learn	tell

EXAMPLE *1. Some boys and girls play different kinds of ballgames.*
2. They play every day.

Linking Verbs

(2) A ***linking verb*** is a verb that expresses a state of being. A linking verb connects the subject of a sentence with a word in the predicate that explains or describes the subject.

Not all verbs express mental or physical action. Some verbs help make a statement by linking the subject of a sentence with a word in the predicate.

EXAMPLES Sandra Cisneros **is** a writer. [The verb *is* connects *writer* with the subject *Sandra Cisneros.*]
The firefighters **appeared** victorious. [The verb *appeared* connects *victorious* with the subject *firefighters.*]

Linking Verbs Formed From The Verb *Be*

am	has been	may be
is	have been	might be
are	had been	can be
was	will be	should be
were	shall be	would have been

Other Linking Verbs

appear	grow	seem	stay
become	look	smell	taste
feel	remain	sound	turn

Some verbs may be either action verbs or linking verbs, depending on how they are used.

ACTION They **sounded** the bell for a fire drill.
LINKING Mom **sounded** happy about her new job. [The verb *sounded* links *happy* with the subject *Mom.*]

ACTION The judge **looked** at my science project.
LINKING Sally Ann **looked** beautiful in her ballerina costume. [The verb *looked* links *beautiful* with the subject *Sally Ann.*]

EXERCISE 4 **Identifying Linking Verbs**

List the ten linking verbs in the following sentences.

GRAMMAR

INTEGRATING THE LANGUAGE ARTS

Writing Link. For students who understand action and linking verbs, you may want to assign independent writing for further practice. Have each student write one paragraph describing someone's personality. Students can consider happiness, sense of humor, friendliness, moodiness, and other traits. Have each student use and underline at least five different linking verbs.

GRAMMAR

ADVANCED STUDENTS

Collect several action pictures from newspapers or magazines. Pass the pictures around the room and ask students to think of a verb suggested by each picture. Then write several of their suggestions on the chalkboard. Discuss whether or not each verb could be used in a sentence about the picture. Discuss which ones most accurately tell about the action in the pictures.

INTEGRATING THE LANGUAGE ARTS

Literature Link. So that students can understand the power of verbs and have a humorous look at using computers, have them read "Think Tank" by Eve Merriam, if it is available in your library. This poem is a string of commands for the computer to obey. Students, especially those who work with computers, will enjoy studying the poem for the different types of verbs used in addressing the computer: commands, polite requests, even impassioned pleas.

GRAMMAR

GRAMMAR

EXAMPLE **1. Peanut soup, a favorite in Guiana, tastes good.**
1. *tastes*

1. Peanuts remain an important crop in many parts of the world.
2. A high-protein food, the peanut is native to South America.
3. Peanuts grow ripe underground.
4. The seeds are the edible part of the plant.
5. Thanks to George Washington Carver, the peanut became one of the major crops of the South.
6. Carver, a scientist who experimented with peanuts and other plants, had been a slave.
7. It may seem strange, but Carver once prepared an entire dinner out of peanuts.
8. The peanut has become an ingredient in over three hundred different products, including wood stains, shampoo, printer's ink, and soap.
9. Of course, roasting peanuts smell wonderful.
10. Peanut butter was the invention of a St. Louis doctor in 1890.

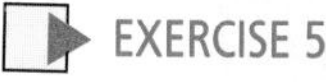

EXERCISE 5 **Identifying Action Verbs and Linking Verbs**

Identify the verb in each of the following sentences as an *action verb* or a *linking verb*.

EXAMPLES **1. One of the most successful businessmen in the United States is John Johnson.**
1. *is—linking verb*

2. Johnson publishes *Ebony, Jet,* and many other magazines.
2. *publishes—action verb*

1. The photograph on the next page shows John Johnson at his most successful.
2. Johnson's life was not always easy.
3. The small Arkansas town of his childhood had no high school.

4. Therefore, Johnson's mother moved to Chicago.
5. In Chicago Johnson attended an all-black high school, with classmates Redd Foxx and Nat King Cole.
6. During the Depression, Johnson's family grew even poorer.
7. However, Johnson studied hard.
8. He soon became an honor student, the class president, and the editor of the high school newspaper.
9. Johnson started his first magazine with borrowed money.
10. Now he is the owner of a publishing empire worth $200 million per year.

GRAMMAR

Helping Verbs

(3) A ***helping verb*** (***auxiliary verb***) helps the main verb to express an action or a state of being.

EXAMPLES **can** speak
will learn
should have been fed

Together the main verb and its helping verb or verbs are called a ***verb phrase.***

EXAMPLES Many students **can speak** Spanish.
I **will learn** all the state capitals tonight.
The dog **should have been fed** by now.

VISUAL CONNECTIONS

About the Subject. Born in 1918 in Arkansas City, Arkansas, John Johnson attended high school and college in Chicago, Illinois. After working for an in-house publication for an insurance company, he went on to found several magazines, including *Ebony* and *Jet.*

GRAMMAR

GRAMMAR

A DIFFERENT APPROACH

Explain that a helping verb always occurs as part of a verb phrase. When a word such as *is* or *does* occurs as a one-word verb, it cannot be a helping verb.

Have students write an action verb with each helping verb listed in the **Helping Verbs** chart. Encourage students to combine more than one helping verb with each action verb.

COMMON ERROR

Problem. Students may confuse prepositional phrases with verb phrases. They may not realize that a modifier in a prepositional phrase is part of the phrase, but a modifier in a verb phrase is separate from the phrase. For example, in the sentence, "He may not be ready to go," students might think that the interrupting word, *not,* is part of the verb phrase, when actually it isn't.

Solution. Point out the distinction between prepositional phrases and verb phrases. In prepositional phrases, the adjectives, adverbs, and articles that come between the preposition and its object are part of the phrase. Only the main verb and helping verbs are included in verb phrases. Interrupting adverbs and nouns are not part of a verb phrase.

GRAMMAR

Helping Verbs

am	were	have	did	can	will
is	be	had	may	could	would
are	been	do	might	shall	
was	has	does	must	should	

Sometimes a verb phrase is interrupted by another part of speech.

EXAMPLES **Suzanne should** not **call** so late at night. [The verb phrase *should call* is interrupted by the adverb *not.*]

Did you **watch** Whitney Houston's new video? [The verb phrase *Did watch* is interrupted by the subject *you.*]

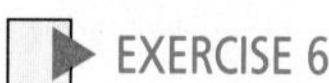

EXERCISE 6 **Identifying Verb Phrases and Helping Verbs**

Identify the verb phrase in each of the following sentences. Then underline the helping verb or verbs.

EXAMPLE **1. We are going to Arizona this summer.**
1. *are going*

1. The Petrified Forest has always attracted many tourists.
2. Their imaginations have been captured by its spectacular beauty.
3. Visitors to the forest can see the Painted Desert at the same time.
4. The colors of the desert do not remain the same for long.
5. Specimens of petrified wood are exhibited at the Visitors' Center.
6. Have you ever seen a piece of petrified wood?
7. A guide will gladly explain the process of petrification to you.
8. Visitors can purchase the wood as a souvenir.

REVIEWS A and B

OBJECTIVE

- To identify verbs in sentences and in a paragraph

9. Walking tours of the Petrified Forest are not recommended for amateur hikers.
10. Hikes must be arranged with park rangers.

GRAMMAR

EXERCISE 7 **Using Helping Verbs in Original Sentences**

Use each of the following word groups as the subject of a sentence with a verb phrase. Make some of your sentences questions. Underline the helping verb in each sentence.

EXAMPLE 1. your neighbor's dog
1. *Can your neighbor's dog do tricks?*

1. my bicycle
2. the astronauts
3. a tiny kitten
4. the hard assignment
5. a famous singer
6. some strange footprints
7. my grandmother
8. the subway
9. a funny costume
10. the refreshments

REVIEW A **Identifying Verbs**

Identify the verb in each of the following sentences. Be sure to include helping verbs.

EXAMPLE 1. Can you form the letters of the sign language alphabet?
1. *Can form*

1. The alphabet chart on the next page will help you.
2. Perhaps you and a friend could practice together.
3. At first, it may be a challenge.
4. Many hearing-impaired people communicate with these letters and thousands of other signs.
5. Different forms of sign language are used by many people in many ways.
6. For example, football signals are sometimes given with sign language.
7. Some stroke victims must learn sign language during their recovery period.

ANSWERS

Exercise 7

Sentences will vary. Make sure students use verb phrases in each sentence and that some of the sentences are questions.

GRAMMAR

COOPERATIVE LEARNING

Have students work in groups of four or five to review the types of verbs they have studied (action, linking, helping, and transitive and intransitive). Have students work with colored markers to make charts clarifying the types of verbs. Transitive and intransitive verbs should be combined on a chart of action verbs. Have students include example verbs and sentences in their charts.

INTEGRATING THE LANGUAGE ARTS

Grammar and Usage. As students proofread their writing, they should check the agreement of each subject and verb. One simple way of checking is to underline subjects once and verbs twice and to study the sentences one by one to be sure the verbs agree with the subjects.

GRAMMAR

GRAMMAR

8. Scientists have even taught a very simple sign language to gorillas and chimpanzees.
9. These animals actually talk to each other and to people in sign language.
10. In this picture, the gorilla on the left and the woman are having a conversation in sign language.

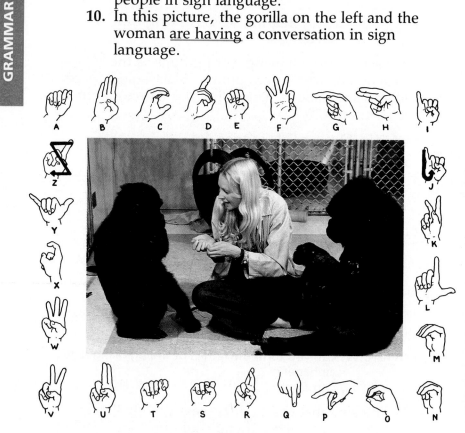

 REVIEW B **Identifying Verbs**

Identify the verbs in the following paragraph. Be sure to include helping verbs.

EXAMPLE [1] Fairy tales are sometimes called "folk tales."
1. *are called*

[1] Long ago, many people could not read. [2] Instead, they would memorize stories. [3] Then, they would tell the stories to their families and friends.

WRITING APPLICATION

OBJECTIVE

- To use the verb *be* as a helping verb and as a linking verb in ten sentences

[4] In this way, the people, or "folk," passed the tales on from generation to generation. [5] Finally, some people wrote the stories down. [6] Two German brothers, Jakob and Wilhelm Grimm, made a famous collection of German folk tales. [7] The brothers had heard many of their tales from older relatives. [8] Their collection of stories became extremely popular all over the world. [9] "Sleeping Beauty," "Cinderella," and "Rumpelstiltskin" were all preserved by the brothers Grimm. [10] In your library, you can find these tales and many others, too.

GRAMMAR

WRITING APPLICATION

Using *Be* as a Helping Verb and a Linking Verb

Can you tell the difference between the helping verb *be* and the linking verb *be*? As a helping verb, a form of *be* is always followed by a main verb. As a linking verb, a form of *be* is the main verb.

HELPING VERB I **am** going to practice my trumpet every day.
LINKING VERB I **am** nicer to my little brother this year.

WRITING ACTIVITY

You and your classmates have decided to list some goals for the coming year. The theme for your lists is "How I Can Make the World a Better Place." Write a list of ten or more goals or resolutions for yourself. Make each of your resolutions a complete sentence. In your list, use the verb *be* at least two times as a helping verb and three times as a linking verb.

Prewriting First, think of some realistic goals you can set for yourself. Could you be more careful about recycling? join a volunteer group? help clean up trash around your neighborhood? List as many goals as you

GRAMMAR

WRITING APPLICATION

The writing assignment gives students practice in composing original, complete sentences. Students will focus on identifying helping verbs and linking verbs and checking to be sure subjects and verbs agree.

CRITICAL THINKING

Analysis

Students may find it helpful to categorize their lists in the prewriting stage so that they can start their writing with specific areas in mind. For example, they might brainstorm goals having to do with schoolwork, social life, homework, or family obligations.

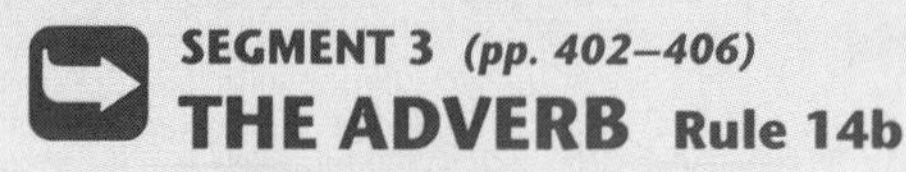

SEGMENT 3 *(pp. 402–406)*

THE ADVERB Rule 14b

OBJECTIVES

- To identify adverbs and the words they modify
- To use appropriate adverbs in sentences

INTEGRATING THE LANGUAGE ARTS

Literature Link. In the first chapter of *All I Really Need to Know I Learned in Kindergarten,* Robert Fulghum includes a list of goals or rules for living that may help students organize their ideas. If the book is available in your library, have students read and discuss the chapter. Then have them copy the list of goals to analyze sentence structure. Point out that many of the sentences in Fulghum's list have *you* (understood) as the subject.

GRAMMAR

Teacher's ResourceBank™

RESOURCES

THE ADVERB

- Adverbs 131

QUICK REMINDER

Write the following sentences on the chalkboard and have students identify the adverb in each sentence:

1. Detergent decays slowly in the environment. [slowly]
2. Detergent often contaminates the air and water. [often]
3. Vinegar and baking soda clean effectively and are safe for the environment. [effectively]

GRAMMAR

can. Some goals may be very simple. For example, you might resolve to do little things like smile at people more or to help out more around the house.

Writing From your list, choose the resolutions that seem the most important and the most manageable. Write each of them as a complete sentence. (For more about complete sentences, see pages 304–305.)

Evaluating and Revising Read through your list. Are your resolutions clear and specific? Will you really be able to keep them? If not, revise or replace some of the resolutions. You may think of some good resolutions that didn't occur to you earlier. Add as many items as you wish. Be sure that you've used a form of the verb *be* as both a helping verb and a linking verb.

Proofreading Make sure that all of your sentences are complete. Do all subjects agree with their verbs? (For more about subject-verb agreement, see pages 457–470.) Identify each helping verb and linking verb. Make sure you've used the verb *be* correctly. Do a final check for errors in grammar, spelling, or punctuation.

The Adverb

14b. An ***adverb*** is a word that modifies a verb, an adjective, or another adverb.

EXAMPLES Reporters **quickly** gather the news. [The adverb *quickly* modifies the verb *gather.*]
The route is **too** long. [The adverb *too* modifies the adjective *long.*]
Our newspaper carrier delivers the paper **very** early. [The adverb *very* modifies another adverb, *early.* The adverb *early* modifies the verb *delivers.*]

An adverb answers the following questions:

Where?	How often?	To what extent?
When?	*or*	*or*
How?	How long?	How much?

EXAMPLES Please put the package **there.** [*There* modifies the verb *put;* it tells *where.*]
I will call you **later.** [*Later* modifies the verb phrase *will call;* it tells *when.*]
Softly I shut my door. [*Softly* modifies the verb *shut;* it tells *how.*]
She **always** reads science fiction novels. [*Always* modifies the verb *reads;* it tells *how often.*]
Would you please **briefly** explain what you mean? [*Briefly* modifies the verb phrase *would explain;* it tells *how long*.]
An owl hooted **very** late last night. [The adverb *very* modifies the adverb *late;* it tells *to what extent.*]
The lemonade was **too** sour. [*Too* modifies the adjective *sour*; it tells *how much.*]

WORDS OFTEN USED AS ADVERBS	
Where?	here there away up outside
When?	now then later soon ago
How?	clearly easily quietly slowly
How often? or How long?	never always often seldom frequently usually forever
To what extent? or How much?	very too almost so really most nearly quite less only

NOTE: The word *not* is an adverb. When *not* is part of a contraction like *hadn't,* the *–n't* is an adverb.

LEP/ESL

General Strategies. You may find some students using the adverbs *very* and *too* interchangeably. Explain that *very* means "a lot," whereas *too* means "more than necessary or desirable." You may want to offer extra practice in completing sentences such as the following ones. Students must supply either *very* and an adjective or *too* and an adjective.

1. Pepperoni pizza is . . . .
2. I find my English class . . . .
3. My best friend is . . . .
4. Rock music is . . . .
5. Summertime can be . . . .

COOPERATIVE LEARNING

Have students work in groups of five or six to make lists of common adverbs. They can begin with the **Words Often Used as Adverbs** chart. You may wish to have them categorize their adverbs, but advise them that many adverbs can be placed in more than one category.

Show the class that most adverbs are formed by adding *–ly* to an adjective (*bad — badly*), but also warn them that not all adverbs end in *–ly* (*well, too,* and *very,* for example) and that not all words ending in *–ly* are adverbs (*lovely, silly*).

A DIFFERENT APPROACH

Explain that just as an adjective modifies a noun or a pronoun, an adverb modifies a verb, an adjective, or another adverb. Write a series of short sentences on the chalkboard, underlining the adverbs. Point out that each underlined word modifies another word in the sentence. Then ask students how it qualifies the word. Does it tell *where, when, how, how often,* or *to what extent*?

1. Dad always walks fast. [how]
2. Please go away. [where]
3. Then she gave me the package. [when]
4. Li won the game easily. [how]
5. Pablo has never played football. [how often or to what extent]

GRAMMAR

ANSWERS

Exercise 8

1. Actually—is (verb)
2. there—grows (verb)
3. very—worried (adjective)
4. seriously—may affect (verb)
5. Very—early (adverb); early—was colonized (verb)

The Position of Adverbs

GRAMMAR

Adverbs may appear at various places in a sentence. Adverbs may come before, after, or between the words they modify.

EXAMPLES **Quietly,** she will tiptoe from the room. [*Quietly* comes at the beginning of the sentence. *Quietly* modifies the verb phrase *will tiptoe.*]

She will **quietly** tiptoe from the room. [*Quietly* comes between *will* and *tiptoe,* the words it modifies.]

She will tiptoe **quietly** from the room. [*Quietly* comes after *will tiptoe,* the verb phrase it modifies.]

She will tiptoe from the room **quietly.** [*Quietly* comes at the end of the sentence.]

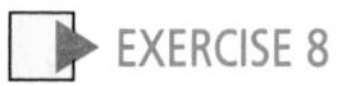

EXERCISE 8 Identifying Adverbs and the Words They Modify

Each of the following sentences contains at least one adverb. Identify the adverb or adverbs. Then give the word each adverb modifies. Be prepared to tell whether the word modified is a verb, an adjective, or an adverb.

EXAMPLE **1.** If you look closely at a world map, you can quite easily find Brazil.
1. *closely—look; quite—easily; easily—can find*

1. Actually, Brazil is the largest country in South America.
2. A large portion of the Amazon rain forest grows there.
3. Many ecologists are very worried about the destruction of the rain forest.
4. The loss of the forest may seriously affect the earth's climate.
5. Very early in the sixteenth century, Brazil was colonized by the Portuguese.

REVIEW C

OBJECTIVE

- To identify adverbs in a paragraph and to tell which words they modify

6. The country later became an independent republic.
7. Brazilians often say *Bom día,* which means "good day" in Portuguese.
8. In Brazil, sports fans can almost always find a soccer game in progress.
9. My aunt travels frequently, but she hasn't been to Brasília.
10. Brasília, the capital of Brazil, is an extremely modern city.

GRAMMAR

REVIEW C **Finding Adverbs in a Paragraph**

Identify the ten adverbs in the following paragraph. Then give the word or words each adverb modifies.

EXAMPLE [1] Williamsburg is a very interesting place.
1. *very—interesting*

[1] Visitors to Williamsburg can truly imagine what life must have been like in the 1700s. [2] As you can see, Williamsburg was carefully built to resemble a small town of the past. [3] On one street a wigmaker carefully makes old-fashioned powdered wigs. [4] Nearby, a silversmith designs beautiful candlesticks, platters, and jewelry. [5] Down the block the bookbinder skillfully crafts book covers out of leather. [6] His neighbor, the blacksmith, was certainly important because he made shoes for horses. [7] In colonial times people could seldom afford new shoes for

6. later — became (verb)
7. often — say (verb)
8. almost — always (adverb); always — can find (verb)
9. frequently — travels (verb); –n't — has been (verb)
10. extremely — modern (adjective)

GRAMMAR

LESS-ADVANCED STUDENTS

You may want to concentrate on the adverb as a modifier of the verb and omit adverbs that modify adjectives or other adverbs.

ADVANCED STUDENTS

To give students further practice using adverbs, have them use adverbs in descriptive paragraphs. Here are possible topics:

1. getting a new pet
2. cooking
3. taking care of a child
4. visiting a zoo

Each student should use at least five adverbs to help make the paragraph clear and interesting. Have students underline the adverbs.

SEGMENT 4 *(pp. 406–410)*

THE PREPOSITION Rule 14c

OBJECTIVES

- To use ten appropriate prepositions in a note
- To identify prepositions and their objects
- To use five words as both prepositions and adverbs in a letter

GRAMMAR

Teacher's ResourceBank™

RESOURCES

THE PREPOSITION

QUICK REMINDER

Use a book or a similar object to give examples of how prepositions show place (which most of them do). Explain the concept visually by placing the book in your hand, beside your hand, above your hand, and so forth. Explain that a preposition shows the relationship between two words in a sentence, as in the sentences on page 407, which show the different relationships between *ball* and *net.*

GRAMMAR

themselves. [8] Nowadays, people enjoy watching this bootmaker at work. [9] Another very popular craftsman makes musical instruments. [10] Williamsburg definitely gives tourists the feeling that they have visited the past.

EXERCISE 9 **Writing Appropriate Adverbs**

Write the following sentences. Fill each blank with an appropriate adverb. Use a different adverb in each sentence. Adverbs will vary.

EXAMPLE **1.** ____ I learned some Spanish words.
1. *Quickly I learned some Spanish words.*

1. I ____ watch TV after school. **1.** never
2. You will ____ bait a hook yourself. **2.** soon
3. My little sister crept down the stairs ____. **3.** quietly
4. Do you think that you can ____ find the answer to the problem? **4.** easily
5. She is ____ eager for lunch. **5.** very

The Preposition

14c. A ***preposition*** is a word that shows the relationship between a noun or a pronoun and some other word in the sentence.

EXAMPLES Your math book is **underneath** your coat. [The preposition *underneath* shows the relationship of *book* to *coat.*]
The one **behind** us honked his horn. [The preposition *behind* shows the relationship of *one* to *us.*]

14c

GRAMMAR

Notice how changing the preposition in the following sentences changes the relationship between *ball* and *net*.

I hit the ball **over** the net.
I hit the ball **into** the net.
I hit the ball **under** the net.

Commonly Used Prepositions

aboard	at	down	off	under
about	before	during	on	underneath
above	behind	except	over	until
across	below	for	past	up
after	beneath	from	since	upon
against	beside	in	through	with
along	between	into	throughout	within
among	beyond	like	to	without
around	by	of	toward	

NOTE: Some prepositions are made up of more than one word. These are called ***compound prepositions.***

Some Compound Prepositions

according to	in addition to	next to
aside from	in place of	on account of
because of	in spite of	out of

EXERCISE 10 **Writing Appropriate Prepositions**

While looking in an old trunk, you found the treasure map shown on the next page. Now, you want to go looking for the buried treasure. Make some notes to help you to plan your route. Think about any special supplies or equipment you'll need. In your notes, use at least ten different prepositions and underline each preposition you use.

LEP/ESL

Spanish. In Spanish, the single preposition *a* is used to denote *in, on,* and *at.* Therefore, you may want to give students extra practice in using prepositions of place. The following rules and examples may prove helpful:

1. Use *in* for cities, states, and countries. (We live in Denver, in Colorado, or in the United States.)
2. Use *on* for streets. (We live on Elm Street.)
3. Use *at* for addresses that include the number. (We live at 112 Elm Street.)

Create a fill-in-the-blank exercise about a family moving from one country to another. Have students fill in the correct prepositions.

LESS-ADVANCED STUDENTS

Allow students to use the **Commonly Used Prepositions** list when they are completing **Exercises 10–12.** Be certain that students understand that for a word to be a preposition, it must have an object.

GRAMMAR

ANSWERS

Exercise 10

Responses will vary. Students' notes should accurately reflect the information in the treasure map.

GRAMMAR

LEARNING STYLES

Auditory Learners. Students can practice using prepositional phrases in sentences by working as a group to create variations on given sentences. One student gives a sentence with a prepositional phrase, such as "The dog walked by the bushes." Other students will create new sentences by changing the preposition or prepositional phrase. Once they have stated several possibilities, the next student should give a sentence with a preposition, and so on.

ADVANCED STUDENTS

Provide students with copies of simple directions found with a recipe, a board game, detergent, or other products. Have the students write *prep.* over the prepositions and *obj.* over the objects. Then discuss how the use of prepositional phrases can make directions more understandable.

GRAMMAR

EXAMPLE *I'll land the rowboat on Mournful Beach and pull it under the cliff, safe from the high tide.*

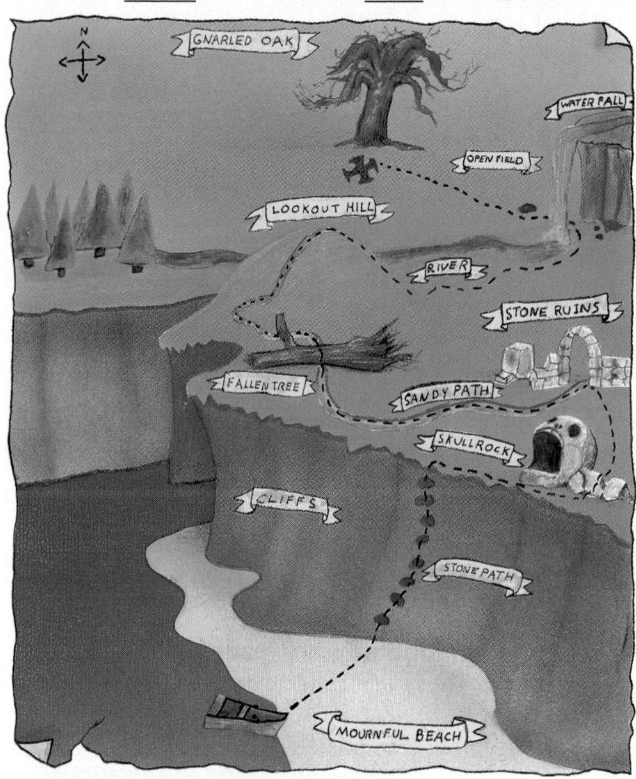

The Prepositional Phrase

A preposition is always followed by at least one noun or pronoun. This noun or pronoun is called the ***object of the preposition.*** The preposition, its object, and the object's modifiers make up a ***prepositional phrase.***

EXAMPLES He poured sauce **over the pizza.** [The preposition *over* relates its object, *pizza,* to *poured.* The article *the* modifies *pizza*.]

The pile **of dry leaves** had grown larger. [The preposition *of* relates its object, *leaves,* to *pile.* The adjective *dry* modifies *leaves*.]

A preposition may have more than one object.

EXAMPLE **The flea collar is for cats and dogs.** [The preposition *for* has the two objects *cats* and *dogs.*]

REFERENCE NOTE: For more about prepositional phrases, see Chapter 15.

EXERCISE 11 **Identifying Prepositions and Their Objects**

Identify the prepositional phrase in each of the following sentences. Underline the preposition and circle its object. There may be more than one object.

EXAMPLE **1. Otters are related to weasels and minks.**
1. *to weasels and minks*

1. Yesterday afternoon, we planted a sapling behind the garage.
2. I bought a pattern for a sari.
3. They live near the airport.
4. My brother wants a guitar for his birthday.
5. The pictures won't be developed until Friday or Saturday.
6. I received a letter from my aunt and uncle.
7. The arctic falcon is the largest of all falcons.
8. Did you have the correct answer to the third question?
9. There are many uses for peanuts.
10. I think that you might need a calculator for that problem.

Prepositions and Adverbs

Some words may be used as prepositions or as adverbs. Remember that a preposition always has an object. An adverb never does. If you can't tell whether a word is used as an adverb or a preposition, look for an object.

GRAMMAR

A DIFFERENT APPROACH

Have students find pictures that show action scenes. Have each student write five sentences containing prepositions describing the scene. Then have two students exchange pictures and sentences. Students should circle prepositions in their partners' sentences and then discuss their findings.

INTEGRATING THE LANGUAGE ARTS

Literature Link. Carl Sandburg's poem "They Have Yarns" is a delightful list of condensed folk tales dealing with subjects such as mosquitoes, snakes, sheep counters, pigs, Paul Bunyan, and John Henry. You may want to have students study and discuss the poem. Help them to see the structure of the poem, which is a lengthy string of prepositional phrases describing types of yarns.

GRAMMAR

GRAMMAR

ANSWERS

Exercise 12

Letters will vary. Students' observations about the castle should accurately reflect the information in the picture.

LESS-ADVANCED STUDENTS

Suggest that students use the following question to help themselves distinguish between prepositions and adverbs:

Is there a single word that explains where, when, or how the action was done (an adverb), or is there a group of words that explains this (a prepositional phrase)?

GRAMMAR

PREPOSITION	Meet me **outside** the gym. [*Gym* is the object of the preposition *outside.*]
ADVERB	Meet me **outside.** [no object]
PREPOSITION	Clouds gathered **above** us. [*Us* is the object of the preposition *above.*]
ADVERB	Clouds gathered **above.** [no object]

EXERCISE 12 Writing Sentences with Prepositions and Adverbs

Your family is on vacation, and you've just spent the whole day exploring this medieval castle. At the castle gift shop, you bought this cutaway drawing to send to your best friend. Write a brief letter to mail along with the drawing. In your letter, use five words as both prepositions and adverbs. Underline these words and be prepared to identify each as a preposition or an adverb.

EXAMPLES *First, I walked completely around the wall.*
Then, I stood on the marshal's tower for a while and looked around.

SEGMENT 5 *(pp. 411–412)*

THE CONJUNCTION Rule 14d

OBJECTIVE

- To identify conjunctions in sentences

14d

GRAMMAR

The Conjunction

14d. A *conjunction* is a word that joins words or groups of words.

The most common conjunctions are the coordinating conjunctions.

Coordinating Conjunctions						
and	but	for	nor	or	so	yet

CONJUNCTIONS JOINING WORDS beans **and** rice / movies **or** television / sad **but** true / Egypt, Italy, **and** Spain

REFERENCE NOTE: For information on using commas in a series of words, see pages 594–595.

CONJUNCTIONS JOINING PHRASES
go for a walk **or** read a book
after breakfast **but** before lunch
cooking dinner **and** fixing breakfast

CONJUNCTIONS JOINING SENTENCES
I wanted to call, **but** it was late.
The deer ran toward the wide river, **for** they smelled smoke from the forest fire.
We knocked on the door, **and** they answered.

REFERENCE NOTE: For information on using commas to join sentences, see pages 307–308.

EXERCISE 13 **Identifying Conjunctions**

Identify the conjunction in each of the following sentences.

EXAMPLE **1.** Lena or I will pitch batting practice.
1. *or*

1. Julio and Roger joined the soccer team.
2. It may rain, but we will be there.

Teacher's ResourceBank™

RESOURCES

THE CONJUNCTION

- Coordinating Conjunctions 134

QUICK REMINDER

Write the following sentences on the chalkboard:

1. I want pizza.
2. I want tacos.

Have students combine the two sentences to create four sentences using the conjunctions *and, but, or,* and *yet.* They may need to add words or otherwise modify the sentences. Have students discuss the differences in meanings of the new sentences.

LEARNING STYLES

Visual Learners. If you are teaching more than one part of speech at one time, a permanent classroom display or poster will probably help students remember the names of the parts of speech. Include the names of the parts of speech being covered, as well as lists of examples from the textbook. You may also want to include model sentences.

GRAMMAR

SEGMENT 6 *(pp. 412–415)*

THE INTERJECTION Rule 14e

OBJECTIVES

- To complete sentences by providing interjections
- To use interjections and conjunctions in writing a report

GRAMMAR

Teacher's ResourceBank™

RESOURCES

THE INTERJECTION

- Interjections 135
- Reviewing the Parts of Speech 136

QUICK REMINDER

List a few out-of-date interjections on the chalkboard. You may want to include *rats, golly, zounds,* and *groovy.*

Ask students to contribute the latest (polite) slang interjections. Explain that most of these words become popular for a time but then are replaced by others.

GRAMMAR

3. I have enough money for popcorn or juice.
4. You warm the tortillas, and I'll melt the cheese.
5. Did Nancy finish her book report, or is she still working on it?
6. He dove for the ball but missed it.
7. For breakfast I usually like to eat pancakes or a bran muffin.
8. The Harlem Boys Choir sang for their friends and families.
9. I have already addressed the envelope but have not mailed it yet.
10. Many Chinese plays include dancing and acrobatics.

The Interjection

14e. An ***interjection*** is a word used to express emotion.

An interjection has no grammatical relationship to the rest of the sentence. Usually an interjection is followed by an exclamation point.

EXAMPLES **Aha!** I knew you were hiding there.
Oops! I punched in the wrong numbers.

Sometimes an interjection is set off by a comma.

EXAMPLES **Oh,** let's just stay home.
Well, what do you think?

Common Interjections

aha	gosh	oops	whew
alas	hey	ouch	wow
aw	hooray	shucks	yikes
goodness	oh	well	yippee

14e

GRAMMAR

EXERCISE 14 **Writing Interjections**

Have you ever heard the expression "an accident waiting to happen"? How many accidents are waiting to happen in the picture below? Write interjections to complete five sentences that the people in the picture might use. Interjections will vary.

EXAMPLE **1.** ____, Vince, have you seen my other skate?
1. *Oh, Vince, have you seen my other skate?*

1. ____! I almost sat on the cat. **1.** Oops
2. ____! Watch out for that book! **2.** Hey
3. ____! Something on the stove is burning. **3.** Uh-oh
4. ____, Lila! Be careful with that milk! **4.** Oh, dear
5. ____, we'll have to get a new cord for our lamp. **5.** Oh, no

Determining Parts of Speech

Remember that you can't tell what part of speech a word is until you know how it is used in a particular sentence. A word may be used in different ways.

VERB Can you **test** the switch?
NOUN Mr. Sanchez assigned a **test** for tomorrow.

LEP/ESL

General Strategies. It is vital that your students understand the function of an interjection. Knowing that such a word is called an interjection is secondary in importance. Explain that this part of speech is used to make language more colorful, to get the listener's attention, and to express strong emotions. Most languages include interjections. You could ask students who speak other languages to share interjections from those languages with the class. Often interjections such as *ouch* are similar in many languages.

ADVANCED STUDENTS

Point out that the term *interjection* does not refer only to words such as *hooray, oh,* and *ouch.* It refers to expressions like *quick* and *for goodness sake.*

You might have advanced students examine the word *interjection.* Have them look up the word *interject* in a dictionary. They will find that in Latin *inter* means "between" and *jacere* means "to throw." From these came the word *interject,* which means "to introduce abruptly." They will also understand why the interjection functions as it does in grammar.

GRAMMAR

REVIEW D

OBJECTIVE

- To identify words in sentences by naming their parts of speech

A DIFFERENT APPROACH

In reviewing parts of speech, emphasize that many words can be used as more than one part of speech. You may want to have students look in dictionaries to find words that can be used as many parts of speech.

List the following words on the chalkboard and have students create example sentences showing these words used as different parts of speech:

1. water [noun, verb, adjective]
2. step [noun, verb, adjective]
3. turn [noun, verb]
4. bridge [noun, verb]

PICTURE THIS

As a prewriting activity, you may want to have the class discuss roller coaster rides they have taken or would like to have taken. They may want to take notes as they listen by listing words that capture the thrill and terror of gravity-challenging dips and climbs. It also will be helpful to briefly discuss ways of rating the imaginary ride in the activity and of justifying the rating with details.

To aid in your evaluation, have students underline and label the interjections and conjunctions.

GRAMMAR

ADVERB	The cat climbed **up.**
PREPOSITION	The cat climbed **up** the tree.
NOUN	We threw pennies in the wishing **well.**
ADJECTIVE	Janice isn't feeling **well.**
INTERJECTION	**Well,** what did he say?

GRAMMAR

REVIEW D **Identifying Parts of Speech**

For each of the following sentences, label the italicized word as a *noun*, a *pronoun*, an *adjective*, a *verb*, an *adverb*, a *preposition*, a *conjunction*, or an *interjection*. Be prepared to give reasons for your answers.

EXAMPLE 1. Some scientists *study* bones.
1. *study—verb*

1. The fans lined up *outside* the stadium. **1.** prep.
2. My mother *drives* to work. **2.** v.
3. Those *plants* grow best in sandy soil. **3.** n.
4. Rhea bought *paper* cups for the party. **4.** adj.
5. *Their* parents own a card store. **5.** pro. [*or* adj.]
6. N. Scott Momaday has written several books, *but* I have read only one of them. **6.** conj.
7. *Oops!* I dropped my backpack. **7.** itj.
8. We play *outdoors* every day until dinnertime. **8.** adv.
9. This videotape looks *interesting*. **9.** adj.
10. You don't sound *too* happy. **10.** adv.

PICTURE THIS

Wow! What a ride! You are a member of the National Roller Coaster Club. You are trying out the new roller coaster shown on the next page and are rating it for the club. Write a brief report for the club newsletter, describing the ride. Tell what you liked best about the coaster, and compare it to others you've heard about

SEGMENT 7 *(pp. 415–417)*

REVIEW: POSTTESTS 1 and 2

OBJECTIVES

- To identify words in sentences as verbs, adverbs, prepositions, conjunctions, or interjections
- To write sentences using words as different parts of speech

or ridden. In your report, use at least three conjunctions and two interjections.

Subject: a roller coaster ride
Audience: members of a roller coaster club
Purpose: to describe and rate the ride; to inform

Review: Posttest 1

Identifying Verbs, Adverbs, Prepositions, Conjunctions, and Interjections

For the following sentences, label each italicized word or word group as a *verb*, an *adverb*, a *preposition*, a *conjunction*, or an *interjection*.

LEP/ESL

General Strategies. Encourage students to use the parts of speech in the same way as they would piece together a puzzle. Have students work in groups. Each group should use colored construction paper to make eight sets of five cards—one set each for nouns, pronouns, adjectives, verbs, adverbs, conjunctions, interjections and prepositions. Each set of cards (each part of speech) should be a different color. Ask the groups to take a minimum of three cards from each set and to create three complete sentences by stringing the parts of speech together appropriately. Students can use extra words, as necessary, but they must make use of all the parts of speech that they select.

EXAMPLE **1. A tornado *is* a terrible *and* violent storm.**
1. *is—verb; and—conjunction*

1. The tornado *struck* our neighborhood *without* warning. 1. v./prep. 2. adv./adv.
2. *Unfortunately*, we do *not* have a basement.
3. I grabbed my dog Muffin *and* ran *into* the bathroom, the safest room in the house. 3. conj./prep.
4. Muffin and I were *tightly* wedged *between* the sink and the tub. 4. adv./prep. 5. v./v.
5. The house *was shaking*, and the air *became* cold.
6. *Suddenly* the roof blew *off*. 6. adv./adv.
7. The sky *was* full *of* loose boards. 7. v./prep.
8. Then everything suddenly *grew* calm—it seemed almost *too* calm. 8. v./adv.
9. I *was* frightened, *but* I was not hurt. 9. v./conj.
10. *Goodness*! Let's build a basement *soon*. 10. itj./adv.

Review: Posttest 2

Writing Sentences Using Words as Different Parts of Speech

Write ten sentences of your own using the following words as directed. Underline the word and give its part of speech after each sentence. Use a variety of subjects and verbs in your sentences.

EXAMPLE **1. Use *down* as an adverb and a preposition.**
1. *We looked down.—adverb*
We looked down the hole.—preposition

1. Use *over* as an adverb and as a preposition.
2. Use *for* as a preposition and as a conjunction.
3. Use *yet* as a conjunction and as an adverb.
4. Use *well* as an interjection and as an adverb.
5. Use *through* as an adverb and as a preposition.

GRAMMAR

ANSWERS

Review: Posttest 2

Sentences will vary. Here are some possibilities:

1. She's coming over. — adverb
   A rainbow arched over the lake. — preposition
2. We had pizza for lunch. — preposition
   Take me home, for I am tired. — conjunction
3. He won't pick up the guitar, yet he plays very well. — conjunction
   She's not ready yet. — adverb
4. Well! The toast is perfect. — interjection
   Neal dances well. — adverb
5. I want to see this project through to the end. — adverb
   Traffic cannot get through the mud. — preposition

SUMMARY OF PARTS OF SPEECH

Rule	Part of Speech	Use	Example
13a	noun	names	His **report** is about **Medgar Evers**.
13b	pronoun	takes the place of a noun	**I** read quietly to **myself**.
13c	adjective	modifies a noun or pronoun	We found **three old Russian** coins in **that yellow** envelope.
14a	verb	shows action or a state of being	She **missed** the test because she **was** ill.
14b	adverb	modifies a verb, an adjective, or another adverb	He **seldom** gets **so** tired, but **today** he practiced **really hard**.
14c	preposition	relates a noun or pronoun to another word	The students **in** the play went **to** the auditorium.
14d	conjunction	joins words or groups of words	Tina **and** Shannon are invited, **but** they can't go.
14e	interjection	shows strong feeling	**Wow!** What great fireworks!

GRAMMAR

SEGMENT 1 *(pp. 418–419)*

DIAGNOSTIC TEST

OBJECTIVE

- To identify adverb phrases and adjective phrases in sentences and to tell what they modify

Teacher's ResourceBank™

RESOURCES

FOR THE WHOLE CHAPTER

- Chapter Review Form A 148
- Chapter Review Form B 149
- Assessment Portfolio
  - Grammar Pretests 447–454
  - Grammar Mastery Tests 471–478

GRAMMAR

CHAPTER OVERVIEW

This chapter begins with an explanation of prepositional phrases, and then goes on to discuss how prepositional phrases are used as adjective phrases and adverb phrases. In the **Writing Application,** students will use prepositional phrases to add detail to their writing. Other exercises are included throughout the chapter to test students' mastery of the prepositional phrase.

USING THE DIAGNOSTIC TEST

Use the **Diagnostic Test** to evaluate your students' mastery of the use of prepositional phrases or to determine problem areas in which additional instruction may be needed.

Going over the answers orally in class may serve as a helpful review for some students, particularly auditory learners.

DIAGNOSTIC TEST

Teaching Note. In sentence number 4, the prepositional phrase *in San Juan, Puerto Rico* could act as either an adjective phrase modifying "grandparents," or an adverb phrase modifying "visit."

GRAMMAR

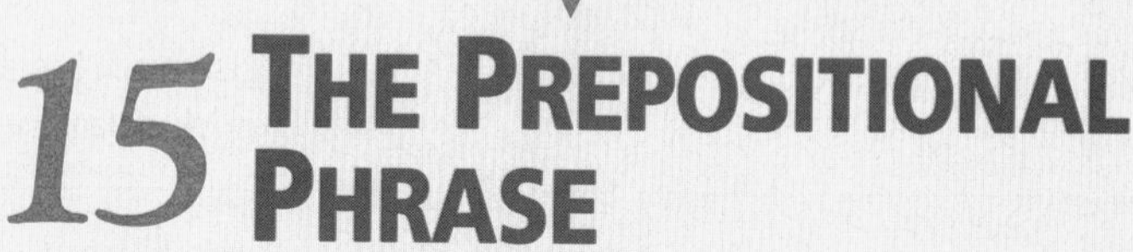

15 THE PREPOSITIONAL PHRASE

Adjective Phrases and Adverb Phrases

Diagnostic Test

Identifying Prepositional Phrases

Identify the prepositional phrase in each of the following sentences and tell whether the phrase is used as an *adjective phrase* or an *adverb phrase.* Then list the word that the phrase modifies.

EXAMPLE 1. We hiked through the woods.
1. *through the woods; adverb phrase—hiked*

1. The crowd waved banners during the game. 1. adv.
2. That book about the Underground Railroad is interesting. 2. adj.
3. A clown handed balloons to the children. 3. adv.
4. We always visit my grandparents in San Juan, Puerto Rico. 4. adj. [*or* visit—adv.]

SEGMENT 2 *(pp. 419–422)*

PHRASES AND PREPOSITIONAL PHRASES Rules 15a, 15b

OBJECTIVES

- To identify groups of words as phrases or sentences
- To identify prepositional phrases and their objects within sentences
- To complete sentences by using prepositional phrases

5. Uncle Eduardo carefully knocked the snow off his boots. 5. adv.
6. Someone left a package on the front porch. 6. adv.
7. Do you have the new CD by Whitney Houston? 7. adj.
8. Have you seen the pictures of the Yamatos' new house? 8. adj.
9. The swings in the park are a bit rusty. 9. adj.
10. Help yourself to some strawberries. 10. adv.

Phrases

15a. A *phrase* is a group of related words that is used as a single part of speech. A phrase does not contain both a subject and a verb.

Phrases cannot stand alone. They must always be used with other words as part of a sentence.

PHRASE **in the box**
SENTENCE **We put the tapes in the box.**

EXERCISE 1 **Identifying Phrases and Sentences**

Identify each of the following groups of words as a *phrase* or a *sentence.*

EXAMPLES
1. in the winter, some people enjoy cross-country skiing
1. *sentence*
2. for many reasons
2. *phrase*

1. ski lifts are used for Alpine skiing 1. sent.
2. down the snowy hills 2. phr.
3. slalom skiers race through gates 3. sent.
4. during the race 4. phr.
5. before the other skiers 5. phr.

Teacher's ResourceBank™

RESOURCES

PHRASES AND PREPOSITIONAL PHRASES

- Prepositional Phrases 145

Write the following sentences on the chalkboard and ask students to fill in the blanks with prepositional phrases. Responses will vary.

1. The book ___ fell ___. [with the blue cover; off the desk]
2. Lucita chased the ball ___. [under the tree]
3. The skinny man ___ ate everything ___. [in the restaurant; in sight]

LEP/ESL

Asian Languages. In some Asian languages such as Japanese and Korean, prepositions come after their objects. For example, "in the house" would be "house in." Other Asian languages, such as Vietnamese, do not always use prepositions, so that "I went to the train station" would be "I go arrive train station."

If your ESL students use similar constructions in English, ask them how the phrases are said in their native languages. Then explain how prepositions are used in English by pointing out the differences in usage.

AT-RISK STUDENTS

Some students maintain a low achievement level due to poor self-esteem and socialization problems. You may want to let them create their own study groups for working with prepositional phrases. You could then give each group a list of prepositions and have the students see how many they can find in the texts of newspaper or magazine articles or even comic books. This will familiarize them with prepositions and make finding prepositional phrases easier for them.

GRAMMAR

GRAMMAR

Prepositional Phrases

15b. A ***prepositional phrase*** is a phrase that begins with a preposition and ends with a noun or a pronoun.

Prepositions show the relationship of a noun or pronoun to another word in the sentence. The noun or pronoun that follows a preposition is called the ***object of the preposition.*** A preposition, its object, and any modifiers of the object are all part of the prepositional phrase.

EXAMPLES I met them **at the corner.** [The noun *corner* is the object of the preposition *at.*]
Did you bring these flowers **for me**? [The pronoun *me* is the object of the preposition *for.*]
We store carrots and potatoes **in our cool, dark basement.** [The noun *basement* is the object of the preposition *in.* The words *our, cool,* and *dark* modify *basement.*]

A preposition may have more than one object.

EXAMPLES Aaron showed his arrowhead collection **to Tranh and her.** [two objects]
The baked chicken came **with a salad, two vegetables, and dessert.** [three objects]

REFERENCE NOTE: For a list of commonly used prepositions, see page 407.

EXERCISE 2 **Identifying Prepositional Phrases**

Identify the prepositional phrase in each of the following sentences. Underline each preposition and circle its object. A preposition may have more than one object.

EXAMPLE **1.** The package was for my brother and me.
1. *for my brother and me*

15b

GRAMMAR

1. The Sahara is a huge desert that lies south of the Mediterranean Sea.
2. We waited until lunchtime.
3. The house across the street has green shutters.
4. Do not make repairs on the brakes yourself.
5. The word *lasso* comes from a Spanish word that means "snare."
6. May I sit between you and him?
7. The woman with the blue uniform is my aunt.
8. The *Cherokee Phoenix* was the first newspaper printed in a Native American language.
9. He is saving money for a stereo and a guitar.
10. The messenger slipped the note under the door.

EXERCISE 3 **Identifying Prepositional Phrases and Their Objects**

For each of the following sentences, identify the prepositional phrase and circle the object or objects of the preposition.

EXAMPLE 1. Dinosaurs and other giant reptiles roamed across the earth sixty-five million years ago.
1. *across the earth*

1. Although some of the dinosaurs were enormous, others were quite small.
2. The drawings on the next page show a triceratops, thirty feet long, and a saltopus, less than three feet long.
3. Many dinosaurs fed on plants and vegetables.
4. Dinosaurs with sharp teeth ate flesh.
5. Can you imagine seeing this flying reptile, the pterodactyl, above you?
6. It once lived in Europe and Africa.
7. Until a few years ago, scientists believed that all dinosaurs were coldblooded.
8. According to recent studies, however, some dinosaurs may have been warmblooded.

A DIFFERENT APPROACH

To give students practice in using prepositional phrases, divide the class into two teams. Set up four chairs, each representing a base in a baseball diamond. The students take turns as batters. As each batter sits at home plate, ask him or her to compose a sentence with a prepositional phrase. The spectators (other students) judge the sentences as being correct or not. (Of course, you are the umpire and will have the final decision.) When sentences are correct, students will move to first base. If a sentence is incorrect, that batter is out. Students continue to compose sentences, gradually sending themselves around the diamond. For each team member who makes it to home plate, the team wins a point. After the first team has three outs, send the second team to bat. The team that gets the most points wins.

GRAMMAR

ANSWERS

Exercise 4

Phrases will vary. Here are some possibilities:

1. at the party
2. after five o'clock
3. at the game
4. across the street
5. over the door

GRAMMAR

9. Many scientists say that birds and crocodiles may be related to dinosaurs.
10. Some people even claim that birds are, in fact, living dinosaurs.

EXERCISE 4 **Writing Appropriate Prepositional Phrases**

Write the following sentences, filling in each blank with an appropriate prepositional phrase.

EXAMPLE **1.** We saw Jason ____.
1. *We saw Jason at the mall.*

1. My favorite comedian will appear ____.
2. That bus always arrives ____.
3. The fans ____ cheered every score.
4. The children ran ____.
5. The light ____ is broken.

SEGMENT 3 *(pp. 423–427)*

ADJECTIVE PHRASES Rule 15c

OBJECTIVES

- To identify adjective phrases and the words they modify
- To complete sentences by adding adjective phrases

15c

GRAMMAR

Adjective Phrases

A prepositional phrase used as an adjective is called an ***adjective phrase.***

ADJECTIVE **Icy chunks fell from the skyscraper.**

ADJECTIVE PHRASE **Chunks of ice fell from the skyscraper.**

REFERENCE NOTE: For more about adjectives, see pages 381–385.

15c. An ***adjective phrase*** modifies a noun or a pronoun.

Adjective phrases answer the same questions that single-word adjectives answer.

What kind? Which one?
How many? How much?

EXAMPLES **Mr. Arnaud ordered a dinner of boiled crawfish.** [The adjective phrase modifies the noun *dinner.* The phrase answers the question *What kind?*]

The one with the big pockets costs more. [The adjective phrase modifies the pronoun *one.* The phrase answers the question *Which one?*]

There was enough room for only three people. [The prepositional phrase modifies the noun *room.* The phrase answers the question *How much?*]

Notice in these examples that an adjective phrase always follows the word it modifies.

EXERCISE 5 **Identifying Adjective Phrases**

Identify the adjective phrase in each of the following sentences. Then give the word that the phrase modifies.

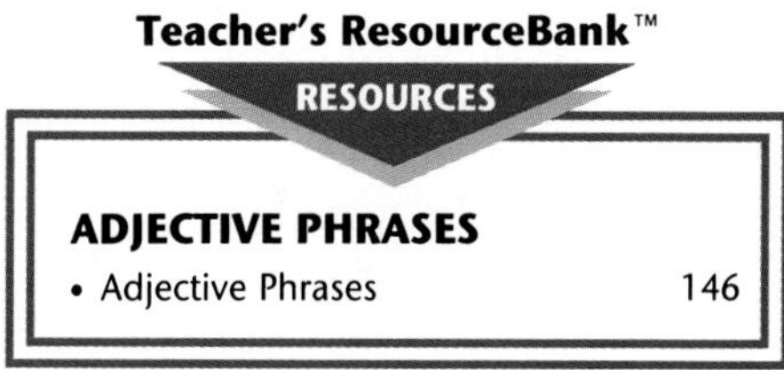

Teacher's ResourceBank™

RESOURCES

ADJECTIVE PHRASES

- Adjective Phrases 146

QUICK REMINDER

Write the following word groups on the chalkboard. Ask students to unscramble each set of words to form sentences and to underline the adjective phrases.

1. the in large The fish is pond [The fish in the pond is large.]
2. received in student class A award an math [A student in math class received an award.]

LEP/ESL

General Strategies. To help students see how adjective phrases can help make descriptions precise, bring several pictures of the same type of object to class and ask students to use adjective phrases to identify and distinguish between the objects. For example, you could bring several magazine advertisements of cars and let the students describe each one with adjective phrases. Or you could bring one picture with lots of cars in it and have the students use adjective phrases to distinguish between the different cars.

GRAMMAR

GRAMMAR

VISUAL CONNECTIONS

About the Artist. Diego Rivera was born in Mexico on December 8, 1886. He began to study art at the age of ten and eventually studied in Spain and in Paris, France. Rivera was one of the leaders of the revolutionary movement in Mexican public wall painting that began in the 1920s. His murals conveyed a message of national identity to the public.

GRAMMAR

EXAMPLE **1.** Diego Rivera was a famous painter from Mexico.
1. *from Mexico—painter*

1. People throughout the world enjoy Rivera's art.
2. The photograph below shows one of his murals.

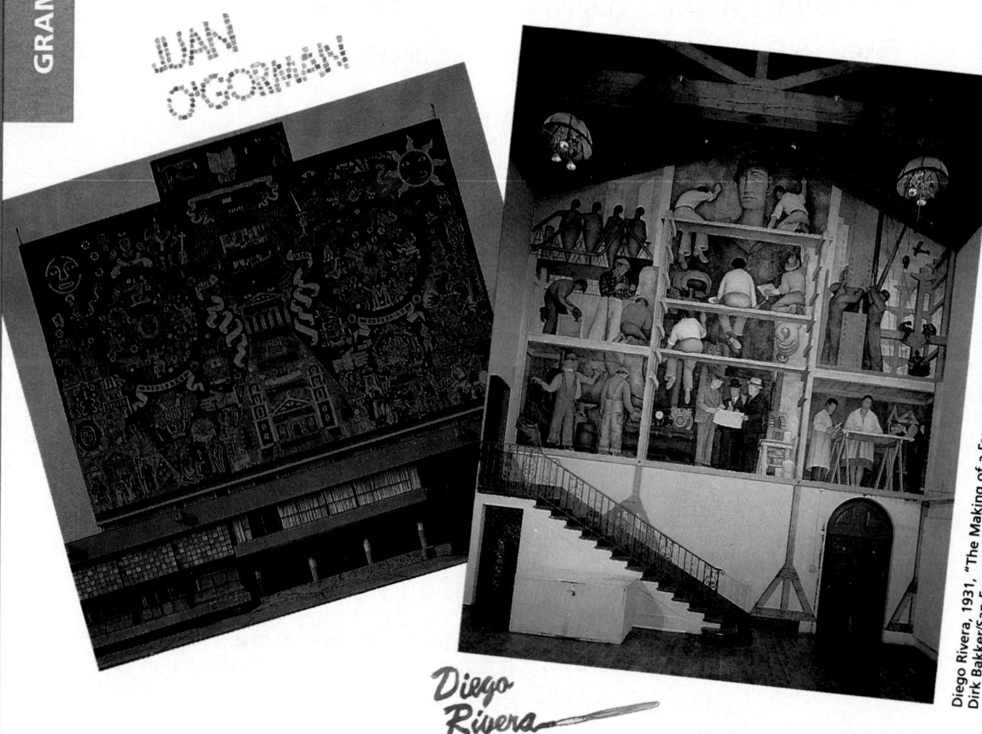

Diego Rivera, 1931, "The Making of a Fre... Dirk Bakker/San F...

3. Rivera painted many murals, which are huge paintings on buildings.
4. His murals are beautiful examples of popular twentieth-century art.
5. Rivera's works express his love for humanity.
6. His work with other Mexican artists was also very important.
7. Rivera was a major influence on another mural artist, Juan O'Gorman.
8. This mural by him decorates a Mexican university library.

9. O'Gorman does not paint his murals; instead, he uses tiny pieces of colored tile.
10. The complicated pattern upon the library walls fascinates everyone who sees it.

More than one adjective phrase may modify the same noun or pronoun.

EXAMPLE **That painting of New England by Edward Bannister is famous.** [The two adjective phrases, *of New England* and *by Edward Bannister,* both modify the noun *painting.*]

An adjective phrase may also modify the object of another adjective phrase.

EXAMPLE **A number of the paintings by that artist are landscapes.** [The adjective phrase *of the paintings* modifies the noun *number.* The adjective phrase *by that artist* modifies *paintings,* the object of the preposition in the first phrase.]

PICTURE THIS

You're the restaurant reviewer for a local newspaper. The Japanese restaurant shown on the next page has recently opened in town, and your job is to report on the food and service there. The server has just brought these colorful, tasty-looking dishes to your table. As you taste each food, write down some notes for your review. Describe how the food looks, tastes, and smells. Also describe the quality of the service. Mention any features of the restaurant that you find particularly interesting. [Note: You can use your imagination to describe features not shown in the photograph.] Decide whether you will or will not recommend this restaurant to your readers. In your notes, use at least five adjective phrases. Be prepared to identify the word or words that each phrase modifies.

GRAMMAR

A DIFFERENT APPROACH

To give students practice in using adjective phrases, bring some magazines to class and let students cut out pictures that are suitable for writing prompts. Ask them to write descriptive paragraphs based on what they see in the pictures. They should include at least one adjective phrase in each sentence. Ask volunteers to read their paragraphs to the class.

GRAMMAR

PICTURE THIS

To help students organize their notes on the food, suggest that they make three lists of adjectives, one each under the headings *looks, tastes,* and *smells,* as a prewriting exercise.

Subject: a new Japanese restaurant
Audience: newspaper readers
Purpose: to inform by describing the food and service; to persuade

EXERCISE 6 **Identifying Adjective Phrases**

In the following sentences, identify each adjective phrase. Then give the noun or pronoun the phrase modifies. [Note: Some sentences contain more than one adjective phrase.]

EXAMPLE 1. This book about birds of North America has won many awards for photography.
1. *about birds—book; of North America—birds; for photography—awards*

1. This book explains the importance of flight in the survival of the bird population.
2. The key to successful flight is the structure of the feather.

GRAMMAR

TIMESAVER

Because **Exercises 5** and **6** are alike, you may want to use **Exercise 6** as an oral review. You could assign only the even-numbered sentences to assess students' progress. For those who still need additional practice, assign the odd-numbered sentences as written work.

3. As you can see below, the shaft and the vane are the two main parts of a feather.
4. The area inside the quill of a feather is hollow.
5. Small barbs on the shaft form a feather's vane.
6. The curves in the vane and notches of the feather permit easy, quick movement.
7. Keratin, the same type of protein that gives strength to hair and nails, makes feathers strong.
8. Feathers on the wings and tails of birds often are quite showy.
9. Fast-flying birds like swifts usually have pointed wings.
10. Have you ever seen any of the birds that have these kinds of feathers?

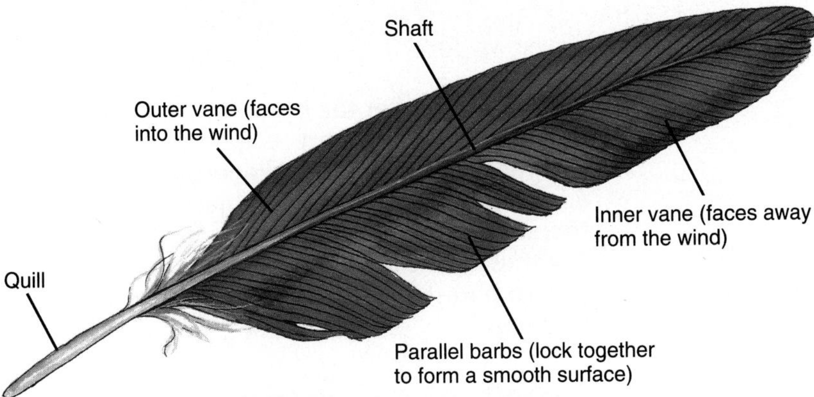

EXERCISE 7 **Writing Adjective Phrases**

Fill in the blank in each of the following sentences with an appropriate adjective phrase.

EXAMPLE **1.** That storm ___ might be dangerous.
1. *That storm from the east might be dangerous.*

1. The shelf ___ is too high to reach.
2. My mariachi costume should win a prize ___.
3. The girl ___ is one of my best friends.
4. The argument ___ really wasn't very important.
5. My favorite birthday present was the one ___.

GRAMMAR

INTEGRATING THE LANGUAGE ARTS

Literature Link. After your students read and discuss Lensey Namioka's humorous short story "The All-American Slurp," ask them to see how many adjective phrases they can locate in the first four paragraphs. Encourage students to discuss ways the story is made more interesting through the use of adjective phrases. [The phrases provide a greater level of detail.]

GRAMMAR

ANSWERS

Exercise 7

Adjective phrases will vary. Here are some possibilities:

1. in the kitchen
2. for imagination
3. in that picture
4. over tickets
5. from Aunt Rita and Uncle Luis

SEGMENT 4 *(pp. 428–433)*

ADVERB PHRASES Rule 15d

OBJECTIVES

- To identify adverb phrases and the words they modify
- To complete sentences by supplying adverb phrases

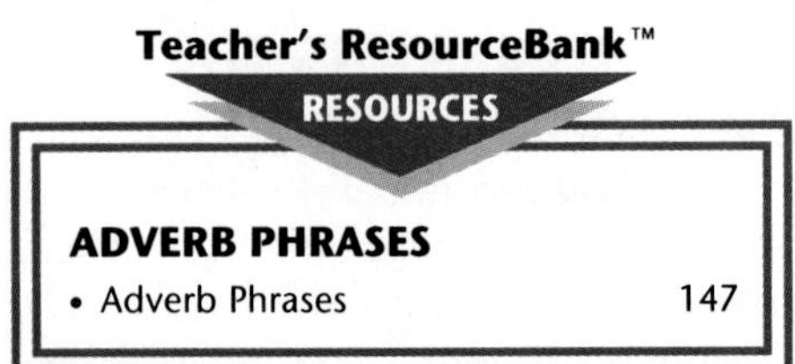

Teacher's ResourceBank™

RESOURCES

ADVERB PHRASES

- Adverb Phrases 147

GRAMMAR

QUICK REMINDER

Write the following sentences on the chalkboard and ask students to identify the adverb phrase in each sentence and the word the phrase modifies:

1. The ballerina fell after her ovation. [after her ovation—fell]
2. We saw the sunrise during breakfast. [during breakfast—saw]
3. Some creative people write with their left hands. [with their left hands—write]

When they are through, point out to the students that because the prepositional phrases modify verbs, they must be adverb phrases.

Adverb Phrases

GRAMMAR

A prepositional phrase used as an adverb is called an *adverb phrase.*

ADVERB We walk **there** every Saturday.
ADVERB PHRASE We walk **along the lake** every Saturday.

15d. An ***adverb phrase*** modifies a verb, an adjective, or an adverb.

Adverb phrases answer the same questions that single-word adverbs answer.

When?	*Why?*
Where?	*How often?*
How?	*How long?*

EXAMPLES **The chorus sang at the hospital.** [The adverb phrase modifies the verb *sang.* It tells *where.*]
Will the rolls be ready by dinnertime? [The adverb phrase modifies the adjective *ready.* It tells *when.*]
Are these jeans long enough for you? [The adverb phrase modifies the adverb *enough.* It tells *how.*]

EXERCISE 8 **Identifying Adverb Phrases**

Identify the adverb phrase used in each of the following sentences. Then write the word or words the phrase modifies.

EXAMPLE **1.** My hamster disappeared for three days.
1. *for three days—disappeared*

1. Dad hung a mirror in the front hall.
2. The cat is afraid of thunderstorms.
3. The acrobat plunged into the net but did not hurt herself.
4. Edward James Olmos will speak at our school.

15d

GRAMMAR

5. Mom discovered several field mice in the cellar.
6. With great courage, Rosa Parks disobeyed the bus driver.
7. He plays well for a beginner.
8. We have planted day lilies along the fence.
9. Soon my shoes were full of sand.
10. Every morning she jogs around the reservoir.

Like adjective phrases, more than one adverb phrase may modify the same word.

EXAMPLE **My teacher said that César Chávez has worked with the United Farm Workers for many years.** [Both adverb phrases, *with the United Farm Workers* and *for many years,* modify the verb phrase *has worked.*]

An adverb phrase may be followed by an adjective phrase that modifies the object of the preposition in the adverb phrase.

EXAMPLE **We went to an exhibit of rare coins.** [The adverb phrase *to an exhibit* modifies the verb *went.* The adjective phrase *of rare coins* modifies *exhibit,* the object of the preposition in the adverb phrase.]

EXERCISE 9 **Identifying Adverb Phrases**

Identify the adverb phrase used in each of the following sentences. After each phrase, give the word or words the phrase modifies.

EXAMPLES
1. On Passover evening, we prepare a Seder, which is a Jewish holiday meal and ceremony.
1. *On Passover evening—prepare*
2. The Passover holiday celebrates a time long ago when Jewish slaves freed themselves from their masters.
2. *from their masters—freed*

1. On Passover, our relatives visit our home.
2. We always invite them for the Seder.
3. Our whole family helps with the preparations.

LEP/ESL

General Strategies. Some students may have problems deciding which preposition to use when writing adverb phrases about transportation. If students are confused about the uses of *in* and *on,* tell them that as a general rule, *on* is used for vehicles that carry only one person: get *on* a motorcycle or bicycle. For vehicles that carry about five people, *in* is used: get *in* the car or canoe. For vehicles that carry about twenty or more people, *on* is again used: get *on* the plane or train.

INTEGRATING THE LANGUAGE ARTS

Literature Link. Ask students to read and discuss Lloyd Alexander's short story "The Stone." Then ask them to identify as many adverb phrases as possible in the first four paragraphs. You may want to read those paragraphs aloud, omitting the adverb phrases to demonstrate how different the story would be without them.

GRAMMAR

GRAMMAR

COOPERATIVE LEARNING

To give students extra practice with adverb phrases, divide the class into groups of three. Provide the groups with some type of text (such as magazine articles, or essays from other classes) and have the groups find as many adverbs as they can. Have them copy the sentences with the adverbs and then rewrite the sentences, substituting prepositional phrases for the adverbs. [For example: "She read the story quickly" might become "She read the story in a minute."]

ANSWERS

Exercise 10

Sentences will vary. Here are some possibilities:

1. We walked down the hall.
2. The mascot stood by them.
3. I saw them in the mall.
4. The ball rolled under the car.
5. She jumped on the diving board.

GRAMMAR

4. Soon, everything is ready for the Seder.
5. In this photograph you can see how beautiful our holiday table is.

6. Holding all the special Passover foods, the Seder plate is displayed in the center of the table.
7. On the plate is a roasted egg representing new life.
8. Horseradish, which represents slavery's bitterness, is placed near the egg.
9. The other carefully arranged foods are also used during the Passover ceremony.
10. Throughout the entire meal, everyone enjoys a variety of delicious foods.

EXERCISE 10 **Writing Sentences with Adverb Phrases**

Write five sentences using the following word groups as adverb phrases. Underline each phrase. Then draw an arrow from the phrase to the word or words it modifies.

EXAMPLE **1.** for the airport

1. *They have left for the airport.*

1. down the hall
2. by them
3. in the mall
4. under the car
5. on the diving board

REVIEWS A–C

OBJECTIVES

- To identify prepositional phrases in sentences as adjective or adverb phrases
- To write sentences using prepositional phrases as adjectives and adverbs

GRAMMAR

REVIEW A **Identifying Adjective and Adverb Phrases**

Each of the following sentences contains a prepositional phrase. Identify each phrase, and label it as an *adjective phrase* or an *adverb phrase*.

EXAMPLE 1. Wilma Rudolph won three gold medals in the 1960 Olympic games.
1. *in the 1960 Olympic games—adverb phrase*

1. Wilma Rudolph did not have the childhood you might expect of a future Olympic athlete.
2. She and her twenty-one sisters and brothers were raised in a needy family.
3. Rudolph suffered from polio and scarlet fever.
4. Back then, illnesses like these were often deadly.
5. For many years afterward, Rudolph used a leg brace when she walked.
6. Yet, she never lost sight of her dreams.
7. She battled the odds against her.
8. With her family's help, she exercised hard every day.
9. All of her hard work made her strong.
10. Years later, she gained fame as a world-class athlete.

REVIEW B **Identifying Adjective and Adverb Phrases**

Each of the following sentences contains at least one prepositional phrase. Identify the phrase or phrases used in each sentence. Label each phrase as an *adjective phrase* or an *adverb phrase*.

EXAMPLE 1. In China, farmers are considered the backbone of the country.
1. *In China—adverb phrase; of the country—adjective phrase*

1. Most of the Chinese people are farmers.
2. They generally work their farms by hand.

GRAMMAR

LESS-ADVANCED STUDENTS

Have students work in pairs or groups of three to do **Review B.** Encourage students to talk about the sentences and any problems they have in comprehending them. You may want to walk about the room, listening to conversations, to verify that the information is being explained adequately.

GRAMMAR

3. Chinese farmers usually use hand tools instead of large machines.
4. Farmland throughout China is carefully prepared, planted, and weeded.
5. Farmers also harvest their crops with great care.
6. In the hills, the Chinese make flat terraces.
7. As you can see below, water from high terraces can flow to lower terraces.
8. Farmers build ridges around them so that they can be flooded during the growing season.
9. In flat sections, water is pumped out of the ground.
10. Other Chinese methods of irrigation are shown in the pictures below.

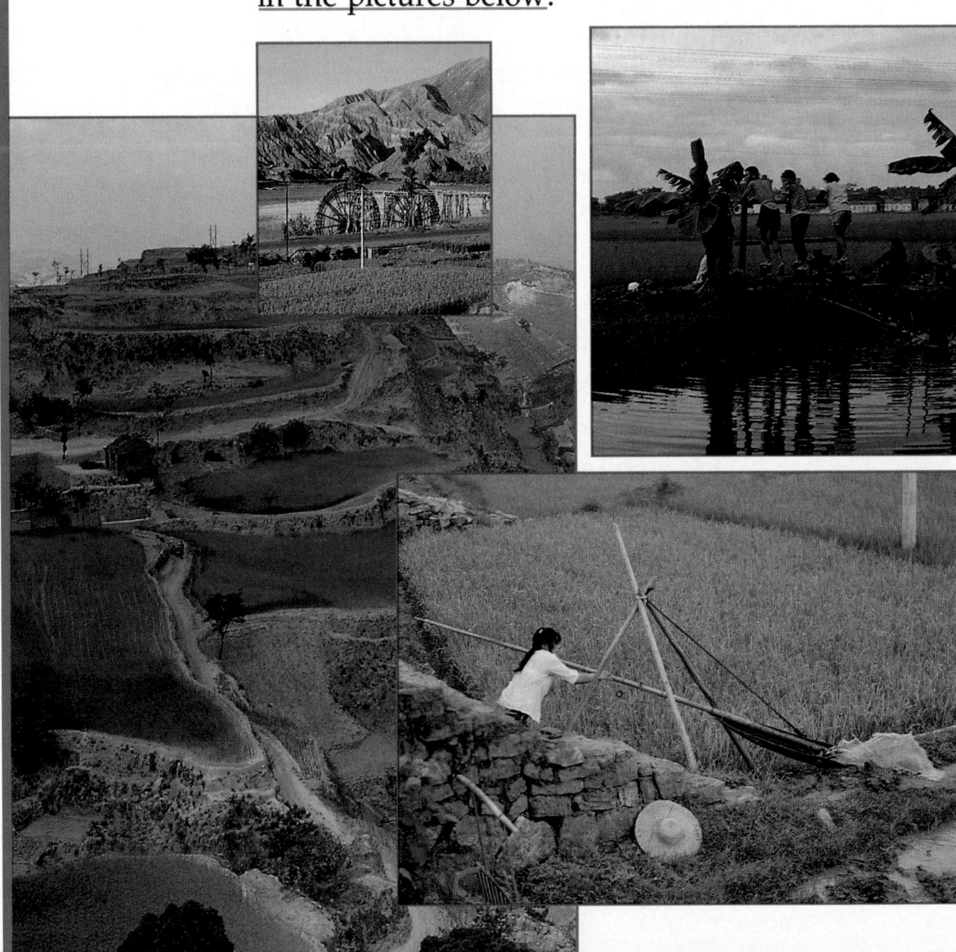

GRAMMAR

WRITING APPLICATION

OBJECTIVE

- To write an expository narrative using adjective and adverb phrases

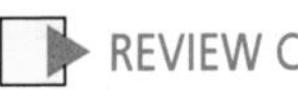

Writing Sentences with Adjective and Adverb Phrases

Use each of the following phrases in two separate sentences. In the first sentence, use the phrase as an adjective. In the second sentence, use the phrase as an adverb.

EXAMPLE 1. in Indiana
1. *The people in Indiana are called "Hoosiers." We once lived in Indiana.*

1. from California
2. in my class
3. along the path
4. under the bridge
5. behind you

GRAMMAR

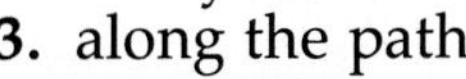

Using Prepositional Phrases to Add Detail

Like one-word adjectives and adverbs, prepositional phrases add information to sentences. Adjective phrases tell *what kind, how many, how much,* and *which one.* Adverb phrases tell *when, where, why, how, how often, how long,* and *to what extent.*

WITHOUT PHRASES I walked my dog.
WITH PHRASES On Saturday I walked my dog on the trail along the river.

WRITING ACTIVITY

The Friends of Animals Society is having a contest for the best true-life pet story. The winner of the contest will have his or her story published in the local newspaper and will receive a fifty-dollar U.S. savings bond. Write a story to enter in the contest. In your story, tell

ANSWERS

Review C

Sentences will vary. Here are some possibilities:

1. The people *from California* came to visit. They moved *from California* last month.
2. A girl *in my class* gave a good report. *In my class* we are studying science.
3. The stream *along the path* is almost dry. We walked *along the path.*
4. The fossils *under the bridge* washed downstream. The kids played *under the bridge.*
5. The man *behind you* is tall. That man stood *behind you* all day.

GRAMMAR

WRITING APPLICATION

Because the writing assignment calls for a narrative, students will need to focus on specific events involving the pets they choose to write about. Remind them that events have beginnings, middles, and ends, and that chronological order is the easiest way to explain an event.

CRITICAL THINKING
Analysis

Students will be required to analyze the characteristics of the pets they are writing about in order to decide what is unique about the animals. The characteristics they focus on could be physical attributes such as unusual coloration, abnormalities, or size; or abilities, whether natural or resulting from training.

PREWRITING

As a prewriting exercise, suggest that each student make a list of the questions that adjective phrases answer [*what kind, how many, how much,* and *which one*] and a list of the questions that adverb phrases answer [*when, where, how, how often,* and *to what extent*] and answer each question with an appropriate adjective or adverb phrase.

GRAMMAR

about an unusual pet that you've known or heard about. Use at least five adjective phrases and five adverb phrases in your story.

Prewriting First, you'll need to choose a pet to write about. Maybe you know of a cat that does clever tricks or a hamster that has a quirky personality. Perhaps you've read about a dog that's especially loyal or brave. Decide which story you want to write. Then jot down details about how the animal looks and how it acts. In your notes, focus on a specific time when the animal did something funny or amazing.

Writing Begin your draft with an attention-grabbing paragraph. Introduce and describe your main character. Be sure that you've included any human characters that play a part in the story. Also, describe the story's setting—for example, your kitchen, your neighbor's backyard, or the woods.

Evaluating and Revising Ask a friend to read your draft. Then ask him or her the following questions:

- Is the story interesting?
- Does it clearly show the animal's personality?
- Are events in the story logically connected?

If the answer to any of these questions is no, you may need to add, cut, or rearrange details. Make sure you've used at least five adjective phrases and five adverb phrases.

Proofreading and Publishing Check your story carefully for errors in grammar, spelling, and punctuation. Use a dictionary or another reference source to make certain that all proper names are spelled and capitalized correctly. You and your classmates may want to collect your stories into a booklet. Along with your stories, you might include pictures or drawings of the pets you've written about.

SEGMENT 5 *(pp. 435–436)*

REVIEW: POSTTEST

OBJECTIVES

- To identify adverb phrases and adjective phrases and the words they modify
- To write sentences with prepositional phrases

Review: Posttest 1

GRAMMAR

Identifying Adjective and Adverb Phrases

Identify the prepositional phrase in each of the following sentences, and tell whether the phrase is used as an *adjective phrase* or an *adverb phrase.* Then give the word or words that the phrase modifies.

EXAMPLE **1.** This newspaper article on weather patterns is interesting.
1. *on weather patterns; adjective phrase—article*

1. The hikers are ready for a break. **1.** adv. phr.
2. Yesterday we rode our bikes through the park. **2.** adv. phr.
3. I always wear heavy woolen socks under my hiking boots. **3.** adv. phr.
4. Jesse Jackson spoke at the convention. **4.** adv. phr.
5. Most children like books with colorful pictures. **5.** adj. phr.
6. Students from both South America and North America attended the meet. **6.** adj. phr.
7. That store has something for everyone. **7.** adj. phr.
8. Joel and Tina are participating in the Special Olympics this year. **8.** adv. phr.
9. I sent it to him this morning. **9.** adv. phr.
10. The road to town is flooded. **10.** adj. phr.
11. The camel is an important animal throughout the Middle East. **11.** adv. phr.
12. I will rake the leaves after lunch. **12.** adv. phr.
13. The plant by the kitchen window is a begonia. **13.** adj. phr.
14. We always camp close to a lake. **14.** adv. phr.
15. The stars of that movie are Rita Moreno and Joan Chen. **15.** adj. phr.
16. She rowed the boat across the lake. **16.** adv. phr.
17. Grandma Moses began painting during her late seventies. **17.** adv. phr.
18. We covered the hot ashes with sand and rocks. **18.** adv. phr.
19. The actors quietly took their places on the stage. **19.** adv. phr.
20. Have you read the book about Sojourner Truth? **20.** adj. phr.

LESS-ADVANCED STUDENTS

If students need additional review before taking the **Posttest,** you may want to give them a little extra study time. Form small study groups of two or three students each. Assign the even-numbered sentences in **Review: Posttests 1** and **2.** Go over the answers orally with the class so that you can identify students who are struggling with the material. When everyone feels confident about the sentences, assign the odd-numbered sentences of **Posttests 1** and **2** as a test.

GRAMMAR

GRAMMAR

ANSWERS

Review: Posttest 2

Sentences will vary. Here are some possibilities:

1. Her report card was found *among the papers.* (was found)
2. She knows *about computers.* (knows)
3. The dirt *under the surface* is hard to get to. (dirt)
4. I like reading *in the afternoon.* (reading)
5. You should exercise *for yourself.* (exercise)
6. The children ran playfully *through the puddles.* (ran)
7. The wire *over the treetops* fell last winter. (wire)
8. *Before dinner,* we washed our hands. (washed)
9. The cat walked *along the fence.* (walked)
10. The dog ran *toward us.* (ran)

GRAMMAR

Review: Posttest 2

Writing Sentences with Prepositional Phrases

Use each of the following prepositional phrases in a sentence. After each sentence, write the word that the prepositional phrase modifies.

EXAMPLE **1. across the street**
1. ***They live across the street.—live***

1. among the papers
2. about computers
3. under the surface
4. in the afternoon
5. for yourself
6. through the puddles
7. over the treetops
8. before dinner
9. along the fence
10. toward us

SEGMENT 1 *(pp. 437–438)*

DIAGNOSTIC TEST

OBJECTIVE

- To identify complements and to classify them as direct objects, indirect objects, predicate nominatives, or predicate adjectives

GRAMMAR

16 COMPLEMENTS

Direct and Indirect Objects, Subject Complements

Diagnostic Test

Identifying Complements

Identify the complement or complements in each of the following sentences. Then label each complement as a *direct object*, an *indirect object*, a *predicate nominative*, or a *predicate adjective*.

EXAMPLE 1. My grandparents sent me some old Moroccan coins.
1. *me—indirect object; coins—direct object*

1. A park ranger told us the history of Forest Park. 1. i.o./d.o.
2. Tuesday is the last day for soccer tryouts. 2. p.n.
3. She made her mother a sari for her birthday. 3. i.o./d.o.
4. These peaches taste sweet and juicy. 4. p.a./p.a.
5. James Baldwin wrote stories, novels, and essays. 5. d.o./d.o./d.o.
6. He handed Amy and me an ad for the concert. 6. i.o./i.o./d.o.
7. Two common desert creatures are the lizard and the snake. 7. p.n./p.n.

Teacher's ResourceBank™

RESOURCES

FOR THE WHOLE CHAPTER

- Chapter Review Form A 157–158
- Chapter Review Form B 159–160
- Assessment Portfolio
  - Grammar Pretests 447–454
  - Grammar Mastery Tests 471–478

GRAMMAR

CHAPTER OVERVIEW

The first part of this chapter asks students to look at incomplete sentences and to evaluate the necessity for a complement to complete the sentences. The second part directs students to specific complements. After treating direct objects, the chapter discusses indirect objects, predicate nominatives, and predicate adjectives.

USING THE DIAGNOSTIC TEST

The **Diagnostic Test** is one way to gauge students' understanding of sentence completeness, especially in regard to the parts of speech that aid in this completeness. The test might be used as a tool for determining the exact nature of problems with students who fail to use complements in their writing, or as a springboard for specific lessons in problem areas.

STUDENTS WITH SPECIAL NEEDS

Some students live in an oral culture; therefore, providing a quiet area for them to read aloud might help them hear sentence incompleteness. However, while students may hear the problem, correcting it may prove more difficult for them.

It might help if students act out sentences like, "I read . . . ," or "The teacher sang . . . ." This action will allow students to hear the necessity for an ending.

COMMON ERROR

Problem. Students often think that a subject and a verb are all that are needed for sentence completion. Therefore, they may write sentences that are lacking necessary complements.

Solution. Give students lists of subjects and verbs and ask them to supply complements to form sentences. Ask students to share their responses and discuss the variety of ways in which they responded.

GRAMMAR

8. My cousin Tena has become an excellent <u>weaver</u> of Navajo blankets. **8.** p.n.
9. Tropical forests give <u>us</u> many helpful <u>plants</u>. **9.** i.o./d.o.
10. The soil in that pot feels <u>dry</u> to me. **10.** p.a.

Recognizing Complements

16a. A ***complement*** is a word or group of words that completes the meaning of a verb.

Every sentence has a subject and a verb. Sometimes the subject and the verb can express a complete thought all by themselves.

EXAMPLES Adriana (S) swam (V).

The baby (S) was sleeping (V).

Often a verb needs a complement to complete its meaning.

INCOMPLETE My aunt (S) found (V) [*what?*]

COMPLETE My aunt (S) found (V) a **wallet** (C). [The noun *wallet* completes the meaning of the verb *found.*]

INCOMPLETE The coach (S) chose (V) [*whom?*]

COMPLETE The coach (S) chose (V) **her** (C). [The pronoun *her* completes the meaning of the verb *chose.*]

INCOMPLETE Raymond (S) seemed (V) [*what?*]

COMPLETE Raymond (S) seemed (V) **tired** (C). [The adjective *tired* completes the meaning of the verb *seemed.*]

SEGMENT 2 *(pp. 439–441)*

DIRECT OBJECTS

OBJECTIVE

- To identify direct objects in sentences

16 a–b

GRAMMAR

Direct Objects

The ***direct object*** is one type of complement. It completes the meaning of a transitive verb.

 REFERENCE NOTE: Transitive verbs are discussed on pages 392–393.

16b. A ***direct object*** is a noun or a pronoun that receives the action of the verb or shows the result of that action. A direct object answers the question *What*? or *Whom*? after a transitive verb.

EXAMPLES **My brother bought a model.** [Bought *what?* Bought a model. The noun *model* receives the action of the verb *bought.*]

He built it. [Built *what*? Built it. The pronoun *it* is the result of the action of the verb *built.*]

A transitive verb may be followed by a compound direct object.

EXAMPLE He needed **glue, paint,** and **decals** for his model. [The compound direct object of the verb *needed* is *glue, paint,* and *decals.*]

A direct object can never follow a linking verb because a linking verb does not express action. Also, a direct object is never included in a prepositional phrase.

LINKING VERB **Julia Morgan was an architect.** [The verb *was* does not express action; therefore, it has no direct object.]

PREPOSITIONAL PHRASE **She studied in Paris.** [*Paris* cannot be the direct object of the verb *studied* because it is the object in the prepositional phrase *in Paris.*]

REFERENCE NOTE: For more about linking verbs, see pages 394–395. For more about prepositional phrases, see Chapter 15.

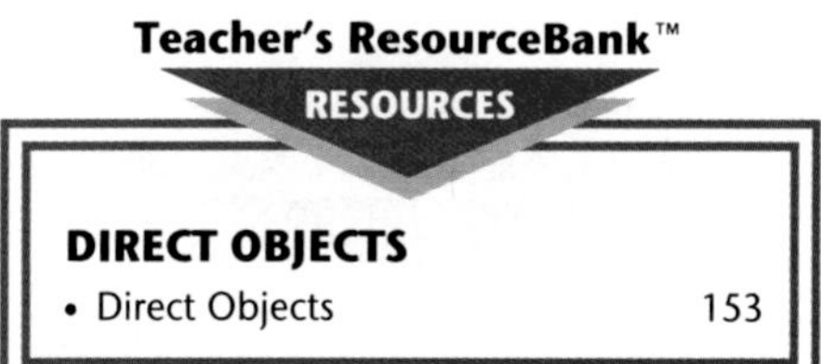

Teacher's ResourceBank™

RESOURCES

DIRECT OBJECTS

- Direct Objects 153

QUICK REMINDER

You may want to review with students the differences between transitive verbs and linking verbs. Unless students feel confident in recognizing these types of verbs, they may become frustrated in their attempts to identify direct objects.

Write the following sentences on the chalkboard and ask students to identify the direct objects and the sentences without direct objects:

1. The dog chewed the bone. [bone]
2. Neal dropped the pencil. [pencil]
3. The car was black. [no object]
4. She gave me a job. [job]
5. The music sounded loud. [no object]

GRAMMAR

MEETING INDIVIDUAL NEEDS

LEP/ESL

General Strategies. To reinforce the fact that a direct object can answer the question *Whom?* as well as *What?*, write the following sentences on the chalkboard and ask students to identify the direct objects and to tell which question they answer:

1. My dog licked me and wagged its tail. [me—whom; tail—what]
2. Melanie hugged her grandmother. [grandmother—whom]
3. Don't tickle her! [her—whom]
4. I can't find David anywhere. [David—whom]

INTEGRATING THE LANGUAGE ARTS

Literature Link. If your literature textbook contains it, have students read and discuss Robert Frost's poem "Blue-Butterfly Day." Have them locate all of the direct objects used in the poem. Discuss how these direct objects create more vivid imagery in the poem. For extra practice, invite students to replace the direct objects in the poem with their own direct objects. Ask students to share their versions with the class.

EXERCISE 1 Identifying Direct Objects

Identify the direct object or objects in each of the following sentences. Remember that a direct object may be compound.

EXAMPLE **1. Do you enjoy books and movies about horses?**
1. *books, movies*

1. Then you probably know some of the stories by Marguerite Henry.
2. Her books about horses have thrilled readers for more than forty years.
3. Henry's most popular books include *Misty of Chincoteague* and *King of the Wind*.
4. Her book *King of the Wind* won the Newbery Medal in 1949.
5. The book tells the adventures of the boy Agba and this beautiful Arabian horse.

SEGMENT 3 *(pp. 441–446)*
INDIRECT OBJECTS

OBJECTIVES

- To identify direct and indirect objects
- To write sentences with direct and indirect objects

6. Agba fed milk and honey to the newborn colt.
7. Sometimes the playful colt bit Agba's fingers.
8. The head of the stables often mistreated Agba and the colt.
9. Later, they both left their home and travelled to England.
10. To find out how the story ends, read *King of the Wind*.

Indirect Objects

The ***indirect object*** is another type of complement. Like the direct object, the indirect object helps to complete the meaning of a transitive verb. If a sentence has an indirect object, it also has a direct object.

16c. The ***indirect object*** is a noun or a pronoun that comes between the verb and the direct object. It tells *to whom* or *to what,* or *for whom* or *for what,* the action of the verb is done.

Teacher's ResourceBank™

RESOURCES

INDIRECT OBJECTS

- Indirect Objects 154

QUICK REMINDER

Write the following sentences on the chalkboard and have students fill in the blanks with names:

1. Don bought ____ a new bike.
2. Mrs. Walker brought ____ new pencils.
3. The salesman showed ____ his new car.

Explain to students that the names they supplied are indirect objects because they tell for whom the action of the verb is done.

LEP/ESL

Spanish. In Spanish, use of the indirect object is far more explicit than in English. That is, the indirect object is always clearly marked by the preposition *a.* For example, consider the following sentences:

1. I gave the cat to my sister.
2. I gave the cat a toy.

Although *cat* changes from direct to indirect object, there is nothing in the words used to indicate this shift. Compare the Spanish translations:

1. Le di un gato **a** mi hermana.
2. Le di un juguete **al** gato.

The marker *a* automatically signals that what follows is an indirect object. Therefore, Spanish speakers may need extra help in identifying indirect objects in English.

GRAMMAR

GRAMMAR

EXAMPLES I gave that **problem** some thought. [The noun *problem* is the indirect object of the verb *gave.* It answers the question "*To what* did I give some thought?"]

Dad bought **himself** some peanuts. [The pronoun *himself* is the indirect object of the verb *bought.* It answers the question "*For whom* did Dad buy peanuts?"]

Do not mistake the object of a preposition for an indirect object.

OBJECT OF A PREPOSITION We sent the sombrero to **her.** [*Her* is the object of the preposition *to.*]

INDIRECT OBJECT We sent **her** the sombrero. [*Her* is the indirect object of the verb *sent.*]

Like a direct object, an indirect object can be compound.

EXAMPLE She gave **Ed** and **me** the list of summer activities. [*Ed* and *me* are the indirect objects of the verb *gave.* They answer the question "*To whom* did she give the list?"]

EXERCISE 2 Identifying Direct and Indirect Objects

Identify the *direct object* and *indirect object* in each of the following sentences. Remember not to confuse objects of prepositions with direct objects and indirect objects. [Note: Some sentences do not have an indirect object.]

EXAMPLE **1. Gabriel sent me a postcard from Ecuador.**
1. *me—indirect object; postcard—direct object*

1. In Ecuador, Gabriel visited many of his relatives.
2. His aunt and uncle showed him the railroad in San Lorenzo.
3. They also visited the port in Esmeraldas.
4. Ecuador exports bananas and coffee.
5. Gabriel's cousin showed him some other sights.
6. She told Gabriel stories about Ecuadoran heroes.

7. Gabriel and his relatives rode a train into the mountains.
8. They took photos from the train four thousand feet up the Andes Mountains.
9. Gabriel enjoyed his visit to Ecuador.
10. He brought us some unusual souvenirs.

GRAMMAR

EXERCISE 3 **Writing Sentences with Direct and Indirect Objects**

You and a friend see the advertisement below for a clothing sale at the neighborhood thrift store. Each of you has saved twenty dollars, so you decide to purchase a few items for yourselves and your families. Using information in the ad and five of the verbs listed below, write five sentences about what you and your friend will buy. Include a direct object and an indirect object in each sentence. Underline the indirect object once and the direct object twice. Be sure to stay within your twenty-dollar budget!

bought	found	paid	showed
gave	sold	owed	asked

EXAMPLE **1.** *Sue bought her mother a necklace.*

ANSWERS

Exercise 3

Sentences will vary. Here are some possibilities:

1. Trudy bought me a hat.
2. I found Dad a shirt.
3. The clerk sold me a coat.
4. Carla showed Bill her new belt.
5. I asked the clerk a question.

GRAMMAR

WRITING APPLICATION

OBJECTIVE

- To write a paragraph containing direct and indirect objects

WRITING APPLICATION

The **Writing Activity** requires that students write paragraphs about their hobbies. Students may need further elaboration on what constitutes a hobby. You can tell them that a hobby is anything someone does on a regular basis for enjoyment.

CRITICAL THINKING

Analysis

To write paragraphs about their hobbies, students will need to analyze the processes they go through when practicing their hobbies. For example, if they collect things, they will need to discuss where or how the things are obtained and how the collections are kept or displayed.

PREWRITING

Because students' paragraphs are to contain direct and indirect objects, it might be helpful to have students make up lists of transitive verbs that they feel are appropriate for describing their hobbies.

GRAMMAR

GRAMMAR

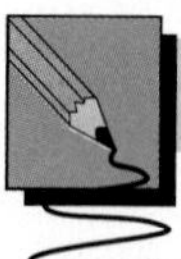

WRITING APPLICATION

Using Direct and Indirect Objects

Many sentences contain action verbs. Often, more information is needed to complete the meaning of these verbs. Direct objects answer the questions *What?* or *Whom?* after transitive verbs. Indirect objects tell *to whom* or *to what,* or *for whom* or *for what.*

INCOMPLETE I collect. [I collect *what*?]
COMPLETE I collect **stamps** from all over the world. [direct object]

INCOMPLETE My pen pal sends many unusual stamps. [My pen pal sends stamps *to whom*?]
COMPLETE My pen pal sends **me** many unusual stamps. [indirect object]

WRITING ACTIVITY

For National Hobby Month, students in your class are making posters about their hobbies. Each poster will include drawings or pictures and a written description of the hobby. Write a paragraph about your hobby to go on your poster. Use at least three direct objects and two indirect objects in your paragraph.

Prewriting Choose a topic for your poster project. You could write about any collection, sport, craft, or activity that you enjoy in your free time. You could also write about a hobby that you're interested in starting. Freewrite about the hobby. Be sure to tell why you enjoy it or why you think you would enjoy it. If the hobby is new to you, find out more about it from another hobbyist or from the library.

Writing Begin your paragraph with a main-idea sentence that clearly identifies the hobby or special interest. (For more about main-idea sentences, see pages

REVIEW A

OBJECTIVE

- To identify direct and indirect objects in sentences

61–63.) Check your prewriting notes often to find details you can use in describing the hobby.

Evaluating and Revising Read your paragraph aloud. Does it give enough information about your hobby? Would someone unfamiliar with the hobby find it interesting? Add, cut, or rearrange details to make your paragraph easier to understand. Identify the transitive verbs in your paragraph. Have you used at least three direct objects and two indirect objects? You may need to revise some sentences.

Proofreading and Publishing Read over your paragraph for spelling, grammar, and punctuation errors. Check carefully for sentence fragments and run-on sentences. (For more about writing complete sentences, see pages 304–305 and 340–341.) You and your classmates may want to make posters using your paragraphs and some pictures. Cut pictures out of magazines and brochures or draw your own. Then attach your writing and art to a piece of poster board.

REVIEW A **Identifying Direct and Indirect Objects**

Identify the *direct object* and *indirect object* in each of the following sentences. [Note: Some sentences do not have indirect objects.]

EXAMPLE **1.** Have you ever given board games much thought?
1. *thought—direct object; games—indirect object*

1. For centuries, people have enjoyed war games.
2. This interest in war games has given us chess and checkers.
3. My brother showed me a book about different kinds of board games.

GRAMMAR

PROOFREADING AND PUBLISHING

If you have students construct posters, the finished products could be displayed in the classroom, the school cafeteria, or the school library.

SEGMENT 4 *(pp. 446–452)*

SUBJECT COMPLEMENTS

OBJECTIVES

- To identify predicate nominatives and predicate adjectives in sentences
- To write a movie review containing predicate adjectives
- To write a paragraph containing predicate adjectives

GRAMMAR

Teacher's ResourceBank™

RESOURCES

SUBJECT COMPLEMENTS

- Predicate Nominatives 155
- Predicate Adjectives 156

QUICK REMINDER

Write the following sentences on the chalkboard. Ask students to identify the subject complements and to tell whether they are predicate nominatives or predicate adjectives.

1. The dog is wet. [wet—p.a.]
2. Mr. Gregg is a nurse. [nurse—p.n.]
3. Carmona sounds hoarse. [hoarse—p.a.]
4. Lucinda became a soldier. [soldier—p.n.]

GRAMMAR

4. Board games reflect many different interests, such as earning money, buying property, and collecting things.
5. Some games may teach players lessons for careers and sports.
6. Of course, word games can give people hours of fun.
7. During the more difficult word games, Mrs. Hampton sometimes helps Chen and me.
8. Do you like quiz or trivia games?
9. Sharon's uncle bought Ronnie and her one of the new quiz games.
10. A popular television show inspired the game.

Subject Complements

16d. A ***subject complement*** completes the meaning of a linking verb and identifies or describes the subject.

EXAMPLES Mrs. Suarez is a helpful **neighbor.** [The subject complement *neighbor* identifies the subject *Mrs. Suarez.*]
The airport in Atlanta is very **busy.** [The subject complement *busy* describes the subject *airport.*]

Subject complements always follow linking verbs, not action verbs.

Common Linking Verbs

appear	become	grow	remain	smell	stay
be	feel	look	seem	sound	taste

There are two kinds of subject complements—the *predicate nominative* and the *predicate adjective.*

Predicate Nominatives

16e. A ***predicate nominative*** is a noun or a pronoun that identifies or explains the subject of the sentence.

EXAMPLES Seaweed is **algae.** [The noun *algae* is a predicate nominative following the linking verb *is. Algae* identifies the subject *seaweed.*]

My secret pal was really **he**! [The pronoun *he* is a predicate nominative following the linking verb *was. He* identifies the subject *pal.*]

Be careful not to mistake a direct object or the object of a preposition for a predicate nominative.

DIRECT OBJECT My brother admired the **acrobat.**

OBJECT OF A PREPOSITION My brother spoke to the **acrobat.**

PREDICATE NOMINATIVE My brother became an **acrobat.**

A predicate nominative may be compound.

EXAMPLE Maya Angelou is a great **poet** and **storyteller.** [*Poet* and *storyteller* are predicate nominatives. They identify the subject and follow the linking verb *is.*]

NOTE: Expressions such as *It's I* and *That was she* sound awkward even though they are correct. In conversation, many people say *It's me* and *That was her.* Such expressions may one day become acceptable in writing, also. For now, however, it is best to follow the rules of standard English in your writing.

 EXERCISE 4 **Identifying Predicate Nominatives**

Identify the predicate nominative in each of the following sentences. [Note: A sentence may have a compound predicate nominative.]

GRAMMAR

MEETING INDIVIDUAL NEEDS

LEP/ESL

General Strategies. You may want to write the following sentences on the chalkboard to remind students that a few of the linking verbs listed (*smell, sound, taste,* and *feel*) can also be used as transitive or action verbs:

1. She smelled fresh bread in the kitchen.
2. He sounded the gong at five o'clock.
3. Taste this sauce!
4. I could feel a cool breeze.

Make it clear that not all sentences using these verbs contain complements.

LESS-ADVANCED

It might benefit students to improve their familiarity with linking verbs before they begin studying subject complements. To this end you can send them on a linking-verb hunt. Bring newspaper or magazine articles to class and have students see how many linking verbs they can find in them.

GRAMMAR

COOPERATIVE LEARNING

To help students learn the difference between predicate nominatives and predicate adjectives, divide the class into groups of three and ask each group to make a list of words that describe the classroom. Then have the groups make lists of different types of rooms. Finally, have students share their words by completing the sentence "The room is . . . ." When one group offers a word to complete the sentence, ask volunteers from other groups to identify the word as a predicate adjective or a predicate nominative. You may want to point out that their predicate nominatives are usually preceded by the articles *a, an,* or *the.*

GRAMMAR

EXAMPLE **1. Mount Rushmore is a national memorial.**
1. *memorial*

1. Was the author Chaim Potok or Amy Tan?
2. Her mother will remain president of the P.T.A.
3. Athens, Greece, has long been a center of art and drama.
4. The platypus and the anteater are mammals.
5. San Juan is the capital of Puerto Rico.
6. The peace pipe, or calumet, was a symbol of honor and power among Native Americans.
7. Quebec is the largest province in Canada.
8. In 1959, Hawaii became our fiftieth state.
9. That bird must be an eagle.
10. The fourth planet from the sun is Mars.

Predicate Adjectives

16f. A ***predicate adjective*** is an adjective that follows a linking verb and describes the subject of the sentence.

EXAMPLES **By 9:30 P.M., I was very tired.** [The adjective *tired* describes the subject *I.*]
The baseball field looks too wet. [The adjective *wet* describes the subject *field.*]

Like a predicate nominative, a predicate adjective may be compound.

EXAMPLE **The blanket felt soft and fuzzy.** [Both *soft* and *fuzzy* describe the subject *blanket.*]

EXERCISE 5 Identifying Predicate Adjectives

Identify the predicate adjective in each of the following sentences. [Note: A sentence may have a compound predicate adjective.]

EXAMPLE **1. The porpoise seemed friendly.**
1. *friendly*

1. Everyone felt ready for the test.
2. Those fresh strawberries smell delicious.
3. The front tire looks flat to me.
4. Everyone appeared interested in the debate.
5. That scratch may become worse.
6. She is talented in music.
7. During the movie, I became restless and bored.
8. Van looks upset about his grades.
9. Queen Liliuokalani was quite popular with the Hawaiian people.
10. The computer program does not seem difficult.

GRAMMAR

EXERCISE 6 **Writing Sentences with Predicate Adjectives**

You've been asked to write a movie review for your class newspaper. Think about a movie you've seen recently. Then write a review that tells why you think other students should or should not go to see the movie. In your review, include at least five sentences that contain predicate adjectives. Underline each predicate adjective.

EXAMPLE 1. *Keanu Reeves is believable as the young attorney.*

PICTURE THIS

As you step outside one night, you are greeted by the fantastic starry night shown on the next page. You are amazed by the swirling light of the stars and moon, and you're surprised by the feeling the scene gives you. You want to remember exactly what you see and feel, so you decide to write about the night in your journal. Write a paragraph describing the night and your feelings about it. In your paragraph, use at

GRAMMAR

ANSWERS

Exercise 6

Reviews will vary. Here is a possibility:

The movie *Batman,* directed by Tim Burton, tells the story of a troubled crime fighter. The mood of the movie is dark and somber. Michael Keaton is believable as the lonely hero who is troubled by his past. Jack Nicholson as the Joker is wonderfully evil. Kim Basinger plays the reporter who falls in love with Batman. The special effects were fantastic. The designs of Batman's vehicles were especially interesting. This is a movie worth watching again and again.

PICTURE THIS

You may want to have a class discussion before students begin writing. Ask students whether they have ever seen a night sky that seemed especially beautiful. How did it make them feel? Have students spend some time looking at the van Gogh reproduction and imagining really seeing such a sky.

REVIEWS B–D

OBJECTIVE

- To identify subject complements as direct objects, indirect objects, predicate nominatives, or predicate adjectives

VISUAL CONNECTIONS

About the Artist. Vincent van Gogh was born on March 30, 1853. His revolutionary and individualistic approach to painting was partly expressionist and partly symbolist. His style was based on dynamic forms and a vigorous use of color and line. Although he was virtually unknown in his lifetime, Van Gogh has exerted a powerful influence on the development of modern painting and is one of the world's most famous artists. He died on July 29, 1890.

least five predicate adjectives. (You may want to refer to the list of Common Linking Verbs on page 446.)

Subject: the night sky
Audience: yourself
Purpose: to remember this scene and your feelings

Vincent van Gogh, *The Starry Night*, collection, The Museum of Modern Art, New York. Acquired through the Lillie P. Bliss Bequest.

REVIEW B **Identifying Subject Complements**

Identify each subject complement in the following sentences as a predicate nominative or a predicate adjective. [Note: A sentence may have more than one subject complement.]

EXAMPLE **1.** The character Jahdu is a magical trickster.
1. *trickster—predicate nominative*

1. A trickster is a character who plays tricks on others.
2. Tricksters have been popular in many folk tales throughout the world.

3. Jahdu, however, is the creation of Virginia Hamilton.
4. Her collections of folk tales, such as *The Dark Way* and *In the Beginning*, are very enjoyable.
5. Jahdu may be her most unusual hero.
6. He certainly seems clever and playful.
7. Even Jahdu's home, a forest on the Mountain of Paths, sounds mysterious.
8. Jahdu can stay invisible by using special dust.
9. He can become any object, from a boy to a taxicab.
10. Why are tricksters like Jahdu always such entertaining characters?

GRAMMAR

REVIEW C **Identifying Complements**

Identify each complement in the following sentences as a *direct object*, an *indirect object*, a *predicate nominative*, or a *predicate adjective*.

EXAMPLE **1. Algonquin, a pony, was a pet of President Theodore Roosevelt's family.**
1. *pet—predicate nominative*

1. Some presidents' pets have become famous. 1. p.a.
2. Someone may have shown you the book by President George Bush's dog. 2. i.o./d.o.
3. Millie, a spaniel, is certainly talented. 3. p.a.
4. With the help of Mrs. Bush, Millie tells us a great deal about her days at the White House. 4. i.o./d.o.
5. President Richard Nixon's best-known pet was Checkers, a cocker spaniel. 5. p.n.
6. Some presidential pets looked quite strange at the White House. 6. p.a.
7. President William Howard Taft kept a pet cow. 7. d.o.
8. Herbert Hoover's family had two alligators. 8. d.o.
9. A pet mockingbird was a favorite companion of Thomas Jefferson. 9. p.n.
10. Calvin Coolidge's raccoon, Rebecca, appeared comfortable at the White House. 10. p.a.

COOPERATIVE LEARNING

Divide students into groups of three and ask each group to compose a set of six sentences that have direct objects. After groups have completed their sentences, have them trade sentences with other groups. The groups can then add indirect objects.

GRAMMAR

A DIFFERENT APPROACH

Provide students with a list of sentences with direct and indirect objects. Ask them each to choose one sentence and to draw a picture depicting the action described in the sentence and showing the direct and indirect objects.

GRAMMAR

GRAMMAR

REVIEW D **Identifying Complements**

Identify each complement in the following sentences as a *direct object,* an *indirect object,* a *predicate nominative,* or a *predicate adjective.* [Note: A sentence may have more than one complement.]

EXAMPLE [1] Have you ever seen a sari or a bindi?
1. *sari, bindi—direct objects*

1. d.o. [1] Many women from India wear these items. [2] A
2. p.n. sari is a traditional Indian garment of cotton or silk.
3. d.o. [3] Women wrap the sari's long, brightly printed cloth
4. p.a./p.a. around their bodies. [4] As you can see, the softly
5. i.o./d.o. draped sari is graceful and charming. [5] Some women
buy themselves cloth woven with golden threads for
6. p.a. an elegant look. [6] As you might imagine, sari
7. d.o. wearers can become quite chilled. [7] In cold climates,
Indian women wear their beautiful, lightweight gar-
8. p.n. ments under sturdy winter coats. [8] Another traditional feature of many Indian women is the colored
9. p.n. dot in the middle of their foreheads. [9] The Indian
10. i.o./d.o. word for the dot is *bindi.* [10] The bindi gives the
wearer a look of beauty and refinement.

SEGMENT 5 *(pp. 453–454)*

REVIEW: POSTTESTS 1 and 2

OBJECTIVES

- To identify complements and to classify them as direct objects, indirect objects, predicate nominatives, or predicate adjectives
- To write sentences with complements

Review: Posttest 1

GRAMMAR

Identifying Complements

Identify each complement in each of the following sentences as a *direct object*, an *indirect object*, a *predicate nominative*, or a *predicate adjective*. [Note: A sentence may have more than one complement.]

EXAMPLE 1. Many forests are cold and snowy.
1. *cold—predicate adjective; snowy—predicate adjective*

1. The home of the former president is now a library and museum. **1.** p.n./p.n.
2. The sun disappeared, and the wind suddenly grew cold. **2.** p.a.
3. We made our parents a family tree for their anniversary. **3.** i.o./d.o.
4. The newspaper published an article and an editorial about Mayor Sharon Pratt Dixon. **4.** d.o./d.o.
5. My uncle gave my sister and me ice skates. **5.** i.o./i.o./d.o.
6. After the long hike, all of the scouts felt sore and sleepy. **6.** p.a./p.a.
7. Leaders of the Ojibwa people held a meeting last summer. **7.** d.o.
8. I wrote my name and address in my book. **8.** d.o./d.o.
9. Your dog certainly appears healthy. **9.** p.a.
10. They always send us grapefruit and oranges from Florida. **10.** i.o./d.o./d.o.
11. Most stars in our galaxy are invisible to the human eye. **11.** p.a.
12. Did the workers really capture an alligator in the sewer system? **12.** d.o.
13. Our trip on the Staten Island ferry soon became an adventure. **13.** p.n.
14. The air show featured balloons and parachutes. **14.** d.o./d.o.
15. The maples in the park are becoming gold and red. **15.** p.a./p.a.

COMMON ERROR

Problem. Students often confuse parts of prepositional phrases with direct objects.

Solution. To reinforce that a direct object cannot be part of a prepositional phrase, write a few simple sentences with direct objects on the chalkboard. Ask students to identify the direct objects. After they have done so, add prepositional phrases to the sentences. For example, to the sentence "The boy hit the ball" you could add "over the fence." Explain that direct objects and prepositional phrases are different things that add detail to sentences.

GRAMMAR

ANSWERS

Review: Posttest 2

Responses will vary. Here are some possibilities:

1. My cat is pretty.
2. She bought me a doll.
3. He threw a baseball.
4. Dolly is a singer.
5. Her dog is brown and black.

16. My parents bought themselves several Celia Cruz CDs. **16.** i.o./d.o.
17. Aunt Kathleen gave Ricardo and me tickets for the show. **17.** i.o./i.o./d.o.
18. The two most popular sports at my school are football and baseball. **18.** p.n./p.n.
19. The water in the pool looked clean and fresh. **19.** p.a./p.a.
20. My mother's homemade Sabbath bread tastes delicious. **20.** p.a.

Review: Posttest 2

Writing Sentences with Complements

Write a sentence using each of the following kinds of complements. Underline the complement or complements in each sentence. Use a variety of subjects and verbs in your sentences.

EXAMPLE **1. a compound predicate nominative**
1. *My aunt is a swimmer and a jogger.*

1. a predicate adjective
2. an indirect object
3. a direct object
4. a predicate nominative
5. a compound predicate adjective

SEGMENT 1 *(pp. 455–456)*

DIAGNOSTIC TEST

OBJECTIVE

- To identify the subjects of sentences and to choose the forms of verbs that agree with those subjects

17 AGREEMENT

Subject and Verb

USAGE

Diagnostic Test

Choosing Verbs That Agree in Number with Their Subjects

For each of the following sentences, identify the subject. Then choose the form of the verb in parentheses that agrees with the subject.

EXAMPLE **1. Here (*are, is*) the tickets for the game.**
1. *tickets—are*

1. The flowers in that garden (*need, needs*) water.
2. She and her cousin (*play, plays*) tennis every weekend.
3. Either Paulette or Lily (*attend, attends*) all the local performances of the Alvin Ailey dancers.
4. There (*was, were*) several teachers at the game.
5. My brother and his dog (*has, have*) gone hunting.
6. (*Was, Were*) Liang and his sister born in Taiwan?

Teacher's ResourceBank™

RESOURCES

FOR THE WHOLE CHAPTER

- Chapter Review Form A 169–170
- Chapter Review Form B 171–172
- Assessment Portfolio
  - Usage Pretests 455–462
  - Usage Mastery Tests 479–486

CHAPTER OVERVIEW

The chapter opens with a discussion of number and moves to a treatment of subject-verb agreement. Then several problems in agreement are discussed, including those caused by phrases coming between the subjects and verbs of sentences, indefinite pronouns, compound subjects, the subject coming after the verb, and the use of the contractions *don't* and *doesn't.*

A **Writing Application** feature asks students to use correct subject-verb agreement to write notes, and the chapter closes with a posttest for checking students' mastery of agreement.

USING THE DIAGNOSTIC TEST

The **Diagnostic Test** is one way to gauge students' understanding of subject-verb agreement. It can also be used as a tool for determining the exact natures of problems of students who fail to use correct verbs in their writing.

SEGMENT 2 *(p. 456)*

NUMBER Rule 17a

OBJECTIVE

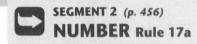

- To identify words as singular or plural

NUMBER

- Number: Singular and Plural 163

QUICK REMINDER

Write the following words on the chalkboard and ask students to supply the plural forms:

1. monkey [monkeys]
2. goose [geese]
3. life [lives]
4. man [men]
5. sky [skies]
6. deer [deer]

Remind students that most words change their spellings when they are made plural.

LEP/ESL

General Strategies. To assist your ESL students in learning the formation of plural nouns, have them record the following rules in their journals:

1. Add *–es* to words ending in *x, sh, ch,* or *s.*
2. When a singular word ends in a consonant followed by *y,* change the *y* to *i* and add *–es.*
3. When a singular word ends in *–fe,* change the *fe* to *v* and add *–es.*

USAGE

7. It (*doesn't, don't*) really matter to me.
8. My best friend at school (*doesn't, don't*) live in our neighborhood.
9. (*Was, Were*) you heating some burritos in the microwave?
10. Here (*come, comes*) Elena and James.

USAGE

Number

Number is the form of a word that shows whether the word is singular or plural.

17a. When a word refers to one person, place, or thing, it is ***singular*** in number. When a word refers to more than one person, place, or thing, it is ***plural*** in number.

SINGULAR	tepee	I	baby	mouse
PLURAL	tepees	we	babies	mice

REFERENCE NOTE: Most nouns ending in *–s* are plural (*igloos, sisters*). However, most verbs that end in *–s* are singular (*sings, tries*). For more about spelling the plural forms of nouns, see pages 644–646.

EXERCISE 1 **Identifying Singular and Plural Words**

Identify each of the following words as singular or plural.

EXAMPLE 1. activities
1. *plural*

1. peach 1. sing.
2. libraries 2. pl.
3. highway 3. sing.
4. knife 4. sing.
5. shelves 5. pl.
6. children 6. pl.
7. they 7. pl.
8. enchiladas 8. pl.
9. women 9. pl.
10. America 10. sing.

SEGMENT 3 *(pp. 457–460)*

AGREEMENT OF SUBJECT AND VERB Rule 17b

OBJECTIVES

- To identify the number of subjects and verbs
- To change the number of subjects and verbs
- To choose verbs that agree in number with their subjects
- To use correct subject-verb agreement in a letter

Agreement of Subject and Verb

17b. A verb agrees with its subject in number.

A subject and verb *agree* when they have the same number.

(1) Singular subjects take singular verbs.

EXAMPLES The **ocean roars** in the distance. [The singular verb *roars* agrees with the singular subject *ocean.*]
Marla plays the violin well. [The singular verb *plays* agrees with the singular subject *Marla.*]

(2) Plural subjects take plural verbs.

EXAMPLES **Squirrels eat** the seeds from the bird feeder. [The plural verb *eat* agrees with the plural subject *squirrels.*]
The **dancers practice** after school. [The plural verb *practice* agrees with the plural subject *dancers.*]

NOTE: The singular pronouns *I* and *you* take plural verbs.

EXAMPLES **You look** puzzled, but **I understand.**

When a sentence has a verb phrase, the first helping verb in the phrase agrees with the subject.

EXAMPLES The **movie is** starting.
The **movies are** starting.

Has Latrice been studying Arabic?
Have they been studying Arabic?

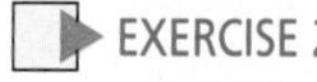

EXERCISE 2 **Identifying the Number of Subjects and Verbs**

Identify each of the following subjects and verbs as either <u>*singular*</u> or <u>*plural*</u>. [Note: All verbs agree with their subjects.]

USAGE

Teacher's ResourceBank™

RESOURCES

AGREEMENT OF SUBJECT AND VERB
- Agreement of Subject and Verb 164

QUICK REMINDER

Write the following subjects and verbs on the chalkboard and ask the students to tell which ones go together:

horses	flies
the ball	turn
the eagle	gallop
wheels	bounces

Remind students that the *–s* ending on a noun indicates that the noun is plural, but the *–s* ending on a verb indicates that the verb is singular.

LEP/ESL

General Strategies. Because *s* serves as a plural marker in English, nonnative speakers may think that a plural noun requires a verb ending in *–s*. Following the same logic, a singular noun would require a verb with no *–s*. However, English operates in just the opposite way.

To provide students practice in subject-verb agreement, have them develop subject-verb pairs like those in **Exercise 2.** You can pair students and have one in each pair suggest subjects and the other suggest verbs that agree with those subjects. For added practice, have students create complete sentences from their subject-verb pairs, as well as from those in **Exercise 2.**

USAGE

EXAMPLE **1. flag waves**
1. *singular*

1. socks match 1. pl.
2. lightning crackles 2. sing.
3. leaves rustle 3. pl.
4. mosquitoes buzz 4. pl.
5. Lyle baby-sits 5. sing.
6. bands march 6. pl.
7. Richelle knits 7. sing.
8. they listen 8. pl.
9. singer practices 9. sing.
10. horses whinny 10. pl.

USAGE

EXERCISE 3 Changing the Number of Subjects and Verbs

All of the subjects and verbs in the following sentences agree in number. Rewrite each sentence, changing the subject and verb to the opposite number.

EXAMPLE **1. The lions roar across the plains of Kenya.**
1. *The lion roars across the plains of Kenya.*

1. Maps show the shape of a country.
2. What countries are highlighted on this map?

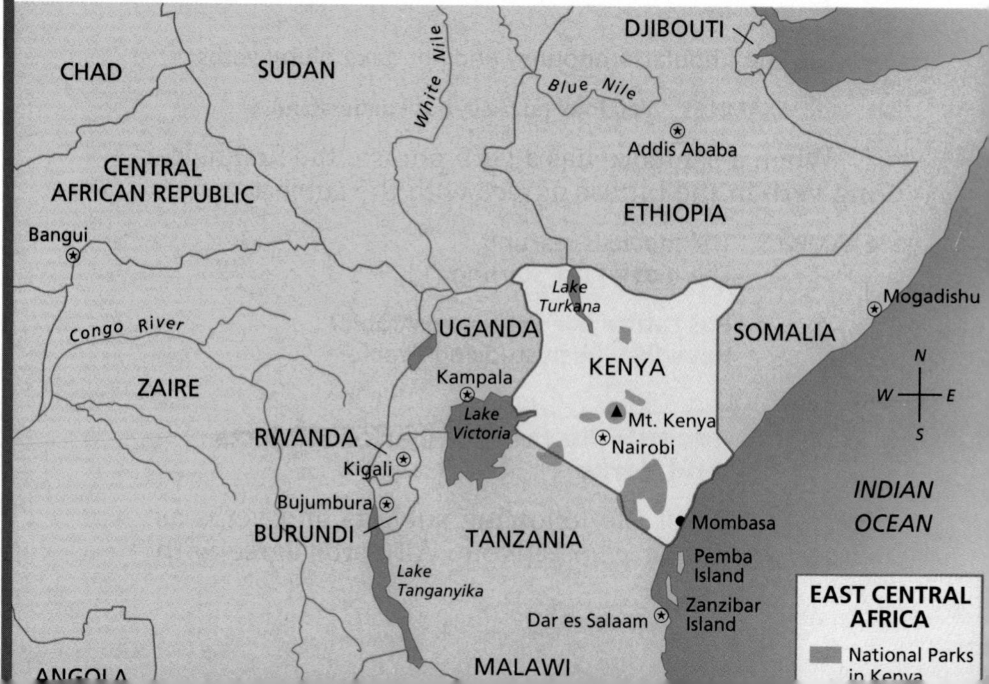

USAGE

ANSWERS
Exercise 3

1. The map shows the shape of a country.
2. What country is highlighted on this map?
3. Do oceans form Kenya's eastern border?
4. A visitor enjoys Kenya's beautiful scenery.
5. Mount Kenya's peak is covered with snow.
6. A wildlife park has been created in Kenya.
7. In the picture below, a ranger patrols a park to protect the animals.
8. He certainly has unusual transportation.
9. An industry is located in Kenya's capital, Nairobi.
10. A Kenyan farmer grows such crops as wheat, corn, and rice.

3. Does an ocean form Kenya's eastern border?
4. Visitors enjoy Kenya's beautiful scenery.
5. Mount Kenya's peaks are covered with snow.
6. Wildlife parks have been created in Kenya.
7. In the picture below, rangers patrol a park to protect the animals.
8. They certainly have unusual transportation.
9. Many industries are located in Kenya's capital, Nairobi.
10. Kenyan farmers grow such crops as wheat, corn, and rice.

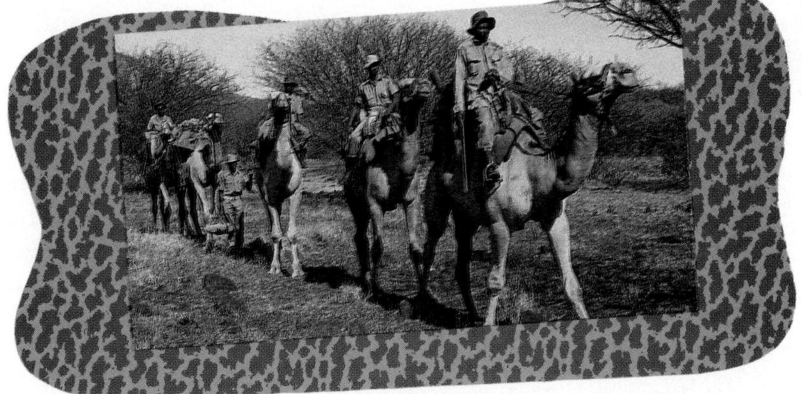

USAGE

EXERCISE 4 Choosing Verbs That Agree in Number with Their Subjects

In each of the following sentences, choose the form of the verb in parentheses that agrees with the subject.

EXAMPLE 1. The kitten (*pounces, pounce*) on the ball.
1. *pounces*

1. Firefighters (*risks, risk*) their lives to save others.
2. The snowplow (*clears, clear*) the road quickly.
3. Some dancers (*like, likes*) reggae music best.
4. St. Augustine, Florida, (*has, have*) many old Spanish buildings.
5. Some students (*chooses, choose*) to play volleyball.
6. At the science fair, the winner (*receives, receive*) a savings bond.

STUDENTS WITH SPECIAL NEEDS

Learning disabled students often have difficulty focusing attention. To help them understand agreement rules, create exercises in which students match subjects and predicates to form complete sentences.

To provide additional practice, write verbs on flash cards and have the students create sentences that contain the verbs.

USAGE

INTEGRATING THE LANGUAGE ARTS

Literature Link. Have students read and discuss a poem such as Pat Mora's "Petals." Then ask them to reread it, to pick out the verbs that end in *–s*, and to identify their subjects. Ask a volunteer to read the poem aloud, first the way it is written and then again, without the *–s* endings from the verbs, so students can hear the difference. Ask them to discuss what happens to the poem when the *–s* endings are removed from the verbs. [In Mora's poem, several clauses have *who* as the subject. Because *who* can be plural or singular, removing the *–s* ending from the verbs following changes the meaning of the poem by obscuring the antecedent of *who*.]

USAGE

PICTURE THIS

You may want to refer students to **Chapter 31: "Letters and Forms"** for the correct format for the letters they are to write.

7. Strong winds (*whistles*, *whistle*) through the old house.
8. Each Saturday, club members (*picks*, *pick*) up the litter in the park.
9. The principal (*makes*, *make*) announcements over the loudspeaker each day.
10. Doctors (*says*, *say*) that listening to loud music can harm people's hearing.

USAGE

PICTURE THIS

You saved up your money for months to order these products from an electronics catalog. Now that your order has arrived, you are dismayed to find that none of these gadgets work! You decide to write to the mail-order company and ask for a refund. Write a letter explaining what's wrong with each product and asking for your money back. Check your writing carefully for any errors in subject-verb agreement.

Subject: faulty products
Audience: a customer relations representative at a mail-order company
Purpose: to explain why you should get a refund

SEGMENT 4 *(pp. 461–472)*

PROBLEMS IN AGREEMENT Rules 17c–17k

OBJECTIVES

- To recognize and choose verbs that agree in number with subjects
- To use correct verbs with compound subjects joined by *or* or *nor*
- To read sentences aloud with stress on the subjects and verbs
- To use *don't* and *doesn't* correctly with subjects

Problems in Agreement

Phrases Between Subject and Verb

17c. The number of a subject is not changed by a phrase following the subject.

EXAMPLES These **shades** of blue **are** my favorite colors.
The smallest **puppy** of the three **is** sleeping in the basket.
The **ballerina** with long black braids **has** been my sister's ballet teacher for two years.

REFERENCE NOTE: For more information about phrases, see Chapter 15.

USAGE

EXERCISE 5 **Choosing Verbs That Agree in Number with Their Subjects**

Choose the form of the verb in parentheses that agrees with the subject in each of the following sentences.

EXAMPLE 1. Islands off the coast (*has, have*) a life of their own.
1. *have*

1. The second largest island of the United States (*is, are*) located in the Gulf of Alaska.
2. The fifteen thousand people on Kodiak Island (*is, are*) mostly of Native Arctic, Russian, or Scandinavian descent.
3. Sacks of mail (*is, are*) flown to the island from the mainland.
4. The citizens of Kodiak (*calls, call*) Alaska the mainland.
5. Industries in the community (*has, have*) suffered in recent years.
6. One cannery on the island (*cans, can*) salmon eggs, or roe.
7. Many residents on the mainland (*considers, consider*) roe a delicacy.

Teacher's ResourceBank™

RESOURCES

PROBLEMS IN AGREEMENT

QUICK REMINDER

Write the following incomplete sentences on the chalkboard and have the students add the proper form of the verb *be:*

1. The largest land animal in the world ____ the African elephant. [is]
2. Most of the people ____ gone. [are]
3. Carrots and broccoli ____ good for you. [are]
4. The desert or the beach ____ where he wants to go. [is]
5. There ____ a cat in the tree. [is]

LEP/ESL

General Strategies. This section of the chapter, with its vast number of rules, is likely to leave ESL students feeling frustrated and overwhelmed. One way to lessen this anxiety is by promoting cooperative learning. Pair ESL students with one or more students who can serve as peer tutors.

USAGE

COMMON ERROR

Problem. Students sometimes make the verb agree with the object of a preposition instead of with the subject of the sentence.

Solution. Write on the chalkboard several sentences that contain prepositional phrases between their subjects and verbs; include both the singular and plural forms of the verb. [Both cars in the yard (leak, leaks) oil.] Show students that if they try reading the sentence with the prepositional phrase removed, they won't confuse the object of the preposition with the subject of the sentence, and it will be easier for them to determine the correct forms of the verbs.

You may want to refer students to **Chapters 14** and **15** for a review of prepositions and prepositional phrases.

USAGE

8. Bears like this one (*catch, catches*) fresh salmon.
9. However, their search for leftovers (*create, creates*) problems for Kodiak.
10. The officials of one town (*has, have*) had to put a special bear-proof fence around the garbage dump.

USAGE

Indefinite Pronouns

Personal pronouns refer to specific people, places, things, or ideas. A pronoun that does not refer to a definite person, place, thing, or idea is known as an ***indefinite pronoun.***

PERSONAL PRONOUNS	she	you	we	them
INDEFINITE PRONOUNS	each	many	anyone	all

17d. The following indefinite pronouns are singular: *each, either, neither, one, everyone, everybody, no one, nobody, anyone, anybody, someone, somebody.*

EXAMPLES **One** of the stars **is** Arsenio Hall.
Each of the tourists **was** given a souvenir.
Does everybody in the restaurant like pita bread?

TIMESAVER

You can save time with the exercises by using the odd-numbered sentences for oral practice and assigning only the even-numbered sentences for independent practice. This will cut your grading time in half.

EXERCISE 6 **Choosing Verbs That Agree in Number with Their Subjects**

In the following sentences, choose the form of the verb in parentheses that agrees with the subject. Remember that the subject is never part of a prepositional phrase.

EXAMPLE **1.** Neither of the teams (*is, are*) on the field.
1. *is*

1. Nearly everybody in Lee's family (*enjoy, enjoys*) bird's nest soup.
2. Neither of them (*was, were*) wearing a helmet.
3. Somebody in the class (*speaks, speak*) French.
4. Nobody in the first two rows (*wants, want*) to volunteer.
5. Each of these tapes (*is, are*) by Natalie Cole.
6. Someone in the crowd (*is, are*) waving a pennant.
7. Everyone in those exercise classes (*has, have*) lost weight.
8. One of the band members (*plays, play*) lead guitar.
9. Either of those salads (*tastes, taste*) delicious.
10. No one (*was, were*) listening to the speaker.

17e. The following indefinite pronouns are plural: *both, few, many, several.*

EXAMPLES **Few** of the guests **are** wearing formal clothes.
Many of the newer houses **have** built-in smoke detectors.

17f. The indefinite pronouns *all, any, most, none,* and *some* may be either singular or plural.

The number of the pronouns *all, any, most, none,* and *some* is determined by the number of the object in the prepositional phrase following the subject. If the pronoun refers to a singular object, the pronoun is singular. If the pronoun refers to a plural object, the pronoun is plural.

USAGE

REVIEW A

OBJECTIVE

- To choose verbs that agree in number with their subjects

AT-RISK STUDENTS

If you have students with low achievement levels stemming from poor self-esteem and socialization problems, you may want to let them work some of the exercises or reviews in groups. They can record their answers on a sheet of paper they have all signed. They will then get equal credit for the work because each of them will have contributed to the completion of the assignment.

LEARNING STYLES

Auditory Learners. Encourage auditory learners to read their work aloud before turning the work in. This will help them hear mistakes that they might miss visually.

Visual Learners. To help visual learners improve their understanding of subject-verb agreement, prepare a variety of sentences with different types of subjects and show students how to tell if a subject agrees with its verb.

USAGE

EXAMPLES **All** of the snow **has** melted. [*All* is singular because it refers to one thing—*snow.* The helping verb *has* is singular to agree with *snow*.]

All of the snowflakes **have** melted. [*All* is plural because it refers to more than one thing—*snowflakes.* The helping verb *have* is plural to agree with *snowflakes*.]

Some of the team **has** left the field. [*Some* is singular because it means "one part" of the team. The helping verb *has* is singular to agree with "one part."]

Some of the players **are** getting on the bus. [*Some* is plural because it refers to more than one player. The helping verb *are* is plural to agree with *players.*]

USAGE

REVIEW A **Choosing Verbs That Agree in Number with Their Subjects**

In the following sentences, choose the correct form of the verb in parentheses.

EXAMPLE **1.** One of these puppies (*needs, need*) a good home.
1. *needs*

1. Most of the balloons (*has, have*) long strings.
2. Everyone in the purple uniforms (*plays, play*) on the softball team.
3. Both of the sneakers (*gives, give*) me blisters.
4. Each of these recipes (*requires, require*) ricotta cheese.
5. Some of the artists (*paint, paints*) landscapes.
6. Neither of those songs (*was, were*) composed by Duke Ellington.
7. None of the apartments (*has, have*) been painted.
8. All of the jewels (*is, are*) in the safe.
9. Many of those designs (*is, are*) found on Navajo rugs.
10. All of the writing (*is, are*) upside down.

Compound Subjects

A compound subject is made up of two or more subjects that are connected by *and, or,* or *nor.* These connected subjects share the same verb.

17g. Subjects joined by *and* take a plural verb.

EXAMPLES **Red** and **blue are** the school's colors.
New **uniforms** and **instruments were** ordered for the marching band.
Mr. Lewis, Mrs. Kirk, and **Ms. Jefferson have** applied for new jobs.

EXERCISE 7 **Choosing Verbs That Agree in Number with Their Subjects**

Identify the compound subject in each of the following sentences. Then choose the form of the verb in parentheses that agrees with the compound subject.

EXAMPLE **1.** Volcanoes and earthquakes (*is, are*) common in that area.
1. *Volcanoes, earthquakes—are*

1. The blanket and the robe (*has, have*) Navajo designs.
2. Wind, hail, and freezing rain (*is, are*) predicted for Thursday.
3. A desk and a bookcase (*was, were*) moved into Ella's room.
4. Savannas and velds (*is, are*) two kinds of grasslands found in Africa.
5. A truck and a car with a trailer (*was, were*) stalled on the highway.
6. A raccoon and a squirrel (*raid, raids*) our garden every night.
7. Mandy and her aunt (*goes, go*) to the Chinese market every Saturday.
8. Eric and Jarvis (*was, were*) asked to introduce the guest speaker.

USAGE

CRITICAL THINKING
Analysis

Remind students that compound subjects aren't always made up of only two elements. There can be a series of three or more elements making up a compound subject. However many elements there are, there will always be a coordinating conjunction, usually *and,* before the last one.

USAGE

REVIEWS B and C

OBJECTIVES

- To choose verbs that agree in number with their subjects
- To proofread a paragraph for incorrect verb forms and to correct those verb forms

9. Mosquitoes and earwigs (*has*, *have*) invaded our back yard.
10. Catsup, onions, and mustard (*goes*, *go*) well on hot dogs and many other sandwiches.

17h. When compound subjects are joined by *or* or *nor*, the verb agrees with the subject nearer the verb.

EXAMPLES A new **statue** or a **fountain has** been planned for the park. [The singular verb *has* agrees with the nearer subject *fountain*.]

A soft **blanket** or warm **booties make** a baby comfortable. [The singular verb *make* agrees with the nearer subject *booties*.]

Neither the **coach,** the **fans,** nor the **players were** happy with the decision. [The plural verb *were* agrees with the nearest subject *players*.]

USAGE

COOPERATIVE LEARNING

Place students in pairs and have them read **Oral Practice 1** and **Oral Practice 2** aloud. Ask each pair to write five sentences of their own using *or* or *nor,* and five sentences using *don't* and *doesn't* correctly.

ORAL PRACTICE 1 Using Correct Verbs with Compound Subjects Joined by *Or* or *Nor*

Read each of the following sentences aloud, stressing the italicized words.

1. Either a *desert* or a *jungle is* the setting for the play.
2. The *table* or the *bookshelves need* dusting first.
3. Neither the *bus* nor the *train stops* in our town.
4. Neither *jokes* nor funny *stories make* Gordon laugh.
5. *Flowers* or a colorful *picture makes* a room cheerful.
6. Either the *story* or the *poems are* by Langston Hughes.
7. *Rice* or *potatoes come* with the tandoori chicken.
8. Neither the *Carolinas* nor *Illinois borders* Texas.

REVIEW B Choosing Verbs That Agree in Number with Their Subjects

For each of the following sentences, choose the form of the verb in parentheses that agrees with the subject.

EXAMPLE **1.** Tara and Chen (*are*, *is*) reading the same book.
1. *are*

1. Many vegetables (*grow*, *grows*) quite large during Alaska's long summer days.
2. His mother (*teach*, *teaches*) math.
3. All of the sailboats in the harbor (*belong*, *belongs*) to the village.
4. You and your cousins (*are*, *is*) invited to the party.
5. Either the wall clock or our watches (*are*, *is*) not accurate.
6. The magazines on the kitchen table (*are*, *is*) for the hospital.
7. My list of favorite singers (*include*, *includes*) Tracy Chapman and Bonnie Raitt.
8. Both my brother and my sister (*deliver*, *delivers*) the morning newspaper.
9. Neither pencils nor an eraser (*are*, *is*) permitted.
10. The clowns and jugglers (*has*, *have*) always been my favorite circus performers.

REVIEW C **Proofreading for Errors in Subject-Verb Agreement**

Most sentences in the following paragraph contain a verb that does not agree in number with its subject. If a sentence is incorrect, give the correct verb form. If a sentence is correct, write *C*.

EXAMPLE [1] Holiday customs throughout the world is interesting to study.
1. *are*

1. celebrate

[1] In Sweden, adults and children ~~celebrates~~ St. Lucia's Day. [2] Everyone there ~~know~~ St. Lucia as the **2.** knows
Queen of Light. [3] Many people eagerly look forward **3.** C
to the December 13 holiday. [4] Girls especially ~~enjoys~~ **4.** enjoy
the day. [5] By tradition, the oldest girl in the family **5.** dresses
~~dress~~ as St. Lucia. [6] The girl in the picture on the **6.** C
next page is ready to play her part. [7] You surely ~~has~~ **7.** have
noticed the girl's headdress. [8] A crown of lighted

USAGE

USAGE

8. is candles ~~are~~ hard to miss! [9] Each of the young Lucias
9. wears also ~~wear~~ a white robe. [10] Early in the morning, the
10. C costumed girls bring breakfast to the adults of the household.

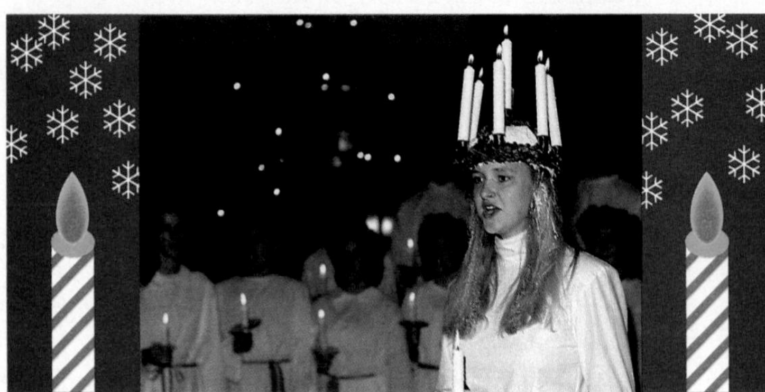

USAGE

Subject After the Verb

17i. When the subject follows the verb, find the subject. Then make sure that the verb agrees with it.

The subject usually follows the verb in sentences that begin with *there* and *here* and in questions.

EXAMPLES There **are** fifty **runners** in the marathon.
There **is** the **winner.**

Here **are** my overdue library **books.**
Here **is** the **book** about reptiles.

Are the **birds** in the nest?
Is the **nest** on a high branch?

NOTE: The contractions *there's* and *here's* contain the verb *is.* These contractions are singular and should be used only with singular subjects.

EXAMPLES There**'s Uncle Max.**
Here**'s your allowance.**

REFERENCE NOTE: For more information about contractions, see pages 629–630.

USAGE

A DIFFERENT APPROACH

For sentences in which the subject comes after the verb, show students how to find the subject by turning the sentence around. Everything that comes after the verb is moved to the beginning, and the order of the verb and any introductory word is reversed. For example:

There are the shoes.
The shoes are there.

17 i–k

EXERCISE 8 **Choosing Verbs That Agree in Number with Their Subjects**

Identify the subject of each sentence. Then choose the form of the verb in parentheses that agrees with the subject.

EXAMPLE **1.** There (*was, were*) a baby rabbit hiding in the grass.
1. *rabbit—was*

1. There (*is, are*) three foreign exchange students at the high school.
2. (*Was, Were*) the fans cheering for the other team?
3. (*Has, Have*) the Washingtons moved into their new home?
4. Here (*is, are*) the tacos and fajitas.
5. (*Has, Have*) the bees left the hive?
6. (*There's, There are*) several correct answers to that question.
7. How long (*has, have*) the Huangs owned this tai chi studio?
8. (*Here are, Here's*) the shells from Driftwood Beach.
9. (*There's, There are*) a pint of strawberries in the kitchen.
10. There (*is, are*) Amy and Wanda in the doorway.

USAGE

The Contractions *Don't* and *Doesn't*

17j. The word *don't* is a contraction of *do not.* Use *don't* with all plural subjects and with the pronouns *I* and *you.*

EXAMPLES		
	I don't have my keys.	**Dogs don't** meow.
	You don't care.	**They don't** know.
	We don't agree.	The **boots don't** fit.

17k. The word *doesn't* is a contraction of *does not.* Use *doesn't* with all singular subjects except the pronouns *I* and *you.*

USAGE

INTEGRATING THE LANGUAGE ARTS

Literature Link. Have students read and discuss a short story such as Elizabeth Enright's "Nancy." Then ask them to reread it to see if they can find examples of the types of sentences discussed in this segment. Can they find examples of sentences with phrases between the subjects and verbs? Sentences with indefinite pronouns or compound subjects? Sentences with subjects following verbs? Sentences using *don't* and *doesn't?* Seeing such sentences in professional writing may reinforce students' comprehension of subject-verb agreement.

INTEGRATING THE LANGUAGE ARTS

Technology Link. If you have access to tape recorders, you can let the students tape each other completing the **Oral Practice** exercises. Or you can let volunteers recite the sentences in the **Oral Practice** exercises with the wrong verb forms so that the other students can hear how incorrect subject-verb agreements sound.

USAGE

EXAMPLES **He doesn't** know you. **She doesn't** care. **It doesn't** work. **Don doesn't** like thunder. The **car doesn't** run. A **penguin doesn't** fly.

ORAL PRACTICE 2 Using *Don't* and *Doesn't* Correctly

Read the following sentences aloud, stressing the italicized words.

1. *He doesn't* want us to give him a party.
2. *Margo* and *Jim don't* have any money left.
3. *Lynna doesn't* remember the capital of Jamaica.
4. The *bus doesn't* stop here.
5. *They don't* believe that old story.
6. *It doesn't* snow here in October.
7. *They don't* sing the blues anymore.
8. That Zuñi *vase doesn't* look very old.

USAGE

EXERCISE 9 Writing *Don't* and *Doesn't* with Subjects

Identify the subject in each of the following sentences. Then choose the contraction, either *don't* or *doesn't,* that agrees with the subject.

EXAMPLE 1. Our cats ___ like catnip.
1. *cats—don't*

1. My parents ___ listen to rap music. 1. don't
2. It ___ seem possible that Leon grew an inch in one month. 2. doesn't
3. I ___ have much homework tonight. 3. don't
4. Jerome ___ play the guitar as well as Angela. 4. doesn't
5. The pizza ___ have enough onions, cheese, or mushrooms. 5. doesn't
6. They ___ permit diving in the pool. 6. don't
7. This bedroom ___ look very neat. 7. doesn't
8. My ski boots ___ fit me this year. 8. don't
9. Matthew enjoys playing lacrosse, but he ___ like to play soccer. 9. doesn't
10. They ___ live on this street anymore. 10. don't

WRITING APPLICATION

OBJECTIVE

- To use correct subject-verb agreement in a note to a neighbor

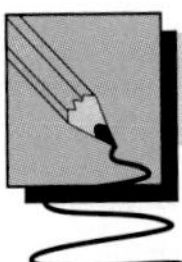

WRITING APPLICATION

Using Subject-Verb Agreement in Writing

Contractions like *there's*, *here's*, and *don't* can make it difficult to spot errors in subject-verb agreement. However, when you spell out these contractions in full, you can easily see whether the verb should be singular or plural.

EXAMPLE There's carrots in the refrigerator. [Spelled out, *There's* becomes *There is.*]

The singular verb *is* doesn't agree with the plural subject *carrots*. The sentence should be revised.

REVISED There **are** carrots in the refrigerator.

WRITING ACTIVITY

Your family is going on a weekend trip. A neighbor has agreed to look after your pet. Write a note giving your neighbor complete instructions for tending the animal. To avoid confusing your reader, make sure the subjects and verbs in your sentences agree.

Prewriting Think about a pet that you've had or that you know about. It might be a rabbit, a cat, a dog, a hamster, or several animals, such as fish or birds. If you've never cared for a pet, talk to someone who has. Take notes on caring for the pet. What does it eat? How much and how often should it be fed? How much water does it need? What other special care does it need?

Writing Now, write a draft of your note. Explain the daily care of the pet step by step. The more specific your instructions are, the better. You can use informal standard English if you're writing to someone you know well. (For more about informal English, see pages 330–331 and 544.)

USAGE

WRITING APPLICATION

Because students will be writing notes that presumably will include lists of activities, you may wish to review **Chapter 23,** which covers the rules for punctuating lists.

CRITICAL THINKING
Analysis

Depending on their familiarity with pets, students may create extensive lists in the prewriting stage. Tell them they must narrow their lists to only those matters that are essential to the well-being of the animals. The focus of the instructions should be on the necessary procedures, not on describing the animals.

USAGE

PREWRITING

Have students make lists of pets they have or have had, and then have each student choose one pet and make a list of everything that must be done for that pet each day. If any student does not have or has never had a pet, ask the student to interview another class member to gather the information needed for this assignment. Have students share their lists with other class members. Ask students to check one another's lists. Are the directions clear? Is anything missing?

REVIEW D

OBJECTIVE

- To proofread sentences for errors in subject-verb agreement and to correct each incorrect verb

A DIFFERENT APPROACH

To give students extra practice with subject-verb agreement, write a list of subjects and a list of verbs on the chalkboard. Ask students to compose sentences showing combinations of various subjects and verbs. You can change the rules from time to time so that students must write sentences of each of the types described in this segment: sentences with compound subjects, sentences with phrases between the subjects and verbs, and sentences with the subjects following the verbs.

USAGE

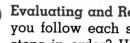

 **Evaluating and Revising** Read your note aloud. Can you follow each step of the instructions? Are all the steps in order? Have you included all the necessary information? If not, revise your note to make it clear and complete.

 **Proofreading** After you've revised your note, check each sentence for subject-verb agreement. Take special care with any verb that is part of a contraction. Check your note for any other errors in grammar, punctuation, or spelling.

USAGE

REVIEW D **Proofreading for Errors in Subject-Verb Agreement**

Most of the following sentences contain a verb that does not agree in number with its subject. Correct each incorrect verb. If a sentence is correct, write *C.*

EXAMPLE **1. Is the people in the picture on the next page worried?**
1. *Are*

1. There ~~is~~ sharks swimming all around them. **1. are**
2. However, the people ~~doesn't~~ seem to care. **2. don't**
3. ~~Has~~ they lost their senses? **3. Have**
4. No, there ~~aren't~~ anything for them to worry about in this shark exhibit. **4. isn't**
5. There's a tunnel right through the shark pool. **5. C**
6. Everyone who visits the exhibit ~~ride~~ a moving walkway through the tunnel. **6. rides**
7. The sharks don't seem to mind the people. **7. C**
8. Actually, sharks in the wild ~~doesn't~~ attack people very often. **8. don't**
9. Of course, sharks ~~does~~ eat almost anything. **9. do**
10. Caution and respect, therefore, ~~needs~~ to be shown by people in shark-inhabited waters. **10. need**

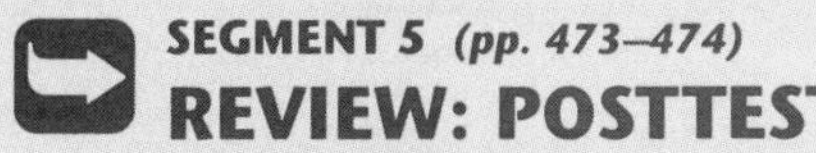

SEGMENT 5 *(pp. 473–474)*

REVIEW: POSTTEST

OBJECTIVE

- To choose verbs that agree in number with the subjects of sentences

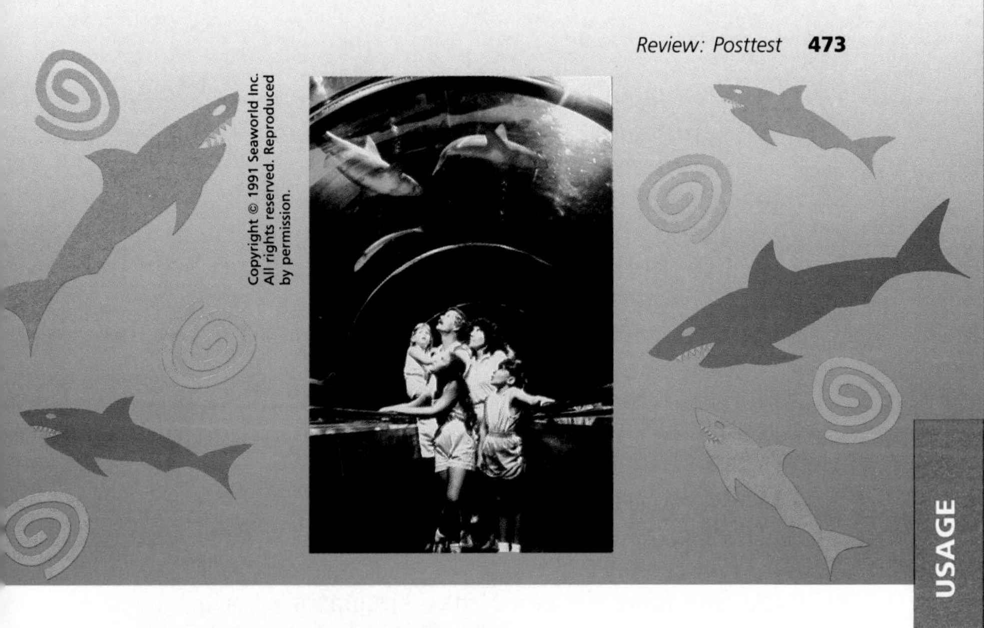

USAGE

Review: Posttest

Choosing Verbs That Agree in Number with Their Subjects

For each of the following sentences, find the subject. Then choose the form of the verb in parentheses that agrees with the subject.

EXAMPLE **1.** Janelle and Brad (*are, is*) in the drama club.
1. *are*

1. Neither the passengers nor the pilot (*was, were*) injured.
2. There (*are, is*) two new rides at the amusement park.
3. That book of Spanish folk tales (*is, are*) selling out.
4. (*Here are, Here's*) some books about Hawaii.
5. Shel Silverstein and Ogden Nash (*appeal, appeals*) to both children and grown-ups.
6. Velma and her little sister (*was, were*) reading a story by Gyo Fujikawa.
7. (*Was, Were*) your parents happy with the results?

USAGE

8. He (*doesn't, don't*) play chess anymore.
9. Why (*doesn't, don't*) she and Megan bring the lemonade?
10. Tickets for that concert (*are, is*) scarce.
11. The dishes on that shelf (*look, looks*) clean.
12. My mother and my brother (*has, have*) been in Florida since Sunday.
13. Either the cats or the dog (*has, have*) upset the plants.
14. Here (*are, is*) the instructions for the microwave.
15. There (*is, are*) ten provinces and two territories in Canada.
16. I (*am, is*) crocheting an afghan.
17. Why (*wasn't, weren't*) you at the scout meeting yesterday?
18. She (*doesn't, don't*) like spectator sports.
19. Several paintings by that artist (*are, is*) now on exhibit at the mall.
20. They (*doesn't, don't*) know how to get to the Juneteenth picnic.

USAGE

USAGE

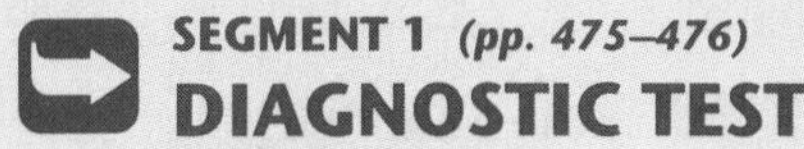

SEGMENT 1 *(pp. 475–476)*

DIAGNOSTIC TEST

OBJECTIVE

- To determine the correct forms and tenses of verbs used in sentences

18 Using Verbs Correctly

Principal Parts, Regular and Irregular Verbs, Tense

USAGE

Diagnostic Test

Using the Correct Forms of Verbs

For each of the following sentences, give the correct form of the verb in parentheses.

EXAMPLE **1. Our family had (*drive*) three hundred miles.**
1. *driven*

1. We had (*ride*) in the car for several hours. 1. ridden
2. Six inches of snow (*fall*) last night. 2. fell
3. I never (*know*) snow was so beautiful. 3. knew
4. The wind had (*blow*) some of it into high drifts. 4. blown
5. As we (*go*) past them, they looked like white hills. 5. went
6. My brother Ernesto (*bring*) some comics to read on the trip. 6. brought
7. I (*lie*) back and looked at the scenery. 7. lay
8. Unfortunately, the car heater had (*break*). 8. broken

Teacher's ResourceBank™

RESOURCES

FOR THE WHOLE CHAPTER

- Chapter Review Form A 184–185
- Chapter Review Form B 186–187
- Assessment Portfolio
  - Usage Pretests 455–462
  - Usage Mastery Tests 479–486

CHAPTER OVERVIEW

This chapter should help students use verbs correctly when they speak and write. The first part of the chapter explains the difference between regular and irregular verbs. It shows how to form the principal parts of regular verbs and offers examples of the present participle, past, and past participle forms of irregular verbs. This chapter also discusses tense and includes a special section on six verbs that often give students problems. A posttest is included at the end of the chapter.

USING THE DIAGNOSTIC TEST

Use the **Diagnostic Test** to determine students' understanding of correct verb forms. The parts of the test that students have trouble with should indicate the areas in which students need help and the sections of the chapter they should concentrate on.

USAGE

Teacher's ResourceBank™

RESOURCES

PRINCIPAL PARTS OF VERBS
- The Principal Parts of Verbs 179

USAGE

QUICK REMINDER

Write the following verb forms on the chalkboard and ask students to identify them as infinitive, present participle, past, or past participle:

1. walked [past]
2. have carried [past participle]
3. throw [infinitive]
4. is speaking [present participle]

LEARNING STYLES

Auditory Learners. It may be easier for some students to identify the correct form of an irregular verb by listening to principal parts of the verb when they are used in sentences. You may wish to read the **Common Irregular Verbs** list (p. 481) aloud and ask for volunteers to use the verbs in sentences. To hold students' attention, suggest sentences that relate to a theme of interest to them.

USAGE

9. We all (*wear*) our heavy coats and mittens. 9. wore
10. However, my ears almost (*freeze*). 10. froze
11. My favorite wool cap had (*shrink*) to a tiny size in the dryer. 11. shrunk
12. During the long ride home, we (*sing*) some songs. 12. sang
13. The clerk (*rise*) and asked if we would like some hot chocolate. 13. rose
14. After lunch, Ernesto (*begin*) to feel sleepy. 14. began
15. We had (*come*) a long way. 15. come
16. I had never (*sit*) so long in a car before. 16. sat
17. I should never have (*drink*) two cups of hot cocoa. 17. drunk
18. When we stopped, Mom and I (*run*) into the gas station. 18. ran
19. At noon, we (*eat*) lunch at a roadside cafeteria. 19. ate
20. All warmed up again, I (*sink*) into a deep sleep. 20. sank

Principal Parts of Verbs

The four basic forms of a verb are called the ***principal parts*** of the verb.

18a. The four principal parts of a verb are the ***infinitive,*** the ***present participle,*** the ***past,*** and the ***past participle.***

Here are the principal parts of two familiar verbs:

INFINITIVE	PRESENT PARTICIPLE	PAST	PAST PARTICIPLE
start	(is) starting	started	(have) started
wear	(is) wearing	wore	(have) worn

Notice that the present participle and the past participle are used with helping verbs (forms of *be* and *have*).

SEGMENT 3 *(pp. 477–489)*

REGULAR AND IRREGULAR VERBS

Rules 18b, 18c

OBJECTIVES

- To read sentences aloud and to stress the verbs
- To form the principal parts of regular verbs and to use them in sentences

As you can see from their names, the principal parts of a verb are used to express time.

PRESENT TIME She **wears** a blue uniform.
Ray **is wearing** a baseball cap.
PAST TIME Yesterday, we **wore** sweaters.
I **had worn** braces for three months.
FUTURE TIME Jessica **will wear** her new dress at the party.
By next spring Joey **will have worn** holes in those shoes.

Because *start* forms its past and past participle by adding *–ed,* it is called a *regular verb. Wear* forms its past and past participle differently, so it is called an *irregular verb.*

USAGE

Regular Verbs

18b. A ***regular verb*** forms its past and past participle by adding *–ed* or *–d* to the infinitive form.

INFINITIVE	PRESENT PARTICIPLE	PAST	PAST PARTICIPLE
wash	(is) washing	washed	(have) washed
hop	(is) hopping	hopped	(have) hopped
use	(is) using	used	(have) used

REFERENCE NOTE: Most regular verbs that end in –e drop the –e before adding *–ing.* Some regular verbs double the final consonant before adding *–ing* or *–ed.* For a discussion of these spelling rules, see pages 640–642.

One common error in forming the past or past participle of a regular verb is to leave off the *–d* or *–ed* ending.

NONSTANDARD Josh was suppose to meet us here.
STANDARD Josh was **supposed** to meet us here.

REFERENCE NOTE: For more about standard English, see pages 329–330.

USAGE

Teacher's ResourceBank™

RESOURCES

REGULAR AND IRREGULAR VERBS

QUICK REMINDER

Write the following infinitives on the chalkboard and have students compose sentences that use the past and past participle forms of each one:

1. bend [She bent the wire into a circle. She has bent the wire into a circle.]
2. put [They put the wheels on the skateboard. They have put the wheels on the skateboard.]
3. meet [He met the tightrope walker. He has met the tightrope walker.]

- To identify the correct forms of irregular verbs in sentences
- To use the past or past participle forms of irregular verbs in notes for a newspaper article

USAGE

ORAL PRACTICE 1 Using Regular Verbs

Read the following sentences aloud, stressing the italicized verb.

1. We are *supposed* to practice sit-ups this morning.
2. With the help of his guide dog, the man *crossed* the street.
3. Carlos and Rita have *ordered* soup and salad.
4. Her family *moved* from Trinidad to Brooklyn.
5. Some Native Americans *used* to use shells for money.
6. They *called* shell money "wampum."
7. Larry has *saved* most of his allowance for the past two months.
8. My grandmother *worked* at the computer store.

EXERCISE 1 Forming the Principal Parts of Regular Verbs

Give the principal parts for each of the following verbs. Remember that some verbs change their spelling when *–ing* or *–ed* is added.

EXAMPLE 1. work
1. *work; (is) working; worked; (have) worked*

1. skate
2. pick
3. live
4. move
5. talk
6. stun
7. enjoy
8. rob
9. laugh
10. love

EXERCISE 2 Using the Principal Parts of Regular Verbs

For each of the following sentences, give the form of the italicized verb that will fit correctly in the blank.

EXAMPLE 1. *paint* Henry Ossawa Tanner ____ many kinds of subjects.
1. *painted*

USAGE

ANSWERS

Exercise 1

1. (to) skate; (is) skating; skated; (have) skated
2. (to) pick; (is) picking; picked; (have) picked
3. (to) live; (is) living; lived; (have) lived
4. (to) move; (is) moving; moved; (have) moved
5. (to) talk; (is) talking; talked; (have) talked
6. (to) stun; (is) stunning; stunned; (have) stunned
7. (to) enjoy; (is) enjoying; enjoyed; (have) enjoyed
8. (to) rob; (is) robbing; robbed; (have) robbed
9. (to) laugh; (is) laughing; laughed; (have) laughed
10. (to) love; (is) loving; loved; (have) loved

1. *create* Tanner ___ images of people, nature, history, and religion. 1. created
2. *learn* What is the boy in this painting ___ to do? 2. learning

Henry Ossawa Tanner, 1893, "The Banjo Lesson," Hampton University Museum, Hampton, Virginia

3. *title* Not surprisingly, Tanner ___ this painting *The Banjo Lesson*. 3. titled
4. *live* The artist, a native of Philadelphia, ___ from 1859 to 1937. 4. lived
5. *move* At the age of thirty-two, Tanner ___ to Paris to study and work. 5. moved
6. *visit* Other African American artists ___ Tanner in France. 6. visited
7. *admire* For years, people have ___ Tanner's paintings. 7. admired
8. *plan* Our teacher is ___ to show us more of Tanner's work. 8. planning
9. *want* I have ___ to see Tanner's portrait of Booker T. Washington. 9. wanted
10. *praise* In his book *Up from Slavery*, Washington ___ Tanner's talent. 10. praised

USAGE

VISUAL CONNECTIONS
The Banjo Lesson

About the Artist. Henry Ossawa Tanner (1859–1937) was born in Pittsburgh, Pennsylvania. He studied at the Pennsylvania Academy and later moved to Paris, France, where he became famous for his symbolist renderings of Biblical scenes. In 1923, Tanner was elected a Knight of the Legion of Honor. He is a major American artist whose work exhibits a blend of conservatism and innovation. *The Banjo Lesson*, one of Tanner's best works, is an oil on canvas painted in 1893.

USAGE

USAGE

LEP/ESL

General Strategies. Emphasize that the past and past participle forms of regular verbs are always the same. Once students have learned the past form, they automatically have command of the past participle.

The **Common Irregular Verbs** list may seem overwhelming to some students. To help them with irregular verbs, make sure that they use the verbs in a personal context. Require students to master only small increments of the material at a time.

Ask each student to choose five irregular verbs and to write an autobiographical paragraph describing an important or unforgettable experience. The paragraph should include the past or past participle forms of each of the five verbs.

LESS-ADVANCED STUDENTS

Remind students that to form the past and past participle forms of regular verbs, they add *–ed* or *–d* to the infinitive form. Write the following verbs on the chalkboard and have students volunteer the past and past participle form for each one:

1. to look [looked]
2. to taste [tasted]
3. to smell [smelled]

USAGE

Irregular Verbs

18c. An ***irregular verb*** forms its past and past participle in some other way than by adding *–d* or *–ed* to the infinitive form.

Irregular verbs form their past and past participles by

- changing vowels *or* consonants

INFINITIVE	PAST	PAST PARTICIPLE
lead	led	(have) led
lend	lent	(have) lent
make	made	(have) made

- changing vowels *and* consonants

INFINITIVE	PAST	PAST PARTICIPLE
catch	caught	(have) caught
draw	drew	(have) drawn
tear	tore	(have) torn

- making no change

INFINITIVE	PAST	PAST PARTICIPLE
cut	cut	(have) cut
hurt	hurt	(have) hurt
won	won	(have) won

NOTE: If you are not sure about the principal parts of a verb, look in a dictionary. Entries for irregular verbs list the principal parts of the verb. If the principal parts are not listed, the verb is a regular verb.

COMMON IRREGULAR VERBS			
INFINITIVE	PRESENT PARTICIPLE	PAST	PAST PARTICIPLE
begin	(is) beginning	began	(have) begun
blow	(is) blowing	blew	(have) blown
break	(is) breaking	broke	(have) broken
bring	(is) bringing	brought	(have) brought
burst	(is) bursting	burst	(have) burst
choose	(is) choosing	chose	(have) chosen
come	(is) coming	came	(have) come
do	(is) doing	did	(have) done
drink	(is) drinking	drank	(have) drunk
drive	(is) driving	drove	(have) driven
eat	(is) eating	ate	(have) eaten
fall	(is) falling	fell	(have) fallen
freeze	(is) freezing	froze	(have) frozen
give	(is) giving	gave	(have) given
go	(is) going	went	(have) gone

ORAL PRACTICE 2 **Using Irregular Verbs**

Read each of the following sentences aloud, stressing the italicized verb.

1. I have *begun* to learn karate.
2. We *chose* to stay indoors.
3. Earline has never *drunk* buttermilk before.
4. We *did* our homework after dinner.
5. Anna and Dee have almost *broken* the school record for the fifty-yard dash.
6. The wind has *blown* fiercely for three days.
7. Last Saturday, Isaac *brought* me a tape of reggae music.
8. The hot-water pipes in the laundry room have *burst* again.

USAGE

COMMON ERROR

Problem. Because there is not a set pattern to follow when forming the past or past participle form of an irregular verb, students may have difficulty remembering how to use irregular verbs correctly.

Solution. Encourage students to memorize irregular verbs. If a student has a question about a particular verb form, tell the student to check it in a dictionary. The more students look up unfamiliar verbs, the easier it will be for students to remember them.

INTEGRATING THE LANGUAGE ARTS

Literature Link. After students have read and discussed a literary selection such as "Life Doesn't Frighten Me" by Maya Angelou, have them list five verbs that the writer uses in the selection. Then ask students to indicate whether the verbs are regular or irregular and have them write the past and past participle forms of each one.

USAGE

COOPERATIVE LEARNING

A team race will help students become more familiar with the correct forms of irregular verbs. Make two identical sets of cards with the irregular verbs *come, fall, swim, burst, ring, shrink, write,* and *go.*

Give each team a set of cards and have the teams write as many sentences with the irregular verbs as possible in three minutes. The team with the most correct sentences wins.

USAGE

PICTURE THIS

Because this assignment is presented as a note-taking activity, students' responses can be in the form of a list of sentences. Encourage students to give equal attention to sounds and feelings as well as sights. You may want to have students underline the verbs they use so that you can more easily check their work.

USAGE

EXERCISE 3 **Identifying the Correct Forms of Irregular Verbs**

For each of the following sentences, choose the correct verb form in parentheses.

1. We had (*began, begun*) our project when I got sick.
2. The Ruiz family (*drove, driven*) across the country.
3. Has anyone (*brung, brought*) extra batteries for the radio?
4. I have finally (*chose, chosen*) the orange kitten.
5. The lake finally (*froze, frozen*) hard enough for skating.
6. My father had (*gave, given*) away all my comic books to the children's hospital.
7. It is amazing that no one has ever (*fell, fallen*) off the old ladder.
8. Everyone (*went, gone*) back to the classroom to watch the videotape of the spelling bee.
9. David's whole family (*came, come*) for his bar mitzvah.
10. Have you (*ate, eaten*) at the new Philippine restaurant?

PICTURE THIS

Thrills! Chills! Death-defying feats! You are a newspaper reporter covering an air show. You and the rest of the audience are amazed at what the pilots can make their aircraft do. As you watch the aerial stunts shown on the next page, you take notes to use in your article. Jot down details about what you see, hear, and feel. Remember that your readers can share this experience only through your words. In your notes, use the past or past participle forms of at least five irregular verbs from the list on page 481.

Subject: air-show performance
Audience: yourself
Purpose: to record your impressions for use in a newspaper article

USAGE

MORE COMMON IRREGULAR VERBS			
INFINITIVE	PRESENT PARTICIPLE	PAST	PAST PARTICIPLE
know	(is) knowing	knew	(have) known
ride	(is) riding	rode	(have) ridden
ring	(is) ringing	rang	(have) rung
run	(is) running	ran	(have) run
see	(is) seeing	saw	(have) seen
shrink	(is) shrinking	shrank	(have) shrunk
sing	(is) singing	sang	(have) sung
sink	(is) sinking	sank	(have) sunk
speak	(is) speaking	spoke	(have) spoken
steal	(is) stealing	stole	(have) stolen
swim	(is) swimming	swam	(have) swum
take	(is) taking	took	(have) taken
throw	(is) throwing	threw	(have) thrown
wear	(is) wearing	wore	(have) worn
write	(is) writing	wrote	(have) written

A DIFFERENT APPROACH

Ask students to think about important moments in their lives. Have any of them won prizes, visited interesting places, or switched schools? Have each student write a descriptive paragraph about such a moment. As students write, tell them to pay close attention to the verbs they use. When students are finished, have them circle the verbs in their paragraphs. Then ask them to trade paragraphs with partners and to identify the verb forms used.

USAGE

INTEGRATING THE LANGUAGE ARTS

Speaking Link. Divide the class into small groups and ask each student to name two verbs. Then have the groups make up stories, with each verb in a separate sentence. Tell students that their stories can be serious or silly.

USAGE

ORAL PRACTICE 3 **Using Irregular Verbs**

Read each of the following sentences aloud, stressing the italicized verb.

1. Before the lecture, I had never *known* the difference between cricket and croquet.
2. The school bell *rang* five minutes late every afternoon this week.
3. In New York, Julia *saw* the musical *Cats.*
4. How many sixth-graders have never *ridden* on the school bus?
5. What is the longest distance you have ever *swum*?
6. George *ran* to the corner to see the antique fire engine.
7. Gloria Estefan *sang* on the awards show.
8. Have you ever *written* haiku?

"You don't say 'He taked my chair' . . . it's 'My chair was tooken'."

USAGE

REVIEWS A–C

OBJECTIVES

- To proofread sentences for errors in verb forms and to supply the correct verb forms
- To provide the correct past or past participle verb forms in sentences
- To revise incorrect verb forms in sentences

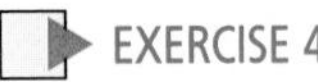 EXERCISE 4 **Identifying the Correct Forms of Irregular Verbs**

For each of the following sentences, choose the correct verb form in parentheses.

1. Who (*ran, run*) faster, Jesse or Cindy?
2. That cute little puppy has (*stole, stolen*) a biscuit.
3. The Harlem Boys Choir has never (*sang, sung*) more beautifully.
4. Jimmy's toy boat (*sank, sunk*) to the bottom of the lake.
5. Have you (*throwed, thrown*) away yesterday's paper?
6. Maria had (*wore, worn*) her new spring outfit to the party.
7. Until yesterday, no one had ever (*swam, swum*) across Crystal Lake.
8. In *Alice's Adventures in Wonderland,* Alice (*shrank, shrunk*) to a very small size!
9. The students have (*wrote, written*) a letter to the mayor.
10. I have never (*spoke, spoken*) to a large audience before.

 REVIEW A **Proofreading for Errors in Irregular Verbs**

Most of the following sentences contain incorrect verb forms. Find each error and write the correct form of the verb. If a sentence is correct, write *C.*

EXAMPLE 1. Many stories have been wrote about the American athlete Jesse Owens.
1. *wrote—written*

1. Owens ~~breaked~~ several sports records during his career. **1. broke**
2. At the Olympic games of 1936, he ~~winned~~ four gold medals. **2. won**

USAGE

USAGE

TIMESAVER

To save time grading the **Review** exercises, have students trade answer sheets. Then read the sentences aloud with the correct answers and have students circle any verbs that are used incorrectly.

VISUAL CONNECTIONS

Exploring the Subject. Born in Oakville, Alabama, on September 12, 1913, Jesse Owens grew up to become one of the United States' greatest track and field athletes. When he was a member of the Ohio State University track team, he tied the world record in one event and broke the world records in three others in one day. At the 1936 Olympics in Berlin, Germany, Owens set new world records in three events and a new Olympic record in a fourth.

USAGE

3. A photographer took this picture of one of Owens's victories. 3. C
4. Owens's career ~~begun~~ in an unusual way. 4. began
5. As a little boy, Owens had been very sick, and later he ~~run~~ to strengthen his lungs. 5. ran
6. In high school, the other boys on the track team did their practicing after school, but Owens had to work. 6. C
7. Owens's coach encouraged him to practice an hour before school and ~~brung~~ him breakfast every morning. 7. brought
8. The coach ~~knowed~~ Owens's parents couldn't afford to send their son to college. 8. knew
9. The coach ~~seen~~ that something had to be done, and he helped Owens's father find a job. 9. saw
10. Later, Owens went to Ohio State University, where he became a track star. 10. C

REVIEW B

Writing the Past and Past Participle Forms of Verbs

For each of the following sentences, give the past or past participle form of the verb that will fit correctly in the blank.

EXAMPLE **1.** *take* Gloria has ___ the last game card.
1. *taken*

1. *do* Has everyone ___ the assignment for today? 1. done
2. *burst* Suddenly, the door ___ open. 2. burst
3. *drive* We have ___ on Oklahoma's Indian Nation Turnpike. 3. driven
4. *eat* Have you ___ lunch yet? 4. eaten
5. *speak* Who ___ at this year's Hispanic Heritage awards ceremony? 5. spoke 6. blew
6. *blow* She ___ out the candles on the cake. 7. fallen
7. *fall* One of the hikers had ___ into the river.
8. *give* Mrs. Matsuo ___ me a copy of the book *Origami: Japanese Paper-Folding.* 8. gave
9. *freeze* The water in the birdbath has ___ again. 9. frozen 10. chosen
10. *choose* Which play have they ___ to perform?
11. *wear* The Highland School Band has always ___ Scottish kilts. 11. worn 12. knew
12. *know* Noriko ___ the way to Lynn's house.
13. *write* Ms. Brook has ___ letters to all of us.
14. *shrink* My sweater ___, so I gave it to my little sister. 13. written 14. shrank 15. rang
15. *ring* Who ___ the doorbell a moment ago?
16. *drink* The puppy has ___ all the water in the dish. 16. drunk 17. stole
17. *steal* David ___ third base in the ninth inning.
18. *swim* Have you ___ in the new pool at the park? 18. swum
19. *see* We had never ___ a koala before. 19. seen
20. *come* Jerome ___ early to help us with the decorations. 20. came

USAGE

COOPERATIVE LEARNING

Divide the class into groups of three or four and have each group write a story. Each story should contain at least six verbs from **Review B.** Each student will be responsible for using two verbs. Tell students that they must use the past or the past participle forms of the verbs they choose. Tell them that their stories can be funny, frightening, exciting, or serious. When the groups finish their stories, have students check their verb forms carefully to make sure that the correct forms are used. Then ask students to share the stories with their classmates.

USAGE

 REVIEW C

Revising Incorrect Verb Forms in Sentences

Read each of the following sentences. If the form of a verb is wrong, write the correct form. If the sentence is correct, write *C*.

EXAMPLE 1. Dr. Seuss knowed how to please readers of all ages.
1. *knew*

1. seen **1.** Have you ever ~~saw~~ either of the wacky characters shown below?

2. C **2.** The imagination of Dr. Seuss brought both of them to life.

3. burst **3.** You may have ~~bursted~~ out laughing at the Cat in the Hat, Horton the elephant, the Grinch, or the Lorax.

4. stole **4.** In one story, the mean Grinch ~~stoled~~ Christmas.

5. gave **5.** In another, a bird ~~gived~~ Horton an egg to hatch.

6. C **6.** The Lorax spoke out in support of the trees and the environment.

USAGE

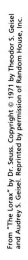

VISUAL CONNECTIONS

About the Artist. Dr. Seuss is the pen name of Theodor Seuss Geisel (1904–1991), an American writer and illustrator of many popular and humorous children's books.

USAGE

SEGMENT 4 *(pp. 489–491)*

TENSE Rule 18d

OBJECTIVE

- To write sentences with different verb tenses

7. The Cat in the Hat has always ~~wore~~ his crazy hat. **7.** worn
8. During his lifetime, Dr. Seuss must have ~~wrote~~ about fifty books with unusual characters. **8.** written
9. Many children have ~~began~~ reading with his books. **9.** begun
10. Dr. Seuss ~~choosed~~ *The Lorax* as his own favorite book. **10.** chose

Tense

18d. The ***tense*** of a verb indicates the time of the action or the state of being expressed by the verb.

Every verb has six tenses.

Present	Past	Future
Present Perfect	Past Perfect	Future Perfect

The following time line shows the relationships between tenses.

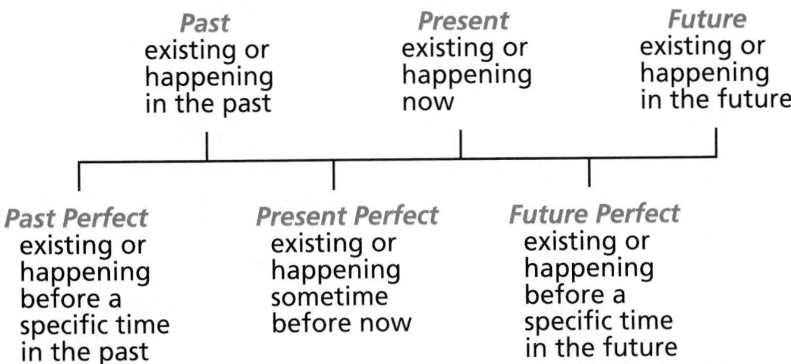

Listing all the forms of a verb is called ***conjugating*** the verb.

USAGE

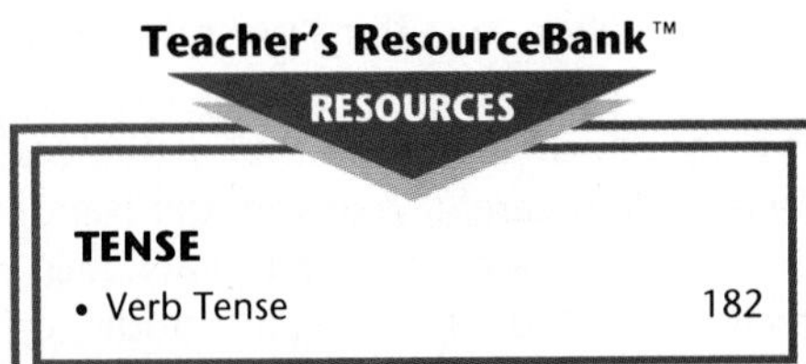

QUICK REMINDER

Write the following verbs on the chalkboard and have the students write the six tenses of each:

1. break [break, broke, will break, have broken, had broken, will have broken]
2. walk [walk, walked, will walk, have walked, had walked, will have walked]
3. grow [grow, grew, will grow, have grown, had grown, will have grown]

Point out the consistent use of auxiliary verbs in some tenses.

USAGE

LEP/ESL

General Strategies. Some students may not write or pronounce the endings for present tense, third-person singular verbs, as in the sentence "She miss the bus almost every day." Similarly, there is a tendency to omit the *–ed* ending for past tense verbs, as in "She miss the bus yesterday." To give students practice with such endings, create sentences containing these forms. Ask students to underline all of the present-tense endings for third-person verbs. Then tell students to circle the past-tense endings and to read the sentences aloud. Listen carefully and model standard pronunciation when necessary. Reinforce the idea that their mode of expression is not wrong; rather, it is helpful for them to learn the standard mode so that they are able to shift back and forth appropriately.

USAGE

USAGE

CONJUGATION OF THE VERB *WEAR*	
PRESENT TENSE	
SINGULAR	***PLURAL***
I wear	we wear
you wear	you wear
he, she, or it wears	they wear
PAST TENSE	
SINGULAR	***PLURAL***
I wore	we wore
you wore	you wore
he, she, or it wore	they wore
FUTURE TENSE	
SINGULAR	***PLURAL***
I will (shall) wear	we will (shall) wear
you will wear	you will wear
he, she, or it will wear	they will wear
PRESENT PERFECT TENSE	
SINGULAR	***PLURAL***
I have worn	we have worn
you have worn	you have worn
he, she, or it has worn	they have worn
PAST PERFECT TENSE	
SINGULAR	***PLURAL***
I had worn	we had worn
you had worn	you had worn
he, she, or it had worn	they had worn
FUTURE PERFECT TENSE	
SINGULAR	***PLURAL***
I will (shall) have worn	we will (shall) have worn
you will have worn	you will have worn
he, she, or it will have worn	they will have worn

EXERCISE 5 Writing Sentences with Different Tenses

Do you ever make up stories about pictures or paintings? Look at this painting by Norman Rockwell. What is the story behind this scene? Write five sentences telling what you think is happening, has happened, and will happen in this winter scene. Use a different tense in each sentence. Be prepared to tell what tenses you've used. If you wish, give names to the man, the boy, and the dog.

EXAMPLE 1. *The boy and his dog have hidden from the man.*

Norman Rockwell, "Man and Boy," © Brown & Bigelow, 1950, Snow Sculpturing GRAND PALS™ Series

USAGE

ANSWERS

Exercise 5

Sentences will vary. Here are some possibilities:

1. The man carries a basket. [present]
2. The man has found the boy and the dog. [present perfect]
3. The boy had thrown a snowball at the man. [past perfect]
4. The boy and the dog built the snowman. [past]
5. The snowman will melt when the sun shines. [future]

VISUAL CONNECTIONS
Man and Boy

About the Artist. Norman Rockwell (1894–1978) was a popular American illustrator whose work depicted idealized, nostalgic, everyday scenes of middle-class America.

USAGE

SEGMENT 5 *(pp. 492–500)*

SIX CONFUSING VERBS

OBJECTIVE

- To use the verbs *sit* and *set, rise* and *raise,* and *lie* and *lay* correctly in sentences

Teacher's ResourceBank™

RESOURCES

SIX CONFUSING VERBS

QUICK REMINDER

Write the six problem verbs *sit, set, rise, raise, lie,* and *lay* on the chalkboard and ask the students to use each one in a sentence. Ask volunteers to share their sentences with the class. Point out that *set, raise,* and *lay* usually have objects, while *sit, rise,* and *lie* do not.

USAGE

LEP/ESL

General Strategies. Some students may need to be reminded that there are two strategies for deciding which of these troublesome verbs to use. The first strategy, as stated in the textbook, is to look for an object directly following the verb. If the object is there, then most likely *lay, set,* or *raise* is the appropriate verb. Students can also look for a preposition or an adverb following the verb. The presence of a preposition or an adverb generally indicates that there is no object and thus *lie, sit,* or *rise* is probably the correct verb.

Six Confusing Verbs

Sit and *Set*

The verb *sit* means "to be seated" or "to rest." *Sit* seldom takes an object.

The verb *set* means "to place (something)" or "to put (something)." *Set* usually takes an object. Notice that *set* has the same form for the infinitive, past, and past participle.

USAGE

INFINITIVE	PRESENT PARTICIPLE	PAST	PAST PARTICIPLE
sit	(is) sitting	sat	(have) sat
set	(is) setting	set	(have) set

EXAMPLES I **will sit** in the easy chair. [no object]
I **will set** the book on the counter. [I will set what? *Book* is the object.]

Shannon **has sat** there for an hour. [no object]
The workers **have set** their equipment aside. [The workers have set what? *Equipment* is the object.]

NOTE: If you don't know whether to use *sit* or *set* in a sentence, try substituting *put.* If the sentence makes sense with *put,* use *set.*

ORAL PRACTICE 4 **Using the Forms of *Sit* and *Set* Correctly**

Read each of the following sentences aloud, stressing the italicized verb.

1. Josie *set* two loaves of French bread on the kitchen table.
2. The clown *sat* on the broken chair.
3. Let's *sit* down and rest awhile.
4. Did you *set* your bracelet on the night stand?

5. The Clarks' car has *sat* in the driveway for a week.
6. My little brother *sits* still for only a few seconds at a time.
7. The teacher *sets* the best projects in the display case.
8. The librarian *set* the book about Michael Jordan on the table.

EXERCISE 6 **Writing the Forms of *Sit* and *Set***

For the blank in each of the following sentences, give the correct form of *sit* or *set*.

EXAMPLE **1. The twins ___ together on the porch swing.**
1. *sat*

1. At the party yesterday, we ___ the birthday presents on the coffee table. **1. set**
2. Then we ___ on the floor to play a game. **2. sat**
3. Alana always ___ next to Rosa. **3. sits**
4. The Jiménez twins never ___ together, even on their birthday. **4. sit**
5. Mrs. Jiménez ___ a large cake on the table in the dining room. **5. set**
6. Mr. Jiménez had already ___ party hats and favors around the table. **6. set**
7. One of the twins ___ on a hat by mistake. **7. sat**
8. Mr. Jiménez ___ out another one. **8. set**
9. At every party we always ___ quietly while the birthday person makes a wish. **9. sit**
10. Yesterday we ___ still twice as long for the Jiménez twins! **10. sat**

Rise and *Raise*

The verb *rise* means "to go upward" or "to get up." *Rise* never takes an object.

The verb *raise* means "to lift (something) up." *Raise* usually takes a direct object.

USAGE

LEARNING STYLES

Visual Learners. To help visual learners understand the differences between the six verbs, you could demonstrate the definitions of the verbs. To begin, you could stand up and then sit down on a chair. As you sit down, you might say aloud, "I sit on the chair." After sitting, you could lift a book and set it on a desk, saying aloud, "I set the book on the desk."

To demonstrate the verbs *rise* and *raise,* you could sit down for a few moments and stand up saying, "I rise." Then pick up a pencil and say, "I raise the pencil."

To demonstrate the verbs *lie* and *lay,* you could pick up a notebook and place it on a desk saying, "I lay the notebook on the desk." Then point to the notebook and say, "The notebook lies on the desk."

USAGE

COOPERATIVE LEARNING

Divide the class into small groups and give each group five minutes to write as many sentences using *raise* and *rise* as they can. When students complete their sentences, have the groups share the sentences with the rest of the class.

USAGE

INFINITIVE	PRESENT PARTICIPLE	PAST	PAST PARTICIPLE
rise	(is) rising	rose	(have) risen
raise	(is) raising	raised	(have) raised

EXAMPLES The full moon **is rising.** [no object]
The winner **is raising** her arms in triumph. [The winner is raising what? *Arms* is the object.]

The kite **rose** quickly in the wind. [no object]
Congress **raised** taxes again. [Congress raised what? *Taxes* is the object.]

USAGE

ORAL PRACTICE 5 **Using the Forms of *Rise* and *Raise* Correctly**

Read each of the following sentences aloud, stressing the italicized verb.

1. The audience had *risen* from their seats to applaud Whitney Houston.
2. They *raised* the curtains for the play to start.
3. Dark smoke *rose* from the fire.
4. They always *rise* early on Saturday mornings.
5. The wind will *raise* the Chinese dragon kite high above the trees.
6. Has the sun *risen* yet?
7. The huge crane can *raise* the steel beams off the ground.
8. Bread dough *rises* very slowly in a cold room.

EXERCISE 7 **Writing the Forms of *Rise* and *Raise***

For the blank in each of the following sentences, supply the correct form of *rise* or *raise.*

EXAMPLE **1.** If our team wins, we will ____ the victory flag.
1. *raise*

1. raised

1. Before the game the color guards ____ the flag.
2. The fans ____ for the national anthem. **2.** rose

3. The pitcher ___ his arm to throw the ball. 3. raised
4. The baseball seemed to ___ above the batter's head. 4. rise
5. Someone in front of me ___ and blocked my view. 5. rose
6. I have ___ my voice to cheer a hundred times during one game. 6. raised
7. If the sun ___ too high, the players can't see the high fly ball. 7. rises
8. Whenever someone hits a home run, the fans ___ their mitts to catch the baseball. 8. raise
9. Yesterday everyone ___ when Marcus Jackson hit a home run. 9. rose
10. As soon as the ninth inning was over, we ___ to leave. 10. rose

Lie and *Lay*

The verb *lie* means "to recline," "to be in a place," or "to remain lying down." *Lie* never takes an object.

The verb *lay* means "to put (something) down" or "to place (something)." *Lay* usually takes an object.

INFINITIVE	PRESENT PARTICIPLE	PAST	PAST PARTICIPLE
lie	(is) lying	lay	(have) lain
lay	(is) laying	laid	(have) laid

EXAMPLES My new wristwatch **is lying** on the dresser. [no object]

The workers **are laying** the new carpet. [The workers are laying what? *Carpet* is the object.]

These clothes **have lain** in the corner for days. [no object]

They **have laid** the beach blanket under the umbrella. [They have laid what? *Blanket* is the object.]

USAGE

A DIFFERENT APPROACH

Ask students to draw comic strips in which they show the differences between *raise* and *rise.* Have them use the verbs *rise* and *raise* in captions to explain the events taking place. This activity can also be done with the other pairs of troublesome verbs.

USAGE

INTEGRATING THE LANGUAGE ARTS

Technology Link. If students are using word processors, tell them to check their word-processing dictionaries if they have questions about when to use these confusing verbs. Along with giving the correct definition of each verb, the dictionaries will probably provide students with sample sentences they can compare with their own to see if they are using the verbs correctly.

ORAL PRACTICE 6 Using the Forms of *Lie* and *Lay* Correctly

Read each of the following sentences aloud, stressing the italicized verb.

1. The corrected test paper *lay* on the desk.
2. My teddy bear has *lain* under my bed for a long time.
3. Before the sale, the clerk *laid* samples on the counter.
4. Have those toys *lain* outside too long?
5. The Inuit hunter *laid* his harpoon on the ice.
6. Last night, I was *lying* on the sofa and reading *Sounder* when the phone rang.
7. The hero has *laid* a trap for the villain.
8. Finally, the baby *lay* quietly in the crib.

EXERCISE 8 Writing the Forms of *Lie* and *Lay*

For each blank in the following sentences, supply the correct form of *lie* or *lay*.

EXAMPLE 1. Children often ___ their toys and other things in the wrong places.
1. *lay*

1. The remote control for the television is ___ under the chair. 1. lying
2. How long has it ___ there? 2. lain
3. My brother Ramón probably ___ it there last night. 3. laid
4. He was ___ on the floor, watching television. 4. lying
5. Julia, my younger sister, always ___ her toys in front of the television set. 5. lays
6. She has ___ little parts from her games all over the house. 6. laid
7. Whenever Mom and Dad find one of these parts, they usually ___ it on the bookcase. 7. lay
8. Yesterday, Dad ___ down on some hard plastic pieces on the sofa. 8. lay

REVIEWS D and E

OBJECTIVES

- To identify and use the correct forms of *sit* and *set, rise* and *raise,* and *lie* and *lay*
- To proofread for and identify incorrect verb forms and to provide correct verb forms

9. Now those broken bits of plastic ___ at the bottom of the wastebasket. 9. lie
10. Today, Julia has ___ every single toy safely in the toy chest. 10. laid

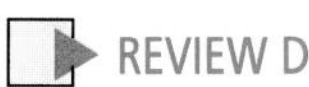 REVIEW D

Identifying the Correct Forms of *Sit* and *Set, Rise* and *Raise,* and *Lie* and *Lay*

For each of the following sentences, choose the correct verb in parentheses.

EXAMPLE 1. Dad (*sat, set*) the pictures from our visit to the Hopi Reservation on the table.
1. *set*

1. Do you know what kind of doll is (*lying, laying*) in this Hopi girl's arms?

2. Someone had (*lain, laid*) down a kachina doll, and this girl picked it up.
3. A Hopi artist probably (*sat, set*) for hours working on this one doll.
4. At the reservation, everyone (*sat, set*) quietly during the Hopi Snake Dance.

USAGE

USAGE

VISUAL CONNECTIONS

Exploring the Subject. The kachina dolls of the Hopi Indians are carved cottonwood figurines. The wooden dolls are intended both as toys and as a means of teaching about ancestral spirits.

INTEGRATING THE LANGUAGE ARTS

Literature Link. After students have read and discussed a poem such as Nikki Giovanni's "Winter Poem," ask them to list the verbs used in the poem and to identify each verb's tense. Ask students how changing the tense of the verbs alters the meaning of the poem.

USAGE

5. One dancer (*rose*, *raised*) a snake above his head for the crowd to see.
6. The growing corn (*rises*, *raises*) high in the Hopi country of Arizona.
7. Hot and tired, I (*lay*, *laid*) on a bench at the Hopi trading post.
8. When we entered the pueblo, a Hopi woman (*rose*, *raised*) from her chair to greet us.
9. Dad had (*rose*, *raised*) his camera to take the woman's picture.
10. Smiling, the woman (*sat*, *set*) a beautiful coiled basket on the shelf behind her.

USAGE

REVIEW E **Proofreading for Correct Verb Forms**

For each of the following sentences, identify the incorrect verb form. Then give the correct form.

EXAMPLE **1. Lately, everyone in our neighborhood has did a lot more to keep physically fit.**
1. *did—done*

1. No one is ~~setting~~ down anymore—except on stationary bicycles. **1. sitting**
2. My mom has ~~rode~~ 150 miles so far. **2. ridden**
3. In addition, I have never ~~knew~~ so many aerobic dancers. **3. known**
4. Yesterday afternoon, I ~~swum~~ twelve laps in the pool myself. **4. swam**
5. Last month, a famous exercise instructor ~~choosed~~ our neighborhood for her new fitness center. **5. chose**
6. Many people ~~seen~~ her interviews on local talk shows. **6. saw**
7. All of a sudden, adults and children have ~~began~~ going to the center. **7. begun**
8. Each person is ~~suppose~~ to use different kinds of equipment. **8. supposed**
9. Last night, I ~~rose~~ fifty pounds of weights. **9. raised**
10. So far, no one has ~~broke~~ a leg on the cross-country ski machine. **10. broken**

WRITING APPLICATION

OBJECTIVE

- To write descriptive paragraphs that contain correct verb forms and tenses

WRITING APPLICATION

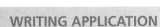

Using Verb Forms Correctly to Make Writing Clear

A sentence without a verb is like a sailboat without a sail. Just as a sail moves a sailboat forward, a verb carries a sentence forward. If you use the wrong form or tense of a verb, your sentence won't go where you want it to go. Look at the two pairs of sentences below.

CONFUSING In the future, people will have wore different clothes than they did now. The clothes are made of a shiny, dirt-resistant fabric.

CLEAR In the future, people **will wear** different clothes than they **do** now. The clothes **will be made** of a shiny, dirt-resistant fabric.

WRITING ACTIVITY

Many scientists and writers make predictions about the future. They base their predictions on past and present trends. You've decided to write a story set in the future. First, you need to imagine what the future will be like. Write a paragraph or two describing how an everyday item such as a car, a house, a home appliance, or a school might be different one hundred years from now. In your description, be sure to use the correct forms and tenses of verbs.

Prewriting Choose a topic that interests you, such as "video games" or "skyscrapers." Based on what you already know about the topic, make some predictions about the future. Jot down as many details as you can think of. For example, if you're writing about cars of the twenty-first century, tell what the cars will look like, how fast they will go, and what kind of fuel they will use.

Writing Begin your draft by telling what time period your predictions are for. Then use your notes to write a

USAGE

WRITING APPLICATION

Before students begin the **Writing Activity,** remind them that they are each to write about only one item. Because this exercise is presented as a prewriting activity for a story set in the future, you may want to limit your assessment to how well students use verb forms and tenses.

CRITICAL THINKING
Analysis

If students have problems speculating about a future one hundred years distant, you can help them by getting them to look at the past. This can be done in a general sense; for example, in the hundred years between 1869 and 1969, humankind went from the horse and buggy to spaceflight and a visit to the moon. Or students can be more specific in their study of the past by concentrating on the histories of the items they have chosen to write about.

USAGE

SEGMENT 6 *(pp. 500–501)*

REVIEW: POSTTEST

OBJECTIVE

- To revise incorrect verb forms in sentences

COOPERATIVE LEARNING

For added review, divide the class into groups of three or four. Give each group a paragraph written in the past tense. Then have the groups rewrite the paragraphs twice by using two other tenses of their choice.

USAGE

clear, vivid description of something in that future time. You may want to compare a present-day example of the item with your prediction of what the item will be like in the future.

Evaluating and Revising Ask a friend to read your description. Is it clear and believable? Do the details help your reader picture the item you've described? If not, you'll need to add, cut, or revise details. Make sure you've used the correct tense for each of your verbs.

Proofreading Read your paragraph carefully to check for errors in grammar, spelling, or punctuation. Take special care with the forms of verbs. Use a dictionary to check the forms of any verbs you're not sure about.

USAGE

Review: Posttest

Revising Incorrect Verb Forms in Sentences

Most of the following sentences contain an error in the use of a verb. If a verb is incorrect, give the correct verb form. If the sentence is correct, write *C*.

EXAMPLE **1.** The last movie I seen was terrible.
1. *saw*

1. My friends and I have ~~set~~ through several bad movies. **1.** sat
2. Has anyone ever ~~wrote~~ a letter to complain about how many bad movies there are? **2.** written
3. Last Saturday they ~~run~~ two bad movies! **3.** ran
4. My friends J.D. and Conchita had ~~went~~ with me to our neighborhood theater. **4.** gone
5. We had hoped we would enjoy *Out of the Swamp*. **5.** C

6. In the beginning of the movie, a huge swamp creature ~~raised~~ out of the muddy water. **6.** rose
7. It ~~begun~~ to crawl slowly toward a cow in a field. **7.** began
8. The cow had been ~~laying~~ under a tree. **8.** lying
9. She never even ~~seen~~ the swamp monster. **9.** saw
10. I ~~sunk~~ back in my seat, expecting the monster to pounce. **10.** sank
11. Then the lights ~~come~~ back on. **11.** came
12. What a disappointment—the film inside the projector had ~~broke~~! **12.** broken
13. It ~~taked~~ a long time before the machine came back on. **13.** took
14. Some children got bored and ~~throwed~~ popcorn up in the air. **14.** threw
15. Others ~~drunk~~ noisily through their straws. **15.** drank
16. I had ~~sat~~ my popcorn on the floor, and someone kicked it over. **16.** set
17. Finally, the theater manager ~~choosed~~ another movie to show us, but it was only a silly cartoon about a penguin. **17.** chose
18. The penguin wore a fur coat it had ~~stole~~ from a sleeping polar bear. **18.** stolen
19. The bear awoke, ~~become~~ angry, and chased the penguin. **19.** became
20. Finally, the penguin gave back the coat and ~~swum~~ to Miami Beach to get warm. **20.** swam

USAGE

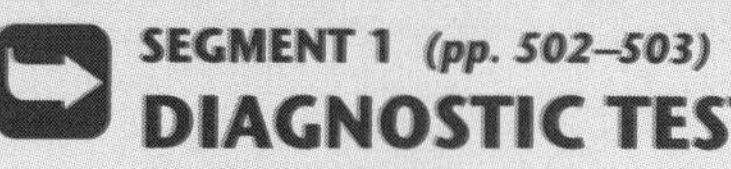

SEGMENT 1 *(pp. 502–503)*

DIAGNOSTIC TEST

OBJECTIVE

- To identify correct pronoun forms

Teacher's ResourceBank™

RESOURCES

FOR THE WHOLE CHAPTER

• Chapter Review Form A	196–197
• Chapter Review Form B	198–199
• Assessment Portfolio	
Usage Pretests	455–462
Usage Mastery Tests	479–486

CHAPTER OVERVIEW

The material in this chapter is organized into four main sections. First, the forms of personal pronouns (subject and object) are explained. Then subject forms and object forms are discussed at length in their own sections. Lastly, the chapter addresses special problems students face with the pronouns *who* and *whom* and with appositives. All the information, reinforced by multiple exercises and activities, challenges students to use pronouns correctly in their speech and writing.

USING THE DIAGNOSTIC TEST

The **Diagnostic Test** can help you determine problem areas in which additional instruction may be beneficial. Going over the answers orally may serve as a helpful review for some students, particularly your auditory learners.

USAGE

19 USING PRONOUNS CORRECTLY

Subject and Object Forms

Diagnostic Test

Identifying Correct Pronoun Forms

For each of the following sentences, choose the correct form of the pronoun in parentheses.

EXAMPLE **1. Our parents and (*they, them*) play tennis together.**
1. *they*

1. Could it be (*she, her*) at the bus stop?
2. The guest speakers were Sandra Cisneros and (*he, him*).
3. Are you and (*they, them*) going to the basketball game?

SEGMENT 2 *(pp. 503–505)*

THE FORMS OF PERSONAL PRONOUNS

OBJECTIVE

- To classify pronouns as having the subject or object form

4. You and (*I*, *me*) have been friends for a long time.
5. Sometimes, even our parents cannot tell (*we*, *us*) twins apart.
6. (*We*, *Us*) players surprised the coach with a victory party.
7. (*Who*, *Whom*) is bringing the holiday turkey?
8. Latisha lent my sister and (*I*, *me*) the new Paula Abdul CD.
9. Mr. Lee will divide the money between you and (*I*, *me*).
10. To (*who*, *whom*) is the envelope addressed?

USAGE

The Forms of Personal Pronouns

The form of a personal pronoun shows its use in a sentence. Pronouns used as subjects and predicate nominatives are in the ***subject form.***

EXAMPLES **He** and **I** went to the post office. [subject]
The winner of the marathon is **she.** [predicate nominative]

Pronouns used as direct objects and indirect objects of verbs and as objects of prepositions are in the ***object form.***

EXAMPLES Mr. García helped **him** and **me** with yesterday's homework. [direct objects]
The clerk gave **us** the package. [indirect object]
When is Theo going to give the flowers to **her?** [object of a preposition]

The ***possessive form*** (*my, your, his, her, its, their, our*) is used to show ownership or relationship.

REFERENCE NOTE: For more about possessive forms, see pages 376 and 624–628.

Teacher's ResourceBank™

RESOURCES

THE FORMS OF PERSONAL PRONOUNS

QUICK REMINDER

Ask each of your students to write two sentences with pronouns in the subject form and two sentences with pronouns in the object form. Ask them to underline the pronouns. [Students' sentences will vary. Here are some possiblities:

1. We and he are planning to go to the soccer game.
2. The master of ceremonies is he.
3. The answers were provided by them.
4. Gina gave him the watch.]

USAGE

LEP/ESL

Spanish. Some students may require extra practice with the possessive pronoun forms *his, her, its,* and *their* because the possessive pronoun *su* is used in Spanish to indicate all of these forms. Therefore, *su llegada* may mean "his arrival," "her arrival," "its arrival," or "their arrival," depending on the context of the sentence. Because Spanish adjectives generally agree in gender with the nouns that follow, students may transfer this strategy to English to create expressions such as *his husband* or *her wife.*

LEARNING STYLES

Auditory Learners. If time permits and if equipment is available, build a tape library of students enunciating sentences in the **Oral Practice** exercises in the textbook. Auditory learners can listen to themselves and their classmates repeatedly to learn the sound of correct usage.

USAGE

PERSONAL PRONOUNS			
SUBJECT FORM		OBJECT FORM	
Singular	**Plural**	**Singular**	**Plural**
I	we	me	us
you	you	you	you
he, she, it	they	him, her, it	them

Notice that the pronouns *you* and *it* are the same in the subject form and object form.

EXERCISE 1 Classifying Pronouns

Classify each of the following pronouns as the *subject form* or *object form.* If the pronoun can be either the subject form or the object form, write *either.*

EXAMPLE **1.** they
1. *subject form*

1. o. **1.** him 3. e. **3.** it 5. s. **5.** she 7. e. **7.** you 9. o. **9.** her
2. o. **2.** me 4. s. **4.** we 6. o. **6.** them 8. s. **8.** I 10. o. **10.** us

EXERCISE 2 Classifying Pronouns in Sentences

In the following sentences, identify each pronoun in italics as either a *subject form* or an *object form*.

EXAMPLE **1.** Ever since *he* could remember, Edward Bannister had wanted to be an artist.
1. *subject form*

1. *He* had to work hard to reach his goal.
2. *We* consider Bannister an American artist, but he was born in Canada.
3. Bannister's parents died when *he* was young.
4. The little money *they* had was left to their son.
5. The young Bannister couldn't afford paper, so *he* drew on barn doors and fences.

SEGMENT 3 *(pp. 505–512)*

THE SUBJECT FORM Rules 19a, 19b

OBJECTIVES

- To read sentences aloud and to stress the pronouns
- To identify the correct forms of pronouns in sentences
- To write sentences with pronouns used as predicate nominatives
- To identify the correct pronouns used as predicate nominatives in sentences

6. Later, Bannister met Christiana Cartreaux and married *her*.
7. *She* was from Rhode Island, where her people, the Narragansett, lived.
8. In 1876, a Philadelphia artistic society recognized Bannister by awarding *him* a gold medal for the painting shown below.
9. Bannister treasured his prize and regarded *it* as a great honor.
10. What do *you* think of the painting?

Oak Trees

Edward Banister, "Oak Trees," 1876. Oil on canvas. 33 7/8 × 60 1/4. Art Resource/National Museum of American Art, Smithsonian Institution, Gift of the Frank Family.

USAGE

The Subject Form

19a. Use the subject form for a pronoun that is the subject of a verb.

EXAMPLES **I walked to school.** [*I* is the subject of the verb *walked.*]

He and **she** live on the Tigua reservation in El Paso, Texas. [*He* and *she* are the compound subject of the verb *live.*]

VISUAL CONNECTIONS
Oak Trees

About the Artist. Edward Bannister (1833–1901) was one of the first African American regional painters to achieve public notice. In 1871, he helped found the Providence Art Club, which became the Rhode Island School of Design.

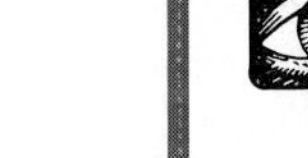

Teacher's ResourceBank™

RESOURCES

THE SUBJECT FORM

- The Subject Forms 192

QUICK REMINDER

Write the following sentence on the chalkboard and ask students to identify the correct pronoun:

Neither Juan nor (me, I) will be able to go to the concert.

Tell your students that one way to identify the correct pronoun in constructions such as this is to try each pronoun in question as the subject of the sentence. "Me will be able to go to the concert" is obviously not correct, but "I will be able to go to the concert" is. Therefore, *I* is the correct pronoun.

USAGE

STUDENTS WITH SPECIAL NEEDS

Learning disabled students often have poor decoding skills. This means that they may read a different word in place of the one written. The words they insert may be similar to the ones written in one or more ways: configuration, sound, definition, and linguistic function. Such substitution may or may not affect students' comprehension, but you should monitor them closely when they are doing the **Oral Practice** exercises.

USAGE

LEP/ESL

Spanish. Because Spanish verbs have endings that indicate the subject, pronouns are often omitted in Spanish. For example, in the sentence *Yo hablo español,* the subject *Yo* (*I*) is rarely used, as the *–o* ending on the verb *hablo* identifies the subject. Students may therefore have difficulty with the subject form of pronouns in English. Especially when the subject of the English sentence is *it,* the Spanish speaker may tend toward omission, creating sentences such as "Is too hard for me." Point out that verbs in English do not have endings that indicate their subjects, and therefore subject pronouns are essential.

There is also a tendency to overcompensate for this subject omission. The student may add an unnecessary subject pronoun, as in "The teacher she is a nice person." Monitor students' written and oral expressions and offer guidance in this area when necessary.

USAGE

ORAL PRACTICE 1 Using Pronouns as Subjects

Read the following sentences aloud, stressing the italicized pronouns.

1. *She* and Ahmed solve crossword puzzles.
2. *They* are very hard puzzles to solve.
3. Dad and *I* finished putting together a jigsaw puzzle last night.
4. *We* worked for three hours!
5. Finally, *you* and *he* found the missing pieces.
6. *He* and *I* liked the completed picture of flamenco dancers.
7. *They* are gypsies from Spain.
8. *We* would like to see a colorful gypsy dance.

To test if a pronoun is used correctly in a compound subject, try each form of the pronoun separately.

EXAMPLE: Tina and (*he, him*) always win.
He always wins.
Him always wins.
ANSWER: **Tina** and **he** always win.

EXAMPLE: (*She, Her*) and (*I, me*) practiced hard.
She practiced hard.
Her practiced hard.
I practiced hard.
Me practiced hard.
ANSWER: **She** and **I** practiced hard.

EXERCISE 3 Identifying the Correct Forms of Pronouns

For each of the following sentences, choose the correct form of the pronoun in parentheses.

EXAMPLE **1.** Brad and (*me, I*) wrote a skit based on the myth about Pygmalion.
1. *I*

19b

1. (*Him*, *He*) and I thought the myth was funny.
2. (*We*, *Us*) asked Angela to play a part in the skit.
3. Neither (*she*, *her*) nor Doreen wanted to play a statue that came to life.
4. Finally Brad and (*me*, *I*) convinced Doreen that it would be a funny version of the myth.
5. (*Him*, *He*) and I flipped a coin to see who would play the part of Pygmalion.
6. The next day (*we*, *us*) were ready to perform.
7. Doreen and (*me*, *I*) began giggling when Brad pretended to be the beautiful statue.
8. In the skit, when Pygmalion returned from the festival of Venus, (*him*, *he*) and the statue were supposed to hug.
9. Instead of hugging, (*they*, *them*) laughed too hard to say the lines correctly.
10. Doreen, Brad, and (*I*, *me*) finally took a bow, and the class applauded.

19b. Use the subject form for a pronoun that is a predicate nominative.

A ***predicate nominative*** follows a linking verb and explains or identifies the subject of the sentence. A pronoun used as a predicate nominative usually follows a form of the verb *be* (such as *am, are, is, was, were, be, been,* or *being*).

EXAMPLES The next singer is **she.** [*She* follows the linking verb *is* and identifies the subject *singer.*]
The first speakers might be **he** and **I.** [*He* and *I* follow the linking verb *might be* and identify the subject *speakers.*]

NOTE: Expressions such as *It's me* or *That's him* are acceptable in everyday speaking. In writing, however, such expressions should be avoided.

REFERENCE NOTE: For more information about predicate nominatives, see page 447.

USAGE

LESS-ADVANCED STUDENTS

If students are having difficulty understanding subject pronouns, you may want to use the odd-numbered items of **Exercise 3** as an oral practice. Have students refer to the **Subject Form** list in the **Personal Pronouns** chart (p. 504) as they answer. Ask volunteers to explain the correct choices, and then have them write the sentences so they can see the correct answers in context.

USAGE

INTEGRATING THE LANGUAGE ARTS

Literature Link. In her short story "Jody's Discovery," Marjorie Kinnan Rawlings skillfully uses subject pronouns to create unity. Have your students read and discuss Rawlings's story. Then have them search the first four or five paragraphs of the story for subject pronouns used either as subjects or as predicate nominatives.

ANSWERS

Exercise 4

Responses will vary. Here are some possibilities:

1. he, she

2. he, she

3. they, we

4. she, he

5. I, he, she

USAGE

ORAL PRACTICE 2 **Using Pronouns as Predicate Nominatives**

Read the following sentences aloud, stressing the italicized pronouns.

1. The stars of *The Man from Snowy River* were *he* and *she.*
2. The actors from Australia must be *they.*
3. Of course, the mountain man is *he.*
4. Was the actress really *she?*
5. The director could have been *he.*
6. The villains are *he* and *they.*
7. The movie's biggest fans may be *you* and *I.*
8. The next ones to rent the film will be *we.*

EXERCISE 4 **Writing Sentences with Pronouns Used as Predicate Nominatives**

For the following sentences, supply pronouns to fill in the blanks. Use a variety of pronouns, but do not use *you* or *it.*

EXAMPLE **1. The people in the silliest costumes were ____.**
1. ***she and they***

1. The person in the gorilla suit must be ____.
2. The next contestants will be ____ and ____.
3. The winners should have been ____.
4. Can that singer be ____?
5. It was ____ sitting in the back row.

EXERCISE 5 **Identifying Pronouns Used as Predicate Nominatives**

For each of the following sentences, choose the correct form of the pronoun in parentheses.

1. Was that (*he, him*) at the door?
2. The winners are you and (*me, I*).
3. The cooks for the traditional Vietnamese meal were (*them, they*).

REVIEW A

OBJECTIVE

- To identify correct pronoun forms in sentences

4. Could it have been (we, us)?
5. Every year the speaker has been (her, she).
6. That was Carl and (they, them) in the swimming pool.
7. The volleyball fans in our family are Dad and (she, her).
8. First on the Black History Month program will be (us, we).
9. It might have been (he, him).
10. Last year, the class treasurer was (he, him).

USAGE

REVIEW A **Identifying the Correct Use of Pronouns**

For each of the following sentences, choose the correct form of the pronoun in parentheses.

EXAMPLE **1. Last summer Carl, Felicia, and (*we, us*) went to San Antonio.**
1. *we*

1. Carl and (she, her) took these photographs.
2. Early one morning (he, him) and (she, her) visited the Alamo.

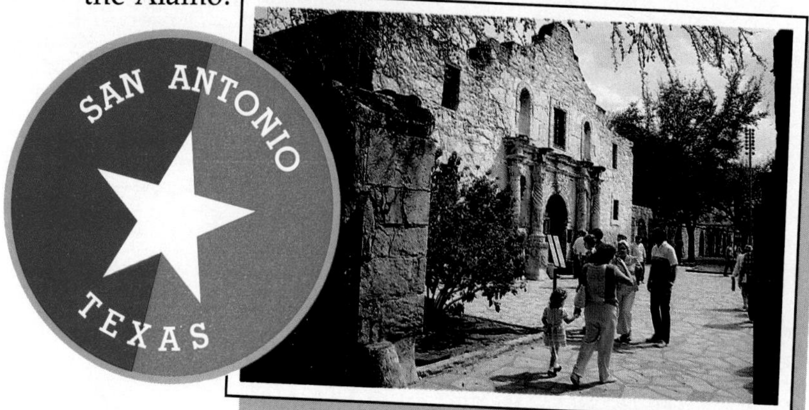

3. That could be (he, him) in the crowd outside the Alamo.
4. Felicia and (I, me) listened to a mariachi band on the Riverwalk.

COOPERATIVE LEARNING

You may want to pair students for **Review A.** One student will be responsible for the even-numbered sentences, and the other student will work with the odd-numbered sentences. Tell them to write the sentences in sequence but to answer alternately. Then they should check each other's work.

USAGE

WRITING APPLICATION

OBJECTIVE

- To use correct pronoun forms in writing

USAGE

WRITING APPLICATION This writing assignment provides students with an opportunity to develop descriptive paragraphs in which they will use correct pronoun forms.

USAGE

5. Of course, the guitar players in the picture below are (*they*, *them*).
6. Don't (*they*, *them*) look as though they're having a good time?
7. Carl and (*I*, *me*) enjoyed visiting the Spanish Governor's Palace.
8. Felicia, Carl, and (*we*, *us*) particularly liked this adobe building.
9. In fact, the first guests there that morning were (*us*, *we*).
10. Maybe you and (*they*, *them*) will get a chance to visit San Antonio someday.

WRITING APPLICATION

Using Correct Pronoun Forms in Writing

When you write a story or a report, you want your writing to be its best. Read the following two sentences. Which would be better to use in a report for school?

Luisa and me will dress up as giant toothbrushes for the skit.

Luisa and I will dress up as giant toothbrushes for the skit.

You might hear the first sentence spoken in a casual conversation. However, the second sentence is better to use in a report. In school or in any other formal situation, your audience usually expects you to follow the rules and guidelines of formal English.

WRITING ACTIVITY

Health Awareness Week is coming up soon. Your class has been chosen to perform a skit on a health-related topic for the rest of the school. Your teacher has asked each class member to write down an idea for an entertaining, informative skit. Write a paragraph or two describing a skit that your class could perform. Be sure to use correct pronoun forms in your description.

Prewriting First, you'll need to decide on a topic for the skit. Think about the health concerns of people your age. For example, you might plan a skit about the dangers of smoking or the importance of regular dental check-ups. After you choose a topic, brainstorm some ideas for a simple, entertaining skit. Be sure to list any props or costumes your class will need.

Writing Use your notes to help you write your draft. First, tell what the skit is about and why it is appropriate for Health Awareness Week. Then, explain what happens in the skit from beginning to end. Be sure to tell in a general way what each character does and says. Describe the props and costumes that your class can make or bring from home.

Evaluating and Revising Ask a classmate to read your paragraph. Is the information given in the skit correct? Does the skit sound entertaining? Is it clear which character does and says what? If not, revise your paragraph. Add details that will make the skit more fun and

USAGE

CRITICAL THINKING
Evaluation

Ask students to avoid falling into the trap of criticizing their work to the point of stifling creativity. Encourage them instead to be objective about each sentence in their paragraphs. Tell them to examine each sentence separately from the others and to use the following criteria:

1. Does the sentence have a subject and a verb and express a complete thought?
2. Does the sentence say exactly what you want it to say?
3. Does the sentence support the topic sentence?
4. Does the sentence contain a subject pronoun or an object pronoun?

WRITING

Remind students that the most important aspect of this stage of writing is simply to put their thoughts on paper. Corrections and improvements will be handled later. You may suggest they write on every other line of notebook paper to have sufficient space for revisions.

USAGE

SEGMENT 4 *(pp. 512–518)*

THE OBJECT FORM Rules 19c–19e

OBJECTIVES

- To read sentences aloud and to stress the pronouns
- To identify the correct forms of pronouns used as direct objects, indirect objects, and objects of prepostitions

USAGE

Teacher's ResourceBank™

RESOURCES

THE OBJECT FORM

• The Object Forms	193

QUICK REMINDER

Write the following sentences on the chalkboard and ask students to identify the pronouns and to note how they're used (as direct objects, indirect objects, or objects of prepositions):

1. Laurie gave him this picture. [i.o.]
2. Mr. Rodriguez presented the award to us. [o. p.]
3. Chuck picked me for his campaign manager. [d.o.]
4. Marco stood by us and them. [o. p.; o. p.]

interesting. Check your sentences to be sure you've used pronouns correctly and clearly.

Proofreading and Publishing Read through your description carefully to check for errors in grammar, spelling, or punctuation. Use this chapter to help you check for errors in pronoun forms. Your class may want to hold a contest for the best skit idea. Using the best idea, work together to develop the skit in more detail. Then, with your teacher's permission, give a performance of the skit for other classes.

USAGE

The Object Form

19c. Use the object form for a pronoun that is the direct object of a verb.

A ***direct object*** follows an action verb and tells *whom* or *what* receives the action of the verb.

EXAMPLES The teacher thanked **me** for cleaning the chalkboard. [*Teacher* is the subject of the verb *thanked.* The teacher thanked whom? The direct object is *me.*]

The answer surprised **us.** [*Answer* is the subject of the verb *surprised.* The answer surprised whom? The direct object is *us.*]

Fred saw **them** and **me** last night. [*Fred* is the subject of the verb *saw.* Fred saw whom? The direct objects are *them* and *me.*]

To help you choose the correct pronoun in a compound object, try each pronoun separately in the sentence.

EXAMPLE: Ms. Stone praised Alonzo and (*we*, *us*).
Ms. Stone praised *we*.
Ms. Stone praised *us*.
ANSWER: Ms. Stone praised Alonzo and **us**.

REFERENCE NOTE: For more about direct objects, see page 439.

ORAL PRACTICE 3 **Using Pronouns as Direct Objects**

Read the following sentences aloud, stressing the italicized pronouns.

1. Kathy found *them* and *me* by the fountain.
2. Mr. Winters took *us* to the rodeo.
3. Did you see *her* and *him* at the Cajun restaurant?
4. Tyrone frightened *us* with his rubber spider.
5. Ellis invited Luis, Jiro, and *me* to his party.
6. The mayor met *them* at Howard University.
7. Uncle Ken thanked *her* for the gift.
8. The fans cheered Anthony and *her*.

EXERCISE 6 **Identifying Pronouns Used as Direct Objects**

For each of the following sentences, choose the correct form of the pronoun in parentheses.

1. Mrs. Freeman invited Leroy and (*I*, *me*) to a Kwanzaa party.
2. The spectators watched (*we*, *us*) and (*they*, *them*).
3. The shoes don't fit either (*her*, *she*) or (*I*, *me*).
4. Sean called Marco and (*he*, *him*) on the telephone.
5. Our new neighbors asked (*we*, *us*) for directions to the synagogue.
6. The new neighbors hired Tía and (*us*, *we*) to rake their yard.
7. The puppy followed Louis and (*he*, *him*) all the way home.

USAGE

LEP/ESL

Spanish. Some students may have difficulty positioning direct and indirect pronouns within sentences. For example, "Lalo gave it to me" is expressed in Spanish as *Lalo me lo dio.* Object pronouns come before verbs in Spanish.

USAGE

INTEGRATING THE LANGUAGE ARTS

Literature Link. To illustrate the value of object pronouns in literature, have your students read "All Summer in a Day" by Ray Bradbury. Then have them identify as many object pronouns as possible on the first page. You may want to read those paragraphs aloud and omit the object pronouns to demonstrate how different the language would sound without them. Ask volunteers to express the grammatical value of object pronouns in literature. [Without object pronouns, the names of the objects would have to be repeated over and over. This would lead to awkward, tedious sentences.]

USAGE

8. Last week, friends from Panama visited (<u>*us*</u>, *we*).
9. Odessa thanked (<u>*her*</u>, *she*) and (<u>*me*</u>, *I*) for helping.
10. The usher showed Greg and (<u>*them*</u>, *they*) to their seats.

19d. Use the object form for a pronoun that is the indirect object of a verb.

An ***indirect object*** comes between an action verb and a direct object. The indirect object tells *to whom* or *to what* or *for whom* or *for what* something is done.

USAGE

EXAMPLES Scott handed **me** a note. [Scott handed what? *Note* is the direct object. To whom did he hand a note? The indirect object is *me.*]

Coretta baked **them** some muffins. [*Coretta* baked what? *Muffins* is the direct object. For whom did Coretta bake muffins? The indirect object is *them.*]

Elizabeth sent **him** and **me** some oranges from Florida. [Elizabeth sent what? *Oranges* is the direct object. To whom did Elizabeth send oranges? The indirect objects are *him* and *me.*]

ORAL PRACTICE 4 **Using Pronouns as Indirect Objects**

Read the following sentences aloud, stressing the italicized pronouns.

1. Mr. Krebs showed Bill and *them* the rock collection.
2. Paco told *me* the answer to the riddle.
3. Mr. Thibaut gives *us* lacrosse lessons.
4. We bought Mother and *him* an anniversary present.
5. The artists drew *us* and *them* some pictures.
6. The server brought *me* a bagel with cream cheese.
7. A pen pal in Hawaii sent *her* some shells.
8. My uncle Shannon told *us* a funny story about leprechauns.

REVIEW B

OBJECTIVE

- To revise incorrect pronoun forms in sentences

EXERCISE 7 Identifying the Correct Forms of Pronouns Used as Indirect Objects

For each of the following sentences, choose the correct form of the pronoun in each set of parentheses.

EXAMPLE **1.** At the start of class, Mr. Chou assigned (*we, us*) new seats.
1. *us*

1. The store clerk gave (*they, them*) a discount.
2. For lunch, Anthony fixed (*he, him*) and (*she, her*) bean burritos.
3. Would you please show (*her, she*) and (*me, I*) that Navajo dream catcher?
4. Those green apples gave both Earl and (*he, him*) stomachaches.
5. The waiter brought (*us, we*) some ice water.
6. Why don't you sing (*she, her*) a lullaby?
7. Have they made (*we, us*) the costumes for the play?
8. An usher handed (*me, I*) a program of the recital.
9. The Red Cross volunteers showed (*we, us*) and (*they, them*) a movie about first aid.
10. Please send (*I, me*) your new address.

REVIEW B Revising Incorrect Pronoun Forms in Paragraphs

In most of the sentences in the following paragraphs, at least one pronoun has been used incorrectly. Identify each incorrect pronoun and give the correct form. If all of the pronouns in a sentence are correct, write C.

EXAMPLE [1] Ms. Fisher took several of my friends and I to the museum.
1. *I—me*

[1] At the Museum of Natural History, Luisa and ~~me~~ wanted to see the Native American exhibit. [2] The 1. I

A DIFFERENT APPROACH

Create flashcards that state the number, person, and form of a pronoun on one side and the corresponding pronoun on the reverse side. (For example, a card might read "First Person Singular—Subject Form/*I*.") Prepare twelve cards, one for each subject and object pronoun form. (For *you* and *it*, you can include all the combinations on the descriptive side of the card. Be sure to include the gender of third-person pronouns in your descriptions.)

Show the descriptive sides of the cards and let volunteers name the correct pronouns. To increase the level of difficulty, have students compose sentences with the pronouns.

INTEGRATING THE LANGUAGE ARTS

Usage and Writing. As an alternative exercise, ask each of your students to write a brief descriptive paragraph about a pet or favorite animal. Students should include object pronouns in each sentence. When they finish their first drafts, tell them to exchange their papers with partners who will check the correctness of the object pronouns.

VISUAL CONNECTIONS

Exploring the Subject. The funeral mask of Tutankhamen is made of solid gold with lapis lazuli eyelids, quartz and obsidian eyes, and blue glass stripes in the headdress. The fact that Tutankhamen was king of both upper and lower Egypt is symbolized by the vulture and cobra on the forehead.

USAGE

2. her/me museum guide showed ~~she~~ and ~~I~~ the displays of Hopi
3. C pottery and baskets. [3] Both she and I were especially
4. C interested in the kachina dolls. [4] After half an hour,
5. she Ms. Fisher found us. [5] Then Luisa, ~~her~~, and I joined
6. C the rest of the group. [6] Another guide had been giving Ms. Fisher and them information about the Masai
7. They/we people in Africa. [7] ~~Them~~ and ~~us~~ decided to see the ancient Egyptian exhibit next.

8. us [8] A group of little children passed Ms. Fisher and
9. they ~~we~~ on the stairway, going to the exhibit. [9] It was
10. C ~~them~~ who reached the exhibit first. [10] Jeff, the jokester, said that they wanted to find their "mummies."
11. we [11] Ms. Fisher and ~~us~~ laughed at the terrible pun.
12. C [12] She gave him a pat on the back. [13] We asked her
13. C not to encourage him. [14] The museum guide led
14. us the children and ~~we~~ to the back of the room. [15] There,
15. them he showed us and ~~they~~ a model of a pyramid.
16. he [16] Then Ms. Fisher and ~~him~~ explained how the Egyp-
17. she tians prepared mummies. [17] It must have been ~~her~~
18. C who asked about King Tutankhamen. [18] Of course, Luisa and I recognized this golden mask right away.
19. us [19] As we were leaving, the guide gave the children and ~~we~~ some booklets about King Tut and other
20. me famous ancient Egyptians. [20] The ones he handed Luisa and ~~I~~ were about the builders of the pyramids.

19e

19e. Use the object form for a pronoun that is the object of a preposition.

A *prepositional phrase* begins with a preposition and ends with a noun or a pronoun, called the *object of the preposition.*

EXAMPLES above **me** beside **us** with **them**
for **him** toward **you** next to **her**

REFERENCE NOTE: For a list of prepositions, see page 407.

When a preposition is followed by two or more pronouns, try each pronoun alone to be sure that you have used the correct form.

EXAMPLE: The puppy walked behind Tom and (*I, me*).
The puppy walked behind I.
The puppy walked behind me.
ANSWER: The puppy walked behind Tom and **me.**

EXAMPLE: Carrie divided the chores between (*they, them*) and (*we, us*).
Carrie divided the chores between they.
Carrie divided the chores between them.
Carrie divided the chores between we.
Carrie divided the chores between us.
ANSWER: Carrie divided the chores between **them** and **us.**

ORAL PRACTICE 5 **Using Pronouns as Objects of Prepositions**

Read the following sentences aloud, stressing the italicized pronouns.

1. The lemonade stand was built by Chuck and *me.*
2. The younger children rode in front of *us.*
3. Just between *you* and *me,* that game wasn't much fun.
4. Everyone has gone except the Taylors and *them.*
5. Give the message to *him* or *her.*
6. Were those pictures of Amish families taken by *him?*

USAGE

AT-RISK STUDENTS

For students who maintain low achievement levels due to poor self-esteem and socialization problems, you may want to let them create their own story circle. Tell them to make up a group story that contains subject and object pronouns. The first student will start by identifying the protagonist, antagonist, and setting in narrative form. The next student will continue the story by revealing conflicts and developments. The story goes around the circle, with each student adding his or her thoughts. The last student in the circle will end the story and resolve all plot issues.

Listen carefully to the story. Students may reveal much about themselves and their lives that might help you in meeting their unique needs.

USAGE

SEGMENT 5 *(pp. 518–523)*

SPECIAL PRONOUN PROBLEMS

OBJECTIVES

- To read sentences aloud and to stress the pronouns
- To identify the correct forms of *who* and *whom* and pronouns with appositives
- To write a story that contains subject and object forms of pronouns

7. Why don't you sit here beside *me*?
8. Donna went to the Cinco de Mayo parade with *them*.

EXERCISE 8 **Identifying the Correct Forms of Pronouns Used as Objects of Prepositions**

For each of the following sentences, choose the correct form of the pronoun in parentheses.

EXAMPLE 1. Someone should have sent an invitation to (*they, them*).
1. *them*

1. In the first round, Michael Chang played against (*he, him*).
2. Did you sit with Martha or (*her, she*) at the game?
3. Peggy sent homemade birthday cards to you and (*them, they*).
4. There is a bee flying around (*he, him*) and you.
5. If you have a complaint, tell it to Mr. Ramis or (*she, her*).
6. Ms. Young divided the projects among (*us, we*).
7. This secret is strictly between you and (*me, I*).
8. Can you believe the weather balloon dropped in front of (*we, us*)?
9. Please don't ride the Alaskan ferry without Jim and (*I, me*).
10. One of the clowns threw confetti at us and (*they, them*).

USAGE

Teacher's ResourceBank™

RESOURCES

SPECIAL PRONOUN PROBLEMS

Special Pronoun Problems

Who and *Whom*

The pronoun *who* has two different forms. *Who* is the subject form. *Whom* is the object form.

When you are choosing between *who* or *whom* in a question, follow these steps:

STEP 1: Rephrase the question as a statement.
STEP 2: Identify how the pronoun is used in the statement—as subject, predicate nominative, direct object, indirect object, or object of a preposition.
STEP 3: Determine whether the subject form or the object form is correct according to the rules of standard English.
STEP 4: Select the correct form—*who* or *whom.*

EXAMPLE: (*Who, Whom*) rang the bell?
STEP 1: The statement is (*Who, Whom*) *rang the bell.*
STEP 2: The pronoun is the subject, the verb is *rang,* and the direct object is *bell.*
STEP 3: As the subject, the pronoun should be in the subject form.
STEP 4: The subject form is *who.*
ANSWER: **Who** rang the bell?

EXAMPLE: (*Who, Whom*) do you see?
STEP 1: The statement is *You do see (who, whom).*
STEP 2: The subject is *you,* and the verb is *do see.* The pronoun is the direct object of the verb.
STEP 3: A direct object should be in the object form.
STEP 4: The object form is *whom.*
ANSWER: **Whom** *do you see*?

EXAMPLE: To (*who, whom*) did you give the gift?
STEP 1: The statement is *You did give the gift to (who, whom).*
STEP 2: The subject is *you,* the verb is *did give,* and the pronoun is the object of the preposition *to.*
STEP 3: The object of a preposition should be in the object form.
STEP 4: The object form is *whom.*
ANSWER: To **whom** did you give the gift?

NOTE: The use of *whom* is becoming less common in spoken English. When you are speaking, you may correctly begin any question with *who.* In written English, however, you should distinguish between

USAGE

QUICK REMINDER

Write the following list on the chalkboard. Ask volunteers to compose original sentences using each word or phrase. Possible sentences are provided.

1. who [Who came for the tickets?]
2. whom [For whom was the call intended?]
3. we cheerleaders [We cheerleaders ate all the apple dumplings.]
4. us drummers [The practice was especially helpful for us drummers.]

USAGE

LEP/ESL

General Strategies. When you are guiding your LEP/ESL students, it is important to always look for a simpler way of expressing rules and to avoid linguistic labeling whenever possible. Differentiating the use of *who* and *whom* is an arduous task, even for a proficient English speaker. Students need as much direct information as they can get.

To help students learn to use *who* and *whom* properly, tell them these simple rules:

1. *Whom* is always used after a preposition.
2. With any form of the verb *be,* always use the subject, not the object, pronoun.

USAGE

who and *whom. Who* is used as a subject or a predicate nominative, and *whom* is used as an object.

ORAL PRACTICE 6 **Using Pronouns Correctly in Sentences**

Read the following sentences aloud, stressing the italicized pronouns.

1. *Who* owns the boat?
2. To *whom* did you throw the ball?
3. *Whom* did Miguel marry?
4. *Who* was the stranger?
5. For *whom* did you knit that sweater?
6. *Who* is the author of *The Jackie Robinson Story*?
7. *Whom* did Josh choose as his subject?
8. By *whom* was this work painted?

USAGE

Pronouns with Appositives

Sometimes a pronoun is followed directly by a noun that identifies the pronoun. Such a noun is called an ***appositive.*** To help you choose which pronoun to use before an appositive, omit the appositive and try each form of the pronoun separately.

EXAMPLE: (*We, Us*) boys swam in the lake. [*Boys* is the appositive identifying the pronoun.]
We swam in the lake.
Us swam in the lake.
ANSWER: **We** boys swam in the lake.

EXAMPLE: The director gave an award to (*we, us*) actors. [*Actors* is the appositive identifying the pronoun.]
The director gave an award to *we.*
The director gave an award to *us.*
ANSWER: The director gave an award to **us** actors.

REFERENCE NOTE: For more information about appositives, see pages 599–600.

REVIEW C

OBJECTIVE

- To revise incorrect pronoun forms in sentences

EXERCISE 9 **Identifying the Correct Forms of Pronouns in Sentences**

For each of the following sentences, choose the correct form of the pronoun in parentheses.

EXAMPLE 1. (*Who, Whom*) can do the most jumping jacks?
1. *Who*

1. (*We*, *Us*) baseball players always warm up before practice.
2. (*Who*, *Whom*) knows how to stretch properly?
3. Coach Anderson has special exercises for (*us*, *we*) pitchers.
4. To (*who*, *whom*) did the coach assign thirty sit-ups?
5. (*Who*, *Whom*) do you favor for tomorrow's game?

REVIEW C **Revising Incorrect Pronoun Forms in Sentences**

Identify each incorrect pronoun in the following sentences. Then write the correct pronoun. If a sentence is correct, write *C*.

EXAMPLE 1. At first Karen and me thought that Lucy was imagining things.
1. *me, I*

1. Lucy told Karen and ~~I~~ that space creatures had landed. 1. me
2. She was certain it was ~~them~~ at the park. 2. they
3. ~~Whom~~ would believe such a ridiculous story? 3. Who
4. ~~Us~~ girls laughed and laughed. 4. We
5. Lucy looked at ~~we~~ two with tears in her eyes. 5. us
6. Karen and I agreed to go to the park to look around. 6. C
7. Lucy walked between Karen and me, showing the way. 7. C
8. In the park she and ~~us~~ hid behind some tall bushes. 8. we
9. Suddenly a strong wind almost blew ~~we~~ three down. 9. us

USAGE

PICTURE THIS

Remind students that the exaggerations of tall tales are usually of three types: exaggeration of physical attributes, exaggeration of capabilities, and exaggeration of exploits.

USAGE

USAGE

10. A green light shined on Karen and ~~I~~, and a red one shined on Lucy. **10.** me
11. ~~Whom~~ could it be? **11.** Who
12. One of the creatures spoke to us girls. **12.** C
13. Very slowly, Karen, Lucy, and ~~me~~ stepped out from behind the bushes. **13.** I
14. "You almost scared ~~they~~ and me silly!" shouted a creature, pointing at the others. **14.** them
15. Neither Karen nor ~~her~~ could speak, and I could make only a squeaking noise. **15.** she
16. Then the man inside the costume explained to ~~we~~ three girls that a movie company was filming in the park. **16.** us
17. They and we could have been in an accident. **17.** C
18. The fireworks hidden in the bushes might have hurt one of ~~we~~ girls. **18.** us
19. Lucy told the director and ~~he~~ about being afraid of the space creatures in the park. **19.** him
20. If you see the movie, the short purple creatures under the spaceship are ~~us~~ three girls. **20.** we

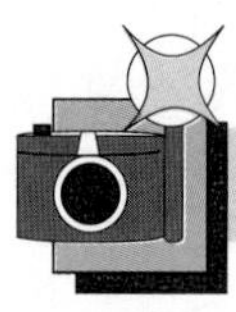

PICTURE THIS

You and some friends are on your way to a weekend campsite. From the car you see the surprising sign shown on the next page. The sign gives you an idea for a tall tale—a humorous, highly unlikely story that stretches the facts. Using the sign to spark your imagination, write a tall tale to tell your friends around the campfire. In your tale, use at least five subject forms and five object forms of pronouns.

Subject: surprising road sign
Audience: friends gathered around a campfire
Purpose: to entertain

SEGMENT 6 *(pp. 523–524)*

REVIEW: POSTTEST

OBJECTIVE

- To revise incorrect pronoun forms in sentences

USAGE

Review: Posttest

Revising Incorrect Pronoun Forms in Sentences

Most of the following sentences contain an incorrect pronoun form. If a pronoun is used incorrectly, write the incorrect form of the pronoun and give the correct form. If a sentence is correct, write *C*.

EXAMPLE **1.** The police officer complimented us and they on knowing the rules of bicycle safety.
1. *they—them*

1. The members of our bicycle club are Everett, Coral, Jackie, and ~~me~~. **1.** I
2. ~~Us~~ four call our club the Ramblers, named after a bicycle that was popular in the early 1900s. **2.** We

USAGE

TIMESAVER

Ask students to circle subject pronouns and to label them as either subjects (s.) or predicate nominatives (p.n.). Then they should underline object pronouns and label them as direct objects (d.o.), indirect objects (i.o.), or objects of prepositions (o.p.).

3. Mrs. Wheeler gave an old three-speed bike to ~~we~~ four. **3.** us
4. ~~Whom~~ explained the special safety course? **4.** Who
5. Our cousins gave Coral and ~~I~~ their old ten-speed bikes. **5.** me
6. Each of ~~we~~ Ramblers rides after school. **6.** us
7. Sometimes we ride with the members of the Derailers, a racing club. **7.** C
8. On Saturday mornings, we and ~~them~~ meet at the school. **8.** they
9. Who told us about the bike trail along the river? **9.** C
10. Everett warned ~~we~~ three to be careful because sometimes the Derailers are reckless. **10.** us
11. He saw other riders and ~~they~~ at an intersection. **11.** them
12. A car almost ran over two of them! **12.** C
13. When the Ramblers ride with the Derailers, it is ~~us~~ who obey all the safety rules. **13.** we
14. Everett, Coral, Jackie, and I entered a contest. **14.** C
15. Other clubs and ~~us~~ competed for a tandem bike. **15.** we
16. Everett and ~~her~~ taught Jackie how to ride it and shift gears. **16.** she
17. One by one, ~~us~~ riders went through the course. **17.** we
18. Of all of ~~we~~ contestants, the most careless were the members of the Derailers. **18.** us
19. Jackie and ~~me~~ were nervous as the judges were deciding. **19.** I
20. Finally, the judges announced that the winners of the safety contest were ~~us~~ Ramblers. **20.** we

USAGE

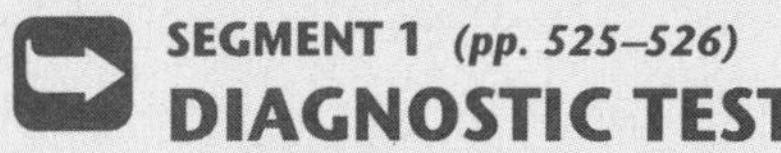

SEGMENT 1 *(pp. 525–526)*

DIAGNOSTIC TEST

OBJECTIVES

- To identify the correct forms of modifiers
- To identify and revise sentences containing double negatives

20 USING MODIFIERS CORRECTLY

USAGE

Comparison of Adjectives and Adverbs

Diagnostic Test

A. Identifying the Correct Forms of Modifiers

In each of the following sentences, choose the correct form of the modifier in parentheses.

EXAMPLE **1.** We felt (*sleepy, sleepily*) after lunch.
1. *sleepy*

1. Cool water tastes (*good, well*) on a hot day.
2. The wind howled (*fierce, fiercely*) last night.
3. Who is (*taller, tallest*), Marcus or Jim?
4. *Forever Friends* is the (*bestest, best*) book I've read this year.
5. Sergio has always played (*good, well*) during an important match.
6. The roses in the vase smelled (*sweet, sweetly*).
7. They could view the eclipse (*more clear, more clearly*) than we could.
8. Which of the two winter coats is the (*better, best*) value?

Teacher's ResourceBank™

RESOURCES

FOR THE WHOLE CHAPTER

CHAPTER OVERVIEW

The chapter begins with a discussion of the degrees of comparison of adjectives and adverbs, both regular and irregular. This is followed by sections on the use of *well* and *good,* on the use of adjectives after linking verbs, and on avoiding double comparisons. The chapter concludes with material on avoiding double negatives.

USING THE DIAGNOSTIC TEST

You can use the **Diagnostic Test** to pinpoint specific problems your students have with the correct use of adjectives and adverbs. There are three types of items in the first part of the test: adjectives modifying nouns, adjectives following linking verbs, and adverbs modifying verbs. If your students show a particular weakness in one of these uses of modifiers, you can skip to the relevant part of the chapter.

The second part of the **Diagnostic Test** deals with double negatives. You can use either section of the chapter as part of a lesson on revision for one of the composition chapters.

USAGE

9. Of all the days in the week, Friday goes by (*more slowly*, *most slowly*).
10. Ernesto felt (*good*, *well*) about volunteering to help collect money for the homeless.
11. Is this the (*darker*, *darkest*) copy of the three?
12. The (*faster*, *fastest*) runner is the captain of the track team.
13. Mr. Chen told them to be (*better*, *more better*) prepared tomorrow.
14. Joni's way of solving the math puzzle was much (*easier*, *more easier*) than Kadeem's.
15. Some people think that *Voyager* is the (*most amazing*, *amazingest*) space probe launched by the United States.

B. Correcting Double Negatives

Most of the following sentences contain errors in the use of negative words. If the sentence is incorrect, write it correctly. If the sentence is correct, write ***C.*** [Note: In some cases a double negative can be corrected in more than one way.]

EXAMPLE **1.** Mr. Gómez didn't give us no homework today.
1. *Mr. Gómez didn't give us any homework today.*
or
Mr. Gómez gave us no homework today.

16. None of us knows ~~nothing~~ about Halley's comet.
17. Willie can hardly wait to see Bobby McFerrin in concert. **16.** anything **17.** C
18. Kristin ~~hasn't never~~ heard of the Navajo art of sand painting. **18.** hasn't ever [*or* has never]
19. Last night we ~~could not see no~~ stars through our binoculars. **19.** could not see any [*or* could see no]
20. Whenever I want fresh strawberries, there are ~~never none~~ in the house. **20.** never any [*or* none]

SEGMENT 2 *(pp. 527–531)*

COMPARISON OF ADJECTIVES AND ADVERBS Rule 20a

OBJECTIVES

- To write the comparative and superlative forms of modifiers
- To use comparative and superlative forms of modifiers correctly in sentences

Comparison of Adjectives and Adverbs

A ***modifier*** is a word or a phrase that describes or limits the meaning of another word. The two kinds of modifiers—adjectives and adverbs—may be used to make comparisons. In making comparisons, adjectives and adverbs take special forms. The form that is used depends on how many things are being compared.

20a. The three degrees of comparison of modifiers are the *positive*, the *comparative*, and the *superlative*.

(1) The ***positive degree*** is used when only one thing is being described.

EXAMPLES *Felita* is a **good** book.
Shawn runs **quickly.**

(2) The ***comparative degree*** is used when two things are being compared.

EXAMPLES In my opinion, *Nilda* is a **better** book than *Felita.*
Juanita runs **more quickly** than Shawn.

(3) The ***superlative degree*** is used when three or more things are being compared.

EXAMPLES *Nilda* is one of the **best** books I've read.
Which member of the track team can run **most quickly?**

NOTE: In conversation you may hear such expressions as *Put your best foot forward.* This use of the superlative is acceptable in spoken English. In your writing, however, you should follow rule 3.

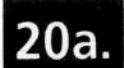

REFERENCE NOTE: For a discussion of standard usage, see pages 329–330.

USAGE

Teacher's ResourceBank™

RESOURCES

COMPARISON OF ADJECTIVES AND ADVERBS

QUICK REMINDER

Ask a student to find the word *modify* in a dictionary and to write the definition on the chalkboard [modify: to change slightly]. Ask students how a word can modify another word. [A modifier changes the meaning slightly by giving more information about the word.]

Ask students to write modifiers for the following words:

1. man [tall, angry, bald, kind]
2. chicken [small, fried, live]
3. tree [large, dead, colorful]

Then ask students to fill in the blanks in the following sentences with a form of the given word.

1. tall—I met a ___ man at school. [tall]
2. small—My chicken is ___ than yours. [smaller]
3. large—This is the ___ tree in the forest. [largest]

USAGE

* To use correctly irregular forms of comparative and superlative modifiers in sentences

LEP/ESL

Spanish. In Spanish, the comparative is formed by using the word *más* (more) before the adjective. Students might therefore adhere to forms such as *more loud* or *more happy* instead of using forms like *louder* or *happier.* Another possible error may result from the fact that Spanish uses the word *que* (translated as *than* or *that*) with comparisons. Students might substitute *that* for *than,* resulting in sentences such as "My brother is more athletic *that* my sister." Give these students as much practice as possible with the comparative form.

LEARNING STYLES

Visual Learners. You can help students understand the difference between the comparative and superlative degrees by letting them use concrete objects to establish comparisons. Bring to class a grape, a lemon, and a large orange. Working with students in a small group, ask them to tell which is the biggest [orange]. Take away the orange and then ask which is bigger [lemon]. Explain that *biggest* is used when there are three or more objects and that *bigger* is used when there are only two.

USAGE

Regular Comparison

Most one-syllable modifiers form the comparative degree by adding *–er* and the superlative degree by adding *–est.*

POSITIVE	COMPARATIVE	SUPERLATIVE
dark	dark**er**	dark**est**
sad	sad**der**	sad**dest**
cute	cut**er**	cut**est**
bright	bright**er**	bright**est**

Some two-syllable modifiers form the comparative degree by adding *–er* and the superlative degree by adding *–est.* Other two-syllable modifiers form the comparative degree by using *more* and the superlative degree by using *most.*

POSITIVE	COMPARATIVE	SUPERLATIVE
fancy	fanc**ier**	fanc**iest**
lonely	lonel**ier**	lonel**iest**
cheerful	**more** cheerful	**most** cheerful
quickly	**more** quickly	**most** quickly

Whenever you are unsure about which way a two-syllable modifier forms its degrees of comparison, look in a dictionary.

REFERENCE NOTE: For guidelines on how to spell words when adding *–er* or *–est,* see pages 641–642.

Modifiers that have three or more syllables form their comparative and superlative degrees by using *more* and *most.*

USAGE

POSITIVE	COMPARATIVE	SUPERLATIVE
difficult	**more** difficult	**most** difficult
interesting	**more** interesting	**most** interesting
clumsily	**more** clumsily	**most** clumsily
skillfully	**more** skillfully	**most** skillfully

EXERCISE 1 **Writing Comparative and Superlative Forms**

Give the comparative form and the superlative form for each of the following modifiers. Use a dictionary if necessary.

EXAMPLE **1.** calm
1. *calmer, calmest*

1. nervous **2.** great **3.** hot **4.** funny **5.** noisy **6.** easily **7.** poor **8.** young **9.** swiftly **10.** intelligent

EXERCISE 2 **Using the Comparative and Superlative Forms Correctly in Sentences**

For each blank in the following sentences, give the correct form of the modifier in italics. Use a dictionary if necessary.

EXAMPLE **1.** *large* As the illustration on the next page shows, the moon appears ____ during the full-moon phase.
1. *largest*

1. *near* The moon is the earth's ____ neighbor in space. **1.** nearest
2. *close* At its ____ point to the earth, the moon is 221,456 miles away. **2.** closest
3. *bright* Seen from the earth, the full moon is ____ than the new moon. **3.** brighter

USAGE

LESS-ADVANCED STUDENTS

Your less-advanced students may benefit from learning a mnemonic device for the comparative and superlative degrees. Point out to them that the comparative degree is often formed by adding two letters (*–er*) to a word and is used when two objects are compared. The superlative degree adds three letters (*–est*) and is used when three or more objects are compared.

COOPERATIVE LEARNING

You may want to let your students work in pairs for **Exercise 1.** Let one member of the pair be responsible for the comparative form and the other member for the superlative form. To ensure that both members of the pairs do equal work, you can have them initial their individual contributions.

ANSWERS

Exercise 1

1. more nervous, most nervous
2. greater, greatest
3. hotter, hottest
4. funnier, funniest
5. noisier, noisiest
6. more easily, most easily
7. poorer, poorest
8. younger, youngest
9. more swiftly, most swiftly
10. more intelligent, most intelligent

USAGE

USAGE

COMMON ERROR

Problem. Students may confuse *less* and *fewer.* Some nouns, known as count nouns, must be modified by *fewer* instead of *less.* Nouns of this type refer to objects that can be considered one at a time, instead of in a mass that can't be separated into individual parts. For example, words like *dollars, houses,* and *examples* are count nouns and must be used with *fewer.*

Solution. Explain that if a plural word can be used in the singular with *a* or *an* before it, it is a count noun and must be modified by *fewer.* If a word has to be used in the singular with *some* before it, it must be modified by *less.*

A DIFFERENT APPROACH

When adjectives end in *–e,* drop the *e* before adding the comparative or superlative ending. You can help your students arrive at this rule inductively by asking them to spell the comparative and superlative forms for the following words on the chalkboard:

1. close [closer, closest]
2. rare [rarer, rarest]
3. wide [wider, widest]
4. large [larger, largest]
5. gentle [gentler, gentlest]

USAGE

4. *small* — The moon appears ___ during the crescent phase.
4. smallest

5. *difficult* — It is ___ to see the new moon than the crescent moon.
5. more difficult

6. *common* — The word *crescent* is ___ than the word *gibbous,* which means "partly rounded."
6. more common

7. *frequently* — We notice the moon ___ when it is full than when it is new.
7. more frequently

8. *big* — Do you know why the moon appears ___ on some nights than on others?
8. bigger

9. *fast* — The changes in the moon's appearance take place because the moon travels ___ around the earth than the earth travels around the sun.
9. faster

10. *slowly* — The moons of some other planets move ___ than our moon.
10. more slowly

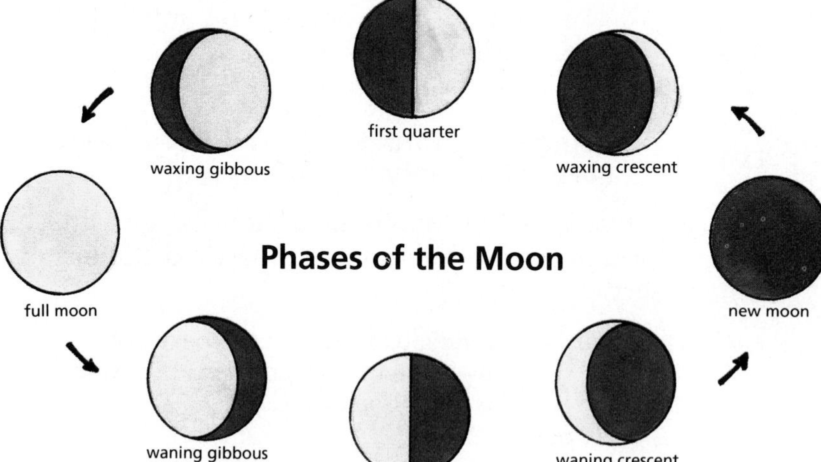

Irregular Comparison

Some modifiers do not form their comparative and superlative degrees by using the regular methods.

POSITIVE	COMPARATIVE	SUPERLATIVE
good	better	best
well	better	best
bad	worse	worst
many	more	most
much	more	most

NOTE: You do not need to add anything to an irregular comparison. For example, *worse,* all by itself, is the comparative form of *bad. Worser* and *more worse* are nonstandard forms.

EXERCISE 3 **Using Irregular Comparative and Superlative Forms**

For each blank in the following sentences, give the correct form of the italicized modifier.

EXAMPLE **1.** *many* Let's see which team can wash the ___ cars.

1. *most*

1. *bad* This is the ___ cold I've ever had. **1.** worst
2. *much* We have ___ homework this year than we had last year. **2.** more
3. *well* Derrick feels ___ today than he did last night. **3.** better
4. *good* This peach has a ___ flavor than that one. **4.** better
5. *well* Of all the instruments he can play, Shen Li plays the banjo ___. **5.** best
6. *much* Catherine ate ___ enchilada casserole on Monday than she had on Sunday. **6.** more
7. *many* Doreen has collected the ___ donations for the animal shelter. **7.** most
8. *bad* Our team played the ___ game in history. **8.** worst
9. *good* The judges will now award the prize for the ___ essay. **9.** best
10. *many* I have ___ baseball cards than John does. **10.** more

USAGE

INTEGRATING THE LANGUAGE ARTS

Dictionary Link. The standard practice of most dictionaries is to give the comparative and superlative degrees for adjectives and adverbs only when there is some irregularity in the spelling of these forms. If comparative and superlative forms aren't given after the entry word, students should assume the word follows the standard pattern.

TIMESAVER

One way to save time grading **Exercise 3** is to have students do the exercise orally. You can add a little variety to this exercise by asking the student who answers the first item to call on someone for the second and for that person to call on someone else for the third, and so on.

USAGE

SEGMENT 3 *(pp. 532–536)*

SPECIAL PROBLEMS IN USING MODIFIERS Rules 20b–20d

OBJECTIVES

- To write sentences with the correct forms of *good* and *well*
- To write the correct modifiers after linking verbs and action verbs

Teacher's ResourceBank™

RESOURCES

SPECIAL PROBLEMS IN USING MODIFIERS

QUICK REMINDER

Write the following expressions on the chalkboard and ask students to select the correct modifier for each:

1. slow, slowly
a ___ stream [slow]
a stream runs ___ [slowly]

2. quick, quickly
to eat ___ [quickly]
a ___ lunch [quick]

3. mad, madly
a ___ dash [mad]
to dash ___ [madly]

Point out to students that an adverb modifies a verb, an adjective, or another adverb, while adjectives modify nouns and pronouns.

AT-RISK STUDENTS

Some at-risk students might resist using standard forms in oral language because of peer pressure to "sound tough." Point out to these students that speech and writing are different forms of communication. Students can express themselves in speech one way and in writing a different way.

USAGE

Special Problems in Using Modifiers

20b. The modifiers *good* and *well* have different uses.

(1) Use *good* to modify a noun or a pronoun.

EXAMPLES The farmers had a **good** crop this year. [The adjective *good* modifies the noun *crop.*]
The book was **better** than the movie. [The adjective *better* modifies the noun *book.*]
Of all the players, she is the **best** one. [The adjective *best* modifies the pronoun *one.*]

Good should not be used to modify a verb.

NONSTANDARD N. Scott Momaday writes good.
STANDARD N. Scott Momaday writes **well.**

(2) Use *well* to modify a verb.

EXAMPLES The day started **well.** [The adverb *well* modifies the verb *started.*]
The team played **better** in the second half. [The adverb *better* modifies the verb *played.*]
Bill Russell played **best** for the Boston Celtics. [The adverb *best* modifies the verb *played.*]

Well can also mean "in good health." When *well* has this meaning, it acts as an adjective.

EXAMPLE Does Sherry feel **well** today? [The adjective *well* modifies the noun *Sherry.*]

EXERCISE 4 **Writing Sentences with the Correct Forms of *Good* and *Well***

You are a famous chef and the host of the popular TV cooking show *Food, Food, Food.* You are preparing for next Friday's program. For this episode, you have decided to show viewers how to get more value for their dollar by shopping wisely. As you look at the

• To write a letter that contains comparative and superlative forms of modifiers

grocery ad below, write five sentences you might use on your show. In each sentence, use one of the words in the following list.

EXAMPLE **1. good**
1. *Thrifty shoppers look for good buys like this bargain on strawberries.*

1. good **2.** best **3.** well **4.** better **5.** well

BARGAIN
Turkey
89¢ lb.
SPECIAL
Strawberries
79¢ pint
SALE
Orange Juice
95¢ gal.
Chicken .... $1.15 lb.
Ocean Perch $1.75 lb.
Milk .... $1.15 1/2 gal.
Fresh Cantaloupe .. 95¢ for 3
Fresh Broccoli .... 79¢ a bunch
Fresh Green beans . 75¢ lb.
The Corner Market
Sale good through Saturday

20c. Use adjectives, not adverbs, after linking verbs.

Linking verbs, such as *look, feel,* and *become,* are often followed by predicate adjectives. These adjectives describe, or modify, the subject.

EXAMPLES Jeanette looked **alert** (not *alertly*) during the game. [The predicate adjective *alert* modifies the subject *Jeanette.*]
Mayor Rodríguez should feel **confident** (not *confidently*) about this election. [The predicate adjective *confident* modifies the subject *Mayor Rodríguez.*]

NOTE: Some linking verbs can also be used as action verbs. As action verbs, they may be modified by adverbs.

EXAMPLE Jeanette looked **alertly** around the gym. [*Alertly* modifies the action verb *looked.*]

USAGE

COOPERATIVE LEARNING

You may want to let students work in groups of two or three on **Exercise 4.** You may also want to consider requiring them to write two or three sentences for each of the words in the exercise. Ask each student in each group to explain why the group chose to use the word the way it did.

ANSWERS

Exercise 4

Sentences will vary. The criteria for evaluating the sentences are the students' adherence to the prescribed topic and their accuracy in using the prescribed words.

A DIFFERENT APPROACH

Linking verbs that are forms of the verb *be* are relatively easy to identify, but some others may not be. You can point out to your students that a verb is a linking verb if the word *seem* can be substituted for it without significantly changing the meaning of the sentence. For example, one could change "This milk tastes sour" to "This milk seems sour." *Tastes* is therefore a linking verb.

USAGE

TIMESAVER

You can save time grading papers for **Exercise 5** by having students do the exercise orally in class. This will also help you identify students who may be having difficulty with the correct use of modifiers after verbs, and it will give you an opportunity for reteaching, if necessary.

USAGE

REFERENCE NOTE: For a complete list of linking verbs, see page 395.

EXERCISE 5 **Writing the Correct Modifiers After Linking Verbs and Action Verbs**

For each of the following sentences, give the correct modifier of the two in parentheses.

EXAMPLE **1.** Murray's matzo ball soup tasted (*delicious, deliciously*).
1. *delicious*

1. The band became (*nervous, nervously*) before the show.
2. You will likely get a higher score if you can remain (*calm, calmly*) while taking the test.
3. We (*eager, eagerly*) tasted the potato pancakes.
4. Peg looked at her broken skate (*anxious, anxiously*).
5. The mariachi band appeared (*sudden, suddenly*) at our table.
6. Sylvia certainly looked (*pretty, prettily*) in her new outfit.
7. The plums tasted (*sour, sourly*).
8. Mr. Duncan was looking (*close, closely*) at my essay.
9. Erica was (*happy, happily*) to help us.
10. One by one, they felt the contents of the big mystery bag (*cautious, cautiously*).

20d. Avoid double comparisons.

A ***double comparison*** is the use of both *–er* and *more* or *–est* and *most* to form a single comparison. When you make a comparison, use only one of these forms, not both.

NONSTANDARD That is Raul Julia's most scariest role.
STANDARD That is Raul Julia's **scariest** role.

NONSTANDARD The kitten is more livelier than the puppy.
STANDARD The kitten is **livelier** than the puppy.

USAGE

REVIEWS A and B

OBJECTIVES

- To write the correct comparative and superlative forms of modifiers in sentences
- To proofread a paragraph to identify and correct errors in the use of modifiers

20d

PICTURE THIS

The people in your neighborhood are sick and tired of looking at this vacant lot. The lot has been a hazard and an eyesore for years. Now, you and your neighbors would like the city to clean up the lot to make it safer and more attractive. Write a letter to the city planning board, explaining why it should sponsor such a project. In your letter, use a total of at least five comparative and superlative forms of modifiers. Underline each comparative or superlative modifier that you use.

Subject: cleaning up a vacant lot
Audience: members of the city planning board
Purpose: to persuade

USAGE

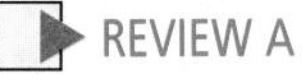

REVIEW A **Writing Comparative and Superlative Forms in Sentences**

For each blank in the following sentences, give the correct form of comparison for the italicized word.

EXAMPLE **1.** *noisy* This is the ____ class in school.
1. *noisiest*

PICTURE THIS

Have students look at the picture that accompanies the feature in the text and list reasons the lot should be cleaned up. You can conduct this brainstorming session with the whole class by writing ideas on the chalkboard as they are presented by students. After several ideas are listed, ask students to select the ones they like best and to list them in order, with the most important reason first.

Because this is a business letter, you may want to review the proper form for a business letter.

LEP/ESL

General Strategies. For the **Picture This** activity, give students the option of selecting situations that actually exist in their city or community. You may want small groups to write letters rather than having students tackle the task independently.

USAGE

1. *bad* Yesterday was the ___ day of my entire life.
1. worst
2. *good* Tomorrow should be ___ than today was.
2. better
3. *old* The ___ Native American tepee in the world can be seen at the Smithsonian Institution.
3. oldest
4. sooner
4. *soon* Your party ended ___ than I would have liked.
5. funniest
5. *funny* That is the ___ joke I've ever heard.
6. *rapidly* Which can run ___, the cheetah or the lion?
6. more rapidly
7. *beautifully* This piñata is ___ decorated than the other one.
7. more beautifully
8. *well* The test had three sections, and I did ___ on the essay questions.
8. best
9. *joyfully* Of all the songbirds in our yard, the mockingbirds sing ___.
9. most joyfully
10. *strange* This is the ___ book I have ever read!
10. strangest

REVIEW B **Proofreading for Correct Forms of Modifiers**

Most of the sentences in the following paragraph have at least one error in English usage. If a sentence contains an error, identify it and then write the correct usage. If a sentence is correct, write *C*.

EXAMPLE [1] You may not recognize the man in the picture on the next page, but you probably know his more famous characters.
1. *more famous—most famous*

1. popular [1] This man, Alexandre Dumas, wrote two of the most ^~~popularest~~ books in history—*The Three*
2. C *Musketeers* and *The Count of Monte Cristo.* [2] Born in France, Dumas was poor but had a good education.
3. quickly [3] As a young playwright, he rose^~~quick~~ to fame. [4] In
4. cheerful person, Dumas always seemed ^~~cheerfully~~. [5] Like
5. C their author, his historical novels are colorful and
6. rapidly full of adventure. [6] Their fame grew^~~rapid~~, and the

USAGE

USAGE

SEGMENT 4 (pp. 537–541)

DOUBLE NEGATIVES Rule 20e

OBJECTIVE

- To revise sentences by eliminating double negatives

public demanded more of them. [7] In response to this demand, Dumas hired many assistants, who probably wrote ~~most~~ of his later books than he did. 7. more
[8] Dumas's son, Alexandre, was also a writer and became ~~famously~~ with the publication of *Camille*. [9] At that time, the younger Dumas was often thought of as a ~~more~~ better writer than his father. [10] Today, however, the friendship of the three musketeers remains ~~aliver~~ than ever in film, print, and even comic books. 8. famous 10. more alive

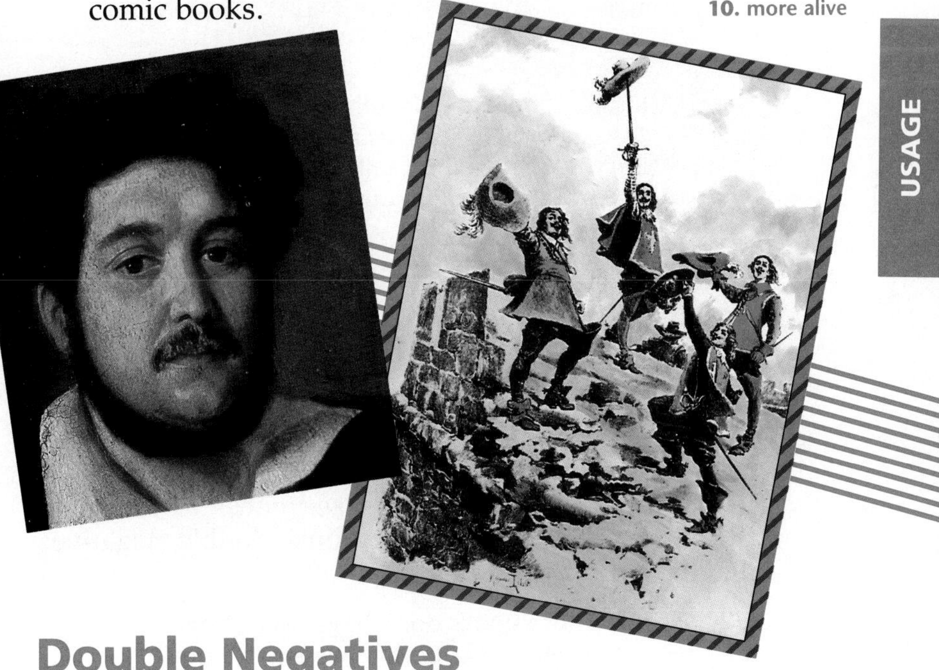

USAGE

Double Negatives

Negative words are a common part of everyday speaking and writing. These words include *no, not, never*, and *hardly*. Notice how negative words change the meaning of the following sentences.

POSITIVE We can count in Spanish.
NEGATIVE We can**not** count in Spanish.

POSITIVE They ride their bikes on the highway.
NEGATIVE They **never** ride their bikes on the highway.

USAGE

Teacher's ResourceBank™
RESOURCES

DOUBLE NEGATIVES
- Double Negatives 209

QUICK REMINDER

Write the following sentences on the chalkboard and ask students to make as many negative sentences as they can:

1. I caught the fish. [I caught no fish. I didn't catch any fish.]
2. She likes to paint. [She doesn't like to paint. She never likes painting.]
3. José bought a new car. [José bought no new car. José didn't buy a new car.]

Point out that there are usually two or more ways to make a sentence negative, but that each of the negative sentences contains only one negative word.

LEP/ESL

Some students who use double negatives in speech may be curious about why they should avoid them. You can point out that double negatives in informal, everyday speech can be effective in adding emphasis, but speakers and writers of English have agreed over the years that they're unnecessary in formal speech and writing. Double negatives state the same thing twice. Also, they can sometimes be confusing to careful readers. For example, a speaker may say, "I don't want no pie," and mean that he or she would prefer not to have pie. In writing, though, a reader may be confused into thinking the speaker wants pie.

USAGE

USAGE

20e. Avoid the use of double negatives.

A ***double negative*** is the use of two negative words to express one negative idea.

Common Negative Words			
barely	never	none	nothing
hardly	no	no one	nowhere
neither	nobody	not (–n't)	scarcely

NONSTANDARD Sheila didn't tell no one her idea. [The two negative words are *–n't* and *no.*]
STANDARD Sheila **didn't** tell anyone her idea.
STANDARD Sheila told **no one** her idea.

NONSTANDARD Rodney hardly said nothing. [The two negative words are *hardly* and *nothing.*]
STANDARD Rodney **hardly** said anything.
STANDARD Rodney said almost **nothing.**

EXERCISE 6 **Revising Sentences by Eliminating Double Negatives**

Revise each of the following sentences to eliminate the double negative. [Note: Some double negatives may be corrected in more than one way.]

Revisions may vary.

EXAMPLE **1.** Those books don't have no pictures.
1. *Those books don't have any pictures.*
or
Those books have no pictures.

1. The Native Americans of the Plains did not waste ~~no~~ part of the buffalo. **1.** any
2. Ms. Wooster never tries ~~nothing~~ new to eat. **2.** anything
3. Movie and TV stars from Hollywood never visit ~~nowhere~~ near our town. **3.** anywhere
4. Until last summer, I didn't know ~~nothing~~ about Braille music notation. **4.** anything

WRITING APPLICATION

OBJECTIVE

- To use the stages of the writing process to write a friendly letter with negative words used correctly

5. By Thanksgiving, the store didn't have ~~none~~ of the silver jewelry left. **5.** any **6.** can
6. I'm so excited I ~~can't~~ hardly sit still. **7.** anything
7. No one brought ~~nothing~~ to eat on the hike.
8. Strangely enough, Freida hasn't ~~never~~ tasted our delicious Cuban bread. **8.** ever
9. There isn't ~~no~~ more pudding in the bowl. **9.** any
10. Our dog never fights with ~~neither~~ one of our cats. **10.** either

WRITING APPLICATION

Using Negative Words in Writing

Negative words are powerful. Just one of them can change the whole meaning of a sentence. Two negative words can create confusion.

EXAMPLE I never see nobody in that store. [What does the writer mean? Is the store always empty, or is it busy? The sentence needs to be revised to eliminate the confusion.]

REVISED I never see anybody in that store.

or

I always see someone in that store.

WRITING ACTIVITY

Everyone has a bad day now and then. Yesterday, it was your turn. You were late for school because your alarm clock didn't go off. From then on, things just got worse. Write a letter to a friend giving a comical description of your unlucky day. Make sure that you use negative words correctly.

Prewriting Jot down some notes about a real or imaginary bad day in your life. List at least five things that

INTEGRATING THE LANGUAGE ARTS

Literature Link. Sometimes authors use double negatives on purpose in stories to give a special flavor to their writing. Ask your students to read the Uncle Remus tale "He Lion, Bruh Bear, and Bruh Rabbit," as retold by Virginia Hamilton (or any of the other Uncle Remus tales of Joel Chandler Harris). As the students read, ask them to make note of the double negatives the narrator and the characters use. What effects do the double negatives have? [They make the story seem more like a tale that a person is telling orally, and they reflect the speech of the people in the story.]

WRITING APPLICATION

Ask your students to write down their basic ideas of a bad day. You can let them share these ideas with a peer response group, or you can circulate among them to spot-check what they're working on.

You may need to review the form for a friendly letter with the class. You can point out that students should pick real people as the audience of their letters, and they should think about how much information they will have to give the people so they will get a full picture of what the bad day was like.

REVIEW C

OBJECTIVE

- To proofread sentences for correct use of modifiers

CRITICAL THINKING

Analysis

Most bad days happen because an event, often a mistake, causes another event, which in turn causes another event, and so on. Your students will have to analyze the causes of the bad things that happened to them on their bad days. You can try asking them to start at the end of the day and to think back to what caused the last bad thing to happen, what caused the bad thing before that, and so on.

EVALUATING AND REVISING

Students may tend to write quickly, without paying close attention to whether they're fully explaining events in their bad days. As they evaluate their drafts, ask them to focus on whether a particular sentence or group of sentences is clear. If there's doubt about clarity, let them share their drafts with other students for second opinions about clarity. If something isn't clear, encourage students to add details to make it clear.

USAGE

went wrong during the day. The events can be big or small. Tell how you felt when one thing after another went wrong.

Writing Before beginning your first draft, you may want to look at pages 707–708 for tips on writing a friendly letter. In your letter, explain the events of your day in the order they happened. Describe each event in detail. Also describe your reactions to the events. You may want to exaggerate some details for a humorous effect.

Evaluating and Revising Ask a friend to read your letter. Have you described the events clearly? Do your descriptions give a vivid, humorous picture of your day? If not, add or revise details. Be sure that your letter follows the correct form for a friendly letter.

Proofreading Proofread your letter carefully for errors in grammar, spelling, or punctuation. Read through each sentence one more time to check that negative words are used correctly.

REVIEW C **Proofreading Sentences for Correct Use of Modifiers**

Most of the following sentences contain errors in the use of modifiers. If a sentence is incorrect, write it correctly. If a sentence is correct, write *C*. [Note: Some double negatives may be corrected in more than one way.]

EXAMPLE **1.** Haven't you never made a paper airplane or a paper hat?

1. *Haven't you ever made a paper airplane or a paper hat?*

or

Have you never made a paper airplane or a paper hat?

USAGE

REVIEW C

Teaching Note. There are two ways of correcting the error in number 2, but the first sentence more closely keeps the meaning of the original sentence.

1. Making paper constructions requires some skill, but they are much ~~more~~ easier to make than Japanese origami figures.
2. Origami, the ancient Japanese art of paper folding, ~~wasn't hardly known~~ in the United States until the 1960s. **2.** was hardly known [*or* wasn't known]
3. Now, many Americans know how to fold the ~~most~~ cleverest traditional origami animals.
4. In true origami, artists ~~do not never~~ cut or paste the paper. **4.** do not ever [*or* never]
5. A beginner doesn't need ~~nothing~~ but a sheet of paper to create an origami figure. **5.** anything
6. With a bit of patience, anyone can ~~quick~~ make a folded-paper figure. **6.** quickly
7. Even kindergarteners can do a good job making the simple sailboat shown in this diagram. **7.** C
8. Other origami figures require ~~more~~ greater time and patience than this sailboat.
9. Today, there probably ~~isn't no one~~ better at origami than Akira Yoshizawa. **9.** isn't anyone [*or* is no one]
10. Even the most difficult figure is not too hard for him, and he has invented many beautiful new figures. **10.** C

USAGE

USAGE

SEGMENT 5 *(p. 542)*

REVIEW: POSTTEST

OBJECTIVE

- To revise sentences by correcting errors in the use of modifiers

USAGE

Review: Posttest

Revising Sentences by Correcting Errors in the Use of Modifiers

Most of the following sentences contain errors in the use of modifiers or negative words. If a sentence has an error, rewrite the sentence correctly. If a sentence is correct, write *C*.

Revisions of double negatives may vary.

EXAMPLE **1.** Your bruise looks more worse today.
1. *Your bruise looks worse today.*

USAGE

1. best — **1.** Of the students in class, Odelle writes ~~better~~.
2. faster — **2.** Can you type ~~fastest~~ on a word processor or on a typewriter?
3. C — **3.** Juan seemed glad that we had visited him.
4. anything — **4.** No one knew ~~nothing~~ about the tornado.
5. regularly — **5.** Throughout history, many people have written ~~regular~~ in their diaries.
6. C — **6.** The Englishman Samuel Pepys wrote about the small events of his daily life.
7. wonderful — **7.** The bread smelled ~~wonderfully~~ when it came out of the oven.
8. well — **8.** Wynton Marsalis plays the trumpet ~~good~~.
9. C — **9.** If you don't feel well today, you shouldn't go out.
10. C — **10.** Mai is one of the most persistent people I know.
11. sad — **11.** I felt ~~sadly~~ at the end of *Old Yeller*.
12. carefully — **12.** Pedro, please look ~~careful~~ as I wrap this tamale.
13. any — **13.** It doesn't make ~~no~~ difference to Brian.
14. better — **14.** I'm not sure which I like ~~best~~, CDs or tapes.
15. nice — **15.** Arthurine's piano playing sounds very ~~nicely~~.
16. suddenly — **16.** The storm appeared so ~~sudden~~ that it surprised us.
17. C — **17.** Tanya is the youngest of my brothers and sisters.
18. older — **18.** Lena and Ivan are twins, but Lena is the ~~oldest~~.
19. could — **19.** We ~~couldn't~~ hardly believe the news!
20. good — **20.** Miyoko looks ~~well~~ in her new kimono.

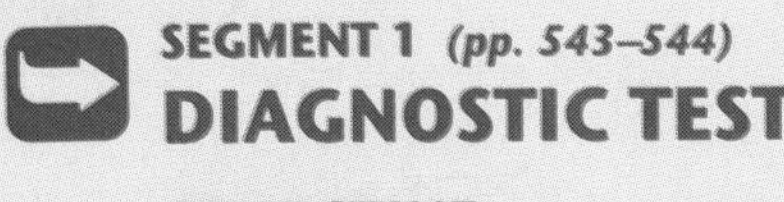

SEGMENT 1 *(pp. 543–544)*

DIAGNOSTIC TEST

OBJECTIVE

- To revise sentences by correcting errors in usage

21 A Glossary of Usage

Common Usage Problems

Diagnostic Test

Revising Sentences by Correcting Errors in Usage

In each of the following sets of sentences, choose the letter of the sentence that contains an error. Then write the sentence correctly, using standard English.

EXAMPLE **1. a.** Did you read this book?
b. It's almost time for dinner.
c. My sister learned me how to do that.
1. *c. My sister taught me how to do that.*

1. a. Everyone was at the meeting except Diego.
b. Is that you're dog? **1.** your
c. Andy waited outside the dentist's office.

2. a. The landfill smelled badly. **2.** bad
b. No one knew whose knapsack that was.
c. We could hardly wait for the rain to stop.

3. a. How come Ginger can't go? **3.** Why/Ginger
b. I feel rather tired today.
c. The team played well in the last game.

USAGE

Teacher's ResourceBank™

RESOURCES

FOR THE WHOLE CHAPTER

- Chapter Review Form A 220–221
- Chapter Review Form B 222–223
- Assessment Portfolio
  - Usage Pretests 455–462
  - Usage Mastery Tests 479–486

CHAPTER OVERVIEW

This chapter completes the review of usage begun in **Chapter 17.** It covers usage problems including those involving adjective-adverb selection, pronoun use, word choice, and verb selection. It is arranged alphabetically and includes several reviews for students to practice what they have learned.

Material in this chapter can be used with an entire class as a unit of study in conjunction with the composition chapters. It can also be used with individual students when problems surface in their compositions.

USING THE DIAGNOSTIC TEST

The results of the **Diagnostic Test** will tell you which students are able to recognize and correct nonstandard usage, but it will not necessarily help students to avoid errors in writing. You might wish to assign a short informative paragraph as a part of the test or use existing writing samples as aids in evaluation.

USAGE

4. a. Nina can run faster than he can.
   b. Anna would have finished, but she was interrupted.
   c. Be sure to bring ~~a~~ extra pencil with you. 4. an
5. a. The cow and its calf stood in the meadow.
   b. The team members were proud of ~~theirselves~~.
   c. What is the difference between these brands of basketball shoes? 5. themselves
6. a. We did as we were told.
   b. Everyone was ~~already~~ to go. 6. all ready
   c. I used to enjoy playing tennis. 7. take
7. a. Penny, ~~bring~~ this book when you go home.
   b. Ms. Mishima told us our plan was all right.
   c. Julie said that it's already time to go.
8. a. The team had fewer fouls in the last game.
   b. They looked everywhere for him.
   c. Do you know where he is ~~at~~?
9. a. Water-skiing is more fun than I thought.
   b. We hiked a long way before we pitched camp.
   c. Try ~~and~~ get to the meeting on time, please.
10. a. Their team has never beaten your team. 9. to
    b. A pop fly is ~~when~~ a ball ~~is~~ batted high in the air into the infield.
    c. I finished my homework; then I called Duane.

This chapter contains an alphabetical list, or glossary, of common problems in English usage. You will notice throughout the chapter that some examples are labeled *standard* or *nonstandard*. ***Standard English*** is the most widely accepted form of English. It is used in *formal* situations, such as in speeches and compositions for school. It is also used in *informal* situations, such as in conversations and everyday writing.

Nonstandard English is language that does not follow the rules and guidelines of standard English.

REFERENCE NOTE: For more discussion of standard English, see pages 329–330.

USAGE

SEGMENT 2 *(pp. 545–552)*
A, AN—HOW COME

OBJECTIVE

- To identify and correct common errors in usage

a, an Use *a* before words beginning with a consonant sound. Use *an* before words beginning with a vowel sound. The first letter in a word does not always determine the sound that the word begins with. The first letter in the words *herb* and *honor* is the consonant *h*. However, both words begin with a vowel sound.

EXAMPLES The airplane was parked in **a** hangar.
She lives on **a** one-way street.
They arrived **an** hour early.
My father works in **an** office.

accept, except *Accept* is a verb. It means "to receive." *Except* may be either a verb or a preposition. As a verb, it means "to leave out." As a preposition, *except* means "excluding," or "but."

EXAMPLES The winners of the spelling bee proudly **accepted** their awards.
Because Josh had a sprained ankle, he was **excepted** from gym class. [verb]
All the food was ready **except** the won-ton soup. [preposition]

ain't Avoid this word in speaking and writing. It is nonstandard English.

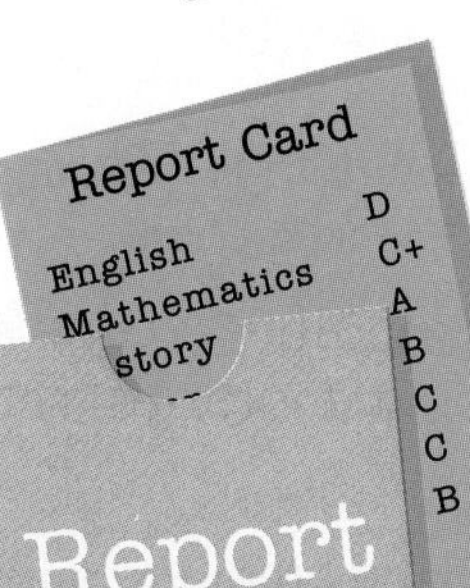

"Beats me why I ain't gettin' no better marks in English."

USAGE

Teacher's ResourceBank™

RESOURCES

A, AN—HOW COME
- Common Usage Problems A 217

QUICK REMINDER

To emphasize that following the rules of standard English usage will help to make communication more effective, write *among* and *between* on the chalkboard. Explain that although the two words are similar in meaning, they are not interchangeable. Draw two sets of four parallel horizontal lines on the chalkboard. Over one set, print "Write between the lines." Over the other, print "Write among the lines." Then follow your own directions. The sillier you make your example, the more likely your students are to remember the point.

LEP/ESL

General Strategies. In presenting *a* and *an,* avoid using the terms *vowel* and *consonant.* Instead, emphasize the initial sound of each noun, so that students understand more clearly which article is appropriate to use. You might want to have students hold up various objects and identify them by saying, "It's a/an . . . ," or you can hold up pictures cut out of a magazine and ask students to identify the objects shown. Write any new vocabulary on the chalkboard.

USAGE

COMMON ERROR

Problem. Students frequently write *all ready* when they mean to use *already*.

Solution. Make the point that *all ready* indicates "ready to do something that has not been done" and that *already* indicates "something that has been done in the past." To help students remember this, you might want to make the analogy of two trains. The *all ready* train is preparing for a destination while the *already* train has reached its destination, as can be seen by the accident it had when its brakes were applied too suddenly as it came to a stop. The quick stop jammed the two *l*'s together, so that one *l* is lying on top of the other. Quick line drawings on the chalkboard can illustrate this point.

USAGE

USAGE

all right *All right* can be used as an adjective that means "satisfactory" or "unhurt." As an adverb, *all right* means "well enough." *All right* should always be written as two words.

EXAMPLES This tie looks **all right** with that blue shirt. [adjective]
The baby squirrel had fallen out of its nest, but it was **all right.** [adjective]
Lorenzo and I did **all right** on the pop quiz. [adverb]

a lot *A lot* should always be written as two words.

EXAMPLE I can make **a lot** of my mom's recipes.

already, all ready *Already* means "previously." *All ready* means "completely prepared" or "in readiness."

EXAMPLES We looked for Jay, but he had **already** left.
The players were **all ready** for the big game.
I had studied for two hours on Sunday night and was **all ready** for the test on Monday.

among See **between, among.**

anywheres, everywheres, nowheres, somewheres Use these words without the final *–s.*

EXAMPLE They looked **everywhere** [not *everywheres*] for the missing puzzle piece.

at Do not use *at* after *where.*

NONSTANDARD Where is the Chinese kite exhibit at?
STANDARD Where is the Chinese kite exhibit?

bad, badly *Bad* is an adjective. It modifies nouns and pronouns. *Badly* is an adverb. It modifies verbs, adjectives, and adverbs.

EXAMPLES The milk smelled **bad.** [The predicate adjective *bad* modifies *milk.*]
Before I took lessons, I played the piano **badly.** [The adverb *badly* modifies the verb *played.*]

NOTE: The expression *feel badly* has become acceptable in informal English.

INFORMAL Beth felt badly about hurting José's feelings.
FORMAL Beth felt **bad** about hurting José's feelings.

between, among Use *between* when you are referring to two things at a time. The two things may be part of a group consisting of more than two.

EXAMPLES Kim got in line **between** Lee and Rene.
Be sure to weed **between** all ten rows of carrots. [Although there are ten rows of carrots, the weeding is done *between* any two of them.]
Alicia can't see much difference **between** the three pictures. [Although there are more than two pictures, each one is compared with each other one separately.]

Use *among* when you are referring to a group rather than to separate individuals.

EXAMPLE The four winners divided the prize **among** themselves.

EXERCISE 1 **Identifying Correct Usage**

Choose the correct word or words in parentheses in each of the following sentences.

EXAMPLE 1. The picture on the next page is titled *After Supper, West Chester,* but the scene could be almost (*anywhere, anywheres*).
1. *anywhere*

1. This colorful work was painted by (*a, an*) artist named Horace Pippin, who lived from 1888 to 1946.
2. By the time Pippin was in elementary school, he was (*already, all ready*) a talented artist.
3. In fact, he had won a drawing contest and had eagerly (*accepted, excepted*) the prize, a box of crayons and watercolor paints.

USAGE

LEP/ESL

General Strategies. When contrasting the usage of *bad* and *badly,* you may want to list the verbs *sound, feel, taste, smell,* and *look* on the chalkboard, emphasizing that when used to show a sensory experience, these verbs are always followed by adjectives, not adverbs. Give students extra practice with this feature by asking them to complete the following sentences with a sensory verb and adjective(s):

1. Chocolate candy bars . . . .
2. The thorn on a rosebush . . . .
3. Before a thunderstorm, the sky . . . .
4. The inside of a garbage dumpster usually . . . .
5. During Marie's first piano lesson, her music . . . .

USAGE

4. In World War I, Pippin was once caught (*among*, *between*) American troops and the enemy.
5. During this battle (*somewheres*, *somewhere*) in France, Pippin's right arm—the arm he painted with—was seriously wounded.
6. For a long time, Pippin felt (*bad*, *badly*) about his disability, but he was determined to paint again.
7. (*Among*, *Between*) the many ways of painting he tried, the most successful was to hold up his right hand with his left arm.
8. It (*ain't*, *isn't*) surprising that one of his first paintings after the war was a battle scene.
9. When Pippin painted *After Supper, West Chester,* in 1935, he was remembering the small town in Pennsylvania (*where he was born*, *where he was born at*).
10. I think that the painter of this peaceful scene must have felt (*all right*, *alright*) about his work and about himself.

VISUAL CONNECTIONS
After Supper, West Chester

About the Artist. Horace Pippin (1888–1946) loved to draw when he was young but worked at various jobs to earn his living. While serving in the infantry during World War I, he suffered a wound that caused paralysis of his right arm. Because he had very limited use of the arm, he returned to his old love, painting. He would burn a design into a board with a poker that had been heated in a fire. Then he would fill in the design with paint.

Horace Pippin, 1935, "After Supper, West Chester". Gridley/Graves © 1991/Collection Leon Hecht and Robert Pincus-Witten, New York City.

bring, take *Bring* means "to come carrying something." *Take* means "to go carrying something." Think of *bring* as related to *come*. Think of *take* as related to *go*.

EXAMPLES Make sure that you **bring** your book when you come to my house.
Take your coat when you go outside.

could of Do not write *of* with the helping verb *could*. Write *could have*. Also avoid *ought to of, should of, would of, might of,* and *must of.*

EXAMPLES Yvetta wished she could **have** [not *of*] gone to the movie.
We should **have** [not *of*] asked your mom for permission.

don't, doesn't See pages 469–470.

everywheres See **anywheres,** etc.

except, accept See **accept, except.**

fewer, less *Fewer* is used with plural words. *Less* is used with singular words. *Fewer* tells "how many." *Less* tells "how much."

EXAMPLES This road has **fewer** stoplights than any of the other roads.
This road has **less** traffic than any of the other roads.

good, well *Good* is always an adjective. Never use *good* to modify a verb. Use *well,* which is an adverb.

NONSTANDARD Heather sings good.
STANDARD Heather sings **well.**

Although it is usually an adverb, *well* may be used as an adjective to mean "healthy."

EXAMPLE Keiko went home today because she didn't feel **well.**

USAGE

INTEGRATING THE LANGUAGE ARTS

Literature Link. Show students that although standard English is the form used in formal writing, nonstandard English is often used to establish character in writing dialogue in works of fiction. Any selection from Mark Twain's work can be used as an example of such writing. Read aloud some of the dialogue from the selection with your students and discuss why Twain uses such nonstandard English.

USAGE

Good is often used in conversation as an adverb but should not be used as an adverb in writing.

NOTE: *Feel good* and *feel well* mean different things. *Feel good* means "to feel happy or pleased." *Feel well* means "to feel healthy."

EXAMPLES I feel **good** when I'm with my friends.
Rashid had a cold, and he still doesn't feel **well.**

had of See **of.**

had ought, hadn't ought The verb *ought* should never be used with *had.*

NONSTANDARD They had ought to be more careful.
You hadn't ought to have said that.
STANDARD They **ought** to be more careful.
You **oughtn't** to have said that.
or
You **shouldn't** have said that.

hardly, scarcely The words *hardly* and *scarcely* are negative words. They should never be used with other negative words.

EXAMPLES Pedro **can** [not *can't*] **hardly** wait for the fiesta.
The sun **has** [not *hasn't*] **scarcely** shone today.

hisself, theirself, theirselves These words are nonstandard English. Use *himself* and *themselves.*

EXAMPLES Mr. Ogata said he would do the work **himself** [not *hisself*].
They congratulated **themselves** [not *theirselves*] on their victory.

how come In informal English, *how come* is often used instead of *why.* In formal English, *why* is always preferred.

INFORMAL How come she can leave early?
FORMAL **Why** can she leave early?

USAGE

REVIEW A

OBJECTIVE

- To proofread a paragraph for correct usage

 EXERCISE 2 **Identifying Correct Usage**

Choose the correct word or words in parentheses in each of the following sentences.

EXAMPLE **1. There might be (*fewer, less*) accidents if people were more alert around small children.**
1. *fewer*

1. Everyone knows that children are not always as careful as they (*ought, had ought*) to be.
2. However, young children (*can hardly, can't hardly*) be blamed for being curious and adventurous.
3. Recently, I was involved in a situation that (*could of, could have*) led to a serious accident.
4. After I (*brought, took*) my little brother Gerald home from a walk, I called my friend Latoya.
5. Before I knew it, Gerald had wandered off by (*hisself, himself*).
6. I don't know (*how come, why*) he always disappears when I'm on the phone.
7. I found Gerald climbing on the stove, and in (*fewer, less*) than a second I lifted him down.
8. I (*might have, might of*) scolded him more, but he seemed sorry for what he had done.
9. He said he would be (*good, well*) from now on.
10. Although the experience was frightening, it turned out (*good, well*).

USAGE

 **Proofreading a Paragraph for Correct Usage**

Each of the sentences in the following paragraph has at least one error in English usage. Identify each error. Then write the correct usage.

EXAMPLE **[1] The game of soccer has proved to be more popular than the king of England hisself.**
1. *hisself—himself*

[1] Derby, England, may have been the town where soccer was first played at. [2] Sometime around the

USAGE

A DIFFERENT APPROACH

Before assigning **Review A,** have a poster contest. Divide the class into pairs or small groups and have each group illustrate two or three of the rules from the list of common usage problems. Each poster must include a rule and an illustration. The original work can be done on typing paper and then transferred to poster board. Prizes such as privileges or extra points may be given to those students whose work is voted best by the class, and all work can be prominently displayed.

USAGE

Teacher's ResourceBank™

RESOURCES

ITS, IT'S–THEM

- Common Usage Problems B 218

QUICK REMINDER

Write the following sentences on the chalkboard and have students choose *lie* or *lay* to complete the sentences correctly.

1. Neal likes to ___ on the sofa when he reads. [lie]
2. Tell Trudy to ___ the dishes on the table. [lay]
3. My cat likes to ___ in the sunshine. [lie]
4. Our hens ___ eggs in the henhouse. [lay]
5. Please don't ___ on my towel. [lie]

Remind students that *lie* means "to rest" or "recline." *Lay* means "to put or place something." *Lay* can also mean "to produce eggs."

SEGMENT 3 ***(pp. 552–556)***

ITS, IT'S–THEM

OBJECTIVES

- To identify correct usage in a paragraph
- To use standard English usage in recording information during an interview

2. between
3. Anywhere
4. fewer/well
5. already
6. themselves
7. all right/an
8. didn't obey [*or* hardly obeyed]
9. bad
10. accept

USAGE

third century, an early version of the game was played ~~among~~ two towns. [3] ~~Anywheres~~ from fifty to several hundred people played in a match. [4] Back then, soccer had ~~less~~ rules than it does today, and the participants probably didn't behave very ~~good~~. [5] By the fifteenth century, the government had ~~all ready~~ outlawed the sport. [6] The king said that young people ~~had~~ ought to train ~~theirselves~~ in archery instead of playing soccer. [7] According to the king, archery practice was ~~alright~~ because bows and arrows could be used against ~~a~~ enemy. [8] Obviously, many people ~~didn't hardly obey~~ the king's rule, because soccer continued to grow in popularity. [9] Perhaps later kings felt ~~badly~~ about outlawing soccer. [10] Eventually the government had to ~~except~~ that soccer had become the most popular sport in England.

its, it's *Its* is the possessive form of the personal pronoun *it*. *Its* is used to show ownership. *It's* is a contraction of *it is* or *it has*.

EXAMPLES The raccoon washed **its** face in the stream. [possessive pronoun]
My grandparents have a dog; **it's** a collie. [contraction of "it is"]
It's been sunny and warm all day. [contraction of "it has"]

kind of, sort of In informal English, *kind of* and *sort of* are often used to mean "somewhat" or "rather." In formal English, however, it is better to use *somewhat* or *rather*.

INFORMAL That story is kind of funny.
FORMAL That story is **rather** funny.

learn, teach *Learn* means "to gain knowledge." *Teach* means "to instruct" or "to show how."

EXAMPLES The students from Vietnam are **learning** English.
Ms. Sanita is **teaching** them.

less See **fewer, less.**

lie, lay See page 495.

might of, must of See **could of.**

nowheres See **anywheres,** etc.

of Do not use *of* with prepositions such as *inside, off,* and *outside.*

EXAMPLES Mrs. Cardona waited **outside** [not *outside of*] the office.
The child jumped **off** [not *off of*] the swing.
We heard a noise **inside** [not *inside of*] the engine.

Of is also unnecessary with *had.*

EXAMPLE If we **had** [not *had of*] known it was the Purim holiday, we would have planned a costume party.

REFERENCE NOTE: For more about using *of* with helping verbs, see *could of.*

ought to of See **could of.**

rise, raise See pages 493–494.

should of See **could of.**

sit, set See page 492.

somewheres See **anywheres,** etc.

sort of, kind of See **kind of, sort of.**

take, bring See **bring, take.**

than, then Do not confuse these words. *Than* is a conjunction. *Then* is an adverb.

EXAMPLES This cheese is tastier **than** that one.
First the phone rang, and **then** someone knocked at the door.

that there See **this here, that there.**

USAGE

LEP/ESL

General Strategies. To help students differentiate more clearly between *than* and *then,* point out that *than* always involves a contrast. For example, "Lisa is taller than Alberto." On the other hand, *then* specifies a point in time. For example, "She ate breakfast; then she went to school."

USAGE

their, there, they're *Their* is the possessive form of *they*. It is used to show ownership. *There* is used to mean "at that place" or to begin a sentence. *They're* is a contraction of *they are.*

EXAMPLES The children played with **their** toys.
We are going over **there.**
There are twelve members in our club.
They're going to have a Juneteenth picnic.

theirself, theirselves See **hisself,** etc.

them *Them* should not be used as an adjective. Use *these* or *those.*

EXAMPLE How much do you want for **those** [not *them*] baseball cards?

USAGE

PICTURE THIS

You are the health reporter for your classroom's monthly newsletter. While researching your story on dental care, you've discovered something that many people share. They are afraid of going to the dentist. To help these people overcome their fear, you decide to write about why they need not dread a visit to the dentist. In gathering information for your article, you have interviewed the young patient shown on the next page. Write your notes from this interview. Be sure to record both your questions and the patient's responses. In your notes, use at least five of the following terms correctly:

all right	ought
bad	less
badly	fewer
good	it's
well	who's

USAGE

PICTURE THIS

Remind students that because they are interviewing for a newsletter, they should be sure that they ask the standard newspaper questions: *who, what, when, where,* and *why.* Students must also, however, add questions that elicit answers about the patient's attitude before and after the visit. Students might ask the patient what advice she has for other patients.

A DIFFERENT APPROACH

You may want to take the **Picture This** activity one step further and have students interview each other. Most students have visited the dentist and can therefore comment on their experiences. Interviewing allows students to participate in the four basic skill areas of listening, speaking, reading (their own notes), and writing.

Subject: a visit to the dentist
Audience: yourself and readers of a classroom newsletter
Purpose: to record information

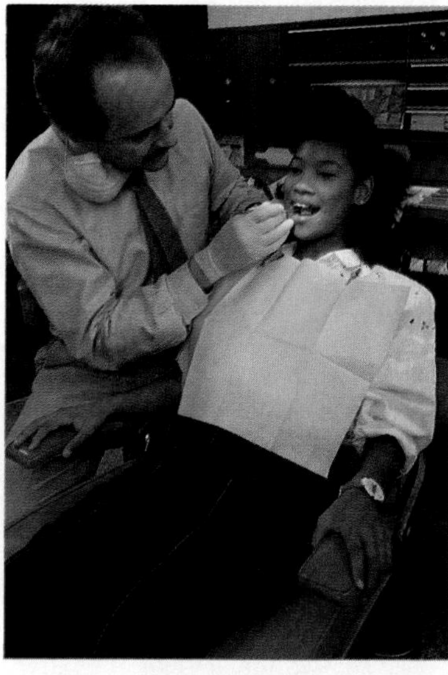

USAGE

EXERCISE 3 **Identifying Correct Usage**

Choose the correct word or words in parentheses in each of the following sentences.

EXAMPLE [1] For years, scientists have studied Mayan writing on temples and (*inside of, inside*) caves.
1. *inside*

[1] Some scientists are *(learning, teaching)* themselves how to understand this writing. [2] The Maya didn't use an alphabet to write *(there, their, they're)* language. [3] Instead, they drew symbols like *(them, these)* small pictures shown on the next page. [4] As you can see, the sign for *jaguar* looked *(rather, sort of)* like a jaguar. [5] At times, it could be *(kind of, rather)* difficult to tell what a picture stood for. [6] *(Its, It's)* meaning was made clear by the use of another small symbol.

USAGE

SEGMENT 4 *(pp. 556–561)*

THIS HERE–YOUR, YOU'RE

OBJECTIVE

- To identify correct usage in a paragraph

VISUAL CONNECTIONS

Exploring the Subject. The Maya were experts in mathematics and developed the most advanced system of record keeping in the world at the time. They also invented and used a calendar that some experts say was better than anything used then in Europe. Ask students to imagine trying to write an assignment in tiny pictures.

Teacher's ResourceBank™

RESOURCES

THIS HERE–YOUR, YOU'RE

- Common Usage Problems C 219

QUICK REMINDER

Write the following sentences on the chalkboard and have the students write the word that correctly completes each one:

1. (Whose, Who's) coming to the movie? [Who's]
2. (You're, Your) expecting a letter, aren't you? [You're]
3. We drove a short (way, ways) down the road. [way]
4. (Whose, Who's) cup is this? [Whose]
5. (You're, Your) camera is at my house. [Your]

[7] *(There, Their, They're)* is an example of this technique in the illustration below. [8] If a scarf symbol was added to the symbol for *man, (then, than)* the picture meant "lord." [9] Mayan writing contained other symbols that were more like syllables *(then, than)* entire words. [10] *(Its, It's)* clear we still have a great deal to learn about this beautiful, ancient language.

this here, that there The *here* and *there* are not necessary after *this* and *that.*

EXAMPLE Do you want **this** [not *this here*] book or **that** [not *that there*] one?

try and In informal English, *try and* is often used for *try to.* In formal English, *try to* is preferred.

INFORMAL Pat will try and explain the problem.
FORMAL Pat will **try to** explain the problem.

use to, used to Be sure to add the *–d* to *use. Used to* is in the past tense.

EXAMPLE Dr. Chang **used to** [not *use to*] live next door to us.

way, ways Use *way,* not *ways,* when referring to a distance.

EXAMPLE We traveled a long **way** [not *ways*] today.

well, good See **good, well.**

when, where Do not use *when* or *where* incorrectly in writing a definition.

NONSTANDARD A *phrase* is when a group of words is used as a part of speech.
STANDARD A *phrase* is a group of words that is used as a part of speech.

Do not use *where* for *that.*

EXAMPLE I read **that** [not *where*] the concert has been canceled.

whose, who's *Whose* is the possessive form of *who.* It shows ownership. *Who's* is a contraction of *who is* or *who has.*

EXAMPLES **Whose** dog is that? [possessive pronoun]
Who's the bravest person you ever met? [contraction of *who is*]
Sarah is the only student **who's** turned in a report. [contraction of *who has*]

would of See **could of.**

your, you're *Your* is the possessive form of *you.* *You're* is the contraction of *you are.*

EXAMPLES Do you have **your** watch with you? [possessive pronoun]
You're late today. [contraction of *you are*]

EXERCISE 4 **Identifying Correct Usage**

Choose the correct word or words in parentheses in each of the following sentences.

EXAMPLE [1] For (*your, you're*) best camping trip ever, take along a trail map.
1. *your*

[1] A trail map is (*when a map shows,* *a map that shows*) trails, campsites, and geographical features.

LEP/ESL

General Strategies. Some students may need practice in determining the correct use of *used to.* You may want to have them record the following information in their journals:

Used to + *verb* refers to an action that happened repeatedly in the past, but which no longer occurs, or a past condition that no longer exists at all.

For example, "Before I learned English, I used to feel shy around new friends" or "I used to have a red bicycle; now I own a blue one." To provide further practice, pair your ESL students. Have them interview each other about things they used to do before coming to the United States.

USAGE

INTEGRATING THE LANGUAGE ARTS

Technology Link. You may wish to enter one of the exercises into a word processor. Ask students to run the spell-check program and to report what they find. [They should find that the spell-check program cannot help them with usage choices; it will tell them only whether or not words are spelled correctly.]

USAGE

[2] For a safe camping trip, a map like (*this here*, *this*) one can be very important. [3] Hikers who are not (*used to*, *use to*) an area often lose their way. [4] Every year, you can read reports (*where*, *that*) some campers were lost for several days. [5] If you don't want to be one of them, (*try and*, *try to*) get a good trail map. [6] In fact, every hiker in your group (*who's*, *whose*) able to read a map should have one. [7] With the map, you can choose a (*good*, *well*) location for your campsite. [8] When you begin your hike, mark where (*your*, *you're*) campsite is on the map. [9] If you go quite a (*way*, *ways*) from your campsite, note your path on the map, too. [10] As (*your*, *you're*) walking, your trail map can help you figure out exactly where you are.

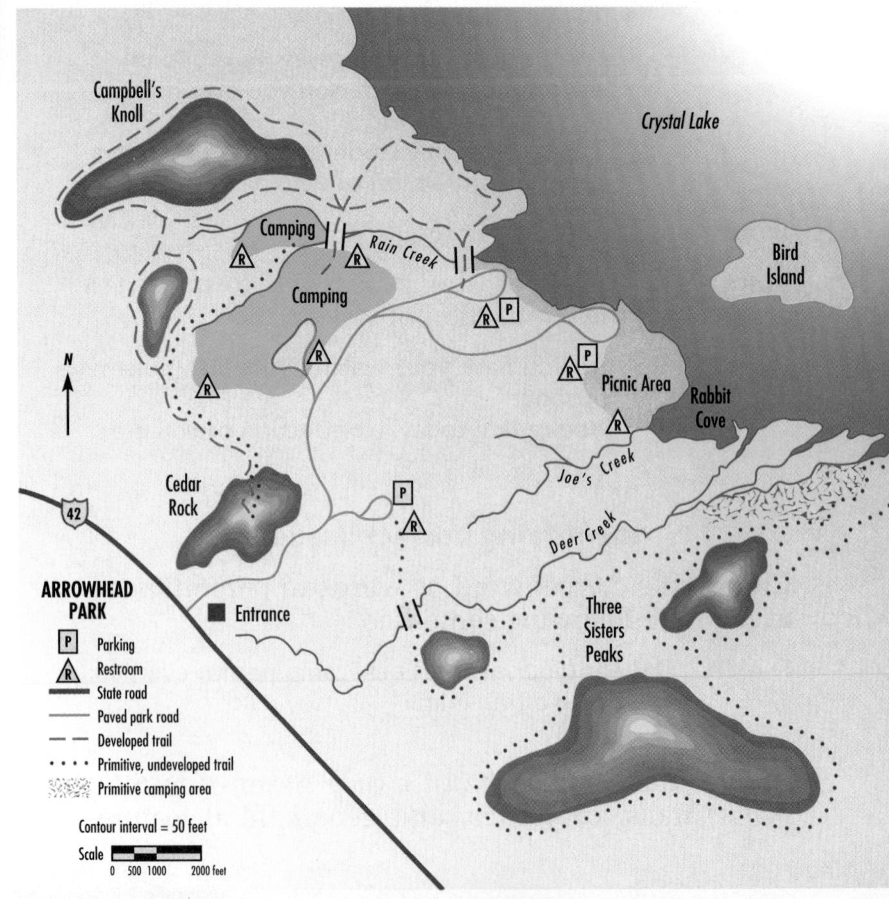

WRITING APPLICATION

OBJECTIVES

- To use specific rules for standard English in writing
- To write an informative letter using the four stages of writing

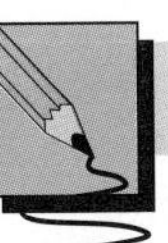

WRITING APPLICATION

Using Formal English in Writing

Standard, formal English isn't necessarily the "best" or the "right" form of English. It's simply the most appropriate kind of English to use in most formal situations. These situations include essays, speeches, reports, and business letters. This chapter gives you a number of guidelines for using formal, standard English.

INFORMAL	I feel badly about not being able to baby-sit tonight.
FORMAL	I feel **bad** about not being able to baby-sit tonight.
INFORMAL	How come this remote-control airplane won't fly?
FORMAL	**Why** won't this remote-control airplane fly?

WRITING ACTIVITY

You are an after-school helper at a day-care center. The teachers at the center plan to take the children on a field trip. One of the teachers has asked you to write a letter to send to the children's parents. The letter should tell where the children will visit and describe some of the things they will do there. The letter should also list any special items the children need to bring. Use this **Glossary of Usage** and other parts of the **Handbook** to help you write the letter in formal, standard English.

Prewriting First, decide where the children will go on their field trip. They might go to a library, a park, a museum, or a fire station. Then, list the kinds of activities the children might participate in there. Note how the children will travel—for example, by bus or car. Also note any special clothing or other things they might need for the field trip. List all the details you can think of.

USAGE

WRITING APPLICATION

The writing assignment gives students an opportunity to use the rules they have learned in this chapter. The rules are numerous, so you might wish to review two or three of those that cover errors common to your class.

Because students are writing informative letters, you might also wish to review material from **Chapter 6: "Writing to Inform."**

CRITICAL THINKING

Analysis

To help students think critically and to help them generate writing ideas, ask them to work together to prepare a questionnaire focusing on young children's interests. After students have composed the questionnaire, distribute copies and ask students to fill them out. Read the results to the class and allow them to write their letters, using any of the ideas.

USAGE

REVIEW B

OBJECTIVE

- To proofread a paragraph for correct usage

COOPERATIVE LEARNING

To help students learn what is required in evaluating and revising, divide the class into small groups. Each person in the group should be made responsible for checking the groups' letters for one or more specific usage problems. Each group member could also be asked to check the clarity of the letter. Students can then revise their letters if revisions are necessary.

USAGE

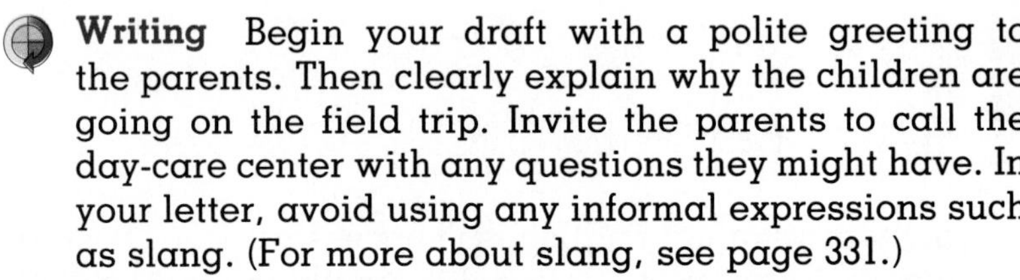

Writing Begin your draft with a polite greeting to the parents. Then clearly explain why the children are going on the field trip. Invite the parents to call the day-care center with any questions they might have. In your letter, avoid using any informal expressions such as slang. (For more about slang, see page 331.)

Evaluating and Revising Ask a friend or a classmate to read your letter. Does your reader understand the information in the letter? Does the letter follow the guidelines for a proper business letter? Revise any details that are not clear. Also, insert additional information where it is needed. (For more information about writing business letters, see pages 709–713.)

Proofreading Read your work carefully. Check for correct spelling, punctuation, and grammar. Pay extra attention to the punctuation of the greeting and closing of your letter.

USAGE

REVIEW B **Proofreading a Paragraph for Correct Usage**

Most of the following sentences contain errors in usage. If a sentence is incorrect, write it correctly. If a sentence is correct, write C.

EXAMPLE [1] Do you know someone who can learn you how to dance the Texas Two-Step?

1. *Do you know someone who can teach you how to dance the Texas Two-Step?*

1. it's

[1] Country music lovers like the ones shown on the next page enjoy the two-step because ~~its~~ fun to dance. [2] If you don't know anyone who can teach you the two-step, you can use this ~~here~~ diagram to

learn the basic steps. [3] So, grab ~~you're~~ partner and get ready. [4] First, listen closely to ~~them~~ musicians. [5] Try ~~and~~ catch the rhythm of the music with a small double shuffle step. [6] Remember, men, ~~your~~ always starting with the left foot; women, you do just the opposite. [7] The man steps to the left, touches his left shoe with his right foot, and then steps to the right and does the same thing. [8] Then, he takes two ~~kind of~~ quick steps forward followed by two slow shuffle steps. [9] You can dance the same steps for a ~~ways~~, or you can try doing a sidestep or a turn. [10] ~~Their~~ you have one version of the Texas Two-Step.

3. your
4. the
5. to
6. you're
7. C
8. rather
9. way
10. There

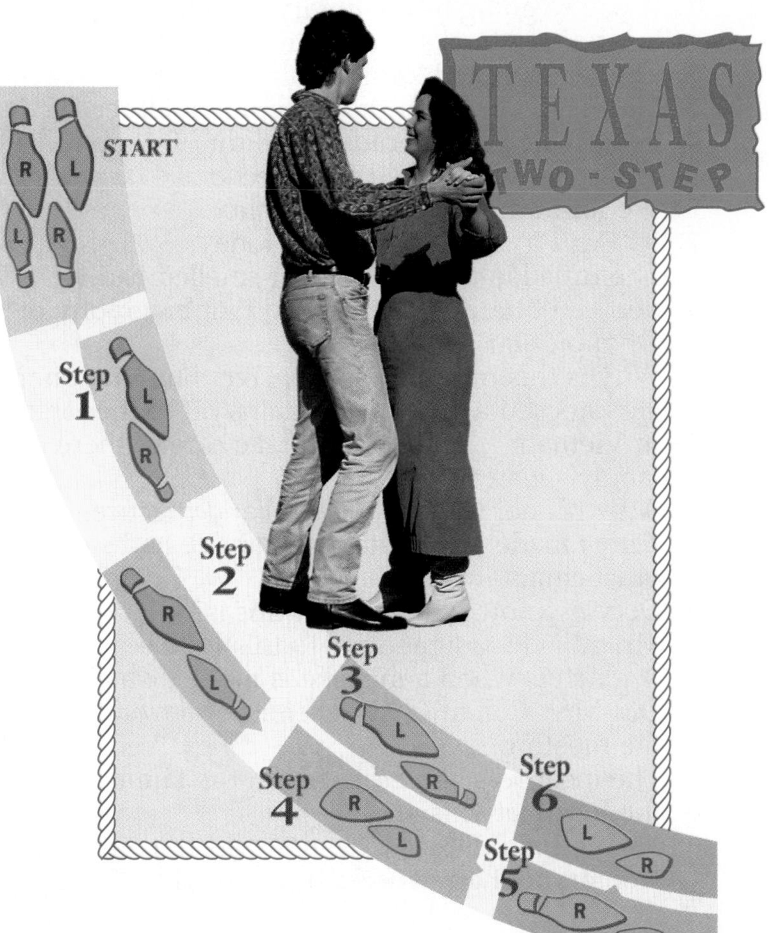

STUDENTS WITH SPECIAL NEEDS

Learning disabled students with a visual-processing deficit tend to become overwhelmed when faced with a page of text to read and correct. Enlisting a peer helper to read the text to the student will draw upon that student's auditory strengths. Have the students answer verbally and then have them write their responses on paper.

SEGMENT 5 *(p. 562)*

REVIEW: POSTTEST

OBJECTIVE

- To revise sentences by correcting errors in usage

Review: Posttest

Revising Sentences by Correcting Errors in Usage

Each of the following sentences contains an error in usage. Write each sentence correctly, using standard, formal English.

EXAMPLE **1.** I knew all the answers accept the last one.
1. *I knew all the answers except the last one.*

1. If you're going to the library, would you please bring these books back there for me? **1.** take
2. The water tasted kind of salty. **2.** rather
3. Has Jamila finished the assignment all ready? **3.** already
4. Leon took a nap because he didn't feel good. **4.** well
5. They should of asked for directions. **5.** have
6. We found nothing but a old shoe. **6.** an
7. Bao will try and fix her bike today. **7.** to
8. The tuna looked all right but smelled badly. **8.** bad
9. Bert can't hardly wait to read that biography of Olympic star Jesse Owens. **9.** can't wait [*or* can hardly wait]
10. Why is this mitt more expensive then that one? **10.** than
11. He knocked a bowl of plantains off of the table.
12. In Vietnam, children often take care of there family's water buffalo. **12.** their
13. After school we use to have band practice. **13.** used
14. Tanya made less mistakes after she had started practicing. **14.** fewer
15. Do you know who's pencil this is? **15.** whose
16. Mr. Abeyto assigned me to this here seat.
17. A glitch is when a mistake is made by a computer.
18. Did Mrs. Cohen say how come she won't be at the meeting? **18.** why
19. The meat was shared between the families of the Innupiat village. **19.** among
20. At one time, Bessie Coleman was the only black woman pilot anywheres in the world. **20.** anywhere

USAGE

USAGE

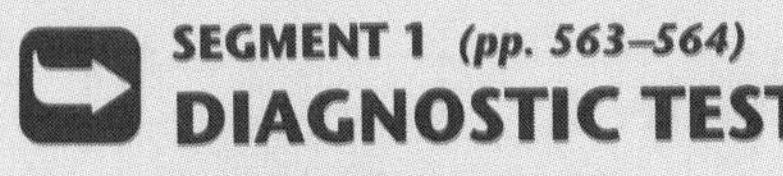

SEGMENT 1 *(pp. 563–564)*

DIAGNOSTIC TEST

OBJECTIVE

- To proofread sentences for correct capitalization

22 CAPITAL LETTERS

Rules for Capitalization

Diagnostic Test

Proofreading Sentences for Correct Capitalization

For each of the following sentences, find each word that has an error in the use of capital letters. Write the word correctly. Words that should be capitalized or lower-cased are underscored.

EXAMPLE **1. Did president Lincoln deliver his Gettysburg Address during The Civil War?**
1. *President, the*

1. Shawn's dog, Ransom, is a german shepherd.
2. Our Spring break begins on march 26.
3. Write to me at 439 Walnut street.
4. Do you know why the *titanic* sank?
5. In 1991, aung san suu kyi of burma won the Nobel peace prize.
6. As soon as i finish my English homework, i'll call you.
7. I would like to go to College someday.
8. We watched a scene from *Romeo And Juliet*.

MECHANICS

Teacher's ResourceBank™ RESOURCES

FOR THE WHOLE CHAPTER

- Chapter Review Form A 230–231
- Chapter Review Form B 232–233
- Assessment Portfolio
  - Mechanics Pretests 463–470
  - Mechanics Mastery Tests 487–494

CHAPTER OVERVIEW

This chapter provides rules for the correct use of capitalization. It includes rules for marking the beginnings of sentences, the pronoun *I*, proper nouns and adjectives—including names of languages and of school subjects followed by a course number, abbreviations, and titles.

This chapter stresses the importance of capitalization in writing and can be referred to during any writing assignment.

This chapter also may be used with the study of common and proper nouns and proper adjectives in **Chapter 13: "The Parts of Speech: Noun, Pronoun, Adjective."**

USING THE DIAGNOSTIC TEST

You may use the **Diagnostic Test** to identify areas in which students need instruction and practice in capitalization. You may wish to take the diagnosis one step further by evaluating actual writing samples to identify students who need more work in this area.

MECHANICS

SEGMENT 2 *(pp. 564–574)*

FIRST WORDS, THE PRONOUN *I*, PROPER NOUNS Rules 22a–22c

OBJECTIVES

- To proofread sentences for correct capitalization
- To write proper nouns, using correct capitalization

Teacher's ResourceBank™

RESOURCES

FIRST WORDS, THE PRONOUN *I*, PROPER NOUNS

- Using Capital Letters A 227

QUICK REMINDER

Write the following sentences on the chalkboard for students to read silently:

1. our team wants little, rice, and bean.
2. we always hear the green twins cheer when bowls makes a strike.

Ask students if the sentences make sense to them. Then tell them that some of the words should have capital letters and ask them to identify the capitalization errors. [**1.** Our team wants Little, Rice, and Bean. **2.** We always hear the Green twins cheer when Bowls makes a strike.]

Have students discuss the problems that arise when reading sentences without capital letters. Most will say that not having capitals makes reading slower and more confusing. Confirm that the visual clues of capitalization make understanding much easier.

MECHANICS

MECHANICS

9. Eric's orthodontist is dr. Chun.
10. On saturday my aunt is taking us to jones beach.
11. Dad used the general Electric waffle iron to make breakfast.
12. have you seen my copy of *sports illustrated*?
13. The Peace corps volunteers helped build a bridge.
14. The capital of Peru is lima.
15. The age of Reason brought many changes to european society.
16. The *viking* space probes landed on mars.
17. Tranh's brother is a buddhist monk.
18. The storm is coming from the North.
19. Are you taking spanish or art this year?
20. The gulf of Mexico lies west of Florida.

22a. Capitalize the first word in every sentence.

EXAMPLES **M**y sister has soccer practice after school. **T**hen she has to do her homework.

The first word of a direct quotation should begin with a capital letter, whether or not the quotation starts the sentence.

EXAMPLE Kameko asked, "**H**ave you finished your report?"

Usually, the first word of every line of poetry begins with a capital letter.

EXAMPLE
Let the rain kiss you.
Let the rain beat upon your head with silver liquid drops.
Let the rain sing you a lullaby.

The rain makes still pools on the sidewalk.
The rain makes running pools in the gutter.
The rain plays a little sleep-song on our roof at night—

And I love the rain.

"April Rain Song," Langston Hughes

- To recognize the correct use of capitalization
- To correct sentences by using capital letters correctly

22 a–c

NOTE: Some poets do not follow this style. When you quote from a poem, use capital letters exactly as the poet uses them.

REFERENCE NOTE: For more about using capital letters in quotations, see page 616.

22b. Capitalize the pronoun *I*.

EXAMPLES When **I** returned home, **I** walked the dog.

EXERCISE 1 **Proofreading Sentences for Correct Capitalization**

If a sentence has an error in capitalization, write correctly the word or words that should be capitalized. If a sentence is correct, write *C*.

EXAMPLE **1.** What time should i call?
1. *I*

1. the library report for social studies is due at the end of next month.
2. My sister memorized the limerick that begins, "a tutor who tooted a flute."
3. Aren't you glad tomorrow is a holiday? 3. C
4. Mary Elizabeth said, "we need to buy some more shampoo."
5. My parents let me watch television only after i have finished all my chores.

22c. Capitalize proper nouns.

A ***proper noun*** names a particular person, place, or thing. Proper nouns are always capitalized. A ***common noun*** names a kind or type of person, place, or thing. A common noun is not capitalized unless it begins a sentence or is part of a title.

REFERENCE NOTE: For more information about proper nouns and common nouns, see page 369.

MECHANICS

INTEGRATING THE LANGUAGE ARTS

Literature Link. To support the textbook statement that the first word of any line of poetry usually begins with a capital letter, have students study poems in their literature textbooks. For example, T. S. Eliot in "The Rum Tum Tugger" and Carl Sandburg in "Phizzog" begin all lines with capitals—even, in Eliot's case, when the words are conjunctions.

You may want to challenge students to find poems that are exceptions and have first words *not* beginning with capitals.

LEP/ESL

General Strategies. In some languages, such as Serbo-Croatian and Vietnamese, it is customary to capitalize only the first word of a geographical name that contains two or more words, while in English we capitalize all the words in the name. For example, *Thai binh duong* means *Pacific Ocean* in Vietnamese. Also, the name of a person's nationality is not capitalized in Spanish, Portugese, Romanian, and Russian; thus, *a Russian* is *un ruso* in Spanish and *ruskii* in Russian. You may wish to emphasize these two points and give students examples to reinforce these differences between English and their native languages.

MECHANICS

LEARNING STYLES

Visual Learners. At the beginning of the lesson, you may want to go through the chapter with students and read each rule, to give an overview of capitalization use. Call students' attention to the **Summary Style Sheet** at the end of the chapter; this summary can be used for review purposes during proofreading. You may want to have students make a similar style sheet of the main rules in the chapter to display on a bulletin board.

COOPERATIVE LEARNING

Organize the class into groups of five. Have the students from each group divide up the ten subsections of **Rule 22c** so that each student is responsible for two subsections. Then have students regroup so that all of those having the same two subsections are working together. These groups should study their categories and then generate example sentences for practice. After this, have the original groups reassemble. Each student should explain his or her two subsections and then have others in the group tell what should be capitalized in the example sentences.

MECHANICS

PROPER NOUNS	COMMON NOUNS
Fairview **S**chool	middle school
November	month
Toni **M**orrison	woman
Red **S**ox	team
Kenya	country

(1) Capitalize the names of persons.

EXAMPLES **K**azue **S**awai, **J**esse **J**ackson, **G**olda **M**eir, **H**eitor **V**illa-**L**obos, **P**aul **B**unyan

(2) Capitalize geographical names.

TYPE OF NAME	EXAMPLES	
Continents	**A**sia **A**ustralia	**N**orth **A**merica **E**urope
Countries	**D**enmark **B**urkina **F**aso	**T**hailand **C**osta **R**ica
Cities, Towns	**M**inneapolis **H**avana	**N**ew **D**elhi **S**an **D**iego
States	**M**aryland **W**est **V**irginia	**M**ississippi **O**regon
Islands	**H**awaiian **I**slands **L**eyte	**B**lock **I**sland **K**ey **W**est
Bodies of Water	**Y**angtze **R**iver **H**udson **B**ay	**L**ake **O**keechobee **C**aribbean **S**ea
Streets, Highways	**F**ront **S**treet **C**helmsford **R**oad **F**ifth **A**venue	**M**ichigan **A**venue **D**arryl **D**rive **I**nterstate 55

MECHANICS

NOTE: In a hyphenated street number, the second part of the number is not capitalized.

EXAMPLE **F**orty-**n**inth **S**treet

TYPE OF NAME	EXAMPLES	
Parks	Mammoth **C**ave San **A**ntonio **M**issions	Yellowstone **N**ational **P**ark
Mountains	**A**dirondacks Pine **M**ountain	**M**ount **K**ilimanjaro **A**ndes
Sections of the Country	the **S**outh **C**orn **B**elt	the **N**orthwest **N**ew **E**ngland

NOTE: Words such as *east, west, northeast,* or *southwest* are not capitalized when the words indicate a direction.

EXAMPLES Turn **e**ast when you reach the river. [direction]
My cousin goes to college in the **E**ast. [section of the country]

EXERCISE 2 **Writing Proper Nouns**

For each common noun given below, write two proper nouns. You may use a dictionary and an atlas. Be sure to use capital letters correctly.

EXAMPLE **1.** lake
1. *Lake Louise, Lake Ontario*

1. river **4.** park **7.** island **9.** country
2. street **5.** friend **8.** state **10.** ocean
3. actor **6.** singer

EXERCISE 3 **Recognizing the Correct Use of Capital Letters**

If a sentence contains an error in capitalization, write correctly the word that should be capitalized. If the sentence is correct, write *C*.

EXAMPLE **1.** Huge rigs pump oil from beneath the North sea.
1. *Sea*

MECHANICS

LESS-ADVANCED STUDENTS

In your approach to this chapter, you may want to use the **Summary Style Sheet** at the end of the chapter. As you teach each rule, have students write the related examples from the style sheet in their notebooks. For practical application, have students add to their style sheets, using names of persons, places, and things from their own town or particular locale.

STUDENTS WITH SPECIAL NEEDS

Students with a visual-processing deficit may have the greatest difficulty in differentiating between a proper noun and a common noun in written text. It may be helpful, when involved in class discussion on this topic, to pay special attention to these students by asking them to make up a proper noun name for a given common noun. Once you are sure they understand the information, read each sentence in **Exercise 3** aloud. Tell the students to state which words are proper nouns and need capitalization. Finally, instruct students to copy down the sentence correctly. Using the students' auditory strength will reinforce their visual skills.

ANSWERS

Exercise 2

Responses will vary. If possible, have dictionaries, geography books, or atlases available for students to use.

MECHANICS

A DIFFERENT APPROACH

Divide the class into two teams to play a game using capital letters. Make up broad categories based on the subsections of **Rule 22c** (such as names of nearby schools, names of nearby towns and cities, names of teams, names of favorite singers, names of businesses in a nearby mall, and so on). Write one category on the chalkboard. Have two or three students from each team work at opposite ends of the chalkboard to write as many capitalized names in the category as they can in three minutes. The team with the most correct examples gets a point. Repeat for other categories and with different team members.

LEARNING STYLES

Kinetic Learners. Challenge students to construct a sentence poster that illustrates each of the subsections of **Rule 22c.** Each student (or small group of students) should write one long sentence on poster board or large paper. Then they should label the capitalized words; for example, they would write *team* over the capitalized name of a team. Students could add artwork to the posters and display them on a bulletin board.

1. María Ayala and eileen Barnes are going to Chicago.
2. Our neighbor Ken Oshige recently moved to canada.
3. Midway island is in the Pacific Ocean.
4. We could see mount Hood from the airplane window.
5. After you turn off the highway, head north for three miles. 5. C
6. During the sixteenth century, Spanish explorers brought the first horses to the west.
7. Several of us in the youth group went canoeing on blue River.
8. My closest friend just moved to ohio.
9. Hawaii Volcanoes National park is on the island of Hawaii.
10. The store is located on Maple street.

(3) Capitalize the names of organizations, teams, businesses, institutions, and government bodies.

TYPE OF NAME	EXAMPLES	
Organizations	**M**ath **C**lub **B**oy **S**couts	**O**akdale **C**hamber of **C**ommerce
Teams	**N**ew **Y**ork **M**ets **R**iverside **R**aiders	**L**os **A**ngeles **R**ams **P**ine **H**ill **J**ets
Businesses	**J.** and **J. C**onstruction, **I**nc. **U**ptown **S**hoe **S**tore **G**rommet **M**anufacturing **C**ompany	
Institutions	**U**niversity of **O**klahoma **K**ennedy **M**iddle **S**chool **M**ount **S**inai **H**ospital	
Government Bodies	**L**eague of **A**rab **S**tates **D**epartment of **E**ducation **F**ederal **B**ureau of **I**nvestigation	

NOTE: Do *not* capitalize words such as *hotel, theater,* or *high school* unless they are part of a proper name.

EXAMPLES **F**remont **H**otel — the hotel
Apollo **T**heater — a theater
Ames **H**igh **S**chool — that high school

REFERENCE NOTE: The names of government bodies are often abbreviated. For information on abbreviations, see pages 589–591 and 602.

(4) Capitalize the names of special events, holidays, and calendar items.

TYPE OF NAME	EXAMPLES	
Special Events	**W**orld **S**eries **N**ew **Y**ork **M**arathon	**P**arade of **R**oses **T**ulip **F**estival
Holidays	**T**hanksgiving **L**abor **D**ay	**M**artin **L**uther **K**ing **D**ay
Calendar Items	**S**unday **F**ather's **D**ay	**D**ecember **A**pril **F**ools' **D**ay

NOTE: Do *not* capitalize the name of a season unless it is part of a proper name.

EXAMPLES a **w**inter storm, the **W**inter **F**estival

(5) Capitalize the names of historical events and periods.

TYPE OF NAME	EXAMPLES	
Historical Events	**B**oston **T**ea **P**arty **B**attle of **H**astings **W**ar of 1812	**N**ew **D**eal **F**all of **R**ome **R**enaissance
Historical Periods	**B**ronze **A**ge **R**eformation	**G**reat **D**epression **M**esozoic **E**ra

MECHANICS

STUDENTS WITH SPECIAL NEEDS

You may want to provide a questionnaire for students that personalizes the application of capitalization rules for proper nouns. This could be a list of questions or a form asking each student to provide the following information:

1. complete names of parents or guardians
2. complete names of friends
3. date of birth
4. city, county, and state of residence
5. favorite singer or musical group
6. favorite cereal

LEP/ESL

General Strategies. In English, the names of days of the week and months of the year are capitalized. Speakers of some languages, such as Czech, French, Polish, Portuguese, Romanian, Russian, Spanish, and Vietnamese write them with small letters. For example, *Saturday* is *samedi* in French, *simbata* in Romanian, *sabado* in Spanish, *subbota* in Russian, and *thu bay* in Vietnamese. You may need to remind students who speak such languages to capitalize these words in English.

MECHANICS

WRITING APPLICATION

OBJECTIVE

- To write an essay about a historical place using capital letters correctly

MECHANICS

WRITING APPLICATION

The writing assignment gives students practice in using capital letters correctly in an essay. Since they will be writing to explain where they would like to go and why, you may wish to review **Chapter 6: "Writing to Inform."**

CRITICAL THINKING

Analysis

To ensure effective essays, students should analyze their travel interests. Their reasons for choosing their destinations will serve as topics for their writing and will determine the details included.

 EXERCISE 4 **Correcting Errors in the Use of Capital Letters**

In each of the following sentences, find the word or words that should be capitalized but are not. Then write the word or words correctly.

EXAMPLE **1.** Hart middle school is having a book fair.
1. *Middle School*

1. Would you like to go to the movies on friday?
2. The special Olympics will be held in our town this year.
3. What plans have you made for easter?
4. My sister and I were born at memorial Hospital.
5. The Rotary club donated equipment for our school's new gym.
6. Did dinosaurs live during the stone Age?
7. My favorite baseball team is the Atlanta braves.
8. Lionel works at the Beattie box company.
9. Congress is made up of the senate and the house of representatives.
10. Did you see any fireworks on the fourth of July?

MECHANICS

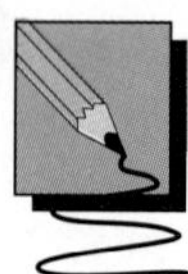

WRITING APPLICATION

Using Capital Letters Correctly

Using capital letters correctly helps your readers understand your meaning. For example, read these two sentences:

> I would like to go hiking in the rocky mountains.
> I would like to go hiking in the Rocky Mountains.

The capital letters in the second sentence make it clear that *Rocky Mountains* is the name of a particular mountain range, not just a description of mountains that are rocky.

WRITING ACTIVITY

Would you like to visit Washington, D.C.? Cairo, Egypt? the Great Wall of China? Your social studies teacher has asked you to write about a vacation you'd like to take to a historical place. Write an essay telling where you'd like to go and why you'd like to go there. In your essay, use at least five proper nouns. Include at least two geographical names and two personal names. Be sure to capitalize each proper noun you use.

Prewriting First, brainstorm a list of historical places that interest you. (You might want to look in a social studies textbook, an atlas, or an encyclopedia for ideas.) Which of these places would you most like to visit? After you choose a place, think about what monuments and other historical sights you would see there. What events in history do these landmarks mark? Jot down notes about what you would do during your visit.

Writing Begin your rough draft by stating where you'd like to go and why. Explain what historical event(s) happened at that place. Then tell what particular areas or landmarks you would visit. Tell what you think you'd most enjoy about your vacation. Be sure to use at least five proper nouns naming places, events, and people.

Evaluating and Revising Use an encyclopedia or other reference source to check any names and facts you're not sure about. Then have a friend read your draft. Have you clearly identified the place you want to visit? Can your friend understand why you want to go there? If not, you'll probably need to give additional specific details.

Proofreading Proofread your essay carefully for any errors in grammar, spelling, or punctuation. Be sure that you have capitalized each proper noun correctly and have not misspelled any names.

MECHANICS

PREWRITING

You may want to provide students with travel brochures to use as references for their work.

This writing application provides an opportunity for cooperative learning. Organize students who choose the same destination into small groups to brainstorm together and share reference works.

MECHANICS

ADVANCED STUDENTS

Students who have a firm grasp of **Rules 22a–22c** may want to examine some works by writers who use capitalization in creative or unusual ways. Students should collect examples, analyze the effects of the creative capitalization, and discuss their findings with the class. Students should be prepared to give their opinions about why the authors choose to break or bend the rules. Possible writers to study include Rudyard Kipling and E. E. Cummings.

MECHANICS

(6) Capitalize the names of nationalities, races, and peoples.

TYPE OF NAME	EXAMPLES	
Nationalities	**M**exican	**S**wiss
Races	**M**icronesian	**C**aucasian
Peoples	**C**herokee	**B**antu

NOTE: The words *black* and *white* may or may not be capitalized when they refer to people.

EXAMPLE During the Civil War, many **B**lacks [*or* **b**lacks] joined the Union forces.

(7) Capitalize the brand names of business products.

EXAMPLES **G**oodyear tire, **W**hirlpool washer, **F**ord truck [Notice that names of types of products are not capitalized.]

(8) Capitalize the names of ships, trains, airplanes, spacecraft, buildings and other structures, and monuments and awards.

TYPE OF NAME	EXAMPLES	
Ships	***S**anta **M**aria*	***M**onitor*
Trains	***M**etroliner*	***C**ity of **M**iami*
Airplanes	***C**oncorde*	***S**pirit of **S**t. **L**ouis*
Spacecraft	***C**olumbia*	***R**anger 7*
Buildings and Other Structures	**F**latiron **B**uilding **W**orld **T**rade **C**enter	**H**oover **D**am **G**olden **G**ate **B**ridge **A**strodome
Monuments and Awards	**L**incoln **M**emorial **S**tatue of **L**iberty	**P**ulitzer **P**rize **M**edal of **H**onor

MECHANICS

(9) Capitalize the names of religions and their followers, holy days, sacred writings, and specific deities.

TYPE OF NAME	EXAMPLES	
Religions and Followers	**B**uddhism **T**aoism	**C**hristian **J**ew
Holy Days	**P**urim **C**hristmas	**R**amadan **P**otlatch
Sacred Writings	**D**ead **S**ea **S**crolls **B**ible	**K**oran **T**almud
Specific Deities	**A**llah **G**od	**V**ishnu **J**ehovah

NOTE: The word *god* is not capitalized when it refers to a god of ancient mythology. The names of specific gods *are* capitalized.

EXAMPLE The Roman **g**od of the sea was **N**eptune.

(10) Capitalize the names of planets, stars, and other heavenly bodies.

EXAMPLES **M**ars, **P**luto, **N**orth **S**tar, **B**etelgeuse, **M**ilky **W**ay, **B**ig **D**ipper, **U**rsa **M**inor

NOTE: The word *earth* is not capitalized unless it is used along with the names of other heavenly bodies. The words *sun* and *moon* are never capitalized.

EXAMPLES China is home to one fourth of the people on **e**arth.
How far is Saturn from **E**arth?
The **s**un rose at 7:09 this morning.

EXERCISE 5 **Correcting Sentences by Using Capital Letters Correctly**

For each of the following sentences, write correctly the word or words that should be capitalized.

MECHANICS

REVIEW A

OBJECTIVE

- To correct sentences by capitalizing proper nouns

INTEGRATING THE LANGUAGE ARTS

Technology Link. You may want to have students find information on capitalization from a computer program that checks style and grammar. As students ask questions and receive information from the program, point out that the information in the computer reinforces the rules in the textbook.

EXAMPLE **1.** We went to the leesburg library to learn more about african american history.
1. *Leesburg Library, African American*

1. The methodist minister quoted a verse from the bible.
2. Bob has a chevrolet truck.
3. On a clear night, you can see venus from earth.
4. Last summer, my history teacher took a cruise on the *song of Norway*.
5. Meet me in front of the Woolworth building.
6. Pilar received the Junior Achievement award.
7. Otis made a detailed scale model of *gemini* for his science project.
8. Helga wrote a poem about the greek god zeus.
9. Some navajo artists make beautiful silver jewelry.
10. Who were the first europeans to settle in Mexico?

REVIEW A **Correcting Sentences by Capitalizing Proper Nouns**

For each of the following sentences, write correctly the word or words that should be capitalized.

EXAMPLE **1.** In the late nineteenth century, henry morton stanley explored an area of africa occupied by ancestors of the bambuti.
1. *Henry Morton Stanley, Africa, Bambuti*

1. The bambuti live in the ituri forest, which is in northeast zaire.
2. This forest is located almost exactly in the middle of africa.
3. It lies east and just north of kisangani, as shown in the boxed area on the map on the next page.
4. The bambuti, also known as twides, aka, or efe, have lived there for many thousands of years.
5. The earliest record of people like the Bambuti is found in the notes of explorers from egypt about 2500 B.C.

MECHANICS

MECHANICS

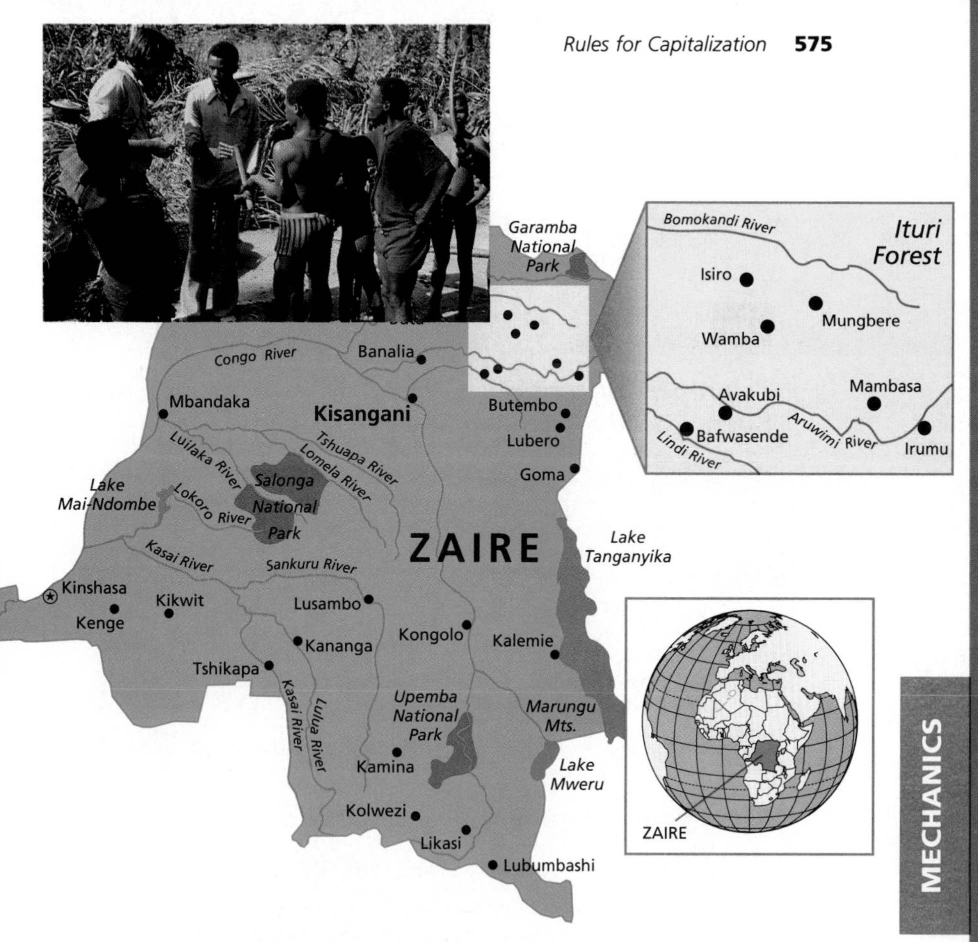

6. Other early reports of these people are found on colorful tiles in italy and in the records of explorers from portugal.
7. Stanley met the bambuti, but he didn't write much about them.
8. In the 1920s, paul schebesta went to africa to learn more about them.
9. He learned that the bambuti are very different from the bantu and their other neighbors.
10. In fact, the bambuti were likely the first people in the tropical rain forest that stretches across zaire from the atlantic ocean on the west coast to the grasslands in the east.

MECHANICS

MECHANICS

SEGMENT 3 *(pp. 576–582)*

LANGUAGES AND SPECIFIC COURSE NAMES, PROPER ADJECTIVES, ABBREVIATIONS, AND TITLES Rules 22d–22g

OBJECTIVES

- To correct sentences by capitalizing words and titles
- To write titles for imaginary works and to capitalize them correctly

Teacher's ResourceBank™

RESOURCES

LANGUAGES AND SPECIFIC COURSE NAMES, PROPER ADJECTIVES, ABBREVIATIONS, AND TITLES

- Using Capital Letters B 228
- Using Capital Letters C 229

QUICK REMINDER

Write the following lists on the chalkboard and have students change the proper nouns on the left to proper adjectives to fill in the blanks on the right:

Proper Noun	Proper Adjective
Navy	____ Academy
Vietnam	____ cooking
Spain	____ dancing
China	____ vase
Poland	____ sausage

[The answers are Naval, Vietnamese, Spanish, Chinese, Polish.]

MECHANICS

22d. Do *not* capitalize the names of school subjects, except languages and course names followed by a number.

EXAMPLES **s**ocial **s**tudies, **s**cience, **h**ealth, **a**rt, **S**panish, **E**nglish, **W**oodworking **I**, **C**onsumer **E**ducation **I**

22e. Capitalize proper adjectives.

A ***proper adjective*** is formed from a proper noun. Such adjectives are usually capitalized.

PROPER NOUN	PROPER ADJECTIVE
Mexico	**M**exican carvings
King **A**rthur	**A**rthurian legend
Judaism	**J**udaic laws
Mars	**M**artian landscape

MECHANICS

22f. Capitalize certain abbreviations.

Many abbreviations are capitalized.

EXAMPLES **M.D., Mr., Ms., Mrs., FBI, TV, UN, U.S., NAACP**

However, some abbreviations, especially those for measurements, are not capitalized.

EXAMPLES **in., yd, cu. ft., lb., etc., cc, ml, mm**

 REFERENCE NOTE: Some of the abbreviations in the two sets of examples above are followed by periods and some are not. For information on when to use periods with abbreviations, see rule 23e on pages 589–591.

Capitalize both letters in a two-letter abbreviation for a state name. Do not place a period after the abbreviation.

EXAMPLES **VA NY TX RI**

 REFERENCE NOTE: For more on using abbreviations for state names, see pages 590 and 602.

- To write a description of an imaginary place, using capital letters correctly

22g. Capitalize titles.

(1) Capitalize the title of a person when the title comes before a name.

EXAMPLES **J**udge O'Connor **P**rincipal Walsh
Mayor Santos **D**octor Nakamura
Senator Topping **P**resident Truman

(2) Capitalize a title used alone or following a person's name only when the title refers to someone holding a high office.

EXAMPLES The **S**ecretary of State flew to Madrid.
Judy Klein, club **p**resident, led the meeting.

A title used alone in direct address is usually capitalized.

EXAMPLES Can the cast come off today, **D**octor?
Good morning, **M**a'am. [*or* **m**a'am]

(3) Capitalize a word showing a family relationship when the word is used before or in place of a person's name.

EXAMPLES Are **U**ncle Carlos and **A**unt Rosa here yet?
I wrote to **G**randpa Wilson yesterday.
Either **M**om or **D**ad will drive us to the show.

Do not capitalize a word showing a family relationship when a possessive comes before it.

EXAMPLES My **c**ousin Dena and her **n**iece Leotie made these baskets.

EXERCISE 6 **Correcting Sentences by Capitalizing Words**

For each of the following sentences, write correctly the word that should be capitalized but is not. If a sentence is correct, write *C*.

MECHANICS

A DIFFERENT APPROACH

To provide extra practice for **Rule 22e**, divide the class into two teams. Each team is to make up sentences containing the names of school subjects—both specific (History II) and general (history). The opposing team is to write the sentences made up by the other team as they are dictated. Then have the teams switch assignments.

ADVANCED STUDENTS

Have students work in small groups to analyze the types of changes made in the spellings of adjectives based on proper nouns. They could develop categories giving examples of the various types of changes. [Examples include adding *–n:* Cuban, American; *–ese:* Portuguese, Japanese; and *–ian:* Egyptian, Laotian.]

After students have completed the activity, you may want to discuss with them similarities in the ways of forming proper adjectives.

MECHANICS

REVIEW B

OBJECTIVE

- To correct sentences by using capital letters correctly

CRITICAL THINKING

Analysis

Assign two capitalization rules to each student. Then ask students to find examples of each use of the rule in newspapers or magazines. Have the students cut out the examples and use them to assemble a bulletin-board display of capitalization rules and examples.

While searching for their examples, students might find examples that contradict the capitalization rules they have learned. Explain that newspapers and magazines often use their own styles, which may differ from the standard use.

COMMON ERROR

Problem. Students are sometimes confused about how to capitalize compound proper adjectives.

Solution. Tell students to remember that usually only the word that is formed from a proper noun should be capitalized. Write these phrases on the chalkboard and ask students to supply correct capitalization:

1. japanese-speaking students [Japanese-speaking students]
2. northern-italian cooking [northern-Italian cooking]
3. hawaiian-style music [Hawaiian-style music]

MECHANICS

EXAMPLE 1. I like french bread with onion soup.
1. *French*

1. Velma is taking biology 100 and typing.
2. Reuben's mother, mrs. Santos, owns the new restaurant.
3. Will your uncle be at the party? 3. C
4. Well, doctor Sakamoto, do I need braces?
5. Danish, Yiddish, Icelandic, and Flemish are all germanic languages.
6. The recipe calls for a few slices of swiss cheese.
7. I wonder why *lb.* is the abbreviation for *pound*. 7. C
8. On Saturday afternoon, aunt Latisha will arrive from Savannah.
9. Does professor Jones teach American history?
10. I learned to swim at grandpa Brown's cottage on the lake.

MECHANICS

REVIEW B

Correcting Sentences by Using Capital Letters Correctly

For each of the following sentences, write correctly the word or words that should be capitalized but are not. If a sentence is correct, write *C.*

EXAMPLE 1. The Civil war is sometimes called the war between the states.
1. *War, War Between the States*

1. There is a fountain in the middle of lake Eola.
2. dr. jones teaches at York high school.
3. Some of these folk songs are mexican.
4. the atlantic ocean borders all the states from maine to florida.
5. Someday i would like to bicycle through europe.
6. all of my friends came to the party.
7. Have you visited the Washington monument?
8. Our history class wrote letters to president bush.
9. There's a long detour on highway 50 just east of brooksville, dad.
10. Our first fall camping trip will be in october.

PICTURE THIS

This white rabbit led Alice to Wonderland, but where will he lead you? Racing right behind this scatter-brained, watch-watching rabbit, you follow him to another fantastic place. Write a description of this other wonderland for a child that you know. You can follow the rabbit underground, above ground, or out of this world. Name the land itself, three of its inhabitants, and at least six different structures, geographical features, or other landmarks that you discover. Capitalize all geographical and personal names.

Subject: a fantastic, imaginary place
Audience: a child you know
Purpose: to entertain

MECHANICS

PICTURE THIS

As a prewriting activity, divide the class into small groups to brainstorm possible imaginary places and people. You may wish to read a passage from a favorite fantasy to inspire creative thinking.

For assessment, check to see that students' descriptions address the proper audience and include proper capitalization for all geographical and personal names.

INTEGRATING THE LANGUAGE ARTS

Technology Link. If your students use style or grammar checkers on computers to find grammatical errors, remind them that these programs, although useful, do make mistakes and may incorrectly question the correct use of capital letters in the middle of a sentence.

VISUAL CONNECTIONS

About the Artist. Ralph Steadman is a British cartoonist and illustrator. His distinctive and ingenious work has appeared in newspapers, magazines, and dozens of books, including Flann O'Brien's *The Poor Mouth.*

MECHANICS

COMMON ERROR

Problem. Students may be confused about when to use underlining (italics) or quotation marks with titles.

Solution. Have students study the examples given in the lesson and generate their own rules based on them. [Underlining is used for the titles of books, magazines, newspapers, movies, plays, television programs, works of art, and long musical compositions. Quotation marks are used for the titles of poems, short stories, and individual songs.]

MECHANICS

(4) Capitalize the first and last words and all important words in titles of books, magazines, newspapers, poems, short stories, plays, movies, television programs, works of art, and musical works.

Unimportant words in a title include

- articles (*a, an, the*)
- coordinating conjunctions (*and, but, for, nor, or, so, yet*)
- prepositions of fewer than five letters (such as *by, for, into, with*)

REFERENCE NOTE: For a list of prepositions, see page 407.

TYPE OF NAME	EXAMPLES	
Books	*The Horse and His Boy* *Dust Tracks on a Road*	
Magazines	*Essence* *Reader's Digest*	*Sports Illustrated for Kids*
Newspapers	*Detroit Free Press*	*Tulsa Tribune*
Poems	"The City Is So Big"	"For a Poet"
Short Stories	"The Six Rows of Pompons" "The Day the Sun Came Out"	
Plays	*Once on This Island*	*A Chorus Line*
Movies	*In the Heat of the Night* *An American Tail: Fievel Goes West*	
Television Programs	*A Different World* *Step by Step*	*Star Trek: The Next Generation*
Works of Art	*Delfina and Dimas*	*Forever Free*
Musical Works	"Oh, What a Beautiful Morning" *Peter and the Wolf*	

MECHANICS

REFERENCE NOTE: For guidelines on using italics (underlining) and quotation marks with titles, see pages 613–614 and 622.

REVIEW C

OBJECTIVE

- To proofread a paragraph to correct errors in capitalization

NOTE: The article *the* before a title is not capitalized unless it is the first word of the title.

EXAMPLES Do you read the *Sacramento Bee?*
Grandmother showed me an article in *The Workbasket.*

EXERCISE 7 **Writing Titles for Imaginary Works**

Create a title for each item described below. Be sure each title is capitalized correctly.

1. a movie about a Native American detective who solves a murder mystery
2. a magazine for people interested in video games
3. a book about choosing the best breed of dog as a pet for your family
4. a song about saving the rain forests
5. a painting about life in the United States

EXERCISE 8 **Correcting Sentences by Capitalizing Titles**

For each of the following sentences, correct any errors you find in the capitalization of a title. If a sentence is correct, write *C*. Words that should be capitalized or lower-cased are underscored.

EXAMPLE 1. Mom gave me an article called "The Importance Of Fitness."
1. *"The Importance of Fitness"*

1. "Heart <u>And</u> Soul" is the only piano duet we can play.
2. Do you read *National <u>geographic</u> World*?
3. My little sister loves *<u>the</u> Cat in the Hat.*
4. I saw *Around the World <u>In</u> Eighty Days* on television.
5. We enjoyed *The Cosby <u>show</u>* last night.

REVIEW C **Proofreading a Paragraph to Correct Errors in Capitalization**

Proofread the following paragraph, correcting any errors in capitalization. Words that should be capitalized or lower-cased are underscored.

MECHANICS

ANSWERS

Exercise 7

Answers will vary. Titles should be capitalized correctly. Here are some possibilities:

1. *Detective Echohawk*
2. *Video Riddles*
3. *How to Choose Your Dog*
4. "Save the Trees"
5. *Hometown, USA*

A DIFFERENT APPROACH

Have students write sentences about titles with which they are familiar. They should each write one sentence about each of these topics:

1. a favorite television show
2. a favorite book
3. a favorite movie
4. a movie I don't like
5. a song I like
6. a newspaper
7. a short story I've read

Instruct students to write complete sentences and capitalize titles correctly.

MECHANICS

AT-RISK STUDENTS

You may want to suggest that students use the following topics to involve their families in a naming activity:

1. a well-known poem
2. a favorite magazine
3. a newspaper
4. a famous painting
5. a favorite song

Students could ask family members for their responses to each category. Have students use capital letters correctly to record responses.

EXAMPLE [1] what a huge ship the *titanic* was!
1. *What, Titanic*

[1] This magnificent ocean liner sank on april 15, 1912. [2] For more than seventy years, the *Titanic* lay untouched in the icy waters of the atlantic ocean. [3] Then, on September 1, 1985, Dr. Robert Ballard of the woods hole oceanographic institution and his crew found the ship. [4] To view the ocean floor, the scientists used the remote-controlled vehicle *argo*, shown here being prepared for launching. [5] Once they discovered the ship, they attached a special underwater Sled to *Argo*. [6] The sled, with its lights and camera, provided dr. Ballard with more than twenty thousand photographs of the *Titanic*. [7] In 1986, Dr. Ballard and his team returned to explore the wreck of the british ocean liner once more. [8] Using a mini-submarine, the Team was able to explore the sunken ship. [9] after years of wondering about the *Titanic*, underwater explorers finally found the wreck and uncovered the truth about its fate. [10] In his book *The discovery of the Titanic*, Dr. Ballard tells about his underwater adventures.

THE DISCOVERY OF THE
Titanic

Woods Hole Oceanographic Institution

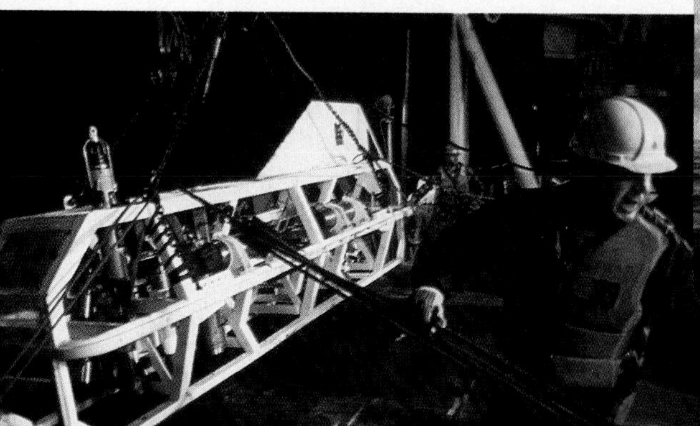

Painting by Ken Marshall from "The Dis of the Titanic" by Dr. R. Ballard, publish Warner-Madison Press.

SEGMENT 4 *(p. 583)*

REVIEW: POSTTEST

OBJECTIVE

- To correct sentences by capitalizing words

COOPERATIVE LEARNING

After students have completed the **Posttest,** have them work in small groups to compare their answers.

When they have finished discussing the sentences, you may want to have students correct their papers by writing the rule that applies to each error made, then writing the correction.

Review: Posttest

Correcting Sentences by Capitalizing Words

For each of the following sentences, write correctly the word or words that should be capitalized but are not.

EXAMPLE **1.** our guest speaker will be mayor Masella.
1. *Our, Mayor*

1. Today i learned the song "simple gifts" from my friend amy, who is a quaker.
2. "Hansel and gretel" is a well-known fairy tale.
3. The kane county fall carnival will be held on saturday, october 19.
4. The trip to japan was led by dr. fujikawa.
5. Let's ask the club treasurer, ms. lee.
6. Have you met professor martínez, rondelle?
7. Luis valdez filmed *the shepherd's play*, a traditional mexican play, for tv. 7. TV
8. The greek god of war was ares.
9. My mother wrote to senator smith about the closing of the base.
10. members of congress often debate issues.
11. Our class pictures will be taken on tuesday.
12. Have you seen any of Mary cassatt's paintings?
13. I didn't know that there are mummies in the american museum of natural history.
14. A venezuelan exchange student will live with our family for eight months.
15. The graduation ceremony at Newberry college was held last week.
16. When is the jewish holiday yom kippur this year?
17. Grandma asked me what i want for my birthday.
18. That movie is about World war II.
19. Next spring uncle William is going to take me on a hiking trip to mount Elbert.
20. Darnell took a raft trip on the Colorado river.

MECHANICS

MECHANICS

SUMMARY STYLE SHEET

Names of Persons

Mae Jemison	an astronaut
Gary Soto	a writer
Maria Tallchief	a dancer

Geographical Names

Levittown	a town in New York
Fayette County	a county in Kentucky
Hawaiian Islands	islands in the Pacific Ocean
Israel	a country
in the West	heading west
Rhine River	a river in Germany
Twenty-first Street	a busy street
Everglades National Park	a park in Florida
the Green Mountains	camping in the mountains

Names of Organizations, Teams, Businesses, Institutions, Government Bodies

the Rotary Club	a service club
Texas Longhorns	a baseball team
General Mills	a large company
Largo High School	my dad's high school
Department of Agriculture	a department of the government

Names of Historical Events and Periods, Special Events, Holidays, Calendar Items

the Revolutionary War	a long war
the Stone Age	an age long ago
Fourth of July	a national holiday
the Super Bowl	a football game
March	a rainy month

Names of Nationalities, Races, Peoples, Religions

Vietnamese	a nationality
Mohawk	a Native American people
Caucasian	a race
Christianity	a religion
God	gods in Greek myths

(continued)

MECHANICS

SUMMARY STYLE SHEET *(continued)*

Brand Names

Cheerios	a **b**owl of **c**ereal
Schwinn	a ten-speed **b**icycle

Names of Ships, Airplanes and Spacecraft, Buildings, Monuments, and Awards

***Q**ueen **M**ary*	a **s**hip
***E**nola **G**ay*	an **a**irplane
***A**pollo*	a **s**pacecraft
Plaza **H**otel	a **h**otel
Nobel **P**rize	a **p**rize
Civil **R**ights **M**emorial	a **m**onument

Names of Heavenly Bodies

Mars, **E**arth	from the **e**arth to the **s**un
Ursa **M**ajor	a **c**onstellation
the **M**ilky **W**ay	our **g**alaxy

Names of Languages, School Subjects

Art I	an **a**rt class
Spanish	a modern **l**anguage
World **H**istory II	a **h**istory course

Titles

Governor Wilder	the **g**overnor of Virginia
the **P**resident of the United States	the **p**resident of the club
Aunt Janell	my favorite **a**unt
***J**ulie of the **W**olves*	a **n**ovel
***T**ime*	a **m**agazine
the ***N**ashville **B**anner*	a **n**ewspaper
"**T**he **M**edicine **B**ag"	a **s**hort story
"**F**ire and **I**ce"	a **p**oem
***P**laces in the **H**eart*	a **m**ovie
***G**et a **L**ife*	a television **p**rogram
***Y**oung **W**oman with a **W**ater **J**ug*	a **p**ainting
*"**T**o a **W**ild **R**ose"*	a **s**ong

MECHANICS

SEGMENT 1 *(pp. 586–587)*

DIAGNOSTIC TEST

OBJECTIVE

- To insert end marks, commas, semicolons, and colons as needed in sentences

Teacher's ResourceBank™

RESOURCES

FOR THE WHOLE CHAPTER

- Chapter Review Form A 246
- Chapter Review Form B 247
- Assessment Portfolio
  - Mechanics Pretests 463–470
  - Mechanics Mastery Tests 487–494

CHAPTER OVERVIEW

The first part of this chapter discusses end marks and abbreviations. The **Writing Application** asks students to write monologues that use punctuation to express feelings. Then comma rules are presented, followed by rules for the use of semicolons and colons. The **Review: Posttest** at the end of the chapter offers students the opportunity to test their mastery of punctuation marks.

This chapter can be integrated with any composition chapter, especially during the proofreading stage of writing assignments.

MECHANICS

23 PUNCTUATION

End Marks, Commas, Semicolons, Colons

MECHANICS

Diagnostic Test

Using End Marks, Commas, Semicolons, and Colons to Punctuate Sentences Correctly

Punctuation marks are missing in the following sentences. Write the word before each missing punctuation mark and add the correct mark.

EXAMPLE **1.** I read my library book studied my spelling words and finished my math homework
1. *book, words, homework.*

1. Flora, please pass the salsa.
2. Do you think it will rain tomorrow, Fred?
3. We are learning about meteorology, the study of weather.
4. The shirts come in the following colors: blue, green, brown, and red.

SEGMENT 2 *(pp. 587–593)*

END MARKS Rules 23a–23e

OBJECTIVES

- To add the appropriate end marks to sentences and abbreviations
- To correct paragraphs by adding the proper end marks to sentences

23a

5. Yasunari Kawabata won the 1968 Nobel Prize in literature; he was the first Japanese writer to win the prize.
6. Watch out!
7. I wish I could go to camp this summer, but I have to stay home to watch my brother.
8. The scouts will swim, ride horses, and play tennis.
9. I taught Zachary how to swim.
10. Mrs. Sanchez is our substitute teacher, for Mr. Arico is on jury duty.
11. My youngest sister was born on April 12, 1990.
12. She is a bright, lively child.
13. His address is 2330 River Rd., Sterling, VA 22170.
14. The Mandan and Hidatsa peoples in North Dakota harvested wild rice, and they traded it for buffalo hides and dried meat.
15. Have you ever been to San Francisco, California?
16. Well, my favorite actress is Jasmine Guy.
17. Connie Chung, a national newscaster, was born in Washington, D.C.
18. I get up at 6:00 A.M. on school days.
19. Yes, a taco is a fried, folded tortilla.
20. The meeting will be held Sunday, February 28, 1993, at 2:00 P.M.

MECHANICS

End Marks

An ***end mark*** is a punctuation mark placed at the end of a sentence. *Periods, question marks,* and *exclamation points* are end marks. Periods are also used after some abbreviations.

23a. Use a period at the end of a statement.

EXAMPLES French and Creole are the official languages of Haiti.
I will write to you soon.

USING THE DIAGNOSTIC TEST

Use the **Diagnostic Test** to determine students' understanding of the correct use of punctuation. Keep in mind that students who can punctuate the test correctly may not transfer this knowledge to their writing. Thus, it may be necessary to examine students' writing to determine which types of punctuation study would be helpful for the class.

You can use the results of the test to decide which segments to teach directly and which ones to assign to cooperative-learning groups.

MECHANICS

Teacher's ResourceBank™

RESOURCES

END MARKS

QUICK REMINDER

Write the following examples of the four types of sentences on the chalkboard and ask students to supply the appropriate punctuation:

1. Where are you going[?] (question)
2. She likes broccoli[.] (statement)
3. That's a great idea[!] (exclamation)
4. Shut the door[.] (command)

Point out to students that the period and exclamation point are sometimes interchangeable, depending on the emotion expressed in the sentence.

LEP/ESL

General Strategies. In most languages, punctuation is generally the same as in English, but some differences do exist. A period is a vertical line in Hindi, a circle in Japanese, and four dots in Aramaic. In many languages, such as Greek, Korean, Persian, and Arabic, the period is slightly raised. The Greek question mark looks like an English semicolon, and Spanish questions and exclamations have end marks at both ends of the sentence, with the first end mark inverted. Differences such as these could cause ESL students to make errors when using English end marks.

MECHANICS

23b. Use a question mark at the end of a question.

EXAMPLES Have you heard Gloria Estefan's new song**?**
Where should I meet you**?**

23c. Use an exclamation point at the end of an exclamation.

EXAMPLES What a cute kitten that is**!**
This egg-drop soup is delicious**!**

23d. Use either a period or an exclamation point at the end of a request or a command.

EXAMPLES Please sit down**.** [a request]
Sit down**!** [a command]

MECHANICS

EXERCISE 1 **Correcting Sentences by Adding End Marks**

Write the last word of each sentence, and add a period, a question mark, or an exclamation point.

EXAMPLE **1.** What time is it
1. *it?*

1. When does the bus come?
2. What a great game that was!
3. Did you bring your lunch today?
4. Hyo was born in Korea.
5. I don't understand the assignment.

EXERCISE 2 **Correcting Paragraphs by Adding Capital Letters and End Marks**

Decide where the sentences in the following paragraphs begin and end. Rewrite each paragraph, providing the needed capital letters and end marks.

EXAMPLE what an ancient art weaving is
What an ancient art weaving is!

23 b–e

have you ever been to Hawaii?the first Europeans who landed there found chiefs dressed in beautiful feather cloaks feathers for cloaks like the one on the left came from thousands of birds different colored feathers were arranged in royal designs then the feathers were attached to a base of woven fibers cloaks were worn into battle and ceremonies most of the islanders did not wear such fine garments

nowadays colorful prints like the ones on the right are worn by all kinds of people on the islands every Friday is Aloha Friday on that day many people wear Hawaiian prints and live flowers wouldn't it be fun if all the students in our school wore clothes to show their heritage once a week?

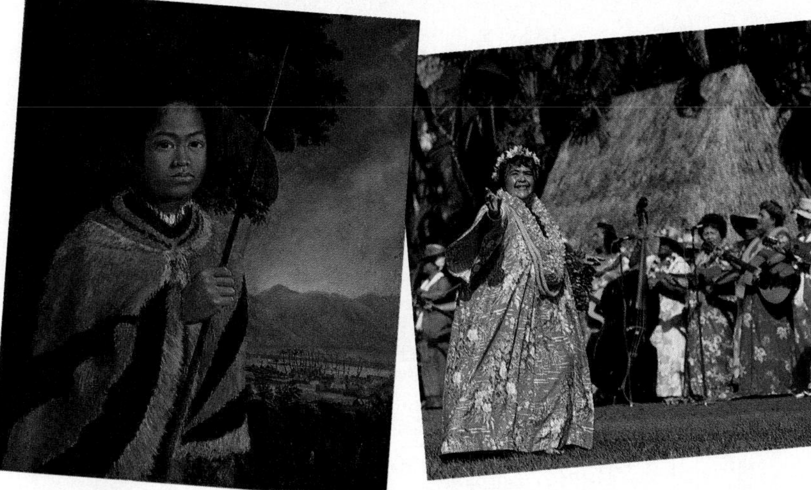

Mrs. Heston Wrenn, in memory of Dr. C. Montague Cooke, Jr.

23e. Use a period after certain abbreviations.

TYPES OF ABBREVIATIONS	EXAMPLES
Personal Names	I. M. Pei N. Scott Momaday Vicki L. Ruíz
Titles Used with Names	Mr. Mrs. Ms. Jr. Dr.
Organizations	Assn. Co. Corp. Inc.

MECHANICS

STUDENTS WITH SPECIAL NEEDS

Students with language problems need to learn to identify and generate statements, questions, exclamations, and requests or commands orally before being required to make written corrections.

Present several examples of each kind of sentence orally. Include as much body language and as many facial expressions as you can to reinforce the meaning of each sentence. Then ask for student volunteers to present example sentences to the class.

LEARNING STYLES

Auditory Learners. It may be easier for some students to hear the differences in the sentence types than it is for them to recognize them visually. Give students oral examples of each sentence type and have them identify the types and their proper end marks.

MECHANICS

A DIFFERENT APPROACH

To give students practice in using end marks and abbreviations, ask volunteers to go to the chalkboard to write specific types of sentences containing specific types of abbreviations.

MECHANICS

NOTE: Abbreviations for government agencies and some widely used abbreviations are written without periods. Each letter of such abbreviations is capitalized.

EXAMPLES ASPCA, CIA, CNN, GI, NAACP, PC, RFD, SOS, TV, YMHA

TYPES OF ABBREVIATIONS	EXAMPLES		
Addresses	Ave. P.O. Box	Blvd. Rd.	Ct. St.
Geographical Names	Ark. St. Paul	Colo. P.R.	D.C. U.S.

NOTE: A two-letter state abbreviation without periods is used only when it is followed by a ZIP code. Both letters of the abbreviation are capitalized. No mark of punctuation is used between the abbreviation and the ZIP code.

EXAMPLES Washington, **DC** 20013
San Juan, **PR** 00904

MECHANICS

TYPES OF ABBREVIATIONS	EXAMPLES			
Times	A.M. P.M.	B.C. A.D.	Aug. Sat.	
Units of Measure	ft.	gal.	lb.	sq. mi.

NOTE: Abbreviations for metric units of measure are usually written without periods.

EXAMPLES cc, kg, ml

If you're not sure whether to use periods with an abbreviation, look in a dictionary, an encyclopedia, or another reliable reference source.

WRITING APPLICATION

OBJECTIVE

- To write a monologue and to use correct end marks to express feelings

NOTE: When an abbreviation that has a period ends a sentence, another period is not needed. However, a question mark or an exclamation point is used in such situations if it is needed.

EXAMPLES The game lasted until 8:30 P.M.
Did it start at 5:00 P.M.?

REFERENCE NOTE: For more information on using capital letters for abbreviations, see page 576.

EXERCISE 3 **Correcting Sentences by Adding Punctuation**

Write the following sentences, adding end marks where they are needed.

EXAMPLE 1. Some caterpillars become butterflies
1. *Some caterpillars become butterflies.*

1. Will Mr Highwater be teaching the science course
2. Just after 3:00 P M the sun came out
3. The letter from Ms E J Hunter was dated Fri, Nov 12
4. How heavy the traffic was on First Avenue
5. Do your measuring cups show both ml and oz

MECHANICS

WRITING APPLICATION

Using End Marks Correctly

End marks let your readers understand your purpose at a glance. Compare the following examples. Which end mark shows that the writer is pleased and excited?

This is great news.
This is great news!
This is great news?

ANSWERS

Exercise 3

1. Will Mr. Highwater be teaching the science course?
2. Just after 3:00 P. M. the sun came out.
3. The letter from Ms. E. J. Hunter was dated Fri., Nov. 12.
4. How heavy the traffic was on First Avenue!
5. Do your measuring cups show both ml and oz.?

MECHANICS

WRITING APPLICATION

This activity calls for a script; however, because the script is to include only what one person will say, there is no need to develop any special form for it, as for a dialogue. A single paragraph will do.

CRITICAL THINKING
Application

The exclamation point is the punctuation mark most associated with expressing feeling, but other punctuation marks can express feeling as well. If students overuse the exclamation point, it will make the feeling seem contrived, not real, and will make the punctuation ineffective. Remind students that the assignment calls for a variety of end marks and challenge the students to convey feeling with what is said, as well as with punctuation.

PREWRITING

It might help students if they were to make lists of the potential emotions experienced by their characters (such as surprise, disbelief, ecstasy, and so on). Remind students that people are different. After receiving one million dollars, some might cry, some might laugh out loud, some might shout, and some might not be able to do much of anything.

MECHANICS

The period at the end of the first sentence tells the reader that the writer is simply making a statement. The question mark at the end of the third sentence indicates that the writer questions whether the news is "great." Only the exclamation mark at the end of the second sentence signals the writer's excitement and happiness.

WRITING ACTIVITY

You are a script writer for a popular TV show. You're writing a scene in which one of the characters wins one million dollars in a sweepstakes. Write down the character's response when he or she hears the good news. Use a variety of end marks to help express the character's feelings.

Prewriting First, you'll need to choose a character. You can either make up a character or use one from a TV show you've seen. Next, put yourself in the place of the character. How would that person feel if he or she won a million dollars? Jot down some notes on how you think your character would react. Would he or she give some or all of the money to charity? put it in a bank? buy a boat? fly around the world?

Writing Using your prewriting notes, write a draft of what your character will say. Make your draft at least one page long. Use end punctuation to help express the character's emotions.

Evaluating and Revising Read your character's response aloud. Does it sound realistic? If not, revise it to make it sound more like what a person would actually say. Check to make sure you've used a variety of end marks to express your character's feelings.

Proofreading Check your writing for any errors in grammar, spelling, or punctuation. Be sure that all proper names are correctly spelled and capitalized.

REVIEW A

OBJECTIVE

- To add the appropriate end marks to sentences

COMMON ERROR

Problem. Students often have trouble deciding whether to use a period or an exclamation point at the end of an imperative sentence.

Solution. Remind students that the presence of the word *please* does not differentiate a request from a command. In addition, not all commands require exclamation points. Advise your students to analyze the emotional level or urgency of the sentence. For example, "Feed the dog" does not carry the weight of "Don't drop the baby!"

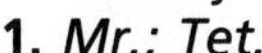 REVIEW A **Using End Marks Correctly**

For each of the following sentences, write the word or words that should be followed by an end mark. Add the proper end mark after each word.

EXAMPLE **1. My neighbor Mr Nhuong showed me this picture of people celebrating the Vietnamese holiday Tet**
1. *Mr.; Tet.*

1. Unlike our New Year's Day, which is always on Jan. 1, Tet can fall on any day late in January or early in February.
2. Moreover, Tet isn't just one single day; the celebration lasts a whole week.
3. Wouldn't you like a week-long holiday?
4. Even here at 8420 Beaconcrest Ave., the Nhuong family still enjoy their traditions.
5. According to Mr. Nhuong, the name of the first person to visit a house can bring good or bad luck to the family.
6. Since my nickname is Lucky, the Nhuongs asked me to be their first visitor and to arrive by 7:00 A.M.
7. Please don't be late.
8. One of the Nhuongs' relatives had flown in from Santa Barbara, Calif., just that morning.
9. Mrs. Nhuong prepared a huge breakfast, and we all sat down to enjoy it.
10. What a great meal that was!

MECHANICS

MECHANICS

Teacher's ResourceBank™

RESOURCES

COMMAS

- Commas with Items in a Series 238
- Commas with Adjectives Before a Noun 239
- Commas with Compound Sentences 240
- Commas with Interrupters 241
- Commas with Introductory Elements 242
- Other Uses of Commas 243

QUICK REMINDER

Write the following sentences on the chalkboard without commas and have your students suggest places where commas should be added:

1. We bought games[,] balloons[,] streamers[,] and colored lights for the party.
2. The students drew pictures[,] framed them for display[,] and waited for the judges.
3. The most talented[,] obedient[,] beautiful[,] and intelligent dog will win the contest.

Remind students that commas not only reinforce natural breaks in sentences but also help make complicated sentences clearer.

MECHANICS

SEGMENT 3 *(pp. 594–604)*

COMMAS Rules 23f–23j

OBJECTIVES

- To proofread sentences and to add commas when necessary
- To write a journal entry with commas used correctly
- To write sentences containing appositives or appositive phrases correctly set off with commas
- To correct dates, addresses, and salutations by adding commas

Commas

End marks separate complete thoughts. Commas separate words or groups of words *within* a complete thought.

Items in a Series

23f. Use commas to separate items in a series.

A ***series*** is three or more items written one after the other. The items may be single words or groups of words.

WORDS IN A SERIES
Sugar, bananas, and citrus are grown in Jamaica. [nouns]
Yesterday I dusted, vacuumed, and mopped. [verbs]
The day was wet, cold, and windy. [adjectives]
GROUPS OF WORDS IN A SERIES
At the beach we swam, built sand castles, and played volleyball. [predicates]
I searched for the lost contact lens in the sink, on the counter, and on the floor. [prepositional phrases]

NOTE: Some writers do not use the comma before *and* in a series. It's a good idea always to use that comma, however. Sometimes the comma is needed to make your meaning clear. Notice how using a comma before *and* changes the meaning in these examples.

EXAMPLES Grandma, Mom, and Dad came to the game. [Three people were at the game.]
Grandma, Mom and Dad came to the game. [Grandma is being told who came to the game.]

MECHANICS

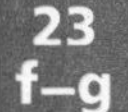
23 f–g

Always be sure that there are at least three items in a series before you add commas. Two items do not need a comma between them.

INCORRECT Today is sunny, and warm.
CORRECT Today is sunny and warm.

When all the items in a series are joined by *and* or *or,* do not use commas to separate them.

EXAMPLES I've seen snakes **and** lizards **and** toads in our yard.
Shall we go bowling **or** rent a movie **or** listen to tapes?

EXERCISE 4 **Proofreading Sentences for the Correct Use of Commas**

Most of the following sentences need commas. If a sentence needs commas, write the word before each missing comma; then add the comma. If a sentence is correct, write *C*.

EXAMPLE **1.** Cora Jack and Tomás all entered the contest.
1. *Cora, Jack,*

1. I finished my dinner, brushed my teeth, and ran out the door.
2. The nurse checked the patient's pulse, took his temperature, and gave him a glass of water.
3. For lunch we had milk, a tuna sandwich, and pears.
4. Jennifer Lawson, La-Doris McClaney, and Sharon Pratt Dixon won Candace Awards in 1991.
5. Marcus plays the piano and the guitar and the drums. 5. C

23g. Use commas to separate two or more adjectives that come before a noun.

EXAMPLES Pita is a round**,** flat bread of the Middle East.
James Earl Jones certainly has a deep**,** strong**,** commanding voice.

MECHANICS

LEP/ESL

General Strategies. In some languages, such as Japanese, Persian, and Arabic, the comma is raised above the line of writing and inverted or reversed. You may find that some of your ESL students will do this when they write in English. Remind them that they should place the comma level with the bottom of the letters, with the tail opening down and curving left.

STUDENTS WITH SPECIAL NEEDS

Students with processing problems have difficulty taking in too many new concepts at one time. The numerous rules of comma usage presented in this chapter might be frustrating if presented simultaneously. Be prepared to spend ample time on each rule before proceeding to the next.

MECHANICS

A DIFFERENT APPROACH

Have each of your students write a series of descriptive sentences on an endangered animal. Emphasize the use of vivid, colorful adjectives. Remind students to use commas correctly when separating adjectives in their sentences. Have the students proofread each other's papers for the proper use of adjectives and commas.

TIMESAVER

When students do the exercises in this chapter, you could have them write the words in one color of ink and then use a different color for punctuation, or you could have them alternate pencil and ink in the same manner. This process will make the punctuation visually striking and easier to check.

MECHANICS

Do not place a comma between an adjective and the noun immediately following it.

INCORRECT I found an old, rusty, bicycle.
CORRECT I found an old, rusty bicycle.

Sometimes the last adjective in a series is closely connected in meaning to the noun. In that case, do not use a comma before the last adjective.

EXAMPLES The tall pine tree swayed in the wind. [not *tall, pine tree*]
Kimchi is a spicy Korean dish made with pickled cabbage. [not *spicy, Korean dish*]

To see whether a comma is needed, add *and* between the adjectives (*tall and pine*, for example). If *and* sounds awkward, don't use a comma.

MECHANICS

EXERCISE 5 Proofreading Sentences for the Correct Use of Commas

For each of the following sentences, write the word that should be followed by a comma; then add the comma. If a sentence is correct, write *C*.

EXAMPLE 1. Mrs. Hirata taught us several beautiful old Japanese folk songs.
1. *beautiful,*

1. His calm, wrinkled face told a story.
2. François Toussaint L'Ouverture was a brilliant, patriotic Haitian leader.
3. The huge, lively kingfish wriggled off the hook.
4. There's a sleek, shiny bicycle in the store window.
5. The sound of the soft, steady rain put me to sleep.
6. We read Chief Black Hawk's moving farewell speech. 6. C
7. After our hike I washed in the cold, clear spring water.
8. May I have some more of that cold, delicious gazpacho soup?

23h

9. The old diary had ragged, yellowed pages.
10. The crowded dining room is filled with people celebrating my parents' anniversary. **10.** C

23h. Use a comma before *and, but, for, or, nor, so,* and *yet* when they join the parts of a compound sentence.

EXAMPLES Theo will bring the potato salad**,** and Sarah will bring the apple juice.
Congress passed the bill**,** but President Bush vetoed it.
I went to bed early**,** for I had a big day ahead of me.

REFERENCE NOTE: If you're not sure that you can recognize a compound sentence, review pages 318 and 357.

In many cases, a very short compound sentence does not need a comma before *and, but,* or *or.*

EXAMPLE I'm tired and I'm hungry.

NOTE: Don't confuse a compound sentence with a simple sentence containing a compound verb. No comma is needed between the parts of a compound verb.

COMPOUND SENTENCE We ran relay races first, and then we ate lunch.
COMPOUND VERB We **ran** relay races first and then **ate** lunch.

REFERENCE NOTE: For more about compound verbs, see pages 353–355.

EXERCISE 6 **Correcting Compound Sentences by Adding Commas**

Some of the following sentences are compound and need to have commas added. If a sentence needs a comma, write the word before the missing comma; then add the comma. If a sentence is correct, write C.

MECHANICS

LEARNING STYLES

Visual Learners. To help students distinguish a compound sentence from a simple sentence with a compound verb, write the following sentence pairs on the chalkboard:

1. Fred loves to eat yet hates meat.
   Fred loves to eat, yet he hates meat.
2. Pam swims often and jogs daily.
   Pam swims often, and she jogs daily.
3. Maria reads books but sees no movies.
   Maria reads books, but she sees no movies.

Underline the subjects with chalk of one color and underline the verbs with another color. Circle the comma in each compound sentence and emphasize that compound sentences have two independent clauses, each of which has a subject and a verb. Therefore, the clauses are separated with a comma and a coordinating conjunction.

MECHANICS

EXAMPLE **1. The storm brought a lot of rain but a tornado did the most damage.**

1. *rain,*

1. At the Native American Heritage Festival, Mary Johns wove baskets from sweet grass, and Alice Billie made rings from beads.
2. The sailboat was almost hidden by the fog, yet we could see part of the mast.
3. Salvador Garcia of Mexico won the 1991 New York City Marathon, and he dedicated his victory to the Mexican people.
4. Would you like to play checkers, or shall we go to the mall instead?
5. I called my friends and told them the news. 5. C
6. Jim practiced the piano piece for hours, for he wanted to do well at the recital.
7. The African American festival Kwanzaa begins the day after Christmas, yet the two holidays are celebrated in very different ways.
8. Neither the students nor their science teacher could make the experiment work. 8. C
9. The old oak tree shaded the house, but the shade kept the grass from growing.
10. The lake contains large fish, and it is also home to several alligators.

MECHANICS

PICTURE THIS

The year is 1910. You are one of the immigrants shown on the next page. You are about to land on Ellis Island, and the Statue of Liberty stands majestically before you. Quickly, before the boat docks, write a journal entry expressing your first impressions of your new country. How does the statue make you feel? What are your hopes and dreams for your new life? In your journal entry, correctly use at least five commas.

MECHANICS

PICTURE THIS

Remind students that the journal entries they are to write for this activity should describe their feelings and not what they see. They may want to use some of the end punctuation covered earlier in the chapter, but as this is an exercise on comma use, students should not be penalized if they misuse end punctuation.

23i

Subject: the Statue of Liberty
Audience: yourself
Purpose: to record your impressions and feelings

Interrupters

23i. Use commas to set off an expression that interrupts a sentence.

Two commas are needed if the expression to be set off comes in the middle of the sentence. One comma is needed if the expression comes first or last.

EXAMPLES My favorite gospel singers, BeBe and CeCe Winans, were on TV last night.
Yes, I'll call back later.
How did you do in karate class today, Kami?

(1) Use commas to set off appositives and appositive phrases that are not needed to understand the meaning of a sentence.

MECHANICS

COMMON ERROR

Problem. Many students will omit the comma that should follow an interrupting expression. This is a particular problem if it involves an appositive that identifies the subject, and the verb directly following makes the sentence sound complete.

Solution. Make a large sentence strip for a sentence containing an appositive phrase. Cut the strip in two places and remove the appositive phrase to show students that the sentence can stand alone without it. Emphasize that when the phrase is reinserted, it must be set off from the sentence by commas. Suggest that students underline or highlight appositive phrases in their written work to make sure the phrases are set off with commas.

MECHANICS

An ***appositive*** is a noun or a pronoun that identifies or explains another noun or pronoun beside it. An ***appositive phrase*** is an appositive with its modifiers.

EXAMPLES **A gymnast, Mrs. Shaw, will coach us.** [The appositive *Mrs. Shaw* identifies who the gymnast will be.]

This book is about geology, the science of the earth and its rocks. [*The science of the earth and its rocks* is an appositive phrase that explains the word *geology.*]

Do not use commas when an appositive is needed to understand the meaning of a sentence.

EXAMPLES **My cousin Roberto lives in Puerto Rico.** [I have more than one cousin and am using his name to identify which cousin I mean.]

My cousin, Roberto, lives in Puerto Rico. [I have only one cousin and am using his name as extra information.]

MECHANICS

EXERCISE 7 **Writing Sentences with Appositives**

In the painting on the next page, young people are enjoying themselves at an outdoor party. Some of the people are dancing. Others are talking or having refreshments. Write five sentences about the people at the party. In your sentences, use five of the following groups of words as appositives. Insert commas wherever they are needed.

Eliza Wolcott	the happiest couple on the dance floor
the best dancer	the girl in the striped dress
the sounds of people having fun	a beautiful place for a party
a quiet spot for conversation	
a refreshing drink	

EXAMPLE *You can hear the murmuring voices and bursts of laughter, the sounds of people having fun.*

MECHANICS

ANSWERS

Exercise 7

Sentences will vary. Here are some possibilities:

1. The woman leaning over the bench, the best dancer, is taking a break.
2. Several people are sitting around the table, a quiet spot for conversation.
3. The dancers on the left, the happiest couple on the dance floor, seem to be posing.
4. The person in the foreground, the girl in the striped dress, is enjoying the party.
5. Everyone likes the *Moulin de la Gallette,* a beautiful place for a party.

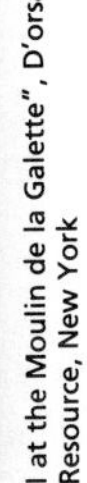

Pierre-Auguste Renoir, "Ball at the Moulin de la Galette", D'orsay Musee, Paris. Giruadon/Art Resource, New York

(2) Use commas to set off words used in direct address.

Using the name of the person to whom you are speaking is using ***direct address.*** Commas are used to set off words used in direct address.

EXAMPLES Ms. Jacobs, please explain the assignment.
Do you know who Santa Anna was, Beth?
You're right, Inés, he was a Mexican general.

(3) Use a comma after such words as *well, yes, no,* and *why* when they begin a sentence.

EXAMPLES Well, I'll help you.
Yes, the table is set.
Why, there's Yoko!

EXERCISE 8 Correcting Sentences by Adding Commas

For each of the following sentences, write each word that should be followed by a comma; then add the comma.

MECHANICS

VISUAL CONNECTIONS
Ball at the Moulin de la Galette

About the Artist. Pierre Auguste Renoir (1841–1919) was one of the innovators of French Impressionism. Among his innovations is the use of pure, unmixed colors—an integral element of impressionist technique.

COOPERATIVE LEARNING

To give students extra practice in punctuating phrases and clauses, separate the class into groups of three to four students. Give each group five blank index cards and ask them to write a phrase or a clause on each card. You could write the following examples on the chalkboard:

1. who found a million dollars
2. which made him scream
3. with no one else in sight
4. looking around carefully
5. that she discovered

Have the groups exchange their sets of cards to use the phrases and clauses on their acquired sets to write correctly punctuated stories. You may want to have one member of each group read the group's story to the rest of the class.

MECHANICS

INTEGRATING THE LANGUAGE ARTS

Literature Link. You may want to have students read a short story such as "President Cleveland, Where Are You?" by Robert Cormier. Have your students find and identify in the story the commas used in compound sentences, introductory expressions, phrases, and so forth. You may want to pair students for this activity.

Next, you can explain to students that authors use punctuation stylistically. Have students choose another short story from their textbooks and have the students analyze the use of commas in a similar way. Ask for volunteers to offer their findings.

MECHANICS

EXAMPLE 1. Will Ruben her oldest brother meet us at the park tomorrow?
1. *Ruben, brother,*

1. Wood Buffalo National Park, the world's largest national park, is in Canada.
2. The park was named for the wood buffalo, a species slightly smaller than the plains buffalo.
3. Michi, will you read the haiku you wrote?
4. Why, you and I were born on the same day!
5. If you mow the lawn, Kelly, I'll rake the clippings.
6. I read about whooping cranes in *Natural History*, a magazine about nature.
7. Did you bring the tickets, Jorge?
8. Yes, I have them right here.
9. Well, I'm glad you didn't forget them.
10. My cousin Velma, my favorite relative, wants to visit Ghana.

MECHANICS

23j. Use commas in certain conventional situations.

(1) Use commas to separate items in dates and addresses.

EXAMPLES Bill Cosby was born on July 12, 1937, in Philadelphia, Pennsylvania.
Saturday, May 10, will be the day of the soccer playoff.
My aunt lives at 41 Jefferson Street, Northfield, Minnesota.

Notice that a comma separates the last item in a date or in an address from the words that follow it. However, a comma does *not* separate a month and a day (*July 12*) or a house number and a street name (*41 Jefferson Street*).

NOTE: Use the correct ZIP code on every envelope you address. No punctuation is used between the state abbreviation and the ZIP code.

EXAMPLE Cerritos, CA 90701

REVIEW B

OBJECTIVE

- To proofread a letter for comma errors and to correct those errors

A DIFFERENT APPROACH

Have groups of students use a television and a VCR to tape several small portions of dialogue that they will then transcribe, or students could use a radio and a tape recorder. Have the students then punctuate the dialogue. To shorten this assignment, you could also specify that each group concentrate on only one portion of dialogue. Groups can then present their tapes and punctuated transcriptions to the class. Ask if others in the class can suggest variations.

(2) Use a comma after the salutation of a friendly letter and after the closing of any letter.

EXAMPLES **Dear Grandma and Grandpa,** **Love,**
Dear Tyrone, **Sincerely,**

EXERCISE 9 **Using Commas Correctly in Conventional Situations**

Write the following items and sentences, inserting commas where they are needed.

1. Yours truly,
2. Shirley Chisholm was born on November 30, 1924.
3. The first woman principal chief of the Cherokee Nation is Wilma Mankiller, who was born near Rocky Mountain, Oklahoma.
4. Write to me at 327 Adams Way, Darrouzett, TX 79024.
5. The Harvest Carnival is on Friday, October 29, 1993.

REVIEW B **Proofreading a Letter for the Correct Use of Commas**

The following letter contains ten errors in the use of commas. Rewrite the letter, adding or deleting commas as needed.

EXAMPLES **[1] July, 6, 1993**
1. ***July 6, 1993***
[2] Dear Tom
2. ***Dear Tom,***

[1] Well, on July 4, 1993, Aunt Lil kept her promise and took me up in her airplane. [2] Wow! What a view of the canyons, valleys, and plateaus we had! [3] We were lucky, and saw a small herd of mustangs on a hill. [4] Aunt Lil circled above the horses, the plane's shadow frightened the stallion, and the whole herd stampeded. [5] Tails, and manes and hooves flew in a storm of dust all the way down into the valley. [6] One

MECHANICS

MECHANICS

SEGMENT 4 *(pp. 604–606)*

SEMICOLONS Rule 23k

OBJECTIVE

- To identify sentences needing semicolons and to use semicolons correctly

tiny black colt trailed behind, but his swift, sturdy mother soon nudged him onward. [7] In a moment the mustangs, descendants of the fiery steeds of the Spanish conquistadors, were galloping into the woods. [8] I wish you could have seen them, Tom! [9] At least I remembered my camera; so here is a picture of those beautiful horses.

[10] Yours truly,

Sal

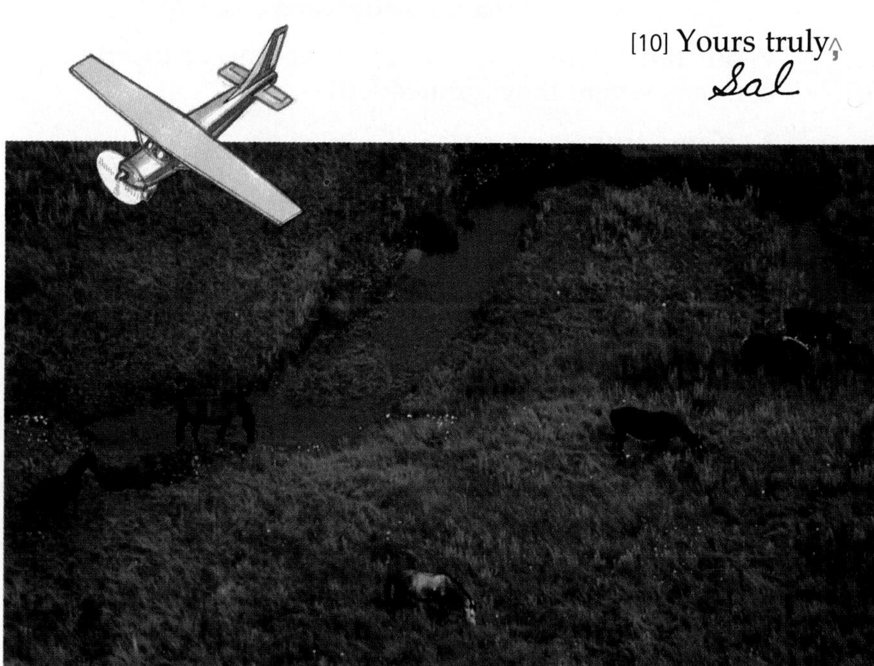

Semicolons

A semicolon is part period and part comma. Like a period, it separates complete thoughts. Like a comma, it separates items within a sentence.

23k. Use a semicolon between parts of a compound sentence if they are not joined by *and, but, or, nor, for, so,* or *yet.*

SEMICOLONS

- Semicolons 244

MECHANICS

23k

EXAMPLES Todd's report is on Arizona**;** mine is on Utah.
The rain clouds are moving in quickly**;** let's head home.

NOTE: Don't overuse semicolons. Sometimes it is better to separate a compound sentence into two sentences rather than to use a semicolon.

ACCEPTABLE Parrots make interesting pets; some can learn to repeat whole sentences or whistle tunes.
BETTER Parrots make interesting pets. Some can learn to repeat whole sentences or whistle tunes.

EXERCISE 10
Proofreading Sentences for the Correct Use of Semicolons

Most of the following sentences have commas where there should be semicolons. If a sentence needs a semicolon, write the words before and after the missing semicolon; then insert the semicolon. If a sentence is correct, write *C*.

Carets indicate placement of semicolons.

EXAMPLE 1. Mary Vaux treasured her box of watercolor paints, she took it with her everywhere she went.
1. *paints; she*

1. On family holidays each year, Mary Vaux visited the Canadian Rockies, and there she began to paint wildflowers. 1. C
2. She loved mountain climbing,^ she often crossed rugged areas to find new wildflowers.
3. She painted her flowers from life, for she did not like to rely on pencil sketches. 3. C
4. You can see five of her paintings on the next page,^ aren't they beautiful?
5. Painting A shows a western red lily,^ it withers quickly when it is picked.
6. Painting B is of a bottle gentian,^ a fall flower, it grows in bogs and swamps. 6. [*or* flower; it]

MECHANICS

QUICK REMINDER

Write the following sentences on the chalkboard and have your students indicate where semicolons should be placed to make the sentences correct:

1. That new movie was a flop[;] it didn't appeal to teenagers.
2. Mara went to see it[;] she said it was really boring.
3. I don't go to the movies often[;] the price of tickets is too high.

LEP/ESL

General Strategies. In English, two independent clauses cannot be separated with only a comma; a semicolon or a comma plus a conjunction is needed. However, in some other languages, such as Arabic, Russian, and Turkish, a comma may set off two independent clauses. You may find that some of your ESL students will use a comma where they should use a semicolon.

MECHANICS

LEARNING STYLES

Auditory Learners. It is often easier for students to identify the two complete thoughts in a run-on sentence when the sentence is heard, rather than read. When you introduce run-on sentences, first read them orally and ask students where they think one complete thought ends and another begins. Point out that the semicolon would be inserted at that point.

MECHANICS

7. American wisteria is a climbing plant, and you can see in Painting C that it has many showy flowers. 7. C
8. Painting D shows blossoms of the American waterlily opening in early morning, their aroma draws insects.
9. In Painting E is the vine of Carolina jessamine, it spreads its fragrant flowers through treetops.
10. Mary Vaux is known as the "Audubon of North American wildflowers," for she painted more than seven hundred species. 10. C

MECHANICS

D

Mary Vaux Walcott/National Museum of American Art

SEGMENT 5 *(pp. 607–609)*

COLONS Rules 23l–23n

OBJECTIVE

- To correct sentences by adding colons

Colons

A colon usually signals that more information follows.

23l. Use a colon before a list of items, especially after expressions such as *the following* and *as follows.*

EXAMPLES These are the winners of the poetry contest**:** Carmen Santiago, Justin Douglass, and Steven Yellowfeather.

Pack the following items for your overnight trip**:** a toothbrush, toothpaste, and your hairbrush.

The order of the colors seen through a prism is as follows**:** red, orange, yellow, green, blue, indigo, violet.

Never use a colon immediately after a preposition or a verb. Instead, either omit the colon or reword the sentence.

INCORRECT My report includes: a table of contents, three chapters, illustrations, and a list of sources.

CORRECT My report includes a table of contents, three chapters, illustrations, and a list of sources.

CORRECT My report includes the following parts**:** a table of contents, three chapters, illustrations, and a list of sources.

23m. Use a colon between the hour and the minute when you write the time.

EXAMPLES 8**:**55 A.M., 9**:**15 P.M., 6**:**22 this morning

23n. Use a colon after the salutation of a business letter.

EXAMPLES Dear Sir or Madam**:** Dear Mrs. Jordan**:**
Dear Sales Manager**:** To Whom It May Concern**:**

Teacher's ResourceBank™

RESOURCES

COLONS

QUICK REMINDER

To show students that colons often precede lists of items or statements that explain other statements, write the following sentences on the chalkboard and omit the colons. Ask students to indicate where colons should be placed in the sentences.

1. The list of items needed for the trip is as follows[:] a flashlight, a sleeping bag, and a compass.
2. She reminded the first-grader of the rules for crossing streets[:] Stop, look, and listen.
3. He followed Ben Franklin's advice[:] "A penny saved is a penny earned."
4. The school is divided into three classes[:] sixth, seventh, and eighth grades.

MECHANICS

REVIEW C

OBJECTIVE

- To proofread a letter for errors in punctuation and to rewrite the letter by inserting correct punctuation where needed

LEP/ESL

General Strategies. Some students might confuse the colon and the semicolon or think that they are interchangeable. Tell your students that a colon usually indicates the part of the sentence the writer wants to emphasize, whereas a semicolon helps the reader avoid confusion.

You may want to make and display a poster illustrating the uses of the colon and the semicolon. Students can refer to the poster throughout the year.

LESS-ADVANCED STUDENTS

Some students will make the error of using a colon between a verb and a series of items. To illustrate that a colon is not used between a verb and a series of items, write the following sentences on the chalkboard:

1. I have the following classes: math, English, and history.
2. My classes are as follows: math, English, and history.
3. My classes are math, English, and history.

Point out that the first two sentences need colons, but that a colon is not needed in the third sentence.

MECHANICS

EXERCISE 11 **Using Colons Correctly**

If one of the following items needs a colon, copy the word the colon should follow; then add the colon. For numbers, write the entire number and insert the colon. If a sentence is correct, write *C*.

EXAMPLE **1. Bring the following items to class your notebook, a pencil, and your textbook.**
1. *class:*

1. We visited the following cities: Bayamón, Ponce, and San Juan.
2. A good baby sitter should have the following qualities: promptness, an interest in children, and common sense.
3. To stay healthy, you should not smoke or chew tobacco. 3. C
4. Add these items to your shopping list: tissues, toothpaste, and shampoo. 5. C
5. A good friend must be loving, loyal, and honest.
6. The first bell rings at 8:10 A.M.
7. Your homework includes studying your spelling words, reading one chapter, and working on your composition. 7. C
8. The recipe for Brunswick stew called for these ingredients: lamb, carrots, potatoes, and onions.
9. The next show begins at 6:00 P.M.
10. Dear Sir or Madam:

MECHANICS

REVIEW C **Proofreading a Letter for the Correct Use of End Marks, Commas, Semicolons, and Colons**

Proofread the following letter for errors in punctuation. Rewrite the letter, adding the necessary end marks, commas, semicolons, and colons.

EXAMPLE [1] **1200 E Halifax Avenue**
Baltimore, MD 21213
1. *1200 E. Halifax Avenue*
Baltimore, MD 21213

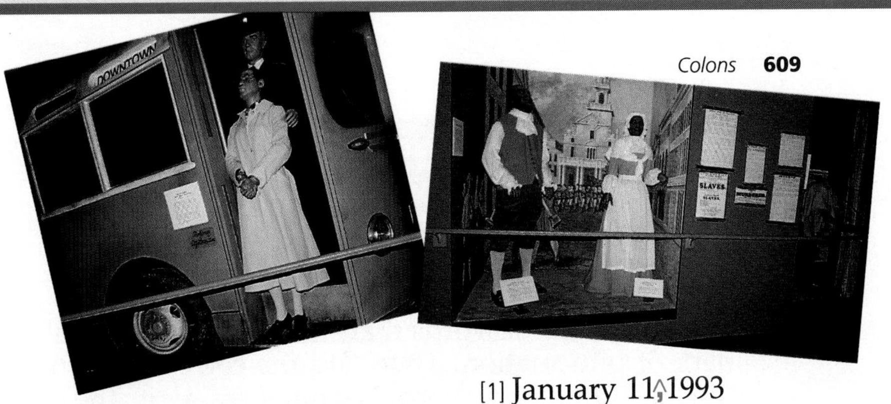

[1] January 11, 1993

Superintendent of Schools
Baltimore City Board of Education
200 E. North Avenue
Baltimore, MD 21202

[2] Dear Superintendent:

[3] Would your students be interested in visiting an African American wax museum? [4] The only one of its kind is right here in Baltimore. [5] The Great Blacks in Wax Museum features life-size wax models of famous African Americans. [6] These wax images include leaders in education, civil rights, and science. [7] The museum displays statues of the following people: Rosa Parks, Phillis Wheatley, and Crispus Attucks (shown in the enclosed publicity photographs), Carter G. Woodson, Dred Scott, Harriet Tubman, Booker T. Washington, Frederick Douglass, and many others.

[8] During Black History Month, our company offers students and teachers discount tours of the museum; tours of other historic attractions are also available. [9] For more information, please call me between 8:30 A.M. and 5:30 P.M.

[10] Yours truly,

Jane Lee Harper

Jane Lee Harper
President
Uhuru Guided Tours

MECHANICS

INTEGRATING THE LANGUAGE ARTS

Mechanics and Speaking. To reinforce the use of colons in statements that introduce quotations and to give students practice in speaking before a group, have them select quotations that they like. If they need help, refer them to Bartlett's *Familiar Quotations* or *Poor Richard's Almanac.* Then have them write sentences containing the quotations. [For example, "I'll never forget Patrick Henry's stirring words: 'Give me liberty or give me death!'"]

Have students write their sentences on the chalkboard. Then have students read the quotations and tell why they chose those quotations. Check sentences for correct colon usage.

MECHANICS

SEGMENT 6 *(pp. 610–611)*

REVIEW: POSTTEST

OBJECTIVE

- To correct sentences by adding end marks, commas, semicolons, and colons

COOPERATIVE LEARNING For additional review, divide the class into two teams. Read sentences to each team and ask for the appropriate end marks. Limit the time each team has per sentence. Team members who give the correct answer get another turn. If a team member misses the answer, the opposing team gets to try the sentence.

MECHANICS

Review: Posttest

Using End Marks, Commas, Semicolons, and Colons Correctly

Write the word or words that should be followed by a mark of punctuation. Then add the correct punctuation mark after each word. For numbers, write the entire number and insert the correct punctuation mark.

EXAMPLE **1.** Mr. Cotton my next-door neighbor asked me to pick up his mail while he is away
1. *Cotton, neighbor, away.*

1. The mangos and papayas and avocados will make a good fruit salad.
2. Ms. Jee gave a short, clear history of Korea.
3. Ray Charles, the popular singer and musician, became blind at the age of seven.
4. I have registered for classes in photography, ceramics, and weaving.
5. When will dinner be ready?
6. Ted mowed the lawn, cleaned the garage, and painted the shed.
7. Here comes a tornado!
8. Cheryl will take gymnastics; Eddie will take piano lessons.
9. Would 6:30 P.M. be too early?
10. This Zuni ring was made in Santa Fe, NM.
11. I finished the letter, but I haven't proofread it yet.
12. Sincerely,
13. We will learn about the U.S. court system; then we will visit the county courthouse.
14. Sara, Eric, and Manuel can speak both Spanish and English.
15. Hurry, get me some ice!
16. Yes, I did clean my room.
17. When you go cross-country skiing, bring the following items: skis, boots, poles, and ski wax.

MECHANICS

18. Shall we leave at 9:00 A.M.?
19. Mr. Pak, when is the Chinese New Year?
20. The Scouts' Annual Dinner will be held February 19, 1993.

SUMMARY OF USES OF THE COMMA

23f Use commas to separate items in a series—words and groups of words.

23g Use commas to separate two or more adjectives that come before a noun.

23h Use a comma before *and*, *but*, *for*, *or*, *nor*, *so*, and *yet* when they join the parts of a compound sentence.

23i Use commas to set off an expression that interrupts a sentence.

(1) Use commas to set off appositives and appositive phrases that aren't needed to understand the meaning of a sentence.

(2) Use commas to set off words used in direct address.

(3) Use a comma after words such as *well*, *yes*, *no*, and *why* when they begin a sentence.

23j Use a comma in certain conventional situations.

(1) Use commas to separate items in dates and addresses.

(2) Use a comma after the salutation of a friendly letter and after the closing of any letter.

MECHANICS

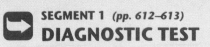

SEGMENT 1 *(pp. 612–613)*

DIAGNOSTIC TEST

OBJECTIVE

- To proofread and revise sentences for the correct use of underlining (italics), quotation marks, apostrophes, and hyphens

Teacher's ResourceBank™

RESOURCES

FOR THE WHOLE CHAPTER

- Chapter Review Form A 261–262
- Chapter Review Form B 263–264
- Assessment Portfolio
  - Mechanics Pretests 463–470
  - Mechanics Mastery Tests 487–494

CHAPTER OVERVIEW

This chapter provides students with practice in using several marks of punctuation. The section following the **Diagnostic Test** explains the use of underlining (italics) for titles. The next section helps students to distinguish between indirect and direct quotations, to punctuate and capitalize direct quotations, and to use quotation marks with titles of short works. The final section before the **Review: Posttest** explains the use of apostrophes in possessives, in contractions, and in the plural forms of letters, numerals, signs, and words used as such.

You may want to integrate the section on direct and indirect quotations with **Chapter 5: "Creative Writing."** Likewise, you may want to teach the sections on punctuating titles when you teach **Chapter 8: "Writing About Literature."**

USING THE DIAGNOSTIC TEST

To avoid unnecessary reteaching, analyze students' responses and assign specific sections to individuals or groups. For students who do exceptionally well on the **Diagnostic Test,** you may want to assign only **Reviews A** and **B, Picture This,** and **Writing Application.**

MECHANICS

24 PUNCTUATION

Underlining (Italics), Quotation Marks, Apostrophes, Hyphens

Diagnostic Test

Using Underlining (Italics), Quotation Marks, Apostrophes, and Hyphens

Each of the following sentences contains one error in the use of underlining (italics), quotation marks, apostrophes, or hyphens. Write each sentence correctly.

The ‸ symbol indicates a hyphen.

EXAMPLE **1.** "Its important for everyone to vote," Jesse Jackson said.
1. *"It's important for everyone to vote," Jesse Jackson said.*

1. I like to sing "This Land Is Your Land."
2. Washington's largest city is named for Chief Seattle.

SEGMENT 2 *(pp. 613–615)*

UNDERLINING (ITALICS) Rule 24a

OBJECTIVE

- To use underlining (italics) correctly in sentences

24a

3. "The Siamese Cat."

3. Chapter Two is called The Siamese Cat.
4. I haven't read the book Treasure Island yet.
5. "I remember making a barometer in the fourth grade. "I had to start over twice before it would work," I said.
6. "Deva, will you please show me how to make a weather vane"? asked Todd.
7. "It took me only forty five minutes to make a sundial," Carlos remarked.
8. We built a model airplane, but it crashed on it's test flight.
9. All student's projects are due next Friday.
10. "Everyones project must be in on time," Mrs. Tolliver said.

Underlining (Italics)

Italics are printed letters that lean to the right—*like this.* When you write or type, you show that a word should be *italicized* by underlining it. If your writing were printed, the typesetter would set the underlined words in italics. For example, if you typed

Zora Neale Hurston wrote Mules and Men.

the sentence would be printed like this:

Zora Neale Hurston wrote *Mules and Men.*

NOTE: If you use a personal computer, you can probably set words in italics yourself. Most word processing software and many printers can produce italic type.

24a. Use underlining (italics) for titles of books, plays, periodicals, films, television programs, works of art, long musical works, ships, aircraft, and spacecraft.

MECHANICS

Teacher's ResourceBank™

RESOURCES

UNDERLINING (ITALICS)
- Italics (Underlining) 253

QUICK REMINDER

Write the following list on the chalkboard:

1. Leigh Botts
2. Dances With Wolves
3. Beverly Hills 90210
4. A fantasy novel
5. The Hobbit
6. Shel Silverstein's poem "Sick"
7. Elements of Writing

Ask students what all the underlined groups of words have in common. [Students should recognize that each is a title.] Explain that the underlined titles are longer works such as books, movies, or television shows.

MECHANICS

LEP/ESL

General Strategies. Write the following incomplete sentences on the chalkboard:

1. My favorite television programs include . . . .
2. Two movies that I saw this year are . . . .
3. A book that I would like to read is . . . .

Have students copy this information and supply responses. Remind them to underline all entries.

INTEGRATING THE LANGUAGE ARTS

Literature Link. Have students write a one-page review of a book such as *The Adventures of Tom Sawyer; Summer of the Swans; Dear Mr. Henshawe; The Lion, the Witch, and the Wardrobe; Julie of the Wolves; Island of the Blue Dolphins;* or *Roll of Thunder, Hear My Cry!*

In writing their reviews, students should answer these questions:

1. What is the theme of the book?
2. How is the theme developed through plot, character, setting, and mood? (Have students choose one or two.)
3. Did you enjoy the book? Why or why not? Would you recommend it to a friend?

MECHANICS

TYPE OF NAME	EXAMPLES
Books	*Number the Stars* *To Kill a Mockingbird* *House Made of Dawn*
Plays	*Song of Sheba* *The Sound of Music* *Life with Father*
Periodicals	the *Sioux City Journal* *Latin American Literary Review* *Highlights for Children*
Films	*A Passage to India* *The Last Emperor* *The Learning Tree*
Television Programs	*Under the Umbrella Tree* *Fun with Watercolors* *Reading Rainbow*
Works of Art	*The Old Guitarist* *Gamin* *Confucius and Disciples*
Long Musical Works	*Chôros* *Treemonisha* *A Little Night Music*
Ships	*Flying Cloud* USS *Lexington*
Aircraft	*Solar Challenger* *Spirit of St. Louis*
Spacecraft	*Pioneer 13* *Discovery*

MECHANICS

NOTE: The article *the* before the title of a magazine or a newspaper is not italicized or capitalized when it is part of a sentence rather than part of the title.

EXAMPLES I deliver the *Evening Independent.* [*The* is part of the sentence, not part of the title.]
Is that the latest issue of *The New Yorker?* [*The* is part of the magazine's title.]

REFERENCE NOTE: For examples of titles that use quotation marks instead of italics, see page 622.

SEGMENT 3 *(pp. 615–624)*

QUOTATION MARKS Rules 24b–24k

OBJECTIVES

- To use punctuation and capitalization correctly in quotations
- To recognize indirect quotations and to rewrite them as direct quotations
- To write a tall tale that includes two titles of books and three or more lines of dialogue

24b

 EXERCISE 1 **Using Underlining (Italics) Correctly**

For each of the following sentences, write each word or item that should be printed in italics, and underline it.

EXAMPLE 1. We saw Rodin's famous work The Thinker.
1. *The Thinker*

1. The magazine Popular Science reports news about science.
2. Have you ever seen the movie The Shaggy Dog?
3. My favorite painting is Morning of Red Bird by Romare Bearden.
4. We read a scene from the play The Piano Lesson.
5. How do you like the new fashions in the latest issue of Seventeen?
6. Tcheky Karyo starred in the 1988 movie The Bear.
7. Have you read today's Chicago Sun-Times or the Chicago Tribune?
8. My sister watches Sesame Street every day.
9. Apollo 11 landed on the moon on July 20, 1969.
10. The book The Path Between the Seas is about the Panama Canal.

MECHANICS

Quotation Marks

24b. Use quotation marks to enclose a ***direct quotation***—a person's exact words.

EXAMPLES Gymnast Lanna Apisukh said, "I always wanted to be the best."
"Let's go home," Jeanne suggested.

Do not use quotation marks for an ***indirect quotation***—a rewording of a direct quotation.

DIRECT QUOTATION Juan said, "The bus is late." [Juan's exact words]
INDIRECT QUOTATION Juan said that the bus was late. [not Juan's exact words]

Teacher's ResourceBank™

RESOURCES

QUOTATION MARKS

QUICK REMINDER

Write on the chalkboard the following two sentences:

1. "Did you go to the football game last night?" LaKeitha asked.
2. Tal replied that he had not gone to the game.

Ask students to explain the difference between the two sentences. Students should be able to explain that the first sentence tells what LaKeitha said in her own words, while the second sentence only reports what Tal said. Point out that the first sentence is a direct quotation, whereas the second sentence is an indirect quotation. Tell students that they will be learning more about direct quotations in this lesson.

MECHANICS

STUDENTS WITH SPECIAL NEEDS

Students with a visual processing deficit may have difficulty determining how to identify the words that make up a direct quote, especially if a quoted sentence is interrupted. It is hard for them to separate a passage solely by reading the sentence.

Have the learning disabled student copy the sentence. Next, assign to the student a partner who can read the sentence aloud. Tell the learning disabled student to repeat the dialogue section only and place the quotation marks accordingly.

MECHANICS

24c. A direct quotation begins with a capital letter.

EXAMPLES Mrs. Talbott said, "**P**lease get a pencil."
Kristina asked, "**I**s it my turn?"

24d. When a quoted sentence is divided into two parts by an expression that identifies the speaker, the second part of the quotation begins with a small letter.

EXAMPLE "Will you take care of my lawn," asked Mr. Franklin, "**w**hile I'm on vacation next month?"

When the second part of a divided quotation is a new sentence, it begins with a capital letter.

EXAMPLE "Yes, we will," I said. "**W**e can certainly use the extra money."

24e. A direct quotation is set off from the rest of the sentence by a comma, a question mark, or an exclamation point, but not by a period.

Set off means "to separate." If a quotation comes at the beginning of a sentence, a comma follows it. If a quotation comes at the end of a sentence, a comma comes before it. If a quoted sentence is interrupted, a comma follows the first part and comes before the second part.

EXAMPLES "I think that dogs make better pets than cats do**,**" said Frank.
Maria asked**,** "What makes you say that?"
"Oh**,**" Donna commented**,** "he's just saying that because he's never had a cat."

When a quotation ends with a question mark or an exclamation point, no comma is needed.

EXAMPLES "Does Frank have a dog**?**" Todd asked.
"He has three of them**!**" Donna exclaimed.

MECHANICS

24 c–g

EXERCISE 2 **Punctuating and Capitalizing Quotations**

For each of the following sentences, add commas, end marks, quotation marks, and capital letters where they are needed. If a sentence is correct, write *C*.

EXAMPLE **1. We're going tubing next Saturday said Carlos.**
1. *"We're going tubing next Saturday," said Carlos.*

1. "May I go with you?" I asked.
2. "We'd like to go, too," added Barbara and Tranh.
3. Barbara asked, "Who will bring tubes for everyone?"
4. Jim said, "I'll bring them."
5. I offered to bring sandwiches and lemonade.
6. "My dad will drive," Carlos said. "He has a van."
7. "The river is fed by a glacier," Tranh stated.
8. "That means," Barbara said, "that the water will be cold."
9. "It should feel good," I pointed out, "if Saturday is as hot as today is."
10. Carlos told all of us to meet him at his house at 8:30 A.M. **10. C**

24f. A period or a comma should always be placed *inside* the closing quotation marks.

EXAMPLE **"I can't wait to see Michael Jackson's new video," James said. "It's supposed to come out next week."**

24g. A question mark or an exclamation point should be placed *inside* closing quotation marks when the quotation itself is a question or an exclamation. Otherwise, it should be placed *outside.*

EXAMPLES **"What time will you be home from work, Mom?" asked Michael.** [The quotation is a question.]
Who said, "All the world's a stage"? [The sentence, not the quotation, is a question.]

MECHANICS

LEP/ESL

General Strategies. Many students learn best by manipulation of the content being introduced. Keeping this in mind, you may want to select those sentences from **Exercise 2** that require only insertion of quotation marks and commas. (Changes in capitalization need to be made only in numbers 3 and 6.) Write each sentence on two pieces of stiff cardboard; the first piece will contain the quotation itself and the second piece will contain the speaker(s) and accompanying verb. For example, write "I'd like to go with you" on one card and "I said" on the second card. Then create extra cards: two large open quotation marks, two large closing quotation marks, and two large commas, and one large period. Ask students to come to the front of the class to create the correct arrangement for each of the sentences.

MECHANICS

LEARNING STYLES

Kinetic Learners. Using a tactile material such as felt, cut out two or three sets of quotations marks and single quotation marks, two or three commas, and a set of capital letters. Attach some sticky material to the backs of these marks and letters. Then write the sentences from **Exercises 3, 4,** or **5** on large posterboard or on the chalkboard. Then have students work as teams to correctly punctuate and capitalize the sentences using the cut-outs.

LESS-ADVANCED STUDENTS

Some students should be able to create dialogues without any trouble, and yet they may not be used to thinking of speech as material to be written and punctuated. You might have students work in pairs, trying to pair each less-advanced student with an advanced, writing-oriented student. Have the less-advanced student dictate some dialogue to the advanced student. Then have the advanced student punctuate the dialogue and discuss the punctuation with the less-advanced student.

MECHANICS

INTEGRATING THE LANGUAGE ARTS

Mechanics and Speaking. Read aloud the sentences from **Exercise 3.** Listening for natural pauses and inflections should help students place quotation marks accurately.

"Stop**!**" yelled the crossing guard. [The quotation is an exclamation.]
What a surprise to hear Susana say, "We're moving back to Puerto Rico in June"**!** [The sentence, not the quotation, is an exclamation.]

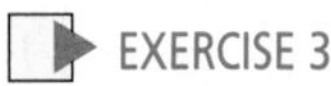

Punctuating and Capitalizing Quotations

Rewrite each of the following sentences correctly, inserting punctuation and adding capitalization where needed.

EXAMPLE **1.** Clementine Hunter was born in 1887 said María and she died in 1988.
1. *"Clementine Hunter was born in 1887," said María, "and she died in 1988."*

1. Staci said, "Here is a photograph of this self-taught American artist."
2. "Clementine Hunter was born in Natchitoches, Louisiana," Staci remarked.
3. "She started working on a plantation when she was only fourteen," María added.
4. "When she was fifty-three years old," said Staci, "Hunter decided to do what she loved most—paint."
5. Staci continued, "She began painting on almost any surface that would hold the paint!"

MECHANICS

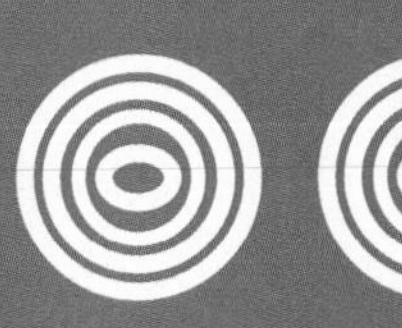

Clementine Hunter, (c. 1945), Photo from the Mildred Bailey Collection, Natchitoches, Louisiana.

6. "Her early pieces were painted on brown paper bags and cardboard boxes," María remarked, "and then on canvas, wood, and paper."
7. "Hunter used bright colors," Mike explained, "to paint everyday scenes like this one, called *Wash Day*."

Clementine Hunter, "Wash Day," Courtesy of the Association for the Preservation of Historical Natchitoches, Melrose Plantation.

8. "It may surprise you to learn," added Mike, "that her paintings sold for only twenty-five cents in the 1940s!"
9. "But," he continued, "in the 1980s her paintings sold for thousands of dollars."
10. "Moreover," Staci concluded, "Clementine Hunter's paintings have been exhibited throughout the United States."

EXERCISE 4 Revising Indirect Quotations to Create Direct Quotations

Revise each of the following sentences by changing the indirect quotation to a direct quotation. Be sure to use capital letters and punctuation marks where they are needed. [Note: Although the example gives two revisions, you need to write only one.]

MECHANICS

AT-RISK STUDENTS

To increase students' self-esteem, choose one or two students to be your helpers or graders for selected exercises in the chapter. Pass around the responsibilities so that each student feels needed and important. It will save you grading time, but it will also make students feel important and help them learn from the reinforcement of checking other students' work.

VISUAL CONNECTIONS *Wash Day*

About the Artist. Born in 1885, the daughter of slaves, Clementine Hunter dropped out of school after three years to work in the cotton fields of Melrose Plantation near Natchitoches, La. In her late 50s, Hunter became a house servant.

The mistress of Melrose, an amateur painter, often entertained artists. One evening Hunter found some discarded tubes of paint and created her first painting on an old window shade.

Hunter went on to paint thousands of canvases–colorful representations of African-American life on a Southern plantation. Her paintings celebrate life and depict only her happy memories. Internationally renowned in her lifetime, Hunter lived to be 101 years old.

MECHANICS

ANSWERS

Exercise 4

Revisions will vary.

1. The cashier replied, "I'm not allowed to make change unless a purchase is made."
2. "I need a new pen," I said.
3. "It costs seventy-nine cents," the cashier said.
4. I said, "I will give you $1.79."
5. "I can then give you change for a dollar," she said.

INTEGRATING THE LANGUAGE ARTS

Literature Link. Some excellent dialogue for discussion can be found in the "Riddles in the Dark" chapter of J.R.R. Tolkien's *The Hobbit.* Illustrate how Tolkien uses dialogue to characterize by reading aloud several examples and by asking your students to identify the speaker as Bilbo or Gollum. Ask students to identify places where Tolkien's use of punctuation contributes to meaning.

MECHANICS

EXAMPLE 1. I asked the cashier for change for a dollar.

1. *"May I please have change for a dollar?" I asked the cashier.*

or

I asked the cashier, "Would you please give me change for a dollar?"

1. The cashier replied that she wasn't allowed to make change unless a purchase was made.
2. I said that I needed a new pen.
3. The cashier told me that it cost seventy-nine cents.
4. I said that I would give her $1.79.
5. She told me that she could then give me change for a dollar.

24h. When you write dialogue (conversation), begin a new paragraph every time the speaker changes.

MECHANICS

EXAMPLE In Khanabad, Mulla Nasrudin was sitting in a teahouse when a stranger walked in and sat down beside him.

The newcomer said:

"Why is that man over there sobbing his heart out?"

"Because I have just arrived from his hometown and told him that all his winter camel fodder was lost in a fire."

"It is terrible to be a bearer of such tidings," said the stranger.

"It is also interesting to be the man who will shortly tell him the good news," said Nasrudin. "You see, his camels have died of a plague, so he will not need the fodder after all."

Idries Shah, "Camel Fodder"

24i. When a quotation consists of several sentences, put quotation marks only at the beginning and the end of the whole quotation.

EXAMPLE **"**Will you help with the scenery for our play, Bao? Zachary and Pia have offered to make costumes,**"** Aaron said.

24j. Use single quotation marks to enclose a quotation within a quotation.

EXAMPLES "Read the chapter 'Comets and Asteroids,'" stated Mr. Mendoza.
"Mrs. Engle distinctly said, 'Your book reports are due Thursday,'" Krista told me.

PICTURE THIS

Your class is holding a contest to see who can write an unlikely story that stretches the facts. You get an idea for a great tall tale when you see this scene. Write a brief tall tale about cows waiting for a bookmobile. In your tale, include at least two titles of books that these cows might check out. Also include three or more lines of dialogue. Be sure to use italics and quotation marks correctly.

Subject: cows waiting for a bookmobile
Audience: your teacher and classmates
Purpose: to entertain

MECHANICS

PICTURE THIS

To give students some ideas for their dialogues, write on the chalkboard the names of several varieties of cows:

1. Dairy cows: Holstein, Jersey, Guernsey, Brown Swiss, Ayrshire
2. Beef cows: Hereford, Brahman, Angus, Charolais

Encourage students to use words associated with cows. For example, they might write about a young couple named Bull Holstein and Daisy Holstein. Daisy could check out a cookbook entitled *Udderly Delicious* and a crafts book called *Sewing Jerseys*. And their children could select books titled *Island of the Blue Cows* and *Dear Miss Bessie.*

MECHANICS

COOPERATIVE LEARNING

Divide the class into groups of three or four and give them lists of books, plays, stories, articles, and poems taken from the table of contents of your literature textbook. Working with fellow group members, have students decide whether each kind of title should be underlined or placed in quotation marks. Refer students to **Rules 24a** and **24k.**

TIMESAVER

Prepare on an overhead transparency a key to **Exercise 5.** Have students check their work while you circulate through the room to answer questions and to make sure students understand the items they have missed. You can use this technique with many of the exercises in this chapter.

MECHANICS

24k. Use quotation marks to enclose the titles of short works such as short stories, poems, newspaper or magazine articles, songs, episodes of television programs, and chapters and other parts of books.

TYPE OF NAME	EXAMPLES
Short Stories	"Raymond's Run" "Two Kinds" "Amigo Brothers"
Poems	"Jetliner" "Mother to Son" "Song of the Sky Loom"
Articles	"Celebrating Our Heritage" "The Giants of Easter Island" "Pollen"
Songs	"Aloha Oe" "Georgia on My Mind" "America the Beautiful"
Episodes of Television Programs	"Kali the Lion" "Soul of Spain" "The Trouble with Tribbles"
Chapters and Other Parts of Books	"Energy from the Stars" "I Go to Sea" "Behind the Cotton Curtain"

REFERENCE NOTE: For examples of titles that use italics instead of quotation marks, see pages 613–614.

EXERCISE 5 **Punctuating Quotations**

Write each of the following sentences, adding single or double quotation marks where they are needed.

EXAMPLE **1.** I just finished the chapter The Circulatory System in our health book, Dell told me.

1. *"I just finished the chapter 'The Circulatory System' in our health book," Dell told me.*

MECHANICS

REVIEW A

OBJECTIVE

- To use quotation marks and other marks of punctuation in a dialogue

1. Diane is learning the song Tarantella for her piano recital.
2. Angelo, can we meet after school tomorrow? We need to practice our presentation, Sam said.
3. I'm sure I heard the announcer say, Schools are closed because of the storm, I said.
4. I can pronounce all the words in Lewis Carroll's poem Jabberwocky Nina told Lou.
5. Ted said, My dad will pick us up on Saturday at 7:30 A.M. After the race, he is taking us to Lucy Ho's for lunch. Do you like Chinese food?

REVIEW A **Punctuating Paragraphs in a Dialogue**

Rewrite the following paragraphs, using capital letters, as well as quotation marks and other marks of punctuation, where they are needed. [Note: The punctuation marks already in the exercise are correct.]

EXAMPLE [1] **What are you writing my grandfather asked.**
1. ***"What are you writing?" my grandfather asked.***

[1] Grandpa I said I'm writing a report about your hero Octaviano Larrazolo. Can you tell me how he helped Mexican Americans?

[2] Grandpa got out his scrapbook. Octaviano did many things for our people he began. In 1912, New Mexico became a state. Octaviano and other Hispanic leaders wanted to be sure that Mexican Americans could hold political office. They wanted to make certain that they would always be allowed to vote. When New Mexico's new constitution was written, Octaviano and the other leaders fought for these rights.

[3] How did Mr. Larrazolo know how to protect the rights of people?

[4] Grandpa replied he had studied law. His knowledge of the law helped him understand the constitution. It also helped him later when he became interested in politics.

MECHANICS

SEGMENT 4 *(pp. 624–634)*

APOSTROPHES AND HYPHENS Rules 24l–24t

OBJECTIVES

- To write the singular and plural possessives of nouns
- To use apostrophes to write the possessive case forms of indefinite pronouns
- To use apostrophes correctly in contractions

[5] "When did Mr. Larrazolo become involved in politics?" I asked.

[6] "In 1916, he campaigned for Ezequiel Cabeza de Baca for governor," said Grandpa. "De Baca was elected, but he died a month later. Another election was held and Larrazolo became New Mexico's governor."

[7] I asked, "What are some things that Mr. Larrazolo felt strongly about?"

[8] He answered, "Octaviano believed that public schools should teach children about Mexican American culture. He also was in favor of both English and Spanish being spoken in schools. Here is a picture of him with his daughters."

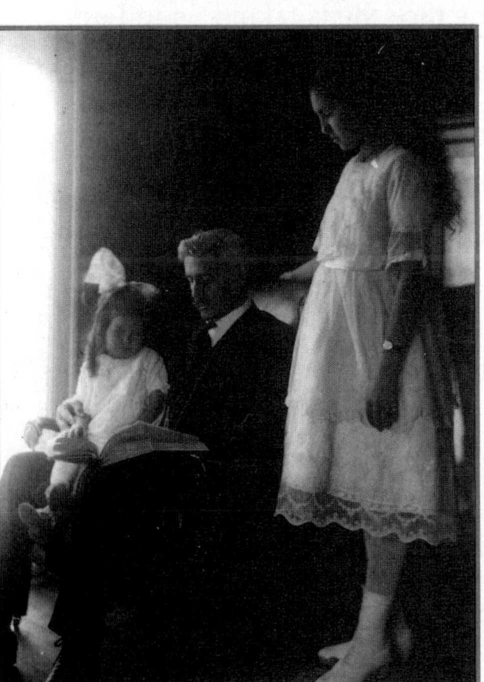

Wesley Bradfield/Courtesy Museum of New Mexico #47760.

[9] "What else should I know about Octaviano Larrazolo?" I asked.

[10] "Octaviano was elected to the United States Senate in 1928," Grandpa said. "He continued to work hard for the rights of Hispanic Americans until he died."

VISUAL CONNECTIONS

Ideas for Writing. Octaviano Larrazolo is obviously a hero to Grandpa. Ask students to write brief essays about their own heroes. Students can write about someone they know or about a historic person. Tell students to answer these questions in their essays:

1. Who is your hero?
2. What heroic actions has this person performed?
3. What heroic qualities does this person have?
4. Will others consider this person a hero? Why or why not?

MECHANICS

MECHANICS

Teacher's ResourceBank™

RESOURCES

APOSTROPHES AND HYPHENS

Apostrophes

Possessive Case

The ***possessive case*** of a noun or a pronoun shows ownership or relationship.

OWNERSHIP	RELATIONSHIP
Heidi's comb **his** jacket **our** dog	**no one's** fault a **week's** vacation **my** stepbrother

24l. To form the possessive case of a singular noun, add an apostrophe and an *s*.

EXAMPLES a student**'s** grant Tanaka**'s** store
the child**'s** toy Tess**'s** painting

NOTE: A proper noun ending in *s* may take only an apostrophe to form the possessive case if adding *'s* would make the name awkward to say.

EXAMPLES Kansas**'** climate
Ms. Morales**'** class

EXERCISE 6 **Using Apostrophes for Singular Possessives**

For each of the following sentences, identify the word that needs an apostrophe. Then write the word correctly punctuated.

EXAMPLE 1. Kenyans celebrate 1963 as the year of their countrys independence.
1. *country's*

1. Soon the young nation's athletes were setting records in international sports.
2. Leading Kenya's world-class distance runners was Kipchoge Keino, shown here with his Olympic medals.

24l

MECHANICS

QUICK REMINDER

Write on the chalkboard the following lists:

List A
1. the skaters' prizes [b.]
2. the skaters won the prize [a.]
3. the skater's prize [d.]
4. the skater's gone [c.]

List B
a. plural
b. plural possessive
c. contraction
d. singular possessive

Ask each of four volunteers to select one item from list A and to draw a line from it to the appropriate description in list B. Explain that this lesson will give students practice with the use of apostrophes in possessives and contractions.

VISUAL CONNECTIONS

Exploring the Subject. The modern Olympic Games are based on the ancient Olympic Games, first recorded in 776 B.C. The ancient games were held at the stadium at Olympia, which lies at the foot of Mt. Olympus, reputed home of the Greek gods. The pure amateur spirit was lost as rules were relaxed and professional athletes were hired for the ancient games. The ancient games officially ended in A.D. 394.

LEP/ESL

Spanish. Students may have difficulty using possessives correctly because in Spanish, there is no possessive ending that resembles *–'s.* The most common way of expressing possession is with the Spanish preposition *de* (*of*). Students may, therefore, generate phrases such as *the book of Lisa,* or they may use correct English word order but simply omit the possessive suffix, resulting in *Lisa book.* You may want to create an exercise such as the following one that combines practicing the possessive *–'s* with review of contractions:

1. That pen belongs to Felipe.
   That is [Felipe's pen].
   [That's] Felipe's pen.
2. This suitcase belongs to Martha.
   It is [Martha's suitcase].
   [It's] Martha's suitcase.

LESS-ADVANCED STUDENTS

Select or borrow several specific and recognizable objects from members of the class. For example, you might choose a purse, a jacket, and so forth. Be sure that students will recognize the ownership of each object. Then hold the objects up in front of the students and have them identify each object correctly on paper.

MECHANICS

3. Keino trained in his homeland's mountains by running many miles in the thin air.
4. In 1965, he burst into his sport's top ranks by setting world records for both the 3,000-meter race and the 5,000-meter race.
5. His training in the mountains helped Keino win his first gold medal at Mexico City's 1968 Olympics.
6. His record in that year's 1,500-meter race stood until 1984.
7. In fact, the Kenyan team's runners took home a total of eight medals in 1968.
8. In the 1972 Olympics, Keino's performance won him a second gold medal, this time for the 3,000-meter steeplechase.
9. A silver medal in the 1,500-meter race marked his career's remarkable completion.
10. His victories not only won Keino the world's praise but also set new standards for runners everywhere.

MECHANICS

24m. To form the possessive case of a plural noun that does not end in *s*, add an apostrophe and an *s*.

EXAMPLES geese**'s** feathers men**'s** clothing
children**'s** books feet**'s** bones

24n. To form the possessive case of a plural noun ending in *s*, add only the apostrophe.

EXAMPLES boxes**'** lids ten minutes**'** time
beetles**'** shells the Ozawas**'** address

NOTE: Do not use an apostrophe to form the *plural* of a noun. Remember that the apostrophe shows ownership or relationship.

INCORRECT Two boys' left their books here.
CORRECT Two **boys** left their books here.

EXERCISE 7 **Writing Possessives**

Rewrite each of the following expressions by using the possessive case. Be sure to add an apostrophe in the right place.

EXAMPLE 1. the speeches of the politicians
1. *the politicians' speeches*

1. the books of the children
2. the prize of the winner
3. the bed of the kittens
4. the home of my friend
5. the streets of the city

EXERCISE 8 **Writing Plural Possessives**

For each sentence, identify the word that needs an apostrophe. Then write the word correctly punctuated.

EXAMPLE 1. Wild creatures survival depends on their ability to adapt.
1. *creatures'*

1. Animals ways of dealing with cold are fascinating.
2. At night, chickadees feathers are fluffed over the soft down next to their skin.
3. In addition, the birds breathing rates and heartbeats slow, and their body temperatures fall, saving energy.
4. Deers winter coats, with their hollow hairs filled with air, keep body heat from escaping.
5. Soft undercoats of fine hair are many animals thermal underwear.
6. In this picture, you can see how squirrels tails, flattened against their backs and necks, keep them warm when they leave their nests.

4. [*or* Deer's]

MECHANICS

ANSWERS

Exercise 7

1. the children's books
2. the winner's prize
3. the kittens' bed
4. my friend's home
5. the city's streets

COMMON ERROR

Problem. Students often use an apostrophe where the meaning calls for a plural noun, as in "The two dog's played."

Solution. Have students work in pairs to identify apostrophes in their partners' writing. Have students highlight each usage. For each apostrophe, have partners ask one another if the phrase can be turned around to read the ____ of ____. For example, the phrase *the two dogs' bone* can be turned around to read *the bone of the two dogs.* However, *the two dog's played* cannot be turned around to read *the played of the two dogs.* Since this second rephrasing does not work, the usage is incorrect.

MECHANICS

MECHANICS

7. The picture above shows how red foxes' tails are used as muffs curled around their heads while they sleep.
8. On grouse's toes are comblike structures that make walking easier.
9. In cold weather, fur grows on the bottom of snowshoe hares' feet for protection.
10. Traits like these make possible wild creatures' survival during freezing temperatures and snow.

24o. Do not use an apostrophe with possessive personal pronouns.

EXAMPLES Is this pencil **yours** or **mine**?
Our apartment is smaller than **theirs.**
Her enchiladas are spicier than **his.**

24p. To form the possessive case of some indefinite pronouns, add an apostrophe and an *s.*

EXAMPLES either**'s** topic
everyone**'s** favorite
somebody**'s** notebook

 REFERENCE NOTE: For more about possessive personal pronouns, see page 503. For more about indefinite pronouns, see page 377.

MECHANICS

INTEGRATING THE LANGUAGE ARTS

Grammar and Punctuation. **Rules 24o** and **24p** explain the use of possessive pronouns. To help students distinguish between the punctuation of personal possessive and indefinite possessive pronouns, give them the practice exercise below and ask them to insert apostrophes where needed. Remind students that personal possessive pronouns do not require apostrophes whereas indefinite possessive pronouns do.

theirs	anybodys ['s]
everyones ['s]	ours
his	everybodys ['s]
yours	eithers ['s]
someones ['s]	hers
nobodys ['s]	anothers ['s]

 EXERCISE 9 **Writing the Possessive Case of Indefinite Pronouns**

Rewrite each of the following expressions by using the possessive case. Be sure to add an apostrophe in the correct place.

EXAMPLE **1.** the speeches of everybody
1. *everybody's speeches*

1. the wishes of everyone **1.** everyone's wishes
2. the fault of nobody **2.** nobody's fault
3. the answer of no one **3.** no one's answer
4. the album of someone **4.** someone's album
5. the guess of anybody **5.** anybody's guess

Contractions

 **24q.** Use an apostrophe to show where letters, numerals, or words have been left out in a contraction.

A ***contraction*** is a shortened form of a word, a number, or a group of words. The apostrophe in a contraction shows where letters, numerals, or words have been left out.

Common Contractions

I am	I'm	they have	they've
1994	'94	here is	here's
let us	let's	you are	you're
of the clock	o'clock	she is	she's
he would	he'd	you will	you'll

The word *not* can be shortened to *n't* and added to a verb. The spelling of the verb usually does not change.

MECHANICS

LEARNING STYLES

Visual Learners. Have students prepare a poster or a display with pairs of confusing possessive pronouns and contractions. Here are some pairs students can use:

PRONOUNS	CONTRACTIONS
its	it's
their	they're
theirs	there's
your	you're
whose	who's

Tell students to refer to this display when they are writing or completing exercises.

COMMON ERROR

Problem. When writing sentences, students often confuse contractions and possessive pronouns that sound alike.

Solution. Tell students to read the sentence aloud and to substitute the appropriate subject and verb. If the subject and verb phrase makes sense, the sentence needs a contraction. If it does not make sense, the sentence needs a possessive pronoun with no apostrophe. Examples:

1. The baby elephant wanted its mother. [The phrase *it is* does not make sense, so no apostrophe is needed.]
2. The band members say that they're learning a new marching song. [The phrase *they are* does make sense, so the contraction *they're* is correct.]

MECHANICS

INTEGRATING THE LANGUAGE ARTS

Literature Link. Select an example of literary dialogue from your textbook or from a book such as *The Lion, the Witch, and the Wardrobe; A Wrinkle in Time;* or *Roll of Thunder, Hear My Cry!* Be sure that the passage contains several contractions. Read the passage aloud as it is written. Then read it aloud again, substituting phrases for the contractions. Ask students which version they like and why. Lead into a discussion about the importance of representing oral language realistically in dialogue.

MECHANICS

EXAMPLES	is not . . . . is**n't**	has not . . . . has**n't**
	are not . . . . . are**n't**	have not . . . . . have**n't**
	does not . . . does**n't**	had not . . . . had**n't**
	do not . . . . do**n't**	should not . . should**n't**
	was not . . . . . was**n't**	would not . . . would**n't**
	were not . . were**n't**	could not . . . . could**n't**
EXCEPTIONS	will not . . . . . **won't**	cannot . . . . **can't**

Don't confuse contractions with possessive pronouns.

CONTRACTIONS	POSSESSIVE PRONOUNS
It's raining. [*It is*] **It's** been a long day. [*It has*]	**Its** tires are flat.
Who's your coach? [*Who is*] **Who's** been in my room? [*Who has*]	**Whose** watch is this?
You're welcome. [*You are*]	**Your** sister won.
They're late. [*They are*] **There's** the bell. [*There is*]	**Their** house is next door. That car is **theirs.**

EXERCISE 10 Using Apostrophes in Contractions

For each of the following sentences, write the word requiring an apostrophe, and add the apostrophe. If a sentence is correct, write *C.*

EXAMPLE **1.** Well be leaving soon.
1. *We'll*

1. Youve been a big help.
2. Its time to leave for the party.
3. Whose umbrella is this? 3. C
4. Were having a fund-raiser for the homeless.
5. I cant find my skate key.
6. He promised hed wear his seat belt.
7. Lets get tickets to see Los Lobos.
8. Youd better hurry up.
9. Its too late now.
10. Ill wash the car tomorrow morning.

EXERCISE 11 Writing Contractions

For each of the following sentences, write the contraction of the italicized word or words.

EXAMPLE **1. *We will* see a performance of the puppet theater when we visit the Japan America Theatre in Los Angeles.**
1. *We'll*

1. *Have not* you always wondered what goes on backstage at a puppet show? 1. Haven't
2. *Here is* an illustration that takes you behind the scenes at a seventeenth-century puppet theater in Japan. 2. Here's
3. The audience *cannot* see all the backstage action because of the curtain. 3. can't
4. The men *who are* handling the puppets are very highly trained. 4. who're
5. They *do not* speak the characters' lines, though. 5. don't
6. *It is* the man sitting on the right on the table who narrates the play. 6. It's
7. As you can see, *he is* accompanied by a musician. 7. he's
8. On the right are more puppets; *they have* been hung there for future use. 8. they've
9. In the box at the top, *that is* the Japanese word that means "puppet." 9. that's
10. As *you will* notice, the Japanese system of writing is very different from ours. 10. you'll

MECHANICS

WRITING APPLICATION

OBJECTIVES

- To write a letter to a friend describing a week at camp
- To use apostrophes correctly in a written letter

WRITING APPLICATION

Students learn a concept more fully when they apply it to their own writing. Thus, this assignment is designed to give students the opportunity to use apostrophes in a writing situation.

CRITICAL THINKING

Analysis

This assignment gives students practice in collecting and organizing details in a letter format. Have students brainstorm a list of the activities they might participate in at summer camp. Their lists will probably include activities such as swimming and making crafts. Encourage students to add to their lists specific details such as learning the backstroke and finger painting. Then have students analyze their brainstorming lists. They should circle items that they want to write about. Have them pick out two or three major ideas to write about.

Synthesis

After students have done their initial brainstorming, have them synthesize their material by drawing lines to connect related items such as swimming and learning the backstroke. Tell students to use a separate paragraph in their letters for each set of related ideas.

MECHANICS

Plurals

24r. Use an apostrophe and an *s* to form the plurals of letters, numerals, and signs, and of words referred to as words.

EXAMPLES The word *Mississippi* has four *i*'**s**, four *s*'**s**, and two *p*'**s**.
Your *1*'**s** and *7*'**s** look alike.
You wrote +'**s** instead of x'**s** on all these math problems.
Try not to use so many *you know*'**s** when you talk.

WRITING APPLICATION

Using Apostrophes Correctly to Make Writing Clear

MECHANICS

Important information can come in small packages. For instance, punctuation marks don't take up much room in your writing, yet they express a great deal in meaning. Compare the following sentences:

Well, go see what's going on.
We'll go see what's going on.

WRITING ACTIVITY

You've been so busy at summer camp that you haven't had time to write to your best friend. Write a letter to your friend, telling about your first week at camp. Be sure to use apostrophes correctly to make your meaning clear.

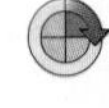

Prewriting Jot down some notes on your activities at summer camp. Use your experience or your imagination to describe activities such as sports, crafts, and hiking trips. Also make some notes about the camp itself. Is it near a lake or an ocean? What plants and animals live in the area?

Where do you sleep? What do you eat? If you've never been to a summer camp, get information from a friend who has.

Writing Before beginning your first draft, you may want to look at page 707 for tips on writing a personal letter. Include specific details about the natural setting and special or daily activities at the camp. Tell your friend what you've enjoyed most. You may also want to mention new friends you've made and new things you've learned. Try to give your friend a clear, vivid picture of your first week.

Evaluating and Revising Ask a friend or a family member to read your letter. Can he or she imagine the activities you've described? If not, revise your letter to make it clearer and more descriptive. Be sure you've used the correct form for friendly letters.

Proofreading As you proofread your letter, take extra care with apostrophes. Check your use of contractions and pronouns like *its, it's, your, you're, their,* and *they're*. Also look for any other errors in grammar, spelling, and punctuation.

MECHANICS

Hyphens

24s. Use a hyphen to divide a word at the end of a line.

When you divide a word at the end of a line, remember the following rules:

(1) Divide a word only between syllables.

INCORRECT Uncle Payat, Aunt Nina, and Ayita will journey eighty miles to join us.

CORRECT Uncle Payat, Aunt Nina, and Ayita will journey eighty miles to join us.

EVALUATING AND REVISING

Have students work in pairs to evaluate and revise their letters. Tell students to pretend to be the people who are receiving the letters. Are their letters interesting? Do they tell their friends all the friends might want to know about summer camp? What else do the letters need to include?

PROOFREADING AND REVISING

Have students work with the same partners that they worked with in the evaluating and revising stage. Tell them to concentrate on the use of apostrophes by identifying every word that uses an apostrophe or ends in an *–s*. Tell students to review **Rules 24l–24t** and then to double check these words to be sure that apostrophes are used correctly.

MECHANICS

REVIEW B

OBJECTIVE

- To use apostrophes and hyphens correctly

INTEGRATING THE LANGUAGE ARTS

Literature Link. In his poetry, E. E. Cummings often uses hyphens and compound words to contribute to his meaning. For example, in "hist whist" he makes up the compound *ghostthings* and uses hyphens in the words *tip-toe, twinkle-toe,* and *hob-a-nob.* If it is available in your library, read this poem aloud to your students, carefully quickening your speed when you get to these words to indicate the poet's rhythmic intention. Then ask students what effect he achieves by using these hyphenated words.

COOPERATIVE LEARNING

Give each student a list of ten to twenty words and have the class work in groups of three or four to determine which words can be divided and to divide them correctly with hyphens. Include one or two one-syllable words that cannot be divided. Provide a dictionary for each group of students. Possible words are *carpet, kitchen, basketball, desk, tortilla, poster, sweater, pencil, football,* and so forth.

MECHANICS

(2) Do not divide a word of one syllable.

INCORRECT They are bringing a salad, ham, and rye bre-ad.
CORRECT They are bringing a salad, ham, and rye bread.

(3) Do not divide a word so that one letter stands alone.

INCORRECT Is that your family's brand-new car parked a-cross the street?
CORRECT Is that your family's brand-new car parked across the street?

24t. Use a hyphen with compound numbers from *twenty-one* to *ninety-nine.*

EXAMPLE Until 1959, the United States had only forty-eight states.

MECHANICS

REVIEW B **Using Apostrophes and Hyphens Correctly**

For each of the following sentences, write the word or term that needs an apostrophe or a hyphen. Add the missing punctuation mark. The ‸ symbol indicates a hyphen.

EXAMPLE **1.** Where**s** my history book?
1. *Where's*

1. Do you know where the atlases and the diction-aries are?
2. There are two r's in *tomorrow.*
3. He can't tie a square knot.
4. The tiger cubs aren't on view yet.
5. Is that one of Issaye Miyake's new designs?
6. I have several of Tina Turner's albums.
7. Forty-nine students signed the get-well card.
8. The men's chorus gave a great performance.
9. Who's going to the fair this weekend?
10. It's almost time to leave.

SEGMENT 5 *(p. 635)*

REVIEW: POSTTEST

OBJECTIVE

- To proofread and revise sentences for the correct use of underlining (italics), quotation marks, apostrophes, and hyphens

Review: Posttest

Proofreading Sentences for the Correct Use of Underlining (Italics), Quotation Marks, Apostrophes, and Hyphens

Each of the following sentences contains at least one error in the use of underlining (italics), quotation marks, apostrophes, or hyphens. Write each sentence correctly.

The ‸ symbol indicates a hyphen.

EXAMPLE **1. We havent finished dinner yet.**
1. ***We haven't finished dinner yet.***

1. Melba built a model of the Santa Maria for extra credit in social studies.
2. My teachers house is being painted.
3. Each classroom has thirty four desks.
4. This recipe calls for fresh greens, potatoes, car rots, and onions.
5. The pots boiling over!
6. Whos going to sample this dish?
7. Dont forget the soy sauce.
8. The three chefs recipes were prepared by the chefs themselves on television.
9. Jiro's last name has two *l*s.
10. Have you seen Faith Ringgolds storyquilts?
11. We could hear the flapping of the geeses wings.
12. Isn't your favorite poem The Unicorn?
13. "Wasn't that a song? asked Carrie."
14. I think a folk singer wrote it, answered Tony.
15. Juanita said that "she would hum a bit of it."
16. Brad commented, "I think my parents have a copy of it".
17. "Can you bring it to class"? Elena asked.
18. "Who said, Time is money"? Gerald asked. **18.** money'?"
19. "Benjamin Franklin wrote it," answered Karen, "in a book called Advice to a Young Tradesman."
20. "I think, said Theo, that you're right."

MECHANICS

MECHANICS

SEGMENT 1 *(pp. 636–644)*

GOOD SPELLING HABITS AND SPELLING RULES Rules 25a–25g

OBJECTIVES

- To spell correctly words that contain the letters *ei* or *ie*
- To add prefixes and suffixes to words

Teacher's ResourceBank™

RESOURCES

FOR THE WHOLE CHAPTER

• Chapter Review Form A	277–278
• Chapter Review Form B	279–280
• Assessment Portfolio	
Mechanics Pretests	463–470
Mechanics Mastery Tests	487–494

CHAPTER OVERVIEW

The chapter begins with a discussion of three methods students can use to improve their spelling. It then presents a series of basic spelling rules, including rules for adding prefixes and suffixes and for forming the plurals of nouns. Exercises are provided to reinforce the understanding of the spelling rules. The chapter also contains lists of homonyms and other words that are often confused and concludes with two lists: **50 Commonly Misspelled Words** and **100 Spelling Words.**

Teacher's ResourceBank™

RESOURCES

GOOD SPELLING HABITS AND SPELLING RULES

• Using a Dictionary	269
• Using Spelling Rules A	270
• Using Spelling Rules B	271
• Using Spelling Rules C	272

25 SPELLING

Improving Your Spelling

Good Spelling Habits

The following techniques can help you spell words correctly.

1. **To learn the spelling of a word, pronounce it, study it, and write it.** Pronounce words carefully. Mistakes in speaking can cause mistakes in spelling. For instance, if you say *ad•je•tive* instead of *ad•jec•tive,* you will probably spell the word wrong.
   - First, make sure that you know how to pronounce the word correctly, and then practice saying it.
   - Second, study the word. Notice any parts that might be hard to remember.
   - Third, write the word from memory. Check your spelling.
   - If you misspelled the word, repeat the three steps of this process.

2. **Use a dictionary.** If you are not absolutely sure about the spelling of a word, look it up in a dictionary. Don't guess about the correct spelling.
3. **Spell by syllables.** A ***syllable*** is a word part that can be pronounced by itself.

EXAMPLES ear • ly [two syllables]
av • er • age [three syllables]

Instead of trying to learn how to pronounce a whole word, break it into its syllables whenever possible. It's easier to learn a few letters at a time than to learn all of them at once.

4. **Keep a list of your spelling errors.** Whenever you misspell a word, add it (correctly spelled) to your list. Review your list often.
5. **Proofread for careless spelling errors.** Always proofread your written work carefully to correct misspellings.

Spelling Rules

ie and *ei*

25a. Write *ie* when the sound is long *e*, except after *c*.

EXAMPLES chief, believe, brief, receive, ceiling
EXCEPTIONS either, neither, weird, seize

Write *ei* when the sound is not long *e*, especially when the sound is long *a*.

EXAMPLES neighbor, weigh, reindeer, sleigh, height, foreign
EXCEPTIONS friend, fierce, ancient, mischief

This verse may help you remember the *ie* rule:

I before e
Except after *c*,
Or when sounded like *a*,
As in *neighbor* and *weigh*.

QUICK REMINDER

Write the following list of words on the chalkboard and have students divide the words into syllables:

1. biography [bi•og•ra•phy]
2. classify [clas•si•fy]
3. ignition [ig•ni•tion]
4. millipede [mil•li•pede]
5. nuclear [nu•cle•ar]
6. rearrange [re•ar•range]

Ask other students to check the words in a dictionary for accuracy. When all the words are correctly divided, have the students pronounce the words aloud, and tell them to note how pronunciation follows syllable breaks. Explain that this is a way to break difficult words into manageable parts to figure out their spellings and pronunciations.

LEP/ESL

General Strategies. English spelling is complicated because some single letters represent more than one sound, whereas in most other languages one letter generally stands for one, and only one, sound. To help students remember English spelling rules, explain them and then give periodic informal, oral quizzes, so that students will think about the rules repeatedly.

STUDENTS WITH SPECIAL NEEDS

Learning disabled students typically have difficulty learning to spell contractions and nonphonetic words. For most students, repeated exposure through reading enhances spelling ability. To improve students' spelling abilities, copy misspelled words taken from their writing assignments. Ask students to write each such word correctly at least three times and to use the words in sentences. Constant repetition in writing, as well as increased exposure to silent reading, can strengthen spelling ability.

MECHANICS

MECHANICS

 EXERCISE 1 **Writing Words with *ie* and *ei***

Complete the following letter by adding the *ie* or *ei* to each numbered word.

EXAMPLE I wrote Aunt Han a [1] br____f thank-you note.
1. *brief*

November 12, 1993

Dear Aunt Han,

Thank you very much for the [1] sl_ei_gh you sent me. I [2] rec_ei_ved it on the [3] _ei_ghth of this month, just in time for our first big snowstorm. Here's a picture to show you how much I am enjoying your gift. My new [4] fr_ie_nds and I also have great fun pulling each other across the [5] f_ie_lds in it. The [6] n_ei_ghbor's dog races alongside us, barking [7] f_ie_rcely all the way.

Thank you again for your thoughtfulness. So far, I like living here in Vermont, but I can't quite [8] bel_ie_ve how different everything is from life in California.

Your loving [9] n_ie_ce,

Mai

P.S. If only we had some [10] r_ei_ndeer to pull us!

25b

Prefixes and Suffixes

25b. When adding a prefix to a word, do not change the spelling of the word itself.

A ***prefix*** is a letter or a group of letters added to the beginning of a word to create a new word that has a different meaning.

EXAMPLES dis + satisfy = **dis**satisfy
mis + lead = **mis**lead
over + due = **over**due
pre + view = **pre**view

EXERCISE 2 **Spelling Words with Prefixes**

Combine each of the following prefixes and words to create a new word.

EXAMPLE **1.** mis + place
1. *misplace*

1. fore + word	**5.** un + common	**9.** dis + loyal
2. un + fair	**6.** im + patient	**10.** over + coat
3. in + dependent	**7.** pre + historic	
4. mis + use	**8.** mis + spell	

EXERCISE 3 **Spelling Words with Prefixes**

Create five words by combining the prefixes given below with the words listed beside them. (You may use each prefix and each word more than once.) Check each of your new words in a dictionary. Then use each word in a sentence.

Prefixes			Words			
un–	mis–	dis–	able	do	judge	place
pre–	over–	re–	cover	trust	pay	informed

EXAMPLE **1.** *repay—I'll repay you when I get my allowance.*

MECHANICS

LEARNING STYLES

Auditory Learners. Encourage students to spell and pronounce new or problem words aloud as they practice writing the words. Some students might need to hear syllable division in the pronunciation of words. Tell them to pronounce problem words syllable by syllable and to pause slightly after each syllable before spelling the words.

ANSWERS

Exercise 2

1. foreword
2. unfair
3. independent
4. misuse
5. uncommon
6. impatient
7. prehistoric
8. misspell
9. disloyal
10. overcoat

ANSWERS

Exercise 3

Words and sentences will vary. Here are some possibilities:

1. unable—The cat was unable to catch the mouse.
2. misplace—My parents always misplace their keys.
3. overdo—Some athletes overdo their workouts.
4. discover—I wonder what secrets the scientist will discover.
5. replace—Please replace the can opener when you are through with it.

MECHANICS

COMMON ERROR

Problem. Students often have problems spelling words with double consonants not related to prefix or suffix formation.

Solution. Tell students that double consonants within words often indicate a certain pronunciation rule. The double consonant often indicates a short vowel sound, as in *latter.* Call out the pairs of words below to the class, telling them that one word in each pair will contain a double consonant. Ask students to write the words side by side.

1. bone, bonnet
2. bore, borrow
3. mane, manner
4. coma, comma
5. cuter, cutter
6. diner, dinner
7. filer, filler

After you have gone through the list, write the pairs on the chalkboard so students can check their spelling.

MECHANICS

25c. When adding the suffix *–ness* or *–ly* to a word, do not change the spelling of the word itself.

A ***suffix*** is a letter or a group of letters added at the end of a word to create a new word that has a different meaning.

EXAMPLES kind + ness = kind**ness**
sincere + ly = sincere**ly**

EXCEPTIONS For most words that end in *y,* change the *y* to *i* before *–ly* or *–ness.*

happy + ly = happ**ily**
friendly + ness = friendl**iness**

25d. Drop the final silent e before a suffix beginning with a vowel. ***Vowels*** are the letters *a, e, i, o, u,* and sometimes *y.* All other letters of the alphabet are ***consonants.***

EXAMPLES cause + ing = caus**ing**
reverse + ible = revers**ible**
strange + er = strang**er**

EXCEPTIONS Keep the silent e in words ending in *–ce* and *–ge* before a suffix beginning with *a* or *o.*

change + able = change**able**
courage + ous = courage**ous**

MECHANICS

PEANUTS reprinted by permission of UFS, Inc.

25e. Keep the final silent *e* before a suffix beginning with a consonant.

EXAMPLES hope + less = hope**less**
agree + ment = agree**ment**
force + ful = force**ful**

EXCEPTIONS argue + ment = argu**ment**
judge + ment = judg**ment**
true + ly = tru**ly**

 EXERCISE 4 **Spelling Words with Suffixes**

Combine each of the following words and suffixes to create a new word.

EXAMPLE **1.** sudden + ness
1. *suddenness*

1. active + ity
2. sure + ly
3. state + ment
4. locate + ion
5. gentle + er
6. silly + ness
7. suspense + ful
8. little + est
9. decorate + ed
10. breathe + ing

25f. For words ending in a consonant plus *y*, change the *y* to *i* before any suffix that does not begin with *i*.

EXAMPLES cry + ed = **cried** lonely + est = lone**liest**
pretty + er = **prettier** lazy + ness = **laziness**

Keep the *y* if the suffix begins with an *i*.

EXAMPLE carry + ing = **carrying**

Keep the *y* if the word ends in a vowel plus *y*.

EXAMPLES stay + ed = **stayed** key + ed = **keyed**

25g. Double the final consonant before adding *–ing, –ed, –er*, or *–est* to a one-syllable word that ends in a single vowel followed by a single consonant.

EXAMPLES beg + ing = **begging** sad + er = sa**dder**
quiz + ed = **quizzed** big + est = **biggest**

MECHANICS

ANSWERS

Exercise 4

1. activity
2. surely
3. statement
4. location
5. gentler
6. silliness
7. suspenseful
8. littlest
9. decorated
10. breathing

A DIFFERENT APPROACH

Word games can help students learn to spell. Write a long word on the chalkboard and have students make as many other words of four or more letters as they can by using letters from the word. Allow them to use dictionaries.

Encourage students to play other word games, including crossword puzzles, word-searches, and manufactured games.

MECHANICS

REVIEWS A and B

OBJECTIVE

- To proofread sentences and a paragraph for correct spelling and to correct any misspelled words

ANSWERS

Exercise 5

1. saying
2. slimmer
3. squeaking
4. rainiest
5. steadiness
6. beating
7. relying
8. easily
9. chopped
10. stepping

MECHANICS

LEP/ESL

Asian Languages. Many Asian languages, such as Chinese, Thai, and Vietnamese, have no affixes. Others, such as Japanese and Korean, do not have many affixes that function as affixes do in English. For ESL students who are speakers of such languages, you may wish to review what an affix is and give examples on the chalkboard to show what effect adding the affix has on the root word. You may wish to point out that affixes and some roots are not words because they cannot stand alone, but they still have meaning.

When a one-syllable word ends in two vowels followed by a single consonant, do *not* double the consonant before adding *–ing*, *–ed*, *–er*, or *–est*.

EXAMPLES sleep + ing = slee**ping** cool + er = coo**ler**
treat + ed = trea**ted** fair + est = fai**rest**

EXERCISE 5 Spelling Words with Suffixes

Combine each of the following words and suffixes to create a new word.

EXAMPLE 1. creep + er
1. *creeper*

1. say + ing
2. slim + er
3. squeak + ing
4. rainy + est
5. steady + ness
6. beat + ing
7. rely + ing
8. easy + ly
9. chop + ed
10. step + ing

MECHANICS

REVIEW A Proofreading Sentences for Correct Spelling

Most of the following sentences contain misspelled words. Write each misspelled word correctly. If a sentence is correct, write *C*.

EXAMPLE 1. My grandma often says, "Let sleepping dogs lie."
1. *sleeping*

1. It's ~~unnusual~~ weather for this time of year. 1. unusual
2. In 1990, Lithuania ~~regainned~~ its independence. 2. regained
3. With Sacagawea's help, Lewis and Clark ~~maped~~ out the Northwest. 3. mapped
4. Now that Bao Duc is on the team, our ~~hiting~~ has gone up. 4. hitting
5. Serita and I can ~~easyly~~ make enough burritos for the entire class. 5. easily
6. We visited my grandmother in the Dominican Republic during the ~~rainyest~~ month of the year. 6. rainiest
7. Please ~~resstate~~ the question. 7. restate

8. My sister has the loveliest voice I've ever heard. **8.** C
9. Astronaut Sally Ride is known for her courage and ~~steadyness~~. **9.** steadiness
10. The temperature has ~~droped~~ ten degrees in the last hour. **10.** dropped

 REVIEW B **Proofreading a Paragraph for Correct Spelling**

For each sentence in the following paragraph, write correctly the word or words that are incorrectly spelled. If a sentence is correct, write *C.*

EXAMPLE [1] My cousin Chris was very couragous after she was baddly hurt in a car accident.
1. *courageous; badly*

[1] After the accident, Chris found that she ~~truely~~ needed other people. [2] Her friends, family, and ~~nieghbors~~ gladly helped her. [3] However, Chris liked the idea of ~~geting~~ along on her own as much as possible, so she was ~~disatisfied~~. [4] ~~Fortunatly~~, she was able to join an exciting program called Helping Hands. [5] This program provides monkeys like this one as friends and helpers for people with disabilities. [6] Chris said that the baby monkeys are raised in ~~lovving~~ foster homes for four years, and then they go to Boston to ~~recieve~~ special training. [7] There, they

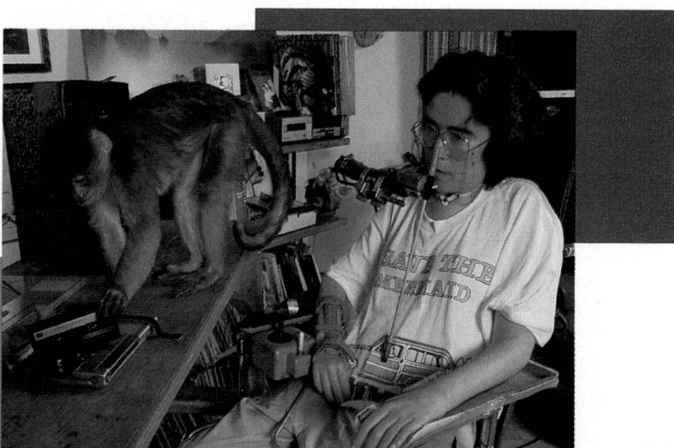

MECHANICS

 **INTEGRATING THE LANGUAGE ARTS**

Literature Link. If your literature book contains it, have students read aloud Shel Silverstein's "Sarah Cynthia Sylvia Stout Would Not Take the Garbage Out." Ask students to look at the word at the end of each line, and ask if any of these words conform to the spelling rules the class has just studied [*ceiling, pie*]. Next, ask the students to look at the words at the ends of lines 40 through 45 and ask if a pronunciation rule could be derived from the spellings of these words. [An *a* coming between two consonants will usually have a long sound if the second consonant is followed by an *e*.] To test the rule, divide the class into two teams and give each team a dictionary. Ask one team to list as many words as they can find that follow the rule, and ask the other to find as many exceptions as they can [*cadet, dare, mare,* and so on]. If the team looking for exceptions finds as many—or almost as many—words as the other team, the rule must be declared invalid or must be further qualified, perhaps by restricting it to words of one syllable or excepting words in which the second consonant is an *r*.

ANSWERS

Review B

1. truly
2. neighbors
3. getting; dissatisfied
4. Fortunately
5. C
6. loving; receive

MECHANICS

SEGMENT 2 *(pp. 644–648)*

FORMING THE PLURAL OF NOUNS Rule 25h

OBJECTIVE

- To spell the plural and singular forms of nouns

7. closing; putting
8. happily
9. retrieves; dropped
10. joking; writing

Teacher's ResourceBank™

RESOURCES

FORMING THE PLURAL OF NOUNS

- Forming the Plural of Nouns 273

MECHANICS

QUICK REMINDER

Write the following words on the chalkboard and ask students to change them to their plural forms:

1. radio [radios]
2. sheriff [sheriffs]
3. child [children]
4. igloo [igloos]
5. potato [potatoes]
6. fungus [fungi]
7. goose [geese]
8. mouse [mice]

Remind students that some words are used only in the plural. Some examples are *scissors, trousers,* and *pliers.*

learn how to do tasks on command, such as opening and ~~closeing~~ doors, turning lights on and off, and ~~puting~~ tapes into a VCR or tape player. [8] Chris has been ~~happyly~~ working with her own monkey, Aldo, for six months now. [9] Aldo ~~retreives~~ anything that Chris has ~~droped~~, works the TV remote control, and even scratches Chris's back when it itches! [10] Chris is always ~~jokeing~~, "Pretty soon Aldo will be ~~writting~~ my book reports for me!"

MECHANICS

Forming the Plural of Nouns

25h. Follow these rules for spelling the plural of nouns:

(1) To form the plural of most nouns, add *–s.*

SINGULAR	snack	oven	heap	valley	organization
PLURAL	snacks	ovens	heaps	valleys	organizations

(2) Form the plural of nouns ending in *s, x, z, ch,* or *sh* by adding *–es.*

SINGULAR	glass	fox	buzz	patch	bush
PLURAL	glasses	foxes	buzzes	patches	bushes

NOTE: Proper nouns usually follow this rule, too.

EXAMPLES the Cruzes the Joneses

EXERCISE 6 **Spelling the Plural of Nouns**

Spell the plural form of each of the following nouns.

EXAMPLE 1. scratch
1. *scratches*

1. taxes
2. dishes
3. addresses
4. lenses
5. boxes
6. branches
7. losses
8. peaches
9. waltzes
10. radishes

1. tax
2. dish
3. address
4. lens
5. box
6. branch
7. loss
8. peach
9. waltz
10. radish

(3) Form the plural of nouns ending in a consonant plus *y* by changing the *y* to *i* and adding *–es.*

SINGULAR	country	puppy	berry
PLURAL	countr**ies**	pupp**ies**	berr**ies**

EXCEPTION With proper nouns, just add *–s:* the Shelby**s**, the Mabry**s**.

(4) Form the plural of nouns ending in a vowel plus *y* by adding *–s.*

SINGULAR	boy	turkey	holiday
PLURAL	boy**s**	turkey**s**	holiday**s**

(5) Form the plural of nouns ending in a vowel plus *o* by adding *–s.*

SINGULAR	rodeo	patio	stereo
PLURAL	rodeo**s**	patio**s**	stereo**s**

(6) Form the plural of nouns ending in a consonant plus *o* by adding *–es.*

SINGULAR	tomato	echo	veto	torpedo
PLURAL	tomato**es**	echo**es**	veto**es**	torpedo**es**

EXCEPTIONS auto—auto**s** Chicano—Chicano**s** silo—silo**s**

NOTE: Form the plural of musical terms ending in *o* by adding *–s.*

SINGULAR	piano	trio	soprano	cello
PLURAL	piano**s**	trio**s**	soprano**s**	cello**s**

EXERCISE 7 **Spelling the Plural of Nouns**

Spell the plural form of each of the following nouns.

EXAMPLE 1. story
1. *stories*

1. cargo
2. apology
3. valley
4. laundry
5. piano
6. potato
7. emergency
8. chimney
9. radio
10. video

MECHANICS

LEP/ESL

General Strategies. Some of your ESL students might speak languages such as Chinese or Vietnamese, which have no plural forms. Others might speak languages such as Portuguese, Spanish, or Turkish, which have very regular plurals. These students might find English irregularities (such as *wife—wives*) and seemingly arcane rules (such as changing a final *y* to *i* between a consonant and a suffix beginning with a vowel) difficult to master. Remind the students a few times on different days of the importance of the rules.

LESS-ADVANCED STUDENTS

Students might confuse collective nouns with noun plurals. Remind them that collective nouns refer to groups of objects when it is necessary to refer to those objects as a unit. Be sure to explain that collective nouns have plurals, too.

MECHANICS

ANSWERS

Exercise 7

1. cargoes *or* cargos
2. apologies
3. valleys
4. laundries
5. pianos
6. potatoes
7. emergencies
8. chimneys
9. radios
10. videos

A DIFFERENT APPROACH

Have sudents work in small groups to generate lists of the plurals of the last names of students in the class. They may need to refer to the rules in this segment to complete the activity. After each group has a complete list, go over it to make certain each name is correct.

As an alternative to this activity, provide phone books or other directories and have groups list twenty-five names and their plurals.

MECHANICS

ANSWERS

Exercise 8

1. Sioux — singular; Sioux — plural
2. fish — singular; fish — plural
3. woman — singular; women — plural
4. child — singular; children — plural
5. tooth — singular; teeth — plural
6. Japanese — singular; Japanese — plural
7. moose — singular; moose — plural
8. deer — singular; deer — plural
9. sheep — singular; sheep — plural
10. game — singular; game — plural

(7) The plural of a few nouns is formed in irregular ways.

SINGULAR	woman	mouse	foot	man	child
PLURAL	women	mice	feet	men	children

(8) Some nouns are the same in the singular and the plural.

SINGULAR AND PLURAL **salmon Sioux deer fowl sheep**

(9) Form the plural of numerals, letters, signs, and words referred to as words by adding an apostrophe and *–s.*

SINGULAR	1990	A	+	*and*
PLURAL	1990's	A's	+'s	*and*'s

NOTE: In your reading, you may notice that these plurals are sometimes written with no apostrophe, as in *1990s.* Leaving out the apostrophe can cause confusion in some cases. Therefore, it is a good idea for you always to use the apostrophe.

MECHANICS

EXERCISE 8 **Spelling the Singular and Plural Forms of Nouns**

Spell the singular form and the plural form of each italicized word in the following sentences. [Note: A word may have more than one correct plural form.]

EXAMPLES
1. We use strong line to fish for *salmon.*
1. *salmon—singular; salmon—plural*
2. Field *mice* invaded the food supplies in the tent.
2. *mouse—singular; mice—plural*

1. Our guide Robert Tallchief, a *Sioux,* knows llamas.
2. Robert and his father use llamas like the ones shown on the next page to carry equipment people need for hiking and for catching *fish.*
3. The trips are very popular with both men and *women.*

REVIEW C

OBJECTIVE

- To proofread sentences for correct spelling and to correct any misspelled words

4. *Children* especially are fascinated by the sure-footed llamas.
5. However, the llama has one very disagreeable habit—if upset, it bares its *teeth* and spits.
6. The Tallchiefs' llama trips have attracted tourists from all over the world, including many *Japanese*.
7. One highlight of these trips is viewing *moose* in their natural habitat.
8. *Deer* thrive in this area of the Northwest.
9. In addition, families of mountain *sheep* clamber up the steep cliffs.
10. Most people who go on the llama trips take many pictures of the wild *game*.

REVIEW C **Proofreading Sentences for Correct Spelling**

For each sentence in the following paragraph, write correctly the word or words that are incorrectly spelled. If a sentence is correct, write *C*.

EXAMPLE **1. Aunt Dorothy Kelly talks mostly in expressions from the 1930s and earlyer.**
1. ***1930's; earlier***

1. When we want something because our friends have it, Aunt Dorothy says we're trying to keep up with the ~~Jones'~~. **1.** Joneses
2. If we get into mischief, she exclaims, "You little ~~monkies~~!" **2.** monkeys
3. When my ~~brother's~~ run through the house, she shakes her head and mutters, "Boys will be boys." **3.** brothers
4. Every time she can't find her eyeglasses, Aunt Dorothy says, "I've beaten the bushes, looking for them." **4.** C

MECHANICS

COMMON ERROR

Problem. Students are often confused when they look up a word in a dictionary and more than one spelling is given.

Solution. Allow time in class for students to become familiar with the dictionaries they use. Have them study the introductory material that explains the policy regarding multiple spellings. For example, the first spelling given is usually the one most commonly used. If two spellings are joined by the word *or*, both may be equally correct.

INTEGRATING THE LANGUAGE ARTS

Literature Link. Authors often use misspelling and nonstandard grammar to create dialects for characters. Have students read a story such as Marjorie Kinnan Rawlings's "Jody's Discovery" and discuss at least five examples of misspellings used to indicate dialect.

MECHANICS

SEGMENT 3 *(pp. 648–661)*

WORDS OFTEN CONFUSED

OBJECTIVE

- To identify often-confused words and to use them correctly

5. Aunt Dorothy believes that there are only two things in life that are certain: death and ~~taxs~~. **5.** taxes
6. We've heard her say "There's no use crying over spilled milk" and "~~Wishs~~ won't wash ~~dishs~~" about a thousand times apiece. **6.** Wishes/dishes
7. Aunt Dorothy's old-time sayings are ~~echos~~ of her childhood. **7.** echoes
8. Sometimes we get tired of hearing these little bits of folk wisdom, especially when Aunt Dorothy and all the little ~~Kellies~~ come over to visit for the holidays. **8.** Kelleys
9. However, Aunt Dorothy is so lovable that we just smile and listen to her proverbs and ~~storys~~. **9.** stories
10. Sometimes she says something really worthwhile, like "There are only two things that money can't buy—true love and home-grown ~~tomatos~~." **10.** tomatoes

MECHANICS

Words Often Confused

People often confuse the words in each of the following groups. Some of these words are ***homonyms.*** They are pronounced the same, but they have different meanings and spellings. Others have the same or similar spellings.

already	*at an earlier time* The show has *already* begun.
all ready	*all prepared; completely prepared* The floats are *all ready* for the fiesta.
altar	[noun] *a table or stand used for religious ceremonies* My uncle Chee wove the cloth for the *altar*.
alter	[verb] *to change* A flood can *alter* a riverbed.

MECHANICS

Teacher's ResourceBank™

RESOURCES

WORDS OFTEN CONFUSED

QUICK REMINDER

A good way to help students master confusing words is to point out that similar words often function as different parts of speech. Write the following words on the chalkboard and ask the students to supply the corresponding parts of speech:

1. affect [verb]; effect [noun, verb]
2. accept [verb]; except [preposition, verb]
3. advice [noun]; advise [verb]

altogether	*entirely* I'm *altogether* lost.
all together	*everyone or everything in the same place* Let's sit *all together* at the movie.
brake	[noun] *a device to stop a machine* The front *brake* on my bike squeaks.
break	[verb] *to fracture; to shatter* Try not to *break* your promises.

EXERCISE 9 **Choosing Between Words Often Confused**

From each pair in parentheses, choose the word or words that will make the sentence correct.

EXAMPLE **1.** Can the artist (*altar, alter*) the design?
1. *alter*

1. Did you help (*brake, break*) the piñata, Felipe?
2. Who arranged the flowers on the (*altar, alter*)?
3. I've (*all ready, already*) seen that movie.
4. My mom was (*all together, altogether*) pleased with my report card.
5. Don't forget to set the emergency (*brake, break*).

capital	*a city, the location of a government* Havana is the *capital* of Cuba.
capitol	*building; statehouse* Our state *capitol* is made of granite.
cloths	*pieces of cloth* My aunt brought these kente *cloths* home from Ghana.
clothes	*wearing apparel* Bob irons his own *clothes*.

MECHANICS

LEP/ESL

General Strategies. Homonyms might seem strange to many ESL students whose native languages lack or have few such pairs of confusing words. Ask the students to find in their native languages the equivalent words of the English homonyms that give them trouble. The corresponding words in their native languages may serve as mnemonics to help them remember which homonym to use in any given situation.

LESS-ADVANCED STUDENTS

Some students might need extra help to master homonyms. Write the following pairs of words on the chalkboard and ask volunteers to circle the syllables or letters that differentiate each pair. Have other volunteers look up the words in a dictionary and report on the different definitions.

1. compliment, complement [*i, e*]
2. stationary, stationery [*a, e*]
3. their, there [*eir, ere*]
4. threw, through [*ew, ough*]
5. weak, week [*a, e*]
6. capital, capitol [*a, o*]

MECHANICS

COOPERATIVE LEARNING

Divide the class into three teams and give each team a different list of ten homonyms. Then challenge the teams to find the homonym(s) of each word on their lists by using a dictionary if necessary. You may want to recognize the team that finishes first and the team with the most homonyms.

A DIFFERENT APPROACH

The following memory tricks can help some students with confusing words:

1. all right—If it's not *all right,* it's all wrong.
2. dessert—When this is served, we often want two (two *s*'s).
3. hear—We do this with our *ears.*
4. piece—A *pie* contains this.
5. stationery—You move a pen across this.

MECHANICS

coarse	[adjective] *rough, crude, not fine* Some cities still use *coarse* salt to melt snow on streets and roads.
course	[noun] *path of action; series of studies* [also used in the expression *of course*] What *course* should we follow to accomplish our goal? The counselor suggested several *courses* for us to take. I can't, *of course,* tell you what to do.
desert [des'ert]	[noun] *a dry, sandy region; a wilderness* Plants and animals of the *desert* can survive on little water.
desert [de•sert']	[verb] *to abandon, to leave* Don't *desert* your friends when they need you.
dessert [de•sert']	[noun] *the final course of a meal* What's for *dessert* tonight?

EXERCISE 10 **Choosing Between Words Often Confused**

From each pair in parentheses, choose the word that will make the sentence correct.

EXAMPLE 1. The sand on the beach is (*coarse, course*).
1. *coarse*

1. The Mojave (*Desert, Dessert*) is located in southeastern California.
2. Juan packed lightweight (*clothes, cloths*) for his trip to Mexico.
3. The sailor set a (*coarse, course*) for the port of Pago Pago.
4. When was the (*capital, capitol*) built, and how long has the state legislature been meeting there?
5. For (*desert, dessert*) we had pears and cheese.

REVIEW D

OBJECTIVE

- To proofread sentences for spelling errors and to correct the words that are misspelled

INTEGRATING THE LANGUAGE ARTS

Technology Link. You may want to discuss the use of spell-check features for students who use word processors. Explain that the computer will search for words not in its dictionary, ask about them, and suggest alternative spellings. Be careful to remind students of the danger of depending entirely on computers for spelling. Most spell-check programs will not recognize the misuse of a homonym. Discuss the responsibilities of careful proofreading in addition to using spell-check features.

 REVIEW D

Proofreading Sentences to Correct Spelling Errors

For each of the following sentences, write correctly the word or words that are misspelled.

EXAMPLE **1. The students are already for the Fall Festival.**
1. *all ready*

1. Throughout history, most societies and cultures from the hot ~~dessert~~ regions to the cold northern regions have celebrated the harvest. **1.** desert
2. The Jewish celebration of Sukkot marks the time when the harvest was gathered and the people were ~~already~~ for winter. **2.** all ready
3. The most important tradition of Sukkot called for the family to live ~~altogether~~ in a temporary shelter called a sukkah. **3.** all together
4. Today, of ~~coarse~~, Jews still celebrate Sukkot, but they simply eat a meal outdoors under a shelter like this one. **4.** course

5. Native Americans believed that without the help of the gods there would be a ~~brake~~ in their good fortune. **5.** break

MECHANICS

MECHANICS

COOPERATIVE LEARNING

For a class project, have students compile a thesaurus from the confusing words listed in this chapter plus any they might discover for themselves. Divide the class into teams of two or three and assign each team confusing words from this chapter.

Give each team a stack of index cards. Instruct the teams to write one word on each card, followed by synonyms found in dictionaries, usage books, thesauruses, or from their own knowledge.

Once the cards have been completed, proofread, and corrected, ask for volunteers to alphabetize the cards. Enter them on a word processor and print a copy of the finished thesaurus for each member of the class.

MECHANICS

6. During their planting ceremonies, most Native Americans honored their gods by wearing special ~~cloths~~ like those shown here. **6.** clothes
7. To thank their harvest gods, the Chinese and Japanese placed wheat on ~~alters~~. **7.** altars
8. The Japanese today do not ~~altar~~ this tradition much. **8.** alter
9. In most Japanese cities, including the ~~capitol~~, the people hold parades to thank the ocean for the food it provides. **9.** capital
10. Many families in the United States celebrate Thanksgiving by sharing a special holiday meal, often with pumpkin pie for ~~desert~~. **10.** dessert

MECHANICS

hear [verb] *to receive sounds through the ears*
When did you *hear* the news?
here [adverb] *in this place*
The mail is *here*.

its [possessive form of *it*]
You cannot judge a book by *its* cover.
it's [contraction of *it is* or *it has*]
It's your turn, Theresa.
It's been a long day.

lead [lēd]	[verb, present tense, rhymes with *need*] *to go first, to be a leader* Will you *lead* the singing, Rachel?
led	[verb, past tense of *lead*] *went first* The dog *led* its master to safety.
lead [lĕd]	[noun, rhymes with *red*] *a heavy metal; graphite used in pencils* *Lead* is no longer used in household paints. Use a pencil with a softer *lead* if you want to draw dark, heavy lines.
loose	[adjective, rhymes with *moose*] *not tight* *A loose* wheel on a bike is dangerous.
lose	[verb] *to suffer loss* That sudden, loud noise made me *lose* my place.

MECHANICS

EXERCISE 11 **Choosing Spelling Words to Complete Sentences**

From each pair in parentheses, choose the word that will make the sentence correct.

EXAMPLE 1. Rabbi Epstein (*lead, led*) our group during our tour of Israel.
1. *led*

1. We could (*hear, here*) the clanking of the heavy (*lead, led*) gates.
2. A kimono is a (*loose, lose*) Japanese garment with short, wide sleeves and a sash.
3. Mom said that (*its, it's*) your turn to wash the dishes tonight.
4. (*Hear, Here*) is a good article about Black History Month.
5. I hope the team doesn't (*loose, lose*) (*its, it's*) opening game.

TIMESAVER

Any of the exercises in this segment can be quickly graded by having the students exchange papers and mark corrections as you write the answers on the chalkboard.

MECHANICS

passed	[verb, past tense of *pass*] *went by* We *passed* you on the way to school this morning.
past	[noun] *that which has gone by;* [preposition] *beyond;* [adjective] *ended* You can learn much from the *past.* The band marched *past* the school. The *past* week was a busy one.
peace	*quiet, order, and security* People all over the world long for *peace.*
piece	*a part of something* I had a delicious *piece* of spinach pie at the Greek festival.
plain	[adjective] *simple, common;* [noun] *a flat area of land* Raul's directions were *plain* and clear. The coastal *plain* was flat and barren.
plane	[noun] *a flat surface; a tool; an airplane* A rectangle is a four-sided *plane* with four right angles. Wood shavings curled from the *plane* to the workshop floor. The *plane* flew nonstop to Atlanta.
principal	[noun] *the head of a school;* [adjective] *chief, main* The middle-school *principal* visited the high school. The committee's *principal* task is preserving the park.
principle	[noun] *a rule of conduct; a general truth* Freedom of speech is one of the *principles* of democracy.

MECHANICS

REVIEW E

OBJECTIVE

- To proofread a paragraph for spelling errors and to correct the words that are misspelled

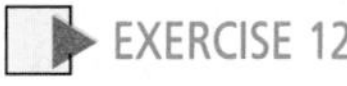

EXERCISE 12 **Choosing Between Words Often Confused**

From each pair in parentheses, choose the word that will make the sentence correct.

EXAMPLE **1.** Florence Griffith-Joyner quickly (*passed, past*) the other runners.
1. *passed*

1. The Old Order Amish wear (*plain, plane*) clothes.
2. Many Americans believe that the golden rule is a good (*principal, principle*) to live by.
3. The trees are just (*passed, past*) their most beautiful fall colors.
4. One (*peace, piece*) of the puzzle was missing.
5. Komako used a (*plain, plane*) to smooth the rough edge of the door.

REVIEW E **Proofreading a Paragraph to Correct Spelling Errors**

For each sentence in the following paragraph, write correctly the word or words that are misspelled.

EXAMPLE [1] Often, people don't know how precious something is until they loose it.
1. *lose*

[1] Several months ago, my aunt had what we all thought was a ~~plane~~ old cold. [2] In the ~~passed~~ her doctor had said there was no cure for a cold, so my aunt didn't even seek treatment. [3] No one knew that she had an ear infection that would ~~led~~ to a hearing loss in one ear. [4] Soon, my aunt realized that she was hearing only ~~peaces~~ of conversations, and could no longer hear out of her left ear. [5] When she went to the doctor, he explained that an infection had caused her to ~~loose~~ hearing in that ear. [6] The doctor gave her a chart like the one on the next page, showing the ~~principle~~ types of hearing aids. [7] He suggested the in-the-canal hearing aid because ~~its~~ barely

MECHANICS

ANSWERS

Review E

1. plain
2. past
3. lead
4. pieces
5. lose
6. principal
7. it's
8. Its
9. course
10. hear

MECHANICS

noticeable when in place. [8] ~~It's~~ small size really surprised me. [9] The doctor told my aunt, of ~~coarse~~, that new advances in hearing technology are being made every day. [10] Some people who could not ~~here~~ at all before can now be helped.

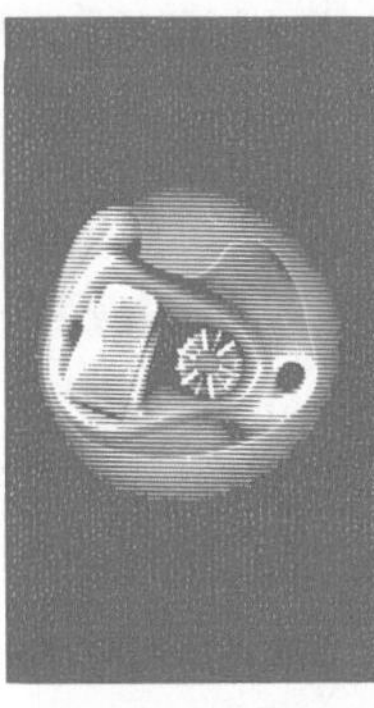
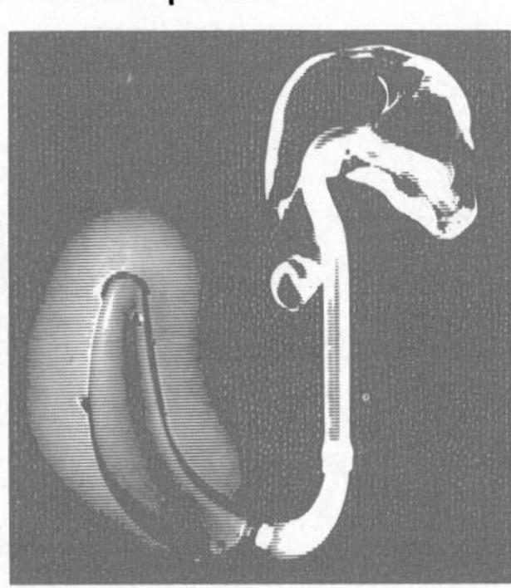

stationary	[adjective] *in a fixed position* The desks are *stationary,* but the chairs can be moved.
stationery	[noun] *writing paper* Sarah designs her own *stationery.*
their	[possessive form of *they*] *Their* pitcher struck out six players.
there	[adverb] *a place* [also used to begin a sentence] I'll see you *there.* *There* are more than two million books in the Harold Washington Library in Chicago.
they're	[contraction of *they are*] *They're* right behind you.
threw	[verb, past tense of *throw*] *hurled* Zack *threw* the ball to me.
through	[preposition] Let's walk *through* the park.

MECHANICS

EXERCISE 13 Choosing Between Words Often Confused

From each group in parentheses, choose the word that will make the sentence correct.

EXAMPLE **1. (*Their, They're, There*) goes the space shuttle!**
1. *There*

1. The 100-yard dash will begin over (*their, there, they're*).
2. The girls (*threw, through*) everything into (*their, there, they're*) lockers and ran onto the field.
3. Earth was once thought to be (*stationary, stationery*) in space.
4. (*Threw, Through*) the door bounded a large dog.
5. Are you sure (*their, there, they're*) not coming?

to	[preposition] We drove *to* Mexico City.
too	[adverb] *also; more than enough* Am I invited *too*? Your poem has *too* many syllables to be a haiku.
two	*one plus one* Ms. Red Cloud's last name is *two* words.
weak	[adjective] *feeble; not strong* People with *weak* ankles have difficulty ice-skating.
week	[noun] *seven days* The club meets once a *week.*
who's	[contraction of *who is* or *who has*] *Who's* wearing a watch? *Who's* seen Frida Kahlo's paintings?
whose	[possessive form of *who*] I wonder *whose* backpack this is.

MECHANICS

INTEGRATING THE LANGUAGE ARTS

Mechanics and Writing. If students are having problems finding misspelled words as they proofread, suggest that they go over their work backwards. Tell them to pay attention to each word and to circle any word they are uncertain about. After they have gone over their papers, they should check each circled word in a dictionary.

MECHANICS

REVIEWS F and G

OBJECTIVES

- To identify and use correctly often-confused words
- To proofread a paragraph for spelling errors and to correct the words that are misspelled

your	[possessive form of *you*] Rest *your* eyes now and then when you read.
you're	[contraction of *you are*] *You're* my best friend.

EXERCISE 14 **Choosing Between Words Often Confused**

From each group in parentheses, choose the word that will make the sentence correct.

EXAMPLE **1.** I wonder (*who's, whose*) won the election.
1. *who's*

1. (*Who's, Whose*) story did you like best?
2. Walking (*to, too, two*) the store, he began to feel (*weak, week*).
3. Does (*your, you're*) dad work there (*to, too, two*)?
4. It took me a (*weak, week*) to complete my project.
5. If (*your, you're*) not making that noise, (*who's, whose*) doing it?

MECHANICS

REVIEW F **Choosing Between Words Often Confused**

From each group in parentheses, choose the word or words that will make the sentence correct.

EXAMPLE **1.** Don't (*loose, lose*) your house key.
1. *lose*

1. Which of these (*to, too, two*) boxes of (*stationary, stationery*) do you like better?
2. The Israelis and the Palestinians met in Madrid, the (*capital, capitol*) of Spain, for the (*peace, piece*) talks.
3. (*Principal, Principle*) Wong raised his hand for silence, and the students waited to (*hear, here*) what he would say.

MECHANICS

4. These curtains will likely be hard to (*altar*, *alter*) because the fabric is so (*coarse*, *course*).
5. (*Its*, *It's*) (*all together*, *altogether*) too easy to confuse similar words.
6. Ruth vowed to (*lead*, *led*) the life of an exile rather than to (*desert*, *dessert*) Naomi.
7. Can that (*plain*, *plane*) (*brake*, *break*) the sound barrier?
8. We're (*all ready*, *already*) for the big game this (*weak*, *week*).
9. (*Your*, *You're*) next chore is to dust; the (*clothes*, *cloths*) are on the counter.
10. The (*to*, *too*, *two*) friends (*passed*, *past*) the time pleasantly reading (*there*, *their*, *they're*) books.

REVIEW G Proofreading a Paragraph to Correct Spelling Errors

For each sentence in the following paragraph, write correctly the word or words that are misspelled. If a sentence is correct, write *C*.

EXAMPLE [1] Its time to test you're knowledge of South American history.
1. *It's; your*

[1] Starting about A.D. 1200, people known as the Incas began ~~too~~ take over the western portion of South America. [2] Look at the map on the next page, and you'll see that ~~thier~~ territory included mountains, seacoasts, river valleys, and ~~desserts~~. [3] The ~~capitol~~ of the Incan empire was Cuzco. [4] The Incas created an impressive road system that connected Cuzco with the rest of ~~there~~ empire. [5] These hard-working people also built storehouses and ~~developped~~ large irrigation projects. [6] To help them manage their huge empire, they used a device called a *quipu* as their ~~principle~~ method of keeping records. [7] The quipu (shown on the next page) is a series of knotted, colored cords. [8] With it, the Incas recorded such information as the number of people ~~liveing~~ in an

MECHANICS

ANSWERS
Review G
1. to
2. their; deserts
3. capital
4. their
5. developed
6. principal
7. C
8. living
9. mid-1500's
10. break

MECHANICS

LEP/ESL

General Strategies. If it is available, software that teaches spelling can be very helpful for ESL students. Pair ESL students with native speakers of English, so that the native speakers can model pronunciation, an integral part of spelling skill.

LESS-ADVANCED STUDENTS

Some long words may confuse students when the students see the words written. It might help students to see that many long words are made up of combinations of letters that by themselves may also be words—words the students can already spell and pronounce. Write the following words on the chalkboard and ask students to copy them. Then have the students find the small words within the longer words by covering parts of the longer word—in both directions—one syllable, or even one letter, at a time.

1. peppermint [pep, pepper, mint]
2. breakfast [break, fast]
3. another [an, other, her]
4. careless [car, are, care, less]
5. together [to, get, her]

MECHANICS

area, the movements of the planets, and the amount of goods in storage. [9] The Incan civilization lasted until the Spanish arrived in the mid~~-1500s~~. [10] In only a short time, Spanish conquistadors were able to defeat the Incas and ~~brake~~ up their empire.

MECHANICS

50 Commonly Misspelled Words

As you study the following words, pay special attention to the letters in italics. These letters usually cause the biggest problems in spelling the words correctly.

a*ch*e	col*o*r	fr*ie*nd	p*ie*ce	te*a*r
ag*ai*n	cou*gh*	g*u*ess	re*a*dy	tho*ugh*
a*l*ways	cou*l*d	ha*l*f	s*ai*d	thr*ough*
an*gle*	c*ou*ntry	ho*u*r	s*a*ys	toni*gh*t
ans*w*er	doct*o*r	inst*ea*d	se*e*ms	tro*u*ble
bri*e*f	do*e*s	*k*new	sho*e*s	we*a*r
b*u*ilt	do*n't*	l*ai*d	sin*c*e	w*h*ere
b*u*sy	*ea*rly	min*ute*	stra*igh*t	w*o*men
b*u*y	ea*s*y	of*t*en	s*u*gar	wo*n't*
ca*n't*	ev*e*ry	*on*ce	s*u*re	*w*rite

100 Spelling Words

absence
achieve
adjective
advertisement
against
aisles
announce
apologize
arithmetic
assignment

autobiography
average
background
bacteria
ballad
benefit
brilliant
business
career
ceased

century
choice
communicate
conservation
constitution
courteous
criticism
curiosity
decimal
delicate

dinosaur
disguise
divide
ecology
eighth
embarrass
environment
equipment

especially
excellent

experience
explanation
fantasy
faucet
fourth
gasoline
gene
genuine
grammar
height

humorous
imitation
immediately
jewelry
legislature
liter
magazine
medicine
message
musician

myth
neighbor
nuclear
occurrence
ounce
passage
physical
poisonous
popularity
population

practice
preferred
prejudice
probably
pyramid
recipe

remainder
rescue
resources
review

rumor
seize
separate
shiny
similar
solar
solemn
species
surface
surprise

temporary
theme
tomorrow
tragedy
treasure
trial
valuable
vegetable
weapon
wrestle

MECHANICS

MECHANICS

PART THREE

RESOURCES

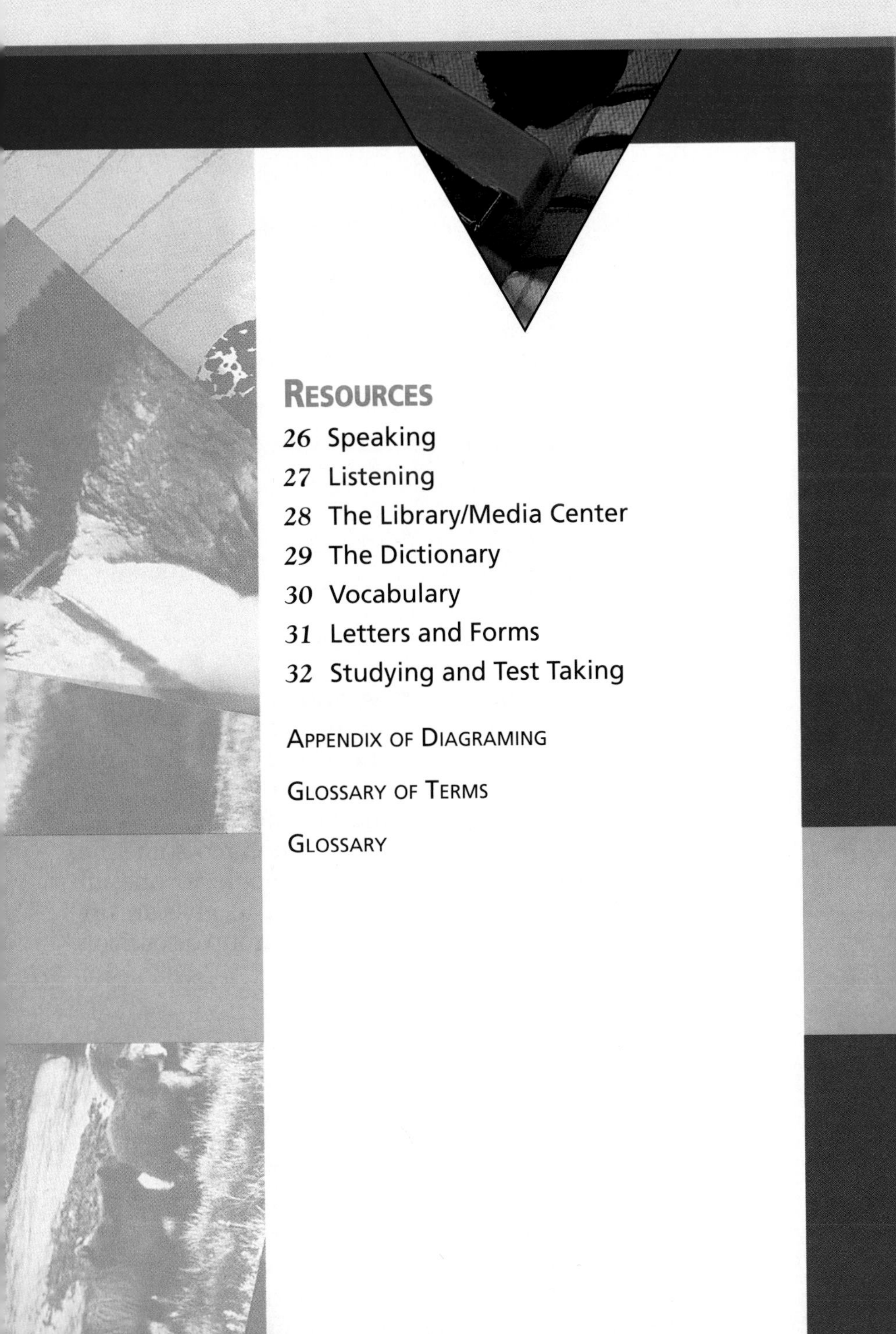

RESOURCES

SPEAKING *(pp. 664–675)*

OBJECTIVES

- To write a brief telephone dialogue
- To prepare directions or instructions for a given situation
- To explain how certain introductions would be made
- To choose a topic for, gather information on, and present a short report ☛

Teacher's ResourceBank™

RESOURCES

SPEAKING

CHAPTER OVERVIEW

This chapter includes informal speaking strategies for having conversations, using the telephone, giving directions and explanations, and making introductions. This chapter also offers instructions for preparing formal speeches. It provides help with selecting topics, gathering information, and organizing and delivering speeches. A section titled **Special Speaking Occasions** deals with making announcements and introductions to presentations. The section on group discussions gives students specific strategies for participating in groups. The chapter concludes with instructions for developing material for oral interpretations.

RESOURCES

26 SPEAKING

Skills and Strategies

You probably enjoy chatting with your friends and others you know well. Sometimes you will find yourself speaking to others in new and different situations. For example, you may need to give a message on the telephone to someone you don't know well. You may give directions or instructions to someone. You may need to introduce two people to one another. Or, in school, you may need to give an oral report to your class or to take part in a group discussion.

RESOURCES

Communicating with Others

Communication is a two-way process. First, a person speaks, telling ideas or feelings to one or more listeners. Then the listeners react or respond to what the speaker says. This response is called ***feedback.***

Listeners may respond in many ways. They may say something to the speaker, or they may communicate a message without words. For example, it's easy for a speaker to judge the meaning of feedback from listeners when they smile or applaud.

- To plan a group discussion
- To present an oral interpretation of a piece of literature

Speaking Socially

In many social situations, remember to speak politely and clearly.

Speaking on the Telephone

It is important to use the telephone courteously. Here are some suggestions.

GUIDELINES FOR TELEPHONING

1. Be sure to dial the correct number. If you get a wrong number, apologize for the error.
2. Call at a time that is convenient for the person you are calling.
3. Speak clearly. Say who you are when the person answers. If the person you're calling isn't there, you may wish to leave your name and number and perhaps a short message.
4. Don't stay on the telephone too long.

Giving Directions or Instructions

You may be asked to give directions or explain how to do something. Make sure your directions or instructions are clear and complete. Here are some pointers.

HOW TO GIVE DIRECTIONS OR INSTRUCTIONS

1. Before you give information, plan what you want to say. Think of the information as a series of steps.
2. Explain the steps to your listener in order. Be sure you haven't skipped any steps or left out any necessary information.
3. If necessary, repeat all of the directions or instructions so your listener can rehearse them.

QUICK REMINDER

Have the class brainstorm a list of characteristics of good speakers and write them on the chalkboard. To prompt students, ask questions such as the following ones: Whom do you enjoy listening to? How do they present information and ideas? Do they use jokes or stories as examples? What kind of language do they use? Do they use hand gestures? What do they look at while speaking? What kinds of facial expressions do they use?

Tell students to keep their ideas about good speaking in mind for comparison with the methods and ideas presented in the chapter.

RESOURCES

STUDENTS WITH SPECIAL NEEDS

Some of the activities in this chapter may be stressful for students with emotional disabilities or with expressive-language problems. You may want to use cooperative-learning groups for those activities that may create problems. Encourage all students to participate in group discussions, but do not force a student to speak in front of the class. Students can contribute in other ways. For example, one student might provide the visuals for group presentations.

Also, it may be helpful to make a chart on which students can record the number and nature of interactions with others. This will help them become more aware of their social interactive behavior.

COOPERATIVE LEARNING

Divide the class into groups of four or five to make various types of introductions to small groups. Each group member will receive a different introduction task chosen randomly from the following possibilities:

1. Introduce one member of your group to another member of the group.
2. Introduce yourself to the group.
3. Introduce a member of your group to a member of the group who will play the part of an adult.
4. Introduce one member of the group to each member individually.
5. Introduce the president of the United States to your group.

RESOURCES

Making Introductions

Sometimes you may need to introduce other people who know you but not each other. Or, at other times, if no one present knows you or if no one is making introductions, you may need to introduce yourself. Here are suggestions for making introductions politely.

HOW TO MAKE INTRODUCTIONS

- When you introduce friends your own age, you can usually use first names. (For example, you can simply say, "Gina, this is Takai.")
- When you introduce a younger person to an older person, say the older person's name first. (For example, you might say, "Dad, I'd like you to meet my language arts teacher, Mrs. Schultz. Mrs. Schultz, this is my father, Michael Rozetti.")
- Introduce yourself to others if no one introduces you first. Start a conversation by mentioning something the person might talk to you about. (For example, "Hi, my my name is Monica. I just moved here from Ohio. What's your name?")
- Don't present someone to a roomful of people all at once. Instead, introduce the person to small groups at a time. (For example, "Jamie, Suzette, Kim—I'd like you to meet Chris Polivka." Or, "Hey, group, this is our new classmate, Rico Morelos. Rico, here are Anya, Sharria, and Li.")
- When you're introduced to someone your own age, you can offer a handshake if you think it is appropriate or friendly. If an older person extends a hand, it's polite for you to shake hands.
- If you are introducing two people and you know that there's something they have in common, you might mention it so that they have something that they can talk about. (For example, "Juana, this is my cousin Bill. Bill, Juana likes to play tennis, just like you do.")

RESOURCES

Speaking Formally

Formal speaking is speaking that is planned. This means that a specific time and place are set aside for someone to speak. The purpose for this type of speaking is to inform, persuade, or entertain the audience. The most common types of formal speaking that you hear around you in school every day are announcements, introductions to a presentation, and oral reports.

Making Announcements

At times, you may need to make an *announcement.* An ***announcement*** is a short, formal speech that provides information to a group of listeners. An announcement often includes instructions about a situation or an event. An announcement should be clear and easy to understand.

HOW TO MAKE ANNOUNCEMENTS

1. Include all important facts that your audience will need to know. Most announcements include the following information:
   - the kind of event or occasion
   - who is involved
   - the time
   - the location where the event will take place
   - why the event is important
   - any special information, such as the amount of an admission fee
2. Add interesting details that will catch your listeners' attention.
3. Announce your message slowly, clearly, and briefly.
4. If necessary, repeat the most important facts.

INTEGRATING THE LANGUAGE ARTS

Technology Link. To help students note the differences between the speaking techniques of professional speakers, celebrities, and public figures, record or have students record parts of political speeches or interviews from news broadcasts. Playing these tapes in the classroom will help students study the styles and effectiveness of different speakers.

COMMON ERROR

Problem. Sometimes speakers stare at the floor, their hands, or the back wall. Other speakers will choose one person in the audience and deliver their speeches to that person alone.

Solution. Remind students to keep their eyes moving and to try to make eye contact at least once with everyone in the audience.

COOPERATIVE LEARNING

Have students work in pairs to write speeches introducing famous people. Possible subjects can include political candidates, historical figures, rock musicians, and so on. This activity can be integrated with a lesson on the library because some research may be needed. When the speeches are written, both students in each pair should share the presentation.

INTEGRATING THE LANGUAGE ARTS

Literature Link. To give students practice in delivering a speech, have them select a portion of a famous speech, such as Lincoln's Gettysburg Address or John F. Kennedy's inauguration speech, to deliver to the class. Before they deliver their speeches, make sure students study their selections for elements they think need to be stressed and to decide on the best way to present the speech to the class.

Making an Introduction to a Presentation

An introduction is a special kind of announcement. An introduction is sometimes given to prepare an audience for a speaker's presentation. If you are introducing a speaker, you will need to attract your listeners' attention and provide brief information about the speaker or the speech topic. This information might include details about the speaker's background, experience, or accomplishments. Keep your introduction brief. Your introduction is meant to prepare the audience to hear what the speaker has to say.

Making an Oral Report

From time to time, you may be asked to give a short speech, or report. You might tell an interesting story, talk about a book you have read, or inform others how to do something. Sometimes the topic for your talk may be chosen for you. On other occasions, you may be allowed to choose your own topic.

Planning Your Report

Giving a successful oral report requires careful planning and preparation.

RESOURCES

HOW TO PREPARE AN ORAL REPORT

1. *Choose a topic that will work well for your speech.* The best topic to choose is one that you are interested in talking about and that you think your audience is interested in hearing about.
2. *Make your topic as specific as possible.* Most oral reports have a time limit. This means you have to limit your topic to fit the time you're allowed.

(continued)

HOW TO PREPARE AN ORAL REPORT *(continued)*

3. *Think about your audience.* Before preparing a talk, ask yourself what your listeners already know about your topic. If they don't know very much about this topic, you'll need to give some background information. However, if they know a lot about your topic, you may need to talk only about information about the topic that you think they'd be less familiar with.
4. *Consider your purpose.* Think about *why* you are speaking. Do you want to *inform* your audience about some situation or process? Would you like to *persuade* them to accept your opinions or take some action? Or, maybe you want to *entertain* them by telling an amusing story.
5. *Gather information for your talk.* Look for material about your topic. Read books, newspapers, or magazines. Talk to people who know about the topic.

 REFERENCE NOTE: For more instructions on gathering information, see pages 281–285.

Organizing Your Report

When you have decided the purpose and the length of your oral report, you can use the information you have gathered to organize and prepare your report. Organizing your ideas for an oral report is almost like writing them. Your best suggestions on deciding what you want to say can be found in the chapters of this textbook that help you write your ideas according to your purpose.

For example, if the purpose of your report is to inform, see pages 182–183 for ideas and suggestions about how to organize information. Or, if you plan to persuade your audience, you should see pages 202–232 for ideas about persuasive techniques.

A DIFFERENT APPROACH

Ask students to draw detailed maps of the routes from their houses to school. Encourage students to include important landmarks and to show the distance between points as accurately as possible. Labeling streets, buildings, and intersections will make their maps easier to follow.

After they have completed their maps, have each student explain the correct route to another student, to a group, or to the class by using their maps as visuals. Encourage listeners to ask questions about any part of the oral directions or the maps that is unclear or confusing.

RESOURCES

Preparing Your Report

Once you have decided exactly what you want to say, you can prepare for giving your report. Make a few notes on 3″ × 5″ note cards and refer to them while you are giving your report. Each note card should have one main idea, and perhaps a few notes about details you plan to mention. Number your note cards to help you keep them in order. Then practice giving your report, using your note cards until you are comfortable referring to them while you are speaking.

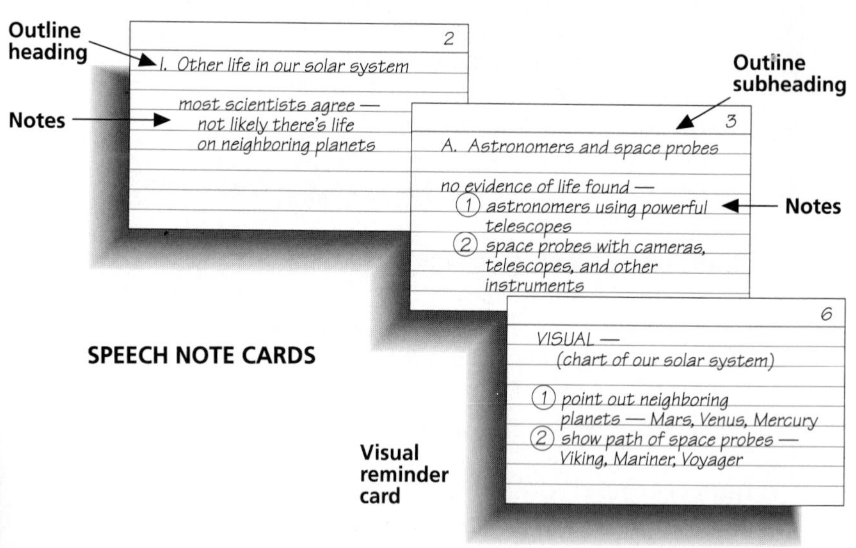

SPEECH NOTE CARDS

Giving Your Report

Most people feel nervous before speaking to an audience. Practice your talk until you feel confident with the material and your note cards. If you feel especially nervous before you speak, take a slow, deep breath. Hold it, then slowly let it out. Above all, pay attention to what you're saying.

RESOURCES

LESS-ADVANCED STUDENTS

Students who do not feel confident about their speaking abilities or who have had little practice in speaking before the class might be nervous and unable to do their best. You might allow these students to practice speaking to the class first from their seats, then seated in front of the class, and finally, standing in front of the class.

HOW TO GIVE A REPORT

1. *Be confident.* Stand up straight but not stiffly. Look as if you're alert and interested in what you're saying.
2. *Look at your audience.* Try to make direct eye contact with your listeners. Speak directly to your audience.
3. *Use your voice effectively.* Use your voice to express your ideas. The way you speak adds interest to your talk and meaning to your message.
   - Speak loudly enough for everyone to hear.
   - To keep your listeners interested, your voice should rise and fall naturally as you speak.
   - Speak at a comfortable, relaxed rate. Pause for a moment before you go on to a different thought.
   - Pronounce your words clearly and carefully. Use a dictionary to find the pronunciation of unfamiliar words.

Group Discussions

Setting a Purpose

In many of your classes you probably work in groups. The purpose of group discussions is to accomplish a specific task or goal. This goal may be

- to discuss and share ideas
- to cooperate in group learning
- to solve a problem
- to arrive at a decision or to make a specific recommendation

To help your group decide about your purpose, identify what you'll need to accomplish within the time you are allowed.

COMMON ERROR

Problem. Many students fall into the trap of asking too many closed-ended questions. If the purpose of communication is to initiate conversation, open-ended questions will produce better results. Asking questions that can elicit only yes or no responses does not initiate conversation.

Solution. Explain to students that open-ended questions elicit details or explanations and prompt the other person to share feelings and ideas. This sharing of personal insight is the goal of interviews, but it will not occur unless the interviewer asks questions that can lead to a lengthy conversation.

RESOURCES

LEP/ESL

General Strategies. Students from cultures that stress collective rather than individual thought are often apprehensive about expressing private opinions that might vary from the group's position. However, role-playing can provide a protective mask behind which they can speak more comfortably.

You may want to assign various roles and topics to students to help them relax when they are expressing opinions in front of others.

RESOURCES

Assigning Roles

Each person involved in a group discussion has a role to play. Each role has special responsibilities. For example, your group may choose a chairperson to help keep the discussion moving smoothly. Someone else may be selected as the secretary, or reporter (recorder), who has the responsibility of taking notes during the discussion.

GUIDELINES FOR GROUP DISCUSSIONS

1. *Prepare for the discussion.* If you know what your group will talk about, spend some time before the discussion gathering information about the topic.
2. *Listen to what others say.* Be willing to learn from what other group members have to offer. Don't interrupt when others are speaking. Speak only when it's your turn to speak.
3. *Do your part.* Contribute to the discussion and share your ideas openly. Take only your fair share of time to talk. Be friendly and polite when it's someone else's turn to speak.
4. *Stay on the discussion topic.* Try not to wander away from the discussion topic. If necessary, politely remind others to stick to the subject.
5. *Ask questions.* If you don't understand something, ask questions.

RESOURCES

Oral Interpretation

The purpose of an *oral interpretation* is to entertain. Sometimes, instead of talking about material you have written, you might be required to give an oral interpretation. An ***oral interpretation*** is a lively reading of someone else's written material.

Choosing a Selection

Short stories, novels, plays, and poems can provide you with good material for oral interpretation. Here are suggestions for finding a literary work that you can use for an oral interpretation.

SELECTIONS FOR ORAL INTERPRETATION

TYPE OF LITERATURE	DESCRIPTION OF POSSIBLE SELECTION
poem	a poem that ■ tells a story, such as an epic or a narrative poem ■ has a speaker (using the word *I*) ■ has a conversation between characters ■ is expressive of a particular emotion
short story	a brief story, or portion of a story, with ■ a beginning, middle, and end ■ characters whose words are expressed in a way that you can act out (such as a narrator who tells the story or characters who talk to one another, using dialogue in quotation marks)
play	a short play, or a scene from a play, with ■ a beginning, middle, and end ■ one or more characters with dialogue

When you choose a selection, think about the occasion. Determine how much time you will have for your presentation. Finally, consider your listeners. How will they respond to your selection? Will your audience find the selection interesting? Will they understand the meaning of your selection?

You may need to write an introduction for your interpretation. See page 668.

RESOURCES

Adapting Material

Sometimes you need to shorten a short story, a long poem, or a play for an oral interpretation This shortened version is called a ***cutting.*** To make a cutting, follow these suggestions.

1. Decide where the part of the story you want to use should begin and where it should end.
2. Cut out parts that don't have anything to do with the portion of the story you are telling.
3. From a short story, cut dialogue tags such as *he growled angrily.* Instead, use these clues to tell you how to act out the characters' words.

Presenting an Oral Interpretation

When you've chosen the piece of literature that you want to present, you can prepare a *reading script.* A ***reading script*** is a typed or neatly written copy of the selection that you can mark to show exactly how you want to present the material to your audience.

HOW TO MARK A READING SCRIPT

1. Underline any words or phrases you wish to stress.
2. Use a slash (/) to indicate a pause.
3. Make notes in the margin to show when you should vary the volume of your voice, show a special gesture, or suggest a particular tone.

Rehearse your selection carefully. Practice reading the material aloud, using voice tone, movements, and dramatic emphasis. Remember to make the meaning of your selection clear to your audience. Use a practice audience, or stand and practice in front of a mirror until you are satisfied with the way you plan to give your presentation.

COOPERATIVE LEARNING

To illustrate the importance of nonverbal communication, have students work in pairs to develop pantomimes. They might use short scenes from their literature books or create their own scenes depicting sports or hobby activities. As an alternative, suggest that each student create a scene that shows a relationship between two people, such as a scene in which an adolescent is asking a parent for permission to go to a friend's house or in which a parent is trying to feed a toddler. The rest of the class can evaluate the pantomimes on the basis of originality and on how clearly the actors illustrate the activity or relationship.

TIMESAVER

To evaluate the telephone dialogues students write for **Exercise 1,** make extra copies so students can read their dialogues to the class with partners. You can then evaluate the dialogues as they are presented.

RESOURCES

Review

EXERCISE 1 Practicing Telephone Dialogue

Write down a brief telephone dialogue for this situation: A friend calls to ask for help with a class project. Your mother needs the phone first.

EXERCISE 2 Giving Directions or Instructions

Prepare directions for this situation: Your parents plan to pick up a homework assignment you left in your locker at school. Explain how to find your locker, open it, and find the right paper.

EXERCISE 3 Making Introductions

Explain what you might say in this situation: Your cousin Nick is visiting your English class. Introduce him to your teacher, then to a classmate.

EXERCISE 4 Preparing and Giving a Report

Choose a topic for a short, three- to five-minute report on a topic that interests you. Gather information on your topic and make note cards. Then give your report.

EXERCISE 5 Participating in a Group Discussion

Plan a group discussion on a topic provided by your teacher. Set a purpose and a time limit for your discussion. Try to accomplish your goal in the time allowed.

EXERCISE 6 Presenting an Oral Interpretation

Select a piece of literature (a short story or play) that contains a scene with one or two characters. Prepare a reading script for a three-minute oral interpretation. Write a brief introduction.

ANSWERS

Exercise 1

Telephone dialogues will vary, but all should be based on the suggested situation.

ANSWERS

Exercise 2

Directions or instructions will vary, but all should be based on the suggested situation.

ANSWERS

Exercise 3

Introductions will vary, but all should be based on the suggested situation.

ANSWERS

Exercise 4

Reports will vary depending on subjects, but each should be no shorter than three and no longer than five minutes.

ANSWERS

Exercise 5

Students' discussions should be consistent with the chosen topic and purpose.

ANSWERS

Exercise 6

Oral interpretations will vary depending on the piece of literature involved. Interpretations should be consistent with the literature.

RESOURCES

LISTENING *(pp. 676–683)*

OBJECTIVES

- To make up questions and to read them aloud to the class
- To prepare interview questions to ask a famous person
- To listen to a speech and to respond to questions about the speech
- To identify propaganda techniques

Teacher's ResourceBank™

RESOURCES

LISTENING

CHAPTER OVERVIEW

This chapter introduces students to the idea that listening is a skill that involves using special strategies and developing good habits for hearing and understanding the spoken word. The strategies include techniques for courteous listening, for purposeful listening, and for understanding instructions. The LQ2R study method (**L**isten, **Q**uestion, **R**ecite, **R**e-listen) is presented as a way to increase understanding and retention of spoken information, and the steps in preparing and conducting an interview are outlined.

This chapter also offers a **Guidelines for Listening Critically** feature to help students learn to evaluate a speaker's ideas and to make decisions based on what is said. A section on **Common Propaganda Techniques** familiarizes students with how speakers and advertisers try to manipulate them.

RESOURCES

27 LISTENING

Strategies for Active Listening

Listening may sound easy, but it's not as simple as it seems. To listen carefully, you must keep your mind on what is being said.

Good listening habits are important to develop. Being a good listener is not just polite. Listening actively will help you to learn more easily and then to remember what you hear.

RESOURCES

Listening with a Purpose

You will be a more effective listener if you remember your purpose for listening. Some common purposes for listening are

- for enjoyment or entertainment
- for information or explanation
- for understanding
- for deciding or evaluating ideas

Listening for Information

Listening for Details

When you're listening to details, try to sort out information that answers the basic *5W-How?* questions: *Who? What? When? Where?* and *How?* As you listen, try to identify answers to these questions.

Listening to Instructions

It's important to listen carefully when you are given assignments, instructions, or directions. Follow these guidelines when listening to instructions.

1. Listen to each step. Listen for words that tell you when each step ends and the next one begins, such as *first, second, next, then,* and *last.*
2. Listen for the number of steps required and the order to follow. Take notes if necessary.
3. Make an outline of the steps to follow in your own mind. Then picture yourself completing each step in order.
4. Make sure you have all the necessary information and understand the instructions. Ask questions if you are unclear about any step.

Listening Politely

Follow these guidelines to be a courteous and effective listener.

1. *Look at the speaker.* Keep your eyes on the person who is speaking. Your attention tells the speaker that you're interested in what he or she is saying.
2. *Respect the speaker.* As a listener, you should evaluate what the speaker has to say. Be tolerant of the speaker's personality or background (including accent, clothing, customs, race, or religion).

RESOURCES

QUICK REMINDER

Ask students to pretend that they are secret agents and have to relay the following message as part of their mission. Be sure to warn students that the secret message may be given only once.

"Dr. Jones has invented a new bomb detector. He is hiding in the fourth house on Mulberry Street and is waiting to be taken to a safe place."

After you have read the message to them, ask students to answer the following questions:

1. What is the doctor's name? [Jones]
2. What street is he hiding on? [Mulberry]
3. Which house is he in? [fourth]
4. Where does he want to go? [to a safe place]

LEP/ESL

General Strategies. ESL students are at a disadvantage as far as listening skills are concerned because listening skills are based on prior knowledge of language and cultural contexts. Prior knowledge can enable a native speaker to comprehend information reasonably well without actively listening, but ESL students must depend solely on their limited knowledge of the language. This can put extra stress on them when they receive spoken information. Encourage students to speak up when they hear something they don't understand. Tell them it's better to ask questions than to miss important information.

RESOURCES

COOPERATIVE LEARNING

To give students practice in listening to instructions, pair students and give a copy of the following instructions to one student per pair. Have those students read the instructions to their partners. If the partners follow the instructions, the answer will be 3.

1. Pick any number between 1 and 10.
2. Multiply that number by 3.
3. Add 9.
4. Multiply by 2.
5. Divide by 6.
6. Subtract the original number.

3. *Don't interrupt the speaker.* Save your comments and questions until the speaker has finished.
4. *Pay attention.* Don't miss what is being said or keep others from being able to pay attention.
5. *Listen before you judge.* Listen to the speaker's entire message before you evaluate the speech.

Using the LQ2R Method

The LQ2R study method is especially helpful when you are listening to a speaker who is giving information or instructions.

L *Listen* carefully to information as it is being presented. Focus your attention on the speaker.

Q *Question* yourself as you listen. Make a list of your questions as you think of them.

R *Recite* to yourself in your own words the details of the information as the speaker presents them. Summarize information in your mind or jot down notes as you listen.

R *Re-listen* as the speaker concludes the presentation. Major points may be repeated.

Taking Notes

Taking notes can help you remember what a speaker says. Don't try to write down every word. Just put down a few key ideas and important details.

Interviewing

An ***interview*** is a special listening situation. When you need firsthand information for a project or a report, set up an interview with someone who knows about your topic.

Follow these suggestions for effective interviews.

Preparing for the Interview

1. Contact the person you would like to interview. Make arrangements to meet for the interview at a specific time and place.
2. Decide what information you most want to know from the person you are interviewing.
3. Make a list of questions to ask. Avoid questions that require simple yes or no answers.

Conducting the Interview

1. Be on time for the interview.
2. Listen carefully. Be courteous and patient. Show respect for what the person has to say, even if you disagree with the person's opinion.
3. Take notes. If you don't understand something, ask questions.
4. As you finish, thank the person for granting you the interview.

Following the Interview

1. Go over your notes to be sure they are clear.
2. Write a summary of the interview as soon as you can, so you'll remember clearly what was said.

Listening Critically

When you listen carefully, you can make decisions based on what you hear. Evaluating what you hear is known as ***critical listening.*** Critical listening is especially important when a speaker is trying to convince you to do something or to think in a certain way. The main purpose of critical listening is to be able to evaluate a speaker's ideas.

INTEGRATING THE LANGUAGE ARTS

Literature Link. To give students practice in listening to details, read the class a short story, such as Mark Twain's "The Story of the Bad Little Boy." After you have finished reading, ask the class a series of questions like these: Who were the main characters in the story? What was the setting of the story? What happened to the main character?

RESOURCES

A DIFFERENT APPROACH

Have students read and discuss the sections titled **Guidelines for Listening Critically** and **Common Propaganda Techniques.** When students have a thorough understanding of the difference between fact and opinion and understand the meaning of the terms *bias, motive,* and *propaganda,* read to them an editorial from a newspaper or a magazine. Have them listen carefully for signs of the author's bias. When you have finished reading, lead students in a discussion with the following questions:

1. How do you think the author feels about this issue?
2. How does the author make his or her opinion known?
3. What facts did the author use to support the opinion?

GUIDELINES FOR LISTENING CRITICALLY

1. *Listen for main ideas.* Identify the most important points. Listen for clue words, such as *major, minor, most important,* or similar words that help you to identify key ideas.
2. *Distinguish between facts and opinions.* Decide which of a speaker's remarks report facts and which express feelings or opinions. A ***fact*** is a statement of information that can be proved to be true. (For example, the saguaro is the state flower of Arizona.) An ***opinion*** is a belief or judgment about something. It cannot be proved to be true. (For example, if you say that chocolate is a better flavor than maple, that's an opinion, not a fact. It's a statement that can't be proved to be true.)
3. *Listen for the speaker's point of view.* Speakers may lean toward one point of view. They may sometimes present only one side of an issue and may not have enough real evidence to back up what they are saying.
4. *Determine the speaker's purpose.* A speaker may have a particular ***motive,*** or underlying reason, for persuading you. If a speaker has something to gain from convincing you to accept his or her opinions, weigh the speaker's arguments very carefully before you agree.

Understanding Propaganda Techniques

To get you to believe in something or to take some action, speakers may use common *propaganda techniques. **Propaganda techniques*** are ways of making an opinion seem very appealing. These techniques are often used in advertising in the mass media because they usually work. If you learn about these techniques, however, you are less likely to be swayed by speakers using them. You'll know the tricks!

COMMON PROPAGANDA TECHNIQUES	
Bandwagon	You are urged to "jump on the bandwagon" because "everyone's doing it." This technique works when people like to join the crowd. ■ "Four out of five teens prefer Teen Scene jeans."
Testimonial	Well-known people sometimes give an endorsement of a product or idea. However, the person might not know much about that particular product. ■ "I'm football hero Joe Manly, recommending Whoosh brand vacuum cleaners."
Emotional appeals	This technique uses words that appeal to your emotions instead of your logic or reasoning. ■ "My political opponent is a dirty, rotten crook!"
"Plain folks"	People who seem to be like you may be used to persuade you. This technique works because people tend to trust those like themselves. ■ "Hey, folks! Come on down and see your friendly neighbors at Hometown Auto Sales."
False cause and effect	This technique is used to suggest that because one event happened first, it caused a second event to occur. However, the two events may not actually be related in any way. ■ "I'm sure the only reason I didn't win the prize was because I walked under a ladder in the parking lot."

RESOURCES

STUDENTS WITH SPECIAL NEEDS

Some students will understand ideas more clearly when they participate in a related experience. To help students understand the **Common Propaganda Techniques** chart, videotape television commercials to show to the class. Ask them to decide which propaganda techniques are being employed.

RESOURCES

RESOURCES

Review

EXERCISE 1 Listening for Information

Make up five questions similar to the numbered items that follow. Read your questions aloud to your classmates, pausing about five seconds after reading each question to allow your listeners time to write down their answers. Then have your listeners check their answers to see how accurately they listened.

Students' questions will vary.

1. Here is a series of letters: *e–g–l–p–w*. What is the second letter? 1. g
2. Here is the order for pairs: first, Delmont and Rolo; then, Lucretia and Velma; last, Ling and Delia. What group is Rolo in? 2. first
3. Here is a list of colors: *blue, green, purple, orange, red*. What is the third color? 3. purple
4. The White Mountains are in New Hampshire, the Great Smoky Mountains are in Tennessee, and the Cascade Mountains are in Washington. Where are the White Mountains? 4. New Hampshire
5. Here is a list of starting times for movies and the theaters where they are showing: 6:30 at the Ritz, 7:15 at the Cinema West, 6:45 at the Film Palace, and 7:10 at the Movie Barn. What time is the show at the Film Palace? 5. 6:45

EXERCISE 2 Preparing Interview Questions

Think of someone famous (either living or dead) that you would like to interview. What specific topic or area of knowledge is this person an expert about? Prepare ten questions that you would like to ask in an interview with the person you have selected. Make sure that your questions require the person you're interviewing to give you more than a simple yes or no answer.

RESOURCES

ANSWERS

Exercise 2

Questions will vary, but they should require more than yes or no answers.

EXERCISE 3 **Listening to a Speech**

Listen to a short speech presented by your teacher in class. Take brief notes. Then respond to the following questions about the speech.

1. What are the main ideas of the speech?
2. Does the speech contain details that support the main ideas in the speech? If so, identify several of them.

EXERCISE 4 **Identifying Propaganda Techniques**

Identify the propaganda technique used in each of the following items.

1. Margo Lane for Bubble-O Bath Oil: "I'm always grateful for two things: all the little people who have made me a star and Bubble-O, the bath oil no tub should be without." **1.** testimonial
2. "Our mayor is a hard worker, just like you. He may be the mayor, but he's just an ordinary guy." **2.** "plain folks"
3. "Don't be out of touch! Listen to 905.5, the radio station more listeners tune in to." **3.** bandwagon
4. "Our rivals use bad material to make their products." **4.** emotional appeals
5. "Jolene wore a green dress on Tuesday. I told her it would bring bad luck. Sure enough, she lost her watch on Thursday. I told her that green was an unlucky color." **5.** false cause and effect

RESOURCES

ANSWERS

Exercise 3

Answers will vary depending on the speech given.

A DIFFERENT APPROACH

Record three messages of varying time lengths (one, two, and three minutes) on a cassette tape. Ask students to listen to the first message and then to paraphrase the information. When students have successfully mastered taking the one-minute message, have them move on to the second and, finally, to the third.

A message might include a list of items a parent would ask a child to purchase, instructions for duties to be performed, or directions and times for meetings, appointments, or parties.

RESOURCES

THE LIBRARY/MEDIA CENTER *(pp. 684–693)*

OBJECTIVES

- To list books in the order that they would be shelved in the library
- To use sample *Readers' Guide* entries to answer questions about articles
- To use the card catalog to find author, title, and subject information

Teacher's ResourceBank™

RESOURCES

THE LIBRARY

CHAPTER OVERVIEW

This chapter tells students how to find information in the library by explaining the arrangement of fiction and nonfiction, the use of the card and on-line catalogs, the kinds of information contained in different parts of a book, the use of reference materials such as the *Readers' Guide,* the organization of materials in the vertical file, and the use of other general references.

RESOURCES

28 THE LIBRARY/ MEDIA CENTER

Finding and Using Information

In the library, or media center, information on all kinds of subjects is collected. To find and use this information, learn about the library's contents and how they are arranged.

The Contents of the Library

The information in a library takes many forms. The resource you use depends on the type of information you need.

BOOKS	
Fiction	Stories (novels and short stories)
Nonfiction	Factual information about real people, events, and things; includes biographies and "how-to" books
Reference books	General information about many subjects

- To indicate which parts of a book contain specific types of information
- To identify the reference tools used to find specified information

QUICK REMINDER

Write these categories on the chalkboard: Sports, Music, Science, and Art. In random order below these categories, write *biology, watercolor, piano, zoology, sculpture, football, jazz,* and *basketball.*

Tell students to imagine that the categories are written on folders in a filing cabinet. Then ask students to identify the items in the second list that should be filed in each of the category folders [Sports—football, basketball; Music—piano, jazz; Science—biology, zoology; Art—watercolor, sculpture].

Suggest to the class that the library is like a huge filing cabinet—the shelves are like labeled folders, and the books are the items that have been arranged in the folders according to category.

OTHER PRINTED MATERIALS	
Magazines and newspapers	Current events, commentaries, and important discoveries
Pamphlets	Brief summaries of facts about specific subjects
Audiotapes, records, films, filmstrips, slides, videotapes	Stories (narrated, illustrated, or acted out); music, instructions and educational material, facts and information about many specific subjects
Computers	Information stored electronically, allowing for easy access and frequent updates
Maps, globes, atlases, and almanacs	Geographic information, facts, dates, and statistics

The Arrangement of a Library

You can usually find a number and letter code on the spine of every book contained in a library. This code is a ***call number.*** The call number identifies the book and tells you where to find it on the shelves of the library.

Arrangement of Nonfiction

Most school libraries arrange nonfiction books using the *Dewey decimal system.* The ***Dewey decimal system*** assigns a number to each nonfiction book. These numbers are assigned according to the book's subject. Using this system of arrangement, books that contain factual information about similar subjects are placed near each other on the library shelves.

RESOURCES

LEP/ESL

General Strategies. Some students may need a hands-on opportunity to help them understand how to use the information in a library. The information in this chapter should be presented on a concrete level, and students will benefit from having a personally meaningful focus to help them assimilate the information.

Suggest that students choose as a subject for research individuals whom they admire. Then plan a trip either to the school library or to the public library. Show students the location of the card or on-line catalog and have them use it to access biographies or autobiographies concerning their subjects. As students read their books, encourage them to identify the books' parts and to note specific information from each part.

LESS-ADVANCED STUDENTS

To give students direction in their exploration of the library, you might have them do personal inventories of their favorite sports, hobbies, kinds of music, and so on before going to the library to find books on those topics.

RESOURCES

When a library assigns a Dewey decimal number to a book, the first step is to place the book in one of ten subject categories. Each of these ten categories has its own range of numbers, as shown in the following chart.

DEWEY DECIMAL SYSTEM
MAJOR SUBJECT CATEGORIES OF NONFICTION

NUMBERS	SUBJECT AREAS	EXAMPLES OF TOPICS
000–099	General Works	encyclopedias and reference books (Some libraries use an *R* with the call number for reference books.)
100–199	Philosophy	ideas about life, theories, personality
200–299	Religions	world religions, mythology
300–399	Social Sciences	government, law, business, education
400–499	Language	dictionaries, grammar books
500–599	Science	general science, chemistry, biology, mathematics
600–699	Technology	"how-to" books, applied sciences (such as engineering and aviation)
700–799	Arts and Recreation	music, art, sports, hobbies
800–899	Literature	poems, plays, essays
900–999	History	events, geography, travel

RESOURCES

Biographies are books that describe the lives of real people. Most libraries place biographies in a separate section. The call number of a biography usually begins with *92* or the letter *B.* Biographies are arranged on the library's shelves in alphabetical order according to the last name of the person the book is about. Two or more biographies about the same person are put in alphabetical order according to the last name of the author.

Arrangement of Fiction

Fiction books are not organized by subject like nonfiction books. Instead, fiction books are arranged alphabetically according to the last name of the author. For example, a novel by Maya Angelou would be arranged alphabetically before a novel by Ernesto Galarza. (Names of authors that begin with *Mc* and *St.* are alphabetized as if they were spelled out: *Mac* and *Saint.*)

If the library has more than one fiction book written by the same author, all these books are grouped together under the author's name. Then these books are arranged alphabetically by their titles. (Remember not to count the first word if it's *A, An,* or *The.*) Collections of short stories are usually kept separate from other works of fiction. Short story collections are sometimes marked with the letters *SC.*

The Card Catalog

The easiest way to locate a specific book in the library is to look it up in the library's *card catalog.* The ***card catalog*** is a cabinet of small drawers. Each drawer holds many small file cards. There are cards in this file for every book in the library.

Cards in the card catalog are arranged in alphabetical order by title, author, or subject. Each fiction book has at least two cards in the catalog—a *title card* and an *author card.* A nonfiction book will have a third card—a *subject card.* Occasionally, you may find "see" or "see also" cards. These cards tell you where to go in the card catalog to find other books about the same subject.

An ***on-line catalog*** is like a card catalog except that the information is stored on a computer. It has the same information and is arranged the same way as a card catalog. The computer version is usually faster in finding the information.

RESOURCES

STUDENTS WITH SPECIAL NEEDS

A library can be an intimidating place for learning disabled students who have difficulties reading. It may be helpful to give some students private tours. Familiarize students with the card catalog by looking up a particular nonfiction book and cross-referencing it with its subject and author cards. If your library has an on-line catalog, be sure to give students ample time to experience that system with helpful supervision. Guide students to the book sections that contain the books they have looked up and help them find those books.

Problem. Sometimes students start their search for a book in the card catalog and don't immediately find the book because they are looking in the wrong section.

Solution. Remind students that card catalogs in most libraries have three sections: one that lists authors, one that lists titles, and one that lists subjects.

RESOURCES

INTEGRATING THE LANGUAGE ARTS

Technology Link. If you do not have an on-line catalog at your school library, you may want to take students on a field trip to the local library or to a nearby university library to use computerized book catalogs and newspaper and magazine indexes.

COOPERATIVE LEARNING

Have students work in teams of three to compete in a scavenger hunt for the call numbers of the following books:

1. a book by Robert Louis Stevenson
2. a travel book
3. a book of poetry by Shel Silverstein
4. a biography of Abraham Lincoln
5. a book about rocks
6. a book about insects
7. a book by Mark Twain
8. a book by E. B. White
9. a book about animals

RESOURCES

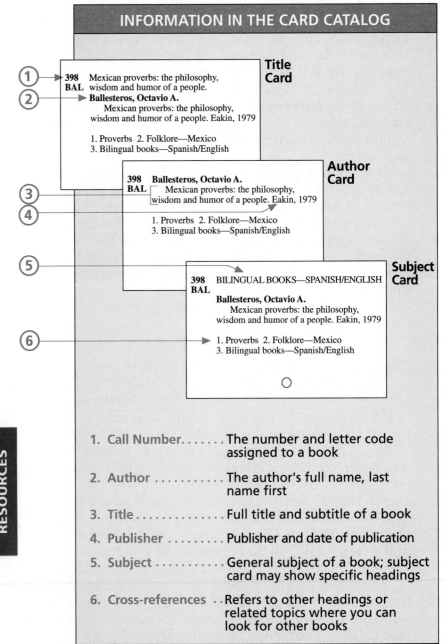

INFORMATION IN THE CARD CATALOG

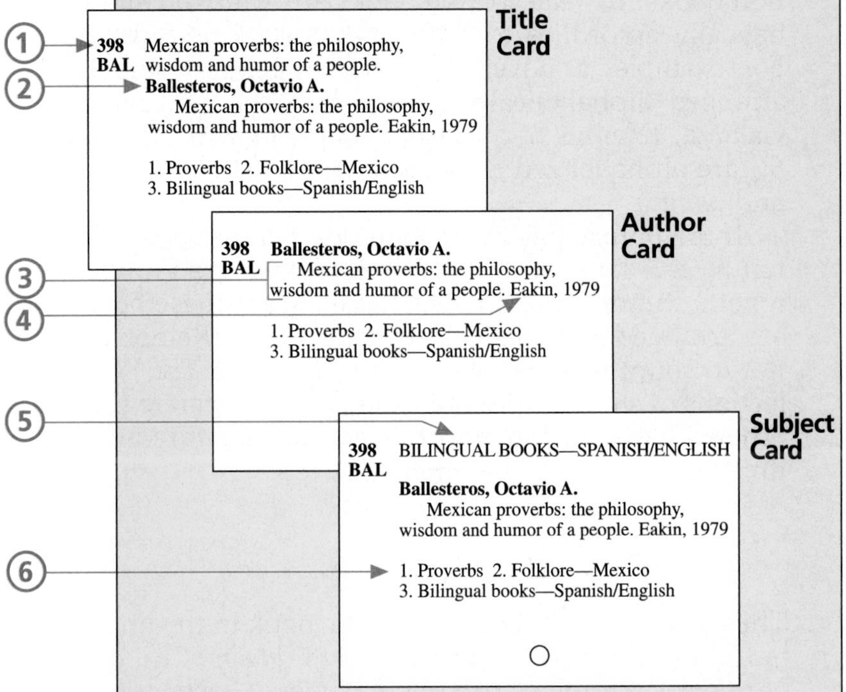

Title Card

(1) 398 BAL Mexican proverbs: the philosophy, wisdom and humor of a people.
(2) **Ballesteros, Octavio A.**
Mexican proverbs: the philosophy, wisdom and humor of a people. Eakin, 1979

1. Proverbs 2. Folklore—Mexico
3. Bilingual books—Spanish/English

Author Card

398 BAL **Ballesteros, Octavio A.**
(3) Mexican proverbs: the philosophy, wisdom and humor of a people. (4) Eakin, 1979

1. Proverbs 2. Folklore—Mexico
3. Bilingual books—Spanish/English

Subject Card

398 BAL (5) BILINGUAL BOOKS—SPANISH/ENGLISH
Ballesteros, Octavio A.
Mexican proverbs: the philosophy, wisdom and humor of a people. Eakin, 1979

(6) 1. Proverbs 2. Folklore—Mexico
3. Bilingual books—Spanish/English

1. Call Number	The number and letter code assigned to a book
2. Author	The author's full name, last name first
3. Title	Full title and subtitle of a book
4. Publisher	Publisher and date of publication
5. Subject	General subject of a book; subject card may show specific headings
6. Cross-references	Refers to other headings or related topics where you can look for other books

RESOURCES

Parts of a Book

Many books that you can use as sources are packed full of information. The specific information that you might need can sometimes be hard to find. You will find information more easily if you know how to use every part of a book. The following chart shows the types of information you will find in different parts of a book.

INFORMATION FOUND IN PARTS OF A BOOK	
PART	INFORMATION
Title page	gives the full title, the name of the author (or authors), the publisher, and the place of publication
Copyright page	gives the date of the first publication of the book and the date of any revisions
Table of contents	lists titles of chapters or sections of the book and their starting page numbers
Appendix	provides additional information about subjects found in the book; sometimes contains tables, maps, and charts
Glossary	defines, in alphabetical order, various difficult terms or important technical words used frequently in the book
Bibliography	lists sources used to write the book; provides names of books about related topics
Index	lists topics mentioned in the book, along with the page or pages on which they can be found; sometimes lists the page where a certain illustration may be found

RESOURCES

A DIFFERENT APPROACH

To introduce students to the section on the parts of a book, write the following questions on the chalkboard and have students find the answers in their literature textbooks:

1. On what page is the title, name, and location of the publisher? [title page]
2. What kind of information is on the back side of the title page? [copyright information]
3. What is the list of chapter titles and page numbers called? [table of contents]
4. In what part of the book is the appendix found? [back]
5. What is the listing of words with definitions in the back of the book called? [glossary]
6. Where can an alphabetical list of the stories and authors in the book be found? [index]

RESOURCES

LEARNING STYLES

Visual Learners. To help visual learners become familiar with the layout of the school library, have students draw a floor plan of the library and label the various sections. Students could color-code the sections and indicate the sections they are interested in exploring. Emphasize that while all libraries might not have the same floor plan, they all contain the same basic elements and an arrangement of similar books and materials.

Kinetic Learners. Some students will better internalize the information about finding books in the library if they are actually led through the process.

RESOURCES

SELECTION AMENDMENT

Description of change: excerpted

Rationale: to focus on the concept of using the *Readers' Guide to Periodical Literature* presented in this chapter

Using Reference Materials

The *Readers' Guide*

You can find the most current information about many subjects in magazine or journal articles. You can locate these articles by using the *Readers' Guide to Periodical Literature,* an index to articles printed in more than 150 magazines. Articles are indexed in the *Readers' Guide* alphabetically both by author and by subject. Each entry has a heading printed in boldfaced capital letters. In the front of the *Readers' Guide* is a guide to abbreviations that are used in entries.

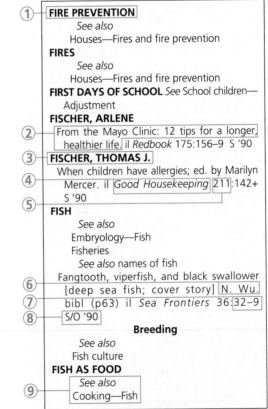

(1) **FIRE PREVENTION**
See also
Houses—Fires and fire prevention
FIRES
See also
Houses—Fires and fire prevention
FIRST DAYS OF SCHOOL *See* School children—Adjustment
FISCHER, ARLENE
(2) From the Mayo Clinic: 12 tips for a longer, healthier life. il *Redbook* 175:156–9 S '90
(3) **FISCHER, THOMAS J.**
When children have allergies; ed. by Marilyn
(4) Mercer. il *Good Housekeeping* 211:142+
(5) S '90
FISH
See also
Embryology—Fish
Fisheries
See also names of fish
(6) Fangtooth, viperfish, and black swallower [deep sea fish; cover story] N. Wu.
(7) bibl (p63) il *Sea Frontiers* 36:32–9
(8) S/O '90
Breeding
See also
Fish culture
FISH AS FOOD
(9) *See also*
Cooking—Fish

(1) **Subject entry**
(2) **Title of article**
(3) **Author entry**
(4) **Name of magazine**
(5) **Volume number of magazine**
(6) **Author of article**
(7) **Page reference**
(8) **Date of magazine**
(9) **Subject cross-reference**

RESOURCES

The Vertical File

Many libraries have a ***vertical file,*** a filing cabinet containing up-to-date materials such as newspaper clippings, booklets, and pamphlets.

Reference Works

Most libraries devote an entire section to reference books. These books contain information about a great number of subjects.

REFERENCE WORKS		
TYPE	DESCRIPTION	EXAMPLES
ENCYCLOPEDIAS	■ many volumes ■ articles arranged alphabetically by subject ■ good source for general information	*Collier's Encyclopedia* *Compton's Encyclopedia* *The World Book Encyclopedia*
GENERAL BIOGRAPHICAL REFERENCES	■ information about birth, nationality, and major accomplishments of outstanding people	*Current Biography* *Dictionary of American Biography* *The International Who's Who* *Webster's New Biographical Dictionary*
ATLASES	■ maps and geographical information	*Atlas of World Cultures* *National Geographic Atlas of the World*

(continued)

RESOURCES

INTEGRATING THE LANGUAGE ARTS

Literature Link. If the story is available in your library, you might read aloud to the class Bernard Malamud's "A Summer's Reading." After you have read the story to the class, ask students to respond with their personal feelings about the story and their feelings about the main character—whether they sympathized with him, and so on. Ask them also to comment on the benefits the boy in the story might have derived from the reading habits he finally developed.

A DIFFERENT APPROACH

The encyclopedia, the atlas, the thesaurus, and the almanac will be important reference sources for students in their school years and later in life. You may want to show the class an example of each reference work, reading some interesting bit of information from each book as you explain the kind of information found in the book. After you have shown students an example of each type of reference work, ask the class to think about situations outside of the school environment in which information from the books could be valuable.

RESOURCES

COOPERATIVE LEARNING

To introduce students to the wealth of interesting information found in almanacs, divide the class into small groups and have the groups use almanacs to write trivia questions about categories such as historical events, geography, movie awards, and sports. Then have the teams pair off against each other, with members taking turns asking the other team the questions. A scorekeeper can be designated to write down points for correct answers.

REFERENCE WORKS *(continued)*		
TYPE	DESCRIPTION	EXAMPLES
ALMANACS	■ up-to-date information about current events, facts, statistics, and dates	*The Information Please Almanac, Atlas and Yearbook* *The World Almanac and Book of Facts*
BOOKS OF SYNONYMS	■ lists of more interesting or more exact words to express ideas	*Roget's International Thesaurus* *Webster's New Dictionary of Synonyms*

Newspapers

Newspapers have many different types of reading materials that are often contained in several separate sections. As a reader, you probably read the various parts of a newspaper for different reasons.

WHAT'S IN A NEWSPAPER?		
TYPE OF WRITING/ EXAMPLES	READER'S PURPOSE	READING TECHNIQUE
informative news stories sports	to gain knowledge or information	Ask yourself the *5W-How?* questions (page 32).
persuasive editorials comics reviews ads	to gain knowledge, to make decisions, or to be entertained	Identify points you agree or disagree with. Find facts or reasons the writer uses.
creative or expressive comics columns	to be entertained	Identify ways the writer interests you or gives you a new viewpoint or ideas.

Review

EXERCISE 1 Using the Library

Answer the following questions about the information resources in the library.

1. Tell the order in which these fiction books would be arranged: *Big Red* by Jim Kjelgaard and *Bronzeville Boys and Girls* by Gwendolyn Brooks.
2. Using the sample *Readers' Guide* entry on page 690, find the article edited by Marilyn Mercer. In what magazine did this article appear?
3. Using the sample *Readers' Guide* entry on page 690, tell what heading you should look for if you want to find information about how to prevent house fires.
4. Use the card catalog or the on-line catalog in your library to find a nonfiction book. Write the title of the book, the author's name, and the call number.
5. What part of a book would you look in to find the meaning of a word you didn't understand?

EXERCISE 2 Using Reference Tools

Answer the following questions about using reference resources in the library.

1. What kind of reference book might show you the number of miles between two cities?
2. What kind of reference book might tell you a list of words that mean the same as the word *large*?
3. What kind of reference book might tell you the population of the United States according to the most recent census?
4. What kind of reference book might you use to find information about pyramids?
5. What is your favorite part of a newspaper? Identify the type of writing and explain why you like to read this specific part of the newspaper.

ANSWERS

Exercise 1

1. *Bronzeville Boys and Girls* by Gwendolyn Brooks would come before *Big Red* by Jim Kjelgaard.
2. *Good Housekeeping*
3. Houses—Fires and fire prevention
4. Responses will vary.
5. glossary

TIMESAVER

Students can check their own answers for **Exercise 2** by actually using the reference tool named to find a title for each of the items on the list. You might allow students to work in pairs on this activity, sharing the titles and information they find.

ANSWERS

Exercise 2

1. atlas
2. books of synonyms
3. almanac
4. encyclopedia
5. Responses will vary.

RESOURCES

THE DICTIONARY *(pp. 694–697)*

OBJECTIVES

- To check pronunciation of words in a dictionary
- To divide words into syllables
- To write examples for each part of speech listed for a word in a dictionary

Teacher's ResourceBank™

RESOURCES

THE DICTIONARY

CHAPTER OVERVIEW

This chapter will familiarize students with the arrangement of dictionaries and the types of information that can be found in a dictionary. A sample entry word illustrates how alphabetical order and guide words are used to find a specific word. Types of information available in dictionaries are explained with suggestions for the effective use of information. The exercises at the end of the chapter require the students to apply dictionary skills beyond simply locating a word.

The material in this chapter can be effectively integrated with **Chapter 30: "Vocabulary."**

RESOURCES

29 THE DICTIONARY

Arrangement and Contents

A dictionary contains information about words. This information includes

- the meanings of a word
- how to spell a word
- how to pronounce, or say, a word
- how to use a word in speaking or writing

RESOURCES

Arrangement of a Dictionary

Words found in a dictionary are called ***entries.*** Word entries in a dictionary are listed in alphabetical order. Each page of word entries in the dictionary has ***guide words*** to help you follow the alphabetical order. The first guide word tells you the first entry word found on that page. The second guide word tells you the last entry word found on that page.

A SAMPLE ENTRY

cloud [kloud] *noun, plural* **clouds. 1.** a white, gray, or dark mass floating high in the sky. Clouds are made of tiny drops of water or ice hanging in the air. ♦ A **cloudburst** is a sudden, heavy rainfall. **2.** any mass or grouping of things like a cloud: a *cloud* of dust. A *cloud* of insects swarmed around the streetlight. —*verb,* **cloud-ed, clouding. 1.** to cover or become covered with clouds: The morning sky was clear, but by noon it *clouded* over. **2.** to make or become darker or less clear: His face *clouded* when he heard the bad news. (6) (7)

(8)

cloud The majestic thunderhead, or *cumulonimbus* [kyo͞om′yə lō nim′bəs] cloud hanging over the woods is a sign that a storm is coming. (9)

Contents of a Dictionary Entry

When you look up a word in a dictionary, you will find helpful information about how the word is used.

1. **Entry word.** The entry word is printed in boldface (dark) letters. It shows the way the word should be spelled and how to divide the word into syllables. It may also show if a word should be capitalized or if the word can be spelled in other ways.

RESOURCES

QUICK REMINDER

Display a dictionary page on an overhead projector and ask volunteers to locate the types of information found in a dictionary. [Students should locate the entry word, guide words, part-of-speech labels, definitions, phonetic and diacritical markings, syllable divisions, definitions, and related word forms.]

You may want to show students other types of resource books, such as telephone books, encyclopedias, and thesauruses, that are arranged in alphabetical order and that feature guide words.

LESS-ADVANCED STUDENTS

Some students may have trouble with alphabetical order, a concept necessary for efficient use of dictionaries and other resource books. Ask students to write the following word list in alphabetical order:

1. energy [6]
2. express [7]
3. extract [8]
4. edible [2]
5. emit [4]
6. elate [3]
7. endeavor [5]
8. abate [1]

Have students write out the alphabet and keep it as a reference during the practice exercise.

A DIFFERENT APPROACH

You could have each student use the phonetic spellings of words to write a coded message to a partner. Then ask the partners to exchange papers and decode the messages.

RESOURCES

INTEGRATING THE LANGUAGE ARTS

Literature Link. You may want to allow time during a lesson on *The Adventures of Tom Sawyer* or other reading selections for students to use context to guess the meanings of new words they encounter in the story. Ask volunteers to identify new words and to read the sentence or passage in which each such word appears. After class discussions about possibilities of meanings, ask students to look up the definitions in a dictionary.

COOPERATIVE LEARNING

Divide the class into groups of three to five students and ask each student in the group to find a word in a dictionary that interests him or her and copy the complete word entry. Then ask each group to collaborate in using each group member's word correctly in a sentence. Have the groups exchange sentences and guess the meanings of the words from the context of the sentence.

The goal is for the students to write sentences that clearly establish a context for the chosen words, so you may want to award a point for each word the class correctly defines.

RESOURCES

2. **Pronunciation.** The pronunciation of an entry word is shown with symbols. These symbols help you pronounce the word correctly. In the sample entry, look at the *k* symbol. It shows you that the *c* in *cloud* sounds more like the *c* in *can* than the *c* in *ice.* Special letters or markings that are used with letters to show a certain sound are called ***phonetic symbols. Accent marks*** show which syllables of the word are said more forcefully. Look in the front of your dictionary for an explanation of the symbols and marks your dictionary uses.
3. **Part-of-speech labels.** Some words may be used as more than one part of speech. For each meaning of a word, the dictionary shows the part of speech. In the sample entry, *cloud* can be used as a noun or as a verb, depending on the meaning.
4. **Other forms.** Sometimes your dictionary will show you how to spell other forms of the word. These may include the plural form of nouns, verb tenses, or adjective and adverb forms.
5. **Definitions.** The different meanings of a word are numbered. To help you understand the different meanings, dictionaries often include a sample phrase or sentence after a numbered definition.
6. **Related word forms.** Sometimes the dictionary may show forms of the entry word created by adding suffixes, prefixes, or other combining forms. Once you know the meaning of the main word (*cloud*), you can usually understand the meaning of the related word (*cloudburst*).
7. **Examples.** Examples show how the entry word is used in a sentence. The examples are often in the form of phrases or sentences using the word in context.
8. **Illustrations.** Sometimes dictionaries include pictures that show what a word means.
9. **Captions.** Illustrations may have a ***caption,*** a label that explains the picture or drawing. A caption may also give an example of how the word is used.

RESOURCES

Review

EXERCISE 1 Dividing Words into Syllables

Divide the following words into syllables. Use the same method to show syllable division that your dictionary uses. Answers may vary according to the dictionary used. These are from *Webster's New World Dictionary,* Third College Edition.

1. manual 1. man|u · al
2. region 2. re · gion
3. familiar 3. fa · mil · iar
4. composure 4. com · po · sure
5. incredible 5. in · cred · i|ble

EXERCISE 2 Using the Dictionary to Check Pronunciation

Answers may vary according to the dictionary used. These are from *Webster's New World Dictionary,* Third College Edition.

Look up the following words in a dictionary. Write the pronunciation of the word the same way that your dictionary shows it.

1. next 1. nekst
2. hyphen 2. hī′fən
3. poncho 3. pän′chō
4. signature 4. sig′nə chər
5. designate 5. dez′ig nāt′

EXERCISE 3 Finding Part-of-Speech Labels

Look up each of the following words in a dictionary. Give all the parts of speech listed for each word. Then write an example of how the word is used as each part of speech.

EXAMPLE 1. graduate
1. *verb—He will graduate from high school. noun—He is a graduate of the state university.*

1. flood
2. link
3. protest
4. beam
5. stack

RESOURCES

EXERCISE 1

Teaching Note. You may want to explain to students that some dictionaries indicate where a word can and cannot be acceptably divided at the end of a line. For example, the vertical lines in the first and fifth words indicate places where the words should not be divided at the ends of lines. Encourage students to check their classroom dictionaries for such information.

STUDENTS WITH SPECIAL NEEDS

Students with visual-processing deficits tend to have problems with pronunciation due to a difficulty in the processing of words into sounds.

A helpful addendum to **Exercise 2** may be to ask the students to refer to the pronunciation key at the front of their dictionaries to find a second word with the same first-syllable vowel sound.

ADVANCED STUDENTS

Ask students to locate the dictionary definitions for the words in **Exercise 2** and to write the definitions in their own words.

ANSWERS

Exercise 3

Examples given will vary, but parts of speech for each will be one noun and one verb. You may want to extend **Exercise 3** by asking students to identify the words that have more than one meaning as a noun or a verb. Then have each student write a sentence for each different meaning.

RESOURCES

VOCABULARY *(pp. 698–705)*

OBJECTIVES

- To use context clues to select word meanings
- To identify and choose appropriate synonyms, antonyms, and homographs in the contexts of sentences
- To form new words by adding prefixes and suffixes

Teacher's ResourceBank™

RESOURCES

VOCABULARY

CHAPTER OVERVIEW

This chapter provides suggestions and exercises that should help students learn the meanings of new words and use them effectively in sentences. The first part of this chapter explains the types of context clues that may be used to determine word meanings and also defines synonyms, antonyms, and homographs. Parts of words (base words, roots, prefixes, and suffixes) are explained, and examples are provided to illustrate each part.

The material in this chapter may be referred to when teaching any literature or composition chapter, and may also be used in conjunction with **Chapter 29: "The Dictionary."**

QUICK REMINDER

Ask students to identify the words that do not fit the contexts of the following sentences and to suggest words that do fit:

1. The car is parked in the roof.
2. Juan took several pictures with his bicycle.
3. Felicia ate three books for lunch.

RESOURCES

RESOURCES

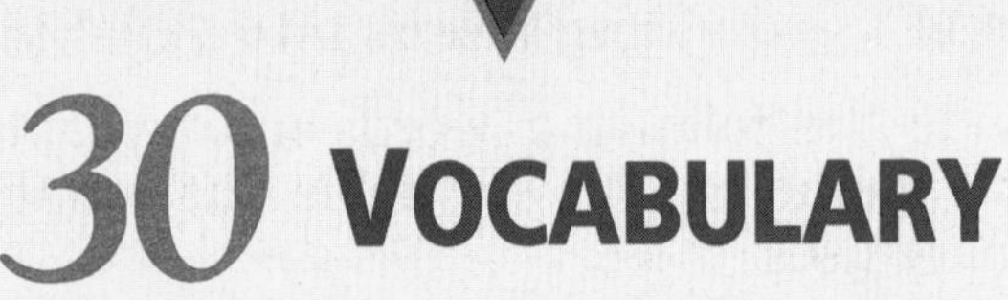

30 VOCABULARY

Learning and Using New Words

You come across new words all the time. You hear new words when you talk with others and even when you listen to people talking in movies, on TV, or on the radio. You also see new words when you read books, magazines, or papers. You will see as you read this chapter that you can learn the meanings of new words in many ways.

Start a Word Bank

A good way to learn new words is by keeping a word bank. This can be as simple as making a vocabulary list in your notebook. When you read or hear an unfamiliar word, include the word and its definition in your list. Then look it up in the dictionary to be sure you have the correct meaning.

Using Words in Context

A dictionary is one of the best sources to find out the meaning of an unfamiliar word. However, when you read or listen, you can probably guess the meanings of many unfamiliar words from the *context,* or the way they are used. The ***context*** of a word includes all the other words and sentences that surround it. These surrounding words often provide clues to the word's meaning.

HOW TO USE CONTEXT CLUES	
TYPE OF CLUE	EXPLANATION
Definitions or Restatements	Look for words that can help you define an unfamiliar word or that restate the meaning of the unknown word, using terms that you already know. ■ Amado someday hopes to become an *architect*, a person who designs buildings. [The clues show you that *architect* can be defined as "a person who designs buildings."]
Examples	Look for one or more examples that show the meaning of an unfamiliar word. ■ Items of *apparel,* including sweaters, vests, pants, and gowns, were found in the old trunk. [The examples show that *apparel* means "clothing."]
Synonyms	Look for clues that show an unfamiliar word is similar in meaning to a more familiar word. ■ From the beginning, I always thought he was a faker, an *impostor!* [The clues show that *impostor* is similar in meaning to *faker.*]

(continued)

LESS-ADVANCED STUDENTS

Read aloud the types of clues listed under **How to Use Context Clues.** Then have students develop an example of each type. Write the words *remedy, valor,* and *beverage* on the chalkboard. Have students suggest a sentence for each one, using the five techniques to provide context clues.

ADVANCED STUDENTS

Photocopy from a social studies or science textbook a short selection that uses one or more of the five types of context clues. Ask students to circle each unfamiliar word and then to underline surrounding words that give clues to its meaning.

STUDENTS WITH SPECIAL NEEDS

When students encounter new words, help them integrate these words into their knowledge base by relating it to something they already know. If possible, provide mnemonic devices to enhance memory. Then have students record the new words on flash cards with definitions or synonyms on the back. Allow students to work in pairs to practice with their flash cards.

INTEGRATING THE LANGUAGE ARTS

Literature Link. Selections from Frances Hodgson Burnett's *The Secret Garden* can offer students a variety of new vocabulary words. In an oral exercise, allow students to choose a few words from the selection and explain their meanings from context clues. Then ask students to find the dictionary meanings, synonyms, and antonyms for the words.

COMMON ERROR

Problem. Students might use general, imprecise words in their writing.

Solution. Organize students in groups of three of four with varying levels of ability in each group. Have them use dictionaries and thesauruses to brainstorm lists of synonyms for the words *said, great,* and *a lot.* You could also have students make lists for other overused words. After lists are completed, each student should make a copy to use as a reference when writing.

RESOURCES

HOW TO USE CONTEXT CLUES *(continued)*	
TYPE OF CLUE	EXPLANATION
Antonyms	Look for clues that show an unfamiliar word is opposite in meaning to a more familiar word. ■ On the tennis court, Elmore and Palani are *adversaries,* but off the court they are good friends. [The clues show that *adversaries* means the opposite of *good friends.*]
Cause and Effect	Look for clues that an unfamiliar word is related to the cause—or is the result—of an action, feeling, or idea. ■ Since the disease was easily spread, people in the stricken city had to be *quarantined.* [You can see that to *quarantine* people must mean to keep them away from others so they won't catch, or spread, a disease.]

RESOURCES

Using the Dictionary

You may not always be able to figure out a word's meaning from its context. You may often need to look up the word in a dictionary. In the dictionary, you may find several meanings listed for a particular word. Then you'll need to read all the meanings to find the one that best fits the context of your sentence.

Synonyms and Antonyms

Synonyms are words that have nearly the same meaning, such as *happy* and *glad.* ***Antonyms,*** by contrast, are words that have nearly the opposite meaning, such as *bold* and *shy*. You can sometimes find synonyms in a dictionary, listed after the definitions for an entry word. Less often, dictionaries list antonyms for an entry word.

The best source to use to find synonyms is a *thesaurus*. A ***thesaurus*** is a special kind of reference book that has word entries like a dictionary. However, instead of definitions, a thesaurus lists synonyms—and sometimes antonyms—for its entry words.

Homographs

Homographs are words that are spelled the same but have different meanings. Although the words look the same, they may not be pronounced the same. To discover the meaning of a homograph in a sentence, you will need to use context clues. Or, you can read all the meanings listed for each homograph in a dictionary. Then choose the one that best fits the context of your sentence.

Using Word Parts

Many words in English can be divided into parts. Sometimes you can figure out the meaning of an unfamiliar word if you know the meaning of each one of its parts.

A word part added to the beginning of a word is called a ***prefix.*** A word part added to the end of a word is called a ***suffix.*** Prefixes and suffixes are not whole words. They must be added to other words or word parts to create words.

A ***base word*** is a complete word all by itself. However, other word parts may be added to a base word to make new words.

RESOURCES

A DIFFERENT APPROACH

Have students look in newspapers or magazines for ten unfamiliar words that can be added to their word banks. Ask them to look in a dictionary and a thesaurus for synonyms and antonyms. Then have them use the words in original sentences. Tell students to go over their notes frequently and to attempt to use the new words they have learned in their speaking and writing.

LEP/ESL

General Strategies. Introduce students to the following homographs:

1. *ad*dress—ad*dress*
2. *con*flict—con*flict*
3. *con*tent—con*tent*
4. *per*mit—per*mit*
5. *pre*sent—pre*sent*
6. *pro*duce—pro*duce*

When the words are used as nouns, the stress is on the first syllable. When the words are used as verbs, the stress falls on the second syllable. Model the correct pronunciation for each word and have students repeat it after you. Ask students to work with partners to create one or more sentences using both words.

RESOURCES

COOPERATIVE LEARNING

Divide the class into groups of three to five. Ask each group to use prefixes and suffixes to create as many new words as possible from the following word list:

1. courage
2. date
3. appreciate
4. agree
5. place
6. change
7. care
8. match

Allow students ten minutes to complete the assignment and award one point for each correctly spelled new word. You may want to give bonus points if the groups identify the parts of speech of the new words.

RESOURCES

PREFIX	BASE WORD	SUFFIX	NEW WORD
dis–	grace	–ful	disgraceful
re–	place	–ment	replacement
un–	read	–able	unreadable

Roots, like prefixes and suffixes, are not whole words. A root is the base a word is built on. It contains the word's core meaning. Roots must combine with one or more word parts to form words.

ROOT	MEANING	EXAMPLE
–ped–	foot	pedal
–port–	carry	portable
–spec–	look	spectator
–struct–	build	structure

COMMON PREFIXES		
PREFIX	MEANING	EXAMPLE
bi–	two	bicycle
dis–	away, opposing	disagree
in–	not	incomplete
mis–	wrong	misspell
non–	not	nonhuman
over–	above, too much	overdone
pre–	before	precook
re–	again	replace
semi–	half	semicircle
sub–	under	subtitle
un–	not	unhappy

RESOURCES

 REFERENCE NOTE: For guidelines on spelling when adding prefixes, see page 639.

COMMON SUFFIXES		
SUFFIX	MEANING	EXAMPLE
–able	able	respectable
–en	make	deepen
–ful	full of	stressful
–ion	action, condition	inspection
–less	without	penniless
–ly	characteristic of	quickly
–ness	quality	togetherness
–ous	characterized by	luxurious

REFERENCE NOTE: For guidelines on spelling when adding suffixes, see pages 640–642.

Review

EXERCISE 1 Using Context Clues

Use context clues to choose the word or phrase that best fits the meaning of each italicized word.

- **a.** simple
- **b.** life's work
- **c.** easily broken
- **d.** movement
- **e.** attack
- **f.** hard to locate
- **g.** beautiful
- **h.** earlier

1. The *migration,* or relocation, of the settlers moving to new lands was a terrible struggle. 1. d
2. Zane likes to work with his hands and wants a *career* as a carpenter or an auto mechanic. 2. b
3. Since we learned that rule in a *previous* lesson, we won't go over it again. 3. h
4. The brave men and women in the fort fought off the sudden *onslaught* of their enemies. 4. e
5. The vase was *fragile,* unlike the shatterproof plates. 5. c

RESOURCES

LEP/ESL

Spanish. Encourage students to look for similarities between Spanish and English whenever possible. For example, in Spanish many nouns are written alike except for an additional end vowel: *pilot, piloto*; *caramel, caramelo.* Many words with *–ive* endings in English correspond to words that end in *–ivo* in Spanish: *fugitive, fugitivo; sensitive, sensitivo.* Many *–tion* English words match Spanish *–ción* words: *invitation, invitación; interruption, interrupción.*

RESOURCES

EXERCISE 2 **Choosing the Best Synonym**

For each of the following sentences, write the word in parentheses that better fits the context of the sentence. Use a dictionary to check exact meanings.

1. In order to get a good night's sleep, Estelle asked everyone not to (*disturb, upset*) her until morning.
2. Shing certainly has a (*sincere, hearty*) appetite.
3. The police found a briefcase full of (*counterfeit, copied*) money in the car.
4. It is (*doubtful, suspicious*) that I will win the national spelling competition.
5. Oily rags in the basement are a fire (*risk, hazard*).

EXERCISE 3 **Choosing Antonyms**

Select the antonym that is more appropriate for the italicized word in each sentence.

1. Vince felt *lazy*, but Kenesha felt (energetic, sleepy).
2. A child's first set of teeth is (temporary, important); the second set is *permanent*.
3. Paulo remained *calm* during the thunderstorm, but his little sister became (homesick, frantic).
4. In our national elections, we don't vote *publicly;* we cast our ballots (privately, separately).
5. The lion became a fierce *hunter;* a young antelope was her intended (partner, prey).

EXERCISE 4 **Identifying Homographs**

Each of the following sentences contains a pair of homographs. Write a meaning for each homograph. You may use a dictionary to find exact meanings.

1. Tony will get a chance to *conduct* the chorus if his *conduct* in class improves.
2. The guide will *lead* us to the *lead* mine.

ANSWERS

Exercise 4

Answers may vary.

1. conduct — *vt.* be the leader of; direct
   conduct — *n.* the way that one acts; behavior; deportment
2. lead — *vt.* to show the way to, or direct the course of, by going before or along with
   lead — *n.* a heavy, soft, malleable, bluish-gray metallic chemical element used in batteries and in numerous alloys and compounds

3. The ship's *bow* was decorated with a bright red *bow.*
4. When his well ran dry, the prospector was forced to *desert* his home in the *desert.*
5. The winter *wind* can somehow *wind* throughout the entire house.

EXERCISE 5 **Making New Words with Prefixes**

Combine each of the following words with the prefix whose meaning is shown in parentheses after the word. Use the prefix chart on page 702 to choose an appropriate prefix. Then write the new word you have formed.

EXAMPLE **1. view (before)**
1. *preview*

1. monthly (two)
2. expensive (not)
3. historic (before)
4. handle (wrong)
5. organize (again)
6. marine (under)
7. locate (away)
8. fire (wrong)
9. place (again)
10. direct (not)

EXERCISE 6 **Making New Words with Suffixes**

Combine each of the following base words with the suffix that follows the plus sign. Write the new word. Use a dictionary to check your spelling.

EXAMPLE **1. victory + ous**
1. *victorious*

1. hope + less
2. love + able
3. demonstrate + ion
4. fury + ous
5. happy + ness
6. light + en
7. forget + ful
8. honorable + ly

RESOURCES

3. bow — *n.* the front part of a ship, boat, or airship; prow
bow — *n.* a bowknot or a decorative knot, as of ribbon, with two or more loops
4. desert — *vt.* to forsake (someone or something that one ought not to leave); abandon
desert — *n.* an uncultivated region without inhabitants; wilderness
5. wind — *n.* air in motion
wind — *vt.* to make one's way in a winding or twisting course

ANSWERS
Exercise 5

1. bimonthly
2. inexpensive
3. prehistoric
4. mishandle
5. reorganize
6. submarine
7. dislocate
8. misfire
9. replace
10. indirect

ANSWERS
Exercise 6

1. hopeless
2. lovable (also loveable)
3. demonstration
4. furious
5. happiness
6. lighten
7. forgetful
8. honorably

RESOURCES

LETTERS AND FORMS *(pp. 706–715)*

OBJECTIVES

- To write a friendly letter about real experiences
- To write a social letter for a given situation
- To write a business letter for a given situation

Teacher's ResourceBank™

RESOURCES

LETTERS AND FORMS

CHAPTER OVERVIEW

This chapter includes letter-writing activities that provide opportunities for students to learn appropriate forms of personal, social, and business letters, as well as guidelines for addressing envelopes and filling out forms. The exercises at the end of the chapter involve consideration of audience as well as selection and organization of contents. You may want to refer to this chapter when teaching any of the composition chapters, especially lessons on narrative writing and persuasive writing.

QUICK REMINDER

Tell students that in many areas of our lives we find that we cannot use the telephone to accomplish what a letter can. Many businesses prefer written correspondence because they want a written record of communications.

Have students brainstorm all the reasons they might have for wanting to write someone. [to order something, to complain, to get information, to express an opinion on an issue, or to wish someone well]

RESOURCES

RESOURCES

31 LETTERS AND FORMS

Style and Contents

Do you like to receive mail? Most people do. That's why you'll find it important to develop good letter-writing skills for social and business letters.

Kinds of Letters

There are several different kinds of letters. All of them have a purpose and an audience.

LETTERS		
TYPE OF LETTER	YOUR PURPOSE FOR WRITING	YOUR PROBABLE AUDIENCE
Personal	to tell about your ideas or feelings	close friends or relatives
Social	to be polite, to thank someone, or to tell someone about a planned event	friends or social acquaintances
Business	to inform a business about a service you need or how a service was performed	a business or organization

Writing Letters

Personal Letters

A ***personal letter,*** also called a friendly letter, is a good way to communicate with a friend or relative. A friendly letter is like a conversation, only much better. Conversations may be interrupted or forgotten, but a friendly letter is often treasured and read many times.

A friendly letter is a token of friendship. It usually contains a personal message from you, the sender, to the person you are writing to, the receiver. For example, you might write a friend to send congratulations for receiving a school award. Or, you might write to tell a friend your reaction to news that the friend's family will be moving away. When you're sending a friendly letter, remember to write about a subject that interests both you and the person you're writing to.

Social Letters

Sometimes, to be very polite, you should write a social letter rather than use the telephone or speak to someone in person. A ***social letter*** is usually a courteous response to a specific event or occurrence. The kinds of social letters people write most often are thank-you letters, invitations, or letters of regret.

Thank-you Letters

When you receive a gift or a favor, you should write a thank-you letter. The purpose of a thank-you letter is to express your appreciation when someone has spent time, trouble, or money to do something for your benefit. In addition to thanking the person, you might include a paragraph or so of personal news or friendly, chatty information. Try to think of something about the person's effort or gift that made it special to you.

AT-RISK STUDENTS

Students may have difficulty getting a personal letter started because they think they do not have anything to write about. You may want to conduct a brainstorming session in which you ask volunteers to suggest subjects that may be of interest to specific audiences, such as friends and relatives. [Responses may include hobbies or school activities, personal feelings and opinions, and family news.] You may want to combine this activity with a lesson on writing narratives. Remind students that prewriting is an essential element in the writing process.

RESOURCES

ADVANCED STUDENTS

You may want to assign a letter-writing project that involves the entire class in the production of a monthly letter to parents, reporting on class activities for the past month and plans for the coming month. This long-term project provides ongoing opportunities for students to develop prewriting and writing skills.

INTEGRATING THE LANGUAGE ARTS

Literature Link. Combine a book-report assignment with a letter-writing activity by asking students to write a friendly letter addressed to a main character in a book of their choice. The letter should follow the guidelines for personal letters and should include the students' impressions of the main character's situation. Suggested books are *Sounder, The Diary of a Young Girl,* and *Anne of Green Gables.*

A DIFFERENT APPROACH

Have students write individual invitations in which they request that a specific person attend a function at school, such as an open house, a carnival, a play, or another program. Students might also draw pictures and designs that illustrate the nature of the upcoming event. Stress the importance of correct form with accurate spelling and punctuation.

RESOURCES

9300 Leon St.
Burlington, VT 05401
October 6, 1993

Dear Grandpa,

Thank you so much for the wonderful beagle puppy you brought down from the farm. She must have been the smartest one in the litter. She already knows her name after only two days. We named her Pocahontas—Poci for short. She's the greatest gift, Grandpa. Thanks!

Love,
Rita

Invitations

You write an invitation to ask someone to an event you're planning. Include specific information about the occasion, such as the type of event, time and place, and any other information your guests might need to know (such as how to dress and what to bring, if anything).

Letters of Regret

You will need to write a letter of regret whenever you receive an invitation to an event that you will not be able to attend. You should always respond in writing to invitations that include the letters *R.S.V.P.* (These letters are an abbreviation for the French words that mean "please reply").

RESOURCES

Business Letters

The Parts of a Business Letter

Business letters usually follow a standard form or style. There are six parts of a business letter:

(1) the heading
(2) the inside address
(3) the salutation
(4) the body
(5) the closing
(6) the signature

Block Style

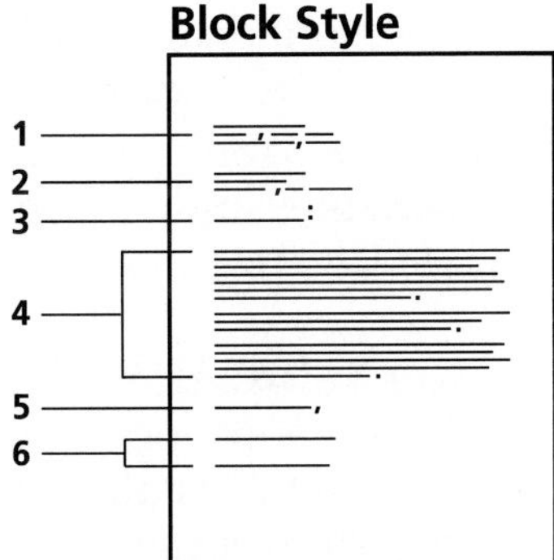

These six parts may be arranged in one of two styles.

In the ***block form,*** every part of the letter begins at the left margin of the page. A blank line is left between paragraphs, which are not indented.

In the ***modified block form,*** the heading, the closing, and your signature are placed to the right of an imaginary line down the center of the page. The middle parts of the letter begin at the left margin. Paragraphs are indented.

Modified Block Style

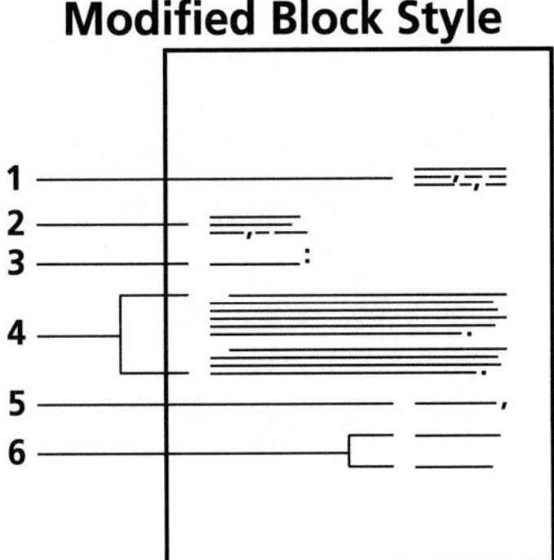

The Heading. The heading of a business letter has three lines:

- your street address
- your city, state, and ZIP code
- the date you are writing the letter

RESOURCES

LEP/ESL

General Strategies. Many students will need extra practice with the abbreviations used in addresses because the terms will be unfamiliar to them. You could make a chart for students of common abbreviations: abbreviations (postal and standard) for states; abbreviations for types of streets; and abbreviations for other words commonly used in addresses, such as titles and companies' names. Explain how each is used on an envelope and in a letter.

RESOURCES

COMMON ERROR

Problem. Students may have difficulty achieving the correct tone in their business letters.

Solution. Tell students to assume that business letters will be received by a busy person who needs a straightforward but complete presentation. Tell them to pretend they work in a department of the businesses they wrote to and are now the recipients of the letters. Then have them reread and revise with this perspective in mind.

RESOURCES

The Inside Address. The inside address gives the name and address of the person you are writing.

- If you're directing your letter to someone by name, use a courtesy title (such as *Mr., Ms., Mrs.,* or *Miss*) or a professional title (such as *Dr.* or *Professor*) in front of the person's name. After the person's name, include the person's business title (such as *Principal* or *Business Manager*).
- If you don't have a person's name, use a business title (such as *Refunds Department* or *Editor in Chief*).

The Salutation. Your salutation is your greeting to the person you're writing. In a business letter, the salutation usually ends with a colon (such as in *Dear Professor Garcia:*).

If you are writing to a specific person, you can begin with the word *Dear,* then use a courtesy title (*Mr., Miss, Ms., or Mrs.*) or a professional title (*Dr., Senator,* or others like these). If you don't have a specific name, use a general greeting (such as *Dear Sir or Madam:* or *Ladies and Gentlemen:*). You can also use a business title instead (*Dear Committee Leader:*).

The Body. The body contains the message of your letter. Leave a blank line between paragraphs in the body of the letter.

The Closing. Conclude your letter politely. The closing of a business letter often uses one of several common phrases (such as *Sincerely, Yours truly,* or *Respectfully yours*). Capitalize only the first word. End the closing with a comma.

The Signature. Sign your first and last name in ink directly below the closing. For a business letter, your name should be typed or printed neatly just below your signature.

RESOURCES

Types of Business Letters

The Request or Order Letter. In a ***request letter,*** you ask for specific information about a product or service. An ***order letter*** tells a business about a product or service you want (such as a free brochure). Be sure to include all important information (such as the item number, size, color, brand name, and price).

The Complaint or Adjustment Letter. When you write a ***complaint*** or ***adjustment letter,*** you state a problem and how you think it should be corrected. For example, if you are unhappy with a product you bought, you might write a letter like the one below.

3400 Werner Drive
Asheville, NC 28814
June 23, 1993

Customer Service Department
Barton Educational Products
1632 5th Street
Asheville, NC 28801

Dear Sir or Madam:

I am returning science kit #609 that was delivered yesterday. It arrived with a broken microscope.

Please replace the kit or refund my purchase price of $69.95 plus $4.30 that I paid for postage and handling.

Yours truly,

Lee Chin

Lee Chin

LESS-ADVANCED STUDENTS

You may want to teach only one type of business letter to some students. If you choose to teach the letter of request, you could find out what reports students are writing in their social studies classes and help them send letters for information they need.

INTEGRATING THE LANGUAGE ARTS

Technology Link. When students are writing business letters to several sources to request information, the process can be simplified by using a computer. Many word processing programs have well-designed business letter formats included. Most of these programs allow the user to quickly and easily replace salutations, addresses, and texts as they vary from letter to letter. Remind students to carefully proofread each letter to make sure all the necessary changes have been made.

TIMESAVER

Remind students that writing effective letters requires editing and revision. Ask them to proofread their letters for correct spelling, punctuation, and capitalization. Remind them to double-check all names and addresses. Ask them to reread the letters and revise any sentences that may be confusing.

RESOURCES

The Appreciation Letter. Whenever you write an ***appreciation letter,*** you tell people in a business or organization that they did a good job. Give details about what they did that you liked. For example, perhaps a waiter or waitress gave you especially good service at a restaurant, and you want to tell the manager that you appreciate such good service.

GUIDELINES FOR WRITING BUSINESS LETTERS

1. *Decide on your purpose.* Are you ordering or returning merchandise? Or, are you asking for someone to send you information?
2. *Include all necessary information.* Your purpose for writing should be very clear to your readers. Be brief and get to the point quickly, but don't leave out any important details.
3. *Write your letter in a timely manner.* If you are requesting something, make your request well in advance. If you have a complaint, send your letter as soon as possible.
4. *Think about your choice of words.* A business letter should be clear, polite, and reasonable. If you have a complaint, tell what's wrong, but be courteous.

RESOURCES

Appearance of a Business Letter

As your representative, your business letter should look its best. Use the following guidelines when writing a business letter.

- Use unlined $8\frac{1}{2}'' \times 11''$ white paper.
- Type your letter or write it neatly in blue or black ink. Always check your letter for errors, smudges, and misspellings.
- Center your letter on the paper to make the margins even all around.
- Do not write on the back. Use a second sheet of paper if necessary.

Addressing an Envelope

Your letter has a much better chance of arriving at its intended destination if you take care to address the envelope neatly and correctly.

- Place your return address in the top left-hand corner of the envelope.
- Write the name and address of the person to whom the letter is being sent in the center of the envelope. (For a business letter, the name and address on the envelope should match the inside address that is written on the business letter.)
- Use standard two-letter postal abbreviations for state names, followed by the ZIP code.

Sudi Foster
63 Washington Ave.
Santa Clara, OR 70501

Aola Washington
2119 Brushcreek Ave. #302
Independence, MO 64055

Completing Printed Forms

You are often required to fill out forms about yourself. You must fill out a form to get a library card, register for school, apply for membership in a club or organization, and for many other reasons.

The following guidelines will help you complete different types of forms.

RESOURCES

LEP/ESL

General Strategies. To provide students with practice in filling out forms, photocopy actual forms such as an application for a library card, a new-patient form for a clinic or doctor's office, a magazine subscription form, an entry form for a contest, and so forth. Go over each section of the forms and help students who have trouble with the required information. Stress the importance of providing complete answers and proofreading for spelling errors.

RESOURCES

HINTS FOR FILLING OUT FORMS

1. Read all instructions before you begin. Look for special instructions to see whether you should use a pen or pencil.
2. Read each item carefully.
3. Print neatly all the information that is requested.
4. Proofread the form to make sure you didn't leave anything blank. Also, check for errors and correct them neatly.
5. Mail the form to the correct address or give it to the correct person.

Review

EXERCISE 1 Writing a Social Letter

Write a social letter for one of the following situations. Make up your own situation if you prefer.

1. Your soccer team has just won its first game. Write a thank-you letter to your grandparents, thanking them for coming to the game.
2. You have been invited to spend a few days at the house of an out-of-town friend. Unfortunately, you cannot go because your family has already planned a vacation for that time.
3. You are planning a joint birthday party for two friends at your house. Write a letter of invitation, including all the information your guests will need to know.

EXERCISE 2 Writing a Business Letter

Write a business letter for one of the situations that follow. Use white, unruled typewriter paper. Use

ANSWERS

Exercise 1

Letters will vary but should follow guidelines for writing a friendly letter.

1. Letters should follow guidelines for writing thank-you letters.
2. Letters should follow guidelines for writing letters of regret.
3. Letters should follow guidelines for writing invitations.

RESOURCES

RESOURCES

your own return address, but make up any other information you need to write the letter. Address an envelope for your letter, but don't actually mail it.

1. You would like historical information about a city. Write to its Chamber of Commerce, requesting a pamphlet or brochure.
2. Write a letter to a nearby museum, asking for a schedule of exhibits. Tell why you are interested in this information.
3. Write a letter of appreciation to your city council, explaining why you are happy with a city service or program, such as a new park or an after-school recreation program for the young people in your community.

EXERCISE 3 **Completing a Form**

For each of the numbered blanks on the following form, write what you would put on that blank line if you filled out this form. Responses will vary.

INFORMATION FORM

NAME (1) ____________________

NICKNAME (2) __________ PHONE # (3) __________

ADDRESS (4) ____________________

____

PARENT OR GUARDIAN (5) ____________________

RESOURCES

ANSWERS

Exercise 2

Students' letters will vary.

1. Letters should follow guidelines for letters of request.
2. Letters should follow guidelines for letters of request.
3. Letters should follow guidelines for letters of appreciation.

A DIFFERENT APPROACH

Expand **Exercise 3** to include an assignment to find out the names of city officials and their business addresses and the names and addresses of museums in the region.

RESOURCES

SEGMENT 1 *(pp. 716–719)*

USING SKILLS AND STRATEGIES

OBJECTIVES

- To choose appropriate reading rates for particular reading purposes
- To apply the SQ3R reading method

Teacher's ResourceBank™

RESOURCES

FOR THE WHOLE CHAPTER

- Chapter Review Form A 368–369
- Chapter Review Form B 370–371

CHAPTER OVERVIEW

This chapter provides students with guidelines for developing both study and test-taking skills. Since these skills are essential to student success, you may want to teach this chapter early in the academic year and review the material as necessary.

Teacher's ResourceBank™

RESOURCES

USING SKILLS AND STRATEGIES

- Reading Rates 355
- The Learning Log 356
- SQ3R 357

QUICK REMINDER

Students will benefit from analyzing their study habits prior to working through this lesson. You might begin by telling students about a fictitious student who has a great deal of work to do in the next week. List the student's assignments and their due dates on the chalkboard. Ask students to pretend that they are required to do the work on schedule; then ask how they would approach the task.

RESOURCES

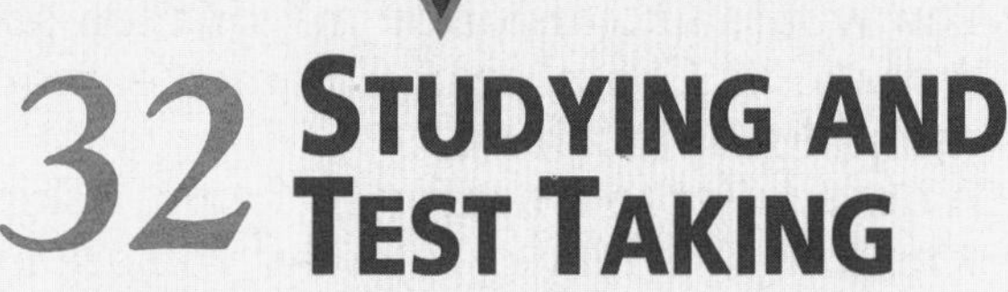

32 STUDYING AND TEST TAKING

Using Skills and Strategies

Good study habits usually result in better grades. However, studying better doesn't always mean you have to study longer. You can learn ways to make every minute of your study time count.

Planning a Study Routine

Set up a study schedule that will help you earn the grades you want. Decide on a schedule and stick to it. Here are some suggestions.

1. *Know your assignments.* Write down your assignments and when each one is due. Be sure you understand the instructions for each assignment.
2. *Plan to finish your work on time.* Break larger assignments into smaller steps. Keep track of when you should be finished with each step.
3. *Study.* Set aside a time and a place to study. Focus your attention only on your assignments.

RESOURCES

Strengthening Study Skills

Reading and Understanding

You read differently depending on what you're reading and why you are reading it. You should read at the rate that fits your purpose for reading. Here are some common purposes for reading.

READING RATES AND THEIR PURPOSE		
READING RATE	PURPOSE	EXAMPLE
Scanning	Reading for specific details	Looking in your English textbook for a poem by Gwendolyn Brooks
Skimming	Reading for main points or important ideas	Reviewing words in boldface or italics in a science chapter to prepare for a test on the parts of a flower
Reading for mastery	Reading closely to understand and remember	Reading a chapter in your history textbook to prepare an oral report on the ancient Incas

Writing to Learn

Writing can be a great tool for exploring ideas. Writing helps you organize your thoughts. In the process of writing, you can solve a problem or make a plan. The following chart shows some kinds of writing that can help you learn.

COMMON ERROR

Problem. Some students read all material at a slow pace.

Solution. Model reading for various purposes. For example, you might bring a cookbook to class to show students how to scan the book in order to find a broccoli casserole recipe, how to skim the recipe in order to make a grocery list, and how to read closely in order to follow the recipe directions.

A DIFFERENT APPROACH

Before students read and discuss the **Writing to Learn** section, design a series of assignments to allow them to experience the benefits of using writing as a learning tool. The assignments need not be elaborate. For example, you might ask students, "What would you like to do during summer vacation?" Allow two or three students to give verbal responses; then encourage the class to freewrite for three to five minutes in response to the question. Encourage students to discuss what they learned from the activity.

Students might also be encouraged to keep a personal journal or diary. You might ask them to record a funny story they've heard. You'll want to help them to focus on the kind of writing that leads to self-awareness.

For an autobiographical paper, have students answer the question, "Who are you?"

RESOURCES

LEP/ESL

General Strategies. When presenting the information concerning word processors, plan a field trip either to the school's computer lab or to a nearby facility (perhaps a high school or community college) where equipment is available, so that students can gain hands-on experience. Guide each student through the procedures of opening a new file and naming it, creating a short document and saving it, and printing out a hard copy.

General Strategies. Understanding oral directions for assignments can be difficult for some students. Encourage them to listen carefully and to write down what they understand the assignment to be. You may need to review with individual students their written versions of the assignment.

INTEGRATING THE LANGUAGE ARTS

Technology Link. To help students recognize the advantages of using computers, have them try invisible writing. Ask them to turn the brightness knob down so that letters no longer appear on the screen and have students enter ideas freely without thinking about organization, grammar, usage, or mechanics. Have students restore the brightness level and show them how to use the appropriate word processing features to organize, revise, and edit their entries.

RESOURCES

TYPE OF WRITING	PURPOSE	EXAMPLE
Freewriting	To help you focus your thoughts	Writing for ten minutes to plan the plot of a short story
Autobiographies	To help you examine the meaning of important events in your	Writing what you learned when you took on the responsibility for a new pet
Diaries	To help you recall thoughts and express your feelings	Writing your feelings when a good friend changed schools
Journals and Learning Logs	To help record observations, descriptions, and questions	Jotting notes after reading a poem, noting difficult parts
	To help you define or analyze information, or propose a solution	Listing and defining words you learned in Spanish class

RESOURCES

Using a Word Processor as a Writing Tool

The word processor is a tool for writing. It can help you plan, draft, and edit your work. Every step of the writing process is easier using a word processor.

WRITING STEP	WORD PROCESSOR BENEFITS
Prewriting	easy to type in rough notes
Writing a First Draft	easy to write, revise, and rearrange parts of what you're writing
Evaluating	easy to try out different versions

(continued)

WRITING STEP	WORD PROCESSOR BENEFITS
Revising and Proofreading	easy to edit and make changes; some processors check spelling
Writing a Final Version	easy to print one or more clean, final copies

Using the SQ3R Method

SQ3R is the name of a study method. It is a series of steps for improving your ability to understand and remember learning materials. Developed by Francis Robinson, an educational psychologist, the SQ3R study method includes five simple steps.

S *Survey* the entire assignment. For example, if you're studying a new chapter in a textbook, look quickly at the chapter headings, subheadings, terms in boldface and italics, charts, outlines, illustrations, and summaries.

Q *Question* yourself. Make a list of questions that you want to be able to answer when you have finished reading.

R *Read* the material carefully to find answers to all the questions you have listed. Take notes as you read.

R *Recite* answers to each of your questions in your own words.

R *Review* the material by rereading quickly, looking over your questions, and recalling the answers.

The SQ3R method will help you identify the most important information in what you read. Also, you are more likely to remember what you read when you ask yourself questions and analyze the material as you read it.

RESOURCES

COOPERATIVE LEARNING

Ask students to apply the SQ3R method to a chapter in their literature textbook or to a chapter in a textbook from another class. After students have completed their work, ask them to share in small groups what they discovered about the chapters. Students will benefit particularly from discussing the kinds of questions they asked and answered. You may also ask each group to design a test on the material in a group member's selected chapter.

RESOURCES

SEGMENT 2 *(pp. 720–732)*

INTERPRETING AND ANALYZING INFORMATION

OBJECTIVES

- To analyze details in a passage
- To draw conclusions and make inferences
- To interpret graphic information

Teacher's ResourceBank™

RESOURCES

INTERPRETING AND ANALYZING INFORMATION

QUICK REMINDER

If your students are familiar with topic sentences, they should have little difficulty with the concept of main idea. You might begin by writing on the chalkboard a short paragraph without its topic sentence.

Ask students to supply a topic sentence for the paragraph. Explain that when the topic sentence is missing the paragraph has an implied main idea, but when the topic sentence is provided the paragraph has a stated main idea.

LEP/ESL

General Strategies. Students will gain a better understanding of the information in the **Finding Relationships Among Details** chart if each strategy is applied to the reading selection that follows. After students read the passage, write the five strategies on the chalkboard. Then, as a whole-class activity, ask students to supply the correct information.

RESOURCES

Interpreting and Analyzing Information

You can find patterns of organization in everything you read. You will better understand what you read if you can understand how the material is organized and how the ideas relate to one another.

Stated Main Idea. The main idea of a passage is the most important point the writer is making. The main idea may be stated. This means the author may write the main idea plainly in one or two sentences.

Implied Main Idea. Sometimes the main idea is not stated. The writer's major point may not be found in one or two specific sentences. Instead, the main idea may be implied. Look for clues to find the central idea that ties all the other ideas together.

HOW TO FIND THE MAIN IDEA

- Skim the passage. (What topic do the sentences have in common?)
- Identify the topic. (What is the passage about?)
- Identify what the passage says about the topic. (What's the message of the passage as a whole?)
- State the meaning of the passage in your own words.
- Review the passage. (If you have correctly identified the main idea, all the other ideas in the passage will support it.)

REFERENCE NOTE: For additional information on finding a main idea, see pages 61–63.

Recognizing Relationships Among Details

To understand the meaning of a reading passage, you need to understand the main idea. Then you need to understand the relationship of details to the main idea and to each other.

- To analyze a note-taking method
- To identify classifications
- To organize information visually
- To paraphrase a poem

FINDING RELATIONSHIPS AMONG DETAILS	
Identify specific details.	What details answer questions such as *Who? What? When? Where? Why?* and *How?* (These are *5W-How?* questions.)
Distinguish between fact and opinion.	What statements can be shown to be true or false? (facts) What statements express a person's beliefs? (opinions)
Identify similarities and differences.	How are the details similar to one another? How are they different?
Understand cause and effect.	Do earlier events affect later ones?
Identify an order of organization.	In what kind of order are the details arranged? Are they in time order, order of importance, spatial order, or some other pattern of organization?

Reading Passage

In 1990, Antonia Novello became the first Hispanic and the first woman to be Surgeon General of the United States. Antonia Novello was born in Puerto Rico in 1945 with a serious health problem. Because of her illness, Antonia spent two weeks in the hospital every summer. At age eight, she was told that she could have surgery to correct her condition. However, the nearest hospital was too far away. For many years

Sample Analysis

DIFFERENCE: How is Antonia Novello different from past Surgeon Generals?
ANSWER: *No other Surgeon General has been either Hispanic or a woman.*

FACT: Where was Antonia Novello born?
ANSWER: *She was born in Puerto Rico.*

INTEGRATING THE LANGUAGE ARTS

Composition Link. Remind students that writers need to make main ideas and relationships among details clear to their readers. Ask each student to analyze one of his or her recent paragraphs or essays using the techniques suggested in this lesson. You might also encourage students to practice the techniques when they act as peer evaluators.

COOPERATIVE LEARNING

Ask students to work in small groups to identify the main ideas in several nonfiction passages from their literature textbooks. Students in each group might then choose a passage and apply the techniques suggested in the **Finding Relationships Among Details** chart.

RESOURCES

INTEGRATING THE LANGUAGE ARTS

Literature Link. Although reading literature and reading factual material are different tasks, they do have some elements in common, and students can benefit from discussing the similarities and differences. You might begin by listing on the chalkboard the titles of two short selections—one fictional and one nonfictional—that your students have read. Ask the class to consider what the theme of each might be. How is theme similar to main idea? Why are specific details important in each of the selections? Do cause-and-effect relationships play an important role in fiction? Is understanding similarities and differences sometimes important?

CRITICAL THINKING

Analysis

After students have read the passage that begins on p. 721, ask them to determine what the main idea of the passage is. [In many ways, Antonia Novello brought a unique point of view to the post of Surgeon General.] Ask them to determine whether the main idea is stated or implied [stated].

RESOURCES

Antonia didn't have surgery. Her experiences made her interested in becoming a doctor and helping others, especially young people, who had health problems.

Antonia Novello entered the University of Puerto Rico when she was eighteen. Finally, she was able to have her surgery. Some problems that developed made a second surgery necessary. This time the surgery was successful.

Antonia missed a semester during her surgeries and her recovery, but she returned to school the very next semester. She graduated from the University of Puerto Rico School of Medicine in 1970. She then went to the University of Michigan, where she was chosen "Intern of the Year." Later, when she had already become a doctor, she went to graduate school, specializing in children's medicine and public health care.

Antonia Novello started working as a children's doctor with the U.S. Public Health Service (PHS) in 1978. There she learned skills in leadership that would help her as Surgeon General. Antonia's experience of living with sickness for many years made her determined to help people who needed health care but weren't getting it. As Surgeon General, she is especially concerned with the health problems of young people.

OPINION: Why do you think Antonia Novello cared so much about health problems of youth?
ANSWER: *As a child, she experienced health problems herself. This may have given her a special sympathy for young people with health problems.*

CAUSE AND EFFECT: Why did Antonia miss a semester of medical school?
ANSWER: *She had two surgeries to correct a health problem.*

DETAILS: What award did Antonia win in college?
ANSWER: *She was named "Intern of the Year."*

ORDER: In what kind of order are the details in this passage organized?
ANSWER: *They are in chronological (or time) order.*

RESOURCES

Applying Reasoning Skills

To understand what you read, you have to think carefully about the ideas and details in the material you are reading. These are like clues, and you have to act like a detective to analyze all the evidence that you find in your reading. When you think critically as you read, you may draw *conclusions*. ***Conclusions*** are decisions based on facts and evidence that you find in your reading.

Sometimes important clues are hard to find. In some cases, this means that you must make *inferences*. ***Inferences*** are decisions you make that are based on evidence that may be only hinted at, or implied, in what you have read.

For example, when you analyze the reading passage on pages 721–722, you might draw conclusions or make inferences such as these:

> The health problem Antonia Novello had was serious. (Evidence: It required two surgeries to correct the problem, and her recovery made her miss a whole semester of college.)
>
> Antonia Novello is very dedicated to her profession. (Evidence: She won an award for her hard work as an intern. After she became a doctor, she returned to college for additional graduate study.)

A ***valid conclusion*** is one that is firmly supported by facts, evidence, or logic. However, a conclusion that is not supported by facts, evidence, or logic is called ***invalid.*** For example, it is invalid to conclude that Antonia Novello could not succeed until her health problem was cured. This conclusion can't be drawn from facts in the reading passage. Antonia Novello had already completed high school despite ten years of having to go to the hospital for two weeks every summer. She was already in college before she had her surgery.

RESOURCES

COOPERATIVE LEARNING

Ask students to work together in small groups to create short narratives involving some kind of mystery, such as a kidnapped cockatoo or the sudden appearance of an extra encyclopedia volume in the library. Each group should provide clues that will allow readers to arrive at the solution of the mystery, but the group's narrative should not reveal the solution. When the groups have completed the assignment, ask them to exchange papers and practice drawing conclusions and making inferences as they try to solve other groups' mysteries.

RESOURCES

LESS-ADVANCED STUDENTS

To provide students with practice in drawing conclusions and making inferences, ask them to discuss detective stories they are familiar with, either from books, from film, or from television. Help students determine when and how detectives draw conclusions and make inferences. Help students see the connection between a detective examining clues and a reader studying details in a text. Students might also enjoy discussing examples of invalid conclusions that some detectives have reached.

RESOURCES

HOW TO DRAW CONCLUSIONS	
Gather all the evidence.	What facts or details have you learned about the subject?
Evaluate the evidence.	What do the facts and details you have gathered tell you about the subject?
Make appropriate connections.	What can you reasonably conclude from the evidence?

Analyzing Graphics and Illustrations

Many books and articles include visual information contained in diagrams, maps, graphs, and illustrations. Visual information is often clearer and easier to understand than information that is written.

A paragraph full of details can be difficult to understand. With graphics and illustrations, many of the relationships among sets of facts are more clear. For example, the following chart shows information about the depth of the world's oceans.

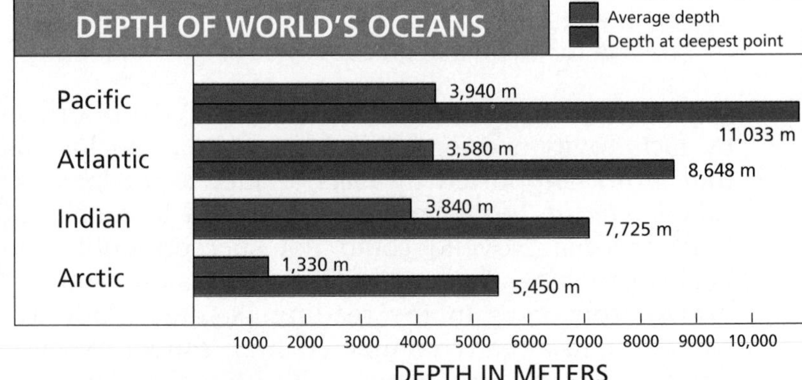

This chart quickly shows you information, such as which of the oceans has the greatest average depth or which ocean has the deepest point.

Applying Study Methods

There are many different ways you can study, because there are many different ways you can organize and handle information. Some of the most common are

- taking notes
- classifying
- organizing information visually
- outlining
- paraphrasing
- summarizing
- memorizing

Taking Notes

Taking accurate notes is worth the extra effort. As you read at home or listen in class, your detailed information will be recorded in your notebook. Then you will be ready to study for even the most challenging tests.

HOW TO TAKE STUDY NOTES

1. Identify and write down the main ideas in class or your reading. These main ideas should be the headings in your notes. In class, listen for key words and phrases, such as *first, most important,* or *therefore.* These words often introduce main ideas and tell you how ideas are related. In a textbook, chapter headings and subheadings usually contain key ideas.
2. Keep your notes brief. Use abbreviations and sum up source material in your own words.
3. Include brief examples or details from the source material. Important examples or details can help you recall the key ideas more easily.
4. Look over your notes soon after you write them to be sure you have included the most important information.

MEETING INDIVIDUAL NEEDS

LEP/ESL

General Strategies. Taking notes while listening to lecture material can prove frustrating because students might not be able to ask the speaker to slow down, to repeat, or to clarify. Students concerned about missing something important may attempt to record the lecture verbatim—an impossible task that inevitably leads to further frustration. To help students master note-taking skills, allow them to work with peer tutors.

A DIFFERENT APPROACH

Before assigning the material on taking notes, ask students to take notes on a passage in one of their textbooks. After students have read and discussed the **Taking Notes** section, ask them to take notes on the same passage and then to compare their first and second efforts.

RESOURCES

Here's an example of careful study notes about the reading passage on pages 721–722. The notes show the main ideas as headings. Underneath each main heading, you will find a group of important details that relate to that heading.

Dr. Antonia Novello

Childhood

- 1945—born in Puerto Rico
- Had serious health problem—2 wks. in hospital every yr.
- At 8 yrs. old—told she needed surgery
- Did not have surgery—hospital too far
- Decided to become a doctor to help others who had health problems

Education

- Graduated from Puerto Rico School of Med., 1970
- Chosen as "Intern of the Year" at Univ. of Mich.

Career

- 1978—started at Public Health Service (PHS) as children's doctor
- 1990—became Surgeon General (1st Hispanic & 1st woman)

Influences

- PHS → skills in leadership
- childhood illness → desire to help others
- children's doctor → concern with health problems of young people

RESOURCES

RESOURCES

Classifying

Classifying is arranging information into categories or groups. When you classify items, you sort them so that the items in each category or group are related. The name or description of the category shows the relationship between the items in the group.

EXAMPLE What do these creatures have in common? giraffe, leopard, ladybug, Dalmatian
ANSWER They all have spots.

You also use classification techniques when you identify patterns. For example, look at the relationship between the following sequence of numbers.

What's the next number in the series?

1 5 9 13 ___?___

ANSWER The first number in this series is *1*. The difference between the first number, *1*, and the second number, *5*, is *4*. Add *4* to the second number to make the third number, *9*. Add *4* to the third number to get the fourth number, *13*. The pattern is to add *4* to each number in the series to get the next number. Therefore, to produce the next number in the series after *13*, you would again add *4*. The answer is *17*.

Organizing Information Visually

If you are learning new information, you may find it easier to understand if you organize it visually. A map, diagram, or chart is often easier to understand than a paragraph.

For example, the passage that follows compares Alaska and Hawaii.

CRITICAL THINKING
Evaluating

To give students additional practice in classifying and in thinking critically, ask them to work in small groups to make lists of all the ways in which they can classify or group the pupils in the room. Discourage physical classifications by suggesting categories such as common interests or future careers. Combine the information from the groups into one list on the chalkboard. Ask the groups to discuss what the purpose might be for each classification and to decide what the advantages and disadvantages might be to classifying students in that fashion.

LEARNING STYLES

Visual Learners. Some students may find it helpful to use color to organize relationships among details in reading assignments. To encourage students, give them copies of the passage comparing Hawaii and Alaska and show them how to sort the information in the passage using different highlighters. For example, have students mark information pertaining only to Hawaii in yellow. Information pertaining only to Alaska could be marked in blue, while information relating to both states could be marked in pink.

COOPERATIVE LEARNING

Ask students to work together in pairs to draw a map, diagram, or chart to visually organize the material in a nonfiction selection from their literature textbook. After students have completed their work, ask that they explain their choices to other pairs of students in the class.

RESOURCES

In some ways, Alaska and Hawaii are extremely different from each other. In other ways, the two states are more like each other than they are like the other forty-eight states.

Alaska is the largest state and the farthest north. One third of Alaska lies north of the Arctic Circle. By contrast, Hawaii is the fourth smallest state and the farthest south. Hawaii is located south of the Tropic of Cancer.

Yet Alaska and Hawaii have some similarities. They are the two newest states. Alaska was the forty-ninth state and Hawaii was the fiftieth. Both are located far from the other forty-eight states. Both states also have unique ethnic mixes. Alaska's population is about one-third Native American. Hawaii has great numbers of people with Japanese and Filipino ancestry, along with many native Polynesians. Both states are very expensive places to live, because many of their goods are shipped at great cost from the main body of states.

If you read this passage and tried to remember all the details, it would not be easy to compare the two states. However, making a chart like the one below would make the information easier to remember.

RESOURCES

ALASKA	HAWAII
largest state	fourth smallest state
most northern state	most southern state
$\frac{1}{3}$ north of Arctic Circle	south of Tropic of Cancer
49th state	50th state
isolated from other 48 states	isolated from other 48 states
unique ethnic mix	unique ethnic mix
high cost of living	high cost of living

Outlining

An *outline* is another way to organize important information. When you make an outline, you arrange the ideas to show which are the main ideas and which are smaller parts of the main ideas. In this way, outlines make the relationship of ideas clear.

Sometimes you may need to use different types of outlines. For example, for a report you might use a formal outline, with Roman numerals for headings and capital letters for subheadings. However, when you take notes in class, an informal outline is easier and faster.

FORMAL OUTLINE FORM

I. Main Point
  A. Supporting Point
    1. Detail
      a. Information or detail

INFORMAL OUTLINE FORM

Main Idea
  Supporting detail
  Supporting detail
  Supporting detail

RESOURCES

Paraphrasing

When you *paraphrase,* you express another person's ideas in your own words. A paraphrase can help you understand readings that are complicated or written with poetic or elaborate words.

A written paraphrase will usually be about the same length as the original. Therefore, paraphrasing is not very practical for long passages of writing. However, you may sometimes be asked (usually in language arts classes) to paraphrase a short passage, such as a poem.

LEARNING STYLES

Kinetic Learners. One way to reinforce the concepts of outlining for kinetic learners is to write each element of an outline on a separate strip of paper and then to ask the students to arrange the strips in logical order.

A DIFFERENT APPROACH

Ask students to make an informal outline of the last paragraph of the passage comparing Hawaii and Alaska. To help students get started, model on the chalkboard the first steps in outlining the passage.

RESOURCES

INTEGRATING THE LANGUAGE ARTS

Study Skills and Mechanics. You may want to remind students that while paraphrased material does not always contain direct quotations from the original source, credit is still given to the original writer. If words or phrases from the original source are used verbatim, they must be enclosed in quotation marks.

COOPERATIVE LEARNING

Students might work in pairs to paraphrase one or two poems. Selections from T. S. Eliot's *Old Possum's Book of Practical Cats* are often found in literature textbooks and lend themselves particularly well to this type of activity.

RESOURCES

SELECTION AMENDMENT
Description of change: excerpted
Rationale: to focus on the concept of *paraphrasing* presented in this chapter

Here is an excerpt from a poem.

from A Poison Tree
by William Blake

I was angry with my friend
I told my wrath, my wrath did end.
I was angry with a foe:
I told it not, my wrath did grow.

As an example, here is a possible paraphrase of this verse of the poem.

The speaker in the poem was upset with a friend and told the friend about the problem. Before long, the speaker wasn't angry any more. However, the speaker was mad at an enemy and kept the anger inside. As a result, the speaker's bad feelings just kept getting worse.

Use these guidelines when you write a paraphrase.

RESOURCES

HOW TO PARAPHRASE

1. Read the selection carefully before you begin.
2. Be sure you understand the main idea of the selection. Look up any unfamiliar words in a dictionary.
3. Determine the tone of the selection. (What is the attitude of the writer toward the subject of the selection?)
4. Identify the speaker in fictional material. (Is the poet or author speaking, or is it a character?)
5. Write your paraphrase in your own words. Shorten long sentences or stanzas. Use your own, familiar vocabulary, but keep the ideas in the same order as in the selection.
6. Be sure that the ideas in your paraphrase match the ideas expressed in the original.

Another common situation when you may find paraphrasing useful is when you are writing a research report. For example, whenever you get a set of facts from an encyclopedia and restate them in your own words, you are paraphrasing the encyclopedia's information. Make sure to name the source you paraphrase. It's very important to give credit for a quote or for a specific idea that you borrowed from someone else.

REFERENCE NOTE: For more about giving credit to your sources when you are writing reports, see pages 283–286.

Summarizing

A ***summary*** is a brief restatement of the main ideas expressed in a piece of writing. A summary is similar to a paraphrase because when you summarize, you express another person's ideas in your own words. However, a summary is usually shorter than a paraphrase. Whenever you summarize, you shorten the original material and present only the most important points.

You think critically whenever you summarize. When you condense material, you make decisions and draw conclusions about what to include in the summary and what to leave out.

HOW TO SUMMARIZE

1. Skim the selection you wish to summarize.
2. Read the passage again closely. Look for main ideas and supporting details.
3. Write your summary in your own words. Include only the main ideas and the most important supporting points.
4. Evaluate and revise your summary. Check to see that you have covered the most important points. Make sure that the information is clearly expressed and that the reader can follow your ideas.

RESOURCES

INTEGRATING THE LANGUAGE ARTS

Literature Link. To give students practice in summarizing a story ask them to write a summary of a story in their literature texts, such as John Gardner's "Dragon, Dragon."

RESOURCES

Here's a sample summary of the reading passage found on pages 272–274.

> Water striders are insects that look similar to daddy longlegs. However, water striders live on the water. They walk, feed, breed, and are even born on the water. Water striders seek land only when the water is choppy or freezing. Their bodies repel water, so they don't absorb water and sink from the weight. Their legs are long and widely spaced to spread their weight. Water striders' lower legs and feet are covered with waterproof hairs that trap air bubbles to help keep them afloat. Water striders are also helped by the film that forms on the surface of water.

Memorizing

There are many times when you need to memorize information for tests and quizzes. It is not a good idea to "cram" information you are trying to memorize. You are more likely to remember the information more accurately and for a longer time if you practice recalling it in frequent, short, focused sessions. Here are some hints for memorizing effectively.

HOW TO MEMORIZE	
Memorize only the most important information.	Whenever possible, condense the material you need to remember.
Practice the material in different ways.	Copy the material by hand. Recite the material out loud.
Invent memory games.	Form a word from the first letters of important terms. Or, make up rhymes that help you remember facts and details.

RESOURCES

COOPERATIVE LEARNING

To give students practice in memorizing information, choose one of the charts in this chapter and assign students the task of memorizing the steps in the chart. Ask students to work in small groups to decide what specific information must be memorized and to invent memory games to help them memorize the information.

LEARNING STYLES

Kinetic Learners. Suggest that students move around when they are memorizing something. For example, if they are memorizing poetry, advise students to walk back and forth repeating the material aloud, adding movements and gestures that they deem appropriate to the poem and referring to the text less and less often. They may connect the movement with the material and later recall a sense of motion that, through association, will help them recapture the words.

RESOURCES

SEGMENT 3 *(pp. 733–744)*

IMPROVING TEST-TAKING SKILLS

OBJECTIVE

- To analyze essay questions

Improving Test-Taking Skills

Preparing for Different Kinds of Tests

Nervousness before a test is normal. However, all the energy that comes from being nervous can help you do well on the test. Your attitude is the key.

HOW TO PREPARE FOR A TEST

Plan for success. Do everything you can to help you do your best on the test. Know what information will be covered on the test. Make a plan that gives you enough time to take notes, study, and review the material.

Be confident. If you have studied thoroughly, you know you are prepared. During the test, pay attention only to reading and answering the test questions.

Keep trying. Be determined to keep improving. Your commitment to keep learning will help you improve your study effectiveness.

Objective questions and *essay questions* are two basic ways that your knowledge can be tested. There are ways that you can prepare for each type of question.

Objective Tests

There are several kinds of objective test questions. Some examples are multiple-choice, true/false, matching, reasoning or logic, or short-answer questions. ***Objective questions*** always ask you for specific information. They may test you on information such as names, terms, dates, or definitions. Most objective test questions have only one correct answer. To prepare for objective tests, you will need to review specific information. The study skills listed earlier in this chapter will help you prepare for objective tests.

RESOURCES

Teacher's ResourceBank™

RESOURCES

IMPROVING TEST-TAKING SKILLS

- Taking a True/False Test 366
- Taking an Essay Test 367

QUICK REMINDER

Encourage students to freewrite for ten minutes in response to the following questions.

1. How do you feel when you find out you are going to have a test?
2. What are your thoughts and feelings when you sit down to take a test?
3. How do you prepare for a test?
4. What strategies do you use to help yourself do well on tests?

After students respond to the questions, invite volunteers to share their responses.

LEP/ESL

General Strategies. Arrange to help students work through several sample test booklets before you administer standardized tests. Make sure that students understand how to follow the directions. Reassure students that failure to complete a section does not necessarily mean failure on the test, and remind them not to begin a section without a signal from the monitor.

RESOURCES

COMMON ERROR

Problem. When recording answers for an objective test on a separate answer sheet, an inexperienced test-taker may not be careful to check that the number beside the answer he or she is marking matches the number of the question being answered. Often this occurs because a student skips a question, planning to come back to it later, but fails to leave a blank space on the answer sheet.

Solution. Remind students to keep careful track of the numbers beside the questions and the numbers on the answer sheet. Tell students that if they save a particularly tough question for later they should be sure to make a special mark—perhaps a star—beside the corresponding number on the answer sheet. Marking the answer sheet will help a student remember to leave the space blank until he or she can come back to it.

RESOURCES

HOW TO STUDY FOR OBJECTIVE TESTS

1. Identify important terms or facts in your textbook and class notes.
2. Review the information in more than one form. For example, you may need to learn the definitions for scientific terms. Make flashcards. Practice identifying the definition from the term, then the term from the definition.
3. Practice and repeat information to remember it. Go over difficult information more than once.
4. If possible, briefly review all the information shortly before the actual test.

You may change your study strategies for each type of objective test. For example, you might use flashcards to study definitions. Or, to study for a problem-solving type of test, you could work out practice problems and check them with your textbook.

Taking Different Kinds of Objective Tests

When you begin an objective test, quickly look over the questions. If you know the number of items on the test, you can decide how to budget your time for each item. Other strategies for handling specific kinds of objective test questions follow.

RESOURCES

Multiple-Choice Questions. With a multiple-choice question, you will need to select a correct answer from a number of items that are provided for you.

EXAMPLE **1.** Antonia Novello was born in

A Mexico
(B) Puerto Rico
C El Salvador
D Italy

HOW TO ANSWER MULTIPLE-CHOICE QUESTIONS	
Read the question or statement carefully.	■ Make sure you understand the question or statement before you begin to look at the answer choices. ■ Look for words such as *not* or *only.* These words limit your choice of answers.
Read all the choices before selecting an answer.	■ Rule out all of the choices that you know are incorrect. ■ Think carefully about all of the remaining choices. Select only the one that makes the most sense.

True/False Questions. True/false questions ask you to decide whether the statement you are given is true or false.

EXAMPLE **1.** T Ⓕ Hawaii is the smallest state in the United States.

HOW TO ANSWER TRUE/FALSE QUESTIONS	
Read the statement carefully.	■ The whole statement is false if any part of the statement is false.
Look for word clues.	■ Words such as *always* or *never* limit the range of possibilities of a statement. ■ A statement is true only if it is entirely and always true.

LESS-ADVANCED STUDENTS

Provide students with scoring sheets so they can practice filling them in. Remind them of the following rules for successful test-taking:

1. Fill in only one answer per question.
2. Erase carefully and completely when changing an answer.
3. Erase all stray marks from the score sheet.

STUDENTS WITH SPECIAL NEEDS

Some students suffer from severe test anxiety and are unable to do their best work in a test situation. Some signs of test anxiety are trembling hands, expressions of fear, self-belittling, preoccupation with unrelated tasks, or watching what others do instead of tackling the test itself.

Class discussion about test anxiety may prove beneficial to the students, particularly if their classmates are able to suggest some strategies for relieving nervousness. You may also want to allow students to practice test-taking often in situations in which they have a good opportunity for success.

RESOURCES

Matching Questions. Matching questions ask you to match the items in one list with the items in another list.

Directions: Match the name of the ocean in the left-hand column with the depth at its deepest point in the right-hand column.

C 1. Indian — A 8,648 meters
A 2. Atlantic — B 11,033 meters
D 3. Arctic — C 7,725 meters
B 4. Pacific — D 5,450 meters

HOW TO ANSWER MATCHING QUESTIONS	
Read the directions carefully.	Sometimes you may be told that you won't use all the items listed in one column. Other times items may be used more than once.
Scan the columns.	If you match items you know first, you'll have more time to think about difficult items you are less sure of answers for.
Complete the rest of the matching.	Make your best guess on remaining items.

RESOURCES

Reasoning or Logic Questions. Reasoning or logic questions don't test your knowledge of a particular subject. These types of questions test your reasoning skills. A reasoning or logic question may ask you to identify the relationship between several items (usually words, pictures, or numbers).

Reasoning questions might ask you to identify a pattern in a number sequence (as in the example on page 727). Or you might be asked to predict the next item in a sequence.

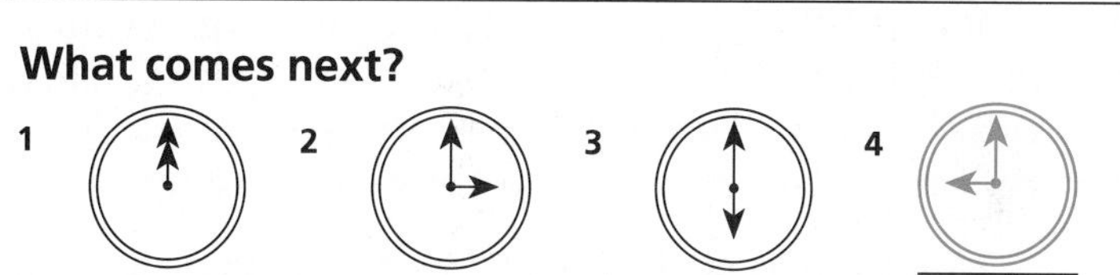

In this sequence of drawings, the time on the clock starts at noon and moves three hours forward each time. In the fourth position it will have reached the nine o'clock position.

HOW TO ANSWER REASONING OR LOGIC QUESTIONS	
Be sure you understand the instructions.	Reasoning or logic questions are often multiple-choice. On some tests, however, you may need to write a word or phrase, complete a number sequence, or even draw a picture for your answer.
Analyze the relationship implied in the question.	Look at the question carefully to gather information about the relationship of the items.
Draw reasonable conclusions.	Evaluate the relationship of the items to decide your answer.

Short-Answer Questions. Short-answer questions require you to give brief, precise responses. Instead of choosing from among several choices, you must write the answer yourself.

Some short-answer questions ask you to give a

STUDENTS WITH SPECIAL NEEDS

Studying for a test that covers multiple chapters can be overwhelming for a student with learning disabilities.

When students first acquaint themselves with each chapter, instruct them to write down the bold faced title of each section. Next, tell them to make notes on the pertinent facts in each section and to pay special attention to all italicized areas. Once this process is completed, students can use the notes for study.

ADVANCED STUDENTS

Have students create reasoning and logic questions for the rest of the class to answer. They may work independently, in pairs, or in small groups.

LESS-ADVANCED STUDENTS

Reasoning and logic questions may seem difficult to students who are not experienced in finding patterns. You might encourage advanced students to explain to the other students the pattern in each question. Once all students have grasped the basic principle of each question, ask them to create reasoning and logic questions of their own.

INTEGRATING THE LANGUAGE ARTS

Literature Link. Choose a selection from the literature textbook and ask students to work in groups of four or five to design a series of test questions for the selection. You might ask students to write four of each type of objective question. Encourage students to make the test fair and ask them to discuss why they selected the questions they did. You may want to point out that professional test-makers think carefully about the questions they are designing.

RESOURCES

label or fill in a blank. This type of question can be answered with one or just a few words. However, other types of short-answer questions ask for a written response that may be several sentences in length.

EXAMPLE **Why do Alaska and Hawaii both have a high cost of living?**

ANSWER ***Both states are isolated from the rest of the United States. Both need to have almost everything shipped to them from far away.***

HOW TO RESPOND TO SHORT-ANSWER QUESTIONS	
Read the question carefully.	Some questions have more than one part, so be sure to answer each part of the question in order to answer the entire item correctly.
Plan your answer.	Briefly decide what you need to include in the answer.
Be as specific as possible in your answers.	Write a full, exact answer.
Budget your time.	Begin by answering those questions you are sure you know. Save time for more difficult items.

RESOURCES

Essay Tests

Essay tests require you to think critically about material you have learned. Then you express your understanding in your own words. Essay tests show how well you understand a subject. Essay answers are usually a paragraph or more in length.

HOW TO STUDY FOR ESSAY TESTS

1. Read the assigned material carefully.
2. Make an outline of the main points and important details.
3. Invent your own essay questions and practice writing out the answers.
4. Evaluate and revise your practice answers by checking your work against your notes and textbook. Also review the writing section of this textbook for help in writing.

Taking Essay Tests

Before you begin to answer an essay question, there are certain steps you should take. First, you should quickly scan the test questions. How many questions are you required to answer? Which of the questions do you think you can answer best? Next, you should plan how much time you can afford to spend on each answer. Then, as you begin to write your responses, stick with your plan.

Read each question carefully. Be sure you understand exactly what the question calls for before you plan your response. Remember that the question may be asking you to write an answer that contains several different parts.

Pay attention to important terms in the question. You always need to complete a specific task to answer an essay question well. You can tell what the task is by looking at the key verb that appears in the essay question.

If you know some of the key verbs and what answer pattern each one calls for, you can write a better essay response. Look at the list of key verbs in the following chart and pay attention to the task that each one asks you to perform.

COOPERATIVE LEARNING

Divide the class into four groups. Give each group copies of the same textbook pages to read. Then assign each group a type of test question (multiple choice, true or false, short answer, or essay) and ask the groups to prepare tests on the textbook material and to provide answer keys for the tests. Groups should present their questions for the class to answer.

A DIFFERENT APPROACH

To assist students in understanding the **Essay Test Questions** chart, encourage them to give further examples of sample questions.

CRITICAL THINKING

Comparing and Contrasting

Ask students to discuss how writing an essay test is similar to writing a composition. [Both use the the writing process; the criteria for a good essay answer are the criteria for a good composition.] How is taking an essay test different from writing a composition? [Responses will vary. On an essay test, one need not worry about catching the reader's interest. Multiple drafts are not possible. Time constraints are a more serious problem. Drafting, revising, and editing have to be done simultaneously.]

RESOURCES

RESOURCES

ESSAY TEST QUESTIONS

KEY VERB	TASK	SAMPLE QUESTION
argue	Give your opinion about an issue and supply reasons to support this opinion.	Argue whether or not students who litter should have to clean up after school.
analyze	Examine something piece by piece to see how each part works.	Analyze the bad effects that smoking can have on people's health.
compare	Point out ways that things are alike.	Compare an apple and a crabapple.
contrast	Point out ways things are different.	Contrast the aliens in *E.T.* and *Cocoon.*
define	Give specific details that make something unique.	Define the term *simile.*
demonstrate	Give examples to support a point.	Demonstrate how water affects the frog's life cycle.
describe	Give a picture in words.	Describe the main characters in *Charlotte's Web.*
explain	Give reasons.	Explain how hail is formed.
identify	Point out specific characteristics.	Identify the three kinds of rocks.
list	Give all steps in order or all details about a subject.	List the food groups that make up a balanced diet.
summarize	Give a brief overview of the main points.	Summarize the story told in "Peter and the Wolf."

Use prewriting strategies. After you identify the key verbs in the question, jot down a few notes or an outline to help you decide what you want to say. Write notes or a rough outline on scratch paper.

Evaluate and revise as you write. You may not be able to redraft your whole essay, but you can edit your essay to strengthen it.

QUALITIES OF A GOOD ESSAY ANSWER

- The essay is well organized.
- The main ideas and supporting points are clearly presented.
- The sentences are complete and well written.
- There are no distracting errors in spelling, grammar, or punctuation.

Review

EXERCISE 1 **Choosing an Appropriate Reading Rate**

Identify the reading rate that best fits each of the following situations.

1. You want to record a song on your new tape deck, so you start reading your owner's manual. 1. mastery
2. You are looking through an encyclopedia for information on Confucius. 2. scanning
3. You are looking for the chart of prime numbers in your math book. 3. scanning
4. You are reading Alfred Noyes' poem "The Highwayman" for an oral report tomorrow. 4. mastery
5. You need to write a summary of the two pages in your social studies textbook on the Ogallala Aquifer. 5. mastery

LESS-ADVANCED STUDENTS

Students may be confused about how essay tests are evaluated. Tell students that usually the grader has a list of main ideas and details that should be included in each answer. A point value is assigned to each idea and to each detail, and the essay is graded according to the completeness of the answer. Sometimes points may be deducted for sloppiness or distracting errors in spelling, punctuation, or grammar.

RESOURCES

ANSWERS
Exercise 2

Responses will vary. Make sure the questions are appropriate for each student's selection.

ANSWERS
Exercise 3

1. two weeks
2. 1970
3. eighteen
4. She started working as a children's doctor with the U. S. Public Health Service.
5. two

ANSWERS
Exercise 4

Answers may vary.

1. She was chosen "Intern of the Year."
2. She went on to graduate school after she had already become a doctor.
3. It was her own experience as a patient that influenced her decision to pursue a career in medicine.

RESOURCES

EXERCISE 2 Applying the SQ3R Method

Use the SQ3R method while reading a newspaper article or a chapter that you need to study for a class. List at least five questions and write a brief answer to each one.

EXERCISE 3 Analyzing Details in a Passage

Answer the following questions about the reading passage on pages 721–722.

1. Before her surgery, how long did Antonia Novello stay in the hospital each summer?
2. In what year did Antonia Novello graduate from medical school in Puerto Rico?
3. How old was Antonia when she had her surgery?
4. What did Antonia do in 1978?
5. How many surgeries did Antonia have to correct her health problem?

EXERCISE 4 Drawing Conclusions and Making Inferences

Using the reading passage on pages 721–722, identify the evidence or reasoning you might use to make the following inferences or draw the following conclusions.

1. Antonia Novello earned other people's respect.
2. Education is important to Antonia Novello.
3. As a doctor, Antonia Novello is sensitive to the patient's feelings.

RESOURCES

EXERCISE 5 Interpreting Graphic Information

Using the graph on page 724, answer the following questions.

1. Which ocean is the deepest? **1.** Pacific **2.** 4,280 meters
2. What is the average depth of the Pacific Ocean?
3. Which ocean is the most shallow? **3.** Arctic

4. What is the difference between the Atlantic's average depth and the Pacific's? 4. 360 meters
5. How deep is the Pacific at its deepest point? 5. 11,033 meters

EXERCISE 6 **Analyzing Your Note-Taking Method**

Select a homework assignment your teacher has given you recently. Take study notes for this assignment, following the guidelines on page 725. Be prepared to share your notes in class and to explain how you took notes.

EXERCISE 7 **Identifying Classifications**

For each of the following groups, identify the category.

1. dog, cat, parakeet, goldfish 1. pets
2. rose, daisy, lily, iris 2. flowers
3. Arabian, Clydesdale, appaloosa, mustang 3. horses
4. country, jazz, classical, rap 4. music
5. Lincoln, Washington, Kennedy, Roosevelt 5. presidents

EXERCISE 8 **Applying Visual Organization**

After reading the paragraph below, make a numbered list of the steps in the metamorphosis of an insect.

From birth to adulthood, most insects experience what is called complete metamorphosis. First, an adult insect produces an egg. Next, the egg hatches to produce the insect in its immature, larval stage. After spending a period of time as a larva, the insect becomes inactive. This inactive insect is called a pupa. While the insect is inactive, it begins its transformation. After the insect completes its metamorphosis, it emerges as a mature adult insect.

RESOURCES

ANSWERS

Exercise 6

Students' notes should indicate that they have followed the guidelines given in the textbook.

ANSWERS

Exercise 8

Answers may vary slightly.

1. The adult produces an egg.
2. The egg produces an insect in its larval stage.
3. The larva eventually becomes an inactive pupa.
4. The pupa undergoes a transformation.
5. The mature insect emerges.

RESOURCES

ANSWERS

Exercise 9

Students' paraphrases will vary but should meet all the criteria suggested in the lesson. A sample paraphrase follows: The eagle stands alone, high on a mountain cliff and then swoops quickly downward toward the sea.

EXERCISE 9 **Paraphrasing a Poem**

Read the following poem. Then, using the instructions for paraphrasing on page 730, write a paraphrase of the poem. Look in a dictionary for the meanings of unfamiliar words. (For example, a *crag* is a cliff, and *azure* means "sky blue.")

The Eagle
by Alfred, Lord Tennyson

He clasps the crag with crooked hands;
Close to the sun in lonely lands,
Ringed with the azure world, he stands.

The wrinkled sea beneath him crawls;
He watches from his mountain walls,
And like a thunderbolt he falls.

ANSWERS

Exercise 10

1. Give a word picture of Melissa's personality.
2. Give a brief overview of the main points in the process of photosynthesis.
3. Give reasons for the changes experienced by Wilbur and Marion.
4. Point out specific characteristics of the major industries.
5. Point out the ways in which a butterfly differs from a moth.

EXERCISE 10 **Analyzing Essay Questions**

Identify the key verb that states the specific task in each of the following essay questions. Do not write an essay. Just state briefly what you would need to do to answer the question. [Hint: Look at the middle column of the chart on page 740.]

1. Describe the personality of Melissa, the narrator of "The Glad Man" by Gloria Gonzalez.
2. Summarize the process of photosynthesis.
3. Explain the changes experienced by Wilbur and Marion, the main characters in "The Bear Hunt" by Gene Caesar.
4. Identify the major industries in the Republic of China.
5. Contrast a butterfly with a moth.

RESOURCES

RESOURCES

APPENDIX

DIAGRAMING SENTENCES

A ***sentence diagram*** is a picture of how the parts of a sentence fit together. It shows how the words in the sentence are related.

Subjects and Verbs (pages 342–357)

To diagram a sentence, first find the simple subject and the simple predicate, or verb, and write them on a horizontal line. Then separate the subject and verb with a vertical line. Keep the capital letters but leave out the punctuation marks.

EXAMPLES **Dogs bark.** **Children were singing.**

Dogs | bark

Children | were singing

The preceding examples are easy because each sentence contains only a simple subject and a verb. Now look at a longer sentence.

EXAMPLE **My older brother is studying Arabic in school.**

To diagram the simple subject and the verb of this sentence, follow these three steps.

Step 1: Separate the complete subject from the complete predicate.

complete subject | complete predicate

My older brother | is studying Arabic in school.

Step 2: Find the simple subject and the verb.

simple subject	verb
brother	is studying

Step 3: Draw the diagram.

brother | is studying

EXERCISE 1 **Diagraming Simple Subjects and Verbs**

Diagram the simple subject and verb in each of the following sentences. Remember that simple subjects and verbs may consist of more than one word.

EXAMPLE **1.** Aunt Carmen is teaching me to cook.

1. Aunt Carmen | is teaching

1. My family goes to the store together every Saturday.
2. We shop the grocery store at the corner of our street.
3. I select the red beans, rice, meat, and cheese.
4. Grandma López must have written the shopping list.
5. Rosita is buying the chile peppers and cilantro.

Compound Subjects (pages 351–352)

To diagram a compound subject, put the subjects on parallel lines. Then put the connecting word (the conjunction, such as *and* or *but*) on a dotted line between the subject lines.

EXAMPLE **Koalas** and **kangaroos** are found in Australia.

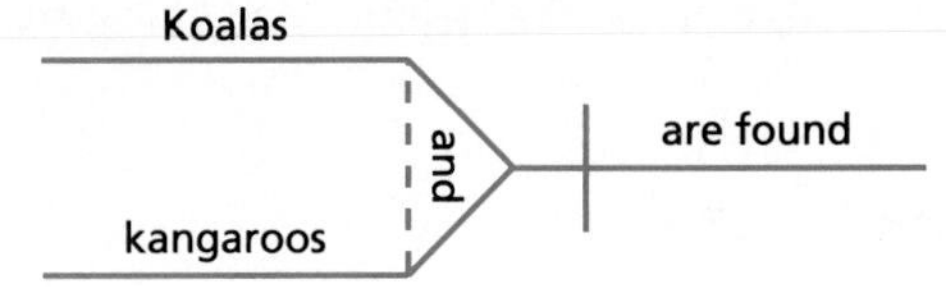

Compound Verbs (page 353)

To diagram a compound verb, put the two verbs on parallel lines. Then put the conjunction on a dotted line between the verbs.

EXAMPLE Giraffes **look** skinny but **may weigh** five tons.

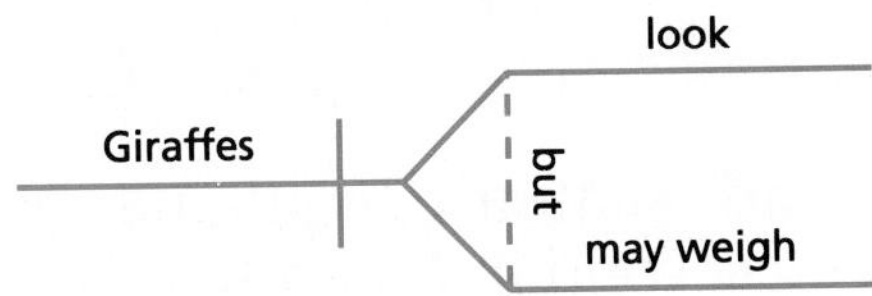

Compound Subjects and Compound Verbs (pages 351–353)

A sentence with both a compound subject and a compound verb combines the two patterns.

EXAMPLE The **cat** and her **kittens ate** and then **slept.**

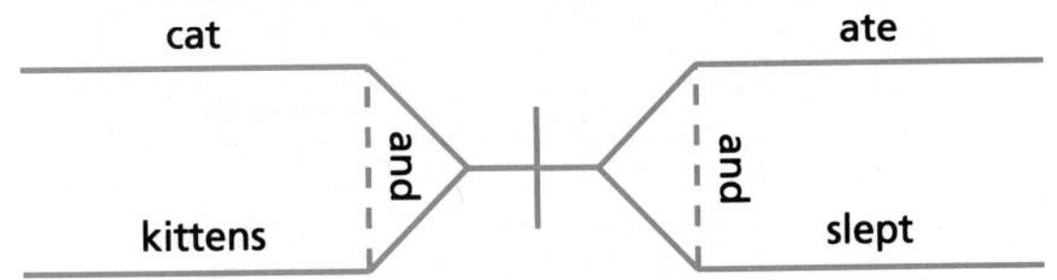

EXERCISE 2 Diagraming Compound Subjects and Compound Verbs

Diagram the simple subjects and verbs in the following sentences.

EXAMPLE 1. Spike Lee and Robert Townsend made and released movies last year.

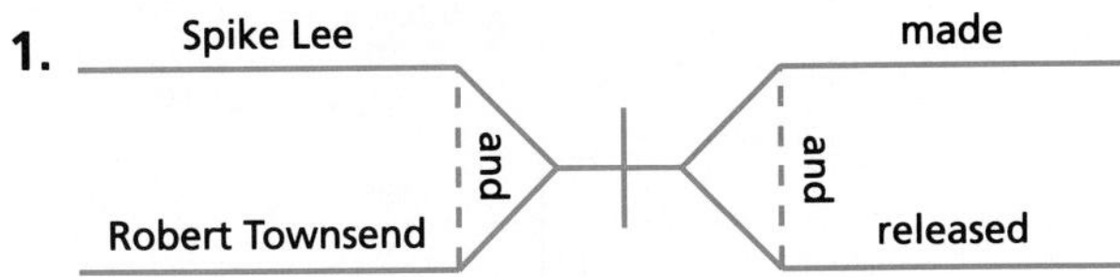

1. Ursula LeGuin and Nicholasa Mohr are my favorite authors.
2. Ms. Sánchez and Mr. Charles teach Spanish.

3. Bill Russell first played and later coached for the Boston Celtics.
4. The students and the teacher visited the museum but did not have time for a complete tour.
5. My friends and I hurried home and told our parents the news.

Compound Sentences (page 357)

A compound sentence contains two independent clauses. The second independent clause is diagramed below the first in the following way.

EXAMPLE **Ostriches seem** clumsy, but **they can run** fast.

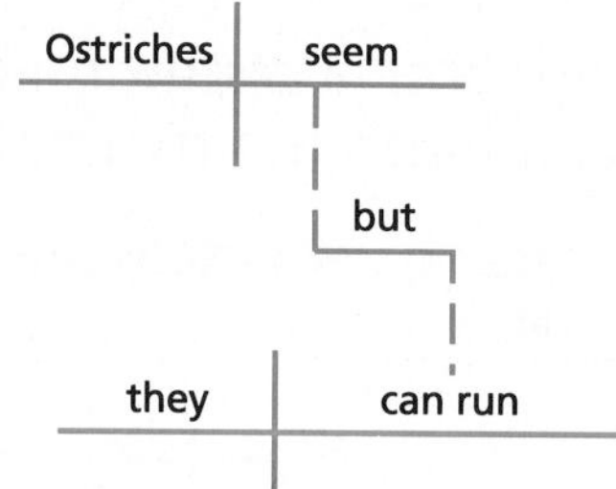

EXERCISE 3 Diagraming Compound Sentences

Diagram the simple subjects and verbs in the following compound sentences.

EXAMPLE **1.** Genna went to the mall, but I stayed home.

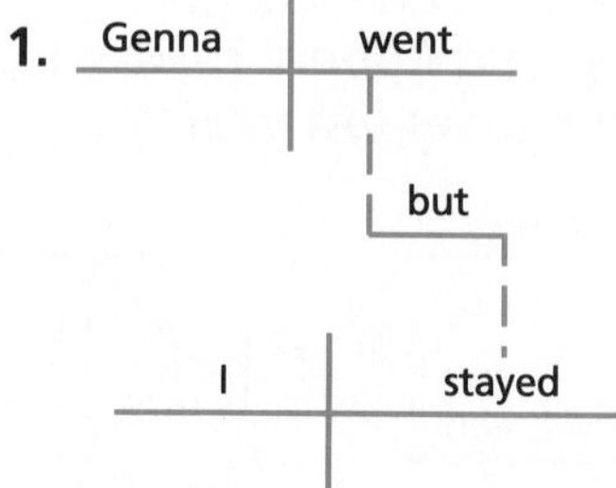

1. Chinese immigrants worked on the railroads in the West, but Irish immigrants built the railroads in the East.

2. Lisa likes roller-skating, but I prefer ice-skating.
3. Jewel will be class president, and Aaron will be vice-president.
4. Cactuses are desert plants, yet they can grow well in milder climates.
5. Gabriela Mistral is a poet, but she has also written essays.

Questions and Commands (page 360)

Questions (page 360)

To diagram a question, first make the question into a statement. Then, diagram the sentence. Remember that in a diagram, the subject always comes first, even if it does not come first in the sentence.

EXAMPLE Can all insects fly? [question]
All insects can fly. [statement]

Notice that the diagram uses the capitalization of the original sentence.

Commands (page 360)

In an imperative sentence, or command, the subject is always understood to be *you*. Place the understood subject *you* in parentheses on the horizontal line.

EXAMPLE Look over there.

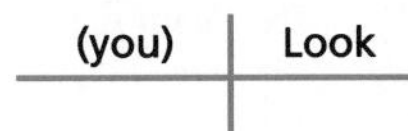

EXERCISE 4 **Diagraming Questions and Commands**

Diagram the simple subjects and verbs in the following sentences.

EXAMPLE **1.** Please wash the dishes, Jerome.

1. (you) | wash

1. Eat the rest of your jambalaya.
2. Do you know much about the Jewish holidays?
3. Where is the driver going?
4. Please help me with these cartons.
5. Why are they standing in line?

Adjectives and Adverbs (pages 381–385 and 402–404)

Adjectives and adverbs are written on slanted lines connected to the words they modify. Notice that possessive pronouns are diagramed in the same way adjectives are.

Adjectives (pages 381–385)

EXAMPLES **yellow** bird **a playful** puppy **her best** blouse

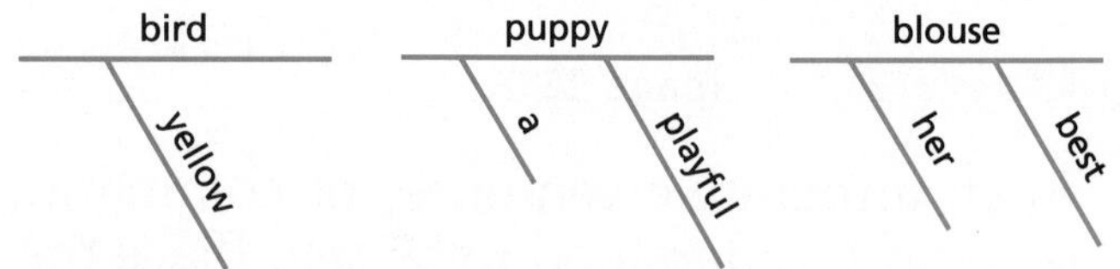

 EXERCISE 5 **Diagraming Sentences with Adjectives**

Diagram the subjects, verbs, and adjectives in the following sentences.

EXAMPLE **1. A strong, cold wind blew all night.**

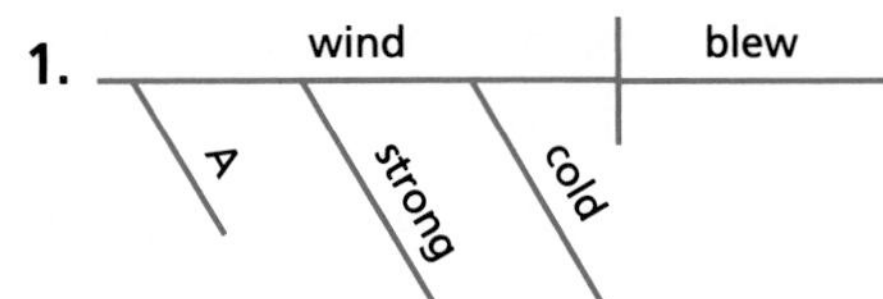

1. My favorite new rock group is coming to town.
2. The long, grueling hike was almost over.
3. The best album of the year is by Michael Jackson.
4. The two brave astronauts stepped into space.
5. A funny movie is playing downtown.

Adverbs (pages 402–404)

When an adverb modifies a verb, it is placed on a slanted line below the verb.

EXAMPLES wrote **quickly** walked **there slowly**

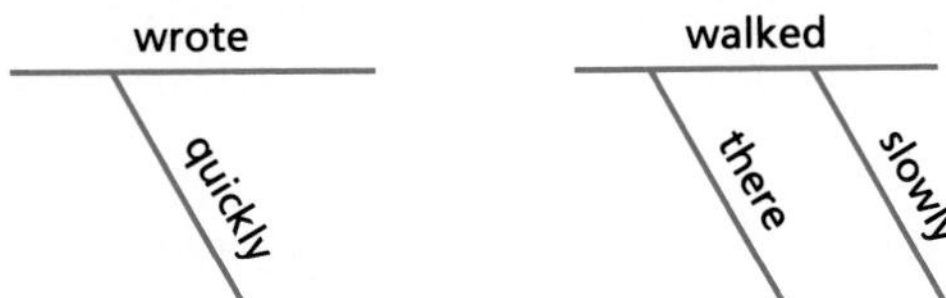

When an adverb modifies an adjective or another adverb, it is placed on a line connected to the word it modifies.

EXAMPLES **incredibly** large poster runs **very** fast

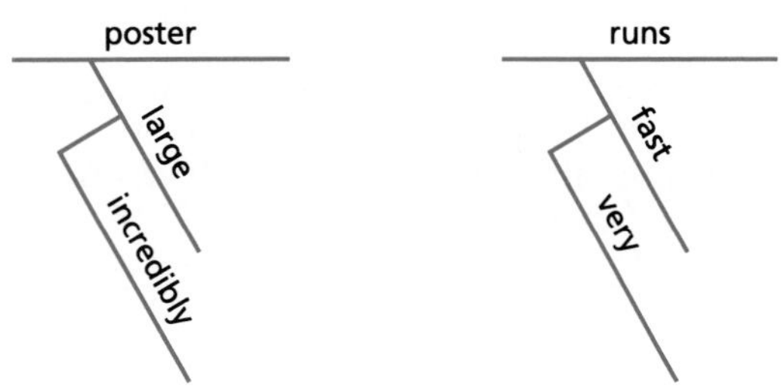

EXERCISE 6 **Diagraming Sentences with Adverbs**

Diagram the subjects, verbs, adjectives, and adverbs in the following sentences.

EXAMPLE **1. We almost always recycle newspapers.**

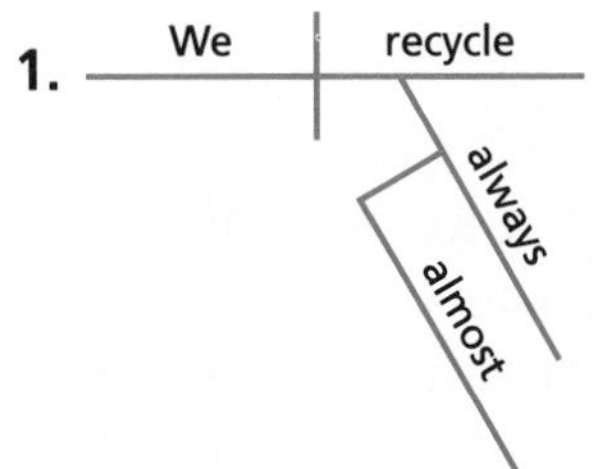

1. This lovely song was recorded by Lena Horne.
2. That new band plays very loudly.
3. The busy librarian almost never leaves early.
4. Her two brothers visited Chinatown yesterday.
5. An extremely unusual program will be broadcast tonight.

Prepositional Phrases (pages 420–429)

Prepositional phrases are diagramed below the words they modify. Write the preposition on a slanting line. Then write the object of the preposition on a horizontal line connected to the slanting line. Notice that the slanting line extends a little way beyond the horizontal line.

Adjective Phrases (pages 423–425)

EXAMPLES time **of day** customs **of the Amish**

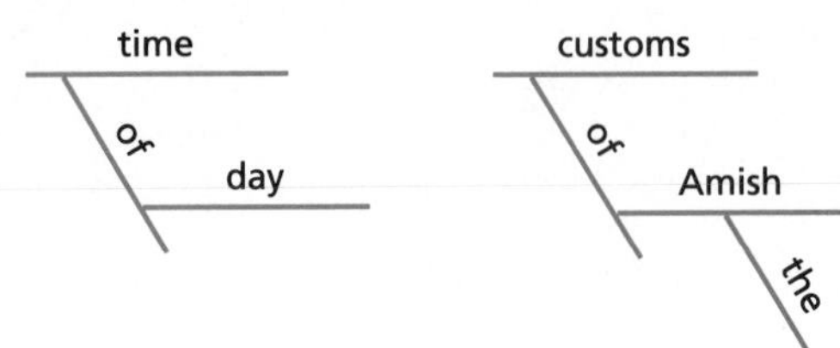

Adverb Phrases (pages 428–429)

EXAMPLES walked **on the moon** looked there **for Skip**

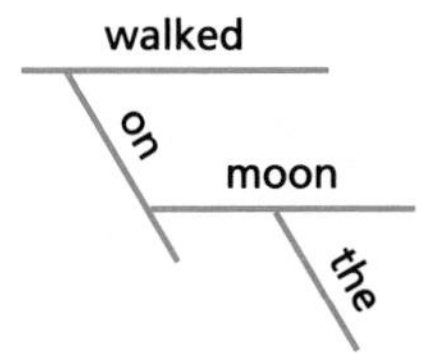

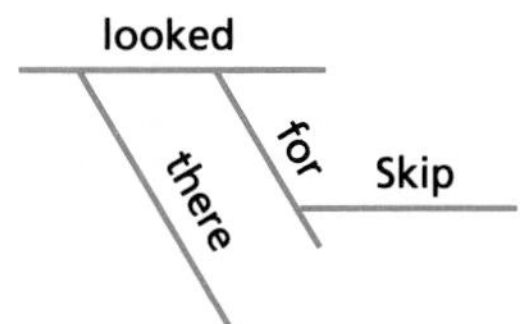

EXERCISE 7 **Diagraming Sentences with Prepositional Phrases**

Diagram the following sentences.

EXAMPLE **1.** The freighter slowed for the first lock.

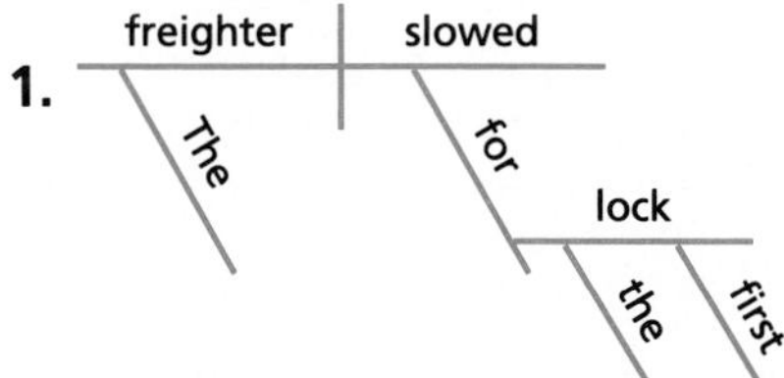

1. Olympia Dukakis and John Travolta starred in that new movie.
2. Tamales are wrapped in corn husks.
3. My friend from India wears a sari.
4. The students in Jill's class went to the library.
5. The soccer team from Brazil ran onto the field.

Direct and Indirect Objects (pages 439–442)

Direct Objects (page 439)

A direct object is diagramed on the horizontal line with the subject and verb. A short vertical line separates the direct object from the verb.

EXAMPLE We have been playing **tapes.**

We | have been playing | tapes

Compound Direct Objects (page 439)

EXAMPLE Rachel enjoys **soccer** and **basketball.**

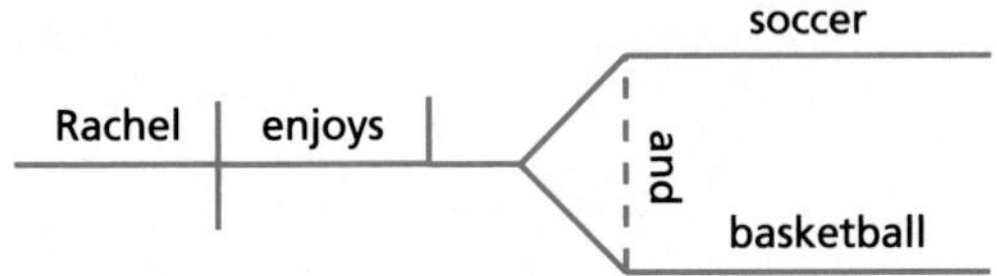

Indirect Objects (pages 441–442)

The indirect object is diagramed on a horizontal line beneath the verb. The verb and the indirect object are joined by a slanting line.

EXAMPLE Dad fixed **us** some spaghetti.

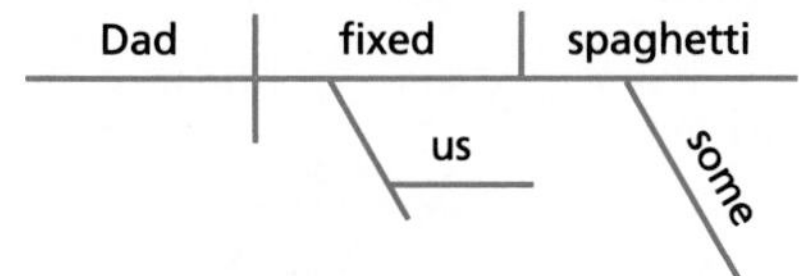

Compound Indirect Objects (page 442)

EXAMPLE Marisa gave her **brother** and **me** some grapes.

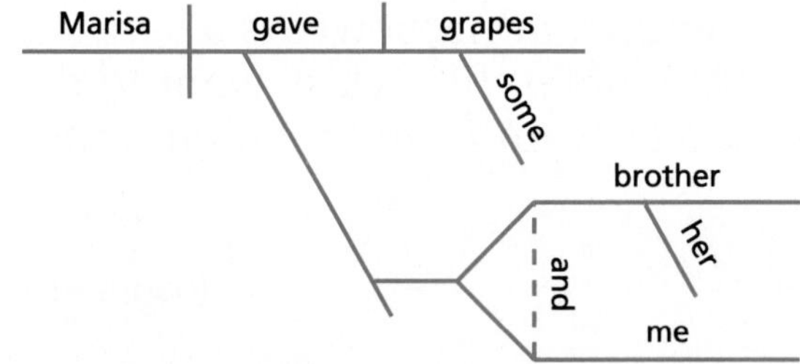

EXERCISE 8 **Diagraming Direct Objects and Indirect Objects**

Diagram the following sentences.

EXAMPLE **1.** He handed her the report.

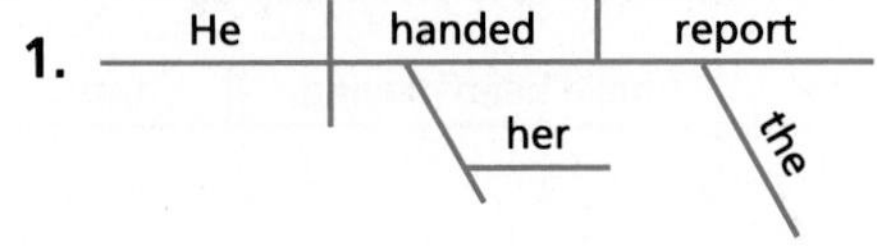

1. Marilyn won a bronze medal in the Special Olympics.
2. I bought Jolene and her sister a present.
3. My grandmother knitted me a sweater.
4. Marcus made a touchdown.
5. Amy Tan wrote that book.

Subject Complements (pages 446–448)

A subject complement is diagramed on the horizontal line with the subject and the verb. The complement comes after the verb. A line slanting toward the subject separates the subject complement from the verb.

Predicate Nominatives (page 447)

EXAMPLE Mickey Leland was a famous **congressman** from Texas.

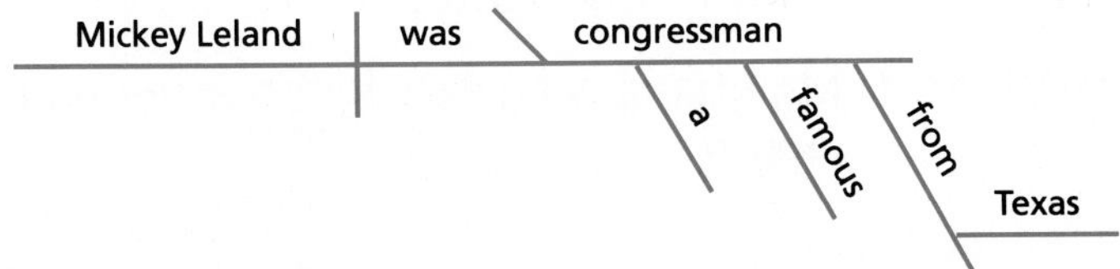

Compound Predicate Nominatives (page 447)

EXAMPLE Paula Abdul is a **singer** and a **dancer.**

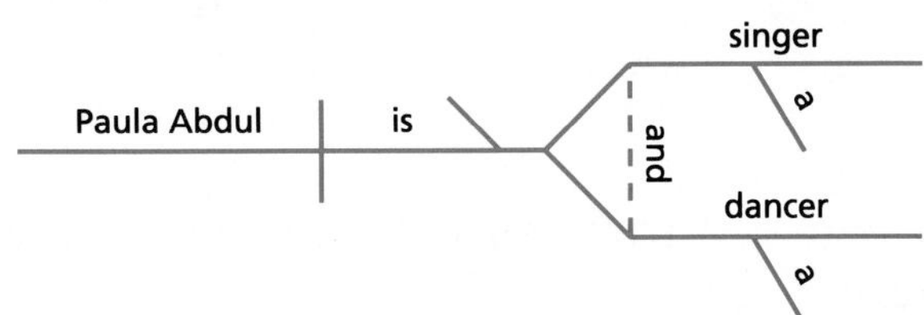

Predicate Adjectives (page 448)

EXAMPLE The guitarist was very **skillful.**

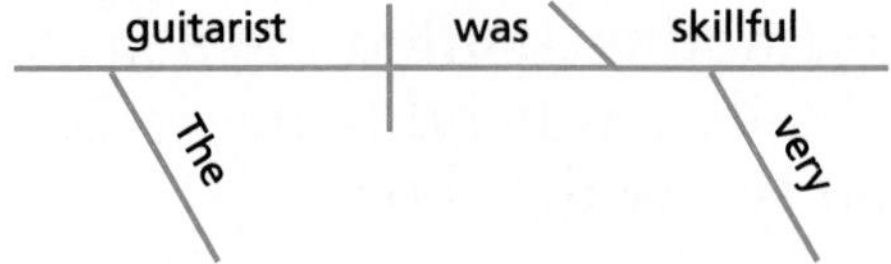

Compound Predicate Adjectives (page 448)

EXAMPLE They were **weary** but **patient.**

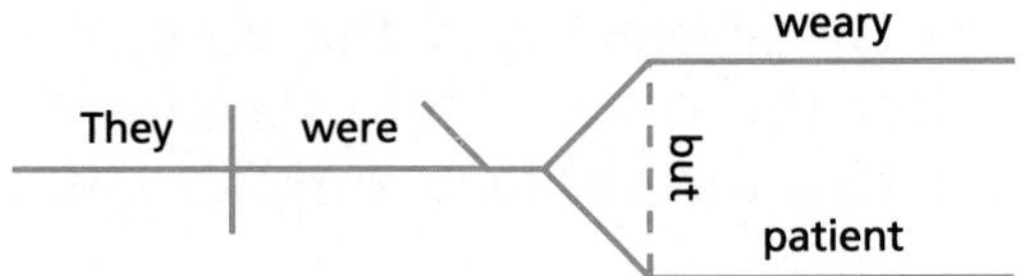

EXERCISE 9 Diagraming Sentences with Subject Complements

Diagram the following sentences.

EXAMPLE 1. Ms. Chang is an excellent teacher and a fine lawyer.

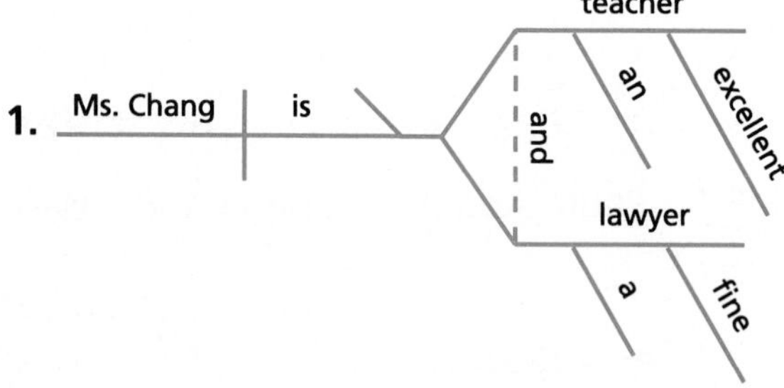

1. Coyote is a trickster in Native American mythology.
2. The library is full of interesting books.
3. These CDs are oldies but goodies.
4. Ossie Davis is an actor and a playwright.
5. Your little brother looks quite sleepy.

Glossary of Terms

A

Action verb An action verb is a verb that expresses physical or mental action. (See page 391.)

Adjective An adjective is a word that modifies a noun or a pronoun. (See page 381.)

Adjective phrase An adjective phrase is a prepositional phrase that modifies a noun or a pronoun. (See page 423.)

Adverb An adverb is a word that modifies a verb, an adjective, or another adverb. (See page 402.)

Adverb phrase An adverb phrase is a prepositional phrase that modifies a verb, an adjective, or another adverb. (See page 428.)

Aim An aim is one of the four basic purposes, or reasons, for writing. (See pages 7 and 24.)

Antecedent An antecedent is a noun or pronoun to which a pronoun refers. (See page 373.)

Appositive An appositive is a noun or a pronoun that explains or identifies another noun or pronoun. (See pages 520 and 600.)

B

Brainstorming Brainstorming is a way a writer finds ideas for writing by listing all thoughts about a subject without stopping to judge the ideas. (See page 29.)

C

Chronological order Chronological order is a way of arranging details according to when events or actions take place. (See page 39.)

Clustering Clustering, or **webbing** or **making connections,** is a way a writer finds writing ideas and gathers information by breaking a large subject into its smaller parts, using circles and lines to create a diagram of his or her thoughts. (See page 30.)

Comparing Comparing means telling how things are alike. (See page 73.)

Complement A complement is a word or group of words that completes the meaning of a verb. (See page 438.)

Complex sentence A complex sentence is made of two sentences joined by a connecting word that shows their special relationship to each other. (See page 318.)

Compound sentence A compound sentence consists of two or more simple sentences, usually joined by a connecting word. (See pages 318 and 357.)

Conjunction A conjunction is a word that joins words or groups of words. (See page 411.)

Contrasting Contrasting means telling how things are different from one another. (See page 73.)

Creative writing Creative writing is writing that aims at creating something new with language: stories, poems, songs, and plays. (See pages 7 and 24.)

D

Declarative sentence A declarative sentence makes a statement and is followed by a period. (See page 360.)

Description Description is a way a writer develops a paragraph or composition by using sensory details to describe something. (See page 69.)

Direct object A direct object receives the action of a transitive verb. (See page 439.)

Double negative A double negative is the use of two negative words to express one negative idea. (See page 538.)

E

Evaluating Evaluating is the stage in the writing process in which a writer goes over a draft, making judgments about it. (See pages 6 and 25.)

Evaluation Evaluation is a way a writer develops a paragraph or composition by making judgments, telling what is good or bad about a subject. (See page 75.)

Exclamatory sentence An exclamatory sentence shows excitement or expresses strong feeling and is followed by an exclamation point. (See page 360.)

Expressive writing Expressive writing is writing that aims at expressing a writer's feelings and thoughts. (See pages 7 and 24.)

F

***5W-How?* questions** The *5W-How?* questions—*Who? What? Where? When? Why? How?*—are questions a writer uses to collect information about a subject. (See page 32.)

Freewriting Freewriting is a way of finding ideas for writing in which a writer writes for a few minutes on whatever comes to mind. (See page 27.)

H

Helping verb A helping, or **auxiliary,** verb helps the main verb to express action or a state of being. (See page 397.)

"How-to" process writing "How-to" process writing is a step-by-step story of how to do something. (See Chapter 6.)

I

Imperative sentence An imperative sentence gives a command or makes a request and is followed by either a period or an exclamation point. (See page 360.)

Indirect object An indirect object is a noun or pronoun that comes between the verb and the direct object. (See page 441.)

Inference An inference is a decision that is made based on clues the writer supplies. (See page 250.)

Infinitive An infinitive is one of the four principal, or basic, parts of a verb. (See page 476.)

Informative writing Informative writing is writing that aims at giving facts or information, or explaining something. (See pages 7 and 24.)

Interjection An interjection is a word used to express emotion. (See page 412.)

Interrogative sentence An interrogative sentence asks a question and is followed by a question mark. (See page 360.)

Intransitive verb An intransitive verb expresses action (or tells something about the subject) without passing the action to a receiver. (See page 393.)

L

Linking verb A linking verb is a verb that expresses a state of being and connects the subject of a sentence with a word in the predicate that explains or describes the subject. (See page 394.)

Logical order Logical order is a way of grouping related ideas by what makes sense. (See pages 39 and 73.)

M

Main idea A main idea is the idea that a paragraph or composition is organized around. (See pages 6 and 24.)

Modifier A modifier is a word or a phrase that describes or limits the meaning of another word. (See page 527.)

N

Narration Narration is a way a writer develops a paragraph or composition by telling about events or actions as they change over a period of time. (See page 71.)

Noun A noun is a word that names a person, place, thing, or idea. (See page 368.)

O

Object of the preposition The noun or pronoun that ends a prepositional phrase is the object of the preposition that begins the phrase. (See pages 408 and 420.)

Order of importance Order of importance is a way of arranging details in a paragraph or composition according to the details' importance. (See pages 39 and 75.)

P

Personal narrative A personal narrative is a form of writing in which an author explores and shares the meaning of an experience that was especially important to him or her. (See Chapter 3.)

Persuasive essay A persuasive essay is a form of writing in which a writer supports an opinion and tries to persuade an audience. (See Chapter 7.)

Persuasive writing Persuasive writing is writing that aims at convincing perople to think or act in a certain way. (See pages 7 and 24.)

Phrase A phrase is a group of related words that is used as a single part of speech and does not contain both a subject and a verb. (See page 419.)

Predicate The predicate is the part of a sentence that says something about the subject. (See page 345.)

Predicate adjective A predicate adjective is an adjective that follows a linking verb and describes the subject of a sentence. (See page 448.)

Predicate nominative A predicate nominative is a noun or pronoun that identifies or explains the subject of a sentence. (See page 447.)

Preposition A preposition is a word that shows the relationship between a noun or pronoun and some other word in the sentence. (See page 406.)

Prepositional phrase A prepositional phrase begins with a preposition and ends with a noun or a pronoun. (See pages 408 and 420.)

Prewriting Prewriting is the first stage in the writing process. In this stage, a writer thinks and plans, decides what to write about, collects ideas and details, and makes a plan for presenting ideas. (See pages 6 and 25.)

Pronoun A pronoun is a word used in place of a noun or more than one noun. (See page 373.)

Proofreading Proofreading is the stage of the writing process in which a writer carefully reads a revised draft to correct mistakes in grammar, usage, and mechanics. (See pages 6 and 25.)

Publishing Publishing is the last stage of the writing process. In this stage, a writer makes a final, clean copy of a paper and shares it with an audience. (See pages 6 and 25.)

Purpose Purpose, or **aim,** is the reason for writing or speaking. (See pages 7, 37, and 76.)

R

Report A report is a form of writing in which a writer presents factual information that he or she has discovered through reading and asking questions about a topic. (See Chapter 9.)

Revising Revising is the stage of the writing process in which a writer goes over a draft, making changes in its content, organization, and style in order to improve it. (See pages 6 and 25.)

Run-on sentence A run-on sentence is two or more complete sentences run together as one. (See page 307.)

S

Sentence A sentence is a group of words that expresses a complete thought. (See pages 304 and 340.)

Sentence fragment A sentence fragment is a group of words that looks like a sentence but does not express a complete thought. (See pages 304 and 340.)

Simple sentence A simple sentence has one subject and one verb. (See page 357.)

Spatial order Spatial order is a way of arranging details in a paragraph or composition by ordering them according to their location—from near to far, left to right, and so on. (See pages 39 and 69.)

Subject The subject is the part of a sentence that tells who or what the sentence is about. (See page 342.)

Subject complement A subject complement completes the meaning of a linking verb and identifies or describes the subject. (See page 446.)

T

Topic sentence A topic sentence is the sentence that states the main idea of a paragraph. (See page 61.)

Transitional words and phrases Transitional words and phrases connect ideas in a paragraph or composition by showing why and how ideas and details are related. (See page 66.)

Transitive verb A transitive verb is an action verb that expresses an action directed toward a person, place, or thing. (See page 392.)

V

Verb A verb is a word that expresses an action or a state of being. (See page 391.)

Verb phrase A verb phrase contains one main verb and one or more helping verbs. (See pages 349 and 397.)

W

"What if?" questions Asking "What if?" questions can help a writer spark his or her imagination to explore ideas for writing. (See page 33.)

Writer's journal A writer's journal is a written record of what happens in a person's life, and how he or she feels and thinks. (See page 26.)

Writing Writing is the stage in the writing process in which a writer puts his or her ideas into sentences and paragraphs, following a plan for presenting the ideas. (See pages 6 and 25.)

Writing process The writing process is the series of stages or steps that a writer goes through to develop ideas and to communicate them clearly in a piece of writing. (See pages 6 and 25.)

Glossary

This glossary is a short dictionary of words found in the professional writing models in this textbook. The words are defined according to their meanings in the context of the writing models.

Pronunciation Key

Symbol	Key Words	Symbol	Key Words
a	asp, fat, parrot	b	bed, fable, dub, ebb
ā	ape, date, play, break, fail	d	dip, beadle, had, dodder
ä	ah, car, father, cot	f	fall, after, off, phone
e	elf, ten, berry	g	get, haggle, dog
ē	even, meet, money, flea, grieve	h	he, ahead, hotel
		j	joy, agile, badge
i	is, hit, mirror	k	kill, tackle, bake, coat, quick
ī	ice, bite, high, sky	l	let, yellow, ball
ō	open, tone, go, boat	m	met, camel, trim, summer
ô	all, horn, law, oar	n	not, flannel, ton
oo	look, pull, moor, wolf	p	put, apple, tap
o͞o	ooze, tool, crew, rule	r	red, port, dear, purr
yo͞o	use, cute, few	s	sell, castle, pass, nice
yoo	cure, globule	t	top, cattle, hat
oi	oil, point, toy	v	vat, hovel, have
ou	out, crowd, plow	w	will, always, swear, quick
u	up, cut, color, flood	y	yet, onion, yard
ʉr	urn, fur, deter, irk	z	zebra, dazzle, haze, rise
ə	a in ago	ch	chin, catcher, arch, nature
	e in agent	sh	she, cushion, dash, machine
	i in sanity	th	thin, nothing, truth
	o in comply	*th*	then, father, lathe
	u in focus	zh	azure, leisure, beige
ər	perhaps, murder	ŋ	ring, anger, drink

Abbreviation Key

adj.	adjective	*pl.*	plural
adv.	adverb	*prep.*	preposition
conj.	conjunction	*vi.*	intransitive verb
n.	noun	*vt.*	transitive verb

A

al • gae [al′jē] ***n.*** Simple plants with no root system that grow in damp places.

Aston Martin [as′tən märt″n] ***n.*** An expensive sports car.

B

be • hest [bē hest′] ***n.*** A command or order.

buoy [boi] ***vt.*** To keep afloat.

C

churl [churl] ***n.*** A selfish, mean person.

con • do • min • i • um [kän′də min′ē əm] ***n.*** An apartment building.

cre • ma • tion [krē mā′shən] ***n.*** The burning of a dead body.

cur • mudg • eon [kər muj′ən] ***n.*** A rude, bad-tempered person.

D

de • lin • quent [di liŋ′kwənt] ***adj.*** Not obeying the law.

dike [dīk] ***n.*** A barrier made of dirt to keep water in or out of an area.

dour [do͝or] ***adj.*** Severe; sullen.

dredge [drej] ***vt.*** To clear out the bottom of a river or other waterway.

driv • el [driv′əl] ***n.*** Silly or meaningless talk.

du • ly [do͞o′lē] ***adv.*** As required or expected.

E

en • crust • ed [en krust′id] ***adj.*** Covered with a hard coating.

er • go [er′gō] ***conj.*** Therefore.

F

feat [fēt] ***n.*** An act showing unusual skill.

foi • ble [foi′bəl] ***n.*** A fault.

for • get-me-not [fər get′mē nät′] ***n.*** A plant with clusters of small pink, white, or blue flowers.

G

gall [gôl] ***vt.*** To annoy.

H

heir [er] ***n.*** One who receives property from a relative who dies.

hog • fish [hôg′fish′] ***n.*** A fish whose head resembles a pig.

I

in • stinc • tive • ly [in stiŋk′tiv lē] ***adv.*** Done in a natural way, without thinking.

M

man • a • tee [man′ə tē′] ***n.*** A large sea cow that lives in warm, shallow tropical waters.

mem • oir [mem′wär] ***n.*** The story of one's life written by oneself.

min • gy [min′jē] ***adj.*** Mean and stingy.

N

nom • i • nal [näm′ə nəl] ***adj.*** Small, compared to what is expected.

P

par · a · site [par'ə sīt] ***n.*** A plant or animal that lives on another plant or animal and takes food from it.

par · si · mo · ni · ous [pär' sə mō'nē əs] ***adj.*** Being over-careful about one's money; stingy.

plod [pläd] ***vi.*** To walk heavily with great effort.

prey [prā] ***n.*** An animal killed for food by another animal.

pum · ice [pum'is] ***n.*** A light rock full of tiny holes made from hardened volcanic lava.

quea · sy [kwē'zē] ***adj.*** Feeling as if one might vomit.

re · gard · less [ri gärd'lis] ***adv.*** Anyway; no matter what.

re · past [ri past'] ***n.*** A meal.

score [skôr] ***vt.*** To partly cut lines in something for easy tearing.

se · rum [sir'əm] ***n.*** The part of an animal's blood often used for preventing diseases in humans.

skin · flint [skin'flint'] ***n.*** A stingy person.

tat · ty [tat'ē] ***adj.*** Shabby; in bad condition.

tax [taks] ***vt.*** To question in an accusing way.

Trans · vaal [trans väl'] ***n.*** A territory in the northeastern part of South Africa.

u · nan · i · mous [yo͞o nan'ə məs] ***adj.*** Everyone agreeing.

u · su · rer [yo͞o'zhər ər] ***n.*** A person who lends money and expects much more in return.

Index

A

INDEX

B

INDEX
765

INDEX

INDEX

INDEX

D

E

INDEX

INDEX

F

INDEX

INDEX

INDEX

INDEX
772

M

INDEX

INDEX

INDEX

775

INDEX

INDEX

INDEX

INDEX

INDEX

INDEX

T

U

V

INDEX

W

Z

INDEX

784

Acknowledgments

For permission to reprint copyrighted material, grateful acknowledgment is made to the following sources:

Rudolfo A. Anaya: From *Tortuga,* a novel by Rudolfo A. Anaya. Copyright © 1979 by Rudolfo A. Anaya. Distributed by University of New Mexico Press, Albuquerque, N.M. 87131.

Atheneum Publishers, an imprint of Macmillan Publishing Company: "How Can Water Striders Walk on Water?" from *How Do Ants Know When You're Having a Picnic?* by Joanne Settel and Nancy Baggett. Copyright © 1986 by Joanne Settel and Nancy Baggett.

Ballantine Books, Inc., a division of Random House, Inc.: From "The Journey to Anar" from *The Sword of Shannara* by Terry Brooks. Copyright © 1977 by Terry Brooks. Map from *The Sword of Shannara* by Terry Brooks, illustrated by The Brothers Hildebrandt. Illustration Copyright © 1977 by Random House, Inc.

Bradbury Press, an Affiliate of Macmillan, Inc: From "Survivors and Colonizers" from *Volcano: The Eruption and Healing of Mount St. Helens* by Patricia Lauber. Copyright © 1986 by Patricia Lauber. "Boar Out There" from *Every Living Thing* by Cynthia Rylant. Text Copyright © 1985 by Cynthia Rylant.

Cobblestone Publishing, Inc.: From "Making a Flying Fish" by Paula Morrow from *Faces,* December 1990 issue: *Happy Holidays.* Copyright © 1990 by Cobblestone Publishing, Inc., Peterborough, NH 03458.

Compton's Encyclopedia: From the entry "Lava and Magma" from *Compton's Encyclopedia and Fact-Index.* Copyright © 1992 by Compton's Learning Company.

Crown Publishers, Inc., a division of Random House, Inc.: From *The Art of the Japanese Garden* by Tatsuo Ishimoto. Copyright © 1958 by Crown Publishers, Inc.

Dial Books for Young Readers, a division of Penguin Books USA Inc.: "Brer Billy Goat Tricks Brer Wolf" from *Further Tales of Uncle Remus,* by Julius Lester. Copyright © 1990 by Julius Lester.

Donadio & Ashworth, Inc: from *Extreme Magic* by Hortense Calisher. Copyright © 1964 by Hortense Calisher.

Doubleday, a division of Bantam Doubleday Dell Publishing Group, Inc.: From "The Sky Is Gray" from *Bloodline* by Ernest J. Gaines. Copyright © 1963 by Ernest J. Gaines.

Mary Facklam: From *Wild Animals, Gentle Women* by Margery Facklam. Copyright © 1978 by Margery Facklam.

Farrar, Straus and Giroux, Inc.: "The Toaster" and from "The Old Man from Okefenokee" from *Laughing Time: Collected Nonsense* by William Jay Smith. Copyright © 1990 by William Jay Smith.

Harcourt Brace Jovanovich, Inc.: From Riddle #11 by James Berry from *When I Dance.* Copyright © 1991, 1988 by James Berry. Entry for "cloud" from *The Lincoln Writing Dictionary,* edited by Christopher Morris. Copyright © 1989 by Harcourt Brace Jovanovich, Inc. From *The Pride of Puerto Rico: The Life of Roberto Clemente* by Paul Robert Walker. Copyright © 1988 by Harcourt Brace Jovanovich, Inc.

HarperCollins Publishers: From *Women Who Made America Great* by Harry Gersh. Copyright © 1962 by Harry Gersh. From *The Land I Lost: Adventures of a Boy in Vietnam,* by Huynh Quang Nhuong. Copyright © 1982 by Huynh Quang Nhuong.

Henry Holt and Company, Inc.: From *Scissor Cutting for Beginners* by Cheng Hou-tien. Copyright © 1978 by Cheng Hou-tien.

785

Alfred A. Knopf, Inc.: "April Rain Song: and "Poem" from *The Dream Keeper and Other Poems* by Langston Hughes. Copyright © 1932 by Alfred A. Knopf, Inc. and renewed 1960 by Langston Hughes.

Lothrop, Lee and Shephard Books, a division of William Morrow & Company, Inc.: From "Man and Manatee" from *Manatee on Location* by Kathy Darling. Copyright © 1991 by Kathy Darling.

Julian Messner, a division of Silver Burdett Press, Inc., Simon & Schuster, Englewood Cliffs, NJ: From "The Outsider" from *The Lost Garden* by Laurence Yep. Copyright © 1991 by Laurence Yep.

Morrow Junior Books, a division of William Morrow & Company, Inc.: From *A Girl From Yamhill, A Memoir* by Beverly Cleary. Copyright © 1988 by Beverly Cleary.

William Morrow and Company, Inc./ Publishers, New York: From "Picky-picky" from *Ramona Forever* by Beverly Cleary. Copyright © 1984 by Beverly Cleary. From *A Cat's Body* by Joanna Cole. Copyright © 1982 by Joanna Cole.

Naomi Shihab Nye: From "The Rider" and Poet's Comment from *The Place My Words Are Looking For* by Naomi Shihab Nye, selected by Paul B. Janeczka. Copyright © 1990 by Naomi Shihab Nye.

The Octagon Press, London: "Camel fodder" from *The Subtleties of the Inimitable Mulla Nasrudin* by Indries Shah. Copyright © 1983 by Designist Communications.

Agnes T. Pratt: "Fragments of Spring" and "So Quickly Came the Summer" by Agnes T. Pratt from *The Whispering Wind: Poetry by Young American Indians*, edited by Terry Allen. Copyright © 1972 by Agnes T. Pratt.

Roberta Pryor, Inc.: From *Expecting the Unexpected* by Donald M. Murray. Copyright © 1989 by Donald M. Murray. Published by Boynton Cook Publishers, a Division of Heinemann Educational Books, Inc.

The Putnam Publishing Group: From *Oral History* by Lee Smith. Copyright © 1983 by Lee Smith.

Random House, Inc.: From "Banana Surprise" from *Mr. Wizard's Supermarket Science* by Don Herbert. Text copyright © 1980 by Don Herbert.

Larry Sternig Literary Agency: From "Zoo" by Edward D. Hoch. Copyright © 1958 by King Size Publications.

John Updike: Quotation by John Updike.

Viking Penguin, a division of Penguin Books USA Inc.: From *Henry Reed, Inc.* by Keith Robertson. Copyright © 1958 by Keith Robertson, renewed © 1986 by Keith Robertson. From "You Can't Take It With You" from *Escape If You Can* by Eva-Lis Wuorio. Copyright © 1977 by Eva-Lis Wuorio.

Walker and Company: From *How Did We Find Out About Coal?* by Isaac Asimov. Copyright © 1980 by Isaac Asimov.

Wayland (Publishers) Limited, 61 Western Road, Hove, East Sussex BN3 1JD, England: From "Which are Rabbits and Which are Hares?" from *Rabbits and Hares* by Ralph Whitlock. Copyright © 1974 by Priory Press Ltd.

H. W. Wilson Company: Entries for "Fire Prevention" through "Fish as Food" from *Readers' Guide to Periodical Literature*, October 25, 1990, Vol. 90, No. 12. Copyright © 1990 by The H. W. Wilson Company.

The World Book, Inc.: From "Massasoit" from *The World Book Encyclopedia*. Copyright © 1991 by World Book, Inc.

PHOTO CREDITS

Abbreviations used: (t) top, (c) center, (b) bottom, (l) left, (r) right

COVER: Ralph J. Brunke Photography; Yellowstone photos courtesy of National Park District, Department of the Interior.

TABLE OF CONTENTS: Page vii, HRW Photo by Michael Lyon; ix, HRW Photo by Joe Jaworski; xi(t), H. Lanks/Superstock; xi(b), E. Streichan/SuperStock; xiv, Phil Degginger/AllStock; xv, L. Willinger/SuperStock; xvii, Millard/Stills/Retna Ltd.; xx, Chris Sorensen; xxi, Chris Sorensen; xxii, K. Scholz/H. Armstrong Roberts; xxiii, Andrew A. Wagner; xxv, Mary Kate Denny/PhotoEdit; xxvi, Charles Gupton/AllStock; xxviii, Nickelodeon; xxix(l), Margaret Miller/Courtesy William Morrow & Company; xxix(c), K. Yep/Harper Collins Publishers; xxix(r), HBJ.

INTRODUCTION: Page 2–3, Jon Feingersh/The Stock Market; 4, Rivera Collection/SuperStock; 5, Steve Chenn/Westlight; 6, Jeffrey W. Myers/The Stock Market; 7, Gabe Palmer/The Stock Market.

CHAPTER 1: Page 22, Photo by Michael Nye; 28, Lisa Davis; 30, HRW Photo Research Library; 32(l), Tim Haske/ProFiles West; 32(r), © John A. Sawyer/ProFiles West; 34, Lewis Hine/The George Eastman House Collection/HRW Photo Research Library; 36(t), David R. Frazier Photolibrary; 36(b), The Stock Market; 38, Joel Salcido; 43, R. Llewellyn/SuperStock; 45, Fred Ward/Black Star; 46(t), G. Ziesler/Peter Arnold, Inc.; 46(b), George D. Lepp/Comstock; 47(l), Tony Stone Worldwide; 47(r), Jeffry W. Myers/The Stock Market; 52, Scot Hill Photography; 55, © Bob Daemmrich Photography.

CHAPTER 2: Page 58, 59, Todd Powell/ProFiles West; 61, Dr. Jane Goodall/The Jane Goodall Institute; 62, Charles P. Cushing/H. Armstrong Roberts; 63, Yoav Levy/Phototake; 65(l), Milt Putnam/The Stock Market; 65(r), © George Dillon/Stock Boston; 67(l,c,r), FPG International; 68, © Joe Bator/The Stock Market; 70, The Stock Market; 72, HRW Photo by Michael Lyon; 74(l), Ken Vinyard/ProFiles West; 74(r), Animals Animals; 77, Mark Antman/ImageWorks; 78 (clockwise), Robert Pearcy/Animals Animals; Bruce Davidson/Animals Animals; Wallace Kirkland/Animals Animals; A. Briere/SuperStock; M.A. Chappell/Animals Animals; John Nees/Animals Animals; 80, Dandry/The Stock Market; 81, © Dough Hoke/ProFiles West.

CHAPTER 3: Page 89(tl), Robert Neuman/The Stock Market; 89(tr), Bob Winsett/ProFiles West; 89(bl), Kevin Forest/The Image Bank; 89(br), Charles Gupton/AllStock; 93, Ted Horowitz/The Stock Market; 95, Mary Kate Denny/PhotoEdit; 96, Texas Highways; 98, Margaret Miller/Courtesy of William Morrow & Company; 102, Bob Daemmrich Photography; 105, Freda Leinwand; 106, Bob Daemmrich Photography; 110(t), FPG International; 110(b), Culver Pictures, Inc.

CHAPTER 4: Page 119, Nita Winter; 121, Everett Collection; 122, E.F. Productions/SuperStock; 123(l), Stephen Dalton/AllStock; 123(r), Tom McHugh/AllStock; 125, Lisa Davis; 128, HRW Photo by Michael Lyon; 129, 132, HRW Photo by Joe Jaworski; 133, Muriel Orans Horticultural Photography, Corvallis, Oregon; 134, Scot Hill Photography; 135(tl, tc, tr), Tony Freeman/PhotoEdit; 135(b), Kevin Schafer/Peter Arnold, Inc.; 136, Comstock; 137, HRW Photo by William Hubbell; 139, Bryan Peterson/The Stock Market; 139(inset), James Blank/The Stock Market; 141(t), Wiley/Wales/ProFiles West; 141(b), Bob Daemmrich Photography.

CHAPTER 5: Page 148(l), Dan Abernathy/ProFiles West; 148(lc), B. Bavdet/SuperStock; 148(c), Schuster/SuperStock; 148(rc), © Bob Daemmrich Photography/People Picture Agency; 148(r), Allen Russell/ProFiles West; 149, Lisa Davis; 150(t), David W. Hamilton/The Image Bank; 150(c), Joel W. Rogers/Index Stock Photography, Inc.; 152(l), Michael J. Howell/ProFiles West; 152(c), AllStock; 152(r), Thomas Ives/The Stock Market; 155, Lisa Davis; 157, Freda Leinwand; 165, 167, 169, Lisa Davis; 173(tl), Culver Pictures, Inc.; 173(tr), Paul J. Sutton/Duomo; 173(bl), David R. Phillips Collection/FPG International; 173(br), Newsworld/NY Tribune.

CHAPTER 6: Page 176, Nickelodeon; 180, Richard Hutchings/Info Edit; 181, 184, Lisa Davis; 187, E. Strerchan/SuperStock; 188, H. Lanks/SuperStock; 190, Lightwave; 194, HRW Photo by Michael Lyon; 196, Spencer Grant/New England Stock Photo; 198, From "The Sword of Shannara" by Terry Brooks, illustrated by The Brothers Hildebrandt, Ballentine Books, NY/Photographed by Eric Beggs; 200, HBJ.

CHAPTER 7: Page 210(t), Joseph Drivas/The Image Bank; 210(b), Zerschung/Photo Researchers, Inc.; 211, Tony Freeman/PhotoEdit; 212, Mary Kate Denny/PhotoEdit; 214, Charles Gupton/AllStock; 215, D. Cavagnaro/DRK Photo; 216, Henley & Savage/The Stock Market; 219, Tom Campbell/Adventure Photo; 220, W. Gregory Brown/Animals Animals; 221, Rhoda Sidney/PhotoEdit; 225, David J. Sams/Texas Inprint; 226, Paul Conklin/PhotoEdit; 229, Mary Kate Denny/PhotoEdit; 233, Gabe Palmer/The Stock Market.

CHAPTER 8: Page 238(t), 238(b), Photographed by Eric Beggs; 239, K. Yep/HarperCollins Publishers; 251, Lisa Davis; 252, Addison Geary/Stock Boston; 266, Bob Daemmrich Photography; 267(tl), S. Barrow/SuperStock; 267(tr), Bob Daemmrich Photography; 267(b), Art Phaneuf/New England Stock Photo.

787

CHAPTER 9: Page 273, G.I. Bernard/Animals Animals; 277, National Baseball Library, Cooperstown, NY; 278(c), Bob Daemmrich Photography; 278(r), David Woods/The Stock Market; 280, Guido A. Rossi/The Image Bank; 282, Armando Jenik/The Image Bank; 284, Lisa Davis; 286, Culver Pictures; 290, Phil Degginger/All-Stock; 291, P. Turner/The Image Bank; 292, G. Brad Lewis/Gamma-Liaison; 298(t), 298(b), FPG International; 301, Scot Hill Photography.

CHAPTER 10: Page 304, David Wheelock/F-Stock; 306, Zig Leszczynski/Animals Animals; 307, NASA/FPG International; 311, L. Willinger/SuperStock; 313, Archive Photos; 316, Photographed by Eric Beggs.

CHAPTER 11: Page 326, Klonsky/The Image Bank.

CHAPTER 12: Page 342, Neil C. Ramhorst; 347, Comstock; 351, Tony Stone Worldwide; 355, Millard/Stills/Retna Ltd; 359(t), Hans W. Silverster/Photo Researchers, Inc.; 359(b), Chuck O'Rear/Westlight; 363(l), Phil Degginger; 363(insert), Spencer Swanger/Tom Stack & Associates; 363(r), G. Ahrens/SuperStock.

CHAPTER 13: Page 370, Orion Press, Japan; 372, Bob Daugherty/Wide World Photos; 383, Comstock; 385 (1), 385 (r), Jaime Villaseca/The Image Bank; 387, S. Vidler/SuperStock.

CHAPTER 14: Page 392(l), Courtesy: The Heard Museum, Phoenix/Jerry Jacka Photography; 392(r), Jerry Jacka Photography; 397, Johnson Publishing Company, Inc.; 400, © Dr. Ronald H. Cohn/The Gorilla Foundation; 405, Lionel Delvingne/Stock Boston; 406, Bruce Roberts/Photo Researchers, Inc.; 415, Larry Dale Gordon/Image Bank West.

CHAPTER 15: Page 424(l), Art Resource, New York; 426(l), 426(r), 430, Lisa Davis; 432(l), A./ Tessore/SuperStock; 432(insert), Photo Researchers, Inc.; 432(tr), Bill Mares/Monkmeyer Press; 432(br), Photo Researchers, Inc.

CHAPTER 16: Page 440, 441, Photographed by Eric Beggs; 452, H. Kanus/SuperStock.

CHAPTER 17: Page 459, Gerald Cubitt, South Africa; 462, David Falconer/David R. Frazier Photolibrary; 468, Joe Viesti/Viesti Associates, Inc.

CHAPTER 18: Page 483(l), 483 (r), Chris Sorensen; 486, UPI/Bettmann.

CHAPTER 19: Page 509, Mike Okoniewski/The Image Works; 510(l), HRW Photo by Joe Jaworski; 510(r), Bob Glander/SuperStock; 516, K. Scholz/H. Armstrong Roberts; 523, HRW Photo by Joe Jaworski.

CHAPTER 20: Page 535, HRW Photo by Joe Jaworski; 537(l), Giraudon/Art Resource, New York; 537(r), The Bettmann Archive.

CHAPTER 21: Page 555, Bob Daemmrich Photography; 561, HRW Photo by Michelle Bridwell.

CHAPTER 22: Page 575, Anthro-Photo File; 579, Photographed by Eric Beggs.

CHAPTER 23: Page 589(r), S. Vidler/SuperStock; 593, Michael Newman/PhotoEdit; 599, Culver Pictures, Inc.; 604, Alex S. Maclean/Landslides; 606 (a,b,c,d,e), Vic Krantz/Smithsonian; 609(l), 609(r), Andrew A. Wagner.

CHAPTER 24: Page 621, McAllister of Denver; 625, Neil Leifer/Sports Illustrated.

CHAPTER 25: Page 638, Toshi/SuperStock; 643, C. Brown/Sipa Press; 647, Alon Reininger/Photo Network; 656(l, c, r), FDA Consumer; 660(r), Robert & Marcia Ascher/Quipu in the Collection of the Harvard Peabody Museum.

ILLUSTRATION CREDITS

Kate Beetle—116, 265

Linda Blackwell—241

Keith Bowden—150, 155, 192, 201, 332, 408, 424

Rondi Collette—xxiv, 117, 134, 174–175, 183, 400, 410, 427, 516, 530, 541, 631

Chris Ellison—13, 15, 16, 242, 243, 244, 245, 258, 452, 497

Richard Erickson—52, 91, 97, 111, 137, 149, 159, 161, 327

Janice Fried—xi, 187, 188, 236, 239, 351, 651

Gerhold/Smith—202–203

Tom Gianni—266, 460, 556

John Hanley—64, 627, 628, 647

Mary Jones—178, 232, 331

Linda Kelen—163, 164, 171, 230, 231, 255, 261, 302, 324, 394, 413, 523

Susan Kemnitz—vi, ix, 20, 21, 22, 99, 100, 114–115, 129

Rich Lo—xii, xix, 30, 36, 121, 167, 181, 184, 185, 194, 204, 205, 206, 207, 221, 347, 422, 443, 533, 555, 604

Yoshi Miyake—xvii, xxiv, 355, 631

Richard Murdock—x, 145

Precision Graphics—458, 558, 575, 660

Jack Scott—xvi, 320, 322, 334, 335

Steve Shock—viii, 84–85, 86, 87

Chuck Solway—xiii, 237

Nancy Tucker—42, 304, 306, 319, 695

Acknowledgments

For permission to reprint copyrighted material in the Annotated Teacher's Edition, grateful acknowledgment is made to the following sources:

Amereon Ltd.: Quotation by Aldous Huxley from *Eyeless in Gaza XXII.*

E. L. Doctorow: An unpublished quotation by E. L. Doctorow.

Donadio & Ashworth, Inc.: From *Extreme Magic* by Hortense Calisher. Copyright © 1964 by Hortense Calisher.

Lord St. John of Fawsley: Quotation by Lord St. John of Fawsley from the "Scourge of Teleprompters" by Jack Valenti from *The New York Times,* July 10, 1984.

Esquire Magazine and John Gregory Dunne: Quotation by John Gregory Dunne from *Esquire,* October 1986. Copyright © 1986 by Esquire Associates.

Estate of Andre Gide: Quotation by Andre Gide from *The Faber Book of Aphorisms* (1964).

William Golding: From *Freefall* by William Golding. Copyright © 1959 by William Golding.

The Guardian: Quotation by Robert Rauschenberg from *The Guardian,* 1965. Copyright © 1965 by The Guardian.

Harvard University Press: From "The Raison d'Etre of Criticism in the Arts" has appeared in this country under the title of "On Criticism in the Arts, Especially Music" in *Music and Criticism: A Symposium,* edited by Richard Frederic French. Copyright © 1948 by The Harvard University Press.

Hippocrene Books, Inc.: Quotation by H. L. Mencken from *Prejudices.* Copyright 1919 by Hippocrene Books, Inc.

Houghton Mifflin Company: From *The Way of Words: An Informal Logic* by Ronald Munson. Copyright © 1976 by Houghton Mifflin Company.

Alex Jackinson: From "Creating Television Stories and Characters" from *Writing for Film and Television* by Stewart Bronfeld. Copyright © 1981 by Stewart Bronfeld.

Kansas City Times: From a quotation by Alfred Adler from *Kansas City Times,* 109:14C, January 24, 1977. Copyright © 1977 by Kansas City Times.

Alfred A. Knopf, Inc.: From "Miss Jewett" from *Not Under Forty* by Willa Cather. Copyright © 1936 by Willa Cather. Quotation by John Cheever accepting Edward MacDowell Medal, September 8, 1979. Copyright © 1979 by John Cheever.

Vernon Law: From "How to Be a Winner" by Vernon Law from *This Week,* August 14, 1960. Copyright © 1960 by Vernon Law.

Macmillan Publishing Company, Inc.: From "Elementary Principles of Composition" from *The Elements of Style,* 3rd edition, by William Strunk, Jr., edited by E. B. White. Copyright © 1979 by Macmillan Publishing Company, Inc.

William Morris Agency, Inc., on behalf of Gore Vidal: From an interview with Gore Vidal from *The New York Times,* February 24, 1976. Copyright © 1976 by Gore Vidal.

The National Observer, a publication of Dow Jones & Company, Inc.: From an article by Robert Penn Warren from *The National Observer,* March 12, 1977. Copyright © 1977 by Dow Jones & Company, Inc. All Rights Reserved Worldwide.

The New York Review of Books: Quotation by Jorge Luis Borges from *The New York Review of Books,* 1971. Copyright © 1971 by The New York Review of Books.

The New York Times: Quotation by Brian Orser from *The New York Times,* March 12, 1987. Copyright © 1987 by The New York Times Company. From "The Scourge of Teleprompters" by Jack Valenti from *The New York Times,* July 10, 1984. Copyright © 1984 by The New York Times Company. From "Interview with Gore Vidal" from *The New York Times* February 24, 1976. Copyright © 1976 by The New York Times Company.

Harold Ober Associates, Inc.: From *Letters of Sherwood Anderson,* edited by Howard Mumford Jones. Copyright © 1953 by Sherwood Anderson.

People Weekly: "Hell on Wheels" from the "Up Front" section of *People Weekly,* September 16, 1991, vol. 36, no. 10. Copyright © 1991 by People Weekly. Quotation by Marilyn Van Derbur from *People Weekly,* December 13, 1976, vol. 6, no. 23. Copyright © 1976 by People Weekly.

Prentice-Hall, Inc.: From *Writing with style: Conversations on the art of writing* by John R. Trimble. Copyright © 1975 by Prentice-Hall, Inc., Englewood Cliffs ,NJ.

The Putnam Publishing Group: From *If You Want to Write* by Brenda Ueland. Copyright © 1938 by Brenda Ueland.

Lois Rosenthal: Quotation by Nikki Giovanni from "Nikki Giovanni" by Lois Rosenthal. Copyright © 1989 by Lois Rosenthal.

John Roskelley: Quotation by John Roskelley from *The New York Times,* August 10, 1986.

Running Press Publishers: Quotation by E. M. Forster and Allen Ginsberg from *Writers on Writing,* selected and edited by Jon Winokur. Copyright © 1986, 1987, 1990 by Jon Winokur.

Charles Scribner's Sons, an imprint of Macmillan Publishing Company: Quotation by Henry James from *A Backward Glance* by Edith Wharton. Copyright © 1933, 1934 by Charles Scribner's Sons. From *By-Lines: Ernest Hemingway,* edited by William White. Copyright 1934 by Ernest Hemingway, copyright renewed © 1962 by Mary Hemingway.

Simon & Schuster, Inc.: From "Creating Television Stories and Characters" from *Writing for Film and Television* by Stewart Bronfeld. Copyright © 1981 by Stewart Bronfeld.

The Sunday Times, London: Quotation by Sir Isaiah Berlin from *The Sunday Times,* 1962. Copyright © 1962 by The Sunday Times. Quotation by John Fowles from *The Sunday Times,* 1977. Copyright © 1977 by The Sunday Times.

Rosemary Thurber: From *Fables for Our Time* by James Thurber. Copyright © 1940 by James Thurber, copyright © 1968 by Helen Thurber.

Times Books, a division of Random House, Inc.: Quotation by James Michener from *Good Advice* by William Safire and Leonard Safir. Copyright © 1982 by William Safire and Leonard Safir.

Union College Press: Quotation by John Dos Passos from an interview from *The Idol.* Copyright © 1969 by *The Idol,* Union College, Schenectady, NY. Quotation by Robert Penn Warren from an interview from *The Idol.* Copyright © 1972 by *The Idol,* Union College, Schenectady, NY. Quotation by John Updike and quotation by Robert Penn Warren from *First Person: Conversations on Writers & Writing,* edited by Frank Gado. Copyright © 1967, 1969, 1971, and 1972, respectively, by The Idol, Union College, Schenectady, New York.

John Van Doren: From *Liberal Education* by Mark Van Doren. Copyright © 1960 by Holt, Rinehart and Winston.

Van Nostrand Reinhold, a division of Thomas Publishing Corporation: From *Toward A Psychology of Being,* Second Edition by Abraham H. Maslow. Copy-right © 1968 by Litton Educational Publishing, Inc.

Vogue: From "The Art of Skepticism" by Rebecca West from *Vogue,* Novem-ber 1, 1952. Copyright © 1952, 1980 by The Condé Nast Publications Inc.

The Writer, Inc.: From "Suspense Writing" by Mary Higgins Clark, from "Writing Nonfiction Books for Young Readers" by James Cross Giblin, from "Don't Think: Write!" by Madeleine L'Engle, and from "Erasing the Blue-Pencil Blues" by David Petersen from *The Writer's Handbook,* edited by Sylvia K. Burack. Copyright © 1988 by The Writer, Inc.

PHOTO CREDITS *(Annotated Teacher's Edition)*

Abbreviations used: (t) top, (c) center, (b) bottom, (l) left, (r) right.

COVER: Ralph J. Brunke Photography

TABLE OF CONTENTS: Page T6(l), Larry Ford; (tr) Dennis Carlyle Darling; (c) Larry Ford; (br) J. Alexander Newberry; T8, HRW Photo by Michael Lyon; T10, HRW Photo by Joe Jaworski; T12(t), H. Lanks/SuperStock; T12(b), H. Lanks/SuperStock; T15, Phil Degginger/AllStock; T16, L. Willinger/SuperStock; T18, Millard/Stills/Retna Ltd.; T20, © Dr. Ronald H. Cohn/The Gorilla Foundation; T22, H. Kanus/SuperStock; T23, Gerald Cubitt, South Africa; T24(t), Chris Sorenson; T24(b), Chris Sorenson; T25(l), HRW Photo by Joe Jaworski; T25(r), Bob Glander/SuperStock; T26, K. Scholz/H. Armstrong Roberts; T28(t), Andrew Wagner; T28(br), S. Vidler/SuperStock; 30, Mary Kate Denny/PhotoEdit; T32, Charles Gupton/AllStock; T33, Richard Hutchings/Info Edit; T34, Nickelodeon; T35(l), Margaret Miller/Courtesy William Morrow and Co.; T35(c), K. Yep/HarperCollins Publishers; T35(r), HBJ.

PROFESSIONAL ESSAYS: Page T36–T77, border by M. Angelo/Westlight; T36(t), Dennis Carlyle Darling; T36(c), T36(b), T37(tl), Larry Ford; T37(tr), J. Alexander Newberry; T37(cl), Larry Ford; T37(cr) Dennis Carlyle Darling; T37(bl), T37 (br), James Newberry; T38, T39, T42, Dennis Carlyle Darling; T45, T47, T48, Larry Ford; T51, Dennis Carlyle Darling; T53, T55, Larry Ford; T57, Dennis Carlyle Darling; T62, T65, J. Alexander Newberry; T66, T67, T68, T69, James Newberry; T72, T73, Larry Ford.

ILLUSTRATION CREDITS: *(Annotated Teacher's Edition)*

Jane Thurmond Design—Page 13A, 61A, 103A, 131A, 165A, 201A, 247A, 283A, 321A, 361A, 405A, 420A, 440A

Edd Patton—Page T39, T40, T41, T44, T46, T49, T50, T53, T54, T57, T58, T59, T60, T61, T63, T64, T66, T67, T69, T71, T72, T74, T75, T76, T77